East Coast Australia

Ryan Ver Berkmoes

Peter Dragicevich, Justin Flynn, Paul Harding, Cath Lanigan
Rowan McKinnon, Alan Murphy, Olivia Pozzan

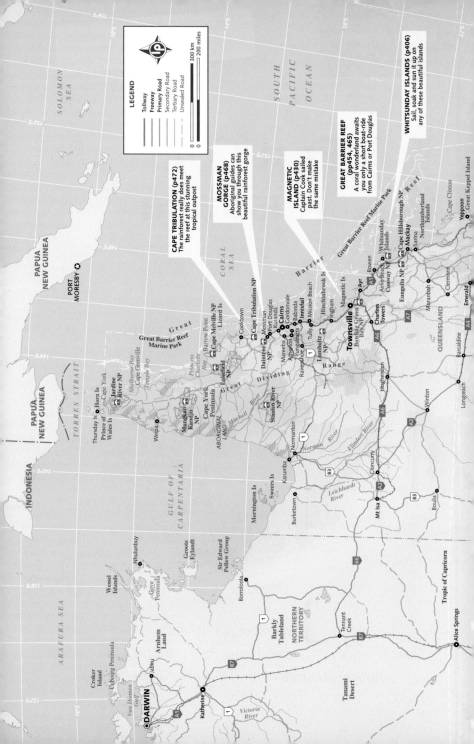

LEGEND
Tollway
Freeway
Primary Road
Secondary Road
Tertiary Road
Unsealed Road

0   300 km
0   200 miles

CAPE TRIBULATION (p472)
The rainforest really does meet the reef at this stunning tropical outpost

MOSSMAN GORGE (p468)
Aboriginal guides can show you through this beautiful rainforest gorge

MAGNETIC ISLAND (p430)
Captain Cook sailed past. Don't make the same mistake

GREAT BARRIER REEF (pp454, 465)
A coral wonderland awaits you only a short boat-ride from Cairns or Port Douglas

WHITSUNDAY ISLANDS (p406)
Sail, soak and sun it up on any of these beautiful islands

SOLOMON SEA

SOUTH PACIFIC OCEAN

PAPUA NEW GUINEA

PORT MORESBY

CORAL SEA

Barrier

Great Barrier Reef Marine Park

PAPUA NEW GUINEA

TORRES STRAIT

Thursday Is
Horn Is
Prince of Wales Is
Cape York

Jardine River NP
Cape York Peninsula
Weipa

Munkan Kandju NP

ABORIGINAL LAND

Mitchell

Lakefield
Lakefield NP

Staaten River NP

GULF OF CARPENTARIA

Mornington Is
Sweers Is
Burketown
Karumba
Normanton

Leichhardt River

Burketown

Mt Isa
Cloncurry

Boulia

83

Shelburne Bay
Cape Grenville
Temple Bay
Princess Charlotte Bay

Barrow Point
Cape Melville NP
Lizard Is

Cooktown
Cape Tribulation NP
Daintree NP
Mossman
Port Douglas
Kuranda
Cairns
Mareeba
Atherton
Gordonvale
Yungaburra
Babinda
Innisfail
Tully
Mission Beach
Ravenshoe
Hinchinbrook Is
Ingham
Limbholtz NP
Townsville
Magnetic Is
Bowling Green Bay NP
Ayr
Charters Towers
Hughenden

Great Dividing Range

Normanton

Norman River

Flinders River

Winton
Longreach
Barcaldine
Emerald

QUEENSLAND

A7

A6

A2

83

1

Bowen
Whitsunday Islands
Airlie Beach
Conway NP
Eungella NP
Mackay
Sarina
Northumberland Islands
Cape Hillsborough NP

Great Barrier Reef Marine Park

Clermont
Moranbah

Yeppoon
Great Keppel Island
Cape Clinton

INDONESIA

ARAFURA SEA

Nhulunbuy
Wessel Islands
Gove Peninsula
Groote Eylandt
Sir Edward Pellew Group

Croker Island
Cobourg Peninsula
Van Diemen Gulf

DARWIN

Jabiru
Katherine
Victoria River
Arnhem Land

Borroloola

NORTHERN TERRITORY

Barkly Tableland

Tennant Creek

Tanami Desert

Alice Springs

Tropic of Capricorn

87

66

1

A1

1

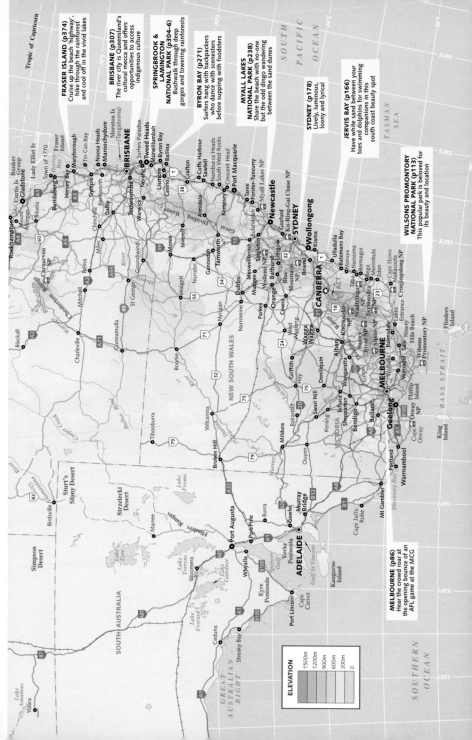

FRASER ISLAND (p374)
Cruise up the beach 'highway', hike through the rainforest and cool off in the vivid lakes

BRISBANE (p307)
The river city is Queensland's cultural mecca and offers opportunities to access indigenous culture

SPRINGBROOK & LAMINGTON NATIONAL PARK (p304-6)
Bushwalk through deep gorges and towering rainforests

BYRON BAY (p271)
Surfers hang with backpackers who dance with scenesters before supping with foodsters

MYALL LAKES NATIONAL PARK (p238)
Share the beach with no-one but the odd dingo wandering between the sand dunes

SYDNEY (p178)
Lively, luminous, loony and lyrical

JERVIS BAY (p166)
Have white sand between your toes and dolphins for swimming companions in this south coast beauty spot

WILSONS PROMONTORY NATIONAL PARK (p113)
This popular park is beloved for its beauty and location

MELBOURNE (p86)
Hear the crowd roar at the opening bounce of an AFL game at the MCG

ELEVATION
1500m
1200m
900m
600m
300m
0

Tropic of Capricorn

SOUTH PACIFIC OCEAN

TASMAN SEA

BASS STRAIT

GREAT AUSTRALIAN BIGHT

SOUTHERN OCEAN

SOUTH AUSTRALIA

NEW SOUTH WALES

VICTORIA

QUEENSLAND

ADELAIDE

CANBERRA

MELBOURNE

BRISBANE

SYDNEY

Newcastle

Wollongong

Geelong

Rockhampton

Birdsville

Simpson Desert

Sturt's Stony Desert

Strzelecki Desert

Flinders Island

King Island

Kangaroo Island

On the Road

RYAN VER BERKMOES
Coordinating author
See that little dot way up there where the sand almost vanishes? That's me. Really. Look harder – I'm there. This is one of the endless beaches at Wooyung Nature Reserve (p279) just up the coast from Byron Bay (p271). This is what the North Coast beaches of New South Wales are about: getting lost so nobody can find you.

PETER DRAGICEVICH Another day, another blissfully deserted, seemingly endless surf beach. One day I spotted a sole dingo wandering a similar beach and another time there were dozens of kangaroos. However on this day, at Middle Beach in Mimosa Rocks National Park (p149), it was just me and a whole lot of nothing.

JUSTIN FLYNN The clouds were coloured like asphalt and the wind and tropical rain strong enough to rip two big branches off the tree next to my room in Mission Beach (p440). 'Just drizzle', the lodge owner said to me as she busily went about removing the branches. I'd hate to see a downpour!

PAUL HARDING Cassowaries, crocs, koalas, stingers...lots of yellow-diamond signs warn you of things to look out for in Far North Queensland. At the entry to Cow Bay (p470) on the beautiful rainforest road to Cape Tribulation (p472) this sign warns of cassowaries crossing. It wasn't long after that I spotted a real one, fortunately not crossing the road.

CATH LANIGAN I'd just finished eating a perfectly cooked salmon fillet and was sitting on the pub deck contemplating the slow revolution there's been in pub food in Gippsland (p107) in the past decade. No more fried everything, the food coming out of some pub bistros is some of the area's best.

ROWAN MCKINNON This is a special place for me – St Andrews Beach, neighbour to the more famous Gunnamatta (p105). I got my best-ever tube ride here as a young surfer when the swell was big and I was fearless. Now, half a lifetime later, I look on and think I should take up surfing again.

ALAN MURPHY With crystal-clear waters lapping against powder-white beaches and stunning bushland areas that are ideal for walking, boredom on Straddie (p330) is not an option. Here I'm trekking through Blue Lake National Park, which is made up of dense Australian bush, and looking forward to a dip in the deep, cool waters of the lake.

OLIVIA POZZAN Noosa's (p345) deeply ingrained surfing culture lured me onto a board and into the surf. There were no hang-tens or smooth moves, but in the warm sunshine and natural beauty of Little Cove, I found my inner surfer-chick.

For full author biographies see p512.

East Coast Australia Highlights

Here at Lonely Planet, we think we know East Coast Australia. Our head office is in Melbourne, after all. When we have holidays, most of our favourite destinations are right here in this book: Wilson's Prom for an easy hike; the Great Ocean Road for Sunday lunch; Sydney for a romantic weekend away; and just about anywhere in Queensland when the winter blues set in down south. Here our staff and authors share a few of their top spots. But we like your own suggestions as much as you like ours. So we asked our travellers – you – about your favourites. Yes, it's subjective. No, you shouldn't read too much into those ratings. Did we miss your own secret highlight? Share it with our community of travellers at lonelyplanet.com/australia.

CAROL WILEY

① BONDI BEACH

Bondi (p194) is as famous for its lifeguards as it is for its swell. A T-shirt from Bondi will have you going home looking like you've just stepped off the set of Baywatch, but with a touch more class.

Kate West, Perth, Western Australia

FRASER ISLAND, QUEENSLAND

Is it just a big sand-dune island (p374)? It may be, but it's also beautiful, and the chance to share a jeep and tent with nine strangers for two days is not to be missed!

Fiona O'Sullivan, Dublin, Ireland

HOLGER LEUE

2

CROAJINGALONG NATIONAL PARK

Bask in the serenity that exudes from Mallacoota (p137). Walk along isolated beaches in surrounding Croajingalong National Park (p139) and catch some surf, or maybe some fish. Explore the lakes on your own, or on a wooden boat that's been ferrying travellers for nigh on a century.

Cath Lanigan, Lonely Planet author

PAUL SINCLAIR

3

THE WHITSUNDAYS, QUEENSLAND

Everyone knows how beautiful the Whitsundays are (p396). They live up to their reputation. But by far the best thing I did there was take a sea-kayaking trip to see turtles. We floated around on water like a millpond, spotting green turtles as they surfaced for air. After we'd had our fill of turtles, we paddled out to a tiny, uninhabited island for lunch and a swim. It was a beautiful way to experience the area away from the resort crowds.

Janet Brunckhorst, Lonely Planet staff, Melbourne, Victoria

HOLGER LEUE

4

GREAT OCEAN ROAD, VICTORIA

This is really a great trip with some spectacular views along the way (p105). Let the surfers blow your mind catching massive waves on Bells Beach, enjoy the pretty villages along the way, or take a helicopter rider over the Twelve Apostles to get the best photo.

Fiona O'Sullivan, Dublin, Ireland

RODNEY HYETT

5

WILSONS PROMONTORY, VICTORIA

Only 2½ hours drive from Melbourne is the pristine wilderness of Wilson's Promontory National Park (p113). Book a couple of nights at one of the historic lighthouse cottages and enjoy the walk in with friends, followed by a glass of red while you watch the sun set. Or take a lighthouse tour.

Marg Haycroft, Foster, Victoria

RICHARD I'ANSON

6

BRISBANE

Check out the best of Brisbane's indoor attractions (p311). The Museum of Brisbane, Queensland Museum South Bank and the newly constructed Gallery of Modern Art are just three that are free to enjoy all year round (except for some exhibitions of course).

Kelly Tohill, Brisbane, Queensland

RICHARD I'ANSON

MUSEUM

7

TIM BARKER

8

SYDNEY HEDONISM

OMG! This city has everything! Beautiful beaches (p194), loads of cool shopping hot spots (p212), and everything else for having a good time!

'Turbz' (online name), traveller

GREG ELMS

LAKES DISTRICT

Ninety Mile Beach (p121) marks the end of a journey through Victoria's High Country and along the rivers past Lake Wellington to the sea. There's nothing like sleeping on the beach and waking up to a sunrise where nature stretches on to eternity in all directions.

'Littlemisslau' (online name), traveller

10

CHRIS MELL

9

NIMBIN, NSW

This is hippy central (p283). People are very friendly and readily offer herbal enhancements to strangers. Not too much to see here, but it's pleasant and you can get high (if that's your kind of thing) by simply breathing the air.

'Ash_jordan' (online name), traveller

RICHARD I'AN

11

BYRON BAY, NSW

Byron (p271) certainly has its fair share of interesting characters, a large proportion left over from the age of Aquarius. The beaches are beautiful, the shopping is great and the pace is chilled out. The perfect gateway to the hinterland towns that surround this magnetic place.

Victoria Downey, Brisbane, Queensland

BLUE MOUNTAINS, NSW

Stock up on trail-mix and head to the Blue Mountains (p216), a wilderness escape just a stone's throw from Sydney. If the hazy blue vistas of this ancient range lull you too deeply, smarten up with an adrenalin-stirring rock-climb.

'Peskyfeminist' (online name), traveller

MTMEDIA

12

SURFERS PARADISE, QUEENSLAND

The most famous beach in Australia after Bondi, the name says it all (p295). Soft sand that leads you to some great surf is frequented by everyone from sporting stars to the average Aussie family. Popular for beach volleyball and ironman comps.

'Cassie19' (online name), traveller

CLAVER CARROLL

13

RICHARD I'ANSON

14 THE DAINTREE, QUEENSLAND

Take a walk in the oldest rainforest on earth (p469). Tread quietly and you'll see a brush turkey; be alert and you'll encounter a lizard or two; look up and spy a sea eagle or wedge tail. Look around and enjoy ferns of all shapes and sizes, orchids, strangler figs, native fruits, wait-a-while trees and more. Just imagine the dinosaurs.

Colin Burton, Bungendore, New South Wales

NOOSA NATIONAL PARK, QUEENSLAND

If you prefer to see your koalas in trees rather than zoos, try the short walk at Noosa National Park (p345) or a slightly longer, less touristed option on Magnetic Island (p430). You'll improve your odds significantly if you are prepared to crane your neck!

'Sueintheus' (online name), traveller

15

RICHARD I'ANSON

WALHALLA, VICTORIA

Walhalla (p120) oozes history – take it in walking the main street, where buildings have been painstakingly restored, on a tour of one of Australia's most prolific gold mines, or off-road on a 4WD tour to a deserted mine. Take the Saturday night ghost tour to immerse yourself in the lore of this old gold mining town and then sleep soundly in a stylish hotel built in the 19th century.

Cath Lanigan, Lonely Planet author

CHRISTOPHER GROENHOUT

16

OLIVER STREWE

17

HUNTER VALLEY, NSW

The Hunter Valley is absolutely one of the best locations if you're into your wines (p231). The wineries are just picture perfect and the wines taste really great too. Best of all, if you take a bus tour, they do all the driving for you.

Jacqueline Davies, Brisbane, Queensland

CAFÉ CULTURE, MELBOURNE

The great thing about Melbourne is that almost any place you go, you're sure to find a happening café hub. Café culture is part of the scenery in Melbourne. Well-known restaurant and café locations in the inner city include the CBD, Docklands and Southbank (all p95), as well as Lygon St in Carlton, Brunswick St in Fitzroy, and Acland St in St Kilda (all p96).

Sandra Taranto, Melbourne, Victoria

PHIL WEYMOUT

JERVIS BAY, NSW

Take the cycle track through Booderee National Park (p167). There's a stretch where you ride along the beach for about 5km. Amazing! Make sure you time it with low tide though.

'Unknown' (online name), traveller

MARK KIRBY

JULIET COOMBE

MELBOURNE SHOPPING

Melbourne *is* shopping (p99)! Chapel St and Bridge Rd are the place to be for boutiques and bargains. If you're after factory outlets, head to Smith Street in Collingwood. And let's not forget the CBD!

Sandra Taranto, Melbourne, Victoria

ST KILDA, VICTORIA

Hire a bike for the day and pedal along the smoothly paved beach path. Soak up the sun, cool off with a swim in the bay, enjoy a picnic lunch and watch the clouds roll by. Feel happy being a part of the buzzing energy of St Kilda (p88).

Kristen Davison, Thornbury, Ontario, Canada

22

JAMES BRAUND

21

CAROL WILEY

SUNSHINE COAST, QUEENSLAND

The Sunshine Coast is brilliant for catching waves (p71). Noosa has a reputation for the best point breaks in Queensland and the strip from Sunshine Beach to Coolum has world-class beach breaks.

Rowan Roebig, Lonely Planet staff, Melbourne, Victoria

RICHARD I'ANSON

23

ATHERTON TABLELAND, QUEENSLAND

The Atherton Tableland is a cool break from the sweaty coast (p449). Misty dawn light hangs over mountains, and other travellers all seem to have been left behind in the sea. The tea grown here is sensational, and it's worth picking up some local homemade jam. Mango, rosella (the fruit, not the bird) and berry varieties are all available. It's a fantastic detour to a beautiful spot for a chill-out.

Janet Brunckhorst, Lonely Planet staff, Melbourne, Victoria

LEONARD ZEL

24 GREAT BARRIER REEF, QUEENSLAND

Snorkelling the Great Barrier Reef is like entering another world (p387). It is like swimming in Earth's womb. The colours of the reef and fish take your breath away, and when the reef ends and there is a sheer drop into deep ocean, it feels like you're skydiving from the highest mountain.

Ursula Hogan, Graz, Austria

Contents

Regional Map Contents

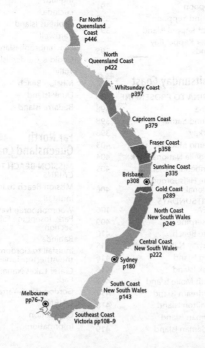

Far North Queensland Coast p446

North Queensland Coast p422

Whitsunday Coast p397

Capricorn Coast p379

Fraser Coast p358

Sunshine Coast p335

Brisbane p308

Gold Coast p289

North Coast New South Wales p249

Central Coast New South Wales p222

Sydney p180

South Coast New South Wales p143

Melbourne pp76–7

Southeast Coast Victoria pp108–9

Destination East Coast Australia

It's all about the water. The East Coast of Australia bangs into the Pacific Ocean for some 4000km (almost five times that if you measure every notched crag and every sinuous strand). Or maybe it's the other way around: the Pacific bangs into the coast. Given the number of surfers riding those breaks, it's probably the latter.

Life here revolves around water and so will your trip, often in ways you might not imagine. Take Melbourne: one of its great joys is its café culture, which entices you to nurse a long black for hours. What's key to that coffee you're drinking? Water. Move up the coast a bit along to southeastern Victoria. What's at the heart of those misty, fern-filled temperate rainforests? Water. The same can be said for southern New South Wales, although as the weather becomes warmer, the form of water focused on is the ocean. Like amphibians in an eternal spring, the surfers and divers increasingly shed their wetsuits as you go north.

Sydney and water are inextricably linked. The harbour. The bridge over the harbour. The people taking the bridge over the harbour to get to some of the most beautiful urban beaches in the world. North of Sydney, philosophers at the many beaches can spend a lifetime pondering the question: if a wave breaks on a beach and there's no one there to hear it, does it make a noise?

Astonishingly long stretches of sand are backed by national parks along the north coast of New South Wales. If you're getting sick of being around people, this is the place for you. In the far north, the water isn't just breaking against the land, it's *part* of the land. Mighty rivers such as the Clarence drain inland rainforests and their vast and lacy deltas support fishing and sugar-cane industries, and in and around Byron Bay are some of the most exquisite organic farms in the country.

If the water south of the Queensland border is a bit of a hippy – fertile, shambolic, untamed – then north of the border it's a starlet. The Gold Coast and the Sunshine Coast beyond are brash, glitzy and, like many a Hollywood-wannabe, possibly over-developed.

As the kilometres click past as you head north from the clean swimming pool–like charms of Brisbane, water simply becomes omnipresent. Hervey Bay is the spring-break home to thousands of humpback whales having a romp before the long slog to Antarctica. North of Rockhampton, water is merely the backdrop for one of the world's natural wonders: the Great Barrier Reef. (Although like any good supporting cast, the water spiffs itself up with an incredible shade of blue.)

By the time you hit Cairns, the water supports a rainforest that cloaks the land with a dripping blanket of green. Up here, whether you go crashing down a vine-strewn path or dive into the brackish depths to discover a living treasure, you're going to get wet and love every minute of it.

And as inescapable an element that water is along the East Coast, you might be surprised to know that the lack of it is what dominates the news year in and year out. Even as people are drawn to the East Coast by its waters they may not have enough once they get there. Droughts of biblical proportions have plagued the region for years, especially Melbourne and parts of Victoria and New South Wales. Watering restrictions, climate change, wildfires, desalinisation schemes and more have dominated discussions.

FAST FACTS

East Coast population: 15.5 million (75% of Australia's total)

Length of coastline: 17,996km (30% of Australia's total)

Inflation rate: 3%

Unemployment rate: 4%

Victoria's official mammal and fish: Leadbeater's possum, weedy seadragon

NSW's official mammal and fish: platypus, blue groper

Queensland's official mammal and fish: koala, barrier reef anemone fish

Favourite brand of beer in all three states: Victoria Bitter (VB)

Favourite East Coast food: fish & chips

Favourite thing to do on the beach: sit

And even when the skies opened up over some parts of the coast in 2008, it was a case of moving from one extreme to another as places such as Mackay in Queensland experienced the worst floods in 100 years.

There were floods of tears along the coast, and indeed across Australia, when Prime Minister Kevin Rudd stood in parliament and said 'sorry' to the stolen generations (p40). His speech was seen by many as a uniting moment for all Australians; others have reserved their judgement until any action transpires. Either way, the speech and its wider implications are the subject of much discussion.

Like the churning surf on an empty East Coast beach, that simple word 'sorry' carried a clarity and purity that won't wash away the past but may begin a transformation for the future.

Getting Started

If you're undecided about whether or not to bring an item from home, you can probably just leave it at home. It's hard to imagine a more traveller-friendly place than Australia's East Coast. You can get anything you need (including sunscreen to replace the big tube you had that was seized at the airport), prices are not outrageous, it's easy to get around and if you can read this, they speak your language (at least in some form). Plus it's amazingly gorgeous, a whole lot of fun and you'll meet lots of people whose dispositions match the weather: sunny.

WHEN TO GO

Any time is a good time to be *somewhere* along the East Coast. When it's cold down south, it's magnificent in the north, and when it's too hot and sweaty up north, Victoria is at its finest. In Victoria and along the south coast of NSW, summer (December to February) offers warm weather and longer daylight hours tailor-made for swimming and outdoor activities. From Sydney to Brisbane, summer temperatures hover around a balmy 25°C – perfect for any activity (or inactivity). In the far north of Queensland, summer is the wet season, when the heat and humidity can be pretty uncomfortable. To make things worse, swimming in the sea isn't possible due to the deadly 'stingers' (box jellyfish) frequenting the waters at this time (see the boxed text, p381).

Winter in the south is from June to the end of August, with temperatures dropping the further south you travel – not surprisingly it's the time when many travellers head north, where the humidity of the wet season has subsided and the temperature is highly agreeable (the Dry lasts roughly from April to September, and the Wet from October to March, with the heaviest rain falling from January onwards). Autumn (March to May) and spring (September to November) are characterised by a lack of climatic extremes along the entire coast.

The other major consideration is school holidays – the high seasons for domestic travel when prices rise and vacancies plummet in the major destinations. In the south, as with the entire country, the Easter (April) and Christmas (December to January) breaks are considered to be the high season. In Queensland, the main tourist season stretches from April to November, and the official high season is June to September. See p488 for more information on holidays. Also note the dates of schoolies, the weeks in late November or December when Australian teens finish high school and head to the beach and drink themselves into oblivion.

See Climate (p482) for more information.

COSTS & MONEY

Prices in Australia will seem familiar if you're coming from the USA (the days of Oz as a bargain destination will remain a memory until the US dollar shows signs of life). From Britain or continental Europe it will seem quite affordable – which makes up for the airfare. Generally you'll find reasonably

---

DON'T LEAVE HOME WITHOUT...

- Sunscreen, sunglasses and a hat to deflect ultra-fierce UV rays (p509)
- A travel insurance policy specifically covering you for any planned high-risk activities (p488)
- Extra-strength insect repellent to fend off merciless flies and mosquitoes (p484)
- An empty hand as there's no reason to overpack – travel light on the East Coast

priced transport and accommodation, and excellent-value food and wine. Like everywhere fuel is soaring and is unlikely to moderate much in price. (Check prices at www.motormouth.com.au.)

Of course, your holiday can be as cheap or as expensive as your tastes demand. A midrange traveller planning to hire a car, see the sights, stay in midrange B&Bs or hotels and indulge in a slap-up restaurant meal in the evening should expect to be out of pocket by at least $180 per day ($120 to $150 per person if travelling as part of a pair or a couple).

At the low-cost end, if you camp or stay in hostels, cook your own meals, avoid big nights out in the pub and catch public transport everywhere, you could probably manage on $50 per day; for a budget that realistically enables you to have a good time and the occasional splurge, set aside at least $75.

Travellers with a demanding brood in tow will find there are many ways to keep kids inexpensively satisfied, including beach and park visits, camping grounds and motels equipped with pools and games rooms, restaurants with discounted kids' meals and child/family concessions for attractions. For more information on travelling with children see p482.

TRAVELLING RESPONSIBLY

Since our inception in 1973, Lonely Planet has encouraged our readers to tread lightly, travel responsibly and enjoy the magic independent travel affords. International travel is growing at a jaw-dropping rate, and we still firmly believe in the benefits it can bring – but, as always, we encourage you to consider the impact your visit will have on both the global environment and the local economies, cultures and ecosystems.

Generally, environmental awareness is on the upswing along the East Coast. Some businesses now make it part of their marketing. And you'll find many of these listed in the back of this book in the GreenDex, see p532.

Here's some top tips from the authors of this book on reducing your impact.

- Buy food at the plethora of local markets: you get the best of the region and support local growers.
- Use local transport; tough yes in some rural areas, but the only way to go in cities such as Sydney and Melbourne.
- If a business says they are environmentally friendly, ask them specifically how. There's no points awarded for the 'green' hotel that's sole initiative is not washing towels.
- Fresh water is an issue in much of the East Coast. Try to use as little as possible. But conversely, don't ration yourself as you need to drink a lot of water in the tropical areas. Refill plastic water bottles from taps.
- Properly dispose of your trash, using recycling bins whenever possible.

PREDEPARTURE READING

Before heading up or down the coast, grab a couple of inspiring, thought-provoking or just plain entertaining books to help put you in the picture.

Tim Flannery's *The Birth of Melbourne* (2002) contains first-hand accounts of the city from 1802 to 1903. That the title subject of *The True History of the Kelly Gang* by the incomparable Peter Carey is an icon for many might be insight enough into country Victoria. *Jackson's Track* (2000) by Daryl Tonkin and Carolyn Landon is a powerful reminiscence by a white bush logger of his interactions with Aboriginal people and the rapidly changing environment.

Utterly contemporary, *The Unknown Terrorist* (2006) by Richard Flanagan is a timely thriller set in Sydney's seamy side. For an unvarnished nonfiction look at the same sleaze, try *Leviathan: The Unauthorised Biography of*

HOW MUCH?

Fish & chips $10

Snorkel gear rental $30

Night in a hostel dorm $25-30

Night at a beachfront hotel from $150

Use of Bondi Beach free

Use of Bondi Beach lifeguard free

TOP 10

FESTIVALS & EVENTS

Aussies love any excuse for a celebration, and flock to the festivals and big sporting events that seem to cram every weekend of the year. These are our top 10 reasons to get festive on the East Coast – more events are listed on p486 and throughout this book.

1 Sydney Gay & Lesbian Mardi Gras (p200) – February

2 Moomba Festival, Melbourne (p91) – March

3 East Coast Blues & Roots Festival (p274) – Byron Bay, Easter

4 Nimbin Mardi Grass (p283) – May

5 Cooktown Discovery Festival (p476) – Queen's Birthday weekend.

6 Brisbane Riverfestival (p320) – September

7 Melbourne Cup (p91) – first Tuesday in November

8 Sydney to Hobart Yacht Race (p200) – from 26 December

9 Boxing Day International Text Match Cricket, Melbourne (p91) – 26 December

10 Woodford Folk Festival (p338) – between Christmas and New Year

MUST-SEE MOVIES

One of the best places to do your essential trip preparation (ie daydreaming) is on a comfy sofa with a bowl of popcorn in one hand and a remote in the other. The following picks range from intelligent and thrilling to stupid yet delightful. See p46 for reviews of some of these and many other locally produced films.

1 *Australia* (2008) directed by Baz Luhrmann

2 *Romper Stomper* (1992) directed by Geoffrey Wright

3 *The Home Song Stories* (2007) directed by Tony Ayres

4 *Rabbit-Proof Fence* (2002) directed by Phillip Noyce

5 *Beneath Clouds* (2002) directed by Ivan Sen

6 *Romulus, My Father* (2007) directed by Richard Roxburgh

7 *The Man who Sued God* (2001) directed by Mark Joffe

8 *Head On* (1998) directed by Geoffrey Wright

9 *Ocean's Deadliest* (2007) directed by John Stainton

10 *Ned Kelly* (2003) directed by Gregor Jordan

TOP READS

The following page-turners have won critical acclaim in Australia and abroad, not least because they have something to reveal to the reader about Australia's cultural evolution and contemporary life. See p47 for reviews of some of these and other books.

1 *It's Raining Mango* (1987) by Thea Astley

2 *The Secret River* (2006) by Kate Grenville

3 *True History of the Kelly Gang* (2000) by Peter Carey

4 *Power Without Glory* (1950) by Frank Hardy

5 *Monkey Grip* (1977) by Helen Garner

6 *Loaded* (1995) by Christos Tsiolkas

7 *Every Move You Make* (2006) by David Malouf

8 *The Brush-Off* (1998) by Shane Maloney

9 *The Harp in the South* (1948) by Ruth Park

10 *My Place* (1987) by Sally Morgan

Sydney (2002) by John Birmingham. Noted novelist Peter Carey gives his own account of his home town in *30 Days in Sydney* (2001). It's quirky, goofy and highly readable.

The Place at the Coast by Jane Hyde is a moving novel looking at a woman's aimless life when she returns to her home in a fading coastal NSW town. It was made into the movie *High Tide* (1987) and filmed in Merimbula and Eden. *Salt Rain* (2004), by Sarah Armstrong, is set in the green hills of the north coast of NSW. It deals with the tough life of a teenage girl who must deal with the strange past life of her mother.

Thea Astley's *It's Raining in Mango* (1987) is an almost tangible taste of Queensland's history. It follows a Sydney family's relocation to Cooktown, and its exposure to the tragic and murderous clash of indigenous and European cultures. David Malouf's 2006 short story collection, *Every Move You Make*, looks at the lives of people from northern Queensland and across the continent.

On a more continental scale, Andrew Bain and wife tackle a circumnavigation by bike with trucks, characters and prevailing headwinds as constant companions in *Headwinds* (2003). Humorist Bill Bryson brings his usual wry voice to the southern nation in *Down Under* (2000), although the pages seem populated by central casting, while *The Fatal Shore* (1987) by Robert Hughes endures as a richly detailed and some say sensationalised tale of England's convicts washing ashore in NSW.

Finally, Tim Flannery writes about the local icon every visitor wants to see in *Chasing Kangaroos: A Continent, a Scientist, and a Search for the World's Most Extraordinary Creature* (2007). The title says it all.

INTERNET RESOURCES

ABC (www.abc.net.au) Australia's public broadcaster has lots of news and information on its website so you can see what's going on before you arrive. Plus there's a full range of great radio shows you can download to your iPod.

Australian Tourist Commission (www.australia.com) Official, federal government-run tourism site with nationwide info for visitors.

Lonely Planet (www.lonelyplanet.com) Great destination summaries, links to related sites and the Thorn Tree bulletin board.

Queensland Holidays (www.queenslandholidays.com.au) Official tourism site, providing comprehensive information on destinations, accommodation, attractions, tours and more.

Tourism New South Wales (www.visitnsw.com.au) The state's tourism site has vast amounts of information on accommodation, activities and much more.

Tourism Victoria (www.visitvictoria.com) Official state tourism site, with excellent sections on festivals and events, accommodation, restaurants, tours and attractions.

Itineraries
CLASSIC ROUTES

EASTCOASTER
One Month to a Lifetime/Sydney to Cairns

The East Coast beckons north of **Sydney** (p178) so it may be hard, but put all the joys of the big smoke behind you and hit the road. Enter the central coast of New South Wales, where there are more beaches and more evidence that people like to live near beaches. **Newcastle** (p225) has swapped its blue collar for Mambo casual, and the pleasantly inebriated **Hunter Valley** (p231) lures from upriver. Don't make the mistake of many and think of this as a long day-trip from Sydney; you want to tipple happily and then get tucked right into bed. Back on the coast, reclusive types may find themselves searching out less developed gems such as **Seal Rocks** (p238) and **Myall Lakes** (p238).

That warm tingly feeling you're noticing is the approaching tropics. Northern NSW basks in subtropical glory. Take in the views at **Hat Head** (p251), go diving at **South West Rocks** (p251), which has a fascinating position overlooking the wave-tossed coast to the north. Halfway between Sydney and Brisbane, **Bellingen** (p254) is a charming town at the base of the mountains with its own delightful beat (lots of folk musicians live here). Carry on up the hill on the beautiful **Waterfall Way** (p258), which is lined with what the name suggests. Further north, you pass some sensational, untouched beaches that

You'll cover at least 3000km by the time you sample the best that this route has to offer. Many of the gems are just off the highway, and around every corner is another beach, another food experience, another tempting detour.

stretch to the horizon; check out those near little wild **Wooli** (p263). **Byron Bay** (p271) is inescapable: don't resist this mellow yet groovin' beach town where surfer meets hipster meets hippy. Nearby towns such as **Bangalow** (p278) are alive with the many palette pleasures of the region. Meditating in Byron's verdant hinterland is the once alternative, still delightful **Nimbin** (p283). From here you've got inland options aplenty through the dense green of several national parks on the **Rainforest Way** (p284).

It will feel like you're in a new country when you pop through into Queensland. Not only is it likely that the time has changed (there's no summer time here because they think it's always summer), but you'll also need to remember how you ordered a beer in Victoria. Gold chains (for both sexes) are the uniform for the **Gold Coast** (p288). The kids can go berserk at the **theme parks** (p303) while you grab a long board or bungee cord. **Brisbane** (p307) has gone glitzy – it still surprises even the locals – and yet nature persists, with wild dolphins to feed at **Tangalooma** (p332) on Moreton Island. The coast now picks up a new alluring name – Sunshine – and the cuisine turns to fusion without confusion at style-setting **Noosa** (p345). There are whales to watch in **Hervey Bay** (p363) – they're lounging around getting ready for the long haul down to Antarctica (trust us, that's worse than even some stretches of the Pacific Hwy). And don't leave the world's largest sand thing, **Fraser Island** (p374), without taking some of it home between your toes after a roll in the huge dunes.

You can watch Australia's favourite rum being distilled in **Bundaberg** (p370), and tiny loggerhead turtles hatching at **Mon Repos Beach** (p372). Chill out at **Town of 1770** (p380) and get your board waxed – this is one of the last places you'll be surfing on this trip. You can get a taste of the coral wonders of the big reef at **Lady Musgrave Island** (p372). Wear a big hat, watch someone riding a bull or join them devouring a steak at beef city, **Rockhampton** (p386), which surprises many with a vibrant art culture you'll find beneath the bull. Explore the trails and sample the beaches of **Great Keppel Island** (p393); it's pure tropical beach bliss. Get even more remote slightly further north at **Byfield National Park** (p393) where streams flow with water so clear you don't even realise it's there. Get another dose of art in the tropics at **Mackay** (p398). And it may be the official mammal of NSW, but you'll spot platypuses aplenty at peaceful **Eungella National Park** (p404).

Your next stop is bustling **Airlie Beach** (p410), gateway to the magical **Whitsunday Islands** (p406), where you can party, dive, sail and snorkel to your heart's content, all while bobbing through the azure waters of your holiday dreams. There are islands and reefs galore up this way. **Townsville** (p424) will put a pause in your action. The place bubbles with diver shops offering **Great Barrier Reef** (p427) explorations of every kind; you'll want an expert just to sort out where to begin in this kaleidoscopic, living breakwater and world unto itself. Next up, walkers should not miss the Thorsborne Trail on magnificent **Hinchinbrook Island** (p438). Adrenaline junkies can take to the white water on the mighty Tully River and you may spot a cassowary at **Mission Beach** (p440) before it spots you. When you reach the tourist town of **Cairns** (p450) you can shout yourself a trip to the reef and a slap-up meal. And you'll find no shortage of fellow travellers here who you can one-up with your coastal tales of adventure.

AROUND THE BEND   Two to Three Weeks/Melbourne to Sydney

You've had so many long blacks that you've almost jumped in front of a tram (twice!) in **Melbourne** (p74). It's getting chilly so now's the time to take your jangled nerves and head north. But the kids (of all ages…) want to see a penguin, so you head south to **Phillip Island** (p106), where penguins, seals and wetsuited surfers frolic in the bracing briny. Next stop, **Wilsons Promontory** (p113). Yes, we are still going south, and yes it is…cool. And clean, and wild and beautiful. And there's nowhere further south to go (sorry Tasmania), so suck in that fresh air and head northeast through the forests, farms and **Gippsland lakes district** (p117) to Victoria's first and last seaside town, **Mallacoota** (p137). Now turn that corner. Things, you will have noticed, are heating up.

Time constricts on the south coast of NSW – distances between towns are noticeably shorter. Each town has a river or an estuary, a golf club and three or four or more golden-sand beaches. People have been known to arrive and never leave – you have been warned. Watch a whale at **Eden** (p144), drop a line at **Narooma** (p151) and take a photo (everybody does) of **Tilba** (p150).

Eventually you'll reach blue-collar **Wollongong** (p172) and the sprawling suburbs, followed by the dazzling lights of **Sydney** (p178). How long you need here depends on your love or loathing of heaving metropolises, and your budget. Escapes to the **Blue Mountains** (p216) are *de rigueur* for frazzled Sydneysiders and overwhelmed travellers alike.

This 1500km trip takes you from the multicultural Victorian capital of Melbourne to Australia's biggest showgirl, Sydney. You travel south-east to Wilsons Promontory before heading northeast around the bend into NSW.

COOKTOWN CIRCLE   One to Two Weeks/Cairns to Cooktown to Cairns

There are two routes from lively Cairns to languorous Cooktown, so if you can organize a 4WD you can make this excellent loop through tropical rainforest and dry savannah, with perhaps a look at Lizard Island.

Leaving **Cairns** (p450), wend your way north on the Captain Cook Hwy through several pretty beach communities including **Holloways Beach** (p460), **Yorkeys Knob** (p461) and, perhaps the best of all, **Palm Cove** (p461). You'll be lured in by good food and reef tours and the lazy local lifestyle at **Port Douglas** (p463), just a short drive off the highway. At unassuming **Mossman** (p468) the main attraction is the magnificent gorge and the **Daintree National Park** (p469), which is best seen near **Cape Tribulation** (p455). From Cape Trib the 4WD **Bloomfield Track** (p474) carves its way through dense rainforests and mountains for 80km. It emerges just south of **Cooktown** (p474), a fascinating outpost of civilisation. From here you can organise a tour to **Lizard Island** (p477), the most northerly Great Barrier Reef resort. Return to Cairns via the inland route, passing the Annan River Gorge to **Lakeland** (p474) – turn right here for the tip of Australia, a mere 700-odd kilometres away. Further along this lonely road there's the Palmer River Roadhouse and the former mining town of **Mt Carbine** (p474), before you reach the farming hub of Mareeba. Turn east here towards the very popular mountain village of **Kuranda** (p462) before descending to the steamy coast and Cairns.

This loop combines the lovely coast north of Cairns, the salubrious hamlet of Port Douglas and the rainforest of Cape Tribulation with the frontier aspect of Cooktown. The 280km trip north takes several days as you lap up the sights.

TAILORED TRIPS

INDIGENOUS CULTURE

The East Coast is the most heavily settled and developed region of Australia, so tangible examples of indigenous culture are not immediately obvious to the traveller. Several cultural centres do, however, welcome visitors and provide guided tours and insights into traditional life. In addition, there are numerous middens, bora rings and other cultural sights protected in national parks and reserves.

Krowathunkoolong Keeping Place (p123) in Bairnsdale is a Gunai Aboriginal space that delivers some truths about the white settlement of southeast Victoria. The NSW south coast, near Bermagui, has the excellent **Umbarra Aboriginal Cultural Centre** (p150), where traditional life including bush tucker can be explored with guides. **Canberra** (p157) has large state museums with extensive displays and exhibits on Aboriginal culture and art.

Sydney (p189) is loaded with sights, museums, shops and tours. Just north, **Ku-Ring-Gai Chase National Park** (p222), just north of Sydney, protects an extensive array of engravings.

The most accessible place in Queensland is the **Dreamtime Cultural Centre** (p388) in Rockhampton, which offers guided tours and boomerang throwing. There are excellent self-guided walks, made with help from the indigenous community, at **Cape Hillsborough National Park** (p406) and **Conway National Park** (p415). For more recommended places, see p45.

Conway
National Park

Cape Hillsborough
National Park

Rockhampton

Ku-Ring-Gai Chase
National Park

Canberra

Sydney

Bermagui

Bairnsdale

FOLLOW THE GREEN

Much of the East Coast is already green, but that's nature's work not man's. However in recent years that's changing as humans are beginning to put a green stamp on natural places that for many years were being stamped out.

In southeast Victoria at **Errinundra National Park** (p133), locals are working at a grassroots level to replace logging jobs with positions in the tourism industry. In the south of NSW, you can get a tour focusing on the ecology of **Mimosa Rocks National Park** (p149) and its protected coastline. Wine-making has never been synonymous with ecological practice (all those critters want the grapes) but many vineyards in the **Hunter Valley** (p233) have sustainable practices.

Byron Bay (p271) and its surrounds are home to oodles of organic farms and sustainable food producers. Visit any of the many markets (p277) to see the local philosophy in action.

In Queensland, you can tour the rich forests of the **Sunshine Coast Hinterland** on eco-themed tours (p354). **Fraser Island** is another good place for a tour (p368) with its unique, sandy ecology. Turtles are threatened around the world, but at **Mon Repos** (p372) near Bundaberg, you can see these gentle creatures in their habitat. Finally, in **Cairns** (p450) there are numerous tours and exhibits on the freshwater rivers and the reefs offshore.

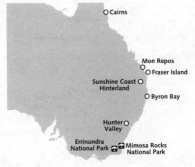

Cairns

Mon Repos
Fraser Island

Sunshine Coast
Hinterland

Byron Bay

Hunter
Valley

Errinundra
National Park

Mimosa Rocks
National Park

NATURE'S BOUNTY

The East Coast is not the Australia of red sand, big rocks and seemingly endless lonely roads across a moonscape. It's the Australia of long golden beaches and verdant rainforests, of the platypus, migrating whales, frolicking dolphins and a plethora of colourful bird life.

Jutting out from the Victorian coast is **Wilsons Promontory** (p113, where wildlife, water and squeaky-clean sand converge on mainland Australia's southern extremity. Further along the coast you can take a multiday coastal hike at **Croajingalong National Park** (p139) before entering the realm of the tall eucalypts of the **Erinundra Plateau** (p133). You can dive with seals, watch whales, point at penguins, and drop a line at **Montague Island** (p152). For a breath of mountain air, discover what all the fuss is about in the popular **Blue Mountains** (p216). There are bottlenose dolphins to hand feed at **Tangalooma** (p332), and migrating whales to gaze upon at **Hervey Bay** (p363). Watch tiny turtles hatch at **Mon Repos Beach** (p372), stroll the metallic beach at **Cape Hillsborough National Park** (p406) with bounding kangaroos, and be astounded by the bright, white arc of **Whitehaven Beach** (p420) on Whitsunday Island. Along the north Queensland coast there are numerous options for getting acquainted with the myriad of colourful denizens of the **Great Barrier Reef National Park** (p387). Take to the classic Thorsborne Trail on mountainous **Hinchinbrook Island** (p438) and be consumed by the dense tropical rainforests of **Cape Tribulation** (p472).

ARE WE THERE YET?

You see the minivan tooling down the road with little windows alive with little faces. Meanwhile outside the windows is a cinematic spectacle. There's much to enthral the kids here. Spoon-feed it to them and plan ahead.

The East Coast has enough diversions to distract the brightest minds, and activities aplenty to soak up the energy of the most boundless youth.

Feed inquiring minds at Melbourne's **Scienceworks** (p90), Sydney's **Powerhouse Museum** (p191) and Brisbane's **Sciencentre** (p311). These are museums where kids can fiddle and interfere with techno gadgets and learn all about all sorts of things.

Melbourne's **Luna Park** (p90) and Sydney's **Luna Park** (p88) are old-style theme parks of the candyfloss and laughing-clown variety, but for ultimate, screaming, what-mind-would-have-designed-this? rides head for the **Gold Coast theme parks** (p303).

Take them snorkelling (but make sure they can swim first) on the **Great Barrier Reef** (p387) or the **Whitsunday Islands** (p406). Instil a deep appreciation of Australia's unique natural heritage by taking them on a **bushwalk** (p64), and reward (or bribe) their gutsy efforts with American-style junk food – the East Coast has oodles of outlets.

And if there's a whimper from the back seat threaten them with the **Big Banana** (p260) at Coffs Harbour, the awfully bloated potato, the truly frightening fibreglass crayfish and the huge…

And if all that fails, leave them at home with a sitter and the TV.

History Michael Cathcart

INTRUDERS

By sunrise, the storm had passed. Zachary Hicks was keeping sleepy watch on the British ship *Endeavour* when suddenly he was wide awake. He summoned his captain, James Cook, who climbed into the brisk morning air to a miraculous sight. Ahead of them lay an uncharted country of wooded hills and gentle valleys. It was 19 April 1770. In the coming days, Cook began methodically to draw the first European map of Australia's eastern coast. He was mapping the end of Aboriginal supremacy.

> Michael Cathcart presents history programs on ABC TV and teaches history at the Australian Centre, University of Melbourne.

CONVICTS

Eighteen years later, in 1788, the English were back to stay. They numbered 751 ragtag convicts and children, and around 250 soldiers, officials and their wives. This motley 'First Fleet' was under the command of a humane and diligent naval captain, Arthur Phillip. By a small cove, in the idyllic lands of the Eora people, Phillip established a British penal settlement. He renamed the place after the British Home Secretary, Lord Sydney.

Robert Hughes' bestseller, *The Fatal Shore* (1987), depicts convict Australia as a terrifying 'Gulag' where Britain tormented rebels, vagrants and criminals. But other historians point out that powerful men in London saw transportation as a scheme for giving prisoners a new and useful life. Indeed, with Phillip's encouragement, many convicts soon earned their 'ticket of leave', a kind of parole that gave them the freedom of the colony and the right to seek work on their own behalf.

> It's east to see some ancient Eora Aboriginal rock engravings (p195) north of the beach uphill near the cliffs at the Bondi Golf Club.

However, the convict system could also be savage. Women (who were outnumbered five to one) lived under constant threat of sexual exploitation. Female convicts who offended their gaolers languished in the depressing 'female factories'. Male re-offenders were cruelly flogged, and could even be hanged for minor crimes such as stealing. In 1803 English officers established

---

50,000 YEARS BEFORE COOK *Ryan Ver Berkmoes*

Little is known about how the first people came to Australia. Even the dates are broadly debatable and seem measured more in geological rather than human terms: 50,000 to 70,000 years ago. What is known is that people came to the continent from Asia during times when the earth was much cooler and water levels much lower. This made it possible for them to walk across Torres Strait from New Guinea. Migrations are thought to have occurred at various times since, with the last major one 5000 years ago. By Cook's arrival in 1770, the continent had a rich and varied culture of indigenous communities.

TIMELINE

60,000 BC	43,000 BC	6,000 BC
Aborigines settle in Australia, according to most experts.	A group of original Australians sit down in the Nepean Valley near current-day Sydney and make some stone tools. Archaeological sites like this have been found across Australia.	Rising water levels due to global warming force many indigenous groups off their fertile flatlands homes along the coasts. Sections of land rivalling today's New South Wales in area are lost.

a second convict settlement at Hobart in Van Diemen's Land (later called Tasmania). Soon male re-offenders filled the grim prison at Port Arthur on the beautiful and wild coast. Others endured the senseless agonies of Norfolk Island in the remote Pacific.

At first Sydney and these smaller colonies depended on supplies brought in by ship. Anxious to develop productive farms, the government granted land to soldiers, officers, and emancipated convicts. After 30 years of trial and error, their farms began to flourish. The most irascible and ruthless of these landholders was John Macarthur. Along with his spirited wife Elizabeth, Macarthur pioneered the breeding of merino sheep on his verdant property near Sydney.

For some indigenous sites of particular interest on the East Coast, see p45.

RUM

John Macarthur was also a leading member of the Rum Corps, a clique of powerful officers which bullied successive governors and grew rich by controlling much of Sydney's trade, notably rum. But its racketeering was ended in 1810 by a tough new governor named Lachlan Macquarie. Under Macquarie's administration the major roads of modern-day Sydney were constructed, some fine public buildings built (many designed by talented convict architect Francis Greenway) and the foundations for a more civil society were laid.

Macquarie also championed the rights of freed convicts, granting them land and appointing several to public office. But this tolerance was not shared by the 'exclusives'. These large landholders, middle-class snobs and senior British officials observed a rigid expatriate class system. They shunned ex-prisoners, and scoffed at the distinctive accent and the easy-going manners of these new Australians.

Sydney's 1816 Mint and Parliament House (p190) were originally wings of the infamous Rum Hospital, which was built by two Sydney merchants in 1816 in return for a monopoly on the rum trade.

By now word was reaching England that Australia offered cheap land and plenty of work, and adventurous migrants took to the oceans in search of their fortunes. At the same time, the British government transported more and more prisoners. In 1825 a party of soldiers and convicts established a penal settlement in the territory of the Yuggera people, close to modern-day Brisbane. Before long this hot, fertile region attracted free settlers, who were soon busy farming, grazing, logging and mining on Aboriginal land.

SHEEP

In the cooler grasslands of Tasmania, the sheepmen were also thriving, and they too were hungry for new pastures. In 1835 an ambitious young squatter named John Batman sailed to Port Phillip Bay on the mainland. On the banks of the Yarra River, he chose the location for Melbourne, famously announcing that 'This is the place for a village.' Batman then worked a staggering swindle: he persuaded local Aborigines to 'sell' him their traditional lands (a whopping 250,000 hectares – roughly 100 sq miles) for a crate of blankets,

3000 BC	1607 AD	1616
The last known large immigration to the continent from Asia occurs (at least until about 1970). Over 250 languages are spoken among the myriad groups living in Australia.	Spanish explorer Luis Torres manages to sail between Australia and New Guinea and not discover the rather large continent to the south. The strait bears his name today.	Dutch voyager Dirk Hartog lands on the coast of western Australia. Like several of his brethren in the 17th century he doesn't enjoy the local way of life (or probably the food) and promptly leaves.

flour, knives and knick-knacks. Back in Sydney, Governor Burke declared the contract void, not because it was unfair, but because the land officially belonged to the British Crown. Burke proved his point by granting Batman some prime acreage near Geelong.

LAND

Each year, settlers pushed deeper into the Aboriginal territories in search of pasture and water for their stock. These men became known as squatters (because they 'squatted' on Aboriginal lands), and many held this territory with a gun. In the USA the conflict between settlers and the indigenous people formed the basis for a rich mythology known as 'the Wild West'. But in Australia the conflict has largely passed from white memory, so white historians now disagree about the extent of the violence. But Aborigines still recount how their water holes were poisoned and their people massacred. Some of the bitterest struggles occurred in the remote mining districts of central Queensland. In Tasmania the impact of settlement was so devastating that today, no 'full blood' Aborigines survive; all of the island's Aborigines are of mixed heritage.

On the mainland many of the squatters reached a truce with the defeated tribes. In remote regions it became common for Aborigines to take low-paid jobs on farms, working on sheep and cattle stations as drovers, rouseabouts, shearers and domestics. In return, those lucky enough to be working on their traditional lands adapted their cultures to the changing circumstances. This arrangement continued in outback pastoral regions until after WWII.

GOLD & REBELLION

Transportation of convicts to eastern Australia ceased in the 1840s. This was just as well: in 1851 prospectors discovered gold in New South Wales and central Victoria. The news hit the colonies with the force of a cyclone. From every social class, young men and some adventurous women headed for the diggings. Soon they were caught up in a great rush of prospectors, entertainers, publicans, sly-groggers, prostitutes and quacks from overseas. In Victoria the British governor was alarmed – both by the way the Victorian class system had been thrown into disarray, and by the need to finance law and order on the goldfields. His solution was to compel all miners to buy an expensive monthly licence, in the hope that the lower orders would return to their duties in town.

But the lure of gold was too great. In the reckless excitement of the goldfields, the miners initially endured the thuggish troopers who enforced the government licence. But after three years the easy gold at Ballarat was gone, and miners were toiling in deep, water-sodden shafts. They were now infuriated by a corrupt and brutal system of law that held them in contempt. Under the leadership of a charismatic Irishman named Peter Lalor, they

'...in 1851 prospectors discovered gold in New South Wales and central Victoria. The news hit the colonies with the force of a cyclone.'

1770	1776	1788
Like Columbus before him, James Cook proves that the spoils of 'discovery' go to the person most adept at self-publicity. He draws the first European map of Australia's eastern coast.	The 13 British colonies in the US declare independence, leaving the King's government without a place to ship undesirables and convicts.	The Eora people of Bunnabi discover they have new neighbours; 11 ships arrive bearing soldiers and convicts, and drop anchor in what is the new arrivals call Botany Bay.

raised the flag of the Southern Cross and swore to defend their rights and liberties. They armed themselves and gathered inside a rough stockade at Eureka, where they waited for the government to make its move.

In the predawn of Sunday 3 December 1854, a force of troopers attacked the stockade. In 15 terrifying minutes, they slaughtered 30 miners and lost five soldiers. The story of the Eureka Stockade is often told as a battle for nationhood and democracy – as if a true nation must be born out of blood. But these killings were tragically unnecessary. The eastern colonies were already in the process of establishing democratic parliaments, with the full support of the British authorities. In the 1880s Lalor himself became Speaker of the Victorian Parliament.

The gold rush also attracted boatloads of prospectors from China. The Chinese prospectors endured constant hostility from whites, and were the victims of ugly race riots on the goldfields at Lambing Flat (now called Young) in NSW in 1860–61. Chinese precincts developed in the backstreets of Sydney and Melbourne and, by the 1880s, popular literature indulged in tales of Chinese opium dens, dingy gambling parlours and oriental brothels. But many Chinese went on to established themselves in business and particularly in market gardening. Today the busy Chinatowns of Sydney and Melbourne, and the ubiquitous Chinese restaurants in country towns, are reminders of Chinese vigour.

Gold and wool brought immense investment and gusto to Melbourne, Sydney and a swath of Queensland. By the 1880s they were stylish modern cities, with gaslights in the streets, railways and that great new invention: the telegraph. In fact, the southern capital became known as 'Marvellous Melbourne', so opulent were its theatres, hotels, galleries and fashions.

Meanwhile, the huge expanses of Queensland were remote from the southern centres of political and business power. It was a tough, raw frontier colony, in which money was made by hard labour – in mines, in the forests and on cattle stations. In the coastal sugar industry, southern investors grew rich on a plantation economy that exploited tough Pacific Island labourers (known as 'Kanakas'), many of whom had been kidnapped from their islands.

Many white Queenslanders still embody the gritty, independent, egalitarian yet racist attitudes that were the key elements of the so-called 'Australian legend'. The legend reached its classic form at the end of the 19th century, when nationalist writers idealised 'the bush', its people and their code of 'mateship'. The great forum for this bush nationalism was the massively popular *Bulletin* magazine. Its politics were egalitarian, democratic, republican…and white.

But while writers were creating national legends the politicians of Australia were devising the framework for a national constitution.

NATIONHOOD

On 1 January 1901 Australia became a federation. When the bewhiskered members of the new national Parliament met in Melbourne, their first aim

Wool was the wealth that built Queensland. Today you can still get close to sheep and also learn ranching skills such as shearing at the Woodstock Trail Rides (p426). You can even be a cowpoke and herd cattle.

1791	1808	1813
The 'Second Fleet' arrives and nascent Sydney gets an injection of petty criminals and a few Irish. For centuries thereafter, descendants claim as much birthright as those from the First Fleet, although few people buy it.	William Bligh does it again. As governor, he takes on the corrupt ruling military mob of the Rum Corps. They rebel and just like on the *Bounty* in 1789, there's a mutiny and he loses power.	The natural barrier of the Blue Mountains west of Sydney is finally conquered by a group of what today would be called extreme adventurers.

was to protect the identity and values of a European Australia from an influx of Asians and Pacific Islanders. Their solution was what became known as the White Australia policy. It became a racial tenet of faith in Australia for the next 70 years. For those who were welcome to live in Australia (ie whites), this was to be a model society, nestled in the skirts of the British Empire.

Just one year later, white women won the right to vote in federal elections. In a series of radical innovations, the government introduced a broad social welfare scheme and protected Australian wage levels with import tariffs. Its mixture of capitalist dynamism and socialist compassion became known as 'the Australian settlement'.

Meanwhile, most Australians lived on the coastal 'edge' of the continent. So forbidding was the arid inland, that they called the great dry Lake Eyre 'the Dead Heart' of the country. It was a grim image. But one prime minister, the dapper Alfred Deakin, was determined to overcome the tyranny of the climate. Back in the 1880s, Deakin championed a scheme by two Canadian engineers to develop irrigated farming on the Murray River at Mildura. The region developed a prosperous grape and dried-fruit industry. (Today this massively productive region is facing an ecological crisis, as salinity and overuse threaten to kill the Murray River.)

WAR & THE GREAT DEPRESSION

Living on the edge of this forbidding land, and isolated from the rest of the world, most Australians took comfort from the idea that they were still a part of the British Empire. When war broke out in Europe in 1914, thousands of Australian men rallied to the Empire's call. They had their first taste of death on 25 April 1915, when the Australian and New Zealand Army Corps (the 'Anzacs') joined British and French troops in an assault on the Gallipoli Peninsula in Turkey. It was eight months before the British commanders acknowledged that the tactic had failed, but by then 8141 young Australians were dead. Soon the Australian Imperial Force was fighting in the killing fields of Europe. By the time the war ended, 60,000 Australian men had been slaughtered. Ever since, on 25 April, Australians have gathered at war memorials around the country and at Gallipoli for the sad and solemn services of Anzac Day.

Australia careered wildly through the 1920s, continuing to invest in immigration and growth, until the economy collapsed into the abyss of the Great Depression in 1929. Unemployment brought its shame and misery to one in three houses. For those who were wealthy – or who had jobs – the depression was hardly noticed. In fact, the fall in prices actually meant that the purchasing power of their income was enhanced.

HEROES

In the midst of the hardship, sport brought escape to a nation in love with games and gambling. Champion racehorse Phar Lap won an effortless and

Lake Burley Griffin in Canberra honours the Chicago architect hired to design the new Australian capital in 1912. Much of Griffin's striking and radical design was never implemented.

Melbourne (p86) and Sydney (p189) have large and impressive memorials to the sacrifices of the 20th century's two World Wars. There are also scores of others, such as the stoic little memorial at the crossroads in NSW's Uki (p284).

graceful victory in the 1930 Melbourne Cup ('the horse race that stops a nation'). In 1932 the great horse travelled to the racetracks of America where he mysteriously died. In Australia the gossips insisted that the horse had been poisoned by envious Americans. And the legend was established of a sporting hero cut down in his prime.

Phar Lap was stuffed and is an exhibit revered by some and reviled by others at the Melbourne Museum (p87).

The year 1932 also saw accusations of treachery on the cricket field. The English team, under its aloof captain Douglas Jardine, employed a violent new bowling tactic known as 'Bodyline'. Jardine's aim was to unnerve Australia's star batsman, the devastating Donald Bradman. The bitterness of the tour became part of the Australian legend. And Bradman batted on – achieving the unsurpassed career average of 99.94 runs.

That same year, the radical Premier of NSW, Jack Lang, officiated at the opening of the great Sydney Harbour Bridge. Before anyone knew what was happening, a man in military uniform rode forward on a skittish horse, drew a sabre and cut the ceremonial ribbon in the name of the King. He was Francis de Groot, a member of the fascist New Guard, who accused Lang of being a closet communist. The Bridge survived the controversy to become a great symbol of hope and optimism, uniting a divided city.

WWII

As the economy began to recover, the whirl of daily life was hardly dampened when Australian serviceman sailed off to Europe for a new war, in 1939. Though Japan was menacing, Australians took it for granted that the British navy would keep them safe. In December 1941 Japan bombed the US Fleet at Pearl Harbor. Weeks later the 'impregnable' British naval base in Singapore crumbled, and soon thousands of Australians and other Allied troops were enduring the savagery of Japan's prisoner of war camps.

As the Japanese swept through Southeast Asia and into Papua New Guinea, the British announced that they could not spare any resources to defend Australia. But the legendary US commander General Douglas MacArthur saw that Australia was the perfect base for American operations in the Pacific. In a series of savage battles on sea and land, Allied forces gradually turned back the Japanese advance. Importantly, it was the USA, not the British Empire, which came to Australia's aid. The days of the British alliance were numbered.

Melbourne's 1858 Customs House is now the Immigration Museum (p83), which takes a fascinating look at the multitudes of immigrants from the early 19th century onwards.

VISIONARY PEACE

As the war ended, a new slogan rang through the land: 'Populate or Perish!' The Australian government embarked on an ambitious scheme to attract thousands of immigrants. With government assistance, people flocked from Britain and from non-English-speaking countries. They included Greeks, Italians, Slavs, Serbs, Croatians, Dutch, Poles, Turks, Lebanese among others. These 'new Australians' were expected to assimilate to a suburban stereotype known as 'the Australian way of life'.

1871	1880	1901
Aboriginal stockman Jupiter discovers gold in Queensland and the rush is on. Within 10 years Brisbane has made its fortune from both gold and wool.	The first issue of the Republican journal for the masses, the *Bulletin*, is published. Its pages are filled with populist fodder. Notable writers include Henry Lawson and 'Banjo' Paterson.	The Australian colonies federate; federal Parliament meets for the first time in Melbourne.

This was the great era of the nuclear family in which Australians basked in the prosperity of a 'long boom'. Many migrants found jobs in manufacturing, where companies such as General Motors and Ford operated with generous tariff support. At the same time, there was growing world demand for Australia's primary products: metals, wool, meat and wheat. In time, Australia even became a major exporter of rice to Japan.

This era of growth and prosperity was dominated by Robert Menzies, the founder of the modern Liberal Party and Australia's longest-serving prime minister. Menzies had an avuncular charm, but he was also a vigilant opponent of communism. As the Cold War intensified, Australia and New Zealand entered a formal military alliance with the USA – the 1951 Anzus security pact. And when the USA hurled its righteous fury into a civil war in Vietnam, Menzies committed Australian forces to the conflict. The following year Menzies retired, leaving his successors a bitter legacy. The antiwar movement split Australia.

There was a feeling among artists, intellectuals and the young that Menzies' Australia had become a dull, complacent country, more in love with American popular culture and British high arts than with its own talents and stories. Australia, they said, had 'an inferiority complex'. In an atmosphere of youth rebellion, and new-found nationalism, Australians began to embrace their own history and culture. The arts blossomed. Universities flourished. A distinctive Australian film industry made iconic movies, mostly funded by government subsidies.

At the same time, increasing numbers of white Australians believed that the Aborigines had endured a great wrong that needed to be put right – and from 1976 until 1992, Aborigines won major victories in their struggle for land rights. Australia's imports with China and Japan increased – and the White Australia policy became an embarrassment. It was officially abolished in the early 1970s, and Australia became a leader in the campaign against the racist 'apartheid' policies of white South Africa.

By the 1970s, over one million migrants had arrived from non-English-speaking countries, filling Australia with new languages, cultures, foods and ideas. At the same time, China and Japan began to outstrip Europe as Australia's major trading partners. As Asian immigration increased, Vietnamese communities became prominent in Sydney and Melbourne. In both those cities a new spirit of tolerance and diversity known as 'multiculturalism' became a particular source of pride.

A powerful dissenting voice in this time of liberal progress was the irascible Joh Bjelke-Petersen, premier of Queensland for 21 years from 1968. Kept in office by a blatant gerrymander (he never won more than 39% of the vote), he was able to impose his policy of development-at-any-price on the state. Forests were felled. Heritage buildings were demolished. Aborigines were cast aside. Protesters were bashed and jailed. But in the late 1980s a series of

> To see some of the immigrant faces of today's Australia, catch the train in Sydney out to Cabramatta, where you can get caught up in a market swirl that could be the heart of Hanoi or Shanghai.

1915	**1918**	**1923**
Anzac legend born when Australian troops join Allied invasion of Turkey.	The Great War ends. Out of a country of 4.9 million, 320,000 were sent to war in Europe and almost 20% were killed. Cracks begin to appear in the ties Australians feel to Britain.	Vegemite, a savoury, yeasty breakfast spread is invented in Melbourne. Given it is a byproduct of brewing that had gone to waste, it is a modern marketing triumph.

SORRY *Ryan ver Berkmoes*

On 13 February 2008, Prime Minister Kevin Rudd stood up and said 'sorry' to the stolen genera-tion. That it was an emotional moment is one of those trite understatements. Just saying 'sorry' had been debated by various political factions and parties for years, although once the speech was made many were surprised at the pent-up emotions that were released. Even some who had opposed the move as unnecessary pandering were caught up in the moment.

Here's the opening statement of Rudd's speech:

'I move:

That today we honour the indigenous peoples of this land, the oldest continuing culture in human history.

We reflect on their past mistreatment.

We reflect in particular on the mistreatment of those who were stolen generations – this blem-ished chapter in our nation's history.

The time has now come for the nation to turn a new page in Australia's history by righting the wrongs of the past and so moving forward with confidence to the future.

We apologise for the laws and policies of successive Parliaments and governments that have inflicted profound grief, suffering and loss on these our fellow Australians.

We apologise especially for the removal of Aboriginal and Torres Strait Islander children from their families, their communities and their country.

For the pain, suffering and hurt of these stolen generations, their descendants and for their families left behind, we say sorry.

To the mothers and the fathers, the brothers and the sisters, for the breaking up of families and communities, we say sorry.

And for the indignity and degradation thus inflicted on a proud people and a proud culture, we say sorry.

We the parliament of Australia respectfully request that this apology be received in the spirit in which it is offered as part of the healing of the nation.

For the future we take heart; resolving that this new page in the history of our great continent can now be written.

We today take this first step by acknowledging the past and laying claim to a future that embraces all Australians.

A future where this parliament resolves that the injustices of the past must never, never happen again.

A future where we harness the determination of all Australians, indigenous and non-indigenous, to close the gap that lies between us in life expectancy, educational achievement and economic opportunity.

A future where we embrace the possibility of new solutions to enduring problems where old approaches have failed.

A future based on mutual respect, mutual resolve and mutual responsibility.

A future where all Australians, whatever their origins, are truly equal partners, with equal opportunities and with an equal stake in shaping the next chapter in the history of this great country, Australia.'

1927	1941	1967
Federal Parliament moves to the new national capital in Canberra.	The Japanese bomb Towns-ville. The war in the Pacific is on. Hundreds of thousands of Australian troops pour out to battlefields worldwide. Thousands of American troops pour in and drink a lot of beer.	Popular referendum over-whelmingly gives Aborigines the status of full citizens.

investigations revealed that Bjelke-Petersen presided over a system that was rotten. His favoured police commissioner was jailed for graft and it became clear that the police force, which Joh had used as a political hit-squad, was largely racist, violent and corrupt. Yet even today there are voters, especially in his old political base among rural white conservatives, who insist that 'Joh was good for Queensland'.

CHALLENGES

Today Australia faces new challenges. Since the 1970s the country has been dismantling the protectionist scaffolding that allowed its economy to develop. Wages and working conditions, which used to be fixed by an independent authority, are now much more uncertain. And two centuries of development have placed great strains on the environment – on water supplies, forests, soils, air quality and the oceans. The country is closer than ever to the USA. Some say that this alliance protects Australia's independence. Others insist that it reduces Australia to a fawning 'client state'.

Though many Australians pride themselves on their tolerance, under popular conservative Prime Minister John Howard there was increasing resistance and discontent over the boatloads of asylum seekers arriving in Australian waters, many living indefinitely in detention camps.

Howard's 11-year reign came to a crashing end in the federal election of 2007 when the Liberal Party was defeated, and Howard lost his own parliamentary seat. Just weeks after taking office, Kevin Rudd's new Labor government delivered an apology to the Aboriginal peoples known as the Stolen Generations (indigenous children removed from their communities and placed with white families during the 19th and 20th century), and ratified the Kyoto Agreement on climate change.

1972	1989	2000
The Aboriginal Tent Embassy is erected on the lawns of Parliament House in Canberra. Over the next decades it serves as a reminder that indigenous peoples have been denied sovereignty to their land.	Joh Bjelke-Petersen finishes his run as premier of Queensland, during which time he used the state police as political enforcers and changed tax laws that resulted in the over-development of the Gold Coast.	Sydney hosts the Summer Olympics. The city shows off to the world and the trouble-free games help burnish the nation's image as a 'cool' place in the 21st century.

The Culture

REGIONAL IDENTITY

Okay, so the East Coast has gorgeous water, great surf, fine diving, beautiful and lush parks, lots of cool little towns and some really big and fascinating ones, but that's about it in the shared attributes department. Sure you'll hear people using 'mate' from Melbourne to Cairns, but as you travel the 4000km of grand and glorious coast covered in this book you'll find more differences than similarities in both the land and the people.

Melbourne, the capital of Victoria, has a stylish European flavour – almost half of Melbourne's population hails from other shores, importing the best cuisine, fashion and culture from their respective nations. It's a city of rich coffee and languid cafés and it can be forgiven if, like second cities everywhere, the locals seem to spend just a tad too much time disparaging Sydney.

Moving up the coast, the misty hills of ferns and dark forests are the backdrop for a rural culture that extends right up into the south of New South Wales (NSW). People here need to be self-sufficient, especially in winter when they have to hunker down against storms blowing up from Antarctica. It's an outpost of individualism, reinforced by it being well and truly off the beaten path.

Somewhere past Jervis Bay, the pace noticeably quickens. It's the Sydney effect and like radiation after an A-bomb blast, the effects are both insidious and widespread. Sydney may be Australia's oldest city, but she's far beyond staid, instead fizzing and popping with sybaritic energy. Sydney loves a party (think Mardi Gras, p200). And with the harbour as a daily reminder that the city is indeed special, who can blame her for wanting to celebrate? Parts of town seem to have more in common with Los Angeles, New York and London than the rest of Australia.

North of Sydney, coastal New South Wales never quite slows down. Well that's not true, everybody slows down because the Pacific Hwy (the main road to Brisbane) is a two-lane coagulation. All the coastal areas see a lot of traffic and in the far north around Byron Bay you find a unique blending of cultures that's rather appealing. Take one part leftover hippy from the hinterlands, add in a dose of surf culture mixed with some urbanism that fell off a passing truck and you have a delightful mix of the creative, laid-back and inventive.

Cross into Queensland and the laid-back goes poof! This land of bland weather (it's pretty much sunny and warm all the time – damn) is Australia's holiday haven. Many people mistake their first glimpse of Surfers Paradise (no one believes in irony here) for Brisbane. As if. It's all glitz and go-go-go right from the Gold Coast to the Sunshine Coast (again, irony not allowed). It's only once you've gotten to the Fraser Coast that things calm down (the lack of a brand-driven regional name here should be a big clue). Here's where you find the Australian cliché of sun, surf and smiles backed by a thick and impenetrable drawl.

When you reach Cairns, you're been in the thick of a place where for some time the men have wrestled crocs and the women have cooked 'em. This land of swaying palms and a certain tropical torpor couldn't be further from the urban frenzy of Sydney or the Continental moods of Melbourne, yet it's all under the same flag.

LIFESTYLE

Residents of the three states are unified in their suburban desire for the Aussie dream: to own a home, produce an average of 1.7 kids and have a mutt doing

Crikey (www.crikey.com .au), a scurrilous, hugely irreverent indie-news service, was started by former Victorian government aide Stephen Mayne. Motto: 'Taking a long spike to bloated egos.'

Talkback radio is the Australian equivalent of talk radio elsewhere. But you'll hear the same fed-up suburbanites ranting about the government and lefties while right-wing hosts scream outrage. Sydney's two big talkback stations, 2GB and 2UE, can be heard nationwide.

something naughty to the lawn out front. But then that's the story in much of the First World – and the developing world for that matter.

Most Victorians live in Melbourne, enjoying a variety of cultural and sporting events, lush green gardens and parks. In keeping with its vague Old World airs, Melbourne loves tradition, including annual events that see scads of women dress up with big, silly hats. Despite the state's hilariously unpredictable weather, the beach holiday is still a priority for many Vics. Families flock to the coastal regions to follow the sun, or else migrate to Queensland resort areas such as Noosa and the Sunshine Coast when the fickle climate plays up.

In contrast, Sydneysiders see no reason to leave the city limits. The balmy weather, the long stretches of beach, the well-preserved waterfront, the strong, ever-growing economy – all these ingredients make Sydney work for its residents. It's a vibrant urban place with plenty of plastic surgeons to keep things buff and a famously lurid nightlife: it's Australia's gay mecca. When people from Sydney leave, it's often to go just far enough to 'get away from the crowds'.

Ignoring the herbal patch of alternative lifestyles in the far north, the rest of NSW is a pretty hunkered down, down-to-earth place. After all, there's that lawn to mow.

In Queensland, most people live in the coastal suburban sprawl between Coolangatta and Cairns. Inexorable development continues, especially in the densely populated southeast, and, although some in Brisbane might moan about the rising property prices, they're still chuffed that they live in one of the country's fastest-growing regions.

Historically, Queensland has been one of Australia's great bastions of conservatism, and even today that attitude is still hard to shake. Given that the current prime minister is both from Queensland and leader of the left-of-centre Labour Party, there's an element of irony here that most locals would find foreign.

POPULATION

Australia's population is 20.2 million. NSW, the most populous state, has 6.7 million people, while Victoria has 5 million and Queensland 3.9 million. Sydney (4.1 million) and Melbourne (3.6 million) are the largest Australian cities.

The first immigrants were mostly British, Irish and Scottish, but the Chinese came after the discovery of gold in the 1850s, and many Italians migrated here to work in the NSW and Queensland sugar industry, and on southeastern Victorian farms.

After WWII mass-immigration policies brought more Italians, as well as migrants from New Zealand, the former Yugoslavia, Greece, Germany, the Netherlands, Vietnam, China and other countries. In 2006 Australia accepted 177,600 immigrants, with 54,900 settling in NSW, 47,200 in Victoria and 33,500 in Queensland.

Although most population growth tends to occur on the Melbourne and Sydney fringes, a lot of movement is occurring north of NSW, making Queensland's east coast the country's fastest-growing region. Development is also rampant on the central coast of NSW. In Queensland, much of the state's population lives within 150km of Brisbane.

An estimated 460,000 (about 2% of Australia's population) identify themselves as Aboriginal, Torres Strait Islanders or of indigenous origin. NSW has Australia's largest indigenous population (around 135,000), with most residing in and around Sydney. Queensland has the country's second-largest indigenous population (126,000), focused in Brisbane but also with large

Culture.gov.au is a website of the Australian government with a vast number of articles and links relating to all forms of Australian culture. It's fully up-to-date and searchable.

Andrew McGahan's award-winning novel *Praise* (1991) stuns with its dark take on mis-matched love in Brisbane. Sex and drugs attempt to enlighten, but modern life proves exceedingly dull and pointless. Later made into a 1998 film.

populations around Townsville and Cairns. More than half of Australia's 42,000 Torres Strait Islanders, from the islands between Cape York and Papua New Guinea, live in northern Queensland and on the islands of the strait itself.

INDIGENOUS AUSTRALIANS

The NSW-based Bangarra Dance Theatre (www .bangarra.com.au) combines 40,000 years of Aboriginal and Torres Strait Islands performance with contemporary, bold choreography.

Around 100,000 Aborigines lived in Victoria before Europeans arrived; by 1860 there were just 2000 left. Now more than half of Victoria's 28,000-strong indigenous population lives in Melbourne. Victorian Koories (Aborigines from southeastern Australia) lived in 38 dialect groups speaking 10 languages; each group was divided into clans and subclans. 'Dispersion' and 'assimilation' policies eradicated the purely traditional lifestyle, but today some Victorian groups are attempting to revive their cultures.

When the British first arrived at Sydney Cove, there were approximately 3000 Aborigines, using three main languages encompassing several dialects and subgroups around what is now Sydney. Today more Aboriginal peoples live in Sydney than in any other Australian city – the region has more than 30,000 indigenous inhabitants, most descended from migratory inland tribes, including a small number of Torres Strait Islanders. The Sydney suburbs of Redfern and Waterloo have large Aboriginal populations.

The first Australian cricket team to tour England was 100% Victorian Aboriginal – in 1868. The subsequent 'whiteness' of the sport in Australia meant that this achievement was unheralded until recently.

Indigenous people of many tribes inhabited the area encompassing Queensland for tens of thousands of years before European settlement. By the turn of the 19th century, the Aborigines who had survived the bloody settlement of Queensland had been run off their lands and the white authorities had set up ever-shrinking reserves to contain the survivors. Today Murri is the term used to refer to the indigenous people of Queensland.

The current status of indigenous peoples in Australia is in stark contrast to the rest of the population. A few – depressing – facts for comparison: school drop-out rates are one-third higher, binge-drinking occurs twice as often, and life expectancy is 17 years fewer than for non-Aboriginal Australians (59 for men and 65 for women).

SPORT

All three East Coast states can stake legitimate claims to the title of Australia's sporting mecca, which should give an indication of just how sports-mad the place is. Passions vary, however. Up north is the gladiatorial arena of rugby ('thugby') while down south is the smouldering cauldron of Aussie Rules football ('aerial ping pong'). Cricket ('watching paint dry') is a nationwide obsession in summer.

Creeping up in popularity is soccer, which is gaining a toehold in all states – the game has progressed from when it was strictly for 'sheilas, wogs and poofters' (as memorably articulated by one prominent soccer identity).

Other popular sports on the coast include basketball, netball, motor sports, driving the porcelain bus, hockey, farnarkling, tennis, elbow bending, horse racing, chundering and surfing. Competitive swimming has a culture all its own.

Australian Rules Football

Melbourne is the spiritual home of that weird hybrid sport, Australian Rules football (a sort of cross between rugby and Gaelic football), from where the **Australian Football League** (AFL; www.afl.com.au) administers the national competition. Traditionally, most big games are played at the Melbourne Cricket Ground (MCG; p99). During the season (March to September), Victorians go footy-mad, entering tipping competitions, discussing groins and hamstrings and savouring the latest loutish behaviour (on and off the field).

EXPLORING THE EAST COAST'S INDIGENOUS CULTURE

As you explore the East Coast, you'll find many ways to learn more about the lives of Australia's first residents. Cultural sites and exhibits are many; some highlights include:

- **Krowathunkoolong Keeping Place** (p123) In Victoria's Bairnsdale, this place explores Gunai (or Kurnai) life from the Dreamtime until after white settlement.
- **Gulaga National Park** (p152) Encompassing the mountain of the same name, this park is jointly managed by the indigenous community and protects a sacred Yuin spot.
- **Canberra** (p157) The capital's large state museums have extensive displays and exhibits on Aboriginal culture and art.
- **Sydney** (p189) Many sights, museums, shops and tours.
- **Ku-ring-gai Chase National Park** (p222) Some 24km from Sydney, the park preserves more than 800 indigenous sites, including rock paintings, middens and cave art.
- **Minjungbal Aboriginal Cultural Centre** (p281) In Tweed Heads, NSW, the displays detail how the Minjungbal people were able to live in harmony with the land.
- **Mt Beerwah** (p336) With neighbouring peaks, this Queensland mountain is an important part of local Aboriginal lore.
- **Scrub Hill Community Farm** (p364) Run by the local Aboriginal community, there are tours, exhibits and feasts.
- **Townsville Cultural Centre** (p426) An interactive Aboriginal dance and interpretive centre in the north of Queensland.
- **Tjapukai** (p453) One of many excellent Aboriginal sights in the far north of Queensland, this is a cultural extravaganza in Cairns.
- **Mossman Gorge Gateway** (p468) A cultural and visitor centre with excellent rainforest walks led by indigenous guides.

Rugby

In NSW and Queensland, rugby league (the 13-a-side version) is king, and is administered by the **National Rugby League** (NRL; www.nrl.com). Queensland has three teams in the Sydney-dominated competition (p212): the Brisbane Broncos; the North Queensland Cowboys, which plays in Townsville; and the Gold Coast Titans.

The most anticipated event in the league calendar is the State of Origin series held every June/July, when Queensland's Maroons (or Cane Toads) take on arch rivals NSW, known as the Blues (or Cockroaches).

Rugby union (the 15-a-side variant) is almost as popular, especially now that it's turned professional. It's run by the **Australian Rugby Union** (www.rugby .com.au). Historically, union was an amateur sport played by posh gits, and its century-long rivalry with rugby league's professional, working-class oiks was a real battle of ideologies.

Russell Crowe spent part of his childhood in Sydney. Today he's part-owner of the Rabbitohs, the 100-year-old South Sydney team in the National Rugby League.

Cricket

Despite behaviour that has generated a lot of negative media coverage, Australia's team continues to dominate cricket, as it has done for the better part of a decade. It won its third consecutive World Cup in 2007. The sport is administered by **Cricket Australia** (www.cricket.com.au).

ARTS

Aussies are supposed to be sports-mad and arts-shy, yet statistics tell otherwise: attendance figures for galleries or performing arts are almost double

It's said by some cynics that more Australians know cricket legend Don Bradman's Test batting average (99.94) than know the year Captain Cook first bobbed around the coast (1770).

The Australian Film Institute (AFI; www.afi .org.au) promotes Oz flicks and sponsors annual awards for films and TV shows. Its best film for 2007 was *Romulus, My Father*.

that for all football codes. Cinema is the top pastime, with around two-thirds of the population taking in at least one movie annually. Aussie bookworms cough up around $1 billion for books each year, around 25% of Australians attend a music concert annually and 21% visit a gallery.

Cinema

All three major capitals of the East Coast have film production studios feeding Australian TV, producing movies for general release and doing contract work for Hollywood.

The big noise recently in Australian film has been the rather grandly titled *Australia,* a classic epic/action film in which Nicole Kidman plays a English rancher who saves her cows from Japanese bombs during WWII with the help of hunky Hugh Jackman. It was shot on location in NSW and Queensland in 2007. See p423 for more details.

Notable Aussie films made in NSW include Ray Lawrence's *Bliss* (1985), a kooky, sexual romp about Sydney advertising exec Harry Joy, and *Lantana* (director Ray Lawrence; 2001) examines a small suburban community where action breeds reaction, senses are deadened and paranoia is rife. Bruce Beresford's classic *Puberty Blues* (1981), which examines south Sydney's surf culture in all its sordid glory. Some 16 years later, *Bra Boys* is an unflinching documentary about the south Sydney surf gang called – you guessed it – the Bra Boys. Made by the members themselves, it shows a violent world far removed from the mellow surfer cliche.

A sighting of Nicole Kidman in Sydney is right up there with sharing a meat pie with Russell Crowe. When she's in town – she grew up here and owns a house in Darling Point with hubby Keith Urban – the tabloids cover her every move.

In Sydney, Fox Studios is at the heart of NSW's healthy film industry, with many American productions drawn there by relatively low costs. Big-budget extravaganzas, financed with overseas money and made for the international market, include *The Matrix* (1999) and *Mission Impossible II* (2000). Sydneysider Baz Luhrmann's *Moulin Rouge* (2001) was also made there.

Set in Melbourne, *The Home Song Stories* (2007) is a widely acclaimed story about the tribulations that await a single Hong King nightclub singer who moves to Australia with her kids in the 1970s. *Noise* (2007) takes a multifaceted look at the aftermath of a mass killing on a train to the suburb of Sunshine (don't say you weren't warned…). Fifteen years earlier, Russell Crowe exploded onto the screen as a violent Melbourne skinhead in *Romper Stomper* (1992).

Also shot in Victoria, *Romulus, My Father* (2007) is based on the Raimond Gaita book about a immigrant boy's struggle to cope with two deeply flawed parents.

Other notable Victorian features include silly-billy comedy *The Castle* (1997), which pokes mild fun at Aussie stereotypes; the gutsy *Head On* (1998), featuring a gay Greek-Australian as the lead character; and perennial fave *Ned Kelly* (2003). The super-stylised film *Chopper* (2000) presents Melbourne celebrity crim Mark 'Chopper' Read as both victim and exploiter of media hype, with black-as-coal humour.

Kenny (2006) is a mockumentary about a battler in the portable toilet business who soldiers on fighting rear guard actions in society's machinery.

There's also a gritty short-film scene in Victoria, perhaps the country's best, including Adam Elliot and his Oscar-winning claymation, *Harvie Krumpet* (2003).

Benchmark Victorian films from the 1970s include Peter Weir's *Picnic at Hanging Rock* (1975), featuring nubile Anglo schoolgirls mysteriously 'absorbed' into the primitive Aussie landscape; and Dr George Miller's apocalyptic *Mad Max* (1979), starring a raw, prefame Mel Gibson as Max, decimating his enemies in a stylised orgy of violence.

Queensland also has a role in the Australian film industry. Commercial production is based around the Warner Roadshow studios on the Gold

Coast, which has produced successful family-orientated films including *Scooby Doo* (2002).

Other titles filmed in the state include *The Thin Red Line* (1998), Terence Malick's critically acclaimed tale of WWII soldiers in the Pacific, and *Crocodile Dundee* (1986), the original and many would say the definitive version of Paul Hogan's studies of Queensland societal mores and habits.

Local films include *Gettin' Square* (2003), a funny/dark tale of two low-rent crims; *Swimming Upstream* (2002), about Anthony Fingleton, a Queensland swimmer in the 1960s; and *Blurred* (2002), which follows five teenagers during schoolies (p297) week.

> It's generally agreed that Victoria produced the world's first feature-length fiction film, *The Story of the Kelly Gang* (1906), a hit with Australian and British audiences. And the first of approximately 3694 filmings of the story.

Literature

Victoria has produced a raft of classic works, including *The Getting of Wisdom* (1910), by Henry Handel (Florence Ethel) Richardson, about a girl's coming of age; *The Songs of a Sentimental Bloke* (1915), by CJ Dennis, poetic verse about a good Aussie bloke who likes beer, fighting and the love of a good woman; *For the Term of His Natural Life* (1927), by Marcus Clarke, a powerful account of Australia's convict era; *My Brother Jack* (1964), by George Johnston, the moving story of two brothers between two world wars; and *Picnic at Hanging Rock* (1967), by Joan Lindsay.

Former Victorian Peter Carey is probably the state's best-known contemporary writer; he now lives in New York. He won the Booker Prize in 1988 for *Oscar & Lucinda,* a lush 19th-century tale of a couple who gamble on love and life, culminating in their quest to transport a glass church across the Aussie landscape; and again in 2002 for *True History of the Kelly Gang,* based on the letters of Ned Kelly and controversial (to say the least, given

> The Miles Franklin Award is given every year to a novel or play that presents aspects of Australian life. Worth over $40,000, it was awarded in 2007 to *Carpenteria* by Alexis Wright.

MUST-SEE AUSSIE TV

Plopped down in the hostel common room or sequestered in your suite, there's plenty to see on Oz TV that may keep you inside longer than you thought. Here are five current hits.

- **Summer Heights High** (ABC) The perils and joy of Australian high school life will be familiar to teenage-years-survivors everywhere. Shot in a fake documentary style, *Summer Heights High* is filled with the sorts of stock characters that have universal familiarity. It's the creation of comedian Chris Lilley.

- **Kath & Kim** (Ch 7) Kath has a sunny disposition, just like the woman who chats to you while you're in the supermarket queue buying milk. Her daughter Kim is the type who always whines in line for a drink at a pub. It's genre-busting, as its awards for both drama and comedy show. One episode was the highest rated program on Oz TV in 2007.

- **Spicks & Specks** (ABC) Hosted by popular comedian Adam Hills, this rollicking musical romp pits two teams of both Australian and international musicians (singers, orchestra conductors etc) against each other in a competition to see who can answer obscure musical questions. There's also a niche offshoot on SBS, *Rockwiz*, which is filmed every Tuesday at the legendary Espy in Melbourne (p97).

- **The Chaser's War on Everything** (ABC) Remember the fake cavalcade that almost made it into George Bush's hotel in Sydney, despite the fact that they were dressed as Osama Bin Laden? Well it was these guys and they have a very popular show that pokes fun at everyone but mostly politicians.

- **Enough Rope** (ABC) Under the premise that everyone has a story, Andrew Denton weaves a fascinating program that breaks out of the vacuous clichés of the chat show. The interviews mix big names (Cate Blanchett, Bill Clinton) with the ordinary (the scone-baking champion was a classic).

John McManus, otherwise known simply as Rove, is a hugely popular TV host who breezily makes the jump between prime-time game shows and an eponymous Melbourne-based chat show in which notables sit down on his couch and, well, chat.

that Kelly is a roguish icon for many) for its suggestion that the Kelly gang were transvestites.

Books with NSW settings include award-winning *The Secret River* (2006) by Kate Grenville, a morality tale of pioneers, compromises and indigenous people. Her *The Idea of Perfection* (1999) is about the ideological clash that occurs when a Sydney museum curator goes to rural NSW to save an old bridge. *Eucalyptus* (1998), by Murray Bail, is a fairy tale set among iconic gum trees. It was going to be a Russell Crowe–Nicole Kidman movie, then it wasn't, then it was, then it wasn't… *The Harp in the South* (1948), by Ruth Park, is an account of an impoverished family's life in Surry Hills when the suburb was a crowded slum.

David Malouf, a Lebanese-Australian who is one of Queensland's most recognised writers, is responsible for evocative, often bitter tales of Brisbane boyhood, including *Johnno* (1975).

His Gold Coast novel, *Fly Away Peter* (1982), tells the story of a returned soldier struggling to come to terms with ordinary life. His 2006 short story collection, *Every Move You Make,* looks at the lives of people from northern Queensland and across the continent.

Thea Astley's work includes *Hunting the Wild Pineapple* (1979), set in the rainforests of northern Queensland. More recently, Brissie bad boy John Birmingham has enjoyed success, notably with *He Died with a Felafel in his Hand* (1994), later made into a film by Richard Lowenstein.

The Chaser (www.chaser .com.au), like America's Onion, utilises 'mocku-mentary' to undermine mass culture. Warning: 'Not recommended in places that restrict freedom of speech, or Queensland.'

Australia's best-known Aboriginal poet and writer is Oodgeroo Noonuccal (Kath Walker), who was born on North Stradbroke Island in 1920. Herb Wharton, an Aboriginal author from Cunnamulla, has written a series of novels and short stories about the lives of the Murri stockmen, including *Unbranded* (1992) and *Cattle Camp* (1994).

Most of the big issues in Aboriginal Australia are covered in contemporary Aboriginal writing. James Miller's *Koori: A Will to Win* (1985), examines the history of European settlement in Australia from a Koori perspective; *My Place* (1987), Sally Morgan's prize-winning autobiography, traces her discovery of her Aboriginal heritage; *The Fringe Dwellers* (1961), by Nene Gare, describes what it's like to be an Aborigine growing up in white society; and Sam Watson's *The Kadaitcha Sung* (1990) combines science fiction, crime fiction, fantasy, social analysis and historical references, and enjoys a cult following.

Music

In the East Coast capitals and touristy locales, there are plenty of emcees, DJs and bedroom boffins producing hip-hop, house, techno, drum 'n' bass, breaks, ambient, electro and trance. Melbourne's Avalanches blend hip-hop, sampledelica, breaks, disco, funk and sweaty live performances. Melbourne also boasts a lineage of experimental 'sound design', with leading practitioners including Philip Brophy, Ollie Olsen and David Thrussell.

Melbourne's pub-rock scene in the late '80s/early '90s was superlative, throwing up such true originals as the scarifying Birthday Party, starring Nick ('the Stripper') Cave as a full-blown madman.

Jammed (2007) is a thriller that takes an unflinching look at sex-trafficking in Melbourne. It generated a fair bit controversy both in and out of the film world.

More sedate Melbourne-based artists include troubadours Paul Kelly and Stephen Cummings, South Australian expat Dave Graney (the self-styled King of Pop), grunge godfather Kim Salmon and folksy Lisa Miller. Jet, Melbourne's answer to the Strokes, sells millions of songs and indie-rocker band Augie March picks up prizes between hits.

The 'Singing Budgie' herself, Kylie Minogue, no longer lives here. Neither does Mr Cave. Nor do gloom-rock merchants, the violin-led Dirty Three.

In the late 1970s Sydney could also claim a ripper pub-rock scene, when incendiary bands such as Radio Birdman and the Screaming Tribesmen trod the boards. These days clubs and DJs rule, although there's still some solid rock and pop action to be found. Local performers include long-time faves the Whitlams, whose Sydney-centric tunes have converted into Australia-wide acclaim, and Faker, a popular alt-rock band. Newcastle spawned today's chart-topping rock band Silverchair back in 1992 when they were first called Innocent Criminals.

Avant-jazz trio The Necks were originally based in Sydney, but have since dispersed overseas; their hypnotic, glacial pieces take their sweet time to unfurl and are utterly compelling.

Queensland has produced some outstanding indigenous musicians, including Christine Anu, a Torres Strait Islander from Cairns who blends Creole-style rap, Islander chants and traditional languages with English. Other regional artists include Torres Strait Islander Rita Mills and Maroochy Barambah of the Sunshine Coast.

Brisbane's pub-rock scene from the late '70s produced one of Australia's greatest bands, the rowdy Saints, who went on to bigger things in Sydney and London. More recently, Powderfinger has played a dominant role in the music industry. Alternative Queensland bands with loyal followings include Regurgitator and Custard.

Melbourne, Sydney and Brisbane have vibrant classical scenes but most of the state orchestras tour the East Coast's major centres, too.

Visual Arts

In the 1880s a group of young artists developed the first distinctively Australian style of watercolour painting, capturing the unique qualities of Australian life and the bush. Their work is generally referred to as the Heidelberg School. In Sydney a contemporary movement worked at Sirius Cove.

Both groups were influenced by the French plein-air painters, whose practice of working outdoors to capture the effects of natural light led directly to Impressionism. The main artists were Tom Roberts, Arthur Streeton, Frederick McCubbin, Louis Abrahams, Charles Conder, Julian Ashton and, later, Walter Withers.

In the 1940s, under the patronage of John and Sunday Reed in suburban Melbourne, a new generation of artists (the Heide movement) redefined the direction of Australian art, including some of Australia's most famous contemporary artists, such as Sir Sidney Nolan and Heide associate Arthur Boyd.

More recently the work of painters such as Fred Williams, John Olsen and Brett Whiteley has made an international impression. Whiteley is certainly Sydney's (and probably Australia's) best-known modern artist; he died in 1992. Other notable Sydney artists include Ian Fairweather, Keith Looby, Ian Grant and Judy Cassab. Sydney painter Del Kathryn Barton won the 2008 Archibald prize, Australia's most prestigious art award. Administered by the Art Gallery of New South Wales in Sydney, this annual prize for portraiture stirs up strong emotions. (Let's put it this way: the people's choice award and the juried award seldom agree.)

Contemporary Melbourne artists such as Ricky Swallow, Bill Henson, Nick Mangan, Juan Ford and Christian Capurro explore the relationship between reality and representation across multiple disciplines. Patricia Piccinini takes cues from the technological world, exploring ethical dilemmas with often disturbing results.

Queensland is a rich centre of traditional and contemporary Aboriginal art. Judy Watson and Gordon Bennett have both won the Moët & Chandon Prize for contemporary artists.

Government-funded Triple J is a national radio station of the ABC (Australia Broadcasting Corporation) that emphasizes new and Australian music. Although its ratings pale compared to screaming commercial stations, its influence on Oz pop music is huge.

The best-selling album ever in Australia is Shania Twain's *Come on Over*, having been bought by over 5% of Australians since it was released in 1997. Meaningful tracks include *Don't Be Stupid* and *Honey I'm Home*.

The surreal, tragicomic work of photographer and filmmaker Tracey Moffatt seeks to understand Aboriginality via a white media lens, and is well worth seeking out.

Theatre & Dance

Melbourne's main theatre troupe, the **Melbourne Theatre Company** (p98), is Australia's oldest, staging around a dozen annual performances at the Victorian Arts Centre (p98). These include works by the leading contemporary Australian playwright, Sydney-based David Williamson, whose dissection of middle-class rituals began in 1971 with *The Removalists* and *Don's Party*. The city has many more cultural institutions,

Sydney has a vibrant performing arts scene and a glittery venue (the Opera House) and some glittery names to give it flash. The **Sydney Theatre Company** (p212) includes Cate Blanchett among its artistic directors.

Australia's national ballet company, the **Australian Ballet** (www.australianballet .com.au), is among the world's finest. It tours locally and internationally and has a diverse repertoire bolstered by renowned guest choreographers.

Australia's innovative modern-dance scene is typified by the **Sydney Dance Company** (www.sydneydance.com) and Melbourne's **Chunky Move** (www.chunkymove.com).

'Australia's national ballet company, the Australian Ballet... is among the world's finest.'

Food & Drink Matthew Evans

Born in convict poverty and raised on a diet heavily influenced by Great Britain, Australian cuisine has come a long way. Australia is now one of the most dynamic places in the world to have a feed, thanks to immigration and a public willing to give anything new and better a go. Sydney and Melbourne can claim to be destinations worthy of touring gourmands from New York to Paris. More importantly, real people, including travellers, feel the effects of a blossoming food culture across the country.

This, however, has only been because of recent history. Australia, despite its world-class dining opportunities, doesn't live to eat. As a nation we're new to the world of good food, of being mesmerised by the latest TV chef, devouring cookbooks and subscribing to foodie magazines in the hundreds of thousands. The eating along the East Coast has never been better, and it's improving by the day. Take a few bites out of the food culture of Byron Bay and its hinterlands and you'll be hooked.

Yet, despite our fascination with tucker, at heart we're still mostly a nation of simple eaters, with the majority of Australians still novices in anything beyond meat and three veg. This is changing, though, as the influx of immigrants (and their cuisine) has found locals trying (and liking) everything from lassi to laksa. This passionate minority has led to a rise in dining standards, better availability of produce and a frenetic buzz about food in general. It's no wonder Australian chefs, cookbooks and food writers are so sought after overseas.

We've coined our own phrase, Modern Australian, to describe our cuisine. If it's a melange of East and West, it's Modern Australian. If it's not authentically French or Italian, it's Modern Australian – our attempt to classify the unclassifiable. Cuisine doesn't alter between regions, but some influences are obvious, such as the Greek migration to Sydney.

Dishes aren't usually too fussy, the flavours often bold and interesting. Spicing ranges from gentle to extreme, coffee is great (though it still reaches its greatest heights in the cities), and the meats are tender, full flavoured and usually reasonably priced.

STAPLES & SPECIALITIES

The East Coast's best food comes from the sea. Nothing compares to this region's seafood, harnessed from some of the purest waters you'll find anywhere, and usually cooked with care.

Connoisseurs prize Sydney rock oysters (a species living along the New South Wales coast) and sea scallops from Queensland. Rock lobsters are fantastic and fantastically expensive, and mud crabs, despite the name, are a sweet delicacy. Another odd-sounding delicacy is 'bugs' – like shovel-nosed lobsters without a lobster's price tag; try the Balmain and Moreton Bay varieties. Yabbies, the smaller cousins of crayfish, can be found throughout the southeast. The prawns are incredible, particularly the sweet school prawns or the eastern king (Yamba) prawns found along northern NSW.

Add to that countless wild fish species and we've got one of the greatest bounties on earth. In fact, the Sydney Fish Market (p191) trades in several hundred species of seafood every day, second only to Tokyo.

Despite their greatness, not many actual dishes can truly lay claim to being uniquely Australian. Even the humble 'pav' (pavlova), the meringue dessert with cream and passionfruit, may be from New Zealand. Ditto for lamingtons (large cubes of cake dipped in chocolate and rolled in desiccated coconut).

Matthew Evans was originally a chef before crossing to the dark side as food writer and restaurant critic. After five years as chief reviewer for The Sydney Morning Herald, he has opted out, growing chooks and making Berkshire pork sausages in foodies paradise, Tasmania.

The Cook's Companion by Stephanie Alexander is Australia's single-volume answer to Delia Smith. If it's in here, most Australians have probably seen it or eaten it.

For a comprehensive list of markets where you can buy the best East Coast produce, see the Australian Farmers' Markets Association website (www.farmersmarkets .org.au).

AVOIDING PISS ON THE EAST COAST

Slang for beer, piss is what you get when you order beer on the East Coast. Sadly, all too often it's the near-literal truth. Bland, nearly frozen lagers – the Carltons, VBs, XXXXs and Toohey's et al of the world – are too common in the pubs from Cairns to Melbourne. But there is hope. Brewers of quality beer, or craft beers as it's referred to in the industry, are appearing and in many pubs you'll find at least one or two excellent choices, including the following:

■ **James Squire** – a Sydney brewer with wide distribution and a range of several craft beers, the IPA is superb.

■ **St Arnou** – a micro-micro brewery in NSW, it has an excellent Belgian-style white beer, St Cloud.

■ **Northern Rivers Brewing Co** – a full range of craft beers from a small brewery near Byron Bay, Ruby Raspberry is a popular postbeach treat

■ **Mountain Goat** – brewed right in the Melbourne suburb of Richmond, the Hightale Ale is an English-style ale that makes a perfect pint

■ **Piss** – a beer from Victoria that takes the piss out of piss… (once you're past the puns, it's an excellent, rich lager)

Finally, it's not East Coast–based, but Coopers of Adelaide makes excellent beers that are probably the easiest to find among Australia's quality brews.

Anything another country does, Australia does, too. Vietnamese, Indian, Fijian, Italian – it doesn't matter where it's from, there's an expat community and interested locals desperate to cook and eat it. Dig deep enough, and you'll find Jamaicans using scotch bonnet peppers and Tunisians making *tagine*. And you'll usually find their houses are the favourite haunts of their locally raised friends. Yum cha (the classic southern Chinese dumpling feast) has found huge popularity with urban locals in recent years, particularly on weekends.

A great website for Australian food and wine is www.campionandcurtis .com. It's written by two talented writers who've also trained as chefs. It has reviews, awards and much more.

Almost everything we eat from the land (as opposed to the sea) was introduced. The fact that the country is huge (similar in size to continental USA) and varies so much in climate, from the tropical north to the temperate south, means that there's an enormous variety of produce on offer.

In summer, mangoes are so plentiful that Queenslanders actually get sick of them. Lamb from Victoria's lush Gippsland is highly prized. And there's a brilliant farmhouse cheese movement, hampered by the fact that all the milk must be pasteurised (unlike in Italy and France, home of the world's best cheeses). Despite that, the results can be great.

DRINKS

The closest region to Sydney, the Hunter Valley (p231) first had vines in the 1830s, and does a lively unwooded Semillon that is best aged. Further inland, there's Canberra, Cowra, Orange and Mudgee. Just out of Melbourne are the Mornington (p104) and Bellarine Peninsulas, Mt Macedon and the Yarra Valley. There's even a wine region in Queensland, though not all of it is good.

Plenty of good wine comes from big producers with economies of scale on their side. However, the most interesting wines are usually made by small wineries where you pay a premium; the gamble means the payoff in terms of flavour is often greater. Much of the cost of wine (nearly 42%) is due to a high taxing programme imposed by the Australian government.

In terms of coffee, Australia is leaping ahead, with Italian-style espresso machines in virtually every café, boutique roasters all the rage and, in urban areas, the qualified *barista* (coffee maker) virtually the norm. Expect the best coffee in Melbourne, decent stuff in most other cities, and a chance of good coffee in many rural areas. Melbourne's café scene rivals the most vibrant in the world; the best way to immerse yourself is by wandering the city centre's café-lined lanes.

Fresh fruit juice is extremely popular along the coast and a healthy way to beat the heat. Fresh-fruit-juice bars that specialise in all sorts of yummy concoctions pepper the landscape, but you can also get good versions at cafés and ice-cream stores.

CELEBRATIONS

Celebrating in the Australian manner often includes equal amounts of food and alcohol. A birthday could well be a barbecue (barbie) of steak (or prawns), washed down with a beverage or two. Weddings are usually a big slap-up dinner, though the food is often far from memorable. Christenings are more sober, mostly offering home-baked biscuits and a cup of tea.

Many regions and cities now hold food festivals. Melbourne, for instance, has a month-long food and wine festival in March (p91). There are harvest festivals in wine regions, and various communities hold annual events.

For many an event, especially in the warmer months, Australians fill the car with an Esky (an insulated ice chest, to keep everything cool), folding tables and chairs, a cricket set or a footy, and head off for a barbie by the lake/river/beach. If there's a total fire ban (which occurs increasingly each summer), the food is precooked and the barbie becomes more of a picnic, but the essence remains the same.

Christmas often finds the more traditional (in a European sense) baked dinner being replaced by a barbecue, full of seafood and quality steak, in a response to the warm weather. Prawn prices skyrocket, chicken may be eaten with champagne at breakfast, and the main meal is usually in the afternoon, after a swim and before a really good, long siesta.

Various ethnic minorities have their own celebrations. Tongans love an *umu*, where fish and vegetables are buried in an earthen pit and covered with coals; Greeks may hold a spit barbecue; and Chinese go off during their annual Spring Festival (Chinese New Year) every January or February (it changes with the lunar calendar).

WHERE TO EAT & DRINK

Oftentimes the best value in cities can be found in simple cafés. What's better is that newer ones are often run by talented young chefs on their way up in the culinary world. Inventive and trend-setting, you can enjoy their fare for a modest fare – at least until the first cookbook comes out.

Typically, a restaurant meal along the East Coast is a relaxed affair. It may take 15 minutes to order, another 15 before the first course arrives, and maybe half an hour between entrées and mains. The upside of this is that any table you've booked in a restaurant is yours for the night, unless you're told otherwise. So sit, linger and live life in the slow lane.

Competitively priced places to eat are clubs or pubs with counter meals. Returned Servicemen's League (RSL) clubs are prolific along the coast, and while the décor can be pretty chintzy, the tucker is normally excellent.

The other species of club you're bound to cross is the Surf Life Saving Club. Most coastal towns have at least one, sometimes up to three. They're similar to RSL clubs, but many now compete with finer restaurants, and their bistros stock inventive fare. Additionally, they're almost always perched on the beachfront so the views tend to be worth a visit alone.

Other clubs to look for are bowls clubs, Irish clubs and sports clubs.

Victoria Bitter (aka VB) is Australia's best-selling beer, even in Queensland, once the domain of strong XXXX beer. Despite the name, it's really just another watery lager and is owned by Foster's.

The *Australian Wine Annual* by Jeremy Oliver is a must-read for those who want the lowdown tipple by tipple, vineyard by vineyard.

Does the winelist in that simple café seem a little too slick? It probably is. Huge liquor merchants such as Foster's supply many eateries with all their wines (most owned or imported by Fosters) and toss in slick, generic winelists.

Solo diners find that cafés and noodle bars are welcoming; good fine-dining restaurants often treat you like a star but, sadly, some midrange places may still make you feel a little ill at ease.

Most restaurants open around noon for lunch and from 6pm or 7pm for dinner. Australians usually eat lunch shortly after noon, and dinner bookings are usually made for 7.30pm or 8pm, though in major cities some restaurants stay open past 10pm.

Quick Eats

There's not a huge culture of street vending, though you may find a pie or coffee cart in some places. Most quick eats traditionally come from a milk bar, which serves old-fashioned hamburgers (with bacon, egg, pineapple and beetroot if you want) and other takeaway foods. Fish and chips is still hugely popular, most often made from a form of shark (often called flake; don't worry, it can be delicious) dipped in heavy batter, and eaten at the beach on a Friday night.

The Australian Vegetarian Society's website (www.veg-soc.org) lists a number of vegie-friendly places to eat around the country.

American-style fast food has taken over recently, though many Aussies still love a meat pie, often from a milk bar, but also from bakeries, kiosks and some cafés. If you're at an Aussie Rules football match, a beer, a meat pie and a bag of hot chips are as compulsory as wearing your team's colours.

Pizza has become one of the most popular fast foods; most pizzas that are home-delivered are of the American style (thick and with lots of toppings) rather than Italian style. That said, more and more wood-fired oven, thin Neapolitan-style pizza can be found, even in country towns. In the city, Roman-style pizza (buy it by the slice) is becoming more popular, but you can't usually buy the other pizza in anything but whole rounds.

There are some really dodgy mass-produced takeaway foods, bought mostly by famished teenage boys, including the dim sim (a bastardisation of the dim sum dumplings from China) and the Chiko Roll (opposite).

VEGETARIANS & VEGANS

You're in luck. Most cities have substantial numbers of local vegetarians, which means you're well catered for. Cafés seem to always have vegetarian options, and some of our best restaurants have complete vegetarian menus. Take care with risotto and soups, though, as meat stock is often used.

Vegans will find the going much tougher, but local Hare Krishna restaurants or Buddhist temples often provide relief, and there are usually dishes that are vegan-adaptable at restaurants.

EATING WITH KIDS

Dining with children is relatively easy. Avoid the flashiest places and children are generally welcomed, particularly at Chinese, Greek or Italian restaurants. Kids are usually more than welcome at cafés; bistros and clubs often see families dining early. Many fine-dining restaurants don't welcome small children (assuming they're all ill-behaved).

The number of Australian organic food producers is growing daily; many are based on the East Coast. The Organic Federation of Australia (www.ofa.org .au) has details.

Most places that do welcome children don't have separate kids' menus, and those that do usually offer everything straight from the deep fryer – crumbed chicken and chips, that kind of thing. It can be better to find something on the menu (say a pasta or salad) and have the kitchen adapt it slightly to your children's needs.

The best news for travelling families, weather permitting, is that there are plenty of free or coin-operated barbecues in parks. Beware of weekends and public holidays when fierce battles can erupt over who is next in line for the barbecue.

See p482 for more information about travelling with children.

DOS AND DON'TS

Do...

■ show up for restaurant dinner reservations on time. Not only may your table be given to someone else, staggered bookings are designed to make the experience more seamless.

■ take a small gift, and/or a bottle of wine to dinner parties.

■ offer to wash up or help clear the table after a meal at a friend's house.

■ ring or send a note (even an email) the day or so after a dinner party, unless the friends are so close you feel it unnecessary. Even then, thank them the very next time you speak.

■ offer to take meat and/or a salad to a barbecue. At the traditional Aussie barbie for a big group, each family is expected to bring part or all of their own tucker.

■ shout your group to drinks on arrival at the pub.

■ tip (up to 15%) for good service, when in a big group or if your kids have gone crazy and trashed the dining room.

Don't...

■ freak out when the waiter in a restaurant attempts to 'lap' your serviette (napkin) by laying it over your crotch. It's considered to be the height of service. If you don't want them doing this, place your serviette on your lap before they get a chance.

■ ever accept a shout unless you intend to make your shout soon after.

■ expect a date to pay for you. It's quite common among younger people for a woman to pay her own way.

■ expect servile or obsequious service. Professional waiters are intelligent, caring equals whose disdain can perfectly match any diner's attempt at contempt.

■ ever tip bad service.

HABITS & CUSTOMS

At the table, it's good manners to use British knife-and-fork skills, keeping the fork in the left hand, tines down, and the knife in the right, though Americans may be forgiven for using their fork like a shovel. Talking with your mouth full is considered uncouth, and fingers should only be used for food that can't be tackled another way.

'Shouting' is a revered custom where people rotate paying for a round of drinks. Just don't leave before it's your turn to buy! At a toast, everyone should touch glasses.

Australians like to linger a bit over coffee. They like to linger a really long time while drinking beer. And they tend to take quite a bit of time if they're out to dinner (as opposed to having takeaway).

Smoking is banned in most eateries in the nation, so sit outside if you love to puff. And never smoke in someone's house unless you ask first. Even then it's usual to smoke outside.

EAT YOUR WORDS

Australians love to shorten everything, including people's names, so expect many other words to be abbreviated. Some words you might hear:

barbie – a barbecue, where (traditionally) smoke and overcooked meat are matched with lashings of coleslaw, potato salad and beer

Chiko Roll – a fascinating, large spring roll-like pastry for sale in takeaway shops. Best used as an item of self-defence rather than eaten

Esky – an insulated ice chest to hold your *tinnies*, before you transfer them to your *tinny holder*.

middy – a midsized glass of beer (NSW)

pav – pavlova, the meringue dessert topped with cream, passionfruit and kiwifruit or other fresh fruit

pot – a medium glass of beer (Vic)

rat coffin – a meat pie; the traditional ones are made with minced beef. Compulsory eating (with White Crow tomato sauce) at footy matches.

sanger/sando – a sandwich

schooner – a big glass of beer (NSW), but not as big as a pint

snags – sausages (aka surprise bags)

snot block – a vanilla slice

Tim Tam – a commercial chocolate biscuit that lies close to the heart of most Australians. Best consumed as a Tim Tam shooter, where two diagonally opposite corners of the rectangular biscuit are nibbled off, and a hot drink (tea is the true aficionado's favourite) is sucked through the fast-melting biscuit. Ugly but good.

tinny – usually refers to a can of beer, but could also be the small boat you go fishing for mud crabs in (and you'd take a few *tinnies* in your *tinny*, in that case).

tinny holder – insulating material that you use to keep the *tinny* ice cold, nothing to do with a boat

Environment Tim Flannery

Australia's plants and animals are just about the closest things to alien life you are likely to encounter on Earth. That's because Australia has been isolated from the other continents for a very long time – at least 45 million years. The other habitable continents have been able to exchange various species at different times because they've been linked by land. Just 15,000 years ago it was possible to walk from the southern tip of Africa right through Asia and the Americas to Tierra del Fuego. Not to Australia, however. Its birds, mammals, reptiles and plants have taken their own separate and very different evolutionary journey, and the result today is the world's most distinct – and one of its most diverse – natural realms.

The first naturalists to investigate Australia were astonished by what they found. Here the swans were black – to Europeans this was a metaphor for the impossible – while it was discovered that mammals such as the platypus and echidna lay eggs. It really was an upside-down world, where many of the larger animals hopped, where each year the trees shed their bark rather than their leaves, and where the 'pears' were made of wood.

If you are visiting Australia for a short time, you might need to go out of your way to experience some of the richness of the environment. Australia is a subtle place, and some of the natural environment – especially around the cities – has been damaged or replaced by trees and creatures from Europe. Places such as Sydney, however, have preserved extraordinary fragments of their original environment that are relatively easy to access. Before you enjoy them though, it's worthwhile understanding the basics about how nature operates in Australia. There's nowhere like Australia, and once you have an insight into its origins and natural rhythms, you will appreciate the place so much more.

A UNIQUE ENVIRONMENT

There are two really big factors that go a long way towards explaining nature in Australia: its soils and its climate. Both are unique. Australian soils are the more subtle and difficult to notice of the two, but they have been fundamental in shaping life here.

In recent geological times, on other continents processes such as volcanism, mountain building and glacial activity have been busy creating new soil – just think of the glacier-derived soils of North America, north Asia and Europe. They feed the world today, and were made by glaciers grinding up rock of differing chemical composition over the last two million years. The rich soils of India and parts of South America were made by rivers eroding mountains, while Java in Indonesia owes its extraordinary richness to volcanoes.

All of these soil-forming processes have been almost absent from Australia in more recent times. Only volcanoes have made a contribution, and they cover less than 2% of the continent's land area. In fact, for the last 90 million years, beginning deep in the age of dinosaurs, Australia has been geologically comatose. It was too flat, warm and dry to attract glaciers; its crust was too ancient and thick to be punctured by volcanoes or folded into mountains.

Under such conditions no new soil is created and the old soil is leached of all its goodness by the rain, and is blown and washed away. Even if just 30cm of rain falls each year, that adds up to a column of water 30 million km high passing through the soil over 100 million years, and that can do a great

Tim Flannery is one of Australia's leading thinkers and writers. A resident of Adelaide, he was the recipient of the Australian of the Year Award in 2007.

The first platypus sent to England for study was dismissed as a hoax. Evidently a critter with a duck's bill and a beaver's tail that also laid eggs yet suckled its young was considered an impossibility.

In *The Weather Makers: How Man Is Changing the Climate and What It Means for Life on Earth*, Tim Flannery shows how humans are both causing global warming and can stop it.

THE OVERSUBSCRIBED EAST COAST ENVIRONMENT *Ryan Ver Berkmoes*

When a $15.7 million house in Byron Bay is bought purely as a tear-down, you know things may be out of hand. Indeed all along the East Coast the desire to be part of this beautiful place is fuelling growth that could well obviate the very appeal that's so attractive. From Melbourne to Cairns, once sleepy coastal towns are dealing with newfound popularity, with locals quick to promise that their town won't become another overdeveloped strip like the hell that is Surfer's Paradise. Still you see signs everywhere. Melbourne is creeping up the southeast coast of Victoria, Sydneysiders are willing to drive for hours to nab a beach cottage, and few timeshare sellers ever go hungry on the Gold or Sunshine Coasts.

How this rapid growth will play out won't be known for decades. Some places have the red carpet out for the money and jobs made possible by development. Other places like Byron Bay have elected left-of-centre councils that try to squelch all development. But this only results in multi-million-dollar tear-downs as the addictive lure of the East Coast continues.

---

deal of leaching! Almost all of Australia's mountain ranges are more than 90 million years old, so you will see a lot of sand here, and a lot of country where the rocky 'bones' of the land are sticking up through the soil. It is an old, infertile landscape, and life in Australia has been adapting to these conditions for aeons.

Australia's misfortune in respect to soils is echoed in its climate. In most parts of the world outside the wet tropics, life responds to the rhythm of the seasons – summer to winter, or wet to dry. Most of Australia experiences seasons – sometimes very extreme ones – yet life does not respond solely to them. This can clearly be seen by the fact that although there's plenty of snow and cold country in Australia, there are almost no trees that shed their leaves in winter, nor do any Australian animals hibernate. Instead there is a far more potent climatic force that Australian life must obey: El Niño.

The cycle of flood and drought that El Niño brings to Australia is profound. Our rivers – even the mighty Murray River, the nation's largest river, which runs through the southeast – can be miles wide one year, yet you can literally step over its flow the next. This is the power of El Niño, and its effect, when combined with Australia's poor soils, manifests itself compellingly.

Australian icon Steve Irwin died while shooting Ocean's Deadliest, *a 2007 documentary he produced with Philippe Cousteau, Jr. It features all sorts of deadly critters from Queensland's waters but not the ray that stung Irwin.*

Birds

Because of the lack of climate stability, relatively few of Australia's birds are seasonal breeders, and few migrate. Instead, they breed when the rain comes, and a large percentage are nomads, following the rain across the breadth of the continent.

So challenging are conditions in Australia that its birds have developed some extraordinary habits. In your travels you're likely to come across kookaburras, magpies and blue wrens, to name just a few. These birds have developed a breeding system called 'helpers at the nest'. The helpers are the young adult birds of previous breedings, which stay with their parents to help bring up the new chicks. Just why they should do this was a mystery, until experts realised that conditions in Australia can be so harsh that more than two adult birds are needed to help feed the nestlings. This pattern of breeding is very rare in places like Asia, Europe and North America, but it is common in many Australian bird species.

The Australia Bush Heritage Fund (www .bushheritage.asn.au) and the Australian Wildlife Conservancy (www .australianwildlife.org) are two groups dedicated to preserving Australia's wildlife and habitat.

Marsupials

Australia is, of course, famous as the home of the kangaroo (roo) and other marsupials. Unless you visit a wildlife park, such creatures are not easy to come across as most are nocturnal. Their lifestyles are exquisitely attuned to Australia's harsh conditions. Have you ever wondered why kangaroos, alone among the world's larger mammals, hop? It turns out that hopping is the most efficient way of getting about at medium speeds. This is because the energy of the bounce is stored in the tendons of the legs – much like in a pogo stick – while the intestines bounce up and down like a piston, emptying and filling the lungs without needing to activate the chest muscles. When you travel long distances across a sparse landscape to find meagre feed, such efficiency is a must.

Marsupials are so energy-efficient that their nutritional requirements are one-fifth less than that of equivalent-sized placental mammals (everything from bats to rats, whales and ourselves). However, some marsupials have taken energy efficiency much further. If you visit a wildlife park or zoo you might notice that faraway look in a koala's eyes. It seems as if nobody is home – and this in fact is near the truth. Several years ago biologists announced that koalas are the only living creatures that have brains that don't take up the capacity of their skulls. Instead they have a shrivelled walnut-sized brain that rattles around in a fluid-filled cranium. Other researchers have contested this finding, however, pointing out that the brains of the koalas examined for the study may have shrunk because these organs are so soft. Whether soft-brained or empty-headed, there is no doubt that the koala is not the Einstein of the animal world, and it is now believed that the koala has sacrificed its brain to energy efficiency. Brains cost a lot to run – our brains typically weigh only 2% of our body weight, but use 20% of the energy we consume. Koalas eat gum leaves, which are so toxic to their systems that koalas use 20% of their energy just detoxifying this food. This leaves little energy for brain function, and living in the tree tops where there are so few predators means that they can get by with few wits at all.

The peculiar constraints of the Australian environment have not made every creature dumb. The koala's nearest relative, the wombat (of which there are three species), has a large brain compared to other marsupials. Wombats live in complex burrows and can weigh up to 35kg, making them the largest herbivorous burrowers on Earth. Because their burrows are effectively air-conditioned (it's far cooler underground), they have the neat trick of turning down their metabolic activity when they are in residence. One physiologist, who studied their thyroid hormones, found that biological activity ceased to such an extent in sleeping wombats that, from a hormonal point of view, they appeared to be dead! Wombats can remain underground for a week at a time, and can get by on just one-third of the food needed by a sheep of equivalent size, yet Australian farmers still keep sheep! At the moment farming wombats isn't possible; the largest of the wombat species, the northern hairy-nose, is one of the world's rarest creatures, with only around 100 surviving in a remote nature reserve in central Queensland.

Among the more common marsupials you might catch a glimpse of in the national parks around Australia's major cities are the species of *Antechinus*. These nocturnal, rat-sized creatures lead an extraordinary life. The males live for just 11 months, the first 10 of which consist of a concentrated burst of eating and growing. Like teenage males, the day comes when their minds turn to sex, and in the *Antechinus* this becomes an obsession. As they embark on their quest for females they forget to eat and sleep. Instead they gather in logs and woo passing females by serenading them with squeaks. By the end of August – just two weeks after they reach 'puberty' – every male is dead, exhausted by sex and by carrying around swollen testes. This extraordinary life history may also have evolved in response to Australia's trying environmental conditions. It seems likely that if the males survived mating, they would compete with

Koalas make cats look like omnivores when it comes to being finicky eaters. They may reject more than 20 or 30 types of eucalyptus tree before deciding one is just right for a snack.

Chasing Kangaroos: A Continent, a Scientist, and a Search for the World's Most Extraordinary Creature is Tim Flannery's 2007 ode to Australia's icon.

During the Pleistocene period ancestors of the kangaroo stood 3m tall.

the females as they tried to find enough food to feed their growing young. Basically, *Antechinus* dads are disposable. They do better for *Antechinus* posterity if they go down in a testosterone-fuelled blaze of glory.

The Great Barrier Reef is considered one of the world's most endangered treasures due to rising ocean temperatures that cause bleaching. Other threats include overfishing and agricultural pollutant run-offs from land.

One thing you will see lots of in Australia are reptiles. Snakes are abundant, here and they include some of the most venomous species known. Where the opportunities for them to feed are few and far between, it's best not to give your prey a second chance – the venom is potent for a reason! Around Sydney and other parts of Australia you are far more likely to encounter a harmless python than a dangerously venomous species. Snakes will usually leave you alone if you don't fool with them. Observe, back quietly away and don't panic, and most of the time you'll be OK.

Some visitors mistake lizards for snakes, and indeed some Australian lizards look bizarre. One of the more abundant species is the sleepy lizard.

MAKING A POSITIVE CONTRIBUTION TO THE REEF *Alan Murphy*

The Great Barrier Reef is incredibly fragile and it's worth taking some time to educate yourself on responsible practices while you're here. The following are a few of the more important sustainable practices, but this is by no means an exhaustive list – see the websites later for more comprehensive information.

■ Whether on an island or a boat, take all litter with you – even biodegradable material like apple cores – and dispose of it back on the mainland.

■ Remember that it is a legal offence to damage or remove coral in the marine park.

■ Don't touch or harass marine animals and be aware that if you touch or walk on coral you'll damage it (it can also create some nasty cuts). Never rest or stand on coral.

■ If you have a boat be aware of the rules in relation to anchoring around the reef, including 'no anchoring areas'. Be very careful not to damage coral when you let down the anchor.

■ If you're diving, check that you are weighted correctly before entering the water and get your buoyancy control well away from the reef. Ensure that equipment such as secondary regulators and gauges aren't dragging over the reef.

■ If you're snorkelling (and especially if you are a beginner) practice your technique away from coral until you've mastered control in the water.

■ Watch where your fins are – try not to stir up sediment or disturb coral.

■ Do not enter the water near a dugong, including when swimming or diving.

■ Note that there are limits on the amount and types of shells that you can collect.

If you're a regular user of the reef you can be part of a program that makes a positive contribution towards its future survival. BleachWatch is a community initiative of the Great Barrier Reef Marine Park Authority and involves regular users of the reef monitoring and reporting signs of coral bleaching. If you'd like to get involved, email bleachwatch@gbrmpa.gov.au.

If you want a deeper understanding of the issues facing the Reef, as well as information on minimising your impact, try clicking on the following:

■ Great Barrier Reef Marine Park Authority (www.gbrmpa.gov.au)

■ Reef Teach (www.reefteach.com.au)

■ Cooperative Research Centre for the Great Barrier Reef World Heritage Area (www.reef.crc.org.au)

■ Australian Conservation Foundation (www.acfonline.org.au)

■ Coral Reef Alliance (www.coralreefalliance.org)

■ Australian Research Centre (ARC) Centre of Excellence for Coral Reef Studies (www.coralcoe .org.au)

These creatures, which are found throughout the southern arid region, look like animated pine cones. They are the Australian equivalent of tortoises, and are harmless. Other lizards are much larger. Unless you visit the Indonesian island of Komodo you will not see a larger lizard than the desert-dwelling perentie. These beautiful creatures, with their leopardlike blotches, can grow to more than 2m long, and are efficient predators of introduced rabbits, feral cats and the like.

If you are very lucky, you might see a honey possum. This tiny marsupial is an enigma. Somehow it gets all of its dietary requirements from nectar and pollen. No one, though, knows why the males have sperm larger even than those of the blue whale, or why their testes are so massive. Were humans as well endowed, men would be walking around with the equivalent of a 4kg bag of potatoes between their legs!

Plants

Australia's plants can be irresistibly fascinating. The best flowers grow on the arid and monotonous sand plains, and the blaze of colour produced by the banksias and similar native plants can be dizzying. The sheer variety of flowers is amazing – the diversity of prolific flowering plants has long puzzled botanists. Again, Australia's poor soils seem to be the cause. The sand plain is about the poorest soil in Australia – it's almost pure quartz. This prevents any one fast-growing species from dominating. Instead, thousands of specialist plant species have learned to find a narrow niche, and so coexist. Some live at the foot of the metre-high sand dunes, some on top, some on an east-facing slope, some on the west and so on. Their flowers need to be striking in order to attract pollinators, for nutrients are so lacking in this sandy world that even insects such as bees are rare.

WATCHING WILDLIFE

Some regions of Australia offer unique opportunities to see wildlife.

For those intrigued by the diversity of tropical rainforests, Queensland's World Heritage sites are well worth visiting. Birds of paradise, cassowaries and a variety of other birds can be seen by day, while at night you can search for tree-kangaroos (yes, some kinds of kangaroo do live in the tree tops). In your nocturnal wanderings you are highly likely to see curious possums, some of which look like skunks, and other marsupials that today are restricted to a small area of northeast Queensland. Fossils from as far afield as western Queensland and southern Victoria indicate that such creatures were once widespread.

The fantastic diversity of Queensland's Great Barrier Reef is legendary, and a boat trip out to the reef from Cairns or Port Douglas is unforgettable.

Even if your visit extends only as far as Sydney, You'll still see plenty of Australian nature. The Sydney sandstone – which extends approximately 150km around the city – is one of the most diverse and spectacular regions in Australia. In springtime, spectacular red waratahs abound in the region's parks, while the woody pear (a relative of the waratah) that so confounded the early colonists can also be seen, alongside more than 1500 other species of flowering plants. Even in a Sydney backyard you're likely to see more reptile species (mostly skinks) than can be found in all of Great Britain – so keep an eye out!

NATIONAL & STATE PARKS

Australia has more than 500 national parks – nonurban protected wilderness areas of environmental or natural importance. Each state defines and runs its own national parks, but the principle is the same throughout Australia.

Cane toads are the rabbits of the reptile world. This introduced species crowds out native Aussie frogs and deprives the little battlers of food. Even when they've croaked, the toads are a menace: their bodies are poisonous.

Of the 700 varieties of eucalyptus, 95% are native to Australia. Think about that the next time you suck on a cough drop.

Hervey Bay in Queensland is a holiday spot for humpback whales who rest here by the thousands from August to early November before they continue on the long haul to Antarctica.

National parks include rainforests, vast tracts of empty outback, strips of coastal dune land and rugged mountain ranges.

Public access is encouraged as long as safety and conservation regulations are observed. In all parks you're asked to do nothing to damage or alter the natural environment. Camping grounds (often with toilets and showers), walking tracks and information centres are often provided for visitors. In most national parks there are restrictions on bringing in pets.

Some national parks are so isolated, rugged or uninviting that you wouldn't want to go there unless you were an experienced bushwalker or 4WD traveller. Other parks, however, are among Australia's major attractions.

State parks and state forests are other forms of nature reserves; owned by state governments they have fewer regulations than national parks. Although state forests can be logged, they are often recreational areas with camping grounds, walking trails and signposted forest drives. Some permit horses and dogs.

Websites for national parks authorities in each East Coast state are: New South Wales (www.nationalparks.nsw.gov.au), Queensland (www.epa.qld.gov.au/parks_and_forests) and Victoria (www.parkweb.vic.gov.au).

East Coast Australia Outdoors

Not only can you do a lot to get wet on the East Coast – whether from sweat, surf, sea or otherwise – but you have world-class places to do it. The Great Barrier Reef off Queensland is known worldwide for its diving, Sydney's harbour is a natural for yachties as are the Whitsundays in Queensland, the Blue Mountains team with climbers, huge swaths of the entire coast pound with surf breaks and it's all laced together by a myriad of walking and hiking trails through the bush.

BOATING

After surfing, boating is the number one activity in many East Coast towns. It has its own distinct marina culture that you'll find in towns with large ports and even its own migratory patterns: during the southern winter boaties and yachties migrate towards the warmer north. (Note: a yachtie can be a boatie but never the other way around, mate.)

There are plenty of opportunities for safe inshore boating and adventurous exploration on the high seas. Always check with the local coast guard and maritime authorities about regional conditions and take note of weather forecasts and warnings broadcast on marine radio.

> Charterguide Australia (www.charterguide.com.au) has comprehensive links to yachts and boats for rent plus aquatic tours of all kinds.

New South Wales

For its entire length the NSW coastline is kinked and wrinkled with bays, inlets and estuaries; ideal water for motorboats and yachts alike. Sydney Harbour is, of course, the jewel in the crown, and on weekends it's a swirling kaleidoscope of huge colourful sails moving to and fro. The simplest boating activity would have you resting your bum on a harbour cruise (p200), but this city's greatest natural asset is an ideal setting to learn to sail (p198). Just about every coastal town south and north of Sydney has a small harbour protecting a flotilla of yachts, and a boat ramp that bursts with activity on weekends. Some of the more popular boating areas include Port Stephens (p236), Myall Lakes National Park (p238) and Jervis Bay (p166). In the north, the broad Clarence River Valley (p265) has hundreds of kilometres of lazy waterways you can navigate in rented houseboats, while Ballina is good for boat hire (p268).

Queensland

Queensland's waters team with seamen and seawomen of all skills, with some of the most stunning sailing locations in the world. The postcard-perfect Whitsunday Islands (p407) are prime waters and can be accessed by charter craft based in Airlie Beach (p410).

You can also explore the Great Barrier Reef and some of the islands off the Far North Queensland coast on board a chartered boat or cruise from Cairns (p450) or Port Douglas (p465), where the yacht club offers free sailing on Wednesdays.

> 100 Magic Miles of the Great Barrier Reef – The Whitsunday Islands, by David Colfelt, is sometimes referred to as the bible of Whitsunday sailing. It contains charts with descriptions of all boat anchorages as well as articles on the islands, resorts, dive sites and marine life.

Victoria

Victoria's southeast coast boasts a couple of expansive bays and some pretty estuaries where boating is popular. City-based yachties tend to gravitate to the many sailing clubs around Port Phillip Bay. Other popular boating areas include the sprawling Gippsland Lakes (see Metung, p125), and the lovely Mallacoota Inlet (p137) near the NSW border.

BUSHWALKING

The East Coast of Australia has a smorgasbord of landscapes and coastline that are laced with amazing bushwalks of every length, standard and difficulty imaginable. Vast rural areas outside of the cities are preserved in an easily accessible network of coastal and hinterland national parks and reserves.

Bushwalking is enjoyed year-round along the East Coast. Summer, however, is the most popular time, particularly in the southeast. It is also the most dangerous period for the major hazard of bushfires (see p485 for more information). Regardless of what time of year it is and no matter how short the walk, you should always take plenty of drinking water. It can get very hot over summer, particularly from the Capricorn Coast north, so consider local conditions before you head out. Rescuing bushwalkers – especially travellers caught out woefully unprepared – is a common occupation for volunteers throughout the region. See the safety guidelines (opposite) for more information.

Many of NSW's national parks hold guided walks on the coast and in the bush. See www .nationalparks.nsw.gov for details. Or ask rangers at the parks.

New South Wales

Opportunities for bushwalking abound in coastal NSW, with a variety of standards, lengths and terrains. In Sydney, try the breathtaking (but hardly wilderness) Bondi to Coogee Coastal Walk, which combines coastal panoramas with opportunities for a surf or a coffee, or the numerous popular bushwalks in the Blue Mountains (p217), Ku-ring-gai Chase (p222) and Royal (p177) National Parks.

For an extended traverse that encompasses the environment around Sydney, the Great North Walk (p222), from Sydney to Newcastle, can be walked in two weeks, or sampled in sections. For superb coastal vistas, wildflowers and short but rugged hikes, the ascents of Pigeon House Mountain (p165), on the NSW south coast, and Mt Warning (p284), on the NSW north coast, can't be beaten. The verdant valleys of Dorrigo National Park (p257) are naturals for walkers and boast many cooling waterfalls.

HEY! A FAMOUS MARSUPIAL!

Bushwalking on the East Coast means you'll see a lot more than just vast numbers of shrubs. You will very likely get a chance to see many of the iconic species that are the symbols of Australia (and big moneymakers for the plush-toy industry).

Here's some of the critters that may provide thrills – and chills – on your adventure:

- Kookaburra – You'll hear the classic cackling laugh before you see this otherwise small white-and-brown bird, found sitting in gum trees new and old.

- Kangaroo – From the tails of planes to the bumpers of buses to the plates of trendy cafés, the star marsupial seems to be everywhere. Fortunately there are millions in the bush and it is not uncommon to see a batch go bounding by at sunset.

- Koala – Thick in the trees of the East Coast south of the tropical regions, these undeniably adorable-looking marsupials require patience to spot. Not known for their activity, you need to look for sedentary lumps high up in the eucalyptus trees.

- Crocodiles – The nasty character of this bunch and just one of many dangerous reptiles in Australia (see also p508 for information on treating snake bites). Salties (salt-water crocodiles) are literally big in Queensland where the late Steve Irwin built an empire on their leathery backs. Watch for warning signs and listen to the advice of locals when in croc country.

SAFETY GUIDELINES

Before embarking on a bushwalking trip, consider the following points to ensure a safe and enjoyable experience:

■ Be sure you are healthy and feel comfortable walking for a sustained period.

■ Obtain reliable information about physical and environmental conditions along your intended route (eg from park authorities).

■ Before tackling a long or remote walk, tell someone responsible about your plans and arrange to contact them when you return.

■ Walk only in regions, and on tracks, within your realm of experience.

■ Boil all water for 10 minutes before drinking it.

■ Be aware that weather conditions and terrain vary significantly from one region, or even from one track, to another. Seasonal changes can significantly alter any track. These differences influence the way walkers dress and the equipment they carry.

■ Before you set out, ask about the environmental characteristics that can affect your walk and how local, experienced walkers deal with these considerations.

Queensland

National parks favoured by bushwalkers include Springbrook (p304) in the Gold Coast hinterland, and D'Aguilar Range National Park (p318), which is a popular escape from the city. More good parks for bushwalking include the Cooloola section of Great Sandy National Park (p352), just north of the Sunshine Coast, and Wooroonooran National Park (p447), south of Cairns, which contains Queensland's highest peak, Mt Bartle Frere (1622m).

The Great Walks of Queensland is a project of the state government to develop iconic walks across the state. They include the Fraser Island Great Walk (p376) which has numerous portions that stretch for a total of 87km across the island's rainforest interior.

In northern Queensland the 32km Thorsborne Trail (p438) on Hinchinbrook Island traverses remote beaches, lush rainforests and crystal-clear creeks. Finally, there are sensational views on Lizard Island (p477).

Victoria

In Victoria's national parks and state forests, walkers enjoy everything from short walks through cool temperate rainforests to more challenging hikes that climb mountains or trace the wilderness coastline. The infrastructure is usually excellent, with marked trails, camp grounds with fireplaces, toilets and fresh water, and park information centres.

For coastal treks, head down to Wilsons Promontory National Park (p113) in Gippsland, with marked trails from Tidal River and Telegraph Bay that can take anywhere from a few hours to a couple of days. Expect squeaky white sands and clean aquamarine waters, pristine bushland and stunning coastal vistas. Further east, and almost tipping over into NSW, the Croajingolong National Park (p139), near Mallacoota in East Gippsland, offers rugged inland treks and easier coastal walks past historic lighthouses and over sand dunes.

Resources

There are numerous bushwalking guidebooks that can help you prepare for the bush and choose a trail. Resources include Tyrone Thomas' *50 Walks in North Queensland* (for walks on the beach or through the rainforest areas of the World Heritage–listed Wet Tropics), *70 walks in Southern NSW and ACT*,

Queensland publishes some excellent information on walks along the coast, from those aimed at history buffs to full-on outdoor explorers; see the list at www.epa.qld .gov.au/shop/.

RESPONSIBLE BUSHWALKING

To help preserve the ecology and beauty of East Coast Australia please consider the following when bushwalking:

- Stay on established trails, avoid cutting corners and taking short cuts (which cause erosion), and stay on hard ground where possible.

- When camping, always use designated camp grounds where provided. When bush camping, look for a natural clearing and avoid camping under large eucalypts, which have a tendency to drop branches without warning.

- Keep your vehicle on existing tracks or roads.

- Pay any fees and possess any permits required by local authorities.

- Do not feed the wildlife as this can lead to animals becoming dependent on hand-outs, and to unbalanced populations and diseases.

- Take all your rubbish out with you – don't burn or bury it.

- Avoid polluting lakes and streams – don't wash yourself or your dishes in them, and keep soap and detergent at least 50m away from waterways.

- Use toilets where provided – otherwise, bury human waste at least 100m away from waterways (taking a hand trowel is a good idea).

- Don't bring dogs or other pets into national parks.

- Take a gas or fuel stove and fuel for cooking.

- Don't light fires unless necessary; if you do need to light a fire, keep the fire small, use only dead fallen wood and ensure you use an existing fireplace. Make sure the fire is completely extinguished before moving on. On total fire ban days, don't (under any circumstances) light a fire.

- Be aware of local laws, regulations and etiquette about wildlife and the environment.

---

and *50 Walks: Coffs Harbour & Gold Coast Hinterland* (covering Tamborine Mountain, Springbrook and Lamington National Parks). *Take a Walk in Queensland's National Parks Southern Zone*, by John and Lyn Daly, provides a comprehensive guide to walks across the southern stretch of the state.

One of the best ways to find out about bushwalking areas is to contact a local bushwalking club. To find a local bushwalking club check the websites of the **Confederation of Bushwalking Clubs NSW** (www.bushwalking.org.au), the **Federation of Victorian Walking Clubs** (www.vicwalk.org.au) and the **Queensland Federation of Bushwalking Clubs** (www.geocities.com/qfbwc).

CANOEING, KAYAKING & WHITE-WATER RAFTING

Canoes and kayaks let you paddle into otherwise inaccessible areas, poking in and out of dense mangroves and estuaries, river gorges, secluded island beaches and remote wilderness inlets. Surf kayaking lets you surge ashore in a whirl of foam and spray. White-water rafting, on the other hand, may not give you as much time to look around as you negotiate yet another rapid, but the adrenaline factor is cranked right up.

For information on events and courses for canoeing and kayaking in NSW, Queensland and Victoria click onto www
.nswcanoe.org.au, www
.canoeqld.org.au and
www.canoevic.org.au,
respectively.

New South Wales

A good place to have your first sea-kayaking adventure is right in Sydney Harbour (p197); although it is busy and can be challenging for a novice, instruction and guiding is easily arranged. Many of the state's numerous rivers are suitable for canoeing and kayaking, with adventurous swift-flowing runs, and long, lazy paddles. Going north, the twin towns of Foster and

Tuncurry (p240) and Coffs Harbour (p260) are good bases for river and ocean adventures. Yamba (p266) is also good and Byron Bay (p273) is great.

In the south, there's plenty of action around Jervis Bay (p167) and Narooma (p151). In Royal National Park (p177), just south of Sydney, you can hire all manner of boats.

Queensland

Not surprisingly, the drenched tropical regions boast some renowned white-water rafting locations: the mighty Tully, North Johnstone, Barron and Russell Rivers between Townsville and Cairns top the list. The Tully (p439) is the most popular and has 44 rapids up to grade three to four. You can do day trips from Cairns (p454) to the Tully but avoid the roads and base yourself close by.

Sea kayaking in the warm Queensland waters is understandably very popular, and there are numerous operations that offer expeditions along the sandy southeast coast, through the calm Barrier Reef lagoon, and among the offshore islands. The protected waterways of the Cooloola section of the Great Sandy National Park (p352) and the inviting beaches of North Stradbroke Island (p330) make for ideal kayaking destinations. Way north, glitzy Palm Cove (p461) is also good.

You can rent kayaks and canoes or join tours in several places along the coast, among them Noosa (p347), Mission Beach (p441) and around the Whitsunday Islands (p407).

Victoria

Melbourne's Yarra River is popular with paddlers, with its gentle lower reaches suitable for families while more exciting rapids of about grade three can be found in the higher reaches. Keen paddlers hankering for multiday trips can try the classic canoe or raft trip down the Snowy River (see boxed text, p134) from MacKillops Bridge to a pull-out point near Buchan. This is some of the best inland canoeing and kayaking in Australia.

Get the low-down on the thrills when huge breaks meet paddles at surfkayaks.com.au.

CYCLING

With enough time you could make all your friends jealous by cycling the entire length of the East Coast. Such an adventure is limited only by your endurance and imagination. Fortunately for most, you can still have plenty of shorter rides that will be the envy of others. The East Coast was largely settled on the principle of not having more than a day's horse/coach ride between pubs, so it's possible to tackle lengthy tours or any number of segments and still clean up, fuel up and drink up at the end of each day.

Casual riders can sample the great cycling routes for a day or extended weekend. There are helpful bicycle organisations in each of the East Coast states that have lots of maps and useful tips and advice; see the following sections and p497 for details of these organisations and for further information on planning, regulations, and purchasing and hiring bikes.

Other good cycling organisations ready to offer advice include the excellent web resources **Bicycles Network Australia** (www.bicycles.net.au) and also **Bicycling Federation of Australia** (www.bfa.asn.au), with links to cycling clubs and organisations throughout Australia.

Bike Paths Safe Escapes (www.bikepaths.com.au) is a comprehensive guide to Victoria's best cycling tracks, both in the city and in country.

Victoria

Melbourne (see p88) has an excellent network of long urban bike trails, and in country areas you'll find thousands of kilometres of diverse cycling terrain, much of it readily accessible by public transport. Highlights include the Great Ocean Road (p105), one of the world's most spectacular coastal roads (though a detour from the East Coast); and the popular annual cycling events. Along the southeast coast there are many opportunities for road riding and much more rugged pedalling in the mountains. One place for the latter is Errinundra National Park (see boxed text, p134), where you can have multi-day adventures.

Excellent sources of information include **Bicycle Victoria** (☎ 03-8636 8888; www .bv.com.au) and the **Melbourne Bicycle Touring Club** (☎ 03-9517 4306; www.mbtc.org.au).

New South Wales & Canberra

Urban bike paths continue to spread through the cities in response to the ever-growing popularity of cycling. Sydney (p197) has an excellent recreational bike-path system and useful bike-hire places. Canberra's Lake Burley Griffin (p159) is another good place for cycling, with a large network of bike paths.

The NSW coast is an obvious choice for cycle touring, with parks, beaches and little towns constantly providing reasons to dismount. Royal National Park (p177) is good as is Byron Bay (p278). The Hunter Valley (see Hunter Valley Cycling, p235) and Blue Mountains (see Velo Nova, p220) provide terrain that is both challenging and beautiful (and at the former you can always drown your saddle-itch at a tasting room).

Pedalling Around Southern Queensland, by Julia Thorn, has tour notes and mud maps for numerous bike rides in the south of the state.

Queensland

There are possibilities for some great rides in Queensland but as with bushwalking, the best time is outside of Queensland's hottest months. Basic safety precautions such as taking plenty of water with you are vitally important here lest you end up as road kill.

There are excellent bike trails around Brisbane (p319). The lush and fertile Atherton Tableland is the destination of cycling tours out of Cairns (p454). You can also do some excellent mountain biking in and around Noosa (see Adventure Activities, p347).

Click on to the website of **Bicycling Queensland** (www.bq.org.au) for information on bike shops and rentals, cycling events and other useful information. The **Queensland Department of Transport** (www.transport.qld.gov.au/cycling) has maps and other resources, including information on road rules.

DIVING & SNORKELLING

For divers around the world, a trip to the Great Barrier Reef is a life goal. And many divers have found that exploring this wonder of the world fills a lifetime. Fortunately both here and elsewhere along the East Coast there are oodles of ways to get a taste of the incredible diving and snorkelling that can only lead to further adventures.

Every major town along the coast has one or more diving schools, but standards vary. Diving professionals are notoriously fickle and good instructors move around from company to company; ask around to see which ones are currently well regarded. **PADI** (Professional Association of Diving Instructors; www.padi.com) open-water courses typically cost $300 to $700 for four or five days, depending on how many dives are done from a boat. Note that with all certified PADI courses you'll need to provide a medical certificate, which costs about $60, and usually you will have to show you can tread water for 10 minutes and swim at least 200m. Dive shops can usually send you off to nearby clinic for your certificate.

Trips and equipment hire are available just about everywhere. You'll need evidence of your qualifications, and some places may also ask to see your log book. Renting gear or going for a day dive generally costs $60 to $100. You can also hire a mask, snorkel and fins from a dive shop for around $30 to $45.

New South Wales

There are many good options for shore-based and boat-based dives around Sydney (p198), including the Gordons Bay Underwater Nature Trail, north of Coogee. Elsewhere in NSW, the protected waters of the Cape Byron Marine Park around Byron Bay (p273), the Solitary Islands Marine Park (p264) and Seal Rocks and the waters around Forster-Tuncurry (p240). In the south, Jervis Bay (p167) has good dives off its pristine parks while near Narooma, spectacular Montague Island (p152) offers diving in waters teaming with mammals such as seals.

Queensland

It's no secret that the Queensland coast has the pick of spectacular dive sites. The Great Barrier Reef provides some of the world's best diving and snorkelling and there are scores of operators vying to teach you or provide you with the ultimate dive experience. There are also some 1600 shipwrecks along the Queensland coast, providing vibrant habitats for marine life. Most cruises to the Great Barrier Reef and through the Whitsunday Islands include free snorkel gear and these are some of the loveliest waters to float in.

During the wet season, usually January to March, floods can wash a lot of mud out into the ocean and visibility for divers and snorkellers is sometimes affected. All water activities, including diving and snorkelling, are affected by the box jellyfish, which line the Queensland coast from the Capricorn Coast up. See p381 for more information on the potentially deadly stingers.

Learning to dive here is fairly inexpensive and you can usually choose to do a good part of your learning in the warm waters of the Great Barrier Reef itself. If you are choosing a course here, look carefully at how much of your open-water experience will be out on the reef. Many of the budget courses only offer a few boat dives. At the other end of the price scale, the most expensive courses tend to be aboard a boat or yacht for several days.

Cairns (p453) and Port Douglas (p465) have plenty of dive companies that operate in the waters of the Great Barrier Reef. Further south, the SS *Yongala* shipwreck, just off Townsville (p432), has been sitting beneath the water for over 90 years and is now home to a teeming marine community. From Airlie Beach (see p407) you can organise dives in the azure waters surrounding the Whitsundays and the Great Barrier Reef.

The spectacular southern Great Barrier Reef has perhaps the best locations of all. Here astraddle the tropic of Capricorn you'll find scores of operators and towns whose symbiosis with the reef is purely one way (reef to land). See p387 for a range of options.

Possibly one of the best locations for low-key (and low-cost) diving instruction in Queensland is the hamlet of Bargara, where there's superb coral viewing (see p372). Rainbow Beach (p359) is another good place to learn about diving and it has some spectacular rock formations that teem with turtles, rays and sharks.

You can snorkel just about everywhere in the warm waters of this state; it requires minimum effort and anyone can do it. Most of the previously mentioned locations are also relevant and popular snorkelling sites. There are coral reefs off some mainland beaches, and not far from Brisbane are the brilliant Tangalooma Wrecks (p332). Backpacker hostels along the coast often provide free use of snorkel gear for their guests.

Whether you're snorkelling or diving on the Great Barrier Reef it's important to remember how vulnerable the ecology is. Most coral damage occurs

> The entire Great Barrier reef is 2000km long and in places is 500m wide.

SAFETY GUIDELINES FOR DIVING

Before embarking on a scuba-diving, skin-diving or snorkelling trip, carefully consider the following points to ensure a safe and enjoyable experience:

■ If scuba diving, possess a current diving certification card from a recognised scuba-diving instructional agency.

■ Be sure you are healthy and feel comfortable diving.

■ Obtain reliable information about physical and environmental conditions at the dive site (eg from a reputable local dive operation).

■ Be aware of local laws, regulations and etiquette about marine life and the environment.

■ Dive only at sites within your realm of experience; if available, engage the services of a competent, professionally trained dive instructor or dive master.

■ Be aware that underwater conditions vary significantly from one region, or even site, to another. Seasonal changes can significantly alter any site and dive conditions. These differences influence the way divers dress for a dive and what diving techniques they use.

■ Ask about the environmental characteristics that can affect your diving and how local trained divers deal with these considerations.

when divers accidentally cut or break it with their fins. Be aware of where your feet are and never stand on the coral; if you need to rest find sand to stand on or use a rest station.

Victoria

Great Barrier Reef Online (www.great-barrier-reef .au.com) is a Cairns-based agent representing dozens of tours for landlubbers to diving experts.

Plug the holes in your wetsuit as the often chilly waters of Victoria offer excellent diving. Port Phillip Bay, right on Melbourne's doorstep, has several good sites, including pods of dolphins and friendly seals, and most weekends see a legion of beginners learning the ropes at places such as the pier at Portsea on the Mornington Peninsula. Other good bases include Flinders and Sorrento (p104), also on the Mornington Peninsula. Bunurong Marine Park (p110) is a seemingly mellow spot until you get to the teaming waters below. Even less developed, Cape Conran Coastal Park (p135) is a hidden diving gem.

EXTREME SPORTS

Maybe it's all that beauty or maybe it's the food or perhaps it's just all those pubs but the East Coast is loaded with places to get your heart pounding and glands working.

Abseiling, Canyoning & Rock Climbing
NEW SOUTH WALES

Near Sydney, the Blue Mountains (p217), especially around Katoomba, are fantastic for abseiling and canyoning, with numerous professionals able to set you up with equipment and training.

VICTORIA

Climbing Australia (www .climbing.com.au) has excellent info on rock climbing.

With a name like Wilsons Promontory you just know there are going to be some rock faces to abseil (see First Track Adventures, p115). Another good place is around the beautiful and legendary Snowy River (see Karoonda Park, p133).

Bungee Jumping & Skydiving

There are plenty of opportunities for adrenaline-junkies to get a hit in the big holiday destinations of the East Coast. A bungee jump generally costs around $100. Prices depend on the height of your jump. Most folk start with a jump of 10,000ft, which provides 35 to 40 seconds of free fall and costs around $200 to $300.

NEW SOUTH WALES
Tandem skydiving is a popular way to try your first plunge to earth. Byron Bay is a popular place to make your first leap (see Skydive Byron Bay, p274).

QUEENSLAND
Something about Queensland makes people want to jump out of air-planes. Caloundra (p338), Hervey Bay (p365), Rainbow Beach (p359), Airlie Beach (p410), Mission Beach (p441) and Cairns (p454) all have skydiving operators.

Surfers Paradise is something of a bungee mecca, offering brave partici-pants a host of creative spins on the original (see p297).

Hang-gliding, Paragliding & Parasailing
Hang-gliding and paragliding are popular at many places along the East Coast.

For information on scores of ways to take to the air without a fixed wing, check out the offerings of the Hang Gliding Federa-tion of Australia (www .hgfa.asn.au).

NEW SOUTH WALES
Great spots to take to the air include Stanwell Park (p176), south of Sydney, which is also ideal for spectators. As always, there's a lot going on around Byron Bay, especially if you want to hang-glide (p274).

QUEENSLAND
Parasailing is a resort staple on the Gold Coast (see p301), Airlie Beach and many other spots in Queensland.

SURFING
The southern half of the East Coast is jam-packed with sandy surf beaches and point breaks. North of Agnes Water in Queensland, the waves disappear thanks to the Great Barrier Reef shielding the coast from the ocean swells. Many trav-ellers who come to the East Coast want to learn to surf, and you'll find plenty of good waves, board hire and lessons available all along the coast. Two-hour lessons cost around $40 to $60 and five-day courses for the really keen go for around $180, although for a bit more you can often enjoy a surf camp.

New South Wales
It's simply hard to go wrong finding a break in NSW. Those endless beaches are battered by beautiful waves much of the year and there's simply so many places to surf that crowds at all but the trendiest spots are rare. Of course for trendy, there's Sydney's Bondi Beach (p194), which for many worldwide is synonymous with surfing. Less fabled but no less good, Manly Beach (p197) is another prime spot.

For definitive surfing information throughout the East Coast, plus surf cams, events and where to learn to stand up on your board, surf, as it were, to www.surfing australia.com or www .coastalwatch.com.

Elsewhere in the state, top highlights in the south include Merimbula (p146), Batemans Bay (p155), Booderee National Park (p167) and Wollongong (p173). Going north, Newcastle is a major spot for surfing and is home to champion surfer Mark Richards (see boxed text, p228). From here to Queensland it is easier to name places with no surfing, but consider Crescent Head (p250), Coffs Harbour (p260) and Lennox Head (p270) for starters. Byron Bay (p274) has a surf culture to rival Bondi.

Queensland
From a surfer's point of view, Queensland's Great Barrier Reef is one of nature's most tragic mistakes – a 2000km-long breakwater! Mercifully, there

are some great surf beaches in southern Queensland. Starting right at the border, Coolangatta (p290) is a popular surfing haunt, particularly at Kirra Beach. Nearby Burleigh Heads (p292) has a serious right-hand barrel, which rewards those with experience.

The Atlas of Australian Surfing, Travellers Edition, by legendary surfer Mark Warren, reveals the biggest waves and the best-kept secret surf in Australia. Features include maps and plenty of practical advice, including warnings about monster waves, sharks and unfriendly locals.

Further north, the swanky resort of Noosa (p345) is a popular hang-out for long-boarders. Near Brisbane, North Stradbroke Island (p330) also has good surf beaches, as does Moreton Island. Queensland's most northern surf beaches are at Agnes Water (p380), just south of Gladstone.

Victoria

With its exposure to the relentless Southern Ocean swell, Victoria's rugged southern coastline provides plenty of quality surf, while the southeast coast is a little more gentle. The usually chilly water (even in summer) has the hardiest surfer reaching for a wetsuit. A full-length, up-to-7mm-thick wetsuit is the standard for winter.

Eastern Victoria's best surf is at Phillip Island (p106), especially at Woolami Beach. Other good surfing spots include Wilsons Promontory (p115) and at Cape Conran Coastal Park (p135).

Victoria

PHIL WEYMOUTH

Melbourne

Melbourne is a city you need to get to know. It might not immediately take your breath away and its many charms aren't always apparent on first meeting, but there's no doubt this city will get under your skin.

Few cities grew as fast and furiously as this one, as it launched itself onto the world stage with an arriviste swagger and a gold-tinted twinkle in its eye. With its Victorian streetscapes and genteel demeanour, Melbourne was considered the most British of Australian cities. These days, it possesses both an adopted European grace and a nonstop energy more akin to the urban hubs of Asia.

Melbourne's citizens look as diverse as they are. It's a city of immigrants whose backgrounds usually span multiple ethnicities. They're good-looking too, though that can be more about culture than nature. Melbournians are passionate about enjoying life: food, fashion, sport and socialising are cherished. Its many bars, cafés and restaurants draw on the best from Europe and Asia, whilst retaining an easy-going, quintessentially Australian feel.

Melbourne is brainy, industrious, imaginative and creative: prolific in architecture, performance, live music and the visual arts, but endlessly self-deprecating. It's one of the world's youngest cities yet also one of the longest-inhabited places on Earth. Melbourne is a city worth exploring: let it win you over.

HIGHLIGHTS

- Visit the world-class **Melbourne Zoo** (p87) and **Royal Botanic Gardens** (p86)

- Sip a latte and watch the eclectic crowd on **Brunswick St** (p87)

- Head to seaside **St Kilda** (p88) for cafés, stylish nightlife, a soak in the **St Kilda Sea Baths** (p88) or a cake on Acland St

- Catch a movie at ACMI in **Federation Square** (p81) or check out the Australian art at the **Ian Potter Centre: National Galley of Victoria Australia** (p81)

- Get caught-up in the roar of the crowd at a footy match at the **Melbourne Cricket Ground** (p99)

- Immerse yourself in the **Queen Victoria Market** (p83)

- Get seriously fashionable in the city's **boutiques** (p99)

- TELEPHONE CODE: 03
- POPULATION: 3.5 million
- www.melbourne.vic.gov.au

MELBOURNE IN...

Two Days

Start at **Federation Square** (p81) and take our **walking tour** (p88) ending with lunch at **Journal Canteen** (p95). In the afternoon, visit the esteemed **Ian Potter Centre: National Galley of Victoria Australia** (p81) or catch a film at **ACMI** (p81). Take a stroll through **Chinatown** (p82) and chow-down on some Cantonese before an evening of **bar-hopping** (p97) around the city laneways.

On the second day visit the bustling **Queen Victoria Market** (p83) and wander around **Melbourne Museum** (p87) before heading to **Brunswick St** (p87) to drink proper coffee, have dinner at **Añada** (p96) and settle into an evening of rowdy music at the **Tote** (p98).

Four Days

Same first two days. On day three visit the **Royal Melbourne Zoo** (p87) or the **Royal Botanic Gardens** (p86). Have lunch in one of the city's arcades and follow it up with a **Melbourne River Cruise** (p90) and see the city from the Yarra. Catch a performance at the **Victorian Arts Centre** (p86) before or after dinner and drinks at **Cookie** (p95).

On your fourth day head to **St Kilda** (p88), Soak in the **St Kilda Sea Baths** (p88), savour a cake in **Acland St**, stroll along **St Kilda Pier,** have some fish and chips and then enjoy the tradition that is the **Espy** (p97).

One Week

A full week will allow you to squeeze in the **Immigration Museum** (p83), have a monster shop along **Chapel St** (p100) and visit the **Dandenongs** (p103).

ORIENTATION

Melbourne hugs the shores of Port Phillip, with the city centre on the north bank of the Yarra River, about 5km inland from the bay. Most of the attractions covered in this chapter are within the city and inner-suburban areas, accessible by public transport.

The inner suburbs that surround the city centre, which is known as the central business district (CBD), are like a ring of urban villages. Beside the Yarra River, on the corner of Swanston and Flinders Sts, is Flinders St station, the main station for suburban trains. The other major station, for country and interstate services, is Southern Cross station (formerly Spencer St station), at the western end of Bourke St.

Maps

You can pick up a free copy of the *Melbourne Visitors Map* at the Melbourne visitors centre (p81) at Federation Sq or at the Melbourne visitors booth (p81) in Bourke St Mall. Street directories are detailed and extremely handy if you're driving. They can be purchased from newsagents and bookshops for around $50. Lonely Planet's *Melbourne City Map* provides excellent coverage.

INFORMATION
Bookshops

Borders (Map p92; ☎ 9824 2299; www.borders.com .au; Jam Factory, 500 Chapel St, South Yarra; ☼ 10am-11pm) This bookstore chain has seven stores in Melbourne with huge selections and late opening hours.

Metropolis (Map pp78–9; ☎ 9663 2015; www .metropolisbookshop.com.au; Level 3, Curtin House, 252 Swanston St; ☼ 10am-6pm Mon-Thu & Sat, 10am-7pm Fri, 10am-5pm Sun) Lovely bookish eyrie with a particular focus on art, architecture, fashion and film.

Readings (www.readings.com.au) Carlton (Map pp84-5; ☎ 9347 6633; 309 Lygon St; ☼ 9am-11pm Mon-Sat, 10am-11pm Sun); St Kilda (Map p92; ☎ 9525 3852; 112 Acland St; ☼ 10am-10pm) A potter around this defiantly prospering indie bookshop can occupy an entire afternoon if you're so inclined.

Emergency

In an emergency, dial ☎ 000 – a free call from any phone. Your call will be diverted to either the police, ambulance service or fire brigade.
Lifeline Counselling (☎ 13 11 14; www.lifeline.org.au; ☼ 24hr)
Police station (Map pp78-9; ☎ 9247 5347; www.police .vic.gov.au; 228-232 Flinders La; ☼ 24hr)

(Continued on page 80

MELBOURNE

MELBOURNE

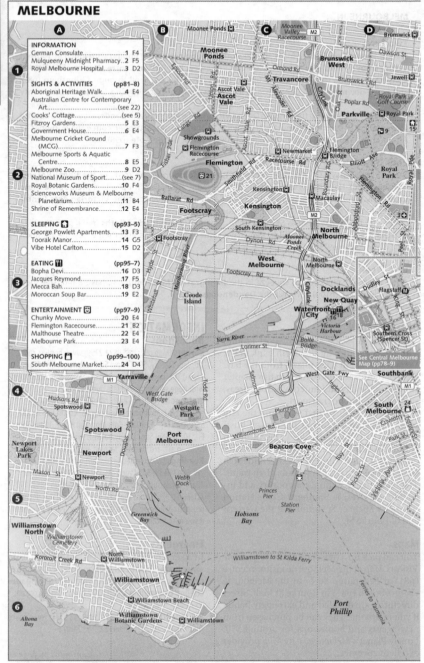

CENTRAL MELBOURNE

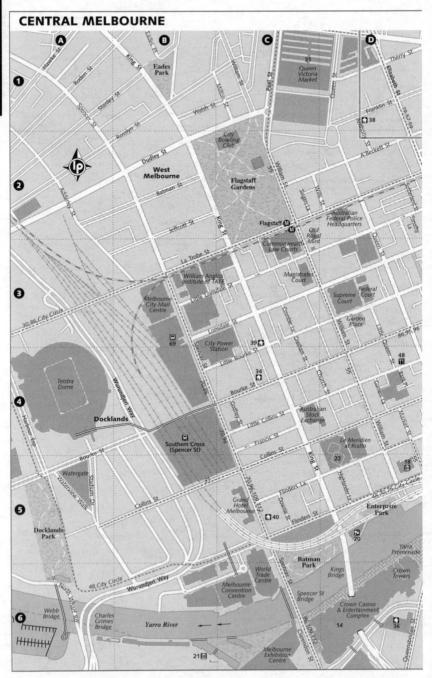

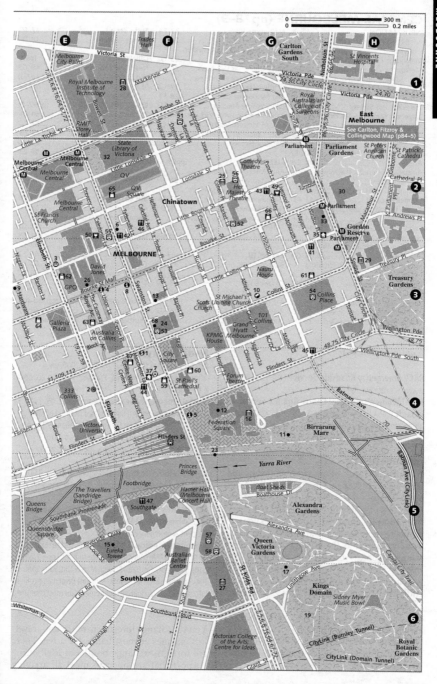

(Continued from page 75)

RACV Emergency Roadside Service (☎ 13 11 11; www.racv.com.au; ☽ 24hr)
Royal Women's Hospital Centre Against Sexual Assault (CASA House; Map pp84–5; ☎ 9344 2201; www .thewomens.org.au/sexualassault; Royal Women's Hospital, 132 Grattan St, Carlton; ☽ 24hr)

Internet Access

Internet cafés are common in Melbourne, and wi-fi access is available in many public places as well as hotels. Melbourne Airport offers wi-fi for a pay-as-you-go fee. Hotel rates vary from complimentary to ludicrously expensive daily fees. Expect to pay around $2 per hour at an internet café. Public libraries, including the State Library of Victoria, usually offer a free service but you'll probably need to book. A couple of good internet cafés:

E:fiftyfive (Map pp78-9; ☎ 9620 3899; 55 Elizabeth St; ☽ 9am–1am Mon & Tue, to 2am Wed & Thu, to 3am Fri, noon-3am Sat, noon-11pm Sun) Coffee, beer and snacks available, and DJs playing nightly.
World Wide Wash (Map pp84–5; ☎ 9419 8214; 361 Brunswick St, Fitzroy; ☽ 9.30am-10pm) A laundrette and cybercafé in one.

Medical Services

Alfred Hospital (Map p92; ☎ 9276 2000; www .alfred.org.au; Commercial Rd, Prahran; ☽ 24hr accident & emergency)
Dental Emergency Service (Map pp84-5; ☎ 9341 1040; www.dhsv.org.au; Royal Dental Hospital of Melbourne, 720 Swanston St, Carlton; ☽ 8.30am-9.15pm)
Mulqueeny Midnight Pharmacy (Map pp76-7; ☎ 9510 3977; cnr Williams Rd & High St, Prahran; ☽ 9am–midnight)
Royal Melbourne Hospital (Map pp76-7; ☎ 9342 7000; www.mh.org.au; Grattan St, Parkville; ☽ 24hr accident & emergency)
St Vincent's Hospital (Map pp84-5; ☎ 9288 2211; www.svhm.org.au; 41 Victoria Pde, Fitzroy; ☽ 24hr accident & emergency)
Travellers' Medical & Vaccination Centre (Map pp78-9; ☎ 9602 5788; www.traveldoctor.com.au; Level 2, 393 Little Bourke St; ☽ 9am-8.30pm Mon & Thu, 9am-8pm Tue, 9am-5pm Wed & Fri, 9am-1pm Sat) Dispenses excellent information on vaccination requirements for most countries.

Money

You can change foreign currency and travellers cheques at most banks for a fee. There are foreign-exchange booths at Melbourne Airport that are open to meet all arriving international flights. There are also numerous booths in central Melbourne's mains streets and arcades. Large hotels will change currency or travellers cheques but at a poorer rate.

American Express (☎ 1300 139 060; www.ameri canexpress.com; 233 Collins St) Commission-free service if you're using its travellers cheques.

Post

Branches of Australia Post can be found everywhere.

Melbourne GPO (General Post Office; Map pp78-9; ☎ 13 13 18; www.auspost.com.au; cnr Little Bourke & Elizabeth Sts; ☉ 8.30am-5.30pm Mon-Fri, 9am-4pm Sat, 10am-4pm Sun)

Tourist Information

Melbourne visitors booth (Map pp78-9; ☉ 9am-5pm Mon-Fri, 10am-5pm Sat & Sun) A small information booth in the Bourke St Mall with helpful staff.

Melbourne visitors centre (Map pp78-9; ☎ 9658 9658; Federation Sq; ☉ 9am-6pm) An excellent source of information about Melbourne events and attractions. Multilingual assistance is available for booking tours and accommodation. Also offers the Melbourne Greeter Service pairing visitors with volunteers for half-day city walking tours (book ahead).

Travellers' Aid Society of Victoria (Map pp78-9; ☎ 9654 2600; www.travellersaid.org.au; Level 2, 169 Swanston St; ☉ 8am-5pm Mon-Fri, 11am-4pm Sat & Sun) Offers free assistance for stranded travellers, as well as information, advice, showers and wheelchair-accessible toilets. There are also support services for disabled and aged people.

SIGHTS

Central Melbourne (the CBD) is compact enough to cover on foot, and navigable by the trams that criss-cross the area (see p102). Other neighbourhoods that attract visitors include the riverfront precincts of Southbank and Docklands, while north of town you'll find Carlton, Fitzroy and Collingwood. South-of-the-city attractions can be found in South Yarra, Prahran and St Kilda.

Central Melbourne
FEDERATION SQUARE

The ugly old Gas & Fuel Building and the railyards that once stretched along the Yarra River have now been replaced by a riotous explosion of steel, glass and abstract geometry known as **Federation Sq** (Map pp78-9; 9655 1900; www .fedsq.com.au), an ambitious move by city planners to create a focal point for Melbourne

and to connect the centre of the city with the Yarra River.

Federation Sq is centred on its **plaza**, a spacious, open courtyard that extends from Princes Bridge. Next along is the dramatic glass-and-steel **atrium** and the adjoining 450-seat **amphitheatre**. The atrium functions as an undercover walkway between Flinders St and the Yarra side of the complex, with a number of cafés and restaurants lining the promenade.

The city's cultural heart also contains the awkwardly named **Ian Potter Centre: National Gallery of Victoria Australia** (NGVA; Map pp78-9; ☎ 8662 2222; www.ngv.vic.gov.au/ngvaustralia; Federation Sq; admission free; ☉ 10am-5pm Mon-Thu, to 9pm Fri, to 6pm Sat & Sun), a dramatic building at the eastern end of Federation Sq. The centre houses the National Gallery of Victoria's impressive collection (over 25,000 pieces) of Australian art from must-see indigenous art to colonial and modern periods.

Also at Fed Square you'll find the innovative **Australian Centre for the Moving Image** (ACMI; Map pp78-9; ☎ 8663 2200; www.acmi.net.au; Federation Sq; ☉ 10am-6pm), a fascinating gallery and cinema space dedicated to film, TV and digital media. Riverside **Birrarung Marr** ('river of mists' in Wurundjeri) is the newest addition to Melbourne's parkland fringe, thoughtfully planned and planted entirely with indigenous flora.

SWANSTON STREET

Swanston St (Map pp78–9) is a semipedestrian mall by day (trams and taxis still move through here), but is open to general traffic after 7pm. Much of the lower stretch of the street is decidedly low-rent in tone.

Melbourne Town Hall (Map pp78-9; ☎ 9658 9779; www .melbournetownhall.com.au; cnr Swanston & Collins Sts; tours free; ☉ tours 11am & 1pm Mon-Fri), built between 1870 and 1880, is a fine civic building (don't miss the beautiful wood-panelled Council Chamber and the magnificent 10,000-pipe organ). Phone for guided tour bookings (also available on the first Saturday of each month at 11am, noon and 1pm).

The **State Library of Victoria** (Map pp78-9; ☎ 8664 7000; www.slv.vic.gov.au; 328 Swanston St; admission free; ☉ 10am-9pm Mon-Thu, to 6pm Fri-Sun), between Little Lonsdale and Latrobe Sts, was built in stages from 1854 and boasts a Classical Revival façade. The library collection includes a 4000-year-old Mesopotamian tablet and the

MELBOURNE

IT'S EASY BEING GREEN

Officially opened in August 2006, the design of **Council House 2** (Map pp78-9; ☎ 9658 9658; 218-242 Little Collins St; tours free; ☻ tours 2pm Tue & Thu) is based on 'biomimicry', reflecting the complex ecosystem of the planet. The building utilises the sun, water and wind in combination with a slew of sustainable technologies. These include a basement water-mining plant, a lovely façade of solar-powered wooden louvres that track the sun, and air-circulation ducts that absorb heat or draw fresh air from the roof. The foyer includes a Janet Laurence installation evoking the hydrology at work beneath the floor. Bookings are required for tours.

records from the infamous Burke and Wills expedition. See the magnificent domed La Trobe Reading Room. The library has regular exhibitions. **Mr Tulk** (☎ 8660 5700; cnr La Trobe St & Swanston St; mains $10-18; ☻ breakfast & lunch Mon-Sat) serves coffee, wine and excellent food.

COLLINS STREET

Collins St (Map pp78-9) is central Melbourne's most elegant streetscape. The western end (from Elizabeth to Spencer St) is home to bankers and stockbrokers; while the eastern end, the 'Paris end' as it's known, has five-star hotels and exclusive fashion boutiques.

Stunning **Block Arcade**, which runs between Collins and Elizabeth Sts, was built in 1891 and is a beautiful, 19th-century shopping arcade with intricate, mosaic-tiled floors, marble columns, Victorian window surrounds and magnificently detailed plasterwork on the upper walls.

On the 55th floor of the **Rialto Towers** is the **Melbourne Observation Deck** (Map pp78-9; ☎ 9629 8222; www.melbournedeck.com.au; 525 Collins St; adult/child/family $14.50/8/39.50; ☻ 10am-10pm), which offers spectacular 360-degree views of Melbourne's surrounds. You can get to the top by the stairs (more than 1250 of them) or take the ear-popping lift. For wheelchair access, use the Collins St entrance to the building.

BOURKE STREET

The area around central Bourke St (Map pp78-9) has the city's main department stores. The **Bourke St Mall** section between Swanston and Elizabeth Sts is closed to vehicular traffic,

and is shared between pedestrians, buskers and trams (beware of the latter!).

Royal Arcade (www.royalarcade.com.au), built between 1869 and 1870, is Melbourne's oldest arcade. Lined with shops, it retains the exquisite detail of the original upper walls and arched ceiling. The tall figures of **Gog** and **Magog** stand guard and have been striking the hour (with their hammers) on the clock since 1892.

SPRING STREET

At the eastern end of Collins St is Spring St (Map pp78-9) and the **Old Treasury Building** (Map pp78-9; ☎ 9651 2233; www.oldtreasurymuseum.org.au; Spring St; adult/concession/family $8.50/5/18; ☻ 9am-5pm Mon-Fri, 10am-4pm Sat & Sun), one of Australia's most elegant 19th-century buildings. Built in 1862, it has huge basement vaults built to store much of the $200 million-worth of gold dug from the Victorian goldfields. It houses permanent exhibitions in the **Gold Treasury Museum**.

Between Bourke and Little Collins Sts is the marvellous 1883 **Windsor Hotel** (Map pp78-9; ☎ 9633 6000; www.thewindsor.com.au; 103 Spring St; ☻ 24hr). Extensive refurbishments in the 1980s abundantly reaffirmed the Windsor's title of the city's grandest hotel.

Opposite the Windsor Hotel, the **Parliament House of Victoria** (Map pp78-9; ☎ 9651 8568; www.parliament.vic.gov.au; Spring St; 30min tours free; ☻ tours 10am, 11am, noon, 2pm, 3pm & 3.45pm Mon-Fri) building was started in 1856, and is still the city's most impressive public building. Its beautiful classical lines and exuberant use of ornamental plasterwork, stencilling and gilt reflect gold-rush-era pride and optimism. Australia's first federal parliament sat here from 1901, before moving to Canberra in 1927. Tours run only when parliament isn't in session.

CHINATOWN

Centred on **Little Bourke St**, Melbourne's Chinatown (Map pp78-9) is the only area of continuous Chinese settlement in the country, and one of Melbourne's most intact 19th-century streetscapes. In the 1850s the Chinese set up their shops here, alongside brothels, opium dens and boarding houses. Today the area is dominated by restaurants and discount traders.

The interesting **Museum of Chinese Australian History** (Map pp78-9; ☎ 9662 2888; www.chinesemuseum.com.au; 22 Cohen Pl; adult/concession $7.50/5.50; ☻ 10am-5pm) documents the long history of Chinese people in Australia. The entrance is guarded by the 218kg Millennium Dragon, which snakes its way through the city streets during Chinese New Year.

QUEEN VICTORIA MARKET

This fabulous **market** (Map pp78–9; ☎ 9320 5822; www.qvm.com.au; 513 Elizabeth St; ☺ 6am-2pm Tue & Thu, 6am-6pm Fri, 6am-3pm Sat, 9am-4pm Sun) is the mother of all Melbourne markets. It was saved from demolition in the 1970s and has been around for more than 130 years. Many of the sheds and buildings are registered by the National Trust.

OLD MELBOURNE GAOL

A bleak bluestone monument to 19th-century (in)justice at Russell St's northern end, Melbourne's old gaol is now a **museum** (Map pp78–9; ☎ 9663 7228; www.oldmelbournegaol.com.au; Russell St; adult/child/family $18/9.50/44; ☺ 9.30am-5pm). It was built in 1841 and used until 1929. In all, 135 prisoners were hanged there. Spooky displays include Ned Kelly's iconic armour, death mask and the gallows from which he hanged. Take a **night tour** (☎ 13 28 49; http://premier.ticketek.com.au; adult/child $30/22.50) by candlelight .

IMMIGRATION MUSEUM

Multimedia displays at this **museum** (Map pp78–9; ☎ 9927 2700; www.museumvictoria.com.au/immigrationmuseum; 400 Flinders St; adult/concession & child $6/free; ☺ 10am-5pm) give a moving account of Melbourne's immigrants from the early 19th century onwards. The museum is in the Old Customs House. Make sure you see the Long Room, an extraordinary example of Renaissance Revival architecture.

MELBOURNE AQUARIUM

On the river's edge, across from Crown Casino, is this **aquarium** (Map pp78–9; ☎ 9620 0999; www.melbourneaquarium.com.au; cnr Queenswharf Rd & King St; adult/child/family $25/15/70; ☺ 9.30am-6pm Feb-Dec, 9.30am-9pm Jan). Giant rays, gropers and sharks cruise around a 2.2-million-litre tank, watched closely by visitors inside a see-through tunnel which traverses the aquarium floor.

FITZROY GARDENS

These **gardens** (Map pp76–7; www.fitzroygardens .com; btwn Wellington Pde, Clarendon, Lansdowne & Albert Sts; ☺ 24hr) divide the city centre from East Melbourne and serve as a verdant retreat from city life. James Sinclair, formerly Russian Tsar Nicholas I's gardener, created a rambling blend of elm and cedar avenues, fern gullies, flower beds, lawns and fountains (many dry due to water restrictions). **Cooks' Cottage** (☎ 9419 4677; www.cookscottage.com .au; adult/child/family $4.50/2.20/12; ☺ 9am-5pm) was shipped here from Yorkshire in 1934. There's also a delightful early 20th-century floral **conservatory** (☺ 9am-5pm).

Southbank & Docklands

These riverside locales were once gritty industrial areas, but they've been transformed into playgrounds of leisure. Southbank (Map pp78–9) sits across the Yarra from Flinders St. **Southgate** (Map pp78-9, www.southgate-melbourne.com .au) is a large, airy shopping mall with fabulous views and an eclectic mix of shops, bars and restaurants. Behind here you'll find the city's major arts precinct; the NGV International, the Victorian Arts Centre and the Australian Ballet. Back down by the river, the promenade stretches to the Crown Casino & Entertainment Complex, where you can lose your shirt 24/7. To the city's west lies Docklands (Map pp78–9).

AUSTRALIAN CENTRE FOR CONTEMPORARY ART

This contemporary **gallery** (ACCA; Map pp76–7; ☎ 9697 9999; www.accaonline.org.au; 111 Sturt St; admission free; ☺ 10am-5pm Tue-Fri, 11am-6pm Sat & Sun) is one of Australia's most exciting, and exhibits some works specially commissioned for the space. The building's rusty metallic exterior and slick, soaring interior, designed to house often massive artworks, is fittingly sculptural.

NATIONAL GALLERY OF VICTORIA INTERNATIONAL

Beyond the water-wall at the front of this **gallery** (NGV; Map pp78–9; ☎ 8620 2222; www.ngv.vic.gov .au; 180 St Kilda Rd, Southbank; admission free; ☺ 10am-5pm Wed-Mon) you'll find international art, from the ancient to the contemporary. Key works include a Rembrandt, a Tiepolo and a Bonnard, and there are galleries featuring impressive collections from the Middle Ages to the present day. This is the place where big international blockbuster shows are hung. The building was designed by modernist Roy Grounds with a recent interior renovation overseen by Mario Bellini – don't miss the Great Hall ceiling.

MELBOURNE

CARLTON, FITZROY & COLLINGWOOD

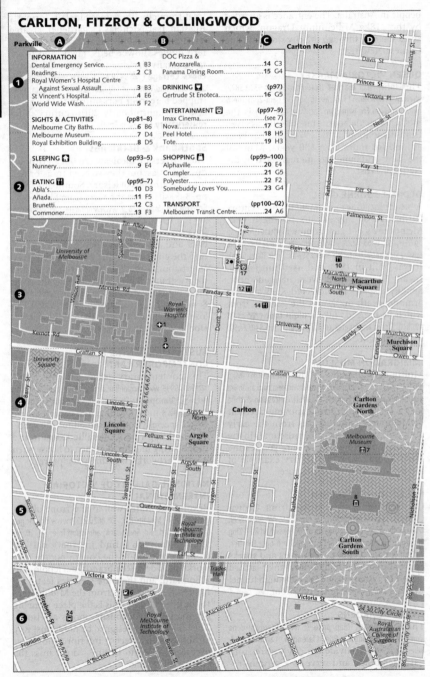

INFORMATION	
Dental Emergency Service	1 B3
Readings	2 C3
Royal Women's Hospital Centre	
Against Sexual Assault	3 B3
St Vincent's Hospital	4 E6
World Wide Wash	5 F2

SIGHTS & ACTIVITIES	(pp81–8)
Melbourne City Baths	6 B6
Melbourne Museum	7 D4
Royal Exhibition Building	8 D5

SLEEPING	(pp93–5)
Nunnery	9 E4

EATING	(pp95–7)
Abla's	10 D3
Añada	11 F5
Brunetti	12 C3
Commoner	13 F3

DOC Pizza &	
Mozzarella	14 C3
Panama Dining Room	15 G4

DRINKING	(p97)
Gertrude St Enoteca	16 G5

ENTERTAINMENT	(pp97–9)
Imax Cinema	(see 7)
Nova	17 C3
Peel Hotel	18 H5
Tote	19 H3

SHOPPING	(pp99–100)
Alphaville	20 E4
Crumpler	21 G5
Polyester	22 F2
Somebuddy Loves You	23 G4

TRANSPORT	(pp100–02)
Melbourne Transit Centre	24 A6

MELBOURNE

EUREKA SKYDECK 88

A wild elevator ride – 88 floors in less than 40 seconds – takes you to the top of Skydeck 88 atop **Eureka Tower** (Map pp78-9; ☎ 9693 8888; www .eurekaskydeck.com.au; Riverside Quay, Southbank; adult/ child/family $16.50/9/39, the Edge extra $12/8/29; ☽ 10am-10pm), completed in 2006. This is (for now) the tallest residential building in the world. If you find the vertiginous views less than satisfying, there's the **Edge** – not a U2 guitarist, but a slightly sadistic, horizontal glass-cube elevator that dangles you out over the side of the building.

VICTORIAN ARTS CENTRE

Hamer Hall at this **arts complex** (Map pp78-9 ☎ 9281 8000; www.theartscentre.com.au; 100 St Kilda Rd, Southbank; tours adult/concession/family $11/8/28; ☽ tours noon-2.30pm Mon-Sat), the circular building closest to the Yarra, features mostly symphonic concerts and opera. The Theatres Building (with the spire) houses the State Theatre, Playhouse and George Fairfax Studio. The famous Spiegeltent – a vintage Belgian mirror-tent – sets up in the forecourt for the Melbourne International Arts Festival (p91). Across in Kings Domain is the Sidney Myer Music Bowl.

CROWN CASINO & ENTERTAINMENT COMPLEX

A nonstop cavalcade of excess, this **casino** (Map pp78-9; ☎ 9292 8888; www.crowncasino.com.au; Southbank; ☽ 24hr) was for a moment the world's largest. There's a luxury hotel here, plus nightclubs, cinemas, a 900-seat showroom, speciality and luxury stores, dozens of cafés and restaurants. Like every Melburnian, you'll either love it or hate it.

MELBOURNE MARITIME MUSEUM

The old iron-hulled, three-masted *Polly Woodside* is the centrepiece of this **museum** (Map pp78-9; ☎ 9699 9760; www.pollywoodside.com.au; Lorimer St E, Southbank) which is undergoing re-development and is due to reopen in 2009. She was built in Belfast in 1885, and carried coal and nitrate between Europe and South America. She was bought by the National Trust in the 1970s and restored by volunteers. Call to check new prices and opening hours.

Kings Domain

Kings Domain (Map pp78–9) is an area of parkland across from the Melbourne arts precinct that contains the wonderful Royal Botanic Gardens, as well as the Shrine of Remembrance, Governor La Trobe's Cottage and the Sidney Myer Music Bowl.

Government House (Map pp76-7; ☎ 9656 9800; Government House Dr; tours adult/child $15/10/30; ☽ tours 10.30am Mon, Wed & Fri) is the home of the Victorian Governor. It's a copy of Queen Victoria's palace on England's Isle of Wight. Built in 1872, it's one of the country's best examples of Italianate style. Entry is by guided tour; bookings are essential. The tour price includes entry to La Trobe's Cottage.

Beside St Kilda Rd stands the massive **Shrine of Remembrance** (Map pp76-7; ☎ 9654 8415; www.shrine .org.au; St Kilda Rd; admission free; ☽ 10am-5pm), built as a memorial to Victorians killed in WWI.

Certainly the finest gardens in Australia and among the world's best, the **Royal Botanic Gardens** (Map pp76-7; ☎ 9252 2300; www.rbg.vic.gov.au; Birdwood Ave; admission free; ☽ 7.30am-8.30pm Nov-Mar, to 5.30pm Apr-Oct) are a must-see. With a prime riverside location, the beautifully laid-out gardens feature lakes, wildlife and plants from around the world. The **visitors centre** (☎ 9252 2429; Observatory Gate, Birdwood Ave; ☽ 9am-5pm Mon-Fri, 9.30am-5pm Sat & Sun) stocks self-guided tour leaflets (also available at garden entrances), which change with the seasons. Also here is the **Ian Potter Foundation Children's Garden** (see p90).

East Melbourne & Richmond

East Melbourne (Map pp76–7) features sedate streets lined with double-fronted Victorian terraces, Italianate mansions and Art Deco apartment blocks. Locals here walk to the city across the Fitzroy Gardens, and to the Melbourne Cricket Ground for a footy or cricket match. Richmond (Map pp76–7), once a raggle-taggle collection of worker's cottages, is now also rather genteel, although it retains many old pubs and has a thriving Vietnamese community along **Victoria St**. Shoppers swarm to the **Bridge Rd** and **Swan St** outlet stores seven days a week, and **Church St** is where fashionable Melbourne comes to buy bathroom fittings.

The 100,000-capacity **Melbourne Cricket Ground** (MCG; Map pp76-7; ☎ 9657 8888; www.mcg.org .au; Brunton Ave) is the temple in which sports-mad Melburnians worship their heroes. It's one of the world's great sporting arenas, full of tradition and atmosphere. The first game of football was played here at 'the G' in 1858, and in 1877 the first test cricket match between Australia and England. The roar at the opening bounce of a sold-out football game makes your hair stand on end! If you want to make a pilgrimage, **tours** (☎ 9657 8879; adult/concession/family $15/11/45; ☽ every 30min 10am-3pm nonmatch days) take you through the stands, coaches' areas, the MCC (Melbourne Cricket Club) museum, and out onto the ground. Tickets for AFL games can be purchased through Ticketmaster7 (p97). Carn Carlton!

The new **National Museum of Sport** (Map pp77-8; ☎ 9657 8856; www.mcg.org.au; Olympic Stand, Gate 3, MCG, Brunton Ave; general admission adult/concession/family $15/11/45, with MCG tour $22/15/50; ☽ 10am-5pm) features five permanent exhibitions. Choice objects on display include hand-written notes outlining the AFL's first rules from 1859, Bradman's baggy green cap, olive branches awarded to Australia's first Olympian in 1886, and our Cathy's famous Sydney Olympics swift suit.'

Carlton, Fitzroy & Collingwood

Carlton (Map pp84–5) and adjacent **Parkville** (Map pp76-7) are divided by the tree-lined Royal Pde. A huge chunk of Parkville is devoted to the enormous 188-hectare **Royal Park**. Carlton is Melbourne's Italian quarter. Many Italian migrants who came to Melbourne after WWII settled here and **Lygon St** became the focal point of their community. Day and night it is filled with people promenading, dining, drinking coffee and shopping. In October, Lygon St hosts the lively four-day **Lygon St Festa**.

Melbourne's first suburbs – Fitzroy (Map pp84–5) and Collingwood (Map pp84–5) – have a rough-around-the-edges feel despite rapid gentrification in the '80s. **Brunswick St** sports a straggle of interesting cafés, restaurants and shops, and its backstreet pubs have managed to stay out of the developers' clutches. Although most of the artists have moved on in search of cheap studio space, you'll still find a number of galleries and arts-related shops here. The rise and rise of **Gertrude St** continues apace, and Collingwood's **Smith St** has a *jolie-laide* charm.

ROYAL MELBOURNE ZOO

Set in spacious landscaped gardens, Melbourne's **zoo** (Map pp76-7; ☎ 9285 9300; www.zoo .org.au; Elliot Ave, Parkville; adult/child/family $21/11.50/53; ☽ 9am-5pm) aims to simulate natural habitats. Walkways pass through the enclosures; you can stroll through the bird aviary, cross a bridge over the lions' park or enter a tropical butterfly hothouse. There's also a large collection of native animals in bush settings.

In summer the zoo hosts **twilight concerts** (www .zoo.org.au/melbourne/twilights.htm). Established in 1861, this is the oldest zoo in Australia and the third-oldest in the world.

CARLTON GARDENS

These **gardens** are home to the historic **Royal Exhibition Building** (Map pp84–5; ☎ 9270 5000; www .museum.vic.gov.au/reb; Nicholson St). Built for the International Exhibition in 1880, and winning Unesco World Heritage status in 2004, this beautiful Victorian edifice symbolises the glory days of the industrial revolution, empire and 19th-century Melbourne's economic supremacy. Australia's first parliament was held here in 1901; a hundred-plus years later everything from trade fairs to dance parties take place. **Tours** (☎ 1300 130 152; adult/child $4/2; ☽ 2pm) happen daily – phone for bookings.

MELBOURNE MUSEUM

This postmodern **museum** (Map pp84–5; ☎ 13 11 02; www.melbourne.museum.vic.gov.au; 11 Nicholson St, Carlton; adult/concession & child $6/free; ☽ 10am-5pm) mixes old-style object displays with themed interactive display areas, providing a grand sweep of Victoria's natural and cultural histories. **Bunjilaka** presents indigenous stories and history told through objects and Aboriginal voices. There's a hands-on children's area and an **Imax Cinema** (☎ 9663 5454; www.imaxmelbourne.com.au).

South Melbourne, Port Melbourne & Albert Park

The main thoroughfare in South Melbourne (Map pp76–7) is **Clarendon St**, which is dissected by laid-back shopping strips on **Coventry St** and **Park St**. In Albert Park (Map pp76–7) there's **Victoria Ave**, lined with cafés, restaurants and shops. The regeneration of Port Melbourne (Map pp76–7) has come more slowly, but now **Bay St** rivals Victoria Ave for style. The common thread is **Canterbury Rd**, which is rebadged as **Ferras St** at Albert Park. The **beachfront** footpath is always full of joggers, dog walkers, roller-bladers and cyclists taking in the sea air.

Elegant black swans give their bottoms-up salute at man-made **Albert Park Lake**, whose perimeter road hosts the **Australian Formula One Grand Prix** (p91).

South Yarra, Prahran & St Kilda

The **Chapel St** strip in South Yarra (Map p92) still parades itself as a must-do fashion

MELBOURNE

destination, but has seen better days; it's been taken over by chain stores and tacky bars. Over Commercial Rd, Prahran (Map p92) and **Windsor** (Map p92) are much more interesting. **Hawksburn** (Map pp76–7) up the hill and High St **Armadale** (Map pp76–7) make for stylish shopping sorties. Cute **Greville St** runs off Chapel and has good nightlife, eating and shopping. **Commercial Rd** is Melbourne's pink zone and home to the excellent Prahran Market.

Bayside St Kilda (Map p92) is one of Melbourne's most cosmopolitan areas, and was Melbourne's favourite 19th-century playground. It's gone in and out of fashion since then. The '80s-era druggies and transvestites have been shooed away from **Fitzroy St**, which has been reborn with stylish bars, restaurants and cafés. Further south, **Acland St** between Carlisle and Barkly Sts, famed for its continental cake shops and delicatessens, is another favourite restaurant strip. St Kilda's halcyon days live on via the grand **George Hotel** (125 Fitzroy St) and the gorgeous **Palais Theatre** (☎ 9525 3240, www.palaistheatre.net.au; Lower Esplanade) where you can see ballet or a touring rock band.

St Kilda Pier and breakwater is a favourite spot for strollers. On the foreshore south of the pier, the **St Kilda Sea Baths** (right) is a Moorish-inspired bathing pavilion.

Luna Park (Map p92; ☎ 9525 5033; www.lunapark .com.au; Lower Esplanade; adult/child 1-ride ticket $7/5.50, unlimited-ride ticket $36/26; ☒ 11am-6pm Sat & Sun) opened in 1912 and retains the feel of an old-style amusement park. There's a heritage-listed scenic railway and a beautifully rococo carousel with hand-painted horses, swans and chariots. See the website for extended hours in summer and school holidays.

ACTIVITIES
Cycling
Many Melburnians take advantage of the city's extensive network of bike paths and scant hills. There's a dynamic club scene (see www .bicycles.com.au) with weekend rides followed by lycra-clad café breakfasts.

Many of Melbourne's cycling paths are constructed in the green belts along rivers and are marked in the *Melway Greater Melbourne Street Directory*. There are also many on-road bike lanes. You can get maps from the visitors centre at Federation Sq (p81) or from the website of VicRoads (www.vicroads.vic.gov.au). **Bicycle Victoria** (☎ 8636 8888; www.bv.com.au) is a self-funded community organisation and

the state's peak cycling body. Its website lists bike-hire operators.

Swimming
Melbourne Sports & Aquatic Centre (Map pp76-7; ☎ 9926 1555; www.msac.com.au; Albert Rd, Albert Park; adult/child $6/4.50; ☒ 6am-10pm) has a fantastic 10-lane, 75m indoor pool, several smaller pools, water slides, a spa/sauna/steam room and spacious common areas.

Melbourne City Baths (Map pp84-5; ☎ 9663 5888; www.melbournecitybaths.com.au; cnr Swanston & Victoria Sts; adult/child/family $5/2.50/11; ☒ 6am-10pm Mon-Thu, 6am-8.30pm Fri, 8am-6pm Sat & Sun) is a stately 1903 heritage-listed swimming hall with a 30m indoor pool plus spas, saunas and gym.

St Kilda Sea Baths (Map p92; ☎ 9525 4888; www .southpacifichc.com.au; 10-18 Jacka Blvd, St Kilda; adult/child $12/6) isn't the cheapest swimming option in town, but it's brilliant, with a 25m indoor sea-water pool, a hydrotherapy pool and a steamroom that can work miracles.

WALKING TOUR
Arcades, Laneways & Street Art
Start at **Federation Sq** (1; p81) at the corner of Swanston and Flinders Sts and admire the vista towards circa-1891 **St Paul's Cathedral** (2) across the street. Cross over Swanston St and head west along Flinders St noting the magnificent **Flinders St station** (3), one of the few Edwardian baroque buildings in Melbourne. Turn right into skinny **Degraves St** (4), named after entrepreneur William Degraves who built a steam-powered flourmill on this site in 1851. This is one of Melbourne's favourite café strips, known for its tiny hole-in-the-wall coffeeshops. At the end of Degraves St on the other side of Flinders La is the beautiful 1920s Spanish-inspired **Majorca Building** (5). Cross over Flinders La and go into the even-skinnier **Centre Pl** (6). Just before the steps on your left is a small alcove where lightboxes illuminate the ephemeral and ever-changing **graffiti and stencil artwork** (7) of local and international artists. Atop the stairs is the **Centre Way** (8) arcade in one of the city's earliest steel-

---

WALK FACTS

Start Federation Sq
Finish Flinders St
Distance 5km
Duration two hours

frame buildings (1913), lined with boutiques and specialty stores.

Centre Way empties onto fashionable Collins St. Cross the road, turn left and walk down to **Block Arcade (9)**, with exquisite mosaic-tiled floors, marble columns and plasterwork. It wends its way around to **Block Pl (10)** – more cafés and casual eateries. Block Pl brings you to Little Collins St and a dilemma: turn right and either go down the superb, Victorian-era **Royal Arcade (11)** with its celebrated Gog and Magog statues watching over the passers-by; or continue east along Little Collins St until you come to **Union La (12)**, another of the city's council-designated street-art sites (you could do a loop and take in both).

You're now at Bourke St Mall. Turn left and walk down to Elizabeth St past Simon Perry's **Public Purse sculpture (13)** in front of the grand 1859-1919 **GPO** (**14**; p100), now refitted as a shopping mall, and turn right into Elizabeth St. The **underground public toilets (15)** here are heritage-listed. The men's dates from 1910; women had to wait until 1927 to piss in… er… under, the street. Turn left into Little Bourke St and walk west past two laneways on your right until you arrive at **Niagara La (16)**. Here you can see the historic 1887 red-brick warehouses with their American barrel-hoists.

Niagara La empties onto Lonsdale St. Here you turn right and walk a block-and-a-half east to **Caledonian La (17)**, which features yet

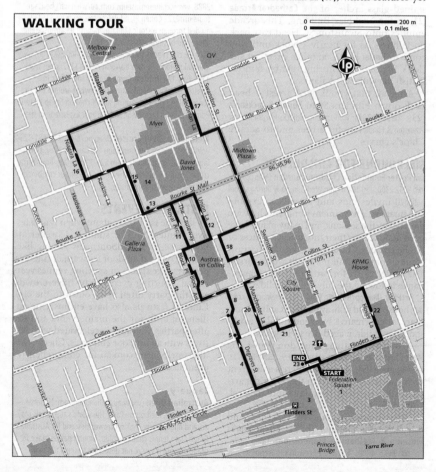

WALKING TOUR

0 —————— 200 m
0 —————— 0.1 miles

more of Melbourne's famed graffiti and stencil art (and St Jerome's, Melbourne's coolest bar; see p97). Turn left into Little Bourke St, right into Swanston St and walk over Bourke St, turning right into Little Collins St. A little way down on your left is broad, L-shaped **Howey Pl (18)**, which has a dim, left-hand extension. This enters the glorious, marble-lined, Art Deco **Manchester Unity Arcade (19)** in the sumptuous 1932 Manchester Unity Building. Though not very large, this arcade is superb (see the timberwork and domed lights in the elevators).

Walk down Collins St, through **Manchester La (20)** and left along Flinders La (once the rag-trade centre of Melbourne) until you come to the steps leading up to the ornate, stained-glass arches of the **Cathedral Arcade (21)** in the Nicholas Building. This arcade empties onto Swanston St. Head east back up Flinders La for nearly a block until you come to **Hosier La (22)**, another street-art site (look for the parachuting rats by famous British guerrilla artist Banksy).

After all that you'll need a rest – head back down Flinders St to **Young & Jackson's (23**; ☎ 9650 3884; www.youngandjackson.com.au; cnr Swanston & Flinders Sts) for a beer and to admire Chloe's curves.

MELBOURNE FOR CHILDREN

Ian Potter Foundation Children's Garden (Map pp78-9; ☎ 9252 2300; ☽ 10am-4pm Wed-Sun, daily during school holidays) invites kids and parents to explore and imagine. The minienvironments here are directed by the seasons, and many plants have been included for their intrinsic weirdness or strong colours. Children can dig, climb, crawl through tunnels and play with worm farms. The garden closes for two months for maintenance following the July school holidays.

ArtPlay (Map pp78-9; ☎ 9664 7900; www.artplay.com.au), housed in old railway buildings at Birrarung Marr, offers creative weekend/holiday workshops for children aged five to 12 years.

Around Christmas time don't miss the **Myer Christmas Windows** (Map pp78-9; ☎ 9661 1111; Myer, Bourke St Mall). Each year there's a different theme as artists transform the Myer department store shopfront windows into magical, animated worlds.

Other options include **Luna Park** (p88) and the **Melbourne Museum** (p87). **Scienceworks Museum & Melbourne Planetarium** (Map p76-7; ☎ 9392 4800; www.scienceworks.museum.vic.gov .au; 2 Booker St, Spotswood; adult/concession $6/free, incl Planetarium show $12.50/5; ☽ 10am-4.30pm) is popular with kids with its many hands-on exhibits.

TOURS

There's a huge array of tours on offer in and around Melbourne. The free monthly *Melbourne Events* guide, available at visitors centres and hotels, has an extensive tours section.

Aboriginal Heritage Walk (Map p76-7; ☎ 9252 2300; www.rbg.vic.gov.au; Royal Botanic Gardens; adult/child/family $18/9/50; ☽ 11am Thu & Fri, 10.30am every 2nd Sun) The Royal Botanic Gardens are on the ancestral lands of the Boonwurrung and Woiworung people. This tour takes you through their story for 90 fascinating minutes.

Chinatown Heritage Walk (Map pp78-9; ☎ 9662 2888; www.chinesemuseum.com.au/whatson_heritage_ tours.html; 22 Cohen Pl; adult/concession from $15/12) Be guided through historic Chinatown, with its atmospheric alleys and bustling vibe.

City Circle Trams (Map pp78-9; ☎ 1800 800 166; www .metlinkmelbourne.com.au/route/view/1112; rides free; ☽ every 12min 10am-6pm) These trams offers free services (clockwise and counterclockwise) around the city centre, along Flinders, Spring and Nicholson Sts to Victoria Pde, and along Latrobe St and Harbour Esplanade in the Docklands.

Melbourne River Cruises (Map pp78-9; ☎ 9681 3284; www.melbcruises.com.au; Vault 11, Banana Alley, Docklands; adult/child/family from $22/11/50) One-hour Yarra cruise upstream or downstream, or a 2½-hour combined upstream/downstream cruise.

FESTIVALS & EVENTS

Melbourne isn't fussy about when it gets festive. Winter chills or summer's swelter are no excuse, with Melbournians joining like-minded types at outdoor festivals, in cinemas, performance spaces or sporting venues year-round. Sporting events draw huge crowds, and the party often spills out into the city. Cultural festivals also have enthusiastic audiences, both for the main events and the after-parties. Summer is celebrated with festivals with an outdoor emphasis. Check www .thatsmelbourne.com.au for comprehensive event listings.

January

Australian Open (www.australianopen.com; National Tennis Centre, Melbourne Park) The world's top tennis players and huge, merry-making crowds descend for Australia's Grand Slam tennis championship. Ground passes make for a grand day out if you're not desperate to see a top seed.

Midsumma Festival (www.midsumma.org.au) Melbourne's annual gay-and-lesbian arts festival features over 100 events from mid-January to mid-February, with a Pride March finale. Expect everything from film screenings to a high-camp rowing regatta, history walks and dance parties.

Big Day Out (www.bigdayout.com) The national rock-fest comes to town at the end of January. Big names are guaranteed, but the local Lily Pad lads often steal the show.

Chinese New Year (www.melbournechinatown.com .au; Little Bourke St, Chinatown) Melbourne has celebrated the Chinese lunar new year since Little Bourke St became Chinatown in the 1860s. Time to touch the dragon falls sometime towards the end of January or early February.

February

St Kilda Festival (www.stkildafestival.com.au; Acland & Fitzroy Sts, St Kilda) This week-long festival ends in a suburb-wide street party on the final Sunday. The crowds are large and laidback, if not as uniformly bohemian as they once were.

St Jerome's Laneway Festival (www.lanewayfestival .com.au) Indie kids delight in their natural laneway habitat, with a line-up of international and local acts loving the intimate atmosphere. Held at the end of February.

Melbourne Fashion Festival (www.mff.com.au) This week-long style-fest from the end of February into March features salon shows and parades showcasing established designers' ranges. Join the airkiss set or get down with the up-and-comings at one of the many off-shoot happenings.

Melbourne Food & Wine Festival (www.melbourne foodandwine.com.au) Market tours, wine tastings, cooking classes and presentations by celeb chefs take place at venues across the city in February and/or March. Chew the gastronomic fat or just eat your fill.

March

Moomba Waterfest (www.thatsmelbourne.com.au; Alexandra Gardens, Birrarung Marr & Waterfront City Piazza, Docklands) Moomba's had something of a new millennium makeover, with the action focussed around the Yarra and Victoria Harbour. The old favourite is the wacky Birdman Rally, where competitors launch themselves into the drink in homemade flying-machines.

Australian Formula One Grand Prix (www.grandprix .com.au; Albert Park) The 5.3km street circuit around normally tranquil Albert Park Lake is known for its smooth, fast surface. The buzz, both on the streets and in your ears, takes over Melbourne for four days of rev-head action.

April

Anzac Day Parade (www.shrine.org.au; Shrine of Remembrance, St Kilda Rd, Kings Domain) On 25 April Australians remember the WWI Australian and New Zealand Army Corps (Anzac) defeat at Gallipoli, and honour all those who have served in war. Melbourne has a dawn service at the Shrine of Remembrance and a veterans parade along St Kilda Rd.

International Comedy Festival (www.comedyfestival .com.au) An enormous range of local and international comic talent hits town with 3½ weeks of stand-up comedy, cabaret, theatre, street performance, film, TV, radio and visual arts.

May

Melbourne Jazz (www.melbournejazz.com) International jazz cats head to town and join locals for gigs at Hamer Hall, The Regent Theatre and the Palms at Crown Casino.

July

Melbourne International Film Festival (www.mel bournefilmfestival.com.au) Midwinter movie love-in brings out black-skivvy-wearing cinephiles in droves. It's held over two weeks at various cinemas across the city in July and August. The music doco programme is a particular treat.

August

Melbourne Writers' Festival (www.mwf.com.au) Beginning in the last week of August, the writers' festival features 10 days of forums and events at various venues, celebrating reading, writing, books and ideas.

September

AFL Grand Final (www.afl.com.au; MCG) It's easier to kick a goal from the boundary line than to pick up random tickets to the Grand Final, but it's not hard to get your share of finals fever anywhere in Melbourne. Pubs put on big screens and BBQs (often accompanied by a spot of street kick-to-kick at half-time). For the truly devoted, there's also the Grand Final Parade on the preceding Friday.

Melbourne Fringe Festival (www.melbournefringe .com.au) The Fringe takes place in September and October and showcases experimental theatre, music and visual arts.

October

Melbourne International Arts Festival (www.mel bournefestival.com.au) Held at various venues around the city, this festival features a thought-provoking programme of Australian and international theatre, opera, dance, visual art and music.

November

Melbourne Cup (www.springracingcarnival.com.au) Culminating in the prestigious Melbourne Cup, the Spring Racing Carnival is as much a social event as a sporting one. The Cup, held on the first Tuesday in November, is a public holiday in Melbourne.

December

Boxing Day Test (www.mcg.org.au; MCG) Boxing Day is day one of Melbourne's annually scheduled international

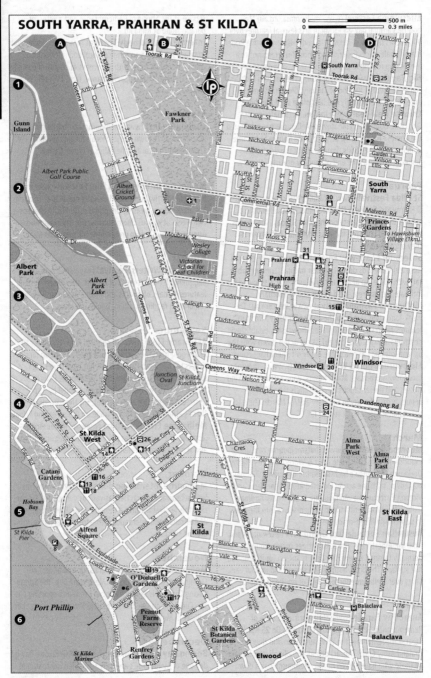

SOUTH YARRA, PRAHRAN & ST KILDA

0 — 500 m
0 — 0.3 miles

SOUTH YARRA, PRAHRAN & ST KILDA (p92)

text cricket match, drawing out the cricket fans. Expect some shenanigans from Bay 13.

New Year's Eve (www.thatsmelbourne.com.au) Fireworks light up the Yarra at 9pm and midnight.

SLEEPING

The city centre is convenient and close to theatres, museums, transport and nightlife, while suburbs such as St Kilda, East Melbourne, South Yarra, Carlton and Fitzroy are good alternatives.

Budget

There are backpacker hostels in the city centre and inner suburbs. Larger hostels often have courtesy buses that pick up from the bus and train terminals, and most offer discounts for longer stays.

CENTRAL MELBOURNE

Melbourne Connection Travellers Hostel (Map pp78-9; ☎ 9642 4464; www.melbourneconnection.com; 205 King St; dm $22-28, d $67-80; 🖳) This little 79-bed charmer follows the small-is-better principle. It offers simple, clean and uncluttered budget accommodation with modern facilities, basement lounge area and well-organised staff.

Hotel Discovery (Map pp78-9; ☎ 9329 7525; www.hotel discovery.com.au; 167 Franklin St; dm $25-28, d from $85; 🖳) Housed in a grand old building, the Discovery offers standard hostel rooms with extras such as a rooftop garden and 'cinema' near Victoria Market. There are also lounge areas, pool tables, a bar and a café, which makes for a very social atmosphere. Family rooms and en suite doubles also available.

Greenhouse Backpacker (Map pp78-9; ☎ 9639 6400; www.friendlygroup.com.au; 6/228 Flinders La; dm/s/d incl breakfast $30/65/80; 🖳) Well-run Greenhouse has a low-key, relaxed vibe. Freebies include daily half-hour internet access, pancakes on Sunday, rooftop BBQs, luggage storage and activities. There are spic-and-span facilities and double-bed bunks for couples in the mixed dorms.

CARLTON, FITZROY & COLLINGWOOD

ourpick **Nunnery** (Map pp84-5; ☎ 9419 8637; www .nunnery.com.au; 116 Nicholson St, Fitzroy; incl breakfast dm $28-32, s $70-80, d $95-115) The Nunnery oozes atmosphere, with sweeping staircases and many original features. The walls are dappled with religious artworks and ornate stained-glass windows. Give thanks for comfortable lounges and communal areas. Apart from the main building there's also the Nunnery Guesthouse, which has larger rooms in a private setting.

SOUTH YARRA, PRAHRAN & ST KILDA

Coffee Palace (Map p92; ☎ 9534 5283; www.coffeepal acebackpackers.com.au; 24 Grey St, St Kilda; dm from $20, d from $60; 🖳) This rambling, old-school backpackers has lots of rooms, lots of activities and lots of years behind it. It has a travel desk, communal kitchen, bar, pool tables, lounge and TV room, plus a rooftop terrace with bay views. Dorms (some women-only) sleep from four to 10. There are also private rooms with shared bathrooms.

ourpick **Base** (Map p92; ☎ 9536 6109; www.base backpackers.com; 17 Carlisle St, St Kilda; dm/r from $30/99; 🖳) St Kilda's flashest hostel fronts Carlisle St with a bold, red feature wall, and has streamlined dorms (each with en suite) or slick doubles. There's also a 'sanctuary' floor for female travellers, a bar and a full range of leisure options (including a pool table) to complete the package. A good-time party atmosphere prevails.

MELBOURNE

Olembia Guesthouse (Map p92; ☎ 9537 1412; www
.olembia.com.au; 96 Barkly St, St Kilda; dm/s/d $30/80/100)
Olembia offers impeccably presented (if
slightly fusty) rooms at backpacker prices.
The small, elegant old house also has a cosy
lounge and a spacious, leafy courtyard out
front. Bookings are advised, especially for the
upstairs family room.

Midrange
CENTRAL MELBOURNE
Pensione Hotel (Map pp78-9; ☎ 9621 3333; www.pensione
.com.au; 16 Spencer St; r from $90; ✳ 🖳) The Pensione
isn't being cute christening some rooms 'petit
double'. What you don't get in size is made up
for in style, room extras and rates. This recent
refurb and rebranding is a welcome jolt to the
Melbourne hotel scene.

City Centre Hotel (Map pp78-9; ☎ 9654 5401; www
.citycentrebudgethotel.com.au; 22 Little Collins St; r from $90;
✳ 🖳) Intimate, independent and inconspic-
uous, this 38-room hotel is a find. It's located
at the city's prettier end in an unassuming
building. All rooms share bathroom facilities,
but the accommodation is light-filled (with
working windows), there's free wi-fi and a
laundry. On the roof there are swing-seats
and banana lounges. The service is genuine
and genial, and everyone is accommodated,
from solo travellers to families.

Alto Hotel on Bourke (Map pp78-9; ☎ 9606 0585; www
.altohotel.com.au; 636 Bourke St; r/apt from $135/160;
✳ 🖳) This is an award-winning, purpose-
built 'green' hotel that's fitted with water-
savings showers, energy-efficient light globes
and double-glazed windows that open. In-
room recycling is promoted. Rooms are
well-equipped, light and neutrally decorated.
Apartments (from one bed and up) have
kitchens, LCD TVs and some have spas.

EAST MELBOURNE & RICHMOND
George Powlett Apartments (Map pp76-7; ☎ 9419
9488; www.georgepowlett.com.au; cnr George & Powlett
Sts, East Melbourne; studio apt from $95; ✳ 🖳) These
older-style rooms have kitchenettes and
are a 10-minute walk from town through
the fabulous Fitzroy Gardens. The low-rise
complex, located in the shadows of the MCG
light towers, has 45 compact rooms, some
with balconies.

CARLTON, FITZROY & COLLINGWOOD
Vibe Hotel Carlton (pp76-7; ☎ 9380 9222; www.vibehotels
.com.au; 441 Royal Pde, Parkville; r from $150; ✳ 🖳 🐾)
This 1960s motel was once noted for its glamorous, high-Californian style. Vibe hasn't
made the most of it, but some period charm
shines through. Rooms have floor-to-ceiling
windows and clean lines. Its Parkville location
is pretty (and close to the zoo), the city is a
short tram-ride away, and the Brunswick or
Carlton North cafés aren't too far by foot.

SOUTH YARRA, PRAHRAN & ST KILDA
Albany (Map p92; ☎ 9866 4485; www.thealbany.com
.au; cnr Toorak Rd & Millswyn St, South Yarra; r from $125;
✳ 🖳) Out the front of this eccentric hotel is
an 1890s mansion with high-ceilinged rooms
and a penthouse that recalls late-'60s swinging
London. Out the back is a motel-style wing.

Tolarno Hotel (Map p92; ☎ 9537 0200; www.hotel
tolarno.com.au; 42 Fitzroy St, St Kilda; r from $145; ✳ 🖳)
Tolarno was once the site of Georges Mora's
seminal gallery Tolarno. The fine-dining restaurant downstairs now bears the name of
his artist wife Mirka, as well as her original
paintings. Rooms upstairs aren't quite so chic,
but are brightly coloured with good beds and
crisp white linen. Those at the front might be
noisy but have balconies.

Toorak Manor (Map pp76-7; ☎ 9827 2689; www.toorak
manor.net; 220 Williams Rd, Toorak; r from $155; ✳) This
graceful old mansion sports frills and flowing
chiffon in its 18 period-style rooms. Some of
the décor is looking a bit tired but you're in a
top spot near happening Hawksburn Village,
and its only about 10 minutes into the city
from the quaint train station.

Top End
SOUTHBANK & DOCKLANDS
Crown Promenade Hotel (Map pp78-9; ☎ 9292 6688; www
.crownpromenade.com.au; 8 Whiteman St, Southbank; r from
$245; ✳ 🖳) Crown's 'other' hotel is linked to
the mothership by an air bridge. It is much
more laidback than Crown Towers and offers
large, modern and gently masculine rooms
with luxurious bathrooms, big windows, flat
screens and Sony Playstations. Views vary but
many are as breathtaking as the Towers.

SOUTH YARRA, PRAHRAN & ST KILDA
Prince (Map p92; ☎ 9536 1111; www.theprince.com.au;
2 Acland St, St Kilda; r from $260; ✳ 🖳) The Prince
is Melbourne's best-known 'design' hotel.
The small lobby is suitably dramatic and the
rooms are an interesting mix of the original pub's proportions, natural materials and
pared-back aesthetic. Larger rooms and suites

feature some key pieces of vintage modernist furniture. Onsite 'facilities' are some of the city's best: Circa restaurant, the Aurora day spa, bars, band rooms and a fabulous wine shop downstairs. Be prepared for weekend nightclub-noise seepage.

EATING

Melbourne has a fine foodie culture thanks to its self-assured bohemianism and rich ethnic melting pot. There are fine-dining menus that follow a contemporary French direction, but you're more likely to encounter thoughtful pan-Mediterranean cuisine and a constantly reinvented grab-bag of styles we call Mod Oz. Italian is done well, as is Eastern Mediterranean food. Along with the Queen Victoria Market and its suburban counterparts in South Melbourne and Prahran, there's a weekly rota of **farmers markets** (www.mfm.com.au), which bring fresh produce to town.

The *Age* newspaper publishes a Tuesday food-and-wine supplement, the annual *Good Food Guide* and its companion *Cheap Eats*.

Central Melbourne

our pick **Bar Lourinhã** (Map pp78-9; ☎ 9663 7890; 37 Little Collins St; tapas $8-20; ☻ lunch & dinner Mon-Fri, dinner Sat) Matt McConnell's wonderful northern-Spanish/Portuguese specialties have the swagger and honesty of an Iberian shepherd, but with a cluey, metropolitan touch. There's an intriguing wine list sourced from the region too. Come Friday night, the sardines are not just on the plate; but a lone spoonful of the house *crema* (espresso foam) is worth the squeeze.

Journal Canteen (Map pp78-9; ☎ 9650 4399; 253 Flinders La; mains $15-25; ☻ lunch Mon-Fri) Journal Canteen, tucked away up an obscure flight of stairs off the CAE building foyer, is no secret. It's packed to the rafters each lunchtime with diners lapping up Rosa Mitchell's sensational Sicilian-style antipasto plates, pastas, roasts and ragouts. Be spared the agony of choice: Rosa bases her few offerings on what is fresh and seasonal the day.

Supper Inn (Map pp78-9; ☎ 9663 4759; 15 Celestial Ave; mains $15-30; ☻ dinner) If you like to find out where the chefs eat when they finish a shift, then look no further. Open till very late (2.30am), it serves some of the best late-night congee, noodles, dumplings and other yummies to a mixed crowd.

Cookie (Map pp78-9; ☎ 9663 7660; 1st fl, 252 Swanston St; mains $17-30; ☻ lunch & dinner) The Thai menu

at this crowd-pleasing beer hall is a pleasant surprise. Grab a spritzer to go with your snapper curry or prawn-and-lemongrass coconut custard, then head up to the Rooftop Bar for Melbourne's best view.

Press Club (Map pp78-9; ☎ 9677 9677; 72 Flinders St; mains $26-35; ☻ lunch Sun-Fri, dinner daily) Melbourne's mod-Greek scene is thriving, and George Columbaris' grand city space gives it the glamour it richly deserves. There's no fusion fussing, just a respect for the basics and a very 'now' sensibility. Think dolmades stuffed with roast quail; salmon cooked slowly in tzatziki and served with almond *skordalia*; or the 'Santorini breakfast' dessert (honey sorbet, yoghurt jelly and walnut biscuit).

Ginger Boy (Map pp78-9; ☎ 9662 4200; 27-29 Crossley St; mains $28-33; ☻ lunch & dinner Mon-Fri, dinner Sat) Brave the aggressively trendy surrounds and weekend party scene for talented Teague Ezard's flash hawker cooking. Flavours pop in dishes such as scallops with green chilli jam, or coconut kingfish with peanut and tamarind dressing. There are two dinner sittings; bookings required.

our pick **Vue De Monde** (Map pp78-9; ☎ 9691 3888; 430 Little Collins St; 5-course degustation menu $150; ☻ lunch & dinner Tue-Fri, dinner Sat) Melbourne's favoured spot for occasion dining isn't stuffy; though set in a 19th-century barrister's chamber, the space is starkly luxe. This is degustation dining with a capital D: you choose how much gastronomic immersion you're up for and courses will be tailored accordingly. Book ahead.

Southbank & Docklands

Bopha Devi (Map pp76-7; ☎ 9600 1887; 27 Rakaia Way, Docklands; mains $16-24; ☻ lunch & dinner) The modern Cambodian food here is a delightful mix of novel and familiar Southeast Asian flavours and textures. Herb-strewn salads, noodles and soups manage to be both fresh and filling.

our pick **Mecca Bah** (Map pp76-7; ☎ 9642 1300; 55a New Quay Promenade, Docklands; mains $17-21; ☻ lunch & dinner) This opulent, hexagon-shaped restaurant serves Turkish pizza and a selection of *meze* (bite-size delights) all day. Their mains – mostly *tagines* (Middle Eastern stews) and grills – are hearty and spicy, most welcome when the wind is whipping up the bay outside.

Tutto Bene (Map pp78-9; ☎ 9696 3334; Mid-level Southgate, Southbank; mains $17-36; ☻ lunch & dinner) There are other *primi piatti*, but the main

MELBOURNE

event here is risotto. Choices range from a simple Venetian *risi e bisi* (rice and peas) to some fabulously luxe options involving truffles, roast quail or aged balsamic. Fine housemade gelato is the requisite desert; you can drop in just for a *coppa* (cup) scooped from the outside servery.

Carlton, Fitzroy & Collingwood

Añada (Map pp84–5; ☎ 9415 6101; 197 Gertrude St, Fitzroy; tapas $4-16 ☺ dinner) Dishes such as mackerel with orange-blossom and pistachio are alive with hearty Spanish and Muslim Mediterranean flavours. There are big and little plates and a good selection of Iberian wines.

our pick **Moroccan Soup Bar** (Map pp76–7; ☎ 9482 4240; 183 St Georges Rd, Fitzroy North; mains $10-15; ☺ dinner Tue-Sun) Nab a table and prick up your ears: the chatelaine of this fabulous, down-to-earth restaurant hardly draws breath as she rattles off a list of soups, starters and heavenly North African *tagines* before telling you what you're getting. The food is divine and authentically Moroccan.

Brunetti (Map pp84–5; ☎ 9347 2801; 198 Faraday St, Carlton; café dishes $3-7, restaurant mains $12-23; ☺ breakfast, lunch & dinner) A stalwart of Italian culinary obsessions, Brunetti is a haven for those who want excellent coffee, exquisite *dolci* (sweets), and mouth-watering Roman-influenced dishes.

our pick **DOC Pizza & Mozarella** (Map pp84–5; ☎ 9347 2998; 295 Drummond St, Carlton; mains $14-23; ☺ dinner daily, lunch & dinner Sun) DOC has jumped on the Milanese-led mozzarella-bar trend and serves up the milky white balls – your choice of local or imported buffalo – as entrees, in salads or atop fabulous pizzas. Other pizza toppings include creamy broccoli puree and prosciutto, bitter-sweet *cicoria* (chicory) and lemon, and the litmus-test margarita. The buffalo milk gelato is a delight.

Abla's (Map pp84–5; ☎ 9347 0006; 109 Elgin St, Carlton; mains $14-25; ☺ lunch Thu & Fri, dinner Mon-Sat) Abla Amad is the motherly matriarch of Melbourne's best Lebanese restaurant. She's been cooking here for 30 years and has inspired a whole generation of Lebanese chefs. Bring a bottle of your favourite plonk and settle in for the compulsory side-splitting banquet on Friday and Saturday nights.

Panama Dining Room (Map pp84–5; ☎ 9417 7663; Level 3, 231 Smith St, Fitzroy; mains $15-22; ☺ dinner Wed-Sun) The Franco-Fitzroy pub-grub on offer here is great value, and just right over

a bottle or two while gawping at the ersatz Manhattan views. The large space also does double-duty as a bar, so come early or be prepared for some happy hubbub with your frites and rillettes.

Commoner (Map pp84–5; ☎ 9415 6876; 122 Johnston St, Fitzroy; dinner mains $17-33; ☺ breakfast & lunch Sat & Sun, dinner Wed-Sun) If you need to be convinced of this off-strip restaurant's serious intent, the house-roasted goat offered up for Sunday lunch should do it. There's a nice, neat wine list and posh beer to compliment the Eastern-Med–inflected dishes.

South Yarra, Prahran & St Kilda

Galleon (Map p92; ☎ 9534 8934; 9 Carlisle St, St Kilda; meals $7-16; ☺ breakfast, lunch & dinner) Just off Acland St, Galleon has fuelled the creative juices of St Kilda's arts community for years with simple and inexpensive café-style food and fantastic hot breakfasts. We love it!

Mama Ganoush (Map p92; ☎ 9521 4141; 56 Chapel St, Windsor; mains $17-32; ☺ dinner Mon-Sat) Middle Eastern food that remains true to its roots whilst being modern and new. The space is full of delicate arabesque screens; the *kibbes* (Middle Eastern ground-lamb dishes), *tagines* and puddings are full of thought, passion and flavour.

Borsch, Vodka & Tears (Map p92; ☎ 9530 2694; 173 Chapel St, Windsor; mains $19-23; ☺ breakfast, lunch & dinner) Come here for spruced-up Polish food and an impressive variety of everyone's favourite white spirit, vodka. *Przekazki* (Polish-style tapas) spreads let you sample; the dumplings, herrings and blintzes are top-notch.

our pick **Cicciolina** (Map p92; ☎ 9525 3333; 130 Acland St, St Kilda; mains $22-32; ☺ lunch & dinner) This is where Renée Zellweger eats when she comes to Melbourne (we sat at the next table). This St Kilda institution is one of the city's great casual restaurants – a warm room of dark wood and subdued lighting. The menu is smart and generous; the service affable. It doesn't take bookings, so eat early or while away your wait in the moody little back bar.

Cafe di Stasio (Map p92; ☎ 9525 3999; 31 Fitzroy St, St Kilda; mains $29-42; ☺ lunch & dinner) Capricious, white-jacketed waiters, a tenebrous Bill Henson photograph and a jazz soundtrack set the mood. The Italian menu has the appropriate drama and grace. Weekly fixed-price lunch menus (two courses and a glass of wine) are great value. The best Italian restaurant in Melbourne. Sublime.

Circa (Map p92; ☎ 9536 1122; 2 Acland St, St Kilda; mains $38-48; ☯ breakfast & dinner daily, lunch Sun-Fri) This dining room has a persistent, pervading glamour and produces some of the city's finest food. Exec chef Andrew McConnell no longer mans the stoves nightly (at the time of writing he was busy relocating his famed Carlton restaurant 312 to Gertrude St, Fitzroy), but his stamp is all over the menu with its precise, intense tastes and eclectic influences. Bookings required.

Jacques Reymond (Map pp76-7; ☎ 9525 2178; 78 Williams Rd, Prahran; 7-course degustation menu $150; ☯ lunch Thu & Fri, dinner Tue-Sat) Housed in a Victorian terrace mansion, Reymond was a local pioneer of degustation dining and still encourages you to eat this way (there's a much-lauded vegetarian version). Expect a French-influenced, Asian-accented menu with lovely details such as house-churned butter. Mod Oz at its best.

DRINKING

When liquor-licensing laws were liberalised in the late 1980s, bars began to spring up everywhere and there are now blurry boundaries between what constitutes a restaurant, bar or café. Bars reviews can be found on the *Age* website and at www.threethousand.com.au.

New Gold Mountain (Map pp78-9; ☎ 9650 8859; www.newgoldmountain.org; 1st fl, 21 Liverpool St) Unsignposted, New Gold Mountain has an intense Chinoiserie interior, which comes as a shock. Two upstairs floors are filled with tiny screen-shielded corners, with decoration so delightfully relentless you feel as if you're trapped in an art-house dream sequence. Sours are the thing here, though they do a great vodka *sharlotka* (vodka and apple juice) too. Harbin heaven.

St Jerome's (Map pp78-9; no phone; 7 Caledonian La) Tiny St Jerome's does great coffee and toasties all day for the students that flock here. Come sundown, its time for longnecks and beats in the cloistered back alley. It's also time for Shit Town, its twisted next-door sister, to open the door (actually a hole in the wall). Here the '80s crackhouse aesthetic is fully realised and the music's loud and leftfield.

Gertrude St Enoteca (Map pp84-5; ☎ 9415 8262; 229 Gertrude St; Fitzroy) The Fitzroyalty regulars don't mind sharing the banquette space, or there are tables out the back among the wine. The wine list at this svelte wine bar-bottle shop favours European grapes, with erudite

advice on same. Bar snacks are sourced from Victoria's top suppliers; you can easily make a meal of them.

ourpick Esplanade Hotel (Map p92; ☎ 9534 0211; 11 The Esplanade, St Kilda) Rock-pigs rejoice! 'The Espy' remains gloriously shabby and welcoming to all. Bands play most nights and there's a spruced-up kitchen out the back. And for the price of a pot you get front-row sunset seats.

Carlisle Wine Bar (Map p92; ☎ 9531 3222; www.carlislewinebar.com.au; 137 Carlisle St, Balaclava) Locals love this often rowdy, wine-worshiping former butcher's shop. The staff will treat you like a regular and find you a glass of something special, or effortlessly throw together a cocktail amidst the weekend rush. The rustic Euro food is good too.

ENTERTAINMENT

Melbourne has a thriving nightlife, a lively cultural scene and great nightclubs – see the lift-out *EG Entertainment Guide*, published in the *Age* on Friday. Visit www.melbourne.vic.gov.au/events and www.melbourne.citysearch.com.au for listings and reviews. Pick up free street-press mags *Beat* and *Inpress* from cafés, pubs and bars. The main ticketing agencies are:

Half Tix (Map pp78-9; ☎ 9650 9420; www.halftixmelbourne.com; Melbourne Town Hall, cnr Swanston & Collins Sts; ☯ 10am-2pm Mon & Sat, 11am-6pm Tue-Thu, 11am-6.30pm Fri) Sells half-price tickets on the day of the performance.

Ticketek (Map pp78-9; ☎ 13 28 49; www.ticketek.com.au; 225 Exhibition St; ☯ 9am-5pm Mon-Fri, 9am-1pm Sat)

Ticketmaster7 (Map pp78-9; ☎ 1300 136 166; www.ticketmaster7.com; Theatres Bldg, Victorian Arts Centre, 100 St Kilda Rd, Southbank; ☯ 9am-9pm Mon-Sat)

Live Music

Melbourne is Australia's rock-music capital, where bands such as AC/DC, Nick Cave & the Bad Seeds and Jet took their first tentative steps. There are also a few great jazz joints. Expect to pay between zilch and $35 for a cover charge, but generally you'll get away with about $10 to $15 for a local act.

Bennetts Lane (Map pp78-9; ☎ 9663 2856; www.bennettslane.com; 25 Bennetts La) Hidden down a narrow lane off Little Lonsdale St (between Exhibition and Russell Sts), this quintessentially dim jazz venue is well worth searching out. It's *the* jazz joint in Melbourne – most big acts that come to town perform here.

Ding Dong Lounge (Map pp78-9; ☎ 9662 1020; www
.dingdonglounge.com.au; 18 Market La) Raucous, grotty
and everything a classic rock-and-roll bar
should be (but no longer smoky!). Local and
international bands play here.

Tote (Map pp84-5; ☎ 9419 5320; www.thetotehotel
.com; 71 Johnston St, Collingwood) The Tote's carpet is not so much sticky as overlaid with
a hardened tar of blackened beer-filth. This
tiny '80s-punk-scene relic is legendary, and
playing here confers more grunge-cred on a
muso than any other gig in Melbourne. Both
local and international acts feature; live music
is on every night except Monday.

Prince Bandroom (Map p92; ☎ 9536 1111; www
.princebandroom.com.au; 29 Fitzroy St, St Kilda) The Art
Deco Prince has been a fixture of the St Kilda
scene for years. The downstairs bar is good
for shooting pool; the band room upstairs
plays host to local and international acts and
popular DJ events.

Nightclubs
Melbourne's ever-changing club scene is a
mixed bag, with clubs ranging from barn-
sized discos to small, exclusive places. Cover
charges range from $5 to $20 and most places
have dress codes. Avoid the King St clubs in
the CBD, full of yobbos.

Lounge (Map pp78-9; ☎ 9663 2916; 243 Swanston St;
Ⓨ Wed-Sat) Café by day, relaxed, down-beat
club by night – this is a good place for a night
out in central Melbourne. The crowd is an
interesting all-comers mix and music crosses
the genres from retro to electro and hip-hop.
The balcony is great on hot summer nights.

Revolver (Map p92; ☎ 9521 5985; www.revolver
upstairs.com.au; 229 Chapel St, Prahran; Ⓨ Mon-Sun)
Revolver is a popular venue with Prahran's
mixed-age bohemian crowd. With art- and
stencil-covered surfaces and a packed program featuring DJs, bands, film nights and
spoken word, there's a lot to like.

Gay & Lesbian Venues
Melbourne's gay and lesbian scene is more
understated than raucously out-and-proud
Sydney's, but it thrives regardless. While there
are pink neighbourhoods, demarcation isn't a
big thing and most inner-city venues are mixed
and completely nondiscriminatory. Commercial
Rd in South Yarra is most gay visitors' first port
o' call. For up-to-date listings pick up the free
Melbourne Star (www.bnews.net.au) and *MCV* (www
.mcv.e-p.net.au) from cafés and clubs.

Girl Bar (Map p92; ☎ 9536 1177; www.princeband
room.com.au; 29 Fitzroy St, St Kilda; cover charge $15) The
Prince Bandroom (left) hosts this monthly
dyke night. Below, in the Prince of Wales
proper, the saloon bar has a queer-friendly
jukebox, with lip-syncing comps and half-
price beer on Mondays.

Greyhound Hotel (Map p92; ☎ 9534 4189; www
.thegreyhoundhotel.webs.com; 1-3 Brighton Rd, St Kilda) The
Greyhound has weekend drag nights and ca-
ters to a very eclectic mix of bikers, transvestites and grungesters.

Peel Hotel (Map pp84-5; ☎ 9419 4762; www.thepeel
.com.au; cnr Peel & Wellington Sts, Collingwood) Perennial
gay-boy favourite.

Cinema
Cinemas are spread throughout Melbourne
city and the suburbs and usually belong either
to the **Hoyts** (http://hoyts.ninemsn.com.au), **Dendy** (www
.dendy.com.au), **Village** (www.villagecinemas.com.au) or
the **Greater Union** (www.greaterunion.com.au) chains;
see their websites for details. Our favourite
cinemas for art-house releases include:

Astor (Map p92; ☎ 9510 1414; www.astor-theatre
.com; cnr Chapel St & Dandenong Rd, St Kilda)

Kino (Map pp78-9; ☎ 9650 2100; www.dendy.com.au;
45 Collins St)

Nova (Map pp84-5; ☎ 9347 5331; www.cinemanova
.com.au; 380 Lygon St, Carlton)

Palace Como (Map p92; ☎ 9827 7533; www.palace
cinemas.com.au; cnr Toorak Rd & Chapel St, South Yarra)

Palace George (Map p92; ☎ 9534 6922; www
.palacecinemas.com.au; 135 Fitzroy St, St Kilda)

Theatre & Dance
Victorian Arts Centre (Map pp78-9; ☎ 9281 8000; www
.vicartscentre.com.au; 100 St Kilda Rd, Southbank) This is
Melbourne's major venue for the performing
arts (see p86).

Malthouse Theatre (Map pp76-7; ☎ 9685 5100; www
.malthousetheatre.com.au; 113 Sturt St, South Melbourne)
The Malthouse Theatre Company is dedicated

NEW THEATRES

At time of going to press the construction
gangs were hard at work on the corner of
Sturt St and Southbank Blvd in Southbank.
This will be the site of the new 1000-seat
Dame Elisabeth Murdoch Melbourne Recital
Hall for chamber music, and the 500-seat
permanent home for the Melbourne Theatre
Company. Both are slated to open in 2009.

to developing and promoting contemporary Australian works, so it's worth checking out for some local content. It's housed in an atmospheric old factory (yes, a malt-house), and shares a courtyard with the Australian Centre for Contemporary Art (p83).

Chunky Move (Map pp76-7; ☎ 9645 5188; www .chunkymove.com; 111 Sturt St, Southbank) The state's acclaimed contemporary dance company performs diverse, poppy pieces at its sexy venue behind the Australian Centre for Contemporary Art.

Sport

Underneath the cultured chat and designer threads of your typical Melbournian, you'll find a heart that truly belongs to one thing: sport. You can book tickets for sporting events through Ticketek (p97) or Ticketmaster7 (see p97).

Understanding the basics of **Australian Rules Football** (AFL or 'footy'; www.afl.com.au) is definitely a way to get a local engaged in conversation, especially during the winter season. Melbourne is the spiritual home of Australian Rules Football and the Melbourne Cricket Ground (see p86) is its holiest temple.

The popularity of **soccer** is on the rise; Melbourne Victory plays **A-League** (www.a -league.com.au) games at **Telstra Dome** (Map pp78–9) in Docklands. The Melbourne Storm **rugby league** team won the 2007 **National Rugby League** (www.nrl.com.au) trophy.

Melbourne's summer love is **cricket** (www .cricket.com.au) and the Boxing Day Test (p91) is bigger than Christmas.

Horse racing is held at the Flemington, Caulfield, Moonee Valley and Sandown Racecourses. The two-mile (3.2km) Melbourne Cup (p91), one of the world's greatest horse races, is the Melbourne's Spring Racing Carnival feature event; it's held at **Flemington Racecourse** (Map pp76-7; ☎ 1300 727 575; www.vrc.net.au; 400 Epsom Rd, Flemington) on the first Tuesday in November and brings Australia to a standstill for three minutes.

Melbourne hosts the **Australian Formula One Grand Prix** (p91) around Albert Park Lake in March, and the Australian round of the **World 500cc Motorcycle Grand Prix** (www.grandprix .com.au/bikes) on nearby Phillip Island (see p106) in October.

SHOPPING

Melbourne offers the best shopping in Australia; the widest array of shops is in the CBD. The suburbs are home to a growing legion of factory outlets (try Bridge Rd and Swan St in Richmond) and shopping malls, plus some off-beat boutiques and specialist stores.

Central Melbourne

Alice Euphemia (Map pp78-9; ☎ 9650 4300; www.alice euphemia.com; Shop 6/37, cnr Swanston St & Flinders La) At the more experimental end of Melbourne fashion, with inventive fabrics, cuts and fin-

---

TO MARKET, TO MARKET

Melbourne's world-famous markets allow you to experience the city in all its multicultural glory, as locals shop, socialise and converse in an array of tongues. Following are some of Melbourne's best markets:

- **Camberwell Market** (off Map pp76-7; Station St, Camberwell; ☷ 6am-2.30pm Sun) One of the most popular trash-and-treasure markets, this has hundreds of stalls piled with everything – get there early to fight the fashionistas for the best retro gear.

- **Prahran Market** (Map p92; www.prahranmarket.com.au; 163-185 Commercial Rd, Prahran; ☷ dawn-5pm Tue & Sat, dawn-6pm Thu & Fri, 10am-3pm Sun) This may be the best food market in the city, with several organic-produce stores, a fresh-pasta store, great delis and a wing devoted to fresh fish and meat.

- **Queen Victoria Market** (Map pp78-9; ☎ 9320 5822; www.qvm.com.au; cnr Victoria & Elizabeth Sts; ☷ 6am-2pm Tue & Thu, to 6pm Fri, to 3pm Sat, 9am-4pm Sun) There are more than 500 stalls here, selling everything under the sun, including fruit and vegetables (organic produce can be found), meat, fish, jeans, furniture, budgies and sheepskin products.

- **South Melbourne Market** (Map pp76-7; ☎ 9209 6295; cnr Cecil & Coventry Sts, South Melbourne; ☷ 8am-4pm Wed, Sat & Sun, 8am-6pm Fri) This general market covers most bases, with delis, foodstuffs and a legendary dim-sim stall that attracts a permanent queue.

ishes that aim to make you look more interesting than you might actually be. There's a great range of rings, brooches and earrings on display, too.

Calibre (Map pp78-9; ☎ 9663 8001; www.calibreclothing .com.au; 45 Collins St, Melbourne) Specialises in high-end men's fashion and classic-contemporary suits, shirts and accessories.

GPO (Map pp78-9; ☎ 9663 0066; www.melbournesgpo .com; 350 Bourke St) A 2001 postfire restoration and reinvention of Melbourne's General Post Office has given the town a whole new postbox of reasons to wander in. The top floor houses fashion heavyweights Akira Isogawa and Belinda. Local screenprint star Spacecraft is also here, and the wonderfully individual jewellery and collectables dealer Gallery Freya. On the mid- and ground levels are a smattering of Melbourne's most fascinating outlets: Gorman, Fat and Metallicus.

Anna Schwartz Gallery (Map pp78-9; ☎ 9654 6131; www.annaschwartzgallery.com; 185 Flinders La) Leader of the pack when it comes to high-profile modern-art exhibitions in a blindingly white, sometimes chilly space.

Marais (Map pp78-9; ☎ 9639 0314; www.marais.com .au; 1st fl, Royal Arcade, 314 Little Collins St) On a stealthily signposted upper floor of the workaday Royal Arcade, this shop evokes its Parisian namesake with raven-stained parquetry and glossy, white-panelled walls. International mens and womenswear labels include fashion darlings Preen and Lavin. Local talent is represented by Sri Lankan born, Melbourne-bred, London-trained Dhini.

Self Preservation (Map pp78-9; ☎ 9650 0523; www .selfpreservation.com.au; 70 Bourke St) Iron cases hold a range of jewels from local artisans and from long ago, and there's a small gallery space out back. Not only can you shop for a gold and silver, you can sit down for a coffee or a glass of wine while you decide. Multitasking never was nicer.

Shag (Map pp78-9; ☎ 9663 8166; Shop 20, Centre Way) Super stylist-ordained vintage pieces, including shoes, furs and bags, plus a great, well-priced collection of fashion-forward Asian-sourced dresses, jackets and tops.

QV (Map pp78-9; ☎ 9658 0100; cnr Swanston & Lonsdale Sts) Features all sorts of populist commercial outlets and a few cool international options.

Missing Link (Map pp78-9; ☎ 9670 8208; www.miss inglink.net.au; Basement, 405 Bourke St) Indie music's most famous Melbourne record store and a haven for grungesters, goths and experimentalists. CDs, vinyl and DVDs from Anus Tumor to Z-Gun.

Carlton, Fitzroy & Collingwood

Crumpler (Map pp84-5; ☎ 9417 5338; www.crumpler .au; cnr Gertrude & Smith Sts, Fitzroy) For the ultimate Melbourne souvenir, visit Crumpler. This local company started out making tough-as-nails bags for bicycle couriers – now a must-have fashion accessory.

Alphaville (Map pp84-5; ☎ 9416 4296; www.alpha60.com .au; 179 Brunswick St, Fitzroy) Alphaville keeps the cool kids of both genders happy with Alpha '60s sharp clothes. Look out for tilts to Jean-Luc Godard and other filmic favourites (we loved the body-bagged Laura Palmer pillow slips).

Somebuddy Loves You (Map pp84-5; ☎ 9415 7066; 193 Smith St, Fitzroy) Announced by the sneaker-draped power lines on neighbouring Charles St, Somebuddy does local variations on the global hipster theme: ironic T-shirts, cult-brand jeans, scenster-in-training babywear and kidult toys.

Polyester (Map pp84-5; ☎ 9419 5137; 387 Brunswick St, Fitzroy) Polyester is a fave indie record store for discerning north-of-the-river listeners.

South Yarra, Prahran & St Kilda

Chapel St Bazaar (Map p92; ☎ 9529 1727; 217-223 Chapel St, Prahran) Calling this a 'permanent undercover collection of market stalls' won't give you any clue to what's tucked away here. This old arcade is a retro-obsessive riot. It doesn't matter if Italian art-glass or Noddy eggcups are your thing, you'll find it here.

Provider (Map p92; ☎ 9529 2629; www.provider.com .au; 114 Greville St, Prahran) If the term 'Air Max' flips your burger, you'll love this trainer temple that stocks Nike to New Balance and what's known as street apparel.

Greville Records (Map p92; ☎ 9510 3012; www.gre villerecords.com; 152 Greville St, Prahran) Our favourite Melbourne record stock of a select stock of CDs, vinyl and DVDs – everything from classic Miles Davis, Can, Buffalo Springfield and Sonic Youth to Deerhoof and Aussie darlings the Drones.

GETTING THERE & AWAY

Air

International and interstate flights operate out of **Melbourne International Airport** (Map p103; ☎ 9297 1600; www.melair.com.au) at Tullamarine and some interstate flights operate from **Avalon Airport** (Map p103; ☎ 1800 282 566; www.avalonairport.com.au).

Bus

Long-distance bus services for **V/Line** (☎ 13 61 96; www.vline.com.au) and **Firefly** (☎ 1300 730 740; www.fireflyexpress.com.au) coaches operate from the **Southern Cross coach terminal** (Map pp78–9) on Spencer St. **Greyhound** (☎ 1300 473 946; www .greyhound.com.au) services operate from the **Melbourne Transit Centre** (Map pp84-5; 58 Franklin St). Basic one-way adult fares from Melbourne to Sydney cost between $65 and $76 (12 hours); and to Brisbane from $196 (24 hours). Carriers offer backpacker, student and pensioner fares and other discounts on these prices. There are at least six departures per day to these cities.

Car & Motorcycle

The quickest and easiest way in and out of Melbourne heading for the East Coast is via CityLink – follow the blue signs. If you want to avoid the tolls, jump on at Toorak Rd. CityLink becomes the Princes Hwy, the road you need to be on!

Train

Long-distance trains depart from **Southern Cross station** (Map pp78–9) on Spencer St. **V/ Line** (☎ 13 61 96; www.vline.com.au) has daily serv- ices from Melbourne to many destinations including Bairnsdale ($25, 3½ hours, three daily) stopping at all major towns along the Princes Hwy in west Gippsland.

Countrylink (☎ 13 22 32; www.countrylink.info) runs XPT (express) trains between Melbourne and Sydney (one-way economy/1st class/1st-class sleeper $130/183/271, 11 hours), with one morning and one evening departure daily in each direction (note that sleeper cabins can- not be booked over the internet). There are discounts of about 30% for bookings made seven or 14 days in advance for travel outside peak times (eg school holidays).

GETTING AROUND
To/From the Airport

Melbourne Airport is at Tullamarine, 22km northwest of the city centre. If you're driving, take the Tullamarine Fwy from the airport to the CityLink (right) toll road, which will take you into town. A 24-hour Tullapass costs $4.10.

A taxi between the airport and the city centre costs around $40 (including the cost of the tollway). **Skybus** (☎ 9335 2811; www.skybus .com.au) operates a 24-hour shuttle-bus service (one way $16, 20 minutes) between the air-

port and the city every 30 minutes between 6am and midnight (hourly otherwise) in both directions. Buses to Avalon airport are run by **Sunbus** (☎ 9689 6888; www.sunbusaustralia.com .au), which operates from Southern Cross bus terminal. **Frankston & Peninsula Airport Shuttle** (☎ 9783 1199; www.fapas.com.au) runs a dozen buses daily (fewer on weekends) to the airport from Rosebud on the Mornington Peninsula through the southeastern bayside suburbs (adult one-way from St Kilda $18).

Car & Motorcycle

If you're lucky enough to find city street park- ing you'll pay from $2 an hour. Check parking signs for restrictions and times, and watch for clearway zones that operate during peak hour. There are more than 70 commercial car parks in the city. Drivers should treat trams with caution – you must *always* stop behind a tram when it drops off or collects passengers. Melbourne's notorious **hook turn** is designed to allow trams through city intersections without being blocked by turning cars. To turn right at hook-turn city intersections, you pull over to the left, wait until the light of the street you're turning into changes from red to green, then complete your turn ahead of the traffic coming from your left. These intersections are identified by black-and-white hook signs that read 'Right Turn from Left Only.'

All the big car-rental firms are repre- sented in Melbourne and have desks at the airport. For disabled travellers, **Avis** (☎ 13 63 33; www.avis.com.au) rents hand-controlled vehicles. The **Yellow Pages** (www.yellowpages.com .au) lists lots of other firms, including some cheaper operators.

TOLL ROADS

CityLink (☎ 13 26 29; www.citylink.com.au) consists of two main sections: the Western Link, which runs from the Calder Hwy intersection of the Tullamarine Fwy down the western side of the city to join with the Westgate Fwy; and the Southern Link, which runs from Kings Way on the southern edge of the CBD, through the Domain and Burnley tunnels to the Malvern section of the Monash Fwy. Both are tollways.

A CityLink account is a prepaid account where tolls are debited electronically as over- head toll-points read transponders (e-Tags) mounted within a vehicle. If you want to use CityLink without an e-Tag, purchase a day pass (valid for 24 hours from your first

MELBOURNE

trip) or a weekend pass (valid from noon Friday to midnight Sunday). Either pass costs $11.55. If you want to go from the airport to Flemington Rd, buy a Tullapass for $4.10. Motorcycles use CityLink for free. If you've inadvertently found your way onto the CityLink toll roads without an e-Tag or appropriate pass you have until midnight the following day to call CityLink and arrange payment. If you do not make reparations you'll incur a $100 fine.

Public Transport

The Met incorporates buses, trains and Melbourne's famous trams. The 750 trams operate up to 20km from the centre. Buses ply routes that trams don't. Trains radiate from the city to the outer suburbs, and cease around midnight. On Friday and Saturday night (ie Saturday and Sunday morning), hourly NightRider buses depart from **City Square** (Map pp78–9) on Swanston St from 12.30am to 4.30am for suburban destinations. Metcard tickets are valid for NightRider buses.

For information contact the **Metlink Information Centre** (☎ 13 16 38; www.metlinkmelbourne.com.au) or visit the **MetShop** (Map pp78-9; ☎ 13 16 38; Town Hall, cnr Swanston & Collins Sts; ☒ 8.30am-5.30pm Mon-Fri, 9am-1pm Sat), which also sells tickets.

TICKETING

Metcards allow you travel on any Melbourne bus, train or tram service, and transfer from one type to another. They're available from Metcard vending machines, train stations, on trams (coins only), from retailers displaying the Metlink flag, and the MetShop. You can purchase tickets directly from the driver on bus services.

The metropolitan area is divided into two zones. Zone 1 covers both the city and inner-suburban areas. Adult fares are as follows:

Zones	Two hours	All day	Weekly
1	$3.50	$6.50	$28
2	$2.70	$4.60	$19.20
1 & 2	$5.50	$10.10	$47.40

BUS

Melbourne's bus network generally links train and tram networks. Buses also go to places not reached by other services, such as hospitals, universities, suburban shopping centres and the outer suburbs.

TRAIN

Trains cover the Melbourne metropolitan area. **Flinders St station** (Map pp78–9), the main city terminal, has a separate platform for each suburban line. The famous row of clocks above the entrance on the corner of Swanston and Flinders Sts indicates the next departing train on each line. On weekdays, trains start at 5am, finish around midnight and run about every 10 minutes during peak hour, every 15 to 20 minutes at most other times, and every 30 minutes after 7pm. On Saturday they run every half-hour from 5am to midnight, and Sunday every 40 minutes from 7am to 11.30pm. The city includes a handy underground service called the **City Loop**, including Parliament, Melbourne Central, Flagstaff, Southern Cross and Flinders St stations.

Bicycles can be carried for free on all trains inside the last door of the last carriage.

TRAM

Melbourne's trams cover the city and inner suburbs. Trams run along most routes every six to eight minutes during peak hour, and every 12 minutes at other times. They share the roads with cars and trucks, so can be delayed by traffic. Services are less frequent on weekends and late at night.

Be extremely careful when getting on and off a tram; by law, cars are supposed to stop when a tram stops to pick up and drop off passengers, but that doesn't always happen.

See p90 for details on the free City Circle tram service.

Taxi

All Melbourne taxis are yellow. The main CBD ranks are outside major hotels and Flinders St and Southern Cross train stations. Finding an empty taxi in the city on Friday or Saturday night can be difficult.

Flagfall is $3.10, and the rate is $1.465 per kilometre thereafter. The tariff is 20% higher between midnight and 5am. Telephone bookings incur a $1.30 surcharge. CityLink tolls ($3.50 for Southern and Western Links, $5.60 for both) are added to the fare.

Yellow Cabs and Silver Top Taxis have cars with wheelchair access, or phone ☎ 1300 364 050. To book a taxi, phone any of the following companies:

Embassy Taxis (☎ 13 17 55)
Silver Top Taxis (☎ 13 10 08)
Yellow Cabs (☎ 13 19 24)

AROUND MELBOURNE

There are some lovely day trips out of Melbourne accessible by public transport, but they're much better when you have a vehicle. The Dandenong Ranges and Mornington Peninsula can be reached in a

little over an hour from Melbourne; Phillip Island takes a little more getting-to.

THE DANDENONGS

On a clear day, you can see the **Dandenong Ranges** from Melbourne. The 633m summit of Mt Dandenong is the highest peak – watch the sun set over the city from the lookout. The

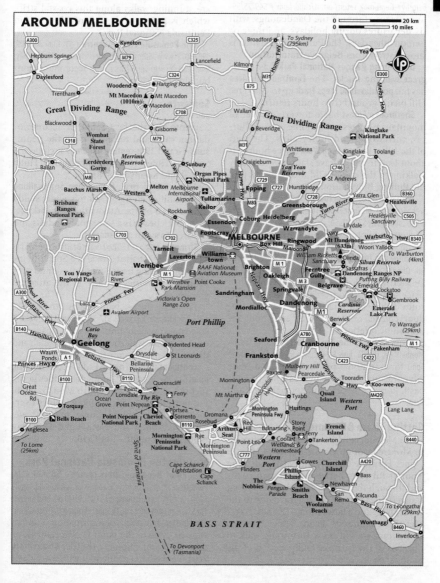

AROUND MELBOURNE

lush hills are about 35km (an hour's drive) east of the city. The **Dandenong Ranges & Knox visitors centre** (☎ 9758 7522; www.dandenongranges tourism.com.au; 1211 Burwood Hwy, Upper Ferntree Gully; ☺ 9am-5pm) is outside the Upper Ferntree Gully train station.

A restored steam train, **Puffing Billy** (☎ 9754 6800; www.puffingbilly.com.au; Old Monbulk Rd, Belgrave; Belgrave-Gembrook return adult/child/family $49/25/99) toots its way through the Dandenongs, with six departures during holidays, and three or four on other days. The Puffing Billy station is short a stroll from Belgrave train station.

Dandenong Ranges National Park has many great walking tracks. The **Ferntree Gully Area** has the popular **1000 Steps Track** up to One Tree Hill picnic ground (two hours return).

Sherbrooke Forest has a towering cover of mountain ash trees and is home to kookaburras, currawongs and honeyeaters. The start of the 10km **Eastern Loop Walk** (three hours), is about 1km from Belgrave station, accessed by walking to the end of Old Monbulk Rd past the Puffing Billy station.

William Ricketts Sanctuary (☎ 13 19 63; www.park web.vic.gov.au; Mt Dandenong Tourist Rd, Mt Dandenong; adult/child/family $7/3/16.50; ☺ 10am-4.30pm) features Ricketts' sculptures, inspired by years spent living with Aboriginal people.

Ranges at Olinda (☎ 9751 2133; 5 Olinda-Monbulk Rd, Olinda; lunch mains $14-22, dinner mains $22-29; ☺ breakfast & lunch daily, dinner Tue-Sat) is a stylish place featuring Mod Oz food. Pasta and risotto dishes, and pita wraps filled with tandoori chicken or Mexican beef are among the lunchtime offerings.

Stop at **Pie in the Sky** (☎ 9751 2128; 43 Olinda-Monbulk Rd, Olinda; pies $4-6, lunch $8-12; ☺ 9.30am-5pm) for traditional pie favourites and more adventurous combos such as tomato-and-basil, korma chicken, and spinach, rice and feta.

Getting There & Around

From Melbourne, drive along Canterbury Rd to Montrose, or go via the Burwood Hwy to Upper Ferntree Gully – the Mt Dandenong Tourist Rd runs between these two roads and through the ranges. The Met's suburban trains (p102) run on the Belgrave line to the foothills of the Dandenongs (Zones 1 & 2 Met ticket required). From Upper Ferntree Gully train station it's a 10-minute walk to the start of the Ferntree Gully section of the national park.

MORNINGTON PENINSULA

The Mornington Peninsula has been a favourite summer destination since the 1870s, when paddle steamers carried holidaying Melburnians to Sorrento.

The calm 'front beaches' are on the Port Phillip and Western Port sides. The rugged ocean 'back beaches' face Bass Strait – there are stunning walks along this coastal strip, which is protected as part of Mornington Peninsula National Park.

The **Peninsula visitors centre** (☎ 1800 804 009, 5987 3078; www.visitmorningtonpeninsula.org; Nepean Hwy, Dromana; ☺ 9am-5pm) has a free accommodation-booking service.

Sorrento
pop 1500

Sorrento has the best range of accommodation, cafés and restaurants on the peninsula. Grand **19th-century buildings** include the Sorrento Hotel (1871), the Continental Hotel (1875) and Koonya (1878).

There are plenty of **swimming** and **walking** opportunities along Sorrento's wide, sandy beaches and bluffs. At low tide, the **rock pool** at the back beach is a safe spot for adults and children to swim and **snorkel**.

Stringer's (☎ 5984 2010; 2 Ocean Beach Rd; sandwiches & snacks $4-8; ☺ breakfast & lunch) is a Sorrento institution, serving house-made meals and with Mornington wines for sale in the attached grocery shop.

Formerly the sea baths, **Baths** (☎ 5984 1500; 3278 Point Nepean Rd; mains $17-30; ☺ breakfast, lunch & dinner) does excellent breakfast cook-ups served on its fantastic waterfront decking. Lunch and dinner get more sophisticated.

Continental Cafe (☎ 5984 2201; 1 Ocean Beach Rd; mains $17-26; ☺ breakfast, lunch & dinner) does gourmet fish and chips and stylish Mod Oz grub. Eat outside at weathered picnic tables overlooking the bay, or in the funky and cosy café. Tuesday is pizza-and-pasta night; Thursday is 300g steak night – both $15.

Mornington Peninsula National Park

The **Point Nepean visitors centre** (☎ 5984 4276; Point Nepean; walk or bicycle admission adult/child/family $7/4/19.50, ind return transport $16/9.50/41.50, bike hire per 3hr $17; ☺ 9am-6pm Jan, to 5pm Feb-Apr & Oct-Dec, 10am-5pm May-Sep) has stacks of information. You can walk or cycle to the point (12km return), or take the Point Explorer shuttle. **Observatory Point** is a sheltered picnic spot with wheelchair

---

DETOUR: GREAT OCEAN ROAD

The **Great Ocean Rd** (B100), which runs between Anglesea and Warrnambool, is Australia's most spectacular coastal road. The most famous section cuts through Port Campbell National Park, with its amazing natural rock sculptures – the Twelve Apostles, London Bridge and Loch Ard Gorge – carved out of the limestone headlands by fierce ocean waves.

There are visitors centres in Torquay, Lorne, Apollo Bay, Port Campbell, Warrnambool, Port Fairy and Portland.

Several companies offer organised tours of the Great Ocean Rd, including the following:

■ **Autopia Tours** (☎ 1800 000 507; www.autopiatours.com.au)

■ **Go West Tours** (☎ 1300 736 551; www.gowest.com.au)

■ **Goin South** (☎ 1800 009 858; www.goinsouth.com.au)

■ **Otway Discovery** (☎ 9654 5432; www.otwaydiscovery.com.au)

■ **Wayward Bus** (☎ 1300 653 510; www.waywardbus.com.au)

Accommodation here is heavily booked during school holidays. There are camping grounds right along the coast. For accommodation check out www.greatoceanroad.stays.com.au.

Trains from Melbourne's Southern Cross station travel to Geelong ($9, one hour, frequently). **V/Line** (☎ 13 61 96; www.vline.com.au) buses cruise along the Great Ocean Rd from Geelong to Apollo Bay ($13, 2¼ hours) via Torquay ($2.50, 30 minutes) and Lorne ($8.50, 1¼ hours) several times daily. There are daily V/line trains that continue from Geelong to Warrnambool ($18, 2¼ hours). On Monday, Wednesday and Friday there are V/Line bus services from Geelong to Port Campbell ($23, 5¼ hours) via Apollo Bay ($13, 2¼ hours).

McHarry's Bus Lines (☎ 5223 2111; www.mcharrys.com.au) has services from Geelong towards Lorne ($8.50, 1¼ hours).

---

access from Gunners car park – en route, take a look at the **graves** of shipwreck victims and Victoria's first settlers.

Cheviot Beach is where prime minister Harold Holt disappeared in 1967. **Fort Nepean** played an important Australian-defence role from the 1880s to 1945. There are two historic **gun barrels** here, which fired the first Allied shots in WWI and WWII.

There are beautiful and rugged **ocean beaches** at Portsea, Sorrento, Rye, Gunnamatta and Cape Schanck. Swimming is dangerous at these beaches: currents are severe and drownings occur – only swim between the flags at the lifeguard-patrolled areas at Gunnamatta and Portsea.

Built in 1859, **Cape Schanck Lightstation** (☎ 0500 527 891, 5988 6184; museum only adult/child/family $10/8/30, museum & lighthouse $14/11/38, parking $4; ☼ 10.30am-4pm) is an operational lighthouse, with a kiosk, museum and visitors centre. From the lightstation, descend the boardwalk steps towards the craggy cape with its outstanding views. Longer **walks** include tracks to **Bushrangers Bay**, which can be approached from Cape Schanck or the Bushrangers Bay

car park on Boneo Rd – about 40 minutes each way.

Getting There & Around

The Moorooduc Fwy becomes the Mornington Peninsula Fwy, which is the main entry point to the peninsula. The Point Nepean Hwy joins the Mornington Peninsula Fwy.

Met trains (buy a Zones 1 & 2 ticket) run from Flinders St station to Frankston station. From there, **Portsea Passenger Service** (☎ 5986 5666; www.grenda.com.au) bus 788 runs to/from Portsea ($5; 90 minutes; half-hourly Monday to Saturday, two-hourly Sunday), via Mornington, Dromana and Sorrento.

Queenscliff-Sorrento Car & Passenger Ferries (☎ 5258 3244; www.searoad.com.au; one-way foot passenger adult/child $9/7, 2 adults & car standard/peak $58/64) runs hourly services every day between Sorrento and Queenscliff on the Bellarine Peninsula.

Inter Island Ferries (☎ 9585 5730; www.interisland ferries.com.au; return adult/child/bike $20/10/8; ☼ every 30min 8.30am-5pm, plus 7pm Fri) runs daily between Stony Point and Cowes (on Phillip Island) via French Island.

PHILLIP ISLAND & THE PENGUIN PARADE

pop 7500

Phillip Island is home to the world-famous Penguin Parade. Excellent surf beaches bring day-tripping boardriders from Melbourne, while there are calmer kid-friendly beaches on the island's north side. The **Phillip Island visitors centre** (☎ 1300 366 422, 5956 7447; www.phillipisland.net.au; Phillip Island Rd, Newhaven; ☻ 9am-5pm) sells the Three Parks Pass (adult/child/family $34/17/85), granting admission to the Penguin Parade, Koala Conservation Centre and Churchill Island.

The **Penguin Parade** (☎ 5951 2800; www.penguins.org.au; Summerland Beach; adult/child/family $20/10/50; ☻ 10am-last penguin show) attracts more than 500,000 visitors a year. Amphitheatres hold up to 3800 people who coo over the penguins as they emerge from the sea after sunset.

From the elevated treetop boardwalks at the **Koala Conservation Centre** (☎ 5952 1307; Phillip Island Rd; adult/child/family $10/5/25; ☻ 10am-5pm) you can watch koalas chewing eucalyptus leaves.

Small **Churchill Island** (☎ 5956 7214; off Phillip Island Rd; adult/child/family $10/5/25; ☻ 10am-4.30pm), connected by a bridge to Phillip Island, is an historic working farm.

The Nobbies are a rock formation on the island's southwest tip. Beyond them are **Seal Rocks**, inhabited by Australia's largest fur-seal colony. The **Nobbies Centre** (☎ 5951 2816; admission free; tours adult/child $10/5; ☻ 10am-8pm Dec-Feb, 10am-5pm Mar-May, 10am-4pm Jun-Aug; 10am-6pm Sep-Nov) offers great views. You can peer through boardwalk binoculars or the centre's underwater cameras.

The island's south-side ocean beaches include **Woolamai**, which has rips and currents and is only suitable for experienced surfers. Beginners and families can go to **Smiths Beach**, which is often teeming with surf-school groups. Both beaches are patrolled in summer. Around the Nobbies, **Cat Bay** and **Flynns Reef** will often work when the wind is blowing onshore at the Woolamai and Smiths areas. **Island Surfboards** (☎ 5952 3443; www.islandsurfboards.com.au; 65 Smiths Beach & 147 Thompson Ave, Cowes; lessons $50) runs surfing lessons and hires gear.

White Salt (☎ 5956 6336; 7 Vista Pl, Woolamai; ☻ lunch & dinner Thu-Mon) serves gourmet fish and chips. The bench seats are usually packed, but you can make off for the beach with a parcel under your arm.

Madcowes (☎ 5952 2560; 17 The Esplanade, Cowes; mains $6-15; ☻ breakfast & lunch) is a stylish café-foodstore.

Getting There & Around

Travelling by car from Melbourne, take the Monash Fwy (M1) and get off at the Phillip Island exit onto the South Gippsland Hwy (M420).

V/Line (☎ 13 61 96; www.vline.com.au) runs a direct Melbourne-Cowes bus ($10, 3¼ hours, five weekly) departing Melbourne's Southern Cross station at 3.50pm Monday to Friday.

Inter Island Ferries (☎ 9585 5730; www.interislandferries.com.au; return adult/child/bike $20/10/8; ☻ every 30min 8.30am-5pm, plus 7pm Fri) runs daily between Stony Point and Cowes (on Phillip Island) via French Island.

Southeast Coast Victoria

If you want unspoilt wilderness areas and stunning beaches, head this way. The star attraction is the much-loved Wilsons Promontory National Park, but venture further into the sparsely populated corner pocket of this region and discover national parks with rugged mountains, pristine rainforests, raging rivers, isolated beaches and few other travellers. This is Gunai (Kurnai) traditional land, and the Bataluk Cultural Trail that snakes its way through the region leads you to some incredibly beautiful and significant places.

Expect to be impressed by South Gippsland with its lush, green rolling hills and rural back roads, and some of the best scuba diving and snorkelling in Australia along its rugged and spectacular coastline. You can get a glimpse of the wilderness feast to come at Tarra-Bulga National Park, covered in towering mountain ash and valleys of giant tree ferns.

The Lakes District is huge – it's Australia's largest inland waterway system, a rich haven for birds, and a favourite for boating, fishing and swimming. It's separated by coastal dunes from the long stretch of Ninety Mile Beach, which has some superb isolated beaches. The whole region is dotted with small, laid-back towns. Some sleepy little hamlets with only a general store, and some more sophisticated with a range of sleeping, eating and activity options. These towns go off during summer school holidays when holidaying hordes arrives.

And there's some sensational food to be had – fish straight off fishing boats, and plenty of places to stop for locally produced wines, cheeses and fruit.

HIGHLIGHTS

- Hiking in wilderness areas and along squeaky beaches at **Wilsons Promontory** (p115)

- Eating dinner lakeside at **Metung** (p125) and chartering a boat to explore the Gippsland Lakes

- Rock hopping, diving and snorkelling at **Bunurong Marine & Coastal Park** (p110)

- Walking, swimming and camping at beautiful **Cape Conran Coastal Park** (p135)

- Exploring the ancient rainforests of **Errinundra National Park** (p133)

- Discovering the idyllic tiny former gold-mining town of **Walhalla** (p120)

- Rafting down the magnificent **Snowy River** (p133)

- Relaxing on the deck of the lighthouse keepers' cottages at **Point Hicks** (p140) and watching migrating whales

---

■ TELEPHONE CODE: 03   ■ www.gippslandtourism.com.au   ■ www.lakesandwilderness.com.au

SOUTHEAST COAST VICTORIA

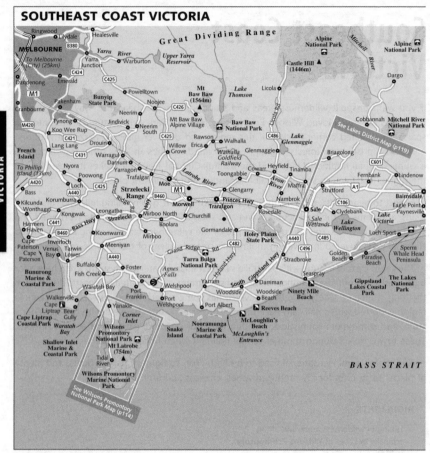

Getting There & Around

There's a good supply of public transport from Melbourne as far as Bairnsdale; after that you're limited to a few bus options. You'll get the most out of this region with a car, to check out the national parks and small towns. A 2WD will get you everywhere except the more remote parts of national parks.

BUS

There are daily services from Melbourne heading up the east coast.

V/Line (☎ 13 61 96; www.vline.com.au) buses pick up where the train leaves off. V/Line has daytime bus services that go along the Princes Hwy (A1) from Bairnsdale to Batemans Bay ($43, 11 hours) three times a week, and as

far as Narooma ($43, 10 hours) every other day. Three times a week another service follows the Princes Hwy as far as Cann River, then veers north to Canberra ($43, 10 hours). **Premier Motor Services** (☎ 13 34 10; www.premierms .com.au) has a daily overnight service/three-month pass ($79/75) from Melbourne to Sydney along the Princes Hwy, though if you're stopping along the way it means you'll be arriving and leaving in the middle of the night.

Away from the main routes bus services are limited, though Bairnsdale is reasonably well serviced with private buses north to Buchan and south to Paynesville. **Buchan Bus 'n' Freight** (☎ 5155 0356; www.buchanbusnfreight.com.au) operates a service on Monday, Wednesday and Friday

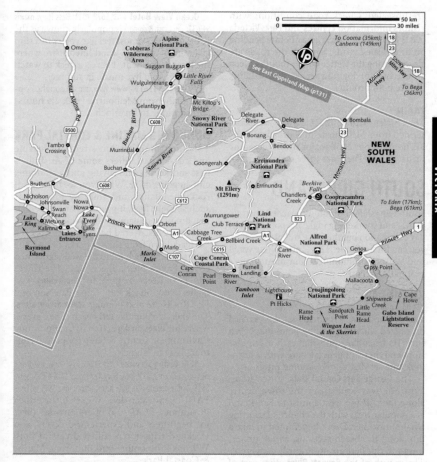

from Bairnsdale to Gelantipy (one way $16) via Lakes Entrance, Nowa Nowa, Buchan and W Tree. **Paynesville Bus Lines** (☎ 0418-516 405) runs daily (except Sunday) services between Bairnsdale train station and Paynesville via Eagle Point (one way $8).

V/Line also has buses running from Traralgon to Sale via Maffra; Melbourne to Yarram, stopping along the South Gippsland Hwy; and Melbourne to Inverloch and Phillip Island, along the Bass Hwy.

Oz Experience (☎ 1300 300 128; www.ozexperience .com) is a hop-on, hop-off backpackers bus with a party atmosphere, travelling via Wilsons Promontory to Lakes Entrance and Gelantipy before going on to Sydney. A Melbourne-to-Sydney pass costs $240.

CAR & MOTORCYCLE

The two major routes through Gippsland are the Princes Hwy (which joins the M1 in Melbourne) and the South Gippsland Hwy. The Princes Hwy is the quickest route through the region, but takes you through Gippsland's unimpressive industrial heartland. The scenic South Gippsland Hwy is the quickest route to Wilsons Promontory. Turn off the South Gippsland Hwy for the Bass Hwy with some stunning ocean views. The South Gippsland Hwy rejoins the Princes Hwy at Sale.

Some areas of national parks and other off-the-beaten-track spots in Gippsland require a 4WD (although 2WD access is often possible during the summer months) as many roads are unsealed. Check road conditions with visitors information centres and **Parks Victoria** (☎ 13 16 93; www.parkweb.vic.gov.au) before heading on to unsealed roads. Some of the roads are closed during the wetter winter months. Keep an eye out for logging trucks and wildlife; they're both prolific.

TRAIN
The efficient **V/Line** (☎ 13 61 96; www.vline.com.au) service from Melbourne to Bairnsdale ($25, 3½ hours) stops at all major towns along the Princes Hwy. There are three daily services.

SOUTH GIPPSLAND

South Gippsland's fabulous beaches, surfing, diving and snorkelling make it a popular holiday destination but there are still places where you can find solitude. This is also where you'll find Wilsons Promontory – one of Australia's best national parks.

KILCUNDA
☎ 03 / pop 270
Tiny Kilcunda has a dramatic setting, perched on rugged cliffs overlooking pounding ocean surf. Its legendary pub makes it a popular stop, and there's a general store with a retro-look café serving up wholesome meals.

The **George Bass Coastal Walk**, a two-hour, 7km one-way walk from the town centre along the cliff top west almost to San Remo is a popular trek, with the chance of spotting whales in winter. Don't be tempted to take a dip along the beach sections, as the undertows and rips here are notoriously dangerous. The mouth of the **Powlett River**, 3km east of Kilcunda, enclosed by high sand dunes, is also worth exploring.

Across the road from the pub, **Kilcunda Oceanview Holiday Retreat** (☎ 5678 7260; www .kilcundacaravanpark.com.au; Bass Hwy; unpowered/powered sites $25/27, cabins d $65-120) is a caravan park with sensational ocean views from its cabins and some of the grassy camp sites. There's a path down to the beach where there's a safe children's swimming area and lots of rock pools to explore.

Billowing curtains frame 180-degree ocean views at **Ocean Walk B&B** (☎ 5678 7419; oceanwalk@ waterfront.net.au; 8-14 Gilbert St; s & d from $155, cottages $200). The light-filled rooms each have their own spa, and it's a short stroll down to the beach.

Ocean View Hotel (☎ 5678 7011; Bass Hwy; mains $19-31; ☽ lunch & dinner) is popularly known as the Killy Pub. You almost feel like you're in a ship galley in this narrow, wood-lined bistro where the food is excellent. There's a deck to watch the sunset, and live music in summer.

V/Line (☎ 13 61 96; www.vline.com.au) coaches operate daily from Melbourne ($10, 2½ hours) and continue to Inverloch.

BUNURONG MARINE & COASTAL PARK
This unassuming 12km stretch of marine and coastal park offers some of Australia's best snorkelling and diving and a stunning, cliff-hugging drive. When you see the ancient rocky headlands and amazing formations such as **Eagles Nest**, it's not so hard to believe that dinosaur remains dating back 120 million years were discovered here.

Head down from the car parks along Cape Paterson-Inverloch Rd to the well-signposted coves. Eagles Nest, Shack Bay, The Caves and Twin Reefs are great for **snorkelling**, and Eagles Nest, Shack Bay, Cape Paterson and Flat Rocks are also popular **scuba diving** sites. The Oaks is a popular **surf** beach. The Caves is where the **dinosaur dig** action is; the Bunurong Environment Centre & Shop (opposite) runs tours here in January.

SEAL Diving Services (☎ 5174 3434; www.sealdiving services.com.au; 7/27 Princes Hwy, Traralgon; PADI 4-day course $575, 1-day double dive $80, introductory dive $99) offers PADI open-water dive courses in Inverloch in summer. SEAL also offers one-day dives for beginners and experienced divers, and weekend trips for certified divers at both Wilsons Promontory and Bunurong Marine & Coastal Park.

INVERLOCH
☎ 03 / pop 4140
Fabulous surf, calm inlet beaches, outstanding diving and snorkelling and some top-notch restaurants – ever-expanding Inverloch is understandably popular. The population explodes in summer when visitors flock to the ocean **surf beaches** along the road to Cape Paterson, and families swamp the inlet beaches close to town. Inverloch also draws the crowds when it hosts the popular **Inverloch Jazz Festival** (☎ 5674 3141; www.inverlochjazzfest.org.au) on the Labour Day long weekend each March.

The staff at the very helpful **Inverloch visitors centre** (☎ 1300 762 433; www.visitbasscoast.com; 39 A'Beckett St; ☽ 9am-5pm; ☐) will make accommodation bookings for free. Internet is available for $1.50 per hour (or free in the library across the road). The **Bunurong Environment Centre & Shop** (☎ 5674 3738; www.sgcs.org.au; cnr The Esplanade & Ramsey Blvd; ☺ 10am-4pm Fri-Mon), home to the South Gippsland Conservation Society, has an abundance of books and brochures on environmental and sustainable living topics, and runs environmental tours during school holidays. The volunteer staff are a fabulous source of knowledge about local environmental issues.

Coffee and light lunches are available in the café section of **Sandsford Antiques** (☎ 5674 3339; 13 A'Beckett St; wi-fi). Wireless internet costs $4 for 30 minutes.

Activities
Screw Creek Nature Walk starts from the Inverloch Foreshore Camping Reserve car park and is an easy 40-minute return walk via dunes, swamps and grasslands with views from the bluff of the town and across to Eagles Nest.

You can take lessons with **Learn to Surf Offshore Surf School** (☎ 5674 3374; www.surfingaustralia .com.au; 32 Park St; 2hr lesson $45) at the main surf beach at Inverloch. Everything is provided – you just need to book and turn up at the beach.

Sleeping & Eating
Inverloch Foreshore Camping Reserve (☎ 5674 1236; www.inverlochholidaypark.com.au; cnr Esplanade & Ramsay Blvd; unpowered/powered sites $21/24) There's shade and privacy here and it's only a short toddle over the scrub-covered dunes to the beach. The reserve is managed by the neighbouring Inverloch Holiday Park.

Moilong Express (☎ 0439 842 334; www.basscoast .info/moilong; 405 Inverloch-Venus Bay Rd; d/f $100) These railway guards' vans, complete with traditional wood panelling and the station railway clock, have been converted into very comfortable accommodation with a kitchen and palatial queen-sized beds. The carriages accommodate up to six people and have soul-lifting views over Anderson's Inlet.

Lofts (☎ 1300 762 4335; www.theloftapartments.com .au; Scarborough St; apt from $150; ✖) Spread out in these sleek, multilevel apartments with high ceilings and their name-sake lofts. They're handily adjacent to the park, beach and shops. Some of these designer apartments have water views and most have a spa. They're managed by several real estate agents so it's easiest to book through the Inverloch visitors centre.

Kiosk (☎ 5674 3611; 2-4 Abbott St; meals $4-17.50; ☺ breakfast & lunch) Opposite the beach, 1km from the town centre, this is the perfect breakfast spot. Grab your newspaper and plonk down out the front, or join the chattering patrons inside this little red retro café, complete with bright orange lamps, for a generous breakfast and delicious juices.

Cafe Pajez (☎ 5674 1516; 27 A'Beckett St; lunch $5-12, dinner $17-22 ☺ lunch & dinner Wed-Sun) The wafting aroma of speciality curries will entice you into this warm, earthy café festooned with rugs. Choose your own level of heat with the five-star curry rating system.

Cafe Gabriel (☎ 5674 1178; 9a A'Beckett St; mains $21-32; ☺ lunch Sat & Sun, dinner Thu-Sun) Adding an upmarket option to the Inverloch scene is this classy restaurant and bar with a window opening to the street. The tone here is refined – signs advise you to take crying babies outside.

Farmers Market (☎ 5664 0096; The Glade, opposite the Inlet Hotel; ☺ 8am-1pm) For some fresh local produce, try this market on the third Sunday of each month.

Getting There & Away
V/Line (☎ 13 61 96; www.vline.com.au) coaches to/from Melbourne stop on Beach Rd ($13, 2¾ hours).

VENUS BAY
☎ 03 / pop 510
This sparsely populated but sprawling holiday settlement by Cape Liptrap Coastal Park is popular for its five surf beaches. Watch out for rips if you're swimming here; only one beach, No 1, is patrolled during summer. Families with young children can play at the state's longest spit of sand at nearby Anderson Inlet. Immerse yourself among the teeming bird life here on the **Anderson Inlet Walk** (4km return, starts Lees Rd, 8km from the town shops), which passes alongside the inlet through mudflats and mangroves – home to zillions of crabs.

Operating with typical Dutch efficiency, **Venus Bay Caravan Park** (☎ 5663 7723; www.venus baycaravanpark.com.au; 113a Jupiter Blvd; unpowered/ powered sites $20/26, cabins d $62-95; ☒ ☐ ; wi-fi) is a well-run, family-friendly park, only 800m from the patrolled surf beach, with some off-beat touches such as a giant chess board. Internet access, including wireless, is $6 for 30 minutes.

WORTH A TRIP: KOONWARRA

This tiny township on the South Gippsland Hwy has a fantastic general store with its own café, a shop selling organic produce, an organic cooking school and a winery.

Koonwarra Food, Wine & Produce Store (☎ 5664 2285; South Gippsland Hwy; items $6-34; ☁ breakfast & lunch daily, dinner Fri) is a destination in its own right. Local produce and wines are on sale in the renovated timber building. Also here is a renowned café that serves simple food with flair, and prides itself on using organic, low-impact suppliers and products. Soak up the ambience and bustle in the wooded interior or relax at a table in the shaded cottage gardens, also home to the Outside Bit, a quirky little nursery.

Peaceful Gardens Organic Cooking School (☎ 5664 2480; www.peacefulgardens.com.au; Koala Dr), Victoria's first certified organic cooking school, offers inspired courses in making cakes, bread, traditional pastries and pasta, and runs cooking classes for kids.

Koonwarra Day Spa (☎ 5664 2332; www.koonwarraspa.com.au; 9 Koala Dr; most 30min treatments $50) is a new centre offering spas, saunas and body treatments ranging from a 30-minute mineral spa ($30) to a six-hour pamper package ($465).

The popular **Lyre Bird Hill Winery & Guest House** (☎ 5664 3204; www.lyrebirdhill.com.au; 370 Inverloch Rd; guesthouse s/d $100/175, cottage d $120; ☁ winery 10am-5pm Wed-Mon; ☒) has an old-fashioned B&B with light-filled rooms overlooking the garden. There are also rooms in a faded country cottage. A three-course dinner can be arranged ($60) accompanied by house wines.

The timber-lined wooden **Koonwarra Cottages** (☎ 5664 2488; hayward@dcsi.net.au; South Gippsland Hwy; s/d $110; ☒) with spa and wood heater have a cosy, country kitchen feel. They're spotlessly clean and run by friendly owners.

There's a **Farmers Market** (☎ 6569 8208; ☁ 8am-1pm) at Memorial Park on the first Saturday of each month featuring organic everything (fruit, vegetables, berries, coffee) plus hormone-free beef and chemical-free cheeses.

To get here from Inverloch, take the Inverloch-Leongatha Rd for 11km. Take the turn-off for Koonwarra and drive another 10km to reach the township on the South Gippsland Hwy.

The aroma of essential oils wafts through **Sundowner Lodge Guesthouse** (☎ 5663 7099; www.venusbaygetaways.com.au; 128 Inlet Rd; d $175), a boutique guesthouse that is now also a day spa. The spacious rooms overlook the outdoor hot tub and neighbour the treatment room where massages, private spa or a complete detox are on offer. The guesthouse has its own fully licensed restaurant featuring local seafood.

Never mind the bland décor at **Kenko Bar** (☎ 5663 7899; 114a Jupiter Blvd; lunch $7-13, dinner $20-35; ☁ lunch Thu-Mon, dinner Fri & Sat, daily Dec-Feb) – the smoothies, juices and focaccias served up at lunchtime are worth stopping by for.

WARATAH BAY, WALKERVILLE & BEAR GULLY

Peaceful Waratah Bay has a couple of quiet and remote holiday townships and some wonderful long stretches of white-sand beach. The calm bay beaches are popular with families, and there's also some good surf. Lessons are available with the Learn to Surf Offshore Surf School (p110). Food supplies are limited to a few basics at the caravan parks, so come prepared.

The friendly, well-treed **Waratah Bay Caravan Park** (☎ 5684 1339; www.waratahbaycp.com.au; Freycinet St; unpowered/powered sites $20/25, cabins d $75-115) abuts the coastal park and has surfboard and boogie board hire and a library of books to borrow.

Overlooking Waratah Bay, and part of **Cape Liptrap Coastal Park**, is pretty Walkerville with holiday houses scattered across the hills. There are some great beach walks in this area – check out the historic lime kilns at the Walkerville South beach – and drive to the lighthouse at **Cape Liptrap**.

Vegetation provides privacy at the free Parks Victoria–operated **Bear Gully Camp Site** (BYO water), by the beach in Walkerville South. Just pitch your tent if there's a spot available.

Wake up to a view of Wilsons Promontory in the stylish, self-contained **Bear Gully Coastal Cottages** (☎ 5663 2364; www.beargullycottages.com.au; 33 Maitland Ct, Walkerville South; d from $230). The light-wooden furnishings and fresh yellow and cream walls give an airy, seaside feel. The

VOLUNTEERING

Interested in doing some volunteer work? National parks and organic farms are two options for travellers.

Parks Victoria (☎ 13 16 93; www.parkweb.vic.gov.au) operates a programme for volunteers at u Promontory National Park, Buchan Caves Reserve and Croajingolong National Park during the Christmas and Easter holidays. Volunteers act as camp ground hosts for a minimum of two weeks and are involved in the day to day operations of the park assisting visitors and rangers. Volunteers camp for free; tents can be provided. Apply through Parks Victoria.

Willing Workers On Organic Farms (WWOOF; ☎ 5155 0218; www.wwoof.com.au; 2615 Gelantipy Rd, W Tree) is a national organisation with its base in East Gippsland. Volunteers work on organic farms that are members of the WWOOF association, in exchange for their meals and accommodation.

cottages front onto a lush green lawn, and it's a few minutes walk down a private track to the beach.

FISH CREEK
☎ 03 / pop 730

You know you've arrived in one quirky, fun little town when you see the giant fish lying on top of the pub (the locals will likely tell you it was washed up in the last flood). The shops have names such as Fishy Tales (a book store), and the park tables and street seats are shaped like fish.

Known as the Fishy Pub (of course), the **Promontory Gate Hotel Motel** (☎ 5683 2404; Old Waratah Rd; s/d hotel $25/45, motel $45/65; ⌘) is a budget traveller's delight. The pub rooms are Spartan but clean and have had a relatively recent décor makeover, so the ancient shared bathroom comes as a surprise. The motel rooms (tacked-on in the 1970s) are serviceable and have air-con. The bistro food is excellent.

The sunny **Flying Cow Cafe** (☎ 5683 2338; 9 Falls Rd; lunch $5-15; ⌘ lunch Fri-Mon) has made a break from the fish theme, and the owners' friends have done an extraordinary job collecting cow mementos for them. Light lunches, and cuppas are served in mandatory cow mugs.

There's a **V/Line** (☎ 13 61 96; www.vline.com.au) bus service from Melbourne ($14.50, 2½ hours).

YANAKIE
☎ 03 / pop 280

The nearest settlement to Wilsons Promontory, Yanakie – an Aboriginal word meaning 'between waters' – is a tiny place with many indulgent sleeping options.

You can take in glorious views of the Prom without leaving your very-comfortable bed

at **Black Cockatoo Cottages** (☎ 5687 1306; www.black cockatoo.com; 60 Foley Rd; d $140) – private, stylish, black-timber, self-contained cottages.

The new, luxury, self-contained accommodation at **Limosa Rise** (☎ 5687 1135; www .limosarise.com.au; 40 Dalgleish Rd; d $200-270; ⌘) has already won regional and state awards. Not surprising, given the contemporary design of the three tastefully-appointed cottages with their full-length glass windows taking full advantage of sweeping views across Corner Inlet.

You need a car to get to Yanakie, which is 25km from Foster.

WILSONS PROMONTORY NATIONAL PARK

With more than 80km of walking tracks, wonderful beaches for swimming and surfing, and abundant wildlife, 'the Prom' is one of the most popular national parks in Australia. The park caters to day-trippers looking for short walks, experienced hikers wanting a wilderness experience, and everyone in between. The wildlife around Tidal River is incredibly tame: kookaburras and rosellas lurk expectantly (but you're not allowed to feed them), and wombats nonchalantly waddle out of the undergrowth.

Wilsons Promontory was an important area for the Kurnai and Boonwurrung Aborigines, and middens have been found in many places along the west coast. The southernmost part of mainland Australia, the Prom was once part of a land bridge that allowed people to walk to Tasmania.

Information

The helpful **Parks Victoria** (☎ 1800 350 552, 13 19 63; www.parkweb.vic.gov.au; ⌘ 8am-4.30pm) office in Tidal River books all accommodation in the

SOUTHEAST COAST
VICTORIA

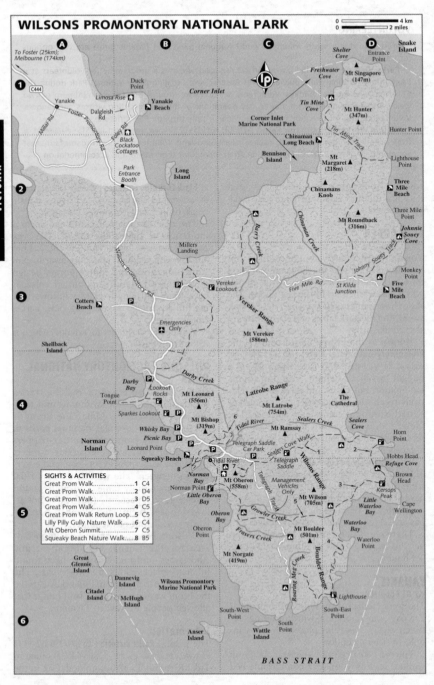

WILSONS PROMONTORY NATIONAL PARK

0 ———— 4 km
0 ———— 2 miles

To Foster (25km);
Melbourne (174km)

Duck Point

Limosa Rise

Yanakie

Dalgleish Rd

Foley Rd

Black Cockatoo Cottages

Park Entrance Booth

Yanakie Beach

Corner Inlet

Shelter Cove

Snake Island

Entrance Point

Freshwater Cove

Mt Singapore (147m)

Tin Mine Cove

Corner Inlet Marine National Park

Bennison Island

Chinaman Long Beach

Mt Hunter (347m)

Tin Mine Track

Hunter Point

Long Island

Mt Margaret (218m)

Lighthouse Point

Chinamans Knob

Three Mile Beach

Millers Landing

Barry Creek

Chinaman Creek

Mt Roundback (316m)

Three Mile Point

Johnnie Souey Cove

Vereker Lookout

Five Mile Rd

St Kilda Junction

Johnny Souey Track

Monkey Point

Cotters Beach

Vereker Range

Five Mile Beach

Emergencies Only

Mt Vereker (586m)

Shellback Island

Darby Creek

Latrobe Range

The Cathedral

Darby Bay

Lookout Rocks

Mt Leonard (556m)

Mt Latrobe (754m)

Sealers Creek

Sealers Cove

Tongue Point

Sparkes Lookout

Mt Bishop (319m)

Sealers Cove Walk

Horn Point

Whisky Bay

Picnic Bay

Tidal River

Mt Ramsay

Wilsons Range

Hobbs Head

Refuge Cove

Norman Island

Leonard Point

Telegraph Saddle Car Park

Telegraph Saddle

Brown Head

Squeaky Beach

Kersops Peak

Norman Bay

Tidal River

Management Vehicles Only

Mt Wilson (705m)

Little Waterloo Bay

Cape Wellington

Norman Point

Mt Oberon (558m)

Telegraph Track

Little Oberon Bay

Oberon Bay

Growler Creek

Waterloo Bay

Waterloo Point

Oberon Point

Frasers Creek

Mt Boulder (501m)

Boulder Range

Mt Norgate (419m)

Roaring Meg Creek

Lighthouse

Great Glennie Island

Dannevig Island

Wilsons Promontory Marine National Park

Citadel Island

McHugh Island

South-West Point

South Point

South-East Point

Anser Island

Wattle Island

BASS STRAIT

SIGHTS & ACTIVITIES
Great Prom Walk...................1	C4
Great Prom Walk...................2	D4
Great Prom Walk...................3	D5
Great Prom Walk...................4	C5
Great Prom Walk Return Loop...5	C5
Lilly Pilly Gully Nature Walk......6	C4
Mt Oberon Summit................7	C5
Squeaky Beach Nature Walk.....8	B5

TOP FIVE PROM WALKS

The Prom's delights are best discovered on foot. Times and distances include walking back.

Sealers Cove Walk

This is the best overnight walk to do at the Prom. Start from the Telegraph Saddle car park and walk down Telegraph Track (it's better than returning uphill via this gnarly track), and stay overnight at beautiful Little Waterloo Bay (12km, 4½ hours). The next day walk on to Sealers Cove via Refuge Cove and return to Telegraph Saddle car park (24km, 7½ hours).

Great Prom Walk

This is the most popular long-distance hike, a moderate 45km circuit across to Sealers Cove, down to Refuge Cove, Waterloo Bay, the lighthouse and back. Allow two to three days and coordinate your walks with tide times, as creek crossings can be hazardous. By prior arrangement with the Parks Victoria office it's possible to visit or stay at the lighthouse.

Lilly Pilly Gully Nature Walk

It's an easy walk (5km, two hours) through heathland and eucalypt forests, with lots of wildlife. Or take the longer route through stringybark forests (6km, two to three hours).

Mt Oberon Summit

Starting from Telegraph Saddle car park, this moderate to hard walk (7km, 2½ hours) is rewarded by excellent panoramic views from the summit. From November to Easter a free shuttle bus operates between Tidal River car park and Mt Oberon car park (a gentle way to start the Great Prom Walk).

Squeaky Beach Nature Walk

Another easy stroll of 5km (two hours) returning through coastal tea trees and banksias to a sensational white-sand beach. Go barefoot on the beach to find out where the name comes from.

park and issues permits for camping away from Tidal River. Bookings can be made up to 12 months in advance.

The only access road into the park leads to **Tidal River**, which has the Parks Victoria office, an education centre, petrol, general store with internet facilities and an open-air cinema (in summer only). A medical centre operates for limited hours in high season. Day entry to the park is $10 per car (included in the overnight charge if you're camping).

Activities

BUSHWALKING

There's an extensive choice of walking tracks that take you through swamps, forests, marshes, valleys of tree ferns, and long beaches lined with sand dunes. The Parks Victoria office has details of walks, from 15-minute strolls to overnight and longer hikes. For some serious exploration, buy a copy of *Discovering the Prom* ($15).

The northern area of the park is much less visited – most walks in this wilderness area are overnight or longer, and are mainly for experienced bushwalkers. Wood fires are not permitted anywhere in the park.

SURFING & DIVING

SEAL Diving Services (p110) offer dives for certified divers, and **Learn to Surf Offshore Surf School** (p111) run surfing lessons here.

Tours

Bunyip Tours (☎ 1300 286 947, 9650 9680; www .bunyiptours.com; 1-/3-day tours $110/$160) One-day guided tours to the Prom, departing from Melbourne, with the option of staying another two unguided days. Camping costs and gear are included in the three-day trip. There's a discount for YHA members.

First Track Adventures (☎ 5634 2761; www.first trackadventures.com.au; per day $99, overnight $189, incl meals) This Gippsland based company organises bushwalking and abseiling trips to the Prom.

Hiking Plus (☎ 9431 1050; www.hikingplus.com; 5-day hikes $1420-1712) This tour company organises hikes to the Prom from nearby Foster where it has comfortable guesthouse accommodation (including spa) for the start and end of each trip. Packages include two- to three-day hikes, meals, a massage and spa.

Sleeping

TIDAL RIVER & AROUND

The following accommodation (huts, cabins, camp sites and cottages) should be booked well in advance through **Parks Victoria** (☎ 1800 350 552, 13 19 63; www.parkweb.vic.gov.au).

Camp Sites (unpowered sites per car & 3 adults (or 2 adults & 2 children) $21.50, extra adult/child/car $5/2.50/6.50) Tidal River has 480 camp sites. For the Christmas school holiday period there's a ballot for sites (apply online by 31 July at www.parkweb.vic.gov.au). For this peak time Parks Victoria reserves some sites for overseas and interstate visitors; there's a two-night maximum stay for these, and the sites can be booked in advance. There are another 11 bush-camping areas around the Prom, all with pit or compost toilets, but nothing else in the way of facilities; you need to carry in your own drinking water. Overnight hikers need camping permits (adult/child $7.50/3.50 per night), which should be booked ahead through Parks Victoria.

Huts & Cabins (4-/6-bed huts $60/92, cabins d $158) Tidal River's cosy wooden huts have bunks and kitchenettes but no bathroom. There are also spacious and private self-contained timber cabins here, with large sliding-glass doors and decking overlook the bush or river. They're simple but ultra-comfortable, and have the luxury of a bathtub. The smaller 1960s motel-style units have been bulldozed and will be replaced with more contemporary units from 2010.

Safari Tents (d/f $240/280) Nestled in bushland at Tidal River, these plush tents (which sleep up to four) are the latest addition to the park's accommodation. Besides comfortable queen-size beds, they also have bathrooms, and there's a shared tent kitchen.

Lighthouse Keepers' Cottages (8-12-bed cottage per person $47-74) Magnificent, heritage-listed, 1850s cottages with thick stone walls, on a pimple of land that juts out into the wild ocean. Kick back after the 19km hike here and watch ships or whales passing by. You can usually visit the lighthouse itself, depending on ranger availability. Prices increase 50% on Saturday nights.

FOSTER

Prom Coast Backpackers (☎ 5682 2171; www.yha.com.au; 40 Station Rd; dm/d/f $25/60/80; 🖳) There are no hostels in the park, but nearby Foster has this cosy renovated cottage with contemporary wooden furnishings that sleeps 10. It's close to the shops and across the road from a good playground. The friendly owners can usually organise a lift to the Prom for $20. Prices are about 10% higher for non-YHA members.

Warrawee Holiday Apartments (☎ 5682 2171; www.gippsland.com/web/warraweeholidayapartments; d/f $120/130; 🐾) Next door to Prom Coast Backpackers and under the same management are these comfortable, two-bedroom apartments, some with air-con.

Eating

Stock up in Foster, which has supermarkets and a fruit shop, on your way to the Prom. In Tidal River, the general store has supplies of all the basics, there's a takeaway shop and the recent addition of a **café** (mains $12-19; ☽ breakfast, lunch & dinner), serving light lunches and bistro-style meals.

Getting There & Away

There isn't any direct public transport between Melbourne and the Prom, though there are day trips and organised tours.

There is a new **bus service** (☎ 0428-672 833) operating on Friday evenings from Foster to Tidal River via Fish Creek ($6.30, 1¼ hours) at 7pm, with a return service on Sundays (departs 2.35pm). Each service connects with V/Line's Melbourne service at Fish Creek.

PORT ALBERT

☎ 03 / pop 250

Port Albert is still a quaint old fishing village, but it's fast reinventing itself with old buildings being converted into contemporary accommodation, cafés and galleries. Port Albert proudly pronounces itself as Victoria's first established port. The many historic timber buildings in the main street date from its busy 1850s port days – each has a brass plaque outlining its history.

Maritime Museum (☎ 5183 2520; Tarraville Rd; adult/child $5/1; ☽ 10.30am-4pm daily Sep-May, Sat & Sun Jun-Aug) The enthusiasm of the volunteer staff here is contagious, as they give you some quick highlights of Port Albert's maritime history before leaving you to your own devices. Check out stories of shipwrecks, the town's whaling and sealing days, and local Aboriginal legends.

Port Albert Hotel/Motel (☎ 5183 2212; fax 5183 2429; 37 Wharf St; s/d $55/75; 🐾) Victoria's oldest continually licensed pub still draws the crowds.

Not surprisingly, with its friendly staff, quality bistro (mains $15 to 30) and takeaway fish and chips (just ring the bell at the outdoor counter and someone will take your order). The motel rooms are clean but faded.

Rodondo (☎ 5183 2688; susan333@optusnet.com.au; 74 Tarraville Rd; cottage $75, B&B d/f $140/160) The contemporary blends seamlessly with the historic in this 1871 renovated home. Crisp white linen and comfortable furnishings give the rooms a homely but luxurious feel, and the friendly hospitality adds to the satisfaction of staying here. There's also a cosy self-contained cabin in the former wash-house.

Port Albert Wharf Fish & Chips (☎ 5183 2434, Port Albert Wharf; meals from $6; ☽ lunch & dinner) The fish and chips here are renowned, and are also available eat-in at their new wharfside restaurant (which should be open by the time you read this).

General Store (☎ 5183 2291; 71 Tarraville Rd; mains $10-22; ☽ breakfast & lunch Tue-Sun) This café-gallery inside an 1856 general store has fast attracted a following. People travel a long way for the (limited) gourmet menu complemented with Gippsland wines (try the Gippsland cheese platter with crusty bread, marinated olives and fig relish). The Asian-influenced gallery stocks unexpected treasures such as Chinese peasant chairs and wooden croaking frogs, while the shop sells an eclectic range of books and gourmet local produce.

V/Line (☎ 13 61 96; www.vline.com.au) coach drop-off is possible at the turn-off to Port Albert on the South Gippsland Hwy, but it's another 7km to Port Albert.

MCLOUGHLIN'S BEACH
☎ 03 / pop 290

Somehow tourism development seems to have bypassed this tiny holiday-shack settlement. Surprisingly, there's not a single accommodation option or shop here – just a sleepy town edged by the salt marshes, mangroves, low-lying scrub and quiet waters of Nooramunga Marine & Coastal Park.

There's a lovely 40-minute return **walk** to Ninety Mile Beach. From the jetty take the boardwalk across an area of salt marsh and mangroves. Look out for orange-bellied parrots flying through the air and birds wading in the mudflats. Cross the wide arm of the inlet at an old wooden bridge to meet a sandy track that passes through banksia forest, then down steep sand dunes to the ocean.

The banksia track intersects with a walk east to **Reeve's Beach** (13km, four hours return) on Ninety Mile Beach (where bush camping is possible); or west to **McLoughlin's Entrance** (6km, two hours return).

WEST GIPPSLAND – TYNONG TO YARRAGON

This is the quickest route from Melbourne to Sale, though it's easy to get distracted stopping at creative Yarragon, detouring to historic Walhalla or along Grand Ridge Rd. Drive straight through and you'll see Gippsland's industrial heartland with the smoking chimney stacks that power most of Victoria.

YARRAGON
☎ 03 / pop 1,140

Yarragon has taken advantage of the highway passing through and evolved into something of a mecca for gifts and gourmet goodies. Innovative glassware and woodwork are a feature of the **Town & Country Gallery** (☎ 5634 2229; www.townandcountrygallery.com.au; 111 Princes Hwy; ☽ 10am-5pm), showcasing some of Gippsland's finest artists. **Gippsland Food & Wine** (☎ 5634 2451; http://gippsland.com/web/GippslandFoodWine/; 123 Princes Hwy; ☽ 7.30am-5pm) has a wide selection of local wines and produce, including a large deli. It's also a visitors centre.

Sticcado (☎ 5634 2101; The Village Walk; breakfast $7-16, lunch mains $5.50-22; ☽ breakfast & lunch Wed-Mon) offers the best food in town and specialises in beef dishes from its own cattle farm.

Signposted off the highway from nearby Trafalgar South is **Sunny Creek Fruit & Berry Farm** (☎ 5634 7526; 69 Tudor Rd; Childers; ☽ 9am-5pm Sat & Sun Nov-Jul). It's a beautiful 7km drive from the highway through some remnant rainforest to pick a bucketful of organic raspberries, strawberries or gooseberries.

LAKES DISTRICT

The Gippsland Lakes comprise the largest inland waterway system in Australia. There are three main lakes that interconnect: Lake King, Lake Victoria and Lake Wellington. The 'lakes' are actually shallow lagoons, separated from the ocean by a narrow strip of sand dunes known as Ninety Mile Beach. Despite nearby bustling Bairnsdale and the Princes Hwy, the 400 sq km Lakes District is remote, with just a half-dozen access points, including Metung, Paynesville, Loch Sport and Lakes

---

DETOUR: GRAND RIDGE ROAD

The spectacular 132km mostly gravel Grand Ridge Rd winds along the top of the Strzelecki Ranges, running from midway between Warragul and Korumburra to midway between Traralgon and Yarram, providing a fabulous excursion through fertile farmland that was once covered with forests of giant mountain ash trees. There are still valleys of tree ferns – you'll likely see more on this drive than you will the rest of your life. If you're going to travel the length of the road, allow the best part of a day – it makes a good alternative to the Princes Hwy. Pick it up south of Warragul, then leave it and travel through the Tarra-Bulga National Park to Yarram on the South Gippsland Hwy, then pick up the main east coast route again.

Only 3km in from the Princes Hwy, you could make your first stop the excellent **Wild Dog Winery** (☎ 5623 1117; www.wilddogwinery.com.au; Warragul-Korumburra Rd; ☼ 10am-5pm), one of Gippsland's first wineries. It produces a great range of wines, all grown and bottled on its 30 acres, and has fabulous views across the Strzeleckis. The only place of any size along the route is the pretty township of **Mirboo North**, home to Gippsland's only brewery, the award-winning **Grand Ridge Brewery & Restaurant** (☎ 5668 2222; www.grand-ridge.com.au; Main St; mains $16-29; ☼ lunch & dinner) producing chemical- and preservative-free beer. The restaurant food is fresh and prepared from local produce, including steaks from the local beef farm. Vegetarians are catered for too – try the slow-cooked lentil curry, made from scratch each time.

You'll pass through the rainforest gully of **Tarra-Bulga National Park,** one of the last remnants of the magnificent forests that once covered all of South Gippsland. There are some good short walks here, including the **Tarra Valley Rainforest Walk** (1.5km, 35 minutes return) to **Cyathea Falls**. Also here is a **visitors centre** (☎ 5196 6166; ☼ 10am-4pm Sat & Sun) and the easy **Fern Gully Nature Walk** (750m, 15 minutes return). Camping is not permitted in the park, but you can stay at the nearby **Tarra Valley Tourist Park** (☎ 5186 1283; www.tarra-valley.com; 1906 Tarra Valley Rd; unpowered/powered sites $24/28; cabins with/without bathroom from $100/75), nestled in rainforest with camping in a pretty riverside setting or cabin accommodation.

For sheer indulgence, make your last stop the **Tarra Valley Rainforest Retreat** (☎ 5186 1313; www.tarravalleyrainforestretreat.com; 1788 Tarra Valley Rd; s/d 145/170; ☒). This elegant Swiss chalet–style accommodation doubles as a chocolate school. Chocolate appreciation courses with the resident Swiss chocolatier cost $50/55 for guests/nonguests.

Entrance. You need a boat to truly appreciate this remarkable lakes system. Part of the 17,200-hectare Gippsland Lakes Coastal Park includes the Lakes National Park, which protects 2400 hectares of native habitat (p122).

SALE

☎ 03 / pop 13,340

Sale is the gateway to the Lakes District and a great lunch spot. For those who'd like to linger longer, there's also some fabulous accommodation and classy restaurants and bars here, and a striking entertainment centre.

Information

Central Gippsland visitors centre (☎ 5144 1108; www.tourismwellington.com.au; 8 Foster St; ☼ 9am-5pm) Has internet facilities and a free accommodation booking service.

Parks Victoria (☎ 13 19 63; www.parkweb.vic.gov.au; 1 Lacey St; ☼ 9.30am-noon & 1-3.30pm Tue & Fri) Turn right at Foster St into Guthridge St then right into Lacey St.

Sights & Activities

The 4km **Sale Wetlands Walk**, which skirts around Lake Guthridge and Lake Guyatt, incorporates an Indigenous Art Trail commemorating the importance of the wetlands to the local Gunai/Kurnai population. Stop off for a coffee overlooking the lake, or take a dip, at the new state-of-the-art **Aqua Energy** (☎ 5142 3700; 1 McIntosh Dr; pool admission adult/child $4.70/3.20; ☼ 6am-9pm Mon-Fri, 9am-6pm Sat & Sun) with its six swimming pools. For the kids, take the extended trail past a very cool playground and a fauna park with furry favourites.

Sale Common, a 300 hectare wildlife refuge with bird hides, an observatory, waterhole, boardwalks and other walking tracks is part of an internationally recognised wetlands system. The wildlife refuge is 2km south of Sale on the South Gippsland Hwy. The best time to see lots of bird life is early morning or late evening (wear some mosquito repellent).

The **Gippsland Art Gallery** (☎ 5142 3372; www .wellington.vic.gov.au/gallery; Civic Centre, 68 Foster St; adult/ child $3/1.50; ◷ 10am-5pm Tue-Fri, 1-5pm Sat & Sun) is always worth a look, exhibiting work by locally and nationally renowned artists and hosting touring exhibitions.

Sleeping & Eating

Free camping is permitted (no facilities) in the Lake Wellington wetlands area (excluding Sale Common), as long as you're at least 20m away from the water.

Cambrai Hostel (☎ 5147 1600; www.maffra.net.au /hostel/backpackers.htm; 117 Johnson St, Maffra; dm/d incl breakfast $25/60; 🖳) There are no backpackers in Sale, but in nearby Maffra this place is a budget haven. It's in a 120-year-old building that was once a doctor's residence and is now a relaxed hostel with licensed bar, open fire and pool table in the cosy lounge. There's a tiny self-catering kitchen and clean, cheerful rooms. Between October and April, loads of backpackers seize the opportunity to work on local vegetable farms. Book well ahead if you want a double or family room as they're snapped up by the long-termers.

minnies (☎ 5144 3344; www.minnies.com.au; 202 Gibsons Rd; s/d $150/160; ✗) It takes some flair to make an outlandish purple-and-green colour scheme not only work but look inspired. This modern B&B does both in its huge lounge area. Choose between the funky green room and the more traditional rose room, with its antique-look bed head complete with rose imprints.

Relish@the Gallery (☎ 5144 5044; Gippsland Art Gallery, 68-70 Foster St; dishes $4-30; ◷ breakfast & lunch daily, dinner Wed-Sat) Take a table by the window and check out the old port of Sale while you tuck into dishes such as the salmon, spinach, capers, red onion and goats cheese omelette in this bustling café. There's an extensive kids menu, and baby change facilities are available.

bis cucina (☎ 5144 3388; Wellington Entertainment Centre, 100 Foster St; breakfast & lunch $6-22, dinner $19-34; ◷ breakfast Sat & Sun, lunch daily, dinner Tue-Sat) Relaxed and attentive service combined with carefully chosen modern Australian cuisine makes this a fine choice for both the serious foodie and the theatre goer wanting a quick pre-show meal. Sit on the deck with a glass of wine from

SOUTHEAST COAST VICTORIA

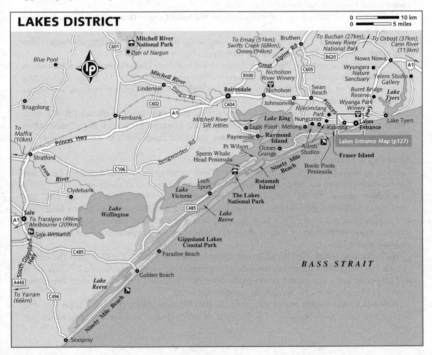

DETOUR: WALHALLA

☎ 03 / pop 18

Tiny Walhalla, 46km northeast of Moe, is one of Victoria's most historic and charming towns. Gold was discovered here in 1862 by Ned Stringer and the population exploded. However, by the time the railway from Moe came into service in 1910, the gold supplies and population were (and still are) in decline. There's still plenty to see in Walhalla, and the drive up to the town is beautiful. Stringers Creek runs through the centre of the town, which is in an idyllic valley encircled by a cluster of historic buildings set into the hillsides. Online, check out www .walhalla.org.au.

Sights & Activities

Many of Walhalla's attractions are open year-round, but there's more happening on weekends and during high season. The best way to see the town is on foot – take the **circuit walk** (45 minutes) anticlockwise from the information shelter as you enter town. This passes the main sights before climbing up the hill to follow the old timber tramway, then heads back down to the car park. The tramway also leads to the **Australian Alps Walking Track** (www.australianalps .deh.gov.au/parks/walktrack), which leads all the way to Canberra. There are other walks to Thomson Bridge, Poverty Point or on to the Baw Baw Plateau.

Guided tours of the **Long Tunnel Extended Gold Mine** (☎ 5165 6259; adult/child/family $15/12/36; ꙮ tours 1.30pm Mon-Fri, noon, 2pm & 3pm Sat & Sun), off Walhalla-Beardmore Rd, give you a look at Cohens Reef, once one of Australia's top reef gold producers.

You can take a very scenic 20-minute ride between Thomson Station (on the main road 3.5km before Walhalla) and Walhalla on the **Walhalla Goldfields Railway** (☎ 9513 3969; return adult/child/ family $17/12/37; ꙮ from Thomson station 11.40am, 1.40pm & 3.40pm, from Walhalla station 12.10pm, 2pm & 3.50pm, Wed, Sat & Sun). The train snakes along Stringers Creek Gorge, passing lovely forested gorge country and crosses a number of trestle bridges.

Back in town, steps lead up a steep hillside to **Walhalla Cricket Ground**, a spectacular place to hit a six.

Walhalla Cemetery gives a more sombre insight into the history of the area; the terrain here is so steep that some souls were buried sideways!

There's a group of restored shops on the main street, including **Walhalla Post Office & Museum** (☎ 5165 6250; admission $2; ꙮ 10am-4pm), which offers ghost tours ($22, 1¼ hours) on the first three Saturdays of each month (7.30pm April to October, 8.30pm October to April) and shares some of the local legends.

For some seriously rugged mountain adventuring, **Mountain Top Experience** (☎ 5134 6876; www.mountaintopexperience.com; adult & child $20, family $60) operates a 1½-hour 4WD Copper Mine Adventure trip most weekends and Wednesdays, along old coach roads to a disused mine.

Sleeping & Eating

Camping in Walhalla is free, and there are good bush camping areas along Stringer's Creek and the designated North Gardens camping area with toilets at the top of the town.

Windsor House (☎ 9882 5985, 5165 6237; www.windsorhouse.com.au; Main Rd; d from $160) The clock turns back more than a century when you step into this B&B with four-poster beds, fires and a library of old books. This 1878 building was a guesthouse during Walhalla's heyday and has been restored to its former glory. It's only open weekends and school holidays. No children under 12.

Walhalla Star Hotel (☎ 5165 6262; www.starhotel.com.au; Main Rd; s & d $199, tr $229) The rebuilt historic Star Hotel offers stylish boutique-hotel accommodation with sophisticated designer décor and king-sized beds. The hotel has an equally upmarket restaurant, Parker's, for some fine dining (mains $25 to $27, open for dinner). No children under 12.

Walhalla Lodge Family Hotel (☎ 5165 6226; Main Rd; mains $14-22; ꙮ lunch & dinner Wed-Mon) A cosy one-room pub decked out with prints of old Walhalla, and serving reasonable pub grub.

BATALUK CULTURAL TRAIL

The Princes Hwy forms the backbone of the **Bataluk (Lizard) Cultural Trail** (www.maffra.net .au/bataluk/sites.htm), which follows a network of Gunai/Kurnai sites of significance. The trail was designed by the Gunai/Kurnai community in Gippsland to offer a greater appreciation and understanding of their traditional and contemporary lifestyles. The **Ramahyuck District Aboriginal Corporation** (☎ 5143 1644; www.ramahyuck.org; 117 Foster St, Sale; ☺ 9am-5pm Mon-Fri) has an information brochure on the trail.

Sites along the Bataluk Cultural Trail include:

Sale Wetlands (p118)
Knob Reserve (p122)
The Den of Nargun (p124)
Howitt Park (p123)
Krowathunkoolong Keeping Place (p123)
Legend Rock (p126)
Buchan Caves (p130)
Burnt Bridge Reserve This reserve adjoins the Lake Tyers Aboriginal Reserve and has information boards about the reserve's history. When it was declared in 1971, it was the first time a State Government had given unconditional freehold title to residents of an Aboriginal reserve.
Salmon Rocks (p135)

All the sights are signposted from the Princes Hwy.

---

the extensive wine list. The bis has the most sumptuous children's menu in Gippsland with offerings such as organic chicken.

Drinking & Entertainment

Kaz Bah Lounge (☎ 5143 3324; 118 Raymond St; ☺ 5pm-midnight Wed-Thu, 5pm-3am Fri, 7pm-3am Sat) Pull up a bar stool and admire the ceiling murals, massive pillars and chandelier in this Art Deco building while you wait for your cocktail.

Wellington Entertainment Centre (☎ 5143 3200; www.wellington.vic.gov.au/entertainment; 100 Foster St; tickets $28-50) Top-class state and national theatre productions, comedy shows and music performances make brief appearances at the centre.

Getting There & Away

V/Line (☎ 13 61 96; www.vline.com.au) has seven train and train/coach services daily between Melbourne and Sale ($20, 2½ hours).

NINETY MILE BEACH

Isolated Ninety Mile Beach is a long, narrow strip of beach backed by dunes, swamplands and lagoons, stretching from McLoughlin's Beach to Marlo. Beaches are great for surf-fishing and walking, though they can be dangerous for swimming, except where patrolled at Seaspray, Woodside and Lakes Entrance.

From Seaspray to Lakes Entrance is the Gippsland Lakes Coastal Park with oodles of low-lying coastal shrubs, banksias and tea tree, and bursts of native wildflowers in spring. It's also home to plenty of kangaroos and black wallabies, so take it easy when driving, especially at night.

The main access roads are from Yarram to Woodside Beach, and from Sale to Seaspray, Golden Beach and Loch Sport. Stock up on supplies in Sale or Yarram, as the townships along here are small and facilities are limited.

If you're interested in the challenge of hiking the length of the Ninety Mile Beach, permission for remote camping can be obtained from **Parks Victoria** (☎ 13 19 63; www.parkweb.vic.gov.au).

At the western end of Ninety Mile Beach, **Reeves Beach** has a camping ground with pit toilets. For a retro blast, go to **Seaspray** (population 190), which has somehow escaped the rampant development along the coast and is packed full of old holiday shacks – it's how Victorian coastal towns used to be in the 1970s. There's one shop that acts as the takeaway, minisupermarket and post office. The long narrow strip of caravans and camp sites in the main street comprises the **Seaspray Caravan Park** (☎ 5146 4364; Main St; unpowered & powered sites $20), and it's a short stroll over the dunes to the patrolled beach. **Ronnie's Tea Rooms** (☎ 5146 4420; 13 Trood St; Devonshire teas $7; ☺ morning & afternoon tea Sat & Sun) offers respite from the beach scene. A cuppa and a scone often come accompanied with a chat with Ronnie in the sunny tea room overlooking his neat garden.

On the road between Seaspray and Golden Beach, there are free Parks Victoria **camp sites**, nestled in on the beach side and shaded by tea tree – they're hugely popular over summer. Some sites have barbecues and pit toilets, but you need to bring your own water and firewood. Hot showers are available at Golden Beach for $2.

Loch Sport (population 780) is a small, bushy town sprawling along a narrow spit of land with a lake on one side and the ocean on the other. There are some good swimming areas here for children. The **Marina Hotel** (☎ 5146 0666; mains $15-23; ☒ lunch & dinner) is perched by the lake and has a friendly vibe and superb sunset views. The bistro menu, featuring fish, isn't bad either. A Loch Sport real estate agent manages 40 **holiday houses** (☎ 5146 0411; www .garypowersrealestate.com; Lot 217, Lake St; houses per night $110-250), ranging from ordinary to luxury, available for nightly or weekly rental.

90 Mile Beach Holiday Retreat (☎ 5146 0320; www.90milebeachholidayretreat.com; Track 10, off Golden Beach-Loch Sport Rd; unpowered/powered sites $26/28, caravans/bunk rooms d $60/75, lodge & cottage d & f $155-165) on a huge chunk of land a few kilometres from Loch Spot, has 2.4km of pristine beach frontage. It's separated from the rest of the world by 6km of dirt track, leading off the road from Golden Beach to Loch Sport. There are plenty of shady, grassy areas for camping, small ex-Melbourne Olympic Village bunk-rooms and spacious, light and airy lodges. The comfortable self-contained cottage is nestled into the dunes, and only a minute from the beach. Take insect repellent to ward off the mosquitoes.

The Lakes National Park

This narrow strip of coastal bushland is surrounded by lakes and ocean. It's a beautiful and quiet little spot to set up camp, except in January when everyone else has the same idea. You can reach this national park by road from adjoining Loch Sport, or by boat from Paynesville (5km).

Banksia and eucalypt woodland abound with areas of low-lying heathland and some swampy salt-marsh scrub. In spring the park is carpeted with native wildflowers and has one of Australia's best displays of native orchids. You're likely to spot kangaroos, as well as wallabies, possums, emus and possibly koalas. There's plenty of bird life too – more than 190 species have been sighted, includ-

ing the rare white-bellied sea eagle and the endangered little tern.

A loop road through the park provides good car access, and there are well-marked **walking trails**, including some short walks, and several picnic areas (BYO water). **Point Wilson**, at the eastern tip of the mainland section of the park is the best picnic spot and a popular gathering spot for kangaroos (no feeding them of course). The only camping is at **Emu Bight** (sites up to 6 people $11.50), nestled in bushland with pit toilets and fireplaces available; BYO water. Sites can be booked through the Sale office of Parks Victoria (p118).

STRATFORD

☎ 03 / pop 1440

Stratford is a pretty little town on the Princes Hwy, a 15-minute drive north from Sale, and has retained its authenticity and appeal without going tourist-kitsch. There's an amazing diversity of shops here: a Turkish rug shop, hobby shop for train lovers, and a lolly shop. The contemporary **Red River Designs Gallery** (☎ /fax 5145 6769; Tyers St; ☒ 10am-4.30pm Fri-Sun) is worth a browse for some distinctive local jewellery and woodwork. The **Shakespeare on the River Festival** (☎ 5145 6133; www.stratfordshake speare.com.au) is held here annually in April/ May, with community and professional theatre productions, and some fabulous activities for children as well as adults.

One of the stops of the Bataluk Cultural Trial, the forested **Knob Reserve**, on a bend in the River Avon, has a deeply calming effect. It feels a world away from the buzz of the highway and has sensational views across the river flats. It was once a meeting place for local Aboriginal clans who gathered here for corroborees and ceremonies. There are lots of picnic tables and a refreshingly old-style playground. The reserve is signposted from the highway.

At **Overland Gold Adventures** (☎ 5145 6701; www .maffra.net.au/overlandgoldadventures; 15 Dawson St; day trip for up to 6 people incl lunch $330), Graham, a friendly third-generation gold miner, operates 4WD tours exploring the gold-mining areas of Gippsland, tailor-made to suit the needs of the group. Visit old mines and prospect for gold. Overnight trips are also possible.

Sleeping & Eating

Tranquil B&B (☎ 5145 6094; bethrip@s140.aone.net.au; 4 Merrick St; r $95) The accommodation in this historic home is quirky and vibrant, a bit like its friendly owner Beth, a local identity. The artistic multicoloured rooms are uplifting, and one has its own bathroom and kitchen.

Stratford Bakehouse (☎ 5145 6003; 35 Tyers St; items $2-6; ✆ 6am-6pm Mon-Fri, 6am-4pm Sat-Sun) Justifiably popular for its pies and cakes (try the 'pear slam'), this is a nice no-frills spot for a quick bite or espresso.

Wa-De-Lock Cellar Door (☎ 5145 7050; 76 Tyers St; dishes $3-13; ✆ breakfast & lunch, dinner by appointment) Kick back with a glass of Gippsland chardonnay in the leafy wine garden while you're served up Wa-De-Lock's own focaccias or pizza bases topped with gourmet local produce. Save room for some of the handmade truffles, and as you toddle out, pick up some Gippsland cheeses, wines and jams.

BAIRNSDALE
☎ 03 / pop 11,290
On the banks of the Mitchell River, Bairnsdale is East Gippsland's commercial hub with a bustling main street and a sprinkling of attractions. Here you'll find an absorbing insight into Aboriginal history, art galleries and the Macleod Morass wetlands – a real contrast to the hubbub of the main street.

Information
Bairnsdale visitors centre (☎ 1800 637 060, 5152 3444; www.lakesandwilderness.com.au; 240 Main St; ✆ 9am-5pm; 🖳)
East Gippsland Shire Library (☎ 5152 4225; Service St; ✆ 10am-5pm Mon, 10am-1pm Tue, 9am-6pm Wed & Fri, 9am-7pm Thu, 9.30am-12pm Sat; 🖳) Free internet access.
Parks Victoria (☎ 5152 0600; www.parkweb.vic.gov.au; 73 Calvert St; ✆ 8.30am-5pm Mon-Fri)

Sights & Activities
Krowathunkoolong Keeping Place (☎ 5152 1891; 37-53 Dalmahoy St; adult/child $3.50/2.50; ✆ 9am-5pm Mon-Fri) It's almost impossible not to be stirred by this Koorie cultural exhibition space that explores Gunai/Kurnai life from the Dreamtime until after white settlement. The exhibition traces the Gunai/Kurnai clan from their Dreamtime ancestors, Borun the pelican and his wife Tuk the musk duck. Also covered is life at Lake Tyers Mission, east of Lakes Entrance, which is now a trust privately owned by Aboriginal shareholders. Items such as an impressive 2.5m bark canoe and a trumpet-like eel-and-fish basket reveal the Kurnai's skill in fishing the waterways of the area. The unmitigated mas-

sacres of the Kurnai during 1839–49 are also detailed. The Keeping Place is signposted from the highway and is behind the train station.

On the edge of town (signposted from the highway at the roundabout as you arrive in Bairnsdale from the west) the **MacLeod Morass Boardwalk** is a stunning internationally recognised wetland reserve with walking tracks and bird hides.

East Gippsland Aboriginal Arts Corporation (☎ 5153 1002; www.australiacouncil.gov.au; 222 Nicholson St; admission free; ✆ 9am-5pm Mon-Fri) is an art gallery featuring the work of local Aboriginal artists.

East Gippsland Art Gallery (☎ 5153 1988; www .eastgippslandartgallery.org.au; 2 Nicholson St; admission free; ✆ 10am-4pm Tue-Fri, 10am-2pm Sat) is a bright, open space that has regular exhibitions, mostly the work of East Gippsland artists.

The grand red-brick **St Mary's Catholic Church** (☎ 5152 3106; Princes Hwy; tours 1pm Mon-Fri, 2.30pm Sat & Sun) towers over the western end of the shopping strip, beside the visitors centre, and is notable for its opulent ceiling murals of rosy-cheeked cherubs.

Howitt Park is a popular playground stop on the highway with a flying fox and giant slide. Just near the slide is a **Scarred Tree**, significant to the local Aboriginal community, which has had bark removed to make canoes or food and infant carriers. Across the road from the park is the starting point for the popular bike and walking track, the **East Gippsland Rail Trail** leading northeast 95km to Orbost. You can also detour and take the **Discovery Trail** via state forest to Lakes Entrance.

About 4km northeast of the town of Nicholson and signposted from the highway, **Nicholson River Winery** (☎ 5156 8241; www.nicholson riverwinery.com.au; 57 Liddells Rd, Nicholson; ✆ 10am-4pm), best known for its award-winning whites, has tastings in a garden with a brilliant location overlooking its namesake river ($2 per person refundable with purchase). Phone ahead in winter and nonholiday times to make sure it is open.

Sleeping & Eating
There are numerous motel options on the highway (Main St).

Mitchell Gardens Holiday Park (☎ 5152 4654; www .mitchellgardens.com.au; unpowered/powered sites $20/23, cabins d $50-86; 🐾) East of the town centre on the banks of the Mitchell River, this is a friendly park with plenty of shade for cabins and a little for tents. The deluxe cabins overlook the river.

> **WORTH A TRIP: MITCHELL RIVER NATIONAL PARK**
>
> About 42km northwest of Bairnsdale, this park has some beautiful green valleys, rocky outcrops, camping areas and lovely hiking, including the two-day, 18km **Mitchell River Walking Track**. Its best-known feature is the **Den of Nargun**, a small cave that, according to Aboriginal stories, is haunted by a strange, half-stone creature, the Nargun.
>
> Access tracks lead into the park off Dargo Rd. There are four free camp sites (all with toilets) within the park, but bring your own drinking water and firewood. Park notes are available at www.parkweb .vic.gov.au, or from the Parks Victoria office in Bairnsdale.

Riversleigh Country Hotel (☎ 5152 6966; www.rivers leigh.info; 1 Nicholson St; s/d incl breakfast from $112/122; ❄) This Victorian-era boutique hotel offers elegant rooms with heritage furnishings. Breakfast is served in the sunny conservatory and there's a formal restaurant here as well (mains $10 to $33, open for lunch and dinner Monday to Saturday), maximising the use of local ingredients in inventive modern cuisine. Disabled facilities are available.

Peppers (☎ 5152 3217; 222 Main St; fish & chips $8; ☾ 8.30am-8.30pm) This contemporary fish-and-chip shop adds flair to the usual offerings. Try its popular fish souvlaki ($6.50) smothered with *tzatziki*.

Gourmet Deli (☎ 5152 1544; 144 Main St; dishes $6-10; ☾ lunch Mon-Fri) They take their coffee seriously here, and you're encouraged to specify precisely how you like it. Tea lovers are also well catered for. Gourmet sandwich ingredients are on display in their deli and served up in thick crusty bread.

River Grill (☎ 5153 1421; 2 Wood St; mains $27-36; ☾ lunch & dinner Mon-Sat) You know you're in for an indulgent experience when you walk into this renovated 1880s building and see the white linen, balloon wine glasses and the four-page menu (with three pages of wine). The newest addition to East Gippsland's culinary scene, River Grill offers contemporary fine dining with Mediterranean flair.

Getting There & Away

Bairnsdale's **V/Line** (☎ 13 61 96; www.vline.com.au) station is on McLeod St, one block south of the town centre. There are three daily train services between Melbourne and Bairnsdale ($25, 3½ hours). From Bairnsdale, **V/Line buses** (☎ 5152 1711) operate daily to Lakes Entrance ($5.50, 30 minutes) and Orbost ($13, 1¼ hours).

EAGLE POINT

☎ 03 / pop 950

The small hamlet of Eagle Point is humbly home to the natural wonder of the 8km-long **Mitchell River Silt Jetties**, the second longest silt jetties in the world (after the Mississippi). You can view them from **Eagle Point Lookout**, and take a drive out on to them as well. The area is a prime fishing and bird-watching spot and a favourite with families for the safe swimming along the lakeside beach. There's also the 6-hectare **Eagle Point Reserve**, which is great bushland for walks and wildlife spotting.

Eagle Point Caravan Park (☎ /fax 5156 6232; Bay Rd; unpowered/powered sites $17/18, cabins $58-78; ❄) The caravan park is well-positioned with camp sites and deluxe cabins right by the lake, bordered on one side by Eagle Point Reserve. The park has the town's only shop.

Beachside Loft (☎ 5156 6345; beachside_loft@big pond.com; cnr Bay & Boatramp Rd; r $140; ❄) This self-contained loft accommodation has a modern, airy, seaside feel with views over the water. A basket of breakfast goodies is provided.

Eagle Point is a 10km drive from Bairnsdale. Follow the signs from Bairnsdale to Paynesville and then take the Eagle Point turn-off. **Paynesville Bus Lines** (☎ 0418-516 405) runs daily (except Sunday) services from Bairnsdale train station and will drop off at Eagle Point Caravan Park on request (one way $7).

PAYNESVILLE & RAYMOND ISLAND

Paynesville (population 2980) is a relaxed little boating town starting to sprawl in a suburban way – everyone seems to be discovering what a great spot it is from which to explore the Gippsland Lakes. The popular **Paynesville Jazz Festival** (www.paynesvillejazzfestival.com.au) happens on the last weekend in February.

You can take your own laptop along or use the terminals at **Clasiqe Computers** (☎ 5156 6448; 29 The Esplanade; 9am-5pm Mon-Fri, 9am-noon Sat; ▢) for $8 per hour.

Sights & Activities

Bull's Cruisers (☎ 5156 1200; www.bullscruisers.com.au; 54 Slip Rd; motor boat 4 nights 4-/8-berth $1087/2022) has motor cruisers sleeping from two to 10 people. Boats must be hired for a minimum of two nights, though it's only about 20% more to take the four-night option. **Mariners Cove Motel** (☎ 5156 7444; cnr Esplanade & Victoria St; hire per 4/8hr $100/160) have the cheapest day boats for hire. No boat licences are required.

You're almost guaranteed to spot a koala at peaceful **Raymond Island** (population 480), a five minute ferry ride across McMillan Strait. There's a large colony of them that was relocated from Phillip Island in the 1950s. The small island has large areas of bush, with some good **walking tracks**. **Clydesdale Carriage Tours** (☎ 0413 029 084; adult/child $9/6; ☺ tours 10.30am-3pm Sat & Sun, or by appointment) offers a koala-spotting drive by horse and cart.

Sleeping & Eating
Paynesville Hotel (☎ 5156 6442; 75 The Esplanade; s/d/f $55/77/87) The rooms above this local's pub will give you '70s flashbacks, but two have brilliant views overlooking the water.

Mariners Cove (☎ 5156 7444; www.marinerscove resort.com; motel d/f $135/165, apt $160/205; ☒) These bright, sunny waterside motel-style units are well located at the end of the shopping strip.

Gippsland Lakes Escapes (☎ 5156 0432; www.gipps landlakesescapes.com.au; 87 The Esplanade; d per 2 nights from $340) This business offers a booking service for more than 60 holiday homes in Paynesville, Raymond Island and beyond.

Lake Gallery B&B (☎ 5156 0448; www.lakegallery bedandbreakfast.com; 2a Backwater Ct; r $195) This stylish B&B is perched on the water's edge and each room has its own original art work, king-sized bed and en suite spa, as well as dreamy views and private balconies. The B&B also has a small art gallery accessible to guests and open to the public occasionally for exhibitions.

Paynesville Seafoods (☎ 5156 6080; 67a The Esplanade; fish & chips $7.50; ☺ lunch & dinner) The menu here is limited, but the fish is local and fresh. On a fine day, it's hard to beat sitting on the foreshore with your white paper package of fish.

Fisherman's Wharf Pavilion (☎ 5156 0366; 70 The Esplanade; mains $6-18; ☺ breakfast & lunch Tue-Sun) The light bounces off the modern artwork and polished wooden floor, but the real attraction is being perched by the water with uninterrupted views of the passing boats and bird life. The food features fresh, local produce such as the delicious homemade toasted muesli with organic Gippsland yoghurt, and slow-roasted seasonal fruit topped with almonds. It serves the best coffee in town and is food allergy-friendly.

Cafe Espas (☎ 5156 7275; Raymond Island Foreshore; mains $26-32; ☺ lunch Fri-Sun; dinner Fri & Sat) Kick back with a glass of wine in hand on the veranda of this waterside café, and savour the perfectly cooked and beautifully presented modern Australian cuisine.

Wine Justice (☎ 5156 1395; 1/85 The Esplanade; ☺ 10am-7pm) Pack a picnic lunch with some of these quality cleanskin wines and gourmet local produce.

Getting There & Away
A car and passenger ferry runs a shuttle service every 30 minutes between Paynesville and Raymond Island (return per car $7, pedestrians free, five minutes) from 8am to 10.30pm Monday to Friday, and slightly later on weekends.

Paynesville Bus Lines (☎ 0418-516 405) runs daily (except Sunday) services between Bairnsdale train station and Paynesville ($8).

METUNG
☎ 03 / pop 730

Metung is the nicest town on the Gippsland Lakes. The unhurried charm of this picturesque village (www.metungtourism.com.au) on Bancroft Bay is contagious; it's an upmarket base for sailing and fishing and its shoreline is dotted with jetties and small wooden craft.

Metung visitors centre (☎ 5156 2969; www.metung accommodation.com.au; 3/50 Metung Rd; ☺ 9am-5pm) has an accommodation booking service and also hires out boats.

Watch the boats bobbing in the Bancroft Bay marina from the bar at **Metung Yacht Club** (☎ 5156 2315; www.metungyachtclub.yachting.org.au; Metung Rd; ☺ bar from 4.30pm Wed-Sun). It also serves dinners from Wednesday to Saturday.

Sights & Activities
At noon each day **pelicans** fly in from all around like bomber planes, swooping on the fish issued outside the Metung Hotel. For a dip, head to the safe **swimming beach** next to Lake King Jetty.

Boats and yachts for cruising, fishing and sailing on the Gippsland Lakes are available from **Riviera Nautic** (☎ 5156 2243; www.rivieranautic .com.au; 185 Metung Rd; motor boat per day $175, yachts per

3 days 4-/8-berth $1170/1980). Fuel and a boating lesson are included – a fabulous way of exploring the lakes. There are countless islands, jetties and stretches of beach around Metung to moor your boat at night.

You can take a 'happy hour' cruise (2½ hours) aboard the **Director** (☎ 5156 2628; adults/child $42/free; ☺ 3pm Tue, Thu & Sat) on to Lakes Entrance. Drink and local cheeses are included. *The Director* management also hires out single and double **sea kayaks**, so you can paddle around to check out the quieter waters of the lakes (from $25 per hour; $65 for four hours).

Opposite Metung Yacht Club on the edge of Bancroft Bay is **Legend Rock**, a sacred Aboriginal site. According to Aboriginal oral histories, the rock represents a hunter who was turned to stone for not sharing the food he had caught. There were originally three rocks; the other two were destroyed during road-construction work, a sad reminder of some of the oblivious attitudes to Aboriginal culture. The remaining one was saved when an injunction was issued, under community pressure. The road into town shaves past the rock.

Providing a focus for the energetic local art scene is **nuart Metung** (☎ 5156 2909; www.nuart metung.com; 69a Metung Rd; ☺ 10am-5pm Thu-Mon), a new contemporary fine art gallery hosting exhibitions and showcasing the work of local artists.

Sleeping

There's little in the way of budget accommodation here.

Metung Holiday Villas (☎ 5156 2306; www.metung holidayvillas.com; cnr Mairburn & Stirling Rds; d $100-150; ☒ ☒) Metung's former caravan park has reinvented itself as a minivillage of luxury cabins. The landscaped bush gardens around them provide some privacy. Linen is provided.

Moorings At Metung (☎ 5156 2750; www.themoorings com.au; 44 Metung Rd; r $140-270; ☒ ☒) In the heart of Metung village, this large, contemporary apartment complex has motel rooms and self-contained units all with water views. It's a luxuriously comfortable option with stylish rooms and a tennis court, indoor and outdoor pools and spa.

Anchorage B&B (☎ 5156 2569; www.anchoragebedand breakfast.com.au; 11 The Anchorage; d $150; closed mid-Jun to mid-Aug; ☒) You'll receive a warm welcome here. Enjoy a sumptuous gourmet breakfast in the sunny guest breakfast room, and kick back in the bush garden and take in the water views. Fluffy towels, crisp sheets and soothing autumn tones make these rooms a very comfortable place to stay.

McMillans of Metung (☎ 5156 2283; www.mcmillan sofmetung.com.au; 155 Metung Rd; cottages s/d $165, villas r $245; ☒ ☒) This lakeside resort has won stacks of tourism awards for its complex of English country-style cottages, set in three hectares of manicured gardens, and has expanded with some modern villas.

Eating

Nina's (☎ 5156 2474; 3/51 Metung Rd; dishes $4-12; ☺ breakfast & lunch Wed-Sun) Don't miss the organic coffee and Mindy's divine home-cooked brownies.

Metung Galley (☎ 5156 2330; 3/59 Metung Rd; lunch $10-18, dinner $19-29; ☺ breakfast & lunch daily, dinner Wed-Mon) Felicity and Richard's city hospitality experience shines through in this friendly, efficient café serving up beautifully presented quality food. The smoked trout, organic goats cheese and rocket tart is delicious.

Metung Hotel (☎ 5156 2206; Kurnai Ave; meals $18-30; ☺ lunch & dinner) Perched on the edge of the lake, and with an outdoor deck, Metung Hotel has had a makeover since top local restaurateur Archie was installed as manager. The bistro food is superb and the best you'll find in a Gippsland pub.

Getting There & Away

V/Line (☎ 13 61 96; www.vline.com.au) has two services daily from Melbourne that stop in nearby Swan Reach (change from train to bus at Bairnsdale; $26, four hours), from where you can call **Metung Taxis** (☎ 5156 2005) for the 5km trip to Metung (around $20).

AROUND METUNG

This little pocket of Gippsland is home to some national and internationally renowned artists with studios open to the public on the weekends from 11am to 4pm. The Metung visitors centre can mark them on a map for you. At the entrance to Metung, turn into Rosherville Rd and then follow the signs to **Daniel Jenkins' Studio** (☎ 5156 2173, 10 Coolavin Rd) to see his garden studio of quirky metal sculptures. **Max Nicolson's Studio** (☎ 5156 2655; 625 Nungurner Rd) is signposted from Metung Rd. He's renowned for his oil and water colour paintings of the Gippsland Lakes. Signposted from Nungurner Rd is the new **oneofftwo** (☎ 5156 3270; 96 Kleinetz

Rd, Nungurner), a studio and workshop showcasing the stunning contemporary jewellery of goldsmith and ceramicist Dore Stockhausen and silversmith Marcus Foley. November to April only.

Ten kilometres east of Metung, signposted off Nungurner Rd, the well-preserved timber homestead at **Nyerimilang Park** (☎ 5156 3253; www .parkweb.vic.gov.au; Metung-Kalimna West Rd; entry by donation; ☽ homestead 9.30am-4pm, park 9am-sunset) was originally built in 1892 as a gentleman's holiday retreat, and is now a minimuseum with some old photographs of the area. It's a lovely spot for a walk or picnic with easy **walking tracks** and some exceptional views across the lakes of Fraser Island and Boole Poole Peninsula. Check out the East Gippsland Garden, which showcases indigenous vegetation.

LAKES ENTRANCE
☎ 03 / pop 4100

Lakes Entrance is the region's main tourist town and greets you with a graceless strip of motels, caravan parks, minigolf courses and souvenir shops lining the Esplanade. It's popular though for its picturesque location on the gentle waters of Cunninghame Arm, backed by sand dunes and fishing boats and just a stroll from a magnificent stretch of ocean beach. This is the place to indulge almost every water-related whim you may have.

Information

Hai Q Computers (☎ 5155 4247; cnr Myer St & The Esplanade; ☽ 9.30am-5pm Mon-Fri, 10am-2pm Sat; ▣ ; wi-fi) Internet access including wireless internet for $7 per hour. A computer business with a quirky gift shop.
Lakes Entrance visitors centre (☎ 1800 637 060, 5155 1966; www.lakes-entrance.com; cnr Princes Hwy & Marine Pde; ☽ 9am-5pm) Accommodation and boat trips booked at no cost.
Library (☎ 5153 9500; 18 Mechanics St; ☽ 8.30am-5pm Mon-Fri; ▣) Free internet access.

Activities

A footbridge crosses the Cunninghame Arm inlet from the east of town to the ocean and **Ninety Mile Beach**. From December to Easter paddle boats, canoes and sailboats can be hired by the footbridge. It's also where the 2.3km **Eastern Beach Walking Track** starts, which takes you down to the entrance artificially

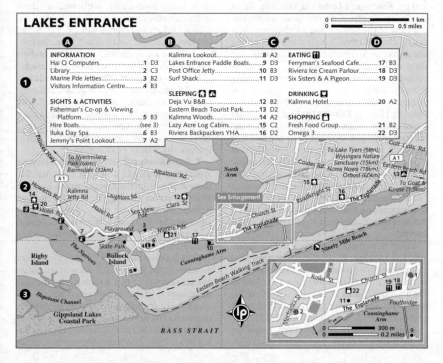

LAKES ENTRANCE

| | | 0 | 1 km |
| | | 0 | 0.5 miles |

INFORMATION
Hai Q Computers........................**1** D3
Library..**2** C3
Marine Pde Jetties....................**3** B2
Visitors Information Centre.......**4** B3

SIGHTS & ACTIVITIES
Fisherman's Co-op & Viewing
   Platform..............................**5** B3
Hire Boats..............................(see 3)
Iluka Day Spa............................**6** B3
Jemmy's Point Lookout............**7** A2

Kalimna Lookout........................**8** A2
Lakes Entrance Paddle Boats....**9** D3
Post Office Jetty.......................**10** B3
Surf Shack.................................**11** D3

SLEEPING ⌂ ⛺
Deja Vu B&B.............................**12** B2
Eastern Beach Tourist Park.......**13** D2
Kalimna Woods.........................**14** A2
Lazy Acre Log Cabins...............**15** C2
Riviera Backpackers YHA..........**16** D2

EATING ⑪
Ferryman's Seafood Cafe.........**17** B3
Riviera Ice Cream Parlour.........**18** D3
Six Sisters & A Pigeon...............**19** D3

DRINKING ▿
Kalimna Hotel............................**20** A2

SHOPPING ⌂
Fresh Food Group......................**21** B2
Omega 3....................................**22** D3

created in 1889 to provide ocean access from the lakes system.

Several companies offer cruises on the lakes:

Corque (☎ 5155 1508; Post Office Jetty, The Esplanade) Popular 4½-hour daily lunch cruise to Wyanga Park Winery (adult $50, child under/over six years $6/25, includes lunch and wine tasting), also weekend dinner cruises and Sunday brunch.

Mulloway Fishing Charters (☎ 0427 943 154, 5155 3304; jetty opposite 66 Marine Pde) Three-hour fishing cruises (adult/child $40/20) on the lake. Rods, tackle, bait and morning or afternoon tea are provided.

Peels Tourist & Ferry Services (☎ 5155 1246; Post Office Jetty, The Esplanade) Daily two-hour lake cruise at 2pm (adult/child $34/17), and four-hour Metung cruise at 11am (adult/child $44/12.50 including lunch, Wednesday to Monday).

To explore the lakes on your own, three companies along Marine Pde offer boats for hire (four/eight hours $90/150).

Surfing lessons are offered by the **Surf Shack** (☎ /fax 5155 4933; 507 The Esplanade; 2hr lesson $45). Qualified instructors lead the surf lessons at Lake Tyers Beach; surf gear is provided.

The **Fisherman's Co-op** (☎ 5155 1688; Bullock Island) viewing platform provides a mesmerising view of the fishing boats unloading their catch. There's often a boat there but phone ahead to check. You'll find the co-op on the right-hand side of Princes Hwy – turn at the roundabout when entering Lakes Entrance from the west.

Also on the western side of town, on the Princes Hwy, is **Kalimna Lookout**, a popular lookout spot. From Kalimna Lookout a **walking track** leads you west through bushland to Kalimna Jetty and along to the North Arm Bridge from where you can walk alongside the highway back to Kalimna Lookout. For a better view of the ocean, lake and entrance (and a quieter location), take the road directly opposite Kalimna Lookout and you'll almost immediately see a sign to **Jemmy's Point Lookout**.

Lakes' newest offering is the blissfully indulgent **Illuka Day Spa** (☎ 5155 3533; www.esplanaderesort .com.au/dayspa; 1 The Esplanade) where therapies range from a 30-minute aromatherapy tub ($60) to the 3¼-hour 'Illuka Dreaming' – a foot treatment, sea wrap (with pearl-and-kelp body mud), and head-to-toe massage ($350).

Guided walks to spot nocturnal wildlife, in the company of an experienced naturalist, are run by **Wildlife at Night** (☎ 5156 5863; Wyungara Nature Sanctuary, Veldens Rd; adult/child/family $22/13/55; ☽ departs sunset Sat) signposted off the Princes Hwy 15km east of Lakes Entrance.

For an air adventure, contact:

Aerial Skydives (☎ 1800 674 276; Great Lakes Airport, Colquhoun Rd; skydives $245) Jump out of a plane with an experienced skydiver and check out the coastline.

Elite Airways (☎ 5155 5777; www.eliteairways.info; Great Lakes Airport, Colquhoun Rd; 20min flight $39) Scenic local flights, or take a 30-minute aerobatic flight (yep, figures-of-eight, barrel rolls and loops) for $220 (including DVD).

Sleeping

Eastern Beach Tourist Park (☎ 5155 1581; www.east ernbeach.com.au; Eastern Beach Rd; unpowered/powered sites $23/27; wi-fi) Close to the beach, this park is refreshingly old-style – it has a bush setting by the Eastern Beach walking track into town (30 minutes one way) and free wireless internet. Prices almost double in peak season.

Riviera Backpackers YHA (☎ 5155 2444; www.yha .com.au; 660-71 The Esplanade; dm $19, s/d/f $30/44/86; 💻 🐾) Part of the Beaches Family Holiday Units complex, the YHA rooms are in old-style brick units, each with two to three bedrooms and a bathroom. There's a big communal kitchen and lounge with pool table and internet access ($2 for 15 mins). Bike and fishing rod hire are available. Non-YHA members pay a few dollars more for accommodation.

Lazy Acre Log Cabins (☎ 5155 1323; www.lazyacre .com; 35 Roadknight St; d/f $105/125; 🐾 🐾) Self-contained small timber cabins are shaded with old gum trees and it's a friendly, relaxed place to stay. There's bicycle hire and a babysitting service. Disabled access is available. Prices increase by 50% in peak season.

Kalimna Woods (☎ 5155 1957; www.kalimnawoods .com.au; Kalimna Jetty Rd; d $115-155, f $145-185; 🐾) Retreat 2km from the town centre to Kalimna Woods, set in a large rainforest-and-bush garden, complete with friendly resident possums and birds. These country-style cottages with either spa or wood fire are spacious and comfortable.

Goat & Goose B&B (☎ 5155 3079; www.goatand goose.com; 16 Gay St; d $140-210) Bass Strait views are maximised at this wonderfully unusual, multistorey, timber pole-framed house. The owners are friendly and all the gorgeously quaint rooms have spas.

Deja Vu B&B (☎ 5155 4330; www.dejavu.com.au; Clara St; d $150-250; 🐾) This imposing, modern, sandstone-coloured home has been cleverly built on the slope of a hill to maximise water views and the bushy garden ensures privacy. Paddle across the North Arm to town in a canoe after a sumptuous breakfast. Two night minimum on weekends.

Eating & Drinking

L'Ocean (☎ 5155 2253; 19 Myer St; ☺ lunch & dinner) With one of Australia's largest commercial fishing fleets, Lakes Entrance is a great place for fresh fish and chips ($8). One of the local favourites is the award-winning L'Ocean, which also caters for the gluten-free crowd and serves delicious fried pumpkin.

Riviera Ice Cream Parlour (☎ 5155 2972; 583 The Esplanade; ice creams $4; ☺ 9.30am-5pm) Organic ice cream – the perfect follow-up to fresh fish and chips.

Six Sisters & a Pigeon (☎ 5155 1144; 567 The Esplanade; meals $6-17; ☺ breakfast & lunch Tue-Sun) On a sunny day, join the locals street-side or by the large open window with your newspaper or magazine. This licensed café adds style to standard café offerings. Try the eggs Atlantic with egg, smoked salmon, baked mushrooms and spinach on Turkish bread. You'll find the best coffee in town here, which goes nicely with the chocolate almond torte.

Ferryman's Seafood Cafe (☎ 5155 3000; Middle Harbour, The Esplanade; mains $10-39; ☺ brunch, lunch & dinner) Perched in the harbour among a flotilla of fishing boats is this café, serving fish with flair. The salmon fillet, encrusted in pistachio nuts, with pomegranate sauce is divine. High chairs, a toy box and friendly staff make it very child-friendly. During business hours you can also buy fresh fish from the shop on the deck below.

Kalimna Hotel (☎ 5155 1202; 1 Hotel Rd, Kalimna; ☺ 11am-1am Mon-Sat, 11am-11pm Sun) For a drink with views, you can't beat this hotel, signposted off the highway on the Melbourne side of Lakes Entrance.

Shopping

Omega 3 (☎ 5155 4344; Shop 5, Safeway Arcade, Church St; ☺ 9am-5pm) This is the shop front for the local Fishermen's Co-op and is the best place to buy fish in East Gippsland.

Fresh Food Group (☎ 5155 4122; 204 Marine Pde; ☺ 9am-5pm Mon-Fri) This fruit-and-vegetable wholesaler and food store sells delicious deli items including jams, chutneys, cheeses, filled pasta and breads.

Getting There & Away

There are two daily **V/Line** (☎ 13 61 96; www .vline.com.au) services between Melbourne and Lakes Entrance (change from train to bus at Bairnsdale; $28, 4¼ hours).

Getting Around

A handy new town bus service loops daily around the town between 11am and 4pm (20 mins, $1.80) leaving from the post office on the hour. The service stops at the backpackers hostel and near the Eastern Beach Tourist Park.

LAKE TYERS BEACH

☎ 03 / pop 550

This small and peaceful settlement is popular with surfers for the good **surf breaks** at Red Bluff, and with families for the options of calm lake waters and ocean beaches. Two-hour **boat cruises** (☎ 5156 5492; adult/child/family $25/15/70; ☺ departs 2pm Mon, Wed, Thu & Sat, 6.30pm Fri) aboard the electric-powered *MV Rumbeena* with the friendly and knowledgeable Bernie include a cuppa and cake in a quiet backwater. Evening cruises with local produce are also available on this century-old boat.

Surfing lessons are offered at Red Bluff by the Surf Shack (opposite).

The camp sites at **Lakes Beachfront Holiday Retreat** (☎ 5156 5582; www.holidayretreats.com.au; 430 Lake Tyers Beach Rd; unpowered/powered sites $30/34, cabins d $95-135, f $119-149, beach cottage d/f $170/184, villas $350; ☒ ☒) are the best in the region outside of national parks. Vegetation offers shade and privacy and it's just a short stroll to the ocean beach. The park is almost totally surrounded by native bush, protecting local flora and fauna. Cabins are spotlessly clean and the luxury cabins are like mini motel rooms, complete with irons and hairdryers. Villas with all mod-cons are the newest addition.

The downstairs bedrooms at **Lake Tyers Beach House** (☎ 5156 5995; www.lakes-entrance .com/beachhouse/house.htm; 3 Larkins Pl; up to 4 people $200) are bright, and the queen-size beds have quality linen, but the real delight here is upstairs: the artistically inspired, hot-pink, retro-chic living area. Wander down the bush garden path to a quiet stretch of ocean beach, or next door to the yoga studio to practise, take a class or some private tuition. Two-night minimum stay.

Waterwheel Tavern (☎ 5156 5530; 557 Lake Tyers Beach Rd; mains $19-35; ☺ lunch & dinner) The

Waterwheel has an inspired bistro menu and brilliant views over the lake.

V/Line (☎ 13 61 96; www.vline.com.au) buses go to Lake Tyers Beach ($29, 4¼ hours) via Lakes Entrance.

NOWA NOWA
☎ 03 / pop 150

Tiny Nowa Nowa, on the north arm of Lake Tyers, is the base for a vibrant arts community that stages regular creative art events (see www.nowanowa.com). Stop by to see what they've been up to. There's also some fabulous, easy short walks – by the wetlands (25 minutes), the sculpture walk (20 minutes), and a walk to Boggy Creek Gorge (20 minutes).

On the site of the original Nowa Nowa settlement, **Mingling Waters** (☎ 5155 7247; 42 Princes Hwy; unpowered/powered sites $22/25, dm $20, cottages d $55-70) offers comfortable accommodation by the lake in rustic, century-old buildings. Mingling Waters café/gallery, with its eclectic timber furnishings, features vegetarian food on the menu (mains $5 to $12; open for breakfast and lunch daily), and Mike makes renowned *ciabattas*. Tourist information is also available.

A few kilometres east of Nowa Nowa, **Yelen's Studio Gallery** (☎ 5155 7277; www.yelen.com; 201 Nelsons Rd; cabin $125), 3km down a dirt road and overlooking Lake Tyers, is home to painter Gary Yelen. Stop by to see his vibrant oil paintings and sensuous sculpture. It's open most days; call to check. You can also stay at Gary's arty-retro cabin by the lake.

EAST GIPPSLAND

This area contains some of the most remote and spectacular national parks in the state – it's a wonderland of dense forests ranging from the coastal wilderness areas of Croajingolong and the rocky gorges of Snowy River, to the lush rainforests of the Errinundra Plateau. Logging in these ancient forests is a hot issue.

The Princes Hwy carves its way through the centre of the region. Unexciting Orbost is the major town and the gateway to the Snowy River and Errinundra National Parks, as well as the magnificent coastal areas of Cape Conran, Mallacoota and Croajingolong, which are all uncrowded, unspoiled and undeveloped.

There are excellent Parks Victoria visitors centres at Cann River and Mallacoota.

BRUTHEN
☎ 03 / pop 630

This energetic little town hosts the annual **Bruthen Blues Festival** (www.bruthenblues.org), billed as the biggest little blues festival in Australia. The festival on the third weekend in February has developed a strong following over the years and features local, national and international blues musicians, as well as music workshops, a community market and an hilarious fundraising duck race.

Le Cafe (☎ 5157 5665; 72 Main St; Devonshire teas $8; ☾ lunch Thu-Sun) is a little place with the best Devonshire teas in East Gippsland, served with lashings of cream and homemade jams. Across the road, the **Bruthen Bakery** (☎ 5157 5554; 69 Main St; pies $4; ☾ 6am-5pm Mon-Fri, 6am-4pm Sat-Sun) is famed for its pies.

BUCHAN
☎ 03 / pop 330

The quiet town of Buchan in the foothills of the Snowy Mountains is famous for its spectacular limestone cave system that has been open to visitors since 1913, and is of significance to the Gunai/Kurnai people. Further up in the mountains is the remote community of W Tree, home to one of Australia's most established Buddhist centres.

Buchan Valley Roadhouse sells petrol, the general store has local tourist information, and internet access is available at the community resource centre.

Sights & Activities

Just over a kilometre from the tiny township is the **Buchan Caves Reserve**. Underground rivers cutting through limestone rock that formed about 300 to 400 million years ago, carved the caves and caverns. The local Aboriginal people lived in them over 18,000 years ago, and have legends associated with them. The reserve itself is also a pretty spot with shaded picnic areas, **walking tracks** and grazing kangaroos. Invigoration is guaranteed dunking your feet or taking a dip in the icy **rook pool** (admission free; ☾ 9am-5pm).

Parks Victoria (☎ 5162 1900; www.parkweb.vic .gov.au), at Caves Reserve, runs guided caves tours (adult/child/family $13/7/33; three to five tours daily), alternating between Royal and Fairy Caves. They're both impressive – Royal has more colour, a higher chamber and extinct kangaroo remains; Fairy has more delicate decorations and fairy sightings have

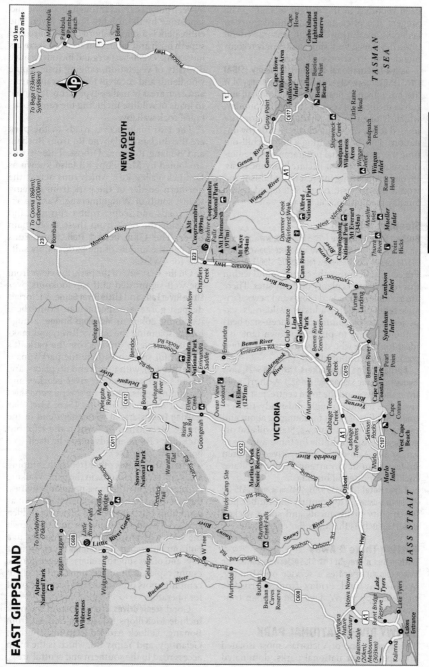

EAST GIPPSLAND

been reported to the delight of many. The rangers also offer hard-hat guided tours to Federal Cave during the high season. Federal is less developed for visitors and is only recommended for those over 12 years.

Sakya International Buddhist Academy (SIBA) (☎ 5155 0329; www.sakya.com.au/siba; 2592 Gelantipy Rd, W Tree) has a divinely beautiful mediation hall and runs a meditation session at 11am on Sunday, which is open to the public. Meditators are invited to say on for lunch afterwards (by donation). For those wanting a longer chill-out time there's an annual programme of meditation retreats in this 40-hectare bushland oasis. If you have a strong interest in Buddhism and would like to visit, or are interested in the Sunday meditation, call ahead.

Sleeping & Eating

Buchan Caves Reserve (☎ 5162 1900; www.parkweb .vic.gov.au; Buchan Caves Reserve; unpowered/powered sites $13/18, cabins $58, wilderness retreats s/d $100/120; 🐾) Edged by state forest, the camp ground within this reserve offers plenty of shady sites. There are a couple of standard cabins and new safari-style tents providing a luxury wilderness experience (think comfortable queen-size bed) without having to pitch your own tent. It's ideal for those who'd love to camp if only it wasn't so uncomfortable.

Buchan Lodge Backpackers (☎ 5155 9421; www .buchanlodge.com; Saleyard Rd; dm $25) A short walk from the caves and the town centre, just by the river, this friendly, rough-and-ready, timber-lined building is great for lounging about and taking in the country views. Staff will also organise a transport shuffle for those wanting to raft or canoe down the Snowy River. Children under 14 can stay by arrangement only. Rates include continental breakfast.

Caves Hotel (☎ 5155 9203; 49 Main St; mains $15-24; ☯ lunch & dinner) This century old timber pub has quality bistro meals and some wicked deserts, such as the *Mars Bar* cheesecake.

Getting There & Away

Buchan Bus 'n' Freight (☎ 5155 0356; www.buchanbusn freight.com.au) operates a service on Monday, Wednesday and Friday from Bairnsdale to Gelantipy via W Tree and Buchan (one way $14).

SNOWY RIVER NATIONAL PARK

This area is one of Victoria's most isolated and spectacular national parks, dominated by deep gorges carved through limestone and sandstone by the mighty Snowy River. The entire park is a smorgasbord of unspoiled and superb bush and mountain scenery. It covers more than 95,000 hectares and includes a huge diversity of vegetation, ranging from alpine woodlands and eucalypt forests to rainforests and even areas of mallee-type scrub. It's home to loads of wildlife including the rare brush-tailed rock wallaby.

The two main access roads to the park are the Buchan-Jindabyne Rd from Buchan, and Bonang Rd from Orbost. These roads are joined by McKillops Rd (also known as Deddick Valley Rd), which runs across the northern border of the park from Bonang to just south of Wulgulmerang. Various access roads and scenic routes run into and alongside the park from these three main roads. The 43km **Deddick Trail**, which runs through the middle of the park, is only suitable for 4WDs.

On the west side of the park, the views from the well-signposted cliff top lookouts over **Little River Falls** and **Little River Gorge**, Victoria's deepest gorge, are spectacular. From there it's about 20km to **McKillops Bridge**, a huge bridge spanning the Snowy River, and making it possible to drive across the park. It's a beautiful spot and where the park's main **camp sites** (free), with toilets and fireplaces, are. There's also some sandy river beaches and swimming spots. There are several good **short walks** around here, and the 15km **Silver Mine Walking Track** starts at the eastern end of the bridge. Be warned: it's worth the trip, but McKillops Rd is an adventure in itself (see boxed text, opposite).

There are various other free bush camping areas and picnic grounds in the park. Walking and canoeing are the most popular activities, but you need to be well prepared for both as conditions can be harsh and subject to sudden change. The classic canoe or raft trip down the Snowy River from McKillops Bridge to a pull-out point near Buchan takes at least four days and offers superb scenery: rugged gorges, raging rapids, tranquil sections and excellent camping spots on broad sand bars. See p134 for operators.

Good **scenic drives** in and around the park include McKillops Rd, Rising Sun Rd from Bonang, Tullock Ard Rd from just south of Gelantipy, and Yalmy Rd, which is the main access road to the southern and central areas,

SOUTHEAST COAST VICTORIA

WING HAGGER

You can do a driving loop through both Snowy River and Errinundra National Parks on McKillops Rd. What's the road like? Oh, it's a goat track! It'll freak you out. It's fine for 2WD though, and it's the one road that's usually passable all year, unless parts of it collapse.

Err, does that happen often? No, heavy rain washed part of it away last year. The road was built in the 1930s, and it's slow work fixing it, so it was closed for a few months.

It's easier now with new technology, right? No, same technology. When they built it in the 1930s, they'd pick and shovel a bit of hill away until it was wide enough for the truck to turn the corner, so they could use the truck to jemmy in the support underneath the road. It's still pretty much the same.

If it's that narrow, what if there's another vehicle coming the other way – do you have to back up? Nah, you can see cars coming a long way ahead, and there are places you can pull over. There's a few more places since the road was rebuilt. Actually, we should have notices up saying, 'Pull over when you see another vehicle.' My wife freaked out the first time I took her along there. It was just after New Year and there were quite a few oncoming vehicles. They all pulled over on the sheer cliff side, and we passed them all on the steep drop side. 'Freaking out mate?' I said to one. He just nodded.

Are there many accidents? Well, none that I've heard about. Nah, it's safe.

Parks Victoria Ranger Wing Hagger works from Parks Victoria's remote office at Bendoc (population 190), just north of Errinundra National Park and close to Snowy River National Park.

---

and places such as Waratah Flat, Hicks Camp Site and Raymond Creek Falls. These roads are unsealed and usually closed during winter.

For information about camping, road conditions and other details contact **Parks Victoria** (☎ 13 16 93; www.parkweb.vic.gov.au).

Sleeping

Karoonda Park (☎ 5155 0220; www.karoondapark.com; Gelantipy Rd; dm/d $28/56, cabins $110; ✎ ▯ ▮) At Gelantipy, 40km north of Buchan, is this cattle and sheep property, home to Snowy River Expeditions, which also has backpacker and cabin accommodation. The backpacker accommodation is in a newish timber lodge. The cabins are comfortable, sleeping six to ten people: some are old and faded; others have been recently renovated. You'll receive a relaxed friendly country welcome here. Rates include breakfast. A three-course home-cooked meal in the large camp kitchen costs $15 to $20; fully catered packages are also available. Activities available include abseiling (per hour $25), horse riding (per hour $35), wild caving (per hour $35), and white-water rafting (see p134).

Getting There & Away

Buchan Bus 'n' Freight (☎ 5155 0356; www.buchanbus nfreight.com.au) operates a bus service to Bairnsdale from Karoonda Park on Monday, Wednesday and Friday (one way/return $16/25).

ERRINUNDRA NATIONAL PARK

The Errinundra Plateau is a misty and verdant wonderland that contains Victoria's largest remaining areas of cool-temperate rainforest. It's one of East Gippsland's most outstanding natural areas and a battleground between environmentalists and loggers. It's also one of the least visited parts of East Gippsland.

The national park coves an area of 25,600 hectares and has three granite outcrops that extend into the clouds, resulting in high rainfall, deep, fertile soils and a network of creeks and rivers that flow north, south and east. The park has several climatic zones – some areas of the park are quite dry, while its peaks regularly receive snow. This is a rich habitat for native birds and animals, which include many rare and endangered species such as the potoroo.

Errinundra is one of the best examples in the world of 'mixed forest' vegetation – it's dominated by southern sassafras and black oliveberry, with tall eucalypt forests providing a canopy for the lower rainforests. Some of the giant trees are many hundreds of years old.

The main access roads to the park are Bonang Rd from Orbost and Errinundra Rd from Club Terrace. Bonang Rd passes on the western side of the park, while Errinundra Rd passes through the centre. Road conditions are variable and the roads are often closed or impassable during the winter months or after floods – check with Parks Victoria offices in

Orbost or Bendoc first. Watch out for logging trucks. Roads within the park are all unsealed but are 2WD accessible. Expect seasonal closures between June and November, though roads can deteriorate quickly at any time of the year after rain.

You can explore the park by a combination of scenic drives, and short and medium-length walks. **Mt Ellery** has spectacular views; **Errinundra Saddle** has a rainforest boardwalk; and from **Ocean View Lookout** there are stunning views down the Goolengook River where you can see as far as Bemm River. The park also has **mountain plum pines**, some of which are more than 400 years old, which are easily accessible from Goonmirk Rocks Rd. For more information contact **Parks Victoria** (☎ 13 16 93, Bendoc ☎ 02-6458 1456, Orbost ☎ 5161 1222; www.parkweb.vic.gov.au).

Nestled on the edge of the forest is tiny **Goongerah** (population 50) where there's a thriving community with two active community environmental organisations. **Goongerah Environment Centre** (GECO; ☎ 5154 0156; www.geco.org.au) organises ongoing protests and blockades in the forest. GECO has detailed information about forest drives and walks on its website. The other community group **Environment East Gippsland** (EEG; ☎ 5154 0145; www.eastgippsland.net.au) lobbies extensively on forest issues and provides people with the chance to explore the forests under the guidance of environmental experts at the **Forests Forever Ecology Camp** (☎ 5154 0145; www.eastgippsland.net.au; per day adult/teenager/child $20/10/free), held each Easter at Ellery Creek camp site in Goongerah. BYO camping gear and food. Ecologists guide you through the forest and hope that you'll be awed by their beauty and complexity, outraged by their destruction, and will spread the word.

Sleeping

Frosty Hollow Camp Site (free) This is the only camping area within the national park (it's on the eastern side). There are also free camping areas on the park's edges – at Ellery Creek in Goongerah, and at Delegate River.

Jacarri (☎ 5154 0145; www.eastgippsland.net.au/jacarri; cnr Bonang Hwy & Ellery Creek Track, Goongerah; s & d $80, f $90) This gorgeous little cottage, made from recycled and plantation timber, is on Jill Redwood's organic farm. It's solar-powered, has a slow combustion stove for heating and cooking, and sleeps four.

ORBOST
☎ 03 / pop 2452

Orbost, by the Snowy River, is just off the highway. It doesn't have a lot to excite the traveller but it's a handy place to stock up if you're heading into the surrounding national Parks.

Orbost visitors centre (☎ 5154 2424; orbostvic@bigpond.com; cnr Nicholson & Clarke Sts; ☉ 9am-5pm) is in an historic 1872 slab hut. **Parks Victoria** (☎ 5161 1222; www.parkweb.vic.gov.au; cnr Nicholson & Salisbury Sts; ☉ 8.30am-5pm) has information on road conditions in the forests.

Orbost Exhibition Centre (☎ 5154 2634; www.orbostexhibitioncentre.org; Clarke St; adult/child $4/free; ☉ 10am-

---

OFF THE BEATEN TRACK

You can't explore most of the Snowy River or Errinundra National Parks with a 2WD, while sections of Croajingolong are only open to a limited numbers of walkers. There are a few companies providing organised trips into this beautiful wilderness area:

An eco-tourism award winner, **Gippsland High Country Tours** (☎ 5157 5556; www.gippslandhighcountrytours.com.au; 5-/7-day tour $1250/1970) is an East Gippsland-based company running easy, moderate and challenging, five- to seven-day hikes in Errinundra, Snowy River and Croajingolong National Parks. The Croajingolong trips include three nights accommodation in the Point Hicks Lighthouse (p140). There's also a five-day bird-watching tour in Snowy River country ($1190).

Rainforest Adventure Services (☎ 5154 0174; www.rainforestadventures.com.au; 2-day walk incl meals $120) runs weekend forest walks in Errinundra National Park with overnight camping.

Take an adventure tour with **Snowy River Expeditions** (☎ 5155 9353; www.karoondapark.com/sre; Karoonda Park, Gelantipy; 1- to 4-day tours per day $135) on a rafting trip of the Snowy or a half-or full-day abseiling or caving trip. Costs include transport, meals and camping gear.

Wilderness Bike Ride (☎ 5154 6637; www.wildernessbikeride.com.au; 3-day ride $310 incl meals & camp fees) runs three- or four-day mountain bike rides in April through the wilds of Errinundra National Park.

4pm Mon-Sat, 10am-1pm Sun) showcases stunning works by local timber artists.

A Lovely Little Lunch (☎ 5154 1303; 125a Nicholson St; mains $7-11; ☺ lunch Mon-Sat) is Orbost's nicest café and has good coffee, a friendly vibe and a baguettes, focaccias and homemade pies for lunch.

MARLO
☎ 03 / pop 340

Sleepy little Marlo sits at the mouth of the Snowy River where the river lazily flows into a large lagoon before entering the sea. You can follow the river as it meanders to the sea along the **French's Narrows Walking Track**, a 20 minute walk just out of town on the Marine Pde-Cape Conran Rd. There's abundant bird life here and the fishing is renowned. There are a couple of caravan parks, pub accommodation and a motel in Marlo. The general store has an ATM and some tourist information.

The **Marlo Hotel & Country Retreat** (☎ 5154 8201; Argyle Pde; mains $16; ☺ lunch & dinner) is Marlo's only sit-down eating option. The food is typically old-style bistro, but the views from the deck overlooking the vast expanse of water are sensational.

CAPE CONRAN COASTAL PARK

This is a blissfully undeveloped part of the coast with some simply beautiful, remote white-sand beaches. The 19km coastal route from Marlo to Cape Conran is particularly pretty, bordered by banksia trees, grass plains, sand dunes and the ocean.

There's good **surfing** at West Cape Beach and you can take lessons here through the Surf Shack (p128).

The Yeerung River is a relaxed spot for swimming, canoeing and fishing. **Cross Diving Services** (☎ 5153 2010; 0407-362 960; per dive $50) offer dives for qualified divers on most weekends at Cape Conran. Equipment hire is available. It's a fabulous spot for **walking** – Parks Victoria can provide a brochure. One favourite is the nature trail that meets up with the East Cape Boardwalk, where signage gives you a glimpse into how indigenous people lived in the Cape area. Take the West Cape Rd off Cape Conran Rd to get to **Salmon Rocks** where there's an Aboriginal **shell midden**, dated at more than 10,000 years old. **Cabbage Tree Palms** can be accessed from a number of points and is a short detour off the road between Cape Conran and the Princess Hwy. This is Victoria's only stand

of native palms – a tiny rainforest oasis. Keep an eye out for bandicoots and potoroos, which have increased in numbers since the park's fox control programme was introduced.

Sleeping

Parks Victoria (☎ 5154 8438; www.conran.net.au) manages the following camping, cabin, and wilderness retreat accommodation at Cape Conran Coastal Park.

Banksia Bluff Camping Area (unpowered sites $16.50) This camp site is right by the foreshore. The generous sites are surrounded by banksia woodlands offering shade and privacy. The camp ground has toilets, cold showers and a few fireplaces, but you'll need to bring drinking water (or purchase from the park office).

our pick **Cape Conran Cabins** (cabin $109) These self-contained cabins, which can sleep up to eight people, are surrounded by bush and are just 200m from the beach. Built from local timbers, the cabins are like oversized cubby houses with lofty mezzanines for sleeping (BYO linen). The cabins have rain water on tap.

Cape Conran Wilderness Retreats (d/f $120/150) Perched in the bush by the sand dunes are these classy safari tents. All the simplicity of camping, but you have comfortable beds, and a deck outside your tent door. Two night minimum stay.

West Cape Cabins (☎ 5154 8296; www.westcapecabins.com.au; 1547 Cape Conran Rd; s & d $175, f $205) Crafted from locally grown or recycled timbers, these self-contained cabins a few kilometres from the national park are a work of art. The timbers are all labelled with their species, and even the queen-size bed bases are tree trucks. An eight-seater outdoor spa adds to the joy. It's a 15-minute walk through coastal bush to the superb beach.

BEMM RIVER
☎ 03/pop 160

If you're into fishing, don't miss Bemm River. This small and friendly holiday hamlet is paradise for fisher folk with a river and inlet seemingly bursting with fish. There's fishing platforms available or you can hire a boat from **Bemm River Holiday Lodge** (☎ 5158 4233; 37-41 Sydenham Pde). The serene Sydenham Inlet is rich with bird life, and sunsets at the nearby coastal beaches are usually impressive.

You'll find basic food supplies and bait here, but no petrol. Accommodation is mostly ageing caravan parks and holiday flats.

The local pub is the **Bemm River Hotel** (☎ 5158 4241; www.bemmriverhotel.com.au; 3-5 Sydenham Pde; d/f $85/120; 🗷), offering the most comfortable accommodation in town. Its newish, beach-hut-style timber cabins are about as stylish as cabins get. Hang out on the pub's wide timber deck overlooking Sydenham Inlet with Baney the pub dog, and munch on homemade pizzas, or tuck into a substantial steak. Fish, of course, also features on the menu (mains $17 to $25; open for lunch and dinner daily).

BEMM RIVER SCENIC RESERVE & LIND NATIONAL PARK

The **Bemm River Scenic Reserve** is just metres from the highway and there's a 45-minute walk through rainforest, crossing two swing bridges. Keep an eye out for lyrebirds.

A few kilometres further along the highway it's worth taking a slight detour to **Lind National Park** for the 6km **nature drive** that follows the Euchre Creek through rainforest back to the Princes Hwy. Some enlightened folk declared this 1370 hectares area of rainforest and bushland as a scenic stopover spot for travellers way back in 1926. You'll see lush valleys, meandering creeks and tall stands of eucalypts. To get there, take the turn-off on the highway to Club Terrace, drive 4km to the township, and turn east at the (faded and small) Euchre Valley Nature Drive signpost.

CANN RIVER

☎ 03 / pop 230

Cann River is a small saw-milling centre with a massive crossroad at the junction of the Princes and Monaro Hwys. The **Parks Victoria** (☎ 5158 6351; www.parkweb.vic.gov.au; Princes Hwy; 🗸 10am-4pm Mon, Tue-Fri when ranger available) office is the main information centre for Croajingolong National Park. Road access information and camping fees are listed on a noticeboard outside the office, along with park notes. When the office is open, overnight hiking and camping permits are available, along with maps and walking guides.

From Cann River, the Monaro Hwy heads north to the Coopracambra National Park (4WD access only) and Canberra, and the unsealed Tamboon Rd heads south to Tamboon Inlet, Thurra River and Mueller Inlet in Croajingolong National Park.

There's nothing to keep you in Cann River beyond a quick bite to eat at one of the cafés or pub, or a stock up at the supermarket, with the delightful exception of **Norinbee Selection Cellar Door** (☎ 5158 6500; 53 Monaro Hwy; mains $23-$26; 🗸 lunch Wed-Sun, dinner Thu-Sat) with wine tastings from its own vineyard and a restaurant menu laced with alcohol. Try the pork fillet in a plum and port wine sauce, or poached pears in your choice of red or white wine. Their truly gourmet pizzas are topped with offerings such as salmon, brie, capers and asparagus. There's also a selection of quilts and other crafts for sale.

About 11km east of Cann River on the northern side of the Princes Hwy is the **Drummer Creek Rainforest Walk**, an easy 45-minute walk that starts at the picnic area and takes you through warm-temperate rainforest. There are some massive grey gums here – kids will love the one with the huge hollow. If you're lucky (and quiet) you might see a Gippsland water dragon sunning itself by the Thurra River. Notes about the rainforest are available at the start of the walk.

COOPRACAMBRA NATIONAL PARK

Remote and undeveloped Coopracambra (38,800 hectares) retains its original ecosystem virtually intact. The landscape is rugged and spectacular, with dramatic deep gorges where the earliest fossil evidence of four-footed creatures was discovered. The only area of the park accessible by 2WD is **Beehive Falls**, an idyllic and scenic spot, with small cascades falling into rock pools shaded by the surrounding bush. Beehive Falls are 2km from the Monaro Hwy, 28km north of Cann River. Beyond the Beehive Falls, the only access through the park is a 4WD track.

The park vegetation is mainly open eucalypt forest, with a few areas of sheltered rainforest, and there are walking tracks to peaks such as Mt Kaye and Mt Denmarsh, though they are only suitable for fit and experienced bushwalkers. **Parks Victoria** (☎ 13 19 63; www.park web.vic.gov.au) can provide further information about extended remote 'off track' walks. It's a fantastic place for bushwalkers who want to escape the crowds, with rewards of sandy beaches and swimming holes. Bush camping is permitted but there are no formal camping or toilet facilities in the park.

GIPSY POINT

Named after the schooner *Gypsy* that tied up here in the 19th century, Gipsy Point is an idyllic settlement at the head of Mallacoota

Inlet. Although it's only 10km off the Princes Hwy, it has a deliciously remote atmosphere – once you're sitting on the jetty looking out over the inlets, you'll feel like you're a million miles from anywhere. A resident mob of eastern grey kangaroos lives in the area and you'll often see them, especially at dusk, as they graze by the water.

Gipsy Point Lodge (☎ 1800 063 556, 5158 8205; www .gipsypoint.com; self-contained cottages d/f $120/140, guesthouse per person r $155 incl dinner & breakfast; ⛄) is a guesthouse in a peaceful setting, surrounded by bush and water. The pastel-green rooms seem to blend with the environment and have glorious water views. Facilities include a tennis court, use of canoe and rowboats, and motor boat hire ($95 per day). Nonguests are welcome for the well-recommended dinner (a three-course set meal for $60 per person), but be sure to book ahead.

The modern, spacious, split-level apartments at **Gipsy Point Lakeside** (☎ 1800 688 200; www.gipsy.com.au; d $240-260; ⛄ ⛄) have king-sized beds and are in a prime location, all designed to maximise the serene water views and your privacy at this luxury boutique resort. There's a guest restaurant, or gourmet hampers and barbecue packs are available. No kids under eight allowed.

MALLACOOTA
☎ 03 / pop 980
Completely surrounded by the internationally acclaimed Croajingolong National Park, Mallacoota is one of the most beautiful spots in the state. Its long, empty, ocean beaches, tidal river mouths and vast inlet are a paradise for swimmers, surfers, anglers and boaties. At Christmas and Easter it's a crowded family holiday spot, but most of the year it's pretty quiet.

Mallacoota has been a haven for travellers since the early 20th century when a camp set up by the poet EJ Brady on the shores of the inlet attracted notable Australian literary figures, such as Henry Lawson and Katherine Susannah Pritchard. It's still an inspirational place.

Information
Lucy's (☎ 5158 0666; 64 Maurice Ave; ☯ 8am-9pm; ▣) Have coffee and cake, or Lucy's homemade rice noodles, while you access the internet ($2 per 15 minutes).
Mallacoota Information Shed (☎ 5158 0800; Main Wharf, cnr Allan & Buckland Dr; ☯ 10am-4pm) Operated by friendly volunteers.

Mallacoota Newsagency (☎ 5158 088; 14 Allan Dr; ☯ 8am-5pm Mon-Sat, 8am-noon Sun; ▣) Internet access for $2.50 per 15 minutes, or you can plug in your own computer.
Parks Victoria (☎ 13 19 63, 5161 9500; www.parkweb .vic.gov.au; cnr Buckland & Allan Drs) Has an information centre opposite the main wharf, with excellent outdoor displays and information on Croajingolong and Mallacoota.

Sights & Activities
CRUISES & BOAT HIRE
One of the best ways to experience the beauty of Mallacoota is by boat. The calm estuarine waters of Mallacoota Inlet are completely surrounded by national park and have more than 300km of shoreline. Cruises are offered and there are many public jetties where you can tie your boat up and come ashore for picnic tables and toilets. Fewer cruises operate in the winter months, so call ahead to check.

MV Loch-Ard (☎ 5158 0764; www.cruisemallacoota .com; Main Wharf; 2hr cruise adult/child $25/10) has been cruising the lakes for almost a century. This old wooden boat also does two- and three-hour trips including one to the far side of the lake where the original Mallacoota settlement once was.

Wilderness Coast Ocean Charters (☎ 0418-553 809; Gabo Island $60, Skerries $120) runs trips to Gabo Island from Bastion Point, leaving early in the morning, with pick-up in the afternoon. The Skerries seal colony trip views these delightful creatures off Wingan Inlet. Whales are sometimes spotted on trips from September to November.

Mallacoota Hire Boats (☎ 0438 447 558; Main Wharf, cnr Allan & Buckland Drs; motor boats per half-/full-day $85/145, canoes per hr $17) is centrally located and hires out canoes and boats; no licence is required. Cash only.

GABO ISLAND LIGHTSTATION RESERVE
The windswept 154-hectare island, 14km from Mallacoota, is home to sea birds and one of the world's largest colonies of Little Penguins. Whales, dolphins and fur seals are regularly sighted off shore. The island has an operating **lighthouse**, built in 1862, which is the tallest in the southern hemisphere; tours are available for $9.50/5 per adult/child. Accommodation is also available (p138). Access to the island is possible by boat (see above) or by air with **Mallacoota Air Services** (☎ 0408-580 806; www.malla cootaairservices.com; return for 3 adults or 2 adults & 2 children $200)

SOUTHEAST COAST VICTORIA

WALKING

There are plenty of great short walks around the town, the inlet, and in the bush, ranging from a half-hour stroll to a four-hour walk. The easy 5km one way **Bucklands Jetty to Captain Creek Jetty Walk** starts about 4km north of the town and follows the shoreline of the inlet past the Narrows. The walk can be extended from Captains Creek via eucalypt forests to either Double Creek (3km) or the Mallacoota-Genoa Rd (3km). The 7km **Mallacoota Town Walk**, which loops around Bastion Point, and combines five different walks, is also popular. Walking notes with maps are available from Parks Victoria and the Information Shed.

BEACHES

For good surf, head to Bastion Point or Tip Beach. There's swimmable surf and some sheltered waters at Betka Beach and it's patrolled during Christmas school holidays. There are also good swimming spots along the beaches of the foreshore reserve, at Bastion Point and Quarry Beach.

VOLUNTEERING

The friendly and relaxed **Bushland Weeding Group** (☎ 5158 0540; Mallacoota Information Shed) meets weekly at the Mallacoota amphitheatre, usually on Fridays from 9am to 11.30am, and warmly welcomes helpers. If you arrive after 9am, directions will be on the amphitheatre blackboard. BYO gloves and weeding tools, or the group can supply these.

OTHER ATTRACTIONS

Mallacoota Air Services (☎ 0408+580 806; www.mallacootaairservices.com scenic flights 3 adults from $80) offers scenic flights over the inlet, to Gabo Island, and as far afield as Eden in NSW.

The **Mallacoota Arts Council** (☎ 5158 0890; www.mallacootaarts.org) organises an annual programme including music events, art exhibitions and a spring festival.

Sleeping

There are plenty of options here, though during Easter and Christmas school holidays you'll need to book well ahead and expect prices to be significantly higher.

Mallacoota Foreshore Caravan Park (☎ 5158 0300; camppark@vicnet.net.au; cnr Allan Dr & Maurice Ave; unpowered/powered sites $17/21, caravan d $65; 🖳) Hundreds of grassy sites extend along the foreshore and

have sublime views of the lake with its resident population of black swans and pelicans. There's free internet access for campers.

Mallacoota Hotel Motel & Backpackers (☎ 5158 0455; inncoota@bigpond.net.au; 51-55 Maurice Ave; dm $22, motel s/d from $65/80; 😵 🖳) The backpackers rooms are a bit shabby but there's a good shared kitchen, use of the motel pool and it's conveniently next door to the pub. Motel and family units overlook the lawn and pool.

Adobe Mudbrick Flats (☎ 5158 0329; www.adobeholidayflats.com.au; 17 Karbeethong Ave; flats $80) These 1970s-built, eco-friendly, comfortable mudbrick flats are about 5km from the town centre and are particularly fun for families, with birds to feed outside your door, a farmyard of ducks, and kangaroos and a lyrebird to look out for. Check out the gorgeous inlet views from the comfort of your hammock. You're encouraged to recycle, compost and conserve water. Linen costs extra.

our pick **Karbeethong Lodge** (☎ 5158 0411; www.karbeethonglodge.com.au; 16 Schnapper Point Dr; d/f $120/150) It's hard not to be overcome by a sense of serenity as you rest on the broad verandas of this early 1900s timber guesthouse with uninterrupted views over Mallacoota Inlet. The large guest lounge and dining room have an open fire and period furnishings, and there's a mammoth kitchen if you want to prepare meals. The pastel-toned bedrooms are small but neat and tastefully decorated. The Lodge is signposted from the Genoa-Mallacoota Rd.

Gabo Island Lighthouse (☎ 5161 9500, 13 19 63; up to 8 people $169) Accommodation is available in the three bedroom Assistant Lighthouse Keeper's residence. Enjoy the extreme isolation (well, along with the 300-plus animal species) and look out for migrating whales in autumn and late spring. Pods of dolphins and seals basking on the rocks are also regular sightings. Two night minimum stay.

Mallacoota Houseboats (☎ 5158 0775; Karbeethong Jetty; 3-night minimum $850) These houseboats are a divine way to explore Mallacoota's waterways. The clean and cosy boats sleep up to six and have kitchen, toilet, shower and barbecue. Prices almost double in peak season.

Eating

Croajingolong Cafe (☎ 5158 0098; Shop 3/14 Allan Dr; mains $5-13; 🕑 breakfast & lunch Tue-Sun) Overlooking the inlet, this is the locals' favourite café to catch up over a coffee on the weekend. Grab your newspaper and settle down to pancakes and wild berries, or the enormous Vegie Brekky. No credit cards.

Mallacoota Hotel Motel (☎ 5158 0455; 51-55 Maurice Ave; mains $15-29; lunch & dinner) The pub bistro provides hearty meals on its varied menu with reliable favourites such as chicken Kiev and vegetable risotto. Bands play at the pub regularly in the summer.

Tide Restaurant (☎ 5158 0100; 70 Maurice Ave; mains $17-29; dinner) The service is attentive at Mallacoota's most upmarket dining option with its prime lakeside setting. The menu featuring seafood is well-presented and the food is similar quality to the pub. No credit cards.

Getting There & Away
Mallacoota is 23km off the Princes Hwy. From Melbourne you can catch a daily **V/line** (☎ 13 61 96; www.vline.com.au) train to Bairnsdale and coach to Genoa ($36, seven hours), then get the **Mallacoota-Genoa Bus Service** (☎ 0408 315 615; one way $4), which meets the V/line coach on Monday, Thursday and Friday. During school and public holidays there's also a Sunday service.

CROAJINGOLONG NATIONAL PARK
Croajingolong is one of Australia's finest national parks, recognised by its listing as a World Biosphere Reserve by Unesco (one of 12 in Australia). This coastal wilderness park covers 87,500 hectares and stretches for about 100km along the easternmost tip of Victoria from Bemm River to the NSW border. Magnificent unspoiled beaches, inlets, estuaries and forests make this an ideal park for camping, walking, swimming and surfing. The five inlets: Sydenham, Tamboon, Mueller, Wingan and Mallacoota, are all popular canoeing and fishing spots. Mallacoota Inlet is the largest and most accessible (see p137).

Two sections of the park have been declared wilderness areas (which means no vehicles, access to a limited number of walkers only, and permits required): the **Cape Howe Wilderness Area**, between Mallacoota Inlet and NSW border, and the **Sandpatch Wilderness Area**, between Wingan Inlet and Shipwreck Creek. The **Wilderness Coast Walk**, only for the well-prepared and intrepid, starts at Sydenham Inlet, by Bemm River and heads along the coast to Mallacoota. You can start anywhere in between. Thurra River is a good starting point, making the walk an easy-to-medium 59km (five-day) hike to Mallacoota. Tony Gray runs

a **car shuttle** (☎ 5158 0472, 0408-516 482; up to six people $212) to Thurra River from Mallacoota: leave your car at Mallacoota airport.

Croajingolong is a bird-watcher's paradise, with more than 300 recorded species, including glossy black cockatoos and the rare ground parrot, while the inland waterways are home to a myriad of water birds such as the delicate azure kingfisher and the magnificent sea eagle. There are many small mammals, including possums, bandicoots and gliders, and some huge goannas. The vegetation ranges from typical coastal landscapes to thick eucalypt forests, with areas of warm-temperate rainforest. The heath land areas are filled with impressive displays of orchids and wild flowers in the spring.

Point Hicks was the first part of Australia to be spotted by Captain Cook and the *Endeavour* crew in 1770 and was named after his first Lieutenant, Zachary Hicks. There's a **lighthouse** here (see p140), which is open for tours recanting tales of dark, stormy nights filled with ghosts and shipwrecks. You can still see remains of the *SS Saros*, which ran ashore in 1937, on a short walk from the lighthouse.

Access roads of varying quality lead into the park from the Princes Hwy. Apart from Mallacoota Rd, all roads are unsealed and can be very rough in winter, so check with Parks Victoria on road conditions before venturing on, especially during or after rain.

Contact **Parks Victoria** (☎ 13 19 63; www.parkweb .vic.gov.au; Cann River ☎ 5158 6351, Mallacoota ☎ 5161 9500) offices in Cann River or Mallacoota for information, road conditions, overnight hiking and camping permits, and track notes. Lonely Planet's *Walking in Australia* has an excellent detailed description of the walk from Thurra River to Mallacoota.

Sleeping
The main camping areas are at Wingan Inlet, Shipwreck Creek, Thurra River and Mueller Inlet. Given their amazing beauty, these campgrounds are surprisingly quiet and bookings only need to be made for the Christmas and Easter holiday periods. Wingan and Shipwreck can be booked through Parks Victoria (see above), and Thurra and Mueller through Point Hicks Lighthouse (p140).

Wingan Inlet (unpowered sites $15.50) Serene and secluded, this site has superb sandy beaches and great walks. The Wingan River Walk (2½ hours return) through rainforest

SOUTHEAST COAST VICTORIA

has great water holes for swimming and cascading rapids.

Shipwreck Creek (unpowered sites $15.50) Only 15km from Mallacoota, this beautiful camping ground is set in forest above a sandy beach. It's a small ground with just five sites and there are lots of short walks to do here.

Mueller Inlet (unpowered sites $16) The calm waters of this inlet are fantastic for kayaking and swimming, and the camp sites are only a couple of metres from the water (not ideal with toddlers). It's a small camping ground with eight sites – three of them walk-in – but it's the only camping ground without fireplaces. There's no vegetation providing privacy, but outside Christmas and Easter holidays it's usually quiet.

Thurra River (unpowered sites $16) This is largest of the park's sites, with 46 well-designed sites

stretched along the foreshore from the river towards the lighthouse. Most of the sites are separated by bush. There's communal fireplaces, and pit toilets with signage reminding you how to look after the environment. Thurra River and Mueller Inlet camping grounds are less than 5km from the lighthouse.

Bush Camping (unpowered sites per person $5) Several other bush-camping sites lie along the Wilderness Coast Walk. BYO drinking water; permits required.

Point Hicks Lighthouse (☎ 5158 4268, 5156 0432; www.gippslandlakesescapes.com.au/Properties/Point HicksLighthouse; up to 6 people $250-295) This remote lighthouse has two comfortable, heritage-listed cottages that originally housed the Assistant Lighthouse Keepers. Each of the cottages have sensational ocean views and wood fires.

New South Wales

OLIVER STREWE

South Coast
New South Wales

Green, luscious and temperate, the New South Wales (NSW) south coast is as pretty a region as you'll find on the island continent. Now that they've stopped harpooning whales, heavy industry doesn't really get a look-in south of Wollongong, leaving the waters unpolluted and spectacularly clear. Dolphins, sensible creatures that they are, have set up shop in the bays, while whales once again visit in numbers on their annual vacations, now that they're less likely to end up with an unfortunate body piercing.

On the drier side of the shoreline vast tracts of national park have been established, ensuring that the remaining virgin coastline continues to look much as it did when Captain Cook cleared customs in 1770. The beachside living is so good in some places that even the kangaroos wander down to the shore for an evening stroll.

Nature doesn't hold all the trumps. Picturesque historic villages dot the hinterlands while Canberra is a textbook of 20th-century architecture and town planning writ life-size. The nation's capital isn't actually on the coast at all, so to compensate, the Australian Capital Territory (ACT) has nabbed arguably the best part of it, Jervis Bay, from NSW.

Part of the south coast's charm is simply a matter of access; where the north coast is on the main highway linking Queensland, NSW and Victoria, the south coast is served by the meandering Princes Hwy, the secondary road from Sydney to Melbourne. For people unwilling to share their coastal wanderings with battalions of trucks, this is a very good thing.

HIGHLIGHTS

- Having kangaroos calling in at your camp site in **Murramarang National Park** (p163)
- Leaving snowy white footprints on the brilliant sands of **Jervis Bay** (p166)
- Marvelling at the dramatic geology of the **Illawarra Escarpment** (p176)
- Watching **Eden**'s whale-human reconciliation play itself out (p146)
- Experiencing village life with the 'quaint' quotient at max in **Central Tilba** (p150)
- Paying respect to the Mother of the Yuin people at sacred **Gulaga** (p152)
- Hanging out with the seals and penguins at **Montague Island** (p152)

Illawarra Escarpment ★

Jervis Bay ★

★ Murramarang National Park

Central Tilba ★ ★ ★ Montague Island
Gulaga ★

★ Eden

■ TELEPHONE CODE: 02   ■ www.southcoast.com.au

SOUTH COAST NSW

SAPPHIRE COAST

Not to be outdone by Queensland's Gold Coast, the southernmost part of NSW considers itself precious too. The moniker is apt, with the coast's pristine water revelling in every shade of blue. You won't see a lot of it from the Princes Hwy, but you can feel confident that taking just about any road east will yield a bit of mostly unblemished coast set in rugged surrounds. This is the start of the traditional lands of the Yuin people.

NADGEE NATURE RESERVE

Continuing over the state border the **Nadgee Howe Wilderness** continues, but its name

changes from Croajingolong National Park (p139) to Nadgee Nature Reserve. Vehicle access is only allowed as far as the ranger station near the Merrica River in the reserve's northern section.

This is the NSW starting point for the 50km **Nadgee Howe Wilderness Walk**, a route suited to experienced hikers. Basic **camp sites** (per adult/child $5/2) – without toilets or drinkable water – are spread along the track. Permits are required before commencing the walk; apply to the National Parks & Wildlife Service (NPWS) in Merimbula (p146).

At the north end of the reserve, the small settlement **Wonboyn**, on the lake, has a store selling petrol and basic supplies.

Wonboyn Cabins & Caravan Park (☎ 6496 9131; www.wonboyncabins.com.au; Wonboyn Rd; camp sites per 2 people $25, cabins $65-112;) is spacious and resonates with bellbird song.

BEN BOYD NATIONAL PARK

The wilderness barely pauses for breath before starting again at 10,709-hectare **Ben Boyd National Park**. Boyd was an entrepreneur who failed spectacularly in his efforts to build an empire around Eden in 1850. This park protects some of his follies, along with a dramatic coastline peppered with isolated beaches. It's split into two sections, with Eden squeezed in between.

The southern section is accessed by mainly gravel roads (per vehicle $7) leading off sealed Edrom Rd, which leaves the Princes Hwy 18km south of Eden. At its southern tip, the elegant 1883 **Green Cape Lightstation** (☎ 6495 5000; www.nationalparks.nsw.gov.au; Green Cape Rd; cottage mid-week/weekend $215/292) copes with its isolation by gazing out at awesome views. There are **tours** (adult/child $7/5; ☽ 1pm & 3pm Thu-Mon) or if you want to share the seclusion, you can spend the night in a lavishly restored keepers' cottage (sleeps six).

Eleven kilometres along Edrom Rd there's a turn-off to the historic **Davidson Whaling Station** on Twofold Bay where you can have a picnic in the rustic gardens of **Loch Gaira Cottage** (1896). Not much whaling paraphernalia remains, but interpretive signs tell the story. It's hard to imagine that until 1929 the peace of this place was rent by the agonised groans of dying whales and the stench of boiling blubber.

Further along is the turn-off for **Boyd's Tower**, an impressive structure indulgently built in the late 1840s with sandstone shipped

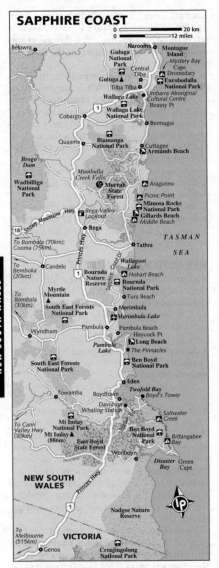

SAPPHIRE COAST

$10/5) along the route at **Saltwater Creek** and **Bittangabee Bay**. Both have vehicle access.

The northern section of the park can be accessed from the Princes Hwy north of Eden. From Haycock Point, where there are good views, a walking trail leads to a headland overlooking the Pambula River. Another good walk is to the **Pinnacles**; this rock formation's white base and red top make it look like a giant jagged slab of coconut ice.

On the edge of the park, near Pambula Lake, is **Monaroo Bobberrer Gudu Aboriginal Cultural Centre** (☎ 6496 1922; Jigamy Farm, Princes Hwy). Call ahead to check whether they've got any tours or cultural activities running.

EDEN

☎ 02 / pop 3006

The first town north of the Victorian border, Eden's a little sleepy place where the only bustle you're likely to find is down at the wharf when the fishing boats come in. Pretty beaches run either side of the town's knobbly peninsula.

For possibly thousands of years this bay has been the site of extraordinary interactions between humans and whales (see p146). Migrating humpback and southern right whales pass so close to the coast that whale-watching experts consider this one of the best places in Australia to observe these magnificent creatures. Often they can be seen feeding or resting in Twofold Bay during their southern migration back to Antarctic waters.

Information

Library (☎ 6496 1687; ☼ 9am-5pm Mon-Fri, 9am-noon Sat) Internet access costs per hour $6.

Post office (☎ 6496 1400; 140 Imlay St; ☼ 9am-5pm Mon-Fri)

Visitors centre (☎ 6496 1953; cnr Imlay & Mitchell Sts; ☼ 9am-5pm)

Sights & Activities

The interesting **Killer Whale Museum** (☎ 6496 2094; www.killerwhalemuseum.com.au; 94 Imlay St; adult/child $7.40/2; ☼ 9.15am-3.45pm Mon-Sat, 11.15am-3.45pm Sun) was established in 1931, mainly to preserve the skeleton of Old Tom (see p146).

Cat-Balou Cruises (☎ 0427 962 027; www.catbalou .com.au; Main Wharf, 253 Imlay St) operates 3½-hour whale-spotting voyages (per person $60) in October and November. At other times of the year, dolphins and seals can usually be seen during the two-hour bay cruise (adult/child $30/17).

from Sydney. It was intended to be a lighthouse but the government wouldn't give Boyd permission to operate it. The twisted red rock formations at its base are striking against the cobalt sea.

The 31km **Light to Light Walk** links Boyd's wannabe lighthouse to the real one at Green Cape. There are **camp sites** (☎ 6495 5000; adult/child

A good **whale lookout** among the many options is at the base of Bass St. When whales are spotted the Killer Whale Museum sounds a siren.

Festivals & Events

Eden comes alive in late October for the **Whale Festival**, with the typical carnival, street parade and stalls plus some innovative local events such as the Slimy Mackerel Throw.

Sleeping

As you enter town from either direction, rows of run-of-the-mill motels and motor parks line the road to greet you.

Eden Tourist Park (☎ 6496 1139; www.edentourist park.com.au; Aslings Beach Rd; camp sites per two people $20, cabins $60-135) Serenely situated on the spit separating Aslings Beach from Lake Curalo, this large well-kept park echoes with birdsong from its sheltering trees.

Twofold Bay Motor Inn (☎ 6496 3111; fax 6496 3058; 164-166 Imlay St; s/d $92/110; ✖ ☎ ; wi-fi) Substantial rooms, some with water views, are the norm at this centrally located motel. There's also a tiny indoor pool.

Gibsons by the Beach (☎ 6496 1414; www.gibsons bythebeach.com.au; 10 Bay St; s/d/tr/q $125/155/190/225; ✖) The beach is a two-minute stroll from the patio door of this self-contained one-bedroom apartment, through lush bushland and the owner's garden.

our pick **Crown & Anchor Inn** (☎ 6496 1017; www.crownandanchoreden.com.au; 239 Imlay St; s $160-180, d $180-200) Awesomely atmospheric, this historic house (1845) has been beautifully restored and furnished with the likes of four-poster beds and claw-foot baths. There's a lovely view over Twofold Bay from the back patio.

Eating

The following eateries are clumped together on the Main Wharf (253 Imlay St) at the bottom of town.

Waterside Café (☎ 6496 1855; mains $5-20; ✆ breakfast & lunch) Decent brekkies, strong coffees and harbourside tables make this a good place to start the day.

Taste of Eden (☎ 6496 1304; mains $9-28; ✆ breakfast & lunch) With décor straight from Davy Jones' locker, this brightly painted café serves delicious local seafood (among other dishes) without any airs or graces. The menu's so fresh it has to be listed on a whiteboard.

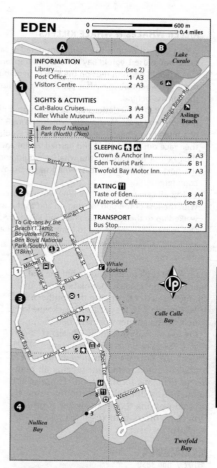

EDEN

INFORMATION	
Library...(see 2)	
Post Office......................................1 A3	
Visitors Centre................................2 A3	

SIGHTS & ACTIVITIES	
Cat-Balou Cruises.............................3 A4	
Killer Whale Museum.......................4 A3	

SLEEPING	
Crown & Anchor Inn........................5 A3	
Eden Tourist Park.............................6 B1	
Twofold Bay Motor Inn....................7 A3	

EATING	
Taste of Eden...................................8 A4	
Waterside Café..............................(see 8)	

TRANSPORT	
Bus Stop..9 A3	

Getting There & Away

Premier Motor Service (☎ 13 34 10; www.premierms .com.au) has two daily buses to Sydney ($66, 10 hours) and one to Melbourne ($53, eight hours). **CountryLink** (☎ 13 22 32; www.countrylink .com.au) runs a daily bus to Canberra ($35, 5¼ hours).

Deanes Buslines (☎ 6495 6452; www.deanesbuslines .com.au) has five buses, Monday to Saturday, to Bega ($13.20, 1¼ hours) via Merimbula ($8.80, 40 minutes).

PAMBULA

☎ 02 / pop 1146

The beautiful drive north from Eden skirts Ben Boyd National Park before passing through the small town of Pambula. Its highway-hugging

---

KILLER WHALES & WHALE KILLERS

Eden's original people, the Yuin, considered orcas (killer whales) to be ancestral beings. Pods of orcas would use Twofold Bay to herd and trap larger migrating whales in the shallows. Aboriginal elders would perform rites on the beach, begging the orcas for a share of the bounty. Amazingly, the orcas would oblige. After consuming the lips and tongue of their victim, they would leave the carcass behind.

After 1830, the relationship was taken up a notch. The Davidson whaling station (p143) employed many local Aboriginals, which was rare for the times. When the orca pod caught sight of a migrating whale, one of their number would head off to alert the whalers. The crew would then race out to the tired and harried victim and finish it off with a handheld harpoon. Keeping their half of the bargain, the whalers would anchor the dead whale and leave it overnight. By the next morning the orcas would have removed the tongue and lips and the contract was complete.

This all came to an end in 1900 when an orca beached itself on Aslings Beach during a hunt. With the rest of the pod looking on and as the whalers rushed to the orca's assistance, a vagrant walked up to the beached animal and killed it. After that, only a few of the older orcas, including Old Tom (p144), continued to hunt with the whaling crews. Shortly after this the last of the Yuin community left Eden for Wallaga Lake.

---

main street is pleasant enough, but the real delight is Pambula Beach (population 655), three kilometres east. Occupying the southern end of Merimbula Bay, it's got a laid-back vibe long gone from its glitzier northern neighbour.

Once a mere oyster kiosk, **Wheeler's** (☎ 6495 6330; Arthur Kaine Dr; takeaway $5-10, mains $22-29; ☾ lunch daily, dinner Mon-Sat) is now an upmarket tourist-oriented restaurant serving all manner of delicious local seafood. Those in the know opt for the takeaway counter and its myriad options. Long an oyster producer, Wheeler's offers **tours** (adult/child $10/5.50, 11am Mon-Sat) of its farm.

MERIMBULA

☎ 02 / pop 3850

Spread around the top end of a gorgeous long golden beach and an appealing inlet (which locals insist on calling a lake), Merimbula is in thrall to holidaymakers and retirees. Not big enough to be interesting and yet weighed down with development, it's hard to muster much enthusiasm for the town centre. As the numerous holiday apartments would suggest, this is one of the few places on the far south coast that really heaves during summer school holidays.

Information

DragNet (☎ 1300 662 344; 11 Merimbula Dr; per hr $6; ☾ 9am-5pm Mon-Fri) Internet access.
NPWS visitors centre (☎ 6495 5000; cnr Merimbula & Sapphire Coast Drs; ☾ 8.30am-4.30pm Mon-Fri)

Post office (☎ 6497 5940; 5 Merimbula Dr)
Visitors centre (☎ 6495 1129; www.sapphirecoast .com.au; 2 Beach St; ☾ 9am-5pm)

Sights

The small **Merimbula Aquarium** (☎ 6495 4446; www.merimbulawharf.com.au; Lake St; adult/child $9.90/5.50; ☾ 10am-5pm) displays the sorts of fish you'll find in the bay. The **Old School Museum** (☎ 6495 2114; Main St; adult/child $2/free; ☾ 2-4.30pm Tue, Thu & Sun) isn't dedicated to ageing rappers. It's one of those volunteer-run museums featuring knick-knackery and displays on local history.

A **nature boardwalk** follows the estuary southwest of the causeway. A plethora of birds and mammals are visible. Pick up the useful brochure at the tourist information centre.

Activities

Diving is popular, with several wrecks in the area including the large *Empire Gladstone*, which sunk in 1950. **Merimbula Divers Lodge**

COWS OR COAST?

From Pambula you've got the option of continuing on the Princes Hwy through Bega or heading to Merimbula and taking Sapphire Coast Drive. While the highway leads through some pretty farmland, the latter option alternates between spectacular beaches and national parks until it rejoins the highway near Tilba Tilba. And it's 5km shorter.

(☎ 1800 651 861; www.merimbuladiverslodge.com.au; 15 Park St) offers basic instruction and one shallow dive from $99, including equipment. It also does snorkelling trips ($40).

True Blue (☎ 6495 1686; Merimbula Marina; www.merimbulamarina.com; adult/child $25/20) offers bargain-priced dolphin-watching cruises in the bay, along with whale-watching from mid-September to November.

Top Lake Boat Hire (☎ 64951987; Lakewood Dr), near the end of the boardwalk, rents out motor boats, pedal boats, kayaks, canoes and rowing boats. **Cycle'n'Surf** (☎ 6495 2171; 18 Marine Pde), south of the lake, hires out bikes (per hour $7), boogie boards (half day $10) and surfboards (per hour $10) as well as carrying out bike repairs.

Sleeping

The isthmus between the beach and the lake is completely overrun with motels and holiday apartments. Self-contained apartments are usually let on a weekly basis, particularly in summer. Letting agents for the area include **Fisk & Nagle** (☎ 6495 3222; www.getawaymerimbula.com .au; cnr Market & Beach Sts).

BUDGET

Merimbula Divers Lodge (☎ 6495 3611; www.merimbuladiverslodge.com.au; 15 Park St; dm $20) No linen is included in the price (not even pillows), but this central place offers clean, bunk-style accommodation split into three separate self-contained apartments, each sleeping eight.

Town Centre Motor Inn (☎ 6495 1163; 8 Merimbula Dr; s/d $75/80; 🖢) A masterpiece of nouvelle retro without even trying, this three-level motel has carpet on the walls, a spew-on ceiling and fabulous 1970s couch fabric. Rooms are tidy but smallish.

MIDRANGE & TOP END

our pick **Seachange B&B** (☎ 6495 3133; www.sapphirecoast.com.au/seachange; 49 Imlay St; s/d $129/149) Adorable hosts with a food and friendliness focus make this comfortable and modern B&B an absolute delight. It has fantastic lake views along with immaculately clean, elegantly furnished rooms with en suite.

Crown Apartments (☎ 6495 2400; www.crownapartments.com.au; 23 Beach St; apt 1-bedroom/2-bedroom $135/165; 🖢 🖢) Eschewing the grim dark brick of so many holiday units, Crown has an airy

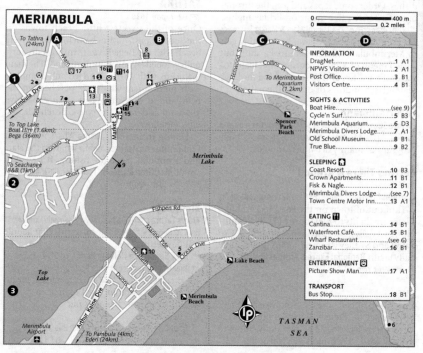

MERIMBULA

0 — 400 m
0 — 0.2 miles

design. Units come with kitchens, balconies and views.

Coast Resort (☎ 6495 4930; www.coastresort.com.au; 1 Elizabeth St; apt 1-bedroom $265, 2-bedroom $275-360, 3-bedroom $375-470; ⌘ ⌘) You could describe the décor of this huge upmarket apartment-style complex as ultramodern, although stark might be more apt. Still, comfort's not a problem and the two pools, tennis court and proximity to the beach are all very appealing.

Eating & Drinking

Waterfront Café (☎ 6495 2211; Beach St; breakfast $5-17, lunch $18-23; ☷ 8am-5pm) Try this place for an excellent coffee or a snack while looking out over the, ahem, lake.

Wharf Restaurant (☎ 6495 4446; Lake St; mains $17-30; ☷ lunch daily, dinner Wed-Sun) With views to make you swoon into your soup, Wharf doesn't drop its informal café vibe until after dark. The aquarium downstairs means you can admire the fish before having their cousins delivered to your plate.

Cantina (☎ 6495 1085; 56 Market St; tapas $10-16, mains $18-30; ☷ lunch & dinner) The changing menu features imaginative Spanish and Mediterranean dishes. Order some tapas and join the throngs outside. There's live music on Friday nights.

Zanzibar (☎ 6495 4038; cnr Main & Market Sts; mains $25-33; ☷ dinner Tue-Sat) As swanky as dining gets in Merimbula, Zanzibar features a short but varied menu of Mod Oz cuisine that leans towards the sea. See and be seen behind the huge plate-glass windows or out on the patio.

Entertainment

Picture Show Man (☎ 6495 3744; www.pictureshowman.com.au; 80 Main St; tickets $8.50-11) Screens a busy program of mainly art-house movies.

Getting There & Around

AIR

Merimbula airport (MIM; ☎ 6495 4211; Arthur Kaine Dr) is 1km out of town on the road to Pambula. There are flights to Melbourne ($170, 90 minutes, two daily), Moruya ($83, 30 minutes, two daily) and Sydney (from $131, 1¾ hours, three daily) with **Regional Express Airlines** (Rex; ☎ 13 17 13; www.rex.com.au).

BUS

Buses stop outside the Commonwealth Bank on Market St. **Premier Motor Service** (☎ 13 34 10; www.premierms.com.au) has two daily buses to Sydney ($64, 9½ hours) via Narooma ($21,

two hours) and one to Melbourne ($53, 9¼ hours) via Lakes Entrance ($26, 3½ hours). **CountryLink** (☎ 13 22 32; www.countrylink.com.au) runs a daily bus to Canberra ($33, 4¼ hours).

Deanes Buslines (☎ 6495 6452; www.deanesbuslines .com.au) provides the local bus service (Monday to Saturday only) that includes Bega ($10, one hour, six daily) and Eden ($8.80, 40 minutes, five daily). **Tathra Bus Service** (☎ 6492 1991; www.tathrabus.com.au) has two buses to/from Tathra ($8.40, 25 minutes) on Tuesdays and Thursdays.

BOURNDA NATIONAL PARK

Taking in most of the coast from Merimbula north to Tathra, **Bournda National Park** (admission per car $7) is a 2590-hectare park with beautiful empty surf beaches, rugged headlands and walking trails through heath, eucalyptus forests and tea-tree. Both fresh- and saltwater lakes support an abundance of bird life, including the threatened Little Tern and Pied Oystercatcher. Camping is permitted at **Hobart Beach** (☎ 6495 5000; camping per adult/child $10/5), on the southern shore of peaceful **Wallagoot Lake**.

TATHRA

☎ 02 / pop 1630

Once of the sweetest little beach towns on the South Coast, Tathra has a long and lovely beach with the Bega River forming a dreamy, undeveloped lagoon at its north end. The main township, with its rough-edged pub (complete with mechanical whale), is perched on the headland at the south end, with expansive views up and down the coast. Beachside, the vibe's mellow.

Dating from 1862, **Tathra Wharf** is the last remaining coastal steamship wharf in the state and a popular place for fishing. It houses a small **Maritime Museum** (☎ 6494 4062; adult/child $2/1; ☷ 10am-4pm).

Sleeping

Elders Tathra (☎ 6494 1087; www.elderstathra.com.au; 34 Bega St) is one of several local agents that handle holiday letting.

Big4 Seabreeze Holiday Park (☎ 6494 1350; www .seabreezetathra.com.au; 41 Andy Poole Dr; sites per 2 people $29-45, cabins $85-170; ⌘ ⌘) Get tropical beneath the palm trees or in the Polynesian cabins at this excellent, friendly park across from the beach.

Sapphire Court (☎ 6494 1980; info@sapphirecourt -holidayunit.com.au; 33 Edna St; apt $110; ⌘) These fully self-contained two-bedroom apartments are terrific value, sleeping six at a squeeze.

our pick Tathra Beach House (☎ 6499 9900; www .tathrabeachhouse.com.au; 57 Andy Poole Dr; apt $125-231; 🖾 🖳) Well designed and lavishly landscaped, this beachside property offers smart apartments, two pools and ocean views.

Eating

Tathra Beach Pickle Factory (☎ 6494 4232; 35 Andy Poole Dr; snacks $3-8; 🕑 8.30am-6pm) Tathra's best breakfast option is this grab-and-run deli-café, with disposable cups and limited seating. The coffee's excellent and the home-baking irresistible.

Fat Tony's Bar & Grill (☎ 6494 4550; 15 Bega St; lunch $14-28, dinner $22-30; 🕑 lunch Thu-Sat, dinner Tue-Sat) Although it sounds like a greasy steak joint, this bistro is actually quite upmarket. Given that all the floor staff seem impressively fit, we can only guess that they hide Tony in the kitchen.

Getting There & Away

Tathra Bus Service (☎ 6492 1991; www.tathrabus.com .au) has three buses to/from Bega ($8.40, 30 minutes) on weekdays and two buses to/from Merimbula ($8.40, 25 minutes) on Tuesdays and Thursdays.

BEGA

☎ 02 / pop 4540

More of a rest stop than a destination in itself, Bega's cheesy delights are an acquired taste. Synonymous in Australia with cheese, it's the service town for the farmers of the rich surrounding dairy country. It may get more interesting when a permaculturally designed ecovillage (complete with composting toilets) opens in the middle of town, but we're not holding our breath.

At the **Bega Cheese Factory & Heritage Centre** (☎ 6492 7762; www.begacheese.com.au; Lagoon St; admission free; 🕑 9am-5pm), north of the river, you can overload on both free tastings and from treats at the café. It also houses the **visitors centre** (☎ 6491 7645; 🕑 9am-5pm), where you can pick up a pamphlet for the self-guided **Bega Heritage Walk**.

The **Bega Pioneers' Museum** (☎ 6492 1453; 87 Bega St; adult/child $5/1; 🕑 10am-4pm Mon-Sat) focuses on local heritage, with particular emphasis on farming and cow-related machinery.

If you're not lactose intolerant and want to explore Bega further, the friendly **Pickled Pear** (☎ 6492 1393; www.thepickledpear.com.au; 60 Carp

St; s/tw $105-120, d $140-170; 🖾 ; wi-fi) has comfortable rooms in a lovely 1870s house near the centre of town.

MIMOSA ROCKS NATIONAL PARK

After leaving Tathra, the road cuts through Mimosa Rocks (5802 hectares), a wonderful coastal park with dense and varied bush, sea caves, lagoons and 20km of beautiful coastline. Unsealed roads lead to **camp sites** (☎ 4476 2888; per adult/child $10/5) at Gillards Beach, Middle Beach, Picnic Point and Aragunnu Beach. The drive to Middle Beach is especially lovely, passing under a canopy of tall eucalypts and palms to the deserted surf beach.

Sapphire Coast Ecotours (☎ 6494 0283; www .sapphirecoastecotours.com.au; tours $30-60) runs highly regarded walks exploring the park's varied ecosystems and may include an Aboriginal guide.

After leaving the park, the road continues through bush and farmland until reaching the coast at **Cuttagee** – like Tathra but with even fewer houses. South of the main beach, Kullaroo St leads to secluded, bush-lined **Armands Bay**, the only clothing-optional beach on the Sapphire Coast.

BERMAGUI

☎ 02 / pop 1300

There's a nice vibe to Bermagui, probably due to the eclectic mix of fisherfolk, surfers, alternative lifestylers and indigenous Australians who call it home. In typical Aussie parlance it's invariably referred to as Bermie (not Berma, or Myanmar).

The Bermagui Community Centre houses the **visitors centre** (☎ 6493 3054; info@bigfoot.com.au; Bunga Rd; 🕑 10am-4pm) and has internet access.

Sights & Activities

You could toss a mullet from the shops and hit **Shelly Beach**, a child-friendly swimming spot. A kilometre's wander around the point will bring you to the **Blue Pool**, a dramatic ocean pool built into the base of the cliffs.

You can wander 6km north along the coast to **Camel Rock** (the camel requires a bit of squinting) and a further 2km around to beautiful **Wallaga Lake**. The route follows **Haywards Beach**, a good surfing spot.

Many of the Yuin people ended up in the reserve on Wallaga Lake's shores after being pushed off their traditional lands. This community runs the excellent **Umbarra Aboriginal Cultural Centre** (☎ 4473 7232; www.umbarra .com.au; 246 Bermagui Rd; ☻ 9am-5pm Mon-Fri, 9am-4pm Sat & Sun), which has interesting historical displays and authentic art for sale. Tours of the lake and cultural sites are offered. It pays to call ahead as family or spiritual *business* takes precedence over tourist operations.

Sleeping

Letting agents for holiday houses include **Fisk & Nagle** (☎ 6493 4255; www.fisknagle.com.au; 14 Lamont St).

Bermagui Motor Inn (☎ 6493 4311; www.acr.net .au/~bmi/; 38 Lamont St; s/d $79/89; ☒) Right in town, this motel may be a classic but it's got new carpets, comfy beds and very friendly owners.

Harbourview Motel (☎ 6493 5213; 56 Lamont St; s $105-110, d $120-130; ☒) Fastidiously tidy, the spacious rooms enjoy private courtyards with their own barbecues. The more expensive ones have sea views.

Bimbimbi House (☎ 6493 4456; bimbimbihouse@big foot.com.au; Nutleys Creek Rd; s $100, d $140-185) Choose between a garden room, a two-bedroom unit or a self-contained cottage on this quiet property, set amid lush gardens. It overlooks the river, 2km from town.

Eating

Cool-O-Cream Gelati (☎ 6493 3555; 1/6 Bunga St; cones $3; ☻ midday-6pm) It's worth taking the coastal route just for this wonderful homemade gelato shop that experiments with barfly-friendly flavours such as 'chocolate grappa' and 'lemon, lime and bitters'.

Cream Patisserie (☎ 6493 5445; 28 Lamont St; items $4-8; ☻ 9am-5pm Mon-Fri, 9am-3pm Sat) A smooth café-style place serving delicious gourmet pies, *focaccia* and cakes.

River Rock Café (☎ 6493 3156; Wallaga Lake Rd; mains $7-15; ☻ 9am-4pm) Nouvelle hippies gravitate to this café just north of the bridge. There are sandwiches, burgers, wraps, *pide* and salads served during the day. Every second Monday it hosts *Spicy Mamas*, an open mic jam night accompanied by an Indian vegetarian feast ($13).

Saltwater (☎ 6493 4328; Lamont St; lunch $16-19, dinner $22-27; ☻ lunch & dinner Wed-Sun, takeaway 11.30am-8pm) Overlooking the marina, the clean lines of Saltwater's interior complement a changing menu of fresh catches. The platter for two is amazing value for $38; or you can get takeaway fish-and-chips for $8.50.

Getting There & Away

Premier Motor Service (☎ 13 34 10; www.premierms .com.au) stops here once a day on the run between Sydney ($55, 8¼ hours) and Eden ($21, 1¾ hours) via Narooma ($9, 40 minutes) and Merimbula ($21, 80 minutes).

EUROBODALLA COAST

Meaning 'Land of Many Waters' this section of coast continues the Sapphire Coast's celebration of all things blue. A fair bit of green gets a look in too, with segments of the disjointed **Eurobodalla National Park** spreading much of its length.

It's an area of sweet little townships, lakes, bays and inlets backed by spotted-gum forests and home to much native wildlife. Part of the Yuin homelands, it includes their sacred mountain, Gulaga (p152).

TILBA TILBA & CENTRAL TILBA

☎ 02 / pop 500

The coastal road from Bermagui rejoins the Princes Hwy just before the loop road leading to these outrageously cute National Trust villages in the shadow of Gulaga (p152).

Tilba Tilba is half the size of its singularly named neighbour, 2km down the road. Gardening freaks will love **Foxglove Spires** (☎ 4473 7375; www.foxglovespires.com.au; Corkhill Dr; admission $7.50; ☻ 10am-4pm), a magical 3½-acre private garden with lots of hidden avenues and bowers.

Central Tilba sits in a nook of a valley that has remained virtually unchanged since the 19th century – except now the main street is jammed with visitors' cars on weekends. Strolling along Bate St, you'll find a string of shops selling the sort of things you'd expect to find in National Trust villages: fudge, boiled lollies, cheese, speciality teas, ice cream, crafts and cafés. Behind the pub, there's a short walk up to a water tower where boulders provide terrific views of Gulaga.

There's information, including a handy town guide, at the **Bates Emporium** (☎ 4473 7290; ☻ 8am-5pm), which also serves as the petrol station, internet café and post office.

The streets are blocked off for the **Tilba Easter Festival** (www.tilba.com.au/tilbafestival.htm), which has lots of music, entertainment and several thousand visitors. The other big event is the acclaimed **Cobargo Folk Festival** (www.cobargofolk

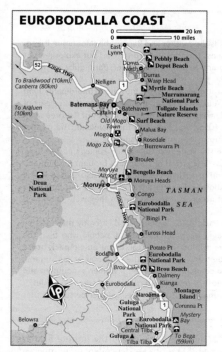

EUROBODALLA COAST

festival.com), held in historic town Cobargo, 20km towards Bega.

A short drive takes you to gorgeously undeveloped **Mystery Bay** and the first pocket of Eurobodalla National Park. At the south end of the main surf beach, a rock formation forms an idyllic natural swimming pool. There's a council-run **camp site** (☎ 0428-622 357; www.mystery baycampground.com; sites per 2 adults & 2 children $13) under the trees near the beach.

SLEEPING & EATING
Dromedary Hotel (☎ 4473 7223; fax 4473 7238; 5 Bate St, Central Tilba; s/d $55/60) There's clean, basic accommodation upstairs in this nice old pub. The walls downstairs are lined with old photos and pictures of prize pumpkins. The bistro (mains $8 to $18) is a rare after-dark eating option.

ourpick Two Story B&B (☎ 4473 7290; www.tilbatwo story.com; Bate St, Central Tilba; s/d $105/120) This atmospheric 1894 former postmaster's residence has plenty of charm and a cosy log fire in winter. Some rooms have en suites.

Green Gables (☎ 4473 7435; www.greengables.com .au; 269 Corkhill Dr, Tilba Tilba; r $140; 🖳) Try to resist the word 'delightful' when describing this gay-

friendly B&B. The 1879 cottage offers three attractive rooms with either en suites or private bathrooms and views over the fields.

Rose & Sparrow Café (☎ 4473 7229; 3 Bate St; mains $5-15; ☯ breakfast & lunch) Serves generous portions of healthy food, including delicious lentil burgers with homemade hot mango chutney.

GETTING THERE & AWAY
Premier Motor Service (☎ 13 34 10; www.premierms .com.au) buses serve the Tilbas daily on the route between Sydney ($54, eight hours) and Eden ($22, 2¼ hours) via Narooma ($3, 20 minutes) and Merimbula ($19, 1¾ hours).

NAROOMA
☎ 02 / pop 3100
Sitting at the mouth of a large, tree-lined inlet and flanked by surf beaches, Narooma is exceedingly pretty. While the commercial centre on the hill is nothing special, the ocean views more than compensate. The locals are a friendly bunch, but with all that pristine water to relax them, why shouldn't they be?

Information
Library (☎ 4476 1164; Field St; ☯ 10am-5pm Mon-Fri, 9.30am-2pm Sat) Free internet access.
NPWS information office (☎ 4476 2888; Burrawang St; ☯ 8.30am-4.30pm Mon-Fri)
Post office (☎ 4476 2049; 106 Wagonga St)
Visitors centre (☎ 4476 2881; Princes Hwy; ☯ 9am-5pm) Has a small museum.

Sights & Activities
The water surrounding Narooma is so exceptionally clear that it's a constant struggle to resist leaping in. The best place for a sheltered swim is over the bridge in the **netted swimming area** at the south end of **Bar Beach**, below the breakwall. There's a surf club at **Narooma Beach**, but the breaks are better at Bar Beach when a southeasterly blows.

If you fancy a stroll, there's a nice walk from Riverside Dr along the inlet to the ocean, and excellent views from **Bar Rock Lookout**. Just below the lookout is **Australia Rock**, a boulder with a bloody great hole in it that vaguely resembles the country (minus Tasmania, of course).

The **Wagonga Princess** (☎ 4476 2665; Riverside Dr; adult/child $33/22) takes a three-hour cruise up the inlet, which includes a stop for a bushwalk and billy tea.

THE MOTHER'S STORY

In Yuin tradition, Gulaga (Mt Dromedary, 806m) is the mother and Barunguba (Montague Island) and Najanuga (Little Dromedary) are her two sons. The sons wanted to head out exploring, but Gulaga thought that Najanuga was too young and kept him at her feet. Barunguba went out alone and was eventually cut off by the water.

The fascinating thing about this story is that it gives an insight into the extraordinarily long and continuous occupation of the area by the Yuin. The mother and her sons were once part of a large volcano, which has long eroded away, leaving only the hardened cores of its three main vents. When sea levels were lower, Montague Island was linked to the mainland. The mother story suggests that the Yuin witnessed its transformation into an island.

These places are highly sacred; holy sites are still visited on Gulaga for *women's business* (secret rituals) and on Barunguba for *men's business*. The arrival of Europeans brought logging and koala-hunting to Gulaga, and the Yuin were horrified. Their continued protests resulted in the mountain being designated the first Area of Aboriginal Significance in Australia and in 2006 it was with great joy that they celebrated the return of their mother, when they were confirmed as the land's legal owners.

The mountain now forms **Gulaga National Park** (4,768 hectares) and is jointly managed by the indigenous community and NPWS. Its walking tracks are open to all people who treat the mountain with respect. Beginning at Pam's Store in Tilba Tilba you can follow an old **pack-horse trail**. The 11km return walk takes about five hours, but don't miss the loop walk at the summit. There's often rain and mist on the mountain, so come prepared. She's a woman's mountain and local lore has it that it's scornful men that get lost or return with grazes and sprained ankles.

Umbarra (p150) runs four-hour **4WD tours** (minimum four people; $60 per person) to sites on the mountain.

If you'd rather set your own pace, **Narooma Marine** (☎ 4476 2126; 31 Riverside Dr) hires kayaks and canoes (per hour $15), pedal boats (per hour $25), tinnies (per two hours $50) and even a 'BBQ boat' (per hour $45).

A good rainy-day option is **Narooma Cinema** (☎ 4476 2352; 94 Campbell St; tickets $9.50-11.50), a picture palace that began showing flicks in 1926 and hasn't changed much since.

MONTAGUE ISLAND (BARANGUBA)

Nine kilometres offshore from Narooma, this small, pest-free island is a spectacular nature reserve, home to many seabirds (shearwaters, sea eagles, peregrine falcons) and hundreds of fur seals. Little penguins nest here and although some remain year-round, there are more than 10,000 at their peak between September and February.

Baranguba, its Aboriginal name, translates as Big Brother (see above), predating both the TV franchise and Orwell by around 8000 years. Sacred sites remain on the island, which only the local Yuin people may access.

The only way to see the island is via extremely interesting three-hour **guided tours** (☎ 4476 2881; www.montagueisland.com.au; adult/child $110/88) conducted by NPWS rangers, which include climbing up the granite **lighthouse** (1881). Trips are dependent on numbers and weather conditions, so book ahead through the visitors centre. The boat voyage takes about 30 minutes and circumnavigates the island if the water's not too choppy. Take the afternoon tour for a better chance of seeing penguins.

NPWS offers the unforgettable opportunity to stay in the solar-powered **lighthouse keepers' cottages** (☎ 03-5330 2600; www.conservationvolunteers .com.au/volunteer/montague.htm; overnight s/d $475-830, 2 nights s/d $670/1100) on the proviso that you take part in conservation work while you're there. That might entail counting and weighing penguins, weeding or planting trees. The cottages are beautifully renovated and very comfortable. Meals are included, but you'll be expected to help with the preparation. Book well ahead.

The clear waters around the island are good for **diving**, especially from February to June. **Island Charters Narooma** (☎ 4476 1047; www .islandchartersnarooma.com) offers diving (double dive $80), snorkelling ($70), whale-watching ($70) and other tours. Attractions in the area include grey nurse sharks, seals and the wreck of the SS *Lady Darling*.

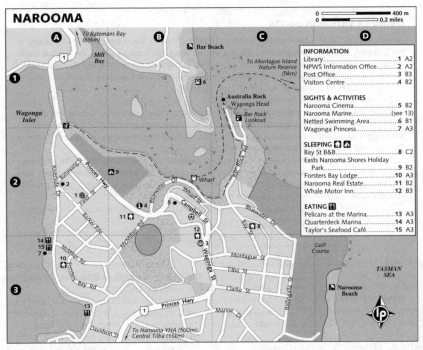

NAROOMA

Festivals & Events

Narooma has a shucking good time during its **Oyster Festival** in mid-May. Grease up your quiff for the **Great Southern Blues & Rockabilly Festival** (www.bluesfestival.tv) on the last weekend of October.

Sleeping

Narooma Real Estate (☎ 4476 3887; www.narooma holidays.com.au; 78 Princes Hwy) deals in the myriad private holiday accommodation options.

our pick **Narooma YHA** (☎ 4476 4440; www.yha .com.au/hostels; 243 Princes Hwy; dm/s/tw $29/61/72, d $68-72; ☐) Although it was obviously once an old-style motel, this super-friendly establishment makes a great hostel. Each room has an en suite for starters. Free bikes and boogie boards are the icing on the stripper-sized cake.

Easts Narooma Shores Holiday Park (☎ 4476 2046; www.easts.com.au; Princes Hwy; sites per 2 people $33-46, cabin $80-230; ☒ ☐ ☐ ; wi-fi) More than 260 camp sites and 43 cabins occupy this lovely spot by the inlet. The friendly managers look after the place well and there's a big pool under the palm trees.

Forsters Bay Lodge (☎ 4476 2319; forstba@acr.net.au; 55 Forsters Bay Rd; d/tr/q $90/100/110) In a quiet spot above pretty Wagonga Inlet, Forsters has six old-fashioned but comfortable self-contained units, scrupulously maintained by an elegant mature hostess.

Whale Motor Inn (☎ 4476 2411; www.whalemotorinn .com; 104 Wagonga St; r $120-190; ☒ ☒) Spot whales from your balcony at this upmarket motel with terrific views and nicely renovated rooms (feel that linen). You can even make like a whale in the spa suites.

Bay St B&B (☎ 4476 3336; 5 Bay St; d $160-180) Up on the hill, this central Narooma home on a quiet street has modern rooms and wide sunny verandas.

Eating

The most evocative eating options are on the marinas of Riverside Dr. They all have heart-melting views over the still, clear waters of the inlet – particularly romantic at sunset.

Quarterdeck Marina (☎ 4476 2723; 13 Riverside Dr; breakfast $4-13, lunch $14-19; ☺ breakfast & lunch Thu-Mon) The only place on the inlet where the décor is even more captivating than the views. Enjoy the

---

LIVING LA VIDA ECOLOGISTA

Annette Turner wasn't born on the south coast; she chose to move here. But unlike others in her position, she isn't a refugee from the big smoke. She came from Avoca on the Central Coast, seeking a place more like the Avoca she was raised in before it was swallowed by suburbia.

'We grew up on the beaches,' she remembers foldly. 'The surf lifesaving club was central to life. Every weekend orientated around a (surf) carnival.'

So what is it that drew her down here?

'I love the diversity of the people. There's a wonderful music community, artistic community, and also an alternative lifestyle community, along with fishermen and dairy farmers. Then there's the wonderful backdrop of national parks,' she adds, 'and beaches where you can go on Christmas Day and not find anyone. It'll never get built up like Avoca.'

Nowadays she gets to see more of those natural delights than most, guiding tours to Montague Island as a part-time Discovery Ranger for NPWS. Juggling that with work as a teacher's aide and preschool teacher, she also lives and volunteers at *The Crossing* in Bermagui, a camp where young people are introduced to practical conservation work.

It seems that the south coast is pretty good place to live out, as Annette puts it, 'a personal passion about the environment'.

As related to Peter Dragicevich

---

excellent breakfasts and seafood lunches under the gaze of dozens of tikis, Chairman Maos and autographed photos of 1950s TV stars.

Taylor's Seafood Café (☎ 4476 2127; 12B Riverside Dr; meals $7-14; ☾ lunch & dinner) The takeaways are a little cheaper, but why miss out on the chance to consume the grilled fish and nongreasy chunky chips while gazing at paradise.

Pelicans at the Marina (☎ 4476 2403; 31 Riverside Dr; breakfast $5-15, lunch $15-25, dinner $22-29; ☾ breakfast & lunch Tue-Sun, dinner Fri & Sat) The simple, elegant interior yields enticing views of the harbour. The menu is also simple and elegant; understandably seafood-focussed with Mod Oz flair.

Getting There & Away

Premier Motor Service (☎ 13 34 10; www.premierms.com .au) buses stop in Narooma on the run between Sydney ($53, 7½ hours) and Melbourne ($62, 11 hours) via Moruya ($10, 35 minutes) and Merimbula ($21, two hours). **Murrays** (☎ 13 22 51; www.murrays.com.au) buses head to Canberra ($37, 4½ hours).

NAROOMA TO MORUYA

From Narooma the highway heads inland to avoid a series of saltwater lakes (inlets, lagoons…call them what you will), leaving a long stretch of little-visited coast clad in sections of **Eurobodalla National Park**. Once again, nearly any right-hand turn can be rewarding, especially if you're a surfer.

The council operates **Dalmeny camp site** (☎ 0428 635 641; sites per two adults & 2 children $17),

close to **Brou Beach**. There's a free, basic **camp site** within the park at **Brou Lake**. **Potato Point** has a decent surf break.

One of the highlights of the national park is the incredible rock formations at **Bingi Point**. It's here that the **Bingi Dreaming Track** commences, a 7½km walk following a spiritually significant Aboriginal route (pick up a brochure from NPWS in Narooma). Keep an eye out for kangaroos, wallabies, bandicoots and goannas. The path finishes at **Congo**, a pretty and peaceful spot, where there's a **camp site** (☎ 4476 2888; per adult/child $10/5) between the estuary and the surf beach

From Congo a dirt road heads through beautiful forest to **Moruya Heads**, where there's a good surf beach and views from Toragy Point. From here it's a 7km drive west along the river to Moruya.

MORUYA

☎ 02 / pop 2430

Its name means black swan but this town is no ugly duckling, with a pleasant collection of Victorian buildings gathered around a broad river. There's a popular weekly **market** (☎ 4474 4106; ☾ 9am-noon Sat) on the south side of Moruya Bridge. **Moruya Library** (☎ 4474 1333; Vulcan St) is also a visitors centre and has free internet access.

The best place to stay is **Post & Telegraph B&B** (☎ 4474 5745; www.southcoast.com.au/postandtel; cnr Page & Campbell Sts; s/d from $100/135), the beautifully restored old post office, which features polished floorboards, iron beds and verandas overlooking gardens. Of the three rooms only one has an en suite.

River (☎ 4474 5505; 16B Church St; mains $26-32; ✇ lunch Wed-Sun, dinner Wed-Sat; ✺) is right on the…you guessed it. The food is proof that rural doesn't mean bumpkin: Mod Oz mixes liberally with international flavours on the ever-changing menu.

Moruya Airport (☎ 4474 2095; George Bass Dr) is 7km from town, near North Head. **Rex** (☎ 13 17 13; www.rex.com.au) flies here from Merimbula ($83, 30 minutes, two daily) and Sydney (from $125, 50 minutes, daily).

Murrays (☎ 13 22 51; www.murrays.com.au) buses head to Canberra ($29, 3¼ hours). **Premier Motor Service** (☎ 13 34 10; www.premierms.com.au) stop on the run between Sydney ($45, seven hours) and Melbourne ($64, 11½ hours) via Narooma ($10, 35 minutes) and Batemans Bay ($8, 30 minutes).

As an alternative to the Princes Hwy, you can turn right after the bridge and follow the coastal George Bass Dr to Batemans Bay.

MOGO
☎ 02 / pop 260

Mogo is a historic strip of wooden shops and houses almost entirely devoted to Devonshire teas, crafts and antiques.

Just off the highway is **Old Mogo Town** (☎ 4474 2123; www.oldmogotown.com.au; James St; adult/child $15/8; ✇ 10am-5pm), a rambling re-creation of a pioneer village, complete with free gold-panning. You can stay in smart **cabins** (dm/s/d/tw/tr/q $25/100/115/155/135/150, ste $110-150; ☑) inside the complex, giving you a good opportunity to play pioneer after dark.

Mogo Zoo (☎ 4474 4930; 222 Tomakin Rd; adult/child $20/10; ✇ 9am-5pm), 2km east off the highway, is a small but interesting zoo where you can get terrifyingly close to the big cats. The stars of the show are the playful and rare white lions.

Suzanne's Coffee House (☎ 4474 3238; 15 Sydney St; meals $9-15; ✇ brunch & lunch) is also a sourdough bakery and organic grocery, so the focus is on delicious sandwiches stuffed full of salad and deli ingredients.

BATEMANS BAY
☎ 02 / pop 10,850

Although Canberra's 150km away, Batemans Bay is effectively its beach, which explains why it's one of the south coast's largest holiday centres. The suburban sprawl along the beaches south of the dreary town centre has

rendered it charmless in comparison to the beautiful coast surrounding it.

Information
Bay Bookshop (☎ 4472 6338; Blandford Centre, Orient St; ✇ 9am-5.30pm Mon-Fri, 9am-4pm Sat, 10am-2pm Sun) Independent store with good selection of local titles.
Post office (☎ 4475 3620; 7 Orient St; ✇ 9am-5pm)
Visitors centre (☎ 4472 6900; cnr Beach Rd & Princes Hwy; ✇ 9am-5pm) Has internet access ($2 per 15 minutes).

Sights & Activities
The **Old Courthouse Museum** (☎ 4472 8993; Museum Place; adult/child $5/1; ✇ midday-3pm Tue & Thu, 8am-noon most Sun), just off Orient St, has displays relating to local history. Just behind the museum is the small **Water Garden Town Park** and a **boardwalk** through wetlands.

Merinda Cruises (☎ 4472 4052; Boatshed, Clyde St; adult/child $27/14) takes a three-hour trip up the Clyde River to Nelligen. **Bluefin Adventures** (☎ 0427 220 238; Main Wharf; adult/child $55/29) heads out to sea where you might see dolphins and penguins at the **Tollgate Islands Nature Reserve** in the bay and, in season, whales.

Birdland Animal Park (☎ 4472 5364; 55 Beach Rd; adult/child $16/8; ✇ 9.30am-4pm), near Batehaven, has the usual collection of cute Aussie critters.

The closest beach to the town centre is **Corrigans Beach**. South of this a series of small beaches dot the rocky shore. There are longer beaches along the coast north of the bridge, leading into Murramarang National Park.

Surfers flock to **Surf Beach**, **Malua Bay**, small **McKenzies Beach** (just south of Malua Bay) and **Bengello Beach**, which has waves when everywhere else is flat. For the experienced, the best surfing is at **Pink Rocks** (near Broulee) when a north swell is running. Locals say the waves are sometimes 6m high. **Broulee** itself has a wide crescent of sand, but there's a strong rip at the northern end.

Sleeping
There are many holiday apartments offering weekly rentals; enquire at **LJ Hooker** (☎ 4472 9294; www.ljhooker.com.au/batemansbay). If your karaoke repertoire stretches to *Proud Mary*, you might want to consider a houseboat. Both **Bay River Houseboats** (☎ 4472 5649; www.bayriverhouseboats.com.au; Wray St) and **Clyde River Houseboats** (☎ 4472 6369; www.clyderiverhouseboats.com.au; Wray St) have eight- and 10-berth vessels available. Prices for three-night rentals start from $510 in the low season but double during the peak.

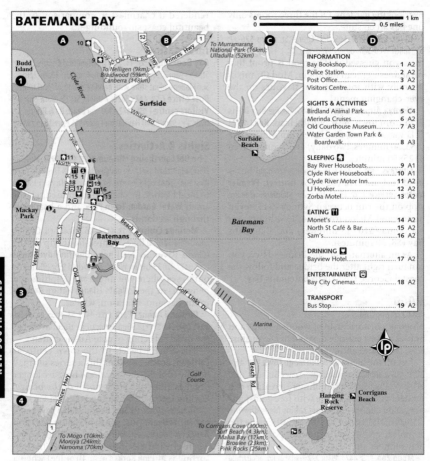

BATEMANS BAY

INFORMATION

Bay Bookshop	1 A2
Police Station	2 A2
Post Office	3 A2
Visitors Centre	4 A2

SIGHTS & ACTIVITIES

Birdland Animal Park	5 C4
Merinda Cruises	6 A2
Old Courthouse Museum	7 A3
Water Garden Town Park & Boardwalk	8 A3

SLEEPING

Bay River Houseboats	9 A1
Clyde River Houseboats	10 A1
Clyde River Motor Inn	11 A2
LJ Hooker	12 A2
Zorba Motel	13 A2

EATING

Monet's	14 A2
North St Café & Bar	15 A2
Sam's	16 A2

DRINKING

Bayview Hotel	17 A2

ENTERTAINMENT

Bay City Cinemas	18 A2

TRANSPORT

Bus Stop	19 A2

Zorba Motel (☎ 4472 4804; www.zorbamotel.com.au; 15 Orient St; s $85-95, d $100-110; ✹) You can't beat the views from Zorba's front rooms. The motel is little changed in decades but continues to offer an old-fashioned Greek welcome.

Clyde River Motor Inn (☎ 4472 6444; www.clyde motel.com.au; 3 Clyde St; s $102-112, d $107-152, q $182; ✹) An older motel on the river in the centre of town, this one's bathed in the sweet smell of jasmine. Rooms are clean and some have views.

Corrigans Cove (☎ 4472 6111; www.corriganscove.com.au; 204 Beach Rd; apt $165-300; ✹ ✹) These flash apartments have all the mod cons (including laundry and dishwashers) and a swimming pool that resembles a giant pac-man.

Eating

Monet's (☎ 4472 5717; 3/1 Orient St; mains $7-20; ✹ breakfast & lunch Mon-Sat) The gentle hues of Monet's waterlilies cover the walls of this snug Mediterranean café. Organic produce and free-range eggs are the norm and there are plenty of vegetarian options available.

our pick North St Café & Bar (☎ 4472 5710; 5 North St; mains $8-20; ✹ 8.30am-4.30pm Mon-Thu, 8.30am-late Fri & Sat) While much of Batemans Bay seems to be stuck in the Golden Age Of Motels, this café is a beacon of modernity – from its shiny counter to its range of organic and gluten-free treats. On Fridays and Saturdays you can kick-start the day with a first-rate coffee and then head back in the evening for cocktails.

Sam's (☎ 4472 6687; Orient St; mains $11-18; ✦ lunch Wed-Fri, dinner Wed-Mon) Grab a seat by the water at this classic old-school Italian, with a devoted following of locals who come for the fresh seafood and unpretentious pasta and pizza.

Drinking & Entertainment

Bayview Hotel (☎ 4472 4522; 20 Orient St; ✦ 10am-midnight) The only real pub in town, it attracts everyone from tourists chilling to yobbos yelling. There's a lively roster of bands, DJs and trivia nights.

Bay City Cinemas (☎ 4472 6009; www.baycitycinemas.com.au; Perry St; tickets $10.50-11.50) Blockbusters for rainy days.

Getting There & Away

The scenic Kings Hwy climbs the escarpment and heads to Canberra from just north of Batemans Bay. Both **Murrays** (☎ 13 22 51; www.murrays.com.au) and the **Surfborder Express** (☎ 6241 0033; www.transborder.com.au) service this route (both $24, 2½ hours).

Premier Motor Service (☎ 13 34 10; www.premierms.com.au) coaches stop on the run between Sydney ($41, six hours) and Melbourne ($68, 12 hours) via Ulladulla ($13, one hour) and Moruya ($8, 30 minutes).

CANBERRA

☎ 02 / pop 322,000

Don't let the dismissiveness of Australians about their capital put you off. Canberra may not be the most riveting city to live in, but it's a fascinating place to visit. Sure, Mussolini would have approved of the grand avenues and triumphal parades, but the geometrical precision of its layout has created a green and spacious city with uplifting vistas at every turn.

When the separate colonies of Australia were federated in 1901, a decision to build a national capital was included in the constitution. American architect Walter Burley Griffin won the competition to design it and in 1908 this site, diplomatically situated between rivals Sydney and Melbourne, was selected. In 1911 the Commonwealth government bought land for the ACT and in 1913 christened the capital Canberra, a name derived from an Aboriginal term for 'meeting place'.

An exploration of Canberra will unearth some of the best examples of modern Australian architecture and some of the grandest public edifices and cultural attractions that taxes can buy.

ORIENTATION

The city is arranged around Lake Burley Griffin. Approaching from the north, the main arterial road, Northbourne Ave, dissects the city centre (aka Civic). The pedestrian malls to its east comprise Canberra's main shopping areas.

Northbourne Ave becomes Commonwealth Ave, which spans Lake Burley Griffin and intersects Capital Circle. This road encircles Capital Hill, the apex of Walter Burley Griffin's parliamentary triangle. Located within and near the triangle are many noteworthy buildings.

Maps

The visitors centre stocks city maps and cartography for bushwalks.

Mapworld (☎ 6230 4097; 65 Northbourne Ave, Civic) Extensive selection of maps and Lonely Planet guidebooks.

NRMA (☎ 6222 7000; Canberra Centre, City Walk, Civic) Information for motorists and road maps.

INFORMATION

The YHA (p161) has a reliable, central internet café.

Canberra Hospital (☎ 6244 2222, emergency dept 6244 2611; Yamba Dr, Garran)

General post office (☎ 13 13 18; 53-73 Alinga St, Civic) Mail can be addressed: poste restante Canberra GPO, Canberra City, ACT 2601.

National Library Bookshop (☎ 6262 1424; Parkes Pl, Parkes) Superb selection of Australian books.

Visitors centre (☎ 1300 554 114; www.visitcanberra.com.au; 330 Northbourne Ave, Dickson; ✦ 9am-5.00pm Mon-Fri, 9am-4pm Sat & Sun)

SIGHTS

Most of Canberra's significant buildings, museums and galleries are scattered around Lake Burley Griffin. You can easily walk here from Civic, Manuka or Kingston. Otherwise any bus heading over the Commonwealth Ave bridge can drop you outside the National Library.

Parliament House

The four-legged, 81m flagpole atop Capital Hill marks the location of **Parliament House** (☎ 6277 5399; www.aph.gov.au; admission free; ✦ 9am-5pm), an accomplished piece of modern architecture in harmony with its environment. The public spaces contain informative displays,

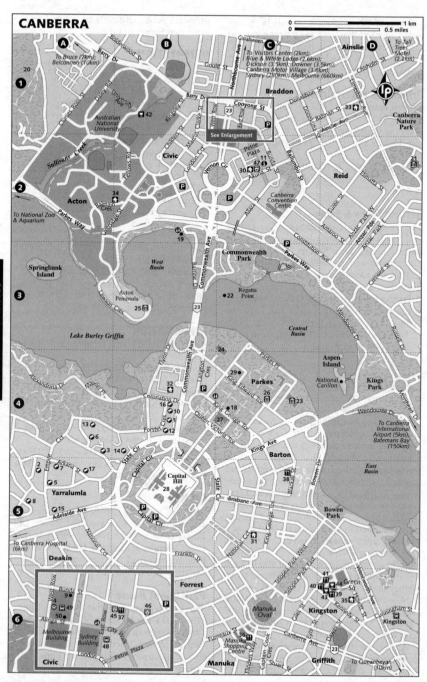

INFORMATION	SIGHTS & ACTIVITIES	EATING 🍴
Canadian High	Aboriginal Tent Embassy.............. **18** C4	Ginseng..........................**36** C6
Commission.....................**1** B4	Acton Park Ferry Terminal...............**19** B2	Milk & Honey.....................**37** B6
Dutch Embassy.......................**2** A5	Australian National Botanic Gardens.**20** A1	Ottoman Cuisine.................**38** C5
French Embassy......................**3** A6	Australian War Memorial...............**21** D2	Pizzazz Café.......................**39** D6
General Post Office.................**4** B1	Captain Cook Memorial Water Jet...**22** C3	Portia's Place.....................**40** D6
German Embassy....................**5** A5	National Gallery of Australia..........**23** C4	Silo Bakery.......................**41** D6
Indonesian Embassy................**6** A4	National Library of Australia............**24** C3	
Irish Embassy........................**7** A5	National Museum of Australia.........**25** B3	DRINKING 🍸
Japanese Embassy..................**8** A5	National Portrait Gallery................**26** C4	ANU Union Bar..................**42** B1
Mapworld.............................**9** A6	Old Parliament House.................**27** C4	B Bar................................**43** D6
National Library Bookshop....(see 24)	Parliament House.......................**28** B5	Filthy McFadden's..............**44** D6
New Zealand High	Questacon – National Science &	
Commission.....................**10** B4	Technology Centre.....................**29** C4	ENTERTAINMENT 🎭
NRMA................................**11** C1		Academy.........................**45** B6
Papua New Guinea High	SLEEPING 🛏	Dendy Canberra Centre......**46** B6
Commission.....................**12** B4	Canberra City YHA................. **30** C2	Ticketek............................**47** C2
Singapore High Commission...**13** A4	Hotel Realm.......................**31** C5	
South African Embassy...........**14** B4	Hyatt Hotel Canberra..............**32** B4	TRANSPORT
Thai Embassy...................... **15** A5	Olims Hotel Canberra...............**33** D1	Civic Bus Interchange..........**48** A6
UK High Commission.............**16** B4	University House.....................**34** B2	Jolimont Centre...................**49** A6
US Embassy..........................**17** A5	Victor Lodge........................ **35** D6	Qantas..............................**50** A6

an excellent collection of Aboriginal art and a 1297 edition of the *Magna Carta*.

Free guided tours (45-minutes on non-sitting days, 20-minutes otherwise) are held every half-hour from 9am to 4pm. You're welcome to find your own way around but you may have to queue to watch parliamentary proceedings from the public galleries. Note that tickets for question time (2pm on sitting days) are free, but must first be booked through the **Sergeant at Arms** (☎ 6277 4889); get them by midday or you may miss out. Tickets aren't required for other sessions in either house. Inside, the red and green of Britain's parliamentary chambers has been transmuted into the pale hues of a eucalyptus forest.

Bus 39 runs to Parliament House from Civic.

Old Parliament House

Elegant **Old Parliament House** (☎ 6270 8222; www .oph.gov.au; King George Tce, Parkes; adult/concession $2/1; 🕙 9am-5pm), the seat of government from 1927 to 1988, is much smaller than its replacement. There's a fascinating, free, 40-minute guided tour (departs every 45 minutes from 9.30am to 11.45am and 12.45pm to 3.45pm), or guide yourself via a free leaflet.

Opposite the main entrance is the **Aboriginal Tent Embassy**, established in 1972 in response to governmental refusal to recognise land rights.

National Gallery of Australia

This excellent **gallery** (☎ 6240 6502; www.nga.gov.au; Parkes Pl, Parkes; permanent collection free; 🕙 10am-5pm)

showcases Australian art, including important paintings by Arthur Boyd, Sidney Nolan and Grace Cossington Smith. Aboriginal works include the wonderful *Aboriginal Memorial* (1988), a forest of 200 burial logs painted by 43 Arnhem Land artists for the bicentenary of colonisation. Of the international pieces featured, perhaps the most famous is Jackson Pollock's *Blue Poles: Number 11, 1952.*

There are all-inclusive guided tours (11am and 2pm), along with one focusing on Aboriginal and Torres Strait Islander art (11am Thursday and Sunday). The gallery often has free lectures and film screenings; phone for details.

National Portrait Gallery

By late 2008 the **National Portrait Gallery** (www.portrait.gov.au; King Edward Tce, Parkes; admission free; 🕙 10am-5pm) should be in a flash new home. Its wonderful collection of painting, sculpture and photos has as its subjects Australians famous and obscure, historical and contemporary. Favourites include a luridly spray-painted Nick Cave by Howard Arkley (1999).

Lake Burley Griffin

Named after Canberra's architect, Lake Burley Griffin was created by damming the Molonglo River in 1963. Swimming is not recommended, but the lake is suitable for boating and great to cycle around. Boats, bikes and in-line skates are available for hire at Acton Park ferry terminal, on the northern shore.

Around the lake's 35km shoreline are many places of interest. The most visible is the **Captain Cook Memorial Water Jet**, built in 1970 for the bicentenary of Captain Cook's landfall.

Australian War Memorial

The colossal **war memorial** (☎ 6243 4211; www.awm .gov.au; Treloar Cres, Campbell; admission free; ☒ 10am-5pm) is set in beautiful grounds at the foot of Mt Ainslie, littered with mature trees, sculpture and big guns. It houses an interesting collection of dioramas, relics and exhibitions. Free 90-minute guided tours are held throughout the day.

Entombed in the glorious **Hall of Memory** is the **Unknown Australian Soldier**, whose remains were returned from a WWI battlefield in 1993. The hall itself is steeped in symbolism, with church-like stained glass and an exquisite 1958 mosaic covering the roof and walls with over six million Italian tiles. It's here that the cult of the Anzac (Australian and New Zealand Army Corps) reaches its apotheosis, the figures haloed like religious icons. Even those uncomfortable with Australia's unquestioning glorification of its military will be impressed.

The view down **Anzac Pde** across the lake to Parliament shows Canberra at its most planned, geometric and grandiose. It's well worth walking to the lake to view the various military memorials stretched along the road like an open-air gallery of 20th-century monument design.

To get to the War Memorial catch bus 33 from Civic.

Australian National Botanic Gardens

Spreading over 90 hectares of the lower slopes of Black Mountain, **Australian National Botanic Gardens** (☎ 6250 9540; www.anbg.gov.au/anbg; Clunies Ross St, Acton; admission free; ☒ 8.30am-5pm) is devoted to the growth, study and promotion of Australian plants. Dedicated trails take in the highlights of the gardens, including sections of rainforest and themed plantings.

Its **visitors centre** (☒ 9am-4.30pm) has maps and is the departure point for free guided walks (11am and 2pm, plus 9.30am in spring and summer).

Bus 81 from Civic will take you directly to the gardens on weekends, public holidays and school holidays. If you're feeling fit, it's a pleasant walk to the gardens through the grounds of the Australian National University.

National Museum of Australia

This **museum** (☎ 6208 5000; www.nma.gov.au; Lawson Cres, Acton Peninsula; admission free; ☒ 9am-5pm), a dramatic modern construction on the northern shore of the lake, showcases the land, nation and people of Australia through Australian eyes and with the aid of interactive gizmos. There are attendants on hand to help you navigate exhibitions on environmental change, indigenous culture, national icons and more, and you can take one-hour guided tours (adult/child $7.50/5.50). First Australians tours are held at 11am and Highlights tours are held at midday, 1.30pm and 3pm.

Bus 34 from Civic runs here.

National Library of Australia

The **National Library of Australia** (☎ 6262 1111; www .nla.gov.au; Parkes Pl, Parkes; admission free; ☒ main reading room 9am-9pm Mon-Thu, 9am-5pm Fri & Sat, 1.30-5pm Sun) is one of the most elegant buildings in Canberra, with an effective use of stained glass in its frontage.

It holds more than six million items, including rare books, paintings, early manuscripts, photographs, oral histories and maps. Bookings are required for the free, 45-minute **Behind-the-Scenes Tour** (☎ 6262 1271; ☒ tour 12.30pm Thu). The **Exhibition Gallery** (admission free; ☒ 9am-5pm) presents thematic displays collated mainly from the library's diverse collections.

Questacon – National Science & Technology Centre

This hands-on **museum** (☎ 6270 2800; www.questa con.edu.au; King Edward Tce, Parkes; adult/child $18/11.50; ☒ 9am-5pm) is educational and great fun. The 200-plus interactive exhibits show how science and technology work in everyday life.

National Zoo & Aquarium

This impressive **zoo** (☎ 6287 8400; www.zooquarium .com.au; Lady Denman Dr, Yarralumla; adult/child $26.50/14.50; ☒ 10am-5pm) is near Scrivener Dam at the western end of Lake Burley Griffin.

Bus 81 from Civic heads to the Zoo before stopping at the Botanic Gardens, but only on weekends, public holidays and school holidays.

Embassies

Being a relatively new capital, many nations have custom-built their embassies. The Yarralumla embassy zone is a fascinating place to explore if you're a fan of 20th-century architecture. Many incorporate elements of their respective cultures. The Papua New Guinea High Commission (Forster Cres) is shaped like a traditional building and decorated with colourful paintings, while New Zealand's has a corrugated-iron cow sculpture.

FESTIVALS & EVENTS

National Multicultural Festival (www.multicultural festival.com.au) Celebrated over 10 days in February.

Royal Canberra Show (www.rncas.org.au/showwebsite/ main.html) The country meets the city (it's not that far to travel) at the end of February.

Celebrate Canberra Festival (www.celebratecanberra .com) Canberra's extended birthday party, held mid-March.

National Folk Festival (www.folkfestival.asn.au) Held Easter weekend.

Floriade (www.floriadeaustralia.com) A month-long celebration of spring flowers, held in September/October.

SLEEPING

This is a government town. There are very few bargains and even shoddy choices dry up when Parliament is sitting. It pays to book ahead. There's hardly any accommodation in the livelier suburbs, such as Manuka and Kingston. Most motels are spread out along Northbourne Ave. The inner city has some options but parking can be a problem.

Budget

Canberra Motor Village (☎ 6247 5466; www.canberra village.com; Kunzea St, O'Connor; camp sites per 2 people $26, cabins $109-175; 🗷 🗩) Dozing in peaceful bush 6km northwest of the centre, the orderly arrangement of tidy cabins and camp sites mirrors Canberra itself.

Canberra City YHA (☎ 6248 9155; canberracity@ yhansw.org.au; 7 Akuna St, Civic; dm $28-34, r/tr $89/112; 🗷 🗩 🗩) This large, bright complex offers plenty of potential to mingle, with its rooftop barbecue area, bar, indoor swimming pool, spa, pool tables and comfy lounge.

Victor Lodge (☎ 6295 7777; www.victorlodge.com .au; 29 Dawes St, Kingston; s/d & tw $69/85; 🗷 🗩 ; wi-fi) Far from flash yet quite presentable, this large house offers clean rooms with shared facilities and a communal kitchen.

Midrange

Blue & White Lodge (☎ 6248 0498; blueandwhitelodge@ bigpond.com; 524 Northbourne Ave, Downer; s/d $95/100; 🗷) Somewhere between a brick-and-tile home and the Parthenon (Ionian columns and pediments) this family-run B&B offers cooked

breakfasts and comfortable, clean rooms. It also has the identical **Canberran Lodge** (528 Northbourne Ave, Downer) a couple of doors down.

Olims Hotel Canberra (☎ 6243 0000; www.olims hotel.com; cnr Ainslie & Limestone Aves, Braddon; r $115-209; 🗷 🗩 ; wi-fi) This 1927 heritage-listed building and its later refurbishments surround a lovely courtyard. The 1st-floor, self-contained 'loft' rooms are more spacious and have balconies overlooking the garden.

Tall Trees Motel (☎ 6247 9200; www.bestwestern .com.au/talltrees; 21 Stephen St, Ainslie; r $119-149; 🗷) The green grounds of this motel and its location in leafy Ainslie lend it a relaxed air. It's a good place to base yourself if you want to be near but not in the centre.

ourpick **University House** (☎ 6125 5211; www .anu.edu.au/unihouse; 1 Balmain Cres, Acton; s $123-136, tw/d $123/136; 🗷 🗩 ; wi-fi) Restored rather than renovated, this glorious 1950s building (with furniture to match), is soothingly positioned amid the rambling university grounds. The rooms are actually minisuites; many have balconies.

Top End

Hotel Realm (☎ 6163 1888; hotelrealm.com.au; 18 National Circuit, Barton; r/ste from $245/275; 🗷 🗩 🗩 ; wi-fi) From its shiny chrome lettering to its cavernous reception void, everything about this large hotel screams modern – albeit in a painfully tasteful grey-on-grey way. You may find it hard to drag yourself out of the comfy beds.

Hyatt Hotel Canberra (☎ 6270 1234; www.canberra .park.hyatt.com; Commonwealth Ave, Yarralumla; r $310-610, ste from $750; 🗷 🗩 🗩 ; wi-fi) Staff zing to attention in plus-fours at this Gatsby-esque, Art Deco hotel. You can almost smell the whiff of past power-plays in the diplomatic suites. The illusion fades in the newer wing, where it's back to the Hyatt world of comfortable normality.

EATING

Most restaurants are in Civic, Kingston, Manuka and Griffith. There's a fantastic Asian strip in Dickson and many other possibilities scattered throughout the suburbs.

Restaurants

Ginseng Restaurant (☎ 6260 8346; 15 Flinders Way, Manuka; lunch mains $11-26; ☽ lunch & dinner) Making up for its shoebox size by spilling onto the street, Ginseng serves modern Chinese dishes and lots of vegetarian options.

Portia's Place (☎ 6239 7970; 11 Kennedy St, Kingston; mains $17-29; ☽ lunch Sun-Fri, dinner daily) The effervescent Portia is very much the host at this popular and accomplished traditional Chinese restaurant. It's a good place to spot politicians.

our pick **Ottoman Cuisine** (☎ 6273 6111; cnr Broughton & Blackall Sts, Barton; mains $29-35; 🕑 lunch Tue-Fri, dinner Tue-Sat) A real sense-of-occasion restaurant, Ottoman is to Turkish what Mod Oz is to meat-and-two-veg. The service is impeccable, there's a good wine list and the mezze plates are amazing.

Cafés & Self-catering

Silo Bakery (☎ 6260 6060; 36 Giles St, Kingston; mains $3-15; 🕑 7am-4pm) Popular to the point of insanity, this legendary bakery and cheese shop has café seating and an excellent breakfast menu.

Milk & Honey (☎ 6247 7722; Garema Pl, Civic; breakfast $5-16, lunch $11-22, dinner $18-29; 🕑 breakfast, lunch & dinner) There are lots of longstanding cafés on this alley but this newcomer has the most interesting food. Try the breakfast trifle or for something more substantial, the truffled scrambled eggs with avocado.

Pizzazz Café (☎ 6239 6200; 41 Kennedy St, Kingston; mains $10-19; 🕑 breakfast & lunch) Although the name sounds like a dodgy 1980s hairdresser, Pizzazz offers an interesting take on café fare with a vaguely Mexican bent.

DRINKING & ENTERTAINMENT

For entertainment listings, see the 'Fly' section of Thursday's *Canberra Times* and the free monthly street mag *bma*. **Ticketek** (☎ 132 849; www.ticketek.com.au; 11 Akuna St, Civic) sells tickets to major events.

B Bar (☎ 6295 1949; 21 Kennedy St, Kingston; 🕑 3pm-late) A slick place to toss back a few cocktails while snacking on tapas.

Filthy McFadden's (☎ 6239 5303; Green Sq, Kingston; 🕑 noon-late) There's a suitably dingy ambience at this better-than-average Irish pub with a big selection of beer on tap.

ANU Union Bar (☎ 6125 3660; www.anuunion.com .au; Union Court, Acton; 🕑 gigs 8pm) Has energetic live music up to three times a week during semester; usually around $10 for local bands, but cover charges can climb to $50.

Academy (☎ 6257 3355; www.academyclub.com .au; Bunda St, Civic; admission $5-15; 🕑 5pm-late Tue-Sat) The original movie screen of this former cinema dominates the crowded dance floor of this nightclub with frenetic, larger-than-life visuals.

Dendy Canberra Centre (☎ 6221 8900; www.dendy .com.au; 148 Bunda St, Civic; adult/child $15/11) A flash new art-house cinema complex.

GETTING THERE & AWAY
Air

Canberra International Airport (☎ 6275 2222; www.can berraairport.com.au) is serviced by four airlines:

Brindabella Airlines (☎ 1300 66 88 24; www .brindabellaairlines.com.au) Services Newcastle (70 minutes) and Albury (45 minutes).

Qantas (☎ 13 13 13; www.qantas.com.au; Jolimont Centre, Northbourne Ave, Civic) Heads to Brisbane (95 minutes), Sydney (50 minutes), Melbourne (one hour), Adelaide (1¾ hours) and Perth (four hours).

Tiger Airways (☎ 03-9335 3033; www.tigerairways .com) Services to/from Melbourne.

Virgin Blue (☎ 136 789; www.virginblue.com.au) Also has services to Sydney, Melbourne and Adelaide, plus the Gold Coast (90 minutes).

Bus

The interstate bus terminal is the **Jolimont Centre** (Northbourne Ave, Civic), which has free phone lines to the visitors centre.

Greyhound (☎ 13 14 99; www.greyhound.com.au; 🕑 Jolimont Centre office 7am-6pm) has frequent services to Sydney ($40, 3½ hours) and Melbourne ($89, nine hours).

Murrays (☎ 13 22 51; www.murrays.com.au; 🕑 Jolimont Centre counter 7am-6pm) has daily services to Sydney ($37, 3½ hours), Batemans Bay ($24, 2½ hours), Narooma ($37, 4½ hours) and Wollongong ($31, 3½ hours).

Surfborder Express (☎ 6241 0033; www.transborder .com.au) connects the capital to Batemans Bay ($24, 2½ hours) and Ulladulla ($35, 3½ hours).

Car & Motorcycle

The quickest route between Canberra and the coast is the Kings Hwy, passing through grazing land before descending the nearly sheer cliffs of the escarpment in a steep, winding, but extremely beautiful road through **Mongo National Park** to Batemans Bay (150km).

If you're fast-tracking it to Sydney (280km), take the Federal then the Hume Hwy. For Melbourne (660km), take the Barton Hwy and then the Hume. For the Victorian Coast, take the Monaro Hwy to Lakes Entrance (420km).

Train

Kingston train station (☎ 6295 1198; Burke Cres), off Wentworth Ave, is the city's rail terminus. Buses 35 and 39 run between here and Civic.

You can book trains and connecting buses inside the station at the **CountryLink travel centre** (☎ 13 22 32; www.countrylink.info; ☺ 6am-4.45pm Mon-Fri). CountryLink trains run to/from Sydney ($40, 4½ hours, two daily). There are no direct trains to Melbourne but you can catch a CountryLink coach to Yass and transfer to a train there but it will take a couple of hours longer than the direct bus.

GETTING AROUND
To/From the Airport
Canberra International Airport is 7km southeast of the city. A taxi to the city costs around $30. **Deane's Buslines** (☎ 6299 3722; www.deanesbuslines.com.au) operates the frequent AirLiner bus (one-way/return $9/15, 20 minutes) between the airport and the city.

Bus
Canberra's public transport provider is **Action** (☎ 131 710; www.action.act.gov.au), with routes that criss-cross the city.

You can purchase single-trip tickets (adult/concession $3/1.50), but a better deal is a daily ticket (adult/concession $6.60/3.30). Prepurchase tickets from Action agents (including the visitors centre and some newsagents) or buy them from the driver.

Taxi
Cab Express (☎ 6260 6011)
Canberra Cabs (☎ 13 22 27)

SHOALHAVEN COAST

The coastal beauty is undiminished in this region, with its great beaches, state forests and numerous national parks, including the huge (190,751-hectare) Morton National Park in the westerly ranges. You're now in striking distance of Sydney, so expect holiday spots to fill up and prices to explode on the weekends and school holidays.

MURRAMARANG NATIONAL PARK
This beautiful 11,978-hectare **coastal park** (admission per car $7) begins just above Batemans Bay and extends to within 20km of Ulladulla. If you haven't seen a kangaroo in the wild yet, here's your chance. At dawn and dusk large numbers of them wander out of the gum- and rainforests to the edges of lovely **Durras Lake**, while colourful parrots fill the trees.

Wasp Head, **Depot**, **Pebbly** and **Merry Beaches** are all popular with surfers and **Myrtle Beach** with nudists. We're not sure where nude surfers go. There are numerous walking trails snaking off from these beaches and a steep but enjoyable walk up **Durras Mountain** (283m).

At the north of the park, **Murramarang Aboriginal Area** encompasses the largest midden on the south coast, its remains suggesting 12,000 years of continual occupation. A self-guided walking track has been laid out with interpretive displays.

Sleeping
NPWS has idyllic **camp sites** (per adult/child $14/7) with showers, flushing toilets and barbecues at **Depot Beach** (☎ 4478 6582), **Pebbly Beach** (☎ 4478 6023) and **Pretty Beach** (☎ 4457 2019). Sites are scarce during school holidays; book ahead. It also rents tidy, self-contained **cabins** ($85-100) at Depot Beach and Pretty Beach, sleeping between four and six people.

Friendly **Durras Lake North Holiday Park** (☎ 4478 6072; www.durrasnorthpark.com.au; 57 Durras North Rd; camp sites per 2 people $20-25, cabins $70-225) has shady camp sites and cute cabins. It's very popular with kangaroos.

Another favourite of the marsupial mob is **EcoPoint Murramarang Resort** (☎ 4478 6355; www.murramarangresort.com.au; camp sites per 2 people $30-74, villas $129-381; ☒). It's a big, modern place with a row of Norfolk pines between it and the beach. Posh extras such as camp sites with en suites and cabins with spas are the norm.

Getting There & Away
The Princes Hwy forms the park's western edge, but it's 10km from the beaches. Many of the roads are pretty rough, but those to Durras, Durras Lake, Depot Beach and Durras North are all sealed, as is Mt Agony Rd to Pebbly Beach (but not Pebbly Beach Rd).

ULLADULLA
☎ 02 / pop 10,300
The harbour is the centre of life in this fishing-focussed town that lets its hair down at Easter for the **Blessing of the Fleet** ceremony. While Ulladulla can be a bit, well, dull, it does have some beautiful beaches.

North of the centre, gorgeous **Mollymook** stretches to over 2km of golden sand. **Narrawallee Beach**, the next one up, ends at a pretty kayak-friendly inlet. Both have beach breaks, although the serious surfers head for

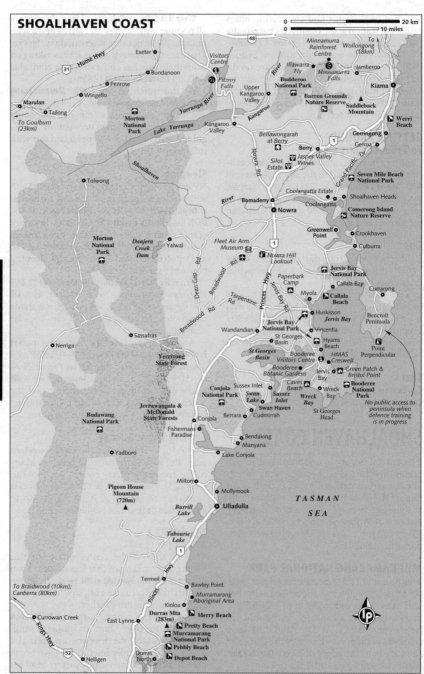

SHOALHAVEN COAST

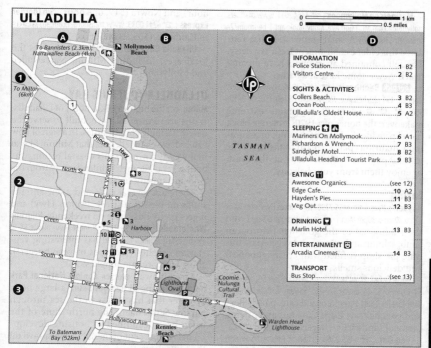

ULLADULLA

INFORMATION
Police Station..................................1 B2
Visitors Centre................................2 B2

SIGHTS & ACTIVITIES
Collers Beach..................................3 B2
Ocean Pool....................................4 B3
Ulladulla's Oldest House....................5 A2

SLEEPING
Mariners On Mollymook.....................6 A1
Richardson & Wrench.......................7 B3
Sandpiper Motel.............................8 B2
Ulladulla Headland Tourist Park..........9 B3

EATING
Awesome Organics........................(see 12)
Edge Cafe...................................10 A2
Hayden's Pies...............................11 B3
Veg Out.....................................12 B3

DRINKING
Marlin Hotel.................................13 B3

ENTERTAINMENT
Arcadia Cinemas...........................14 B3

TRANSPORT
Bus Stop...................................(see 13)

Collers Beach below the golf course, which offers left- and right-hand reef breaks and decent barrels. Immediately south of the harbour is a small beach with a large **ocean pool**.

Information
Post office (Princes Hwy)
Visitors centre (☎ 4455 1269; www.shoalhavenholidays .com.au; Princes Hwy; ☯ 10am-6pm Mon-Fri, 9am-5pm Sat & Sun) Has internet access (per half hour $1.25)

Sights & Activities
The **Coomee Nulunga Cultural Trail** is a 700m walking trail established by the local Aboriginal Land Council. It begins near Lighthouse Oval (take Deering St east of the highway) and follows a path forged by the Rainbow Serpent (an important being in Aboriginal mysticism) from the headland through native bush to the beach.

In comparison to the trail, **Ulladulla's Oldest House** (☎ 4455 6996; www.miltonulladullahistoricalsociety inc.org.au; 275 Green St; admission free; ☯ 9am-5pm Mon & Wed-Fri, 9am-4pm Sat, 10am-3pm Sun) is a youngster, having been built in 1850. It's now a speciality tea shop but gawkers are welcome.

Climbing **Pigeon House Mountain** (720m), in the far south of Morton National Park, is an enjoyable challenge. A road runs close to the summit, from where it's a walk of over three hours and 5km to the top and back. The last stretch features steep steps and ladders. The main access road leaves the highway 5km north of Ulladulla just before Milton, then it's 28km to the car park.

Sleeping
For holiday home rentals try **Richardson & Wrench** (☎ 4455 3999; www.randwulladulla.com.au; cnr Princes Hwy & South St).

Ulladulla Headland Tourist Park (☎ 4455 2457; www.holidayhaven.com.au; South St; camp sites per person $10-20, cabins $70-235; ☒) Not skimping on the 'park' part of the tourist park equation, this headland property has a lovely, leafy setting with ample ocean views. Facilities are good and well-kept.

Sandpiper Motel (☎ 4455 1488; www.sandpiper motel.com.au; 78 Princes Hwy; s/d $70/75; ☒ ☒) Clean rooms, friendly staff, reasonable rates and a large DVD library separates this traditional motel from the other brick-and-tile places.

Mariners on Mollymook (☎ 4454 2011; www.mariners mollymook.com.au; 1 Golf Ave, Mollymook; apt 1-bedroom/2-bedroom $160/180) A smart renovation has rendered this older establishment fresh as a daisy. The self contained apartments have dreamy beach views; some have spa baths.

our pick **Bannisters** (☎ 4455 3044; www.bannisters .com.au; 191 Mitchell Pde, Mollymook; r $260-350, ste $410-560; ❄ ▢ ▣ ; wi-fi) The ultimate extreme makeover: the bones of a 1970s concrete block motel provide the basis of this hip, unassumingly luxurious place. Splash to the lip of the infinity pool for sublime views up the coast, or enjoy them from your balcony.

Eating

Hayden's Pies (☎ 4455 7798; 166 Princes Hwy; pies $3-5; ⏰ 6.30am-5.30pm Mon-Fri, 7am-4.30pm Sat & Sun) From the traditional to the gourmet (Moroccan lamb; salmon and prawn) and vegetarian, this little pie shop is filled with crusty goodness and delicious smells.

Edge Cafe (☎ 4454 3565; cnr Green & Boree Sts; breakfast $4-13, lunch $7-14, dinner $22-26; ⏰ 9am-4.30pm Mon-Thu, 9am-late Fri & Sat) Part licensed café, part gallery and part bakery, Edge Cafe has an enticing menu of sandwiches, bagels, pasta and pizza.

Veg Out (☎ 4455 2266; Bellbrook Arcade, 95 Princes Hwy; mains $5-10; ⏰ 8am-4pm Mon-Fri, 8am-2pm Sat) The awesome coffee may not be conducive to veging out, but the organic, meat-free salads, wraps, quiches and cakes certainly are. Stock up on earth-friendly groceries at **Awesome Organics** (⏰ 9.30am-5pm Mon-Thu, 10.30am-5pm Fri), two doors down.

Bannisters Restaurant (☎ 4455 3044; 191 Mitchell Pde; breakfast $14-17, dinner $29-42; ⏰ breakfast daily, dinner Tue-Sun) Elegantly situated on Bannister's Point, 1km north of town, the Mod Oz fare matches the fine views, showcasing local ingredients in a creative menu.

Drinking & Entertainment

Marlin Hotel (☎ 4455 1999; cnr Princes Hwy & Wason St) There are harbour views from the back bar of this big old pub, and regular bands and DJs.

Arcadia Cinemas (☎ 4454 1224; Rowens Arcade, Boree St; tickets $10-12) Blockbuster and art-house movies make their way here.

Getting There & Away

Premier Motor Service (☎ 13 34 10; www.premierms .com.au) coaches stop on the run between Sydney ($31, five hours) and Melbourne ($76, 12¾ hours) via Batemans Bay ($13, one

hour) and Nowra ($17, one hour). **Surfborder Express** (☎ 6241 0033; www.transborder.com.au) heads to Canberra ($35, 3½ hours).

Ulladulla Bus Lines (☎ 4455 1674) services the local area, including Milton, Narrawallee and Mollymook.

ULLADULLA TO JERVIS BAY

Milton, on the highway 6km north of Ulladulla, is this area's original town, built to serve the nearby farming communities. In a sign of how values have changed, note that Milton, like so many early towns in this coastal region, was built several kilometres inland, away from the cold and stormy coast.

There are several cafés and a few antique shops on the main street (Princes Hwy) and it gets pretty busy here on weekends. **Pilgrims Wholefoods** (☎ 4455 3421; Princes Hwy; meals $5-9; ⏰ breakfast & lunch Mon-Sat) has interesting vegetarian lunches (six types of vege burger!), along with organic supplies.

The highway passes **Conjola National Park** before skirting **St Georges Basin**, a large body of water that has access to the sea through narrow **Sussex Inlet**. The north shore of the basin has succumbed to housing developments reminiscent of the suburban sprawl on the central coast.

JERVIS BAY

One of the most stunning spots on the south coast, this large, sheltered bay is a magical amalgamation of snow-white sand, crystalline waters, national parks and frolicking dolphins. Seasonal visitors include hordes of Sydney holidaymakers (summer and most weekends) and migrating whales (May to November).

To reach the bay you have to pass through sections of **Jervis Bay National Park**, 4854 hectares of low scrub and woodland, which shelter the endangered eastern bristlebird. The bay itself is a marine park.

In 1995 the Aboriginal community won a land claim in the Wreck Bay area and now jointly administers **Booderee National Park** (opposite) at the southern end of the bay. By a strange quirk this area is actually part of the ACT, not NSW.

Most of the development in Jervis Bay is on the western shore, around the settlements of **Huskisson** and **Vincentia** (combined population 3391). The northern shore has less tourist infrastructure. **Callala Bay** (population 2717), despite its close proximity to Huskisson, is cut off by the Currambene Creek – you have to drive back to the highway and head south (which is just the way the locals like it). **Beecroft Peninsula** forms the northeastern side of Jervis Bay, ending in the dramatic sheer wall of appropriately named **Point Perpendicular**. Most of the peninsula is navy land but is usually open to the public.

Sights & Activities

Huskisson (Huskie to her friends) is the centre for most tourist activities.

Lady Denman Maritime Museum (☎ 4441 5675; www.ladydenman.asn.au; cnr Woollamia Rd & Dent St; adult/ child $8/4; ☼ 10am-4pm) has an interesting historic collection as well as the 1912 *Lady Denman* ferry. Also here, **Timbery's Aboriginal Arts & Crafts** sells work produced by one family of artisans. The shop is normally staffed by Laddie, the entertaining patriarch.

Behind the pub, **Huskisson Sea Pool** (admission free; ☼ 7am-6pm Mon-Fri, 10am-5pm Sat & Sun) has salt water but is more like an Olympic pool than the usual ocean pools.

Dolphin Watch Cruises (☎ 4441 6311; www.dolphin watch.com.au; 50 Owen St; adult/child from $20/15) offers several dolphin and whale-watching trips on its custom catamaran.

The marine park is popular with divers, offering the chance to get close to grey nurse sharks and fur seals. **Deep 6 Diving** (☎ 4441 5255; www.deep6divingjervisbay.com; 64 Owen St) charges $100 for two boat dives, plus equipment hire ($150 with full gear).

Jervis Bay Sailing Charters (☎ 4441 8777; www .jervisbaysailingcharters.com.au; 9 Hawke St) offers two- or three-hour cruises on a luxury catamaran. The boat holds 12 passengers and rates vary widely.

Jervis Bay Kayaks (☎ 4441 7157; www.jervisbaykayaks .com; 13 Hawke St) offers rentals (two-hour/day $36/66) or guided half-day paddling and snorkelling trips ($96).

South of Huskisson, **Hyams Beach** is an attractive stretch of sand that is said to be the whitest in the world. It's a little like walking on warm snow.

BOODEREE NATIONAL PARK

Occupying Jervis Bay's southeastern spit, this sublime national park offers good swimming, surfing and diving on both bay and ocean beaches. Much of it is heath land, with some forest, including small pockets of rainforest.

Booderee means 'plenty of fish' and it's easy to see what a bountiful place this must

have been for the indigenous people. For personalised tours with an Aboriginal focus, talk to Wreck Bay identity **Uncle Barry** (☎ 0402-441 168).

There's a good **visitors centre** (☎ 4443 0977; www.booderee.gov.au; ☼ 9am-4pm) at the park entrance with walking-trail maps and information on camping. Inside the park is **Booderee Botanic Gardens** (☎ 4442 1122; ☼ 8.30am-4pm), which is a branch of the Australian National Botanic Gardens in Canberra and includes some enormous rhododendrons.

There are many walking trails around the park. Keep an eye out for the 206 species of bird, 27 species of land mammal and 23 species of reptile. Amphibian enthusiasts can thrill to the 15 species of frogs.

Entry to the park costs $10 per vehicle per 48 hours, or you can buy an unlimited annual pass for $40 (NPWS passes are not valid). There are idyllic camping grounds at **Green Patch** (camp sites $20-45 plus $10/5 per adult/child) and **Bristol Point** (camp sites $20-52 plus $10/5 per adult/child). For a more secluded experience try the basic camping at **Caves Beach** (camp sites $11 plus $10/5 per adult/child). Book through the visitors centre or via the internet up to three weeks in advance at peak times. There's a 24-hour self-registration system at the entrance to the park.

Surfing is good at Caves Beach, but the real drawcard is the **Pipeline** (aka Black Rock, Wreck Bay or Summercloud Bay), an A-grade reef break that produces 12-foot tubes in optimal conditions.

The park is also home to the naval training base HMAS *Creswell*, which is off limits to the public.

Sleeping

There's plenty of accommodation in Huskisson and Vincentia but it still pays to book ahead. Prices skyrocket on weekends. Hyams Beach is a relaxing place to stay, but options are limited to mainly private rentals; try **Hyams Beach Real Estate** (☎ 4443 0242; www .hyamsbeachholidays.com.au; 76 Cyrus St, Hyams Beach).

Huskisson Beach Tourist Resort (☎ 4441 5142; www.holidayhaven.com.au; Beach St; sites per 2 people $30-42, cabins $85-190; ☒) Run by the Shoalhaven Council, this well-equipped camping ground has a great location right on the beach and flash cabins.

Jervis Bay Motel (☎ 4441 5781; www.jervisbaymotel .com.au; 41 Owen St; r $115-165; ☒ ☒) An old-fashioned motel that's been tarted up, you'll find pleasant décor and quality furnishings, as well as lovely views from the upstairs rooms.

Jervis Bay Guesthouse (☎ 4441 7658; www.jervisbay guesthouse.com.au; 1 Beach St; r $175-235; ❇ ▣) This beautifully restored wooden guesthouse is opposite the beach, surrounded by tropical gardens. Most rooms have a beach view and wide verandas.

Paperbark Camp (☎ 4441 6066; www.paperbark camp.com.au; 59 Woollamia Rd; tent $320-450) Camp in ecofriendly style in one of 12 luxurious solar-powered safari tents, with comfy beds, gorgeous en suites and wrap-around decks. It's set in dense bush 3.5km from Huskisson; you can borrow kayaks to paddle up the creek to the bay.

Eating

Supply (☎ 4441 5815; 1/54 Owen St; mains $5-15; ❇ breakfast & lunch) The best of Huskisson's cafés, Supply doubles as a deli. Grab a newspaper and settle into the smart surroundings for a satisfying breakfast.

Hyams Beach Café (☎ 4443 3874; 76 Cyrus St, Hyams Beach; breakfast $8-14, lunch $14-17, dinner $24-29; ❇ breakfast & lunch daily, dinner Fri & Sat) Once a simple beach store, it's now a smart café selling fancy provisions, frilly gifts and copies of *Vogue Living*. The menu is varied and excellent; takeaways are a cheaper option.

Gunyah Restaurant (☎ 4441 7299; 59 Woollamia Rd; mains $29-32; ❇ breakfast & dinner) Sit under the canopy and watch the light change through the trees from the balcony of this acclaimed restaurant at Paperbark Camp (above). The focus is on local ingredients, although ordering 'roo has less appeal when there's a possibility of a live one walking past.

Drinking & Entertainment

Husky Pub (☎ 4441 5001; www.thehuskypub.com.au; Owen St) The funnest place in town has fabulous bay views from indoors and outside at the many picnic tables. There's live music most weekends.

Huskisson Pictures (☎ 4441 6343; www.huskpics .com.au; cnr Sydney & Owen Sts; tickets $8.50-9.50) This tiny picture house leans towards the art house.

Getting There & Away

Being off the highway, Jervis Bay is poorly served by public transport. **Stuart's Coaches** (☎ 4421 0332) runs a school-bus service from Nowra to Callala Bay.

NOWRA

☎ 02 / pop 27,480

From a traveller's perspective, Nowra's more of a means to an end rather than an end in itself. It may be the largest town in the Shoalhaven area but it doesn't have the charm of Berry, 17km northeast, or the beaches of Jervis Bay, 25km southeast. It is, however, the southernmost point that the train from Sydney stops on the east coast. There are some good eateries and when Jervis Bay fills up you can stop here and commute.

Information

NPWS office (☎ 4423 2170; 55 Graham St; ❇ 8.30am- 4.30pm Mon-Fri)

Post office (59 Junction St)

Visitors centre (☎ 4421 0778; www.shoalhaven.nsw .gov.au; cnr Princes Hwy & Pleasant Way; ❇ 9am-5pm) Internet is available ($1 per 15 minutes).

Sights & Activities

The 6.5-hectare **Nowra Wildlife Park** (☎ 4421 3949; www.nowrawildlifepark.com.au; Rock Hill Rd; adult/ child $16/8; ❇ 9am-5pm), on the north bank of the Shoalhaven River, is where you can kiss a cockatoo and meet other native animals. Head north from Nowra, cross the bridge and immediately turn left, then follow the signs.

Nowra Museum (☎ 4421 1228; cnr Kinghorne & Plunkett Sts; adult/child $1/50c; ❇ 1-4pm Sat & Sun) has heaps of old stuff. **Meroogal** (☎ 4421 8150; www .hht.net.au/museums/meroogal/; cnr West & Worrigee Sts; adult/child $8/4; ❇ 1-5pm Sat, 10am-5pm Sun) is a historic 1885 house containing the artefacts accumulated by four generations of women who lived there. Entry is by guided tours, which leave on the hour.

If you're at all interested in military planes and helicopters, **Fleet Air Arm Museum** (☎ 4424 1920; www.navy.gov.au/faam/; 489A Albatross Rd; adult/child $7/free; ❇ 10am-4pm), 10km south of Nowra, has an excellent display. Nearby **Nowra Hill lookout** offers expansive views over the plains to the escarpment.

The visitors centre produces a handy compilation of walks in the area. The relaxing **Ben's Walk** starts at the bridge near Scenic Dr and follows the south bank of the Shoalhaven River (6km return). North of the river, the circular 5.5km **Bomaderry Creek Walking Track** runs through sandstone gorges from a trailhead at the end of Narang Rd.

Shoalhaven River Cruises (☎ 0429 981 007; www.shoal havenrivercruise.com) has tours either up ($25, two

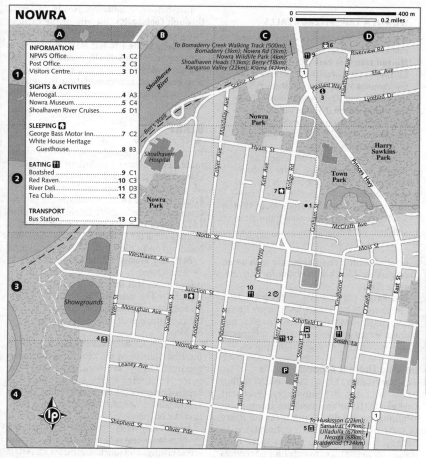

NOWRA

INFORMATION
NPWS Office..................................1	C2
Post Office....................................2	C3
Visitors Centre.............................3	D1

SIGHTS & ACTIVITIES
Meroogal.......................................4	A3
Nowra Museum............................5	C4
Shoalhaven River Cruises..........6	D1

SLEEPING
George Bass Motor Inn................7	C2
White House Heritage	
Guesthouse..............................8	B3

EATING
Boatshed.......................................9	C1
Red Raven...................................10	C3
River Deli....................................11	D3
Tea Club......................................12	C3

TRANSPORT
Bus Station.................................13	C3

SOUTH COAST
NEW SOUTH WALES

hours) or down ($35, three hours) the beautiful Shoalhaven River, leaving from the wharf just east of the bridge. Call ahead for times.

Sleeping

our pick **White House Heritage Guest House** (☎ 4421 2084; www.whitehouseguesthouse.com; 30 Junction St; s $85, d $100-130; ✻) A friendly family runs this beautifully restored guesthouse with comfortable en suite rooms. The light breakfast out on the wide veranda is a great way to start the day.

George Bass Motor Inn (☎ 4421 6388; www.george bass.com.au; 65 Bridge Rd; s $93-115, d $99-125; ✻) An unpretentious but well-appointed single-storey motor inn, the George Bass has clean and sunny rooms. The more expensive ones are slightly newer.

Eating

Boatshed (☎ 4421 2419; 10 Wharf Rd; breakfast $5-12, lunch $13-15, dinner $19-24; ✻ breakfast & lunch Sat & Sun, dinner Thu-Sat) Nowra's most atmospheric eating option is right by the river, almost under the bridge. Enjoy weekend brunch on the terrace or settle into the Mod Oz dinner menu.

River Deli (☎ 4423 1344; 84 Kinghorne St; meals $5-15; ✻ breakfast & lunch Mon-Sat) The smart set gathers at this trendy spot to pour over the stacks of newspapers and savour the array of deli items including filled baguettes and salads. The *barrista* with the Dali-esque moustache makes a mean coffee.

Tea Club (☎ 4422 0900; www.teaclub.com.au; 46 Berry St; breakfast $5-8, lunch $9-10; ✻ breakfast & lunch Mon-Sat) Nowra's bohemian set hangs out at this

---

WORTH A TRIP: FITZROY FALLS

Water falling 81m makes a big roar and that's what you hear at this stunning spot in **Morton National Park** (admission per vehicle $3). Even more spectacular is the view down the Yarrunga Valley from the sheer cliffs of the escarpment. There are various walks in the vicinity where if you're very lucky you might spot a platypus or a lyrebird. The **visitor centre** (☎ 4887 7270; ☼ 9am-5.30pm) has a café and good displays.

From either Nowra or Berry the road is a delight, heading through pretty Kangaroo Valley where the historic town is hemmed in by the mountains. Then it's over castle-like Hampden Bridge, an ostentatious 1898 sandstone affair, before taking the steep climb up the escarpment.

---

comfortable little vegetarian café with a vast back garden. Check its website for interesting live gigs.

Red Raven (☎ 4423 3433; 55 Junction St; lunch $13-20, dinner $20-28; ☼ lunch Tue-Fri, dinner Tue-Sat) Occupying the 1908 fire station, this BYO restaurant serves interesting Italian-influenced dishes with plenty of vegetarian options.

Getting There & Around

The **train station** (☎ 4423 0141; Meroo St) is 3km north of town at Bomaderry. Frequent **CityRail** (☎ 131 500; www.cityrail.info) trains go to Wollongong ($8.60, 75 minutes) via Berry ($3.40, 10 minutes), with connections to Sydney. Local buses link Nowra to the train station on weekdays with only limited services on Saturdays. Or take a **taxi** (☎ 4421 0333).

Premier Motor Service (☎ 13 34 10; www.premierms .com.au) coaches stop on the run between Sydney ($22, 3½ hours) and Melbourne ($76, 13¾ hours) via Ulladulla ($17, one hour).

AROUND NOWRA

East of Nowra, the Shoalhaven River meanders through dairy country in a system of estuaries and wetlands, finally reaching the sea at Crookhaven Heads.

On the north side of the estuary is **Shoalhaven Heads**, where the river once reached the sea but is now blocked by sandbars. Just north of the surf beach here is **Seven Mile Beach National Park** (admission free) stretching up to **Gerroa**.

Just before Shoalhaven Heads you pass through **Coolangatta**, the site of the earliest European settlement on NSW's south coast. **Coolangatta Estate** (☎ 4448 7131; www.coolangatta estate.com.au; s/d & tw $110/130; ☼ winery 10am-5pm) is a slick winery with a golf course, a good restaurant and accommodation in convict-built buildings. Prices nearly double on the weekends.

BERRY
☎ 02 / pop 1490

Berry has the potential to be a chintzy nightmare, yet somehow it maintains its considerable historic graces without folding under the weight of antique shops and Devonshire teas. Founded in the 1820s, it remained a private town on the Coolangatta Estate (above) until 1912. **Queen St**, Berry's short main street, is worth a stroll for its National Trust–classified buildings and a multitude of shops and cafés.

Pottering Around (☎ 4464 2177; 99 Queen St; ☼ 10am-4.30pm) is a gift shop with tourist information and internet access ($3 per 30 minutes). The **museum** (☎ 4464 3097; 135 Queen St; admission free; ☼ 11am-2pm Sat, 11am-3pm Sun), near the post office, is in an interesting 1884 bank building.

The popular **Berry Country Fair** is held on the first Sunday of the month at the showgrounds. On the last Saturday in May the peace is shattered by the caber-tossers and haggis-hurlers of the **Berry Celtic Festival** (☎ 4234 1346; Berry Showground; adult/child $10/5), not to mention the bagpipes.

Jasper Valley Wines (☎ 4464 1596; 152 Croziers Rd; ☼ 10am-4pm Fri-Sun) is 5km south of Berry, and offers tastings and lunches. Nearby, **Silos Estate** (☎ 4448 6082; www.thesilos.com; B640 Princes Highway, Jaspers Brush; lunch $25, dinner $30-33; ☼ lunch Thu-Sun, dinner Thu-Sat) also offers tastings along with an acclaimed restaurant.

Sleeping

Conjuring up images of cosy wood fires, Berry is a popular weekender in winter as well.

Berry Hotel (☎ 4464 1011; www.berryhotel.com.au; 120 Queen St; s/d midweek $45/70, s/d weekend $70/100) This country pub is a rarity – it caters to weekending city slickers without totally losing its status as a local watering hole. The rooms are standard pub bedrooms with bathrooms down the corridor, but large and well presented.

Bunyip Inn B&B (☎ 4464 2064; blakekittle@myoffice .net.au; 122 Queen St; s/d $90/120; ☼) Next to the Berry

---

GRAND PACIFIC DRIVE

In an attempt to distract travellers from charging along the freeway and bypassing their region, the good burghers of the Illawarra region are actively promoting a coastal alternative with the lofty name Grand Pacific Drive.

Start by turning right immediately after the bridge out of Nowra (in decidedly un-grand Bomaderry) and head towards Shoalhaven Heads. The route then passes through Gerroa, Gerringong, Kiama, and on to Wollongong and its northern beaches, before cutting through Royal National Park and rejoining the Princes Hwy above Waterfall.

The most scenic section is north of Wollongong, especially the stunning **Sea Cliff Bridge**, which sinuously curls along the base of the Illawarra Escarpment where it meets the ocean.

The only downside of this route is that it bypasses lovely Berry, but you can rectify that by starting from the dreamy back road from Berry to the coast, which starts as Prince Alfred St.

Hotel, this is an excellent place in one of the town's more impressive buildings: an old bank. There's a variety of spacious rooms, some with spas and all with loads of character.

Berry Village Boutique Motel (☎ 4464 3570; www .berrymotel.com.au; 72 Queen St; r $145-165 Sun-Thu, $175-195 Fri, $215-225 Sat; 🏊 🖳) Large, comfortable rooms are the go at this upmarket place at the edge of the main strip. The tiny pool, just off reception, seems to work more as a water-feature.

Bellawongarah at Berry (☎ 4464 1999; www .accommodation-berry.com.au; 869 Kangaroo Valley Rd, Bellawongarah; r/ste/cottage $200/250/260; 🖳) Misty, magical rainforest surrounds this wonderful place, 8km from Berry on the mountain road leading to Kangaroo Valley. Asian art features in the main house, while nearby an 1868 Wesleyan church has been given a French provincial makeover and is rented as a self-contained cottage for two. The lovely hostess serves up full country breakfasts.

Eating

Berry Woodfired Sourdough Bakery (☎ 4464 1617; 23 Prince Alfred St; mains $5-17; 🕑 breakfast & lunch Wed-Sun) Stock up on delicious bread or sit down for a light meal at this highly esteemed bakery, which attracts foodies from far and wide.

Coach House Restaurant (☎ 4464 1011; 120 Queen St; mains $15-25; 🕑 10am-late) The restaurant at the Berry Hotel offers a nice ambience and meals a cut above usual pub grub. Sit in the large covered beer garden or grab a table in the 1860 Kangaroo Inn, a single room brick building at the back.

Twenty Three (☎ 4464 2323; 85 Queen St; mains $23-25; 🕑 dinner Tue-Sat) There's a small but upmarket and stylish dining room inside as well as a courtyard and garden. The menu is adventurous: Mod Oz with an Asian influence.

Getting There & Away

Frequent **CityRail** (☎ 131 500; www.cityrail.info) trains go to Wollongong ($7.20, one hour) and Nowra ($3.40, 10 minutes) from **Berry station** (☎ 4464 1022; Station Rd), with connections to Sydney.

GERRINGONG
☎ 02 / pop 3590

The lesser of the coast's two Gongs, Gerringong is a pleasant little town surrounded by farmland above the impressive sweep of **Werri Beach**. It's popular with both retirees and surfies.

Just Stuff (☎ 4234 4443; cnr Fern & Belinda Sts; 🕑 9am-5pm) acts as the visitors centre. **Boolarng Nangamai** (☎ 0414 322 142; www.boolarng-nangamai .com; 5/9 Bergin St; 🕑 10.30am-3.30pm Sat & Sun) is an Aboriginal art and culture studio that runs workshops and acts as a gallery for local artists. Take the first left after the train station.

Sleeping & Eating

Tumblegum Inn (☎ 4234 3555; www.tumbleguminn.com .au; 141C Belinda St; s/tw/d $80/100/120) There's three rooms with en suites in this pretty wooden villa with friendly hosts. On sunny days you can enjoy a cooked breakfast on the veranda.

Bellachara Boutique Hotel (☎ 4234 1359; www .bellachara.com.au; 1 Fern St; r midweek $250-550, weekend $295-650; 🏊 🖳) An old motel has been given quite a makeover to turn it into this luxurious complex. The rooms are smartly furnished and the day spa suitably glam.

Gerringong Deli & Café (☎ 4234 1035; 133 Fern St; breakfast $5-14, lunch $10-17; 🕑 8am-5pm) Housed in a nice old wooden building with lots of art on the walls, this deli café has plenty of vego choices, along with sandwiches, wraps, burgers and pasta.

**SOUTH COAST
NEW SOUTH WALES**

Getting There & Away

From **Gerringong station** (☎ 4234 1422; Grey St) regular **CityRail** (☎ 131 500; www.cityrail.info) trains go to Wollongong ($6.60, 56 minutes) and Berry ($3.40, nine minutes), with connections to Sydney.

KIAMA

☎ 02 / pop 12,290

Kiama's a large town with fine old buildings, magnificent mature trees, numerous beaches and crazy rock formations, but it's the **blowhole** that's the clincher. At its most dramatic when the surf's up, the water pounding the cliff explodes out of a gaping fissure in the headland known as Blowhole Point. It's been drawing visitors for a century and is now floodlit at night. The **visitors centre** (☎ 4232 3322; www.kiama .com.au; ☼ 9am-5pm) is nearby, beside the small **Pilot's Cottage Museum** (☎ 4232 1001; adult/child $3/2; ☼ 11am-3pm Fri-Mon).

It's only a couple of feet wide, but **little blowhole** (off Tingira Cres, Marsden Head) rivals its big brother, shooting water in a great jet like a dragon snorting. There's a small enclosed **surf beach** right in town and **Bombo Beach**, 3km north of the centre has a great beach and a CityRail stop near the sand.

From the top of **Saddleback Mountain** you get a great view of the Illawarra Escarpment, the massive sandstone rampart that separates the coastal plain from the Southern Highlands. From Manning St, turn right on to Saddleback Mountain Rd, keeping an eye out for the historic **dry stone walls** lining the road.

By the time this book is published there will also be spectacular views from the **Illawarra Fly** (☎ 1300 362 881; www.illawarrafly.com.au; 182 Knights Hill Rd, Knights Hill; adult/child $19/9; ☼ 9am-5pm), a 500m viewing tower above the rainforest canopy at the top of the escarpment, 25km west of town.

In the same vicinity, **Minnamurra Rainforest Centre** (☎ 4236 0469; car $11; ☼ 9am-5pm, last entry 4pm) is on the eastern edge of **Budderoo National Park**, about 14km inland from Kiama. From the NPWS visitors centre you can take a 1.6km loop walk on a boardwalk through the rainforest following a cascading stream. Keep an eye out for water dragons and some of the most sociable lyrebirds in the country. A secondary 2.6km walk on a beautiful but sometimes steep track leads to the Minnamurra Falls. The visitors centre has a café.

On the way to Minnamurra you'll pass through the old village of **Jamberoo**, which has a nice pub.

Sleeping

Kendalls On The Beach Holiday Park (☎ 4232 1790; www.kiama.net/holiday/kendalls; Bonaira St; sites per 2 people $35-40, cottages $100-300; ☒) Perched on one of Kiama's loveliest beaches this upmarket holiday park has flash cottages facing the beach and good clean facilities for campers.

Bellevue Accommodation (☎ 4232 4000; www.belle vueaccommodation.com.au; 21 Minnamurra St; units $160-200; ☒) Six large modern units with wide porches and good town views have been carved out of this lovely 1890 house, steeped with the scent of jasmine. The décor is plush and units have DVD players and kitchen facilities.

Eating

Chachi's (☎ 4233 1144; 32 Collins St; mains $14-29; ☼ dinner) Located in a historic strip of terraced houses, Chachi's offers casual Italian alfresco dining. The smells wafting onto the pavement are hard to resist.

ourpick 55 On Collins (☎ 4232 2811; 55 Collins St; breakfast $4-13, lunch $12-29, dinner $28-33; ☼ 9am-4pm daily, dinner Mon-Tue & Thu-Sat) Big city culinary creativeness comes to Kiama with this smart place, which combines local produce with eclectic tastes. The wait-staff are so switched on you'd half expect them to know the first names of the animals being served. If you can't justify a dinner splurge, reasonably priced café fare is available during the day.

Every fourth Saturday, the **Kiama Produce Market** (☎ 0409-377 132; Black Beach; ☼ 8am-1pm) offers an array of local organic produce, unusual baked goods and prepared foods.

Getting There & Away

CityRail (☎ 13 15 00; www.cityrail.info) trains hit **Kiama station** (☎ 4223 5613; Railway Pde) on their run between Wollongong ($5.60, 47 minutes) and Bomaderry/Nowra ($4.60, 28 minutes), via Gerringong ($3, nine minutes).

WOLLONGONG

☎ 02 / pop 234,500

Hemmed in by the majestic Illawarra Escarpment, Wollongong sprawls along the coast from Lake Illawarra in the south, to within spitting distance of the Royal National Park. It's a city that gets progressively nicer as you head north, with the southern end dominated by the biggest steelworks in Australia at Port Kembla. The town centre isn't about to be crowned Miss Australia either, but a string of ever prettier surf beaches to the north compensate somewhat, as does the ever-present backdrop of those immense cliffs.

The region is part of the traditional lands of the Dharawal people, which continue north to Botany Bay. It was explored by Europeans in the early 19th century, but apart from timber cutting and dairy farming there was little development until the escarpment's coalfields attracted miners. By the turn of the 20th century Wollongong was a major coal port. Steelworks were developed in the 1920s and today the region is one of Australia's major industrial centres and Wollongong its ninth biggest city.

The Gong's surf ethos is a happy contrast to its blue-collar grit, and the result is genuine locals and a laid-back lifestyle. The city's cuisine measures up to that of any major city and the robust student population ensures that bar staff are never bored for long.

Orientation

Crown St is the main commercial street, and between Kembla and Keira Sts is a two-block somewhat sterile pedestrian mall. Keira St is part of the Princes Hwy, but through traffic bypasses the city on the Southern Fwy.

Information

At the time of research plans were afoot to move the **Wollongong visitors centre** (www.tourism wollongong.com) to the Princes Hwy, Bulli. Addresses and phone numbers hadn't been confirmed, so you're best to check the website. A smaller office may also open in the city itself. There's a post office and banks with ATMs on Crown St Mall.

Network Café (☎ 4228 8686; Upstairs, 157 Crown St; per hr $3.50; ☸ 10am-6pm Mon-Wed, 10am-11.30pm Thu & Fri, 10am-5.30pm Sat) Internet access.

NPWS office (☎ 4223 3000; ground fl, State Government Office Block, Market St; ☸ 8.30am-4.30pm Mon-Fri)

Sights & Activities

Wollongong's fishing fleet is based at **Belmore Basin** at the southern end of the harbour, which was cut from solid rock in 1868. There's a fishing cooperative and an 1872 **lighthouse** on the point. Nearby, on the headland, is the newer **Breakwater Lighthouse**.

North Beach generally has better surf than **Wollongong City Beach** and you can't see the mill. The harbour itself has beaches that are good for children. Others run north up the coast, including the surfer magnets of **Bulli**, **Sandon Point**, **Thirroul** (where DH Lawrence lived during his time in Australia; the cottage where he wrote *Kangaroo* still stands) and pretty **Austinmer**.

The excellent **Wollongong City Gallery** (☎ 4228 7500; www.wollongongcitygallery.com; cnr Kembla & Burelli Sts; admission free; ☸ 10am-5pm Tue-Fri, noon-4pm Sat & Sun) displays a permanent collection of modern Australian, indigenous and Asian art, and diverse temporary exhibits.

Quizzical kids of all ages can indulge their senses at the **Science Centre & Planetarium** (☎ 4286 5000; http://sciencecentre.uow.edu.au; Squires Way, Fairy Meadow; adult/child $10/7; ☸ 10am-4pm). Operated by the University of Wollongong, this interactive science extravaganza covers everything from dinosaurs to electronics. Planetarium shows run through the day ($3 per person).

The utterly serene **Wollongong Botanic Gardens** (☎ 4225 2636; 61 Northfields Ave, Keiraville; admission free; ☸ 7am-5pm Mon-Fri, 10am-5pm Sat & Sun) is a beautiful spot to wind down with a picnic lunch. The gardens represent a range of habitats including tropical, temperate and woodland. During summer, outdoor movies are often played.

Just south of the city, **Nan Tien Temple** (☎ 4272 0600; www.nantien.org.au; Berkeley Rd, Berkeley; admission free; ☸ 9am-5pm Tue-Sun) is the largest Buddhist temple in the southern hemisphere. The custodians of this ornate complex encourage visitors to contemplate the 10,000 Buddhas and participate in meditations and cultural activities. Dress appropriately (no shorts, singlets or flip-flops) and remove your shoes before entering the shrines.

The **Cockatoo Run** (☎ 1300 653 801; www.3801limited .com.au; adult/child/family $40/35/100; ☸ 11am, 2nd Sun of each month) is a heritage tourist train that travels inland across the Southern Highlands to Moss Vale. The route traverses the escarpment, coursing through dense rainforest along the way.

Sleeping

Most of Wollongong's motels seem to have been time-warped in from the 1970s or earlier. Prices leap by around $20 on weekends.

BUDGET

The council runs three **tourist parks** (http://tourist parks.wollongong.nsw.gov.au; camp sites per 2 people $20-25)

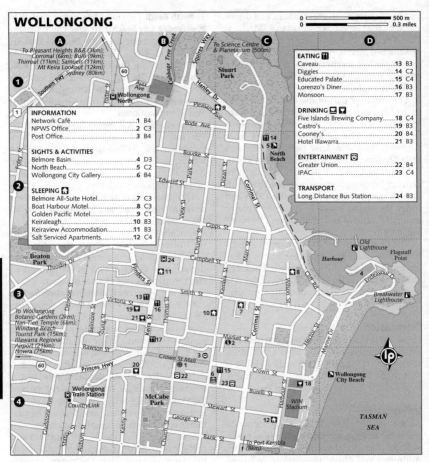

WOLLONGONG

0   500 m
0   0.3 miles

INFORMATION
Network Café..............................**1** B4
NPWS Office...............................**2** C3
Post Office..................................**3** B4

SIGHTS & ACTIVITIES
Belmore Basin.............................**4** D3
North Beach................................**5** C2
Wollongong City Gallery............**6** B4

SLEEPING
Belmore All-Suite Hotel............**7** C3
Boat Harbour Motel...................**8** C3
Golden Pacific Motel..................**9** C1
Keiraleagh................................**10** B3
Keiraview Accommodation.......**11** B3
Salt Serviced Apartments.........**12** C4

EATING
Caveau......................................**13** B3
Diggies......................................**14** C2
Educated Palate.......................**15** C4
Lorenzo's Diner.........................**16** B3
Monsoon...................................**17** B3

DRINKING
Five Islands Brewing Company.......**18** C4
Castro's.....................................**19** B3
Cooney's...................................**20** B3
Hotel Illawarra.........................**21** B3

ENTERTAINMENT
Greater Union...........................**22** B4
IPAC..**23** C4

TRANSPORT
Long Distance Bus Station............**24** B3

on popular beaches: **Windang** (☎ 4297 3166; Fern St; cabins $55-145), **Corrimal** (☎ 4285 5688; Lake Pde; cabins $75-110) and **Bulli** (☎ 4285 5677; 1 Farrell Rd; cabins $55-170).

Keiraleagh (☎ 4228 6765; keiraleagh@backpack.net .au; 60 Kembla St; dm $20-25, s $35, d/tw $55-65) This rambling heritage house is clogged with atmosphere, with pressed metal ceilings, roses in the cornices and festively painted rooms. The basic dorms are out the back, along with a sizeable patio and a BBQ.

Keiraview Accommodation (☎ 4229 1132; www.yha .com.au/hostels; 75-79 Keira St; dm $29-41, tw/d $82/110; 🖵) Modern and clinically clean, this complex contains the YHA hostel, which caters to students and backpackers in tidy four-bed dorms. The double rooms have verandas and kitchenettes.

MIDRANGE
Golden Pacific Motel (☎ 4226 3000; fax 4228 3853; 16 Pleasant Ave, North Beach; r $95-135; 🐾) The friendly owners keep the place so spick-and-span that it seems churlish to giggle over the dated furnishings – although it's hard to resist with the satin and lace draped four-poster in the honeymoon suite.

Boat Harbour Motel (☎ 4228 9166; www.boatharbour -motel.com.au; cnr Campbell & Wilson Sts; s $110-129, d $120-145; 🐾) Dressed like a sailor in white and navy blue trim, this older style motel has nice balconies and comfortable if unmemorable décor.

Belmore All-Suite Hotel (☎ 4224 6500; www.belmore .net; 39 Smith St; apt $139-219; 🐾) All the units (ranging from studios to two bedroom apartments) are spacious in this gracious, conservatively decorated building near the beaches. There are kitchenettes and attractive patios.

TOP END
Salt Serviced Apartments (☎ 4229 6866; www.salt wollongong.com.au; 5 Stewart St; apt $170-240; ❄ ; wi-fi) Extremely schmick, these identical corner apartments are four to a floor in a contemporary block next to the stadium. Compared with the rare thrill of a rugby league view, the ocean views seem mundane.

Pleasant Heights B&B (☎ 4283 3355; www.pleasant heights.com.au; 77 New Mt Pleasant Rd; r $250-450) Eccentrically but stylishly furnished, these three very different rooms are very luxe indeed. Some have awesome views while others have opulent spa baths. All smell very nice.

Eating
North of the mall, Keira St is jammed with eateries of all types and budgets. Other places are spread across town.

BUDGET
Austibeach (☎ 4268 5680; 104 Lawrence Hargrave Dr, Austinmer; breakfast $4-17, lunch $13-20, dinner $17-23; ✷ breakfast & lunch daily, dinner Wed-Sat) Drop in for brunch or a homemade gelato as you're heading up the coast. The views from the terrace look to heaven via Austinmer Beach. There's live music on Saturday nights.

our pick **Diggies** (☎ 4226 2688; 1 Cliff Rd, North Beach; breakfast $5-18, lunch $18-23, tapas $7-11; ✷ breakfast & lunch daily, dinner Fri & Sat, cocktails from 4pm Sun) Sunny service matches the views at this informal café on the beach. Keep an eye on the surf while ordering from the foodie-friendly breakfast menu or just listen to it roar over tapas at night.

Educated Palate (☎ 4225 0100; 87 Crown St; mains $7-17; ✷ breakfast & lunch) Forgive the seriously pretentious name and raid the deli counter for provisions, or let the cooks put in the hard yards over, say, the grilled haloumi and chorizo omelette. The coffee is excellent.

MIDRANGE & TOP END
Monsoon (☎ 4229 4588; 193 Kiera St; lunch $8-10, dinner $15; ✷ lunch Tue-Sat, dinner Tue-Sun) The décor is typically oddball Vietnamese: there's a mirror ball, a Buddha and a cat-headed Egyptian figure. Thankfully the food is also authentic; try the wonderfully fragrant *pho bo* (beef noodle soup).

Samuels (☎ 4268 2244; 382 Lawrence Hargrave Dr, Thirroul; breakfast $9-16, lunch $25, dinner $25-30; ✷ break-fast Sat & Sun, lunch Tue-Fri, dinner Tue-Sun) Well worth the drive out to Thirroul, this excellent restaurant has a lively Mod Oz menu where all the dishes come with a choice of two sides. Sunday nights feature $25 soup-and-roast deals.

Lorenzo's Diner (☎ 4229 5633; 119 Keira St; mains $29-34; ✷ lunch Thu & Fri, dinner Tue-Sat) Seriously nice people run this upmarket modern Italian restaurant. The food matches the excellent service.

Caveau (☎ 4226 4855; 122-124 Keira St; 2 courses $57; ✷ lunch Thu & Fri, dinner Tue-Sat) The top-rated restaurant on the south coast, even with its hip corrugated-iron trim Caveau shrieks 'formal'! The menu is all 'champagne *veloute*' this and 'perigord truffle' that, promising memories that will live on after the credit card pain subsides.

Drinking
Five Islands Brewing Company (☎ 4220 2854; www.five islandsbrewery.com; WIN Entertainment Centre, cnr Crown & Harbour Sts; ❄) Its 10 signature draughts lubricate the crowd, which bursts the seams on weekends. There's a great patio overlooking the sea.

Cooney's (☎ 4229 1911; 234 Keira St) This vast, dark bar has cosy nooks, pool tables and constant tunes. There's also a beer garden and often live music and DJs.

Hotel Illawarra (☎ 4229 5411; cnr Keira & Market) Modernised into the city's swankiest pub complex, the Illawarra has a decent bistro, orange pool tables, regular DJs and a urinal-like waterfall constantly tinkling in the beer garden.

Castro's (☎ 4227 2058; 5 Victoria St; admission free, $10 after 11pm Sat; ✷ 9pm-late Wed-Sat) Wollongong's gay bar-club plays host to a mixed student crowd on Wednesdays and drag shows on Saturdays.

Entertainment
Illawarra Performing Arts Centre (IPAC; ☎ 4226 3366; www.ipac.org.au; 32 Burelli St) This busy venue presents an excellent and continuous stream of theatre, dance and music. It's home to the impressive Merrigong Theatre Co.

Greater Union (☎ 4228 4888; www.greaterunion .com.au; 68 Burelli St) Multiple screens showing Hollywood blockbusters.

Getting There & Away
AIR
Illawarra Regional Airport (☎ 4221 6102; Airport Rd) is 21km south of the centre at Albion Park Rail, a 15-minute walk from Albion Park

Rail station. On weekdays there are flights to/from Melbourne on **QantasLink** (☎ 13 13 13; www.qantas.com.au).

BUS
All long-distance buses leave from **Wollongong City Coach Terminus** (☎ 4226 1022; cnr Keira & Campbell Sts). **Premier Motor Service** (☎ 133 410; www.premierms.com.au) operates buses to/from Sydney ($15, two hours, two daily) and Melbourne ($79, 15 hours, daily). **Murrays** (☎ 13 22 51; www.murrays.com.au) travels to Canberra ($31, 3½ hours, daily).

TRAIN
CityRail (☎ 131 500; www.cityrail.info) trains run frequently from Sydney's Central Station to Wollongong ($9.60, 1¾ hours), continuing south to Kiama ($5.60, 47 minutes) and Bomaderry/Nowra ($8.60, 75 minutes).

Getting Around
Local buses (☎ 131 500) link most suburbs. You can reach most beaches by rail and trains are fairly frequent. Bringing a bike on the train from Sydney is a great way to get around; a cycle path runs from the city centre north to Bulli and south to Lake Illawarra.

For taxis, call ☎ 4229 9311.

AROUND WOLLONGONG
SOUTH OF THE CITY
Just south of Wollongong, **Lake Illawarra** is popular for water sports including windsurfing. There are good ocean beaches on the Windang Peninsula to the east of the lake. Further south is **Shellharbour**, a popular holiday resort, and one of the oldest towns along the coast. Its name comes from the number of shell middens (remnants of Aboriginal occupation) that the European colonists found here.

ILLAWARRA ESCARPMENT STATE CONSERVATION AREA
Rainforest hugs the edge of the ever-eroding sandstone cliffs of the escarpment, which rise to 534m at their peak at **Mt Kembla**. This discontinuous conservation area protects much of it. For wonderful views of the coast, you can drive up to the **Mt Keira lookout** (464m); take the freeway north and follow the signs. There are other lookouts at **Bulli** and **Sublime Point**.

The park is accessible from several roadside car parks; grab the excellent pamphlet

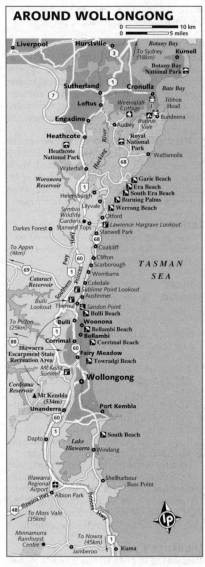

from NPWS (p173), with maps and details of walks.

NORTH OF THE CITY
On the road to the Royal National Park, the **Lawrence Hargrave Lookout** at Bald Hill above Stanwell Park is a superb cliff-top viewing point. Hargrave, a pioneer aviator, made his

SOUTH COAST NEW SOUTH WALES

first attempts at flying in the area early in the 20th century. His obsession has since been picked up by avid hang-gliders. To join in, **HangglideOz** (☎ 0417 939 200; www.hangglideoz .com.au) and **Sydney Hang Gliding Centre** (☎ 4294 4294; www.hanggliding.com.au) offer tandem flights from $199.

Symbio Wildlife Gardens (☎ 4294 1244; www.symbio zoo.com.au; 7-11 Lawrence Hargrave Dr, Stanwell Tops; adult/child $19/9.50; ☼ 9.30am-5pm) has more than 1000 cute and furry critters. Some are native, some are exotic and some are farm animals, but all are popular with kids.

You can hit the trails on the back of a horse at **Darkes Forest Riding Ranch** (☎ 4294 3441; www .horseriding.au.com; 84 Darkes Forest Rd, Darkes Forest; per hr from $40).

ROYAL NATIONAL PARK

The only thing preventing Wollongong from becoming a suburb of Sydney is this wonderful **coastal park** (admission per car $11, pedestrians & cyclists free), which protects 16,300 hectares stretching inland from 32km of beautiful coast. Encompassing dramatic cliffs, secluded beaches, scrub and lush rainforest, it's the oldest national park in the world having been gazetted in 1879. The park has a large network of **walking tracks**, including a spectacular 29km (two day) coastal trail.

There are lots of beautiful beaches, but most are unpatrolled and rips can make them dangerous. **Garie**, **Era**, **South Era** and **Burning Palms** are popular surf beaches and **Werrong Beach** is 'clothing-optional'. The side roads to the smaller beaches are closed at 8.30pm. Cycling is popular but stick to the trails to avoid a fine.

The **visitors centre** (☎ 9542 0648; ☼ 8.30am-4.30pm) is at Audley, 2km inside the north-eastern entrance, off the Princes Hwy. Nearby, you can hire row boats, canoes and kayaks from the **Audley Boatshed** (☎ 9545 4967; per hr/day $20/40; ☼ 9am-5pm Mon-Sat, 9am-5.30pm Sun), as well as mountain bikes (per hour/day $16/34).

The sizeable town of **Bundeena**, on the southern shore of Port Hacking opposite Sydney's southern suburb of Cronulla, is surrounded by the park. From here you can walk 30 minutes towards the ocean to **Jibbon Head**, which has a good beach and interesting Aboriginal rock art. Bundeena is the starting point of the coastal walk.

Sleeping

The only park camping ground accessible by car is at **Bonnie Vale** (camp sites per adult/child $14/7), near Bundeena. Bush camping is allowed in several other areas, but you must obtain a permit (adult/child $5/3) from the visitors centre, where you can get information about current usable camp sites. NPWS also rents out gorgeous **Weemalah Cottage** (cottage winter/summer $190/220), by the river at Warumbul. Once kept for visiting dignitaries, this fully self-contained house has wide verandas and sleeps eight.

Garie Beach YHA (☎ 9261 1111; www.yha.com.au; Garie Beach; dm $16) Secluded behind the dunes, this hostel is near great surf breaks and has no phone, power (apart from solar lighting), showers or other amenities to spoil the rustic mood (OK, there are composting toilets). You need to book, collect a key and get detailed directions from the YHA Membership & Travel Centre (p184) in Sydney.

Beachhaven B&B (☎ 9544 1333; www.beachhaven bnb.com.au; 13 Bundeena Dr, Bundeena; r $275; ☒ ▢) Shaded by palms and with direct access to gorgeous Hordens Beach, there are two swank rooms here. Amenities include DVD players, antiques and a spa overlooking the sand.

Getting There & Away

Cronulla National Park Ferries (☎ 9523 2990; www .cronullaferries.com.au; adult/child $5.40/2.70; ☼ hourly 8.30am-5.30pm) travels to Bundeena from Cronulla, which you can reach by train from Sydney. Hours are longer on weekdays and in summer.

Sydney

It's the first place most people see when they come to Australia and why not? Big, bold, brash and fun, Sydney is a great introduction to the continent. So what if others elsewhere in Oz quibble about this or that with regards to the top city. Ignore 'em; that's what Sydney does.

Sydney is a huge place but is surprisingly manageable for the average visitor. Basically, if it's north of the harbour, you can ignore it. Sure, a couple of million people up there might beg to differ, but trust them that it's a nice place to live and leave it at that. Rather, think of the big green patch of lawn at Hyde Park in the centre of town as your own ground zero. Within a half-hour walk of here in various directions, you can plunge into the edgy vibe of Newtown, travel to Asia in Chinatown, marvel at the iconic Opera House and harbour, get trashed beneath the bright lights of Kings Cross, have a balls out exploration of lifestyles in Darlinghurst and nosh with posh hipsters in Surry Hills. It's that kind of place.

You can mix and match your neighbourhoods and experiences by mood or whim. But the best part is you won't be bored. Ever. When you want to go a bit further, there's the pure pleasure of the ferry to Manly, the ocean plunge at Bondi Beach and the jaw-dropping spectacle of the Blue Mountains.

HIGHLIGHTS

- Strolling from the **Royal Botanic Gardens** (p190) to the **Sydney Opera House** (p184)
- Alternating shopping with cafés in **Paddington** (p213)
- Taking the iconic plunge at **Bondi Beach** (p194) or **Coogee** (p194)
- Catching the ferry to **Manly** (p197) and doing the Manly Scenic Walkway
- Letting Echo Point introduce you to the **Blue Mountains** (p216)
- Finding the perfect meal in **Surry Hills** (p206)

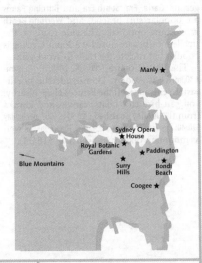

- TELEPHONE CODE: 02
- POPULATION: 4 MILLION
- www.sydney.citysearch.com.au

HISTORY

The Sydney region is the ancestral home of the Eora people (the Kuring-gai, Birrabirragal and Cadi peoples) who possessed an intimate understanding of environmental sustainability, spoke three distinct languages, and maintained sophisticated sacred and artistic cultures. In 1788 Captain Arthur Phillip established Australia's first European settlement, and the Eora were soon stripped of the legal rights to their land, and systematically incarcerated, killed or driven away by force.

Early Sydney bumbled through near-starvation and rum-fuelled political turmoil, but boom didn't arrive until the 1850s gold rush, when Sydney's population doubled in a decade.

In the 20th century, post-WWII immigrants from the UK, Ireland and the Mediterranean brought spirit and prosperity to Sydney. These qualities have endured as the immigrant pool has expanded to include Asia (especially Vietnam and China), the Middle East and Africa. Hosting the 2000 Olympic Games thrust Sydney into the global limelight for celebratory reasons; its glitzy vibe keeps it there.

ORIENTATION

The harbour divides Sydney into north and south, with the Sydney Harbour Bridge and the Harbour Tunnel joining the two shores. The city centre is roughly from Circular Quay to Central Station. To the west is Darling Harbour, while to the east lie Darlinghurst, Kings Cross and Paddington.

Three kilometres further southeast, along the coast, are the ocean-beach suburbs of Bondi and Coogee. Sydney's Kingsford Smith Airport is 10km south of the city centre. West of the centre are the gentrified suburbs of Pyrmont, Glebe and Balmain. The inner west includes Newtown and Leichhardt. Suburbs stretch 20km north and south of the centre, their extent limited by national parks. The suburbs north of the bridge are known collectively as the North Shore. The western suburbs sprawl for 50km to reach the foothills of the Blue Mountains.

Maps

If you're driving around the city for any length of time, a *Sydney UBD* street directory (around $35) is invaluable. Otherwise, you'll find free maps aplenty at the visitor centres. The free city-sponsored themed walking guides are excellent.

Map World (Map pp186-7; ☎ 9261 3601; www .mapworld.com.au; 280 Pitt St; ☯ 9am-5.30pm Mon-Fri, 10am-3.45pm Sat) Maps, atlases, GPS and travel guides.

INFORMATION
Bookshops

Ariel (Map pp186-7; ☎ 9332 4581; www.arielbooks .com.au; 42 Oxford St, Paddington; ☯ 9am-midnight) Art, film, fashion, design and travel guides.
Dymocks (Map pp186-7; ☎ 9235 0155; www.dymocks .com.au; 424-28 George St, Sydney; ☯ 9am-6.30pm Mon-Fri, to 6pm Sat, 10am-5pm Sun) Mainstream titles, stationery and lots of guidebooks and maps.
Gleebooks (Map p196; ☎ 9660 2333; www.gleebooks .com.au; 49 Glebe Point Rd, Glebe; ☯ 9am-9pm) Politics, arts and fiction…just about everything in a classic neighbourhood shop; others are nearby.
Kinokuniya (Map pp186-7; ☎ 9262 7996; www .kinokuniya.com; Level 2, TGV, 500 George St, Sydney; ☯ 10am-7pm Mon-Sat, to 6pm Sun) Over 300,000 titles – Sydney's biggest bookshop.
Travel Bookshop (Map pp186-7; ☎ 9261 8200; www .travelbooks.com.au; 175 Liverpool St, Sydney; ☯ 9am-6pm Mon-Fri, 10am-5pm Sat) Travel books, and lots of them.

Emergency

In the event of an emergency, call ☎ 000 to contact the police, ambulance and fire authorities.
Lifeline (☎ 13 11 14; www.lifeline.com.au) Over-the-phone counselling services, including suicide prevention.
National Roads & Motorists Association (NRMA; Map pp186-7; ☎ 13 21 32; www.nrma.com.au; 74-6 King St, Sydney; ☯ 9am-5pm Mon-Fri) Car insurance and roadside service.
Police Stations Include 132 George St, Sydney (Map pp186-7) and 1-15 Elizabeth Bay Rd, Kings Cross (Map p193).
Rape Crisis Centre (☎ 1800 424 017)

Internet Access

Internet cafés are common in Sydney, especially in Kings Cross, Chinatown and Bondi. Rates are around $3 an hour. Plenty of hostels and hotels offer internet access to their guests.
Global Gossip Kings Cross (Map p193; ☎ 9326 9777; 61 Darlinghurst Rd; per hr $2; ☯ 9am-midnight); Sydney (Map pp186-7; 790 George St); Sydney (Map pp186-7; 415 Pitt St); Bondi (Map p195; 37 Hall St) Traveller-friendly chain.

Internet Resources

For more information on Sydney, check out the following websites:

GREATER SYDNEY & BLUE MOUNTAINS

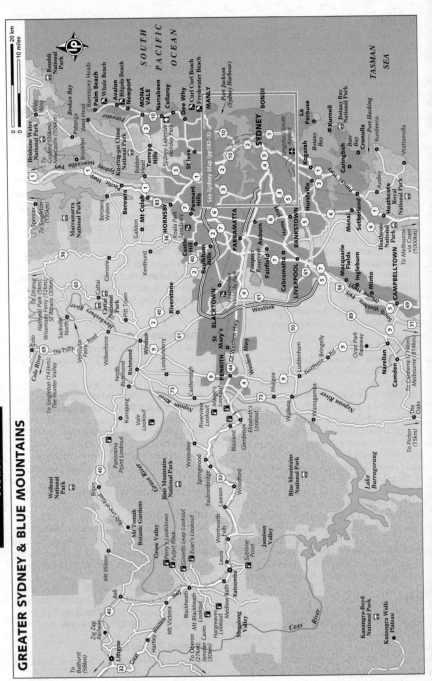

SYDNEY IN...

Two Days
Start your day in Sydney with the walking tour of the **centre** (see boxed text, p199) before scooting off to **Bondi** (p194) and enjoying a dip at Sydney's most famous beach. That night, catch a performance at the **Opera House** (p184), before or after dining at one of Sydney's many fabulous restaurants.

The next day, hop on a slow ferry to **Manly** (p197), where you can enjoy an open-air brunch, followed by a swim or long walk along the 9km Manly Scenic Walkway. If you have time, stop at the **Taronga Zoo** (p197). That night, head out to **Surry Hills** (p206) for dinner and drinks.

Four Days
By the third day, you'll be itching to see Sydney's diverse neighbourhoods. Energise yourself with yum cha in **Chinatown** (p206). In the afternoon, walk around edgy **Newtown** (p195) and **Glebe** (p195), and that night go genteel at a posh pub in **Darlinghurst** (p206) or **Paddington** (p207).

On the fourth day, get out of town by taking the train to the majestic **Blue Mountains** (p216), and join in the sighing as you gaze upon the **Three Sisters** (p218). Have lunch in **Katoomba** (p218) before heading back to Sydney or staying the night in one of the mountain villages.

One Week
Spend your final days filling in the gaps of your sightseeing. Get out on the water on a yacht (p198). Spend a day taking a tour of one of **Sydney Harbour National Park's** (p184) islands. Go nuts in the endless nightlife of **Kings Cross** and **Darlinghurst** (for both, see p211).

Shop till you drop on your last days in Sydney, loading up on fashion and kitsch at **Paddington Market** (p213) or at one of Sydney's many outdoor **crafts markets** (p213).

www.cityofsydney.nsw.gov.au Visitor information, disabled access, parking, history and downloadable walking tours.
www.eatability.com.au User-generated dining and bar reviews.
www.inthemix.com.au What's on in the dance music and club scene.
www.smh.com.au Good for upcoming events, restaurant and bar reviews, and to take the pulse of the city.
www.sydney.citysearch.com.au What's on listings.
www.visitnsw.com.au Neighbourhood by neighbourhood visitors' guide.

Medical Services
Kings Cross Travellers Clinic (Map p193; ☎ 9358 3066; www.travellersclinic.com.au; 13 Springfield Ave, Kings Cross; ◯ 9am-1pm & 2-6pm Mon-Fri, 10am-noon Sat) General medical, dive medicals and morning-after pill scripts; bookings advised.
Sydney Hospital (Map pp186-7; ☎ 9382 7111; www .sesahs.nsw.gov.au/sydhosp; 8 Macquarie St, Sydney; ◯ 24hr emergency)

Money
There are plenty of ATMs throughout Sydney; both **American Express** (Map pp186-7; ☎ 1300 139 060; 175 Liverpool St, Sydney; ◯ 8.30am-5pm Mon-Fri) and

Travelex (Map pp186-7; ☎ 9231 2523; Queen Victoria Bldg, 455 George St, Sydney; ◯ 9am-5pm Mon-Fri, 10am-2pm Sat) have city branches. Seven-day exchange bureaus include:
Central Station (Map pp186-7; Coach Terminal; ◯ 9am-4pm)
Circular Quay (Map pp186-7; Wharf 6; ◯ 8am-9.30pm)
Kings Cross (Map p193; cnr Springfield Ave & Darlinghurst Rd; ◯ 8am-midnight)

Post
Stamps are sold at post offices, Australia Post retail outlets in most suburbs and most newsagents.
General Post Office (GPO; Map pp186-7; ☎ 13 13 18; www.auspost.com.au; 1 Martin Pl; ◯ 8.15am-5.30pm Mon-Fri, 10am-2pm Sat)

Tourist Information
Sydney Harbour National Parks Information Centre (Map pp186-7; ☎ 9247 5033; Cadmans Cottage, 110 George St, The Rocks; ◯ 9.30am-4.30pm Mon-Fri, 10am-4.30pm Sat & Sun) Has maps of walks in different parts of the park and information on tours of the harbour islands.
Sydney visitors centres The Rocks (Map pp186-7; ☎ 9240 8788; www.sydneyvisitorcentre.com; cnr Argyle & Playfair Sts; ◯ 9.30am-5.30pm); Darling Harbour (Map

SYDNEY

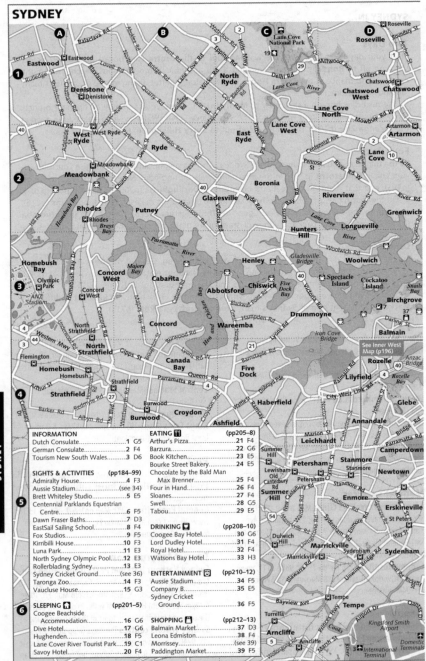

SYDNEY

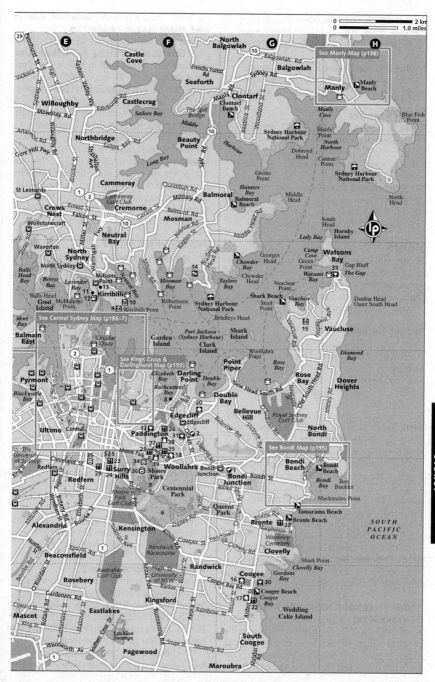

See Manly Map (p198)

See Central Sydney Map (p186-7)

See Kings Cross &
Darlinghurst Map (p193)

See Bondi Map (p195)

SYDNEY

pp186-7; ☎ 9240 8788; www.sydneyvisitorcentre.com; Palm Grove, behind Imax; ☒ 9.30am-5.30pm) Comprehensive; also acts as an accommodation agency. The Rocks location is part gift shop.

Tourism New South Wales (Map pp182-3; ☎ 9667 6050; International Arrivals, Terminal 1, Kingsford Smith Airport; ☒ 5am-11pm) Accommodation and travel advice.

Travel Agencies

Travellers Contact Point (Map pp186-7; ☎ 9221 8744, 1800 647 640; www.travellers.com.au; Level 7, 428 George St; ☒ 9am-6pm Mon-Fri, 10am-4pm Sat) Backpacker agency that holds mail and has a good bulletin board.

YHA Membership & Travel Centre (Map pp186-7; ☎ 9261 1111; www.yha.com.au; 422 Kent St; ☒ 9am-5pm Mon-Wed & Fri, to 6pm Thu, 10am-2pm Sat) Offers travel packages and YHA bookings worldwide.

SIGHTS

Sydney will keep you busy. Much of it doesn't cost a cent, but if you plan on seeing an exceptional number of museums, attractions and tours, check out the **Smartvisit card** (☎ 1300 661 711; www.seesydneycard.com).

Sydney Harbour

Stretching 20km inland to the mouth of the Parramatta River, Sydney Harbour (aka **Port Jackson**) is Sydney's shimmering soul, its beaches, coves, bays, islands and waterside parks providing crucial relief from the ordeals of urban life.

Forming the gateway to the harbour are **North Head** (Map pp182-3) and **South Head** (Map pp182-3). **Watsons Bay** (Map pp182-3) nestles on South Head's harbourside, fostering a salty cottage atmosphere. The harbour beaches are generally sheltered, calm coves with little of the frenzied foam of the ocean beaches. On the south shore is **Camp Cove** (Map pp182-3), a photogenic swimming beach where Arthur Phillip first landed, and the shark-netted **Shark Bay** (Map pp182-3). On the North Shore try **Manly Cove, Reef Beach, Clontarf Beach, Chinamans Beach** and **Balmoral Beach** (all Map pp182-3). Exploring this vast area by ferry (p214) is one of Sydney's great joys.

SYDNEY HARBOUR NATIONAL PARK

This **national park** (Map pp182-3) protects scattered pockets of harbourside bushland with magical walking tracks, lookouts, Aboriginal engravings and historic sites. Its southern side incorporates South Head and **Nielsen Park**; on the North Shore it includes **North Head, Dobroyd Head, Middle Head** and **Ashton Park**.

Five harbour islands are also part of the park: **Clark Island** off Darling Point, **Shark Island** off Rose Bay, **Rodd Island** in Iron Cove, **Goat Island** (Map pp186-7), once a hellish convict gulag, and the small fortified **Fort Denison** (Map pp182-3) off Mrs Macquaries Point.

Except for Goat Island, which is currently off limits, the harbour islands are open to visitors. The NSW National Parks & Wildlife Service (NPWS) runs 2½-hour Fort Denison **tours** (adult/concession $27/24; ☒ 12.15 & 2.30pm, also 10.45am Wed-Sun) – book at the Sydney Harbour National Park Information Centre (p181). You can catch a water taxi (p214) to Rodd and Clark Islands; they incur a $5 landing fee, also payable at Cadman's Cottage.

SYDNEY OPERA HOUSE

The **opera house** (Map pp186-7; ☎ 9250 7111; www.sydneyoperahouse.com; Bennelong Pt, Circular Quay E), designed by Danish architect Jørn Utzon, is Australia's most recognisable icon and essential sight. It's said to have drawn inspiration from orange segments, snails, palm fronds and Maya temples, and has been poetically likened to a 'nun's scrum' and the sexual congress of turtles. It's arresting from any angle (the 67m-high roof features 27,230 tonnes of Swedish tiles – 1,056,000 of them), but the ferry view approaching Circular Quay is hard to beat.

There are four main auditoriums for dance, concerts, opera and theatre events, plus the left-of-centre Studio for emerging artists. The acoustics are superb, the internal aesthetics like the belly of a whale. Two thousand four hundred annual events cost over $40 million to run and keep the Concert Hall organ's 10,500 pipes humming.

Opera house **tours** (☎ 9250 7250; adult/concession $35/24, discounts online; ☒ 1hr tours 9am-5pm) take you from 'front of house' to backstage, excluding theatres in rehearsal use. Let them know in advance if you require wheelchair access.

SYDNEY HARBOUR BRIDGE

Whether they're driving over it, climbing up it, rollerblading across it or sailing under it, Sydneysiders adore their bridge (Map pp186-7). The 1932 bridge links the CBD with the North Sydney business district, spanning the harbour at one of its narrowest points.

The best way to experience the bridge is on foot – don't expect much of a view crossing by car or train. Staircases climb up to the bridge from both shores, leading to a footpath running the length of the eastern side. A cycle way wheels along the western side. You can climb the southeastern pylon to the **Pylon Lookout** (Map pp186-7; ☎ 9240 1100; www.pylonlookout.com.au; adult/child/concession $9.50/4/6.50; ۞ 10am-5pm), or ascend the great arc on a **bridge climb** (see p201).

The Rocks

The Rocks – the site of Sydney's first European settlement – has evolved unrecognisably from its squalid, overcrowded origins. Residents once sloshed through open sewers and alleyways festering with disease, prostitution and drunken lawlessness. Sailors, whalers and rapscallions boozed and brawled shamelessly in countless harbourside pubs.

The Rocks remained a commercial and maritime hub until shipping services left Circular Quay in the late 1800s. A bubonic plague outbreak in 1900 continued the decline. Construction of the Harbour Bridge in the 1920s brought further demolition, entire streets disappearing under the bridge's southern approach.

It wasn't until the 1970s that the Rocks' cultural and architectural heritage was recognised. The ensuing redevelopment saved a lot of old buildings but has turned the area east of the bridge highway into a tourist trap. Kitsch cafés and shops hocking stuffed koalas and bare bum postcards now prevail.

Cadmans Cottage (Map pp186-7; ☎ 9247 5033; www.nationalparks.nsw.gov.au; 110 George St; ۞ 9.30am-4.30pm Mon-Fri, 10am-4.30pm Sat & Sun), built on a buried beach, is Sydney's oldest house (1816). Its namesake, John Cadman, was Government Coxswain. Water police detained criminals here in the 1840s; it was later converted into a home for retired sea captains. Further along George St is the schlock-laden weekend **Rocks Market** (see p213).

The excellent **Rocks Discovery Museum** (Map pp186-7; ☎ 1800 067 676; www.rocksdiscoverymuseum.com; 2-8 Kendall Lane, The Rocks; admission free; ۞ 10am-5pm) digs deep into artefact-laden Rocks history and provides insight into the lives of the Cadi people, the Rocks' original inhabitants.

Beyond the **Argyle Cut** (Map pp186-7), an impressive tunnel excavated by convicts, is **Millers Point**, a charming district of early colonial homes; stroll here to enjoy everything the Rocks is not. **Argyle Place** (Map pp186-7) is an English-style village green on which any

Australian has the legal right to graze livestock. Overlooking it is **Garrison Church** (Map pp186-7), Australia's oldest church (1848).

The 1850s, copper-domed, Italianate **Sydney Observatory** (Map pp186-7; ☎ 9217 0485; www.sydneyobservatory.com.au; Watson Rd; admission free; ۞ 10am-5pm) sits atop Observatory Park. You can look around or enjoy a celestial show in the theatre.

In the old military hospital building nearby, the **SH Ervin Gallery** (Map pp186-7; ☎ 9258 0173; www.nsw.nationaltrust.org.au/ervin.html; Watson Rd; adult/child $6/4; ۞ 11am-5pm Tue-Sun) exhibits Australian art, including the annual Salon des Refusés collection of alternative Archibald Prize entries.

The wharves around Dawes Point are rapidly emerging from prolonged decay. Walsh Bay's Pier 4 houses the renowned **Sydney Theatre Company** (p212) and several other performance troupes. The impressive **Sydney Theatre** (p212) is across the road.

CIRCULAR QUAY

Built around Sydney Cove, Circular Quay is Sydney's public-transport hub, with ferry quays, bus stops, a train station and the **Overseas Passenger Terminal** (Map pp186-7), where cruise ships disgorge their mobs. European settlement grew around the Tank Stream, which now trickles underground into the harbour near Wharf 6. For many years Circular Quay was also Sydney's port, but these days it's more of a recreational space, with harbour walkways, grassy verges, cafés and buskers of varying talent.

The cavernous 1885 **Customs House** (Map pp186-7; ☎ 9242 8555; www.cityofsydney.nsw.gov.au/library; 31 Alfred St; admission free; ۞ 8am-midnight Mon-Fri, 10am-midnight Sat, noon-5pm Sun, library 10am-7pm Mon-Fri, 11am-4pm Sat & Sun) has been recently renovated and houses the Customs House Library. Under the glass floor of the foyer is a way-cool 1:500 model of Sydney.

MUSEUM OF CONTEMPORARY ART

Always ready with something to love or hate, the **MCA** (Map pp186-7; ☎ 9245 2400; www.mca.com.au; 140 George St; admission free; ۞ 10am-5pm) fronts Circular Quay West in a stately Art Deco building. Its constantly changing exhibitions from Australia and overseas range from hip to explicit to disturbing.

Central Sydney

Central Sydney stretches from Circular Quay in the north to Central Station in the south. The rather dull (especially on weekends!) business

CENTRAL SYDNEY

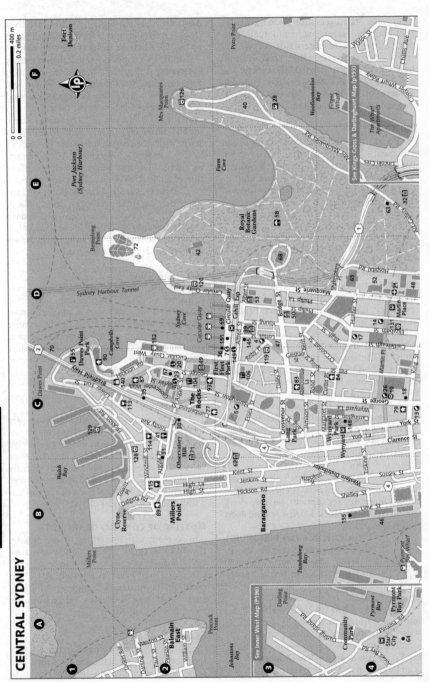

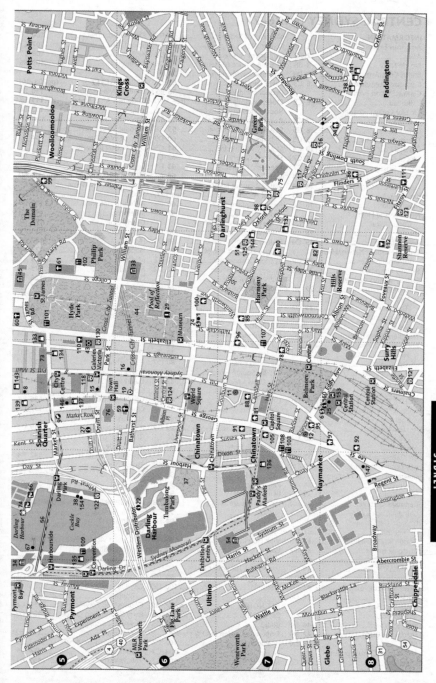

CENTRAL SYDNEY (p186–7)

SYDNEY

INDIGENOUS SYDNEY

Sydney, with its own rich Aboriginal heritage, is a good place to start to explore Aboriginal culture and life both locally and across Australia.

For information on Aboriginal rock carvings around Sydney Harbour – they date back thousands of years – check with the Sydney Harbour National Parks Information Centre (p181). You can also find rock carvings close to Bondi (p194).

A cluster of major cultural institutions, the **Australian Museum** (p190), the **Art Gallery of NSW** (p190) and the **Royal Botanic Gardens** (p190), all have extensive exhibits and programs relating to Aboriginal life and culture.

Many tour companies offer themed itineraries. **Sydney Aboriginal Discoveries** (p201) offers well-regarded walks.

Many shops sell Aboriginal goods, although it's easy to find fake junk that's made in China. Among the places well-regarded for their authentic art and goods are:

Artery (Map p193; ☎ 9380 8234; Shop 2, 221 Darlinghurst Rd, Darlinghurst) Artery deliberately steers away from the glitzy Sydney gallery scene, sourcing its contemporary, original selections from up-and-coming Central Australian artists. Prices are realistic and affordable: modern indigenous jewellery, hand-woven baskets and gorgeous canvasses start at $25.

Gavala (Map pp186-7; ☎ 9212 7232; Shop 131, 1st fl, Harbourside Shopping Centre, Darling Harbour) Gavala is 100% Aboriginal-owned, stirring up an outback vibe with a mind-boggling collation of paintings, boomerangs, didjeridus, artefacts, books, clothing and CDs.

---

hub is towards the northern end, but the southern end is being redeveloped, gradually shifting the city's focus. For a lofty city view, take a trip up **Sydney Tower** (Map pp186-7; 100 Market St).

Sydney lacks a true civic centre, but **Martin Place** (Map pp186-7) comes close. This grand pedestrian mall extends from Macquarie St to George St, and is lined with monumental financial buildings and the Victorian colonnaded General Post Office. There's a cenotaph commemorating Australia's war dead, an amphitheatre for lunchtime entertainment and plenty of places to sit and watch the weekday crowds.

Sydney's 1874 **Town Hall** (Map pp186-7) is a few blocks south of here on the corner of George and Druitt Sts. The elaborate chamber room and concert hall inside match the fabulously ornate exterior. Next door, the Anglican **St Andrew's Cathedral** (Map pp186-7), built around the same time, is Australia's oldest cathedral. Next to St Andrew's, taking up an entire city block, the **Queen Victoria Building** (p212) is Sydney's most sumptuous shopping complex and a real highlight. Running a close second is the elegant **Strand Arcade** (p212) between Pitt St Mall and George St.

Breathing life into the CBD's lacklustre southwestern zone are Sydney's teensy **Spanish Quarter** (Map pp186-7) and thriving **Chinatown** (Map pp186-7), a tight nest of restaurants, shops and aroma-filled alleyways around Dixon St. Chinatown goes berserk

during Chinese New Year in late January/early February – streets throng with sideshows, digitally accompanied musicians and stalls selling everything from good-luck tokens to black-sesame ice-cream burgers (seeing jaunty, fire-breathing paper dragons after eating these is not a hallucinogenic effect).

On the eastern edge of the city centre is the formal **Hyde Park** (Map pp186-7), which has a grand avenue of trees and delightful fountains. Wander into the dignified **Anzac Memorial** (Map pp186-7; ☎ 9267 7668; www.rslnsw.com.au; admission free; ☉ 9am-5pm) here, with an interior dome studded with one star for each of the 120,000 NSW citizens who served in WWI. The pines near the entrance grew from seeds gathered at Gallipoli. **St Mary's Cathedral** (Map pp186-7), with its new copper spires, overlooks the park from the east, while the 1878 **Great Synagogue** (Map pp186-7; ☎ 9267 2477; www.greatsynagogue.org.au; 187a Elizabeth St; adult/child $5/3; ☉ tours noon Tue & Thu) stands to the west.

Macquarie Place & Around

Narrow lanes lead south from Circular Quay towards the city centre. At the corner of Loftus and Bridge Sts is **Macquarie Place** (Map pp186-7), a leafy public square proudly displaying a cannon and an anchor from the First Fleet flagship, HMS *Sirius*, and an 1818 obelisk etched with road distances to various points in the nascent colony.

Inside the old Water Police Station (1858) nearby, the **Justice & Police Museum** (Map pp186-7; ☎ 9252 1144; www.hht.net.au; cnr Albert & Phillip Sts; adult/child/family $8/4/17; ◷ 10am-5pm Sat & Sun, daily Jan) celebrates, as it were, disreputable activities. Does anyone not look guilty in a mugshot?

MUSEUM OF SYDNEY

This thoroughly engaging **museum** (Map pp186-7; ☎ 9251 5988; www.hht.net.au; cnr Bridge & Phillip Sts; adult/child/family $10/5/20; ◷ 9.30am-5pm) is east of Macquarie Place, on the site of Sydney's first (and infamously pungent) Government House (1788). The city's early history (including pre-1788) comes to life here through whispers, arguments, gossip, artefacts and state-of-the-art installations.

MACQUARIE STREET

A crop of early public buildings grace this street, defining the city's edge from Hyde Park to the Opera House. Many of these buildings were commissioned by Lachlan Macquarie, the first NSW governor with a vision of Sydney beyond its convict origins. He enlisted convict architect Francis Greenway to help realise his plans.

Two Greenway gems front onto Queens Sq at Hyde Park's northern end: **St James Church** (Map pp186-7), Sydney's oldest church, having been built in 1819, and the **Hyde Park Barracks Museum** (Map pp186-7; ☎ 8239 2311; www.hht.net.au; adult/child/family $10/5/20; ◷ 9.30am-5pm), also built in 1819. The barracks functioned as quarters for Anglo-Irish convicts (aka Oz pioneers) from 1819 to 1848, an immigrant depot (1848–86) and government courts (1887–1979) before its current incarnation – a window into everyday convict life.

Further down Macquarie St are the deep verandas, formal colonnades and ochre tones of the twin 1816 **Mint** (Map pp186-7; ☎ 8239 2288; www.hht.net.au; admission free; ◷ 9am-5pm Mon-Fri) and **Parliament House** (Map pp186-7; ☎ 9230 2111; www.parliament.nsw.gov.au; admission free; ◷ 9am-5pm Mon-Fri) buildings, originally wings of the infamous Rum Hospital, which was built by two Sydney merchants in 1816 in return for a monopoly on the rum trade.

Next to Parliament House, the **State Library of NSW** (Map pp186-7; ☎ 9273 1414; www.sl.nsw.gov.au; ◷ 9am-6pm Mon-Fri, 11am-5pm Sat & Sun) holds over five million tomes, the smallest being a tablet-sized Lord's Prayer, and hosts innovative exhibitions in its **galleries** (◷ 9am-8pm Mon-Thu, 10am-5pm Fri-Sun).

At the top of Bridge St, the **Sydney Conservatorium of Music** (☎ 9351 1222; www.usyd.edu.au/conmusic; Macquarie St) was the Greenway-designed stables and servants' quarters for Macquarie's planned Government House. Macquarie was usurped as governor before the house could be finished, partly because of the project's extravagance.

Built between 1837 and 1845, the Gothic Revival **Government House** (Map pp186-7; ☎ 9931 5222; www.hht.net.au; admission free; ◷ 10.30am-3pm Fri-Sun, grounds 10am-4pm daily) is just off Macquarie St in the Royal Botanic Gardens. You can only see the overstuffed furnishings on a tour.

The **Domain** (Map pp186-7) is a pleasant grassy area east of Macquarie St that was set aside by Governor Phillip for public recreation. The unfailingly eccentric **Speakers' Corner** (Map pp168-7; ◷ noon-4pm Sun) convenes in front of the Art Gallery – religious zealots, nutters, political extremists, homophobes, hippies and guidebook writers express their earnest opinions.

AUSTRALIAN MUSEUM

Not far from Macquarie St, this **natural history museum** (Map pp186-7; ☎ 9320 6000; www.amonline.net.au; 6-8 College St; adult/child/family $10/5/25; ◷ 9.30am-5pm) stuffed its first animal just 40 years after the First Fleet dropped anchor. There are Aboriginal, native-wildlife and kid-friendly exhibitions, self-guided tours and indigenous performances on Sunday (call for times).

ART GALLERY OF NSW

Highlights at this **gallery** (Map pp186-7; ☎ 9225 1744; www.artgallery.nsw.gov.au; Art Gallery Rd, The Domain; admission free, varied costs for touring exhibitions; ◷ 10am-5pm Thu-Tue, to 9pm Wed, free guided tours 1pm) include 19th- and 20th-century Australian art and Aboriginal and Torres Strait Islander art. The European and Asian art is best for those not leaving Oz anytime soon. The controversial, much-discussed Archibald Prize (www.thearchibaldprize.com.au) exhibits here annually, with portraits of the famous and not-so-famous bringing out the art critic in everyone. There are numerous screenings and special programs.

ROYAL BOTANIC GARDENS

The **gardens** (RBG; Map pp186-7; ☎ 9231 8111; www.rbgsyd.nsw.gov.au; Mrs Macquaries Rd; admission free; ◷ 7am-sunset) were established in 1816 as the colony's vegetable patch. The attitude here is relaxed – signs say, 'Please walk on the grass. We also invite you to smell the roses, hug the trees, talk to the birds and picnic on the lawns'. Take a free **guided walk** (10.30am daily), or an **Aboriginal Heritage Tour** (9231 8134; per person $25; 2pm Fri), both departing from the Gardens Shop.

Highlights include the rose garden, the South Pacific plant collection, the prickly arid garden, the glass pyramid at the **Tropical Centre** (adult/child $4.20/2.20; 10am-4pm) and a herb garden. Management periodically tries to oust the colonies of bats (aka flying foxes) as they destroy things and poop on everything but they just keep hanging around. Amid the hubbub of central Sydney, you may well want to hang around the gardens yourself. The walk from Mrs Macquaries Point to the Opera House is one of Sydney's best.

Darling Harbour

This rambling, purpose-built, waterfront tourist development (www.darlingharbour.com) lining Cockle Bay on the city's western edge was once industrial docklands with factories, warehouses and shipyards. These days it is very commercial and something of a theme park, without a real theme except money.

Hemmed in by an architectural spoil of grotesque flyovers, chain hotels, sculptures and playgrounds are various museums and sights, a plethora of harbour-cruise outlets and the overrated Harbourside Shopping Centre. The flashy **Cockle Bay Wharf** (Map pp186–7) and **King St Wharf** (Map pp186–7) precincts contain cafés, bars and restaurants aimed at the day-tripping masses.

An actual highlight is a stroll across the restored **Pyrmont Bridge** (Map pp186–7), which cuts over this mess with a timeless dignity. It leads to **Pyrmont** (Map p196), home of the Sydney Fish Market (see right) and the **Star City Casino** (Map pp186–7; 9657 8694; www.starcity .com.au; 80 Pyrmont St, Pyrmont; 24hr), where fish of a different type are filleted.

Darling Harbour and Pyrmont are serviced by ferry, monorail, Metro Light Rail (MLR) and the Sydney Explorer bus.

SYDNEY AQUARIUM

Visitors wander about fish-eyed at the ever-popular **aquarium** (Map pp186–7; 8251 7800; www .sydneyaquarium.com.au; Aquarium Pier; adult/child/fam-ily $30/15/70; 9am-10pm, last admission 9pm), celebrating the richness of Australian marine life. Three 'oceanariums' are moored in the harbour: sharks, rays and humungous fish in one; Sydney Harbour marine life and seals in the other two. Don't miss the kaleidoscopic colours of the Great Barrier Reef exhibit, platypuses and crocodiles at the Southern and Northern Rivers exhibits, and the cute penguins in the Southern Oceans section.

SYDNEY WILDLIFE WORLD

Next to the aquarium, this indoor **wildlife zoo** (Map pp186–7; 9333 9288; www.sydneywildlife world.com.au; Aquarium Pier; adult/child/family $30/15/70; 9am-10pm, last admission 9pm) is the place to poke a koala or mount a wallaby (OK, you just get to look at them unless you buy the stuffed versions in the vast gift shop). Unexpectedly intriguing are the displays of ants and other industrious bugs.

AUSTRALIAN NATIONAL MARITIME MUSEUM

Beneath an Utzonlike roof, the thematic **maritime museum** (Map pp186–7; 9298 3777; www.anmm .gov.au; 2 Murray St; admission free, special exhibits adult/ child/family from $10/6/20; 9.30am-5pm) examines Australia's inextricable relationship with the sea. Exhibitions range from Aboriginal canoes to surf culture and the Navy. If you can avoid a trip to the poop deck on the extra-cost ships moored outside, this museum is great value.

POWERHOUSE MUSEUM

Many get a charge out of this eclectic **museum** (Map pp186–7; 9217 0100; www.powerhousemuseum .com; 500 Harris St, Ultimo; adult/child/family $10/5/25, ad-ditional costs for special exhibits; 10am-5pm) inside the former power station for Sydney's defunct tram network. It's a fascinating place with hands-on exhibits on everything from science to how people used to live in Sydney (note the women's work area titled '…never done').

CHINESE GARDEN OF FRIENDSHIP

Built according to the balanced principles of Yin and Yang, these **gardens** (Map pp186–7; 9281 6863; www.chinesegarden.com.au; adult/child/family $6/3/15; 9.30am-5pm) is an oasis of tranquillity in the otherwise hectic Darling Harbour.

SYDNEY FISH MARKET

With over 15 million kilograms of seafood shipped through here annually, the cavernous **fish market** (Map p196; 9004 1122; www.sydneyfish market.com.au; cnr Pyrmont Bridge Rd & Bank St, Pyrmont; 7am-4pm) is the place to introduce yourself to a bewildering array of mud crabs, Balmain

SYDNEY

bugs, lobsters, oysters, mullet, rainbow trout, fat slabs of salmon and more. There are plenty of fishy restaurants, a deli, a wine centre, a sushi bar and an oyster bar. You can picnic on the water. Arrive early to check out the early morning auctions or take a behind-the-scenes **auction tour** (per person $20; 6.50-8.30am Thu) – reservations aren't required, but wear closed-toe shoes. You can also book yourself in for regular seafood cooking classes here at the **Sydney Seafood School** (Map p196; 9004 1111; classes from $75). It's west of Darling Harbour on Blackwattle Bay; the MLR stops outside.

Kings Cross

Riding high above the CBD under the big **Coca-Cola sign** (Map p193) – as much a Sydney icon as LA's Hollywood sign – 'the Cross' is a bizarre, densely populated dichotomy of good and evil. Strip joints, tacky tourist shops and backpacker hostels bang heads with trendy restaurants, funky bars and sybaritic guesthouses. The Cross retains a sleazy, cannibalistic aura, but the vague sense of menace is more imaginary than real. Sometimes the razzle-dazzle has a sideshow appeal; sometimes walking up Darlinghurst Rd promotes pity. Either way, it's never boring.

The gracious tree-lined streets of neighbouring **Potts Point** (Map p193) and **Elizabeth Bay** (Map p193) feature well-preserved Victorian, Edwardian and Art Deco houses and flats.

Possibly the only word in the world with eight 'o's, **Woolloomooloo** (Map p193), down **McElhone Stairs** (Map p193) from the Cross, was once a slum full of drunks and sailors, and drunk sailors. Things are begrudgingly less pugilistic these days – the pubs are relaxed and **Woolloomooloo Wharf** (Map p193) contains scads of restaurants. The infamously lowbrow and exceedingly popular **Harry's Café de Wheels** (see p206) remains. Gulp down a late-night pie and mash.

It's a 15-minute walk to the Cross from the city, or you could hop on a train. Buses 323-7, 324-5 and 333 from the city also pass through here.

Inner East

The pulsing backbone of the Inner East is **Oxford Street** (Map pp182–3), a long string of shops, cafés, bars and clubs that exudes a flamboyance largely attributable to Sydney's gay community. The **Sydney Gay & Lesbian Mardi Gras** (see p200) gyrates through here every

February. **Taylor Square** (Map pp186–7) is gay Sydney's decadent nucleus.

Oxford St runs all the way from Hyde Park to Centennial Park, continuing to Bondi Junction. Confusingly, street numbers recommence east of South Dowling St, the Darlinghurst-Paddington border. Bus 378 from Railway Sq and buses 380, 389 and L82 from Circular Quay run the length of Oxford St.

Wedged between Oxford and William Sts, Darlinghurst is home to the **Sydney Jewish Museum** (Map p193; 9360 7999; www.sydneyjewish museum.com.au; 148 Darlinghurst Rd; adult/child/family $10/6/22; 10am-4pm Sun-Thu, to 2pm Fri, closed Jewish holidays), with evocative, powerful exhibits on Australian Jewish history and the Holocaust.

South of Darlinghurst is **Surry Hills**, a very walkable area where scenesters prowl the pavements and every corner seems to have some perfect little pub or café. It was once the undisputed centre of Sydney's rag trade and print media, and many of its warehouses have been converted to slick apartments. Preserved as a temple to rock and roll artistry, the **Brett Whiteley Studio** (Map pp182–3; 9225 1881; www.brett whiteley.org; 2 Raper St; adult/concession $7/5; 10am-4pm Sat & Sun) exhibits some of Whiteley's most raucous paintings. Surry Hills is a short walk east of Central Station or south from Oxford St. Catch buses 301, 302 or 303 from Circular Quay.

Next door to Surry Hills, **Paddington** (Map pp182–3), aka 'Paddo', is an elegant suburb of restored terrace houses on steep leafy streets. Paddington was built for aspiring Victorian artisans, but the lemminglike rush to the outer suburbs after WWII turned it into Australia's worst slum. Renewed passion for Victorian-era architecture (and the realisation that the outer suburbs were unspeakably boring) fuelled Paddington's 1960s resurgence. By the 1990s, real estate was out of reach and the Victorians terraces (with their iron 'lace' detailing) had never looked better.

The best time to explore Paddington's streets and hibiscus-lined laneways is on Saturday when the **Paddington Market** (p213) is pumping. Join the meandering throngs for a foot massage, a tarot reading or a funky shirt to wear clubbing that night. Many a weekend has been whiled away strolling Oxford St.

Just southeast of Paddington is Sydney's biggest park, the 220-hectare **Centennial Park** (Map pp182–3), which has running, cycling, skating and horse-riding tracks, duck ponds, barbecue sites and sports pitches.

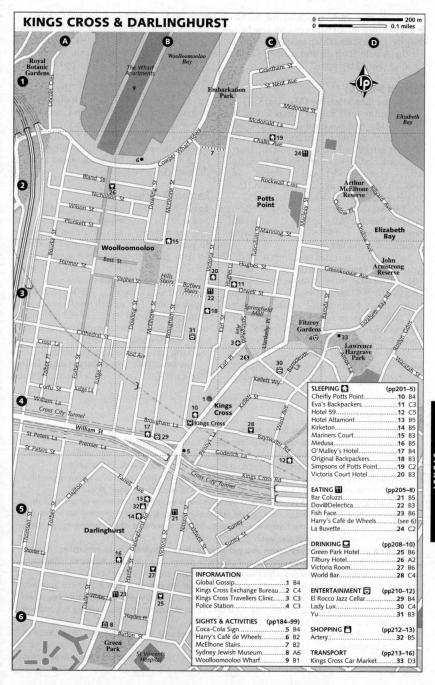

KINGS CROSS & DARLINGHURST

SYDNEY

Near Moore Park, much of the former Sydney Showgrounds has been converted into the private **Fox Studios** (Map pp182–3). Nearby are the Aussie Stadium and Sydney Cricket Ground (both Map pp182–3).

Eastern Suburbs

Handsome **Rushcutters Bay** (Map pp182–3) is a five-minute walk east of Kings Cross; its harbourside park is a great spot for cooped-up travellers to stretch their legs. The eastern suburbs extend out from here – a shimmering, conservative conglomeration of Range Rovers, skinny models and mortgage madness. The harbour-hugging New South Head Rd passes through **Double Bay** (Map pp182–3) and **Rose Bay** (Map pp182–3), and then climbs east into **Vaucluse** (Map pp182–3) and genteel **Parsley Bay** (Map pp182–3), where a platypus is sometimes spotted.

An imposing, turreted specimen of Gothic Australiana, **Vaucluse House** (Map pp182-3; ☎ 9388 7922; www.hht.net.au; Wentworth Rd, Vaucluse; adult/child/family $8/4/17; ⏱ 9.30am-4pm Fri-Sun) is Sydney's last 19th-century harbourside estate. Explorer and political sabre-rattler William Charles Wentworth lived here from 1828 to 1862. The Bondi Explorer bus (see p200) stops outside.

At the entrance to the harbour is **Watsons Bay** (Map pp182–3), a snug community with restored fisherman's cottages, a palm-lined park and a couple of nautical churches. Nearby **Camp Cove** (Map pp182–3) is one of Sydney's best harbour beaches, and there's a nude beach (mostly male) near South Head at **Lady Bay**. **South Head** (Map pp182–3) has great views across the harbour entrance to North Head and Middle Head. The **Gap** (Map pp182–3) is an epic cliff-top lookout where sunrises, sunsets, canoodling and suicide leaps transpire with similar frequency.

Buses 324 and 325 from Circular Quay service the eastern suburbs via Kings Cross. Grab a seat on the left heading east to snare the best views.

Eastern Beaches

Bondi (Map p195) lords it over every other beach in the city, despite not being the best one for a swim, a surf or, damn it, a place to park your bum on a summer weekend. Despite the rather ugly commercial strip, there's an indefinable buzz here which, when combined with the flashy cafés and rugged rocks flanking the sand, gives this place a perceptible aura. The suburb itself has a unique atmosphere due to its mix of old Jewish and other European communities, dyed-in-the-wool Aussies, tourists who never went home, working travellers and budgie-smugglers.

The beautiful, 5km **Bondi to Coogee Clifftop Trail** leads south from Bondi Beach along the

---

BONDI RESCUE

Tom Bunting is a lifeguard at Bondi Beach. As if that job wasn't iconic enough, he's also highly visible on *Bondi Rescue*, the hugely popular reality TV show on Australia's Ten network, which, in typical TV-fashion, has dubbed him 'the smartest lifeguard'. We talked to Tom while he scanned Bondi Beach and the surf from the lifeguard tower smack in the middle of the sand.

How has being on a number-one-rated show changed your life? We're all a lot more popular! Seriously, though, none of us are here for that – we just want to be good at our job.

What are the first clues that someone is likely to need your help? We know before they do – we know where the rips and currents are in relation to where they are swimming, we watch the way they are swimming, their stroke, and not to be racist about it, their nationality, as some nationalities are not used to the water.

What do people usually say when you get them ashore? Anything ever surprising? Usually very little. They are usually embarrassed. About one person in 10 actually thanks us. [There is a pinboard in the tower covered with thank you letters and cards.]

Does it get you dates? Are there lots of fake Bondi lifeguards in the pubs? I'm in a very happy relationship, and about 90% of the lifeguards are in stable relationships too. I've never seen or heard of any fakes, and the council is very strict about our uniform – we are not allowed to give any of our shirts etc to friends.

What would you quit this job to do? I'm about to become a paramedic, but I'll continue to do this part-time.

As related to Ryan Ver Berkmoes

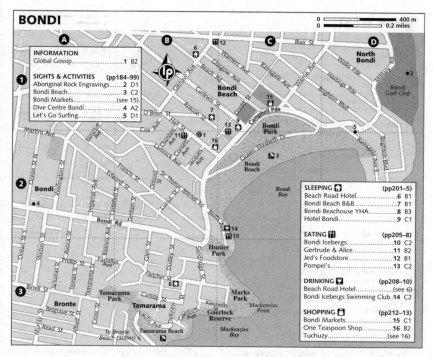

BONDI

cliff tops to Coogee via Tamarama, Bronte and Clovelly Beaches, interweaving panoramic views, swimming spots and foodie delights.

Most of the pubs, bars and restaurants are set back from the beach along daggie Campbell Pde and more-hip Hall St. Nearby are Sunday's **Bondi Markets** (Map p195), and some Eora **Aboriginal rock engravings** (Map p195) north of the beach uphill near the cliffs at the Bondi Golf Club. Look for the fenced areas about 20m southeast of the enormous chimney.

Catch bus 380, 389 or L82 from the city or bus 381 from Bondi Junction to get to the beach.

Inner West

West of the centre is the higgledy-piggledy peninsula suburb of **Balmain** (Map pp182–3). It was once a notoriously rough neighbourhood of dockyard workers but has been transformed into an artsy, middle-class area of restored Victoriana flush with pubs, cafés and trendy shops. Don't miss the Saturday market (see p213). Catch a ferry from Circular Quay, or buses 432/4 from Railway Sq or 441/2 from the QVB.

Cosy, bohemian **Glebe** (Map p196) lies just southwest of the centre, and boasts a large student population, streets lined with BMWs, a tranquil Buddhist temple, yuppies galore and Glebe Point Rd, a wonderful, leafy ramble of shops and cafés amid gentrified workers cottages. Saturday's **Glebe markets** (Map p196) overrun Glebe Public School. Glebe is a 10-minute walk from Central Station along side streets – avoid smoggy Broadway. Buses 431/4 from Millers Point run via George St along Glebe Point Rd. The MLR also services Glebe.

South of Sydney University is **Newtown** (Map p196), a melting pot of social and sexual subcultures, students and edgy boutiques. King St, its relentlessly urban main drag, is full of funky clothes stores, bookshops and cafés. Slowly moving upmarket, Newtown retains an irrepressible dose of grunge and a rockin' live-music scene. Take the train, or bus 422/3, 426 or 428 from Circular Quay to King St.

Southwest of Glebe is predominantly Italian **Leichhardt** (Map pp182–3), increasingly popular with students and yuppies. Norton St is the place for pizza, pasta and slick

SYDNEY

INNER WEST

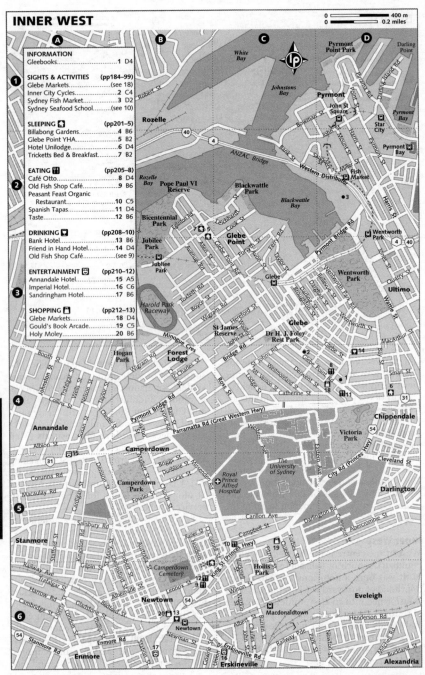

0 — 400 m
0 — 0.2 miles

Mediterranean style. Bus 413 from Wynyard, and buses 435/8 and 440 from Circular Quay service Leichhardt.

North Shore

On the northern side of the Harbour Bridge is **North Sydney** (Map pp182–3), a high-rise office centre with little to tempt the traveller. **McMahons Point** is a low-key, forgotten suburb below the western side of the bridge. There's a row of cheery alfresco cafés on Blues Point Rd, running down to Blues Point Reserve on Lavender Bay.

At the end of Kirribilli Point, just east of the bridge, are **Admiralty House** (Map pp182–3) and **Kirribilli House** (Map pp182–3), the Sydney residences of the Governor General and Prime Minister respectively.

On the eastern shore of Lavender Bay is **Luna Park** (Map pp182–3; ☎ 9922 6644; www.lunapark sydney.com; 1 Olympic Pl, Milsons Point; admission free, multiride passes from $20; ☼ 10am-10pm Sun-Thu, to midnight Fri & Sat), with its sinister chip-toothed clown entry. It's a classic, retro carnival with a Ferris Wheel, Rotor, Flying Saucer, Tumble Bug and other rides guaranteed to shake loose lunch.

East of here are the upmarket suburbs of **Neutral Bay**, **Cremorne** and **Mosman**, all with coves and harbourside parks perfect for picnics. Ferries from Circular Quay service these suburbs. On the northern side of Mosman is improbably pretty **Balmoral**, facing Manly across Middle Harbour.

In a superb harbourside setting, **Taronga Zoo** (Map pp182–3; ☎ 9969 2777; www.zoo.nsw.gov.au; Bradleys Head Rd, Mosman; adult/child/family $37/18/93; ☼ 9am-5pm) has some 4000 critters (from seals to tigers, koalas to giraffes, echidnas to platypuses), all in hillside habitats. Twilight concerts take place in the zoo during February and March. Zoo ferries depart Circular Quay's Wharf 2 at a quarter past and quarter to the hour.

The zoo is really steep, so if you arrive by ferry, consider taking the **Sky Safari cable car** (included in admission) or bus 238 to the top entrance and work your way downhill. A **ZooPass** (adult/child $44/22), sold at Circular Quay and elsewhere, includes return ferry rides and zoo admission.

Manly

Laid-back Manly clings to a narrow isthmus between ocean and harbour beaches near North Head. **North Steyne Beach** was named

Sydney's best in 2008 for its beauty and friendliness; and overall, dare we say it, you'll have a beachier experience here than at Bondi.

The **Manly visitors centre** (Map p198; ☎ 9977 1430; www.manlytourism.com; Manly Wharf; ☼ 9am-5pm Mon-Fri, 10am-4pm Sat & Sun), just outside the ferry wharf, has information on the 9km **Manly Scenic Walkway**, which tracks west from Manly around North and Middle Harbours, past waterside mansions and harbour viewpoints and through rugged Sydney Harbour National Park. At times you'll feel completely isolated in bushland – it's easy to forget you're right in the middle of Sydney.

The **Corso** connects Manly's ocean and harbour beaches – surf shops, burger joints, juice bars and so-so cafés proliferate. A footpath follows the ocean shoreline around a small headland to tiny **Fairy Bower Beach** and the picturesque **Shelly Beach**. On the harbourside, the refurbished **Manly Wharf** offers cafés, pubs and restaurants. West of here is **Oceanworld** (Map p198; ☎ 8251 7879; www.oceanworld.com.au; W Esplanade; adult/child/family $18/10/44; ☼ 10am-5.30pm), a tired 1980s aquarium with underwater transparent tubes where you can see 3m sharks. Next door, the whimsical **Manly Art Gallery & Museum** (Map p198; ☎ 9949 1776; www.manly.nsw.gov.au; admission free; ☼ 10am-5pm Tue-Sun) focuses on Manly's relationship with the beach.

North Head Scenic Dr (Map pp182–3) provides stunning ocean, harbour and city views. At road's end, the 1km **Fairfax Walk** connects three lookouts over the churning waters of the harbour entrance. The bushland scenery isn't half bad, either.

To get to Manly, you could take a bus but the only real way to go is by ferry or JetCat. The ride is one of Sydney's musts.

ACTIVITIES
Canoeing & Kayaking

Natural Wanders (☎ 9899 1001; www.kayaksydney .com; per person from $90; ☼ 9am-1pm) Has exhilarating half-day bridge and island-paddling tours.
New South Wales Canoeing Association (☎ 8116 9730; www.nswcanoe.org.au) For information on canoeing.

Cycling

For information, **Bicycle NSW** (Map pp186–7; ☎ 9281 4099; www.bicyclensw.org.au; level 5, 822 George St) publishes *Cycling Around Sydney*, which details city routes and paths.
Inner City Cycles (Map p196; ☎ 9660 6605; 151 Glebe Point Rd, Glebe; per day/week $33/88; ☼ 9.30am-6pm

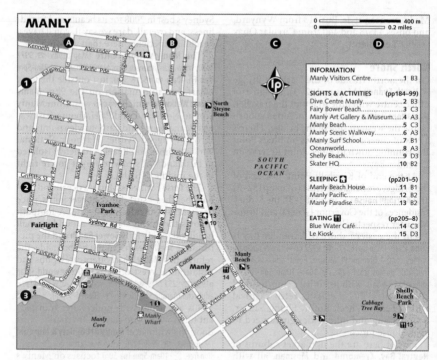

Mon-Wed & Fri, 9.30am-7pm Thu, 9am-4pm Sat, 11am-3pm Sun; 🚌 431-434) Convenient access to the city and to Central Station.

Diving

Sydney's best shore dives are at Gordons Bay, north of Coogee (Map pp182–3); Shark Point, Clovelly (Map pp182–3); and Ship Rock, Cronulla (Map p180). Popular boat-dive sites are Wedding Cake Island off Coogee (Map pp182–3), Sydney Heads (Map pp182–3), and off Royal National Park (Map p180).

Dive Centre Bondi (Map p195; ☎ 9369 3855; www .divebondi.com.au; 198 Bondi Rd, Bondi; 🕑 8.30am-6pm Mon-Fri, from 7.30am Sat & Sun) Four-day PADI course from $425; shore and boat dives, and rentals.

Dive Centre Manly (Map p198; ☎ 9977 4355; www .divesydney.com.au; 10 Belgrave St, Manly; 🕑 8.30am-7pm Mon-Fri, from 7.45am Sat & Sun) Similar rates and offerings as its sister office in Bondi.

Horse Riding

The **Centennial Parklands Equestrian Centre** (Map pp182–3; ☎ 9332 2809; www.cp.nsw.gov.au; Lang Rd, Paddington; per hr incl equipment $70; 🕑 9am-5pm) conducts one-hour, 3.6km horse rides around tree-lined Centennial Park, Sydney's favourite urban green space. Several stables at the centre conduct rides; equine familiarity is not required.

In-Line Skating

The beach promenades at Bondi and Manly and the paths of Centennial Park are the favoured spots for skating.

Rollerblading Sydney (Map pp182–3; ☎ 0411-872 022; www.rollerbladingsydney.com.au; Milsons Point Station; lessons per hr $55; 🕑 7am-9pm Mon-Fri, 8am-6pm Sat & Sun) Rentals, quality skates and protective gear.

Skater HQ (Map p198; ☎ 9976 3833; www.skaterhq .com.au; 2/49 North Steyne, Manly; hire per hr from $15; 🕑 9am-6pm) Excellent blades and gear.

Sailing

Sydney has dozens of yacht clubs and sailing schools. In fact life on the water is an essential part of the Sydney's zeitgeist.

EastSail Sailing School (Map pp182–3; ☎ 9327 1166; www.eastsail.com.au; d'Albora Marina, New Beach Rd, Rushcutters Bay; cruises per person from $100; 🕑 9am-6pm) A sociable outfit offering cruises, and introductory 'Yachtmaster' courses from $500.

Sydney by Sail (Map pp186-7; ☎ 9280 1110; www
.sydneybysail.com.au; Festival Pontoon, National Maritime
Museum, Darling Harbour; courses $425; ☾ 9am-5pm)
Daily harbour sailing tours (three hours, $150) and intro-
ductory weekend sailing courses.

Surfing

On the South Shore, get tubed at Bondi,
Tamarama, Coogee, Maroubra and Cronulla.
The North Shore is home to a dozen gnarly
surf beaches between Manly and Palm Beach,
including Curl Curl, Dee Why, Narrabeen,
Mona Vale and Newport.

Let's Go Surfing (Map p195; ☎ 9365 1800; www
.letsgosurfing.com.au; 128 Ramsgate Ave, Bondi; 2hr
lesson with gear adult/child from $75/39; ☾ 9am-7pm)
Board and wetsuit hire is $30 for two hours.

Manly Surf School (Map p198; ☎ 9977 6977; www
.manlysurfschool.com; North Steyne Surf Club, Manly;
lessons per hr incl board & wetsuit adult/child $55/45;
☾ 9am-6pm) Small-group surf lessons.

Swimming

There are 100-plus public swimming pools in
Sydney, and many beaches have protected rock
pools. Harbour beaches offer sheltered and
shark-netted (but sometimes soupy) swimming, but nothing beats (or cures a hangover
faster than) Pacific Ocean waves. Always swim
within the flagged lifeguard-patrolled areas,
and never underestimate the surf.

Outdoor city pools include:

Andrew 'Boy' Charlton Pool (Map pp186-7; ☎ 9358
6686; www.abcpool.org; 1C Mrs Macquaries Rd, The
Domain; adult/child $5.50/3.80; ☾ 6am-8pm Sep-Apr) A
50m outdoor saltwater pool and harbour-view café.

Dawn Fraser Baths (Map pp182-3; ☎ 9555 1903;
Elkington Park, Glassop St, Balmain; adult/child $4/2;
☾ 7.15am-6.15pm Oct-Nov & Mar-Apr, 6.45am-7pm
Dec-Feb) These magnificently restored late-Victorian baths
(1884) protect swimmers from underwater undesirables.

North Sydney Olympic Pool (Map pp182-3; ☎ 9955
2309; www.northsydney.nsw.gov.au; Alfred St South,
Milsons Point; adult/child $5.50/3; ☾ 5.30am-9pm
Mon-Fri, 7am-7pm Sat & Sun) Next to Luna Park, right on
the harbour. A place of legends – many world records have
been set here.

WALKING TOUR

This walk combines four star sights for a
highly concentrated start on the city.

Start in Hyde Park at the **Anzac Memorial** (**1**;
p189). Walking north, on your right you'll see
the **Australian Museum** (**2**; p190) and, a bit further
on, the impressive **St Mary's Cathedral** (**3**; p189).

Keep going north to reach **Macquarie Street** (**4**;
p190), with its collection of early colonial buildings. If you love gardens, head east through
the **Royal Botanic Gardens** (**5**; p190). Follow the
waterfront path to the spectacular **Sydney Opera
House** (**6**; p184) and **Circular Quay** (**7**; p185). On
the west side of Circular Quay, behind the
Museum of Contemporary Art (**8**; p185), is **the Rocks**
(**9**; p185) – very much worth exploring.

> **WALK FACTS**
>
> **Start** Anzac Memorial
> **Finish** Pylon Lookout
> **Distance** 5km
> **Duration** two to three hours

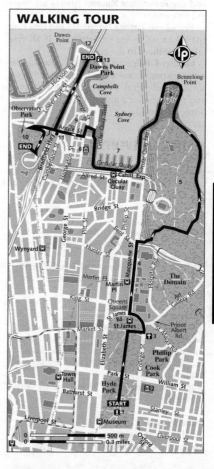

WALKING TOUR

SYDNEY

Work your way up to the **Sydney Observatory** (**10**; p185). If you want to cross the **Harbour Bridge** (**12**; p184), find the **Argyle Cut** (**11**; p185), near Cumberland St, and head up; the views from the bridge are worth every step, especially from the **Pylon Lookout** (**13**; p185). Head back to the Rocks for a refreshing drink (see p208).

SYDNEY FOR CHILDREN

Organised kids' activities ramp up during school holidays (December/January, April, July and September) – check www .sydneyforkids.com.au and the free *Sydney's Child* and *Kid Friendly* magazines for listings. Otherwise, in Darling Harbour, **Sydney Aquarium** (p191), **Sydney Wildlife World** (p191) and the **Powerhouse Museum** (p191) are huge kid favourites.

Elsewhere, **Taronga Zoo** (p197) and **Luna Park** (p197) are sure-fire entertainers. If all else fails, take them to the beach!

Nannies & Helpers (☎ 9363 4221; www.nannies andhelpers.com.au; booking fee $20-33, babysitting per hr $15-20) will send a babysitter to wherever you're staying for a minimum of three hours. Some of the bigger hotels offer their own services.

FESTIVALS & EVENTS

Sydney has plenty of festivals and special goings-on year-round. Visitors centres will be able to advise you what's on when you're in town.

January

Sydney Festival (www.sydneyfestival.org.au) This massive event floods the city with art, including free outdoor concerts in the Domain.

Big Day Out (www.bigdayout.com) Open-air concert featuring many local and international performers and bands.

February

Sydney Gay & Lesbian Mardi Gras (www.mardigras .org.au) Late February. The highlight of this world-famous festival is the over-the-top, sequined Oxford St parade, culminating in a bacchanalian party at the Entertainment Quarter.

Tropfest (www.tropfest.com) The world's largest short-film festival.

March/April

Royal Easter Show (www.eastershow.com.au) Twelve-day agricultural show and funfair at Homebush Bay.

May

Australian Fashion Week (www.mafw.org.au) Early May. At Circular Quay.

June

Sydney Film Festival (www.sydneyfilmfestival.org) A 14-day orgy of cinema held at the State Theatre and other cinemas.

September

Royal Botanic Gardens Spring Festival (www .rbgsyd.gov.au) Spring into spring, with concerts, colourful flower displays and plenty of pollen.

Rugby League Grand Final (www.nrl.com) The two best teams left standing in the National Rugby League (NRL) meet to decide who's best.

October

Manly Jazz Festival (www.manly.nsw.gov.au/manly jazz) Labour Day long weekend. The jazz is mostly free.

December

Sydney to Hobart Boat Race (www.rolexsydney hobart.com) On 26 December Sydney Harbour is a sight to behold as hundreds of boats crowd its waters to farewell the yachts competing in this gruelling race.

TOURS

There are countless tours available in Sydney. You can book most of them at the visitors centres (p181).

City Bus Tours

Bondi Explorer (☎ 13 15 00; www.sydneypass.info; adult/child $39/19; ⊙ 8.45am-4.15pm) Two-hour, hop-on, hop-off, 19-stop loop from Circular Quay to Kings Cross, Double Bay, Rose Bay, Vaucluse, Watsons Bay, the Gap, Bondi Beach and Coogee, returning to the city along Oxford St. Buses depart every 30 minutes; buy your ticket on board or at STA offices.

Sydney Explorer (☎ 13 15 00; www.sydneypass.info; adult/child $39/19; ⊙ 8.40am-5.20pm) The red STA Sydney Explorer bus follows a two-hour, 26-stop hop-on, hop-off loop from Circular Quay through Kings Cross, Chinatown, Darling Harbour and the Rocks, with pithy on-board commentary and discounted entry to attractions. Buses depart every 20 minutes.

Harbour Cruises

Captain Cook Cruises (Map pp186-7; ☎ 9206 1111; www.captaincook.com.au; Wharf 6, Circular Quay; adult/child/family from $25/12/55) Also at Aquarium Wharf, Darling Harbour.

Sydney Ferries (Map pp186-7; ☎ 9246 8300, 131 500; www.sydneyferries.nsw.gov.au; Circular Quay) Has a huge amount of info online and at the info booth that shows you how to tour the harbour by ferry and walk along the shore.

Walking Tours

BridgeClimb (Map pp186-7; ☎ 8274 7777; www
.bridgeclimb.com; 5 Cumberland St, The Rocks; adult $179-295, child $109-195; ☒ 3½hr tours around the clock) Don a headset, an umbilical cord and a naff grey jumpsuit and up you go. Book well in advance.

Sydney Aboriginal Discoveries (☎ 9680 3098, 0405-289 016; www.sydneyaustour.com.au/Abordiscover
.html; per person $65-180; ☒ 2-4hr tours daily) Tours focusing on Aboriginal culture and history, landmarks, sacred sites, a tasty feast of native Australian foods, and a Dreamtime cruise.

SLEEPING

Sydney's well of accommodation seems to never run dry, with everything from budget hostels to cosy B&Bs, comfortable motels, authentic Aussie pubs and deluxe harbour-view hotels. Between November and February, you should expect prices (especially at beach-side hotels) to jump by as much as 40%. Conversely, winter can mean bargains.

Read up on Sydney's neighbourhoods before you decide where to stay: partiers should head for Kings Cross, Darlinghurst, Paddington or Bondi; highlight hunters should shoot for the Rocks, the CBD, Darling Harbour or Chinatown. If you want to feel like a local, try Glebe, Potts Point, Surry Hills or Manly.

In this chapter, a budget room is classified as under $100 per night. Midrange doubles cost between $100 and $180; top-end doubles start at $180 a night. Serviced apartments usually sleep more than two people – good value for groups and families.

Budget

Sydney is a budget traveller's dream. Cheap accommodation can be found across the city.

CITY CENTRE

Wake Up! (Map pp186-7; ☎ 9288 7888; www.wakeup
.com.au; 509 Pitt St; dm from $28, r from $98; ☒ ☐ ; wi-fi) Backpackers sleep soundly in this converted 1900 department store on top of Sydney's busiest intersection. It's a convivial, colourful, professionally run hostel with a tour desk, 24-hour check-in, a sunny café, a bar and more. Dorms have four to 10 beds.

Big Hostel (Map pp186-7; ☎ 9281 6030; www
.bighostel.com; 212 Elizabeth St, Surry Hills; dm $28-32, r

$75-100; ☒ ☐ ; wi-fi) Upmarket and stylish, Big has attractive communal areas, including a cute rooftop terrace. All rooms have TVs and video players. Rates include a light breakfast. Although this bit of Elizabeth St isn't Sydney's most salubrious locale, Central Station's just across the road for a quick escape.

Railway Square YHA (Map pp186-7; ☎ 9281 9666; www.yha.com.au; 8 Lee St; dm $30-40, d $85-100; ☐ ☒) Adjoining Central Station, this hostel's main building is a historic 1904 train shed – some of the dorms are inside old train carriages. Facilities lean to the functional side of fancy but there's really not a bad bed among the 280 here. The more expensive doubles have bathrooms.

Sydney Central YHA (Map pp186-7; ☎ 9218 9000; www.yha.com.au; 11 Rawson Pl; dm from $30, d from $90; ☒ ☐ ☒) Near Central Station this 1913 heritage-listed 556-bed monolith has been massively renovated and now has its own supermarket, cinema and more. Rooms are brightly painted and the kitchens are great, but the highlight is sitting in the rooftop pool feeling at ease with the world.

ourpick Y Hotel (Map pp186-7; ☎ 9264 2451; www
.yhotel.com.au; 5-11 Wentworth Ave; dm $35, r from $80; ☒ ☐ ; wi-fi) A budget place with hotel services, the Y is perfectly located for walking everywhere *and* easy airport train access. Rooms are in a modern high-rise and span the gamut from small dorms to large rooms with en suites and kitchenettes.

Grand Hotel (Map pp186-7; ☎ 9232 3755; www
.merivale.com; 30 Hunter St; r from $80; ☒) One of Sydney's oldest hotels, the Grand is a busy multilevel pub. Up top, though, it has clean rooms with shared bathrooms; some have balconies. Stash a fruity blush wine in the fridge to accompany the fruity décor.

KINGS CROSS

Wooddduck Harbour City Backpackers (Map pp186-7; ☎ 1800 882 922; www.harbourcitybackpackers.com.au; 50 Sir John Young Cres, Woolloomooloo; dm $25, r from $75; ☐) Friendly and funky, this Woolloomooloo hostel is beloved for its roof terrace with Cinerama city skyline views. It's a huge place with 250 beds, but the ceilings are high and rooms airy.

Eva's Backpackers (Map p193; ☎ 9358 2185; www
.evasbackpackers.com.au; 6-8 Orwell St, Potts Point; dm $30, r from $80; ☒ ☐ ; wi-fi) Eva's is a perennial back-packers' favourite, probably because it's far enough out of the Kings Cross fray to maintain

some composure and dignity. Some rooms in this solid old building that looks like a country mercantile have air-con.

Original Backpackers (Map p193; ☎ 9356 3232; www .originalbackpackers.com.au; 160-162 Victoria St, Kings Cross; dm $30, r from $80; 🖳) A hostel for almost three decades, there's something new at the Original: a wing of spiffy doubles with private bathrooms. The true original is a rambling 176-bed affair in two character-filled Victorian houses. The front veranda is a fine place for soaking the always genial pleasures here.

O'Malley's Hotel (Map p193; ☎ 9357 2211; www.omal leyshotel.com.au; 228 William St, Kings Cross; r from $80; 🕱) This jovial Irish pub has 15 traditionally decorated, well-furnished rooms with private heritage-tiled bathrooms. It's surprisingly quiet, given the location. Harbour-view rooms are winners; breakfast is included.

BONDI
Bondi Beachouse YHA (Map p195; ☎ 9365 2088; www .bondibeachouse.com.au; 63 Fletcher St; dm from $25, r from $55; 🖳) A short stroll from the beach, the Art Deco, 94-bed Bondi Beachouse has a pool table, TV rooms, a barbecue, free play stuff (surfboards, snorkels etc) and Tamarama Beach views from the rooftop spa. It's the sort of place where you keep telling the staff 'another night please'. Bus 380 from Circular Quay stops nearby.

Beach Road Hotel (Map p195; ☎ 9130 7247; brh bondi@bigpond.com; 71 Beach Rd; r from $75; 🕱) This chipper hotel with the huge Coopers sign is part of a big, boxy pub two blocks back from the beach. Nautical décor surfs through the bars, eateries and nightclub to the rooms, which are clean and bright with decent bathrooms. Stay here only if you plan to partake of the pleasures below.

COOGEE
Coogee Beachside Accommodation (Map pp182-3; ☎ 9315 8511; www.sydneybeachside.com.au; 178 Coogee Bay Rd; d & tw $75) Beachside offers simple, clean doubles and twins with tidy shared bathrooms in a huge converted house. If you're in Sydney for a while, there are also one-, two- and three-bed apartments for longer stays. Common areas are spartan but clean.

GLEBE & NEWTOWN
Billabong Gardens (Map p196; ☎ 9550 3236; www.billa bonggardens.com.au; 5-11 Egan St, Newtown; dm from $25, r $50-100; 🖳 🏊) This enduring motel/hostel of-

fers a richer experience than most backpacker joints, with travellers, touring rock bands and anonymous others mixing by the jellybean of a pool. Rooms come with or without bathrooms; dorms have up to six beds.

Glebe Point YHA (Map p196; ☎ 9692 8418; www.yha .com.au; 262-264 Glebe Point Rd, Glebe; dm $25-40, r $70-120; 🖳; wi-fi) This 151-bed hostel features colourful, basic rooms and shared bathrooms. The main lure is the rooftop with its barbecue nights and a plethora of party high jinks. Kitchens and bathrooms are solid.

MANLY
Manly Beach House (Map p198; ☎ 9977 7050; www.manly beachhouse.com.au; 179 Pittwater Rd; r from $60; 🖳; wi-fi) Readers recommend this rambling, cheery, good-value option, a four-minute walk from the beach. Polite management prides itself on making *sure* you're comfortable (clean too: washing machines are free). Shared facilities are clean.

Midrange
THE ROCKS & CITY CENTRE
Mercantile Hotel (Map pp186-7; ☎ 9247 3570; www .mercantilehotel.citysearch.com.au; 25 George St, The Rocks; r from $110) The Mercantile's green-tiled exterior hints at the shamrock sympathies emanating from the bar. Upstairs the comfy, pub-style rooms avoid orange and green conflict with neutral colours, shared bathrooms and little fireplaces. Four suites have spas ($140).

Palisade Hotel (Map pp186-7; ☎ 9247 2272; www .palisadehotel.com; 35 Bettington St, The Rocks; r from $125) Standing sentinel-like at peaceful Millers Point, the Palisade Hotel has nine basic rooms with tidy shared bathrooms. The front rooms open onto shared balconies with iconic views of the Harbour Bridge, while others have windows looking over Walsh Bay. The neighbourhood pub downstairs usually shuts at sleep-friendly hours.

our pick Lord Nelson Brewery Hotel (Map pp186-7; ☎ 9251 4044; www.lordnelson.com.au; 19 Kent St, The Rocks; d $130-180; 🕱) Built in 1841, this boutique sandstone pub has its own brewery (try a pint of 'Nelson's Blood') and is just far enough from the Rocks' tourist mobs. The rooms have a graceful elegance and many have walls of the original exposed stone. Bathrooms are regal – even those that are shared.

Russell (Map pp186-7; ☎ 9241 3543; www.therussell .com.au; 143a George St, The Rocks; r from $135; 🕱) Traditionally decorated rooms (think lace and frills), lounge areas with fireplaces, library and a rooftop garden just minutes from Circular Quay make the architecturally chaotic old Russell a popular choice. A generous continental breakfast is included.

B&B Sydney Harbour (Map pp186-7; ☎ 9247 1130; www.bedandbreakfastsydney.com; 142 Cumberland St, The Rocks; r $140-230; ⊠) This century-old guesthouse is close to ferries and the Rocks, should you suddenly feel the need for a souvenir. Rooms (some with private bathroom) have lovely Empire-era furniture you might wish you had at home. Breakfasts are lavish.

Vibe Hotel (Map pp186-7; ☎ 9282 0987; www.vibehotels.com.au; 111 Goulburn St; d from $190; ⊠ ⊑ ⊛) This refurbished old dowager has a pale palette of shades accented by a fruit basket of bright colours, kind of like the walls at a daycare centre. The 190-room boutique chain hotel is the kind of place where the alluring rooftop pool is described as a 'lifestyle' rather than an amenity.

CHINATOWN & DARLING HARBOUR

Pensione Hotel (Map pp186-7; ☎ 9265 8888; www.pensione.com.au; 631-635 George St; r from $100; ⊠ ⊑) This tastefully reworked post office features 68 smart, neutrally shaded rooms with fridges. Mark Rothko prints and a wooden staircase warm the simple, restrained surrounds. Aim for a rear room away from traffic noise.

Capitol Square Hotel (Map pp186-7; ☎ 9211 8633; www.rydges.com/capitolsquare; cnr George & Campbell Sts; r $120-200; ⊠) Near both Chinatown and Darling Harbour, with double-glazed windows to keep out the noise, this heritage hotel is part of the Rydges chain. The rather plain rooms can be tight, although you can escape to the world via high-speed internet access.

Metro Hotel Sydney Central (Map pp186-7; ☎ 9283 8088; www.metrohospitalitygroup.com; 431 Pitt St; r from $150; ⊠ ⊛ ; wi-fi) Centrally located, the high-rise Metro has a brassy lobby, a business centre and 220 comfortable rooms. (Deluxe rooms have designers prints; basic ones have country scenes suitable for jigsaw puzzles.) The rooftop pool puts you above it all.

KINGS CROSS

Hotel 59 (Map p193; ☎ 9360 5900; www.hotel59.com.au; 59 Bayswater Rd, Kings Cross; r from $90; ⊠) Hotel 59 provides good bang for your buck on the quiet part of Bayswater Rd, with nine nouveau-Med rooms that have fridges. Guests get a free run of the tasty café downstairs at breakfast.

Mariners Court (Map p193; ☎ 9358 3888; www.marinerscourt.com.au; 44-50 McElhone St, Woolloomooloo; r $100-160; ⊑) A tucked-away treasure, this ship-shape old place goes for the hat trick of location, price and roominess. All rooms have courtyards or balconies, some with leafy outlooks. There's even a billiards room.

Chiefly Potts Point (Map p193; ☎ 9358 2755; www.cresthotel.com.au; 111 Darlinghurst Rd, Kings Cross; r $145-200; ⊠ ; wi-fi) With the definitive Kings Cross location, the high-rise Chiefly is the rebadged old Crest. The 227 rooms are business standard with a certain anonymity that dirty weekenders and execs on the lam appreciate. Splurge for a harbour view.

Victoria Court Hotel (Map p193; ☎ 9357 3200; www.victoriacourt.com.au; 122 Victoria St, Potts Point; r from $160; ⊠) The Victoria is a 22-room high-end guesthouse filling a pair of three-storey 1881 brick terrace houses. Rooms have private bathrooms and a museum's worth of frills. Some have balconies; all have access to the covered courtyard where breakfast is served.

Simpsons of Potts Point (Map p193; ☎ 9356 2199; www.simpsonspottspoint.com.au; 8 Challis Ave, Potts Point; r from $175; ⊠ ⊑ ; wi-fi) An 1892 red-brick politician's palace, Simpsons has an entrance flanked by palm trees and is on a street of chic cafés. The 14 rooms are restrained but quite elegant and you can get in the mood with a glass of port at check-in. Most rooms have showers although there are a few tubs lurking about.

DARLINGHURST & SURRY HILLS

Macquarie Boutique Hotel (Map pp186-7; ☎ 8262 8844; www.macquariehotel.com; 40-44 Wentworth Ave, Surry Hills; r $90-120; ⊠ ⊑) This pub represents a good deal on a number of fronts – a supercentral location, decent prices, plenty of character and its own microbrewery. The rooms have had a spiffing up of late and now boast high-speed internet. For those who equate pubs with sticky carpets, the polished wood floors will be a nice surprise.

Wattle Hotel (Map pp186-7; ☎ 9332 4118; www.thewattle.com; 108 Oxford St, Darlinghurst; r $100-160; ⊠) There's no handier place to stay if your Sydney itinerary is largely nocturnal and gay. At Mardi Gras be prepared to book a decade in advance and sacrifice your straight sibling's first-born for one of the corner terraces overlooking the parade route. There's a rooftop terrace good for gazing year-round.

City Crown Motel (Map pp186-7; ☎ 9331 2433; www.citycrownmotel.com.au; 289 Crown St, Surry Hills; d from $115;

⊠ ▣) In an unbeatable Surry Hills location, this nondescript three-storey motel has basic rooms with alarmingly striped bed covers. Escape to the balconies and plan your next fun foray.

Hotel Altamont (Map p193; ☎ 9360 6000; www.altamont.com.au; 207 Darlinghurst Rd, Darlinghurst; r from $130; ⊠ ▣ ⊠) The Rolling Stones have stayed in this Georgian pile that's had a postmodern make-over, thus the name Altamont (given the legendary concert turned into a brawl, maybe the Stones skipped paying here). Rooms are sleek and just the thing for a club-heavy visit to Sydney.

Cambridge Park Inn (Map pp186-7; ☎ 9212 1111; www.cambridgeinn.com.au; 212 Riley St, Surry Hills; r $150-180; ⊠ ▣ ⊠) The embodiment of what architect Robin Boyd called the 'Great Australian Ugliness', this hotel is best seen from the inside looking out. Many of the 170 rooms have balconies and are sleekly decorated. You can't beat the location.

Manor House (Map pp186-7; ☎ 9380 6633; www.manorhouse.com.au; 86 Flinders St, Darlinghurst; r from $170; ⊠ ▣) Step off busy Flinders St and step back in time to 1850 as you enter this grand mansion, complete with extravagant chandeliers, moulded ceilings, Victorian tiling and enough brocade for a queen. It's popular at Mardi Gras time, being right on the parade route and staggering distance from the party.

PADDINGTON & WOOLLAHRA

Hughenden (Map pp182-3; ☎ 9363 4863; www.hughendenhotel.com.au; 14 Queen St, Woollahra; r from $150; ⊠ ; wi-fi) A quirky 1870s Italianate guesthouse, the Hughenden is a short walk to legions of genteel pubs. Rooms feature antique bric-a-brac flourishes; some have balconies, all have fridges and access to a reading room and sundeck. Breakfast is included.

Sullivans Hotel (Map pp186-7; ☎ 9361 0211; www.sullivans.com.au; 21 Oxford St, Paddington; r $165-180; ⊠ ▣ ⊠ ; wi-fi) Popular with gay travellers, this well-run 64-room motel in 'Paddinghurst' has tidy rooms in an anonymous package (think plain grey wrapper). Still, the location's great, and the brick-paved central courtyard has a solar-heated pool.

EASTERN SUBURBS

Savoy Hotel (Map pp182-3; ☎ 9326 1411; www.savoyhotel.com.au; 41 Knox St, Double Bay; r $125-200; ⊠) Sitting pretty among the gentrified charms of Double Bay's café strip, the Savoy offers an upscale retreat near the harbour. Catch a ferry to the city. Rooms are motel-standard but do have fridges for chilling the fizz. Try to avoid atrium-view rooms.

BONDI

Hotel Bondi (Map p195; ☎ 9130 3271; www.hotelbondi.com.au; 178 Campbell Pde; r $50-135; ⊠) Let it all hang out at the landmark 'Pink Palace' on Bondi Beach. The 50 rooms seem to come in that many variations: small and cheap singles are just that, and moving up the price scale gets you steadily more room and better views until the entire sweep of the beach is yours (and you have a balcony and air-con).

Bondi Beach B&B (Map p195; ☎ 9365 6522; www.bondibeach-bnb.com.au; 110 Roscoe St; r $95-200) Owners Nadia and Michael go all-out to make this place feel like your own home (only cleaner, and with colours out of a tropical fish tank). Rooms vary greatly, some have cute little terraces with tiny tables outside.

COOGEE

Dive Hotel (Map pp182-3; ☎ 9665 5538; www.divehotel.com.au; 234 Arden St; r $140-220; ⊠ ; wi-fi) Here's your chance to live the cheap-chic Ikea lifestyle without having to screw your furniture together. The smart and simple rooms have kitchenettes and blue-tile bathrooms; some have balconies with beach views. Enjoy the included continental breakfast on the courtyard until 1pm.

GLEBE

Hotel Unilodge (Map p196; ☎ 9338 5000; www.unilodgehotel.com.au; cnr Broadway & Bay St; r from $150; ⊠ ▣ ⊠) The rooms inside this former Grace Bros department store would never have passed muster with a window-designer back in the day – they're very bland in a Best Western–sort-of-way. Still, they are huge, good-value and have kitchenettes and high-speed internet.

Tricketts Bed & Breakfast (Map p196; ☎ 9552 1141; www.tricketts.com.au; 270 Glebe Point Rd; r from $175; ⊠ ▣ ; wi-fi) Inside this carefully restored 1880s merchant's mansion, seven large rooms with private bathrooms are decked out with antiques and Persian rugs. The garden is a verdant wonderland, overlooked by a sumptuous veranda.

MANLY

Manly Paradise (Map p198; ☎ 9977 5799; www.manlyparadise.com.au; 54 North Steyne; motel r $155-210, apt from $280; ⊠ ▣) Spacious *Miami Vice*–era apartments sleep five; some have balconies overlooking Manly's ocean beach. There's a heated, 5th-floor rooftop pool, a spa, a sauna, half-court tennis and more. Motel rooms lack the room for a beach bash.

Top End

THE ROCKS

Park Hyatt (Map pp186-7; ☎ 9241 1234; www.sydney .park.hyatt.com; 7 Hickson Rd, The Rocks; r from $500; ⊠ ▣ ▣; wi-fi) Commanding the opposite tip of the horseshoe of Circular Quay to the Opera House, the Park Hyatt boasts the best location in Sydney. The graciously low-rise building matches the opulence of its position with sandstone, marble and slick contemporary design. The views are mesmerising, but be sure to not cheap out and get a room *without* a balcony.

CITY CENTRE

Blacket (Map pp186-7; ☎ 9279 3030; www.theblacket .com; 70 King St; r from $230; ⊠ ▣; wi-fi) Blacket's 68 stark, dark and stylish rooms blend urban escape with lashings of contemporary cool. Loft suites – all white, caramel and grey – sleep four and have spa, separate lounge, kitchenette and let you share the sounds of your bed experience with those below.

Establishment Hotel (Map pp186-7; ☎ 9240 3100; www.establishmenthotel.com; 5 Bridge Lane; r from $290; ⊠ ▣) Through this door pass discreet celebrities, stylish foreigners, corporate raiders and execs hoping for a nooner with their assistant. The hotel of Sydney's power bar has artful and large rooms that come in two themes that roughly translate as posh and zen. All have high-speed internet.

DARLINGHURST & SURRY HILLS

Kirketon (Map p193; ☎ 9332 2011; www.kirketon.com .au; 229 Darlinghurst Rd, Darlinghurst; r from $220; ⊠ ▣) The Kirketon's 40 designer rooms are as impeccably turned out as its brash young clientele (and hot staff). Stylishly sparse suites are jazzed up with passion-fruit scented toiletries, bright wall colours, retro furnishings, Swiss chocolates, mohair throw rugs and a vague sense of entitlement.

Medusa (Map p193; ☎ 9331 1000; www.medusa.com .au; 267 Darlinghurst Rd, Darlinghurst; r from $270; ⊠ ▣; wi-fi) Medusa the seducer's shocking-pink exterior hints at the vibrant, playful décor inside. Eighteen small, vivid suites with enormous beds, mod-con bathrooms and regal furnishings open onto a tranquil courtyard and reflection pool. Just being in the rooms will make you upgrade your underwear.

MANLY

Manly Pacific (Map p198; ☎ 9977 7666; www.accorhotels .com.au; 55 North Steyne; r from $190; ⊠ ▣ ▣) Right on Manly's ocean beach, this dapper midrise hotel is managed by resort-brand, Novotel. Its 214 rooms may be a quick ferry ride from the CBD but they are closer in holiday spirit to Coffs Harbour or even the Gold Coast. Lounge by the rooftop pool or just hang on your balcony.

Camping

Sydney's caravan parks, most of which also have sites for tents, are a fair way out of town. The following are up to 26km from the city centre. Note that peak seasons (such as Christmas) see rate hikes.

Lane Cove River Tourist Park (Map pp182-3; ☎ 9888 9133; www.lcrtp.com.au; Plassey Rd, North Ryde; unpowered/ powered sites $34/36, cabins from $145; ⊠ ▣) This cheery place in the national park lies 14km north of the city and has good facilities (including over 150 caravan sites, plus cabins). By bus the CBD is a 40-minute trip.

Sydney Lakeside Holiday Park (☎ 9913 7845; www .sydneylakeside.com.au; Lake Park Rd, Narrabeen; unpowered/powered sites from $35/45, cabins from $140; ⊠ ▣) Located 26km north of Sydney, this nifty place occupies prime real estate around the northern beaches.

EATING

Eating out is a pure delight in Sydney. Abundant fresh produce, innovative and highly competitive chefs, and a multicultural melange all combine to make it the number one sport of locals and visitors alike.

City Centre, the Rocks & Circular Quay

The mix of dining options in Sydney's urban core ranges from frenetic lunchtime cafés to some fine establishments. In the centre, weekday surprising lunchtime pleasures abound in mall and arcade food courts along George St.

La Renaissance (Map pp186-7; ☎ 9241 4878; 47 Argyle St; meals $6-14; ☻ breakfast & lunch) Hidden in a maze of inner courtyards within the heart of the Rocks, this authentic French bakery has lovely baguette sandwiches and many other treats, including Orangina. A real find amid the tourist squalor, and the coffee is *très bon*.

Bodhi (Map pp186-7; ☎ 9360 2523; Cook & Phillip Parks, 2-4 College St; yum cha $5-8, mains $6-18; ☽ lunch daily, dinner Tue-Sun) Bodhi scores high for its cool design and leafy disposition. Quick-fire waiters rebound off the minimalist interior and slat-wood tables outside. Yum cha is a daily constant.

Spice I Am (Map pp186-7; ☎ 9280 0928; 90 Wentworth Ave; mains $8-26; ☽ lunch & dinner Tue-Sun) Join legions of local Thais (and Thai cuisine aficionados) wanting an authentic taste of Southeast Asia. Service is speedy, which is good as people queue for a chance to eat the bargain-priced fragrant and spicy dishes.

Bar Quattro (Map pp186-7; ☎ 9267 0299; St James Station; mains $12-25; ☽ 7am-5pm Mon-Fri, 8am-5pm Sat & Sun) Chatting, drinking coffee and choosing items off a traditional Italian menu are the order of the day at this limestone heritage building that was once a public toilet. It's a lovely spot right on Hyde Park.

One Alfred Street (Map pp186-7; ☎ 9241 4636; 1 Alfred St; mains $16-20; ☽ breakfast, lunch & dinner) Look past the fast food neon for this island of fine fare. Australian cuisine gets star treatment morning noon and night. Even the fish and chips are a few cuts above. The menu features many NSW prize foodstuffs, especially cheeses.

Chinatown & Darling Harbour

Chinatown is flush with spicy nooks dishing up fantastic plastic décor and cheap and scrumptious fare, especially around Dixon St. Darling Harbour's developments place an emphasis on views.

Xic Lo (Map pp186-7; ☎ 9280 1678; 215A Thomas St, Haymarket; mains $8-14; ☽ 11am-10.30pm) Serving up authentic favourites such as *pho bo* (beef rice-noodle soup) and rice paper rolls, this slick diner is a Vietnamese temple to budget eating.

Emperor's Garden BBQ & Noodles (Map pp186-7; ☎ 9281 9899; 213 Thomas St, Haymarket; dishes $8-26; ☽ 9.30am-11pm) Barbecued ducks dangling in the window catch your eye, *gow gee* (dumplings) and the delicious softshell crab catch your palette at this barebones Chinatown special.

Marigold Restaurant (Map pp186-7; ☎ 9281 3388; Level 5, 683 George St, Haymarket; 4-5 serves yum cha $15-25; ☽ 10am-3pm & 5.30pm-midnight) So popular it has an extra floor (4th) just for Sunday. This vast yum cha palace is a constant whirl of trolley dollies in silk dresses and waiters in bow ties bustling around the 800 seats.

Zaaffran (Map pp186-7; ☎ 9211 8900; Level 2, 345 Harbourside, Darling Harbour; mains $17-38; ☽ lunch & dinner) For once a Darling Harbour restaurant where the food will divert you from the view. Highly creative and upscale takes on Indian cuisine are a true pleasure. Veggies will beam at the selection.

Kings Cross, Potts Point & Darlinghurst

The Cross has a good mixture of tiny cafés, swanky eateries and fast-food joints with greasy fare to soak up beer, or gargantuan hangover breakfasts if you're a little too late.

Harry's Café de Wheels (Map p193; ☎ 9357 3074; Cowper Wharf Rdwy, Woolloomooloo; mains $5-10; ☽ 8.30am-2.30am Mon-Wed, to 3am Thu, to 4am Fri & Sat, to 1am Sun) For decades, cab drivers, sailors and boozed-up nocturnals have sought relief with pea-and-pie floaters across Harry's famous counter. Sit on a milk crate overlooking the hulking Woolloomooloo warships and commence eating.

Bar Coluzzi (Map p193; ☎ 9380 5420; 322 Victoria St, Darlinghurst; meals $5-10; ☽ 5am-7pm) Legendary Coluzzi has been infusing Darlinghurst with caffeine for over 50 years. It's as simple as a perfect tall black; enjoy people-watching from a stool out front.

La Buvette (Map p193; ☎ 9358 5113; 35 Challis Ave, Potts Point; mains $11-17; ☽ 6am-9pm Sun-Thu, 6am-5.30pm Fri & Sat) Teeny La Buvette is crammed with the beautiful, the famous and the unknown-but-glam. The menu features salads, sandwiches, crepes and excellent coffee. There are a couple other scenester places nearby.

Dov@Delectica (Map p193; ☎ 9368 0600; 130 Victoria St, Potts Point; mains $17-24; ☽ 7.30am-3pm Sun-Tue, 7.30am-10pm Wed-Sat) Opening onto the nicest part of leafy Victoria St, Dov has a vibe that will tempt you to linger all morning. The menu varies throughout the day, starting with reasonably priced brekkie ($5 to $14) and lunch before the evening's serious fare listed on an ever-changing blackboard menu.

Fish Face (Map p193; ☎ 9332 4803; 132 Darlinghurst Rd, Darlinghurst; mains $22-30; ☽ dinner) Sardine-sized Fish Face is in your face with simple, make-no-compromises seafood. From the constant drama of the open kitchen emerges plate after plate of exquisite preparations from sushi to amazing fish and chips to whatever else is fresh.

Surry Hills

Sydney's trendiest neighbourhood rewards culinary explorations. Restaurants and cafés line Crown St north of Cleveland to Oxford St with many more on parallel Bourke St.

Bourke Street Bakery (Map pp182-3; ☎ 9669 1011; 633 Bourke St, Surry Hills; mains $3-7; ☒ 7am-4pm Mon-Fri, 8am-4pm Sat) The fresh baking in this corner spot is impeccable, particularly the sourdough bread. Grab a seat (or a milk crate outside) and an excellent coffee and pick from the alluring array of pizza slices, pies and pastries.

Book Kitchen (Map pp182-3; ☎ 9310 1003; 255 Devonshire St; mains $12-25; ☒ breakfast & lunch Wed-Mon, dinner Wed-Sat) Inspiration? You need inspiration? There's plenty in this stylish former garage that's now a used cookbook shop and bistro. Top NSW produce goes into an array of brekkie specials, salads and sandwiches by day. At night, the fare is fusion.

Tabou (Map pp182-3; ☎ 9319 5682; 527 Crown St; mains $14-25; ☒ lunch Mon-Fri, dinner daily) Settle into a little bentwood chair at this *belle époque* gem of a French restaurant. Classic French such as *pot au feu* (a herby, meaty stew) are presented in a perfect manner that's just so. The steak *frites* always rewards. There are several more places nearby.

Paddington

Paddington and Woolhara just east are dotted with casual places for an excellent meal. This is upscale and precious Sydney and the locals don't settle for the mundane.

Chocolate By The Bald Man Max Brenner (Map pp182-3; ☎ 9357 5055; 437 Oxford St, Paddington; sweets $3.50-5; ☒ 9am-11pm Mon-Thu, 9am-midnight Fri & Sat, 10am-10.30pm Sun) Shiny copper pipes lead to big vats of liquid heaven, while shelves bulge with all sorts of tempting treats to take away. Shudders of delight accompany the hot chocolate on a brisk day.

Sloanes (Map pp182-3; ☎ 9331 6717; 312 Oxford St, Paddington; mains $10-15; ☒ breakfast & lunch) Skip the tiny interior, for the sweet courtyard surrounded by mature trees. The breakfast and coffee are great, and the lunch blackboard is always crammed with fancy pies, salads, wraps and soups. The BLT (bacon, lettuce and tomato sandwich) is a thing of beauty.

Arthur's Pizza (Map pp182-3; ☎ 9332 2220; 260 Oxford St, Paddington; mains $10-25; ☒ lunch Sat & Sun, dinner daily) Pizzas continue to continue to draw the masses for their crispy cheesy goodness. Try the 'Zorro' (olives, ricotta, red onion, spinach and semidried tomato).

Four in Hand (Map pp182-3; ☎ 9362 1999; 105 Sutherland St, Paddington; mains $18-25; ☒ lunch & dinner) You can't go far in Paddington and Woollahra without tripping over some beautiful old pub with amazing food. In this case just don't trip over the dog on the way in. French bistro fare is given a Sydney makeover: look for fresh local seafood served superbly.

Bondi

Rub elbows with models, model-wannabes, model surfers and former model prisoners in lively Bondi. Gould and Hall Sts have more choices than a hunky lifeguard in a singles bar.

Jed's Foodstore (Map p195; ☎ 9365 0022; 60 Warners Ave; mains $5-14; ☒ breakfast & lunch) This sunny corner café is the epitome of slacker cool. It's just out of the Bondi hubbub so you can lounge away with spunky flavoured meals that include baked goods with colour and sambos with flair.

Gertrude & Alice (Map p195; ☎ 9130 5155; 40 Hall St; mains $10-15; breakfast & lunch) You're never at a loss for something to read in this shambling used bookshop-cum-café. The counter up front serves delightful baked goods such as Smartie cookies and a range of Med treats.

Pompei's (Map p195; ☎ 9365 1233; 126 Roscoe St; mains $17-22; ☒ lunch & dinner Tue-Sun) The pizza packs 'em in although the real secret is the northern Italian dishes whipped up by expat George Pompei. The house-made sorbets and gelati go down well at the pavement tables.

Bondi Icebergs (Map p195; ☎ 9365 9000; 1 Notts Ave; mains $38-50; ☒ lunch & dinner Tue-Sun) Poised above the famous swimming pool, iconic Icebergs' equally iconic views sweep across Bondi Beach and the sea. Steak and seafood are prepared with Italian flair and served with old-world finesse. Book early.

Coogee & Bronte

Swell (Map pp182-3; ☎ 9386 5001; 465 Bronte Rd, Bronte; mains $11-28; ☒ breakfast, lunch & dinner) Pull up a bench for seaside Swell's alluring day-turns-to-night Mod Oz menu. This is the perfect reward/draw for the lovely walk from Bondi.

Barzura (Map pp182-3; ☎ 9665 5546; 64 Carr St, Coogee; mains $17-27; ☒ breakfast, lunch & dinner) Frequented by sunglass-clad people with no visible daytime obligations, Barzura has to have the best views of any café in Sydney. The classic café fare includes uncomplicated salads, pasta dishes and generous breakfasts.

SYDNEY

Glebe & Newtown

The inner west is one of Sydney's most condensed melting pots, and global ethnic treats beckon from the main strips. Glebe touts a laid-back, unpretentious atmosphere and good-value food. Funky cafés and multicultural restaurants catering to student budgets line Newtown's King St.

Old Fish Shop Café (Map p196; ☎ 9519 4295; 239a King St; snacks $3; ⊙ 6am-7pm) This almost wall-free corner spot is Newtown's tattooed, dreadlocked hub. Friendly pierced staff will fix you a double shot as you put your feet up on the cushions in the window and watch the Newtown freak show pass onwards to oblivion.

Taste (Map p196; ☎ 9519 7944; 235 King St; meals $5-8; ⊙ lunch & dinner) Middle Eastern food so fresh it almost crackles. Nab one of the eight seats or get a picnic to go. Choose from an array of enticing salads and hot meals displayed like luxury goods behind glass.

Café Otto (Map p196; ☎ 9552 1519; 79 Glebe Point Rd, Glebe; mains $15-20; ⊙ lunch & dinner) A shady respite off the bustling strip, you can dine under trees or inside the airy, woodsy main room. There's good beer on tap, which will ease the process of ploughing through the long menu of burgers, pizza, pasta and salads.

Spanish Tapas (Map p196; ☎ 9571 9005; 26 Glebe Point Rd, Glebe; tapas $10-14, mains $20-23; ⊙ lunch Thu-Sat, dinner daily) This is a good-time restaurant: shared tapas plates, spirited music, raucous diners and waiters who say, 'Yezz, we jave a table forl yo!' Cheap jugs of sangria dissolve party resistance and fire you up for flamenco-dancing displays.

Peasant Feast Organic Restaurant (Map p196; ☎ 9516 5998; 121a King St; mains $20-30; ⊙ dinner Tue-Sat) French and Med fuse here over food that really would please a plutocrat. The menu includes classics such as cassoulet as well as veggie and vegan options such as gluten-free timbale. Cane-bottomed chairs and blackboard menus add charm (although they may not be organic).

Manly

The ferry terminal has some surprisingly nice little stands with fresh fare you can nab coming or going.

Blue Water Café (Map p198; ☎ 9976 2051; 28 South Steyne; mains $15-30; ⊙ 7.30am-10pm) This bustling beach café adorned with surfboards has plenty of company on the Manly shore. Choose between pasta, burgers, wraps, salads and more.

Le Kiosk (Map p198; ☎ 9977 4122; 1 Marine Pde, Shelly Beach; mains $29-37; ⊙ lunch daily, dinner Fri-Sun) 'Le Kiosk' sounds ugly but defines romance – a little sandstone cottage, subtle lighting, an open fireplace and the lull of lapping waves. The food proves a worthy paramour; swoon over snapper fillet with sautéed calamari, bacon, chilli and cauliflower. Vegetarians get a look in, too.

DRINKING

Pubs are a crucial part of the Sydney social scene, and you can down that sweet gold nectar at elaborate 19th-century affairs, cavernous Art Deco joints, modern and minimalist recesses, and everything in-between. Bars are generally more stylish and urbane, often with a dress code.

THE ROCKS

The Rocks is littered with rambling old pubs aimed at mobs. You can have your own pub crawl among three of Sydney's most evocative pubs on the almost-tourist-free north side of the bridge highway.

Harbour View Hotel (Map pp186-7; ☎ 9252 4111; 18 Lower Fort St; ⊙ 11am-midnight Mon-Sat, 11am-10pm Sun) Built in the 1920s, the Harbour View was the main boozer for the Harbour Bridge builders. There's good beer on tap and an exterior as beautiful as the porcelain on your granny's mantle.

Hero of Waterloo (Map pp186-7; ☎ 9252 4553; 81 Lower Fort St; ⊙ 9am-midnight Mon-Sat, noon-10pm Sun) Enter into the roughly hewn stone interior, meet some of the boisterous locals and enjoy the nightly music (piano, folk, jazz or Irish tunes) of this historic, old-time bar.

Lord Nelson Brewery Hotel (Map pp186-7; ☎ 9251 4044; www.lordnelson.com.au; 19 Kent St; ⊙ 11am-11pm Mon-Sat, noon-10pm Sun) Built in 1841, the 'Nello' claims to be Sydney's oldest pub (or is it the Hero of Waterloo down the road?) The on-site brewery produces some of Sydney's best ales; take some to bed… (see p202).

CITY CENTRE

Bambini Wine Room (Map pp186-7; ☎ 9283 7098; 185-187 Elizabeth St; ⊙ noon-10pm Mon, noon-11pm Tue-Fri, 5-11pm Sat) This tiny darkwood-panelled room with a huge chandelier is the sort of place where you might expect to see Oscar Wilde holding court in a corner. There's an extensive wine list (including rarely seen sparkling shiraz) and free almonds and breadsticks.

Establishment (Map pp186-7; ☎ 9240 3000; 252 George St; ✆ 11am-late Mon-Fri, 6pm-late Sat) Establishment's well-healed crush proves the art of swilling cocktails after a hard, city day is not lost. Sit at the majestic marble bar, in the swish courtyard or be absorbed by the leather lounge.

WOOLLOOMOOLOO

Tilbury Hotel (Map p193; ☎ 9368 1955; 18 Nicholson St; ✆ 9am-midnight) Yuppies, yachties, suits, gays and straights populate the light, bright interiors, packing the bistro and 1st-floor terrace at weekends. *The* place on Sunday afternoons.

KINGS CROSS & DARLINGHURST

Twenty-four-hour party people head for Darlinghurst and Kings Cross – denizens of its trashy main drag, Darlinghurst Rd, are more concerned with bar opening times as opposed to closing times.

Victoria Room (Map p193; ☎ 9357 4488; Level 1, 235 Victoria St, Darlinghurst; ✆ 6pm-midnight Tue-Thu, to 2am Fri & Sat, 2pm-midnight Sun) Plush chesterfields, Art Nouveau wallpaper, dark-wood panelling and bamboo screens – this joint is 1920s Bombay gin palace meets Hong Kong opium den.

Green Park Hotel (Map p193; ☎ 9380 5311; 360 Victoria St, Darlinghurst; ✆ 10am-2am Mon-Fri, noon-2am Sat & Sun) Slightly glammed-up old corner boozer where retro chic black linoleum replaces the sticky carpet. Always heaving, watch the passing parade from the pavement tables or hunker down in the beer garden.

World Bar (Map p193; ☎ 9357 7700; 24 Bayswater Rd, Kings Cross; ✆ 1pm-1am Mon, 1pm-4am Tue & Thu, 1pm-3am Wed, 1pm-6am Fri, 1pm-7am Sat, 1pm-3am Sun) Three floors of cool spaces attract the backpacking crowd (especially on Tuesday's Krapp Karaoke night). There's a vast tropical terrace out front, different genre DJs nightly and live local bands on Friday.

SURRY HILLS

Surry is scenester, hipster and yupster central. Wander the streets for a fine variety of pubs.

Cricketers Arms Hotel (Map pp186-7; ☎ 9331 3301; 106 Fitzroy St; ✆ noon-midnight Mon-Sat, to 10pm Sun) The polysexual Cricketers is a favourite haunt of arts students, metrosexuals and turntable boffins. There's tapas on tap and open fires because even people in black sometimes get cold.

Dolphin (Map pp186-7; ☎ 9331 4800; 412 Crown St; ✆ 10am-midnight Mon-Sat, 10am-10pm Sun) This large refurbished pub is as slick as its refurbished locale. The pretty things head upstairs to the is-that-actually-someone's-lounge-room addition, while nonidiot sports fans gravitate to the big screens downstairs.

PADDINGTON & WOOLLAHRA

The little streets between Oxford St and the Harbour shelter a fine range of neighbourhood pubs.

Royal Hotel (Map pp182-3; ☎ 9331 2604; 237 Glenmore Rd, Five Ways, Paddington; ✆ 11am-midnight) One of the points on the five-pointed junction star, the Royal not only is a star but it attracts them as well. This is a fine pub spread over three floors. At the top, the Elephant Bar has views over the harbour. Several good cafés adjoin.

Lord Dudley Hotel (Map pp182-3; ☎ 9327 5399; 236 Jersey Rd, Woollahra; ✆ 11am-11pm Mon-Wed, to midnight Thu-Sat, noon-10pm Sun) Millionaires and tradesfolk rub elbows, leaving one soiled and the other itchy. It's as close as Sydney gets to a ivy-covered English pub, right down to the quality beers by the pint.

WATSONS BAY

Watsons Bay Hotel (Map pp182-3; ☎ 9337 4299; 10 Marine Pde, Watsons Bay; ✆ 10am-midnight) Surrounded by two pricey seafood restaurants (both called Doyles) and a boutique hotel (also called Doyles), this simple boozer with a big terrace has the same views but isn't called Doyles. Avoid weekends.

BONDI & COOGEE

Coogee Bay Hotel (Map pp182-3; ☎ 9665 0000; cnr Coogee Bay Rd & Arden St, Coogee; ✆ 9am-5am Thu-Sat, to midnight Sun, to 3am Mon-Wed) The rambling, rowdy Coogee Bay complex has live music, a beer garden and views across the water. It is vacation time.

Beach Road Hotel (Map p195; ☎ 9130 7247; 71 Beach Rd, Bondi; ✆ 10am-2.30am Mon-Fri, 9am-12.30am Sat, 10am-10pm Sun) Weekends at this big, boxy pub see Bondi types (bronzed, buff and brooding) and woozy out-of-towners playing pool, drinking beer, and digging live bands and DJs. Sleep off your hangover upstairs (p202).

Bondi Icebergs Swimming Club (Map p195; ☎ 9130 3120; 1 Notts Ave, Bondi; ✆ 10am-11pm Sun-Thu, 10am-midnight Fri & Sat) Located just below Bondi Icebergs (p207), this is a more affordable and laid-back place with practically the same views.

SYDNEY

GAY & LESBIAN SYDNEY

Gay and lesbian culture forms a vocal, vital part of the Sydney's social fabric. **Taylor Square** (Map pp186–7) on Oxford St is the centre of arguably the second-largest gay community in the world; Newtown is home to Sydney's lesbian scene.

Sydney's famous **Gay & Lesbian Mardi Gras** (www.mardigras.org.au) draws over 700,000 spectators.

Free gay media includes *SX*. Online resources include www.ssonet.com.au (Sydney's main gay newspaper) and www.lotl.com (Sydney's monthly lesbian magazine).

Most accommodation in and around Oxford St is very gay-friendly. For frolicking, go for a wander along the city end of Oxford Street, or try the following popular faves on for size.

ARQ (Map pp186-7; ☎ 9380 8700; www.arqsydney.com.au; 16 Flinders St, Darlinghurst; Thu/Fri/Sat/Sun free/$10/20/5; ☼ 9pm-7am Thu, 9pm-9am Fri-Sun) This flash megaclub has a cocktail bar, a recovery room and two dance floors with high-energy house music, drag shows and a hyperactive smoke machine.

Imperial Hotel (Map p196; ☎ 9519 9899; www.theimperialhotel.com.au; 35 Erskineville Rd, Erskineville; admission free; ☼ 3-11.30pm Mon, 3pm-midnight Tue & Wed, 3pm-4am Thu, 3pm-6am Fri & Sat, 1pm-midnight Sun) The Art Deco Imperial's drag shows inspired *Priscilla, Queen of the Desert* (the opening scene was filmed here). Any drag queen worth her sheen has played the Cabaret Room.

Midnight Shift (Map pp186-7; ☎ 9360 4319; www.themidnightshift.com; 85 Oxford St, Darlinghurst; video bar free, club $10-20; ☼ noon-4am Mon-Wed, noon-6am Thu & Fri, 2pm-6am Sat & Sun) Sydney's perennial good-time boy palace packs in everyone from beefcakes to drags. The grog is cheap, the patrons messy and Kylie rules.

Oxford Hotel (Map pp186-7; ☎ 9331 3467; 134 Oxford St, Taylor Sq, Darlinghurst; admission free; ☼ 24hr) Big and crimson, the ever-lovin' Oxford is a Taylor Sq beacon. Downstairs it's beer-swilling and mannish, things get more precious as you climb.

Finally, if you simply must bring home a gift, the **Tool Shed** (Map pp186-7; ☎ 9360 1100; 191 Oxford St; ☼ 24hr) has sex toys that will both fascinate and horrify airport screeners.

NEWTOWN & GLEBE

The inner west is a great spot for a low-key schooner – Glebe and Newtown have plenty of decent pubs.

our pick Friend in Hand Hotel (Map p196; ☎ 9660 2326; 58 Cowper St, Glebe; ☼ 10am-late) Drink all the beer you want here, but don't be surprised when the eating competitions, water-pistol fights, crab racing and cheesy piano men distract you from your boozing. That's OK, you can always stroke the cockatoo.

Bank Hotel (Map p196; ☎ 8568 1900; www.bankhotel .com.au; 324 King St, Newtown; ☼ 10am-midnight Sun-Tue, 10am-2am Wed & Thu, 10am-4am Fri & Sat) Your drinking HQ in Newtown is as multifaceted as the streets below – or the crowd around you. Enjoy views from the rooftop terrace or the shade of the beer garden.

ENTERTAINMENT

Sydney has an eclectic and innovative arts, entertainment and music scene. Outdoor cinemas and sports stadiums cater to families, the city's jazz and blues circuit is healthy and dynamic, and live music is everywhere.

Pick up the 'Metro' section in Friday's *Sydney Morning Herald* for comprehensive entertainment details. Free weekly street magazines specialise in gig and club information. Tickets for most shows can be purchased directly from venues or the following distributors:

Moshtix (☎ 9209 4614; www.moshtix.com.au) Servicing alternative music venues.

Ticketek (Map pp186-7; ☎ 132 849; www.ticketek .com.au; 195 Elizabeth St; ☼ 9am-5pm Mon-Wed, to 7pm Thu & Fri, to 4pm Sat) Main booking agency.

Cinemas

First-run cinemas abound; tickets generally cost $15 to $18 for an adult, and $10 to $12 for a child. Most cinemas have a cheap night when tickets are discounted by around a third. Sydney also has a huge following of indie and foreign films.

Academy Twin Cinema (Map pp186-7; ☎ 9331 3457; www.palacecinemas.com.au; 3a Oxford St, Paddington) Art-house enthusiasts roll up for Academy's broad selection of independent Australian and international releases and annual Italian,

Mardi Gras, French and Spanish film festivals (held in February, March, April and May respectively).

Dendy Opera Quays (Map pp186–7; ☎ 9247 3800; www.dendy.com.au; Shop 9, 2 Circular Quay E) A plush cinema, screening first-run, independent world films.

Open Air Cinema (Map pp186–7; ☎ 1300 366 649; www.stgeorgeopenair.com.au; Mrs Macquaries Point, Royal Botanic Gardens; adult/concession $25/23; ⏰ box office 6.30pm, screenings 8.30pm Jan & Feb) Right on the harbour and outside, the three-storey screen here comes with surround sound, sunsets, skyline and swanky food and wine.

Clubs

Arthouse Hotel (Map pp186–7; ☎ 9284 1200; www.thearthousehotel.com.au; 275 Pitt St; ⏰ 11am–midnight Mon & Tue, 11am–1am Wed & Thu, 11am–3am Fri, 5pm–6am Sat) The art-meets-alcohol theme carries throughout this historic multistorey site. Friday nights see live jazz in the Dome Lounge, while on Saturday the whole downstairs becomes Kink (admission $25), one of Sydney's hottest club nights.

Home (Map pp186–7; ☎ 9266 0600; Cockle Bay Wharf, Darling Harbour; admission $25; ⏰ 11pm–6am Fri, 9pm–6am Sat) Welcome to the pleasuredome: a three-level, 2000-capacity timber-and-glass extravaganza, home to a huge dance floor, countless bars, outdoor balconies and an amazing DJ booth. Top-name international DJs spin house; live bands amp it up.

Lady Lux (Map p193; ☎ 9361 5000; www.myspace.com/ladyluxnightclub; 2 Roslyn St; admission $10; ⏰ 10pm–5am Fri–Sun) There's a sophisticated cosiness to this smallish club with its funky floral metallic wallpaper and cushioned couches. Friday nights are for underground house 'from deep to minimal tech', with loads of international DJs. Sundays are huge; there are other clubs nearby.

Yu (Map p193; ☎ 9358 6511; 171 Victoria St, Potts Point; admission $10–20; ⏰ 10pm–6am Thu–Sun) Sydney's best house DJs spin hip-hop, nu-skool, vocal and funky house in three rooms divided by sliding video screens.

Live Music
CLASSICAL

Sydney Opera House (Map pp186–7; ☎ 9250 7111; www.sydneyoperahouse.com; Bennelong Point) Yes, it's more than a landmark. As well as theatre and dance, the Opera House (p184) regularly hosts a number of local classical groups, including:

Opera Australia (☎ 9699 1099; www.opera-australia.org.au)

Sydney Symphony (☎ 8251 4600; www.sydneysymphony.com)

JAZZ & BLUES

Basement (Map pp186–7; ☎ 9251 2797; www.thebasement.com.au; 29 Reiby Pl, Circular Quay; admission $15–50; ⏰ noon–1.30am Mon–Thu, noon–2.30am Fri, 7.30pm–3am Sat, 7pm–1am Sun) Sydney's premier jazz venue presents big touring acts (Taj Mahal) and big local talent (Vince Jones, Mia Dyson). A broad musical mandate also sees funk, blues and soul bands performing, plus the odd spoken-word gig. Book a table by the stage.

El Rocco Jazz Cellar (Map p193; ☎ 9368 0894; 154 Brougham St; admission free–$35; ⏰ 5pm–1am Mon–Fri, 6pm–1am Sat & Sun) Sydney's first jazz club, this was the city's premier bohemian haunt, hosting performances by Frank Sinatra and Sarah Vaughan. Live jazz has now returned to this legendary rock-hewn basement.

Wine Banq (Map pp186–7; ☎ 9222 1919; www.winebanq.com.au; 53 Martin Pl; ⏰ noon–midnight Mon–Fri, 6pm–1am Sat) Sydney's sexiest jazz room adds a brilliant wine list to performers along the lines of Wynton Marsalis, James Morrison and Harry Connick Jr.

ROCK

Tickets to see rock bands can range from free to $50 or more depending on venues and whether you've ever actually heard the band before. Sydney's rock scene produces a lot of home-grown talent you'll hear playing in pubs all over town on weekends.

Annandale Hotel (Map p196; ☎ 9550 1078; www.annandalehotel.com; 17 Parramatta Rd, Annandale; ⏰ 11am–midnight Mon–Sat, 4–10pm Sun) The Yeah Yeah Yeahs and the Dandy Warhols are some of the bigger names to have fired up the stage at this alternative venue that hosts live music from Tuesday to Sunday (tickets $11 to $30). Cult movies screen on Monday nights.

Metro (Map pp186–7; ☎ 9287 2000; www.metrotheatre.com.au; 624 George St; tickets $25–65; ⏰ box office 10am–7pm Mon–Fri, noon–7pm Sat) Big-name indie acts grace the Metro's stage, eg the Eels and well-chosen local rockers such as the Butterfly Effect. It has theatre-style tiers, air-con, and super sound and visibility.

Gaelic Club (Map pp186–7; ☎ 9211 1687; www.thegaelicclub.com.au; 64 Devonshire St, Surry Hills; tickets $10–30; ⏰ varies with shows) Get your earwax blasted out at the Gaelic courtesy of iconic internationals of the likes of the Darkness and the Strokes, or home-grown sonic assailants Wolfmother and silverchair. It's a midsize, split-level, mosh-crazy affair.

Hopetoun Hotel (Map pp186-7; ☎ 9361 5257; 416 Bourke St, Surry Hills; admission free–$12; ☯ 3pm-midnight) Once the uncontested crucible for new Sydney rock bands, the diminutive 'Hoey' is still a launching pad for garage bands with plans. Plus there's Coopers on tap.

Sandringham Hotel (Map p196; ☎ 9557 1254; 387 King St, Newtown; admission free–$10; ☯ 9.30am-midnight Mon-Wed, 9.30am-2am Thu & Fri, 10am-2am Sat, 10am-10pm Sun) You can get rocked from Tuesday to Sunday at the Sando for not much money. There's a beer garden and happy hour (4pm to 7pm).

Spectator Sports
On any given Sydney weekend there'll be all manner of balls being hurled, kicked and batted around. Sydneysiders are excruciatingly passionate about the **National Rugby League** (NRL; www.nrl.com.au; tickets $20-40), the season transpiring at suburban stadia and **Aussie Stadium** (Map pp182-3; ☎ 9360 6601; www.aussiestadium.com; Driver Ave, Moore Park), with September finals.

From March right through to September, 2005's premiership winning Sydney Swans play in the **Australian Football League** (AFL; www.afl.com.au; tickets $20-40) at the **Sydney Cricket Ground** (SCG; Map pp182-3; ☎ 9360 6601; www.sydneycricketground.com.au; Driver Ave, Moore Park) and **ANZ Stadium** (Map pp182-3; ☎ 8765 2000; www.anzstadium.com.au; Olympic Blvd, Homebush Bay).

The **cricket** (www.cricinfo.com) season runs from October to March, the SCG hosting interstate Pura Cup matches and sell-out international test and World Series Cup matches.

Theatre
Sydney gets its share of big productions. Check entertainment listings for what's on.

Company B (Map pp182-3; ☎ 9699 3444; www.belvoir.com.au; 25 Belvoir St, Surry Hills; tickets $32-52) Artistic director Neil Armfield is a bright light of the Sydney theatre world. Stars such as Geoffrey Rush clamour to perform his adventurous interpretations in the Belvoir Street Theatre.

Sydney Theatre (Map pp186-7; ☎ 9250 1999; www.sydneytheatre.org.au; 22 Hickson Rd, Walsh Bay; tickets $65-75) The resplendent Sydney Theatre at the base of Observatory Hill puts 850 bums on seats for specialist drama and dance.

Sydney Theatre Company (Map pp186-7; ☎ 9250 1777; www.sydneytheatre.com.au; level 2, Pier 4, Hickson Rd, Walsh Bay; tickets $73) STC is Sydney's premier theatre company. Major Australian actors perform works by Alan Bennett, David Williamson and Shakespeare. Ask about $20 'Student Rush' tickets. Cate Blanchett and hubby Andrew Upton are the artistic directors.

SHOPPING
Shopping in Sydney is just plain amazing. If you want it, you'll find it. More important are all the things you didn't know you wanted until you make their discovery.

Most stores are open from 9.30am to 6pm Monday to Wednesday, Friday and Saturday, and until 9pm Thursday. Sunday trading is common but expect shorter hours, such as noon to 4pm or 5pm.

Shopping Areas
What follows are a few of the most interesting places to shop in Sydney and what you might find there.

CITY CENTRE
Sydneysiders head cityward if they've got something special to buy or when serious retail therapy is required. The central city's diverse range of mainly upmarket stores – centred on Pitt St Mall, Market St and George St – offers plenty of choice for gifts and treats.

David Jones (Map pp186-7; ☎ 9266 5544; cnr Market & Castlereagh Sts, Sydney) In two enormous city buildings, DJs is Sydney's premier department store. The Market St store has menswear, electrical and a highbrow food court; Castlereagh St has women's and children's wear and a friendly concierge to point you in the right direction. The food halls in the basement are a foodie fantasy.

Queen Victoria Building (QVB; Map pp186-7; ☎ 9265 6869; 455 George St, Sydney) This high-Victorian masterpiece occupies an entire city block, and though there are some inspiring retail offerings, they run a distant second to the magnificent wrought-iron balconies, stained-glass shopfronts and mosaic floors.

RM Williams (Map pp186-7; ☎ 9262 2228; 389 George St, Sydney) Urban cowboys and country folk can't get enough of this hard-wearing outback gear. Favourites include oilskin jackets, Akubra hats, moleskin jeans and leather work boots.

Strand Arcade (Map pp186-7; ☎ 9232 4199; 412 George St & 193-5 Pitt St Mall, Sydney) Constructed in 1891 in a squeezy space between George and Pitt Sts, the Strand Arcade rivals the QVB in the ornateness stakes. Three floors of designer fashions, Australiana and old-world coffee shops will make your short cut through here considerably longer.

Strand Hatters (Map pp186-7; ☎ 9231 6884; Shop 8, Strand Arcade, 412 George St, Sydney) Strand Hatters can top your noggin with a classically Australian Akubra bush hat. Staff block and steam hats to customers' cranial requirements.

PADDINGTON

Oxford St in Paddington is Sydney's premier strip for fashion. Among the choices:

Leona Edmiston (Map pp182-3; ☎ 9331 7033; 88 William St) Exuberantly feminine, flirtatious and fun designs.

Morrissey (Map pp182-3; ☎ 9380 4722; 372 Oxford St) Sexy, high-heeled, high-priced style.

Quick Brown Fox (Map pp186-7; ☎ 9331 3211; 100 Oxford St) Funky vintage fashions, catchy patterns and very hip boots and bags.

Sass & Bide (Map pp186-7; ☎ 9360 3900; www .sassandbide.com; 132 Oxford St) Sassy super-low-cut women's jeans, body-hugging jackets and minidresses.

Scanlan & Theodore (Map pp186-7; ☎ 9380 9388; 122 Oxford St) Beautifully made women's outfits for the evening or the office.

BONDI

As Bondi Beach has gentrified it has attracted its own big-name local designers, mainly based around Gould St.

One Teaspoon Shop (Map p195; ☎ 9365 1290; 86 Gould St) Rising star Jamie Blakey shows off cleavage-revealing dresses, as well as bikinis, belts and shoes.

Tuchuzy (Map p195; ☎ 9365 5371; 90 Gould St) Stocks an edgy collection of local and imported labels for budding male or female rock stars.

SURRY HILLS

The bottom end of Crown St has some great vintage stores.

C's Flashback (Map pp186-7; ☎ 9331 7833; 316 Crown St) Camp secondhand store sells both men's and women's threads.

NEWTOWN

The Inner West is the place to look for anything punky, alternative or in shades of black. King St has an interesting collection of boutiques, secondhand stores and the city's best used bookstores.

Gould's Book Arcade (Map p196; ☎ 9519 8947; 32 King St) Floor-to-ceiling racks and stacks.

Holy Moley (Map p196; ☎ 9550 4033; 325 King St) Very-Newtown murals (Robert De Niro in *Taxi Driver*, a skeleton with a mohawk) are right outside the station. Inside it's punky T-shirts, baby-doll dresses, sexy lingerie and more.

Markets

Balmain Market (Map pp182-3; ☎ 0418-765 736; cnr Darling St & Curtis Rd, Balmain; ⏲ 8.30am-4pm Sat) Set in the shady grounds of St Andrews Congregational, stalls sell arts, crafts, books, clothing, jewellery, plants, and fruit and veg. One of the best locally.

Bondi Markets (Map p195; ☎ 9315 8988; Bondi Beach Public School, cnr Campbell Pde & Warners Ave, Bondi; ⏲ 9am-4pm Sun) The kids are at the beach on Sunday while their school fills up with Bondi characters rummaging through tie-dyed secondhand clothes and books, beads and earrings, aromatherapy oils, candles, old records, and more.

Glebe Markets (Map p196; ☎ 4237 7499; Glebe Public School, cnr Glebe Point Rd & Derby Pl, Glebe; ⏲ 9am-4pm Sat) The best of the west; Sydney's dreadlocked, shoeless, inner-city contingent beats an aimless course to this crowded market.

Paddington Market (Map pp182-3; ☎ 9331 2923; St John's Church, 395 Oxford St, Paddington; ⏲ 10am-4pm Sat) Sydney's most-attended weekend market dishes up vintage clothes and hip fashions, jewellery, books, massage and palmistry. Just as your spirits flag, you'll find something special under a little awning.

Paddy's Markets (Map pp186-7; ☎ 1300 361 589; cnr Hay & Thomas Sts, Haymarket; ⏲ 9am-5pm Thu-Sun) This rollicking carnival of a market has over 1000 stalls specialising (mostly) in stuff that tomorrow will be junk (and at a secondhand market).

Rocks Market (Map pp186-7; ☎ 9240 8717; George St, The Rocks; ⏲ 10am-5pm Sat & Sun) Under a long, white canopy near Sydney Harbour Bridge, the 150 stalls here target tourists with an enormous amount of crap.

GETTING THERE & AWAY
Air

Sydney's Kingsford Smith Airport (code: SYD; Map pp182-3; ☎ 9667 9111; www.sydneyairport.com.au) is Australia's busiest, so don't be surprised if there are delays. It's only 10km south of the city centre, making access relatively easy. The T1 (international) and T2 and T3 (domestic) terminals are a 4km, $5 bus or train ride apart (the airport is privately run so transferring terminals – a service that's free in most of the world – is seen as a profit centre).

You can fly into Sydney from all the usual international points and from within Australia.

Qantas (☎ 13 13 13; www.qantas.com.au), **Jetstar** (☎ 13 15 38; www.jetstar.com.au) and **Virgin Blue** (☎ 13 67 89; www.virginblue.com.au) have frequent flights to other major cities. Smaller Qantas-affiliated airlines fly to smaller Oz destinations.

For further details on air travel within Australia, see p497. For air travel to/from Australia, see p494.

Bus

All private interstate and regional bus travellers arrive at **Sydney Coach Terminal** (Map pp186-7; ☎ 9281 9366; Central Station, Eddy Ave; ☉ 6am-10.30pm). Sample destinations include Brisbane ($120, 16 hours), Byron Bay ($110, 13 hours) and Melbourne ($80, 13 hours). There are lots of discounted fares.

The government's CountryLink rail network is also complemented by coaches. Most buses stop in the suburbs on the way in and out of Sydney. If you hold a VIP or YHA discount card, shop around the major bus companies with offices here:

Firefly (☎ 1300 730 740; www.fireflyexpress.com.au)
Greyhound (☎ 13 14 99; www.greyhound.com.au)
Premier (☎ 13 34 10; www.premierms.com.au)

Train

Sydney's main rail terminus for CountryLink interstate and regional services is the huge **Central Station** (Map pp186-7; ☎ 13 22 32; www.countrylink.info; Eddy Ave; ☉ staffed ticket booths 6am-10pm, ticket machines 24hr). It has a small bookshop that's a train-spotter's dream. CountryLink discounts often nudge 40% on economy fares – sometimes cheaper than buses.

Sample train fares (without discount) include Brisbane ($90, 14 hours) and Melbourne ($90, 11 hours).

GETTING AROUND

Your transport options may be many in Sydney but your journey may not be easy. Spend more than a day in town and you won't be able to miss stories about the dire state of the overpatronised, underfunded system. Just figuring it out is a challenge: there are over 100 different fares types. That the various modes are Balkanised is another problem. Buses, ferries and many trains are operated by the same agency but each seems to operate in blissful ignorance of the others. A trip to the various info booths at Circular Quay will confirm this. (And as an added bone-us, the tram and monorail are not part of the system at all.)

For information on government buses, ferries and trains try the **Transport Infoline** (☎ 13 15 00; www.131500.com.au).

To/From the Airport

One of the easiest ways to get to and from the airport is with a shuttle company such as **Kingsford Smith Transport** (KST; ☎ 9666 9988; www.kst.com.au; one way/return from $12/20; ☉ 5am-11pm), which services central Sydney hotels, and **Manly Airport Bus** (☎ 0500 505 800; one way/return $35/68; ☉ 5am-11pm), from Manly. Bookings are essential for both.

Airport Link (☎ 13 15 00; www.airportlink.com.au; one way/return Central Station to domestic terminal $13/20, to international terminal $14/21; ☉ 5am-midnight) is a strange service: it's a normal commuter line (with dirty cars) but you pay through the nose to use the airport stations (punters going to Wolli Creek, the next stop *beyond* the airport pay $3).

Taxi fares from the airport are approximately $25 to $35 to Circular Quay, $40 to $50 to North Sydney and Bondi, and $60 to Manly.

Boat
FERRY

Sydney transport's most civilised option (and an attraction in themselves) – the harbour ferries, JetCats (to Manly) and RiverCats (to Parramatta) – depart from Circular Quay. Most ferries operate between 6am and midnight; those servicing tourist attractions operate shorter hours. The **Ferry Information Office** (Map pp186-7; ☎ 9207 3170; www.sydneyferries.info; ☉ 7am-5.45pm Mon-Sat, 8am-5.45pm Sun) at Circular Quay has details. Some have connecting bus services.

A one-way inner-harbour ride on a regular ferry costs $5.20/3 adult/concession. A one-way ride to Manly on the JetCat costs $8 (no concession, 15 minutes, half-hourly). A one-way RiverCat ride to Parramatta costs $8/4 adult/concession (50 minutes, hourly).

WATER TAXI

Water taxis ply dedicated shuttle routes; rides to/from other harbour venues can be booked. **Watertours** (Map pp186-7; ☎ 9211 7730; www.watertours.com.au; ☉ 9.30am-11pm) Opera House to Darling Harbour $15/10 adult/child; one-hour Harbour and Nightlights Tours $30/20 adult/child.
Yellow Water Taxis (Map pp186-7; ☎ 9555 9778; www.yellowwatertaxis.com.au; ☉ 7am-midnight) Circular Quay to Darling Harbour $15/10 adult/child; 45-minute Harbour Tours $25/20 adult/concession.

Bus

Sydney buses run to most places but not frequently. Bondi, Coogee and parts of the North Shore are serviced only by bus. Nightrider buses operate skeletally after regular services cease around midnight.

The main city bus stops are Circular Quay, Wynyard Park (York St) and Railway Sq. Buy tickets from newsagents, Bus TransitShops and on buses. Pay the driver as you enter, or dunk prepaid tickets in ticket machines by the door. Fares start at $1.80; most trips are under $3.50. There's a **Bus TransitShop** (Map pp186–7; www .sydneybuses.info; cnr Alfred & Loftus Sts; 7am-7pm Mon-Fri, 8.30am-5pm Sat & Sun) at Circular Quay, and there are others at the Queen Victoria Building (Map pp186–7), Railway Sq (Map pp186–7) and Wynyard Station (Map pp186–7).

Bus routes starting with an X indicate limited-stop express routes; those with an L have limited stops. Most buses depart the city on George or Castlereagh Sts, ploughing down George or Elizabeth Sts on the way back in. Many bus stops lack basic route and schedule information.

Car & Motorcycle

Cars are good for day trips out of town, but driving one in the city is like having an anchor around your neck. Heavy traffic, elusive and very expensive parking (even at hotels, expect $30 per day) and the extra costs just aren't worth the stress.

BUYING OR SELLING A CAR

The secondhand car industry is a minefield of mistrust and dodgy wheelers and dealers, but with a bit of research you can still land yourself a decent deal. Parramatta Rd is lined with used-car lots, and the *Trading Post* (www .tradingpost.com.au), a weekly rag available at newsagents, lists secondhand vehicles. For more information on buying or selling a vehicle, see p500.

The **Kings Cross Car Market** (Map p193; 1800 808 188; www.carmarket.com.au; car park Level 2, cnr Ward Ave & Elizabeth Bay Rd, Kings Cross; 9am-5pm Sun-Thu, to 4pm Fri & Sat) is a good spot to buy and sell a car. It's potentially hit and miss, but always busy.

RENTAL

Major rental agencies with offices in Sydney:
Avis (13 63 33; www.avis.com.au)
Budget (13 27 27; www.budget.com.au)
Europcar (1300 131 390; www.europcar.com.au)

Hertz (13 30 39; www.hertz.com.au)
Thrifty (1300 367 227; www.thrifty.com.au)

The **Yellow Pages** (www.yellowpages.com.au) lists many other car-hire companies, some specialising in renting clapped-out wrecks at rock-bottom prices – read the fine print!

ROAD TOLLS

There's a $3 southbound toll on the Sydney Harbour Bridge and Tunnel. If you're heading from the North Shore to the eastern suburbs, it's easier to take the tunnel. There's a $4 northbound toll on the Eastern Distributor; the infamous Cross City Tunnel costs $3.50 one way. Sydney's main motorways (M1, M2, M4, M5 and M7) are also tolled ($2.50 to $7). There are a few cash booths at toll gates, but the whole system is electronic, meaning that it's up to you to pay your toll through a phone call or website. Watch for signs with phone numbers and websites as you drive so you know who to pay (and they will find your credit card through your car rental agency if you don't). For info, try www.sydneymotorways.com.

Fare Deals

The **SydneyPass** (www.sydneypass.info) offers three, five or seven days' unlimited travel over seven days on STA buses, ferries and the rail network's Red TravelPass zone (inner suburbs). Passes include the Airport Express, Sydney and Bondi Explorer buses, JetCats, RiverCats and three STA-operated harbour cruises. They cost $110/55/275 adult/child/family (three days), $145/70/360 (five days) and $165/80/410 (seven days). Buy passes from STA offices, train stations, Bus TransitShops, the Sydney visitors centre at the Rocks (p181) and from Airport Express and Explorer bus drivers.

TravelPasses offer unlimited rail, bus and ferry rides at cheap weekly rates and can be a far better deal than the SydneyPass. There are various colour-coded grades offering combinations of distance and service. A weekly Red TravelPass (inner suburbs), available at train stations, STA offices, Bus TransitShops and newsagents, costs $35/17.50 adult/concession.

If you're just catching buses or trains or ferries, various TravelTen tickets offer 10 discounted rides but are only good on one mode of transport.

Several good-value transport-plus-entry tickets are available from the Circular Quay Ferry Information Office (p214).

Monorail & Metro Light Rail (MLR)

The privately operated **Metro Monorail** (☎ 9285 5600; www.metromonorail.com.au; single circuit $5; ☽ every 4min, 7am-10pm Mon-Thu, to midnight Fri & Sat, 8am-10pm Sun) claims to offer good sightseeing as it circles Darling Harbour and the city but many of the windows are obscured with advertising.

Run by the same outfit, the **Metro Light Rail** (MLR; ☎ 9285 5600; www.metrolightrail.com.au; Zone 1 adult/concession $3/2, Zone 1 & 2 adult/concession $4/3, day pass adult/concession $9/7; ☽ 24hr, every 15min 6am-midnight, every 30min midnight-6am) is a tram between Central Station and Pyrmont via Chinatown and Darling Harbour. The Zone 2 service beyond Pyrmont to Lilyfield stops at 11pm Sunday to Thursday, midnight Friday and Saturday. The service should be integrated into the rest of the system but isn't. Ticketing is separate; most transit passes aren't valid on the monorail or the MLR and conductors take delight in collecting the fare.

Taxi

Taxis and cab ranks proliferate in Sydney. Flag fall is $3, then it's $1.79 per kilometre (plus 20% from 10pm to 6am). The waiting charge is $0.77 per minute. Passengers must pay bridge, tunnel and road tolls (even if you don't incur them 'outbound', the returning driver will incur them 'inbound').

The four major taxi companies offering phone bookings ($1.60 fee) are:

Arrow Taxis (☎ 13 22 11)
Legion (☎ 13 14 51)
Premier Cabs (☎ 13 10 17)
Taxis Combined (☎ 13 33 00)

Train

Sydney's suburban rail network can be a good way to get around (except to places such as Bondi…) Lines radiate from the underground City Circle (seven city-centre stations) but don't service the northern and southern beaches, Balmain or Glebe. All suburban trains stop at Central Station, and usually one or more of the other City Circle stations too.

Trains run from around 5am to midnight. At weekends and after 9am on weekdays you can buy an off-peak return ticket, valid until 4am the next day, for little more than a standard one-way fare.

Twenty-four-hour ticket machines occupy most stations, but humans are usually available if you need help with the fares. If you have to change trains, buy a ticket to your ultimate destination, but don't exit the transfer station en route or your ticket will be invalid.

For train information, visit the **CityRail Information Booth** (Map pp186-7; ☎ 13 15 00; www.131500.com.au; Circular Quay; ☽ 9.05am-4.50pm).

AROUND SYDNEY

You'll find blasts of fresh ocean air at coastal national parks close to Sydney. Ku-ring-gai Chase National Park (p222) to the north and Royal National Park (p177) to the south are good examples. The Hunter Valley (p231) draws wine lovers north and there are many day trips from Sydney, but it's a fair haul and the long time in a bus may drive you to drink. It's better included as part of your itinerary going north.

BLUE MOUNTAINS

Ooh! That's the constant chorus you hear at the Echo Point Lookout in Katoomba in the heart of the Blue Mountains. This jaw-dropping spectacle of canyons and green hills is Unesco-recognised and it'll make you wonder if anyone even needed to apply. And it's but one of the many wondrous sights in the Blue Mountains (Map p180), a region of astounding scenery, fabulous bushwalks and more gorges, gum trees and gourmet restaurants than seem viable. The slate-coloured haze that gives the mountains their name comes from a fine mist of oil exuded by eucalyptus trees.

The foothills begin 65km inland from Sydney, rising to an 1100m-high sandstone plateau riddled with valleys eroded into the stone over thousands of years. In 1813 Wentworth, Blaxland and Lawson were the first Europeans to traverse the mountains.

There are several national parks in the area. The **Blue Mountains National Park** has some truly fantastic scenery, excellent bushwalks, Aboriginal engravings and all the canyons and cliffs you could ask for. It's the most popular and accessible of the three national parks in the area. Great lookouts include Evan's Lookout and Govett's Leap Lookout near Blackheath – both even more spectacular than Echo Point in Katoomba.

Wollemi National Park, north of the Bells Line of Road, is NSW's largest forested wilderness area and stretches all the way to Denman in the Hunter Valley.

For more information on these parks (including camping) contact the **NPWS visitors centre** (☎ 4787 8877; www.nationalparks.nsw.gov.au; Govetts Leap Rd, Blackheath; ⏰ 9am-4.30pm), about 2.5km off the Great Western Hwy and 10km north of Katoomba. After the beaches of Bondi you may find the hills surprisingly cool. Bring a wrap.

Activities
BUSHWALKING
The roads across the mountains offer tantalising glimpses of the majesty of the area, but the only way to really experience the Blue Mountains is on foot. There are walks lasting from a few minutes to several days. The two most popular areas are Jamison Valley, south of Katoomba, and Grose Valley, northeast of Katoomba and east of Blackheath. The area south of Glenbrook is also good.

The NPWS centre can help you pick a hike or, for shorter walks, ask at the Katoomba Echo Point visitors centre (p218).

ADVENTURE ACTIVITIES & TOURS
Most operators have offices in Katoomba – competition is steep, so shop around for the best deal. If you have a YHA card, ask if you're eligible for a discount.

Australian School of Mountaineering (ASM; Map p219; ☎ 4782 2014; www.asmguides.com; 166 Katoomba St, Katoomba) Rock climbing from $165, abseiling from $145 and canyoning from $165.

Blue Mountains Adventure Company (Map p219; ☎ 4782 1271; www.bmac.com.au; 84A Bathurst Rd, Katoomba) A bit more expensive than ASM; also has bushwalking (from $135) and mountain biking (from $125).

Blue Mountains Walkabout (☎ 0408 443 822; www.bluemountainswalkabout.com) Eight-hour, at times strenuous, bushwalks with Aboriginal themes and spirituality ($95 cash only; 25% donated to Aboriginal causes). Meets at Faulconbridge train station.

Tread Lightly Eco Tours (☎ 4788 1229; www.tread lightly.com.au) Has a wide range of walks that emphasise the ecology of the region.

Getting There & Away
To reach the Blue Mountains by road, leave Sydney via Parramatta Rd. At Strathfield detour onto the Western Motorway tollway (M4;

$2.50), which becomes the Great Western Hwy west of Penrith. This is the main road and passes right through Katoomba, some 100km west of Sydney.

The Bells Line of Rd is north of the Great Western Hwy. It twists and turns through the mountains and can be combined with the Great Western Hwy for a circle route. To reach it, head out on Parramatta Rd, and from Parramatta drive northwest on Windsor Rd to Windsor. The Richmond Rd from Windsor becomes the Bells Line of Rd west of Richmond.

CityRail trains regularly service Leura and Katoomba; see p220 for details.

WENTWORTH FALLS TO LEURA
As you head into **Wentworth Falls**, you'll get your first real taste of Blue Mountains scenery: views to the south open out across the majestic Jamison Valley. Wentworth Falls themselves launch a plume of fraying droplets over a 300m drop – check them out from Falls Reserve. This is also the starting point for a network of walking tracks, which delve into the sublime Valley of the Waters, with waterfalls, gorges, woodlands and rainforests.

Leura is a gracious, affluent town, fashioned around undulating streets, unparalleled gardens, Art Deco houses and sweeping Victorian verandas. The **Mall** is the genteel tree-lined main street with boutiques, galleries and cafés. It is only 2km east of Katoomba.

KATOOMBA
☎ 02 / pop 18,000
The Blue Mountains' crowning urban glory manages to be bohemian and bourgeois all at once. Its steep streets are lined with Art Deco buildings and bathed in often bracing swirling mists. Amid more humdrum shops, you'll find some splendid, notable cafés. And despite its burgeoning tourist industry, it retains a friendly, country town sort of ambience. Katoomba is an ideal day trip from Sydney. The train makes access easy and there's enough to keep you busy for at least a day. If you spend the night, you'll have time to enjoy some walks or other activities in the Blue Mountains.

Information
There are numerous banks and ATMs on Katoomba St.

SYDNEY

Echo Point visitors centre (☎ 4782 9865, 1300 653 408; www.australiabluemountains.com.au) Covers the region.

Katoomba Book Exchange (☎ 4782 9997; 32 Katoomba St; internet access per 30min/1hr $4/7; ☼ 10am-6pm; 🖳) One of several secondhand book stores.

Sights

Katoomba's big-ticket drawcard is **Echo Point**, where a series of sensational viewing platforms transport your gaze out over the Jamison Valley. The impressive **Three Sisters** rock formation towers over a scene of green-clad peaks and orange rocks. Misty ranges stretch into the distance, each a paler shade of blue.

Echo Point attracts profuse serenity-spoiling tourists and idling buses. However, like so many places that draw mobs, a short walk along one of several walkways will rapidly leave 90% of the day-trippers in the dust. Go far enough and you can hear the birds calling from below. When walking here from the town centre, Lurline St is the least dull.

To the west of town is **Scenic World** (☎ 4782 2699; www.scenicworld.com.au; cnr Cliff Dr & Violet St; cable car return adult/child $19/10; ☼ 9am-5pm), with a megaplex vibe and an 1880s railway descending the 52-degree incline to the valley floor. It also has a glass-floored **Scenic Skyway** cable car floating out across the valley.

Sleeping

BUDGET

Katoomba Falls Caravan Park (☎ 4782 1835; www.bmcc.nsw.gov.au; Katoomba Falls Rd; unpowered/powered sites $25/32, cabins from $75) This council-run park lacks atmosphere and gets mixed reviews, but it's Katoomba's only camping option.

No 14 (☎ 4782 7104; www.bluemts.com.au/no14; 14 Lovel St; dm $22, d with/without bathroom $69/59) This colourful hostel feels like a cheery share house. The airy veranda is the perfect spot to relax and polished floorboards make a pleasant change from daggie carpets. Dorms have three beds; attic-style doubles are comfy and private.

Blue Mountains YHA (☎ 4782 1416; www.yha.com.au; 207 Katoomba St; dm/d/f from $24/73/116; 🖳) The austere Art Deco exterior of this popular 200-bed hostel belies its cavernous, sparkling innards. Dorms and family rooms are spotlessly bright. Highlights include a pinball machine, pool tables, open fires, a giant chess set, central heating, barbecues and curry nights. Good place to organise activities.

Katoomba Mountain Lodge (☎ 4782 3933; www.katoombamountainlodge.com.au; 31 Lurline St; s/d from $42/58; 🖳 ; wi-fi) Nonhip retro décor is the price you'll pay for the best-value rooms in town. It's a cheerily run, 90-year-old house right in the middle of town, with astounding views from some of the top-floor rooms.

MIDRANGE

Cecil Guesthouse (☎ 4782 1411; www.ourguest.com.au/cecil.html; 108 Katoomba St; s with/without bathroom $80/75, d $106/84) Generations of Sydneysiders have sought refuge in cool Katoomba and the Cecil bears witness to many of them. Creaky floorboards, unrenovated walls and kooky lounge rooms – put character before glitz. Lawn tennis anyone?

3 Explorers Motel (☎ 4782 1733; www.3explorers.com.au; 197 Lurline St; s/d from $79/90; 🐾 🖳) There's nothing exceptional about this two-storey motel but the 15 rooms are good value and there is easy access to Echo Point, so you can ponder the changing colours at any hour.

Clarendon Guesthouse (☎ 4782 1322; www.clarendonguesthouse.com.au; 68 Lurline St; r from $120; 🖳 🎭) The rambling old Clarendon is light on ceremony and heavy on character. Original rooms (with shared bathrooms) are charmingly old school (and cheap: $90), the newer motel extension has an elusive '50s retro character. We'd pick the 1920s in the main building.

TOP END

Carrington Hotel (☎ 4782 1111; www.thecarrington.com.au; 15-47 Katoomba St; r $145-400) Katoomba's social and architectural high-water mark, the Carrington has been accommodating road-weary travellers since 1880. Every inch has been refurbished, but its historical character remains intact. Throwback amenities include a library, a billiards room and stately gardens.

Eating

Katoomba St has an amazingly tasty selection of places to eat.

Blue Mountains Food Co-op (☎ 4782 5890; Hapenny Lane; ☼ 8am-6pm) The perfect stop for hard-core self-caterers. Organic, vegan and gluten-free are just some of the labels on the mostly local foods and produce. The place to get an odd-ball soda you'll wish they sold at home.

Hominy Bakery (☎ 4782 9816; 185 Katoomba St; snacks from $3; ☼ 6am-5:30pm) Yet another reason you can't help but eat well locally. This organic

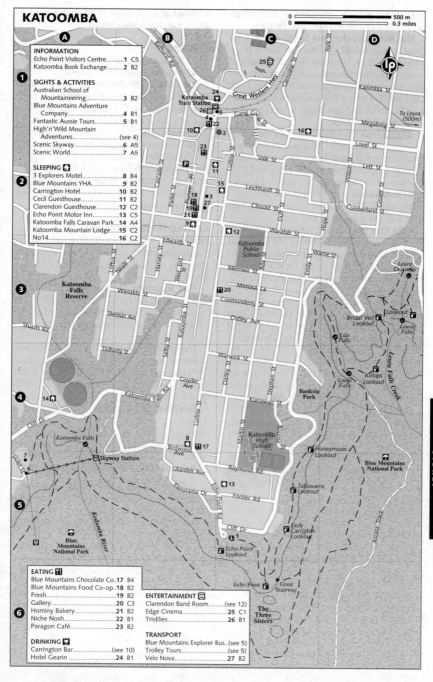

KATOOMBA

0 — 500 m
0 — 0.3 miles

INFORMATION
Echo Point Visitors Centre.......**1** C5
Katoomba Book Exchange.......**2** B2

SIGHTS & ACTIVITIES
Australian School of
Mountaineering.......................**3** B2
Blue Mountains Adventure
Company.................................**4** B1
Fantastic Aussie Tours...............**5** B1
High'n'Wild Mountain
Adventures...........................(see 4)
Scenic Skyway..........................**6** A5
Scenic World............................**7** A5

SLEEPING
3 Explorers Motel.....................**8** B4
Blue Mountains YHA.................**9** B2
Carrington Hotel.....................**10** B2
Cecil Guesthouse.....................**11** B2
Clarendon Guesthouse.............**12** C2
Echo Point Motor Inn...............**13** C5
Katoomba Falls Caravan Park...**14** A4
Katoomba Mountain Lodge.....**15** C2
No14......................................**16** C2

EATING
Blue Mountains Chocolate Co..**17** B4
Blue Mountains Food Co-op..**18** B2
Fresh......................................**19** B2
Gallery...................................**20** C3
Hominy Bakery.......................**21** B2
Niche Nosh.............................**22** B1
Paragon Café..........................**23** B2

DRINKING
Carrington Bar.....................(see 10)
Hotel Gearin **24** B1

ENTERTAINMENT
Clarendon Band Room..........(see 12)
Edge Cinema.........................**25** C1
TrisElies.................................**26** B1

TRANSPORT
Blue Mountains Explorer Bus..(see 5)
Trolley Tours........................(see 5)
Velo Nova..............................**27** B2

SYDNEY

bakery has a daily selection of sourdough breads and exquisite cakes and pastries.

Blue Mountains Chocolate Co (☎ 4782 7071; 176 Lurline St; snacks from $3; ☺ 10am-6pm) Not a place where you'll exclaim 'oh fudge!' but a real candy company that makes exquisite high-end chocolates (the white passion fruit: 'Oh God! Oh God!'). Enjoy a few on the veranda with a coffee drink and you might forget you were headed to Echo Point.

our pick Fresh (☎ 4782 3602; 181 Katoomba St; meals $7-14; ☺ breakfast & lunch) Quite possibly the best breakfast you'll have in Oz. Simply beautiful eggs prepared many ways; all served with wholemeal sourdough toast. Lunch includes great sandwiches on the same bread and interesting salads. There's a full coffee bar, luscious smoothies and tables in and out.

Niche Nosh (☎ 4782 1622; 10 Katoomba St; meals $8-15; ☺ lunch & dinner) A shambling old place that sprawls from one room to the next and out to the footpath. Pick up on the local alternative vibe while enjoying veggie specials made with local produce. Go on, be a poser and join the zillions who love the veggie burger.

Paragon Café (☎ 4782 2928; 65 Katoomba St; mains $10-20; ☺ breakfast & lunch) The heritage-listed 1916 Paragon proclaims its 'Art Deco magnificence'. Sampling coffee and chocolates in the cluttered surrounds is a compulsory Blue Mountains experience. The front window boasts a hodge-podge of junk; the menu leans to standards such as spag bol.

Gallery (☎ 4782 1220; 98 Lurline St; mains $29-32; ☺ dinner Thu-Sun) Chef Barry Sullivan not only knows his chops, he has chops in the kitchen. As the name suggests, there's art aplenty at this quiet spot midway to Echo Point both on the walls and on the plates. The changing menu is global fusion where you might pair a starter of local roast quail with a main of Moroccan lamb with lentils.

Drinking

The Clarendon Guesthouse (p218) has many good regional bands on weekends.

Hotel Gearin (☎ 4782 4395; www.gearinhotel.com; 273 Great Western Hwy; ☺ 7am-2am Mon-Thu, to 3am Fri & Sat, 10am-10pm Sun) The stylish place for a cold one or a game of pool.

Carrington Bar (☎ 4782 1111; www.thecarrington.com .au; 10-16 Katoomba St; admission free; ☺ 9.30am-1.30am Mon-Thu, to 4.30am Fri & Sat, to 11pm Sun) The ceramic-tiled outpost of the upper-crust hotel looks like a tube stop outside. Settle in for a schooner and shoot some pool. There's a nightclub upstairs on Saturday night (admission $5).

Getting There & Around

CityRail (☎ 131 500; www.cityrail.com.au) runs to Katoomba from Sydney's Central Station (one way adult/child $12.20/6.10, two hours, hourly).

Blue Mountains Explorer Bus (☎ 4782 4807; www.explorerbus.com.au; 283 Main St; adult/child $32/16; ☺ 9.45am-5.15pm) offers hop-on hop-off service on an hourly Katoomba/Leura loop, stopping at 30 attractions.

Trolley Tours (☎ 4782 7999, 1800 801 577; www .trolleytours.com.au; 285 Main St; adult/child $15/12; ☺ 9.15am-5pm Mon-Fri, 9.45am-3.45pm Sat & Sun) runs a bus barely disguised as a trolley, with piped commentary.

Velo Nova (☎ 4782 2800; www.velonova.com.au; 182 Katoomba St; half-/full-day $28/50; ☺ 9am-5pm Mon-Sat) rents out hi-tech, 24-speed, all-terrain mountain bikes. Saturday morning group rides run along Cliff Dr, finishing up with a café coffee.

Katoomba-Leura-Wentworth Falls Taxis (☎ 4783 1311) service its monikers.

Central Coast New South Wales

It seems a little redundant in a book about Australia's East Coast to rave about awesome beaches, but the stretch heading north of Sydney has them in truckloads. As national parks play leapfrog with towns and cities all the way, you can choose between completely deserted forest-lined sands where modern life is little more than a worrying rumour and lifesaver-patrolled paradises where a decent coffee is but a short stroll away.

Surfers will be in hang-ten heaven: pile out of your Combi pretty much anywhere the mood takes you and you'll find a decent break. If surf isn't your thing, a series of coastal saltwater lakes allows for a calmer dip.

Fresh seafood, azure water and sand between your toes – these are timeless pleasures that cut across generations and Port Stephens is the exemplar, with its collection of coves that will make grandma swoon, junior squeal and Surfer Joe stub out his joint. A spell of bad weather may not affect the surfies, but for those less bronzed and salty it's the perfect excuse to take refuge in the recesses of the Hunter Valley wine region. Indulgence isn't limited to its liquid form here. The leafy country roads are strewn with producers of chocolate and cheese, and wineries with world-class restaurants.

The Pacific Highway divides the region, a mainline blacktop cable plugged in to the electric climes up north. Many of the sights mentioned are off the highway though, and there's more besides. Maybe just throw the map away every now and then, make a few random right-hand turns, and stop and smell the salt.

HIGHLIGHTS

- Colonising your own empty beach at **Bouddi** (p224), **Booti Booti** (p240) or **Crowdy Bay** (p242) **National Parks**
- Marvelling at the pre-European landscape stretching endlessly from **Crowdy Head** (p242)
- Imagining the Sahara among the rolling dunes of the **Worimi Conservation Lands** (p236)
- Broadening your palate and waistline in the **Hunter Valley** (p231)
- Beach- and bar-hopping in a transformed **Newcastle** (p225)
- Cruising the bucolic country roads around **Wingham** (p241)
- Spotting koalas in **Tomaree National Park** (p236), dingoes in **Myall Lakes National Park** (p238), pythons in **Port Macquarie's rainforest** (p245) and dolphins in **Port Stephens** (p236)

- TELEPHONE CODE: 02
- www.visitnsw.com.au

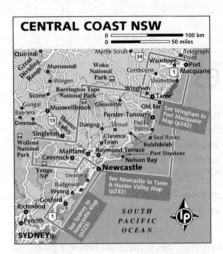

CENTRAL COAST NSW

SYDNEY TO NEWCASTLE

After struggling through the traffic of Sydney's outer suburbs the bushy vistas of Ku-ring-gai Chase and Brisbane Waters National Parks offer an intoxicating shot of paradise. From here the choice is yours whether to motor straight up the freeway to Newcastle or meander along the coast. Truth be known, neither route will be a highlight of your trip, but if you've got time to kill there are some interesting diversions on the coastal road.

KU-RING-GAI CHASE NATIONAL PARK

The exhilarating, 14,928-hectare **Ku-ring-gai Chase National Park** (www.nationalparks.nsw.gov.au; admission per car $11) forms Sydney's northern boundary, 24km from the city centre. It's a classic mix of sandstone, bushland and water vistas, taking in over 100km of coastline along the southern edge of Broken Bay where it heads into the Hawkesbury River.

Ku-ring-gai takes its name from its original inhabitants, the Guringai people, who were all but wiped out just after colonisation through violence at the hands of British settlers or introduced disease. It's well worth reading Kate Grenville's Booker-nominated *The Secret River* for an engrossing but harrowing telling of this story.

Remnants of Aboriginal life are visible today, with the preservation of more than 800 sites, including rock paintings, middens and cave art. West Head Rd offers access to

some of the best places within the park to see them. Nearly at **West Head** is the Resolute picnic area; from here you can amble 100m to **Red Hands Cave** where there are some very faint ochre handprints. About another 500m along **Resolute Track** (after a short steep section) is an engraving site. You can turn around or continue to one more site and make a 3.5km loop that takes in **Resolute Beach**.

Back on West Head Rd, just less than 2km west of the picnic area, is the **Echidna Track**, whose boardwalk provides good disabled access to engravings very near the road. Less than 1km up the road from Echidna is the **Basin Track**, which makes an easy stroll to a good set of engravings.

The **Great North Walk**, a two-week hike from Sydney to Newcastle, passes through Ku-ring-gai. This 14-day odyssey begins from the centre of Sydney and, after a short ferry ride, follows natural bushland almost the entire way to Newcastle.

It's unwise to swim in Broken Bay due to sharks but there is a netted swimming area at **The Basin** (day visit adult/child $3/2), a shallow round inlet perfect for children and easily accessed by ferry from Palm Beach.

Information

Kalkari Discovery Centre (☎ 9472 9300; Ku-ring-gai Chase Rd; ◷ 10am-4pm Mon-Fri, 10am-5pm Sat & Sun) Has displays and videos on Australian fauna and Aboriginal culture.

Ku-ring-gai visitors centre (☎ 9472 8949; Bobbin Inn, Bobbin Head; ◷ 10am-4pm) Has a marina, picnic areas, a café (serving hot meals, coffee and snacks) and a boardwalk leading through mangroves.

Sleeping

Basin camping area (☎ 9974 1011; www.basincamp ground.com.au; sites per adult/child $14/7) Proper toilets and showers are provided. Walk about 2.5km from West Head Rd, or take a ferry or water-taxi from Palm Beach. Book ahead.

   Pittwater YHA (☎ 9999 5748; www.yha.com.au /hostels/details.cfm?hostelid=31; Towlers Bay; dm/d/tw/q $28/72/72/96) Wake up to marvellous bay views at this converted 1920s guesthouse, 15 minutes uphill from Halls Wharf (this is a blissfully car-free zone – you'll need to catch the **Church Point Ferry** (☎ 9999 3492)). The surrounding bushland is dominated by magnificent purple-grey eucalypti, which harbour a welter of cockatoos and wallabies. Book ahead and bring food; demand for this idyllic retreat is high.

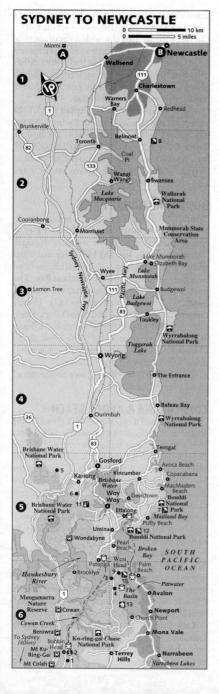

SYDNEY TO NEWCASTLE

Getting There & Away

Access to the park is by ferry or via several through-roads (enter Ku-ring-gai Chase Rd off Pacific Hwy, Mt Colah; Bobbin Head Rd, North Turramurra; or McCarrs Creek Rd, Terrey Hills).

Sydney Buses (☎ 131 500; www.131500.com.au) runs express services to Palm Beach (route L90, $5.80, 1¾ hours) and Church Pt (route E86, $5.80, 1½ hours) from near Central Station. Otherwise you can catch the train to Turramurra ($4.20, 40 minutes) and then the 577 bus to the park entrance on Bobbin Head Rd ($1.80, 10 minutes). From here it's a 4km walk to Bobbin Head.

The **Palm Beach Ferry** (☎ 9974 2411; www .palmbeachferry.com.au; adult/child $6.30/3.20; ☻9am-5pm Mon-Thu, 9am-8pm Fri, 9am-6pm Sat & Sun) runs hourly from Palm Beach to Mackerel Beach, via the Basin. If you want to continue north, it has services to Ettalong via Wagstaffe (adult/child $9.10/4.60).

Palm Beach & Hawkesbury River Cruises (☎ 0414-466 635; adult/child return $35/20) departs Palm Beach for Bobbin Head via Patonga (11am daily, plus 9am and 3.45pm Saturday and Sunday).

BRISBANE WATER NATIONAL PARK

Facing Ku-ring-gai from the northern side of the Hawkesbury River this 11,473-hectare park extends the green belt separating Sydney from the Central Coast, preserving in part the landscape that the Guringai people enjoyed for thousands of years. Their distinctive art also survives here, engraved in Hawkesbury sandstone.

A boardwalk has been created around the **Bulgandry Aboriginal Site**, both protecting and pro-viding access to a collection of engravings that include wallabies, fish and a male figure. The site is 2km along Woy Woy Rd from Kariong. A few kilometres south, **Staples Lookout** has epic views over the park.

The park is known for its wildflowers (especially waratahs), in bloom from July to October. If you're lucky you might spot a koala or tiger quoll.

There are no camping facilities within the park itself, but you can pitch up at the council-run **Patonga Caravan & Camping Area** (☎ 4325 8486; sites per 2 people $30) at **Patonga**, a small fishing village within the southern end of the park.

Similarly tucked within the park's folds is **Pearl Beach**, a sweet National Trust–listed hamlet with an idyllic beach. Its constricted location has saved it from the holiday-house sprawl of the beaches to the north, making the (mainly) wealthy Sydneyites lucky enough to have snaffled up property here that's the envy of all their friends.

Pearl Beach General Store & Café (☎ 4343 1222; 1 Pearl Beach Pde; mains $15-20; ☺ breakfast & lunch daily, dinner Thu-Sat) offers a yummy selection of reasonably priced risotto, pasta and salads. Try **Pearl Beach Real Estate** (☎ 4341 7555; www.pearl beachrealestate.com.au) for holiday apartment and house rentals.

The main road access to the park is via Woy Woy Rd at Kariong, along the Pacific Hwy. **CityRail** (☎ 131 500; www.cityrail.info) trains from Sydney ($7.20, 1¼ hours) or Gosford ($3.80, 20 minutes) stop on request inside the park at Wondabyne. **Busways** (☎ 4368 2277; www.busways .com.au) runs services from Woy Woy station to Patonga (route 50, adult/child $4/2).

For ferry services from Palm Beach, see p223.

GOSFORD
☎ 02 / pop 35,000

You're not going to want to linger in Gosford, but this uninspiring town serves as the transport and services hub for the surrounding beaches. The **visitors centre** (☎ 4325 2835; 200 Mann St; ☺ 9.30am-4pm Mon-Fri, 10am-12.30pm Sat) is near the train station and there's a **National Parks & Wildlife Service (NPWS) office** (☎ 4320 4200; 207 Albany St N; ☺ 8.30am-4.30pm Mon-Fri).

The excellent **Australian Reptile Park** (☎ 4340 1022; www.reptilepark.com.au; adult/child $23/12; ☺ 9am-5pm), well signposted from the Gosford freeway exit, offers a chance to get up close to koalas and pythons, watch funnel-web spiders being milked (for the production of antivenin) and

learn about the plight of the Tasmanian devil (the park serves as a diabolical breeding ark). On our visit we had the added excitement of witnessing a keeper struggling to shake loose a large saltwater crocodile that had gotten rather attached to his finger during feeding. There's also a wonderfully craptastic *Lost Kingdom of Reptiles* Disney-style enclosure.

Gosford has numerous **CityRail** (☎ 131 500; www.cityrail.info) connections to Sydney ($8.60, 1½ hours) and Newcastle ($18, 1½ hours). From Gosford station, **Busways** (☎ 4368 2277; www.busways.com.au) runs frequent services to Terrigal and neighbouring towns and beaches; less often on weekends.

BOUDDI NATIONAL PARK

Bouddi National Park (1532 hectares) extends from the north head of Broken Bay to MacMasters Beach, 12km south of Terrigal. Vehicle access is limited but there are short walking trails leading to wonderfully isolated beaches, including lovely **Maitland Bay**. The park is in two sections on either side of **Putty Beach**, which has vehicle access ($7). There's **camping** (☎ 4320 4203) at **Little Beach** (site per adult/child $10/5), **Putty Beach** (site per adult/child $14/7) and **Tallow Beach** (site per adult/child $10/5); book ahead at busy times. Only the Putty Beach site has drinkable water and flush toilets.

Take **Busways** (☎ 4368 2277; www.busways.com.au) bus 61 from Gosford.

COPACABANA & AVOCA BEACH

☎ 02 / pop 2680 (Copacabana), 6470 (Avoca Beach)

There aren't too many showgirls called Lola in the vicinity and if there were, they'd have to learn how to surf as that's the main entertainment around these parts. Copa (in the local lingo) is particularly beautiful, with two dramatic headlands. The surf can be mountainous, so swim between the flags. There's a viewing platform for whale-spotting; look out for humpbacks from late May to early August.

At **Avoca Beach** there's a lovely curving surf beach, guarded by a string of tall pine trees. It's a low-key little place that also has the charmingly old-school **Avoca Beach Picture Theatre** (☎ 4382 1677; www.avocabeachpicturetheatre.com.au; 69 Avoca Dr; admission before/after 6pm $10/12.50).

Café Sirocco (☎ 4382 6967; 204 Del Monte Pl, Copacabana; mains $7-17; ☺ breakfast & lunch) does a mean breakfast with lots of vegetarian choices and beach views.

Blue Bar & Restaurant (☎ 4381 0707; 85 Avoca Dr, Avoca Beach; mains $32-39; ⏰ lunch & dinner Tue-Sun) offers plenty of skilfully crafted seafood dishes, making it the top-rated restaurant on this part of the coast. Its take on surf'n'turf is beef'n'bugs (Moreton Bay bugs, of course) and the crab and orange ravioli is wonderful.

Busways (☎ 4368 2277; www.busways.com.au) has services to Copacabana (route 66, $4.80) and Avoca (routes 65 or 69, $4) from Gosford.

TERRIGAL

☎ 02 / pop 9750

At Terrigal you'd be forgiven for thinking that Sydney's Northern Beaches had begun again. The beach is awesome and the surf's good, but the surrounding area is very built-up. It gets even more suburban as you head north through **Wamberal**, **Bateau Bay** and **The Entrance.**

Several reefs and wrecks make for good diving. In September 2008, an Australian Navy frigate, the **HMAS Adelaide**, is set to be sunk here for divers to explore. **Terrigal Diving School** (☎ 4384 1219; www.terrigaldive.com.au; The Haven; single/wreck/double dive $45/50/80) is Australia's oldest, having explored these waters for over 39 years.

Ye Olde Miami Guesthouse (☎ 4384 1919; www.miamiguesthouse.com.au; 9 Ocean View Dr; s/d $50/65) offers cramped but clean pine-floored rooms. It's hostel style in that the facilities are shared, but there are no dorms.

Tiarri (☎ 4384 1423; www.tiarriterrigal.com.au; 16 Tiarri Cres; r $110-120 Sun-Thu, $148-168 Fri & Sat; ❄; wi-fi) has seven roomy doubles (all with courtyards) and a hilltop location near the beach. Two suites have spas (there's also a common spa), and all rooms have a TV, VCR and 'nonallergenic' doonas.

Patcinos (☎ 4385 1960; cnr Church St & Campbell Cres; mains $8-17; ⏰ 7am-5.30pm) may be squeezed into a tiny corner but it manages to serve the best coffees in town, along with a limited menu including salads, wraps and hotcakes.

From Gosford, **Busways** (☎ 4368 2277; www.busways.com.au) services run to Terrigal (routes 67 and 68, $4) at least hourly.

LAKE MACQUARIE

☎ 02 / pop 183,140

A series of saltwater 'lakes' spreads up the coast between Bateau Bay and Newcastle, the largest of which, Lake Macquarie, covers four times the area of Sydney Harbour. All of them have channels opening to the sea, so you could easily call them estuaries, inlets or harbours – but in Lake Macquarie's case they go one better and call it a city. A series of pockets of dull suburbia dotted around a body of water hardly a city makes, but it does have some nice pelicans.

The drive between the lakes and the ocean is a pleasant if unspectacular alternative to the freeway, especially once you're past The Entrance. The route takes in stretches of **Wyrrabalong**, **Munmorah** and **Wallarah National Parks**. If you feel like a dip, there's plenty of room to spread your towel at **Nine Mile Beach**.

The enthusiastic **visitors centre** (☎ 1800 802 044; 228 Pacific Hwy, Swansea; ⏰ 9am-5pm Mon-Fri, 9am-4pm Sat & Sun) has a wealth of information on the area and free internet access.

NEWCASTLE

☎ 02 / pop 288,740

Newcastle occupies a bizarre parallel universe to its namesake in northern England. Both were once grim, grimy, industrial mill towns that in recent years have been transformed into vibrant, artsy, thoroughly pleasant places to visit. Both have a fanatical devotion to their local sports teams, albeit in different codes (here it's the Newcastle Knights rugby league squad that sets passions ablaze). And both are awash with lagered-up young people on the weekends.

That's where the similarities end. In this parallel universe it's sunny most of the time and there's a surf beach around every bend.

In 1989 Newcastle suffered Australia's most destructive recorded earthquake; 12 people died. The shake-up both required and enabled the city to start again. Now, in the midst of its tourist-fuelled rebranding, it's in serious danger of becoming cosmopolitan.

But despite the money that's been spent on attracting high-tech business, cleaning up the air, preserving the interesting architecture and greening the foreshore, that famous Hunter larrikin spirit is, thankfully, still present. Newcastle's steely past is not the albatross you might expect, and is helping to shape a confrontational arts and music scene.

ORIENTATION

The city centre is bordered by the Hunter River and the sea. The main shopping strip is Hunter St, a pedestrian mall between Newcomen and Perkins Sts.

INFORMATION

If you've got a laptop with wireless capability, head to Beaumont St in Hamilton where there's free wi-fi broadband. The airport also offers free wireless connections. You'll find banks and ATMs in Hunter St Mall. Most have foreign exchange.

John Hunter Hospital (☎ 4921 3000; Lookout Rd, New Lambton) Has emergency care.

Library (☎ 4974 5300; Laman St) Has internet access (per hour $5.50).

Post office (☎ 13 13 18; 1 Market St)

Visitors centre (☎ 4974 2999; www.visitnewcastle .com.au; 361 Hunter St; ☺ 9am-5pm Mon-Fri, 10am-3.30pm Sat & Sun)

SIGHTS
Museums & Galleries

Newcastle Region Art Gallery (☎ 4974 5100; www.ncc .nsw.gov.au/discover_newcastle/region_art_gallery; 1 Laman St; admission free; ☺ 10am-5pm Tue-Sun) collects works by revered Australian artists (Drysdale, Nolan, Whiteley) and hosts exhibitions by international stars and young local artists.

The **Lock Up** (☎ 4925 2265; www.thelockup.info; 90 Hunter St; admission free; ☺ 10am-4pm Tue-Thu, 10am-5pm Fri-Sun) once held convicts but now incarcerates only the artists-in-residence who create and exhibit in this former police station (1861). There's an interesting law and order museum within the creepy, cramped cells of the old men's block.

If you're visiting after late 2009 a new **Newcastle Regional Museum** (☎ 4974 1400; www .newcastle.nsw.gov.au/discover_newcastle/regional_museum; Honeysuckle Dr) should have opened in the old Honeysuckle rail workshops on the foreshore. Expect lots of scientific gadgets and displays about the earthquake. Phone for more details.

Nearby, the **Newcastle Region Maritime Museum** (☎ 4929 2588; Lee Wharf, 1 Honeysuckle Dr; adult/child 5/2; ☺ 10am-4pm Fri-Sun) celebrates Newcastle's nautical nuances.

Wildlife

Sitting in a tract of bushland with plenty of walking trails, the council-run **Blackbutt Reserve** (☎ 4904 3344; www.newcastle.nsw.gov.au/environment/black butt_reserve; Carnley Ave, Kotara; admission free; ☺ 9am-5pm) has enclosures featuring native critters including koalas, kangaroos and quolls, along with a cacophonic chorus of native birds. Take bus 224 ($3, 30 minutes) from the train station to the park's edge then walk 1km to the entrance.

Hunter Wetlands Centre (☎ 4951 6466; www.wet lands.org.au; Sandgate Rd, Shortland; adult/concession $6/3; ☺ 10am-5pm Mon-Fri, 9am-5pm Sat & Sun) is a swampy wonderland, home to over 200 bird and animal species. You can hire a canoe ($9.90 for two hours) or dip in a net and examine the results under a magnifying glass. Bring mosquito repellent if you don't want to contribute to the ecosystem in ways you hadn't intended. Take the Pacific Hwy towards Maitland and turn left at the cemetery, or catch bus 108 ($3, 40 minutes) from the train station.

Views

Queens Wharf Tower, on the waterfront, and the **obelisk** above King Edward Park provide commanding views of the city and the water. Across the river (about five minutes by ferry) is **Stockton**, a modest settlement with striking views back towards Newcastle and exposed shipwrecks in its waters.

Other Attractions
NOBBY'S HEAD

Nobby's used to be an island until it was joined to the mainland in 1846 to create a singularly pretty sand spit; it was twice its current height before being reduced to 28m above sea level in 1855. The walk along the spit towards the lighthouse and meteorological station is exhilarating, with waves crashing about your ears and joggers jostling your elbows.

FORT SCRATCHLEY

This large **fort** (☎ 4929 3066; www.fortscratchley.org .au; Nobby's Rd) was one of the few gun installations in Australia to fire a gun in anger during WWII. On 8 June 1942 a Japanese submarine suddenly surfaced, raining shells on the city. Fort Scratchley returned fire, negating the threat after just four rounds.

By the time you're reading this, the site should have reopened after four years of restoration. Call ahead for opening times and admission charges.

ACTIVITIES
Swimming & Surfing

At the East End, the needs of surfers and swimmers are sated at **Newcastle Beach**, but if you're irrationally paranoid about sharks, the **ocean baths** are a mellow alternative, encased in wonderful multicoloured 1922 architecture. There's a shallow pool for toddlers and a compelling backdrop of heaving ocean and

NEWCASTLE

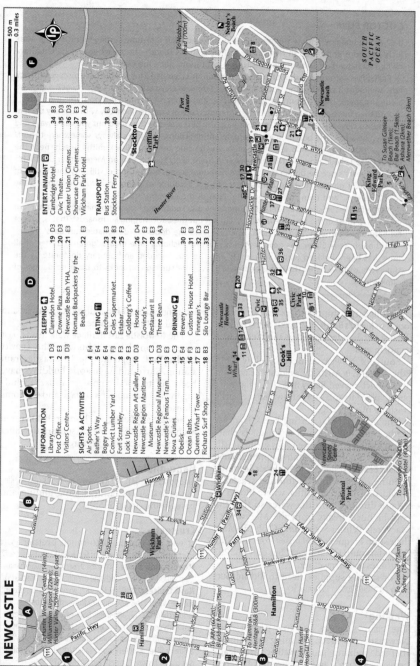

DOCTOR SURF

It's hard to imagine a more thoroughly Newcastle lad than four-time surfing world champ Mark Richards. Born and raised in Newcastle, surfing is in his blood – his beach-loving parents have owned Richards Surf Shop (below), a Newie institution, since the early 1960s.

Richards is enthusiastic about his city's evolution. 'It's changed a lot. People have discovered it. It's now the biggest city after the state capitals, yet I think of Newcastle as halfway between a city and a country town. There's plenty of stuff going on and a vibrant nightlife but no traffic problems.'

And then there are the beaches. As Richards points out, it's rare to find a city with so many brilliant beaches so close to the centre. 'It may not have the best waves in the world but you can always find a wave,' he adds. 'The beach breaks face different directions, so there's always somewhere to surf.'

As a grommet, Richards learnt his craft on the safe breaks at Blacksmiths Beach, near the entrance to Lake Macquarie. Nowadays you're more likely to find him on Merewether Beach. It's been 25 years since he dominated the international scene, but surfing is still very much part of his routine. 'I get up at about 6am and try to get a couple of hours in before heading to the shop,' he says, 'and then sometimes again later in the evening.'

At the family surf shop travellers are sometimes shocked to find Richards behind the counter. 'I'm in the shop most of the time', he laughs, 'if I'm not out the back shaping surfboards'. That is, except for Saturday afternoons and Sundays, when he locks the doors for 'designated surf days'.

Although Kelly Slater has now beaten his record, Richards' title of the 'greatest surfer of all time' has been replaced with a simple 'Dr' after he was awarded an honorary doctorate by the University of Newcastle. His status as Newie's favourite surfing son looks to be in no danger of diminishing.

chugging cargo ships. Surfers should goofy-foot it to **Nobby's Beach**, just north of the baths – the fast left-hander known as the Wedge is at its north end.

South of Newcastle Beach, below King Edward Park, is Australia's oldest ocean bath, the convict-carved **Bogey Hole**. It's an atmospheric place to splash about when the surf's crashing over its edge.

The most popular surfing break is at **Bar Beach**, 1km south. If your swimsuit is chafing, scramble around the rocks at the north end to the (unofficial) clothing-optional **Susan Gilmour Beach**. At nearby **Merewether Beach** the opening of the winter swimming season is heralded at its ocean baths, where blocks of ice are dumped into the water so that the cold-blooded freaks from the Merewether Mackerels Winter Swimming Club can strut their stuff. Frequent local buses from the CBD run as far south as Bar Beach, but only bus 207 continues to Merewether.

For surfing supplies, head to **Richards Surf Shop** (☎ 4961 3088; 755 Hunter St).

Walking

The visitors centre has free pocket-sized Newcastle booklets outlining self-guided themed walking tours. **Bather's Way** leads between Nobby's and Merewether Beaches,

with signs describing indigenous, convict and natural history in between swims.

The **Newcastle East Heritage Walk** heads past many colonial highlights like the **Convict Lumber Yard**, opposite the Newcastle train station. Surrounding historic buildings have been put to good commercial use, including the old paymaster's cottage and Customs House (p230).

Newcastle By Design is a short stroll down and around Hunter St, covering some of the inner city's interesting architecture.

Hang-gliding

Air Sports (☎ 0412 607 815; www.air-sports.com.au; King Edward Park) offers tandem hang-gliding and paragliding (from $165).

Cruises

If you can't make it to much prettier Port Stephens, some boats offer local cruises.

Moonshadow's Cruz (☎ 4984 9388; www.moonshadow.com.au) Offers dinner, lunch and evening cruises (from $15).

Nova Cruises (☎ 0400 381 787; www.novacruises.com.au; Lee Wharf) Has a 90-minute Newcastle Harbour Cruise (adult/child $22/12) and three-hour whale-watching expeditions on the weekends between late May and August. Every month it puts on a lunch cruise (adult/child $49/29), a Hunter River discovery cruise (adult/child $69/49) and a day trip to historic Morpeth (adult/child $79/54).

FESTIVALS & EVENTS

Surfest (www.surfest.com) Hangs-ten in March.

Newcastle Jazz Festival (www.newcastlejazz.com.au) Jammin' late August.

This Is Not Art Festival (www.thisisnotart.org) Alternative cultural festival in early October.

Mattara – Festival of Newcastle (www.mattarafestival .org.au) Celebrates Newcastle with stalls, concerts and a parade in early October.

TOURS

Newcastle's Famous Tram (☎ 4977 2270; www.famous -tram.com.au; Newcastle Station; adult/child $15/6; ☽ 11am & 1pm Mon-Fri) trundles around the East End for 45 minutes, taking in major historical sites. On the weekends it heads to the Hunter Valley for six-hour winery tours (per person $45). How does it do that? It's not actually a real tram – it has regular wheels with tyres.

Run by a local larrikin, **Tex Tours** (☎ 0410-462 540) offers entertaining full-day Hunter Valley winery tours ($50), dolphin and 4WD dune tours to Port Stephens ($65) and bush'n'beach eco-safaris to Myall Lakes ($79).

SLEEPING
Budget

our pick **Newcastle Beach YHA** (☎ 4925 3544; www.yha .com.au/hostels/details.cfm?hostelid=134; 30 Pacific St; dm/s/d from $24/42/60; ☐) This heritage-listed building is a bikini strap away from Newcastle Beach. Inside, it's a bit like an English public school (without the humiliating hazing rituals): grand, high ceilings, plush-leather common room. There's also surfboard hire (per hour $5), pub meals, quizzes, pizza nights, and a barbecue courtyard.

Nomads Backpackers by the Beach (☎ 1800 008 972, 4926 3472; www.backpackersbythebeach.com.au; 34 Hunter St; dm $26-28, d & tw $60-64; ☐) It's not a patch on the YHA but it's clean, small and the staff dispense knowledge on Newcastle nightlife and surfing.

Midrange & Top End

Hamilton Heritage B&B (☎ 4961 1242; colaine@iprimus .com.au; 178 Denison St, Hamilton; s $90, d $120-140) It's all pastels, florals and moulded cornices in this lovely Federation-era home near the Beaumont St café strip. Rooms are reasonably sized and have en suites.

Clarendon Hotel (☎ 4927 0966; www.clarendon hotel.com.au; 347 Hunter St; r $140-170; ☒ ; wi-fi) The Art Deco Clarendon is thickly atmospheric, with stylish furniture and lighting. There's

a bar, brasserie and lashings of conviviality downstairs.

Ashiana (☎ 4929 4979; www.ashiana.com.au; 8 Helen St, Merewether; r $145-165) There's a slightly cluttered hippy sensibility to this nice old cottage near the beach, making it very homey. Two rooms are available; the larger has an en suite, the other a private bathroom.

Crowne Plaza (☎ 4907 5000; www.crowneplaza.com.au; cnr Merewether St & Wharf Rd; r $250-362; ☒ ☐ ☒ ; wi-fi) It's a large, beige modern hotel, but it's right on the waterfront and easily the best in town. With business people as regulars, expect lower rates on the weekend and lots of dark suits.

EATING

Newcastle's transformation has included the addition of some world-class restaurants. Darby and Beaumont are the main eat streets, rammed to the gills with culinary establishments. For self-catering, head to the **Coles supermarket** (☎ 4926 4494; cnr King & National Park Sts).

Restaurants

Govinda's (☎ 4929 6900; 110 King St; all-you-can-eat buffet $11; ☽ lunch Sun-Fri, dinner Tue-Sun) This airy, skylighted eatery serves the usual vegetarian Krishna fare (*pakoras*, rice fancies etc), loaded with taste.

Arrivederci (☎ 4963 1036; 53 Glebe Rd, The Junction; mains $11-25; ☽ dinner) Tony Soprano would probably order the Steak Al Capone at this old-fashioned Italian joint, but you can just drop in for cheap pasta and pizza.

Restaurant II (☎ 4929 1233; 8 Bolton St; mains $33-36; ☽ lunch Fri, dinner Tue-Sat) Restaurant II has more in common with *Terminator 2* than *Grease 2* – it's a sequel that stands up to scrutiny extremely well. An unexpected opening (a chef-provided canapé) leads through an action-packed midsection (try the ocean trout with zucchini flowers) to a satisfying denouement.

our pick **Bacchus** (☎ 4927 1332; 141 King St; tapas $7-11, mains $34-39; ☽ 11.30am-midnight Tue-Fri, 5pm-midnight Sat, 1-10.30pm Sun) A decadent Roman god has transformed this former Methodist church into a very atmospheric place to splurge (not purge – this isn't ancient Rome, after all). The food is exquisite – the squid ink risotto with cured scallops, divine.

Cafés

Estabar (☎ 4927 1222; 61 Shortland Esplanade; mains $6-14; ☽ 7am-10.30pm) Start the day with an excellent coffee or a Spanish-style hot chocolate at this sun-drenched café overlooking Newcastle Beach. When the temperature soars, stop in for gelato.

Goldberg's Coffee House (☎ 4929 3122; 137 Darby St; breakfast $5-16, lunch $7-15, dinner $12-23; ☺ 7am-midnight) A smooth café, European-style with open frontage, but featuring a typically Novocastrian twist: a wrought-iron chandelier descending like an oversize arachnid. Attracts chatty crowds of all persuasions.

Three Bean (☎ 4961 2020; 103 Tudor St (enter Beaumont), Hamilton; breakfast $6-15, lunch $14-18; ☺ 7am-5pm Mon-Fri, 7am-3pm Sat) Serious foodie attention has been paid to the menu, including notes on the provenance of the produce. It offers a welcome change from predictable café fare, although pan-seared wild rabbit livers aren't ever likely to bother our morning coffee schedule.

DRINKING

Finnegan's (☎ 4926 4777; 21-23 Darby St) The place for backpacker meals, trivia, pool competitions and, on the weekends, live bands and DJs.

Brewery (☎ 4929 6333; 150 Wharf Rd) Perched on Queens Wharf; the views and outdoor tables are sought after by both Novocastrian office workers and uni students. Has regular live music and decent food.

Junction Hotel (☎ 4961 4529; cnr Corlette & Kendrick Sts, The Junction) Doubters of Newcastle chic will be amazed by the architecturally impressive make-over of this ageing pub.

Silo Lounge Bar (☎ 4926 2828; 18/1 Honeysuckle Dr) More smart surrounds, this time in the new Honeysuckle quarter on the waterfront. Expect smooth sounds, lots of outdoor seating, chandeliers and flocked wallpaper.

Customs House Hotel (☎ 4925 2585; 1 Bond St) Once HQ for confiscating contraband, this lovely old building with a scenic alfresco patio is now part pub, part bistro.

ENTERTAINMENT
Live Music

Live Sites (www.livesites.org.au) This popular council-led initiative offers a varied line-up of acts (Latin jazz, professional street performers, Indian raga music) in malls, squares and public spaces around town.

Cambridge Hotel (☎ 4962 2459; www.yourcambridge .com; 789 Hunter St) The Cambridge launched silverchair, Newcastle's most famous cultural export, and continues to showcase touring national bands and local acts with live music from Wednesday to Sunday.

Wickham Park Hotel (☎ 4965 3501; www.myspace .com/thewicko; 61 Maitland Rd) Heralding itself as 'the home of the blues', this cosy pub has acoustic shows in the beer garden.

Cinemas
Showcase City Cinemas (☎ 4929 5019; 31 Wolfe St; tickets $12-13) Specialises in foreign and independent flicks.

Greater Union Cinemas (☎ 4926 2233; 185 King St; tickets $14.50) Has mainstream releases.

Theatre
Civic Theatre (☎ 4929 1977; www.civicprecinctnewcastle .com.au; 375 Hunter St) The Civic hosts theatre, musicals, concerts and dance in an evocative building designed by internationally renowned 'picture palace' architect Henry White.

GETTING THERE & AWAY
Air
Newcastle's **airport** (☎ 4928 9800; www.newcastle airport.com.au) is at Williamtown, 23km north of the city.

Virgin Blue (☎ 136 789; www.virginblue.com.au) and **Jetstar** (☎ 131 538; www.jetstar.com) both fly to Brisbane, the Gold Coast and Melbourne. **Tiger Airways** (☎ 03-9335 3033; www.tigerairways.com) also covers Melbourne. **Brindabella Airlines** (☎ 1300 66 88 24; www.brindabellaairlines.com.au) services Brisbane, Coffs Harbour, Port Macquarie and Canberra. If you really hate roads, **Aeropelican** (☎ 13 13 13; www.aeropelican.com.au) will take you to Sydney, as well as Inverell and Tamworth. **Norfolk Air** (☎ 1300 669 913; www.norfolkair.com) has a weekly link to its island home.

Bus
Nearly all long-distance buses stop behind the station in Newcastle. **Greyhound** (☎ 1300 473 946; www.greyhound.com.au) heads to Forster ($38, three hours, daily) and Port Macquarie ($58, four hours, three daily). **Premier Motor Service** (☎ 133 410; www.premierms.com.au) has a daily bus to/from Sydney ($30, 2½ hours) and Brisbane ($70, 13 hours).

Newcastle Buses (☎ 131 500; www.newcastlebuses .info) does the Lake Macquarie run, including Swansea (buses 349 to 351, $3, one hour). **Rover Coaches** (☎ 4990 1699; www.rovercoaches.com .au) heads to Cessnock ($5.80, 1¼ hours) in the Hunter Valley. **Port Stephens Coaches** (☎ 4982 2940; www.pscoaches.com.au) has regular buses between Nelson Bay and Newcastle ($5.80, 1½ hours). **Busways** (☎ 1800 043 263; www.busways .com.au) has services to/from Tea Gardens ($22, 90 minutes, three daily).

Car

ARA (☎ 4962 2488; www.ararental.com.au; 86 Belford St, Broadmeadow) offers rental from $30 a day. Alternatively, Tudor St in Hamilton has the big agencies.

Train

A better option than the buses, **CityRail** (☎ 13 15 00; www.cityrail.info) has frequent trains to Sydney ($18, three hours) via Gosford ($10.60, 90 minutes). A line also heads to Branxton ($7.20, 55 minutes) in the Hunter Valley.

Heading north, **CountryLink** (☎ 8202 2000; www.countrylink.info) services depart from Broadmeadow station to Wingham ($25, three hours, two daily), Coffs Harbour ($55, 6½ hours, three daily) and on to Brisbane ($81, 12 hours, one daily).

GETTING AROUND
To/From the Airport

Port Stephens Coaches (☎ 4982 2940; www.pscoaches .com.au) head to Williamtown airport frequently ($4.80, 40 minutes) en route to Nelson Bay.

Network All Travel (☎ 4956 9299; www.alltravel .com.au) runs a door-to-door shuttle between the airport and the city ($30), Port Stephens ($45) and the Hunter Valley ($65); bookings required. **Taxis** (☎ 131 008) to the city centre cost around $50.

Bus

Newcastle has an extensive and reasonably priced network of **local buses** (☎ 13 15 00; www .newcastlebuses.info). There's a fare-free bus zone in the inner city between 7.30am and 6pm. Other fares are time-based (one-hour/four-hour/all-day $3/5.90/9). The main depot is near the train station.

Ferry

The Stockton ferry ($2.10) goes every half-hour from Queens Wharf, 5.15am until midnight on Friday and Saturday, 11pm Monday to Thursday and 10pm on Sunday.

Train

Services terminate at Newcastle station after stopping at Broadmeadow, Hamilton, Wickham and Civic.

NEWCASTLE TO TAREE & HUNTER VALLEY

From Newcastle you can choose to charge along the freeway, make a detour away from the coast to the Hunter Valley or make a series of meandering diversions along the coast. If you've got time to spare, the last two options are well worth the effort.

LOWER HUNTER VALLEY

A spider's web of pleasant country lanes crisscrosses this verdant valley, but a pleasant country drive isn't the main motivator for visitors. Sheer decadence is. The Hunter Valley is one big gorge-fest: fine wine, boutique beer, chocolate, cheese, olives, you name it. Bacchus would surely approve.

Going on the philosophy that good food and wine has got to up the odds for nookie, the Hunter is a popular naughty weekender for Sydney couples. Every Friday they descend, like a plague of Ralph-Lauren-Polo-shirt-wearing locusts. Prices leap up accordingly.

The Hunter Valley, the oldest wine region in Australia, is known for its Semillon and Shiraz. Vines were first planted in the 1820s and by the 1860s there were 20 sq km under cultivation. A Hunter sparkling made its way to Paris in 1855 and was favourably compared with the French product. However, the wineries gradually declined, and it wasn't until the 1960s that winemaking again became an important industry. If it's no longer the crowning jewel of Australian wine regions, it still turns in some excellent vintages.

The Hunter has an important ace up its sleeve: these wineries are refreshingly attitude-free and welcoming of viticulturists and novices alike. Staff will rarely give you the evil eye if you leadenly twirl your glass once too often, or don't conspicuously savour the bouquet. Even those with only a casual interest in wine should tour around – it's a lovely area, and a great direction to turn to if the weather drives you from the beaches.

Orientation

Most attractions lie in an area bordered to the north by the New England Hwy and to the south by Wollombi/Maitland Rd. The

NEWCASTLE TO TAREE & HUNTER VALLEY

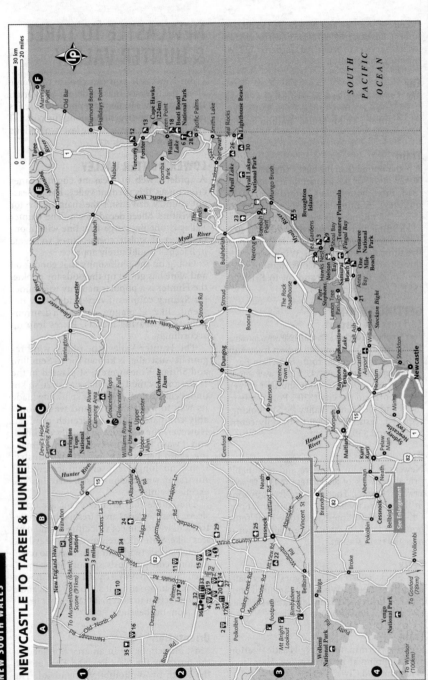

main town serving the area is Cessnock, to the south. Wine Country Dr heads straight up from Cessnock to Branxton, where there's a train station. To confuse matters, the bottom half of this route is sometimes labelled Allandale Rd and the top end Branxton Rd.

Heading north there are further vineyards around Broke, Singleton and the Upper Hunter.

Information

Visitors centre (☎ 4990 0900; www.winecountry .com.au; 455 Wine Country Dr; ☼ 9am-5pm Mon-Sat, 9am-4pm Sun)

Sights & Activities
WINERIES

The valley's 140 wineries range from small-scale family-run affairs to massive architectural extravagances. Most offer free tastings, although a couple of the glitzier ones charge a small fee. Remember that the vineyards don't offer this service out of the goodness of their hearts. It's poor form if you don't buy at least the occasional bottle.

Grab a vineyard map and plot your course or just follow your nose, hunting out the tucked-away small producers. Here are a few picks to get you started:

Audrey Wilkinson Vineyard (☎ 4998 7411; www .audreywilkinson.com.au; DeBeyers Rd; ☼ 9am-5pm Mon- Fri, 9.30am-5pm Sat & Sun) One of the oldies (first planted 1866), it's worth visiting more for its interesting historic display and excellent views (bring a picnic) than for its overcrowded and touristy tasting room.

Brokenwood (☎ 4998 7559; www.brokenwood.com .au; 401-427 McDonalds Rd; ☼ 9.30am-5pm Mon- Sat, 10am-5pm Sun) One of the Hunter's most acclaimed wineries.

Hungerford Hill (☎ 4998 7666; www.hungerfordhill .com.au; 1 Broke Rd; ☼ 9am-5pm Mon-Wed, 9am-7pm Thu & Fri, 10am-7pm Sat & Sun) Shaped like a big barrel, with its 'lid' permanently propped open, this commanding spectacle stands sentinel over the lakes and valleys below.

Macquariedale Estate (☎ 6574 7012; www.mac quariedale.com.au; 170 Sweetwater Rd; ☼ 10am-5pm Fri-Mon) A boutique winemaker that's certified organic and biodynamic.

Moorebank Vineyard (☎ 4998 7610; www.moore bankvineyard.com.au; Palmers Lane; ☼ 10am-5pm) Sustainable winemaking practices and delicious home-made condiments.

Pepper Tree Wines (☎ 4998 7746; www.peppertree wines.com.au; Halls Rd; ☼ 9am-5pm Mon-Fri, 9.30am-5pm Sat & Sun) Set in gorgeous, New England–style gardens. It has won over 200 awards and medals.

Peterson's Champagne House (☎ 4998 7881; www .petersonhouse.com.au; cnr Wine Country Dr & Broke Rd; ☼ 10am-5pm) Lovely jubbly bubbly, including some sparkling reds.

Piggs Peake Winery (☎ 6574 7000; www.piggspeake .com; 697 Hermitage Rd; ☼ 10am-5pm) A proper small-scale winery where the owners get their hands dirty.

Pooles Rock Wines (☎ 4998 7356; www.poolesrock .com.au; DeBeyers Rd; ☼ 9.30am-5pm) A big player, producing the midpriced Cockfighter's Ghost range as well as its excellent flagship wines.

Small Winemakers Centre (☎ 4998 7668; www .smallwinemakerscentre.com.au; McDonalds Rd; ☼ 10am-5pm) Acts as a cellar door for six boutique winemakers.

Tamburlaine (☎ 4998 7570; www.mywinery.com; 358 McDonalds Rd; ☼ 9am-5pm) Another excellent producer focusing on sustainable viticulture with some wines fully organic.

HUNTER VALLEY GARDENS

Although there's something a little Disney about it, this relatively young 24-hectare

CENTRAL COAST
NEW SOUTH WALES

garden (☎ 4998 4000; www.hvg.com.au; Broke Rd; adult/child $20/11; ⏲ 9am-5pm) has impressive floral and landscape displays.

Tours

If no-one's volunteering to stay sober enough to drive, there are plenty of winery tours available. Some will collect you in Sydney or Newcastle for a lengthy day trip. Staff at visitors centres and accommodation providers should be able to arrange a booking that suits your needs. These are but a few of the options:

Hunter Valley Day Tours (☎ 4951 4574; www.huntervalleydaytours.com.au) Wine-and-cheese-tasting tours; prices vary according to group numbers (from $89 per person).

Hunter Valley Tours (☎ 4990 8989; www.huntervalleytours.com.au) Small group local-run boutique tours; from $95 per person for full day including lunch.

Pokolbin Horse Coaches (☎ 4998 7305; www.pokolbinhorsecoaches.com.au; McDonalds Rd) Full (adult/child $60/30) or half-day (adult/child $45/25) vineyard tours in an open-air carriage.

Festivals & Events

During the warm months superstars regularly drop by for weekend concerts at the bigger vineyards. If there's something special on, accommodation gets scooped up well in advance. Check what's on at www.winecountry.com.au.

Hunter Valley Harvest Celebrations Two months of postharvest celebration (late April to early June).

Lovedale Long Lunch (www.lovedalelonglunch.com.au) Eight wineries and chefs produce gut-bursting lunches, served with music and art; May.

Jazz in the Vines (www.jazzinthevines.com.au) October.

Opera in the Vineyards (www.4di.com.au) October.

Sleeping

Prices shoot up savagely on Friday and Saturday nights (expect around 50% higher than we've listed following) and two-night minimum stays are common. It's best to time your trip for midweek when you're less likely to be subjected to endless visions of bourgeois bonding.

BUDGET

Hunter Valley YHA (☎ 4991 3278; www.yha.com.au/hostels/details.cfm?hostelid=235; 100 Wine Country Dr; site per person $10, dm $29-32, s $65-75, d & tw $77-92; 🖳 🛋) In late summer this newish, custom-built hostel is packed to the rafters with

---

SENSIBLE SUPPING

If you are driving, remember that to stay under the blood-alcohol limit of 0.05, men can generally have two standard drinks in the first hour and one every hour after. Women can have one standard drink per hour. Wineries usually offer 20mL tastes of wine – five of these equals one standard drink. To be extra safe: choose a designated driver; sip, then tip the remainder; use the spittoons provided; or take a tour.

---

working-holiday-makers, picking fruit on the vineyards. The reward at the end of a long day is a welcoming pool, clean facilities and plenty of bonhomie. The rooms can get stiflingly hot.

Big4 Valley Vineyard Tourist Park (☎ 4990 2573; www.valleyvineyard.com.au; 137 Mt View Rd; sites per 2 people $30-40, cabins $65-120; 🛋) A spacious, orderly park with a pool and on-site Thai restaurant.

MIDRANGE & TOP END

Hill Top Country Guest House (☎ 4930 7111; www.hilltopguesthouse.com.au; 81 Talga Rd; r $90-180; 🖳 🛋) Hill Top offers great views, horse riding, in-house massage, a pool, 4WD safaris, spa baths, a grand piano, cattle mustering, a billiards room – or just a whole lot of peace and quiet. And you thought you were here for the wine.

Vineyard Hill Country Motel (☎ 4990 4166; www.vineyardhill.com.au; Lovedale Rd; d/tr $118/165; 🖳 🛋) The pleasant self-contained units have decks on which to stretch out and enjoy fine valley views, preferably vino in hand. It's much better than the average motel.

Hunter Country Lodge (☎ 4938 1744; www.shakeytables.com.au; 1476 Wine Country Dr; s/d/tw/tr $110/150/150/205; 🖳 🛋) You'll know you're in the country when kangaroos bounce past your simple but well-furnished wooden room. With the wonderful Shakey Tables (opposite) as its dining room, breakfasts shouldn't be missed. Book the dinner-inclusive package for at least one night.

Peppers Convent (☎ 4993 8999; www.peppers.com.au; Halls Rd; r $198-219; 🖳 🛋 ; wi-fi) This grand Edwardian former nunnery has been moved hundreds of kilometres, planted among the vineyards and thoroughly renovated in a French provincial style. It makes for a lovely, lavish retreat.

Eating

It seems that everyone expects wine lushes to also be gluttons and millionaires, as the Hunter is stuffed full of expensive restaurants. Unbelievably, several local places are pricier than Sydney's best, despite lower overheads and ready access to quality fresh ingredients. That said, there are some truly excellent places to eat.

RESTAURANTS

Oishii (☎ 4998 7051; Tempus Two Winery, cnr Broke & McDonald Rds; mains $16-25; ☻ lunch & dinner) One of the few decent spots for a good meal without causing you to haemorrhage money, this modern place serves a large selection of Thai and Japanese dishes including plenty of vegetarian options.

our pick **Shakey Tables** (☎ 4938 1744; 1476 Wine Country Dr; mains $36; ☻ dinner) The chef's vibrant art is on the walls as well as on the plates of this fabulously eccentric restaurant. Kooky combinations (mining myriad cuisines, even Scottish) are deftly plated into fiddly masterpieces. We were particularly enamoured of the dessert that looked like Elvis' hair – made of pistachio spun sugar and served with lychee ice cream, Turkish delight and rose petals.

Firestick Café & Rock Restaurant (☎ 4998 6968; Pooles Rock Wines, DeBeyers Rd; lunch $18-39, dinner $48-69; ☻ 9.30am-5pm daily, dinner Thu-Sat) The slightly more mild-mannered Firestick by day morphs into the award-winning Rock at night. Both are terrific, albeit terrifically expensive. The delicious daytime-only crispy pizzas are an affordable route to sampling the Hunter's top rated establishment, although you run the risk of caving in once you see the innovative Mod Oz menu on offer.

CAFÉS & PROVIDORES

Australian Regional Food Store & Café (☎ 4998 6800; Small Winemakers Centre, McDonalds Rd; mains $7-20; ☻ 9am-5pm) Like the centre in which it's located, this food store champions 'indie', often organic, produce. The café makes good use of the store's excellent products.

Hunter Valley Cheese Company (☎ 4998 7744; McGuigans Complex, McDonalds Rd; platters $28; ☻ 9am-5.30pm) 'Blessed are the cheesemakers' quotes the staff T-shirts, and the people inside those shirts will chew your ear about cheesy comestibles all day long. There's a bewildering, sinful variety of styles, with free tastings available. Or you can settle down to a cheese platter.

For other yummy stuff:

Hunter Valley Chocolate Company (☎ 4998 7301; Peterson's Champagne House, cnr Broke & Branxton Rds; ☻ 10am-5pm) All manner of cacao derivatives.

Hunter Olive Centre (☎ 4998 7524; Pokolbin Estate Vineyard, McDonalds Rd; ☻ 10am-5pm) Dozens of things to try on little squares of bread – oil, tapanade, *dukkah* (a blend of ground nuts and spices), chutney etc. If you're shameless you could make it lunch.

Drinking

Bluetongue Brewery (☎ 4998 7777; Hunter Resort, Hermitage Rd; ☻ 10am-11.30pm) Sample the creative and refreshing brews using the Tasting Paddle (six beers for $10). Also on offer are pizza, pies, a pool table, tours of the adjacent Hermitage Rd Cellars (11am and 2pm, $5) and a daily wine school (9am, $30).

Harrigan's (☎ 4998 4000; Broke Rd) A comfortable Irish pub with live bands most weekends, trivia competitions and the occasional backpacker barbecue (it's not as sinister as it sounds).

Getting There & Away

Wine Country Xpress (☎ 4990 1699; www.rovercoaches .com.au; one way/return $35/60) leaves Sydney's Central Station at 8.30am daily, returning at 4.40pm (arriving Sydney 7pm). A day pass ($70) combines this service with the Wine Rover (below).

CityRail (☎ 13 15 00; www.cityrail.info) has a line heading through the Hunter Valley from Newcastle ($7.20, 55 minutes), or you can jump on at Sydney ($22, 3¾ hours). The closest station to the vineyards is Branxton.

Greyhound (☎ 1300 473 946; www.greyhound.com.au) runs a daily bus from Sydney ($64, 4½ hours) to Branxton, departing outside Central Station at 2.15pm. **Rover Coaches** (☎ 4990 1699; www.rover coaches.com.au) has regular services between Cessnock and Newcastle ($5.80, 1¼ hours).

Getting Around

Without a car and sober driver your best option is to use the **Wine Rover** (☎ 4990 1699; www .rovercoaches.com.au; all day $20; ☻ 9am-4.45pm), a hop-on/hop-off bus service plying backwards and forwards on two main routes throughout the day. To get to a specific destination, **Vineyard Shuttle** (☎ 4991 3655; www.vineyardshuttle.com.au) offers a door-to-door service for around $10 per trip.

Both **Grapemobile** (☎ 0418 404 039; www.pokol binbrothers.com.au/grapemobile.htm; Pokolbin Brothers Vineyard, Palmers Lane) and **Hunter Valley Cycling**

WORIMI COUNTRY

The area from the Tomaree Peninsula to Forster and as far west as Gloucester is the land of the Worimi people, who have lived in this region for thousands of years. Very little of it is now in their possession, but in 2001 the sand dunes of the Stockton Bight were returned to them, creating the Worimi Conservation Lands (below). The Worimi people in turn entered an agreement to co-manage it with the NPWS.

Sacred places and occupation sites are scattered throughout the region. **Dark Point Aboriginal Place** in Myall Lakes National Park has been significant to the Worimi for around 4000 years. Local lore has it that in the late 19th century it was the site of one of many massacres of Aboriginals at the hands of white settlers, when a group was herded onto the rocks and pushed off.

(☎ 0418 281 480; www.huntervalleycycling.com.au) hire bikes.

PORT STEPHENS

This stunning sheltered bay is about an hour's drive north of Newcastle, occupying a submerged valley that stretches more than 20km inland. Framing its southern edge is the narrow **Tomaree Peninsula**, unfairly blessed with near-deserted beaches, national parks and an extraordinary sand dune system. The main centre, **Nelson Bay** (population 4120), is home to both a fishing fleet and an armada of tourist vessels, capitalising on its status as the 'dolphin capital of Australia'.

Just east of Nelson Bay, and virtually merged with it, is pretty **Shoal Bay** (population 1750), with a long, sheltered beach, lumpy headland and great views across to hilly islands. The road ends a short drive south from here at **Fingal Bay** (population 700), with another lovely beach on the fringes of **Tomaree National Park**. The park stretches west around clothing-optional **Samurai Beach**, a popular surfing spot, and **One Mile Beach**, a gorgeous semicircle of the softest sand and bluest water favoured by those in the know: surfers, beachcombers, idle romantics.

The park ends at the nondescript surfside village of **Anna Bay** (population 2640), but wait till you see what it's backed by – the incredible **Worimi Conservation Lands** (right).

Opposite Nelson Bay, on the north shore of Port Stephens, are the small, pretty towns of **Tea Gardens** and **Hawks Nest** (see p238).

Information

Internet Café (☎ 4984 3225; 106 Magnus St, Nelson Bay; per hr $8)

NPWS office (☎ 4984 8200; www.npws.nsw.gov.au; 12B Teramby Rd, Nelson Bay; ☽ 8.30am-4.30pm)

Visitors centre (☎ 4980 6900; www.portstephens .org.au; Victoria Pde, Nelson Bay; ☽ 9am-5pm)

Sights

The **Worimi Conservation Lands** at Stockton Bight are the longest moving sand dunes in the southern hemisphere, stretching over 35km. The tourist board claims the dunes are *Mad Max*–style, but if you want to talk films, think *Lawrence of Arabia* – more Sahara than outback. In the heart of it, it's possible to become so surrounded by shimmering sand you'll lose sight of the ocean or any sign of life. In short, it's incredibly evocative. At the far west end of the beach, the wreck of the *Sygna* founders in the water.

Thanks to the generosity of the Worimi people (see boxed text, above), whose land this is, you're able to roam around (provided you don't disturb any Aboriginal sites), camp within 100m of the high tide mark (you'll need a portable toilet), drive along the beach (4WD only; permit required) and mash up the sand dunes within the designated recreational vehicle area (permit required). Get your permits from the visitors centre or NPWS office in Nelson Bay ($10 for three days; see left).

Tomaree National Park is a wonderfully wild expanse harbouring several threatened species, including the spotted-tailed quoll and powerful owl. If you keep your eyes peeled you're bound to spot a koala or wallaby. At the eastern end of Shoal Bay there's a short walk to the surf at unpatrolled **Zenith Beach** (beware of rips and strong undercurrents), or you can tackle the strenuous **Tomaree Head Summit Walk** (1km and 80 minutes return). Longer walks are detailed in a pamphlet available from NPWS.

The restored 1875 **Heritage Light House Cottage** (☎ 4984 2505; admission free; ☽ 10am-4pm) at Nelson Head has a small museum with displays on the area's history and a tea room. The views of Port Stephens are suitably inspiring.

Tours

There are dozens of operators offering action-packed ways to spend your day. Inquire and book at the visitor centre in Nelson Bay.

WET STUFF

Anna Bay Surf School (☎ 4981 9919; www.annabay surfschool.com.au; One Mile Beach Holiday Park, Hannah Pde; half-/2-/3-day $75/98/138) Surf lessons and board hire (per hour/day $15/45).

Blue Water Sea Kayaking (☎ 0405 033 518; www .kayakingportstephens.com.au) Offer a range of paddle-powered excursions including hour-long beginner tours ($25), 90-minute champagne sunset tours ($35) and 2½-hour dolphin-seeking tours ($45).

Imagine Cruises (☎ 4984 9000; www.imaginecruises.com .au; Dock C, d'Albora Marina, Nelson Bay) Eco-accredited trips, including 3½-hour Sail, Swim & Snorkel ($45), 90-minute Dolphin Watch cruises ($22), three-hour Whale & Dolphin Watch cruises ($55) and the Sundowner Sail ($25).

Moonshadow (☎ 4984 9388; www.moonshadow.com .au; 35 Stockton St, Nelson Bay) Dolphin-watching ($21), whale-watching ($55), dinner cruises ($65) and seven-hour trips to Broughton Island ($75) on big catamarans. Eco-accredited.

SANDY STUFF

Oakfield Ranch (☎ 0429 664 172; www.oakfieldranch .com; Birubi Pt car park, James Patterson Dr, Anna Bay) Twenty-minute camel rides along the beach on Sundays and school holidays.

Port Stephens 4WD Tours (☎ 4984 4760; www.port stephens4wd.com.au; 35 Stockton St, Nelson Bay; tours $20-75) Drive around the dunes and go sand-boarding.

Quad Bike King (☎ 4919 0088; www.quadbikeking .com.au; tours $85-240) Guided quad-bike forays out on the dunes, or just a sandboarding shuttle ($20).

Sleeping

In Nelson Bay, Government St between Stockton and Church Sts is lined with motels and hotels, but the most memorable accommodation is around Anna Bay and Shoal Bay. There's free camping at Samurai Beach for nudists.

BUDGET

Melaleuca Surfside Backpackers (☎ 4981 9422; www .melaleucabackpackers.com.au; 2 Koala Pl, One Mile Beach; sites per person/dm/d/tw $15/28/80/80; 🖵) Wooden cabins are set amid peaceful scrub inhabited by koalas and wallabies. There's a comfortable lounge area and kitchen, and the camp sites are 'free range' – you pick your own and cars are not allowed near tents.

ourpick Port Stephens YHA Samurai Beach Bungalows (☎ 4982 1921; www.samuraiportstephens .com; Frost Rd, Anna Bay; dm $29, d $77-105, tr/q $108/132; 🖵 🖵 ; wi-fi) These attractively furnished wooden-floored cabins are separated by pleasant koala-populated bushland dotted with Asian sculpture. The central pool is blissful.

Shoal Bay Holiday Park (☎ 4981 1427; www.beach sideholidays.com.au; Shoal Bay Rd, Shoal Bay; sites per 2 people $39-65, d $80-210; 🖾) An excellent camping ground, right on the bay, with top-notch cabins.

MIDRANGE & TOP END

O'Carrollyn's (☎ 4982 2801; www.ocarrollyns.com .au; 5 Koala Pl, One Mile Beach; d $140-215; 🖾 ; wi-fi) Wheelchair-accessible self-contained villas and wheelchair access to a beautiful, near-deserted beach. This is spruce, feel-good accommodation, surrounded by landscaped gardens, teeming with koalas.

Wanderers Retreat (☎ 4982 1702; www.wanderers retreat.com; 7 Koala Pl, One Mile Beach; d $155-270, tr $180-295, q $205-320; 🖾 🖵) Wear your designer frayed jeans and pretend you're Robinson Crusoe in your own luxury treehouse. I bet he didn't have a spa bath, though.

Bali at the Bay (☎ 4981 2964; www.baliatthebay .com.au; 1 Achilles St, Shoal Bay; d/tr/q $230/285/285; 🖾) Two exceedingly beautiful self-contained apartments, chock-full of flower-garlanded Buddhas and carved wood, do a good job of living up to the name. The bathrooms are exquisite and spa treatments are available.

Eating

Anna Bay's a dead loss, so explore Nelson Bay's marina and Shoal Bay's waterfront for further dining options.

Red Ned's Pies (☎ 4984 1355; www.redneds.com.au; Shop 3/17-19 Stockton St, Nelson Bay; pies $5-6; ⏱ 6am-5pm) King piemaker Barry Kelly learnt his trade in top-shelf international hotels and his philosophy is simple: he gets a kick out of watching people stare at his specials board, goggle-eyed (anyone for barbecue-bourbon-and-beef or kangaroo-teriyaki?).

Aquablu (☎ 4984 9999; d'Albora Marina, Nelson Bay; breakfast $5-14, lunch $15-26, dinner $17-34; ⏱ 8am-8.30pm) One of the more reasonably priced and hipper places on the waterfront, Aquablu is a combination café-bar-bistro that suits any time of the day.

Zest (☎ 4984 2211; 16 Stockton St, Nelson Bay; 2 courses $60; ⏱ dinner Tue-Sat) Rhymes with best, which is exactly what this restaurant is on this part of the coast. Its prestigious *Good Food Guide* 'chef's hat' award proves it – you won't find another one before Bellingen. Bravely, for a fishing town, the menu emphasises game over the predictably poisson.

Getting There & Around

Port Stephens Coaches (☎ 4982 2940; www.pscoaches .com.au) regularly zips around Port Stephens' townships heading to Newcastle ($5.80, 1½ hours) and the airport. There's also a daily service to/from Sydney ($33, 3½ hours).

Port Stephens Ferry Service (☎ 0412-682 117) chugs from Nelson Bay to Tea Gardens and back three times a day ($20 return, one hour).

TEA GARDENS & HAWKS NEST

☎ 02 / pop 1980 (Tea Gardens), 1030 (Hawks Nest)
Sporting the most quaintly evocative names on the coast, this duo of towns straddles the mouth of the Myall River, linked by the graceful, curved Singing Bridge. Tea Gardens has a quiet, laid-back charm; it's a river culture here, older and genteel. At Hawks Nest it's all about the beaches. **Jimmys Beach** fronts a glasslike stretch of water facing Nelson Bay, while stunning **Bennetts Beach** looks to the ocean and Broughton Island.

Information

Library (☎ 4997 1265; Marine Dr; ☼ 9am-5pm Mon, Wed & Fri, 10am-12.30pm Sat) Free internet access.
Visitors centre (☎ 4997 0111; www.greatlakes.org.au; Myall St; ☼ 10am-4pm) Near the bridge.

Sleeping

Tea Gardens Hotel Motel (☎ 4997 0203; http://teagardens -hawksnest-hotelmotel.com.au; cnr Marine Dr & Maxwell St; s/d $55/70; 🖳) On the riverfront, this popular watering hole has cute pink and blue rooms set around a garden out back.

Tea Gardens Waterfront B&B (☎ 4997 1688; www .waterfrontbandb.com.au; 117 Marine Dr; r $110-150; 🖳) Has two large spotless studio-rooms set in a leafy courtyard. Breakfast is included in the rates – enjoy it over river views.

Eating

Cornerstone Kitchen (☎ 4997 0666; 83 Marine Dr; mains $5-12; ☼ 7am-5pm) Sandwiches, wraps and salads are the, ahem, cornerstone of this snazzy deli-café. That and delicious coffee.

Nicole's (☎ 4997 2922; 81 Marine Dr, Tea Gardens; breakfast & lunch $5-17, dinner $15-27; ☼ breakfast &

lunch daily, dinner Mon-Sat) Housed in a Victorian cottage, this seriously sweet café doubles as an art gallery and gift shop. The garden is seductive, with trickling water features, bird baths, much greenery and Roman statues. Good cakes, too.

Getting There & Around

While only 5km from Nelson Bay as the cockatoo flies, the drive necessitates returning to the Pacific Hwy near Raymond Terrace and then doubling back – a distance of 83km. The alternative is the Port Stephens Ferry Service (left).

If you're continuing north, take the stunning scenic route through Myall Lakes National Park; it involves a short ferry crossing and 10km is unsealed.

Busways (☎ 1800 043 263; www.busways.com.au) has services to/from Newcastle ($22, 90 minutes, three daily) and Forster ($36, 1¾ hours, two daily) via Blueys Beach ($22, 80 minutes).

MYALL LAKES NATIONAL PARK

On an extravagantly pretty section of the coast, this large park incorporates a patchwork of lakes, islands, dense littoral rainforest and beaches. The lakes support an incredible number and variety of bird life, including bowerbirds, white-bellied sea eagles and tawny frogmouths. There are paths through coastal rainforest and past beach dunes at **Mungo Brush** in the south, perfect for spotting wildflowers and dingoes.

The best beaches and surf are in the north around beautiful, secluded **Seal Rocks**, a bushy hamlet hugging Sugarloaf Bay. It has a great beach, with emerald-green rock pools, epic ocean views and golden sand. Take the short walk to the **Sugarloaf Point Lighthouse** where the views are sublime; there's a water-choked gorge along the way and a detour to lonely **Lighthouse Beach**. At the time of research, NPWS was seeking an interested party to transform the historic stone lighthouse keepers cottages into holiday accommodation.

The path around the lighthouse leads to a lookout over the actual Seal Rocks – islets that provide sanctuary for Australia's northernmost colony of Australian fur seals. During summer breeding, the seals are out in abundance and you'll do well to bring binoculars. **Humpback whales** swim past Seal Rocks during their annual migration and can sometimes be seen from the shore.

THE LAKES WAY OR THE HIGHWAY

An excellent alternative to the Pacific Hwy, The Lakes Way twists through Myall Lakes and Booti Booti National Parks before passing through Forster-Tuncurry. Shortly after leaving the highway, 4km past Bulahdelah, there's a bumpy road heading to the Grandis. At 76m this massive flooded gum is the tallest tree in New South Wales.

Busways (☎ 1800 043 263; www.busways .com.au) takes this route, charging $36 from Newcastle to Forster.

About a half-hour by boat from Nelson Bay, **Broughton Island** is uninhabited except for mutton birds, little penguins and an enormous diversity of fish species. The diving is tops and the beaches are incredibly secluded.

Vehicle access to some parts of the park is $7. At Bombah Broadwater the Bombah Point ferry (per car/pedestrian $6/2.50; five minutes) crosses every half-hour from 8am to 6pm. A 10km section of Bombah Point Rd, heading to the Pacific Hwy at Bulahdelah, is unsealed.

Sleeping

The park is well served with **camp sites** (☎ 4984 8200; www.npws.nsw.gov.au; sites per adult/child $10/5), most of which have composting toilets and water for boiling. There are eight excellent sites along Mungo Brush Rd, between Hawks Nest and the ferry. At the top end of the park, near Seal Rocks, are Yagon camp site (by the surf beach) and Neranie camp site (by the lake). The other 12 sites are mainly dotted around the lake and are accessible either by foot, boat or, in some cases, unsealed roads. Broughton Island also has a site.

Myall Shores EcoPoint Resort (☎ 4997 4495; www.myallshores.com.au; Bombah Pt Rd; sites per 2 people $34, q $72-458; 🗙 🖭) Right on the water, this well-outfitted resort has eco-friendly cabins, a restaurant and bar, petrol, gas and basic groceries. It also hires canoes (one hour $20), bikes (one hour $10), power boats (two hours $65) and catamarans (three hours $200).

Bombah Point Eco Cottages (☎ 4997 4401; www .bombah.com.au; 969 Bombah Pt Rd; d/tr/q $280/285/320; 🖭) Green isn't just chic on St Patrick's Day at this gorgeous, architecturally designed, solar-powered, eco-toileted bush retreat. The six

spiffy self-contained cottages are scattered among the trees.

PACIFIC PALMS
☎ 02 / pop 680

Sneaky Pacific Palms is secluded between Myall Lakes and Booti Booti National Parks. It's one of those places that well-heeled city dwellers slink off to on weekends – which sounds perfectly dreadful, but it's actually very pleasant…and a hell of a lot nicer than Forster up the road. If you're camping in either of the parks you might find yourself here when the espresso cravings kick in.

Most of the houses cling to **Blueys Beach** or **Boomerang Beach**, both long stretches of golden sand. **Elizabeth Beach**, just inside Booti Booti, is the nicest and has lifesavers at peak times.

The volunteer-run **visitors centre** (☎ 6554 8799; Boomerang Dr; 🕑 9am-4pm) has internet access ($2.50 per 15 minutes) and some arts and crafts for sale.

Sleeping & Eating

Blueys by the Beach (☎ 6554 0665; www.blueysbythe beach.com.au; 186 Boomerang Dr; r $110-125; 🗙 🖭) It's closer to the shops than the beach, but that's a minor quibble. This standard but friendly motel has large tidy rooms and is a solid option in a settlement catering mainly to the wealthy in private homes.

Twenty by Twelve (☎ 6554 0452; 207 Boomerang Dr; mains $5-19; 🕑 7.30am-2pm) Camping is all very well, but try getting a coffee like this out of a billy can – let alone a drool-worthy moist muffin from a barbecue. It also sells local organic produce and delicious deli treats.

Hueys at Blueys (☎ 6554 0222; 201 Boomerang Dr; mains $11-15; 🕑 dinner) Dishes up tasty thin-crust pizza and surfer wisdom.

Recky (☎ 6554 0207; The Lakes Way; mains $14-21; 🕑 11am-late) If you want to be formal, it's the Pacific Palms Recreation Club. Yep, it's one of those sign-in clubs with cheap booze and a bistro (serving generous seafood platters). It overlooks lovely Wallis Lake and has a reputation as a live music venue.

Getting There & Around

Busways (☎ 1800 043 263; www.busways.com.au) stops on the way between Tea Gardens and Forster.

Forster Bus Service (☎ 6554 6431; www.forsterbus .au) heads to Forster ($8.60, 25 minutes) twice daily on weekdays.

CENTRAL COAST NEW SOUTH WALES

BOOTI BOOTI NATIONAL PARK

This 1567-hectare **national park** (vehicle admission $7) stretches along a skinny peninsula with **Seven Mile Beach** on its eastern side and **Wallis Lake** on its west. The northern section of the park is swathed in coastal rainforest and topped by 224m **Cape Hawke**. At the Cape Hawke headland there's a **viewing platform**, well worth the sweat of climbing the 420-something steps.

You won't really be darkening the door of a church if you visit the **Green Cathedral** as there is no door. This interesting space (consecrated in 1940) consists of wooden pews under the palm trees, looking to the lake.

There's self-registration camping at the **Ruins** (camping per adult/child 14/7), at the southern end of Seven Mile Beach, with an **NPWS office** (☎ 6554 0446) nearby.

Avoid Forster's motel mania at **Lakeside Escape B&B** (☎ 6557 6400; www.lakesideescape.com.au; 85 Green Point Dr, Green Point; r $155-165; 🖳), seven minutes out of town in the Green Point fishing village. The en suite rooms look over Wallis Lake and there's a spa. Breakfast is included.

FORSTER-TUNCURRY

☎ 02 / pop 18,380

Forster-Tuncurry are twin towns facing off on either side of the sea entrance to Wallis Lake. Forster (pronounced Foster) is like a mini Gold Coast – high-rises everywhere – but even less interesting. Thankfully, the beaches are nice, the lake's pretty and there's an abundance of water sports possible. Dolphins and pelicans seem to like the place, so it can't be too bad.

The **visitors centre** (☎ 6554 8799; www.great lakes.org.au; Little St, Forster; ⏰ 9am-4pm) is by the lakeside. There's internet access at the **library** (☎ 6591 7256; Breese Pde, Forster; ⏰ 10am-6.30pm Tue, 10am-5.30pm Wed-Fri).

Sights & Activities

Imagination doesn't seem to have troubled the early settlers much if the beach names are anything to go by. **Nine Mile Beach** at Tuncurry is consistently the best for surf, but **Forster** and **Pebbly** Beaches can also be good. Further south there's **One Mile Beach**, which is north of **Seven Mile Beach**. The lake is tops for paddling. There are large **ocean pools** at Forster Beach and near the harbour entrance in Tuncurry.

Tobwabba Art (☎ 6554 5755; www.tobwabba.com .au; 10 Breckenridge St, Forster; ⏰ 9am-5pm Mon-Fri) is one of the best known and largest Aboriginal artistic communities in NSW. It's a great place to purchase authentic indigenous art.

The **museum** (☎ 6554 6275; Capel St, Tuncurry; adult/child $3/1; ⏰ 1-2pm Tue & Wed, 1-4pm Sun), off South St, has a set of historic buildings (a windmill, a lock-up etc) and relics from local pioneer families.

Popular dives in the area include the **Pinnacles**, the huge wreck of the **SS Satara** and **Seal Rocks**, where there are grey nurse sharks to cosy up to. **Dive Forster** (☎ 6554 7478; www .diveforster.com.au; Fisherman's Wharf, Memorial Dr) offers double boat dives ($100), equipment hire (an extra $50) and PADI open water courses ($490). It also runs a 2½-hour **Swim With Wild Dolphins Cruise** (swimmers/nonswimmers $60/35) where you're hooked onto a rope while the boat moves through the water and, hopefully, attracts the interest of the dolphins.

Amaroo Cruises (☎ 0419 333 445; www.amaroocruise .com.au; Lakeside, Memorial Dr; adult/child $40/25) offers two-hour cruises most days, touring around Wallis Lake before heading out to the ocean, where you'll usually see dolphins and sometimes whales, sea turtles and sharks.

Most of the marinas along Little St hire out boats, canoes and even aqua bikes.

Sleeping

Forster Beach Caravan Park & Marina (☎ 6554 6269; www.forsterbeachcaravan.com.au; Reserve Rd; sites per 2 people $32, cabins $65-143) This sprawling, well-ordered space – virtually a self-contained village – is backed by the mighty breakwall. Villas and cabins are available.

Dorsal (☎ 6554 8766; www.dorsalhotel.com.au; 1 West St; r $200-260; 🐕) Modern and medium-rise without being hideous, the Dorsal has nicely furnished, spacious rooms with views and balconies. There's also a gym and continental breakfast is provided.

Eating

Coffee Grind (☎ 6557 5155; 59 Wharf St; mains $5-10; ⏰ 9am-4pm) The name says it all: this shiny, tiny place serves the best brew in town.

Sotos Café (☎ 6555 4337; Marine Pde; breakfast & lunch $8-12, dinner $15-20; ⏰ breakfast & lunch daily, dinner Thu-Sat) Tuck into the substantial marinated tofu salad while peering at pelicans on the lake from the terrace of this excellent little café. Vegetarian and vegans are well catered for but carnivores shouldn't worry, there's still bangers and bacon for brekkie.

DETOUR: BARRINGTON TOPS NATIONAL PARK

This 74,000-hectare World Heritage wilderness lies on the rugged Barrington Plateau, which rises to almost 1600m. Northern rainforest butts into southern sclerophyll here, creating one of Australia's most diverse ecosystems, with giant strangler figs, mossy Antarctic beech forests, limpid rainforest swimming holes and pocket-sized pademelons (note: it is illegal to put pademelons in your pocket).

There are many walking trails and lookouts, and camping is permitted at various places, including Devil's Hole (free) and Gloucester River (sites per adult/child $10/5). Be prepared for cold snaps, even snow, at any time. Being a rainforest, it gets a lot of rain – about 1600mm annually. All drinking water must be boiled.

Canoe Barrington (☎ 6558 4316; www.canoebarrington.com.au; 774 Barrington East Rd) runs white-water trips out of its riverside lodge, 14km from Gloucester. Weekend packages including accommodation, food and guide cost $350. Kayaks can be rented from $55 daily, and accommodation starts at $60 per person.

The **Barrington Outdoor Adventure Centre** (☎ 6558 2093; www.boac.com.au) offers one-day ($125) or two-day ($335) kayaking and mountain biking adventures.

The park is vast and can be approached by many routes. There's a beautiful alpine drive between Scone and Gloucester along Barrington Tops Forest Rd, although it's a little rough on the western end. From Newcastle, the road through Morpeth and Paterson to Dungog is dreamy, passing by rolling green fields, historic towns, frolicking horses and stands of silver birch and ghost gums.

There's no public transport to the park; the nearest trains stop in Dungog and Gloucester.

Casa del Mundo (☎ 6554 5906; 8 Little St; mains $19-29; dinner) Authentically Spanish, the chef splits his time between here and his homeland. Expect excellent tapas, wicked sangria and the odd dose of live music.

Getting There & Away

Greyhound (☎ 1300 473 946; www.greyhound.com.au) has a daily service, travelling between Sydney ($61, 5¼ hours) and Brisbane ($88, 10½ hours) via Port Macquarie ($50, 1¾ hours).

Busways (☎ 1800 043 263; www.busways.com.au) has services to Sydney ($55, six hours, daily) and Newcastle ($36, three hours, three daily) via Pacific Palms.

Forster Bus Service (☎ 6554 6431; www.forsterbus.com.au) plies the local streets and heads to Pacific Palms ($8.60, 25 minutes) twice daily on weekdays.

WINGHAM TO PORT MACQUARIE

WINGHAM

☎ 02 / pop 4820

Combining English county cuteness with a rugged lumberjack history, Wingham is a lovely little town serving the upper Manning Valley. Federation-era buildings surround **Central Park**, a large, grassy square that was once the town's common and still hosts cricket matches.

The timber industry is remembered with a 31-tonne brush box log on the edge of the common, testimony to the might of the valley's vanished forests. The 'wing' part of the town's name is evoked by a Vampire Jet mounted nearby, which serves as a war memorial.

Facing the square, the **museum** (☎ 6553 5823; 12 Farquhar St; adult/child $3/1; 10am-4pm) has farm machinery, a reconstructed pioneer bedroom and more, including tourist information.

Just east of the town centre, down Farquhar St, is a picnic spot on a bend in the wide Manning River. Don't miss close-by **Wingham Brush Nature Reserve**, a 10-hectare vestige of dense subtropical flood-plain rainforest, alive with birds. There are wheelchair-accessible boardwalks via the massive buttress roots of huge, otherworldly Moreton Bay figs. Up in the trees you may see the maternity ward and nursery of the grey-headed flying foxes, which spend the summer months here in their thousands.

Wingham's **market**, held on the second Saturday of the month beside Central Park, has fruit and vegetables, handicrafts and nanna's cakes by the dozen.

Near Wingham, **Tinonee** (population 740) is a tiny heritage town. The drive between the two is dotted with art and craft galleries and cafés.

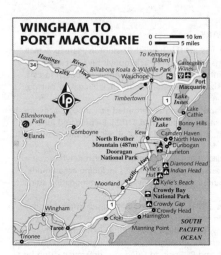

Sleeping & Eating

Australian Hotel (☎ 6553 4511; 24 Bent Sts; s/d $25/45)
Country sorts prop up the bar in this character-filled pub facing Central Park. Meals are around $22. The old-fashioned rooms upstairs share bathrooms, but they're clean enough and open onto an attractive wide balcony.

our pick Bank (☎ 6553 5068; www.thebankandtellers.com.au; 48 Bent St; s/d $120/135; wi-fi) Ever fancied being a bank manager? You won't get to shatter someone's dreams of owning their own home, but you will get to sleep in style in the en suite rooms fashioned from this solid 1929 bank. The original manager's apartment is the biggest, but most have separate sitting rooms. Add an extra $20 on weekends.

Tellers Café & Restaurant (☎ 6553 5068; 48 Bent St; breakfast & lunch $4-16, dinner $24-30; breakfast & lunch Wed-Sun, dinner Thu-Sat) The ebullient hostess

---

DETOUR: ELLENBOROUGH FALLS

If you're fond of country drives, the 40km route from Wingham to the Ellenborough Falls is a doozy. About 10km of it is unsealed and full of potholes but the countryside is bucolic. As the road climbs steeply to the Bulga Plateau, farms give way to native bush once exploited for its cedar. The falls plunge 200m in one dramatic drop into a gorge below. The best view is from The Knoll, an easy short bushwalk. A more strenuous walk leads to the base, taking about 30 minutes down but 45 minutes back up.

---

of the Bank also runs this wonderful place downstairs, serving interesting food with a vaguely Italian slant.

Getting There & Away

CountryLink (☎ 8202 2000; www.countrylink.info) trains stop here twice daily on the journey between Sydney ($67, 5¼ hours) and Coffs Harbour ($32, 3½ hours) via Newcastle ($25, three hours).

HARRINGTON & CROWDY HEAD

☎ 02 / pop 2350

A short detour from the highway follows the Manning River to its mouth where the pleasant fishing village of Harrington is sheltered by a spectacular rocky breakwater and watched over by pelicans. It's the sort of lazy, leisure-orientated hamlet popular with both holiday-makers and retirees – 30% of the population is over the age of 65. An oceanside lagoon provides a safer swimming alternative to the excellent surf beaches nearby.

Big4 Harrington Beach Holiday Park (☎ 6556 1228; www.big4harringtonbeach.com.au; Crowdy Rd; sites per 2 people $42-45, cabins $110-190;) is on the way to Crowdy Head, behind the lagoon. It's large and shaded, with well-kept facilities.

Harrington Hotel (☎ 6556 1205; 30 Beach St; s/d $45/55) is a spruce, spacious pub with a great bistro serving excellent platters and pizza (mains $14 to $27) to patrons blissing out on the large waterside terrace. Live bands perform most weekends. The standard pub-style rooms (shared facilities) are clean enough, and rates include a continental breakfast.

Crowdy Head is an even smaller fishing village 6km northeast of Harrington at the edge of Crowdy Bay National Park. It was supposedly named when Captain Cook witnessed a gathering of Aborigines on the headland in 1770. The views from the 1878 **lighthouse** are absolutely breathtaking – out to the limitless ocean, down to the deserted beaches and back to the apparent wilderness of the coastal plain and mountains. It's like Cook never arrived at all.

Stay at the cute **Crowdy Head Motel** (☎ 6556 1206; www.harrington-crowdy.com/CHM/; 7 Geoffrey St; dm/s/d $35/84/99), an older-style place with friendly service, small but pleasant rooms and chairs outside from which to contemplate the views.

CROWDY BAY NATIONAL PARK

Known for its rock formations and rugged cliffs, 10,001-hectare Crowdy Bay National

---

THE COAST ROAD LESS TRAVELLED

The tiny town of Kew marks the start of this 49km alternative route that passes through forest reserves (and some suburbia), with pockets of splendid coast; it's a much more picturesque route than the section of the Pacific Hwy between Kew and Port Macquarie. Along the way, you'll pass **Dooragan National Park**, dominated by **North Brother Mountain** with lookouts and incredible views. Nearby is **Camden Haven**, a cluster of sleepy villages around the wide sea entrance of **Queens Lake**. **North Haven** is an absolute blinder of a surf beach. North of here, the coast road passes **Lake Cathie** (pronounced cat-eye), a shallow body of water suitable for kids.

Park backs onto a long and beautiful beach that sweeps from Crowdy Head north to **Diamond Head**. There's a lovely 4.8km (two-hour) loop track over the Diamond headland.

The roads running through the park are unsealed and full of potholes, but the dappled light of the gum trees makes it a lovely drive (vehicle entry $7). If you enter the park at Crowdy Head and continue through to Laurieton you can head all the way to Port Macquarie without touching the motorway (see boxed text, above).

There are basic **camp sites** (☎ 6586 8300; site per adult/child $10/5) at Diamond Head, Indian Head, Kylie's Hut, Kylie's Beach and Crowdy Gap, but you need to bring water.

PORT MACQUARIE

☎ 02 / pop 39,220

Pleasure has long replaced punishment as the main purpose of Port Macquarie. Formed in 1821 as a place of hard labour for those convicts who reoffended after being sentenced to Sydney, it was the third town to be established on the Australian mainland. Now Port, as it's commonly known, is overwhelmingly holiday-focused, making the most of its position at the entrance to the subtropical coast.

Comparisons with Newcastle, its slightly older but much bigger sister, are perhaps inevitable: they both sit at the mouth of a river and have beautiful surf beaches at every turn. When Newcastle was covered in soot from heavy industry, Port Macquarie was easily the prettier sibling. But now that Newcastle's

had work done, Port seems a little dull in comparison.

What it does have over Newcastle is a surfeit of reasonably priced accommodation options. And koalas. Enough of them to justify a hospital for the insanely cute tree-huggers.

Orientation

The city centre fronts the mouth of the Hastings River. The beaches begin at the mouth to the river and continue south. Hastings River Dr gets you out to the Pacific Hwy heading north and Oxley Hwy hits the Pacific Hwy heading south.

Information

NPWS office (☎ 6586 8300; 152 Horton St; 9am-4.30pm Mon-Fri)

Port Macquarie Base Hospital (☎ 6581 2000; Wrights Rd)

Port Surf Hub (☎ 6584 4744; 57 Clarence St; per hr $6.50; 9am-6pm Mon-Fri, noon-2pm Sat, noon-4pm Sun) Internet access.

Post office (Palm Court, cnr Short & William Sts)

Visitors centre (☎ 6581 8000; www.portmac quarieinfo.com.au; cnr Gordon & Gore Sts; 8.30am-5pm Mon-Fri, 9am-4pm Sat & Sun)

Sights

BEACHES

Port Mackers is blessed with nine awesome beaches. Surfing is excellent at **Town**, **Flynns** and **Lighthouse Beaches**, all of which have lifeguards in summer. The rainforest runs down to the sand at **Shelly** and **Miners Beaches**, the latter of which is an unofficial nude beach and the closest thing the town has to a gay venue.

It's possible to walk all the way from the Town Wharf to Lighthouse Beach. Along the way, the **breakwater** at the bottom of town has been transformed into a work of community guerrilla art. The elaborately painted rocks range from beautiful memorials for lost loved-ones to 'party hard'-type inanities.

KOALAS

Koalas living near urban areas are at risk from traffic and domestic animals, and more than 200 each year end up at the **Koala Hospital** (☎ 6584 1522; www.koalahospital.org.au; Lord St; admission by donation). You can walk around the wards (open-air enclosures) any time of the day, but you'll learn more during the tours (3pm). Some of the longer-term patients have signs

PORT MACQUARIE

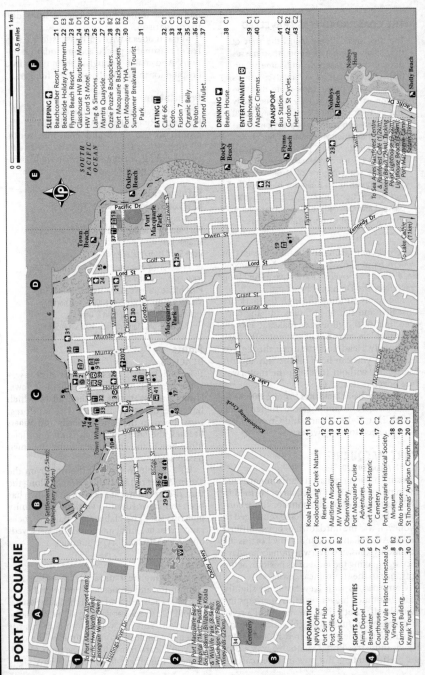

INFORMATION
NPWS Office.............................	1 C2
Port Surf Hub...........................	2 C1
Post Office..............................	3 C1
Visitors Centre........................	4 B2

SIGHTS & ACTIVITIES
Alma Doepel............................	5 C1
Breakwater..............................	6 D1
Courthouse..............................	7 C2
Douglas Vale Historic Homestead & Vineyard........................	8 B2
Garrison Building......................	9 D3
Kayak Tours............................	10 C1
Koala Hospital..........................	11 D3
Kooloonbung Creek Nature Reserve...........................	12 C2
Maritime Museum.......................	13 D1
MV Wentworth..........................	14 C1
Observatory.............................	15 D1
Port Macquarie Cruise Adventures......................	16 C1
Port Macquarie Historic Cemetery......................	17 C2
Port Macquarie Historical Society Museum....................	18 C1
Roto House..............................	19 D3
St Thomas' Anglican Church......	20 C1

SLEEPING
Beachcomber Resort................	21 D1
Beachside Holiday Apartments...	22 E3
Flynns Beach Resort..................	23 E4
Glasshouse HW Boutique Motel..	24 D1
HW Lord St Motel......................	25 D2
Laing & Simmons......................	26 C1
Mantra Quayside.......................	27 C1
Ozzie Pozzie Backpackers...........	28 B2
Port Macquarie Backpackers......	29 B2
Port Macquarie YHA..................	30 D2
Sundowner Breakwall Tourist Park........................	31 D1

EATING
Café 66...................................	32 C1
Cedro.....................................	33 C1
Fusion 7..................................	34 C2
Organic Belly............................	35 C1
Peloton....................................	36 B2
Stunned Mullet.........................	37 D1

DRINKING
Beach House............................	38 C1

ENTERTAINMENT
Glasshouse...............................	39 C1
Majestic Cinemas......................	40 C1

TRANSPORT
Bus Station...............................	41 C2
Gordon St Cycles......................	42 B2
Hertz......................................	43 C2

CENTRAL COAST
NEW SOUTH WALES

detailing their stories. Check the website for details of volunteer opportunities.

For more koala action head to the **Billabong Koala & Wildlife Park** (☎ 6585 1060; 61 Billabong Dr; adult/child $15/10; ☻ 9am-5pm) outside town, just west of the intersection of the Pacific and Oxley Hwys. Make sure you're there for the 'koala patting' (10.30am, 1.30pm and 3.30pm). The park has a koala breeding centre, although if this facility is anything to go by, koala dating requires a lot of sitting around looking stoned. There are heaps of other Australian critters here, along with international visitors such as monkeys.

NATURE RESERVES & PARKS

The **Kooloonbung Creek Nature Park** (cnr Gordon & Horton Sts; admission free) is close to the town centre. Home to many bird species its 50 hectares of bush and wetland can be explored via walking trails and wheelchair-accessible boardwalks. It includes the **Port Macquarie Historic Cemetery** (Gordon St), bizarrely built above what was the early settlement's main water supply.

Sea Acres Rainforest Centre (☎ 6582 3355; www.nationalparks.nsw.gov.au; Pacific Dr; adult/child $8/4; ☻ 9am-4.30pm) protects a 72-hectare pocket of coastal rainforest (a candidate for national park status) alive with birds, goannas, brush turkeys and, so as to be truly authentic, mosquitoes (insect repellent is provided). While there's no charge for wandering through the other paths in the rainforest it's worth paying the admission to the ecology centre and wheelchair-accessible 1.3km-long boardwalk. Fascinating one-hour guided tours by knowledgeable volunteers are included in the price. Call ahead for times of bush tucker tours led by Aboriginal guides.

HISTORIC BUILDINGS & MUSEUMS

Most of Port's historic buildings are in the city centre. The 1835 **Garrison building** (cnr Clarence & Hay Sts) is camouflaged by an uninspiring array of fast-food shops. Next door, the 1836 **Port Macquarie Historical Society Museum** (☎ 6583 1108; 22 Clarence St; adult/child $5/2; ☻ 9.30am-4.30pm Mon-Sat) has fared better, its labyrinth of rooms including a costume gallery. Opposite is an 1869 **courthouse** (☎ 6584 1818; adult/child $2/0.50c; ☻ 10am-3.30pm Mon-Fri).

The 1824, convict-built **St Thomas' Anglican Church** (☎ 6584 1033; Hay St; adult/child $2/1; ☻ 9.30am-noon & 2-4pm Mon-Fri) is one of Australia's oldest and still has its box pews and crenulated tower, echoing the Norman churches of southern England. The walls are over half a metre thick, comprising 365,000 handmade bricks. A spiral staircase heads up the tower to a small collection of historic documents and vestments. From here three ladders continue to the roof and excellent views of the town.

Roto House (☎ 6584 2180; Lord St; admission by gold coin donation; ☻ 10am-4pm Mon-Fri, 9am-1pm Sat & Sun), next to the Koala Hospital in Macquarie Nature Reserve, is a lovely Victorian villa (1891) with interesting displays about its original owners.

Between Miners and Lighthouse Beaches, little **Tacking Point Lighthouse** (1879) commands a headland offering immense views up and down the coast. It's a great spot to watch the waves rolling in to the long beautiful stretch of Lighthouse Beach.

The old pilot house above Town Beach has been converted into a small **Maritime Museum** (☎ 6583 1866; 6 William St; tour adult/child $5/2; ☻ 10am-4pm). There's a small extension of the museum at the wharf, where bookings are taken for the MV *Wentworth* (p246).

While on the maritime theme, you can tour the **Alma Doepel** (☎ 6583 3513; adult/child $3/1; ☻ 9am-5pm), a 1903 three-masted schooner permanently moored near the bottom of Horton St.

OBSERVATORY

Stargazers will enjoy the small **observatory** (☎ 6584 9164; www.pmobs.org.au; Rotary Park, William St; adult/child $8/5; ☻ 7.30-8.30pm Wed & Sun, 8.15-9.15pm during daylight saving).

WINERIES

The Hastings Valley has a long history of wine-making, but the half dozen working vineyards scattered around the area hardly qualify it as a wine region. They're all quite far apart, but if you're in the mood for a country drive, grab a *Wine Trail Guide* from the visitors centre. Semillon and Chambourcin grapes do well here.

Bago Vineyards (☎ 6585 7099; www.bagovineyards.com.au; Milligans Rd; ☻ 10am-5pm) Watch out for wallabies and goannas on the picturesque, partly unsealed forest drive to this vineyard 22km out of town, south of Wauchope. Every second Sunday of the month it hosts live jazz afternoons (adult/child $5/free).

Cassegrain Wines (☎ 6582 8377; www.cassegrainwines.com.au; 764 Fernbank Creek Rd; ☻ 9am-5pm) The best known, with arguably the finest wine. Its restaurant, Ça Marche, is worth the trip.

Douglas Vale Historic Homestead & Vineyard (☎ 6584 3792; www.douglasvalevineyard.com.au; Oxley

Hwy; ☺ 10am-3pm Wed, Sat & Sun) Founded in 1859, wine is produced from remnants of the little-known Isabella grapes planted in the 1860s. It's opposite the TAFE college.

Activities

Port Macquarie Surf School (☎ 6585 5453; www.port macquariesurfschool.com.au) offers a wide range of lessons and prices.

Kayak Tours (☎ 6584 1039; Sea Rescue Shed, Buller St; 2hr trip $35) runs guided trips into the upper reaches of the Hastings River.

Camel rides are available south of town with **Port Macquarie Camel Safaris** (☎ 6583 7650; www.portmacquariecamels.com.au; Matthew Flinders Dr; 20min $20; ☺ 9.30am-1pm Sun-Fri).

Tours

The Maritime Museum runs harbour tours on Tuesdays and Thursdays aboard its restored boat, the **MV Wentworth** (☎ 6584 2987; Clarence St, Town Wharf). A two-hour tour starts at 10.30am (adult/child $15/10), with a one-hour tour at 1pm (adult/child $10/6).

Port Macquarie Cruise Adventures (☎ 1300 555 890; www.cruiseadventures.com.au; 74 Clarence St, Town Wharf; adult/child from $15/10) offers dolphin-watching, whale-spotting, oyster-guzzling, lunch, sunset, river and everglades tours.

Sleeping

Port offers a decent range of boudoir options, ranging from a clutch of tidy hostels to a multitude of apartment-style resorts. Competition among the hostels is fierce, so expect lots of free perks – breakfast, transfers, bikes, boogie boards, internet access etc. A better strategy for some of them would be employing staff who can smile.

For private apartment rentals, get in touch with **Laing & Simmons** (☎ 6583 7733; www.portreal estate.net; cnr Horton & William Sts), which promotes itself as a carbon-neutral agency.

BUDGET

Sundowner Breakwall Tourist Park (☎ 6583 2755; www.sundownerholidays.com; 1 Munster St; dm $25, sites per 2 people $36-42, cabins $95-274; ☐ ☎) With extensive facilities and a roomy feel, this quality place is right by the river mouth. There's a backpackers' area with a separate kitchen and lounge.

Ozzie Pozzie Backpackers (☎ /fax 6583 8133; 36 Waugh St; dm $27, d $65-75; ☐) The clean rooms are bright and there's a range of activities on offer, along with free bikes and boogie boards.

Port Macquarie Backpackers (☎ 6583 1791; www .portmacquariebackpackers.com.au; 2 Hastings River Dr; dm/d/ tr $28/69/84; ☐ ☎) Easily identified by the globe out the front, this heritage-listed house has pressed-tin walls, comfy bunks and the friendliest atmosphere of any hostel in town. The veranda is a popular meeting place. Traffic can be noisy, but loads of freebies compensate.

Port Macquarie YHA (☎ 6583 5512; www.yha.com.au /hostels/details.cfm?hostelid=26; 40 Church St; dm/tw $30/73, d $65-89; ☐) A neat and compact hostel close to Town Beach with tidy, bright rooms.

MIDRANGE

HW Lord St Motel (☎ 6583 5850; www.hwmotel.com.au; cnr Lord & Burrawan Sts; r $90-180; ☒ ☎) At the cheaper end of the motels, this option has reasonable-sized, clean and comfy rooms. The décor's a bit '70s but the bed linen is crisp and new.

Beachside Holiday Apartments (☎ 6583 9544; www.beachsideholidays.com; 48 Pacific Dr; apt from $135; ☒ ☎ ; wi-fi) This fun place is right across the road from Flynns Beach. The units are large, have balconies and face either the ocean or the enticing pool.

Glasshouse HW Boutique Motel (☎ 6583 1200; www.hwmotel.com.au; 1 Stewart St; r $145-165; ☒ ☎) The HW is a renovated older motel with lots of sharp 1970s angles. Many feature balconies with views over Town Beach; deluxe spa units are available.

Beachcomber Resort (☎ 6584 1881; www.beach comberresort.com.au; 54 William St; apt $145-195; ☒ ☎ ; wi-fi) Close to the beach and the centre, the 22 large self-contained units range from studios to two-bedroom apartments, all set around a beautifully landscaped pool.

TOP END

Mantra Quayside (☎ 6588 4000; www.mantraquayside .com.au; cnr William & Short Sts; apt $182-229; ☒ ☎ ; wi-fi) As slick as it gets, the elegant apartments in this central midrise are fully self-contained with all the modern gadgets. The highlight is the heated rooftop pool and barbecue area. The units facing William St have views over St Thomas' Church but penance is provided by rowdy boofheads spilling out of the nightclub across the road.

Flynns Beach Resort (☎ 6583 3338; www.flynns beachresort.com.au; cnr Pacific Dr & Ocean St; apt $224; ☒ ☎ ; wi-fi) Flynns Beach is across the road from this large complex with extensive, lush gardens and a fancy amoeba-shaped pool. All units have two bedrooms, spacious balconies and pleasant living spaces.

Eating

RESTAURANTS & CAFÉS

Stunned Mullet (☎ 6582 8320; 24 William St; breakfast $5-15, lunch $14-30, dinner $29-34; ☯ breakfast, lunch & dinner) Australian idiom lesson: to look like a stunned mullet is to wear an expression of bewilderment. It's exactly the sort of look you might adopt while struggling to choose between the delicious Mod Oz menu items in this chic eatery. For brekkie, try the homemade granola with lemon myrtle-flavoured yogurt. It's better than a poke in the eye with a burnt stick.

Cedro (☎ 6583 5529; 72 Clarence St; breakfast $5-15, lunch $15-17; ☯ breakfast & lunch Mon-Sat) On a sunny day you can sit on the street between the palm trees, order the Bedouin eggs and plan your next nomadic move. The food's excellent and it's not all exotic; those with simpler tastes can opt for fish and chips.

Rainforest Café (☎ 6582 4444; Sea Acres Rainforest Centre, Pacific Dr; mains $8-16; ☯ breakfast & lunch) You may be surrounded by lush foliage but don't expect bush tucker; the talented and gregarious chef is as French as they come. The focus is on healthy sandwiches, salads and pasta constructed from quality ingredients.

Fusion 7 (☎ 6584 1171; 124 Horton St; lunch $10-17, dinner $25-32; ☯ lunch Thu & Fri, dinner Tue-Sat) It's completely surprising that this restaurant: a) isn't exorbitantly expensive; b) doesn't serve wine (but you can bring your own); and c) is in Port Macquarie at all. Chef Lindsey Schwab worked with the father of fusion cuisine Peter Gordon in London, returning to be closer to his family. Expect the unexpected.

Café 66 (☎ 6583 2484; 66 Clarence St; meals $15-29; ☯ breakfast, lunch & dinner) This agreeable, unreconstructed Italian eatery has good coffee and reasonably priced pasta, risotto and grills. Book ahead on Tuesday nights when half of Port tries to squeeze in for two-for-one pasta.

QUICK EATS & SELF-CATERING

Peloton (☎ 6583 6522; 163 Gordon St; snacks $5-10; ☯ 6.30am-3.30pm Mon-Fri, 7.30am-12.30pm Sat) Tucked inside Gordon St Cycles, this excellent little espresso bar's fit and friendly staff will get you on your bike in no time, buzzed up with the town's best coffee and tasty muffins.

Organic Belly (☎ 6582 4495; 2 Murray St; ☯ 10am-5pm Mon, 9am-5pm Tue-Wed & Fri, 9am-6pm Thu, 9am-2pm Sat) The place to stock up on organic and Fair Trade produce.

Drinking & Entertainment

Things can get rowdy on weekends, so the council has imposed a lock-out policy on bars and clubs, which means that if you're not in a venue by 1am, you're not getting in.

Beach House (☎ 6584 5692; 1 Horton St) In the historic Royal Hotel, this place goes off on the weekends. Take in the waterfront view from one of the outside tables.

Majestic Cinemas (☎ 6583 8400; www.portcinemas.com.au; cnr Horton & Clarence Sts; adult/child $11/9) Latest blockbusters and the odd indie flick.

Glasshouse (☎ 6581 8888; www.glasshouse.org.au; cnr Hay & Clarence Sts) At the time of research this centre was still being constructed, but an impressive programme of theatre and opera had already been announced.

Getting There & Away

AIR

Port Macquarie Airport (☎ 6583 1904; Boundary St) is 5km from the centre of town ($10 in a taxi).

Both **Qantas** (☎ 13 13 13; www.qantas.com.au) and **Virgin Blue** (☎ 136 789; www.virginblue.com.au) have daily flights to Sydney. **Brindabella Airlines** (☎ 1300 66 88 24; www.brindabellaairlines.com.au) has services to Brisbane, Coffs Harbour and Newcastle.

BUS

Greyhound (☎ 1300 473 946; www.greyhound.com.au) stop three times daily on its way between Sydney ($64, 6½ hours) and Brisbane ($88, nine hours), via Forster ($50, 1¾ hours).

Premier Motor Service (☎ 133 410; www.premierms.com.au) heads daily to Sydney ($55, 6¼ hours), Newcastle ($43, four hours), Kempsey ($15, 45 minutes) and Brisbane ($62, 8½ hours).

Getting Around

Busways (☎ 6559 7712; www.busways.com.au) runs local bus services.

The Settlement Point ferry (per car $3) operates 24 hours. A 10-minute trip on a flat punt gives you access to North Beach and Pilots Beach.

For car rentals, **Hertz** (☎ 6583 6599; www.hertz.com.au; 102 Gordon St) is one of several agents in town. For bikes, try **Gordon St Cycles** (☎ 6583 3633; www.gordonstreetcycles.com.au; 163 Gordon St; per 2hr/day $15/30).

North Coast New South Wales

A beach interrupted by a few rocks is one way to think of the north coast of New South Wales. And indeed that's not far from the truth. One breathtaking vista after another yields scenes of endless sand pounded by ceaseless Pacific breakers. Not a lot of people live up here, so on some days it may feel like the ratio of beach to people is 500m to 1.

Surfing, diving and just plain lounging are major coastal activities. Byron Bay, the one definite stop on every itinerary, combines all three. It also has energetic nightlife, great restaurants, a languid café culture and enough activities to tempt you out of your hammock. And it's not alone. All along the Pacific Hwy are little towns and parks scattered amid the rich deltas of the mighty Clarence, Richmond and Tweed Rivers.

And after your first experience with a nasty delay on the stress-inducing highway, you'll be happy to know that opportunities to get off it abound. Roads head west into the thick subtropical rainforest and towns such as Bellingen nestle in the lush hills and offer temptations that may have you quickly altering your plans.

In the northern part of NSW, the hinterlands are a celebration of alternative lifestyles and lush organic produce. Little villages boast restaurants that are among the best in the country and creative-minded consumers will find much to enjoy while wandering the backroads of this idiosyncratic corner of the state.

HIGHLIGHTS

- Filling your days and nights in exciting **Byron Bay** (p271)
- Enjoying the artful village charms of **Bellingen** (p254)
- Losing yourself on the untrod beaches near **Wooli** (p263)
- Exploring hinterland villages, including **The Channon** (p282)
- Finding treasures in markets like the one at **Nimbin** (p283)

Nimbin ★
The Channon ★ ★ Byron Bay
Wooli ★
Bellingen ★

- TELEPHONE CODE: 02
- www.visitnsw.com.au

NORTH COAST NSW

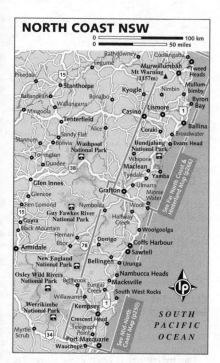

0 ————— 100 km
0 ————— 50 miles

(eg Coffs Harbour) and speed cameras. One local politician has called it a 'national shame'. Of course the rotten road conditions give you yet more reasons to stop and enjoy yourself.

TRAIN

CountryLink (☎ 13 22 32; www.countrylink.com.au) stopped its essential services to Byron Bay in 2004. Trains to/from Sydney stop far inland at the agricultural town of Casino and you have to transfer to a bus to reach Byron, Lismore et al. To the south, the train still serves Coffs Harbour, Nambucca Heads and Kempsey. Other CountryLink buses offer useful services linking towns, especially in the far north.

MID-NORTH COAST

The best thing about the Pacific Hwy driving north from Port Macquarie is all the chances you have to drive off it. On the ocean, Crescent Head and Southwest Rocks bracket beautiful and often deserted beaches; in the hills, the drive through delightful Bellingen and on to Dorrigo plunges into the heart of waterfall-laced rainforest. North, beachy Coffs Harbour defines 'family-friendly' and there's discoveries to be made, inlcuding the natural beauty of Wooli.

Getting There & Around

AIR

Airports along the north coast, including Coffs Harbour, Grafton, Ballina and Lismore, are attracting the service of budget carriers in addition to commuter runs to Sydney. Services fluctuate all the time.

BUS

Greyhound (☎ 13 14 99; www.greyhound.com.au) and **Premier** (☎ 13 34 10; www.premierms.com.au) both offer services three to five times daily linking major – and minor – towns along the Pacific Hwy. The real choice between them may come down to which one you have a bus pass with and which has the schedule you want.

Local bus services are sporadic along the coast and are often timed solely for school runs.

ROAD

The Pacific Hwy (Hwy 1) is an adventure in itself. Parts have been greatly improved (eg north of Byron Bay) with eased curves and dual carriageways. But other stretches remain a minefield of narrow curves, stoplights, traffic

KEMPSEY

☎ 02 / pop 8500

Kempsey is a large agricultural town about 45km north of Port Macquarie serving the farms of the Macleay Valley. The town is the home of the **Akubra hat** (www.akubra.com.au), which screams 'Down under!' from the top of any head sporting one. Although the factory misses tourism opportunities by the busload (it's closed to visitors), you can see the full range at **Barsby's Department Store** (☎ 6562 4870; Main St), an old-fashioned gem in the heart of Kempsey.

The late Slim Dusty, another Oz icon, was born here and he presumably got his inspiration for country-music songs like 'Duncan' from this unassuming town. A long-proposed **Slim Dusty Heritage Centre** (www.slimdustycentre .com.au) remains the attraction with no completion date.

The highly useful regional **visitors centre** (☎ 6563 1555, 1800 642 480; Pacific Hwy; ◷ 9am-5pm Mon-Fri, 10am-4pm Sat & Sun) is at a rest stop on the south side of town. It shares space with a small museum that honours the sacrifice of sheep-shearers, lumber-whackers, cattle-pokers

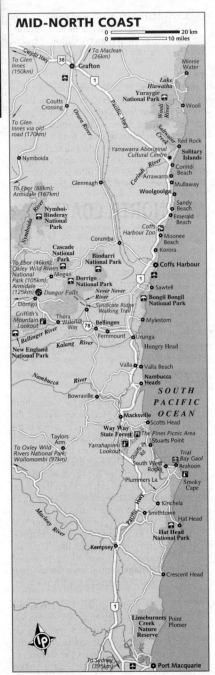

MID-NORTH COAST

and all the others who've made Kempsey an agricultural paradise.

Sleeping & Eating

There's a small string of motels just north of the centre. For camping, the best spots are out on the coast.

Moon River (☎ 6562 8077; www.moonriver.com.au; 157 Pacific Hwy; s/d from $65/75; ⌘ ⌘; wi-fi) Most appealing of the traveller-friendly motels, Moon River may not be as Andy Williams sang, but it does have 33 comfortable, good-sized rooms and a view of the Macleay River.

our pick Fredo Pies (☎ 6566 8226; 75 Macleay St, Frederickton; pies under $4; ⏱ 7am-7pm) Just 6km north of Kempsey look for the iconic statue of Marilyn Monroe as her skirt blows up in the film *The Seven Year Itch*. It's all tasty inside at this equally iconic pie purveyor, where you can sample from up to 50 pie varieties including the 'Truckie' (steak, bacon, onion and cheese).

Getting There & Around

Greyhound (☎ 13 14 99; www.greyhound.com.au) and **Premier** (☎ 13 34 10; www.premierms.com.au) pass through several times a day on their Pacific Hwy runs.

CountryLink (☎ 13 22 32; www.countrylink.com .au) runs a north coast train service that goes north to Coffs Harbour ($13, 1½ hours) and south to Sydney ($59, seven hours).

CRESCENT HEAD

☎ 02 / pop 1200

In surfing circles, this is where the Malibu surfboard gained prominence in Australia during the '60s. Now a third generation continues the surfing legacy this town cherishes. Many come just to watch the longboard riders surf the epic waves of **Little Nobby's Junction** when the swell's up. Crescent Head is a low-key mix of families and surfers. The real attraction here is untrammelled **Killick Beach**, which stretches 14km north.

If you're driving, the direct road to Crescent Head is near the visitors centre in Kempsey. Alternatively, from the north you can take the very scenic Belmore Rd, which leaves the Pacific Hwy at Seven Oaks and follows the sinuous bends of the Belmore River through lush flatlands.

For holiday rentals, try the **Crescent Head Accommodation Bureau** (☎ 6566 0306; www.pointbreak realty.com.au).

WORTH A TRIP: SLIM DUSTY SPECTACULAR

Even if the heritage centre seems jammed on the spindle, this part of NSW is Slim Dusty country. To visit his childhood home, take the Armidale road west of Kempsey for 55km until 2km before the village of Bellbrook, then turn north on Nulla Creek Rd. When the road turns to gravel, it's another 2.2km to what is now a private home but displays by the road put the place into context. Retrace your drive back to Hickey's Creek and take the partially paved road of that name 26km northeast to the fabled **Pub With No Beer** (☎ 6564 2100; Taylors Arm Rd; 🕑 noon-late) in Taylor's Arm. You won't find a dog on the v'randa but inside you'll find a slick operation with its own microbrewery (Murray's) and upscale meals ($10 to $25); see p436 for more details on the song that made this place famous. From here it is 25km east to Macksville and the Pacific Hwy. Note that south of Taylors Arm you can get a feel for the land of Dusty's youth in the old gum forests of the Ngambaa Nature Reserve.

Right at the mouth of the river, **Crescent Head Holiday Park** (☎ 6566 0261; Pacific St; camp sites from $25, cabins from $80) has 156 sites.

Surfaris (☎ 1800 007 873; www.surfaris.com; per person from $85; wi-fi) has a surf camp 3km north of Crescent Head. Rates include beds in dorms or space in a single or double tent, meals and surfing lessons on Killick Beach. Transport options include Sydney, Byron Bay and the bus and train stops in Kempsey.

The nine-room, two-storey **Mediterranean Motel** (☎ 6566 0303; www.crescentheadaccommodation .com.au; 35 Pacific St; r $90-145; 🅿 🏊) is the pick of the handful of motels. Groups of up to eight may enjoy the 'surf shacks' (self-catering cottages) out the back ($90 to $200).

Busways (☎ 1300 555 611; www.busways.com.au) runs two or three times daily Monday to Saturday to/from Kempsey (Belgrave St, $9, 50 minutes).

HAT HEAD NATIONAL PARK

This remote coastal park of 6500 hectares runs north from near Crescent Head almost to South West Rocks. It protects wetlands and some excellent beaches backed by one of NSW's largest sand dunes. Birds are prolific. Rising up from the generally flat landscape is Hungry Hill, near Hat Head, and sloping Hat Head itself. Walking tracks include a 2½-hour loop from the Cap picnic area.

Surrounded by the national park, the village of **Hat Head** is minute. **Hat Head Holiday Park** (☎ 6567 7501; www.4shoreholidayparks.com.au; camp sites from $19, cabins from $70) has 280 tent sites, eight cabins and a beautiful location. You can camp ($5 per person) in the park at Hungry Head, 5km south of Hat Head. There are pit toilets and no showers, and you'll need to take your own water.

The park is accessible from the hamlet of Kinchela, on the pretty road between Kempsey and South West Rocks.

At the north end of the park, **Smoky Cape Lighthouse** has commanding views out to sea, 9km southeast of South West Rocks. Relive the lives of the lighthouse-keepers by staying in one of two large restored self-catering 1891 **cottages** (☎ 6566 6301; www.smokycapelighthouse.com; d $190, cottages from $230), except you won't be screwing in any lightbulbs. Two large bedrooms are also available for B&B accommodation.

SOUTH WEST ROCKS
☎ 02 / pop 4150

Well off the Pacific Hwy, South West Rocks is a little beach town with just enough to keep you busy relaxing for days. Overlooking Trial Bay to the north, the town has a hook shape which affords views back over the water at sunset. Ignore the fringe of suburban blight and make for the centre.

Just getting to South West Rocks may be more than half the fun. The area west of the Pacific Hwy is a rich river delta lined with dense reeds, appealing old farmhouses and vintage shacks built on stilts. It's a great drive; to fully appreciate it, leave the Pacific Hwy at Seven Oaks and take the sinuous 22km road along the Macleay River, which passes through a few quaint fishing villages.

You may feel like the stranger who's walked into a bar in the old west, but once past the suspicious reception at **Boatman's Cottage** (☎ 6566 7099; cnr Ocean Ave & Livingstone St; admission free; 🕑 10am-4pm) you'll be rewarded by a fascinating little museum that shows how life on the coast once revolved around boats as opposed to roads. The building, which dates to 1902, has a small display of tourist info.

Sights & Activities

The waters off South West Rocks are great for divers, especially **Fish Rock Cave**, south of Smoky Cape. **South West Rocks Dive Centre** (☎ 6566 6474; www.southwestrocksdive.com.au; 5/98 Gregory St) offers dive lessons and trips.

Imposing and historic, **Trial Bay** occupies the east headland of South West Rocks. The area has a rather dramatic past: Sydney convicts stole a boat, the *Trial*, in 1816 but their bid for freedom ended up literally on the rocks after a storm sank it. Eventually the government decided that a breakwater was needed to protect boats – stolen or otherwise – taking shelter in the now-named Trial Bay. As a result, the **Trial Bay Gaol** (☎ 6566 6168; admission $5; ⊙ 9am-4:30pm) was built to house convicts charged with the breakwater's construction. However, plans fizzled and except for a brief interlude in WWI when it housed Germans, the gaol has been unoccupied for more than 100 years. It's now a museum.

The **Arakoon State Conservation Area** surrounds the gaol and has a popular campground. From South West Rocks it's a pleasant 4km walk to Trial Bay along the beach; look out for the **love shack**, formerly a fisherman's abode, about halfway between South West Rocks and Trial Bay.

Sleeping & Eating

Trial Bay Camping Area (☎ 6566 6168; camp sites per adult/child $24/9) is beside the gaol and has over 70 sites, some set right on the beach. Amenities include hot showers and coin-powered barbies.

Horseshoe Bay Beach Park (☎ 6566 6370; Livingstone St; camp sites from $35, cabins from $80) Superb position right in town and right on the little namesake beach cove. The 70 sites and 13 cabins are often booked out over the summer holidays.

Seabreeze Hotel (☎ 6566 6909; www.seabreezebeach hotel.com.au; Livingstone St; r $80-120; meals $8-20; ⊙ bistro lunch & dinner; ⌘ ; wi-fi) Tables in the casual Sea Breeze bistro overlook the town's green verge with the ocean beyond. The 28 rooms are motel-style; the better ones have balconies and/or views of the water.

Rock Pool Motor Inn (☎ 1800 180 133; www.rock poolmotorinn.com.au; 45 Mcintyre St; r $90-200; ⌘ ▣ ▣) This 28-room modern motel is right in the centre and a short walk to the beach and shops. The small pool is kid-friendly; rooms are unadorned but have niceties such as fridges.

Heritage Guest House (☎ 6566 6625; www.herit ageguesthouse.com.au; 21-23 Livingstone St; r $115-170;

▣) Proof that tourism has always been important here, this 1887 building is beautifully renovated but still serves its original purpose. The nine rooms have internet and some on the 2nd floor have ocean views from the veranda.

Seaside Café (☎ 6566 9557; 21-23 Livingstone St; meals $6-12; ⊙ 8am-3pm) The old billiard pavilion at the Heritage guest house is now an upscale café where you can enjoy creative breakfasts and lunches at tables inside and out. In every iteration, the pancakes are excellent.

Getting There & Away

Busways (☎ 1300 555 611; www.busways.com.au) runs two or three times daily Monday to Saturday to/from Kempsey (Belgrave St, $12, 50 minutes).

NAMBUCCA HEADS
☎ 02 / pop 6200

Nambucca Heads (nam-*buk*-a) has a workaday centre atop a hill. But get towards the water and you'll be rewarded with wide vistas of the coast. There's a number of nature walks and plenty of beachy walking so you can get fit while you holiday.

The Nambucca Valley (which means 'many bends') was occupied by the Gumbainggir people until European timber-cutters arrived in the 1840s. There are still strong Aboriginal communities in Nambucca Heads and up the valley in Bowraville.

Orientation

The town is just off the Pacific Hwy. Riverside Dr runs alongside the estuary of the Nambucca River, then climbs a steep hill to Bowra St, the main shopping street. A right turn onto Ridge St at the top of the hill leads to the bluffs and the beaches. Wellington Dr follows the river to the V-Wall.

Information

Bookshop Cafe (☎ 6568 5855; cnr Ridge & Bowra Sts; ⊙ 8am-5pm; ▣) Used books and internet access.

Visitors centre (☎ 6568 6954; cnr Riverside Dr & Pacific Hwy; ⊙ 9am-5pm) Very helpful; doubles as the main bus terminal. It has a nice spot on the estuary.

Sights & Activities

At the east end of town, 1.2km from the centre on a high bluff, the **Captain Cook Lookout** is the place to ponder the swath of beaches. A road here leads down to **Shelly Beach**, which has

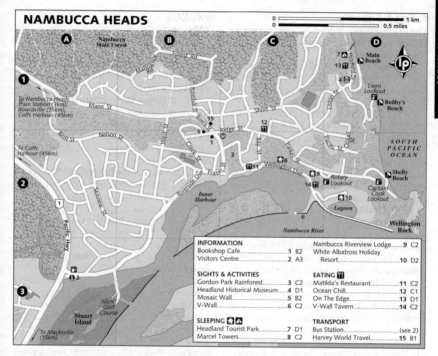

NAMBUCCA HEADS

INFORMATION		Nambucca Riverview Lodge.......**9** C2
Bookshop Cafe.....................**1** B2		White Albatross Holiday
Visitors Centre.....................**2** A3		Resort.........................**10** D2
SIGHTS & ACTIVITIES		EATING 🍴
Gordon Park Rainforest........**3** C2		Matilda's Restaurant...........**11** C2
Headland Historical Museum....**4** D1		Ocean Chill.....................**12** C1
Mosaic Wall.....................**5** B2		On The Edge....................**13** D1
V-Wall...........................**6** C2		V-Wall Tavern..................**14** C2
SLEEPING 🛏️		TRANSPORT
Headland Tourist Park...........**7** D1		Bus Station.....................(see 2)
Marcel Towers...................**8** C2		Harvey World Travel...........**15** B1

tidepools. Going north, it blends into **Beilby's Beach** and then **Main Beach**, which has lots of parking and surf patrols.

Above Main Beach, the **Headland Historical Museum** (☎ 6568 6380; Liston St; adult/child $2/50¢; ☺ 2-4pm Wed, Sat & Sun) has local history exhibits, including a collection of over 1000 photos and displays of maritime equipment.

Wellington Dr leads downhill off Bowra St to the waterfront and the V-Wall breakwater with its mostly well-mannered graffiti by locals and travellers. There's a short but interesting boardwalk through the mangroves here. Various nature trails wander the hillside up to the lookouts; scan the many trees for a sighting of a kookaburra. The **Gordon Park Rainforest** at the start of Wellington Dr is a small but dense patch of trees with several twisting paths.

On Bowra St, the **Mosaic Wall** is a riot of polychromatic tiles and broken crockery that has a wealth of hidden detail.

Sleeping

Nambucca Heads has a loyal cadre of sun-seekers and books out in summer.

Headland Tourist Park (☎ 6568 6547; www.head landtouristpark.com.au; Liston St; camp sites from $16, cabins from $60) Just above Main Beach and close to the museum, this nicely landscaped place has 78 sites under swaying palms.

White Albatross Holiday Resort (☎ 6568 6468; www.white-albatross.com.au; camp sites from $28, cabins from $70) Located near the river mouth with an adjacent lagoon to swim in, this large holiday park surrounds a sheltered lagoon. Beaches and the V-Wall Tavern are all close by.

Nambucca Riverview Lodge (☎ 6568 6386; www .riverviewlodgenambucca.com.au; 4 Wellington Dr; r $80-145; 🐾) Built in 1887, the Riverview has just that from its long veranda out front. This old two-storey wooden charmer has a colourful history the owners will happily share. The eight rooms have fridges; some have stunning views.

Marcel Towers (☎ 6568 7041; www.marceltowers .com.au; 12 Wellington Dr; r $85-250; wi-fi) Overlooking the estuary, this 1970s apartment complex has 11 large units with multiple bedrooms and full kitchens. The balconies have fine views and a recent redecoration trumps the daggie architecture.

Eating & Drinking

The bracing ocean breezes here put people to bed early; the streets are mostly rolled up by 10pm weeknights.

Bookshop Cafe (☎ 6568 5855; cnr Ridge & Bowra Sts; meals $6-10; ☺ 8am-5pm; ☐) The porch tables here are *the* place in town for breakfast. The fruit smoothies are excellent.

On The Edge (☎ 6569 4494; 1 Headland Dr; mains $15-25; ☺ dinner Wed-Sat, brunch Sun) Right by the museum on the head, you can dine on an octagonal terrace to the atmospheric distant roar of the surf. The huge, well-thumbed curry cookbook attests to the popularity of the curry special; other dishes include sprightly seasoned seafood and steaks.

ourpick Matilda's Restaurant (☎ 6568 6024; Wellington Dr; mains $15-35; ☺ lunch & dinner Mon-Sat) A whimsical gem down by the water. The playful theme extends from the colourful birds on the walls to the vegemite-and-toast starter. There's numerous daily specials reflecting what's fresh. Seafood dishes are unpretentious but surprising in their rich flavours and presentation. BYO.

Ocean Chill (☎ 6568 8877; 58 Ridge St; mains $25-30; ☺ dinner Tue-Sat) In a simple little house just east of the centre, the Ocean Chill has a short Mod Oz menu dramatically prepared in an open kitchen. Seafood stars although carnivores appreciate the lamb. BYO.

V-Wall Tavern (☎ 6568 6394; 1 Wellington Dr) A big, modern place with classic water views from its long patio on the upper floor. There's pub food and a bistro with more expensive fishy fare. On weeknights the taps stop pouring their mediocre selection of beer as early as 9pm.

Getting There & Around

Harvey World Travel (☎ 6568 6455; 16 Bowra St) handles transport bookings.

Long-distance buses stop at the visitors centre. **Premier** (☎ 13 34 10; www.premierms.com.au) charges $58 to either Sydney or Brisbane (both eight to nine hours) on the Pacific Hwy. **Greyhound** (☎ 13 14 99; www.greyhound.com.au) is usually somewhat more.

Busways (☎ 1300 555 611; www.busways.com.au) runs two or three times Monday to Saturday from Nambucca Heads to Bellingen ($9, one hour) and Coffs Harbour ($9, 50 minutes) via Urunga.

CountryLink (☎ 13 22 32; www.countrylink.com.au) has three trains north to Coffs Harbour ($5, 40 minutes) and beyond, and south to Sydney ($66, eight hours).

URUNGA

☎ 02 / pop 2750

Urunga is family-friendly, with safe river beaches, good fishing and a perpetual calm, about 20km north of Nambucca Heads. Hungry Head, just south along the coast, is a popular surf spot.

The **Bellingen Shire visitors centre** (☎ 6655 5711; ☺ 9am-5pm Mon-Sat, 10am-2pm Sun) is on the Pacific Hwy, just before you reach the river, and serves the whole area. It has a model that will help you finally make sense of the region's chaotic topography.

Catch a buzz at the **Honey Place** (☎ 6655 6160; Pacific Hwy; ☺ 8.30am-5pm), or maybe just have a sugar high. Hives hum and you can sample a wide variety of honeys produced by busy bees. The New England Blackbutt is significantly better than the name implies: the fruity bouquet is divine. It's 3km south of town.

Have a total getaway at **Hungry Head Nature Reserve Cabins** (☎ 6655 6208; Hungry Head; cabins from $75). Set in a dense forest behind the beach, 5km south of town, the 10 cabins here are very basic but have full kitchens and porches ideal for viewing the many marsupials who hop past.

The most prominent building in Urunga, the **Ocean View Hotel** (☎ 6655 6221; 15 Morgo St; s/d from $40/70; mains $10-15; ☺ breakfast, lunch & dinner) dates to 1927 and offers genteel B&B rooms.

BELLINGEN

☎ 02 / pop 2850

Bellingen is a charming hill town that manages to have a lot of interest without selling itself out with some of the tacky tourism vices found in other places along the coast. There's a delightfully laid-back vibe that's spiced with art and alternative lifestyles. Many of the buildings date from the early 1900s and have cast-iron details. Numerous folk musicians live in the region while the bulletin board at the bus stop features fliers for various forms of yoga, guinea-pig breeding, acoustic-guitar lessons and much more.

The lovely 12km drive off the Pacific Hwy is worth the journey alone and the road continues west to the Waterfall Way. The wide Bellingen River valley here was part of the extensive territory of the Gumbainggir people until European timber-cutters arrived in the 1840s. The first settlement here was at Fernmount, about 5km east of Bellingen, but later the administrative centre of the region was moved to Bellingen. River craft were able

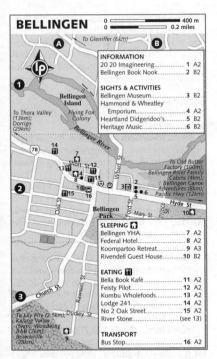

BELLINGEN

0 ——————— 400 m
0 ——————— 0.2 miles

To Gleniffer (6km)

INFORMATION	
20 20 Imagineering	1 A2
Bellingen Book Nook	2 B2

SIGHTS & ACTIVITIES	
Bellingen Museum	3 B2
Hammond & Wheatley Emporium	4 A2
Heartland Didgeridoo's	5 B2
Heritage Music	6 B2

SLEEPING	
Bellingen YHA	7 A2
Federal Hotel	8 A2
Koompartoo Retreat	9 A3
Rivendell Guest House	10 B2

EATING	
Bella Book Kafé	11 A2
Feisty Pilot	12 A2
Kombu Wholefoods	13 A2
Lodge 241	14 A2
No 2 Oak Street	15 A2
River Stone	(see 13)

TRANSPORT	
Bus Stop	16 A2

To Thora Valley (13km); Dorrigo (29km)

Bellingen Island
Flying Fox Colony

Bellinger River

Short St

Wharf St

To Old Butter Factory (100m); Bellingen River Family Cabins (4km); Bellingen Canoe Adventures (8km); Pacific Hwy (12km)

Hyde St

Mary St

Bellingen Park

Church St

Hawson St

Dudley St

To Lily Pily (2.5km); Kalang Valley (5km); Woodgong B&B (7km); Bowraville (28km)

to come up here until the 1940s, when dredging was discontinued. Until tourism boomed at Coffs Harbour in the 1960s, Bellingen was the most important town in this area.

Orientation

The main road from the Pacific Hwy to Dorrigo and the Waterfall Way becomes Hyde St in town. Next to the post office, Wharf St leads across the river to North Bellingen and Gleniffer. There isn't a visitors centre, so stop at the regional centre in Urunga (opposite).

Information

The visitor centres in Urunga on the coast and up the mountain in Dorrigo have Bellingen info. See Eating (p256) for the Bella Book Kafé.

20 20 Imagineering (☎ 6655 0006; Elite Espresso Gallery, 62 Hyde St; ☻ 9am-5pm Mon-Fri, 9am-noon Sat) Full-service internet shop (per hour $8) adjoining a café.

Bellingen Book Nook (☎ 6655 9372; 25 Hyde St; ☻ 10am-4pm Mon-Fri, 9am-3pm Sat market) In a real nook. Lots of books are crammed into this small space. There's always a few itinerant readers lounging around while others gossip.

www.bellingen.com This community website is an excellent resource.

Sights & Activities

To get a feel for the town's past, head to the magnificent **Hammond & Wheatley Emporium** (Hyde St), which looks like a musty old department store until you see the range of stylish goods for sale in the restored 1909-vintage surrounds. There's also an art gallery and a café.

The historic **Old Butter Factory** (☎ 6655 2150; 1 Doepel Lane; ☻ 9.30am-5pm) houses craft shops, a local art gallery, opal dealers and various New Age healers.

Among the dozens of interesting shops, two attest to the importance of music locally: **Heritage Music** (☎ 6655 1611; 23 Hyde St; ☻ 10am-4pm Tue-Sat) and **Heartland Didgeridoo's** (☎ 6655 9881; www.heartdidg.com; 2/25 Hyde St; ☻ 10am-4pm Mon-Sat). The former is an acoustic mecca selling and servicing guitars. You can take lessons from local luminaries and on occasion, a few drop by to perform. The latter is the real deal, with didj's from across Australia, lessons on offer and more.

Bellingen Museum (☎ 6655 1259; Hyde St; adult/child $2/free; ☻ 10am-3pm Tue, 10am-noon Wed & Fri) is one of those places run by enthusiastic volunteers who you suspect hang out there even when it's closed. It has a range of booklets on local walks and history.

For a nature fix, from December to March there's a huge colony of flying foxes on **Bellingen Island**. It's an impressive sight when thousands head off at dusk to feed (best seen from the bridge). There's also an interesting walk to **rope swings** into the river, near the YHA hostel.

About 8km east of town in Fernmount, **Bellingen Canoe Adventures** (☎ 6655 9955; www.canoeadventures.com.au; 4 Tyson St) rents out canoes (from $11) and organises ecofriendly river tours ($45 to $90). You'll see stars on the full moon tour.

On the third Saturday of the month the community **market** takes to the streets and it is a regional sensation, with over 250 stalls. On the second and fourth Saturday of the month there's an **organic market**. Although mobbed, the markets show Bellingen in full blossom.

Festivals & Events

Stamping Ground (☎ 6655 2472; www.stamping ground.com.au) A festival of international dance performances in January.

Bellingen Jazz & Blues Festival (www.bellingenjazz festival.com.au) Features a strong line-up of jazz names in mid-August.

Global Carnival (www.globalcarnival.com) A multicultural mix of music and performances held annually in early October.

Sleeping

Much of the region's accommodation is in small B&Bs and cottages scattered across the hillsides.

Bellingen YHA (☎ 6655 1116; www.yha.com.au; 2 Short St; dm/d from $25/64; 🖵) Once you enjoy the rainforest views from the broad veranda or listen to the flying foxes from a hammock, it's easy to see why this hostel is always popular. A tranquil, engaging atmosphere pervades this renovated weatherboard house. There's a free shuttle to the bus stop and train station in Urunga. Tent sites are $15.

Federal Hotel (☎ 6655 1003; 77 Hyde St; dm $25, r from $45) The basic but clean rooms have access to a wide 2nd-floor veranda with views of the local action. Tiny TVs are mounted up near the wooden ceilings.

Bellingen River Family Cabins (☎ 6655 0499; www .bellingencabins.com.au; 850 Waterfall Way; cabins from $100) Two large two-bedroom cabins overlook the wide river valley on this family farm 4km east of Bellingen. The units are nicely equipped with DVDs and other extras. Make friends with Marilyn the pig and Jack the dog.

Rivendell Guest House (☎ 6655 0060; www.riven dellguesthouse.com.au; 12 Hyde St; r $110-150; 🖵) Unlike many, Rivendell is right in town. The three bedrooms have verandas fronting lush gardens surrounding a freshwater pool. Décor is restrained, always a plus with a B&B.

Koompartoo Retreat (☎ 6655 2326; www.koom partoo.com.au; cnr Lawon & Dudley Sts; r from $145; 🐾) Ferns hang over the wide balconies on the four chalets at this tropical retreat close to town. Each is constructed from local hardwoods and blends right into the hillside. Kitchenettes let you show off your romantic prowess at the cooker.

Woodsong B&B (☎ 6655 9687; www.woodsong .com; 720 Kalang Rd; r $150; 🐾) Made from heavy bricks and timber found on the estate, this cottage stays cool in summer and warm in winter – although the wood fire may light your own fires anyway. Lush grounds surround a freshwater pool.

Lily Pily (☎ 6655 0522; www.lilypily.com.au; 54 Sunny Corner Rd; r $180-220; 🐾) Set on a knoll, this

architect-designed modern complex has three bedrooms overlooking the valleys. It's a high end place designed to pamper with champagne on arrival, lavish breakfasts served until noon, luxurious furnishings and more. It's 3km south of the centre.

Eating & Drinking

The creativity of the locals comes through in the many cafés and restaurants.

Kombu Wholefoods (☎ 6655 9299; 105 Hyde St) An organic grocery-cum-community centre that speaks to the local culture by posting its business philosophy outside.

our pick Feisty Pilot (☎ 6655 0840; 5 Church St; meals $5-10; ☺ 10am-5pm) A Belligen classic: enjoy sushi from the café while you browse busking gear or get your face painted. Get your rave wear here and find out when they're on locally.

Bella Book Kafé (☎ 0413 707 775; 7 Church St; meals under $12; ☺ 9am-4pm Tue-Sun) Excellent brekkies and fresh juices fuel the tummy while the broad assortment of books and games fuel the mind. Sofas are the place to curl up when the rains fall outside.

Federal Hotel (☎ 6655 1003; 77 Hyde St; meals $8-15; ☺ 11am-late) Tragically modernized inside, the town's main pub still has wide porches where you can often hear local musicians jamming.

River Stone (☎ 6655 9099; 103 Hyde St; meals $12-30; ☺ breakfast & lunch daily, dinner Fri & Sat) The Balinese teak furniture at this stylish open-air café hints at the Asian touches on the ever-changing menu. The corn fritters at breakfast are a treat, the *mezze* plate at lunch sumptuous and the prawn *laksa* for dinner divine.

Lodge 241 (☎ 6655 2470; 117-121 Hyde St; mains $16; ☺ breakfast & lunch) Art adorns the walls and there are valley views outside at this bistro set in an old Masonic lodge. Enjoy organic fare such daily pasta specials at large wooden tables inside and out.

No 2 Oak St (☎ 6655 9000; 2 Oak St; mains $28; ☺ dinner Tue-Sat) The bounty of local produce is celebrated at this celebrated restaurant where host Toni Urquart provides the welcome while Ray Urquart works his kitchen magic. A table on the veranda at this 1910 country house is a magical place for the evening.

Getting There & Away

Busways (☎ 1300 555 611; www.busways.com.au) runs two or three times Monday to Saturday from Nambucca Heads ($9, 40 minutes) and

Coffs Harbour ($8, 70 minutes) to Bellingen via Urunga.

Keans (☎ 1800 625 587) has buses west to Dorrigo and Tamworth a pitiful two times a week.

From Bellingen the Waterfall Way climbs steeply 29km to Dorrigo – it's a spectacular drive. From Dorrigo you can continue west to the Armidale–Grafton road. A network of unsealed roads leads south to Bowraville and some tiny mountain settlements.

AROUND BELLINGEN

Explorations of Belligen's lush surrounding valleys are always rewarded. The most accessible is the tiny hamlet of **Gleniffer**, 6km to the north and clearly signposted from North Bellingen. There's a good swimming hole in the **Never Never River**, behind the small Gleniffer School of Arts at the crossroads. Then you can drive around Loop Rd, which takes you to the foot of the New England Tableland – a great drive that words cannot do justice to.

If you want to sweat, tackle the **Syndicate Ridge Walking Trail**, a strenuous 15km walk from Gleniffer to the Dorrigo Plateau following the route of a tramline once used by timber-cutters. There's a very steep 1km climb on the way up. To get to the start of the trail, take the Gleniffer road from Bellingen, turning into Adams Lane soon after crossing the Never Never River. The walking track commences at the first gate.

The **Kalang Valley**, southwest of town, and the **Thora Valley**, about 10km west of town, are also well worth exploring. Feel like you missed the 1960s? They never ended here.

DORRIGO NATIONAL PARK

Layered over sharp peaks and plunging valleys, this is the most accessible of Australia's World Heritage rainforests. The 11,732-hectare park is home to a huge diversity of vegetation owing to its rich soil and subtropical conditions. All those trees mean there's plenty of places for birds to perch and at last count there were over 120 species present.

The **Waterfall Way** climbs the hills between Belligen and Dorrigo and lives up to its name by passing several plunging streams at the roadside. Near the top, 2km south of Dorrigo, the **Rainforest Centre** (☎ 6657 2309; Dome Rd; ☽ 9am-5pm), at the park entrance, has information about the park's many walks and nature displays. The highlight – literally – is

the short **Skywalk** walkway that arches over the rainforest and provides vistas to the valleys below. You can see right down to the ocean on a fine day. The **Wonga Walk** is a three-hour, 6km-return walk on a sealed track through the heart of the rainforest. It's well worth making the drive down to the **Never Never rest area** in the middle of the national park, from where you can walk to waterfalls or begin longer walks.

DORRIGO
☎ 02 / pop 980

The drowsy streets of this agricultural village atop the plateau are starting to see an upscale outpost or two, attesting to its burgeoning popularity. It's sunny and warm up here in contrast to the often misty forests in the national park below.

The **visitors centre** (☎ 6657 2486; 36 Hickory St; ☽ 10am-4pm), in the middle of what passes for the main drag, is run by volunteers who share a passion for the area. Pick up the useful scenic drives brochure ($1). The town's main attraction is **Dangar Falls**, which pound down into a swimming hole – think of it as aquatic massage.

The fire's gone out of a proposed **Steam Railway Museum**, but it's well worth visiting the site: there's a long line of steam engines and lots of old railway paraphernalia scattered about.

In town, **Dorrigo Antiques** (☎ 6657 1000; cnr Waterfall Way & Hickory St), gives artistic presentation (and price tags) to the kinds of old items often found in local attics or country museums. **Pinnata Gallery** (☎ 6657 1668; 69a Hickory St; ☽ 9.30am-4.30pm Tue-Sun) has a good line-up of local art.

Sleeping & Eating

Dorrigo Hotel/Motel (☎ 6657 2017; www.hotelmotel dorrigo.com.au; cnr Cudgery & Hickory Sts; dm $17, r $60-85) This classic country pub is a stately example of 1920s architecture. Rooms span the gamut from restored beauties on the veranda to modern motel jobbies out back. Food is equally, shall we say, timeless: try the chicken nuggets lunch plate.

Gracemere Grange (☎ 6657 2630; www.gracemere grange.com.au; 325 Dome Rd; dm $30, s/d from $40/70) The endearing owner serves a yummy breakfast here. Cosy bedrooms upstairs have slanted, attic-style roofs. It's just 1km east of the centre.

Misty's (☎ 6657 2855; www.dorrigo.com/mistys; 33 Hickory St; r from $95; ☽ lunch Sun, dinner Wed-Sat) Misty's self-contained cottage dates from the 1920s and has a gorgeous antique kitchen and bedroom. The lavish breakfast comes in a hamper. Meals are a treat: the owners serve a changing menu of regional specialties made from mostly organic ingredients. It's right in the centre.

Dorrigo Bakery (☎ 6657 2159; 39 Hickory St; snacks $3; ☽ 8am-4pm Mon-Sat) This traditional bakery is famous for its pies.

Waterfall Way Winery (☎ 6657 1373; 51-53 Hickory St; snacks from $2; ☽ 10am-4pm Mon-Fri, 10am-noon Sat) Right in the centre, owner David Scott creates a range of fortified wines made with local fruit. Buy a bottle, plus some of his deli snacks and you're talking picnic.

Fresh (☎ 6657 2356; 18-20 Cudgery St; mains $10-20; ☽ breakfast & lunch Tue-Fri, dinner Sat) The local foodies' hub, Fresh is a bakery, deli and café set in a chic minimalist space with cream-coloured mismatched chairs at tables scattered front and back. Creative salads, sandwiches, veggie specials and more entice.

Getting There & Away

Keans (☎ 1800 625 587) has buses east to Bellingen and west to Tamworth a pitiful two times a week.

COFFS HARBOUR

☎ 02 / pop 26,600

You can't help but stop in Coffs Harbour: the coagulated Pacific Hwy gives you no choice. This regional centre has a range of protected beaches and attractions that appeal to families. Of course 'family-friendly' can also mean 'dull and predictable' and it seems that some people feel that way about it.

Originally called Korff's Harbour, the town was settled in the 1860s. The jetty was built in 1892 to load cedar and other logs; it fell into disrepair some years ago but is now restored to its former glory. Bananas were first grown in the area in the 1880s, but no-one made much money from them until the railway came to town in 1918.

Banana growing reached its peak in the 1960s; these days tourism is the mainstay of the local economy.

Orientation

The town is split into three areas: the jetty area, the commercial centre with its malls and the beaches. The Pacific Hwy becomes Grafton St and then Woolgoolga Rd on its fume-ridden run through town. The city centre is around the Grafton St and Harbour Dr junction. Note that High St and Harbour Dr are one and the same, with both names used interchangeably by adjoining businesses.

The Pacific Hwy is the best way to access the beaches and resorts to the north. South of Coffs is Sawtell, a sprawl of housing developments fronting some fabulous surf beaches, which merge into Coffs Harbour.

Information

Internet Shop (☎ 6651 9155; Jetty Village, Harbour Dr; per 15min $2.50; ☽ 9am-7pm) Down by the marina; offers broadband laptop connections, wi-fi and CD burning.

Main post office (Ground fl, Palms Centre Shopping Complex) In a mall. There's another outlet at the jetty, opposite the Pier Hotel, and a third at Park Beach Plaza (the large mall off the Pacific Hwy).

Book Warehouse (☎ 6651 9077; 26 Harbour Dr) In the heart of the commercial centre.

Planet Games (☎ 6652 5188; 7/20 Gordon St; ☽ 9am-6pm Mon-Fri, 10am-5pm Sat) Internet access (per 20 minutes $2) a short walk from the bus stop.

Visitors centre (☎ 6652 1522, 1300 369 070; www .coffscoast.com.au; cnr Pacific Hwy & McLean St;

WORTH A TRIP: FOLLOWING THE WATERFALL WAY

Once you've travelled the 41km from the Pacific Hwy through Bellingen to Dorrigo, you've gone pretty far from the coast, although there's still another 124km of the Waterfall Way to go before you reach Armidale. Should you press on, these are the highlights:

■ Forty-eight kilometres past Dorrigo (2km west of Ebor) there's a turn for Ebor Falls, where the Guy Fawkes River takes a big plunge.

■ A further 7km on is Point Lookout Rd, which leads to New England National Park, another World Heritage site. There are numerous walks into this misty rainforest.

■ After another 30km, look for Wollomombi Falls, a highlight of the World Heritage-listed Oxley Wild Rivers National Park. Here the water plunges down 260m.

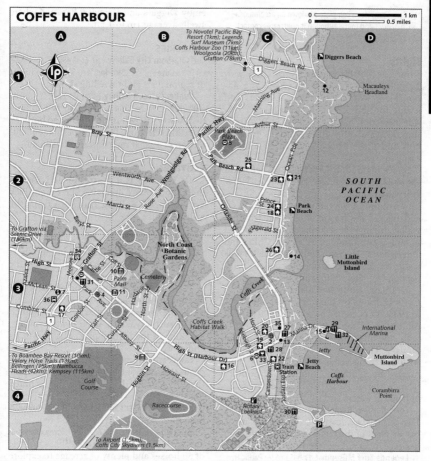

COFFS HARBOUR

⊗ 8am-5pm) Has a complete rundown on accommodation, activities and tours, although it obliterates contact info on brochures with its own.

Sights

Some see the **Big Banana** (☎ 6652 4355; www .bigbanana.com; Pacific Hwy; ⊗ 9am-4.30pm) as a national icon with plenty of appeal, others find it ripe for abuse. This long-running roadside attraction has ice-skating ($12), a snow slope ($5) and other attractions. It's great for kids and those whose sense of style is not easily bruised.

Strolling through **North Coast Botanic Gardens** (☎ 6648 4188; Hardacre St; admission by donation; ⊗ 9am-5pm) you can immerse yourself in the subtropical surrounds. Lush rainforest and numerous endangered species are some of the features, which also include sections devoted to places as faraway and foreign as Africa, China and Queensland. The 6km **Coffs Creek Habitat Walk** passes by, starting opposite the council chambers on Coff St and finishing near the ocean.

Dramatic **Muttonbird Island** was joined to Coffs Harbour by the northern breakwater in 1935. It's occupied by some 12,000 pairs of mutton birds from late August to early April, with cute offspring visible in December and January. The 500m walk to the top rewards with sweeping vistas along the coast. This marks the southern boundary of Solitary Islands Marine Park (p264), a meeting place of tropical waters and southern currents.

Coffs Harbour Regional Museum (☎ 6652 5794; 191a Harbour Dr; adult/child $3/1; ⊗ 10am-4pm Tue-Sat) has displays of the region's nautical and fruit heritage in an old weatherboard house.

Legends Surf Museum (☎ 6653 6536; Pacific Hwy; adult/child $5/2; ⊗ 9am-4pm) lets you smell the wax. Over 160 boards are on display, including ancient ones from, like, 50 years ago, man. Owner Scott Dillon is as salty as the ocean and has a passel of tales, although as he notes: 'Everyone wants to hear shark stories'. It's 500m west of the Pacific Hwy 7km north of town.

BEACHES

Park Beach, which has a picnic ground and is patrolled at busy times, is a long and lovely stretch of sand. It is backed by dense shrubbery and dunes that conceal the urban blight beyond. **Jetty Beach** is more sheltered. **Diggers Beach**, reached by turning off the highway near the Big Banana, has a nude section. Surfers

enjoy Diggers and **Macauleys Headland** where swells average 1m to 1.5m.

GALLERIES

Coffs Harbour City Gallery (☎ 6648 4861; Rigby House, cnr Coff & Duke Sts; ⊗ 10am-4pm Wed-Sat) has exhibits of regional art and travelling shows.

Bunker Cartoon Gallery (☎ 6651 7343; City Hall Dr; adult/child $2/1; ⊗ 10am-4pm Mon-Sat) is a unique institution where humour knows no borders. Rotating selections from the permanent collection of 12,000 cartoons are on display.

Activities

Coffs Harbour is a centre for activities in the region, many involving the ocean. Pick up the useful walking brochure from the visitors centre.

Jetty Dive Centre (☎ 6651 1611; www.jettydive.com .au; 398 Harbour Dr; double dives from $95) offers greatvalue PADI certification; the diving and snorkelling is pretty spectacular as you explore the Solitary Islands Marine Park.

Watery fun of all kinds is on offer at **Liquid Assets Adventure Tours** (☎ 6658 0850; www.surfraft ing.com; 328 Harbour Dr; half-day surf rafting $50), which offers surf-kayaking, white-water rafting, kayaking in the marine park, platypus tours and more.

East Coast Surf School (☎ 6651 5515; www.eastcoast surfschool.com.au; Diggers Beach; lessons from $55) is particularly female-friendly as it is run by noted East Coast surfer Helene Enevoldson. Fellow boardie **Lee Winkler's Surf School** (☎ 6650 0050; Park Beach; lessons from $45) also has a good rep.

Valery Horse Trails (☎ 6653 4301; www.valerytrails .com.au; 758 Valery Rd, Valery; 2hr ride $45) has a stable of 60 horses and plenty of acreage to explore in the hills behind town.

Tours

Mountain Trails (☎ 6658 3333; tours per person from $65) Award-winning ecofriendly 4WD tours. A reader fave.

Festivals & Events

Gold Cup (☎ 6652 1488) Early August. Coffs' premier horse race.

Coffs Harbour International Buskers' Festival (www.coffsharbourbuskers.com) Late September and not to be missed. Tattooed men balance precariously on a unicycle while juggling bearded ladies.

Coffs Harbour Food & Wine Festival Last weekend in October.

Pittwater to Coffs Yacht Race New Year. Starts in Sydney and finishes here.

Sleeping

Motels cluster in two spots: out on the Pacific Hwy by the visitors centre where they can suck in road-trippers, and down by Park Beach where they can comfort beachgoers.

One of many holiday-apartment agents is **Pacific Property & Management** (☎ 6652 1466; www .coffsholidayrentals.com.au; 101 Park Beach Rd). The range of offerings is numbing. The visitors centre has an accommodation booking service.

BUDGET

If you're visiting during peak times, it's good to note that most hostel prices remain consistent all year, but book ahead.

Park Beach Holiday Park (☎ 6648 4888; Ocean Pde; camp sites from $24, cabins from $90; 🖳) Massive, with 332 sites and 55 cabins; ideally located at the beach.

Aussitel Backpackers Hostel (☎ 1800 330 335, 6651 1871; www.aussitel.com; 312 Harbour Dr; dm/d $24/60; 🖳 🗺) On a bluff across from parkland and near the jetty, this delightful hostel has free canoes you can take out on the river plus diving and other activities.

Coffs Harbour YHA (☎ 6652 6462; www.yha.com.au; 51 Collingwood St; dm/d from $24/70; 🖳 🗺) There's 92 beds in spacious dorms and en-suite doubles. It's all very modern and immaculate. Rentals include surf boards and bikes.

Hoey-Moey Backpackers (☎ 6651 7966; Ocean Pde; dm/d $26/60; 🖳 ; wi-fi) Right on the beach, Hoey Moey shares space with a high-volume pub and drive-through bottleshop. Rooms range from singles to four-bed dorms.

MIDRANGE

There's no real reason to stay out by the Pacific Hwy.

Ocean Parade Motel (☎ 6652 6733; 41 Ocean Pde; s/d from $65/70; 🗺 🗺 ; wi-fi) One of the best choices on the motel strip, the 19 units here are kept immaculate. Rooms are large and include fridges, barbeques and views of the salt-water pool.

Ocean Palms Motel (☎ 6651 5594; www.oceanpalms motel.com.au; cnr Park Beach Rd & Ocean Pde; r from $70; 🗺) The mature palms at this mature motel give it a South Seas feel. There's a 12m saltwater pool surrounded by gardens. Rooms are good-sized and you'll stay sweet-smelling thanks to the free laundry.

Bananatown Motel (☎ 6652 4411; cnr Grafton St & Pacific Hwy; r from $70; 🗺 🖳 🗺) The roadside choice for those just blowing through, the Banantown logo of a slacker munching a banana under a palm is hard to resist. Rooms are basic and clean as is the diminutive pool. It's close to the bus stop.

Caribbean Motel (☎ 6652 1500; www.stayincoffs .com.au; 353 High St; r $75-115; 🗺 🖳 🗺) Close to Coffs Creek and the jetty, this 24-unit motel features a breakfast buffet and tables outside. The best rooms have balconies, views, kitchens and spas.

Bo'suns Inn Motel (☎ 6651 2251; www.motelcoffshar bour.com; 37 Ocean Pde; d from $90; 🗺 🗺) The nautical theme here runs from the life-size seaman out the front to the scenes of frigates mounted over the beds. You can almost smell the poop deck. The 12 units are close to Park Beach and have lots of niceties such as microwaves and fridges.

Observatory Holiday Apartments (☎ 6650 0462; www.theobservatory.com.au; 30-36 Camperdown St; apt from $140; 🗺 ; wi-fi) Some have window spas and all have balconies with ocean views. The one-, two- and three-bedroom apartments in this attractive complex are bright and airy, with chef-friendly kitchens.

TOP END

Novotel Pacific Bay Resort (☎ 6659 7000; www.pa cificbayresort.com.au; cnr Pacific Hwy & Bay Dr; r from $190; 🗺 🗺 ; wi-fi) Has all the features of a large resort: tennis courts, a golf course, walking trails, a kids' club, a spa and a fitness centre. The grounds are large and the 180 rooms have balconies, many with kitchens.

Eating

You can eat well down by the jetty. The strip of eateries on Harbour St is a hungry browser's delight.

JETTY

As well as the listings here, you'll find budget Italian, Vietnamese, Indian, and fish and chips. Kitchens start closing around 8.30pm, so come early and make a reservation if you have your heart set on a particular place or a pavement table.

Urban Espresso Lounge (☎ 6651 1989; 384a Harbour Dr; mains $6-16; 🕑 breakfast & lunch) A stylish little java outpost on the strip. Pancakes, fresh fruit and yogurt are some of the breakfast delights. Lunches include a Thai beef and prawn salad and a luscious roast beef sandwich.

Crying Tiger (☎ 6650 0195; 382 Harbour Dr; mains $8-20; 🕑 dinner) Elegant Thai food is served in this stylish open-air restaurant. There's oodles of tables for slurping your noodles; which is good as the place is very popular.

our pick **Caffé Fiasco** (☎ 6651 3000; 368 Harbour Dr; mains $15-30; brunch Sun, dinner Tue-Sun) It doesn't live up to its name. Really, how about Caffé Wonderful? Classic Italian fare is prepared in an open kitchen surrounded by widely spaced tables that flow from inside to out. The gardens are fields with herbs used in the dishes, which include some excellent local seafood.

MARINA

Second to the Jetty in popularity; there is some excellent seafood here.

Fisherman's Co-op (☎ 6652 2006; cnr Marina Dr & Orlando St; mains $8-10; 9am-6pm winter, 9am-8pm summer) Fresh fish right off the boats here includes whiting and chips. Homemade gelato and covered picnic tables complete the joy; there's much here that would make a good picnic at Muttonbird Island.

Tide & Pilot Oyster Bar & Sea Grill (☎ 6651 6888; Marina Dr; café $6-12, mains restaurant $20-30; café breakfast & lunch, restaurant lunch & dinner) Right on the ocean this bifurcated seafood place has casual fare at ground level and exquisite dining on the second level, where tables have views over the jetty. This is the place to bring a date.

Ocean Front Brasserie (☎ 6651 2819; Jordan Esplanade; meals $6-25; lunch & dinner) Located on a knoll at the south end of the marina, the restaurant of the Coffs Harbour Deep Sea Fishing Club does – surprise! – fish well. But you may not notice as the views are panoramic; in season, watch for whales.

CBD

The downtown area is good for lunch, or for coffee all day, but most places are closed in the evening. The pedestrian area opposite Palm Mall (part of High St Pedestrian Mall) has a few pavement cafés.

Swanky's (☎ 6651 5403; City Sq; meals $5-12; breakfast & lunch Mon-Sat) A vine-covered awning shelters the sturdy wood tables at this popular open-air café. There is a full espresso bar and classic Aussie breakfasts, salads and sandwiches.

Drinking & Entertainment

See Thursday's edition of the *Coffs Harbour Advocate* for listings. Clubs change names with the seasons.

Hoey Moey Pub (☎ 6852 3833; Ocean Pde) In the same complex as Hoey Moey Backpackers, this party pub caters to the demanding backpacker and tradies markets and is your best bet for local acts and Journey cover bands. Karaoke nights are an endurance test.

Pier Hotel (☎ 6652 2110; cnr Hood & High Sts) Renovated into a bland band venue, you can find bad beer in a warren of rooms that draw crowds due to the location. Wait! Do I hear Journey?

Plantation Hotel (☎ 6652 3855; Pacific Hwy) Don't let the neon lights, mirrored walls and colourful wedge seating fool you, the Plantation is still a pub at heart, so beer, live rock and the occasional 'Miss Indy' quest are still mainstays. It's near a few other charmers of this ilk.

Getting There & Away

AIR

Coffs Harbour Airport (CFS) is just south of town. **Virgin Blue** (☎ 13 67 89) has flights to Sydney and Melbourne. **QantasLink** (☎ 13 13 13) flies to Sydney.

BUS

Long-distance and regional buses leave from a shelter adjacent to the visitors centre.

Greyhound (☎ 13 14 99; www.greyhound.com.au) has several services a day north, including Byron Bay ($58, four hours) and south to Sydney ($82, nine hours). **Premier** (☎ 13 34 10; www.premierms.com.au) offers similar services in both directions.

Busways (☎ 1300 555 611; www.busways.com.au) runs two or three times daily Monday to Saturday to Nambucca Heads ($9, 70 minutes) and Bellingen ($8, 70 minutes) via Urunga.

TRAIN

CountryLink (☎ 13 22 32; www.countrylink.com.au) has three trains daily all the way north to the nonthriving town of Casino (where the train used to branch off to Byron Bay) and Brisbane ($59, 5½ hours), and south to Sydney ($67, nine hours).

Getting Around

Hostel shuttles meet most long-distance buses and trains.

Coffs Bike Hire (☎ 6652 5102; cnr Orlando & Collingwood Sts; per day from $25; 8.30am-5.30pm Mon-Fri, 9am-2pm Sat & Sun) rents cruisers, mountain bikes and more.

Major car-rental companies are at the airport.

For a cab, **Coffs District Taxi Network** (☎ 13 10 08, 6658 5922) operates a 24-hour service.

COFFS HARBOUR TO GRAFTON

The Pacific Hwy runs near the coast – but not in sight of it – for 30km north of Coffs. Look for turnoffs to small beaches that are often quite uncrowded. The road then turns inland to Grafton, avoiding Yuraygir National Park and the isolated beach town of Wooli.

Woolgoolga
☎ 02 / pop 3800

With a nice beach in a deep cove, Woolgoolga is a less-developed coastal town 20km north of Coffs that is renowned for its surf and sizeable Sikh community. As you drive by on the highway you will notice the impressive **Guru Nanak Temple**, the *gurdwara* (place of worship). Don't confuse it with the **Raj Mahal**, an Indian-influenced decrepit concrete eyesore with two mangled elephant statues out front.

Even if you're not sticking around, drive straight through town up to the point, you'll get a magnificent **view** of the Solitary Islands Marine Park and the coast stretching into the mists north and south.

The **Woolgoolga Beach Caravan Park** (☎ 6654 1373; Beach St; camp sites $24, cabins $60) is a crowded place right on the beach (which affords great walks to flee the mobs).

On the beachfront, **Bluebottles Brasserie** (☎ 6654 1962; cnr Wharf & Beach Sts; mains $10-30; ☽ breakfast & lunch daily, dinner Thu-Sat) is a bistro with fare that includes the mandatory caesar salad, big sandwiches, seafood specials and pasta. On some summer evenings, there's live jazz.

Red Rock
☎ 02 / pop 290

Red Rock, a site that's sacred to the Gunawarri tribe, is a sleepy village 5km off the highway. It has a beautiful inlet and gorgeous surrounds. Soak up the sun or catch a fish while camping at **Red Rock Caravan Park** (☎ 6649 2730; 1 Lawson St; camp sites from $13, cabins from $65).

Yuraygir National Park

Yuraygir (20,000 hectares) protects the longest stretch of undeveloped coast in NSW (60km). It is the southernmost in a chain of coastal national parks and nature reserves

that runs almost all the way north to Ballina. It encompasses forests, heaths, estuaries and wetlands. The beaches are outstanding and there are some bushwalking paths where you can view endangered coastal emus. The park is in three sections, from **Red Rock** to the Wooli River (turn off the highway just north of Red Rock); from the township of **Wooli** to the Sandon River (turn off the highway 12km south of Grafton); and from near **Brooms Head** to **Angourie Point** (accessible from those towns). Together the areas comprise 60km of coast but there is no vehicle access between the sections; on foot you'd have to cross the challenging Wooli and Sandon Rivers.

Walkers can bush-camp and there are basic **camping areas** (per person $10) at Station Creek in the southern section; at the Boorkoom and Illaroo rest areas in the central section; and on the north bank of the Sandon River, and at Red Cliff at the Brooms Head end of the northern section. These are accessible by car; there are also walk-in camp sites in the northern section: Plumbago Headland, Shelly Head and Shelly Beach. Self-service kiosks collect the park's $10 day-use fee.

Wooli
☎ 02 / pop 570

The beauty of this little town is that it is surrounded by the Yuraygir National Park on land and the Solitary Islands Marine Park by sea. This means you are encircled by wildlife and crisp waters.

Just getting here is a treat. The 34km drive from the Pacific Hwy passes through a variety or natural terrain in and out of park. Stands sell produce from the many small farms. The beach is backed by dunes and stretches for eight uninhabited kilometres. The town is on a long isthmus, with a river estuary on one side and the ocean on the other. This only adds to its isolated charm.

On the Queen's Birthday long weekend in June, the locals hold their big event, the **Goanna Pulling Championships**. It's not what some might assume, as contestants wrap a leather strap around their head for a good old-fashioned tug-of-war.

Wooli has a couple of small grocers and a café. Apartments can be booked through **Wooli Holiday Accommodation** (☎ 6649 7540). The **Wooli Camping & Caravan Park** (☎ 6649 7671; North St; camp sites from $20, cabins from $60) is a quiet, compact option on the river and the centre – such as it is. The **Solitary Islands Marine Park Resort** (☎ 6649 7519; www.solitaryislandsresort.com.au; camp sites from $22, cabins from $70) is another pastoral spot, in this case about 2km north of town.

Solitary Islands Marine Park

This group of five islands is the meeting point of warm tropical currents and cooler southern currents, making for a wonderful combination of corals, reef fish and seaweeds. Dubbed the 'rivers of life', this is the best area in North Coast NSW in which to dive or snorkel (look out for extremely rough conditions). The **park** (☎ 6652 0900) protects some 550 species of fish and 90 species of coral. Check at tourism information centres and dive shops for a handy booklet outlining the many rules and regulations designed to preserve the park. Dive shops in Coffs Harbour (p260) organise tours of the park.

FAR NORTH COAST

This is where the coast heats up in activity, hype and temperature. Byron Bay is the centre of all the attention, with its nightlife, stunning location and beach. But there are places with equal beauty that are much quieter. Lennox Head and its surrounds are much more serene than the tourist Babylon to the north, while Yamba offers a bit of colour on its estuary.

Coupled with the beaches and ideal subtropical climate are rivers rich in appeal. The Clarence River vies to be the most beautiful river in NSW, such is its striking blueness. The Richmond and Tweed Rivers sprawl out into rich deltas and provide wide vistas. Many visitors simply come for the weather: warm winters and long, hot summers.

GRAFTON

☎ 02 / pop 17,500

Grafton is a regional agricultural centre that has prominence due to its location on the Pacific Hwy. In fact it will give you a good taste of the vast NSW hinterlands and may well encourage you to keep right on driving. Still it is pretty enough and in season the streets are awash with the purple flowers of Brazilian jacaranda in late October. For the road weary, there's just enough places to offer a choice.

Don't be fooled by the franchises along the highway, the main part of town is

reached over an imposing 1932 doubledecker (road and rail) bridge.

Information

Clarence River visitors centre (☎ 6642 4677; www .clarencetourism.com; cnr Spring & Charles Sts; ☑ 9am-5pm) On the Pacific Hwy south of the town, near the turn-off to the bridge. Tellingly, it shares a parking lot with a McDonald's.
NPWS office (National Parks & Wildlife Service; ☎ 6641 1500; 49 Victoria St; ☑ 8.30am-5pm)

Sights

Victoria St is the focal point of days gone by with the **courthouse** (1862), **Roches Family Hotel** (1870), **Anglican Cathedral** (1884) and the private residence **Istria** (1899) providing glimpses of 19th-century architecture.

Fitzroy St runs parallel to Victoria St. The **Grafton Regional Gallery** (☎ 6642 6996; 158 Fitzroy St; admission free; ☑ 10am-4pm Tue-Sun) is in a slightly grand 1880 house and has works by regional artists. It's a well-curated place and there are regular special exhibitions.

Nearby, **Schaeffer House** (1903) is where you'll find the **Clarence River Historical Society** (190 Fitzroy St; adult/child $3/1; ☑ 1-4pm Tue, Wed, Thu & Sun), with its displays of treasures once littering attics across town.

Festivals & Events

Horse Racing Carnival Every July; this is the richest in country Australia.
Jacaranda Festival In the week joining October and November, Australia's longest-running floral festival sees Grafton come alive in an ocean of mauve.

Sleeping & Eating

Motels line the Pacific Hwy.

Roches Family Hotel (☎ 6644 2866; www.roches .com.au; 85 Victoria St; s/d $30/40) is a historic old corner pub in the town centre with spruced up rooms. Be sure to get one with doors opening onto the veranda. It's a tidy place with new bathrooms.

Jacaranda Motor Lodge (☎ 6642 2833; www.jaca randamotorlodge.com.au; Pacific Hwy; s/d $80/90; ☒ ☑) One of the nicer highway motel options, the Jacaranda knows its market well: there's stabling for horses and pets are welcome. Some of the 25 modern rooms have large, shady balconies.

Courtyard Cafe (☎ 6642 6644; cnr Prince & Fitzroy Sts; meals $9-15; ☑ lunch Mon-Fri) Make your way past a heritage sandstone building to this local favourite. The salads and sandwiches are fresh and varied. More ambitious options include grilled local seafood and steaks.

Georgie's Café (☎ 6642 6996; 158 Fitzroy St; mains $12-20; ☺ lunch Tue-Sun, dinner Tue-Sat) The food here is as artful as the location: the courtyard of the Grafton Regional Gallery. Dishes by day include lovely baked goods, creative salads, thick sandwiches and more. At night it's a serious restaurant with a changing menu depending on what's coming off the local farms.

Getting There & Away

Busways (☎ 1300 555 611; www.busways.com.au) runs to Yamba ($12, 75 minutes, six times daily) and Maclean ($10, 45 minutes).

Greyhound (☎ 13 14 99; www.greyhound.com.au) and **Premier** (☎ 13 34 10; www.premierms.com.au) stop at the train station on their multiple Pacific Hwy runs.

CountryLink (☎ 13 22 32; www.countrylink.com.au) stops here on its north coast route. Sydney is served three times daily ($72, 10 hours).

Near Grafton there are several scenic routes that parallel the Pacific Hwy. Try the north bank of the Clarence route between Grafton and Maclean, which involves a ferry crossing at Lawrence.

CLARENCE RIVER VALLEY

The Clarence River rises in Queensland's McPherson Ranges and runs south through the mountains before thundering down the gorge in the Gibraltar Range west of Grafton.

The Clarence then meanders northeast to the sea at Yamba, giving life to a beautiful and fertile valley along the way.

The delta between Grafton and the coast is a patchwork of farmland in which the now sinuous and spreading Clarence River forms over 100 islands, some very large. If you're driving,

the profusion of small bridges and waterways makes it hard to keep track of whether you're on an island or the mainland.

There are Aboriginal sites throughout the region dating back 4500 years or more. Today it is the start of sugar-cane country and also the beginning of Queensland-style domestic architecture: wooden houses with high-pitched roofs perched on stilts to allow air circulation in the hot summers. The burning of the cane fields (May to December) adds a smoky tang to the air.

Clarence Riverboats (☎ 6647 6232; www.clarence riverboats.com.au; Brushgrove) has cute houseboats that sleep up to six. Meandering amid the dozens of islands and channels defines relaxation. Rates vary widely but three days and two nights costs from $600 – a bargain with a group.

For casual explorations, **Seelands Boat Hire** (☎ 6644 9381; Seelands Hall Rd) is on the Clarence River west of Grafton. Rentals include aluminium outboards (per day $80) and canoes (per day $60).

MACLEAN

☎ 02 / pop 3300

It's never this warm in Scotland. And here the sugar is still growing while there the sugar is in a deep-fried Mars bar. Tartan-clad Maclean takes its Scottish heritage very seriously, so such comparisons are inevitable. That said, the town is set in charming surrounds with the imposing Clarence River beginning its lazy sprawl over the delta. Prawn fishing is popular.

The amazing **Lower Clarence visitors centre** (☎ 6645 4121; Pacific Hwy; ☺ 9am-5pm) is on the southern entry to town in a large building with a riverside café. Internet access is $3 for 15 minutes. There is a staggering amount of local

---

WORTH A TRIP: INLAND FROM GRAFTON

The Clarence River is navigable as far upstream as the village of **Copmanhurst**, about 35km northwest of Grafton. Further upstream the Clarence River descends rapidly from the Gibraltar Range through the rugged **Clarence River Gorge**, a popular and challenging site for white-water canoeing.

Private property flanks the gorge. On the south side the land is owned by the Winters family, who allow day visitors and have cabin accommodation at **Winters' Shack** (☎ 6647 2173; s/d $30/60). Access is via Copmanhurst. It's best to ring first to get permission and to arrange for the gates to be unlocked. On the north side, **Wave Hill Station** (☎ 6647 2145; www.wavehillfarmstay .com.au; camp sites $25, B&B per person from $60) has homestead and accommodation plus 4WD or horse-riding trips to the gorge.

NORTH COAST NEW SOUTH WALES

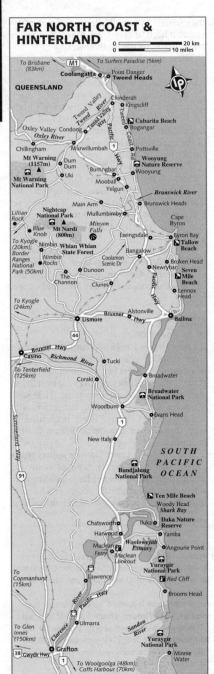

FAR NORTH COAST & HINTERLAND

information here: everything from shipwrecks to markets and all of it excellent. Pick up a copy of *Maclean Heritage Trail*, which gives great detail on this largely preserved river town.

For sweeping views of the river delta, head up the hill to **Maclean Lookout**. The **Maclean Historical Society** (☎ 6645 3416; www.maclean history.org.au; cnr Wharf & Grafton Sts; adult/child $3/1; 1-4pm Wed & Sat, 10am-4pm Fri) gives a good insight into the town's Scottish roots. The complex includes a beautiful 1879 stone cottage.

The centre of Maclean still has a pleasant early 1900s feel. Stroll the riverfront, check out the shops and have a cold one at one of the old hotels.

YAMBA

☎ 02 / pop 5700

The 17km drive from Maclean straight east to Yamba takes in some lush delta scenery and plenty of sugarcane. You don't really need an award for this kind of drive but Yamba is one all the same. Flowing over a head and boasting both river and ocean beaches, this small town is gaining in popularity by the year.

Sights & Activities

The centre sits behind a head, which is indented with small cove beaches. The **Story House Museum** (☎ 6646 2316; River St; adult/child $3/50¢; 10am-4.30pm Tue & Wed, 2-4.30pm Thu, Sat & Sun) has hundreds of photos telling the story of the once pervasive local maritime culture. Check out details of the dozens of shipwrecks. **Arthouse Australia** (☎ 6646 1999; 25 Coldstream St; 9am-5pm Mon-Fri, 10am-2pm Sat) displays works by local artists inspired by the location.

Get a close-up view of the diversity of life in the Clarence estuaries on a tour with **Yamba Kayak** (☎ 6646 1137; www.yambakayak.com.au; tours from $60). Pick up is at Gorman's Restaurant at Yamba Bay. To use the motorised version, the **Hire Hut** (☎ 6646 2194; Blue Dolphin Holiday Resort; full-day, up to 8 people $150) has simple, square boats. It's near the entrance to town.

A **community market** is held at the Ford Park on the fourth weekend of each month. The **Yamba Bookshop** (☎ 6646 3111; 19 Yamba St) has a small but excellent selection.

Sleeping

A much-needed YHA hostel is planned for Yamba. Check www.yha.com.au for details.

Calypso Holiday Park (☎ 6646 2468; Harbour St; camp sites from $22, cabins from $60-150;) The best-located camping place, Calypso is a short walk from the town centre and all the beaches. There are 162 sites and 32 cabins, some quite posh.

Pacific Hotel (☎ 6646 2466; www.pacifichotelyamba .com.au; 1 Pilot St; dm $18-20, r $60-130; 🖵) Gorgeously situated overlooking the ocean, rooms here are as varied as the stories surrounding this historic place. The best ones have balconies overlooking the water. The views are superb, as is the bistro (below).

Surf Motel (☎ 6646 2200; 2 Queen St; r $90-250; 🐾) On a bluff overlooking the main beach, this modern, seven-room place is across from a large green. Rooms are quite big and have balconies and kitchenettes.

Angourie Rainforest Resort (☎ 6646 8600; www .angourieresort.com.au; 166 Angourie Rd; 1-bedroom ste $140-325; 🐾 🖵 🏊) Set in rainforest 1km west of Yamba, management here take an ecological approach to running this 66-unit resort. The rooms have high-speed internet and are spacious. There are pools and a lavish spa.

Eating & Drinking

Caper Berry Café (☎ 6646 2322; cnr Coldstream & Yamba Sts; meals $6-10; 🕑 breakfast & lunch Mon-Sat) This little gem of a corner café has a long and delicious breakfast menu. Lunch includes bargain-priced pastas, sandwiches and various Mediterranean treats.

Yamba Soundlounge (☎ 6646 3909; cnr Coldstream & Yamba Sts; meals $6-12; 🕑 breakfast & lunch; 🖵 ; wi-fi) There's a funky collection of CDs for sale at this idiosyncratic place in the centre. Smoothies, burgers, juices and coffees highlight the menu. There are tables inside and out.

Pacific Hotel (☎ 6646 2466; 1 Pilot St; mains $15-30; 🕑 lunch & dinner) The bistro in this Cliffside classic is a cut above the rest of the hotel, which is pretty pub-standard. The seafood menu changes regularly but always includes at least 10 or 12 items. Oysters are a popular starter.

Yamba Bar & Grill (☎ 6646 1155; 15 Clarence St; mains $26-30; 🕑 dinner Tue-Sun) The stylishly simple interior has a few nautical touches to remind you where you are. Highlights on the short Mod Oz menu include rack of lamb, steaks and cod. Sides are right from the gastropub playbook: chips and rocket salad. There are a couple of other restaurants on this little strip.

Yamba Bowling Club (☎ 6646 2305; 44 Wooli St) For regular live music, check the schedule here.

Getting There & Around

Yamba is 15km east of the Pacific Hwy; turn off at the Yamba Rd intersection just south of the Clarence River. A passenger-only **ferry** (☎ 6646 6423; adult/child $6/3) runs to Iluka, on the north bank of the Clarence River, five times daily.

Busways (☎ 1300 555 611; www.busways.com.au) buses go to Maclean ($6, 30 minutes) and Grafton ($11, 75 minutes, several Monday to Saturday).

CountryLink (☎ 13 22 32; www.countrylink.com.au) buses go to Grafton where you can connect to Byron Bay ($14, three hours, one daily).

Yamba Squash & Cycle (☎ 6646 2237; 35 Coldstream St) is near the bowling club and rents bikes from $20 per day.

AROUND YAMBA

A surf haven where epic breaks beckon, **Angourie Point** lies 5km south of Yamba. There are good views from the small cliffs at the end of the road above the rocky shore.

Iluka is a carbon copy of Yamba but much less developed. You can make a circular visit to both by using buses and the passenger ferry. **Busways** (☎ 1300 555 611; www.busways.com.au) buses go to Maclean ($12, 50 minutes, two Monday to Saturday).

Fishermen love this area as much as nature enthusiasts; the town acts as a gateway to the World Heritage–listed **Iluka Nature Reserve**, a tiny vestige of coastal rainforest close to town. North of here, **Bundjalung National Park** is largely untouched and best explored with 4WD. Highlights include the literally named Ten Mile Beach and the hopefully not-literally named Hell Hole Lagoon.

BUNDJALUNG NATIONAL PARK

Created in 1980, this park comprises almost 4000 hectares of coastal land and includes 38km of unspoilt beaches. The entrance is 60km north of Grafton or 50km south of Ballina and there are four main areas.

The first is the **Gumma Garra** picnic area, with creeks, islands, rainforests and a midden that can be seen by the river. You can get there via Evans Head on the Bundjalung Rd. The second is **Black Rocks** (☎ 6646 6134; camp sites per person $10) picnic area and camping, which is tucked in behind the sand dunes of Ten Mile Beach. You can sit in the shade of a tuckeroo tree.

The third area is the **Woody Head** (☎ 6646 6134; camp sites per person $14) picnic and camping area, which has rock pools and is 6km north of Iluka. The fourth is **Shark Bay**, where you can bushwalk and swim. Smack in the middle of the park is the evocatively named **Hell Hole Lagoon**; try not to fall in.

The day-use fee is $10 per vehicle.

EVANS HEAD
☎ 02 / pop 2614

Evans Head is a low-key little place that eschews charm and instead concentrates on its intense prawn and fishing industry. There are no compelling reasons to visit the town itself, but the 11km road north that joins the Pacific Hwy passes through the unspoiled **Broadwater National Park**.

Extending from north of Evans Head to Broadwater, this small coastal park (3750 hectares) protects an 8km stretch of beach backed by coastal heath. The beach is excellent and you can go kayaking. **Evans River Kayak Adventures** (☎ 6682 6229; www.evansriverkayaks.com) leads a variety of tours (from $25) through he estuaries.

BALLINA
☎ 02 / pop 18,750

Crossing the Richmond River marks the end of the fishing villages and the beginning of the tourist-driven economy. Ballina is a sign of the times, basing its appeal around family holidays and nature activities. Although it likes to tout itself as a quiet alternative to Byron, Ballina is fast-developing along the riverfront.

The Pacific Hwy approaches from the south and turns into River St, the main drag. A bypass due for completion by 2010 will whack off the Pacific Hwy's clogged route through Ballina to the benefit of the town and drivers.

The **visitors centre** (☎ 6686 3484; www.discoverballina.com; cnr Lasbalsas Plaza & River St; � 9am-5pm) has detailed information on surrounding attractions. Pick up the excellent brochure on local birds.

For internet access, try Ice Creamery Internet Café (see opposite).

Sights
Behind the information centre is the large **Naval & Maritime Museum** (☎ 6681 1002; Regatta Ave; admission by donation; �a 9am-4pm). Here you will find the amazing remains of a balsawood raft that drifted across the Pacific from Ecuador as part of the Las Balsas expedition in 1973.

For a good sampling of local history, stroll the length of Norton St, which boasts a number of impressive late 19th-century buildings from Ballina's days as a rich lumber town. For architecture of a different, the

fabled (and faded) **Big Prawn** petrol station is 1km west of town.

White and sandy, like all good beaches, **Shelly Beach** is patrolled. Calm **Shaws Bay Lagoon** is popular with families.

Cruises up the Richmond River are a good way to get away from it all; **Richmond River Cruises** (☎ 6687 5688; Regatta Ave; 2hr trip adult/child $26/13) has good views from its two-deck boat.

Just north of Ballina, the **Thursday Plantation** (☎ 1800 029 000; Pacific Hwy; �a 9am-5pm) is an established vendor of products made with tea tree oil. Its roots go back to local markets. It lures visitors with a large sculpture garden.

Activities
Ballina's many waterways are lined with paths, so it's good for biking and walking. **Jack Ransom Cycles** (☎ 6686 3485; Cherry St; �a 8am-5pm Mon-Fri, 8am-noon Sat), rents bikes from $20 per day.

Ballina Boat Hire (☎ 6681 6115; cnr Brunswick St & Winton Lane; per half-day $90) has tinnies for fishing and catamarans for the more adventurous.

Ballina Ocean Tours (☎ 0408 863 999; www.ballinaoceantours.com; tours from $45) has whale- and dolphin-watching tours, snorkelling and various other exciting aquatic diversions.

Sleeping
River St and the northern approach from the Pacific Hwy both have many motels to choose from. Among the local holiday-rental agents is **Ballina Professionals** (☎ 6686 3511; www.professionalsballina.com.au; cnr Martin & River Sts).

Shaws Bay Caravan Park (☎ 6681 1413; www.bscp.com.au/shawsbay; 1 Brighton St; camp sites from $22, cabins from $54; wi-fi) Right on the lagoon and low-key, it's an easy walk to the centre; there are 123 sites.

Ballina Travellers Lodge YHA (☎ 6686 6737; 36-38 Tamar St; dm/s/d from $25/65/75; ✂ 🖥 🛄) Part hostel, part motel, this quiet one-storey place has modern rooms. Bikes and body boards are available for hire if you want to leave the ink-blot-shaped pool.

Hi-Craft Motel (☎ 6686 8868; hi-craft@bigpond.com; 297 River St; r $65-135; ✂ ; wi-fi) If there's a friendlier motel in town, it's probably been shut by the saccharine police. The welcome here is warm and the 26 rooms in a two-storey block are basic and comfortable.

Ramada Ballina (☎ 1800 826 181; www.ramadaballina.com.au; 2 Martin St; r from $130; ✂ 🛄 ; wi-fi) Part of a flash new development right on the river, the Ramada has large rooms that come with king-sized beds, work desks, spa tubs and balconies

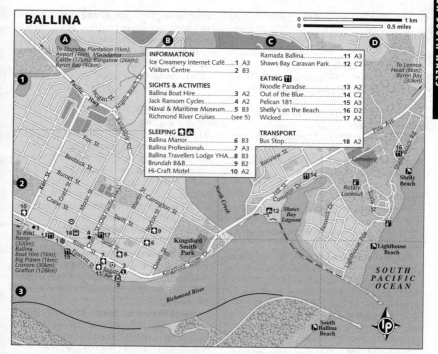

with great views. One-bedroom apartments are available (and you can buy a time-share in one should you feel light-headed). The swish café is popular with local scenesters.

Brundah B&B (☎ 6686 8166; www.babs.com.au/brundah/; 37 Norton St; s/d $145/190; 🐾) This restored 1908 Federation home is completely surrounded by lovely gardens. The three large bedrooms have access to splendid public spaces and a library.

Ballina Manor (☎ 6681 5888; www.ballinamanor.com.au; 25 Norton St; r $165-250; 🐾 ; wi-fi) One of the best places to stay in the region, this boutique hotel began in the 1920s as an Edwardian-style girls' school. The 12 rooms have been beautifully restored and boast many antiques. The small restaurant serves dinner.

Eating & Drinking

Ice Creamery Internet Café (☎ 6686 5783; 178 River St; snacks $3; 🕒 7am-5pm; 🖳) Sip a good banana smoothie or an espresso while you surf the internet ($1 per 5 minutes).

Noodle Paradise (☎ 6686 6632; 216 River St; mains $10; 🕒 lunch & dinner) One of several cheap and cheerful takeaways on this little strip.

Singapore fried noodles with extra peppers and garlic will have you singing.

Shelly's on the Beach (☎ 6686 9844; Shelly Beach Rd; meals $8-15; 🕒 breakfast & lunch) The mist from the surf over the dunes will help perk up your tired cheeks. The fine brekkies and lunchtime sambos will fuel your day.

Pelican 181 (☎ 6686 9181; 12-24 Fawcett St; meals $6-20; 🕒 breakfast, lunch & dinner) A breezy fish-and-chips restaurant and takeaway right on the river. Prawn baguettes are irresistible for many.

Out of the Blue (☎ 6686 6602; 3 Compton Dr; mains $15-25; 🕒 lunch Sun, dinner Wed-Sat) The good views of Shaw's Bay complement the huge variety of fresh seafood and daily specials at this popular restaurant. Lots of daily specials.

Wicked (☎ 6686 2564; 37 Cherry St; mains $24-30; 🕒 dinner Wed-Sun) Global tastes flavour the excellent seafood at this chic open-air bistro. Portuguese *piri-piri* prawns, Boston clam chowder, piquant Thai fish cakes and more delight the nightly crowds.

Getting There & Around

If you're driving to Byron Bay, take the coast road through Lennox Head. It's much prettier than the Pacific Hwy and less traffic-clogged as well.

AIR
Ballina's airport (BNK) is the best way to reach Byron Bay – only 30km to the north. It has car rental desks and plenty of local transport options. Airline service is increasing.

Jetstar (☎ 13 15 38; www.jetstar.com.au) Serves Melbourne and Sydney.

Regional Express (☎ 13 17 13; www.regionalexpress .com.au) Serves Sydney.

Virgin Blue (☎ 13 67 89; www.virginblue.com.au) Serves Melbourne and Sydney.

BUS
Greyhound (☎ 13 14 99; www.greyhound.com.au) stops at the Big Prawn, 1km southwest town. **Premier** (☎ 13 34 10; www.premierms.com.au) stops at the Tamar St bus stop.

Blanch's Bus Service (☎ 6686 2144; www.blanchs .com.au) operates several daily services from the airport and the Tamar St bus stop to Lennox Head ($6, 30 minutes), Byron Bay ($10, 70 minutes) and Mullumbimby ($10, 85 minutes). **Kirklands Buslines** (☎ 6626 1499; www.kirk lands.com.au) offers similar but less frequent service.

CountryLink (☎ 13 22 32; www.countrylink.com.au) has buses connecting to trains at the Casino train station (70 minutes).

CAR RENTAL
Companies with desks at the airport include:

Avis (☎ 6686 7650; www.avis.com)

Ballina Byron Rental Cars (☎ 6687 4009; www.bbrc .com.au)

Budget (☎ 6686 9955; www.budget.com)

Byron Bay RentaCar (☎ 6685 5517)

Hertz (☎ 6686 2143; www.hertz.com)

SHUTTLES
Numerous shuttle companies meet flights and serve Ballina, Byron Bay and other nearby towns. Rates average $15 to $20.

Airport Express (☎ 0414 660 031; www.stevestours .com.au)

Byron Easy Bus (☎ 6685 7447; www.byronbayshuttle .com.au)

AROUND BALLINA
Inland from Ballina, the closely settled country of the north coast hinterland begins with winding, hilly roads running past tropical fruit farms, tiny villages and the occasional towering rainforest tree that has somehow escaped the wholesale clearing of the forest.

Come out of your shell at the **Macadamia Castle** (☎ 6687 8432; Pacific Hwy; ☺ 8.30am-5pm), a classic roadside attraction some 17km north of Ballina. Kids go nuts here.

LENNOX HEAD
☎ 02 / pop 5900
Think of it as Byron Jr. Once sleepy Lennox Head now has the buzz and crowds of its flashier neighbour to the north. A vibrant strip of stylish shops and cafés fronts the long and popular beach. Surfing is part of the local culture and the breaks here have been declared a state surfing reserve, which means planning will include preservation of the local surfing culture, dude. **Seven Mile Beach**, north of Lennox, is a mostly people free.

Lake Ainsworth is a freshwater lake conducive to pleasant swimming and windsurfing. Swimming there can be somewhat beneficial to the skin as the water has a trace of tea-tree oil.

Wind & Water Action Sports (☎ 0419 686 188; www .windnwater.net; sailboard or longboard per day $60) rents boards for surfing or powered by kite or wind. Kitesurfing lessons are $110 per hour.

Sleeping
The **Professionals** (☎ 6687 7579; www.professionalslen noxhead.com.au; 66 Ballina St) is a good agent for holiday rentals.

Lake Ainsworth Caravan Park (☎ 6687 7249; www .bscp.com.au/lakeains; Pacific Pde; camp sites $21, cabins $71) Across from the hostel, this 293-site holiday park is right along the lake and enjoys cool breezes.

Lennox Head Beachouse YHA (☎ 6687 7636; www .yha.com.au; 3 Ross St; dm/d $26/62; 🖳) You'll be in the pink at this rosy-hued 46-bed purpose-built hostel that's only 100m from the beach. You can rent boards, sailboards and bikes or get a massage.

Eating
In The Pink (☎ 6687 5552; 76 Ballina St; cones $3; ☺ 10am-7pm) Serves homemade ice cream; the dreamy passion fruit may cause you to burst your banana hammock.

Red Rock Cafe (☎ 6687 4744; 3/60 Ballina St; mains $10-12; ☺ breakfast, lunch & dinner; wi-fi) A delightful pavement café that gets a loyal following of holidaymakers on their second day. Big brekkies, scrumptious burgers, salads and more are all made with zesty extra touches.

Lime (☎ 6687 7132; 1/70 Ballina St; meals $10-20; ☻ 7am-5pm) A classic Mod Oz café with lots of comfy chairs in a stylish open-air setting across from the beach. Breakfast features plenty of egg dishes bearing the name Benedict; lunch features a BLAST – which takes a BLT and adds avocado and Swiss cheese. Yum!

7 Mile Café (☎ 6687 6210; 41 Pacific Pde; mains $12-24; ☻ lunch & dinner Wed-Sun) Just north of the commercial strip, this simple place offers shady outdoor seating. The menu runs from burgers to pasta to seafood. It's licensed so you can have a snoot while you choose.

Getting There & Away
Blanch's Bus Service (☎ 6686 2144; www.blanchs.com.au) has daily service to Byron Bay and Ballina.

BYRON BAY
☎ 02 / pop 7100

New South Wales doesn't hurt for beaches, in fact go a short distance north and south from Byron Bay and you'll find untrod beaches stretching beyond your vision. Byron's beaches are nice as well, but what makes them special is Byron itself: one of Australia's best beach towns. Low-rise, funky, walkable, relaxed are all good descriptions. It is everything that the overhyped, overdeveloped towns across the border in Queensland are not.

Of course Byron does get crowded, which is in direct conflict with it's mellow charms. Jonson St can seize up like the arteries of a pie addict and the bars can get jammed. Developers would cheerfully turn Byron into a Surfers Paradise given the chance. But locals are dedicated to preserving the essential small-town soul even as everyone wants a piece. The left-wing council is constantly under assault from business interests and property prices are sending residents packing.

The thing to remember about Byron is that under all the glitz it is still at heart a small town. The whole place is set up for the several thousand who live there year-round. So if the roads were widened and new shopping centres built, the charm would be gone.

Byron was a quiet, unassuming little village until 1963. That year surfers discovered 'The Pass' and over the following years the town became a cauldron of artistically minded people. Surfers adore the seven different beachfronts that surround the point, knowing that at least one will always have a break.

Information
In addition to the resources listed here, the website www.byron-bay.com is helpful. The *Pink Guide* is a local publication aimed at gay and lesbian tourists; have a look at its useful website (www.byronbaypinkguide.blogspot.com).

BOOKSHOPS
Byron Book Exchange (☎ 6685 5458; 31A Fletcher St) Lots of used books.
Mary Ryan's (☎ 6685 8183; 21-25 Fletcher St) Good selection, has author signings and a small café.

INTERNET ACCESS
Byron has many internet-access places that cram customers together in tight, sweaty little pods to stare at tiny screens. The Balcony and One One One have wi-fi (see p276).
Global Gossip (☎ 6680 9140; 84 Jonson St; per hr $8; 🖳) Internet access.

LAUNDRY
Coin Laundry (☎ 0427 6685 0427; cnr Jonson & Marvell Sts; load $9; ☻ 7am-7pm)

MEDICAL SERVICES
Bay Centre Medical Clinic (☎ 6685 6206; 6 Lawson St; ☻ 8am-5pm Mon-Fri, 8am-noon Sat) Full- service general surgery.
Byron Bay Hospital (☎ 6685 6200; cnr Wordsworth & Shirley Sts; ☻ 24hr) For medical emergencies.
ChemCoast Pharmacy (☎ 6685 6274; 31 Jonson St; ☻ 8am-8pm)

MONEY
Byron Foreign Exchange (☎ 6685 7787; Central Arcade, 4/47 Byron St; ☻ 9am-5pm Mon-Sat, 10am-4pm Sun; 🖳) Foreign exchange, cash and money transfers, internet access.

TOURIST INFORMATION
Backpackers World (☎ 6685 8858; www.backpackersworld.com.au; Shop 6, 75 Jonson St; ☻ 9.30am-7pm Mon-Fri, noon-6pm Sat & Sun; 🖳) Primarily a travel agent.
Byron Bus & Backpacker Centre (☎ 6685 5517; 84 Jonson St; ☻ 7.30am-7pm) Next to the coach stop; handles bus, train, accommodation and activity bookings. Has left-luggage lockers ($6).
Byron Environmental Centre (Octagonal hut, Jonson St) The hours are highly sporadic but the passions of these local environmentalists are not.

BYRON BAY

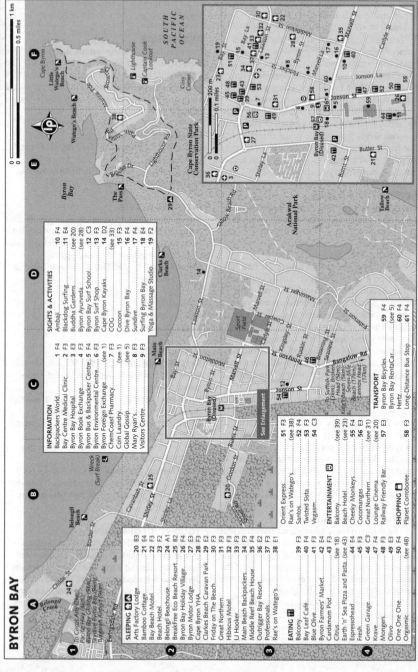

INFORMATION

Backpackers World	1 F4
Bay Centre Medical Clinic	2 F3
Byron Bay Hospital	3 E3
Byron Book Exchange	4 F3
Byron Bus & Backpacker Centre	5 F4
Byron Environmental Centre	6 F3
Byron Foreign Exchange	(see 1)
ChemCoast Pharmacy	7 F3
Coin Laundry	(see 5)
Global Gossip	8 F3
Mary Ryan's	9 F3

SIGHTS & ACTIVITIES

Ambaji	10 F4
Blackdog Surfing	11 E4
Buddha Gardens	(see 20)
Byron Ayurveda	12 C3
Byron Bay Surf School	13 F3
Byron Surf Shop	14 D2
Cape Byron Kayaks	(see 1)
COG	15 F3
Cocoon	16 F4
Dive Byron Bay	17 F4
Sundive	18 E4
Surfing Byron Bay	19 F2
Yoga & Massage Studio	

SLEEPING

Arts Factory Lodge	20 B3
Bamboo Cottage	21 E4
Bay Beach Motel	22 F3
Beach Hotel	23 F3
Belongil Beachouse	24 A1
BreakFree Eco Beach Resort	25 B2
Byron Bay Holiday Village	26 F4
Byron Motor Lodge	27 F3
Cape Byron YHA	28 F3
Clarkes Beach Caravan Park	29 E2
Friday on The Beach	30 F3
Great Northern	31 F3
Hibiscus Motel	32 F3
LJ Hooker	33 F3
Main Beach Backpackers	34 F3
Middle Reef Beach House	35 F4
Outrigger Bay Resort	36 F2
Professionals	37 F3
Rae's on Watego's	38 E1

EATING

Balcony	39 F3
Bay Leaf Café	40 F4
Blue Olive	41 F3
Byron Farmers' Market	42 E4
Cardamom Pod	43 F3
Citrus	(see 18)
Earth 'n' Sea Pizza and Pasta	(see 43)
Espressohead	44 F3
Fresh	45 F3
Green Garage	46 C3
Krave	47 F4
Mongers	48 F3
Olivo	49 E3
One One One	50 F4
Orgasmic	(see 48)
Orient Express	51 F3
Rae's on Watego's	(see 38)
Santos	52 F4
Twisted Sista	53 F3
Vegasm	54 C3

ENTERTAINMENT

Balcony	(see 39)
Beach Hotel	(see 23)
Cheeky Monkeys	55 F4
Cocomangas	56 E3
Great Northern	(see 31)
Lounge Cinema	(see 20)
Railway Friendly Bar	57 E3

SHOPPING

Planet Corroboree	58 F3

TRANSPORT

Byron Bay Bicycles	59 F4
Byron Bay RentaCar	(see 5)
Hertz	60 F4
Long-Distance Bus Stop	61 F4

Visitors centre (☎ 6680 9279; www.visitbyronbay
.com; Stationmaster's Cottage, Jonson St; ⊙ 9am-5pm)
Ground zero for tourist information (and when it's busy
this cramped office feels like it).

Sights

CAPE BYRON

Many think the town is the namesake of
George Gordon Lord Byron, but they're off
by two generations, Captain Cook named this
spot for his grandfather while they were sailing past in the 1770s. (Later bureaucrats as-
sumed it was the poet's grandson who'd been
honoured and planned out streets with names
such as Jonson and Shelley.) Among the
spectacular views, you can see dolphins and
humpback whales, which pass nearby during
their northern (June to July) and southern
(September to November) migrations.

You can drive right up to the picturesque
1901 **lighthouse** (☎ 6685 6585; ⊙ 8am-sunset), but
it'll cost you $7 to park (there's free parking
300m below). There are good displays and
if you like it here, you can stay; see p275 for
details. **Tours** (adult/child $8/6; ⊙ 11am, 12.30 & 2pm Tue
& Sat) are illuminating. There's a 4km circular
walking track round the cape from the **Captain
Cook Lookout** on Lighthouse Rd. You've a good
chance of seeing wallabies, brush turkeys and
feral goats in the final rainforest stretch.

BEACHES

Immediately in front of town, **Main Beach** is as
good for people-watching as for swimming.
At the western edge of town, perfect **Belongil
Beach** avoids many of the crowds and is unof-
ficially clothing optional. At the east end, the
Wreck is a powerful right-hander surf break.

Clarks Beach, at the eastern end of Main
Beach, can have good surf but the best surf
is at the next few beaches going east. **The Pass**
adjoins Clarks. **Watego's** is a wide crescent of
sand with turquoise surf. There's limited parking, so use the 1.1km walk that begins at the
Captain Cook Lookout. Another 400m brings you
to **Little Watego's**, another lovely patch of sand
backed by rocks. Go another 300m east and the
only option to go further is swimming: you've
reached the easternmost point in Australia.

Tallow Beach extends 7km south of Cape
Byron. It's quite an amazing stretch of sand,
backed by Arakwal National Park, and fronting rugged open ocean. The rocks of Cape
Byron are to the north and there are many
good walks near the beach parking area ($2).

This is the place to flee the crowds and its only
a short walk or bike ride from the centre.

Past Tallow Beach, there is a rockier stretch
around **Broken Head** and the nature reserve,
where a succession of small beaches dot the
coast before opening onto **Seven Mile Beach**,
which goes all the way to Lennox Head.

The suburb of **Suffolk Park** (with more good
surf, particularly in winter) starts 5km south
of town. **Kings Beach** is a popular gay beach
and is just off Seven Mile Beach Rd near the
Broken Head Holiday Park.

Activities

Adventure sports abound in Byron Bay and
most operators offer a free pick-up service
from local accommodation. Surfing and diving are the biggest draws.

COG (☎ 6680 7066; 1-3 31 Lawson St) rents bikes
($20 per day), kayaks (half-day $45), surfboards ($25 per day) and other active gear.

Once upon a time you wanted to run away
and join the circus. You can finally make good
on this desire by taking trapeze with **Circus Arts**
(☎ 6685 6566; www.circusarts.com.au; 17 Centennial Circuit),
about 2km west of town. Type A characters
may find the juggling classes useful.

ALTERNATIVE THERAPIES

Healing hippies are just some of the many
characters ready to put your mind and body
at rest in Byron. Bulletin boards are awash in
cards for people with titles like 'Evolutionary
Facilitator'.

Ambaji (☎ 6685 6620; www.ambaji.com.au; 6 Marvell St;
treatments from $65; ⊙ 10am-4pm Mon-Sat, 11am-3pm
Sun) Hawaiian massage, aqua balance healing and more.

Buddha Gardens (☎ 6680 7844; www.buddhagar
dens.com; Arts Factory Village, 21 Gordon St; treatments
from $80; ⊙ 10am-6pm) Balinese-style day spa.

Cocoon (☎ 6685 5711; 6/11 Fletcher St; massage from
$60; ⊙ 9.30am-6pm) Offers 'healthful retreats' from
family holidays.

Byron Ayurveda Centre (☎ 6632 2244; www.ayurve
dahouse.com.au; Shop 6, Middleton St; treatments from
$45; ⊙ 9am-6pm Mon-Sat) It's exfoliation over enemas
at this restful place aimed at the masses.

Yoga and Massage Studio (☎ 0407 807 797; Main
Beach; massage from $40; ⊙ 8am-6pm Mon-Sat) Above
the surf life-saving, offers massage and yoga lessons and
treatments.

DIVING

About 3km offshore, **Julian Rocks** is a meeting
point for cold southerly and warm northerly

currents, attracting a profusion of marine species and divers alike. Much of these waters is protected by the Cape Byron Marine Park. PADI open-water certification costs about $400 locally; snorkelling/dive trips are about $50/80.

Dive Byron Bay (☎ 1800 243 483, 6685 8333; www .byronbaydivecentre.com.au; 9 Marvell St) Rentals, sales, wide range of trips and lessons.

Sundive (☎ 6685 7755; www.sundive.com.au; 8 Middleton St) A good, full-service choice.

FLYING

Byron Airwaves (☎ 6629 0354; www.byronair.cjb.net) Tandem hang-gliding ($145) and courses (from $1500).

Byron Bay Gliding (☎ 6684 7572; www.byronbayglid ing.com; Tyagarah Airport) Glider joy flights over the coast and hinterland from $95 for 20 minutes.

Skydive Byron Bay (☎ 6684 1323; www.skydiveby ronbay.com; Tyagarah Airport) Tandem dives ($214 to 299) are priced depending on altitude and time of freefall (20 to 70 seconds).

KAYAKING

Cape Byron Kayaks (☎ 6680 9555; www.capeby ronkayaks.com; tours from $60) See dolphins and turtles.

SURFING

Most hostels provide free boards to guests, or you can rent equipment. Classes typically start at $65.

Blackdog Surfing (☎ 6680 9828; www.blackdogsurf ing.com; Shop 8, The Plaza, Jonson St) Intimate group lessons and women's courses.

Byron Bay Surf School (☎ 1800 707 274; www .byronbaysurfschool.com; 127 Jonson St; classes from $60) Most students enjoy the lab work.

Byron Surf Shop (☎ 6685 7536; cnr Lawson & Fletcher Sts) Shop selling gear and renting boards (from $30) and wetsuits ($5).

Surfing Byron Bay (☎ 6685 7099; www.gosurfingby ronbay.com; 84 Jonson St) Has courses for kids.

Tours

Numerous operators run tours to Nimbin and other interesting places in the hinterland. See p283 for details. Most tour companies will pick you up from where you're staying.

Mountain Bike Tours (☎ 1800 122 504, 0429-122 504; www.mountainbiketours.com.au; per person from $100) Environmentally friendly bike tours.

Festivals & Events

East Coast International Blues & Roots Music Festival (☎ 6685 8310; www.bluesfest.com.au) Held over

Easter, this international jam attracts high-calibre international performers and local heavyweights. Book early.

Splendour in the Grass (www.splendourinthegrass .com) Held in late July/early August, this indie music festival includes funk, electronica, folk, rock, hip-hop and a host of other genres. Book early.

Byron Bay Writers Festival (☎ 6685 5115; www .byronbaywritersfestival.com.au) In late July/early August, this gathers together top-shelf writers and literary followers from across Australia.

Taste of Byron (www.atasteofbyron.com) Celebration of regional produce, held in late September.

Sleeping

There's every kind of accommodation you could hope for in and around Byron. Just don't be a bonehead and turn up in January without a reservation or you'll join the hordes of backpackers and jet-set models milling around the visitors centre with hang-dog looks because they thought there would be just one more room.

Motels are clustered in town and south along Bangalow Rd. There are scores of B&Bs and apartments all along Belongil Beach.

The **Accommodation booking office** (☎ 1300 465 669, 6680 8666; www.byronbayaccom.net), run by the visitor centre, is a great service for booking in advance.

Holiday houses during low/peak season cost from $400/600 per week and go much, much higher. Rental agents:

LJ Hooker (☎ 6685 7300; www.ljhooker.com; 4/31 Lawson St)

Professionals (☎ 6685 6552; www.byronbaypro .au; cnr Lawson & Fletcher Sts)

BUDGET

Byron has more than 10 hostels; here is a selection.

Cape Byron YHA (☎ 6685 8788, 1800 652 627; www .yha.com.au; cnr Middleton & Byron Sts; dm/d from $25/82; ❌ 🖥 ☎) This two-storey complex is situated close to the town centre and has its own shops and heated pool. It's a modern and tidy place.

Belongil Beachouse (☎ 6685 7868; www.be longilbeachouse.com; Childe St; dm/d from $28/70, self-contained cottages from $160; 🖥) Across from Belongil Beach in a park-like area, this stylish place has excellent self-contained cabins, spartan studio units and comfortable dorms. Pick of the bunch are the cosy, self-contained doubles.

Arts Factory Lodge (☎ 6685 7709; www.artsfactory .com.au; Skinners Shoot Rd; camp sites from $15, dm/d from $30/80; 🖥 ☎) A huge pool set in lush tropical forest is just one of the highlights of this vast complex that includes pubs and a café. Bunk down in a tepee, tent or a dorm. There are free minibuses around town.

OUR PICK Middle Reef Beach House (☎ 6685 5118; www.middlereef.com.au; 13 Marvell St; dm from $20, s/d $50-190; 🅿️ 🅿️ ; wi-fi) Great little residential compound close to everything. Rooms are basic but very comfortable; the cheapest share bathrooms and some have patios. There are shared kitchens and dorm rooms are bunk-free.

Also recommended:

Byron Bay Holiday Village Backpackers (☎ 6685 8888; www.byronbaybackpackers.com.au; 116 Jonson St; dm from $26; 🅿️ 🅿️) Motel-style with a good vibe and lots of freebies.

Clarkes Beach Caravan Park (☎ 6685 6496; clarkes@bshp.com.au; unpowered sites/cabins from $25/120) Tightly packed cabins and sites in a bush setting off Lighthouse Rd.

Great Northern (☎ 6685 6454; Jonson St; s/d $55/65) Basic pub rooms; crash here – with or without a band member from downstairs.

Main Beach Backpackers (☎ 6685 8695; www.mainbeachbackpackers.com; cnr Lawson & Fletcher Sts; dm/d from $18/50; 🅿️ 🅿️ 🅿️) A good quality 94-bed place near the beach. There's a decent-sized pool.

MIDRANGE

Off-season, midrange places offer deals galore.

Bamboo Cottage (☎ 6685 5509; www.byron-bay.com/bamboocottage; 76 Butler St; r from $90) Featuring global charm (French and Japanese is spoken), the cottage has three rooms with a the kind of decor you end up with after several trips across Asia. Hammocks are hard to leave should you feel the call of chores in the shared kitchen.

Byron Motor Lodge (☎ 6685 6522; www.byronmotorlodge.com; cnr Lawson & Butler Sts; s/d from $95/100; 🅿️ 🅿️) This low-key low-rise 14-room motel has a central location near everything. The grounds are simple as are the rooms but everything is in perfect shape.

Hibiscus Motel (☎ 6685 6195; www.byronbayresorts.com/hibiscus; 33 Lawson St; r from $140; 🅿️) Excellent location, right in town and right near Main Beach. The seven rooms are right out of the 1960s; they're clean but there's no wry wink at their retro status.

Outrigger Bay Resort (☎ 6685 8646; www.outriggerbay.com; 9 Shirley St; r from $170; 🅿️ 🅿️ ; wi-fi) This apartment complex has one-, two- and three-bedroom units on a shady site overlooking a pool. The beach is only 50m away. The open kitchens are good for festive food fun.

Bay Beach Motel (☎ 6685 6090; www.baybeachmotel.com.au; 32 Lawson St; r $170-200; 🅿️ 🅿️) A trip to Ikea and you can transform dowdy to chic. This older motel has been given a stylish, clean-lined makeover. The large rooms are comfortable and the beach is right across the street.

BreakFree Eco Beach Resort (☎ 6639 5700; www.breakfree.com.au; 35 Shirley St; ste from $190; 🅿️ 🅿️ 🅿️) One of many holiday apartment complexes and B&Bs on this stretch of Belongil Beach, this 30-unit resort claims its 'eco' label because of the architecture is designed to blend into the surroundings.

Lighthouse Keeper Cottages (3-day rentals from $800) Located right at the Byron Bay Lighthouse (p273), these two historic 1901 cottages have been renovated with polished wood floors and lovely furnishings. The views are swell and you have the place to yourself after dusk. Book through the **Professionals** (☎ 6685 6552; www.byronbaypro.com.au).

TOP END

Friday on the Beach (☎ 1300 554 150, 6685 6373; www.fridayonthebeach.com.au; r from $180; 🅿️ 🅿️ 🅿️ ; wi-fi) Would you get that same sense of languor if it was called Monday at the Beach? This small, older motel overlooking the grassy verge behind Main Beach has been transformed into a stylish little complex. The 19 rooms are a study in taupe, go for ones with private balconies up front.

Beach Hotel (☎ 6685 6402; www.beachhotel.com.au; cnr Jonson & Bay Sts; r $240-700; 🅿️ 🅿️ ; wi-fi) Byron's hub, nothing is more central than this beachfront icon. Ground-floor rooms open onto lush gardens and a heated pool; rooms in the upper storeys have ocean views.

Rae's on Wategos's (☎ 6685 5366; www.raes.com.au; Marine Pde; d $400-1150; 🅿️ 🅿️ 🅿️ ; wi-fi) This dazzlingly white Mediterranean villa was rated by *Condé Nast Traveller* as one of the world's top 25 hotels. Rooms here have an artistic and casual elegance that lets the luxury sneak up on you. The restaurant (p276) is worth the trip alone.

Eating

You can eat well in Byron; there's a huge range of choices and many are excellent.

CAFÉS

Espressohead (☎ 6680 9783; shop 13, 108 Jonson St; snacks $3; ⏰ 8am-5pm) Tucked away behind Woolworths, locals flock to this place for its excellent coffees. See if you can count the number of dodgy vans for sale on the bulletin board.

Orgasmic (☎ 6680 7778; 11 Bay Lane; mains $6-9; ☺ 10am-10pm) Plop your bum on a cube cushion at this alley eatery that's one step above a stall. The exciting Middle Eastern food explains the name.

Twisted Sista (☎ 6680 9100; Shop 1, 4 Lawson St; mains $8-15; ☺ breakfast & lunch) Bounteous baked goods include huge muffins, cheesy casseroles and overstuffed sandwiches on beautiful bread. Outdoor tables finish the deal.

Fresh (☎ 6685 7810; 7 Jonson St; meals $7-22; ☺ breakfast, lunch & dinner) Top spot for breakfast with excellent pancakes. Mod Oz at night is great at the open-air tables. Always popular, the people-watching is half the appeal.

Bay Leaf Café (☎ 6685 8900; Marvell St; mains $10-18; ☺ breakfast & lunch) This tiny wedge-shaped bohemian café has a small but excellent menu prepared in a busy open-kitchen. Aioli and other big flavours figure in the daily changing menu of sandwiches, pastas and more.

RESTAURANTS
Vegasm (☎ 6680 7080; 130 Jonson St; mains $10; ☺ lunch & dinner) Legumes are squirting out all over at this pea-sized vegan eatery. Pizzas with organic crusts are popular as are the lentil pies and salads.

One One One (☎ 6680 7388; 1/111 Jonson St; mains $10-25; ☺ breakfast & lunch daily, dinner Fri & Sat; wi-fi) HQ for slow food devotees locally, the ingredients celebrate regional produce. The menu is mostly vegetarian save for some superb spiced prawns and other seafood. Flavours are mostly Med and plates are good for sharing.

Earth 'n' Sea Pizza & Pasta (☎ 6685 6029; 11 Lawson St; mains $15-20; ☺ lunch & dinner) The pizza list at this old favourite is long and full of flavour (eg the Capriciosa, a ham, pepperoni, mushroom and anchovies gem). Beers include several excellent microbrews from the Northern Rivers Brewing Co.

Balcony (☎ 6680 9666; cnr Lawson & Jonson Sts; dinner $18-30; ☺ breakfast, lunch & dinner; wi-fi) The eponymous architectural feature here wraps around the building and gives you tremendous views of the passing Byron parade and the always clogged traffic circle. The food is Mediterranean fusion, with global influences. The drink list is long.

Orient Express (☎ 6680 8808; 1/2 Fletcher St; mains $20-30; ☺ lunch & dinner) At first you might think you're in a stylish Asian decorator's shop but no, you're in one of the best restaurants in Byron. Unlike some places, the Thai-Vietnamese menu here is fairly brief but, you guessed it, full of flavour. Expect to wait.

Olivo (☎ 6685 7950; 34 Jonson St; mains $25-30; ☺ dinner) The long and narrow brick-walled space here is complemented by beige leather seating. The menu features local produce and is heavily accented by Mediterranean flavours. A steak will come with polenta, roasted fish will be covered in capers etc. The dark chocolate mousse always rewards those with fortitude.

Rae's on Wategos (☎ 6685 5366; Marine Pde; mains $40-45; ☺ lunch & dinner) Exquisite Mod Oz cuisine on a terrace with the sound of surf providing background noise to your witticisms. The menu changes daily but always surprises with its unconventional pairings of ingredients and spices. Book ahead.

QUICK EATS
Krave (3/93 Jonson St; meals from $7; ☺ 10am-10pm) This sparkly storefront serves a profusion of juices and kebabs right off the grill.

Mongers (☎ 6680 8080; 1 Bay Lane; meals $9-15; ☺ lunch & dinner) Tucked behind the Beach Hotel, the region's best fish and chips issue forth to tables of devotes. It's a narrow, back alley space but the quality is all high street.

Cardamom Pod (Shop 8, Pier Arcade, 7 Lawson St; meals $10-16; ☺ lunch & dinner) Tucked off the street, this small vegetarian Indian place is the counterpoint to the donut shop next door.

SELF-CATERING
Blue Olive (☎ 6680 8700; 27 Lawson St; ☺ 10am-5.30pm Mon-Sat, 10am-4pm Sun) Fine cheeses and deli items; enjoy the beautiful prepared foods at shady pavement tables.

Byron Farmers' Market (☎ 6685 9792; Butler St; ☺ 8-11am Thu) This is an open-air temple to the amazing food produced in the region.

Citrus (☎ 6680 7040; 130 Jonson St; ☺ 9.30am-6pm Mon-Fri, 9.30am-4pm Sat) Small deli with tables inside and out.

Green Garage (☎ 6680 8577; 68 Tennyson St; ☺ 7am-7pm) Like an ongoing farmers market; good prepared foods.

Santos (☎ 6685 7071; 105 Jonson St; ☺ 8.30am-6.30pm Mon-Fri, 9.30am-5pm Sat, 10am-4pm Sun) A locally beloved organic food store.

Entertainment
Byron Bay's nightlife is varied and runs late. Check the gig guide in Thursday's *Byron Shire News* or tune into Bay 99.9 FM.

SLOW BUT GOOD

Victoria Cosford writes the weekly food column for the *Bryron Shire Echo*. She's been chronicling the growth of the Slow Food movement in the region (started in Italy, Slow Food puts an emphasis on eating the best local foods from non-industrial suppliers).

What should people seek out to eat in the Byron region? The local growers' markets held regularly, where regional produce is showcased (macadamias, pecans, avocados, coffee, olive oil, blueberries, pineapples – the list goes on).

Why are there so many foodies locally? People have moved up here from places like Melbourne and Sydney bringing with them their expertise, experience and knowledge of food-related issues. There are a lot of very passionate people up here – there are also a lot of people who have money and are retired or semiretired and can indulge the passion.

What does Slow Food mean locally? People think more about the provenance and sustainability of foods – it has heightened people's appreciation of regional foods.

Where should people eat? There's no real getting around the touristy restaurants, but good food can be found – just ask a local where! Which, let's face it, applies to everywhere in the world.

As told to Ryan Ver Berkmoes

CINEMAS

Lounge Cinema (☎ 6685 5833; Gordon St; admission $10) The cinema at the Arts Factory Lodge (p274) shows second-run and arthouse flicks nightly.

CLUBS

Cheeky Monkeys (☎ 6685 5886; 115 Johnson St; ☯ 7pm-3am) Mayhem is the theme at this full-on boozer. Keep your wits so things won't get out of hand.

Cocomangas (☎ 6685 8493; 32 Jonson St; ☯ 9pm-late) This bilevel gay-friendly club thrashes about to indie rock, old school, techno and fusion.

PUBS

Beach Hotel (☎ 6685 6402; cnr Jonson & Bay Sts; ☯ 11am-late) This sprawling beachfront terrace at the hotel of the same name (see p275) draws everyone from model-wannabes to beach bums. There's live music by cover bands many nights.

Balcony (☎ 6680 9666; cnr Lawson & Jonson Sts; ☯ until late) The popular restaurant (see opposite) is also a fine bar. Sit and soak up the view from stools, chairs or sofas while ploughing through the long drinks list.

Great Northern Hotel (☎ 6685 6454; Jonson St) This enormous, boisterous pub has live music and DJs many nights and Coopers ales on tap.

Railway Friendly Bar (☎ 6685 7662; Jonson St; ☯ 11am-late) The railway may have deserted Byron but this bar stays true. It's a vast indoor/outdoor pub with excellent burgers, salads, pasta and more. There's live music many nights and the excellent St Arnou beer on tap.

Shopping

You can while away hours away from the beach in Byron's many shops. Broadly speaking Fletcher St, north of Marvell St, has artsy boutiques; frock shops hover around the Lawson and Fletcher Sts traffic circle; west of here and south on Jonson St you'll find a huge range: everything from lingerie to New Age hokum.

Planet Corroboree (☎ 6680 7884; 1/69 Jonson St) has a huge range of Aboriginal art.

Getting There & Away

AIR

The closest airport is at Ballina (p270) and with its rapidly expanding service it is the best airport for Byron. It also has shuttle services and rental cars for Byron travellers.

Coolangatta airport (see p289) on the Gold Coast has a greater range of services but can involve a traffic-clogged drive. **Airport Express** (☎ 0401-622 228) serves the airport from Byron ($25).

BUS

Long-distance buses for **Greyhound** (☎ 13 14 99; www.greyhound.com.au) and **Premier** (☎ 13 34 10; www.premierms.com.au) stop on Jonson St. Approximate times and fares for both are as follows: Brisbane ($40, three hours), Coffs Harbour ($55, four hours) and Sydney ($110, 12 to 14 hours). Services operate several times daily. Check the boards at the bus stop for other Queensland options.

Blanch's Bus Service (☎ 6686 2144; www.blanchs.com.au) operates several daily services from the airport to Lennox Head ($6, 25 minutes), Ballina (Tamar St stop, $10, 40 minutes) and Mullumbimby ($10, 35 minutes). **Kirklands Buslines** (☎ 6626 1499; www.kirklands.com.au) offers similar but less frequent service.

TRAIN

People still mourn the loss of the popular CountryLink train service from Sydney. In fact a popular movie released in 2008, *Derailed*, documents this transport travesty. **CountryLink** (☎ 13 22 32; www.countrylink.com.au) has buses connecting to trains at the Casino train station (70 minutes). Get full details from the rather forlorn **train station** (☺ 10am-4pm Mon-Fri).

Getting Around

Byron Bay Bicycles (☎ 6685 6067; The Plaza, 85 Jonson St) Hires mountain bikes for $28 per day.

Byron Bay RentaCar (☎ 6685 5517; 84 Jonson St) Rents a wide range of vehicles.

Byron Bay Taxis (☎ 6685 5008) On call 24 hours.

Hertz (☎ 6621 8855; 5 Marvell St) Ask about one-way rentals to Ballina airport.

BANGALOW

☎ 02 / pop 1230

Just a short distance inland from Byron Bay (14km), Bangalow has become a major stop on the foodie circuit. Its sloping main drag (Byron St) is lined with famous and soon-to-be-famous cafés and restaurants. The odd boutique or two gives you something to do between meals.

Riverview Guesthouse (☎ 6687 1317; www.riverviewguesthouse.com.au; 99 Byron St; s/d from $95/145) is a stately Victorian house filled with Federation-period antiques. You can relive the era while soaking in a claw-foot tub.

About 4km north, **Possum Creek Eco Lodge** (☎ 6687 1188; www.possumcreeklodge.com.au; Cedarvale Rd; bungalows from $165; ☒) has views across the lush valleys. The 'eco' in the name is not green-washing – water is recycled, stored from rain and otherwise conserved. Power is partially solar. Two stylish cottages for two and a larger house have broad decks and cooking facilities.

The **farmers market** (Byron St; ☺ 8-11am Sat) is renowned for its selection of local foodstuffs.

The interior at **Utopia** (☎ 6687 2088; 13 Byron St; meals $12-16; ☺ breakfast & lunch daily, dinner Fri & Sat; ☒) is like the foam on a rich latte. The long narrow space is open and airy; piles of stylish magazines provide diversions. The fare is Mod Oz bistro with an em-phasis on local produce. There is live jazz Saturday afternoons.

Satiate (☎ 6687 1010; 33 Byron St; menu $55; ☺ dinner Tue-Sat), on the upper floor of a heritage building, has well-spaced tables sporting white tablecloths. Those out the back look over the valley. Dinner is a five-course meal; diners choose between meat, seafood and veggie and then the fun begins. The same chefs run a literally truncated version downstairs called **Ate** (meals $9-16; ☺ breakfast & lunch Tue-Sat) – deli-café combo. Grab a stool up front or a small table in the tiny rear garden. Blackboards specials can include pancakes with rhubarb or fresh pea risotto.

Another place with a split personality is **Urban** (☎ 6687 2000; 37 Byron St; meals $6-12; ☺ breakfast & dinner). By day it is an upscale corner café with luscious eggs Benedict and other treats. At night, the incense burns and it becomes **Bang Thai** (mains $20-32; ☺ dinner Thu-Sat), an ambitious restaurant with Thai food several cuts above the norm. When's the last time you had spicy prawns wrapped in betel leaves?

Blanch's Bus Service (☎ 6686 2144; www.blanchs.com.au) runs three times weekdays to Byron Bay ($6, 25 minutes) and Ballina ($10, 45 minutes).

MULLUMBIMBY

☎ 02 / pop 3050

The hip and happening are spilling over from Byron and this atmospheric former centre of animal husbandry is seeing trendy cafés and bistros appear along with the beautiful people who are drawn to them.

Burringbar St is the main shopping street and runs off Dalley St, which is the main road through town. Byron Bay is 19km southeast. A good adventure is the 20km Coolamon Scenic Drive south to Bangalow. It twists through the rugged hills and offers a surprise vista around every bend.

Sights & Activities

The best thing to do in Mullumbimby is simply walk around. Besides the interesting commercial streets, there is a trail along the Brunswick River in town that passes through tropical forest and is lined with signs relating Aboriginal stories.

The **Brunswick Valley Historical Society Museum** (☎ 6684 1149; cnr Myocum & Stuart Sts; ☺ 11am-3pm Fri & market Sat) has collections of farm implements housed in the old post office.

Art Piece Gallery (☎ 6684 3446; 105 Stuart St; ☾ 10.30am-4.30pm Mon-Fri, 10.30am-12.30pm Sat) displays art, ceramics and jewellery by many local talented artisans.

Sleeping

Maca's Camping Ground (☎ 6684 5211; Main Arm Rd, Main Arm; camp sites $15) Camping under a macadamia-nut plantation is what Maca's offers and delivers. This otherwise basic place is 12km north of town.

Mullumbimby Motel (☎ 6684 2387; www.mullumbimbymotel.com.au; 121 Dalley St; r from $80; ☒ ; wi-fi) The 10 rooms in this older one-storey building are lushly shaded by gardens. It's clean as a whistle and bits of colour spiff up the grey décor.

Mooyabil Farm Holidays (☎ 6684 1128; 448 Left Bank Rd; r from $95; ☒) Hang with a pony or make friends with a cow at this 100-acre working farm 2km west of town. There are two large two-bedroom units that have access to a 20m-long pool in addition to all the barnyard diversions.

Eating

Santos (☎ 6684 3773; 51-53 Burringbar St; meals $6; ☾ 8.30am-6pm Mon-Fri, 8.30am-2pm Sat, 10am-4.30pm Sun) Withdraw some local organic produce from this grand old bank building that's now a health food market. Deposit yourself on a veranda table for a daily lunch special from the café.

Milk & Honey (☎ 6684 1422; 59A Station St; mains $14-22; ☾ dinner Mon-Sat) Chef Chris Pellen is an artisan when it comes to pizza. The wood-fired thin-crust wonders come with a changing line-up of toppings. Lines form early for the tables inside and out. Pasta specials may well temp you to the fork-side.

Poinciana (☎ 6684 4036; 55 Station St; meals $6-20; ☾ breakfast & lunch daily, dinner Thu-Sat; wi-fi) With a patio shaded by ancient poinciana trees, you may just put down roots for a while (even if you don't join the kids in the sandbox). Tables in a little open-sided house are matched by many more outside. Breakfast choices include buckwheat crepes with fresh local fruit. Later in the day there is more savoury fare with Mediterranean touches. At night there's a long list of tapas and wine.

Getting There & Away

Blanch's Bus Service (☎ 6686 2144; www.blanchs.com.au) operates two to six times daily to Byron Bay ($6, 30 minutes) and Ballina ($10, 75 minutes).

BRUNSWICK HEADS
☎ 02 / pop 1900

Fresh oysters and mud crabs call the Brunswick River home, as do retirees and families, who love this place as a quiet getaway with good beaches and great fishing. Go for a quiet swim on the river and then cross the short bridge to the lively ocean beaches.

The **Visitor Information Centre** (☎ 6685 1003; 7 Park St; ☾ varies, usually 10am-2pm) is a great little resource.

The **Terrace Reserve Caravan Park** (☎ 6685 1233; www.northcoastparks.com.au/terrace; Fingal St; camp sites from $25, cabins from $105), right on the Simpson River and right in town, has 182 sites 500m from the beach. The 11 cabins are posh – they even have cable TV.

Much local life centres on the splendid **Hotel Brunswick** (☎ 6685 1236; www.hotelbrunswick.com.au; Mullumbimby St; s/d $50/80). It has a magnificent beer garden that unfurls beneath flourishing poincianas. On a Sunday, the place jumps. **The Bruns** (mains $15-25; ☾ lunch & dinner) serves good burgers, pasta and more; there's live music on weekends.

Chalet Motel (☎ 6685 1257; www.brunswickvalley.com.au/chaletmotel; 68 Tweed St; r $80-150; ☒ ☒) is one of a handful of motels in town and like the rest is low-key and centrally located. Many of the 9 rooms have kitchenettes.

The **Dolphin Cafe** (☎ 6685 1355; 8 The Terrace; meals $8-12; ☾ breakfast & lunch) is one of several

---

WORTH A TRIP: WOOYUNG NATURE RESERVE

Exit the newish Pacific Hwy dual carriageway at the Wooyung turn. Crossing over a cool little old wooden railway bridge, the road passes through untouched coastal NSW countryside. Drive 5km east to where the sealed road turns north up the coast. You're in the **Wooyung Nature Reserve**, a suitably undeveloped place that features a long, dune-backed beach. Pull off most anywhere for beautiful and deserted seashore. After 8km, you come to Pottsville Beach, your cue to head west back to the highway. North along the coast things only get more developed until you reach the sprawl of Tweed Heads.

excellent places that give the town its own little café culture, replete with buzzy soundtrack. It has a deli and good meals such as creative salads and sandwiches.

Easy to miss in a daggie motel, **Fat Belly Cat** (☎ 6685 1100; 26 Tweed St; mains $6-15; 🕑 dinner Wed-Mon) is a much-lauded Greek restaurant that brings feta-cheese-seekers from afar. You can't get food this good in the Old Country.

CountryLink (☎ 13 22 32; www.countrylink.com.au) has buses to Byron Bay ($5, 30 minutes) and Casino (90 minutes) for the train connection.

TWEED HEADS

Tweed Heads is the butt end of the Gold Coast – and that's not a good place to be. The mirrored-glass high-rises have nothing to do with the cool vibe of the beach towns to the south. But the showy lack of taste at the water pales in comparison to the nightmare of strip malls littering the Pacific Hwy.

Tweed Heads represents the beginning of the Gold Coast strip, the 18m monument at **Point Danger** a testament to the ghastly designs that are apparent along this belt. The border between NSW and Queensland can pass by

---

MARKETS

You can get a real insight to the far north coast and hinterland at one of the myriad markets, which bring together hippies, yuppies and just about anyone else you can imagine. The food offerings are exquisite and diverse and you get a chance to experience the region first-hand.

Expect to find oodles of seasonal organic produce along with other foodstuffs such as farmhouse cheeses, honey and baked goods. There are often vendors selling crafts and it's common to hear some live folk music, especially at the weekend markets. Hours can be erratic, but you're safest aiming to arrive in the morning.

Weekly Markets
Bangalow Farmer's Market (Byron St; 🕑 8-11am Sat) Organic produce.
Byron Farmers' Market (Butler St; 🕑 8-11am Thu)
Lismore Farmers Market (Lismore Showground; 🕑 8am-noon Sat)
Rainbow Region Organic Markets (Lismore Showground; 🕑 8-11am Tue)

First Weekend of the Month
Brunswick Heads (Memorial Park; 🕑 Sat)
Byron Community Market (Butler St; 🕑 Sun)
Lismore Car Boot Market (Lismore Shopping Centre; 🕑 Sun)

Second Weekend of the Month
Alstonville Market (Apex Pavilion, Alstonville Showground; 🕑 Sun)
Channon Craft Market (Coronation Park; 🕑 Sun)
Lennox Head Lakeside Market (Lake Ainsworth Foreshore; 🕑 Sun)

Third Weekend of the Month
Aquarius Fair Markets (Nimbin Community Centre; 🕑 Sun) Produce and art. Live music.
Ballina Markets (Canal Rd; 🕑 Sun)
Lismore Car Boot Market (Lismore Shopping Centre; 🕑 Sun)
Mullumbimby Museum Market (Stuart St; 🕑 Sat)
Uki Buttery Bazaar (Uki Village Buttery; 🕑 Sun)

Fourth Weekend of the Month
Bangalow Village Market (Bangalow centre; 🕑 Sun)
Evans Head Riverside Market (Recreation Reserve; 🕑 Sat)

Fifth Weekend of the Month
Aquarius Fair Markets (Nimbin Community Centre; 🕑 Sun) Produce and art. Live music.
Lennox Head Lakeside Market (Lake Ainsworth Showground; 🕑 Sun)

unnoticed, as there is no river or landmark, but rather an imaginary line and a lot of cars caught in traffic.

Most of the cafés, surfers' bars and motels are just over the border in Coolangatta (Tweed Heads having cornered the market on discount auto-parts stores). See p290 for places to sleep and eat locally.

The **Minjungbal Aboriginal Cultural Centre** (☎ 5524 2109; cnr Kirkwood & Duffy Sts; adult/child $15/7.50; ☺ 9am-4pm Mon-Fri) is set in a grove of old gum trees on the Tweed River. Displays detail how the Minjungbal people were able to live in harmony with the land.

Tweed Heritage Maritime Museum (☎ 5536 8625; Kennedy Dr; adult/child $5/1; ☺ 11am-4pm Tue, Thu & Fri, 1-4pm Sun) has an array of photos documenting the time when locals fished for fish and not tourists.

FAR NORTH COAST HINTERLAND

It's not all beach. Away from the coast, the lush scenery, organic markets and alternative lifestyles inland complement places such as Byron Bay and make the far north coast region one of Australia's most appealing places – for locals and visitors alike. In fact the post-hippy rural lifestyle out here has become so mainstream that the epicentre of Nimbin is almost a theme park.

Twenty-two million years ago, an eruption of lava from Mt Warning created the northern half of the hinterland, flattening the valley and enclosing it with dramatic mountain ranges. The southern end is a maze of steep hills and beautiful valleys, some still harbouring magnificent stands of rainforest. Other parts of the area have been cleared for cattle grazing as well as macadamia-nut, avocado and coffee plantations. The area's three national parks – Border Ranges, Mt Warning and Nightcap – are all World Heritage rainforest.

LISMORE
☎ 02 / pop 27,400
A great base for visiting the hinterland, or even Byron, Lismore is close to rainforest, beaches and the river, has some interesting cafés and bookstores and has a thriving arts scene. The campus of Southern Cross University gives the town a young vibe.

The excellent **visitors centre** (☎ 6622 0122; Ballina St; Internet access per 15min $2.50; ☺ 9.30am-4pm) has a rainforest display ($1). Little kids dig the **Heritage Park** playground, next to the centre, with its skate park and **train rides** ($2; ☺ 10am-2pm Thu, 10am-4pm Sat).

The **Lismore Regional Art Gallery** (☎ 6622 2209; www.lismore.nsw.gov.au/gallery; 131 Molesworth St; admission by donation; ☺ 10am-4pm Tue-Sat) displays the works of many local artists and has an evocative collection of old photos from Nimbin's early hippy days.

The **Koala Care & Research Centre** (☎ 6622 1233; www.friendsofthekoala.org; Rifle Range Rd; admission $3; ☺ 10am & 2pm Mon-Fri, 10am Sat) is home to recovering koalas and well worth a visit (you can view animals from outside anytime). It is 2km east of the centre. To get a glimpse of a platypus, head up the north end of Kadina St and walk up to **Tucki Tucki Creek**; your best bet to witness these animals in the wild is at dawn or dusk.

More than a half dozen used book stores are within a block of the intersection of Carrington and Magellan Sts. Typical is **Noahs Arc** (☎ 6621 8169; 66 Magellan St), which has a large selection in a heritage building.

Sleeping
With a couple of exceptions. Lismore is not a motel mecca. Most people stay in the hinterland's villages or closer to the coast.

Lismore Palms Caravan Park (☎ 6621 7067; 42 Brunswick St; camp sites from $16, cabins from $60; ☒) The best of Lismore's caravan parks, this one is right on the river and has 13 self-contained cabins.

Wilson Motel (☎ 6622 3383; 119 Ballina St; r from $90; ☒ ; wi-fi) The pick of the litter, the Wilson is a low-rise place close to the centre with 25 large and comfortable rooms. The décor may leave you cold but the welcome is warm.

Eating & Drinking
Lismore stages its farmers market every Saturday at the Showground, off Nimbin Rd. Several good cafés make is a good place to pause.

Goanna Bakery & Café (☎ 6622 2629; 171 Keen St; mains $6-10; ☺ breakfast & lunch Mon-Sat) An amazing and inventive bakery makes stupendous treats. Try the house-roasted coffee and some of the enticing veggie meals at tables inside or out.

Left Bank Café (☎ 6622 2338; 133 Molesworth St; mains $8-20; ☺ breakfast & lunch Mon-Sat, dinner Fri &

Sat; wi-fi) The art gallery's café, the Left Bank manages just a touch of Parisian snobbery. Although the Mod Oz meals will put your nose in the air sniffing for more too.

Mega Pizza (☎ 6622 2900; Wyrallah Rd Shopping Centre; meals $11-14; ◷ 4.30pm-late) Chef Barry is the hinterland's pizza sorcerer, cooking up pies with a range of unusual flavours including chicken satay and seafood cocktail. Go for crispy and thin. It's all take-away so you'll have to picnic.

Mecca Café (☎ 6621 3901; 80 Magellan St; meals $8-16; ◷ 7am-5pm Mon-Wed, 7am-late Thu-Sat) A stodgy old caff has been reborn as a retro-hip scenester playground. Lots of local musicians hang out at the pavement tables sipping the excellent coffee by day and jamming till late weekend nights.

Entertainment

Lismore has a number of typical large pubs that literally burst with liquored up rural folks on weekends.

For a total change of pace, try the vintage **Winsome Hotel** (☎ 6621 2283; 11 Bridge St), which sits proudly across the river from the centre and has regular sessions with DJs and bands. There's some outdoor seating, a small bistro and events that are gay- and lesbian-friendly.

Getting There & Away

Lismore may well have the most helpful transit centre in NSW. It's right on Molesworth St by the gallery.

Kirklands (☎ 6622 1499; www.kirklands.com.au) runs to Byron Bay ($15, 50 minutes, two to three times daily). **Waller's** (☎ 6687 8550) school buses run to Nimbin ($10, 70 minutes).

THE CHANNON

The Channon is an intimate village on a detour between Nimbin and Lismore. If you can, time your visit for the second Sunday of each month for a true classic hinterlands craft market. Other times you'll find a café and old pub where you can chill out and find out about the many idiosyncratic B&Bs hidden in the hills.

Eternity Springs B&B (☎ 6688 6385; www.eternitysprings.com; 483 Tuntable Creek Rd; camping per person $12, s/d from $50/80) is a true eco-haven. Choose from cosy 'cubbies' with private verandas and shared bathrooms; en-suite doubles filled with art; or the stylish, self-contained, one-bedroom 'Lotus Room'. Eco features include spring water, solar power, permaculture, flushing compost toilets and organic breakfasts.

Havan's (☎ 6688 6108; www.rainbowregion.com/havan; Lot 1, Lawler Rd; s/d $75/125) is an ecotourist retreat set in the heart of a rainforest. There are numerous walks near the property, including ones where you can see platypus and other exotic creatures plus treks to waterfalls. The owner offers courses in yoga and painting.

NIGHTCAP NATIONAL PARK

South of Murwillumbah, north of Lismore and bordering Nimbin and The Channon is the Nightcap National Park, encompassing 8080 hectares. It was given World Heritage status in 1989.

The park is home to diverse subtropical rainforests and many species of wildlife, notably the bent-winged bat, the wompoo fruit-dove, the masked owl and the red-legged pademelon (a type of wallaby). With the highest annual rainfall in NSW, the park has spectacular waterfalls, gorgeous green gullies and sheer cliff walls. The exposed rock pinnacles of the **Sphinx** can be seen from Lismore.

You can choose from walks, lookouts and picnic spots to enjoy, and **Mt Nardi** (800m) offers a challenging climb. However, most of the access is on unsealed roads and the park is – rightfully – undeveloped.

WHIAN WHIAN STATE FOREST

Timber is still produced in this **state forest** (☎ 6627 0200), which is unfortunate given the beauty of the area. The forest adjoins the southeast side of Nightcap National Park and is home to the Albert's lyrebird. There are plans to develop camping areas.

The spectacular **Minyon Falls** are found here, plunging over 100m into a rainforest gorge and surrounded by a flora reserve with several walking tracks. Take a dip under the falls for an unforgettable experience.

The **Nightcap Track** (16km long) passes through state forest and Nightcap National Park, and was the original track used by postal workers and others in the late 19th and early 20th centuries. **Rummery Park** is not far off the road down from the falls and has a picnic spot with barbecues and cold showers. **Peate's Mountain Lookout**, just on from Rummery Park, gives you a great panoramic view from

Jerusalem Mountain in the north to Byron Bay in the east.

Mud Manor Forest Retreat (☎ 6688 2205; www.mudmanor.com; Fox Rd, Rosebank; r from $120; 🖳 🏊), southeast of the state forest, is a perfect haven for those who just want to get away from the crowds. The building is built of bricks made on site and the two rooms have large decks. It is roughly equidistant by country road from The Channon and Bangalow (20km).

NIMBIN
☎ 02 / pop 500

A true product of the hippy-era and the legendary 1973 Aquarius Festival, Nimbin works so hard at being alternative it's almost mainstream. But not too mainstream. Bra is still an abbreviation for brass here even if the tattoos are still red around the edges and the didgeridoo players went to the best Sydney prep schools. Characters young and old prowl the streets and there are numerous businesses and community centres that attest to the unique culture found locally.

Nimbin is a study in contrasts. At noon when the hordes of bused-in day-trippers from Byron are prowling the streets in gaggles while being hectored by pot dealers it can all seem literally like a bad trip. (This scene took a hit in 2008 when a huge force of heavily armed state police made mass arrests of pot dealers.)

At other times when the true locals are dominant, you get a sense of the real Nimbin, where anyone searching for a real rainbow might just find it.

Orientation & Information
Nimbin is actually a tiny village, easily walked in a few minutes. Most businesses are on Cullen St – and green alert! – there's lots of parking out the back.

Given that some locals would have a hard time answering the question: 'Which came first, Nimbin or the organic farms?', it shouldn't surprise that there are nearly 100 local farms more than happy to host volunteers willing to yank weeds and perform other chores. The international **Willing Workers on Organic Farms** (www.wwoof.com.au) coordinates many such programs.

The **Nimbin Visitors Centre** (☎ 6689 1388; www.visitlismore.com; 80 Cullen St; ⏲ 10am-4pm Mon-Sat) is at the northern end of town and has accommodation options, bus tickets and a wealth

of knowledge. The community website (www.nimbinweb.com.au) is useful. Blow your mind listening to 2NIM 102.3FM.

Sights & Activities
Despite the reticence of many locals to be pinned down on exact opening times, for fear of ruining Nimbin's image, generally everything is open 10am to 6pm.

Nimbin Museum (☎ 6689 1123; 62 Cullen St; admission $2) is an interpretive and expressionistic museum, far more a work of art than of history. Across the street, the **Hemp Embassy** (☎ 6689 1842; www.hempembassy.net; 51 Cullen St) raises consciousness about marijuana legalisation, as well as providing all the tools and fashion items you'll need to get high (or at least attract more police raids). The embassy leads the **Mardi Grass** festival each May. Smokers are welcome at the tiny **Hemp Bar** next door, which is like Haight-Ashbury in a bottle.

There are even more artists than pot dealers and you can find their work on display at the **Nimbin Artists Gallery** (☎ 6689 1444; 47 Cullen St; ⏲ 10am-4pm).

Just 400m down the hill from town and off the Murwillumbah road, the Old Butter Factory is just that. It now incubates a number of little businesses including the **Nimbin Candle Factory** (☎ 6689 1010), which is redolent with wax. Thousands of hand-dipped paraffin candles are on display.

Every third and fifth Sunday, Nimbin has its own **market**, a spectacular affair of produce and art where locals revel in their culture. There's live music.

Sleeping
Rainbow Retreat Backpackers (☎ 6689 1262; www.rainbowretreat.net; 75 Thorburn St; camp sites $10, dm/d $20/45) Very basic, but totally in the age-of-Aquarius spirit. Relax, chill out, sleep in a shack or camp out in the gypsy vans. There's a free courtesy bus from Byron Bay.

Nimbin Rox YHA Hostel (☎ 6689 0022; www.nimbinrox.com; 74 Thornburn St; camp sites $10, dm/d from $24/60; 🖳 🏊) Rox has hammocks, permaculture gardens, craft workshops, live bands, Thai massage, tepees and a heated pool. Check out the website, a trip in itself.

Nimbin Caravan & Tourist Park (☎ 6689 1402; 29 Sibley St; camp sites from $17; 🏊) A simple place with three dozen sites next to the local swimming pool, down Cullen St past the Nimbin Hotel.

WORTH A TRIP: THE RAINFOREST WAY

The **Rainforest Way** (www.rainforestway.com.au) is a touring route that takes in much of the Gondwanan rainforest, the primeval vestiges of the dense forests that covered Australia 50 million years ago when it was part of the supercontinent Gondwana. Today bits of the surviving forest are preserved in a series of Unesco-recognized parks in northern NSW and southern Queensland. These national parks include Nightcap (p282), Mt Warning (below), Border Ranges (p286) and Springbrook (p304).

The driving route has many options; visitor centres have brochures and maps. You can see quite a bit of it by following the portion from Lismore north through Nimbin, Uki and Murwillumbah, then into Queensland, going through Springbrook and rejoining the Pacific Hwy at Nerang.

Nimbin Hotel (☎ 6689 1246; freemasonhotel@bigpond.com; 53 Cullen St; dm $25) The two- and four-bed rooms in the town's veteran pub are tidy and open onto the classic, shaded veranda.

Eating & Drinking

A number of coffee places tenuously exist along the pavement.

Rainbow Café (☎ 6689 1997; 64A Cullen St; mains $4-9; ☺ breakfast & lunch) The original Nimbin institution makes delicious cakes, big breakfasts, avocado-laden burgers and vegetarian fare, and has a big, funky backyard.

Aquarius Bakery/Cafe (☎ 6689 1566; 45 Cullen St; meals $5-8; ☺ 6am-4pm) An excellent mainstream bakery where you can have a tasty sandwich on fresh bread and a delicious coffee out on the patio.

Nimbin Hotel (☎ 6689 1246; Cullen St; meals $7-15) The classic local boozer. A vast covered porch out back overlooks a verdant valley. Inside, artistic photos of regulars grace the walls and there's actually a slight hint of minimalist style. The fare is typical pub grub; there's live music many Friday nights.

Nimbin Trattoria & Pizzeria (☎ 6689 1427; 70 Cullen St; mains $8-16, pizzas $4-23; ☺ dinner daily, lunch Thu-Sun) The sort of top-end place in town is fittingly laid-back. Groovy pizzas vie with salubrious salads for your attention.

Getting There & Around

Several outfits run shuttles and tours for day-trippers from Byron Bay; some include stops in the region at natural wonders such as Minyon Falls (p282). The tours charge $25 to $35 depending on the itinerary and time of year, but most offer a lower rate if you just want to get to or from Nimbin.

Operators include:

Happy Coach (☎ 6685 3996; www.happycoach.com.au) Departs daily.

Jim's Alternative Tours (☎ 6685 7720; www.jimsalternativetours.com; per person $35) Entertaining tours (with free fruit) to Nimbin.

Nimbin Tours & Shuttle Bus (☎ 6680 9189; www.nimbintours.com) Departs Byron at 11am.

Waller's (☎ 6687 8550) For a traditional trip (as it were), Waller's runs school buses run to Lismore ($10, 70 minutes).

UKI

☎ 02 / pop 220

Uki (*uke*-i) is a cute little village tucked between the surging Tweed River and the dominating peak of Mt Warning. It has a couple of galleries and a used bookshop. The **visitor information centre** (☎ 6679 5399; ☺ 10am-3pm Mon-Sat), run by volunteers, has details of the nearby national parks.

This is a stop on the **Rainforest Way** driving route (see above). Note the **memorial** at the town crossroads. The sheer number of names attests to the profound impact the 20th century's world wars had on small country towns.

The fully accessible **Uki Guesthouse** (☎ 6679 5777; www.ukiguesthouse.com.au; Mitchell St; r from $70; 🖳) is in an old weatherboard house overlooking the crossroads. The **Uki Café** (☎ 6679 5351; 1 Rowlands Creek Rd; mains $7-12; ☺ breakfast & lunch daily, dinner Fri & Sat), serves good food on a sweeping veranda, or by a damp-banishing potbelly stove inside.

MT WARNING NATIONAL PARK

Relatively small in size (2380 hectares), this park is the most dramatic feature of the hinterland, with Mt Warning (1156m) towering over the valley. The peak is the first part of mainland Australia to be touched by sunlight each day. Over 60,000 people a year make the 4.4km, five-hour round-trip trek to the top from Breakfast Creek.

Captain Cook aptly named this mountain in 1770 to warn seafarers of the offshore reefs. The Aboriginal people called it Wollumbin, meaning all of these: 'cloud catcher', 'fighting chief of the mountain' and 'weather maker'.

You can't camp at Mt Warning, but the **Mt Warning Caravan Park & Tourist Retreat** (☎ 6679 5120; Mt Warning Rd; camp sites from $18, cabins from $55), on the Mt Warning approach road, is a viable option, with good kitchen facilities and a well-stocked kiosk.

Some 12km west of Uki, **Mount Warning Forest Hideaway** (☎ 6679 7277; www.foresthideaway .com.au; 460 Byrrill Creek Rd; r from $90; 🖵) has simple rooms with kitchenettes in a motel-style building. There are miles of hikes nearby.

For a first, second or unofficial honeymoon, **Wollumbin Palms Retreat** (☎ 6679 5063; www.wol lumbinpalms.com.au) has three individual lodges, each sleeping two people, scattered across its large rainforest estate on the road to the park. Each is a design wonder, with private spas and large open areas where you can immerse yourself in the sounds of the rainforest.

Wallers (☎ 6687 8550) runs infrequently between Nimbin and Murwillumbah via Dum Dum, the town at the turn-off for Mt Warning. Call for schedules.

MURWILLUMBAH
☎ 02 / pop 7596

Sitting on the banks of the wide Tweed River, Murwillumbah bridges the mist-shrouded hills that include Mt Warning to the west and the broad, green fertile river plain to the east.

It's a scenic spot and well worth the detour off the Pacific Hwy. It is also the gateway to the Border Ranges National Park (p286) and is a key point on the Rainforest Way (opposite) driving tour. The compact centre is good for a stroll and a stop in a café.

The **visitors centre** (☎ 6672 1340; www.tweedcool angatta.com.au; cnr Alma St & Tweed Valley Way; ☷ 9am-4.30pm) has national park info and passes, a great rainforest display and a prime position on the Tweed River.

Sights

The exceptional **Tweed River Art Gallery** (☎ 6670 2790; www.tweed.nsw.gov.au/artgallery; cnr Mistral Rd & Tweed Valley Way; admission free; ☷ 10am-5pm Wed-Sun) is an architectural delight and home to some of Australia's finest in a variety of media. Temporary exhibits complement the permanent fixtures. Check out the iconic portrait of Jonathan Aatty by Hui Hai Xie. The gallery is 3km south of town.

The large **Escape Gallery** (☎ 6672 2433; 1 Brisbane St; ☷ 10am-4pm) has rotating exhibits by regional artists, an 'escape corner' where weary tourists can chill out and a sweet little café. The **Murwillumbah Museum** (☎ 6672 1865; 2 Queensland Rd; adult/child $2/1; ☷ 9.30am-4pm Wed & Fri) brings to life the region's long heritage as a sugar producer.

Tropical Fruit World (☎ 6677 7222; www.tropicalfruit world.com.au; Duranbah Rd; adult/child $33/16; ☷ 10am-4.30pm) is a fruit-themed family attraction 12km northeast of Murwillumbah, with an admission price that's a bit ripe. For a more affordable experience with local fruit, check out the **Tweed**

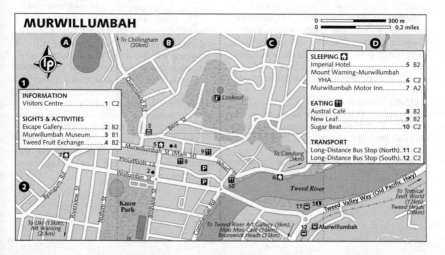

MURWILLUMBAH

| 0 | 300 m |
| 0 | 0.2 miles |

INFORMATION
Visitors Centre........................1 C2

SIGHTS & ACTIVITIES
Escape Gallery........................2 B2
Murwillumbah Museum........3 B1
Tweed Fruit Exchange...........4 B2

SLEEPING 🛏
Imperial Hotel..........................5 B2
Mount Warning-Murwillumbah
YHA.......................................6 C2
Murwillumbah Motor Inn............7 A2

EATING 🍴
Austral Café..............................8 B2
New Leaf...................................9 B2
Sugar Beat...............................10 C2

TRANSPORT
Long-Distance Bus Stop (North)..11 C2
Long-Distance Bus Stop (South)..12 C2

Lookout

To Chillingham (20km)

Queensland Rd

Bent St

Murwillumbah St (Main St)

Proudfoots La

Wollumbin St

Byangum Rd
Riverview St
Nullum St
Brisbane St

Wharf St

To Condong (5km)

Tweed River

Know Park

Commercial Rd

Tweed Valley Way (Old Pacific Hwy)

To Uki (13km); Mt Warning (20km)

To Tweed River Art Gallery (3km); Moo Moo Café (16km); Brunswick Heads (33km)

Murwillumbah

To Tropical Fruit World (12km); Tweed Heads (28km)

Fruit Exchange (☎ 6672 1155; 103 Murwillumbah St), a 68-year-old family business right in town.

Sleeping

Mount Warning-Murwillumbah YHA (☎ 6672 3763; www.yha.com.au; 1 Tumbulgum Rd; dm/d from $26/56) Bohemian airs perfume this colourful waterfront house with eight-bed dorms. There's free ice cream at night plus canoe and bike hire. Tours to Mt Warning are reason enough to bunk down here.

Imperial Hotel (☎ 6672 2777; 115 Murwillumbah St; s/d with shared bathroom $35/45, d $60) These old pub rooms look like they haven't been altered since the opening ceremony – shabby chic without even trying. Still a stay here will you put in the pink, even if it's just the paint outside.

Murwillumbah Motor Inn (☎ 1800 687 224, 1800 023 105; www.murwillumbahmotorinn.com.au; 17 Byangum Rd; s/d $89/99; ✖ ⌘ ; wi-fi) They're a mite frumpy, but all 31 rooms here have cable TV and basic cooking facilities. There's also a pleasant courtyard out the back.

Eating

Austral Café (☎ 6672 2624; 88 Main St; mains $6; ⌣ breakfast & lunch Mon-Sat; ✖) The motto at this 1950s icon is 'a great place to meet and eat'. It dates from 1919 and offers vintage treats such as cupcakes.

New Leaf (☎ 6672 4073; Shop 10, Murwillumbah Plaza; meals $5-10; ⌣ 7.30am-5pm Mon-Fri; ✖) The food here is creative and vegetarian. There are many Middle Eastern dishes such as falafel and hummus. Enjoy inside, out on the courtyard or take away. It now also has an organic grocery.

Sugar Beat (☎ 6672 2330; Shop 2, 6-8 Commercial Rd; mains from $10; ⌣ breakfast & lunch) Park yourself by the sunny window, settle into a corner of the long bench seating or take in the scene from one of the pavement tables. There's café-style fusion fare and locally famous baked goods.

Getting There & Away

Greyhound (☎ 13 14 99; www.greyhound.com.au) and **Premier** (☎ 13 34 10; www.premierms.com.au) have services several times daily on the Sydney to Brisbane route.

Waller's (☎ 6622 6266) has school-day buses to Nimbin (one hour) and Lismore.

BORDER RANGES NATIONAL PARK

The Border Ranges National Park, a World Heritage area of 31,729 hectares, covers the NSW side of the McPherson Range, which runs along the NSW–Queensland border, and some of its outlying spurs. The park's wetter areas protect large tracts of superb rainforest and it has been estimated that a quarter of all bird species in Australia can be found in the park.

The park is made up of three main sections. The eastern section – which includes the escarpments of the massive Mt Warning caldera – is the most easily accessible area. Access it via the Tweed Range Scenic Drive, which begins at Barkers Vale, 40km southwest of Murwillumbah. It's possible to access the smaller central section from Lions Rd, which turns off the Kyogle–Woodenbong road 22km north of Kyogle. The large and rugged western section is almost inaccessible except to well-equipped bushwalkers, but it's possible to get good views of the peaks in the area from the Kyogle–Woodenbong road. The Rainforest Way (p284) skirts the very eastern edge of the park as goes north from Murwillumbah.

To really experience the park, try the rugged **Tweed Range Scenic Drive** – gravel and usable in dry weather – which loops through the park from Lillian Rock (midway between Uki and Kyogle) to Wiangaree (north of Kyogle on the Woodenbong road). The signposting on access roads isn't good (when in doubt take roads signposted to the national park), but it's well worth the effort of finding it. The road is unsuitable for caravans and large vehicles.

The road runs through mountain forest most of the way, with steep hills and breathtaking lookouts over the Tweed Valley to Mt Warning and the coast. The seemingly perilous walk out to the crag called the **Pinnacle** – about half an hour's walk from the road and back – is not for agoraphobics. At **Antarctic Beech** there is, not surprisingly, a forest of Antarctic beeches. Some of these trees are more than 2000 years old. From here, a walking track (about 5km) leads down to **Brindle Creek**, where there is lush rainforest and a picnic area. The road also runs down to Brindle Creek.

Queensland

HOLGER LEUE

Gold Coast

The shimmering ribbon of high rises, theme parks and intensive tourist developments stretching nearly 40km along the beachfront from the tip of South Stradbroke Island to the New South Wales border reflects the insidious glitzy makeover of the once sleepy surfing beaches of the Gold Coast. As the 'bling' capital of Queensland, the Gold Coast offers its four million annual visitors nonstop recreational action and a host of ways to fritter away time and money. But the brash commercialism and relentless pace won't appeal to everyone.

The nerve centre is Surfers Paradise, which, depending on your viewpoint, is either the heart of the action or the place you'll most want to avoid. To escape the crowds and hype of the epicentre you won't need to head far: beach-chic cafés and swish restaurants can be found in Broadbeach and Burleigh Heads, and the laid-back surfie ethos in Coolangatta.

The beaches, the original drawcard, are spectacular and there's excellent surfing at Currumbin, Burleigh Heads, Kirra and Duranbah. While many are drawn by the surf and sun, there's a stunning subtropical, rainforested hinterland less than 30km from the beachfront high rises. The cool mountain landscape has rainforest walks, waterfalls and cosy retreats in Lamington and Springbrook National Parks and the quaint hill-top village of Tamborine Mountain.

HIGHLIGHTS

- Pumping into party overdrive in heady **Surfers Paradise** (p295)
- Waxing it up and barrelling down the huge right-hander at **Burleigh Heads** (p292)
- Bushwalking through deep gorges and towering rainforests in **Springbrook National Park** (p304) and **Lamington National Park** (p306)
- Chilling out on a looong uncrowded beach on **South Stradbroke Island** (p303)
- Joining the après-beach scene at a snazzy café in **Broadbeach** (p294)
- Getting tossed, rolled, wild and wet at the Gold Coast **theme parks** (p303)

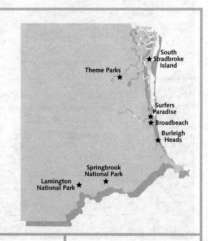

■ TELEPHONE CODE: 07　　　■ www.verygc.com　　　■ www.goldcoastguide.com

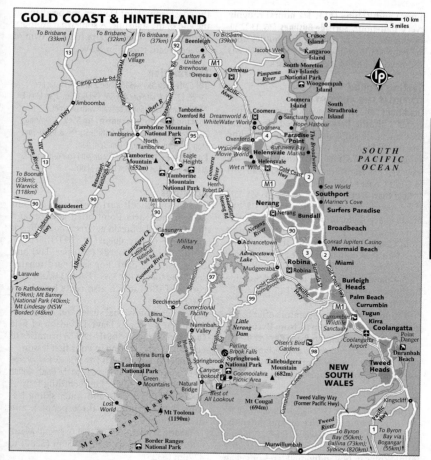

GOLD COAST & HINTERLAND

GOLD COAST

Getting There & Away

AIR

The **Gold Coast Airport** (code: OOL; Coolangatta Airport ☎ 5589 1100; www.goldcoastairport.com.au) at Coolangatta is 25km south of Surfers Paradise. **Qantas** (☎ 13 13 13; www.qantas.com) flies from Sydney (1½ hours) and Melbourne (two hours). **Jetstar** (☎ 13 15 38; www.jetstar.com.au) and **Virgin Blue** (☎ 13 67 89; www.virginblue.com) also fly from Sydney and Melbourne. **Tiger Airways** (☎ 03 9335 3033; www.tigerairways.com) has flights from Melbourne.

BUS

Long-distance buses stop at the bus transit centres in Southport, Surfers Paradise and Coolangatta. **Greyhound Australia** (☎ 1300 473 946; www.greyhound.com.au) has frequent services to/from Brisbane ($20, 1½ hours), Byron Bay ($30, 2½ hours) and Sydney ($154, 15 hours). **Premier Motor Service** (☎ 13 34 10; www.premierms.com.au) serves the same routes and is less expensive. **Kirklands** (☎ 02-6686 5254; www.kirklands.com.au) travels to Surfers Paradise from Byron Bay ($28) and Brisbane ($16), stopping at most Gold Coast towns along the way.

Coachtrans (☎ 3358 9700; www.coachtrans.com.au) runs the Airporter direct services from Brisbane airport (one way $39) to anywhere on the Gold Coast and has services from Brisbane City to Surfers ($28, 1½ hours) or to the theme parks.

TRAIN

Citytrain services link Brisbane to Helensvale station ($8.40, one hour), Nerang ($9.40, 1¼ hours) and Robina ($11, 1¼ hours) roughly every half-hour. **Surfside Buslines** (☎ 13 12 30; www.transinfo.qld.gov.au) runs regular shuttles from the train stations down to Surfers ($3 to $4) and beyond, and to the theme parks.

Getting Around
TO/FROM THE AIRPORT
Coachtrans (☎ 3358 9700; www.coachtrans.com.au) operates a shuttle between Tweed Heads and Brisbane, with stops along the way, including Dreamworld, Movie World and Wet'n'Wild. **Aerobus** (☎ 1300 664 700; www.aerobus.net; one-way tickets $35) has transfers from Brisbane airport to Gold Coast accommodation.

Gold Coast Tourist Shuttle (☎ 1300 655 655, 5574 5111; www.gcshuttle.com.au; adult/child/family $18/9/45) meets every flight into Coolangatta Airport and operates door-to-door transfers to most Gold Coast accommodation. It also offers a Freedom Pass, which includes return transfers to your accommodation plus unlimited theme-park transfers and unlimited Surfside Buslines travel from $58/29/145 per adult/child/family for three days.

A number of private operators offer transfers for the two-hour trip to/from Byron Bay, including **Airport Transfers Byron Bay** (☎ 02-6620 9200; www.airporttransfersbyronbay.com; adult/child $36/18) and Coolangatta Byron Bay Airporter (☎ 0414-608 660; www.byronbayairporttransfers.com.au; per person $35).

BUS
Surfside Buslines (☎ 13 12 30; www.transinfo.qld.gov.au) runs a frequent service up and down the Gold Coast Hwy from Tweed Heads, stopping at Dreamworld, Sanctuary Cove and Paradise Point. You can buy individual fares or get an Ezy Pass for three day's unlimited travel ($26), or a weekly pass ($45).

TAXI
Ring ☎ 13 10 08 for services on the Gold Coast.

COOLANGATTA
☎ 07 / pop 4870
Coolangatta is a laid-back seaside resort proud of its good surf beaches and tight community. Despite a few attempts at a makeover the town retains a 1980s summer-holiday feel and this is its greatest charm. If you want to bypass the glam and party scene of Surfers, catch a few waves and kick back on the beach, you've found the spot. There are good views down

the coast from Point Danger, the headland at the end of the state line. A somewhat arbitrary border divides Coolangatta from its twin of Tweed Heads (p280) in NSW.

Information
3W C@fé (☎ 5599 4536; Shop 2 Griffith Plaza; per 15min $2, wi-fi rate per day $6; ☺ 6.30am-7pm Mon-Fri, 7.30am-6pm Sat & Sun) Cool café with internet.
Coolangatta visitor's centre (☎ 5569 3380; Shop 22, Showcase on the Beach, Griffith St; ☺ 8.30am-5pm Mon-Fri, 9am-3pm Sat, 10am-3pm Sun)
Post office (☎ 13 13 18) Coolangatta (cnr Griffith St & Marine Pde); Tweed Heads (Tweed Mall)

Activities
The most difficult surf break here is Point Danger, but Kirra Point often goes off and there are gentler breaks at Greenmount Beach and Rainbow Bay. **Quigsi** (☎ 5599 1731; 87 Griffith St) hires out surfboards ($30 per day) and bikes ($30 per day). For surfboard repairs, see **Retro Groove** (☎ 5599 3952; 4/33 McLean St), a cool surf shop which also rents boards for $30 per day.

Former professional surfer and Australian surfing team coach Dave Davidson of **Gold Coast Surf Coaching** (☎ 0417-191 629) promises to get you up and surfing in your first lesson.

Accelerate Water Sports (☎ 5536 4074; www.acceleratesport.com.au; Shop 7, Showcase on the Beach, Griffith St; ☺ 9am-5.30pm) offers kite-boarding lessons ($89), wake-boarding and water-skiing lessons ($220; minimum three people), and diving courses.

Tandem Skydive (☎ 5599 1920; Coolangatta Airport) offers tandem jumps from 3050m ($280) to 4270m ($325).

Tours
Catch-A-Crab (☎ 5599 9972; www.catchacrab.com.au; adult/child $55/36) Has great half-day tours along the Terranora Inlet of the Tweed River. The cruise involves mud-crab catching, fishing, pelican feeding and, if the tides permit, yabbie hunting. Lunch is extra.
Rainforest Cruises (☎ 5536 8800; www.goldcoast cruising.com) Has three cruise options ranging from crab catching to surf'n'turf lunches on rainforest cruises along the Tweed River. Cruises start from $32 for two hours.

Sleeping
BUDGET
Coolangatta YHA (☎ 5536 7644; www.coolangattayha .com; 230 Coolangatta Rd, Bilinga; incl breakfast dm $23-28, s/d $33/54; 🖳 🕾) A looong haul from the bustle,

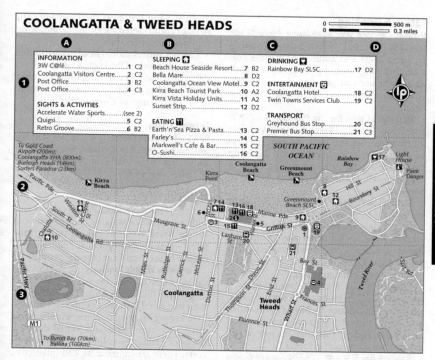

COOLANGATTA & TWEED HEADS

0   500 m
0   0.3 miles

INFORMATION
3W C@fé..............................1 C2
Coolangatta Visitors Centre......2 C2
Post Office...........................3 B2
Post Office...........................4 C3

SIGHTS & ACTIVITIES
Accelerate Water Sports..........(see 2)
Quigsi................................5 C2
Retro Groove.......................6 B2

SLEEPING
Beach House Seaside Resort....7 B2
Bella Mare..........................8 D2
Coolangatta Ocean View Motel..9 C2
Kirra Beach Tourist Park.........10 A2
Kirra Vista Holiday Units........11 A2
Sunset Strip.......................12 D2

EATING
Earth'n'Sea Pizza & Pasta......13 C2
Farley's.............................14 C2
Markwell's Cafe & Bar...........15 C2
O-Sushi.............................16 C2

DRINKING
Rainbow Bay SLSC...............17 D2

ENTERTAINMENT
Coolangatta Hotel................18 C2
Twin Towns Services Club.......19 C2

TRANSPORT
Greyhound Bus Stop.............20 C2
Premier Bus Stop.................21 C3

GOLD COAST

this well-equipped YHA is favoured by surf junkies (of all vintages) who overdose on the excellent breaks across the road. You can also hire boards ($25 per day) and bikes. Courtesy transfers from Coolangatta are available.

Kirra Beach Tourist Park (☎ 5581 7744; www.gctp .com.au/kirra; Charlotte St, Kirra; unpowered sites $25-29, powered sites $27-34, cabins from $104; 🕱 🖳) This large park has plenty of trees and a well-stocked open-air camp kitchen. The modern self-contained cabins are good value. There's also a TV room, BBQs and volleyball and basketball courts. Rates are for two people.

Sunset Strip (☎ 5599 5517; www.sunsetstrip.com.au; 199 Boundary St, Coolangatta; s/d/t/q per person $55/35/35/33, self-contained units from $285, minimum 3 nights; 🖳) There's not much ambience but backpackers will be happy enough with this budget accommodation close to the river and to the beaches. There's a TV lounge and a large, clean kitchen.

MIDRANGE

Coolangatta Ocean View Motel (☎ 5536 8722; oceanviewmotel@bigpond.com; cnr Marine Pde & Clark St, Coolangatta; d $105; 🕱) The facilities are fairly minimal in this small motel but it's all about the location – across the road from Greenmount Beach and close to the Twin Towns Services Club.

Kirra Vista Holiday Units (☎ 5536 7375; www.kirra vista.com.au; 12-14 Musgrave St, Kirra; d $125; 🖳) These self-contained units are looking a bit worn and tired but the owners are friendly and all rooms have ocean views.

Bella Mare (☎ 5599 2755; www.bellamare.com.au; 5 Hill St, Coolangatta; r from $140, 2-bedroom/3-bedroom villas from $175/215, minimum 3 night stay; 🕱 🖳) Adding just a hint of the Mediterranean to Coolangatta, these fancy beachside apartments are set in cool landscaped gardens. All apartments and villas are fully self-contained with private patios or balconies, and it's only 50m to the beach.

Beach House Seaside Resort (☎ 5595 7599; www .classicholidayclub.com.au; 52 Marine Pde, Coolangatta; s/d from $150/180; 🖳) Although it belongs to a holiday club, this apartment complex often has rooms available to nonmembers. The décor is fairly generic, but the units are fully self-contained and sleep up to six people. Also within the complex is a gym, spa and sauna.

Eating & Drinking

O-Sushi (☎ 5563 5455; 66-80 Marine Pde; sushi rolls from $2.50, mains $8-13; ☻ lunch & dinner) Boasting Japanese chefs and authentic Japanese cuisine, this perky sushi bar is about as stylish as a sushi bar can get. Try the *kushi-yaki* (traditional Japanese grill). Sit outdoors for beach views.

Markwell's Café & Bar (☎ 5536 4544; 64 Griffith St; mains $12-30; ☻ breakfast & lunch; ▢ ; wi-fi) With free wireless internet, this has to be your (all day) breakfast choice. It's licensed, and dishes up salads, sandwiches, and a tempting range of seafood such as coconut prawns dipped in beer batter.

Earth'n'Sea Pizza & Pasta (☎ 5536 3477; Marine Pde; mains $14-27; ☻ lunch & dinner) A hot summer night, a balmy sea breeze, a cold beer and a sizzling pizza – what better way to top off a day at the beach? Voted Best Pizza Restaurant on the Gold Coast, it has 21 gourmet pizzas on offer – you can't go wrong.

Farley's (☎ 5536 7615; Beach House Arcade, Marine Pde; mains $17-30; ☻ breakfast, lunch & dinner) From gourmet sandwiches to Mod Oz creations such as Moreton Bay bugs with bok choy and basil pesto, Farley's (opposite the beach) will satisfy your aprés-surf cravings.

Rainbow Bay SLSC (☎ 5536 6390; www.rainbowbayslsc.com; 2 Snapper Rocks Rd) is popular with surfers.

Entertainment

Coolangatta Hotel (☎ 5536 9311; cnr Marine Pde & Warner St) One of the hottest spots on the Gold Coast, the 'Cooly' has legendary Sunday sessions, and the Balcony nightclub attracts some of the biggest acts in the music industry.

Twin Towns Services Club (☎ 5536 1977; Wharf St, Tweed Heads) Has family-oriented shows and regular free movies.

Getting There & Away

The **Greyhound** (☎ 1300 473 946; www.greyhound.com.au) bus stop is in Warner St while **Premier** (☎ 13 34 10; www.premierms.com.au) coaches stop in Bay St. See p289 for further information.

BURLEIGH HEADS & CURRUMBIN

☎ 07 / pop 7610 & 2650

In the chilled-out surfie town of Burleigh Heads, cheery cafés and beachfront restaurants overlook a gorgeous stretch of white sand and a beautiful, tiny national park on the rocky headland. Burleigh is legendary among surfers for the spectacular barrel of its right-hand break off the headland. The strong rip and jagged rocks make this one for experienced surfers only.

Learner surfers should head to Currumbin Alley, 6km south of Burleigh. Currumbin is a sleepy little town, and a great spot for a relaxing family holiday, especially as the kids can swim in the calm waters of Currumbin Creek.

Information

QPWS Information Centre (QPWS; ☎ 5535 3032; 1711 Gold Coast Hwy; ☻ 9.30am-4pm Mon & Wed, 9am-3pm Tue, Thu & Fri, 9am-4pm Sat & Sun) is at the northern end of Tallebudgera Creek.

Sights

Burleigh Heads National Park is crisscrossed with a number of walking tracks. Look out for the basalt columns poking through the forest – they hold considerable cultural significance to the local Kombumerri people.

Currumbin Wildlife Sanctuary (☎ 5534 1266; www.cws.org.au; Gold Coast Hwy, Currumbin; adult/child $32/21; ☻ 8am-5pm) showcases Australian native animals in natural bush and rainforest habitats. Tree kangaroos, koalas, emus, wombats and other cute-and-furries are joined daily by flocks of brilliantly coloured rainbow lorikeets. There are informative and interactive shows throughout the day (did you know the scrub python can swallow four times the size of its head?), and there is also an Aboriginal dance show. Try to see the sanctuary on a Wildnight Tour (adult/child $49/27), when the native nocturnal animals go about their business.

David Fleay Wildlife Park (☎ 5576 2411; West Burleigh Rd; adult/child/senior/family $15.40/7.20/10.30/39.10; ☻ 9am-5pm) is run with the help of the QPWS. With 4km of walking tracks through mangroves and rainforest and plenty of informative shows throughout the day, it's an excellent opportunity to experience Australian fauna. The platypus was first bred in captivity here and the park still runs a research and breeding programme for rare and endangered species.

Activities

The right-hand point break at Burleigh Heads is the best wave here, but it's usually crowded with pro surfers. There are plenty of other waves to practise on along the beach.

Surfing Services Australia (☎ 5535 5557; www.surfingservices.com.au; adult/child $30/20) holds surfing lessons at Currumbin Alley every weekend at

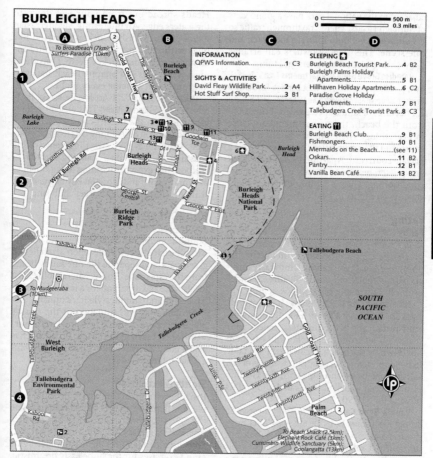

BURLEIGH HEADS

INFORMATION
QPWS Information.................1 C3

SIGHTS & ACTIVITIES
David Fleay Wildlife Park..........2 A4
Hot Stuff Surf Shop................3 B1

SLEEPING
Burleigh Beach Tourist Park.......4 B2
Burleigh Palms Holiday
 Apartments.....................5 B1
Hillhaven Holiday Apartments....6 C2
Paradise Grove Holiday
 Apartments.....................7 B1
Tallebudgera Creek Tourist Park..8 C3

EATING
Burleigh Beach Club................9 B1
Fishmongers......................10 B1
Mermaids on the Beach........(see 11)
Oskars...........................11 B2
Pantry...........................12 B1
Vanilla Bean Café................13 B2

GOLD COAST

8am and 10.30am. Meet on the grass opposite the lifeguard tower.

The **Hot Stuff Surf Shop** (☎ 5535 6899; 1706 Gold Coast Hwy) rents out surfboards for $20/30 per half-/full day.

Sleeping

Burleigh Beach Tourist Park (☎ 5581 7755; www.gctp .com.au/burly; Goodwin Tce, Burleigh Heads; unpowered/powered sites $24/26, cabins $115; 🏊 💻) This council-run park is snug, so get in quick to bag a shady site. The good news is that you can stumble to the beach and there's a saltwater pool just across the road. Rates are for two people.

Tallebudgera Creek Tourist Park (☎ 5581 7700; www.gctp.com.au/tally; 1544 Gold Coast Hwy, Burleigh Heads; unpowered/powered sites $29/32, cabins $125-167;

🏊 💻 🛁) This sprawling park is colossal but it's well laid out with its own road system and sits right on the banks of Tallebudgera Creek. Rates are for two people.

Burleigh Palms Holiday Apartments (☎ 5576 3955; www.burleighpalms.com; 1849 Gold Coast Hwy, Burleigh Heads; 1-bedroom apt per night/week from $120/490, 2-bedroom apt from $140/600; 🛁) Even though they're on the highway these large and comfortable self-contained units, so close to the beach, are solid value. The owner is a mine of information and is happy to recommend places to visit and organise tours.

our pick Hillhaven Holiday Apartments (☎ 5535 1055; www.hillhaven.com.au; 2 Goodwin Tce, Burleigh Heads; d per night $160, minimum 3 night stay) These opulent apartments perched high on the headland

GOLD COAST

adjacent to the national park have a grand view of Burleigh Heads. There's no through traffic so it's ultraquiet yet only 150m to the beach and café scene. The friendly owners can arrange baby-sitting, airport transfers and tours.

Paradise Grove Holiday Apartments (☎ 5576 3833; www.paradisegrove.com.au; 7 West Burleigh Rd, Burleigh Heads; 2-bedroom apt per week from $900; ❇ ⌘) Set on 2.4 hectares of landscaped gardens only 100m from the beach, these apartments are close to everything. There are two pools, a tennis court, and the ground floor apartments have a private courtyard. Apartments down the back are quieter; be sure to specify if you want air-conditioning. There's a minimum three-night stay; seven nights in peak season.

Eating

Pantry (☎ 5576 2818; 15 Connor St, Burleigh Heads; dishes $8-16; ❇ 6am-4.30pm) A looong breakfast menu greets the cappuccino set at this gathering point. For lunch you can tuck into tasty burgers, wraps, melts and salads. Sit alfresco under umbrellas for a spot of people-watching.

Fishmongers (☎ 5535 2927; 9 James St, Burleigh Heads; dishes $8-17; ❇ lunch & dinner) This fishmonger-cum-restaurant is the business. Select your seafood bites from the display and eat them hot down by the beach. Or sit down at a table in the unpretentious restaurant where you can satisfy your heart and hips with the Healthy Heart special – grilled fish, salad and a glass of wine for $13.90.

Vanilla Bean Café (☎ 5576 4707; 31 Connor St, Burleigh Heads; mains $9-14; ❇ 6am-4pm) This busy modern café opposite the Bowls Club dishes up gourmet salads, focaccias, burgers, grills and nachos. Its freshly made cool juices are a great way to start the surf-day.

Burleigh Beach Club (☎ 5520 2972; cnr Goodwin Tce & Gold Coast Hwy, Burleigh Heads; dishes $10-25; ❇ breakfast Wed-Sun, lunch & dinner daily) The fantastic ocean views at this club, sitting directly above the beach, are hard to beat. The fare is typical bistro but it's all tasty and the portions are huge.

Elephant Rock Café (☎ 5598 2133; 776 Pacific Pde, Currumbin; mains $16-30; ❇ breakfast, lunch & dinner) Opposite the beach, this cool café specialising in Mod Oz and 'gourmet vegetarian' cuisine (gluten sufferers will want to head here) morphs from beach-chic by day to ultrachic at night.

our pick Mermaids on the Beach (☎ 5520 1177; 31 Goodwin Tce, Burleigh Heads; mains $23-36; ❇ breakfast, lunch & dinner) Another gem directly on the beach: the beautiful white sands of Burleigh

Heads spread out from your feet down to the waters edge. An interesting Mediterrasian menu produces dishes such as Moreton Bay bugs with chilli parsley black linguine, anchovy crumbs and rocket pesto. Outside of meal hours this is a snappy beach bar with live music and a theme every night.

Oskars (☎ 5576 3722; 43 Goodwin Tce, Burleigh Heads; dishes $25-34; ❇ lunch & dinner) This elegant restaurant (right on the beach) constantly lands a coveted place on best-dining lists from all quarters. Against elevated, sweeping views of the coastline you'll dine on a changing selection of seafood, but expect something along the lines of Yamba prawn and Moreton Bay bug tempura with mesclun greens and sweet chilli jam.

BROADBEACH

☎ 07 / pop 3780

Boutique shops and fashionable cafés line the Broadbeach streets while open stretches of green parkland separate the fine sandy beach from the esplanade. This is where Gold Coast locals wine and dine, and for a taste of the stylish beach-and-sun lifestyle it's exquisite.

Shopaholics will find two of the coast's major shopping centres (Oasis and Pacific Fair) within easy reach of the beach. Broadbeach is also a good alternative to Surfers if you want a peaceful night's sleep.

Sights & Activities

Broadbeach's main claim to fame is the temple to Mammon that is **Conrad Jupiters Casino** (☎ 5592 8100; www.conrad.com.au; Gold Coast Hwy; admission free; ❇ 24hr). The first legal casino in Queensland, it features the usual wallet-lightening exercises for the hopelessly optimistic. Also here is **Jupiters Theatre** (☎ 1800 074 144), with live music and glamorous dinner shows. The casino complex is connected to the Oasis Shopping Centre by a short monorail.

For the ghoulishly inclined, **Dracula's Theatre Restaurant** (☎ 5575 1000; www.draculas.com.au; 1 Hooker Blvd; dinner & show midweek/weekend $74/79) entertains with a vampirish cabaret act and fetishly dressed wait-staff while you sink your fangs into fiendish-sounding dishes including the restaurant's signature diabolical and delicious Death by Chocolate.

Sleeping

Hi-Ho Beach Apartments (☎ 5538 2777; www.hihobeach .com; 2 Queensland Ave; 1-/2-bedroom apt $130/160; ⌘) A great choice, close to the beach and Broadbeach's café scene. Apartments are bright and airy with a favourable northeasterly aspect.

Wave (☎ 5555 9200; www.thewavesresort.com.au; 89-91 Surf Parade; r $269-750, minimum 3 night stay; 🍴 💻 🏊) You can't miss this spectacular high rise with its wave-inspired design towering over Broadbeach's glam central. These luxury apartments make full use of the coast's spectacular views, especially from the sky pool on the 34th floor.

Eating
Broadbeach's culinary scene is a class above Surfers'.

Manolas Brothers Deli (☎ 5538 8223; 19 Albert Ave; dishes $8-25; 🕑 7am-7pm Mon-Sat, to 6pm Sun) Cosmopolitan delicacies fill every nook and cranny on the ceiling-high shelves in this sumptuous gourmet deli-café. Park yourself at the massively long wooden table to better salivate over the juicy olives, antipasti, imported cheeses and decadent homemade cakes and biscuits. Health freaks will love the salads and juices.

Champagne Brasserie (☎ 5538 3877; 2 Queensland Ave; mains $20-35; 🕑 lunch Tue-Fri, dinner Tue-Sat) This lively, unassuming restaurant could have been plucked from a French village. Quail, grain-fed beef and barramundi are worked into tantalizing taste sensations but don't forget to leave room for the crepe suzette.

Koi (☎ 5570 3060; Wave Bldg, cnr Surf Parade & Albert Ave; mains $24-40; 🕑 breakfast, lunch & dinner) For serious people-watching, morning lattes or sunset cocktails, this cruisy café and lounge bar is the happening place. Gourmet pizzas and tapas rub shoulders with an interesting contemporary menu including crocodile tail and kangaroo loin. Live music on Sunday afternoons draw the aprés-beach crowd.

Moo Moo (☎ 5539 9952; Broadbeach on the Park, 2685 Gold Coast Hwy; mains $30-60; 🕑 lunch & dinner) Vegetarians steer clear, this is the mecca for serious carnivores. Moo Moo's signature dish is a 1kg Wagyu rump steak rubbed with spices, char-grilled until smoky then roasted, and carved at the table. Beef connoisseurs will drool over the Master Kobe rib fillet, a luxury beef produced from a long period of grain feeding of Wagyu beef.

SURFERS PARADISE
☎ 07 / pop 18,510
Sprouting out of the commercial heart of the Gold Coast is the signature high-rise settlement of Surfers Paradise. Here the pace is giddy and frenetic, a brash pleasure dome of nightclubs, shopping and relentless entertainment. Surfers is the acknowledged party hub of the Gold Coast, happily catering to all demographics, from 40-somethings getting squiffy on martinis, to Gen Ys dropping pills on the dance floor and schoolies cutting loose on the beach. With so much bling and glitz in your face, be prepared to part with your cash. About the only time you won't is if one of the famous 'meter maids' – pretty young things in gold-lamé bikinis – feeds your expired parking meter.

The density of towering high rises shades the beach from midafternoon so if you're after a suntan or a relaxing beach holiday, head further south.

Orientation
The main thoroughfare, Cavill Ave, runs down to the seafront, ending in a pedestrian mall. Orchid Ave, one block back from The Esplanade, is the nightclub and bar strip. The Gold Coast Hwy splits either side of Surfers, with Surfers Paradise Blvd taking southbound traffic and Remembrance Dr, which then becomes Ferny Ave, taking northbound traffic.

Although Cavill Mall is the recognized centre of Surfers, a new upmarket precinct Circle on Cavill (bounded by Ferny Ave, Cavill Ave and Surfers Paradise Blvd) promotes itself as the 'new heart of Surfers Paradise'.

Information
Email Centre (☎ 5538 7500; Orchid Ave; 🕑 9am-10pm)

Gold Coast Tourism Bureau (☎ 5538 4419; Cavill Ave Mall; 🕑 8.30am-5.30pm Mon-Fri, 8.30am-5pm Sat, 9am-4pm Sun) Information booth; also sells theme-park tickets.

Post office (☎ 13 13 18; Shop 165, Centro Surfers Paradise, Cavill Ave Mall; 🕑 9am-5.30pm Mon-Fri, to 12.30pm Sat)

Surfers Paradise Day & Night Medical Centre (☎ 5592 2299; 3221 Surfers Paradise Blvd; 🕑 7am-11pm) Pharmacy attached.

Travellers Central (☎ 1800 359 830, 5538 3274; www.stayoz.com.au; Surfers Paradise Transit Centre, cnr Beach & Cambridge Rds; 🕑 9am-7pm) This extremely friendly and helpful information desk can help with accommodation and tours for travellers of all budget ranges.

Sights
Surfers' sights are usually spread across beach towels but for a spectacular 360-degree panorama of the Gold Coast and hinterland zip up

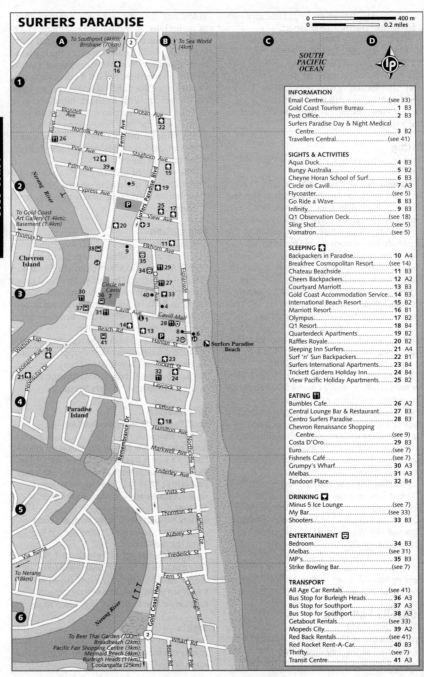

SURFERS PARADISE

SCHOOLIES ON THE LOOSE

Every year in November, hundreds of teenagers flock to Surfers Paradise to celebrate the end of their high-school education in a month-long party that's become known as 'schoolies week'.

Schoolies week started in the early '90s and quickly gained popularity – and notoriety – as an anything-goes party, with drunk and drug-addled teens a common sight in the streets and pubs of Surfers. Although the local authorities have stepped in to regulate the excesses – organising plenty of free entertainment, sections of the beach devoted to drug- and alcohol-free parties, and accessible emergency and counselling services – unruly behaviour is still the norm. Avoid schoolies week if possible (unless you've just finished school!)

For more information visit www.schoolies.com.

---

to the **Q1 observation deck** (☎ 5630 4525; Hamilton Ave; adult/child/family $17.50/10/45; ⏲ 9am-9pm Sun-Thu, 9am-midnight Fri & Sat). On a clear day you can see north to Brisbane and south to Byron Bay. Wander around the glass-enclosed deck and you'll learn other interesting tidbits, like the Q1 is the world's 20th tallest building, the arc lights illuminating the spine can be seen 200km away, and it takes 43 seconds to reach the observation deck on the 77th floor. There's a café and comfy lounge chairs so there's no need to hurry back to earth.

For a spot of culture, the **Gold Coast Art Gallery** (☎ 5581 6567; www.gcac.com.au; Gold Coast Arts Centre, 135 Bundall Rd; ⏲ 10am-5pm Mon-Fri, 11am-5pm Sat & Sun), about 1.5km inland, has an excellent permanent collection featuring many of Australia's finest artists.

The kiddies will like **Infinity** (☎ 5538 2988; www.infinitygc.com.au; Chevron Renaissance, cnr Surfers Paradise Blvd & Elkhorn Ave; adult/child/family $23.90/15.90/67.90; ⏲ 10am-10pm), a walk-through maze cleverly disguised by an elaborate sound and light show.

Activities

You won't be bored in Surfers. Apart from swimming at the beach it's action all the way.

SURFING & KAYAKING

Behind the seemingly impenetrable wall of high rises, the beach here has enough swell to give beginners a feel for the craft of surfing. Surf schools charge between $40 and $50 for a two-hour lesson.

Brad Holmes Surf Coaching (☎ 5539 4068, 0418-757 539; www.bradholmessurfcoaching.com; 90min lessons $75) Also caters to disabled surfers.

Cheyne Horan School of Surf (☎ 1800 227 873, 0403-080 484; www.cheynehoran.com.au; 1hr lessons $45) World Champion surfer Cheyne Horan offers excellent tuition.

Go Ride a Wave (☎ 1800 787 337, 5526 7077; www.gorideawave.com.au; Cavill Ave Mall; surfing/kayaking 2hr lessons from $55; ⏲ 9am-5pm) Also rents out surfboards and kayaks.

Splash Safaris Sea Kayaking (☎ 0407-741 748; www.kayakingaustralia.com.au; tours $59-75) Kayak tours from introductory courses to five-hour safaris include snorkelling, dolphin searching, bushwalking and lunch.

AIRBORNE ACTIVITIES

Both **Balloon Down Under** (☎ 5593 8400; www.balloondownunder.com.au; 1hr flights adult/child $295/200) and **Balloon Aloft** (☎ 5578 2244; www.balloonaloft.net; 1hr flights adult/child $295/200) offer early morning flights over the Gold Coast hinterland, including transfers, and ending with a hot breakfast.

ADRENALINE ACTION

Experience the Broadwater with spins, slides and speed! **Jetboat Extreme** (☎ 5538 8890; www.jetboatextreme.com.au; 1hr rides adult/child $50/35) propels you across the water in a turbo charged, twin-jet-powered, custom-built jetboat.

Almost a rite of passage in Surfers is betting your life on the strength of a giant rubber band at **Bungy Australia** (☎ 5570 4833; cnr Cypress & Ferny Aves; jumps from $99). On the same block, **Flycoaster** (☎ 5539 0474; www.flycoaster.com; rides $39) swings you like a pendulum after you've been released from a hoist 34m up, **Sling Shot** (☎ 5570 2700; rides $30) catapults you into the air at around 160km/h, and **Vomatron** (☎ 5570 200; rides $30) whisks you around in a giant arc at about 120kph. All are open from 10am to 10pm daily from August to April. From May to July opening hours are 2pm to 10pm Monday to Friday and 10am to 10pm Saturday and Sunday.

WHALE-WATCHING

Between June and November, **Whales in Paradise** (☎ 3880 4455; www.whalesinparadise.com; adult/child $85/50) leaves central Surfers for 3½ hours of whale-watching action.

INDYCAR FEVER

Since 1991 Surfers Paradise has been host to what has been dubbed Queensland's biggest party – the Australian leg of the IndyCar series (the US equivalent of Formula One motor racing). Each October the main streets of central Surfers are transformed into a temporary race circuit, around which hurtle some of the world's fastest cars, with drivers who push them up to speeds of more than 300km/h. The champ cars are the main attraction, but plenty of folk come to see Ford and Holden battle out their famous rivalry in the V8 Supercars.

Over the entire four days, when the tracks aren't screeching with races or practice sessions, you can catch motorcycle stunt shows and spectacular air shows. There are also plenty of opportunities to meet the masters for autograph sessions, and revheads can shell out $22 and take a tour through either the Champ Car Pit Lanes or a V8 Supercar Pit Lane.

On a good year, around a quarter of a million spectators descend for the festival. Surfers is fairly over the top at the best of times, but IndyCar gives the town a chance to *really* let its hair down.

General admission charges to the races ranges from $40 to $105 per day at the gate, cheaper if you book. Four-day grandstand seating is between $235 and $570. For more information call ☎ 1800 300 055 or check www.indy.com.au.

HORSE RIDING

Numinbah Valley Adventure Trails (☎ 5533 4137; www .numinbahtrails.com), 30km south of Nerang, and **Gumnuts Horseriding** (☎ 5543 0191; Biddaddaba Creek Rd, Canungra) offer half-day rides from around $70, including pick-ups from the coast.

Tours

A kitschy way to explore Surfers is on the **Aqua Duck** (☎ 5538 3825; 7A Orchid Ave; adult/child $32/26), a semi-aquatic bus (or a boat on wheels) that moves effortlessly from the road to the river and back again.

You can also access the Gold Coast hinterland with a number of tour operators from Surfers Paradise. See p304 for more information.

Festivals & Events

Big Day Out (www.bigdayout.com) Huge international music festival in late January.

Quicksilver Pro-Surfing Competition Some of the world's best surfers ride the waves in mid-March.

Surf Life-Saving Championships Also in mid-March, expect to see some stupidly fit people running about wearing very little.

Gold Coast International Marathon Run in July.

IndyCar October; see the boxed text, above.

Coolangatta Gold The Ironman of Surf Lifesaving, held in October.

Schoolies week November; see boxed text p297.

Sleeping

The **Gold Coast Accommodation Service** (☎ 5592 0067; www.goldcoastaccommodationservice.com; Shop 1, 1 Beach Rd) can arrange and book accommodation.

BUDGET

Surfers has several decent hostels, all of which offer vouchers for the nightclubs in town.

Cheers Backpackers (☎ 1800 639 539, 5531 6539; www.cheersbackpackers.com.au; 8 Pine Ave; dm/d $24/56; 💻 💷) Amid the friendly blur of theme nights, karaoke, pool comps, pub crawls, happy hours and BBQs, you'll also find adequate rooms and good facilities. Cheers is undeniably a party hostel, and a short walk to the clubs

Surf 'n' Sun Backpackers (☎ 1800 678 194, 5592 2363; www.surfnsun-goldcoast.com; 3323 Surfers Paradise Blvd; dm/d $24/60; 💷) A very friendly family-run business that rivals Cheers as party central, this hostel is the best option for Surfers' beach and bars.

Backpackers in Paradise (☎ 5538 4344; www .backpackersinparadise.com; 40 Peninsular Dr; dm/d $26/65; 💷 💻) Aspiring party hostel with basic dorms and en suites.

Sleeping Inn Surfers (☎ 1800 817 832, 5592 4455; www.sleepinginn.com.au; 26 Peninsular Dr; dm $26, d with/ without bathroom $76/66; 💻 💷) This converted motel has modern facilities and a wide choice of rooms but needs a few more bathrooms. A quieter option is the shared apartments nearby. You can watch movies in the pool or in Priscilla (the orange bus out the back).

MIDRANGE

Surfers is riddled with self-contained units. In peak season, rates skyrocket by up to 100% and there's usually a two- or three-night minimum stay. High-season rates are quoted.

International Beach Resort (☎ 1800 657 471, 5539 0099; www.internationalresort.com.au; 84 The Esplanade; apt

$120-165; ⊠ ⊒) Another seafront high rise, this place is just across from the beach, and has good studios and one- and two-bedroom units. The café downstairs is open for breakfast, lunch and cocktails.

Olympus (☎ 5538 7288; www.olympusapartments.com.au; 62 The Esplanade; d $130-180; ⊒ ⊒) Just 200m north of Elkhorn Ave and opposite the beach, this high-rise block has well-kept, spacious apartments with one or two bedrooms.

Quarterdeck Apartments (☎ 1800 635 235, 5592 2200; 3263 Surfers Paradise Blvd; 1-bedroom apt from $134; ⊒) Comfortable one-bedroom apartments but air-con is extra.

Trickett Gardens Holiday Inn (☎ 5539 0988; www.trickettgardens.com.au; 24-30 Trickett St; d $140; ⊠ ⊒) This friendly low-rise block is great for families, with a central location and well-equipped, self-contained units. It's so tranquil it's hard to believe you're close to Surfers' frantic action.

Breakfree Cosmopolitan Resort (☎ 5570 2311; www.breakfree.com.au; cnr Surfers Paradise Blvd & Beach Rd; r from $143; ⊠ ⊒) Set back from the beach a tad but still very central, this complex contains 55 privately owned, self-contained apartments, each uniquely furnished by the owners. There's also a BBQ area, spa and sauna, but it can be noisy at night.

View Pacific Holiday Apartments (☎ 5570 3788; www.viewpacific.com; 5 View Ave; 1-/2-bedroom apt $150/155; ⊒ ⊒) The self-contained units in this wee complex are spacious and offer good value. All contain life's necessities such as washers and dryers (but only some have air-con), and balconies get glimpses of the beach between the surrounding buildings.

Surfers International Apartments (☎ 1800 891 299, 5579 1299; www.surfers-international.com.au; 7-9 Trickett St; 1-/2-bedroom apt from $150/190; ⊒) This high rise, just off the beach, has plush apartments bathed in classy blue hues. Each contains a modern kitchen, sizable bedrooms and full ocean views. The complex comes with a small gym and poolside BBQ. This is a good option, close to everything.

TOP END

Raffles Royale (☎ 5538 0099; www.rafflesroyale.com.au; 69 Ferny Ave; r from $165; ⊒) An unobtrusive, low-rise block with bright and cheerful self-contained units.

Chateau Beachside (☎ 5538 1022; www.chateaubeachside.com.au; cnr Elkhorn Ave & The Esplanade; d/studio/1-bedroom apt $165/180/195; ⊠ ⊒) Right in the heart

of Surfers, this seaside complex has comfortable, spacious units with excellent views.

Courtyard Marriott (☎ 1800 074 317, 5579 3499; www.marriott.com; cnr Surfers Paradise Blvd & Hanlan St; d/ste from $165/235; ⊠ ⊒ ⊒ ; wi-fi) Right in the centre of Surfers, this plush top-end hotel is attached to the Centro Shopping Complex. The top-price suites have spa baths.

Q1 Resort (☎ 1300 792 008, 5630 4500; www.q1.com.au; Hamilton Ave; 1-/2-/3-bedroom apt from $284/444/654; ⊠ ⊒ ⊒) Spend a night in the world's tallest residential tower. This stylish 80-storey resort is a modern mix of metal, glass and fabulous wrap-around views. There's a lagoon-style pool, a fitness centre and a day spa.

Marriott Resort (☎ 5592 9800; www.marriott.com; 158 Ferny Ave; d/ste from $315/575; ⊠ ⊒ ⊒) Just north of the centre, this resort is ridiculously sumptuous, from the sandstone-floored foyer with punka-style fans to the lagoon-style pool, complete with artificial white-sand beaches and waterfall.

Eating

Self-caterers will find supermarkets in **Centro Surfers Paradise** (Cavill Ave Mall), **Chevron Renaissance Shopping Centre** (cnr Elkhorn Ave & Gold Coast Hwy) and **Circle on Cavill** (cnr Cavill & Ferny Ave).

BUDGET

Fishnets Café (☎ 5538 2280; Circle on Cavill, 3/38 Surfers Paradise Blvd; dishes $7-13; ⏱ lunch & dinner) Forget the paper plates and plastic cutlery, the fish and chips, octopus salad and fresh fish fillets at this outdoor eatery in the heart of the Circle are excellent value.

our pick **Bumbles Café** (☎ 5538 6668; 21 River Dr; dishes $11-18; ⏱ 7am-4pm) One of the few tranquil spots in Surfers, this cute café is located in a quiet nook opposite the Nerang River. The menu isn't extensive and the service a bit slow but the food is well worth the wait. For a light lunch try the roasted vegetables with feta and cashew nut pesto.

MIDRANGE

Central Lounge Bar & Restaurant (☎ 5592 3228; 27 Orchid Ave; mains lunch $11-20, dinner $20-32; ⏱ lunch & dinner) Rubbing shoulders with Costa D'oro, this modern restaurant and lounge bar is a cool place to indulge in a long lunch. Tables and chairs spill into the centre of the mall so passers-by can watch you having a good time. Salads, steaks and beer-battered fish and chips are on offer. The resident DJ creates a fusion of cool tunes to smooth you into the weekend club scene.

Euro (☎ 5538 1996; Circle on Cavill, Surfers Paradise Blvd; mains $13-20; ☘ breakfast, lunch & dinner) Dine alfresco in the heart of the Circle with a prime view of the big screen. The gentle splash of the fountain masks the outer-Circle traffic noise. The Mediterranean salad or steak sandwich is a good choice before a night of clubbing.

Beer Thai Garden (☎ 5538 0110; cnr Chelsea Ave & Gold Coast Hwy; mains $13-21; ☘ dinner) Reputed to dish up the best Pad Thai on the coast, this lovely restaurant brims with atmosphere. Two glitzy elephants flank the entrance, and soft lighting makes the most of the outdoor Thai garden bar. Good value and easy on the pocket. It's south down the Gold Coast Hwy.

Tandoori Place (☎ 5538 0808; Aegean Resort, Laycock St; mains $15-20; ☘ lunch & dinner) An Indian restaurant that boasts a swag of awards and is highly recommended by locals has to be a winner. On the extensive menu you'll find seafood, poultry, lamb, beef and hot, hot, *hot* vindaloo roo. Vegetarians are also spoiled for choice.

Costa D'oro (☎ 5538 5203; 27 Orchid Ave; mains $17-29; ☘ lunch & dinner) The Italian village setting painted into the backdrop of this popular restaurant goes nicely with the authentic, if not predictable, pasta, pizzas, salads and mains. It's in a good people-watching possie and if you have a late lunch (or early dinner) between 3pm and 7pm you get 40% off your meal.

TOP END

Melbas (☎ 5592 6922; 46 Cavill Ave; mains $25-38; ☘ breakfast, lunch & dinner) Melbas' revolutionary menu dishes up such surprises as vanilla-roasted duck breast with creamy polenta. Steak and fish feature prominently but unfortunately vegetarian options are limited. Upstairs, Club Melbas is a popular drinking hole.

Grumpy's Wharf (☎ 5531 6177; Tiki Village, Cavill Ave; mains $27-38; ☘ dinner) Right on the water, Grumpy's is a secluded and tranquil retreat serving fine seafood with Asian and Mediterranean touches.

Drinking

Basement (☎ 5588 4000; Gold Coast Arts Centre, 135 Bundall Rd) In the same building as the art gallery (p297), this bar hosts touring performers who excel in jazz, blues and folk. Regular Saturday night sessions specialise in blues, roots and world music courtesy of the resident band.

Minus 5 Ice Lounge (☎ 5527 5571; Circle on Cavill, Cavill Ave; 30min adult/child $30/15; ☘ 11am-midnight) The coolest bar in town – literally. At minus 5°C, everything in the bar is made of ice, including the seats, walls, bar and even your glass. You'll need more than one vodka to warm your innards.

My Bar (☎ 5592 1144; 15 Orchid Ave) In the mega-complex housing Shooters, this new bar is a seductive chill zone. Curtained booths, towering candle-holders, softly lit glass-topped tables and House music create a class venue.

Shooters (☎ 5592 1144; 15 Orchid Ave) This Wild West American saloon bar is where Big Brother evictees immediately come to drown their sorrows. The décor is spot-on so you know there's got to be a cowboy somewhere among the pool tables, big-screen videos, DJs and live acts.

Entertainment

Orchid Ave is Surfers' main bar and nightclub strip. Cover charges are usually between $10 and $20 and Wednesday and Saturday are generally the big party nights.

Take the hassle out of your big night out with **Wicked Club Crawl** (☎ 5580 8422; www.wicked clubcrawl.com.au; tickets $40). Every Wednesday and Saturday the Wicked team organise a club crawl to five nightclubs (including free entry for the rest of the week), a free drink and pizza at each venue, party games and loads of fun.

Backpackers Big Night Out (www.goldcoastbackpack ers.net; tickets $30) hosts a similar club crawl on Wednesdays and Saturdays, exclusively for backpackers. A party bus picks you up from your hostel and that's when the party begins. Tickets are available only through Gold Coast Association hostels and get you free entry into four nightclubs, a free drink and pizza at each venue, and other goodies.

Bedroom (☎ 5592 0088; 26 Orchid Ave) One of the hottest clubs in town brings upmarket funk to the Gold Coast. Softly lit double beds along the walls make this a seriously sexy venue. Throw in high-tech mood lighting, plasma screens in the dance floor, and pumping acoustics and you know you're in for a good time. But before you get too comfy, remember the rules: no smoking, no pillow fights and no jumping on the bed.

Strike Bowling Bar (☎ 1300 787 453; Circle on Cavill, Cavill Ave) Retro meets the future in this hip bowling bar. Forget daggy, when bowling fuses with disco lighting, pumping music and cool cocktails, the effect is striking.

Melbas (☎ 5538 7411; 46 Cavill Ave) Upstairs from the restaurant, Melba's nightclub is a local haunt and gets packed quickly. Aspiring pole-dancers can gyrate to their heart's content.

MP's (☎ 5526 2337; Forum Arcade, 26 Orchid Ave) This popular gay club has cheap drinks and drag shows on Tuesday, Thursday and Sunday. On Friday and Saturday it fills with a happy, mixed crowd soaking up a generic nightclub atmosphere.

Getting There & Away

The transit centre is on the corner of Beach and Cambridge Rds. All the major bus com-panies have desks here. For more information on buses and trains, see p289.

Getting Around

Car hire costs around $30 to $50 per day. Some of the many operators:

All Age Car Rentals (☎ 5570 1200, 0418-766 880; Transit Centre, cnr Beach & Cambridge Rds)

Getabout Rentals (☎ 5504 6517; Shop 9, The Mark, Orchid Ave) Also rents scooters and bikes and organises motorcycle tours of the Broadwater area (from $50 for 30 minutes to $260 per half-day).

Red Back Rentals (☎ 5592 1655; Transit Centre, cnr Beach & Cambridge Rds)

Red Rocket Rent-A-Car (☎ 1800 673 682, 5538 9074; Centre Arcade, 16 Orchid Ave) Also rents scooters (per day $30) and bicycles (per day $12).

Mopeds City (☎ 5592 5878; 103 Ferny Ave) hires out brand new mopeds (per hour/day $30/70).

SOUTHPORT & MAIN BEACH

☎ 07 / pop 24,100

Sheltered from the ocean by a long sandbar, known as the Spit, and the Broadwater estu-ary, Southport is a relatively quiet residential enclave 4km north of Surfers Paradise. There's not much to do here and it's a long way from the beach but it can be a good base if you want to escape the nonstop frenzy of Surfers.

Main Beach, just south of Southport, marks the gateway to the Spit and the high-rise tour-ist developments. The Spit runs 3km north, dividing the Broadwater from the South Pacific Ocean. The ocean side of the Spit is relatively untouched, backed by a long strip of natural bushland, and has excellent beaches and surf. At the southern end of the Spit is the Sea World theme park, while the upmarket shopping complex of Marina Mirage is near Mariner's Cove and the marina, the depar-ture point for cruises and other water-based activities.

Activities

Mariner's Cove is the place to book all water activities. The easiest way to sift through the plethora of operators is to book at the **Mariner's Cove Tourism Information & Booking Centre** (☎ 5571 1711; Mariner's Cove; ⏰ 9am-5pm). Some recom-mended activities include:

Australian Kayaking Adventures (☎ 0412-940 135; www.australiankayakingadventures.com.au; 3hr/half-day tours to South Stradbroke Island $55/75) Includes breakfast on the beach.

Australian Whale Watching (☎ 1300 422 784; www .australianwhalewatching.com.au; adult/child $85/50) Three-hour whale-watching cruise between June and November.

Gold Coast Helitours (☎ 5591 8457; www.goldcoast helitours.com.au; Mariner's Cove Marina) Flights range from five minutes (adult/child $44/33) up to 30 minutes ($203/115). The only company to offer tandem skydiving out of a helicopter at 3050m.

Queensland Scuba Diving Company (☎ 5526 7722; www.queenslandscubadive.com.au; Mariner's Cove Marina; dives from $99)

Paradise Jet Boating (☎ 1300 538 2628; Mariner's Cove Marina; 45min rides $60) Serious speed, spins and beach-blasting on a jet-boat reaching 85km/h.

Tall Ship (☎ 5532 2444; www.tallship.com.au; Mari-ner's Cove Marina; full day cruises adult/child/senior/family from $99/59/89/269) Cruises to South Stradbroke Island on yachts dressed up to look like tall ships. Half-day cruises also available. Combine parasailing with a tall ship experi-ence for $50. Also has whale-watching cruises.

Skydive Queensland (☎ 5528 2777; www.skydiveqld .com.au; Mariner's Cove) Tandem jumps from 3050m ($280) to 4270m ($325).

Tours

Blue Fire Cruises (☎ 5557 8888; www.bluefirecruises .com.au; Marina Mirage) Offers dinner and cabaret cruises (adult/child from $75/55), South Stradbroke Island day cruises (from $75/55) including morning tea, lunch, boom netting and ski boarding, and a whale-watching cruise (adult/child $75/40) from April to November.

Broadwater Canal Cruises (☎ 0410-403 020; adult/ child $32/15) Offers cruises to Tiki Village Wharf in Surfers Paradise. Cruises depart Mariner's Cove at 10.30am, 2pm and 4.30pm and the two-hour tour includes a buffet-style Devonshire tea.

Sleeping

Surfers Paradise YHA at Main Beach (☎ 5571 1776; www.yha.com.au/hostels; 70 Sea World Dr, Main Beach; dm/d & tw $24/66; 🖳) In a great position overlooking

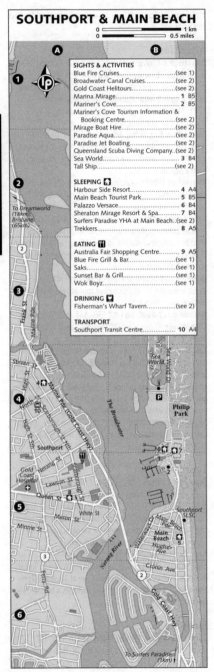

SOUTHPORT & MAIN BEACH

0 — 1 km
0 — 0.5 miles

SIGHTS & ACTIVITIES	
Blue Fire Cruises	(see 1)
Broadwater Canal Cruises	(see 2)
Gold Coast Helitours	(see 2)
Marina Mirage	1 B5
Mariner's Cove	2 B5
Mariner's Cove Tourism Information & Booking Centre	(see 2)
Mirage Boat Hire	(see 2)
Paradise Aqua	(see 2)
Paradise Jet Boating	(see 2)
Queensland Scuba Diving Company	(see 2)
Sea World	3 B4
Tall Ship	(see 2)

SLEEPING	
Harbour Side Resort	4 A4
Main Beach Tourist Park	5 B5
Palazzo Versace	6 B4
Sheraton Mirage Resort & Spa	7 B4
Surfers Paradise YHA at Main Beach	(see 2)
Trekkers	8 A5

EATING	
Australia Fair Shopping Centre	9 A5
Blue Fire Grill & Bar	(see 1)
Saks	(see 1)
Sunset Bar & Grill	(see 1)
Wok Boyz	(see 1)

DRINKING	
Fisherman's Wharf Tavern	(see 2)

TRANSPORT	
Southport Transit Centre	10 A4

To Dreamworld (18km); Brisbane (65km)

To Surfers Paradise (1km)

the marina, here you only have to drop over the balcony to access the plethora of water sports, cruises and tours on offer. BBQ nights are every Tuesday and Friday and the hostel is within staggering distance of the Fisherman's Wharf Tavern.

Trekkers (☎ 1800 100 004, 5591 5616; www.trekkersbackpackers.com.au; 22 White St, Southport; dm/d & tw $26, $68; 🖥 💷) You could bottle the friendly vibes of this beautiful Queenslander and make a mint. Some of the themed doubles have bathrooms and TVS. The communal areas are spotless and homy and the garden is a mini oasis.

Main Beach Tourist Park (☎ 5581 7722; www.gctp.com.au/main; Main Beach Pde, Main Beach; unpowered/powered sites from $29/32, cabins from $129-205; 🖥 💷) Just across the road from the beach, this caravan park is a favourite with families. It's a tight fit between sites but the facilities are good. Rates are for two people.

Harbour Side Resort (☎ 5591 6666; www.harboursideresort.com.au; 132 Marine Pde, Southport; studio $100, 1-/2-bedroom apt $130/170; 🖥 💷) Disregard the overwhelming brick façade and busy road; within this sprawling property you'll find pastel-hued units with oodles of room. The kitchens are well equipped and the complex also has a laundry and tennis courts. In high season there's a minimum five-night stay.

Sheraton Mirage Resort & Spa (☎ 1800 073 535, 5591 1488; www.sheraton.com/goldcoast; Sea World Dr, Main Beach; d from $275, ste $500-650; 🖥 💷 ; wi-fi) If you must have direct beach access this is the only five-star resort on the coast that will do. The rooms are classy and spacious and there's a gym, tennis courts, two restaurants, three bars and a beautiful lagoon-style pool. Spa aficionados will get their fix at the Golden Door Spa & Health Club here.

our pick Palazzo Versace (☎ 1800 098 000, 5509 8000; www.palazzoversace.com; Sea World Dr, Main Beach; d $480-585, ste/condos from $685/1300; 🖥 💷 ; wi-fi) The Palazzo is quite simply pure extravagance, from the sumptuous rooms to the equally indulgent restaurants and bars. Everything from the pool furniture to the buttons on the staff uniforms has Donatella Versace's glamorous mark on it.

Eating

The cheapest place to eat is the food court in the Australia Fair Shopping Centre.

Sunset Bar & Grill (☎ 5528 2622; Marina Mirage, Main Beach; dishes $5-17; ⏲ 7am-6pm) If your wallet has taken a beating at the exclusive boutiques in

---

GOLD COAST THEME PARKS

Test your lung capacity (or better yet, the kids') on the thrilling rides and swirling action at the five American-style theme parks just north of Surfers. Discount tickets are sold in most of the tourist offices on the Gold Coast; the 3 Park Super Pass (adult/child $177/115) covers entry to Sea World, Movie World and Wet'n'Wild.

Dreamworld (Map p289; ☎ 5588 1111; www.dreamworld.com.au; Pacific Hwy, Coomera; adult/child $66/43; ☺ 10am-5pm) Skip breakfast if you plan on tackling the Big 6 Thrill Rides, which include the Claw, a giant pendulum that swings you nine storeys high at 75km/h, and the Giant Drop, a terminal-velocity machine where you free fall from 38 storeys. It's not all rides, though: there's an interactive tiger show and an IMAX theatre. A two-day world pass (adult/child $102/68) lets you jump between Dreamworld and WhiteWater World as often as you like.

WhiteWater World (Map p289; ☎ 5588 1111; www.whitewaterworld.com.au; Pacific Hwy, Coomera; adult/child $43/29; ☺ 10am-5pm) A new addition next door to Dreamworld, this aquatic theme park is the place to take the kids on a hot summer day. There's the Hydrocoaster (a rollercoaster on water), and the Green Room, where you'll spin in a tube through a tunnel then drop 15m down a green water funnel. Get caught in The Rip or splash around in the surging swells in the Cave of Waves.

Sea World (Map p302; ☎ 5588 2222, show times 5588 2205; www.seaworld.com.au; Sea World Dr, Main Beach; adult/child $66/43; ☺ 10am-5pm) See Australia's only polar bears in this aquatic park, along with dugongs, sharks and performing seals and dolphins. There are dizzying rides, of course, but for a unique hands-on experience book an Animal Adventure with a marine-mammal trainer.

Warner Bros Movie World (Map p289; ☎ 5573 8485; www.movieworld.com.au; Pacific Hwy, Oxenford; adult/child $66/43; ☺ 10am-5pm) 'Hollywood on the Gold Coast' boasts more movie-themed rides than movie-set action but the kids will love meeting their favourite movie legends and Loony Tunes characters.

Wet'n'Wild (Map p289; ☎ 5573 2255; www.wetnwild.com.au; Pacific Hwy, Oxenford; adult/child $45/29; ☺ 10am-5pm Feb-Apr & Sep-Dec, 10am-4pm May-Aug, 10am-9pm 27 Dec-25 Jan) If the beach is too sedate, this colossal water-sports park offers plenty of creative ways to get wet. You can launch from a 15m-high platform in a tube and blast down a 40m tunnel, or swirl through the Black Hole, or zoom down Mammoth Falls in a big rubber ring. If all that sounds too energetic, catch a movie in a tube at the Dive'n'Movies.

---

the mall, you'll be glad to find this little place right on the water. Steaks, burgers and seafood dishes are all reasonably priced and all sandwiches are only $5.

Wok Boyz (☎ 5591 6808; Marina Mirage, Main Beach; dishes $14; ☺ lunch daily, dinner Tue-Sat) If the towering, tasty bowls of noodles don't lure you to this tiny noodle bar, maybe the fact that Jessica Alba ate here will.

Blue Fire Grill & Bar (☎ 5557 8877; Marina Mirage, Main Beach; mains $28-42; ☺ breakfast, lunch & dinner) Fancy something totally unexpected? Then try the *churrascaria*. This Brazilian method of flame-grilling and serving meats, chicken and fish (carved at your table) is a theatrical and gastronomic treat. Otherwise the Mediterranean menu will be sure to please as will the stylish décor and water views.

Saks (☎ 5591 2755; Marina Mirage, 74 Sea World Dr, Main Beach; mains $30-50; ☺ lunch & dinner) This smart, salubrious bar and restaurant lures cultured palettes with a brief but sophisticated menu

boasting dishes such as char-grilled eye fillet topped with Moreton Bay bugs, scallops and king prawns. Tall glass windows offer uninterrupted views of the marina.

Drinking

Fisherman's Wharf Tavern (☎ 5571 0566; Mariner's Cove, Main Beach) The famous Sunday Sessions at this styled-up tavern kick off at 3pm with live music on the deck overlooking the Broadwater.

Getting There & Away

Coaches stop at the Southport Transit Centre on Scarborough St, between North and Railway Sts. Catch local Surfside buses from outside the Australia Fair Shopping Centre on Scarborough St.

SOUTH STRADBROKE ISLAND

This narrow, 20km-long sand island is largely undeveloped, and a tranquil contrast to the mainland sprawl of the Gold Coast tourist strip. At the northern end, the narrow channel separating it from North Stradbroke Island is popular for fishing, while at the southern end the tip of the Spit is only 200m away. There are two resorts, a camping ground and plenty of bush, sand and sea to satisfy anglers, surfers, bushwalkers and kayakers. Cars aren't permitted on the island so you'll have to walk or cycle to get around.

The **Couran Cove Island Resort** (☎ 1800 268 726, 5509 3000; www.couran.com; d from $241; ⊗ ⊇) is an exclusive luxury resort with all guests' rooms perched on the water's edge. There are four restaurants to choose from, a day spa, a private marina and guided nature walks. Rates don't include ferry transfers (adult/child $47/25 return) from Hope Harbour at the northern end of the Gold Coast. Ferries leave at 10.30am, 2pm, 4pm and 6pm and return at 9am, noon, 3pm, 5pm and 7pm.

For something less extravagant, you can head to the **Couran Point Island Beach Resort** (☎ 5501 3555; www.couranpoint.com.au; d incl breakfast from $200; ⊇), which has colourful and comfortable hotel rooms, and slightly larger units with kitchenettes. All rates include a continental breakfast and use of nonmotorized facilities but do not include ferry transfers (adult/child $25/20 one way). Day-trippers can access the resort facilities (adult/child/family $65/30/170 includes BBQ lunch). The ferry leaves Marina Mirage daily at 10am and returns at 4pm.

GOLD COAST HINTERLAND

Inland from the surf, sand, and half-naked bods on the Gold Coast beaches, the densely forested and unspoiled mountains of the McPherson Range feel like a million miles away. The range forms a natural barrier between the eastern coastline and the rolling green hills of the Darling Downs, and the national parks here are a subtropical paradise of rainforests, waterfalls, numerous walking tracks, panoramic lookouts and amazing wildlife.

Tours

The only way to access the hinterland without your own wheels is on a tour.

4X4 Hinterland Tours (☎ 1800 604 425, 0429-604 425; www.4x4hinterlandtours.com.au; day tours adult/child $125/60) Specialises in small-group 4WD ecotours.

Australian Day Tours (☎ 1300 363 436; www.day tours.com.au; day tours adult/child $79/44, 2-day tours $350/145). Tours travel via Mt Tamborine and Canungra to O'Reilly's Rainforest Guesthouse in Lamington National Park, where you'll stay on the two-day tour.

Bushwacker Ecotours (☎ 3720 9020; www.bush wacker-ecotours.com.au; day trips adult/child $115/95) Has an extensive array of ecotours to the hinterland including a two-day tour (adult/child $239/199) with an overnight jungle camp.

SPRINGBROOK NATIONAL PARK

An excellent winding drive up from the Gold Coast beaches takes you into a *Jurassic Park* ecosystem of lush subtropical rainforests where closed canopies high overhead protect an amazing array of endangered and protected flora and fauna. The 3425-hectare **Springbrook National Park** consists of three reserves: Springbrook Plateau, Mt Cougal and Natural Bridge.

Like the rest of the McPherson Range, the Springbrook area is a remnant of the huge shield volcano that dominated the region 23 million years ago. From Best of All Lookout (reached via Lyrebird Ridge Rd; see opposite) you can see the once buried volcanic plug, Mt Warning (1156m), in NSW. The southern cliffs of Springbrook and Lamington continue into NSW arcing around in a giant circle, outlining the rim of the ancient volcanic crater.

The park is a mix of subtropical warm and cool temperate rainforest and open eucalypt forest. Hikers will want to make full use of the extensive walking tracks showcasing the weird world of strangler figs, vines, epiphytes, glow-in-the-dark mushrooms and worms, colourful wildlife and spectacular waterfalls and gorges. But be prepared, at 900m the national park can be up to 5°C cooler than the lowlands.

Each section of the park is reached by a long access road, and there are no shortcuts between the sections, so make sure you get on the right road. Coming from Nerang, take Springbrook Rd for the Springbrook section and the Nerang-Murwillumbah Rd for the Natural Bridge section. Take the Currumbin Creek Rd from Currumbin for Mt Cougal.

There's a **ranger's office** (☎ 5533 5147; 87 Carrick Rd; ⊙ 8am-3.30pm Mon-Fri) at Springbrook where you can pick up a copy of the national park's walking tracks.

Springbrook Plateau

The village of Springbrook is balanced right on the edge of the plateau, with numerous waterfalls tumbling down to the coastal plain below. The 'town' is actually a series of properties stretched along a winding road. Understandably, lookouts are the big attraction here, and there are several places where you can get the giddy thrill of leaning right out over the edge.

At **Gwongorella Picnic Area**, just off Springbrook Rd, the lovely **Purling Brook Falls** drop 109m into the rainforest. There are two easily accessed lookouts with views of the lush canopy and towering falls, and a number of walking trails including a 6km-return walk to Waringa Pool, a beautiful swimming hole.

The national park **information centre** is at the end of Old School Rd. A little further south **Canyon Lookout** affords jagged views through the valley all the way to the coast. This is also the start of a 4km circuit walk to **Twin Falls** and the 17km **Warrie Circuit**.

At the end of Springbrook Rd, the pleasant **Goomoolahra Picnic Area** has BBQs beside a small creek. A little further on, there's a great lookout point beside the falls with views across the plateau and all the way back to the coast.

True to its name, the **Best of All Lookout** offers spectacular views from the southern edge of the plateau to the flats below. The 350m trail from the car park to the lookout takes you past a clump of mighty Antarctic beech trees. Take time to admire the gnarled and twisted roots of these ancient giants. You'll only find them around here and in northern NSW.

There's only one camping ground at Springbook, the **Settlement Camp Ground** (☎ 13 13 04; www.epa.qld.gov.au; Carrick's Rd; camp sites per person $4.50), a rather uninspiring camping ground devoid of trees and showers but it does have toilets and electric BBQs.

Most guesthouses are along or signposted off Springbrook Rd.

Across the road from Canyon Lookout, **Rosellas at Canyon Lookout** (☎ 5533 5120; 8 Canyon Pde; s/d incl breakfast from $80/95) is a friendly family-run guesthouse. The three en suite rooms are clean and basic with TVs and bar fridges. There's a lovely **restaurant** (dishes $10-20; ☺ 9am-4pm Fri & Sun, to late Sat), and a smattering of local crafts for sale.

Set on 10 hectares of landscaped gardens is the stately Tudor-style **Springbrook Mountain Manor** (☎ 5533 5344; www.springbrookmountainmanor .com.au; 2814 Springbrook Rd; s/d incl breakfast from $155/210). The rooms are heavy with brocade and period furniture and there's even a bridal suite. The restaurant (open for lunch and dinner) offers fine dining with five-star service.

Springbrook Mountain Chalets (☎ 5533 5205; sm chalets.com.au; 2058 Springbrook Rd; midweek/week end from $170/250) has stylish wooden chalets peppered throughout a thick plot of bush. Cathedral

---

DETOUR: TAMBORINE MOUNTAIN

A mountaintop rainforest community just 45km inland from the Gold Coast beaches, Tamborine Mountain has cornered the chocolate, fudge, and craft cottage industries in a big way. Of the three satellite suburbs (Eagle Heights, North Tamborine and Mt Tamborine), **Gallery Walk** in Eagle Heights is the place to stock up on homemade jams and all things artsy-craftsy but wherever you are on Tamborine Mountain a Devonshire tea is never too far away.

As well as housing a bevy of creative artists and musicians, Tamborine Mountain is home to Queensland's oldest national park. The **Tamborine Mountain National Park** is actually 13 sections of land that stretch across the 8km plateau, offering tumbling cascades and great views of the Gold Coast. Most of the national parks surround North Tamborine and some of the best spots are **Witches Falls, Curtis Falls, Cedar Creek Falls** and **Cameron Falls**.

To get to Tamborine Mountain, turn off the Pacific Hwy at Oxenford or Nerang. The **visitor information centre** (☎ 5545 3200; Doughty Park; ☺ 10am-3.30pm Mon-Fri, 9.30am-3.30pm Sat & Sun) is located in North Tamborine. This is part of the **Rainforest Way**, the scenic route that includes 14 Unesco-recognized parks in Queensland and NSW (see p284).

There are plenty of romantic weekend hideaways in the rainforest including **Songbirds Rainforest Retreat** (☎ 5545 2563; www.songbirds.com.au; Tamborine Mountain Rd, North Tamborine; villas per night from $425). Each of the six luxurious Southeast Asian–inspired villas has a double spa bath with rainforest views, and you can book private massage, meditation or yoga sessions. If you're not staying the night, have lunch at the **St Bernards Hotel** (☎ 5545 1177; 101 Alpine Tce, Tamborine; mains $16-28; ☺ lunch & dinner), a rustic old mountain pub with a large deck that has commanding views of the gorge.

ceilings, large glass doors, spa baths and pot-belly stoves add up to an intimate weekend.

ourpick Hidden in the magical misty woods are the A-frame red-cedar cottages of the **Mouses House** (☎ 5533 5192; www.mouseshouse.com.au; 2807 Springbrook Rd; 2 nights from $385). Soft lighting along rainforest boardwalks leads to 11 enchanted chalets, each with a double spa and wood fire. These ultraprivate fairytale cottages are the ultimate romantic mountain hideaway. Breakfast, lunch and dinner hampers are available on request.

Right by the car park for Purling Brook Falls, **Rainforest Retreat** (☎ 5533 5335; 33 Forestry Rd; dishes $7-14; ☷ 10am-4pm) is a simple tearoom with healthy salads and light meals.

Springbrook Homestead (☎ 5533 5200; 2319 Springbrook Rd; mains $10-29; ☷ lunch daily, dinner Fri) serves ploughman's lunches, soup and damper, and chunky rump pies. You can pick up a walking map here and work out your route over a beer.

LAMINGTON NATIONAL PARK

Australia's largest remnant of subtropical rainforest covers the deep valleys and steep cliffs of the McPherson Range, reaching elevations of 1100m on the Lamington Plateau. The 200-sq-km Lamington National Park is a Unesco World Heritage site and has over 160km of walking trails.

The two most popular and accessible sections of the park are **Binna Burra** and **Green Mountains**, both reached via Canungra. Binna Burra can also be reached from Nerang. Both roads twist and snake their way up the mountain, cutting through encroaching forest and open grazing land. It's a spectacular drive, particularly along the Green Mountain Rd, and well worth the effort.

At Green Mountains, be sure to walk the excellent **tree-top canopy walk** along a series of rope-and-plank suspension bridges 15m above the ground. Serious hikers can tackle the 24km **Border Trail** that links the two sections of the park. Walking trail guides are available from the **ranger stations** (Binna Burra ☎ 5533 3584; ☷ 9am-3.30pm Sat & Sun; Green Mountains ☎ 5544 0634; ☷ 9-11am & 1-3.30pm Mon-Fri).

Binna Burra Mountain Lodge (☎ 1300 246 622, 5533 3622; www.binnaburralodge.com.au; Binna Burra Rd, Beechmont; unpowered/powered sites $24/27, safari tents from $55, d incl breakfast with/without bathroom $250/150) is an excellent mountain retreat with rustic log cabins and camp sites surrounded by forest. **O'Reilly's Rainforest Guesthouse** (☎ 1800 688 722, 5544 0644; www.oreillys.com.au; Lamington National Park Rd; guesthouse s/d from $155/265, 1-/2-bedroom villas from $310/360) at Green Mountains was built in 1926. The guesthouse is looking dated and faded but still manages to retain its old-world rustic charm – and sensational views.

Brisbane

Brisbane appears to be setting the tempo for Australian urban spaces. It's the fastest growing capital city in the country and with that comes an energy, and a get-up-and-go attitude, as evidenced by all the building sites in the CBD. Once these initial conceptions are peeled away however, Brisbane is revealed as an affable place, stacked full of colonial architecture, gracious subtropical gardens and a culture revolving around an outdoor life-style, underneath skies that are rarely anything but blue. A river city at heart, Australia's third metropolis huddles around the Brisbane River. Exploring Brisbane by ferry, and passing under the mighty Story Bridge will give you a wonderful appreciation of this city with its prosperous and sophisticated society. Between the parks, koala sanctuaries, tropical flora and river views is world-class cuisine, heritage pubs, style-cat bars spilling onto sidewalks, museums and galleries and perhaps the best opportunity in urban Australia to access indigenous culture. To top it off artistic festivals set the events calendar ablaze.

The water lapping at the city's doorstep is Moreton Bay, which has about 365 islands (one for every day of the year), around which whales, dolphins and dugongs frolic. On Moreton Island the forest tumbles down to white-sand beaches and snorkelling the Tangalooma Wrecks just offshore means immersing yourself in crystal-clear jade and indigo-blue waters. North Stradbroke is more developed and no less attractive with glorious beaches, pristine lakes, thick bush and lots of activities to build up an appetite for the island's gourmet foodie scene.

HIGHLIGHTS

- Heading into the modish suburb of **New Farm** (p323)
- Washing away that urban grit in leafy **Mt Coot-tha** (p318) where you could spend a day exploring bush tracks, gardens, and a city lookout
- Discovering the river city in the Brisbane River with a **scenic river cruise** (p320)
- Checking out the brazen new **Queensland Gallery of Modern Art** (p316)
- Scaling the floodlit, pink, volcanic cliffs at Kangaroo Point, a premier site for **rock climbing** (p319)
- Beating the heat at Streets Beach in the **South Bank Parklands** (p316)
- Exploring the bush wilderness and startling coloured waters of postcard-perfect **Moreton Island** (p332), right on Brisbane's doorstep
- Kayaking the sublime coastline, surf, swim or just relax on a blissful stretch of beach on **North Stradbroke Island** (p330)

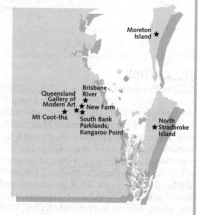

■ TELEPHONE CODE: 07   ■ POPULATION: 1.86 million   ■ www.ourbrisbane.com

BRISBANE

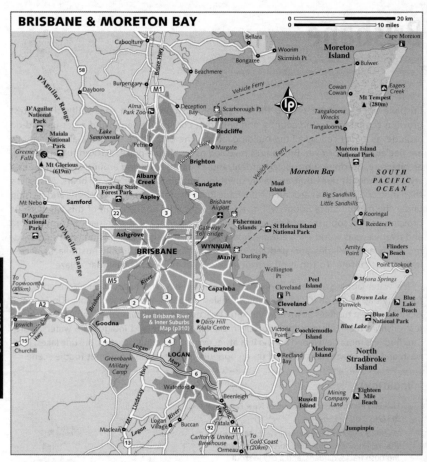

ORIENTATION

Brisbane's central business district (CBD) is bound to the south by a U-shaped loop of the Brisbane River, about 25km upstream from the river mouth. Queen St Mall, which runs down to the Treasury Casino and the Victoria Bridge, is the main shopping district. South across Victoria Bridge is South Brisbane, with the Queensland Cultural Centre and the South Bank parklands, and the hip suburb of West End. Northeast of the city, along Ann St, is Fortitude Valley, with its small Chinatown, alternative scene and lots bars and nightclubs. Southeast of here is New Farm, which has excellent culinary and drinking options.

The Roma St Transit Centre, where you'll arrive if you're coming by bus, train or airport shuttle, is about 500m northwest of the Queen St Mall.

Brisbane airport is about 15km northeast of the city; see p328 for information about getting to/from the airport.

Maps

For a comprehensive and handy map pick up a copy of Lonely Planet's *Brisbane and Gold Coast City Map*. You can pick up free Queensland Tourism maps with coverage of the CBD from one of the visitor centres. For more comprehensive detail, pick up a copy of *Brisbane Suburban Map* by UBD

BRISBANE IN...

Two days

Greet the day with an unhurried breakfast in the trendy **West End** (p324) before strolling to the **South Bank Parklands** (p316) to get acquainted with offerings at the **Queensland Cultural Centre** (p311). Already hungry? Then slip into one of the **riverside cafés** (p323) and watch the city's morning routine. As the day warms up, cool those heels, and everything else, at **Streets Beach** (p316). If it's summer, stick around for an alfresco movie in the park. Looking for dinner? Why not jump on a ferry and head to Eagle St Pier where you can tuck into the best steak in town at **Cha Cha Char** (p323).

On day two stroll downtown through the city's mix of old and new architecture. Explore Brisbane's history at **City Hall** (p311) and enjoy the beautiful old **Treasury Building** (p311), before heading south to the **City Botanic Gardens** (p311). The massive Moreton Bay Figs shade the perfect spot for a lazy picnic. Finish the day with a brew at the **Port Office Hotel** (p325) and enjoy a cool breeze off the river over dinner at **Watt** (p324) in New Farm.

Four Days

On day three check out the cafés in **New Farm** (p323) and delve into the trendy shops and **galleries** (p317) in nearby Fortitude Valley. Spend the afternoon at the lookout at **Mt Coot-tha Reserve** (p318). Take in a short bushwalk and visit the beautiful **Brisbane Botanic Gardens** (p318). Then head back to **Fortitude Valley** (p323) for fine dining, and work it all off in one of the clubs or late night bars. On day four you'll need to give the feet a rest, so take a cruise up the Brisbane River to **Lone Pine Koala Sanctuary** (p319). As you cruise back, watch the city glide past, in all its leafy glory. Recount the day's events over a beer at the **Breakfast Creek Hotel** (p324) and then gravitate to Paddington for a feast at **Sultan's Kitchen** (p323) before collapsing into bed.

($7.95) or *Brisbane and Region* by Hema Maps ($6.50).

INFORMATION
Bookshops

Archives Fine Books (Map pp314-15; ☎ 3221 0491; 40 Charlotte St; ☘ 9am-6pm Mon-Thu, 9am-9pm Fri, 9am-5pm Sat, 10am-5pm Sun) Fantastic range of secondhand books, boasting one million titles.
Borders Bookstore (Map pp314-15; ☎ 3210 1220; 162 Albert St; ☘ 9am-7pm Mon-Thu, 9am-9pm Fri, 9am-6pm Sat, 10am-5pm Sun)
World Wide Maps & Guides (Map pp314-15; ☎ 3221 4330; Shop 30, Anzac Square Arcade, 267 Edward St; ☘ 8.30am-5pm Mon-Thu, 8.30am-7pm Fri, 10am-3pm Sat)

Emergency

Ambulance (☎ 000, 1300 369 003)
Fire (☎ 000, 3247 5539)
Police (☎ 000) City (Map pp314-15; ☎ 3224 4444; 67 Adelaide St); Headquarters (Map pp314-15; ☎ 3364 6464; 200 Roma St); Fortitude Valley (Map pp314-15; ☎ 3131 1200; Brunswick St Mall)
RACQ (☎ 13 19 05, breakdown ☎ 13 11 11) City (Map pp314-15; GPO Bldg, 261 Queen St); St Pauls Tce (Map pp314-15; 300 St Pauls Tce) Roadside service.

Internet Access

Internet cafés are prolific in Brisbane. Rates range from $3 to $5 per hour.
Global Gossip City (Map pp314-15; ☎ 3229 4033; 290 Edward St; ☘ 9am-11pm Mon-Sat, 10am-10pm Sat & Sun); Fortitude Valley (Map pp314-15; ☎ 3666 0900; 312 Brunswick St; ☘ 9am-11pm) Charges $4 per hour with membership; gets cheaper the more you use it.
Internet City (Map pp314-15; ☎ 3003 1221; Level 4, 132 Albert St; per hr $4; ☘ 24hr)
IYSC (Map pp314-15; ☎ 3211 9095; 128 Adelaide St; 60c per 10min, $3 per hr; ☘ 8.30am-8.30pm Mon-Fri, 9.30am-8.30pm Sat & Sun)
State Library of Queensland (Map pp314-15; ☎ 3840 7666; South Bank; ☘ 10am-8pm Mon-Thu, 10am-5pm Fri-Sun; wi-fi) Free, but advance bookings required.

Medical Services

Brisbane Sexual Health Clinic (Map pp312-13; Biala City Community Health Centre; ☎ 3837 5611; 270 Roma St)
Royal Brisbane & Women's Hospital (Map pp312-13; ☎ 3636 8111; cnr Butterfield St & Bowen Bridge Rd, Herston; ☘ 24hr casualty ward)
Travel Clinic (Map pp314-15; ☎ 1300 369 359, 3211 3611; 1st fl, 245 Albert St; ☘ 7.30am-7pm Mon-Thu, 7.30am-6pm Fri, 8.30am-5pm Sat, 9.30am-5pm Sun)

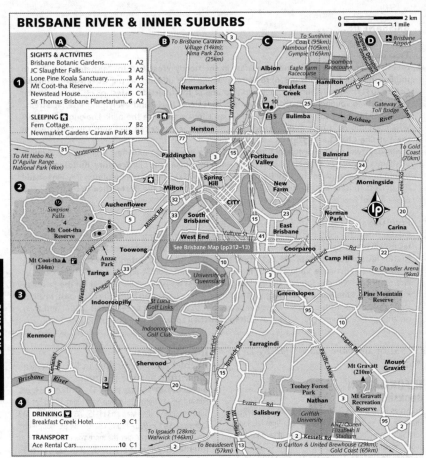

BRISBANE RIVER & INNER SUBURBS

SIGHTS & ACTIVITIES
Brisbane Botanic Gardens............1 A2
JC Slaughter Falls........................2 A2
Lone Pine Koala Sanctuary..........3 A4
Mt Coot-tha Reserve....................4 A2
Newstead House..........................5 C1
Sir Thomas Brisbane Planetarium.6 A2

SLEEPING
Fern Cottage................................7 B2
Newmarket Gardens Caravan Park.8 B1

DRINKING
Breakfast Creek Hotel..................9 C1

TRANSPORT
Ace Rental Cars..........................10 C1

Travellers' Medical & Vaccination Centre (Map
pp314–15; TMVC; ☎ 3815 6900; 75 Astor Tce, Spring Hill;
⊙ 8am-5pm Mon, Tue, Thu & Fri, 8.30am-8pm Wed,
8am-1.30pm Sat)

Money

There are plenty of foreign-exchange bureaus
at Brisbane airport's domestic and interna-
tional terminals, as well as ATMs that accept
most international credit cards. ATMs are
prolific throughout Brisbane.
American Express (Map pp314–15; ☎ 1300 139 060;
Shop 3, 156 Adelaide St)
Interforex Brisbane (Map pp314–15; ☎ 3221 3562;
Shop 255, Wintergarden Centre, 171 Queen St)
Travelex (Map pp314–15; ☎ 3210 6325; Shop 149F, The
Myer Centre, Queen St Mall)

Post

Australia Post (☎ 13 13 18) GPO (Map pp314–15; 261
Queen St; ⊙ 7am-6pm Mon-Fri); Wintergarden (Map pp314–
15; 2nd fl, Wintergarden Centre, 171 Queen St, ⊙ 9am-5pm
Mon-Fri, 9am-1pm Sat) The GPO has poste restante.

Tourist Information

Brisbane Visitor Information Centre (Map pp314–
15; ☎ 3006 6290; Queen St Mall; ⊙ 9am-5.30pm Mon-
Thu, 9am-7pm Fri, 9am-4.30pm Sat, 9.30am-4pm Sun)
Located between Edward and Albert Sts. Great one-stop
info counter for all things Brisbane.
Brisbane Visitors Accommodation Service (Map
pp314–15; ☎ 3236 2020; 3rd fl, Roma St Transit Centre,
Roma St; ⊙ 7.30am-6pm Mon-Sat, 8am-6pm Sun) Privately run outfit specialising in backpacker travel, tours and
accommodation in Brisbane and elsewhere in Queensland.

Naturally QLD (Map pp314-15; ☎ 1300 130 372; 160 Ann St; ☯ 8.30am-5pm Mon-Fri) The QPWS runs this excellent information centre. You can get maps, brochures and books on national parks and state forests, as well as camping information and Fraser Island permits.

South Bank Visitors Centre (Map pp314-15; ☎ 3867 2051; www.visitsouthbank.com.au; Stanley St Plaza, South Bank Parklands; ☯ 9am-5pm)

SIGHTS

A walk through the city will reveal Brisbane's colonial history and architecture, and a ferry ride across the river takes you to the attractions and activities of South Bank. The free *Brisbane's Living Heritage* brochure, available from the visitor centre, highlights many of these sights.

City Centre

Brisbane's **City Hall** (Map pp314-15; ☎ 3403 6586; btwn Ann & Adelaide Sts; admission free; ☯ lift & viewing tower 10am-3pm) is a historic sandstone building overlooking the sculptures and fountains of King George Square, and offers one of the best views across the city. On the ground floor is the **Museum of Brisbane** (Map pp314-15; admission free; ☯ 10am-5pm), which describes the city's historical journey with interactive exhibits, as well as showcasing art and crafts. There are free guided tours of the museum at 11am on Tuesday, Thursday and Saturday. **King George Square**, the city's premier public space, was getting a huge makeover when we passed through. The project incorporates a subtropical design and should definitely be worth a look when complete.

At the western end of the Queen St Mall is the magnificent Italian Renaissance-style **Treasury Building**. Behind the lavish façade you won't find pin-striped bureaucrats and tax collectors, but rather spruikers and an entirely different kind of money spinner: Conrad's 24-hour casino. In the block southeast of the casino, the equally gorgeous former **Land Administration Building** (Map 314-15) has been converted to a five-star hotel (see p323).

Further south along George St is **Parliament House** (Map pp314-15; ☎ 3406 7562; cnr Alice & George Sts; admission free), dating from 1868, where you're free to watch Queensland's law-makers in action on sitting days. Free guided tours are available on demand between 9am and 4pm Monday to Friday, and 10am to 2pm weekends, unless parliament is sitting, in which case you can hang out in the public gallery and watch.

Brisbane's **City Botanic Gardens** (Map pp314-15; ☎ 3403 0666; Albert St; ☯ 24hr) is right on the river and are a mass of green lawns, towering Moreton Bay figs, bunya pines, macadamia trees and other tropical flora, descending gently from the Queensland University of Technology (QUT) campus. Its lawns are popular with lunching office workers, joggers and picnickers.

In the grounds of QUT is the **QUT Art Museum** (Map pp314-15; ☎ 3864 2797; 2 George St; admission free; ☯ 10am-5pm Tue, Thu, Fri, 10am-8pm Wed, noon-4pm Sat & Sun), which has regularly changing exhibits of contemporary Australian art and works by Brisbane art students. Next door is the former **Old Government House**, a beautiful colonnaded building dating from 1860 and now the home of the National Trust.

Built by convicts in 1829, the **Commissariat Stores Building** (Map pp314-15; ☎ 3221 4198; 115 William St; adult/child $4/2; ☯ 10am-4pm Tue-Fri) is one of Brisbane's oldest buildings and houses a museum devoted to Brisbane's convict and colonial history.

South Bank

QUEENSLAND CULTURAL CENTRE

In South Bank, just over the Victoria Bridge from the CBD, is the extensive Queensland Cultural Centre. The austere exterior of the **Queensland Art Gallery** (Map pp314-15; ☎ 3840 7303; www .qag.qld.gov.au; Melbourne St, South Brisbane; admission free; ☯ 10am-5pm Mon-Fri, 9am-5pm Sat & Sun, free guided tours at 11am, 1pm & 2pm Mon-Fri, 11am, 12.30pm & 2pm Sat & Sun) doesn't begin to hint at the fine collection of works by European and Australian artists. The 1st floor is devoted to celebrated Australian artists (1840s–1970s), and you can view works by masters including Sir Sydney Nolan, Arthur Boyd, William Dobell, George Lambert, Margaret Preston and Brett Whitely.

At the back of the complex, the **Queensland Museum** (Map pp314-15; ☎ 3840 7555; www.qmuseum.qld .gov.au; Grey St, South Brisbane; admission free; ☯ 9.30am-5pm) has an eclectic collection of exhibits relating to Queensland's history, including a skeleton of Queensland's own dinosaur *Muttaburrasaurus*, and the *Avian Cirrus*, the tiny plane in which Queensland's Bert Hinkler made the first England to Australia solo flight in 1928. It also has a very good examination of Aboriginal and Torres Strait Islander cultures and artefacts. Within the museum is the excellent **Sciencentre** (Map pp314-15; admission adult/child/family $10/8/29), a hands-on science exhibit with interactive displays and regular film shows.

(Continued on page 316

BRISBANE

BRISBANE

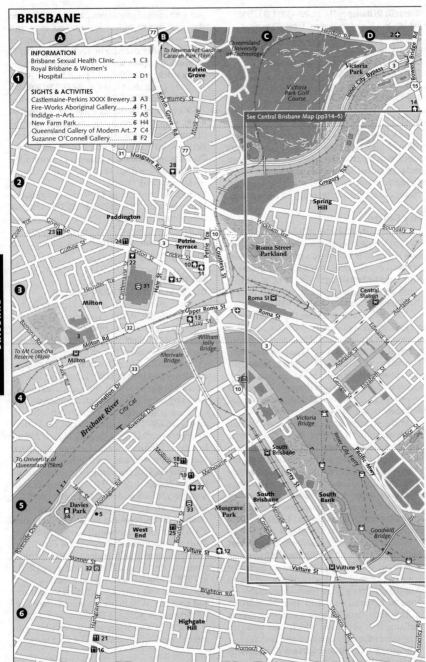

INFORMATION
Brisbane Sexual Health Clinic...........1 C3
Royal Brisbane & Women's
  Hospital....................................2 D1

SIGHTS & ACTIVITIES
Castlemaine-Perkins XXXX Brewery.3 A3
Fire-Works Aboriginal Gallery........4 F1
Indidge-n-Arts.............................5 A5
New Farm Park.............................6 H4
Queensland Gallery of Modern Art..7 C4
Suzanne O'Connell Gallery...........8 F2

See Central Brisbane Map (pp314–5)

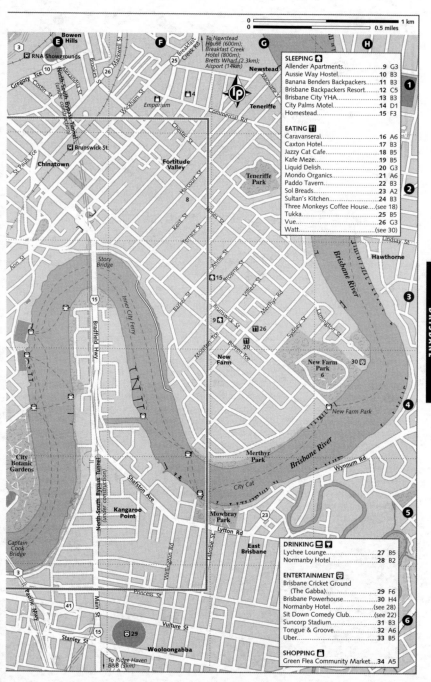

BRISBANE

CENTRAL BRISBANE

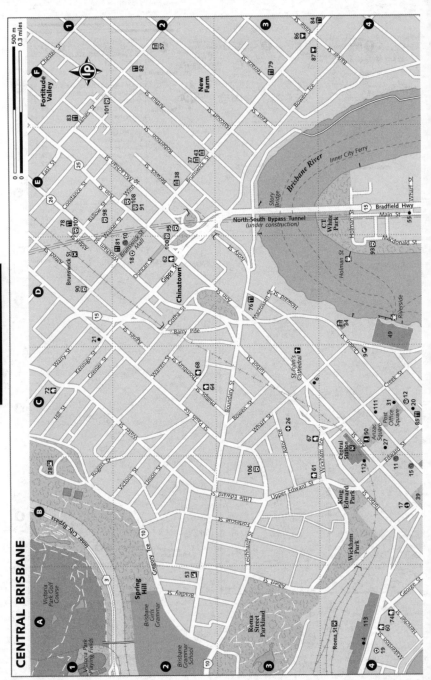

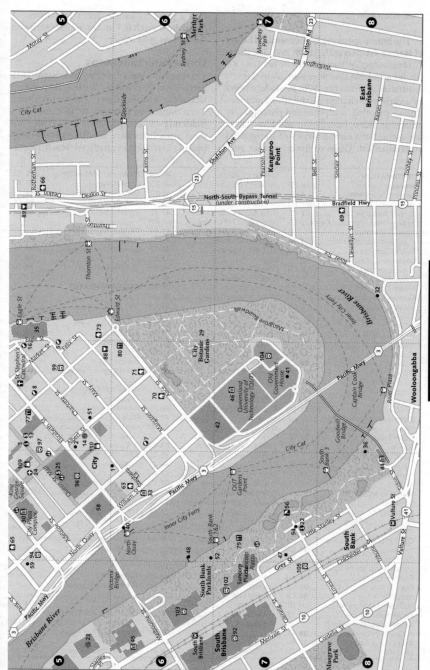

BRISBANE

(Continued from page 311)

The brand-spanking new **Queensland Gallery of Modern Art** (Map pp312-13; ☎ 3840 7350; Stanley Pl; admission free; ☉ 10am-5pm Mon-Fri, 9am-5pm Sat & Sun, free guided tours same times as art gallery) depicts Australian art from the 1970s to modern times in a variety of changing exhibitions and mediums: painting, sculpture and photography alongside video, installation and film. There are some outstanding works of indigenous Australian art. Observe the work that goes

into a piece by Joseph Jurra Tjalpatjarri. A favourite though is Vincent Serico's series on Cooktown gold miners.

SOUTH BANK PARKLANDS

This beautiful smear of green **park** (Map pp314-15; admission free; ☉ dawn-dusk), skirting the western side of the Brisbane River, is home to cultural attractions, fine eateries, small rainforests, hidden lawns and gorgeous flora. The standout attractions here are **Streets Beach** (Map pp314–15), a funky artificial beach resem-

BRISBANE

ACCESSING INDIGENOUS AUSTRALIAN CULTURE IN BRISBANE

Experiencing indigenous culture is a highlight of any visit to Queensland and Brisbane presents some fine opportunities to access, experience and admire the unbroken spiritual legacy of the first Australians.

Art
Fire-Works Aboriginal Gallery (Map pp312-13; ☎ 3216 1250; www.fireworksgallery.com.au; 11 Stratton St, Newstead; ☻ 11am-5pm Tue-Fri, 11am-3pm Sat) is a wonderful centre for contemporary and often quite political Aboriginal art. There are a number of striking pieces of artwork set in a warehouse gallery, some a staggering size, giving insight into the hours of meticulous detail that goes into this wonderful artform – the wildlife depictions in particular are outstanding. There are also giant boomerangs and wire art.

    Suzanne O'Connell Gallery (Map pp314-15; ☎ 3358 5811; www.suzanneoconnell.com; 93 James St; ☻ 11am-4pm Wed-Sat) tucked away in New Farm has stunning works of art from celebrated indigenous artists such as Nancy Nungurrayi. Everything is for sale and prices start around $800. It's a lovely, compact gallery with good lighting and austere surrounds, which enhances the effect of the indigenous works. There are also regular exhibitions from various artists, and it's a good source for information.

Workshops
Tribal Galleries (Map pp314-15; ☎ 1800 806 225; www.indigenousgallery.com.au; 376 George St; ☻ 9am-5pm Mon-Fri) has a mix of Aboriginal art and tourist souvenirs including a hefty range of didjerius – if you're lucky someone instore may demonstrate the didgeridoo for you, or else grab a free lesson at 4pm on Monday, Wednesday or Friday. This place also runs the **Basement** around the corner where you can do a workshop to learn about Australian indigenous culture and craft techniques. Run by traditional Aboriginal artists you can have a go at canvas painting or decorating your own raw boomerang ($30).

    Indidge-n-Arts (Map pp312-13; ☎ 1800 893 896; 270 Montague Rd, West End; ☻ 9am-5pm) also holds workshops including didgeridoo making ($120), bush seed jewellery ($25), basket weaving ($35), as well as hand drumming ($30) and didgeridoo playing ($30) lessons. These people like working with children so chances are yours would be very welcome.

bling a tropical lagoon, and, behind the beach, **Stanley Street Plaza**, a renovated section of historic Stanley St, with shops, cafés and a tourist information centre.

On the eastern edge of the parklands is the **Queensland Maritime Museum** (Map pp314-15; ☎ 3844 5361; Sidon St, South Brisbane; adult/child $7/3.50; ☻ 9.30am-4.30pm), which has a wide ranging display of maritime adventures (and misadventures) along the coast.

The South Bank parklands are also within easy walking distance of the city centre, but CityCat and Inner City Ferries stop at South Bank 1, 2 and 3 jetties if you'd like to go by boat. Alternatively, you can get there by bus or train from Roma St or Central station.

Inner North
For over a decade the alternative neighbourhoods of Fortitude Valley and nearby New Farm have been the hub of all things contemporary and cool, thanks to a confluence of artists, restaurateurs and various fringe types flooding the area.

Between the months of November and February, the alfresco **Moonlight Cinemas** (☎ 1300 551 908; www.moonlight.com.au; adult/child $13/9; ☻ 6pm Wed-Sun) screens movies in New Farm Park.

The **Institute of Modern Art** (Map pp314-15; ☎ 3252 5750; www.ima.org.au; ☻ 11am-5pm Tue-Sat, until 8pm Thu), a noncommercial gallery with an industrial exhibition space, has regular showings by local names. It's housed inside the **Judith Wright Centre for Contemporary Arts** (Map pp314-15; ☎ 3872 9000; www.judithwrightcentre.com.au; 420 Brunswick St, Fortitude Valley).

Other galleries in the area:
Jan Murphy Gallery (Map pp314-15; ☎ 3254 1855; 486 Brunswick St; ☻ 10am-5pm Tue-Sat)
Philip Bacon Galleries (Map pp314-15; ☎ 3358 3555; 2 Arthur St; ☻ 10am-5pm Tue-Sat)

A HELPING HAND

Volunteering is a great way of helping out local communities and you will get to see a slice of the east coast few other visitors experience. Some volunteering can also provide valuable opportunities for training and increase your skill set. A good place to get started is **Volunteering Queensland** (www.volunteeringqueensland.org.au) where you can register to search their database for current placements. Brisbane-based organisations to consider include:

Brisbane ActionWeb for Refugee Collaboration (www.barc.org.au) This umbrella organisation is an excellent information source and can link you up with flexible volunteer placements helping refugees and asylum seekers around Brisbane.

Friends of the Earth Brisbane (www.brisbane.foe.org.au) Provides lots of opportunities to become involved in local environmental issues including campaigns about climate change and their nuclear concerns for Queensland.

Queensland Parks & Wildlife Service (www.epa.qld.gov.au) A government body providing volunteering opportunities all over the state: from counting frogs in tropical rainforest, and nurturing sick and injured wildlife, to restoring degraded land.

Save the Koala (www.savethekoala.com) Runs programs in Queensland and elsewhere in the country including volunteer field-trips and a program where you can foster one of the cuddly bears.

Newstead

North of the centre, on the Brisbane River, is Brisbane's best-known heritage site, the lovely old **Newstead House** (Map p310; ☎ 3216 1846; Breakfast Creek Rd, Newstead; adult/child/family $4/2/10; ⏰ 10am-4pm Mon-Fri, 2-5pm Sun). The historic homestead dates from 1846 and is beautifully fitted out with Victorian furnishings and antiques, clothing and period displays. Surrounded by manicured gardens it sits on a breezy elevated position overlooking the river, giving superb water vistas. First Friday of each month is free admission.

Mt Coot-tha Reserve

A short drive or bus ride from the city, this huge bush reserve and parkland has an excellent botanic garden, a planetarium, eateries and a superb lookout over the city. On a clear day you can see the Moreton Bay islands. The lookout is accessed via Samuel Griffith Dr and has wheelchair access.

Just north of the road to the lookout, on Samuel Griffith Dr, is the turn-off to **JC Slaughter Falls**, reached by a short walking track, plus a 1.5km **Aboriginal Art Trail**, which takes you past eight art sites with works by local Aboriginal artists.

The pleasant **Brisbane Botanic Gardens** (Map p310; ☎ 3403 8888; admission free; ⏰ 8am-5.30pm Sep-Mar, 8am-5pm Apr-Aug; free guided walks 11am & 1pm Mon-Sat) has a plethora of mini ecologies, which include cactus, Japanese and herb gardens, rainforests, and arid zones, making you feel like you're traversing the globe's landscape in all its vegetated splendour.

Also within the gardens, the **Sir Thomas Brisbane Planetarium** (Map p310; ☎ 3403 2578) is Australia's largest planetarium. There's a great observatory here and the shows inside the **Cosmic Skydome** (adult/child/family $12.10/7.10/32.70) will make you feel like you've stepped on board the *Enterprise*. Note you must see a show to access the planetarium; it is not open to the public otherwise.

To get here via public transport, take bus 471 from Adelaide St, opposite King George Sq ($2.80, 30 minutes, hourly Monday to Friday, six services Saturday and Sunday). The bus drops you off in the lookout car park and stops outside the Brisbane Botanic Gardens en route.

D'Aguilar Range National Park

Brisbanites suffering from suburban malaise satiate their wilderness cravings at this 50,000-hectare park in the D'Aguilar Range, 10km north of the city centre. At the park entrance the **Brisbane Forest Park information centre** (☎ 1300 723 684; www.epa.qld.gov.au; 60 Mt Nebo Rd; ⏰ 9am-4.30pm) has information about **camping** (per person $4.50) and maps of the park. If you plan to camp, keep in mind that these are remote, walk-in, bush-camp sites.

Beside the visitors centre is **Walkabout Creek** (adult/child/family $5.30/2.60/13.20; ⏰ 9am-4.30pm), a wildlife centre where you can see a resident platypus up close, as well as turtles, green tree frogs, lizards, pythons and gliders.

To get here catch bus 385 ($3.60, 30 minutes), which departs from the corner of Albert and Adelaide Sts hourly from 8.50am to 3.55pm.

Lone Pine Koala Sanctuary

Just a 35-minute bus ride south of the city centre, **Lone Pine Koala Sanctuary** (Map p310; ☎ 3378 1366; Jesmond Rd, Fig Tree Pocket; adult/child/family $20/15/52; ☺ 8.30am-5pm) is set in attractive parklands beside the river. It is home to 130 or so koalas, as well as kangaroos, possums and wombats. The koalas are undeniably cute and most visitors readily cough up the $15 to have their picture taken hugging one.

To get here catch the express bus 430 ($3.20, 35 minutes, hourly), which leaves from George St. Alternatively, **Mirimar Cruises** (☎ 1300 729 742; incl park entry per adult/child/family $48/27/135) cruises to the sanctuary along the Brisbane River from North Quay, next to Victoria Bridge. It departs at 10am daily, returning from Lone Pine at 1.30pm.

ACTIVITIES

The **Cliffs** (pp314–15) at Kangaroo Point, opposite the Botanic Gardens on the south bank of the Brisbane River, is a rock-climbing venue that's flood-lit at night. Several operators offer climbing and abseiling instruction here, including **Worth Wild Rock Climbing** (☎ 1800 689 453; www.worthwild.com.au) and **K2 Extreme** (☎ 3257 3310; www.k2extreme.com.au; per person $30).

Skatebiz (Map p314-15; ☎ 3220 0157; 101 Albert St; per 2/24hr $13/20; ☺ 9am-5.30pm Mon-Thu, 9am-9pm Fri, 9am-4pm Sat, 10am-4pm Sun) rents out in-line skates and the necessary protective equipment. Some of the best skating areas are the South Bank Parklands, the City Botanic Gardens and the bike paths that follow the Brisbane River.

Brisbane has some 500km of bike trails, all of which are detailed in the *Brisbane Bicycle Experience Guide,* available from visitors centres. The most scenic routes follow the Brisbane River. Bicycles are allowed on Citytrains, except

on weekdays during peak hours. You can also take bikes on CityCats and ferries for free. You can rent a bike from **Riders** (Map pp314-15; ☎ 3846 6200; Shop 9, Little Stanley St, South Bank; per hr/day $12/30; ☺ 8am-5pm Mon-Sat, 10am-4pm Sun).

There are several good swimming pools in Brisbane, including **Centenary Aquatic Centre** (Map pp314-15; ☎ 3831 7665; 400 Gregory Tce, Spring Hill; adult/child $4.60/3.60; ☺ 5.30am-7.30pm Mon-Fri, 6am-6pm Sat & Sun), **Spring Hill Baths** (Map pp314-15; ☎ 3831 7881; 14 Torrington St, Spring Hill; ☺ 6.30am to 8pm Mon-Thu, 6.30am to 7pm Fri, 8am to 5pm Sat, 9am to 5pm Sun, closed May-mid Aug) and the **Streets Beach** lagoon at the South Bank parklands.

You can tandem skydive with the **Brisbane Skydiving Centre** (☎ 5464 6111; www.brisbaneskydive .com.au; tandem skydive from $300), or go ballooning with **Fly Me to the Moon** (☎ 3423 0400; www.flyme tothemoon.com.au; Mon-Fri $300, Sat & Sun $350).

BRISBANE FOR CHILDREN

One of the best attractions for children is the **Queensland Cultural Centre** (p311), where the Queensland Museum runs a range of fantastic hands-on programmes. The incorporated Sciencentre is made for inquisitive young minds and will keep them busy for hours. The Queensland Art Gallery has a Children's Art Centre that runs regular programmes.

Hands On Art (Map pp314-15; ☎ 3844 4589; www.hand sonart.org.au; South Bank; ☺ 10am-5pm Wed-Fri, 10am-5pm Mon-Fri during school holidays) is an art workshop where kids get to unleash their inner Picasso. The **South Bank Parklands** (p316) has the safe and child-friendly Streets Beach and a scattering of jungle gym playgrounds.

The river is a big plus; many children will enjoy a river-boat trip, especially if it's to the **Lone Pine Koala Sanctuary** (left), where they can cuddle up to one of the lovable creatures.

BRISBANE

QUIRKY BRISBANE

It may not be the Melbourne Cup, but Brisbane is mighty proud of the annual **Australia Day Cockroach Races**, held at the Story Bridge Hotel (p325) every 26 January. If racing keeps you on the edge of your seat, then you'll also be in the front row for the annual **Great Brisbane Duck Race**. No, the locals have not figured out a way to train waddling water birds into becoming elite athletes. This is a *rubber* duckie race, an annual event on the Brisbane Riverfestival calendar (see p320). You get to 'adopt a duck' for $5 and spur it down the river (strictly a vocal affair), willing it to defeat its competitors and become the first to cross the line. The competition is fierce – an estimated 20,000 ducks fight for the winner's crown each year. If you happen to be the lucky caretaker of the victor you'll be rewarded for your efforts with a new car! If your duck performed at a substandard level you go home knowing you helped raise funds for the Princess Alexandra Hospital Foundation.

The free monthly booklet *Brisbane's Child* (www.brisbaneschild.com.au) has information about Brisbane for parents.

TOURS

The **City Sights bus tour** (day tickets per adult/child $25/20) is a hop-on-hop-off shuttle taking in 19 of Brisbane's major landmarks. Tours depart every 45 minutes between 9am and 3.45pm from Post Office Sq on Queen St and allow you to get off and on whenever and wherever you want. The same ticket covers you for unlimited use of CityCat ferry services.

Other tours of the city:

Castlemaine Perkins XXXX Brewery (Map pp312-13; ☎ 3361 7597; www.xxxx.com.au; cnr Black & Paten Sts; adult/child $18/10; ⏱ hourly 10am-4pm Mon-Fri & 6pm Wed) Adult tickets include four ales at the end of the tour. The brewery is a 20-minute walk west from the transit centre, or take the Citytrain to Milton station. Wear closed shoes.

Ghost Tours (☎ 3344 7265; www.ghost-tours.com.au; tickets $35-55) Offers something a little different: guided tours of Brisbane's haunted heritage, murder scenes, cemeteries, haunted tunnels and the infamous Boggo Road Gaol. Most tours are on Saturday nights.

River City Cruises (☎ 0428-278 473; www.rivercity cruises.com.au; South Bank Parklands Jetty A; adult/child/family $25/15/60) Has 1½-hour cruises with commentary, departing South Bank at 10.30am and 12.30pm (plus 2.30pm during summer).

Story Bridge Adventure Climb (☎ 1300 254 627; www.storybridgeadventureclimb.com.au) Offers 2½ hours of exhilarating (or terrifying depending on your vertigo quotient) views over Brisbane and beyond from the upper reaches of the city's premier bridge.

FESTIVALS & EVENTS

Information on festivals and events in Brisbane can be found at the visitors centres or at www.ourbrisbane.com/whatson. Major happenings:

Chinese New Year Always a popular event in the Valley in January/February.

Tropfest (www.tropfest.com) This nationwide short film festival is telecast live from South Bank during late February.

Brisbane Pride Festival (www.pridebrisbane.org.au) Brisbane's fabulously flamboyant gay and lesbian celebration, held in June.

Queensland Music Festival (www.queenslandmu sicfestival.com.au) Outstanding celebration of the world of music, held over 17 days in July in odd-numbered years.

Brisbane International Film Festival (www.biff.com .au) Ten days of quality films in August.

Ekka Royal National Agricultural Show (www.ekka .com.au) The country comes to town in early August.

Brisbane Riverfestival (www.riverfestival.com.au) Brisbane's major festival of the arts (see below), with buskers, performances, music and concerts. Held in September.

SLEEPING

Brisbane has an excellent selection of accommodation options that will suit any budget. Most are outside the CBD, but more often than not they're within walking distance or have good public transport connections.

Budget

Most of Brisbane's hostels are concentrated in the inner suburbs of Petrie Terrace, Fortitude Valley, New Farm and the West End.

A CITY CELEBRATES ITS RIVER

Running over 10 days from late August to early September, **Riverfestival** (www.riverfestival.com .au), the city's biggest arts event of the year, celebrates Brisbane's relationship with its river. The common thread between the performances, artistic displays, mini food festivals and cultural celebrations is that they are as intrinsic to Brisbane as its meandering river; continuously shaping and developing with the city's evolving character.

The festival is opened each year with a bang – literally. Staged over the Brisbane River, with vantage points from South Bank, the city and the West End, **Riverfire** is a massive fireworks show with dazzling visual choreography and a synchronised soundtrack. Also a staple is the **Riversymposium**; an international conference on the development of new approaches and methods to preserve the world's waterways. Other events combine Indigenous culture with contemporary performance to pay homage to the river and celebrate cultural collaboration.

Music plays a major role throughout the festival. The **Riverconcert**, held in the City Botanic Gardens, features live acts performing everything from jazz to hip hop to electronic soundscapes. The city's live-music venues also fill their playlist nightly.

Most of the events are free and family-friendly and there's a smorgasbord of activities for the kids. For more information click on to the Riverfestival website.

CITY

Tinbilly (Map pp314-15; ☎ 1800 446 646, 3238 5888; www
.tinbilly.com; 462 George St; 13-/7-/4-bed dm $26/28/29, tw &
d $100; ⚇ 🖳) This sleek hostel flaunts its youth
with a modern interior, excellent facilities and
clinical cleanliness. Downstairs a happy, helpful buzz swims around the job centre, travel
agency and the very popular bar, which is one
big party place.

Annie's Inn (Map pp314-15; ☎ 3831 8684; www.babs.com
.au/annies; 405 Upper Edward St; s/d $60/70, d with bathroom
$80) In a central location and walking distance
to the CBD, this modest B&B feels a little like
a large doll-house. The owners are helpful
and friendly.

FORTITUDE VALLEY & NEW FARM

Homestead (Map pp312-13; ☎ 1800 658 344, 3358 3538; 57
Annie St, New Farm; dm $22-26, d $69; 🖳) In a top New
Farm location, Homestead has four-, six- and
eight-bed dorms, and mixed and female-only
dorms in a great old house. No 6 is the best
double with heaps of space. This backpackers
would suit those looking for a quieter stay,
away from the more institutional options.

Bunk Backpackers (Map pp314-15; ☎ 1800 682 865; www
.bunkbrisbane.com.au; cnr Ann & Gipps St, Fortitude Valley;
dm $26-29, s $70, d & tw $90; ⚇ 🖳) More like a
snazzy hotel than a backpackers, this excellent
hostel has generous dorms with bathrooms,
gleaming kitchens and funky décor. It's extremely secure and the faaaabulous bar and
swimming pool belong on a CD cover.

PETRIE TERRACE

Aussie Way Hostel (Map pp312-13; ☎ /fax 3369 0711; 34
Cricket St, Petrie Tce; dm/s/d $25/45/60; ⚇) A small
and personal hostel housed in a picturesque
Queenslander that feels more like a guesthouse than a hostel. The upstairs balcony is
good for breezy afternoons. Dorms are a tad
more spacious than most.

Banana Benders Backpackers (Map pp312-13;
☎ 1800 241 157, 3367 1157; www.bananabenders.com;
118 Petrie Tce, Petrie Tce; dm $25, tw & d $60; 🖳) This
small and down-to-earth hostel is a great spot
if you're planning to hang your hat for awhile.
A great decking is the real pull of this place
with top city views. The friendly owners can
also help you find work.

Brisbane City YHA (Map pp312-13; ☎ 3236 1004; brisbane
city@yhaqld.org; 392 Upper Roma St, Petrie Tce; dm $29, tw & d
$67-85; ⚇ 🖳) You can't miss the Legoland ex-
terior of this hostel, but inside it's spacious and
comfortable. There are clean three- to 10-bed

dorms and key-card security. It's very popular,
attracting all ages and groups. Refurbishments
were taking place as we went to press.

WEST END

our pick **Brisbane Backpackers Resort** (Map pp312-13;
☎ 3844 9956; www.brisbanebackpackers.com.au; 110 Vulture
St, West End; dm $24-28, d $73; ⚇ 🖳 🏊) The word
'resort' is not in the title of this backpackers by
accident – it's a class act. Perks include TVs,
en suites and private balconies in the dorms,
and a tiled outdoor area around the bar, which
is spacious and has a nice tropical feel.

CAMPING

As all the camping grounds are far from the
centre of town, hostels are generally a better
bet for budget travellers.

Newmarket Gardens Caravan Park (Map p310; ☎ 3356
1458; www.newmarketgardens.com.au; 199 Ashgrove Ave,
Ashgrove; powered/unpowered sites $30/27, caravans $47,
cabins $80-100; ⚇ 🖳) This clean site is just 4km
north of the city centre and is well connected to
town by bus routes and Citytrain (Newmarket
station). The best tent-sites are around Nos
193 and 194, where there are shady spots in
the bottom corner of the park.

Brisbane Caravan Village (off Map p310; ☎ 1800
060 797, 3263 4040; www.caravanvillage.com.au; 763 Zillmere
Rd, Aspley; sites $25-50, cabins $95-110; ⚇ 🖳 🏊) Tidy
and excellent facilities.

Midrange

Brisbane has a good range of midrange city
hotels. Many cater to the business trade and
offer discount rates on the weekend.

CITY & NEW FARM

Allender Apartments (Map pp312-13; ☎ 3358 5832; www
.allenderapartments.com.au; 3 Moreton St, New Farm;
r $100-155; ⚇ ; wi-fi) The yellow-brick façade
may not grab you, but Allender's studios and
one-bedroom apartments are tasteful and immaculate. The cool and shaded interiors are a
fusion of funky décor and homely amenities
and there's plenty of room to spread out.
Allender also own more contemporary apartments that carry a touch of class, on nearby
Villiers St.

Explorers Inn (Map pp314-15; ☎ 1800 623 288, 3211
3488; www.explorers.com.au; 63 Turbot St; r from $110, su-
perior or family $150; ⚇ 🖳) A modern hotel with
very friendly management and a supreme city
centre location; prices do vary and its much
more expensive if booked at the last minute.

BRISBANE

Standard rooms are pretty boxy – the best room in the house is No 316.

Royal on the Park (Map pp314-15; ☎ 1800 773 337, 3221 3411; www.royalonthepark.com.au; cnr Alice & Albert Sts; r $130-300; ✖ 🖳 🛋 🐾) You'll feel like royalty indeed once you've spied the wonderful views of the City Botanic Gardens from the stylish room here. This four-star hotel is very popular with business travellers, so the cheaper rates are for Friday to Sunday nights. The rooms have broadband internet access.

Abbey Apartments (Map pp314-15; ☎ 3236 0600; www.abbeyhotel.com.au; 160 Roma St; 1-bed apt nightly/weekly per night $200/140; ✖ 🖳 🛋 🐾) Consisting of older, self-catering, apartments that have been tastefully and extensively refurbished to give them a very contemporary feel, these are great value CBD apartments. It's opposite the transit centre so very handy for coming and going.

Inchcolm Hotel (Map pp314-15; ☎ 3226 8888; www.inchcolmhotel.com.au; 73 Wickham Tce; r $160-250; ✖ 🐾) Dripping with character, the heritage structure gives this personable hotel much of its charm. Rooms have been renovated extensively and those in the newer wing tend to have more space and more light courtesy of huge windows, while rooms in the older wing have more character. The best deluxe is room is No 112 and the best executive rooms are Nos 101 and 102.

KANGAROO POINT

Paramount Motel (Map pp314-15; ☎ 3393 1444; www.paramountmotel.com.au; 649 Main St, Kangaroo Point; s/d/f $80/95/115; ✖ 🐾) Ignore the 'No Vacancy' sign out the front and check availability with reception at this excellent motel. It has cheery and impeccably clean rooms. Facilities include TVs and fully equipped kitchens making rooms terrific value.

Il Mondo (Map pp314-15; ☎ 3392 0111; www.ilmondo.com.au; 25 Rotherham St, Kangaroo Point; r $115-150, apt $150-350; ✖ 🐾) This postmodern boutique hotel has contemporary three- and four-star rooms that are reminiscent of an Ikea showroom. There's plenty of block colours, minimalist design and space, and the bathrooms are quite blissful. Towering over the Story Bridge the location is excellent.

PADDINGTON

Fern Cottage (Map p310; ☎ 3511 6685; www.ferncottage.net; 89 Fernberg Rd, Paddington; s/d $115/140; ✖ 🖳) Fern Cottage is a beautifully renovated Queenslander with a splash of Mediterranean ambi-

ence. Rooms have a cottage appeal and the burgundy room is the pick of the bunch: it's upstairs, spacious and has a great balcony.

SPRING HILL

our pick Spring Hill Terraces (Map pp314-15; ☎ 3854 1048; www.springhillterraces.com; 260 Water St, Spring Hill; budget/std r $75/100, studio/terrace unit $120/145; ✖ 🖳 🐾) Good old fashioned service and a range of accommodation is provided at this place, just tucked away off Brunswick St. It offers motel-style rooms and units all set in a collage of greenery and a tropical atrium garden very close to the Valley.

City Palms Motel (Map pp312-13; ☎ 3252 1338; www.citypalmsmotel.com; 55 Brunswick St, Spring Hill; standard/deluxe r $90/100; ✖) Fringed by palm trees on busy Brunswick St, this little motel is excellent value with cool, dark rooms that include a kitchenette. Deluxe rooms are bigger and have queen-size beds.

Dahrl Court Apartments (Map pp314-15; ☎ 3830 3400; www.dahrlcourt.com.au; 45 Phillips St, Spring Hill; r per night/week $125/805; ✖) Tucked into a quiet, leafy pocket of Spring Hill, this boutique complex offers outstanding value. The sizable apartments are fully self-contained with stylish bathrooms (including baths), kitchens and heritage aesthetics throughout (two with balconies – popular with smokers). The commodious townhouses are a step up in style and go for $140/910 per night/week.

One Thornbury House (Map pp314-15; ☎ 3839 5334; www.onethornbury.com; 1 Thornbury St, Spring Hill; d $140-170; ✖) Effortlessly dashing and with a hint of debonair, this two-storey Queenslander guesthouse is a classy affair. There are four rooms, three of which are en suite. All are beautifully furnished in warm contemporary décor, which contrasts vividly against rendered brick. Pick of the rooms is No 1 (with king-size bed), which is more like a boutique hotel room.

Top End

Brisbane has several fabulous top-end places, and they often give discounts to walk-in guests, particularly on weekends.

Quay West Suites Brisbane (Map pp314-15; ☎ 1800 672 726, 3853 6000; reservations@qwsb.mirvac.com.au; 132 Alice St; 1-/2-bedroom ste $200/450; ✖ 🐾) This sophisticated hotel has opulent, self-contained units with modern kitchens, fully equipped laundries, numerous TVs, stereos and spectacular views. The refined interiors are worth the price tag and the staff are utterly gracious.

Note that renovations were ongoing at the time of research.

Conrad Treasury (Map pp314-15; ☎ 3306 8888; www.conradtreasury.com.au; 130 William St; r from $215; ✿ 💻) Brisbane's classiest hotel is in the beautifully preserved former Land Administration Building. Every room is unique and awash with heritage features, polished wood, elegant furnishings and marble. If you go for a standard room, nab one on the 4th floor – they're slightly smaller but have brilliant balconies overlooking the city and river.

Stamford Plaza Brisbane (Map pp314-15; ☎ 3221 1999; www.stamford.com.au; cnr Edward & Margaret Sts; r from $220; ✿ 💻 ⚟ ; wi-fi) At the southern end of the city, the Stamford has a historic façade in front of a modern tower. The indulgent rooms have antique touches, large beds and plenty of atmosphere. There are often good package deals up for grabs.

EATING

Brisbane has a sophisticated and varied dining scene, with the best places to be found in New Farm, West End, Petrie Terrace and the CBD. Many eateries take advantage of Brisbane's climate with open-air courtyards or tables out on the pavement.

City Centre & South Bank

Java Coast Cafe (Map pp314-15; ☎ 3211 3040; 340 George St; mains $6-10; ⏱ 7.30am-4pm Mon-Fri) Fancy recapturing your zen while lunching under a canopy of trees in the middle of the CBD? Tables in the leafy rear courtyard here feel a mile away from the busy streets outside at this special city nook. Goodies include giant muffins, bagels, panini and quiche. There are also 20 different varieties of teas and they know how to brew a decent coffee.

Embassy Hotel (Map pp314-15; ☎ 3221 7616; 188 Edward St; light meals $12; ⏱ lunch, dinner) With suave red tones, cubed seating and polished wood, this groovy hotel dishes out some excellent pub nosh (mains $13 to $17) and is popular with city folk and travellers alike.

Café San Marco (Map pp314-15; ☎ 3846 4334; South Bank Parklands; mains $16-28; ⏱ breakfast, lunch & dinner) Swimming in a blithe, balmy atmosphere, this waterfront bistro is the perfect spot for a relaxed feed. It's just the ticket for picky palates and the patter of little feet. Good for families.

E'cco (Map pp314-15; ☎ 3831 8344; 100 Boundary St; starters $22, mains $38; ⏱ lunch Tue-Fri, dinner Tue-Sat) One of the finest restaurants in the state,

award-winning E'cco is a must for any culinary aficionado. Masterpieces on the menu include Margaret River lamb rump, zucchini, eggplant, crisp sage and chickpeas.

Cha Cha Char (Map pp314-15; ☎ 3211 9944; Shop 5, Eagle St Pier; mains $30-40; ⏱ lunch Mon-Fri, dinner daily) Wallowing in awards, many consider this Brisbane's best restaurant. And although you can tuck into fish, veal or duck dishes, this is primarily a steak restaurant – and a supremely good one at that. It's very classy without being pretentious as demonstrated by the diverse clientele.

Il (Map pp314-15; ☎ 3210 0600; cnr Edward & Alice Sts; mains $40-45; ⏱ lunch Mon-Fri, dinner Mon-Sat) This elegant restaurant is agreeable without making too much of a statement – that mission is saved for the food. Dishes include fillet of black Angus beef, bubble & squeak, king brown mushrooms and red wine jus.

Petrie Terrace & Paddington

Sol Breads (Map pp312-13; ☎ 3876 4800; 20 Latrobe Tce; breakfast $8.50; ⏱ 7am-4pm Mon-Sat, 7am-3pm Sun) Vegetarians will love this joint, which is all about fresh, healthy eating. It even makes its own sourdough bread onsite. Breakfast can be bircher muesli, fruit salad or baked eggs with avocado, garden salad and sourdough. The small balcony out the back is perfect for settling restless bubs.

Sultan's Kitchen (Map pp312-13; ☎ 3368 2194; 163 Given Tce, Paddington; dishes $12-17; ⏱ lunch Fri, dinner) If Indian food is your weakness, then this award winner will make you wobble. The service is impeccable and flavours from all corners of the subcontinent are represented on the menu. The nine types of naan are a meal unto themselves.

The bistros at both the **Caxton Hotel** (Map pp312-13; ☎ 3369 5544; 38 Caxton St, Petrie Tce; mains $15-25; ⏱ lunch & dinner; ✿), which has a popular steakhouse, and the **Paddo Tavern** (Map pp312-13; ☎ 3369 0044; 186 Given Tce, Paddington; mains $10-18; ⏱ lunch & dinner; ✿), serve good pub food.

Fortitude Valley & New Farm

Liquid Delish (Map pp312-13; ☎ 3254 4900; 4/893 Brunswick St; turkish sandwich $7.50; ⏱ 6am-3.45pm Mon-Thu, 6am-3pm Fri & Sat, 7am-1pm Sun) Hunt out this star performer in New Farm. It specialises in delicious juices ($6; a meal unto themselves), especially the frappes, and turkish bread sandwiches (fillings are creative and fresh) and salads, all with a Mediterranean feel.

Wok on Inn (Map pp314–15; ☎ 3254 2546; 728 Brunswick St; mains $10-12; ⊗ lunch & dinner) With a lovely shaded front courtyard this industrious and popular noodle bar is the New Farm spot for some fast noodles. Choose your noodle, your cooking style (incl Mongolian) and your meat/veg combo.

Spoon Deli & Café (Map pp314–15; ☎ 3257 1750; 22 James St; breakfast $10-15, mains $14-21; ⊗ 5.30am-7pm Mon-Fri, till 6pm Sat & Sun) Inside James St market, this upmarket deli serves deliciously rich pasta, salads and soup and colossal paninis and focaccias. Diners munch their goodies amidst the deli produce at oversized square tables or low benches skirting the windows, which flood the place with sunlight.

our pick Garuva Hidden Tranquillity Restaurant & Bar (Map pp314–15; ☎ 3216 0124; 324 Wickham St; mains $19; ⊗ dinner) This is no restaurant, it's a dining experience! Garuva's rainforested foyer leads to tables with cushioned seating concealed by walls of fluttering white silk. The menu shows diverse influences including Asian and southern European. There's a very Arabian Nights feel to dining, along with dim lighting, smooth soundtracks and lulled voices, which create a debaucherous air.

Purple Olive (Map pp314–15; ☎ 3254 0097; 79 James St; mains $20-30; ⊗ lunch Fri-Sun, dinner Tue-Sun) With a Mediterranean feel and a diverse continental menu this place fuses the best of southern European cooking with local produce. Dishes such as char-grilled baby octopus in sweet Hungarian smoked paprika or Moreton Bay bug fettuccine work a treat.

Watt (Map pp312–13; ☎ 3358 5464; Brisbane Powerhouse; mains $34; ⊗ lunch & dinner Tue-Sun) On the lower level of the of the Powerhouse Arts precinct, this is riverside dining at its best. The minimalist setup along the river creates a unique dining ambience. The Mod Oz food with Asian and Middle Eastern influences is delightfully presented and the fusion of flavours is a masterclass in cooking.

Also recommended:

Himalayan Cafe (Map pp314–15; ☎ 3358 4015; 640 Brunswick St; dishes $10-16; ⊗ dinner Tue-Sat) The authentic Tibetan and Nepali fare gets rave reviews. Kids welcome.

Vue (Map pp312–13; ☎ 3358 6511; 1/83 Merthyr Rd; mains $12-16; ⊗ 7am-10pm Tue-Sat, 7am-6pm Sun & Mon) Trendy bar-restaurant with gourmet pizza and pasta dishes.

West End

Three Monkeys Coffee House (Map pp312–13; ☎ 3844 6045; 58 Mollison St; dishes $7-16; ⊗ breakfast, lunch & dinner) A far departure from the profusion of minimalist cafés, this laid-back alternative is steeped in pseudo-Moroccan décor and ambience. *The* place to hunker down in the West End on a rainy afternoon.

Jazzy Cat Cafe (Map pp312–13; ☎ 3846 2544; 56 Mollison St; mains $12-23; ⊗ 10am-late Wed-Fri, 8am-late Sat, 8am-3pm Sun) Set in a beautifully restored Queenslander, this restaurant/café is a wee warren of dining nooks, bohemian vibes and friendly staff. The menu is imaginative (all-day veggie breakfasts are popular) with lots of picky entrees.

Mondo Organics (Map pp312–13; ☎ 3844 1132; 166 Hardgrave Rd; mains $28-35; ⊗ lunch Tue-Fri, dinner Tue-Sat) Blow your tastebuds, not your arteries, at this exquisite organic restaurant. In urban timber surrounds diners savour dishes such as lamb backstrap with pumpkin and olive cannelloni, pea puree and roasted garlic.

Tukka (Map pp312–13; ☎ 3846 6333; 145 Boundary St; mains $30-35; ⊗ dinner daily, lunch Sun) The menu at this restaurant reads like a who's who of Australian game: Tasmanian confit possum, paperbark-roasted Cairns crocodile and seared emu fillets. It's amazing what Aussie tucker you can eat in this country and you'll find plentiful samples of it in creative combinations at Tukka. There are also vegie dishes for the timid diners who prefer more standard fare.

Also recommended:

Caravanserai (Map pp312–13; ☎ 3217 2617; 1-3 Dornoch Tce; mains $20-25; ⊗ lunch Thu-Sun, dinner Tue-Sun) Delicious and slightly extravagant Turkish cuisine.

Kafe Meze (Map pp312–13; ☎ 3844 1720; cnr Boundary & Browning Sts; starters $9, mains $27; ⊗ lunch, dinner) Fresh flavours and tastes of the Mediterranean. Where Greek people in Brisbane go to dine out.

Self-Catering

James St Market (Map pp314–15; James St, Fortitude Valley) The produce is pricey but the quality is excellent and there's a good fishmonger here.

There's a great produce market inside **McWhirters Marketplace** (Map pp314–15; cnr Brunswick & Wickham Sts) in Fortitude Valley. The Asian supermarkets in Chinatown mall also have an excellent range of fresh vegies, Asian groceries and exotic fruit.

There's a Coles Express on Queen St, just west of the mall, and a **Woolworths** (Map pp314–15) on Edward St in the city.

DRINKING

our pick Breakfast Creek Hotel (Map 310; ☎ 3262 5988; 2 Kingsford Smith Dr; steaks $16-34; ⊗ lunch & dinner) In a great rambling building dating from 1889, this historic pub is a Brisbane institution. Built in French Renaissance style the best part remains the spacious, art-deco front bar – it's nothing fancy but it reeks of authenticity.

Lychee Lounge (Map pp312-13; ☎ 3846 0544; 2/94 Boundary St, West End) Sink into the lush furniture and stare up at the macabre dolls head chandeliers at this exotic oriental lounge-bar. Mellow beats, mood lighting and an open frontage to Boundary St create an ideal trifecta. Specialises in cocktails.

Story Bridge Hotel (Map pp314-15; ☎ 3391 2266; 196 Main St, Kangaroo Point; ✖) This beautiful old pub beneath the bridge at Kangaroo Point is the perfect place for a pint after a long day sightseeing. You can mingle with the fashionable in the back bar with its floor to ceiling glass, or hunker down in the casual beer garden.

Normanby Hotel (Map pp312-13; ☎ 3831 3353; 1 Musgrave Rd, Red Hill) Opposite the train station of the same name, this rambling hotel is pure Queensland. Without doubt its best feature is the colossal, modern beer garden, which can get a real party atmosphere on weekends. The huge bar upstairs is a mishmash of brick, art deco, sawdust floor and modernist bar design.

Port Office Hotel (Map pp314-15; ☎ 3221 0072; 40 Edward St, City; ✖) The industrial edge of this renovated city pub is spruced up with swathes of dark wood and jungle prints. In the afternoon a table by the open windows is the perfect place to watch city life tick by.

Two New Farm hotspots on opposing street corners are the **Alibi Room** (Map pp314-15; ☎ 3358 6133; 720 Brunswick St; ✖ closed Mon), a quirky bar bucking the fine wining and dining trend, calling itself 'a cultural splinter in the tail end of Brisbane'; and **Gertie's Bar & Lounge** (Map pp314-15; ☎ 3358 5088; 699 Brunswick St; ✖ closed Mon), a more sophisticated affair with comfy seating, cool lighting, cocktails and, on the weekends, acoustic guitar.

ENTERTAINMENT

Brisbane pulls most of the international bands heading to Oz and the city's clubs have become nationally renowned. There's also plenty of theatre and cultural events. Pick up copies of the free entertainment papers *Time Off* (www.timeoff.com.au), *Rave* (www.ravemag.com.au) and *Scene* (www.scenemagazine.com.au) from any café in the Valley. A good website to check out is www.my247.com.au/brisbane.

The *Courier-Mail* also has daily arts and entertainment listings, and a comprehensive 'What's On In Town' section each Thursday.

Ticketek (☎ 13 28 49; http://premier.ticketek.com.au) is an agency that handles phone bookings for many major events, sports and performances.

Nightclubs

Brisbane is proud of its nightclub scene – most clubs are open Thursday to Sunday nights, are adamant about ID and charge between $7 and $25 cover. The alternative scene is centred on the Valley, and attracts a mixed straight and gay crowd.

Family (Map pp314-15; ☎ 3852 5000; 8 McLachlan St, Fortitude Valley) One of Brisbane's best nightclubs, the music scene here is phenomenal. Family exhilarates dance junkies every weekend on four levels with two dance floors, four bars, four funky themed booths and a top-notch sound system.

Monastery (Map pp314-15; ☎ 3257 7081; 621 Ann St, Fortitude Valley) After a sensible refurbishment giving more space to the dance floor and easier access to the bar, Monastery really does look like a monastery inside (apart from the heaving, sweaty hordes churning up the dance floor) with its iconic, plush design and gothic lighting.

Uber (Map pp312-13; ☎ 3846 6680; 100 Boundary St, West End) Brisbane's latest club, Uber is cool indeed with a stylish décor and patrons to match. It's all a bit decadent feeling like an old-style boutique hotel. The music varies but weekends are dedicated to pure main-room house.

Beat MegaClub (Map pp314-15; ☎ 3852 2661; 677 Ann St, Fortitude Valley) Five dance floors, six bars, and hardcore techno equals the perfect place for dance junkies who like their beats hard. It's popular with the gay and lesbian crowd with regular drag performances, but Beat is welcoming to all.

Two places next door to each other on Warner St, popular with the younger set, and in the heart of the Valley are: **Mass** (Map pp314-15; ☎ 3852 3373; 25 Warner St), which is set in an old cathedral and pulls some impressive DJs spinning house and electro; and **Planet** (Map pp314-15; ☎ 3852 2575; 27 Warner St), which has been newly renovated and has a great light and sound set up.

Live Music

In recent years successful acts, including Katie Noonan, Kate Miller-Heidke and Pete Murray have illustrated Brisbane's musical cred. You

BRISBANE

GAY & LESBIAN BRISBANE

Most action, centred in Fortitude Valley, is covered by the fortnightly **Q News** (www.qnews.com.au). *Queensland Pride*, another gay publication, takes in the whole of the state. **Queer Radio** (www .queerradio.org), a radio show on Wednesday from 8.30pm to 10pm on FM102.1, is another source of information on the city.

Major events on the year's calendar include the **Queer Film Festival**, held in late March, which showcases gay, lesbian, bisexual and transgender films, and **Brisbane Pride Festival** in June (see p320). Pride attracts up to 25,000 people every year, and peaks during the parade held midfestival.

Brisbane's most popular gay and lesbian venue is the **Wickham Hotel** (Map pp314–15; ☎ 3852 1301; cnr Wickham & Alden Sts), a classic old Victorian pub with dance music, drag shows and dancers. The Wickham celebrates the Sydney Mardi Gras and the Pride Festival in style. The **Sportsman's Hotel** (Map pp314–15; ☎ 3831 2892; 130 Leichhardt St) is another fantastically popular gay venue, with a different theme or show for each night of the week.

The **Gay & Lesbian Welfare Association of Brisbane** (GLWA; ☎ 1800 184 527; www.glwa.org.au) can offer information on groups and venues and also counselling.

can get in early to see history in the making at any number of venues. Cover charges start at around $5.

Zoo (Map pp314–15; ☎ 3854 1381; 711 Ann St, Fortitude Valley;) The long queues here start early for a good reason and whether you're into hard rock or electronic soundscapes, Zoo has a gig for you. It's one of your best chances to hear some raw, local talent.

Tongue & Groove (Map pp312–13; ☎ 3846 0334; 63 Hardgrave Rd, West End; closed Mon) This funky little venue in the West End hosts everything from jazz, blues, reggae and funk to dance beats from Wednesday to Sunday. All nightlife takes place in the subterranean bar. See tng.net.au to check out their upcoming gigs.

Brisbane Jazz Club (Map pp314–15; ☎ 3391 2006; 1 Annie St, Kangaroo Point) A Brizzie institution for addicts of the swinging and soulful, this club lures jazz purists aplenty from Thursday to Sunday nights. There's usually a cover charge of $15, and anyone who's anyone in the jazz scene plays here when they're in town.

Other live venues:

Arena (Map pp314–15; ☎ 3252 5690; 210 Brunswick St, Fortitude Valley) An industrial-sized venue that attracts local and international rock acts. Big supporter of hip hop.

Brisbane Convention & Exhibition Centre (Map pp314–15; ☎ 3308 3000; Glenelg St, South Bank;) When the big acts are in town they perform at this multi-functional entertainment complex.

Normanby Hotel (Map pp312–13; ☎ 3831 3353; 1 Musgrave Rd, Red Hill) Great venue for live music – Sunday goes off. Bands on Tuesday, Wednesday, Thursday and Sunday night.

Cinema

There are open-air movies screened over summer in the South Bank Parklands (p316) and New Farm Park.

The **Dendy Cinema** (Map pp314–15; ☎ 3211 3244; 346 George St) shows good art-house films.

In the Valley, **Palace Centro** (Map pp314–15; ☎ 3852 4488; 39 James St, Fortitude Valley) also screens good art-house films and has a Greek film festival at the end of November.

South Bank Cinema (Map pp314–15; ☎ 3846 5188; cnr Grey & Ernest Sts, South Bank) is the cheapest cinema for mainstream flicks; tickets cost about a third less than at other places.

Cinemas on Queen St Mall:

Greater Union (Map pp314–15; ☎ 3027 9999; Level A, Myer Centre) Mainstream blockbusters.

Hoyts Regent Theatre (Map pp314–15; ☎ 3027 9999; 107 Queen St Mall) A lovely old cinema worth visiting for the building alone.

Theatre

Brisbane is well stocked with theatre venues, most of them located in the South Bank Parklands. The **Queensland Cultural Centre** (☎ 13 62 46) handles bookings for all the South Bank theatres and publishes *Centre Stage*, the events diary for the complex.

Queensland Performing Arts Centre (Map pp314–15; ☎ 3840 7444; www.qpac.com.au; Queensland Cultural Centre, Stanley St, South Bank;) This centre consists of three venues and features concerts, plays, dance and performances of all genres.

Queensland Conservatorium (Map pp314–15; ☎ 3875 6375; 16 Russell St, South Bank) South of the

Performing Arts Centre, the Conservatorium showcases the talent of attending students.

Brisbane Powerhouse (Map pp312–13; ☎ 3358 8622, box office 3358 8600; www.brisbanepowerhouse.org; 119 Lamington St, New Farm; P ☒) A magnificent conversion from an old powerhouse into a leading place for contemporary culture at a picturesque spot on the Brisbane River. This one-stop venue presents an evolving schedule of theatre, dance, music and workshops.

Metro Arts Centre (Map pp314–15; ☎ 3221 1527; www.metroarts.com.au; 109 Edward St, City; ☒) This progressive venue hosts community theatre, dance and art shows.

QUT Gardens Theatre (Map pp314–15; ☎ 3138 4455; www.gardenstheatre.qut.com; QUT, 2 George St) This university theatre hosts touring national and international productions as well as student performances.

Sit Down Comedy Club (Map pp312–13; ☎ 3369 4466; Paddo Tavern, Given Tce, Paddington; P ☒) The most prominent comedy venue in town, at the Paddo Tavern.

Sport

Like other Australians, Brisbanites are sports-mad. You can see interstate cricket matches and international test cricket at the **Gabba** (Brisbane Cricket Ground; Map pp312–13; ☎ 3008 6166; www.thegabba.org.au) in Woolloongabba, south of Kangaroo Point. If you're new to the game try and get along to a 20/20 match, which is cricket in its most explosive form. The cricket season runs from October to March.

During the other half of the year, rugby league is the big spectator sport. The Brisbane Broncos plays home games at **Suncorp Stadium** (Map pp312–13; ☎ 3331 5000; Castlemaine St, Milton).

Once dominated by Victorian teams, the Australian Football League (AFL) has been challenged by the Brisbane Lions, which has tasted success in recent years. You can watch the team kick the ball and some southern butt at a home game at the Gabba between March and September.

Australia's National Basketball League (NBL) is based on American pro basketball, and the fast-paced NBL games draw large crowds. Brisbane's team, the Brisbane Bullets, is based at the **Brisbane Convention and Exhibition Centre** (Map pp314–15; ☎ 3308 3000; www.bcec.com.au; cnr Merivale & Glenelg Sts, South Brisbane).

Queensland also has a side in the National Netball League – the Queensland Firebirds. Their home stadium is the **Chandler Arena** (off Map p310; Old Cleveland & Tiley Rd, Chandler). You can book tickets through Ticketek, or online at http://firebirds.netballq.org.au.

SHOPPING

See p317 for places to purchase indigenous crafts.

Clothing

For something fashionable, there are plenty of Australian and international boutiques in the upmarket **Elizabeth Arcade** (Map pp314–15), between Elizabeth and Charlotte Sts, and **Brisbane Arcade** (Map pp314–15), between the Queen St Mall and Adelaide St. For club fashions, head to Fortitude Valley around Brunswick, Wickham and Ann Sts.

Markets

Every Sunday, the carnival-style Riverside Centre and Eagle St Pier markets have over 150 stalls, including glassware, weaving, leather work and children's activities.

South Bank Lifestyle markets (Map pp314–15; Stanley St Plaza, South Bank; ☒ 5-10pm Fri, 10am-5pm Sat, 9am-5pm Sun) These popular markets have a great range of clothing, craft, art, handmade goods and interesting souvenirs.

Green Flea Community Market (Map pp312–13; Davies Park, cnr Montague Rd & Jane St; ☒ 6am-2pm Sat) This cosmopolitan flea market has loads of fresh produce, herbs, flowers, organic foodstuff, clothing and bric-a-brac. It's an apt representation of the diverse West End.

King George Square Contemporary Craft & Art Market (Map pp314–15; King George Sq; ☒ 8am-4pm Sun) These markets transform a pocket of the city centre into a bustling arts and crafts fair on the weekends. A nice spot to bring the kids.

GETTING THERE & AWAY
Air

Brisbane's main airport is about 16km northeast of the city centre at Eagle Farm and has separate international and domestic terminals about 2km apart, linked by the Airtrain ($4 per person).

Qantas (Map pp314–15; ☎ 13 13 13; www.qantas.com.au; 247 Adelaide St), has an extensive network, connecting Brisbane with Sydney (1½ hours), Melbourne (2½ hours), Adelaide (2½ hours), Canberra (two hours), Hobart (four hours), Perth (five hours) and Darwin (four hours).

Virgin Blue (☎ 13 67 89; www.virginblue.com.au) also flies between Brisbane and Australian capital cities. **Jetstar** (☎ 13 15 38; www.jetstar.com.au) connects Brisbane with the same cities (except Perth) as well as Cairns.

The new kid on the block, **Tiger Airways** (☎ 9335 3033; www.tigerairways.com.au) is a genuine Singapore-based budget carrier that will hopefully shake-up the airline market in Australia and bring about better budget fares. It currently flies from Melbourne to the Gold Coast and Sunshine Coast but may well have started a Brisbane service by the time you read this.

Qantas, Virgin Blue and Jetstar all fly to towns and cities within Queensland, especially the more popular coastal destinations and the Whitsunday Islands. **Macair** (☎ 1300 622 247; www.macair.com.au) flies to many destinations in the Queensland outback, including Mt Isa (four hours).

Bus

Brisbane's **Roma St Transit Centre** (Map pp314–15), about 500m west of the city centre, is the main terminus and booking office for long-distance buses and trains. The centre has shops, food places, a post office and an accommodation booking service. Bus companies have booking desks on the 3rd level. **Greyhound** (☎ 13 14 99; www.greyhound.com.au) is the main company on the Sydney to Brisbane run; you can either go via the New England Hwy (17 hours) or the quicker Pacific Hwy (16 hours) for $125. **Premier** (☎ 13 34 10; www. premierms.com.au) does the same route and often has slightly cheaper deals.

North to Cairns, Premier Motor Service runs one direct service daily and Greyhound runs four. The approximate fares and journey times to places along the coast are as follows:

Destination	Duration	One-way fare
Noosa Heads	2½hr	$30
Hervey Bay	5½hr	$65
Rockhampton	11½hr	$115
Mackay	16½hr	$165
Townsville	23hr	$215
Cairns	29hr	$255

Car

There are five major routes into and out of the Brisbane metropolitan area, numbered from M1 to M5. The major north-south route, the M1, connects the Pacific Hwy to the south with the Bruce Hwy to the north, but things get a bit confusing as you enter the city.

Coming from the Gold Coast, the Pacific Hwy splits into two at Eight Mile Plains. From here, the South East Freeway (M3) runs right into the centre, skirting along the riverfront on the western side of the CBD, before emerging on the far side as the Gympie Arterial Rd.

All of the major companies – **Hertz** (☎ 13 30 39), **Avis** (☎ 13 63 33), **Budget** (☎ 13 27 27), **Europcar** (☎ 13 13 90) and **Thrifty** (☎ 1300 367 227) – have offices at the Brisbane airport terminals and throughout the city.

There are also several smaller companies in Brisbane that advertise slightly cheaper deals, including **Ace Rental Cars** (Map p310; ☎ 1800 620 408, 3862 2158; www.acerentals.com.au; 35 Sandgate Rd, Albion).

Train

Brisbane's main station for long-distance trains is the Roma St Transit Centre. For reservations and information visit the **Queensland Rail Travel Centre** (☎ 131 617; www.qr.com.au) Central Station (Map pp314-15; ☎ 3235 1323; Ground fl, Central Station, 305 Edward St; ☒ 8am-5pm Mon-Fri); Roma St (Map pp314-15; ☎ 3235 1331; Roma St Transit Centre, Roma St; ☒ 6am-5pm Mon-Fri). You can also make reservations online or over the phone.

CountryLink (☎ 13 22 32; www.countrylink.nsw.gov.au) has a daily XPT service between Brisbane and Sydney (economy/1st class $92/130, 14 hours). The northbound service runs overnight, and the southbound service runs during the day.

Coastal services within Queensland:

Spirit of the Outback (economy seat/economy sleeper/1st-class sleeper $185/245/375, 24 hours) Brisbane–Longreach via Rockhampton ($105/165/255, 10½ hours) twice weekly.

Sunlander ($215/270/415, 30 hours) Departs Tuesday, Thursday and Sunday for Cairns via Townsville.

Tilt Train (business $310, 25hr) Brisbane-Cairns train leaves Brisbane at 6.25pm Monday, Wednesday and Friday, returning from Cairns at 9.15am Sunday, Wednesday and Friday.

Concessions are available to children under 16 years, students with a valid International Student Identity Card (ISIC), and senior citizens. For details contact **Queensland Rail** (☎ 13 22 32; www.traveltrain.com.au).

GETTING AROUND
To/From the Airport

The easiest way to get to/from the airport is the **Airtrain** (☎ 3215 5000; www.airtrain.com.au; per adult/child $13/6.50; ☒ 6am-7.30pm), which runs every 15 to 30 minutes between the airport and the Roma St Transit Centre and Central Station. There are also half-hourly services to the airport from Gold Coast Citytrain stops.

Coachtrans (☎ 3358 9700; www.coachtrans.com.au) runs the half-hourly Skytrans shuttle bus between the Roma St Transit Centre and the airport between 5.45am and 10pm. It costs $12 per adult and $8 per child for the trip from the airport to the city. A taxi into the centre from the airport will cost around $35.

Bicycle

See p319 for information on cycling.

Car

Be warned that Brisbane's peak hour(s) traffic is notorious. There is free two-hour parking on many streets in the CBD and in the inner suburbs, but the major thoroughfares become clearways (ie parking is prohibited) during the morning and afternoon rush hours.

Queensland's motoring association is the RACQ (p309). You can obtain insurance and maps at the city branch.

Public Transport

Information on bus, train and ferry routes and connections can be obtained from the **Trans-Info Service** (☎ 13 12 30; www.transinfo.qld .gov.au). Information is also available at the Brisbane Visitor Information Centre (p310), the **bus station information centre** (Map pp314-15; Queen St Mall; ⏰ 8.30am-5.30pm Mon-Thu, to 8pm Fri, 9am-4pm Sat, 10am-4pm Sun), and the Queensland Rail Travel Centres.

Fares on buses, trains and ferries operate on a zone system. The city centre and most of the inner-city suburbs fall within Zone 1, which translates to a single fare of $2.30/1.20 per adult/child.

If you're going to be using public transport more than once on any single day, it's worth getting a daily ticket. These allow you unlimited transport on all buses, trains and ferries and are priced according to the number of zones you'll be travelling in:

Zone 1 (adult/child $4.60/2.30)
Zone 2 (adult/child $5.40/2.70)
Zone 3 (adult/child $6.40/3.20)

You can also buy cheaper off-peak daily tickets that allow you to do the same thing between 9am and 3.30pm and after 7pm from Monday to Friday and all weekend.

BOAT

Brisbane's CityCat catamarans run every 20 to 30 minutes, between 5.45am and 11pm, from the University of Queensland in the west to Bretts Wharf in the east, and back. Stops along the way include North Quay (for the Queen St Mall), South Bank, Riverside (for the CBD) and New Farm Park. CityCats are wheelchair accessible at all stops except for West End, QUT Gardens Point, Riverside, Bulimba and Brett's Wharf.

Also useful are the Inner City Ferries, which zigzag back and forth across the river between North Quay, near the Victoria Bridge, and Mowbray Park. Services start at about 6am from Monday to Sunday, and run until about 11pm. There are also several cross-river ferries; most useful is the Eagle St Pier to Thornton St (Kangaroo Point) service.

BUS

The Loop is a free bus that circles the city, stopping at QUT, Queen St Mall, City Hall, Central Station and Riverside; it runs every 10 minutes on weekdays from 7am to 6pm.

The main stop for local buses is in the basement of the Myer Centre, where there's a small information centre. You can also pick up most of the useful buses from the colour-coded stops along Adelaide St, between George and Edward Sts.

Useful buses from the city centre include buses 195, 196, 197 and 199 to Fortitude Valley and New Farm, which leave from Adelaide St between King George Sq and Edward St. You can pick up bus 375 to Paddington from opposite the transit centre or on Adelaide St.

Taxi

There are usually plenty of taxis around the city centre, and there are taxi ranks at the transit centre and at the top end of Edward St, by the junction with Adelaide St. The major taxi company here is **Black & White** (☎ 13 10 08). Rivals include **Yellow Cab Co** (☎ 13 19 24) and **Brisbane Cabs** (☎ 13 22 11).

Train

The Citytrain network has seven lines that run as far as Nambour, Cooroy and Gympie in the north (for the Sunshine Coast) and Nerang and Robina in the south (for the Gold Coast). Other useful routes include

Rosewood (for Ipswich) and Cleveland (for the North Stradbroke Island ferry). The lines to Pinkenba, Shorncliffe and Ferny Grove are mainly for suburban commuters.

The Airtrain service (p328) integrates with the Citytrain network in the CBD and along the Gold Coast line. All trains go through Roma St and Central stations in the city, and Brunswick St station in Fortitude Valley.

Trains run from around 4.30am, with the last train to each line leaving Central Station between 11.30pm and midnight. On Sunday the last trains run at around 10pm.

AROUND BRISBANE

MORETON BAY ISLANDS

The patch of water lapping at Brisbane's urban edges is packed full of marine life including whales, dolphins and dugongs. Moreton Bay also has a bunch of startlingly beautiful islands that are very accessible from the mainland. North Stradbroke Island with its nonchalant holiday air and Moreton Island, a stunning patch of wilderness on Brisbane's doorstep, are two of the best.

North Stradbroke Island

Brisbanites are lucky to have such a brilliant holiday island on their doorstep. A mere 30-minute ferry ride from Cleveland, this sand island has a string of glorious powdery white-sand beaches. Inland are two glittering lakes carved out of the surrounding bushland, and

back along the coast quality accommodation and dining options await.

ORIENTATION & INFORMATION

Straddie has three small settlements, Dunwich, Amity Point and Point Lookout, all grouped around the northern end of the island. In the hilly central area is the beautiful Blue Lake National Park, and, while the wild southern half of the island is inaccessible due to mining, Eighteen Mile Beach, which runs clear down the eastern edge of the island, is accessible to 4WDs.

Stradbroke Island visitor information centre (☎ 3409 9555; www.stradbroketourism.com; Junner St; 8.30am-4.30pm) is 200m from the ferry terminal in Dunwich.

SIGHTS & ACTIVITIES

If you're interested in Straddie's art scene, check out the local **Coral Sea Gallery** (Map p330; www.straddieonline.com.au/StraddieOnline/CoralSeaGallery .aspx; Pandamus Palms Resort) where the island's artistic community is well represented.

Straddie's best beaches for both **surfing** and **swimming** are around Point Lookout, where there's a series of points and bays around the headland and long stretches of white sand.

If you're not so keen on the surf, there are a couple of inland lakes worth exploring. If you don't have your own vehicle, you can take a tour or hire a bike, but be warned that there are some punishing hills to be negotiated. Both Brown Lake and Blue Lake are accessed via the sealed Mining Company Rd

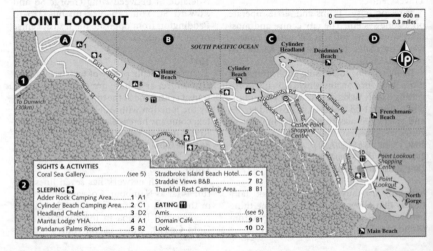

POINT LOOKOUT

0 — 600 m
0 — 0.3 miles

SOUTH PACIFIC OCEAN

To Dunwich (30km)

SIGHTS & ACTIVITIES		Stradbroke Island Beach Hotel.....**6** C1	
Coral Sea Gallery......................(see 5)		Straddie Views B&B........................**7** B2	
		Thankful Rest Camping Area.......**8** B1	
SLEEPING			
Adder Rock Camping Area..........**1** A1		EATING	
Cylinder Beach Camping Area.....**2** C1		Amis...(see 5)	
Headland Chalet.........................**3** D2		Domain Café................................**9** B1	
Manta Lodge YHA........................**4** A1		Look...**10** D2	
Pandanus Palms Resort...............**5** B2			

from Dunwich. The turn-off to **Brown Lake** is reached first after about 3km; the lake is a short distance down a dirt track. The water is indeed brown, and shallow to boot, but it's a decent spot for a picnic and popular with young families.

Blue Lake, accessed from a car park a further 5km along the road, is a different proposition altogether. The centrepiece of Blue Lake National Park, it's reached via a beautiful and winding 2.1km walking track. The lake itself is small, crystal clear and very deep – the bottom drops away quickly and a little alarmingly right by the shore – but it's a serene and very beautiful spot. If you're lucky you'll have it all to yourself, and if you're even luckier you'll spot a rare and shy golden wallaby. There's no camping or drinking water in the park, so come prepared.

The eastern beach, known as **Eighteen Mile Beach**, is open to 4WD vehicles and campers and finishes up at the popular fishing spot of **Jumpinpin** on the island's southern tip. **Straddie Super Sports** (☎ 3409 9252; Bingle Rd; ⏱ 7.30am-5pm Mon-Fri, 7.30am-4pm Sat & Sun) hires out fishing gear from $20 per day (plus deposit of $30). **Manta Lodge & Scuba Centre** (☎ 3409 8888; www.mantalodge .com.au; 1 East Coast Rd), based at the YHA (right), offers snorkelling for $50 inclusive of a two-hour boat trip and all the gear.

Straddie Adventures (☎ 3409 8414; Point Lookout) offers sea-kayaking trips (including snorkelling stops $35) around Straddie, and sandboarding ($25), which is like snowboarding, except on sand.

TOURS

A number of tour companies offer tours of the island. Generally the 4WD tours take in a strip of the eastern beach and several freshwater lakes.

North Stradbroke Island 4WD Tours & Camping Holidays (☎ 3409 8051; straddie@ecn.net.au) Generally, half-day tours cost $30/15 per adult/child.

Point Lookout Fishing Charters (☎ 3409 8353, 0407-376 091) Organises six-hour fishing trips that cost $160 per person.

Straddie Kingfisher Tours (☎ 3409 9502; www .straddiekingfishertours.com.au; adult/child $70/40) Operates ecotours that last for six hours.

SLEEPING

Most accommodation is at Point Lookout, which is strung along 3km of coastline on the northern shore of the island.

Budget

Manta Lodge YHA (☎ 3409 8888; www.mantalodge.com .au; 1 East Coast Rd; dm $28, tw & d $70; 🖳 🖭) This large beachside hostel is clean and well kept, and has excellent facilities, including a dive school right on the doorstep. There are four-, six- and eight-bed dorms Guests can rent surfboards, bodyboards and bikes for $20/35 per half-/full day.

Headland Chalet (☎ 3409 8252; 213 Midjimberry Rd, Point Lookout; d & tw cabins $66, bungalow $110; 🖭) An excellent budget option is this cluster of cabins on the hillside overlooking Main Beach, near the roundabout. The cabins are attractive inside and have good views, and there's a pool, a TV room and a small kitchen.

There are five camping grounds on the island operated by **Straddie Holiday Parks** (☎ 1300 551 253; unpowered sites $13-31, powered sites $28-38, cabins from $75), but the most attractive are the places grouped around Point Lookout. The Adder Rock Camping Area and Thankful Rest Camping Area both overlook lovely Home Beach, while the Cylinder Beach Camping Area sits right on Cylinder Beach, one of the most popular beaches on the island. Sites should be booked well in advance.

Midrange & Top End

Straddie Views B&B (☎ 3409 8875; www.northstrad brokeisland.com/straddiebb; 26 Cumming Pde; r $130-140) This friendly B&B, run by a couple of Straddie locals, has excellent-size rooms – probably double the size of most B&B rooms. Inside you get cane furniture, a breakfast menu and little touches such as wine glasses on the bed filled with choccies awaiting your arrival.

Stradbroke Island Beach Hotel (☎ 3409 8188; www.stradbrokeislandbeachhotel.com.au; East Coast Rd; r from $145; 🅿 🖭 🖭) Straddies' only hotel has been totally revamped. And we mean totally. Razed to the ground, the old hotel was blown aside for this masterclass of contemporary architecture. Rooms have muted, inoffensive tones, large flat-screen TVs and a cool, modern ambience.

Pandanus Palms Resort (☎ 3409 8106; www.panda nus.stradbrokeresorts.com.au; 21 Cumming Pde; apt $180-320; 🖭) Perched high above the beach, with a thick tumble of vegetation beneath, the large two-bed townhouses here are a good size and it is well worth paying the extra and getting one down the front of the complex. No 28 is probably the best – it has been modernised inside and has a large coconut tree in your private courtyard from where you can enjoy the views while cooking on the BBQ.

EATING

There are a couple of general stores selling groceries in Point Lookout, but it's worth bringing basic supplies.

Look (☎ 3415 3390; shop 1, 29 Mooloomba Rd; lunch mains $8-16; ☻ breakfast, lunch & dinner) This seems to be the hub of Point Lookout during the day, with funky tunes in the background and great outdoor seating where you catch the breeze and sublime views over the water. Dinner mains cost $15 to $26.

Domain Café (☎ 3415 0090; East Coast Rd; mains lunch/dinner $16/26; ☻ breakfast, lunch & dinner) Domain is a classy little eatery adjutting the resort of the same name. Dinner mains consist of meat oriented dishes, seafood (such as char grilled reef fish) and pasta.

Amis (☎ 3409 8600; 21 Cummings Pde; entrees $17, mains $31; ☻ dinner Wed-Sun) If you're looking for a special feast, this is the spot to head. This restaurant raises the bar on Straddie, serving delicate concoctions such as Bush to Bay – Queensland kangaroo loin fillet and Moreton Bay bugs with apple and pear risotto, bilberry rose petal sauce and bush herb oil. Many dishes have a north African influence.

GETTING THERE & AWAY

The gateway to North Stradbroke Island is the seaside suburb of Cleveland. Regular **Citytrain** (☎ 13 12 30; www.transinfo.qld.gov.au) services run from Central Station or Roma St to Cleveland station ($4.50, one hour) and buses to the ferry terminals meet the trains at Cleveland station ($1, 10 minutes).

Several ferry companies head across to Straddie. **Stradbroke Ferries** (☎ 3286 2666; www.stradbrokeferries.com.au) runs a water taxi to Dunwich almost every hour from about 6am to 6pm ($17 return, 30 minutes). It also has a slightly less frequent vehicle ferry (per vehicle including passengers $122 return, 45 minutes) from 5.30am to 5.30pm.

The **Stradbroke Flyer** (☎ 3286 1964; www.flyer.com.au) also runs an almost-hourly catamaran service from Cleveland to One Mile Jetty ($17 return, 45 minutes), 1.5km north of central Dunwich.

GETTING AROUND

Local buses (☎ 3409 7151) meet the ferries at Dunwich and One Mile Jetty and run across

to Point Lookout ($9.50 return). The last bus to Dunwich leaves Point Lookout at about 6.45pm, later on Friday. There's also the **Stradbroke Cab Service** (☎ 0408-193 685), which charges $35 from Dunwich to Point Lookout.

Moreton Island

You don't need to head north to find a patch of island paradise in Queensland. Thick foliage tumbles down to white-sand beaches along the coast of Moreton Island. Largely undeveloped, most of the island is national park with walking trails, and the bird life is prolific. The water itself is a patchy jade and indigo colour, and once you're in it, crystal clear, as you'll discover if you go diving or snorkelling around the Tangalooma Wrecks, a shipwreck just off the west coast.

ORIENTATION & INFORMATION

Apart from the Tangalooma resort, the only other settlements are **Bulwer** near the northwestern tip, **Cowan Cowan** between Bulwer and Tangalooma, and **Kooringal** near the southern tip. The shops at Kooringal and Bulwer are expensive, so bring what you can from the mainland.

You can get Queensland Parks & Wildlife Service (QPWS) maps from the vehicle-ferry offices or the Information desk at the **Marine Research & Education Centre** (below) at Tangalooma, which is a very helpful resource. Vehicle permits for the island cost $36 and are available through the ferry operators or from the Naturally Qld office in Brisbane (p311). Ferry bookings are *mandatory* if you want to take a vehicle across; see opposite for operators.

SIGHTS & ACTIVITIES

Tangalooma, halfway down the western side of the island, is a popular tourist resort sited at an old whaling station. The main attraction is the **dolphin feeding**, which takes place each evening around sunset. Usually about eight or nine dolphins swim in from the ocean and take fish from the hands of volunteer feeders. Although you have to be a guest of the resort to participate, onlookers are welcome.

Also here is the **Marine Research & Education Centre** (Tangalooma Resort; ☻ 10am-noon & 1-5pm), which has a display on the amazingly diverse marine and bird life of Moreton Bay. Don't miss the 'Oddities of the Deep' board.

You can pick up a map of the island showing walking trails at the Centre. There's a desert walk (two hours) and a bush walk (1½ hours), both leaving from the resort, as well as a longer walk to Water Point (four hours) on the east coast. It's also worth making the strenuous trek to the summit of Mt Tempest, 3km inland from Eagers Creek.

About 3km south and inland from Tangalooma is an area of bare sand known as the **Desert**, while the **Big Sandhills** and the **Little Sandhills** are towards the narrow southern end of the island. The biggest lakes and some swamps are in the northeast.

At the island's northern tip is a **lighthouse** built in 1857.

You can hire snorkelling gear from **Get Wet Sports** (☎ 3410 6927; Tangalooma Wild Dolphin Resort; per hr/day $6/12) and immerse yourself amid the colourful coral and marine life of the Tangalooma Wrecks.

TOURS

Gibren Expeditions (☎ 1300 559 355; 1-/2-day tours from $140/220) Offers tours of the island with heaps of activities thrown in. The guides are locals and really know the island. The two-day tour means you camp overnight.

Moreton Bay Escapes (☎ 1300 559 355; www .moretonbayescapes.com.au; 1-day tours adult/child from $140/120, 2-day camping tours incl meals from $220) Its itineraries are similar to those of Gibren Expeditions.

Sunrover Expeditions (☎ 1800 353 717, 3880 0719; www.sunrover.com.au; adult/child $120/90) A friendly and reliable 4WD tour operator with good day tours, which include lunch. It also operates two-day camping tours (adult/child $195/150).

SLEEPING

There are a few holiday flats and houses for rent at Kooringal, Cowan Cowan and Bulwer. To see what's on offer including current pricing arrangements go to www.moreton-island .com/accommodation.html.

   Tangalooma Wild Dolphin Resort (☎ 1300 652 250, 3268 6333; www.tangalooma.com; 1-night packages from $200; 🍽 💻 🐬) This luxurious modern resort is the only formal setup on the island. There's a plethora of options available starting with pretty standard hotel-style rooms. A step up are the units and suites – refurbished B and D blocks offer your best options here,

where you'll get beachside access and rooms kitted out in cool, contemporary décor with good facilities.

There are nine (including four on the beach) national park **camping grounds** (sites per person/family $4.50/18), all with water, toilets and cold showers. For information and camping permits, contact the Naturally Qld office in Brisbane (p311) or call ☎ 13 13 04. Camping permits must be arranged before you get to the island.

The shops at Kooringal and Bulwer are expensive, so bring what you can from the mainland.

GETTING THERE & AROUND

A number of ferries operate from the mainland. The **Tangalooma Flyer** (☎ 3268 6333; www .tangalooma.com/tangalooma/transport; per adult/child return day trip $40/25, or from $80/40), a fast catamaran operated by the resort, sails to the resort on Moreton Island daily from a dock at Holt St, off Kingsford Smith Dr (in Eagle Farm). A bus ($10) to the flyer departs the Roma St Transit Centre at 9am. You can use the bus for a day trip (it returns at 9am and 4pm daily as well as at 2pm on Saturday and Sunday) or for camping drop-offs. Bookings are necessary. The trip takes 1¼ hours.

The **Moreton Venture** (☎ 3895 1000; www.more tonventure.com.au; adult/child/vehicle & 2 passengers return $45/30/190; 🕒 8.30am daily, 6.30pm Fri & 2.30pm Sun) is a vehicle ferry that runs from Howard-Smith Dr, Lyton, at the Port of Brisbane, to Tangalooma. It leaves the island at 3.30pm daily, as well as at 8pm on Friday, and 1pm and 4.30pm on Sunday.

The **Combie Trader** (☎ 3203 6399; www.moreton-island.com/how.html; adult/child/vehicle & 4 passengers return $40/25/165; 🕒 8am & 1pm Mon, 8am Wed & Thu, 8am, 1pm & 7pm Fri, 8am & 1pm Sat, 10.30am & 3.30pm Sun) sails between Scarborough and Bulwer and takes about 2½ hours to make the crossing. The Saturday morning crossings are slightly cheaper for pedestrians.

   Moreton Island 4WD Taxi & Tour Services offer a 4WD taxi service and tours of the island – for information click onto www.moretonisland .com.au/product.php?id=67753.

Sunshine Coast

The laid-back beach-chic culture of the Sunshine Coast turns lazy summer holidays into treasured memories of melting ice creams, sand between your toes, and fish and chips on the beach. The natural, unaffected charm of this strip of coastline is one of its greatest attractions.

From Bribie Island, the Sunshine Coast stretches north for one hundred golden kilometres to the Cooloola Coast just beyond the exclusive, leafy resort town of Noosa. Along the coastline, the southern sleepy town of Caloundra gives way to the laconic suburban swell of Mooloolaba with its popular beach, outdoor eateries and cafés. During school holidays the population here mushrooms as Australian families converge en masse. A little further north are the long, uncrowded and unspoilt beaches of Coolum and Peregian.

Forming a stunning backdrop to this spectacular coastline are the ethereal Glass House Mountains, and the forested folds and ridges, gorges and waterfalls, lush green pastures and quaint villages of the Blackall Range.

HIGHLIGHTS

- Hiking along the coastal track around the headland of **Noosa National Park** (p344)
- Sampling gourmet beach fare in one of **Noosa**'s (p350) swish restaurants
- Finding funky treasures at the **Eumundi markets** (p353)
- Walking through cool subtropical rainforests at **Kondalilla Falls** (p356)
- Lapping up the sun and sipping lattés in **Mooloolaba** (p340)
- Visiting the wildlife menagerie at **Australia Zoo** (p337)
- Hiking the volcanic crags of the **Glass House Mountains** (p336)
- Canoeing and exploring the Cooloola Section of the **Great Sandy National Park** (p352)

Great Sandy ★
National Park

Noosa & Noosa
★ National Park

Eumundi
★

Kondalilla
★ Falls

Mooloolaba
★

Australia
★ Zoo

Glass House
Mountains

- TELEPHONE CODE: 07
- www.sunshinecoast.org
- www.sunzine.net/suncoast

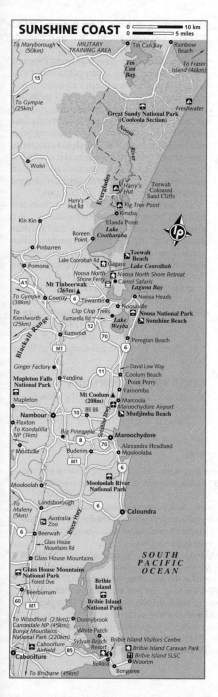

SUNSHINE COAST

Getting There & Away

AIR

The Sunshine Coast's airport (Maroochydore Airport) is at Mudjimba, 10km north of Maroochydore and 26km south of Noosa. **Jetstar** (☎ 13 15 38; www.jetstar.com.au) and **Virgin Blue** (☎ 13 67 89; www.virginblue.com.au) have daily flights from Sydney and Melbourne. **Tiger Airways** (☎ 03-9335 3033; www.tigerairways.com) has less frequent flights from Melbourne.

BUS

Greyhound Australia (☎ 1300 473 946; www.grey hound.com.au) has several daily services from Brisbane to Caloundra ($26, two hours), Maroochydore ($26, two hours) and Noosa ($27, three hours). **Premier Motor Service** (☎ 13 34 10; www.premierms.com.au) also services Maroochydore ($20) and Noosa ($20) from Brisbane.

Getting Around

Several companies offer transfers from Maroochydore Airport and Brisbane to points along the coast. Fares from Brisbane cost $30 to $40 for adults and $15 to $25 for children. From Maroochydore Airport fares are around $10 to $20 per adult and $5 to $10 per child. The following are recommended:

Col's Airport Shuttle (☎ 5450 5933; www.airshuttle .com.au)

Henry's (☎ 5474 0199)

Noosa Transfers & Charters (☎ 5450 5933; www .noosatransfers.com.au)

Sun-Air Bus Service (☎ 1800 804 340, 5477 0888; www.sunair.com.au)

The blue minibuses run by **Sunbus** (☎ 13 12 30) buzz frequently between Caloundra and Noosa. Sunbus also has regular buses from Noosa across to the train station at Nambour ($5, one hour) via Eumundi.

BRIBIE ISLAND

☎ 07 / pop 15,920

This slender island at the northern end of Moreton Bay is popular with young families, retirees and those with a cool million or three to spend on a waterfront property. It's far more developed than Stradbroke or Moreton Islands but the **Bribie Island National Park** on the northwestern coast has some beautifully remote **Queensland Parks and Wildlife Service (QPWS) camping areas** (4WD access only, per person/family $4.50/18).

SUNSHINE COAST

DETOUR: CABOOLTURE

If historical villages take your fancy, exit the Bruce Hwy at Caboolture for the **Caboolture Warplane Museum** (☎ 5499 1144; Hangar 104, Caboolture Airfield, McNaught Rd; adult/child/family $8/5/18; ☽ 10am-4pm), which has a collection of restored WWII warplanes, all in flying order. Then follow the signs through town to the **Caboolture Historical Village** (☎ 5495 4581; Beerburrum Rd; adult/child $10/2; ☽ 9.30am-3.30pm), which has over 70 buildings including a barber shop, a licensed hotel, the original railway station, a maritime museum and more, set on 5 hectares of land. The village is 4km north of Caboolture. After visiting the museum, either return to the Bruce Hwy or continue north on Beerburrum Rd, turn left onto Steve Irwin Way and follow this road a further 13km to Australia Zoo.

There's no 4WD hire on the island and **4WD permits** (per week/year $33.90/105.80) should be purchased from the **Bongaree Caravan Park** (☎ 3408 1054; Welsby Pde). The **rangers station** (☎ 3408 8451) is at White Patch on the southeastern fringes of the park, and you can pick up 4WD maps and other information at the **Bribie Island visitors centre** (☎ 3408 9026; www.bribie .com.au; Benabrow Ave, Bellara; ☽ 9am-4pm Mon-Fri, 9am-3pm Sat, 9.30am-1pm Sun).

A totally unexpected treasure about 25km from Bribie Island, back towards the Bruce

Hwy, is the wonderful **Abbey Museum** (☎ 5495 1652; www.abbeytournament.com; 1 The Abbey Pl; adult/child $8/4.50; ☽ 10am-4pm Mon-Sat). The impressive art and archaeology collection here spans the globe and would be at home in any of the world's famous museums. Once the private collection of Englishman John Ward, the pieces – including neolithic tools, medieval manuscripts and even an ancient Greek foot-guard (one of only four worldwide) – will have you scratching your head in amazement. The church has more original stained glass from Winchester Cathedral than what is actually left in the cathedral. In July, you can make merry at Australia's largest medieval festival, held on the grounds.

The **Inn Bongaree** (☎ 3410 1718; www.innbongaree .com.au; 25 Second Ave, Bongaree; s/d/tr $40/50/60) is a great budget option or you can stay at **Sylvan Beach Resort** (☎ 3408 8300; www.sylvanbeachresort .com.au; d from $170; ☒ ☒), which has comfortable self-contained units across the road from the beach.

Bribie Island SLSC (☎ 3408 4420; Rickman Pde; mains $10-25; ☽ lunch & dinner), at the southern end of the beach, serves up good ol' Aussie tucker.

Frequent **Citytrain** (☎ 13 12 30; www.citytrain. com.au) services run from Brisbane to Caboolture where a Trainlink bus connects to Bribie Island.

GLASS HOUSE MOUNTAINS

The ethereal volcanic crags of the Glass House Mountains rise abruptly from the subtropical plains 20km northwest of Caboolture. In

---

THE WEEPING MOUNTAIN & HIS WAYWARD SON

According to Aboriginal legend, the Glass House Mountains are a family of mountain spirits. Tibrogargan (364m), the father of all tribes, and his wife Beerwah (556m) had several offspring, of whom Coonowrin (377m) was the eldest.

One day, Tibrogargan noticed the sea level rising. Anticipating a flood, Tibrogargan left his eldest son, Coonowrin, to assist Beerwah while he gathered his younger children to safety. But to his dismay Coonowrin fled and abandoned his mother. In a blinding rage, Tibrogargan picked up his *nulla nulla* (club) and struck Coonowrin, dislocating his neck.

Once the floodwaters subsided and the family returned to their home, Coonowrin's siblings teased him about his crooked neck. Ashamed of his actions, Coonowrin sought forgiveness from his father, explaining he abandoned his mother because she was so big he thought she would be able to take care of herself. What he did not realise, however, was that Beerwah was not just big, but heavily pregnant. Coonowrin's siblings began to weep, adding their tears to Tibrogargan's, which in turn formed many streams, some reaching all the way out to sea.

According to the law of the tribe, Tibrogargan could not forgive his son who had disgraced him, so he turned his back on Coonowrin forever. To this day Tibrogargan faces out to sea while his son hangs his crooked neck in shame and cries. As for Beerwah, well, she is still pregnant – it takes a long time to give birth to a mountain.

ECO-WARRIOR

Best known as the Crocodile Hunter, Steve Irwin's zany and daring encounters with venomous snakes, crocs and sharks (the 'big apex predators') made spectacular viewing. But it wasn't an apex predator that killed the charismatic founder of Australia Zoo. In September 2006, while filming the wildlife documentary, *Ocean's Deadliest*, Irwin was fatally pierced in the heart by a stingray's barb.

A legend in his own lifetime, Irwin set up international crocodile rescue projects and supported various research projects worldwide, created Wildlife Warriors (a global conservation network), and established a state-of-the-art animal hospital at his own Australia Zoo. Madly passionate about conservation, having fun while avoiding sharp teeth and deadly fangs was Irwin's way of making wildlife a hip, cool thing. Education through entertainment was never better and an army of little tackers in khaki (crikey!) have sprung up in his wake.

Dreamtime legend these rocky peaks belong to a family of mountain spirits (see boxed text, opposite). It's worth diverting off the Bruce Hwy onto the slower Steve Irwin Way (formerly the Glass House Mountains Rd) to snake your way through dense pine forests and green pastureland for a close-up view of these spectacular volcanic plugs.

The Glass House Mountains National Park is broken into several sections (all within cooee of Beerwah) with picnic grounds and lookouts but no camping grounds. The peaks are reached by a series of sealed and unsealed roads known as Forest Dr, which heads inland from Steve Irwin Way. For more information visit the **QPWS** (☎ 5494 0150; Bells Creek Rd, Beerwah).

Sights & Activities

A number of signposted walking tracks reach several of the peaks but be prepared for some steep and rocky trails. **Mt Beerwah** (556m) is the most trafficked but has a section of open rock face that may increase the anxiety factor. The walk up **Ngungun** (253m) is more moderate and the views are just as sensational, while **Tibrogargan** (364m) is probably the best climb with a challenging scramble and several amazing lookouts from the flat summit. Rock climbers can usually be seen scaling Tibrogargan, Ngungun and Beerwah (for climbing information visit www.qurank.com). **Mt Coonowrin** (aka 'crook-neck'), the most dramatic of the volcanic plugs, is closed to the public.

Just north of Beerwah is – crikey! – **Australia Zoo** (☎ 5494 1134; www.australiazoo.com.au; Steve Irwin Way, Beerwah; adult/child/family $49/29/146; ☼ 9am-4.30pm), one of Queensland's most popular tourist attractions. The unfortunate accident that claimed Steve Irwin's life has only served to increase the zoo's popularity and the zany

celebrity's conservation message (see boxed text, above). Billboards of the khaki-clad Crocodile Hunter welcome you even from the croc-filled afterlife along the highway and into an amazing wildlife menagerie complete with a Cambodian-style Tiger Temple, an Asian-themed Elephantasia, as well as the famous crocoseum. There are macaws, birds of prey, giant tortoises, snakes, otters, camels, and more crocs and critters than you can poke a stick at. Spend a full day at this amazing wildlife park.

Various companies offer tours from Brisbane and the Sunshine Coast (see p354). The zoo operates a free courtesy bus from towns along the coast, and the Beerwah train station (bookings essential).

Sleeping & Eating

With only basic accommodation available, the Glass House Mountains are best visited as a day trip.

Glasshouse Mountains Log Cabin Caravan Park (☎ 5496 9338; logcabin@powerup.com.au; Glasshouse Mountains Tourist Dr, Glasshouse Mountains; unpowered/powered sites $20/24, cabins from $80; ☒ ☒) This park has comfortable, self-contained cabins, pretty sites and spectacular mountain views. Facilities include BBQs, a tennis court and a small café.

Glasshouse Mountains Tavern (☎ 5493 0933; 10 Reed St, Glasshouse Mountains; mains $12-23; ☼ lunch & dinner) Part kit home, part old country tavern, this welcoming pub cooks up good pub nosh. The open fire keeps things cosy during winter and a peppering of outdoor seating is great for a midday middy on sunny days.

CALOUNDRA

☎ 07 / pop 20,140

Straddling a headland at the southern end of the Sunshine Coast, Caloundra is slowly shedding its staid retirement village image without losing its sleepy seaside charm. Excellent fishing in Pumicestone Passage (the snake of water separating Bribie Island from the mainland) and a number of pleasant surf beaches make it a popular holiday resort for both families and water-sports action fans.

Information

Caloundra visitors centre (☎ 5420 6240; 7 Caloundra Rd; ⏰ 9am-5pm) On the roundabout at the entrance to the town.

Hotspot Internet Café (☎ 5499 6644; Shop 8, 51 Bulcock St; per 15min/1hr $2/6; ⏰ 8.30am-5pm Mon-Fri, 8.30am-1pm Sat)

Information kiosk (☎ 5420 8718; 77 Bulcock St; ⏰ 9am-5pm) In the main street.

Sights & Activities

Caloundra's beaches curve around the headland so you'll find a sheltered beach no matter how windy it gets. **Bulcock Beach**, just down from the main street and pinched by the northern tip of Bribie Island, captures a good wind tunnel, making it popular with kite-surfers. **Kings Beach** has a lovely promenade, a kiddie-friendly interactive water feature, and a free saltwater swimming pool on the rocks. Depending on the conditions, **Moffat Beach** and **Dickey Beach** have the best surf breaks. Rent boards from **Beach Beat** (surfboards/body boards per day $35/20; Caloundra ☎ 5491 4711; 119 Bulcock St; ⏰ 9am-5.30pm; Dicky Beach ☎ 5491 8215; 4-6 Beerburrum St; ⏰ 9am-5.30pm). Learn to surf with **North Caloundra Surf School** (☎ 0411-221 730; www.northcaloundrasurfschool.com; 1½hr lesson $70). **Q Surf School** (☎ 0404 869 622; www.qsurfschool .com; 1hr lesson per person private/group $89/35) arranges day trips from Brisbane with transfers, two surf lessons, and lunch for $150 per person.

Caloundra Cruise (☎ 5492 8280; www.caloun dracruise.com; Maloja Ave Jetty; adult/child/concession/family $16/8/15/40) operates cruises in the channel and out to Bribie Island and has a great 2½-hour ecoexplorer cruise.

Active sorts will opt to kayak across the channel to explore the northern tip of Bribie Island National Park on foot with **Blue Water Kayak Tours** (☎ 5494 7789; www.bluewaterkayaktours .com.au; full/half-day tours $130/65, minimum 2 people).

A coastal walk, popular with joggers, cyclists and leisurely strollers, starts from the boat ramp at the northern end of Golden Beach and follows the headland north to Currimundi.

Sunshine Coast Skydivers (☎ 5437 0211; Caloundra Aerodrome; dives from $199) will facilitate any urges to jump out of a plane (tandem) – and film it in the process. Budding aviators may find the **Queensland Air Museum** (☎ 5492 5930; 7 Pathfinder Dr, Caloundra Aerodrome; adult/child/concession $9/6/7; ⏰ 10am-4pm) of passing interest.

Sleeping

Dicky Beach Family Holiday Park (☎ 5491 3342; www .dicky.com.au; 4 Beerburrum St; unpowered/powered sites $24/29, cabins from $67; 🅿 🌊) You can't get any closer to one of Caloundra's most popular beaches. The brick cabins are as ordered and tidy as the grounds and there's a small swimming pool for the kids. Rates are for two people.

Belaire Place (☎ 5491 8688; www.belaireplace.com; 34 Minchinton St; r $120-175; 🅿 🌊) Overlooking Bulcock Beach, these spacious, sunny one-bedroom apartments are great value. Close to cafés and restaurants and with excellent ocean views, you can watch the action on the beach from a balcony big enough to park a truck on.

Rolling Surf Resort (☎ 5491 9777; www.rolling surfresort.com; Levuka Ave, Kings Beach; 1-/2-bedroom apt

---

WOODSTOCK DOWN UNDER

The famous **Woodford Folk Festival** features a huge diversity of over 2000 national and international performers playing folk, traditional Irish, indigenous and world music, as well as buskers, belly dancers, craft markets, visual arts performances, environmental talks and a visiting squad of Tibetan monks. The festival is held on a property near the town of Woodford from 27 December to 1 January each year. Camping grounds are set up on the property with toilets, showers, and a range of foodie marquees but be prepared for a mud bath if it rains. The festival is licensed, so leave your booze at home.

Tickets cost around $79 per day ($94 with camping) and can be bought at the gate or through the **festival office** (☎ 5496 1066). Check online at www.woodfordfolkfestival.com for a programme of performances.

Woodford is 35km northwest of Caboolture. Shuttle buses run regularly from the Caboolture train station to and from the festival grounds.

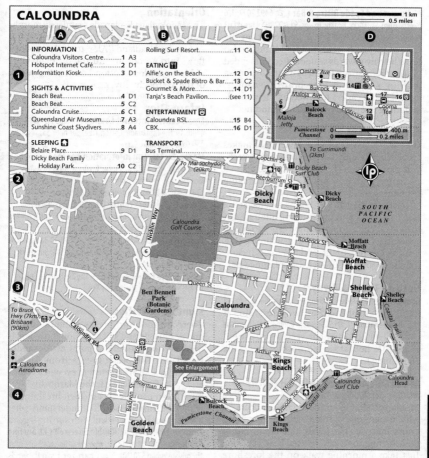

CALOUNDRA

INFORMATION
Caloundra Visitors Centre	**1** A3
Hotspot Internet Café	**2** D1
Information Kiosk	**3** D1

SIGHTS & ACTIVITIES
Beach Beat	**4** D1
Beach Beat	**5** C2
Caloundra Cruise	**6** C1
Queensland Air Museum	**7** A3
Sunshine Coast Skydivers	**8** A4

SLEEPING
Belaire Place	**9** D1
Dicky Beach Family Holiday Park	**10** C2

Rolling Surf Resort	**11** C4

EATING
Alfie's on the Beach	**12** D1
Bucket & Spade Bistro & Bar	**13** C2
Gourmet & More	**14** D1
Tanja's Beach Pavilion	(see 11)

ENTERTAINMENT
Caloundra RSL	**15** B4
CBX	**16** D1

TRANSPORT
Bus Terminal	**17** D1

$180/200;) This ultra-chic resort directly on the beach has *très* modern furnishings, fantastic views and a heated pool. Be king of Kings Beach in the three-bedroom penthouse suite. In high season there's a minimum five-night stay.

Eating

Gourmet & More (☎ 5499 6833; Shop 3, 63 Bulcock St; sandwiches $7; 8.30am-5.30pm Mon-Fri, 9am-2pm Sat) Start the day with a shot of pure caffeine. This delightful deli has over 20 different coffee flavours and a range of organic coffee beans. The rustic wooden benches reflect the rustic-style gourmet sandwiches of prosciutto, pastrami, sun-dried tomato and olives.

our pick Tanja's Beach Pavilion (☎ 5499 6600; 8 Levuka Ave, Kings Beach; mains $12-32; 6.30am-10.30pm) The landmark pavilion of this outdoor café and restaurant hangs directly over the sand on popular Kings Beach. All that salty sea air can really help to work up a hunger. For something light the chilled and grilled fresh seafood with tasty dipping sauces is an excellent choice.

Alfie's on the Beach (☎ 5491 0800; 26 The Esplanade, Bulcock Beach; mains $14-20; breakfast, lunch & dinner) Walk straight off the beach into this cool and casual café. The service can be patchy but the food and the views more than compensate. The macadamia pancake stack is a breakfast winner, while the rest of the day is given over to seafood.

Bucket and Spade Bistro & Bar (☎ 5492 7077; 1/6 Beerburrum St, Dicky Beach; mains $17-27; ☺ breakfast & lunch daily, dinner Fri & Sat) A new baby on the Caloundra beach scene, this trendy bistro also leans heavily towards seafood. Recommended is the chef's special: Sally's pasta marinara starring a sauce of king prawns, snapper, calamari and capers followed by the wicked-sounding ooey gooey chocolate pudding.

Entertainment

CBX (☎ 5439 4555; 12 Bulcock St) Live music makes Queensland's only beer exchange the weekend party scene. The bar works like a stock exchange, with beer prices rising and falling depending on demand.

Caloundra RSL (☎ 5491 1544; 19 West Tce) Some RSLs are small and unassuming affairs – not this one. With enough flamboyance to outdo Liberace, Caloundra's award-winning RSL features two restaurants and three bars including the groovy 1970s-style Lava Lounge Bar.

Getting There & Away

Greyhound (☎ 1300 473 946; www.greyhound.com.au) buses from Brisbane ($26, two hours) stop at the **bus terminal** (☎ 5491 2555; Cooma Tce). **Sunbus** (☎ 13 12 30) has frequent services to Noosa ($5.80, 1½ hours) via Maroochydore ($3.20, 50 minutes).

MOOLOOLABA & MAROOCHYDORE

☎ 07 / pop 10,250 / 16,360

Mooloolaba has seduced many a 'sea-changer' with its sublime climate, golden beach and cruisy lifestyle. The locals here are proud of their surfing roots and relaxed beach culture. Just take a morning walk on the foreshore and you'll find walkers and joggers, suntans and surfboards, and a dozen genuine smiles before breakfast.

Mooloolaba and Maroochydore, along with Alexandra Headland and Cotton Tree, form the Maroochy region. While Maroochydore takes care of the business end, Mooloolaba steals the show. Eateries, boutiques and pockets of low-rise resorts and apartments have spread along the Esplanade transforming this once-humble fishing village into one of Queensland's most popular holiday destinations. In summer Maroochy bursts with families indulging in good fishing and surf beaches, but it quickly reverts back to the tranquil epitome of coastal Oz for the remainder of the year.

Orientation

The Mooloolaba Esplanade seamlessly morphs into Alexandra Pde along the beachfront at Alexandra Headland ('Alex' to the locals) then flows into Aerodrome Rd and the main CBD of Maroochydore. Cotton Tree is at the mouth of the Maroochy River.

Information

Email Central Internet Lounge (Map p341; ☎ 5443 4440; 19 The Esplanade, Cotton Tree; per hour $5; ☺ 9am-6pm Mon-Sat)

Maroochy tourism information booths Mooloolaba (Map p342; ☎ 5478 2233; cnr Brisbane Rd & First Ave, Mooloolaba; ☺ 9am-5pm) Maroochydore Airport (off Map p341; ☎ 5448 9088; Friendship Dr, Marcoola)

Maroochy visitors centre (Map p341; ☎ 1800 882 032, 5459 9050; www.maroochytourism.com; cnr Sixth Ave & Melrose St, Maroochydore; ☺ 9am-5pm)

Post office Mooloolaba (Map p342; ☎ 13 13 18; cnr Brisbane Rd & Walan St) Maroochydore (Map p341; Sunshine Plaza, Horton Pde)

QPWS office (☎ 5443 8940; 29 The Esplanade, Cotton Tree; ☺ 8.30am-4.30pm Mon-Fri)

Sights & Activities

There are good surf breaks along the strip – one of Queensland's best for longboarders is the **Bluff**, the prominent point at Alexandra Headland. The beach breaks from Alex to Maroochydore are consistent even in a southerly while **Pincushion** near the Maroochy River mouth can provide an excellent break in the winter offshore winds. To understand what it's all about book a lesson with surfing legend Robbie Sherwell at **Robbie Sherwell's XL Surfing Academy** (☎ 5478 1337; www.xlsurfingacademy.com; 1hr private/group $70/30). You can rent surfboards from **Beach Beat** (Map p341; ☎ 5443 2777; 164 Alexandra Pde, Alexandra Headland; surfboards/body boards per day $35/25; ☺ 9am-5pm).

The Wharf (Map p342; Parkyn Pde) is a little bit tacky, a little bit kitsch, but showcases one of Mooloolaba's biggest drawcards, **Underwater World** (Map p342; ☎ 5444 8488; www.underwaterworld .com.au; The Wharf, Mooloolaba; adult/child/family $26.50/16/73; ☺ 9am-6pm), the largest tropical oceanarium in the southern hemisphere. You can swim with seals, dive with sharks or simply marvel at the psychedelic fish, stingrays and ocean life outside the 80m-long transparent underwater tunnel. There's a touch tank, seal shows and educational spiels to entertain both kids and adults.

Scuba World (Map p342; ☎ 5444 8598; www.scu baworld.com.au; The Wharf, Mooloolaba; dives from $90;

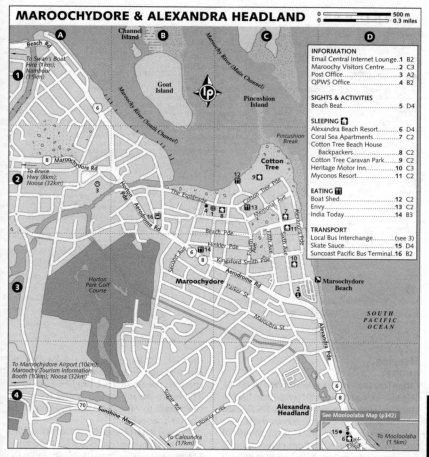

MAROOCHYDORE & ALEXANDRA HEADLAND

INFORMATION
Email Central Internet Lounge..**1** B2
Maroochy Visitors Centre.......**2** C3
Post Office....................**3** A2
QPWS Office..................**4** B2

SIGHTS & ACTIVITIES
Beach Beat....................**5** D4

SLEEPING
Alexandra Beach Resort........**6** D4
Coral Sea Apartments..........**7** C2
Cotton Tree Beach House
    Backpackers...............**8** C2
Cotton Tree Caravan Park......**9** C2
Heritage Motor Inn...........**10** C3
Myconos Resort...............**11** C2

EATING
Boat Shed....................**12** C2
Envy........................**13** C2
India Today..................**14** B3

TRANSPORT
Local Bus Interchange..........(see 3)
Skate Sauce..................**15** D4
Suncoast Pacific Bus Terminal.**16** B2

10am-5pm) arranges shark dives (certified/ uncertified divers $129/165) at Underwater World, coral dives off the coast and a wreck dive of the sunken warship, the ex-HMAS *Brisbane*. Sunk in July 2005, the wreck and its artificial reef is amazingly popular with divers. Beginners can also do a PADI course.

For a leisurely paddle down the Maroochy River, hire canoes or kayaks from **Swan's Boat Hire** (off Map p341; ☎ 5443 7225; 59 Bradman Ave, Maroochydore; per hr $14; 6am-6pm).

Tours
Steve Irwin's Whale One (Map 341; ☎ 1300 27 45 39; www.whaleone.com.au; adult/child/family $125/75/320) offers whale-watching cruises from August to October.

Several outfits offer river cruises along the Mooloolah River, departing from the Wharf in Mooloolaba. Check out the glitterati canal houses with a **Harbour River Canal Cruise** (Map p342; ☎ 5444 7477; www.sunshinecoast.au.nu/canalcruise .htm; The Wharf, Mooloolaba; adult/child/family $15/5/38; 11am, 1pm & 2.30pm) or take a two-hour eco-tour into the Mooloolah River National Park on **Cruiz Away River Tours** (Map p342; ☎ 5444 7477; www.cruizaway.com; The Wharf, Mooloolaba; ecotours adult/ child $45/30, sunset cruise $30).

For the more adventurous, **Aussie Sea Kayak Company** (Map p342; ☎ 5477 5335; www.ausseakayak .com.au; The Wharf, Mooloolaba; 4hr tour $65, 2hr sunset paddle $45) offers sea-kayaking trips including multiday trips to North Stradbroke, Fraser and Moreton Islands.

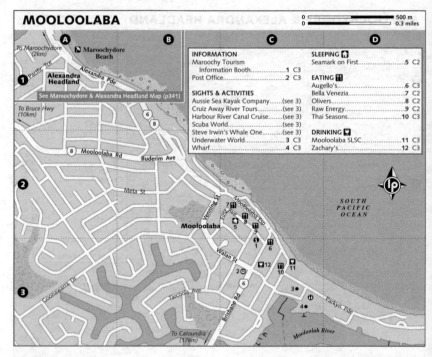

MOOLOOLABA

0 — 500 m
0 — 0.3 miles

To Maroochydore (2km)

Maroochydore Beach

Alexandra Pde

Alexandra Headland

Pacific Tce

See Maroochydore & Alexandra Headland Map (p341)

To Bruce Hwy (10km)

Mooloolaba Rd

Buderim Ave

Meta St

Vanning St

Brisbane Rd

Mooloolaba

Walan St

Tarcoola Ave

Goonawarra Dr

To Caloundra (17km)

Mooloolah River

SOUTH PACIFIC OCEAN

INFORMATION	
Maroochy Tourism	
Information Booth	1 C3
Post Office	2 C3

SIGHTS & ACTIVITIES	
Aussie Sea Kayak Company	(see 3)
Cruiz Away River Tours	(see 3)
Harbour River Canal Cruise	(see 3)
Scuba World	(see 3)
Steve Irwin's Whale One	(see 3)
Underwater World	3 C3
Wharf	4 C3

SLEEPING	
Seamark on First	5 C2

EATING	
Augello's	6 C3
Bella Venezia	7 C2
Olivers	8 C2
Raw Energy	9 C2
Thai Seasons	10 C3

DRINKING	
Mooloolaba SLSC	11 C3
Zachary's	12 C3

Sleeping

BUDGET

Cotton Tree Caravan Park (Map p341; ☎ 1800 461 253, 5443 1253; www.maroochypark.qld.gov.au; Cotton Tree Pde, Cotton Tree; unpowered/powered sites from $25/28, cabins $125-160) A merger of two caravan parks, this baby sits right on the beach at the mouth of the Maroochy River. In summer it resembles a teeming suburb but it's a grassy spot with great facilities. Rates are for two people.

Cotton Tree Beach House Backpackers (Map p341; ☎ 5443 1755; www.cottontreebackpackers.com; 15 The Esplanade, Cotton Tree; dm/d $22/50) The vibe is as warm as the brightly painted common room walls and the atmosphere is as laid-back as the fat labrador lolling on the sofa. Opposite a park and river, this renovated century-old Queenslander is clean and homy and oozes charm along with free surfboards, kayaks and bikes.

MIDRANGE & TOP END

During school holidays most places require a minimum two- or three-night stay.

Heritage Motor Inn (Map p341; ☎ 5443 7355; heri tagemotorinn@hotmail.com; 69 Sixth Ave, Maroochydore; r from $145; 🅿 🌐) Push past the kitsch exterior – as motels go this one's a winner. The spacious rooms are cool, bright and spotless. The hosts are superfriendly and it's only a short walk to Maroochydore Beach and the Cotton Tree cafés.

Myconos Resort (Map p341; ☎ 1800 041 166, 5451 1711; www.myconosresort.com; 45 Sixth Ave, Maroochydore; 1-bedroom apt per 2 nights from $315; 🅿 🌐) From the outside this loud tower looks like every other high-rise, but inside are a multitude of stylish, themed rooms with subtle overtones of Africa, the Middle East and the Mediterranean. And they all come with kitchens, spas and big balconies.

Alexandra Beach Resort (Map p341; ☎ 5475 0600; www.alexandra-beach-resort.com; cnr Alexandra Pde & Pacific Tce, Alexandra Headland; 1-/2-bedroom apt 2 nights $330/442; 🅿 🌐) Directly opposite the beach, these large and comfy apartments open either onto a courtyard or a balcony, but can be quite noisy. The 150m tropical lagoon pool comes with a pool bar!

Seamark on First (Map p342; ☎ 5457 8600; www .seamarkresort.com.au; 29 First Ave, Mooloolaba; 2-/3-bedroom apt per 5 nights $1000/1245; 🅿 🌐) One street back

SUNSHINE COAST

from Mooloolaba's fashionable Esplanade this stylish and modern resort is bright, airy and spacious. Most apartments have ocean views – sit on the balcony and watch the moon rise over the water.

ourpick **Coral Sea Apartments** (Map p341; ☎ 5479 2999; www.coralsea-apartments.com; 35-7 Sixth Ave, Maroochydore; apt per week from $1380; ❀ ▣) These yawning two- and three-bedroom apartments occupy a lovely spot close to Maroochy Surf Club and the beach. Inside you'll find tasteful décor and the balconies are plenty big and breezy.

Eating
BUDGET
Raw Energy (Map p342; ☎ 5444 2111; Shop 3, Mooloolaba Esplanade, Mooloolaba; dishes $6-15; ❀ 6.15am-5pm) In this popular beachside café pretty young things serve up tofu, tempeh and gluten-free items with 'zinger' juices. Muffin addicts will think they've found The One. With the best coffee on the strip and a prime spot for people-watching it's definitely worth the (sometimes long) wait.

Envy (Map p341; ☎ 5443 8494; The Esplanade, Cotton Tree; mains $6-15; ❀ breakfast & lunch daily, dinner Fri) This cosy café serves up chai and soy lattes with a dash of bohemia. The menu features healthy salads, burgers, and thick bread sandwiches and there's a three-course set menu on Friday nights ($40). The local artwork on the walls is a talking point.

Thai Seasons (Map p342; ☎ 5444 4611; 10 Mooloolaba Esplanade, Mooloolaba; mains $10-12; ❀ dinner) The plastic outdoor setting won't win any awards, and you have to grab your own cutlery, but this unpretentious restaurant dishes out the best Thai food in town. If it's crowded, order takeaway and head for the picnic tables overlooking Mooloolaba's main beach.

MIDRANGE
Olivers (Map p342; ☎ 5478 1893; 57 The Esplanade, Mooloolaba; mains $10-22; ❀ breakfast, lunch & dinner) In the heart of the Mooloolaba strip, this outdoor eatery has balmy sea breezes and ocean views. Lunch is a casual affair with *mucho* people-watching and the evening ambience is relaxed and casual. The cosmopolitan menu has dishes such as Thai beef salad and lamb cutlets on couscous and rocket salad.

India Today (Map p341; ☎ 5452 7054; 91 Aerodrome Rd, Maroochydore; mains $13-18; ❀ lunch Thu, Fri & Sat, dinner nightly) You can't miss the masses of fairy lights

decorating this restaurant on Maroochydore's main drag. Be prepared for the brightly and chaotically coloured visual feast of Indian cloths, textiles, paintings and wall hangings waiting inside. The butter chicken with the chef's special sauce is delicious.

Augello's (Map p342; ☎ 5478 3199; cnr Mooloolaba Esplanade & Brisbane Rd, Mooloolaba; mains $15-29; ❀ lunch & dinner) This Mooloolaba institution spoils hungry folk of all ages with outstanding Italian food and a solid reputation. Authentic and prize-winning pizzas join nouveau concoctions such as Moroccan chicken with sundried tomatoes and lime yogurt dressing. Nab an upstairs table for ocean views.

TOP END
Boat Shed (Map p341; ☎ 5443 3808; Mooloolaba Esplanade, Cotton Tree; mains $22-34; ❀ lunch daily, dinner Mon-Sat) A shabby-chic gem on the banks of the Maroochy River, great for sunset drinks beneath the sprawling cotton tree. Seafood is the star of the menu and a must-try is the coconut battered prawns with roasted banana and caramelised rum syrup. After dinner, roll back to the outdoor lounges for dessert and some serious romantic star-gazing.

ourpick **Bella Venezia** (Map p342; ☎ 5444 5844; 95 Mooloolaba Esplanade, Mooloolaba; mains $25-38; ❀ lunch & dinner) This long-established icon has added a wine bar to its arcade cul-de-sac. The menu is exclusively Italian with exquisite dishes such as *ravioli alla sambucca* and *risotto nera* (squid-ink risotto). Has live music on Wednesday nights and fortnightly wine tastings.

Drinking
Zachary's (Map p342; ☎ 5477 6877; 17-19 Brisbane Rd, Mooloolaba) The place to meet for after-work drinks or to fuel up a Friday night on the town. Small booths, floor cushions, low central lounges and a hip DJ set the mood.

Mooloolaba SLSC (Map p342; ☎ 5444 1300; Esplanade, Mooloolaba; ❀ 10am-10pm Sun-Thu, 10am-midnight Fri & Sat) A traditional Aussie icon, the surf club somehow seamlessly morphs from a midweek good-value family outing to a weekend singles pick-up joint where local bands play c 1980s dance music every Friday night.

Getting There & Away
Greyhound Australia (☎ 1300 473 946; www.greyhound .com.au) runs to and from Brisbane ($28, two hours) using the **Suncoast Pacific bus terminal** (Map p341; ☎ 5443 1011; First Ave, Maroochydore; ❀ 7.30am-

4.30pm Mon-Fri, 7.30am-12.30pm Sat). **Premier Motor Services** (☎ 13 34 10; www.premierms.com.au) also has a daily service from Brisbane ($20, two hours).

Getting Around

Sunbus (☎ 13 12 30) has frequent services between Mooloolaba and Maroochydore ($2) and on to Noosa ($5, one hour). The local bus interchange is at the Sunshine Plaza.

Skate Sauce (Map p341; ☎ 5443 6111; 150 Alexandra Pde, Alexandra Headland; 9am-5pm Mon-Sat, 10am-4pm Sun) hires out in-line skates with all the gear as well as bicycles (per hour/day $8/20).

COOLUM

☎ 07 / pop 7180

Coolum is one of the Sunshine Coast's hidden treasures. Rocky headlands create a number of secluded coves before spilling into the fabulously long stretch of golden sand and rolling surf of Coolum beach. With its budding café society and within easy reach of the coast's hot spots it's an attractive escape from the more popular and overcrowded holiday scene at Noosa and Mooloolaba.

For outstanding views of the coast a hike to the top of **Mt Coolum** (200m, one hour return), south of town, is worth the sweat factor. At the base of the mountain, the **Hyatt Regency Coolum** (☎ 5446 1234; www.coolum.regency.hyatt.com; Warran Rd, Coolum Beach; ste per night from $250; wi-fi) is a five-star golf and spa resort set on 150 hectares of rainforest, Australian bushland and lush gardens.

The wee council-run **Coolum Beach Caravan Park** (☎ 1800 461 474, 5446 1474; www.maroochypark.qld.gov.au; David Low Way, Coolum; unpowered/powered sites $24/27) is rudimentary, but it's nudged onto a grassy plot in front of the beach and just across the road from Coolum's main strip.

Hidden behind a cool and leafy veranda, the modest row of bungalows at **Villa Coolum** (☎ 5446 1286; www.villacoolum.com; 102 Coolum Tce, Coolum Beach; r $79;) are kitted out with simple gear, but the rooms are spacious and spotless. This is a good spot for families.

A long stretch of parkland separates the beach from a string of outdoor cafés including **Raw Energy** (☎ 5473 9066; David Low Way; mains $6-14; breakfast & lunch) where the menu reeks of salads, tofu and all things healthy.

For dinner, **My Place** (☎ 5446 4433; David Low Way; mains $15-20; 7am-11pm), opposite the boardwalk, has sensational ocean views and alfresco dining including a daily selection of tapas.

The convivial **Castro's Bar & Restaurant** (☎ 5471 7555; cnr Frank St & Beach Rd; mains $15-30; dinner) satisfies all radicals with dishes such as Tuscan fish stew, tempura-battered wild barramundi fillet, Middle Eastern seared salmon and wood-fired pizza.

Sol Bar (☎ 5446 2333; cnr Beach Rd & David Low Way) is one of the funkiest venues on the coast, hosting some of Australia's biggest bands. The vibe is casual, cool and alternative – like the music.

PEREGIAN & SUNSHINE BEACH

☎ 07 / pop 2800 / 2360

Fifteen kilometres of uncrowded, unobstructed beach stretches north from Coolum to Sunshine Beach and the rocky northeast headland of Noosa National Park. **Peregian** clusters around a small village square with only a few cafés and restaurants, its lack of nightlife a drawcard for holidaying families. This is the place for long solitary beach walks, good surf breaks, fresh air and sunshine – and it's not uncommon to see whales breaching offshore.

A little further north the laid-back latte ethos of **Sunshine Beach** attracts Noosa locals escaping the summer hordes. Beach walks morph into bush walks over the headland; a postprandial stroll through the **Noosa National Park**, taking two hours to Noosa's Laguna Bay. Road access to the park is from McAnally Dr or Parkedge Rd.

Dolphins Beach House (Map p348; ☎ 5447 2100; www.dolphinsbeachhouse.com; 14 Duke St, Sunshine Beach; dm/d/apt $24/60/65;), nestled in a patch of tropical gardens, reflects the Asian and Mexican influences of its well-travelled owner. The rooms are basic and clean, there's plenty of kitchen space, it's close to cafés and the beach, and only a short bus ride from Noosa.

It's only small but you can't miss the electric blue **Pacific Blue Apartments** (☎ 5448 3611; www.pacificblueapartments.com.au; 236 David Low Way, Peregian Beach; r $85-90). Close to the pub the beach, Pacific Blue has cheerful studios and one-bedroom units, all self-contained with a healthy dose of space.

It's hard to book anything less than a two-night stay in Sunshine Beach's holiday apartments. **Andari** (Map p348; ☎ 5474 9996; www.andari.com.au; 19-21 Belmore Tce, Sunshine Beach; 2-/3-bedroom apt $330/400, minimum 2-night stay;) is a quiet retreat of townhouses set in shady, subtropical gardens. The apartments are light and airy, overlook the beach, and are a short stroll to cafés and restaurants.

Peregian's limited eating options are surprisingly good and conveniently located in the central village square. The **Baked Poetry Cafe** (☎ 5448 3500; 218 David Low Way, Peregian Beach; dishes $10-14; ☷ 9am-5pm Mon-Fri, 8am-5pm Sat & Sun) is a minibakery and café, famous for its great coffee and German sourdough bread.

For something unexpected, the Persian restaurant **Qom** (☎ 5448 1665; Shop 5, 4 Kingfisher Dr, Peregian Beach; mains $14.50-18; ☷ breakfast & lunch daily, dinner Mon-Sat), also in the village square, has excellent Middle Eastern food with a twist – mains are vegetarian with side dishes of meat and fish.

Sunshine Beach's café strip lives up to Noosa's exacting standards. **Fratellini** (Map p348; ☎ 5474 8080; 36 Duke St, Sunshine Beach; mains $12-26; ☷ 7am-10pm summer, 8am-9pm winter) is a stylish beach-chic café focused on all things Italian. Local celebs escape here to relax over good coffee and lazy lunches.

The international flavour on the strip continues with **Wasabi** (Map p348; ☎ 5449 2443; cnr Duke & Bryan Sts, Sunshine Beach; mains $30; ☷ dinner Tue-Sun, lunch Fri). Pull up a cushion at the traditional Japanese tables sunk into the floor while feasting on ultrafresh sushi, sashimi and fresh swimmer crabs. Save room for the green tea ice cream.

Raising the bar is the **Marble Bar Bistro** (Map p348; ☎ 5455 3200; 40 Duke St; tapas $12-19; ☷ 11.30am-late daily, breakfast Sun), a cruisy cocktail and tapas bar sans doors or walls. Kick back in a cushioned lounge or perch yourself at one of the marble benches to scope the local beat.

NOOSA

☎ 07 / pop 9110

Gorgeous Noosa is a stylish resort town with a stunning natural landscape of crystalline beaches and tropical rainforests. Designer boutiques and swish restaurants draw beach-elite sophisticates, but the beach and bush are still free, so glammed-up fashionistas simply share the beat with thongs, boardshorts and bronzed bikini bods baring their bits.

Noosa is undeniably developed but its low-impact condos and chichi landscape have been cultivated without losing sight of simple seaside pleasures. On long weekends and school holidays, however, bustling Hastings St becomes a slow-moving file of traffic.

Orientation

Noosa has an amazing number of round-abouts and it's easy to get lost. Broadly speaking, Noosa encompasses three zones: Noosa Heads (around Laguna Bay and Hastings St), Noosaville (along the Noosa River) and Noosa Junction (the administrative centre).

Noosa National Park dominates the headland overlooking the town. The area north of the Noosa River is preserved as the Cooloola Section of Great Sandy National Park and offers great opportunities for 4WD driving, hiking and kayaking.

Information

Adventure Travel Bugs (Map p348; ☎ 1800 666 720, 5474 8530; 9 Sunshine Beach Rd, Noosa Junction; internet access per hr $4; ☷ 8am-8pm Mon-Fri, 9am-7pm Sat & Sun)

Noosa visitors centre (Map p348; ☎ 5430 5020; www .visitnoosa.com.au; Hastings St; ☷ 9am-5pm) Very helpful.

Peterpan Adventure Travel (Map p348; ☎ 1800 777 115, 5455 4747; www.peterpans.com; Shop 3, 75 Noosa Dr, Noosa Junction; Internet access per hr $2; ☷ 9.45am-5.30pm Mon-Fri, 11am-4.30pm Sat & Sun)

Post office (Map p348; ☎ 5473 8591; 91 Noosa Dr)

Urban Mailbox (Map p348; ☎ 5473 5151; Ocean Breeze, Noosa Dr, Noosa Heads; per 15min $3; ☷ 8am-8pm) Super-expensive internet access.

Sights

One of Noosa's best features, the lovely **Noosa National Park**, covering the headland, has fine walks, great coastal scenery and a string of bays with waves that draw surfers from all over the country. The most scenic way to access the national park is to follow the boardwalk along the coast from town. Pick up a walking track map from the **QPWS centre** (Map p346; ☎ 5447 3243; ☷ 9am-3pm), at the entrance to the park. Sleepy koalas are often spotted in the trees near Tea Tree Bay and dolphins are commonly seen from the rocky headlands around Alexandria Bay, an informal nudist beach on the eastern side.

For a panoramic view of the park, walk or drive up to **Laguna Lookout** from Viewland Dr in Noosa Junction.

Activities

SURFING & WATER SPORTS

With a string of breaks around an unspoilt national park, Noosa is a fine place to catch a wave. Generally the waves are best in December and January but Sunshine Corner,

NOOSA

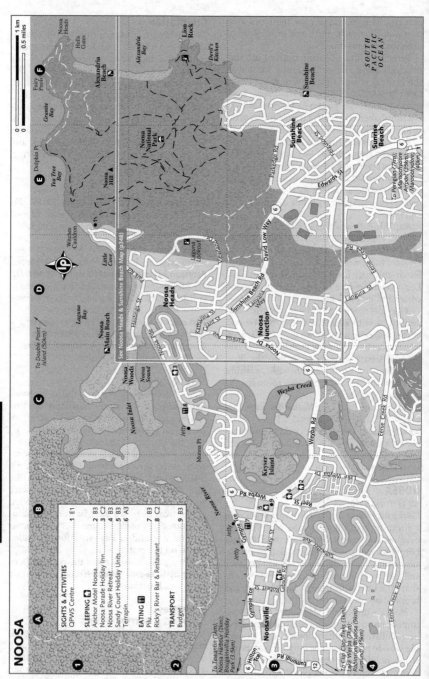

SUNSHINE COAST

SIGHTS & ACTIVITIES
QPWS Centre...............................1 E1

SLEEPING 🛏
Anchor Motel Noosa.....................2 B3
Noosa Parade Holiday Inn............3 C2
Noosa River Retreat.....................4 B3
Sandy Court Holiday Units............5 B3
Terrapin.......................................6 A3

EATING 🍴
Pilu...7 B3
Ricky's River Bar & Restaurant......8 C2

TRANSPORT
Budget..9 B3

See Noosa Heads & Sunshine Beach Map (p348)

at the northern end of Sunshine Beach, has an excellent year-round break, although it has a brutal beach dump. The point breaks around the headland only perform during the summer, but when they do, expect wild conditions and good walls at Boiling Point and Tea Tree, on the northern coast of the headland. There are also gentler breaks on Noosa Spit at the far end of Hastings St, where most of the surf schools do their training.

Kite-surfers will find conditions at the river mouth and Lake Weyba are best between October and January, but on windy days the Noosa River is a playground for serious daredevils.

Recommended companies:

Merrick's Learn to Surf (☎ 0418-787 577; www .learntosurf.com.au; surfing 2/3hr lesson $55/150)

Noosa Adventures & Kite-Surfing (☎ 0438-747 801; www.noosakitesurfing.com.au; 2/8hr kite-surfing lessons $140/$400, equipment rental per hr/day $30/100)

Noosa Longboards (Map p348; ☎ 5447 2828; www.noosa longboards.com; 64 Hastings St, Noosaville; 2hr surfing lesson $55, longboard hire per half-/full day $35/50, surfboard hire $25/40, body-board hire $15/20)

Noosa Surf Lessons (☎ 0412-330 850; www.noosa surflessons.com.au; 1-/3-/5-day lesson from $45/120/170)

CANOEING & KAYAKING

The Noosa River is excellent for canoeing; it's possible to follow it up through Lakes Cooroibah and Cootharaba, and through the Cooloola Section of Great Sandy National Park. The Elanda Point Canoe Company (see p352) rents canoes and kayaks.

Noosa Ocean Kayak Tours (☎ 0418-787 577; www .learntosurf.com; 2hr tours $66, kayak hire per day $55) offers kayaking tours around Noosa National Park and along the Noosa River.

ADVENTURE ACTIVITIES

Pedal & Paddle (☎ 5474 5328; www.pedalandpaddle .com.au; tours $89) Operates great four-hour combo hike, bike and kayak tours. Prices include morning and afternoon tea and local transfers.

Noosa Bike Hire & Tours (☎ 5474 3322; www.noosa bikehire.com; tours $69) Offers half-day mountain bike tours down Mt Tinbeerwah, including morning tea and transfers.

HORSE RIDING & CAMEL SAFARIS

Noosa North Shore Retreat (p352) offers horse riding along bush trails and along the beach. Camel Company Australia (p352) operate camel safaris on the beach and in the bush. **Clip Clop Treks** (off Map p346; ☎ 5449 1254; www .clipcloptreks.com.au; Eumerella Rd, Lake Weyba; 2hr/1-day rides $70/165, 4-day pub treks $1320) Offers horse rides around Lake Weyba and the surrounding bush. Better yet is the all-inclusive four-day pub trek, which takes you through the northern Sunshine Coast hinterland, staying at historic pubs along the way.

Tours
FRASER ISLAND

A number of operators offer trips to Fraser Island via the Cooloola Coast. All include informative commentaries and major Fraser Island highlights.

Fraser Island Excursions (☎ 5449 0393; www .fraserislandexcursions.com.au; tours $189) offers small group day tours in comfortable 4WDs and includes a gourmet lunch and a complimentary wine. **Fraser Island Adventure Tours** (☎ 5444 6957; www.fraserislandadventuretours.com.au; adult/child $159/115) has won several industry awards for its day tours in 4WD minibuses that include a BBQ lunch.

Fraser Explorer Tours (☎ 1800 249 122; www.fraser -is.com; adult/child $135/75) offers less intimate tours but takes in the same sights and stops for lunch at Eurong Beach Resort. **Trailblazer Tours** (☎ 3512 8100; 3-day safaris per person $340) operates small group tours and can pick up and drop off at either Noosa or Rainbow Beach. For more information about tours to Fraser Island, see boxed text, p172.

To do it in style, several companies offer fly-drive packages including flights to Fraser Island and 4WD hire for self-guided day trips. Tours cost $250 to $300 per person:

Air Fraser Island (☎ 1800 247 992; www.airfraser island.com.au)

Fraser Island Heli-Drive (☎ 1800 063 933, 4125 3933; www.fraserislandco.com.au/helidrive.html)

Sunshine Coast Scenic Flights (☎ 5450 0516; www .noosaaviation.com)

EVERGLADES

Several companies run boats from the Noosa Harbour at Tewantin up the Noosa River into the 'Everglades' area (essentially the passage of the Noosa River that cuts into the Great Sandy National Park). Companies include:

Beyond Noosa (☎ 1800 657 666, 5449 9177; www .beyondnoosa.com.au; afternoon tours adult/child $69/45, day tours incl lunch adult/child $84/50, ecotour of everglades & 4WD beach driving adult/child $149/100) All tours include Noosa transfers.

MV Noosa Queen (☎ 5455 6661; 3hr tours per person $45) Lunch cruises up the river.

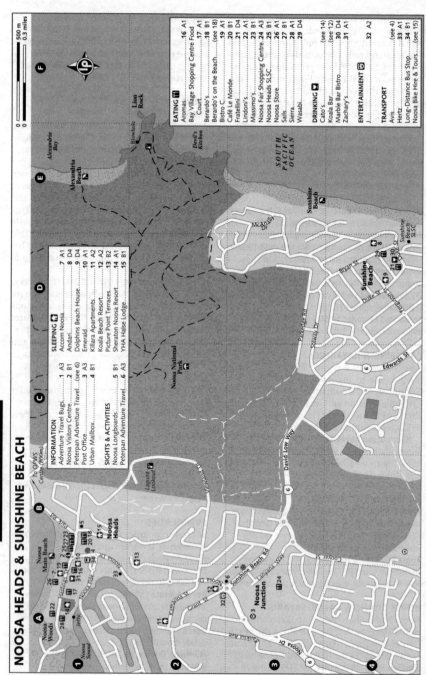

NOOSA HEADS & SUNSHINE BEACH

INFORMATION
Adventure Travel Bugs................1 A3
Noosa Visitors Centre..................2 B1
Peterpan Adventure Travel........(see 6)
Post Office...................................3 A3
Urban Mailbox.............................4 B1

SIGHTS & ACTIVITIES
Noosa Longboards........................5 B1
Peterpan Adventure Travel..........6 A3

SLEEPING
Accom Noosa................................7 A1
Andari...8 D4
Dolphins Beach House..................9 D4
Emerald.......................................10 A1
Killara Apartments......................11 A2
Koala Beach Resort.....................12 A2
Picture Point Terraces.................13 B2
Sheraton Noosa Resort................14 A1
YHA Halse Lodge........................15 B1

EATING
Aromas.......................................16 A1
Bay Village Shopping Centre Food
  Court.......................................17 A1
Berardo's....................................18 B1
Berardo's on the Beach.........(see 18)
Bistro C.......................................19 A1
Café Le Monde.............................20 B1
Fratellini.....................................21 D4
Lindoni's.....................................22 A1
Massimo's....................................23 B1
Noosa Fair Shopping Centre.......24 A3
Noosa Heads SLSC......................25 B1
Noosa Store.................................26 A1
Sails...27 B1
Sierra..28 A1
Wasabi..29 D4

DRINKING
Cato's.....................................(see 14)
Koala Bar................................(see 12)
Marble Bar Bistro.......................30 D4
Zachary's....................................31 A1

ENTERTAINMENT
J..32 A2

TRANSPORT
Avis...(see 4)
Hertz...33 A1
Long-Distance Bus Stop..............34 B1
Noosa Bike Hire & Tours........(see 15)

500 m
0.3 miles

SOUTH PACIFIC OCEAN

For the more adventurous, **Peterpan Adventure Travel** (Map p348; ☎ 1800 777 115; www.peterpans.com; Shop 3, 75 Noosa Dr, Noosa Junction; tours $90) has three-day canoe tours into the park including tents and equipment. Alternatively, the **Elanda Point Canoe Company** (☎ 1800 226 637, 5485 3165; www .elanda.com.au/noosa; Elanda Point; tours adult/child $70/59) offers half-day canoe tours including transfers and morning tea.

Festivals & Events

Noosa Festival of Surfing (www.usmevents .au/noosasurf) A week of longboard action, in March-

Noosa Jazz Festival (☎ 5449 9189; www.noosajazz .com.au) Four-day annual jazz festival in late August and early September.

Noosa Triathlon (☎ 5449 0711; www.usmevents .com.au) Triathlon and week-long sports festival in early November.

Noosa Long Weekend (☎ 5474 9941; www.noosa longweekend.com) Ten-day festival of arts, culture, food and fashion in June/July.

Sleeping

Accom Noosa (Map p348; ☎ 1800 072 078; www.ac comnoosa.com.au; Shop 5, Fairshore Apartments, Hastings St, Noosa Heads) has an extensive list of private holiday rentals that are good for stays of a week or more.

With the exception of backpackers hostels, accommodation prices can rise by 50% in busy times and 100% in the December to January peak season. During these times most places require a minimum two- or three-night stay. High-season prices are quoted.

BUDGET

Bougainvillia Holiday Park (off Map p346; ☎ 1800 041 444, 5447 1712; jsjs@optusnet.com.au; 141 Cooroy-Noosa Rd, Tewantin; unpowered/powered sites from $30/34, cabins $65-135; 🖪 🖳) Neat as a pin and meticulously landscaped, this is the best camping option in the area. The facilities are spotless and there's an on-site café.

YHA Halse Lodge (Map p348; ☎ 1800 242 567, 5447 3377; backpackers@halselodge.com.au; 2 Halse Lane, Noosa Heads; members/nonmembers dm $29/32, d $74/82; meals $9-12; 🖳) Elevated from Hastings St by a steeeep driveway, this splendid colonial-era timber Queenslander is legendary on the backpacker route. The dorms and kitchen are a tad cramped, but the bar is a mix-and-meet bonanza and serves great meals.

Koala Beach Resort (Map p348; ☎ 1800 357 457, 5447 3355; www.koala-backpackers.com; 44 Noosa Dr, Noosa

Junction; dm/d $27/60; 🖳 🖳) One of the Koala chain, this hostel has the usual trademarks – popular bar, central location and party atmosphere. Your buck also buys huge dorms, good facilities and professional staff.

Sandy Court Holiday Units (Map p346; ☎ 5449 7225; smitherines@bigpond.com; 30 James St, Noosaville; d $70-110; 🖳) Down a quiet residential street, these self-contained units offer unbeatable value. The décor is a bit weary and the furnishings and crockery are mix-and-match, but the units are clean and comfortable.

MIDRANGE

Anchor Motel Noosa (Map p346; ☎ 5449 8055; www .anchormotelnoosa.com; cnr Anchor St & Weyba Rd, Noosaville; r from $110; 🖪 🖳) There's no escaping the nautical theme in this colourful motel. Blue-striped bedspreads, porthole windows and marine motifs will have you wearing stripes and cut-offs while grilling prawns on the barbie.

Robinsons@noosa (off Map p346; ☎ 5471 1129; www .robinsonsatnoosa.com; 855 Noosa Eumundi Rd, Doonan; r $120; 🖳) Five rooms span out of a central lounge, kitchen (for guests' use), and winery cellar door at this comfy B&B only 10 minutes from Hastings St. There are no added luxuries but the rooms are large and swimming in sunlight. It's private, quiet and set on 5 hectares of land.

Noosa River Retreat (Map p346; ☎ 5474 2811; www .noosariverretreat.net; cnr Weyba Rd & Reef St, Noosaville; 1-bedroom unit $130; 🖪 🖳 🖳) Your buck goes a long way at this orderly complex, which houses spick, span and spacious units. Onsite are a central BBQ and laundry and the corner units are almost entirely protected by small native gardens.

Noosa Parade Holiday Inn (Map p346; ☎ 5447 4177; www.noosaparadeholidayinn.com; 51 Noosa Pde, Noosa Heads; r $180; 🖪 🖳) Not far from Hastings St, these tiled and spotless apartments are reminiscent of an Ikea showroom. The pleasant and cool interiors are clad in bold colours and face away from the street and passing traffic.

Terrapin (Map p346; ☎ 5449 8770; www.terrapin.com.au; 15 The Cockleshell, Noosaville; 2-bedroom townhouse from $180; 🖳) You can relax out of sight in the courtyard and gardens of these two-storey townhouses. The earthy interiors are lifted by bold furnishings and balconies or gardens. All contain every mod con you need to sustain a serious stay.

Killara Apartments (Map p348; ☎ 5447 2800; www.kil laranoosa.com; cnr Grant St & Banksia Ave, Noosa Junction; 1-/2-bedroom unit $185/264; 🖪 🖳) These functional and modern units have plenty of space and colour. They're in a picturesque street on Noosa Hill, and some come with private BBQs and courtyards. There's a three-night minimum stay.

TOP END

Sheraton Noosa Resort (Map p348; ☎ 5449 4888; www .starwoodhotels.com/sheraton; 14-16 Hastings St, Noosa Heads; r $290-540; ✿ 🖳 ☲) As expected, this five-star hotel has tastefully decorated rooms with suede fabrics, fabulous beds, balconies, kitchenettes and spas. The hotel houses the popular Cato's (see opposite) as well as a day spa.

Emerald (Map p348; ☎ 1800 803 899, 5449 6100; www .emeraldnoosa.com.au; 42 Hastings St, Noosa Heads; 2-bedroom apt from $370; ✿ 🖳 ☲) The stylish Emerald has indulgent rooms bathed in ethereal white and sunlight. Expect clean, crisp edges and exquisite furnishings. All one-, two- and three-bedroom apartments are fully self-contained.

our pick **Picture Point Terraces** (Map p348; ☎ 5449 2433; www.picturepointterraces.com.au; 47 Picture Point Crescent, Noosa Heads; 2-/3-bedroom apt from $445/555; ✿ 🖳 ☲ ; wi-fi) On high ground behind Noosa these ultrachic apartments with all the mod cons have fantastic views over the rainforest to Laguna Bay. The private spa bath on the balcony is the ideal spot for a sunset cocktail. There's a seven-night minimum stay in high season.

Eating

You can eat well for around $10 at the **Bay Village Shopping Centre food court** (Map p348; Hastings St, Noosa Heads). Self-caterers can stock up at the Noosa Fair Shopping Centre (Map p348).

Massimo's (Map p348; ☎ 5474 8022; Hastings St; gelati $2-4; ✆ 9am-10pm) Definitely one of the best *gelaterias* in Queensland, you'll melt over the orgasmic gelati made fresh every day.

Aromas (Map p348; ☎ 5474 9788; 32 Hastings St; mains $10-28; ✆ breakfast, lunch & dinner) This European-style café is unashamedly ostentatious with chandeliers, faux-marble tables and cane chairs deliberately facing the street so patrons can ogle the passing foot traffic. There's the usual array of panini, cakes and light meals but most folk come for the coffee and atmosphere.

Sierra (Map p348; ☎ 5447 4800; 10 Hastings St; mains $15-25; ✆ breakfast, lunch & dinner) This hot little pavement café has great coffee, killer cocktails and an assortment of interesting dishes including grilled prawns with Cajun bananas and black sticky rice. Daiquiri Hour is be-

tween 5pm and 7pm and live music plays on Wednesdays and Sundays.

our pick **Berardo's on the Beach** (Map p348; ☎ 5448 0888; On the Beach, Hastings St; mains $15-30; ✆ lunch & dinner) Reminiscent of the French Riviera, this stylish bistro is only metres from the waves. Classy without being pretentious, this is Noosa in a seashell. The Mod Oz menu has Asian and Italian influences.

Bistro C (Map p348; ☎ 5447 2855; On the Beach, Hastings St; mains $15-32; ✆ breakfast, lunch & dinner) The menu at this yuppie beachfront brasserie is an eclectic blend of everything that seems like a good idea at the time. The egg-fried calamari with chilli lime coriander dip is legendary.

Café Le Monde (Map p348; ☎ 5449 2366; Hastings St; mains $17-28; ✆ breakfast, lunch & dinner) Café Le Monde's enormous menu will satisfy all appetites. The large, open-air patio buzzes with diners digging into burgers, seared tuna steaks, curries, pastas, salads and plenty more. The place rocks with live music nearly every night and is a great venue for a few drinks.

Lindoni's (Map p348; ☎ 5447 5111; Hastings St; mains $20-30; ✆ dinner) Behind the gothic candelabra guarding the entrance, this romantic Italian restaurant has a Mediterranean courtyard for intimate candlelit dining. The cuisine favours the lighter southern Italian style – think Positano and the Amalfi coast – with lashings of *amore*.

Berardo's (Map p348; ☎ 5447 5666; Hastings St; mains $26-35; ✆ dinner) Beautiful Berardo's is culinary utopia, from the sun-dappled setting swimming in elegance to the heavenly food. Soft music from the grand piano and delicate dishes such as quail crepinettes with truffle polenta will lull you into a coma.

Sails (Map p348; ☎ 5447 4235; cnr Park Rd & Hastings St; mains $29-38; ✆ breakfast, lunch & dinner) A culinary gem at the eastern end of Hastings St, there's only a mere swathe of lawn between Laguna Bay and the timber floors of this classy restaurant. The Mod Oz menu favours seafood with such delights as grilled Moreton Bay bugs wrapped in pancetta. The wine list is extensive.

Also recommended:

Noosa Heads SLSC (Map p348; ☎ 5474 5688; Hastings St; mains $10-28; ✆ breakfast Sat & Sun, lunch & dinner daily) Good club grub with perfect beach views from the deck.

Ricky's River Bar & Restaurant (Map p346; ☎ 5447 2455; Noosa Wharf, 2 Quamby Pl; mains $27-36; ✆ lunch & dinner) An elegant restaurant on the water.

Pilu (Map p346; ☎ 5449 0961; 2/257 Gympie Tce, Noosaville; mains $18-28; ⊙ lunch daily, dinner Wed-Sun) The speciality at this award-winning Italian restaurant is *gamberetti*: fresh prawns grilled with garlic and chilli.

Drinking & Entertainment

Zachary's (Map p348; ☎ 5447 3211; 30 Hastings St, Noosa Heads) This is a shabby-chic, 2nd-storey 'gourmet pizza bar' with comfy lounges and Aussie sports memorabilia framed on the walls. The dark red walls, dim lighting and ambient beats make this a social hot spot.

Koala Bar (Map p348; ☎ 5447 3355; 44 Noosa Dr, Noosa Junction) Noosa's backpackers and other free spirits start their nightly revelry at this popular hostel bar. Live rock fills every crevice several nights a week; when it doesn't, the place hums to the harmony of beer jugs and beery banter.

Cato's (Map p348; ☎ 5449 4754; The Sheraton, 16 Hastings St) As well as a decadent cocktail list, Cato's boasts over 30 wines by the glass. The place can get noisy, especially on Friday nights when live music draws the crowds. If you need more than liquid sustenance there's also a hearty buffet and an à la carte menu.

J (Map p348; ☎ 5455 4455; www.thej.com.au; 60 Noosa Dr, Noosa Junction) The J, aka The Junction, showcases a broad range of artistic, cultural and musical performances from world to rock to classical. Check the website for event details.

Getting There & Away

Long-distance buses stop at the bus stop near the corner of Noosa Dr and Noosa Pde (Map p348). **Greyhound Australia** (☎ 1300 473 946; www.greyhound.com.au) has several daily connections from Brisbane ($27, three hours) while **Premier Motor Service** (☎ 13 34 10; www.premierms.com.au) has one ($20, 2½ hours).

Sunbus (☎ 13 12 30) has frequent services to Maroochydore ($5, one hour) and the Nambour train station ($5, one hour).

Getting Around

BICYCLE

Noosa Bike Hire and Tours (☎ 5474 3322; www.noosabikehire.com; per 4hr/day $39/49) hires bicycles out from several locations in Noosa including YHA Halse Lodge (p349). Alternatively, bikes are delivered to/from your door for free.

BOAT

Riverlight Ferry (☎ 5449 8442) operates ferries between Noosa Heads and Tewantin (one

way adult/child/family $12/4/27, all-day pass $17.50/5/39.50, 30 minutes). Tickets include onboard commentary, so the ferry provides a tour as well as being a people-mover.

BUS

During the peak holiday seasons – 26 December to 10 January and over Easter – there are free shuttle buses every 10 to 15 minutes between Weyba Rd, just outside Noosa Junction, travelling all the way to Tewantin, and stopping just about everywhere in-between. Sunbus has local services that link Noosa Heads, Noosaville, Noosa Junction and Tewantin.

CAR

The **Other Car Rental Company** (☎ 5447 2831; www.noosacarrental.com; per day from $49) delivers cars and 4WDs to your door. The big guns are also in town and rent cars from around $50 per day. They include:

Avis (Map p348; ☎ 5447 4933; Shop 1, Ocean Breeze Resort, cnr Hastings St & Noosa Dr, Noosa Heads)

Budget (Map p346; ☎ 5474 2820; 52 Mary St, Noosaville)

Hertz (Map p348; ☎ 5447 2253; Noosa Blue Resort, 16 Noosa Dr, Noosa Heads)

COOLOOLA COAST

Stretching for 50km between Noosa and Rainbow Beach, the Cooloola Coast is a remote strip of long sandy beach backed by the Cooloola Section of the **Great Sandy National Park**. Although it's undeveloped, the 4WD and tin-boat set flock here in droves so it's not always as peaceful as you might imagine. If you head off on foot or by canoe along the many inlets and waterways, however, you'll soon escape the crowds.

From the end of Moorindil St in Tewantin, the **Noosa North Shore Ferry** (☎ 5447 1321; pedestrians/cars one way $1/5; ⊙ 5.30am-12.30am Fri & Sat, 5.30am-10.30pm Sun-Thu) shuttles across the river to Noosa North Shore. If you have a 4WD you can drive along the beach to Rainbow Beach (and on up to Inskip Point to the Fraser Island ferry), but check the tide times before setting out.

On the way up the beach you'll pass the **Teewah coloured sand cliffs**, estimated to be about 40,000 years old.

Lake Cooroibah

A couple of kilometres north of Tewantin, the Noosa River widens into Lake Cooroibah. If you take the Noosa North Shore Ferry, you can drive up to the lake in a conventional vehicle and camp along sections of the beach.

Camel Company Australia (☎ 5442 4402; www .camelcompany.com.au; Beach Rd, North Shore, Tewantin; 1hr rides adult/child $50/40, 2hr rides $70/55) has beach camel rides, overnight trips (adult/child $150/90) and a six-day Fraser Island safari (per person $1100).

Noosa North Shore Retreat (☎ 5447 1706; www .noosanorthshore.com.au; Beach Rd; unpowered/powered sites from $16/21.50, r from $100, cabins from $110; 🕄 🕄) is a sprawling park with a variety of sleeping options. Activities on offer include bushwalking, canoeing, fishing, tennis and horse riding (two-hour bush-and-beach ride $75). As well as a pub and a small shop there's a first-class equestrian centre here and you can bring your own horse (stabling per night $25).

If you want a rugged experience (complete with composting toilets) you could try **Gagaju Backpackers** (☎ 1300 302 271, 5474 3522; www.travo holic.com/gagaju; 118 Johns Dr, Tewantin; unpowered sites/dm $10/15). Recycled materials have been used to build the basic dorms in this riverside wilderness camp. It's isolated, rustic and won't suit everyone's tastes. Bring your own food and mozzie repellent. The Gagaju minibus shuttles to and from Noosa twice a day.

Lake Cootharaba & Boreen Point

Cootharaba is the biggest lake in the Cooloola Section of Great Sandy National Park, measuring about 5km across and 10km in length. On the western shores of the lake and at the southern edge of the national park, Boreen Point is a relaxed little community with several places to stay and eat. The lake is the gateway to the Noosa Everglades, offering bushwalking, canoeing and bush camping.

From Boreen Point, an unsealed road leads another 5km to **Elanda Point**, and the headquarters of the **Elanda Point Canoe Company** (☎ 1800 226 637, 5485 3165; www.elanda.com.au; Elanda Point; hire per day 1 or 2 people $40), which rents canoes, kayaks and camping equipment. It can also arrange permits and Noosa transfers; and transport to Kinaba (one way $65) and Harry's Hut (one way $50, minimum four people) camping grounds but rates are much cheaper if you rent a canoe. **Cooloola Canoes & Kayaks** (☎ 5484 3164; 20 Boreen Point Pde, Boreen Point) also hires out kayaks and canoes.

The two self-contained units at **Lake Cootharaba Gallery Units** (☎ 5485 3153; 64 Laguna St, Boreen Point; r per night/week from $90) are homy and practical. Linen costs extra and there's a minimum two-night stay. The interesting gallery here is a tad on the eccentric side.

On a serene strip by the river, the quiet and simple **Boreen Point Caravan & Camping Area** (☎ 5485 3244; Dun's Beach, Teewah St, Boreen Point; unpowered/powered sites $14/20) is dominated by large gums and native bush. Take a right turn off Laguna St onto Vista St and bear right at the lake.

Apollonian Hotel (☎ 5485 3100; Laguna St, Boreen Point; s/d with shared bathroom $30/50, mains $10-24; 🕙 lunch & dinner) is a gorgeous old pub with sturdy timber walls, shady verandas and a beautifully preserved interior. Rooms are in the Queenslander out the back and the pub grub is tasty and popular.

Great Sandy National Park – Cooloola Section

The Cooloola Section of Great Sandy National Park covers more than 54,000 hectares from Lake Cootharaba north to Rainbow Beach. It's a varied wilderness area with long sandy beaches, mangrove-lined waterways, forest, heath and lakes, all featuring plentiful bird life – including rarities such as the red goshawk and the grass owl – and lots of wildflowers in spring.

The Cooloola Way, which runs from Tewantin up to Rainbow Beach, is open to 4WD vehicles unless there's been heavy rain – check with the rangers before setting out. Most people prefer to bomb up the beach, though you're restricted to a few hours either side of low tide.

Although there are many 4WD tracks to lookout points and picnic grounds, the best way to see Cooloola is by boat or canoe along the numerous tributaries of the Noosa River. Boats can be hired from Tewantin and Noosa (along Gympie Tce), Boreen Point and Elanda Point on Lake Cootharaba.

There are some fantastic walking trails starting from Elanda Point on the shore of Lake Cootharaba, including the 46km Cooloola Wilderness Trail to Rainbow Beach and a 7km trail to an unstaffed QPWS information centre at Kinaba.

The **QPWS Great Sandy Information Centre** (☎ 5449 7792; 240 Moorindil St, Tewantin; 🕙 8am-4pm) can provide information on park access, tide times and fire bans within the park, as well as issuing camping permits for the Great Sandy National Park, and car and camping permits for Fraser Island. You can also book online at www.epa.qld.gov.au.

The park has about 17 camping grounds, many of them along the river. The most popular (and best-equipped) camping grounds are Fig Tree Point (at the northern end of Lake Cootharaba), Harry's Hut (about 4km upstream) and Freshwater (about 6km south of Double Island Point) on the coast. You can also **camp** (per person/family $4.50/18) on the beach if you're driving up to Rainbow Beach. Apart from Harry's Hut, Freshwater, Teewah Beach and Poverty, all sites are accessible by hiking or river only.

EUMUNDI
☎ 07 / pop 490

Sweet little Eumundi is a quaint highland village with a quirky new-age vibe greatly amplified during its famous market days. The historic streetscape blends well with modern cafés, unique boutiques, silversmiths, craftsmen and body artists doing their thing. Once you've breathed Eumundi air don't be surprised if you feel a sudden urge to take up beading or body-painting.

Information
The **Discover Eumundi Heritage and Information Centre** (☎ 5442 8762; Memorial Dr; ☻ 10am-4pm) also houses the **museum** (admission free).

Sights & Activities
The **Eumundi markets** (☻ 6.30am-2pm Sat, 8am-1pm Wed) attract thousands of visitors to their 300-plus stalls and have everything from handcrafted furniture and jewellery to homemade clothes and alternative healing booths.

The town's other claim to fame is Eumundi Lager, originally brewed in the Imperial Hotel. Nowadays it's made down at Yatala on the Gold Coast but you can still sample it on tap at the **Imperial Hotel** (Memorial Dr).

The Aboriginal-owned and operated **Black Fulla Dreaming** (☎ 5479 0533; www.murrawolka.com; 39 Memorial Dr; ☻ 9am-4.30pm Mon-Fri) sells boomerangs and didgeridoos hand-painted by Indigenous artists.

About 10km northwest of Eumundi, the little village of **Pomona** sits in the shadow of looming Mt Cooroora (440m) and is home to the wonderful **Majestic Theatre** (☎ 5485 2330; www .majestic.spiderweb.com.au; 3 Factory St, Pomona; ☻ Thu-Sun nights), one of the only places in the world where you can see a silent movie accompanied

by the original Wurlitzer organ soundtrack. For 21 years (until 2007) the theatre played only one film – Rudolph Valentino's *The Son of the Sheikh*, every Thursday night. A recent spruce-up has seen the addition of a restaurant and the reintroduction of talkies but the focus remains firmly on the silent screen. For a step back in history, catch a **screening** (tickets $15, meal deal $25; ☻ 8pm) of the iconic *The Son of the Sheikh* on the first Thursday of each month.

Sleeping & Eating
Hidden Valley B&B (☎ 5442 8685; www.eumundibed .com; 39 Caplick Way; r $175-195, railway carriage from $105; 🖳) This not-so-hidden retreat is on 1.5 hectares of land only 1km from Eumundi on the Noosa road. Inside this attractive Queenslander you can choose a themed room to match your mood – Aladdin's Cave, the Emperors Suite or the Hinterland Retreat. All have private balconies but there are simpler rooms in the converted railcar in the garden. Cooking courses are also available ($95 for in-house guests).

Harmony Hill Station (☎ 5442 7469; www.leoandco .com.au; 81 Seib Rd; carriage $120; 🖳) Perched on a hilltop in a 5-hectare property this restored and fully self-contained 1912 purple railway carriage is the perfect place to relax or to romance. Share the grounds with grazing kangaroos, watch the sunset from Lover's Leap, share a bottle of wine beneath a stunning night sky…or even get married (the owners are celebrants!). Breakfast and dinner hampers are available on request.

Berkelouw Café (☎ 5442 8422; 87 Memorial Dr; dishes $5-15; ☻ 7.30am-5pm) One of the few cafés to open every day, this is the place for coffee, cakes and muffins. Take your coffee for a browse through Berkelouw Books next door (☎ 5442 8366; open 9am to 5.30pm).

Green Bean Café (☎ 5442 8388; 6/77 Memorial Dr; mains $8-11; ☻ breakfast & lunch Tue-Sat) Directly opposite the markets this funky café serves up wholesome wraps, burgers and light meals. The large window opens onto the main street so you still feel part of the market-day action.

Treefellers Café (☎ 5442 7766; 69 Memorial Dr; mains $16-21; ☻ breakfast Wed, Sat & Sun, lunch Wed-Sun, dinner Thu-Sat) Eumundi's most cosmopolitan eatery was named after Eumundi legend, Dick Caplick, a tree-feller turned eco-friend. The café is famous for its humungous Treefellers 'all day breakfast' (with enough calories to fuel a lumberjack).

LIQUID GLASS

'Glass is alchemic. You mix dirt together, burn it with fire, control it with water, wood, air and steel, but never completely master it. Glass can only be guided, not forced.' Like a medieval magician, master glassblower Lucas Salton conjures trippy triffids, sensuous waves and intriguing acoustic-inspired totems from the earth's base elements. 'I find inspiration in nature...from ripples in the water, the shape of a cloud, the colours in a leaf...but also from the nature of the glass itself.' From the age of 17, Lucas has perfected the glassblowing craft, infusing the swirling colours and shapes of his creations with a living, and seemingly tangible, otherworldly quality. Wandering through his gallery is like strolling through an ethereal elemental garden with waving fields of long-necked plants, colonies of standing water stones, and crystallised sound waves.

Get blown away with Lucas Salton's glass art at the **Liquid Glass Gallery** (☎ 5442 8835; www .liquidglassgallery.com; Imperial Hotel, Memorial Dr, Eumundi; ☽ 9am-5pm Mon-Sat, 10am-3pm Sun).

---

our pick **Spirit House Restaurant** (☎ 5446 8994, 20 Ninderry Rd, Yandina; mains $28-36; ☽ lunch daily, dinner Wed-Sat) is a legendary restaurant at Yandina, 11km south of Eumundi. The subtropical surrounds create an authentic Southeast Asian setting, while the kitchen concocts Thai-infused innovations such as whole crispy reef fish with tamarind and chilli or citrus scallops with fresh coconut. If you feel inspired sign up for a cooking class (☎ 5446 8977; per person $125), which includes all ingredients, recipes, lunch and wine.

Drinking
Joe's Waterhole (☎ 5442 8144; www.musicliveatjoes .com; Memorial Dr) Built in 1891 this old pub has weathered the century to attract big-name national and international musicians. Check the website for details.

Getting There & Away
Sunbus (☎ 13 12 30) runs hourly from Noosa Heads ($3.20, 40 minutes) and Nambour ($4.10, 30 minutes). Alternatively, both **Storeyline Tours** (☎ 5474 1500; www.sunshinecoastday tours.com.au) and **Henry's** (☎ 5474 0199) offer door to door transfers from Noosa accommodation (adult/child $15/10, 30 minutes Wednesday and Saturday), allowing around three hours at the markets.

SUNSHINE COAST HINTERLAND

Reaching to heights of 400m and more, the Blackall Range forms a stunning backdrop to the Sunshine Coast's popular beaches, a short 50km away. A relaxed half- or full-day

circuit drive from the coast follows a winding road along the razorback line of the escarpment, passing through quaint mountain villages and offering spectacular views of the coastal lowlands. The villages (some suffering an overdose of kitschy craft shops and Devonshire tearooms) are worth a visit but the real attraction is the landscape with its lush green pastures and softly folded valleys and ridges, and the waterfalls, swimming holes, rainforests and walks in the national parks. Cosy cabins and B&Bs are popular weekend retreats, especially during winter.

Tours
Plenty of tour companies operate through the hinterland and will pick up from anywhere along the Sunshine Coast.

Off Beat Rainforest Tours (☎ 5473 5135; www .offbeattours.com.au; adult/child $149/99) has 4WD ecotours to Conondale National Park, including morning tea, a gourmet lunch and transfers. **Storeyline Tours** (☎ 5474 1500; adult/child $74/41) has small-group tours to Montville and nearby rainforests, and trips to the Glass House Mountains.

MALENY
☎ 07 / pop 1300
Perched high in the heart of the rolling green hills of the Blackall Range, Maleny is an intriguing melange of artists, musicians and creative souls, the ageing hippy scene, rural 'tree-changers' and cooperative ventures. Its quirky bohemian edge underscores a thriving commercial township that has well and truly moved on from its timber and dairy past without yielding to the tacky heritage developments and ye olde tourist-trap shoppes that have engulfed nearby mountain

villages. The town has a strong community with amazing support for local 'co-ops' and environmental concerns.

There's a small **visitors centre** (☎ 5499 9033; www.tourmaleny.com.au; 23 Maple St; 🕑 9am-3pm) at the Maleny Community Centre.

Mary Cairncross Scenic Reserve (☎ 5499 9907; Mountain View Rd) is a pristine rainforest shelter spread over 52 hectares southeast of town. Walking tracks snake through the rainforest and there's a healthy population of bird life and unbearably cute pademelons.

Sleeping

Ocean View Tourist Park (☎ 1300 769 443, 5494 1171; www.oceanviewtouristpark.com; Maleny–Landsborough Rd; unpowered/powered sites $20/25, cabins $50-95; 🐾) Conveniently close to Australia Zoo, the coast and the hinterland, this tourist park also has magnificent views of the Glass House Mountains and Sunshine Coast beaches. Rates are for two people.

Morning Star Motel (☎ 5494 2944; www.morningstarmotel.com; 2 Panorama Pl; r $88-110; 🖤) The rooms at this comfortable and clean motel have outstanding coastal views, and the deluxe suites also have a spa.

Maleny Lodge Guest House (☎ 5494 2370; www.malenylodge.com; 58 Maple St; s incl breakfast $130-160, d incl breakfast $150-170; 🐾) This rambling B&B boasts a myriad of gorgeous rooms with cushy, four-poster beds and lashings of stained wood and antiques. There's an open fire for cold winter days and an open pool house for warm summer ones.

Obi Eco (☎ 5499 9261; susannehaydon@gmail.com; Nadi Lane; midweek/weekend $249/598; 🖥) This luxurious energy-efficient sustainable two-bedroom cottage is set on 12 hectares in a Land for Wildlife Sanctuary. The spacious deck overlooks Obi Obi Creek and is the perfect place to relax and enjoy the sight of cows grazing in the pasture.

A short stroll takes you to a private picnic area on the creek where platypus frolic in the water. The cottage is secluded yet still only 3km from Maleny's vibrant main street.

Relax at the Cabin (☎ 5499 9377; www.kingludwigs.com.au; cabin $350) Only 3km from Maleny this secluded cabin is set in pine forest on 8 hectares of land. The spa, fireplace and large, comfy bed dominate the living room, and a wall of glass doors open onto a wide timber deck. Your favourite wines, a range of beers and a welcoming cheese platter greet your arrival and little luxuries such as fluffy bathrobes and heated towel-racks are a classy touch. There's a dam on-site so you can bring your horse; and a helicopter pad if you want to arrive in style.

Eating

Monica's Café (☎ 5494 2670; 11/43 Maple St; mains $8-17; 🕑 breakfast & lunch) Snazzy Monica's blackboard menu promises innovative dishes such as gluten-free risotto pots and Balinese beef skewers with kumara paste. Sit outside to soak up the town's cruisy vibe or take a seat at the long wooden table indoors. There's also a cosy nook upstairs.

our pick **Up Front Club** (☎ 5494 2592; 31 Maple St; dishes $9-18; 🕑 breakfast, lunch & dinner) This cosy café injects funk by the bucketful into Maleny's main strip, with organic breads and tofu and tempeh salads. Live music takes to the stage Friday to Sunday nights (cover charge $8 to $10) and you'll catch anything from reggae to a bout of folk. Musicians are welcome to the blackboard sessions on Monday evenings.

Terrace (☎ 5494 3700; cnr Mountain View & Maleny–Landsborough Rds; mains $26-36; 🕑 lunch & dinner) One of Queensland's best, this award-winner serves delectable seafood and has spectacular views of the Glass House Mountains. If you're ravenous try the Moreton Bay bugs,

---

SUGAR & SPICE

The **Big Pineapple** (☎ 5442 1333; Nambour Connection Rd, Nambour; 🕑 9am-5pm) at Nambour is one of Queensland's 39 kitschy 'big things'. You can walk through the 15m-high fibreglass fruit itself for free or take a plantation train tour (adult/child $11.50/9.50), a tour through macadamia orchards and rainforests ($7.50/5), or you can buy a combined ticket (adult/child/family $15.50/11.50). Don't forget to spend more money at the souvenir shop.

In Yandina, on the Bruce Hwy about 7km north of the Big Pineapple, you'll find the **Ginger Factory** (☎ 5446 7100; 50 Pioneer Rd; admission free; 🕑 9am-5pm), a tacky souvenir store and tourist attraction. There are train rides, factory and plantation tours and, of course, a huge range of ginger products and souvenirs on sale.

DETOUR: MONTVILLE & KENILWORTH

It's hard to imagine that the chintzy mountain village of **Montville** with its fudge emporiums, Devonshire tearooms and cottage crafts began life under the dramatic name of Razorback – until you arrive at the town's spectacular ridge-top location 500m above sea level. To work off that excess fudge, take a pleasant rainforest hike to Kondalilla Falls in **Kondalilla National Park,** 3km northwest of town. After a refreshing swim in the rock pool at the head of the falls check for leeches!

Romantics will want to spend a night at **Secrets on the Lake** (☎ 5478 5888; www.secretsonthe lake.com.au; 207 Narrows Rd, Montville; midweek/weekend $320/370; ✱) where boardwalks through the foliage lead to magical, wooden treehouses with sunken spas, log fires and stunning views of Lake Baroon.

From Montville, head to the tiny village of **Mapleton** and turn left on the Obi Obi Rd. After 18km you reach Kenilworth, a small country town in the pretty Mary River Valley. **Kenilworth Country Foods** (☎ 5446 0144; 45 Charles St; ⏰ 9am-4pm Mon-Fri, 10.30am-3pm Sat & Sun) is a boutique cheese factory with creamy yogurt and wickedly good cheese. If you plan to camp in the Kenilworth State Forest or Conondale National Park you'll need a **permit** (☎ 13 13 04; www.epa .qld.gov.au; per person $4.50).

Otherwise, head northeast on the Eumundi–Kenilworth Rd for a scenic drive through rolling pastureland dotted with traditional old farmhouses and floods of jacarandas. After 30km you reach the Bruce Hwy near Eumundi.

king prawns, salmon and mahi mahi served on a sizzling granite tile with vegetable skewers and pilaf rice.

King Ludwigs Restaurant (☎ 5499 9377; 401 Mountain View Rd; mains $26.50-32.50; ⏰ lunch Wed-Sun, dinner Wed-Sat) Klaus and Barbara have a passion for good food, German beer and welcoming Bavarian hospitality. A schnapps (or two) in the rustic Bavarian bar will prime your taste buds for the mouth-watering dishes on the menu including the legendary Bavarian potato cream soup with Frankfurt sausage. The views of the Glass House Mountains are sensational.

Fraser Coast

The sassy, social bustle of the Sunshine Coast diminishes north of Noosa, giving way to the sleepy coastal villages and rural inland towns of the Fraser Coast. The undisputed highlight of the region is Fraser Island, the world's largest sand island. Essentially one long, forest-backed beach, Fraser Island is a land sculpted by wind and surf; a mystical land of giant dunes, ancient rainforests, luminous lakes and endemic wildlife that includes the purest strain of dingo to be found in Australia. Whether on a 4WD camping trip or in five-star luxury, the Fraser experience is not to be missed.

Across the calm waters of the Great Sandy Strait, the mellow coastal community of Hervey Bay is the gateway to Fraser Island, and a chill-out bay for migrating humpback whales. From July to October each year, whales stream into the bay for a few days before continuing on to Antarctica. Further south, tiny Rainbow Beach is a refreshingly unaffected seaside village in a pristine natural setting and is fast gaining popularity as an alternative launch pad to Fraser Island.

Fishing, swimming, boating and camping are hugely popular along this entire stretch of coastline, while further inland dry bushland and agricultural fields surround old-fashioned country towns steeped in history. Bundaberg, the largest city in the region, overlooks a sea of waving cane fields that gives birth to its famous liquid-gold rum – a fiery, gut-churning spirit guaranteed to scramble a few brain cells!

HIGHLIGHTS

- Cruising up the beach 'highway', hiking through the rainforest and cooling off in the vivid lakes of **Fraser Island** (p374)
- Watching the whales play in **Hervey Bay** (p363)
- Witnessing turtles take their first flipper-stumble down the beach at **Mon Repos** (p372)
- Copping an eyeful of the coloured sand cliffs at **Rainbow Beach** (p359)
- Sampling 'liquid gold' at the rum distillery in **Bundaberg** (p371)

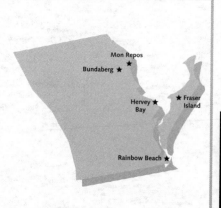

Mon Repos ★
Bundaberg ★
Hervey ★   ★ Fraser
Bay   Island
Rainbow Beach ★

FRASER COAST

- TELEPHONE CODE: 07   - www.seefraserisland.com   - www.frasercoastholidays.info

FRASER COAST

The Fraser Coast runs the gamut from coastal beauty, beachfront national parks and tiny seaside villages to agricultural farms and sugarcane fields surrounding old-fashioned country towns. Mellow Hervey Bay draws the biggest crowds with its easy access to Fraser Island and pumping whale-watching action. Nestled in a picturesque bay south of Hervey Bay, pretty little Rainbow Beach, with its stunning coloured-sand cliffs, is even closer to Fraser and has a good surf beach.

Far removed from the cruisy beach scene, Maryborough and Gympie are inland country towns steeped in history and heritage. A little further north, Bundaberg rises out of a sea of sugarcane fields, fruit orchards and vegetable patches. Seasonal picking and harvesting attract long-staying backpackers, or maybe the pull is Bundaberg's wickedly famous rum!

GYMPIE

☎ 07 / pop 10,933

Gympie's gold once saved Queensland from near-bankruptcy but that was in the 1860s and not much has happened since. A few period buildings line the main street but most travellers on the Bruce Hwy bypass the town centre.

For information on the Fraser Coast region you can stop at one of the three offices of the **Cooloola Regional Development Bureau** (www.cooloola.org.au); Matilda (☎ 5483 5554; Matilda Service Centre, Bruce Hwy; ☽ 9am-5pm); Lake Alford (☎ 5483 6411; Bruce Hwy, Gympie; ☽ 9am-4.30pm); Gympie (☎ 5483 6656; 107 Mary St; ☽ 8.30am-4pm). They also stock the (free) *Heritage Walking Tour Map*, which details Gympie's relics of the gold-mining days.

The **Woodworks Forestry & Timber Museum** (☎ 5483 7691; cnr Fraser Rd & Bruce Hwy; adult/student $4/2; ☽ 9am-4pm Mon-Fri, 1-4pm Sun) on the highway displays memorabilia and equipment from the region's old logging days.

The **Gympie Gold Mining & Historical Museum** (☎ 5482 3995; 215 Brisbane Rd; adult/child/family $8.80/4.40/20; ☽ 9am-4pm) is set up to exhibit a large collection of mining equipment and functioning steam-driven engines, as well as the more traditional exhibits of a historical museum.

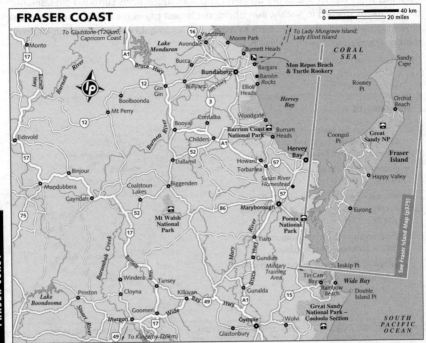

For a scenic tour of the pretty Mary Valley you can chug through the countryside on a restored 1923 steam train, **The Valley Rattler** (☎ 5482 2750; www.thevalleyrattler.com; half-day tours per adult/child $20/10, day tours $36/18). The train leaves from the old Gympie train station on Tozer St every Wednesday and Sunday morning at 10am and steams along to the tiny township of Imbil 40km away. On Saturday, **half-day tours** (⏰ 9.30am, 11.45am & 1.45pm) only go as far as Amamoor, 20km away. Amamoor is the site of the annual **Muster**, a country music hoe-down held over six days in late August each year.

If you don't want to camp at the Muster, the **Cooloola Country B&B** (☎ 5482 5018; cooloolacountry@hotmail.com; 69 Duke St; s/d $95/110) has homey rooms in a classic Queenslander. Otherwise, the **Gympie Muster Inn** (☎ 5482 8666; 21 Wickham St; d $100; ❄ ♒) is a large, central motel with business facilities and a restaurant.

Although Gympie's attractions are somewhat lacking, gourmet travellers will salivate over the lovely **Kingston House Restaurant** (☎ 5483 6733; 11 Channon St; mains $18-29; ⏰ lunch & dinner Wed-Sun). Nestled inside a beautifully renovated, sprawling Queenslander, this restaurant is pure class. The menu features delicious dishes using local produce and has a boutique wine list. Long lunches, tapas nights and a cosy fireplace are worth the trip.

Another novelty in country Gympie is **Emilia's** (☎ 5482 8885; 201 Mary St; mains $8-20; ⏰ 8am-5pm Mon-Fri), an Italian-run deli and café adorned with heavy brocade, ornate gold-framed mirrors, a tempting range of imported deli items – and excellent espressos.

Greyhound Australia (☎ 1300 473 946; www.greyhound.com.au) has numerous daily services from Brisbane ($34, 3½ hours), Noosa ($18, two hours) and Hervey Bay ($28, 1¾ hours). **Premier Motor Service** (☎ 13 34 10; www.premierms.com.au) operates the same routes (once daily). Long-distance coaches stop at the bus shelter in Jaycee Way, behind Mary St. **Polley's Coaches** (☎ 5482 9455; Pinewood Ave) has buses to Rainbow Beach ($15, 1¾ hours), departing from the RSL on Mary St at 1.15pm on weekdays.

Queensland Rail (☎ 1300 131 722; www.traveltrain.com.au) operates the *Tilt Train* (adult/child $39.60/19, 2½ hours) on Sunday to Friday and the *Sunlander* (adult/child $39.60/19, 3¼ hours, three weekly), which travel from Brisbane to Gympie on their way to Rockhampton and Cairns.

RAINBOW BEACH

☎ 07 / pop 999

Gorgeous Rainbow Beach is a smidgeon of a town at the base of the Inskip Peninsula with spectacular multicoloured sand cliffs overlooking its rolling surf and white sandy beach. Still relatively 'undiscovered', the town's friendly locals, relaxed vibe, and convenient access to Fraser Island (only 10 minutes by barge; see p377) and the Cooloola Section of the Great Sandy National Park has made this a rising star of Queensland's coastal beauty spots.

Information

QPWS office (☎ 5486 3160; Rainbow Beach Rd; ⏰ 7am-4pm) Has walking maps and 24-hour vending machines that issue car and camping permits for Fraser Island (credit cards only).

Rainbow Beach visitors centre (☎ 5486 3227; 8 Rainbow Beach Rd; ⏰ 7am-5pm)

Sights & Activities

The town is named for the **coloured sand cliffs**, a 2km walk along the beach. A 600m track along the cliffs at the southern end of Cooloola Drive leads to the **Carlo Sandblow**, a spectacular 120m-high dune.

Double Island Point has a good surf break, but fishing is the most popular activity here. The vast shoreline provides abundant beach fishing and really serious anglers can access

Tin Can Bay (opposite) inlet from either the Carlo Point or Bullock Point Boat Ramps. Both are just north of town.

Beyond Double Island Point is the Cooloola Section of the **Great Sandy National Park** (p352) and with a 4WD it's possible to drive all the way to Noosa. Bushwalkers will find tracks throughout the national park (maps from the QPWS office) including the 46.2km Cooloola Wilderness Trail, which starts at Mullens car park (off Rainbow Beach Rd) and ends near Lake Cooloola.

Rainbow Paragliding (☎ 5486 3048, 0418-754 157; www.paraglidingrainbow.com; glides $150) offers tandem glides above the Carlo Sandblow. If you get hooked you can do a one-day introduction ($220) or an eight-day full licensed course ($1400). **Skydive Rainbow Beach** (☎ 0418-218 358; www.skydiverainbowbeach.com; 2440m/4270m dives $305/400) gets your knees in the breeze and lands on the main beach.

Horsey types can get their equine fix on a beach-and-bush ride with **Rainbow Beach Horse Rides** (☎ 0438 710 530; 1hr ride adult/child $50/40, 1½hr ride $60/50).

Rainbow Beach Dolphin View Sea Kayaking (☎ 0408-738 192; 4hr tours per person $65) operates kayaking safaris and rents kayaks (half day $65), but if you'd rather surf with the dolphins, the company also runs the Rainbow Beach Surf School (one-hour session $55). Board hire is $15 per hour or $40 per day. **Carlo Canoes** (☎ 5486 3610; per half/full day $30/45) hires canoes if you want to do your own exploring.

Teeming with gropers, turtles, manta rays and harmless grey nurse sharks, Wolf Rock, a congregation of four volcanic pinnacles off Double Island Point, is widely regarded as one of Queensland's best scuba-diving sites. The **Wolf Rock Dive Centre** (☎ 5486 8004; www.wolfrockdive.com.au) offers four-day PADI courses ($595) that include two dives at Wolf Rock.

Rainbow Dreaming (☎ 0428-895 576; ☽ by appointment) at Pippies Beach House (right) entertains with cultural talks and Dreamtime legends while you spend half a day fashioning a didgeridoo ($100) or boomerang ($25).

Tours

Surf & Sand Safaris (☎ 5486 3131; www.surfandsandsafaris.com.au; adult/child $80/40) has a combined 4WD and amphibious vehicle tour through the national park, and along the beach to the coloured sands and lighthouse at Double Island Point.

Dolphin Ferry Cruise (☎ 5486 8085, 0428-838 836; www.dolphinferrycruise.com.au; adult/child $18/9, 3hr cruise $35/20; ☽ 7.20am & 9.30am Tue-Sun) run leisurely houseboat cruises from Carlo Point across the inlet to Tin Can Bay. The highlight of the trip is hand-feeding Mystique, a wild Indo-Pacific Humpback dolphin who makes regular breakfast visits to the Tin Can Bay marina (see boxed text, opposite).

Sleeping

Rainbow Beach Holiday Village (☎ 1300 366 596, 5486 3222; www.beach-village.com; 13 Rainbow Beach Rd; unpowered/powered sites from $22/28, cabins from $90; ☒ ☑) This excellent park spreads over 5 acres, overlooking the beach and ocean. The cabins are fully self-contained, and it's extremely popular. Rates are for two people.

Pippies Beach House (☎ 1800 425 356, 5486 8503; www.pippiesbeachhouse.com.au; 22 Spectrum St; dm/d $22/60; ☒ ☑ ☑) With only seven rooms, this small, super-chilled hostel is the place to relax. Learn to fashion a didgeridoo, then play it around the campfire at the free BBQs every Wednesday night. Other bonuses include free breakfasts and water toys, and plenty of space in the garden for tents and vans ($12 per person).

Dingo's Backpackers Resort (☎ 1800 111 126, 5486 8222; www.dingosatrainbow.com; 20 Spectrum Ave; dm/d $22/65; ☒ ☑ ☑) The bar is as lively as the vivacious English manager in this party hostel. There's live music every Wednesday night, a Balinese-style gazebo for recovery, free tours to Carlo Sandblow, free pancake breakfasts, and cheap meals every night.

our pick Debbie's Place (☎ 5486 3506; www.rainbowbeachaccommodation.com.au; 30 Kurana St; d/ste from $69/79; ☒) The charming rooms inside this beautiful timber Queenslander are fully self-contained and have private entrances and private verandas. The effervescent Debbie is a mine of information and makes this a cosy home away from home. Laundry facilities are available and there's a BBQ in the tropical gardens.

Rainbow Sands Holiday Units (☎ 5486 3400; 42-46 Rainbow Beach Rd; d $89, 1-bedroom apt $100; ☒ ☑) This low-rise, palm-fronted complex has neat, appealing motel rooms with poolside glass doors and bar fridges, and self-contained units with full laundries.

Rainbow Shores Resort (☎ 5486 3999; www.rainbowshores.com.au; 12 Rainbow Shores Dr; r from $875 per week, villas & beach houses from $1075 per week; ☒ ☑) The accommodation options in this luxury bush retreat include standard holiday units,

FRASER COAST

DETOUR: TIN CAN BAY

En route from Rainbow Beach to Maryborough, turn north off Rainbow Beach Rd on to Tin Can Bay Rd. After 10km you reach the idyllic and quiet fishing village of Tin Can Bay. Sitting at the southern tip of the Great Sandy Strait, it's the perfect place to escape the beaten track.

Mystique, the resident dolphin, makes regular breakfast visits to the Tin Can Bay marina boat ramp and monitored feeding takes place from 8am to 10am.

On the main road into town, the **Sandcastle Motel** (☎ 5486 4555; Tin Can Bay Rd; d $75; 🍴 🖭) has large rooms with small kitchenettes, or you could live it up at **Dolphin Waters** (☎ 5486 2600; www.dolphinwaters.com.au; 40-1 The Esplanade; d per night/week from $125/700; 🍴 🖭), which has spotless, self-contained units.

The seafood platter at **Codfather Too** (☎ 5486 4400; 1 Oyster Pde; mains $12-30; 🕐 lunch & dinner Wed-Mon) has piles of mud crab, Moreton Bay bugs, prawns, calamari, scallops, and fish and chips; the marina restaurant has lovely water views.

---

funky, individual three-bedroom beach houses and stylish split-level villas. There's a restaurant, nine-hole golf course, tennis courts, BBQs – and a minimum five-night stay in high season.

Also recommended is **Fraser's on Rainbow** (☎ 1800 100 170, 5486 8885; www.frasersonrainbow.com; 18 Spectrum St; dm/d from $22/64; 🖵 🖭). In a nicely converted motel this hostel has clean, roomy dorms and a pleasant, relaxed atmosphere.

Eating
Self-caterers will find a supermarket on Rainbow Beach Rd.

Archies (☎ 5486 3277; 12 Rainbow Beach Rd; mains $7-15; 🕐 breakfast, lunch & dinner) This popular café perfectly encapsulates Rainbow's laid-back surfer chic, serving delicious smoothies, veggie burgers, and fish in various guises.

Waterview Bistro (☎ 5486 8344; Cooloola Drive; mains $23-28; 🕐 breakfast Sun, lunch Wed-Sat, dinner Wed-Sun) Sunset drinks are a must at this swish restaurant with sensational views of Fraser Island from its hilltop perch. Interesting seafood dishes include crumbed garfish fillets and Sandy Straits crab linguini.

Getting There & Around
Greyhound (☎ 1300 473 946; www.greyhound.com.au) has several daily services from Brisbane ($52, five hours), Noosa ($33, 2½ hours) and Hervey Bay ($28, 1½ hours). **Premier Motor Service** (☎ 13 34 10; www.premierms.com.au) has less expensive services. **Polley's Coaches** (☎ 5482 9455) has buses from Gympie ($15, 1¾ hours).

Most 4WD hire companies will also arrange permits, barge costs and hire out camping gear. Some recommended companies:
All Trax 4WD Hire (☎ 5486 8767; Karoonda Rd)

Rainbow Beach Adventure Centre 4WD Hire (☎ 5486 3288; www.adventurecentre.com.au; Rainbow Beach Rd; 🕐 7am-5pm)
Safari 4WD (☎ 1800 689 819, 5486 8188; 3 Karoonda Ct)

Cooloola Coast Realty (☎ 5486 3411; Shop 2, 6 Rainbow Beach Rd; per night $10) rents lock-up garages if you need to leave your own car in town.

MARYBOROUGH
☎ 07 / pop 21,500
Born in 1847, Maryborough is one of Queensland's oldest towns, and its port was the first shaky step ashore for thousands of 19th-century free settlers looking for a better life in the new country. Heritage and history are Maryborough's fortes, the pace of yesteryear reflected in its beautifully restored colonial-era buildings and gracious Queenslander homes.

Orientation & Information
The helpful **Maryborough/Fraser Island visitors centre** (☎ 1800 214 789, 4190 5742; City Hall, Kent St; 🕐 9am-5pm Mon-Fri, 9am-3pm Sat & Sun) has free copies of self-guided walking tours.

Kent St is the main strip but you'll find Portside with most of the museums and the Mary River Parklands along Wharf St.

Sights
Portside in the historic port area beside the Mary River has 13 heritage-listed buildings, parklands and museums. Today's landscaped gardens and tidy colonial-era buildings paint a different story from Maryborough's once-thriving port and seedy streets filled with sailors, ruffians, brothels and opium dens. The **Portside Centre** (☎ 4190 5730; cnr Wharf &

Richmond Sts; ⏰ 10am-4pm) located in the former **Customs House** has interactive displays on Maryborough's history. Part of the centre but a few doors down, the **Bond Store Museum** also highlights key periods in Maryborough's history. Downstairs is the original packed-earth floor and even some liquor barrels from 1864.

To trace your genealogical tree, cross the road to the **Heritage Centre** (⏰ 4123 1842; cnr Wharf & Richmond Sts; ⏰ 9am-4pm) where you'll find colonial immigration records from ships logs; and if dear old great-great-granddaddy arrived in Australia courtesy of Her Majesty's prison system, you'll find convict records as well.

Also on Wharf St, the **Maryborough Military & Colonial Museum** (⏰ 4123 5900; 106 Wharf St; adult/child $5/2; ⏰ 9am-3pm) has the only surviving three-wheeler Girling car. Originally built in London in 1911, this fully restored model zips along at a blistering 29kph. The museum also houses a replica Cobb & Co coach and one of the largest military libraries in Australia.

The **Mary River Parklands** on the riverfront has pleasant walkways and picnic areas. Further down the river is pretty **Queens Park** (heritage-listed) with a profusion of glorious trees, including a Banyan fig that's more than 140 years old.

Lining the streets around Portside are many fine old buildings including Queensland's oldest **post office** (cnr Bazaar & Wharf Sts) built in 1866. On Richmond St is the revival-style **Woodstock House** and the neoclassical **former Union Bank**, birthplace of *Mary Poppins* author, PL Travers. The life-size **Mary Poppins statue** on the street depicts the acerbic character Travers created rather than the saccharine-sweet Disney version. Back on Wharf Street is the **Customs House Hotel** (closed for renovations), one of the oldest portside hotels, which once had an opium den and now has a resident ghost!

You'll have to leave Portside to visit the National Trust–classified **Brennan & Geraghty's Store** (⏰ 4121 2250; 64 Lennox St; adult/child/family $5.50/2.50/13.50; ⏰ 10am-3pm), which traded for 100 years before closing its doors. The museum is filled with tins, bottles and packets, including early Vegemite jars and curry powder from the 1890s, all crammed onto the ceiling-high shelves. Look for the 1885 tea packet from China, the oldest item in the store.

Activities

On a **Tea with Mary** (⏰ 1800 214 789, 4190 5730; per person $10.50) tour of the historic precinct, a costumed guide spills the beans on the town's past. The tour includes morning tea.

Maryborough Riverboat Cruises (⏰ 4123 1523; www.maryboroughrivercruise.com; 1hr tour adult/child $15/8, 2hr lunch cruise $30/15; ⏰ 10am, noon & 2pm Tue-Sun) provide informed commentaries while you cruise past heritage homes and historic buildings along the Mary River.

On the last weekend of each month you can catch an outdoor flick at **Moonlight Movies** in the Mary River Parklands on Friday night; get spooked on a torch-lit tour of the city's grisly murder sites, opium dens, haunted houses and town cemetery with **Ghostly Tours & Tales** (⏰ 1800 214 789, 4190 5742; tour incl progressive 3-course dinner $75) on Saturday night; and top it off with a leisurely morning of food, brass bands, steam train rides and river cruises the next morning at **Sunday in the Park**.

Sleeping

Wallace Caravan Park & Units (⏰ 4121 3970; www .wallacecaravanpark.com.au; 22 Ferry St; unpowered/powered sites $17/22, cabins $35-70; 🐕 🖳) This pleasant park spreads itself across a gentle slope underneath a bevy of towering trees. Modern cabins, self-contained motel units, and camp kitchens cater to all tastes. Rates are for two people.

Royal Centrepoint Motel (⏰ 4121 2241; www .centrepointmotel.com.au; 326 Kent St; s/d $70/75; 🐕 🖳) The faded carpets and 1920s-style corridors give this old building in the town centre a Heartbreak Hotel feel. The rooms and the communal kitchenette are spotless and a continental breakfast is included in the tariff.

Blue Shades Motor Inn (⏰ 4122 2777; www.blue shades.com; 35 Ferry St; r/ste from $86/120; 🐕 🖳 ; wi-fi) A close second to the Parkway, this large motel complex has a range of accommodation, from generic and simple motel rooms to modern executive rooms.

McNevin's Parkway Motel (⏰ 1800 072 000, 4122 2888; www.mcnevins.com.au; 188 John St; r/ste from $99/125; 🐕 🖳 ; wi-fi) This well-run complex is popular with business folk but the rooms are comfortable, regardless of why you are staying. A step up in style and price are the smart executive suites, which have separate bedrooms and spas.

Eating

Toast (⏰ 4121 7222; 199 Bazaar St; dishes $5-7.90; ⏰ 7am-4pm Mon-Sat, 7pm-11pm Fri & Sat) Stainless steel fittings, polished cement floors and excellent coffee (served in paper cups) stamp the metro-chic seal on this groovy café.

Muddy Waters Café (☎ 4121 5011; 71 Wharf St; mains $15-32; 10am-3pm Tue-Fri, 9am-3pm Sat & Sun, dinner Wed-Sat) The shady riverfront deck and summery menu at this classy café will keep you happy with tempting seafood dishes such as Heineken-battered barramundi and salt-and-pepper squid.

Port Residence (☎ 4123 5001; Wharf St; mains $12-25; lunch Wed-Mon, dinner Fri & Sat) An elegant restaurant and tea room in the old Custom House residence. Light meals and traditional Aussie favourites including scones and tea are served on the shady veranda, which has lovely views over the parklands.

Drinking & Entertainment

A few *salutés* and *chin-chins* are in order at the **Post Office Hotel** (☎ 4121 3289; cnr Bazaar & Wharf St), a lovely building designed by an Italian architect, Caradini, in 1889.

For a touch of culture, the strikingly contemporary **Brolga Theatre** (☎ 4122 6060; 5 Walker St) hosts musical and theatrical events.

Getting There & Away

Both the *Sunlander* ($56.10, five hours, three weekly) and *Tilt Train* ($56.10, 3½ hours, Sunday to Friday) connect Brisbane with the Maryborough West train station, 7km west of the centre. There's a shuttle bus from the main bus terminal beside the Maryborough train station on Lennox St.

Greyhound Australia (☎ 1300 473 946; www.greyhound.com.au) and **Premier Motor Service** (☎ 13 34 10; www.premierms.com.au) have buses to Gympie ($25, one hour), Bundaberg ($34, three hours), Hervey Bay ($9, 40 minutes) and Brisbane ($54, 4½ hours).

Wide Bay Transit (☎ 4121 3719) has hourly services between Maryborough and the Urangan Marina in Hervey Bay ($7.60, one hour) every weekday, with fewer services on the weekend. Buses depart Maryborough from outside the City Hall in Kent St.

HERVEY BAY

☎ 07 / pop 41,225

Named after an English Casanova, it's no wonder Hervey Bay's seductive charms are difficult to resist. A warm subtropical climate, long sandy beaches, calm blue ocean and a relaxed and unpretentious local community lures all sorts of travellers – backpackers, families and sea-changing retirees – to its shores. Throw in the chance to see the majestic humpback whales frolicking in the water, and the town's convenient access to the World Heritage–listed Fraser Island and it's easy to understand how this once sleepy fishing village seduces you without even trying.

Don't bother packing a surfboard though: Fraser Island shelters Hervey Bay from the ocean surf and the sea here is shallow and completely flat – perfect for kiddies and postcard summer holiday pics.

Orientation

Hervey Bay covers a string of beachside suburbs – Point Vernon, Pialba, Scarness, Torquay and Urangan – but behind the flawless beachfront and pockets of sedate suburbia, the outskirts of town dissolve into an industrial jungle. Unfortunately, when you enter town on the Maryborough–Hervey Bay Rd, the only way to reach the beach is through this frenzied traffic snarl.

Information

The official tourist office is a fair way from the centre.

Great Adventures (☎ 4125 3601; 408 The Esplanade, Torquay; internet per hr $4; 8.30am-10pm) Located at Koala Beach Resort. Offers internet access and is a booking agent for tours and activities.

Hervey Bay Tourism & Development Bureau (☎ 1800 811 728, 4125 9855; www.herveybaytourism.com.au; cnr Urraween & Maryborough Rds; 9am-5pm) Helpful and professional tourist office on the outskirts of town.

Hervey Bay visitors centre (☎ 1800 649 926, 4124 4050; 401 The Esplanade, Torquay; per hr $4; 8.30am-8.30pm Mon-Fri, 9am-5pm Sat & Sun) Privately run booking office with internet access.

Post office (☎ 4125 1101; 414 The Esplanade, Torquay)

Whale Watch Tourist Centre (☎ 1800 358 595; Urangan Marina, Urangan; 7am-5pm) Privately run and has good information.

Sights

Reef World (☎ 4128 9828; Pulgul St, Urangan; adult/child $16/8, shark dives $60; 9.30am-4.30pm) is a small aquarium stocked with some of the Great Barrier Reef's most colourful characters, including a giant 18-year-old groper. You can also take a dip with lemon, whaler and other nonpredatory sharks.

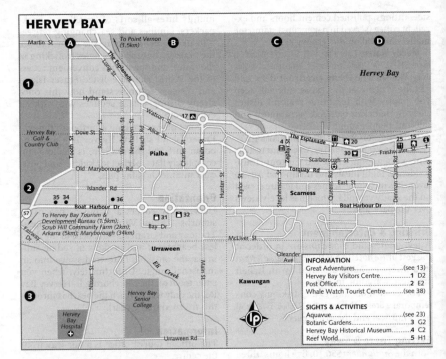

Run by the Korrawinga Aboriginal Community, the **Scrub Hill Community Farm** (☎ 4124 6908; Scrub Hill Rd; tours adult/child $16.50/5.50), about 2km southwest of town, produces organic vegetables, tea-tree oil and excellent art works. Guided tours (call to arrange) detail how the farm operates and the slightly more expensive option (adult/child $25/10) includes bush tucker and a traditional dancing display.

Hervey Bay's pretty **Botanic Gardens** (Elizabeth St, Urangan; ☼ 6.30am-8.30pm) has a few small lagoons, dense foliage and walking tracks. There's also a small but beautiful **orchid house** (admission $2; ☼ 10am-3.45pm Mon-Fri) and an Aboriginal bush-tucker garden.

For a nature walk with a difference, head 5km north along the Burrum Heads Rd to **Arkarra** (☎ 4128 7300; www.arkarra.com.au; 28 Panorama Dr, Dundowran Beach; ☼ 10am-4pm Mon-Fri, 8.30am-4pm Sat & Sun). This popular eco-tourist Balinese tea garden is set on 30 acres of subtropical rainforest, melaleuca wetlands and lagoons. Finish off a walk with lunch or afternoon tea in the authentic thatched-roof Balinese huts overlooking the lagoons.

The **Hervey Bay Historical Museum** (☎ 4128 1064; 13 Zephyr St, Scarness; adult/child $5/0.50; ☼ 1-5pm Fri-Sun) has more than 3000 items on display, but the emphasis is on quantity rather than quality.

Activities
WHALE-WATCHING
Whale-watching tours operate out of Hervey Bay every day (weather permitting) during the annual migrations between late July and early November. Sightings are guaranteed from August to the end of October (with a free return trip if the whales don't show). Off season many boats offer dolphin-spotting tours. Boats cruise from Urangan Harbour out to Platypus Bay and then zip around from pod to pod to find the most active whales. Most vessels offer half-day tours for around $100 for adults and $60 for children, and most include breakfast or lunch. Tour bookings can be made through your accommodation or the information centres.

Some recommended operators:
Blue Dolphin Marine Tours (☎ 4124 9600; www .bluedolphintours.com.au; ☼ 7.30am) Maximum 20 passengers on a 10m catamaran.

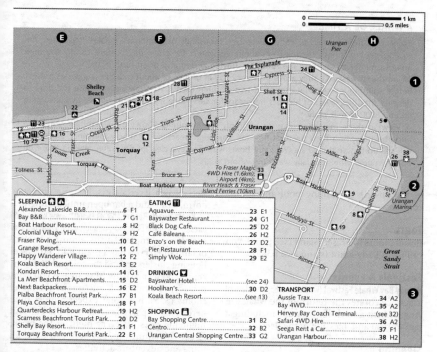

DescaradA (☎ 1800 606 136; www.descarada.com.au; ⏱ 8.30am) Maximum of 30 passengers on a 70ft luxury motor yacht.**MV Tasman Venture** (☎ 1800 620 322; www.tasmanventure.com.au; ⏱ 8.30am & 1.30pm) Maximum of 80 passengers, underwater microphones and viewing windows.
Quick Cat II (☎ 1800 671 977, 4128 9611; www.hervey baywhalewatch.com.au; ⏱ 8am & 1pm) With underwater cameras, a maximum of 80 passengers and wheelchair access.
Whalesong (☎ 1800 689 610, 4125 6222; www .whalesong.com.au; ⏱ 7.30am & 1pm) Maximum of 70 passengers. Caters to disabled travellers.

FISHING

MV Fighting Whiting (☎ 4124 6599; adult/child/family $60/35/160) and **MV Princess II** (☎ 4124 0400; adult/ child $120/85) offer calm-water fishing trips that include lunch. **Lapu Charters** (☎ 4194 2440; www .lapucharters.com.au) can tailor make fishing or diving expeditions.

WATERSPORTS

Aquavue (☎ 4125 5528; www.aquavue.com.au; The Esplanade, Torquay) a beach shed and café on the foreshore rents out jet skis ($40/135 per 15 minutes/hour), kayaks ($20 per hour), fish-ing boats ($80 for two hours) and SeaKarts ($50 per hour).

SCENIC FLIGHTS

Air Fraser Island (☎ 1800 247 992, 4125 3600) operates whale-watching flights and scenic flights over Fraser Island from $70. **MI Helicopters** (☎ 1800 600 345) has a range of scenic flights from 10 minutes ($95) to one hour. Flights of 35 minutes ($255) and longer take you over Fraser Island.

To really feel like a bird, ditch the metal shell and cruise the skies in a microlite with **Fraser Coast Microlites** (☎ 1300 732 801; flights per 20/30/45/70min $75/120/175/230).

OTHER ACTIVITIES

Hervey Bay Skydivers (☎ 1300 558 616, 4183 0119; www .herveybayskydivers.com.au) offers tandem skydives for $250 from 3050m and $270 from 4270m. Add an extra $30 for skydives over the beach.

The **Susan River Homestead** (☎ 4121 6846; www .susanriver.com; Hervey Bay-Maryborough Rd; 2hr bush ride $60), about halfway between Maryborough and Hervey Bay, has popular horse-riding packages ($165/126 per adult/child), which include accommodation, all meals and use

---

A WHALE OF A TIME

Every year, from August to early November, thousands of humpback whales *(Megaptera novaeangliae)* cruise into Hervey Bay's sheltered waters for a few days before continuing their arduous migration south to the Antarctic. Having mated and given birth in the warmer waters off northeast Australia, they arrive in Hervey Bay in groups of about a dozen (known as pulses), before splitting into smaller groups of two or three (pods). The new calves utilise the time to develop the thick layers of blubber necessary for survival in icy southern waters, by consuming around 600L of milk daily.

Viewing these majestic creatures is simply awe-inspiring. Showy aqua-acrobats, you'll see humpbacks waving their pectoral fins, tail slapping, breaching or simply 'blowing', and many will roll up beside the whale-watching boats with one eye clear of the water making those on board wonder who's actually watching whom.

---

of the on-site swimming pool and tennis courts.

Tours

Besides tours to Fraser Island (see p368), you can fly to Lady Elliot Island (see p385).

Festivals & Events

Hervey Bay Whale Festival (www.herveybaywhalefestival .com.au) celebrates the return of the whales in August with a week-long parade including a jazz festival and 'blessing of the fleet'.

Sleeping

BUDGET

Hervey Bay's hostels will usually pick you up from the bus station.

Beachfront Tourist Parks (www.beachfronttourist parks.com.au; unpowered/powered sites $20/26) are appealing council-run parks right on the beach at Pialba (☎ 4128 1399), Scarness (☎ 4125 1578) and Torquay (☎ 4128 1274). Rates are for two people.

Colonial Village YHA (☎ 1800 818 280, 4125 1844; www.cvyha.com; 820 Boat Harbour Dr, Urangan; unpowered/powered sites $18/24; dm/d/cabins from $20/50/80;) This excellent YHA is set on 83hectares of tranquil bushland, close to the marina and only 50m from the beach. It's a lovely spot, thick with ambience, possums and parrots. Facilities include a spa, tennis and basketball courts, and a funky bar. Breakfast is free and dinners cost $8 to $10.

Next Backpackers (☎ 4125 6600; www.nextbackpack ers.com.au; 10 Bideford St, Torquay; dm $22-25, d $65;) Having won the Best Budget Accommodation Award for the Fraser Coast you'd expect this modern hostel to be a cut above the usual suspects. With polished wooden floors, ultra-clean roomy rooms and a well-equipped stainless

steel kitchen, it certainly is. There's a 'girls only' dorm, a café and a bar open until midnight.

Koala Beach Resort (☎ 4125 3601; www.koalaadven tures.com; 410 The Esplanade, Torquay; dm/d $24/60) This sprawling complex covers almost a hectare of land in Hervey Bay's main hub. Low level housing clusters around the colonial-style bar, central pool and shady BBQ area. If you want privacy, you can book into one of the motel rooms ($75), but don't expect a quiet time here. This is party central, and the bar and nightclub goes off every night of the week. Great Adventures (p363) here can book all tours and adventure activities.

Also recommended:

Fraser Roving (☎ 1800 989 811, 4125 6386; www .fraserroving.com; 412 The Esplanade, Torquay; dm $20-25, d with/without bathroom $60/65;) A well-deserved reputation as one of the friendliest hostels in Qld.

Happy Wanderer Village (☎ 4125 1103; www.happy wanderer.com.au; 105 Truro St, Torquay; unpowered/powered sites from $28/32, cabins/villas from $62/116;) The manicured lawns and profuse gum-tree cover at this large park make for great tent sites, and the cabins and villas are clean and roomy.

MIDRANGE

Playa Concha Resort (☎ 4125 1544; www.playaconchare sort.com; 475 The Esplanade, Torquay; r from $88;) This lovely spot across from the beach has clean and airy rooms, masses of trees in the courtyard and a Spanish restaurant with a paella and sangria meal deal for $25.

Boat Harbour Resort (☎ 4125 5079; www.boathar bourresort.net; 651-652 Charlton St, Urangan; r $110-130;) Close to the Hervey Bay marina, these timber studios and cabins are set on attractive grounds. The studios have sizable decks out the front and the roomy villas are great for families.

Kondari Resort (☎ 4125 4445; www.kondarilake sidevillas.com.au; 49-63 Elizabeth St, Urangan; r $120-135; 🔡 🖳 🔁) Set on 20 acres beside a lake this sprawling, low-rise resort has two pools, tennis courts, BBQs and a profusion of native bush. All cabins have private verandas and kitchenettes with limited cooking facilities.

Shelly Bay Resort (☎ 4125 4533; www.shellybay resort.com.au; 466 The Esplanade, Torquay; 1-/2-bedroom units $125/170; 🔡 🔁) The bold, cheerful self-contained units at this complex have slightly dated facilities, but the beach is just across the road and all rooms have water views.

Alexander Lakeside B&B (☎ 4128 9448; www.hervey baybedandbreakfast.com; 29 Lido Pde, Urangan; r $130-160; 🔡) In a quiet street, this warm and friendly B&B offers lakeside indulgence. There's an Asian beach-chic feel, a heated lakeside spa, and all rooms have private bathrooms and TVs. Guests also have access to a kitchen and laundry.

Bay B&B (☎ 4125 6919; www.baybedandbreakfast.com .au; 180 Cypress St, Urangan; s $75, d $135-150; 🔡 🖳 🔁) This cosy and homey B&B is run by a friendly, well-travelled Frenchman. Guest rooms are in a comfy annexe out the back and breakfast is served on an outdoor patio in a tropical garden surrounded with birds and masses of greenery. Families can take over the separate fully self-contained unit.

La Mer Beachfront Apartments (☎ 1800 100 181, 4128 3494; www.lamer.com.au; 396 The Esplanade, Torquay; r per night/week $180/800; 🔡 🔁) Behind the generic façade are fresh and modern luxury apartments with open plans and new mod cons including full laundries, DVDs, cable TV and even coffee plungers.

TOP END

ourpick **Quarterdecks Harbour Retreat** (☎ 4197 0888; www.quarterdecksretreat.com.au; 80 Moolyyir St, Urangan; 1-/2-/3-bedroom villas $160/210/240; 🔡 🔁) These brand-new contemporary villas are fantastic value. Each villa is stylishly furnished with a private courtyard, all the mod cons you could wish for, and little luxuries such as fluffy bathrobes. Backing onto a nature reserve, it's quiet apart from the wonderful bird life, and is only 60m from the beach. Pets welcome.

Grange Resort (☎ 4125 2002; www.thegrange -herveybay.com.au; cnr Elizabeth & Shell Sts, Urangan; 1-/2-bedroom villas $195/225; 🔡 🔁) Reminiscent of a stylish desert resort with fancy split-level condos and filled with life's little luxuries, this place is close to the beach and to town. Glossy kitchens and bathrooms with stainless-steel appliances, plump couches, spacious boudoirs and commodious decks are the norm.

Eating

Enzo's on the Beach (☎ 4124 6375; 351a The Esplanade, Scarness; mains $7-15; 🕥 6.30am-5pm) A shabby-chic outdoor café with a superb beachfront location, you can dine on sandwiches, salads and light meals or just sip a coffee, listen to chill music and wallow in the perfect ocean views.

Aquavue (☎ 4125 5528; www.aquavue.com.au; 415 The Esplanade, Torquay; mains $8-13; 🕥 breakfast & lunch) Another outdoor café on the beachfront offering unbeatable sea views and the usual assortment of sandwiches and light meals. There are plenty of water toys for hire.

Simply Wok (☎ 4125 2077; 417 The Esplanade, Torquay; mains $14-25; 🕥 breakfast, lunch & dinner) Noodles, stir-fries, seafood and curries will satisfy any cravings for Asian cuisine, and there's an all-you-can-eat hot buffet for $13.90.

Black Dog Café (☎ 4124 3177; 381 The Esplanade, Torquay; mains $14-33; 🕥 lunch & dinner) This funky café oozes groove, starting with the chilled funk on the speakers and ending with the East-meets-West inventions on your fork. Sushi, Japanese soup, fresh burgers, club sambos and seafood salads will tame any black dog.

Café Balaena (☎ 4125 4799; Shop 7, Terminal Bldg, Buccaneer Ave, Urangan; mains $10-25; 🕥 breakfast & lunch daily, dinner Thu-Mon) This waterfront café provides expensive views, atmosphere with a laid-back twist, and wallet-friendly prices. The menu is hip café fare – mountainous paninis and salads – with a good dose of fresh seafood.

Pier Restaurant (☎ 4128 9699; 573 The Esplanade, Urangan; mains $20-40; 🕥 dinner Mon-Sat) Although sitting opposite the water the Pier makes little use of its ocean views but this à la carte restaurant has an interesting seafood menu (mud crab claws with chilli mango, and oysters with frozen margarita) and is highly recommended by the locals.

Bayswater Restaurant (☎ 4194 7555; 569 The Esplanade, Urangan; mains $26-39; 🕥 lunch & dinner) This stylish contemporary restaurant in Peppers Pier Resort dishes up modern Australian cuisine with European influences. Signature dishes include crispy-skinned salmon and chilli blue swimmer crab linguini. It's open and airy and the views are sensational.

Drinking & Entertainment

Bayswater Hotel (☎ 4194 7555; 569 The Esplanade, Urangan) Adjacent to The Bayswater Restaurant

SAND SAFARIS

There's a sci-fi other-worldliness to Fraser Island, as 4WDs and buses with towering wheel bases and chunky tyres pull in to refuel against an idyllic beach backdrop of white sand and waving palm trees. The surfeit of sand and the lack of paved roads mean that only 4WD vehicles can negotiate the island. For most travellers there are three transport options: self-drive tours, organised tours or 4WD hire.

Be aware of your environmental footprint. When choosing, bear in mind that the greater the number of individual vehicles driving on the island, the greater the environmental damage.

Self-Drive Tours

Unbeatable on price, these tours are incredibly popular with backpackers. Nine new friends are assigned to a vehicle, given some 4WD instruction, and head off in a convoy for a three-day, two-night camping safari.

Unfortunately, there have been complaints about costly, dodgy vehicle-damage claims upon return, but booking through a local hostel reduces the risk. Either way, check your vehicle beforehand.

Rates hover around $140 and exclude food and fuel. Recommended operators:

- **Colonial YHA** (☎ 1800 818 280, 4125 1844; www.cvyha.com) Hervey Bay.
- **Dingo's Backpacker's Resort** (☎ 1800 111 126, 5486 8200; www.dingosatrainbow.com) Rainbow Beach.
- **Fraser Roving** (☎ 1800 989 811, 4125 6386; www.fraserroving.com.au) Hervey Bay.
- **Koala Adventures** (☎ 1800 354 535, 4125 3601; www.koalaadventures.com) Hervey Bay.

Tours

There are plenty of tours in anything from private 4WDs to large coaches carrying up to 40 passengers. Most include accommodation and all meals, and cover the highlights: rainforests, Eli Creek, Lakes McKenzie and Wabby, the coloured Pinnacles and the *Maheno* shipwreck.

Among the many operators:

- **Footprints on Fraser** (☎ 1300 765 636; www.footprintsonfraser.com.au; 4-/5-day walk $1250/1670) Highly recommended guided walking tours of the island's natural wonders
- **Fraser Experience** (☎ 1800 689 819, 4124 4244; www.fraserexperience.com; 2-day tours $265) Small groups and more freedom about the itinerary.
- **Fraser Explorer Tours** (☎ 4194 9222; www.fraserexplorertours.com.au; day tours adult/child $145/85, 2-day tours $253/170) Overnight at Eurong Beach Resort.
- **Fraser Island Company** (☎ 1800 063 933, 4125 3933; www.fraserislandco.com.au) Offers a range of tour options.
- **Kingfisher Bay Tours** (☎ 1800 072 555, 4120 3333; www.kingfisherbay.com; Fraser Island; day tours adult/child $155/85, 2-/3-day tours $265/355) Ranger-guided ecotours. Multiday tours targeted at 18–35-year-olds.

4WD Hire

You can hire a 4WD from Hervey Bay, Rainbow Beach and even on Fraser Island. All companies require a hefty bond, usually in the form of a credit-card imprint, which you *will* lose if you drive in saltwater – don't even think about running the waves!

A driving instruction video will usually be shown, but when planning your trip, reckon on covering 20km an hour on the inland tracks and 50km an hour on the eastern beach.

Rates for multiday rentals start at around $130 per day and most companies also rent camping gear. See Car & Motorcycle (opposite) and Getting There & Around (p361) for rental companies in Hervey Bay and Rainbow Beach. On the island, **Kingfisher Bay 4WD Hire** (☎ 4120 3366) hires out 4WDs from $250 per day.

at Peppers Pier Resort, this breezy bar and bistro is ultra-cool. Cocktails on the outdoor cane lounges come with the same fantastic ocean views.

Hoolihan's (☎ 4194 0099; 382 The Esplanade, Scarness). Like all good Irish pubs, Hoolihan's is cosy and packed with interesting characters.

Koala Beach Resort (☎ 4125 3601; 410 The Esplanade, Torquay) Backpackers will gravitate to Hervey Bay's party central at Koala's, with loads of drinking and fun every night of the week.

Getting There & Away
AIR
Hervey Bay airport is off Booral Rd, Urangan, on the way to River Heads.

Qantas (☎ 13 13 13; www.qantas.com.au) has several daily flights to/from Brisbane ($140, 45 minutes) and a daily flight to/from Sydney ($186, two hours). **Virgin Blue** (☎ 13 67 89; www .virginblue.com.au) and **Jetstar** (☎ 13 15 38; www.jet star.com) fly daily from Sydney ($110, two hours).

BOAT
Boats to Fraser Island leave from River Heads, about 10km south of town, and Urangan Marina (see p377). Most tours leave from Urangan Harbour.

BUS
Buses depart **Hervey Bay Coach Terminal** (☎ 4124 4000; Central Ave, Pialba). **Greyhound Australia** (☎ 1300 473 946; www.greyhound.com.au) and **Premier Motor Service** (☎ 13 34 10; www.premierms.com.au) have several services to/from Brisbane ($65, 5½ hours), Maroochydore ($46, 3½ hours), Bundaberg ($18, 1½ hours) and Rockhampton ($80, six hours).

Suntours (☎ 4125 2221; www.suntours.net.au) has daily services to Brisbane airport ($55) and the Sunshine Coast airport ($42).

Wide Bay Transit (☎ 4121 3719) has hourly services from Urangan Marina (stopping along The Esplanade) to Maryborough ($7.60, one hour) every weekday, with fewer services on weekends.

Trainlink buses connect Maryborough West train station with the Coach Terminal ($7.50, 45 minutes).

Getting Around
CAR & MOTORCYCLE
Seega Rent a Car (☎ 4125 6008; 463 The Esplanade) has small cars from $30 to $40 a day.

Plenty of choice makes Hervey Bay the best place to hire a 4WD for Fraser Island:

Air Fraser Island (☎ 1800 247 992, 4125 3600; www .airfraserisland.com.au)

Aussie Trax (☎ 1800 062 275; 56 Boat Harbour Dr, Pialba)

Bay 4WD (☎ 1800 687 178, 4128 2981; www.bay4wd .com.au; 52-54 Boat Harbour Dr, Pialba)

Fraser Magic 4WD Hire (☎ 4125 6612; www.fraser -magic-4wdhire.com.au; Lot 11, Kruger Crt, Urangan)

Hervey Bay Rent A Car (☎ 4194 6626) Also rents out scooters ($30 per day).

Safari 4WD Hire (☎ 1800 689 819, 4124 4244; www .safari4wdhire.com.au; 102 Boat Harbour Dr, Pialba)

BICYCLE
Bay Bicycle Hire (☎ 0417-644 814; per half/full day $15/20) rents bicycles from various outlets along The Esplanade, or can deliver bikes to your door.

CHILDERS
☎ 07 / pop 1350

Surrounded by lush green fields and rich red soil, Childers is a charming little town, its main street lined with tall, shady trees and lattice-trimmed historical buildings. Backpackers flock here for fruit-picking and farm work, although, sadly, Childers is best remembered for the 15 backpackers who perished in a fire in the Palace Backpackers Hostel in June 2000. There is now a moving memorial, with poignant images of those who perished, at the **Childers Palace Memorial & Art Gallery** (☎ 4126 1994; 72 Churchill St; ☼ 9am-4pm Mon-Fri, 9am-3pm Sat & Sun). You'll also find the visitors centre here.

Childers' lovely 100-year-old **Federal Hotel** has batwing doors while a bronze statue of two fighting pig dogs sits outside the **Grand Hotel**. On the outskirts of town, the **Isis Historical Complex** (Taylor St; adult/child $2/free; ☼ 9am-noon Mon-Fri) is a mock historical town, with cottages, a general store and a post office.

On the last Sunday in July, Childers' main street is swamped with street performers, musicians, dancers, and global food stalls during its annual **Festival of Cultures**, which draws over 50,000 people.

A little out of town, **Sugarbowl Caravan Park** (☎ 4126 1521; 4660 Bruce Hwy; unpowered/powered sites $20/22, cabins $66; ☐ ☻) has plenty of space and spectacular views over the surrounding countryside. Backpackers will want to stay here for the views, the facilities and the friendly owners who can help with work placement (by prior arrangement) and transport to the farms.

In the centre of town, **Motel Childers** (☎ 4126 1177; 136 Churchill St; s/d $75/85; 🉑) has clean, basic rooms with the usual facilities.

For warm, country hospitality the cute cane-cutter cottages at **Mango Hill B&B** (☎ 4126 1311; www.mangohillcottages.com; 8 Mango Hill Dr; s/d/tr $90/120/140; 🉑), 4km south of town, are decorated with handmade wooden furniture, country décor and comfy beds that ooze charm and romance. A bottle of preservative-free, organic wine from the on-site boutique winery, **Hill of Promise Estate** (cellar door ☢ 10am-4pm, or by appointment), goes well with the picture-pretty views from the cottage veranda.

If you're stopping for lunch, **Kapé Centro** (☎ 4126 1916; 65 Churchill St; mains $9-15; ☢ breakfast & lunch) in the old post office building dishes up light meals, salads and pizzas on the veranda.

A little more upmarket, **Laurel Tree Cottage** (☎ 4126 2911; 89 Churchill St; dishes $10-20; ☢ breakfast & lunch) has an even balance of frills and funk; the interior is very tea shoppe but the gourmet sandwiches, burgers and breakfasts are definitely from this century.

Childers is 50km southwest of Bundaberg. **Greyhound Australia** (☎ 1300 473 946) and **Premier Motor Service** (☎ 13 34 10) stop at the Shell service station north of town and have daily services to/from Brisbane ($75, 6½ hours), Hervey Bay ($18, one hour) and Bundaberg ($18, 1½ hours).

BURRUM COAST NATIONAL PARK

The Burrum Coast National Park covers two sections of coastline, on either side of the little holiday community of Woodgate, 37km east of Childers. The Woodgate section of the park begins at the southern end of The Esplanade; it has attractive beaches, abundant fishing and a **QPWS camping ground** (per person $4) at Burrum Point, reached by a 4WD-only track. Several walking tracks start at the camping ground or Acacia St in Woodgate. There are more isolated bush-camping areas in the Kinkuna section of the park, a few kilometres north of Woodgate, but you'll need a 4WD to reach them. Contact the **park rangers** (☎ 4126 8810) or go online at www.epa.qld.gov.au to book camping permits.

Woodgate Beach Tourist Park (☎ 4126 8802; www.woodgatebeachtouristpark.com; 88 The Esplanade; unpowered/powered sites $20/23, cabins $79-89, beachfront villas $130;

🉑) is a tidy, tranquil park close to the national park and opposite the beach. There's a lovely outdoor café open for breakfast and lunch.

The **Woodgate Beach Hotel-Motel** (☎ 4126 8988; 195 The Esplanade; d $88), at the northern end of The Esplanade, has a block of reasonable motel units just across from the beach and dishes up decent pub grub.

BUNDABERG
☎ 07 / pop 46,961

Boasting a sublime climate, coral-fringed beaches and waving fields of sugarcane, 'Bundy' should feature on the Queensland tourist hit parade. But this old-fashioned country town feels stuck in a centuries-old time-warp and nothing much seems to happen here. The pleasant main strip is a wide, palm-lined street, and the surrounding countryside forms a picturesque chequerboard of rich red volcanic soil, small crops and sugarcane stretching pancake-flat to the coastal beaches 15km away. Born out of these cane fields is the famous Bundaberg Rum, a potent and mind-blowing liquor bizarrely endorsed by a polar bear but as iconically Australian as Tim Tams and Vegemite.

Hordes of backpackers flock to Bundy for fruit-picking and farm work; others quickly pass through on their way to family summer holidays at the nearby seaside villages.

Information

Bundaberg Email Centre (☎ 4153 5007; 197 Bourbong St; per hr $4; ☢ 10am-10pm) Internet access.
Bundaberg visitors centre (☎ 1300 722 099, 4153 8888; www.bundabergregion.info); 271 Bourbong St (☢ 9am-5pm); 186 Bourbong St (☢ 9am-5pm Mon-Fri, 9am-noon Sat & Sun)
Cosy Corner Internet Cafe (☎ 4153 5999; Barolin St; per hr $5; ☢ 8am-7pm Mon-Fri, 9am-5pm Sat, 11am-5pm Sun) Internet access.
Post office (☎ 4151 6708; cnr Bourbong & Barolin Sts)
QPWS (☎ 4131 1600; 46 Quay St)

Sights

From the lookout on top of the **hummock** (96m), an extinct volcano and the only hill in this flat landscape, you see Bundaberg's patchwork fields of sugarcane and small crops spread against an ocean backdrop. During the caneharvest season from July to November, the horizon blazes with spectacular and incredibly quick-lived and furious cane fires.

Bundaberg's biggest claim to fame is the iconic Bundaberg Rum – you'll see the Bundy

Rum polar bear on billboards all over town. At the **Bundaberg Rum Distillery** (☎ 4131 2999; www .bundabergrum.com.au; Avenue St; self-guided tour adult/child $10/7; ☼ 9am-4pm Mon-Fri, 9am-3pm Sat & Sun) tours follow the rum's production from start to finish, and include a tasting.

Not quite as famous (probably because it's nonalcoholic) is Bundaberg Ginger Beer. To see how the ginger is mushed, crushed, brewed and fermented visit **The Bundaberg Barrel** (☎ 4154 5480; www.bundaberg -brew.com.au; adult/child $5/3; ☼ 9am-4.30pm Mon-Sat, 10am-3pm Sun).

The **Botanic Gardens** (Mt Perry Rd; ☼ 5.30am-6.45pm Sep-Apr, 6am-6.30pm May-Aug), 2km north of the centre, is a pleasant oasis of tropical shrubs, towering trees, and flowering gardens

surrounding a few small lakes. Within the grounds are three museums. The **Hinkler House Museum** (☎ 4152 0222; adult/child $5/2; ☼ 10am-4pm) is set inside the house of Bundaberg's most famous son, aviator Bert Hinkler, who made the first solo flight between England and Australia in 1928. The house was painstakingly relocated from Southampton in 1983.

The **Bundaberg & District Historical Museum** (☎ 4152 0101; adult/child $4/2; ☼ 10am-4pm) has plenty of colonial-era antiques such as quaint 1920s handmade quilts. Look for the wedding albums showcasing every Bundy bride since 1974.

At the southern end of the park, the **Fairymead House Sugar Museum** (☎ 4153 6786; adult/child $4/2; ☼ 10am-4pm), set in an old

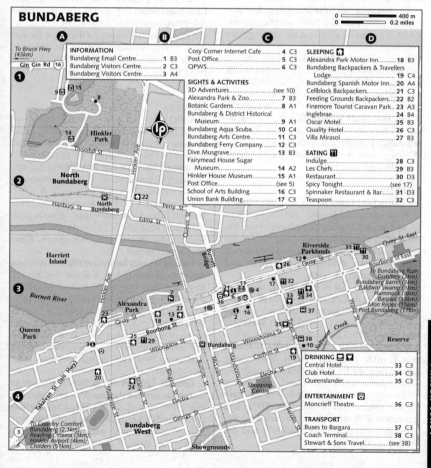

BUNDABERG

0 — 400 m
0 — 0.2 miles

To Bruce Hwy (43km)

Gin Gin Rd (16)

Hinkler Park

North Bundaberg

Thornhill St

Hanbury St

Harriett Island

Burnett River

Queens Park

Alexandra Park

Perry St

Edina St

Quay St

Bourbong St

Woongarra St

Crofton St

Electra St

Shopping Centre

Electra

George St

Bundaberg West

Showgrounds

Quay St East

Bourbong St East

To Bundaberg Rum Distillery (2km); Bundaberg Barrel (3km); Baldwin Swamp (3km); Hummock (8km); Bargara (13km); Mon Repos (15km); Port Bundaberg (17km)

Riverside Parklands

Saltwater Creek

Reserve

Burnett Bridge

Bundaberg

To Country Comfort Bundaberg (2.1km); Reading Cinema (3km); Hinkler Airport (4km); Childers (51km)

To Takalvan St (66 Hwy)

FRASER COAST

TURTLE TOTS

Mon Repos, 15km northeast of Bundaberg, is one of Australia's most accessible turtle rookeries. From November to late March, female loggerheads lumber laboriously up the beach to lay eggs in the sand. About eight weeks later the hatchlings dig their way to the surface, and under cover of darkness emerge en masse to scurry as quickly as their little flippers allow down to the water. The **QPWS visitors centre** (☎ 4159 1652; ☺ 7.30am-4pm Mon-Fri) has nightly tours (adult/child $8.70/4.60) from 7pm during the season. Bookings are mandatory and can be made through the Bundaberg visitors centre (p370) or online at www.bookbundabergregion.com.au. Alternatively, you can take a turtle-watching tour with **Foot Prints Adventures** (☎ 4152 3659; www.footprintsadventures.com.au; adult/child incl transfers $44/22).

Savour your turtle experience with a few laid-back days at **Turtle Sands Tourist Park** (☎ 4159 2340; www.turtlesands.com.au; Mon Repos; unpowered/powered sites $20/22, cabins from $70; ☒), a pretty caravan park with good facilities, daily parrot feeding, and a superb beachfront location.

Queenslander, documents the development of the sugar industry.

The **Alexandra Park & Zoo** (Quay St) is tucked into a green corner on the banks of the Burnett River. It's a pretty spot and the large, grassy park begs for a picnic.

In town, the **Bundaberg Arts Centre** (☎ 4152 3700; www.bundaberg.qld.gov.au/arts; cnr Barolin & Quay Sts; admission free; ☺ 10am-5pm Mon-Fri, 11am-3pm Sat & Sun) has displays of local and travelling exhibitions. Interesting old buildings in town include the ornate **Union Bank building** (Targo St), the **post office** (cnr Bourbong & Barolin Sts), and the **School of Arts Building** (Bourbong St). Pick up a copy of *A Walking Tour of the Bundaberg City Centre* from the visitors centres.

Activities

Bundaberg Ferry Company (☎ 4152 9188; 3 Quay St; 2½-hr tours per adult/child/family $25/13/70; ☺ 9.30am & 1.30pm Tue, Wed, Fri & Sun, 1.30pm Sat) operates the *Bundy Belle*, an old-fashioned ferry that chugs at a pleasant pace to the mouth of the Burnett River. The tour includes a commentary and morning or afternoon tea.

About 16km east of Bundaberg, the small beach hamlet of **Bargara** (p374) has good diving and snorkelling at Barolin Rocks and in the Woongarra Marine Park. Both **Bundaberg Aqua Scuba** (☎ 4153 5761; www.aquascuba.com.au; Shop 1, 66 Targo St) and **3D Adventures** (☎ 4152 4064; 66 Targo St) offer four-day, PADI open-water diving courses for $219, but this only includes shore dives. Advanced open-water dive courses cost from $265. **Dive Musgrave** (☎ 4154 3800; www.divemusgrave.com.au; 239 Bourbong St; per person $678) offers three-day trips for experienced divers to Lady Musgrave and the Bunker group of islands.

Tours

You can fly to Lady Elliot Island with **Lady Elliot Island Resort** (☎ 1800 072 200, 5536 3644; www.ladyelliot.com.au; adult/child $275/146). The day trip includes at least five hours on the Great Barrier Reef, a glass-bottomed boat or snorkel tour, lunch and use of the resort's facilities. See p385 for information about longer stays on the islands.

Sleeping

BUDGET

Bundaberg's hostels cater to working backpackers; most hostels arrange harvest work and stays of one week or longer are the norm.

Finemore Tourist Caravan Park (☎ 4151 3663; www.bundaberg.qld.gov.au/tourism; 33 Quay St; unpowered/powered sites from $16/18, cabins from $55; ☒ ☒) This small, attractive park sits on the banks of the Burnett River. Quite a few long-termers pitch their digs here and it's close to the zoo and walking distance to the town centre. Rates are for two people.

Feeding Grounds Backpacker (☎ 4152 3659; www.footprintsadventures.com.au; 4 Hinkler Ave; dm $23) Sleeping only 18, the smallest hostel in Bundaberg is a friendly, family-run affair in a converted and extended house. The country style kitchen and lounge, four-bed dorms and two bathrooms makes for a very cosy time. The environmentally-conscious owner of the hostel runs Footprints Adventures turtle tours (see above).

Cellblock Backpackers (☎ 1800 837 773; www.cellblock.com.au; cnr Quay & Maryborough Sts; dm per night/week from $25/145, d $66; ☒ ☐ ☒) This arresting hostel in Bundy's heritage-listed former lock-up is a swish resort with plasma screen TVs, a trendy pool bar and clean, modern facilities.

The seven restored jail cells (grab the padded cell!) lack windows (of course) but are great for couples. The hostel arranges harvest work and the bathrooms are remarkably clean considering most backpackers drag farm soil home from a day in the fields.

Bundaberg Backpackers & Travellers Lodge (☎ 4152 2080; bundybackpackers@iinet.com.au; cnr Targo & Crofton Sts; dm per night/week $25/150; ✷ 🖳) The first place you see when you get off the bus. The friendly and genuine owners of this hostel also run Bus Stop Backpackers (at the bus stop, of course!). The rooms are clean, it's fully air-conditioned and has cable TV.

MIDRANGE
Bundaberg Spanish Motor Inn (☎ 4152 5444; www.bundabergspanishmotorinn.com; 134 Woongarra St; s/d $80/90; ✷ 🗟) In a quiet side street off the main drag, this Spanish hacienda-style motel is great value. All units are self-contained and all rooms overlook the central pool.

Oscar Motel (☎ 4152 3666; reception@oscarmotel.com.au; 252 Bourbong St; s/d $83/94; ✷ 🗟) The Oscar offers a range of rooms; smaller digs are functional and warm and the larger rooms are huge. There's a guest laundry and a tour desk, and the proud owners keep the whole place spotless.

Alexandra Park Motor Inn (☎ 1800 803 419, 4152 7255; www.alexandra.com.au; 66 Quay St; d $85-95; ✷ 🗟) A gracious timber exterior, complete with sweeping balcony, greets visitors to this quiet motel off the main road into town. The more expensive rooms upstairs are large and contain kitchenettes. The restaurant and bar is open for dinner and serves up New Orleans and hearty Australian cuisine.

Inglebrae (☎ 4154 4003; www.inglebrae.com; 17 Branyan St; r incl breakfast $100-130; ✷) For old-world English charm in a glorious Queenslander, this delightful B&B is just the ticket. Polished timber and stained glass seep from the entrance into the rooms, which come with high beds and small antiques. Breakfasts are big and hot, and are served on the lovely veranda.

Villa Mirasol (☎ 4154 4311; www.villa.net.au; 225 Bourbong St; s/d/ste $105/120/175; ✷ 🗟) The Mexican theme is evident in this ochre-coloured, central motel. Aztec motifs decorate the rooms and the executive suites come with a spa.

Quality Hotel (☎ 4155 8777; www.flagchoice.com.au; 7 Quay St; r $135-150; ✷ 🗟) This modern pit stop is popular with conferences and travelling business folk, but the good facilities and

décor from the new millennium set it apart from just about every other option in town. The rooms are quite stylish and there's a gym, a sauna, and a licensed restaurant and cocktail bar overlooking the Burnett River.

Eating
Teaspoon (☎ 4154 4456; 10 Targo St; mains $5-8; ⏰ 8am-5pm Mon-Sat) This funky little café with green velvet sofas has the best coffee in town. The cosy vibe is matched with yummy cakes, panini and light meals.

Indulge (☎ 4154 2344; 80 Bourbong St; dishes $9-16; ⏰ breakfast & lunch) With its sophisticated ambience and intoxicating pastries, this narrow café brings a European flavour to country Bundaberg. Has fancy brekkies and sweet indulgences.

Spicy Tonight (☎ 4154 3320; 1 Targo St; dishes $10-19; ⏰ dinner) Bundaberg's spicy little secret combines Thai and Indian cuisine with hot curries, vindaloo, tandoori and a host of vegetarian dishes.

Les Chefs (☎ 4153 1770; 238 Bourbong St; mains $24; ⏰ lunch Mon-Fri, dinner Mon-Sat) One for the carnivores, this upmarket, intimate restaurant goes global, treating diners to duck, veal, seafood, chicken and beef dishes à la Nepal, Mexico, France, India and more.

Restaurant (☎ 4154 4589; cnr Quay & Toonburra St; mains $25-35; ⏰ dinner Mon-Sat) Once used as a rowing shed, this riverside bar and restaurant serves up simple mod Oz cuisine. The interior can be a bit dim but the outdoor tables on the timber deck make a lovely spot for a quiet drink.

Spinnaker Restaurant & Bar (☎ 4152 8033; 1a Quay St; dishes $26-38; ⏰ lunch Tue-Fri, dinner Tue-Sat) Bundaberg's classiest restaurant woos diners with a picturesque perch above the Burnett River where you can nibble on gourmet tapas such as herb-crusted bocconcini, or savour full-flavoured dishes of pasta, seafood and pizza.

Drinking & Entertainment
Central Hotel (☎ 4151 3159; 18 Targo St) is Bundy's hottest nightclub, while **Club Hotel** (☎ 4151 3262; cnr Tantitha & Bourbong Sts) has laid-back lounges and chill-out music. **Queenslander** (☎ 4152 4691; 61 Targo St) hosts live gigs and DJs on weekends and only has red wine by the cask (cold!).

Moncrieff Theatre (☎ 4153 1985; 177 Bourbong St) Bundaberg's lovely old cinema has plays, shows and mainstream movies.

FRASER COAST

Getting There & Around

AIR

Bundaberg's **Hinkler Airport** (Takalvan St) is about 4km southwest of the centre. There are several daily flights to Brisbane ($150, one hour) with **Qantaslink** (☎ 13 13 13; www.qantas.com.au).

BUS

The coach terminal is in Targo St where you'll find **Stewart & Sons Travel** (☎ 4152 9700; 66 Targo St; ☺ 9am-6pm Mon-Fri, 10am-noon Sat). Both **Greyhound Australia** (☎ 1300 473 946; www.greyhound.com.au) and **Premier Motor Service** (☎ 13 34 10; www.premierms.com.au) have daily services connecting Bundaberg with Brisbane ($81, seven hours), Hervey Bay ($18, 1½ hours), Rockhampton ($62, four hours) and Gladstone ($45, 2½ hours).

Duffy's Coaches (☎ 4151 4226) has numerous services every weekday to Bargara ($4.40, 35 minutes), leaving from the back of Target on Woongarra St and stopping around town.

TRAIN

Queensland Rail's (www.traveltrain.com.au) *Sunlander* ($64.90, seven hours, three weekly) and *Tilt Train* ($64.90, five hours, Sunday to Friday) services travel from Brisbane to Bundaberg on their respective routes to Cairns and Rockhampton.

AROUND BUNDABERG

In many people's eyes, the beach hamlets around Bundaberg are more attractive than the town itself. Some 25km north of the centre is **Moore Park**, with wide, flat beaches. To the south is the very popular **Elliot Heads** with a nice beach, rocky foreshore and good fishing. Locals and visitors also flock to **Mon Repos** to see baby turtles hatching from November to March (see boxed text, p372).

Bargara

☎ 07 / pop 5525

Some 16km east of Bundaberg lies the cruisy beach village of **Bargara**, a picturesque little spot with a good surf beach, a lovely esplanade and a few snazzy cafés. Recent years have seen a few high-rises sprout up along the foreshore but the effect is relatively low-key. Families find Bargara attractive for its clean beaches and safe swimming, particularly at the 'basin', a sheltered artificial rock pool.

Bargara Beach Dive (☎ 4159 2663; www.bargaradive.com; Shop 4, 16 See St) hires out equipment and runs PADI open-water dive courses ($495),

as well as local dives ($130) and snorkelling safaris (four-hour snorkel $99).

The large sprawling grounds of the **Bargara Beach Caravan Park** (☎ 4159 2228; www.bargarabeach.com.au; Nielson Park, Bargara; unpowered/powered sites $20/23, cabins $70) covers 16 acres so you're bound to find room to pitch a tent.

Set on five acres of landscaped gardens, **Kelly's Beach Resort** (☎ 1800 246 141; 4154 7200; www.kellysbeachresort.com.au; 6 Trevors Rd, Bargara; cabin weekday/weekend $99/110; ☒ ☒) has large self-contained condos with private decks, and is just a short walk to Kelly's beach.

Kacy's Restaurant & Bar (☎ 4130 1100; cnr See & Bauer Sts, Bargara; mains $12-32; ☺ breakfast & dinner daily, lunch Fri-Sun) on the foreshore is like a fantastic South Pacific oasis with colourful cocktails, delicious seafood and ocean breezes.

FRASER ISLAND

The local Aborigines call it K'Gari or 'paradise'. Sculpted from wind, sand and surf, the striking blue freshwater lakes, crystalline creeks, giant dunes and lush rainforests of this gigantic sandbar form an enigmatic island paradise unlike any other in the world. Created over hundreds of thousands of years from sand drifting off the east coast of mainland Australia, Fraser Island is the largest sand island in the world (measuring 120km by 15km) and the only place where rainforest grows on sand.

Inland, the vegetation varies from dense tropical rainforest and wild heath to wetlands and wallum scrub, with 'sandblows' (giant dunes over 200m high), mineral streams and freshwater lakes opening on to long sandy beaches fringed with pounding surf. The island is home to a profusion of bird life and wildlife, while off-shore waters teem with dugong, dolphins, sharks and migrating humpback whales.

Once exploited for its natural resources – sand and timber – Fraser Island joined the World Heritage list in 1992. At present the northern half of the island is protected as the Great Sandy National Park while the rest of the island comprises state forest, crown land and private land.

This island Utopia, however, is marred by an ever-increasing volume of 4WD traffic tearing down the beach and along sandy inland tracks. With over 350,000 people visiting

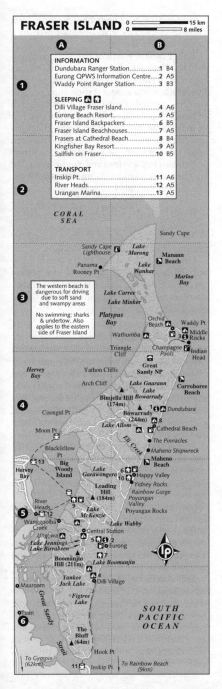

FRASER ISLAND

INFORMATION		
Dundubara Ranger Station	1	B4
Eurong QPWS Information Centre	2	A5
Waddy Point Ranger Station	3	B3
SLEEPING		
Dilli Village Fraser Island	4	A6
Eurong Beach Resort	5	A5
Fraser Island Backpackers	6	B5
Fraser Island Beachhouses	7	A5
Frasers at Cathedral Beach	8	B4
Kingfisher Bay Resort	9	A5
Sailfish on Fraser	10	B5
TRANSPORT		
Inskip Pt	11	A6
River Heads	12	A5
Urangan Marina	13	A5

the island each year, Fraser can sometimes feel like a giant sandpit with its own peak hour and congested beach highway.

Information & Orientation

A 4WD is necessary if you're driving on Fraser Island. General supplies and expensive fuel are available from stores at Cathedral Beach, Eurong, Kingfisher Bay, Happy Valley and Orchid Beach. Most stores stock some camping and fishing gear, and those at Kingfisher Bay, Eurong, Happy Valley and Orchid Beach sell alcohol. There are public telephones at these locations and at most camping grounds.

The main ranger station, **Eurong QPWS Information Centre** (☎ 4127 9128; 10.30am-3.30pm Mon, 8am-3.30pm Tue-Thu, 8am-noon Fri) is at Eurong. Others can be found at **Dundabara** (☎ 4127 9138; hours vary) and **Waddy Point** (☎ 4127 9190; hours vary).

The **Fraser Island Taxi Service** (☎ 4127 9188) operates all over the island. A one-way fare from Kingfisher Bay to Eurong costs \$70.

The tow-truck service is based at **Eurong** (☎ 4127 9449, 0428-353 164).

PERMITS

You must purchase permits from **QPWS** (☎ 13 13 04; www.epa.qld.gov.au) for vehicles (per month/year \$35.40/177.30) and camping (per person/family \$4.50/18) before you arrive. Permits aren't required for private camping grounds or resorts. Permit issuing offices:

Bundaberg QPWS Office (☎ 4131 1600; 46 Quay St)

Great Sandy Information Centre (☎ 5449 7792; 240 Moorinidil St, Tewantin; 7am-4pm) Near Noosa.

Maryborough QPWS (☎ 4121 1800; cnr Alice & Lennox St; 8.30am-5pm Mon-Fri)

Naturally Queensland (Map pp314-5; ☎ 3227 8185; 160 Ann St, Brisbane; 8.30am-5pm Mon-Fri)

Rainbow Beach QPWS (☎ 5486 3160; Rainbow Beach Rd; 7am-4pm) Purchase permits from the 24-hour vending machines – credit card only.

River Heads information kiosk (☎ 4125 8485; 6.15-11.15am & 2-3.30pm) Ferry departure point at River Heads, south of Hervey Bay.

Sights & Activities

Starting at the island's southern tip, where the ferry leaves for Inskip Point on the mainland, a high-tide access track cuts inland, avoiding dangerous Hook Point, and leads to the entrance of the Eastern Beach's main thoroughfare. The first settlement is **Dilli Village**,

FRASER COAST

FRASER ISLAND GREAT WALK

The Fraser Island Great Walk is a stunning way to experience this enigmatic island. The trail undulates through the island's interior for 90km from Dilli Village to Happy Valley. Broken up into seven sections of around six to 16 kilometres each, plus some side trails off the main sections, it follows the pathways of Fraser Island's original inhabitants, the Butchulla people. En route, the walk passes underneath the rainforest canopies, circles around some of the island's vivid lakes and courses through shifting dunes.

Pick up the *Fraser Island Great Walk* brochure from a QPWS office (or download it from www.epa.qld.gov.au under the Parks and Forests heading) and seek updates on the track's conditions.

---

the former sand-mining centre; **Eurong**, with shops, fuel and places to eat, is another 9km north. From here, an inland track crosses to Central Station and Wanggoolba Creek (for the ferry to River Heads).

Right in the middle of the island is the ranger centre at **Central Station**, the starting point for numerous walking trails. From here you can walk or drive to the beautiful **McKenzie, Jennings, Birrabeen** and **Boomanjin Lakes**. Lake McKenzie is spectacularly clear and is ringed by white sand beaches, making it a great place to swim, but Lake Birrabeen sees fewer tour and backpacker groups.

About 4km north of Eurong along the beach is a signposted walking trail, which leads across sandblows (enormous dunes created by wind-blown sand) to the beautiful **Lake Wabby**, the most accessible of Fraser's lakes. An easier route is from the lookout on the inland track. Lake Wabby is surrounded on three sides by eucalypt forest, while the fourth side is a massive sandblow that encroaches on the lake at about 3m a year. The lake is deceptively shallow and diving is very dangerous.

As you drive up the beach you may have to detour inland to avoid Poyungan and Yidney Rocks during high tide before you reach **Happy Valley**, with places to stay, a shop and bistro. About 10km north is **Eli Creek**, a fast-moving, crystal-clear waterway that will carry you effortlessly downstream. About 2km from Eli Creek is the rotting hulk of the **Maheno**,

a former passenger liner blown ashore by a cyclone in 1935 as it was being towed to a Japanese scrap yard.

Roughly 5km north of the *Maheno* you'll find the **Pinnacles** – an eroded section of coloured sand cliffs – and, about 10km beyond, **Dundubara**, with a ranger station and excellent camping ground. Then there's a 20km stretch of beach before you come to the rock outcrop of **Indian Head**. Sharks, manta rays, dolphins and (during the migration season) whales can often be seen from the top of this headland.

Between Indian Head and Waddy Point the trail branches inland, passing **Champagne Pools**, which offer the only safe saltwater swimming on the island. There are good camping areas at **Waddy Point** and **Orchid Beach**, the last settlement on the island.

Many tracks north of this are closed for reasons of environmental protection.

On the island you can take a scenic flight with **MI Helicopters** (☎ 1800 600 345; www.mihelicopters.com.au; 25min flight $240), based at Kingfisher Bay Resort (opposite), or with **Air Fraser** (☎ 1800 600 345; 10min flights from $70).

Sleeping & Eating

Fraser Island Backpackers (☎ 4127 9144; www.fraserislandco.com.au; Happy Valley; dm $39-59; mains $10-20; ⏰ breakfast, lunch & dinner; 🖳 🍺) This wilderness-retreat-turned-backpackers has dorms (sleeping up to seven) in nine timber lodges. The cabins cascade down a gentle slope amid plenty of tropical foliage and there's a bistro and bar on site.

Eurong Beach Resort (☎ 1800 111 808, 4127 9122; www.fraser-is.com; Eurong; r $150, 2-bedroom apt $270, mains $15-30; ⏰ breakfast, lunch & dinner; 🍴 🍺) Bright, cheerful Eurong is the main resort on the east coast and the most accessible for all budgets. At the cheaper end of the market are simple motel rooms and units, while comfortable, fully self-contained apartments are good value for families. On site is a cavernous restaurant, bar, two pools and tennis courts.

Sailfish on Fraser (☎ 4127 9494; www.sailfishonfraser.com.au; Happy Valley; d/f from $220/240; 🍺) Any notions of rugged wilderness and roughing it will be forgotten quick smart at this plush, indulgent retreat. These two-bedroom apartments are cavernous and classy, with wall-to-wall glass doors, spas, mod cons, mod furnishings and an alluring pool.

Kingfisher Bay Resort (☎ 1800 072 555, 4120 3333; www.kingfisherbay.com; Kingfisher Bay; d $285, 2-bedroom villa $380; ✻ ▢ ♈) This elegant eco-resort has smart hotel rooms with private balconies, and sophisticated two- and three-bedroom timber villas that are elevated to limit their environmental impact. The villas are utterly gorgeous and some even have spas on their private decks but there's a three-night minimum stay in high season. The resort has restaurants, bars and shops and operates daily tours of the island (adult/child $149/89).

Fraser Island Beachhouses (☎ 1800 626 230, 4127 9205; www.fraserislandbeachhouses.com.au; Eurong Second Valley; studio per 2 nights $360, 1-bedroom house per 2 nights from $700; ♈) Another luxury option, this complex contains sunny, self-contained units kitted out with polished wood, cable TVs and ocean views. Rates start with studios and climb to $900 for two-bedroom beachfront houses.

CAMPING

Supplies on the island are limited and costly. Before arriving campers should stock up well. Be prepared for mosquitoes and March flies.

Camping permits are required at QPWS camping grounds and any public area (ie along the beach). The most developed **QPWS camping grounds** (per person/family $4.50/18) with coin-operated hot showers, toilets and BBQs are at Waddy Point, Dundubara and Central Station. Campers with vehicles can also use the smaller camping grounds with fewer facilities at Lake Boomanjin, Ungowa and Wathumba on the western coast. Walkers' camps (for hikers only) are set away from the main campgrounds along the Fraser Island Great Walk trail (opposite). The trail map lists the camp sites and their facilities. Camping is permitted on designated stretches of the eastern beach, but there are no facilities. Fires are prohibited, except in communal fire rings at Waddy Point and Dundubara, and to utilise these you'll need to bring your own firewood in the form of untreated, milled timber.

Dilli Village Fraser Island (☎ 4127 9130; Dilli Village; unpowered sites/bunk rooms $10/40, cabins $60-100) Managed by the University of the Sunshine Coast, Dilli Village offers good sites on a softly sloping camping ground. The facilities are neat as a pin and the cabins are ageing but accommodating.

Frasers at Cathedral Beach (☎ 4127 9177; www.fraserislandco.com.au; Cathedral Beach; unpowered/powered sites $27/38, cabins with/without bathroom $140/170) This spacious, privately run park with its abundant flat, grassy sites is a fave with families. The excellent facilities include large, communal BBQ areas and spotless amenities. The quaint, comfortable cabins come with private picnic tables.

Getting There & Away

AIR

Air Fraser Island (☎ 1800 247 992, 4125 3600; www.airfraserisland.com.au) charges $70 for a return flight (20 minutes each way) to the island's eastern beach, departing Hervey Bay airport.

BOAT

Several large vehicle ferries connect Fraser Island to the mainland. Most visitors use the two services that leave from River Heads (about 10km south of Hervey Bay) or from Inskip Point near Rainbow Beach.

Fraser Island Barges (☎ 1800 227 437; pedestrian/vehicle & 4 passengers return $30/150, additional passengers $10.50) make the 30-minute crossing from River Heads to Wanggoolba Creek on the western coast of Fraser Island. It departs daily from River Heads at 9am, 10.15am and 3.30pm, and returns from the island at 9.30am, 2.30pm and 4pm. The same company also operates a service from the Urangan Marina in Hervey Bay to Moon Point on Fraser Island, but car-hire companies won't allow you to drive their cars here so it's limited to car owners and hikers. Rates are the same as for the River Heads to Wanggoolba Creek service.

Kingfisher Vehicular Ferry (☎ 1800 072 555, 4120 3333; vehicle & 4 passengers return $145, additional passengers $10) operates two boats. Its vehicle ferry makes the 45-minute crossing from River Heads to Kingfisher Bay daily, departing at 7.15am, 11am and 2.30pm, and returning at 8.30am, 1.30pm and 4pm. The Kingfisher Fast Cat Passenger Ferry (adult/child return $55/28) makes the 30 to 45 minute crossing between Urangan Marina and Kingfisher Bay at 6.45am, 8.45am, noon, 4pm, 7pm and 10pm daily, returning at 7.40am, 10.30am, 2pm, 5pm, 8pm and 11.30pm daily.

Coming from Rainbow Beach, both **Rainbow Venture** (☎ 5486 3227; pedestrian/vehicle return $10/80) and **Manta Ray** (☎ 5486 8888; vehicle return $85) make the 15-minute crossing from Inskip Point to Hook Point on Fraser Island continuously from about 7am to 5.30pm daily.

Capricorn Coast

Straddling the tropic of Capricorn, Rockhampton is the major hub of the Capricorn Coast, and rates as Australia's brash beef-farming capital, with pub rodeos, steakhouses and oversized bulls dominating the town. A short drive from the cattle capital is the sleepy coastal village of Yeppoon, the launch pad to the easily accessible and beautiful Great Keppel Island. North of Yeppoon the rugged and wild Byfield National Park has several back-to-nature bush retreats.

Further south, the industrial port town of Gladstone is the gateway to the Capricorn Coast's stunning offshore attractions – tropical islands and coral cays fringed with powdery white beaches and clear, turquoise waters. The deserted and sparsely inhabited islands of the southern Great Barrier Reef, especially Heron and Lady Elliot Islands, offers some of the best snorkelling and diving in Queensland. Day trips to the coral cays offer an unforgettable Barrier Reef adventure but to fully experience the magic of the islands, camp overnight on uninhabited Lady Musgrave Island.

Remote beaches and windswept national parks can be found along the entire Capricorn coastline, from Byfield National Park south to the relatively untouched seaside settlements of Agnes Water and the Town of 1770.

HIGHLIGHTS

- Diving the spectacular underwater coral gardens of **Heron Island** (p386) and **Lady Elliot Island** (p385)

- Playing castaway on the deserted islands and coral cays of the **Southern Reef Islands** (p385)

- Tucking into a huge steak in Australia's beef capital, **Rockhampton** (p386)

- Crawling through black holes and tight tunnels in the **Capricorn Caves** (p391)

- Surfing and chilling at Queensland's most northerly surf beach, **Agnes Water** (p380)

- Claiming a tropical beach for the day on **Great Keppel Island** (p393)

Capricorn Caves ★
Rockhampton ★   ★ Great Keppel Island
                    Heron Island ★
                    Southern Reef Islands ★
Agnes Water ★   Lady ★ Elliot Island

■ TELEPHONE CODE: 07   ■ www.capricorncoast.com.au   ■ www.capricorntourism.com.au

CAPRICORN COAST

Crocodiles inhabit rivers and lakes in tropical areas; swimming is not recommended.

Getting There & Away

AIR

Both Rockhampton and Gladstone have major domestic airports.

Jetstar (☎ 13 15 38; www.jetstar.com.au) Connects Rockhampton with Brisbane.

Qantas (☎ 13 13 13; www.qantas.com.au) Connects Rockhampton with Mackay, Gladstone, Brisbane and Sydney. Qantaslink connects Brisbane with Gladstone.

Tiger Airways (☎ 03 9335 3033; www.tigerairways .com) Connects Rockhampton with Melbourne.

Virgin Blue (☎ 13 67 89; www.virginblue.com.au) Connects Rockhampton with Brisbane and Sydney.

BUS

The operators **Greyhound Australia** (☎ 13 20 30; www.greyhound.com.au) and **Premier Motor Service** (☎ 13 34 10; www.premierms.com.au) both have regular coach services along the Bruce Hwy. Greyhound operates regular services to and from Rockhampton, Gladstone and Agnes Water, while Premier Motor Service runs a Brisbane to Cairns route that stops at Rockhampton.

CAR & MOTORCYCLE

The Bruce Hwy runs all the way up the Capricorn Coast and passes through the region's major hub of Rockhampton.

The Burnett Hwy, which starts at Rockhampton and heads south through the old gold-mining town of Mt Morgan, is an interesting and popular alternative inland route to Brisbane.

TRAIN

Queensland Rail (☎ 13 22 32; www.traveltrain.com.au) operates frequent services between Brisbane, Townsville, Cairns and Longreach. The high-speed *Tilt Train* and the more sedate *Sunlander* operate on the coastal route. The *Spirit of the Outback* leaves Brisbane twice weekly and turns inland from Rockhampton to Longreach. For details, see the Getting There & Away sections of the relevant towns and cities.

AGNES WATER & TOWN OF 1770
☎ 07 / pop 1620

Surrounded by national parks and the Pacific Ocean, the twin coastal towns of Agnes Water and Town of 1770 are among Queensland's most appealing seaside destinations. The tiny settlement of Agnes Water has a lovely white-sand beach, the east coast's most northerly surf beach, while the even tinier Town of 1770 (little more than a marina!) marks Captain Cook's first landing in Queensland. The 'Discovery Coast' is a popular nook for surfing, boating, and fishing away from the crowds. To get here, turn east off the Bruce Hwy at Miriam Vale, 70km south of Gladstone. It's another 57km to Agnes Water and a further 6km to the Town of 1770.

Information

At Miriam Vale is the **Discovery Coast visitors centre** (☎ 4974 5428; 🕑 8.30am-5pm Mon-Fri, 9am-5pm Sat & Sun) but you'll also find visitors centres in town.

The **Agnes Water visitors centre** (☎ 4902 1533; Rural Transaction Centre, 3 Captain Cook Rd; 🕑 8.30am-5pm Mon-Fri, 9am-5pm Sat & Sun) is opposite Endeavour Plaza. Next door, the **Agnes Water Library** (☎ 4902 1515; Rural Transaction Centre, Round Hill Rd; 🕑 9am-4.30pm Mon-Fri) has internet access ($4 for 30 minutes).

The **Discovery Centre** (☎ 4974 7002; Shop 12, Endeavour Plaza, cnr Round Hill Rd & Captain Cook Dr, Agnes Water) is a helpful, privately run information service.

Queensland Parks & Wildlife Service (QPWS; ☎ 4974 9350; www.epa.qld.gov.au; Captain Cook Dr, Town of 1770) has information and brochures on the Eurimbula and Deepwater National Parks. Book camp sites through the Bundaberg office (☎ 4131 1600).

Sights & Activities

The **Miriam Vale Historical Society Museum** (☎ 4974 9511; Springs Rd, Agnes Water; admission adult/child $3/free; 🕑 1-4pm Mon & Wed-Sat, 10am-4pm Sun) displays a small collection of artefacts, rocks and minerals, as well as extracts from Cook's journal and the original telescope from the first lighthouse built on the Queensland coast.

Agnes Water is Queensland's northernmost **surf beach**. Learn to surf on the gentle breaks here with the highly acclaimed **Reef 2 Beach Surf School** (☎ 4974 9072, 0402 328 515; www.reef2beachsurf .com; 1/10 Round Hill Rd, Agnes Water; per lesson $55).

Dive 1770 (☎ 4974 9359; www.dive1770.com) and **1770 Underwater Sea Adventures** (☎ 1300 553 889; www.1770underseaadventures.com.au) offer a range of dive courses (Professional Association of Diving Instructors – PADI – Open Water from $250), Great Barrier Reef and wreck dives ($160).

Round Hill Creek at the Town of 1770 is a calm anchorage for boats, and there's good fishing and mudcrabbing upstream. **Fish 1770 Bait & Tackle** (☎ 4974 9227) at the marina hires out aluminium dinghies (half-/full day $65/95).

Charter boats available for fishing, surfing, snorkelling and diving trips to the Great Barrier Reef include the **MV James Cook** (☎ 4974 9422; www.1770jamescook.com.au). The 14m vessel sleeps up to 10 people for tours of up to seven days. **Hooked on 1770** (☎ 4974 9794) has full- and half-day fishing and scenic charters starting from $55 per person.

You can hire kayaks and canoes on the waterfront just north of the marina from **1770 Liquid Adventures** (☎ 0428-956 630; www.liquidadven tures.com.au; 1hr hire kayak/canoe $25/20) or join a 2½-hour sunset tour (from $30), which offers wine and nibblies along with spectacular sunsets.

Adrenaline junkies can wave-jump, surf and slalom run in a surf-racing boat with **ThunderCat 1770** (☎ 0427-177 000; adult/child $45/35) while **Wyndham Aviation** (☎ 0431-399 626; 1¼hr flight per person $85) flies over the headland for aerial views of dolphins and marine life.

Back on land, ride a chopper along back country roads with **Scooteroo** (☎ 4974 7696; www .scooterrootours.com; 21 Bicentennial Dr; 3hr ride $65; 🕑 3pm summer, 2.30pm winter, by appointment). The 60km tour offers scenic views of the coast and hinterland, with plenty of kangaroos and wallabies thrown in. All you need is a car licence as the machines are fully automatic. Wear long pants and closed-in shoes.

Tours

1770 Larc Tours (☎ 4974 9422; www.1770larctours .com.au) Runs fun full-day tours in its amphibious vehicles. The tours leave from the marina on Monday, Wednesday

STINGERS

The potentially deadly Chironex box jellyfish and Irukandji, also known as sea wasps or 'marine stingers', occur in Queensland's coastal waters north of Agnes Water (occasionally further south) from around October to April, and swimming is not advisable during these times. These potentially lethal jellyfish are usually found close to the coast, especially around river mouths. Fortunately, swimming and snorkelling are usually safe around the reef islands throughout the year; however, the rare and tiny (1cm to 2cm across) Irukandji has been recorded on the outer Reef and islands.

The large (up to 30cm across) Chironex box jellyfish's stinging tentacles spread several metres from its body; by the time victims see the jellyfish, they've already been stung. Treatment is urgent and similar for both species: douse the stings with vinegar (available on many beaches or from nearby houses) and call for an ambulance (if there's a first-aider present, they may have to apply CPR until the ambulance arrives). Do *not* attempt to remove the tentacles.

Some coastal resorts erect 'stinger nets' that provide small areas offering good protection against Chironex, but not necessarily the smaller, rarer Irukandji. Elsewhere, you can wear a stinger suit for protection or simply stay out of the sea when stingers are around.

and Saturday and take in Middle Island, Bustard Head and Eurimbula National Park. It costs $121.50/76.50 per adult/child, including lunch. It also runs daily one-hour sunset cruises ($36.50/21.50).

All Aboard 1770 (☎ 0427-597 122) Dishes up pancakes with maple syrup on its 1½-hour breakfast cruises (adult/child $35/20) along Round Hill Creek. It also offer sunset cruises ($30/15) with tea, coffee and nibblies (BYO alcohol). Cruises leave the marina at 8am and 4.30pm.

Lady Musgrave Cruises (☎ 4974 9077; www .1770reefcruises.com; Captain Cook Dr; adult/child $160/80) Has excellent day trips to Lady Musgrave Island aboard the *Spirit of 1770*. It takes 1¼ hours to get there and five hours is spent at the island and its stunning blue lagoon. Coral viewing in a semisubmersible, lunch, morning and afternoon tea, snorkelling and fishing gear are provided on the cruises which depart the Town of 1770 marina at 8am every morning. For an extra cost you can go diving. Island camping transfers are available for $320 per person, and the company runs a shuttle bus from Bundaberg (per person $10 return).

Sleeping

BUDGET

Most backpacker hostels organise pick-ups from the bus drop offs.

1770 Camping Grounds (☎ 4974 9286; campground1770@bigpond.com; Captain Cook Dr, Town of 1770; unpowered/powered sites $24/27) A large but peaceful park with sites right by the beach and plenty of shady trees. Prices are for two people.

Cool Bananas (☎ 4974 7660; www.coolbananas.net .au; 2 Springs Rd, Agnes Water; dm $25; 🖳) This funky Balinese-themed backpackers has roomy six- and eight-bed dorms, open and airy communal areas, and is only a five-minute walk to the beach

and shops. Otherwise, you can laze the day away in a hammock in the tropical gardens.

1770 Southern Cross Tourist Retreat (☎ 4974 7225; www.1770southerncross.com; 2694 Round Hill Rd, Agnes Water; dm/d incl breakfast $25/65, 2 night minimum stay; 🖳 🖳) More of an ecoresort than a backpackers, this excellent retreat is set on 6.5 hectares of bushland 2.5km out of town. The three- and four-bed dorms are clean, airy, timber cabins (all with en suites), there's an open-air meditation *sala* (where you'll sometimes see visiting Buddhist monks), an ultracool communal chill-out zone, kangaroos in the grounds, and a free shuttle bus to town. Bike hire is free or you can hire a scooter, and you can swim or fish in the lake. Highly recommended.

MIDRANGE & TOP END

Mango Tree Motel (☎ 4974 9132; www.mangotreemotel .com; 7 Agnes St, Agnes Water; s/d from $85/95; 🖳) Only 100m from the beach, this good-value motel offers large self-contained rooms (sleeping up to six) with the option of continental breakfast. There's also a licensed restaurant, Beachside Bar & Restaurant, next door (see p382).

Agnes Palms Beachside Apartments (☎ 4974 7200; www.agnespalms.com; Captain Cook Dr, Agnes Water; motel $75, 1-/2-bedroom apt $85/120; 🖳) Another good-value option are these pleasant fully self-contained apartments, which back onto dense rainforest. Each apartment has undercover car parking and private BBQ or you can bunk down in a motel room. A 300m boardwalk through the rainforest leads to the beach.

Sovereign Lodge (☎ 4974 9257; www.1770sovereignlodge .com; 1 Elliot St, Town of 1770; d $120-220; 🖳 🖳) This lovely boutique accommodation has a range of immaculate self-contained rooms, some with excellent views from its hilltop perch. There's also a Balinese 'Body Temple' here where, among other offerings, you can be massaged, wrapped in clay, rubbed with hot rocks and scrubbed with salt.

ourpick Sandcastles 1770 Motel & Resort (☎ 07-4974 9428; www.sandcastles1770.com.au; 1 Grahame Colyer Dr, Agnes Water; d garden villas/beach-home apt from $130/160; ❄ ▢ ☙) Set on 4 hectares of landscaped gardens and subtropical vegetation, Sandcastles has a range of accommodation options from well above average motel-style backpacker dorms ($25) to luxury beach-home apartments and villas. The funky one- to four-bedroom Balinese-themed villas are large and airy and open on to a central courtyard. Some have a private pool. There's also a popular restaurant, Kahunas (see below), here as well as a small café.

Beach Shacks (☎ 4974 9463; www.1770beachshacks .com; 578 Captain Cook Dr, Town of 1770; d from $168) These delightful self-contained tropical 'shacks' are decorated in timber, cane and bamboo. They offer grand ocean views and magnificent private accommodation just a minute's walk from the water.

Eating

ourpick Saltwater Café 1770 & Tree Bar (☎ 4974 9599; Captain Cook Dr, Town of 1770; mains $10-26; ❄ lunch & dinner) This little salt-encrusted waterfront diner has plenty of charm and an atmospheric bar. Seafood is a prime offering – go for the mud crabs – and the pizzas are excellent.

Kahunas Pizza Bar & Grill (☎ 4974 9428; 1 Grahame Colyer Dr, Agnes Water; mains $10-30; ❄ dinner) At Sandcastles, Kahunas is a popular choice, especially for beer and pizza on a hot night. There's plenty of meat on the char-grill and the Moreton Bay bugs come in chilli, citrus, mornay or garlic sauce.

Beachside Bar & Restaurant (☎ 4974 9614; 7 Agnes St, Agnes Water; mains $13-28; ❄ breakfast, lunch & dinner) You can dine alfresco or indoors at this good restaurant next to Mango Tree Motel and the Agnes beach car park. The menu features seafood, poultry, meat and pasta, and the duck risotto is a recommended choice.

Yok Attack (☎ 4974 7454; Shop 22, Endeavour Plaza, cnr Captain Cook Dr & Round Hill Rd, Agnes Water; mains $15-25; ❄ lunch & dinner Thu-Tue) This simple Thai restaurant is very popular with the locals and is highly recommended.

Aggies Restaurant (☎ 4974 9469; Agnes Water Tavern, 1 Tavern Rd, Agnes Water; mains $22-28; ❄ lunch & dinner) The large bistro in the tavern offers massive steaks and classic seafood baskets without much atmosphere but the shaded outdoor dining area is quite nice and the bar is a good place to meet the locals.

Getting There & Away

BUS

Only one of several daily **Greyhound** (☎ 13 20 30; www.greyhound.com.au) buses detours off the Bruce Hwy to Agnes Water; the direct bus from Bundaberg ($24, 1½ hours) arrives opposite Cool Bananas at 6.10pm. Others, including **Premier Motor Service** (☎ 13 34 10; www.premierms .com.au), drop passengers at Fingerboard Rd, where a local **shuttle service** (phone 'Macca' ☎ 4974 7540; $24) meets the bus.

EURIMBULA & DEEPWATER NATIONAL PARKS

South of Agnes Water is Deepwater National Park, an unspoiled coastal landscape with long sandy beaches, freshwater creeks, good fishing spots and two camping grounds. It's also a major breeding ground for loggerhead turtles, which dig nests and lay eggs on the beaches between November and February. You can watch nesting turtles and see emerging hatchlings at night between January and April, but you need to observe various precautions outlined in the QPWS park brochure (obtainable at the office in Town of 1770).

The northern park entrance is 8km south of Agnes Water and is only accessible by 4WD. It's another 5km to the basic camping ground at Middle Rock (no facilities) and a further 2km to the Wreck Rock camping ground and picnic areas, with rain and bore water and composting toilets. Wreck Point can also be accessed from the south by 2WD vehicles via Baffle Creek.

The 78-sq-km Eurimbula National Park, on the northern side of Round Hill Creek, has a landscape of dunes, mangroves and eucalypt forest. There are two basic camping grounds, one at Middle Creek with toilets only and the other at Bustard Beach with toilets and limited rainwater. The main access road to the park is about 10km southwest of Agnes Water.

Middle Rock in Deepwater and Middle Creek in Eurimbula have self-registration stands but you must obtain permits for the other campgrounds from the **Bundaberg QPWS** (☎ 4131 1600).

GLADSTONE

☎ 07 / pop 28,810

On first impression, the industrial town of Gladstone with its busy port, coal- and bauxite-loading terminals, oil tanks, alumina refinery and power station is rather uninspiring. Sometimes first impressions are right. There's little in the way to keep you in town; head straight for the marina, the main departure point for boats to the southern coral cay islands of Heron, Masthead and Wilson on the Great Barrier Reef.

Information

Gladstone City Library (☎ 4976 6400; 39 Goondoon St; 9.30am-5.45pm Mon-Fri, 9.30am-7.45pm Thu, 9am-4.30pm Sat) Free internet access but you must book in advance.

QPWS (☎ 4971 6500; 3rd fl, 136 Goondoon St; 8.30am-4.30pm Mon-Fri) Provides information on all the southern Great Barrier Reef islands, as well as the area's mainland parks.

Visitors centre (☎ 4972 9000; Bryan Jordan Dr; 8.30am-5pm Mon-Fri, 9am-5pm Sat & Sun) Located at the marina.

Sights & Activities

If you have time to spare, drive up to the **Auckland Point Lookout** for views over Gladstone harbour, the port facilities and shipping terminals. A brass tablet on the lookout maps the harbour and its many islands.

The **Toondoon Botanic Gardens** (☎ 4971 4444; Glenlyon Rd; admission free; 9am-6pm Oct-Mar, 8.30am-5.30pm Apr-Sep), about 7km south of town, comprises 83 hectares of rainforest, lakes and Australian native plants. There's a visitor centre, an orchid house, and free one-hour guided tours between February and November (tours can be booked at the gardens or visitors centre). The gardens have wheelchair access.

In the old town hall, the **Gladstone Art Gallery & Museum** (☎ 4976 6766; cnr Goondoon & Bramston Sts; admission free; 10am-5pm Mon-Fri, to 4pm Sat) displays a rolling programme of local and national exhibitions.

The picturesque **Gecko Valley Winery** (☎ 4979 0400; www.geckovalley.com.au; Glenlyon Rd; 11am-4pm Tue-Sun) offers wine tasting in a bush setting adjacent to the botanic gardens.

For those who have even more time in Gladstone, **Sable Chief Marine** (☎ 4972 3006) offers PADI dive courses ($545).

If you're in the area, **market days** (ask the visitors centre for dates) at the **Calliope River Historical Village** (☎ 4975 7428; Dawson Hwy, Calliope; admission $2; 8am-4pm), 26km south of Gladstone, are hugely popular. Held six times a year, the 200-plus stalls of arts, crafts, clothes, jewellery and local produce attracts over 3000 people. While here you can wander around the historical village's restored heritage buildings, including an old pub (licensed on market days), church, schoolhouse and a slab hut.

Tours

Gladstone's various industries, including the alumina refineries, aluminium smelter, power station and port authority, offer free **industry tours**. The one- or 1½-hour tours start at different times on different days of the week. Book at the visitors centre.

Curtis Ferry Services (☎ 4972 6990; www.curtisferryservices.com.au) Has a morning coffee cruise (adult/child $18/10, 10.40am April to October) leaving the marina every Wednesday, taking in the highlights of the Gladstone harbour. It also connects Gladstone with Curtis Island.

MV Mikat (☎ 4972 3415; www.mikat.com.au) Fishing, diving and sightseeing cruises to the Swains and Bunker Island groups are the speciality of the 20m MV *Mikat*. Cruises are a minimum of three days.

ART DETOUR

Cedar Galleries (☎ 4975 0444; enquiries@cedargalleries.com.au; Bruce Hwy; 9am-4pm Thu-Sun) is a tranquil artists' bush retreat where you can watch painters and sculptors at work in the hand-built slab-hut studios. To unleash your creative genius you can take **art classes** (9am-12.30pm Sat; per lesson $10) or just browse the gardens and the gallery. There's also a café, a beautiful hand-crafted wedding chapel, and winery cellar door but no accommodation, although aspiring artists are welcome to pitch a tent or sleep on the floor. If you're here on the first Sunday of the month you can watch local musicians do their thing at the monthly 'rock-star boot camp' (admission $12).

This unique artists' colony (30km south of Gladstone) is signposted off the Bruce Hwy, 7km south of Calliope.

CAPRICORN COAST

DETOUR: CURTIS ISLAND

Curtis Island, just across the water from Gladstone, can't be confused with a resort island. Apart from swimming, fishing and curling up with a good book, its only real drawcard is the annual appearance of rare flatback turtles on its eastern shores between November and January. With advance notice (contact the Gladstone or Bundaberg QPWS), you can accompany the volunteer rangers on their nightly patrols. There's a free council camping ground and basic, self-contained units at **Capricorn Lodge** (☎ 4972 0222; d $90). **Curtis Ferry Services** (☎ 4972 6990; www.curtisferryser vices.com.au; return adult/child/family $28/20/76) connects the island with Gladstone on Monday, Wednesday, Friday, Saturday and Sunday.

Sleeping

Gladstone Backpackers (☎ 4972 5744; gladstoneback packers@aapt.net.au; 12 Rollo St; dm/d $25/55; 🖥 🖭) This fairly central hostel has recently undergone renovations – with more to come. It's a friendly, family-run place in an old Queenslander, with a large kitchen, clean bathrooms and an airy outside deck. There's free use of bicycles and free pick-ups from the marina, bus, train and airport.

Barney Beach Caravan Park (☎ 4972 1366; barney beachqpark@bigpond.com.au; Friend St; unpowered/powered sites $25/26, cabins $60-125; 🏊 🖥 🖭) About 2km east of the city centre and close to the foreshore, this is the most central of the caravan parks. It's large and tidy, with a good camp kitchen and excellent self-contained accommodation. Complimentary transfers to the marina are available for guests visiting Heron Island. Buslink Queensland runs buses here; see opposite.

Auckland Hill B&B (☎ 4972 4907; www.ahbb.com .au; 15 Yarroon St; s/d $120/175; 🏊 🖭) The Auckland is a sprawling, comfortable Queenslander that provides six spacious rooms that come with king-sized beds. Each room is differently decorated: there is a spa suite and one with wheelchair access.

Harbour City Motel (☎ 4976 7100; harbourcitymotel@ yahoo.com.au; 20-24 William St; r $130) This decent motel in the centre of town has large rooms with modern bathrooms, and the motel has a licensed steakhouse.

Eating & Drinking

Gladstone Yacht Club (☎ 4972 8611; 1 Goondoon St; mains $10-19; 🕥 lunch & dinner) With daily buffet specials, the yacht club is a popular place to wine and dine on a budget. Dine on the deck overlooking the water.

Scotties Bar & Restaurant (☎ 4972 9999; 46 Goondoon St; mains $12-35; 🕥 dinner Mon-Sat, lunch Fri only) Thai, Mediterranean, steak, seafood and pasta: this popular restaurant with a decidedly blue theme has an eclectic and always changing menu that includes a couple of vegetarian options. The walls bear interesting local artwork, and you can sit on the outside deck in the main street.

Kapers BYO (☎ 4972 7902; 124b Goondoon St; mains $26-30; 🕥 dinner Mon-Sat) A bright, breezy, offbeat place with hand-painted tables, blackboards scrawled with gems on the meaning of life – including a memo from God – and an imaginative and varied menu.

Flinders (☎ 4972 8322; 2 Oaka Lane; mains $30-40; 🕥 dinner Mon-Sat) This cosy restaurant specialises in seafood with tasty dishes such as steamed mud crabs served with hot butter, or with garlic cream, or Singapore-style chilli.

Bojangles Brasserie & Piano Bar (☎ 4972 2847; 6 Goondoon St) Cocktails and live bands.

Entertainment

Gladstone Entertainment Centre (☎ 4972 2822; 58 Goondoon St; 🕥 box office 8.30am-5.30pm Mon-Fri, 9am-12.30pm Sat) Showcases various visiting live acts.

Players International Nightclub (☎ 4972 6333; Flinders Pde; 🕥 10pm-late) For late-night drinking and dancing.

Getting There & Away

AIR

Qantaslink (☎ 13 13 13; www.qantas.com.au) has several daily flights between Brisbane and Gladstone ($110, 70 minutes) and two flights a day between Rockhampton and Gladstone ($85, 25 minutes). The airport is 7km from the centre.

BUS

Greyhound Australia (☎ 13 20 30; www.greyhound.com .au) has several coach services from Brisbane ($105, 10½ hours), Bundaberg ($45, 1½ hours) and Rockhampton ($34, 2½ hours). The terminal for long-distance buses is at the Mobil 24 Hour Roadhouse, on the Dawson Hwy about 200m southwest of the centre.

BOAT

Curtis Ferry Services (☎ 4972 6990; www.curtisferryservices.com.au) has regular services to Curtis Island (opposite) five days per week. The service leaves from the Gladstone marina and stops at Farmers Point on Facing Island en route. Transport to North West and Masthead Islands can be arranged on request.

You can also access the islands with various charter operators (p383).

If you've booked a stay on Heron Island, the resort operates a launch (adult/child $110/55, two hours) which leaves the Gladstone marina at 11am daily.

TRAIN

Queensland Rail (☎ 13 22 32; www.traveltrain.com.au) has frequent north- and southbound services passing through Gladstone daily. The *Tilt Train* stops in Gladstone from Brisbane ($92.40, 6½ hours) and Rockhampton ($28.60, one hour). The more sedate *Sunlander* and *Spirit of the Outback* trains take far longer.

Getting Around

Gladstone Airport is 7km south-west of town. **Buslink Queensland** (☎ 4972 1670) has four services daily from the airport into town. Catch either bus 2 or 3 and expect to pay from $1 to $3 depending on the route.

In general, public transport to places around Gladstone is severely limited. **Buslink Queensland** (☎ 4972 1670) runs local bus services on weekdays only, including a service along Goondoon St to Barney Point (and the rather unattractive Barney beach), which stops out the front of the caravan park there.

To book a taxi, call **Blue & White Taxis** (☎ 13 10 08).

AROUND GLADSTONE

Tannum Sands & Boyne Island

☎ 07 / pop 4140 & 3690

On the coast, 20km southeast of Gladstone, Tannum Sands is the local beachside hang-out. It's a quiet seaside village with a long stretch of pleasant parkland with BBQs and playgrounds along the foreshore at Millenium Esplanade. Across the Boyne River, Boyne Island is even less developed but both areas are popular with fishing and boating enthusiasts.

Boyne Island Motel & Villas (☎ 4973 7444; www.boynemotel.com.au; 3 Orana Ave; d $85, 1-/2-bedroom villas $115/155; ✠ ▣) has roomy self-contained cabins in tropical gardens close to the beach.

Next door is **Breezes Café** (☎ 4973 3267; 1 Orana Ave; mains $13-27; ⏰ lunch & dinner Wed-Sat, breakfast & lunch Sun), about your only option other than shopping-centre cafés.

Lake Awoonga

Created by the construction of the Awoonga Dam in 1984, Lake Awoonga is a popular recreational area 30km south of Gladstone. Backed by the rugged **Mt Castletower National Park**, the lake has landscaped picnic areas, a café, BBQs, walking trails and bird life. You can hire canoes, boats and fishing gear (the lake is stocked with barramundi) from the **Lake Awoonga Caravan Park** (☎ 4975 0155; barraheaven@hotkey.com.au; Lake Awoonga Rd, Benaraby; unpowered/powered sites $20/25, cabins from $75).

SOUTHERN REEF ISLANDS

If you've ever had 'castaway' dreams of tiny coral atolls fringed with sugary white sand and turquoise blue seas, you've found your island paradise in the southern Great Barrier Reef islands. From beautiful Lady Elliot Island, 80km northeast of Bundaberg, secluded and uninhabited coral reefs and atolls dot the ocean for about 140km up to Tryon Island, east of Rockhampton.

Several cays in this part of the Reef are excellent for snorkelling, diving and just getting back to nature – though reaching them is generally more expensive than reaching islands nearer the coast. Some of the islands are important breeding grounds for turtles and seabirds, and visitors should be aware of precautions to ensure the wildlife's protection, outlined in the relevant QPWS information sheets.

Camping is allowed on Lady Musgrave, Masthead and North West national park islands, and campers must be totally self-sufficient. Numbers are limited, so it's advisable to apply well ahead for a camping permit ($4.50/18 per person/family). Contact the Gladstone **QPWS** (☎ 13 13 04; 4971 6500; 136 Goondoon St) or book online (www.epa.qld.gov.au).

Access is from Bundaberg, Town of 1770, Gladstone, or Rosslyn Bay near Yeppoon.

Lady Elliot Island

On the southern frontier of the Great Barrier Reef, Lady Elliot is a 40-hectare vegetated coral cay popular with divers, snorkellers and nesting sea turtles. The island is a breeding and nesting ground for many species of tropical seabirds but its stunning underwater landscape is the main attraction. Divers can walk straight off the beach to explore an ocean-bed of shipwrecks, coral gardens, bommies (coral pinnacles or outcroppings) and blowholes.

Lady Elliot Island is not a national park, and camping is not allowed. Your only option is the low-key **Lady Elliot Island Resort** (☎ 1800 072 200; www.ladyelliot.com.au; per person tents from $149, rooms from $189). Accommodation at this no-frills resort is in basic tent cabins, simple motel-style units, or more expensive two-bedroom self-contained suites. Rates include breakfast and dinner, snorkelling gear and some tours.

The only way to reach the island is in a light aircraft. Seair (book through the resort) flies guests to the resort from Bundaberg and Hervey Bay for $219/119 per adult/child return. You can also visit the island on a day trip from Bundaberg and Hervey Bay for $275/146 (the price includes lunch and snorkelling gear).

Lady Musgrave Island

This tiny 15-hectare cay 100km northeast of Bundaberg sits on the western rim of a stunning turquoise blue reef lagoon renowned for its safe swimming, snorkelling and diving. A squeaky-white-sand beach fringes a dense canopy of pisonia forest, which brims with roosting bird life, including terns, shearwaters and white-capped noddies.

The entire island is an uninhabited national park and there is a QPWS camping ground on the island's west side. The camping ground has bush toilets but little else and campers must be totally self-sufficient, even bringing their own water. Numbers are limited to 40 at any one time, so apply well ahead for a permit through the **Environmental Protection Agency** (☎ 13 13 04; www.epa.qld.gov.au; per person/family $4.50/18).

Lady Musgrave Cruises (☎ 1800 631 770, 4974 9077; www.1770reefcruises.com; adult/child $160/80) operates transfers and day trips from the Town of 1770 marina (see p381).

Heron & Wilson Islands

With the underwater reef world accessible directly from the beach, Heron Island is famed for superb scuba diving and snorkelling, although you'll need a fair amount of cash to visit. A true coral cay, it is densely vegetated with pisonia trees and surrounded by 24 sq km of reef. There's a resort and research sta-

tion on the northeastern third of the island; the remainder is national park.

Heron Island Resort (☎ 4972 9055, 1800 737 678; www.heronisland.com; s/d incl buffet breakfast from $399/420) covers the northeastern third of the island. Its comfortable accommodation is suited to families and couples; the Point Suites have the best views. Meal packages are extra, and guests will pay $200/100 per adult/child for launch transfer, or $440/270 for helicopter transfer. Both operate from Gladstone.

Wilson Island (www.wilsonisland.com; 2 nights incl all meals s/d from $1530/1980), also part of a national park, is an exclusive wilderness retreat with six permanent tents and solar-heated showers. There are excellent beaches and superb snorkelling. The only access is from Heron Island and you'll need to buy a combined Wilson-Heron package and spend at least two nights on Wilson Island. Transfers between Wilson and Heron are included in the tariff.

ROCKHAMPTON
☎ 07 / pop 60,830

If the wide-brimmed hats, cowboy boots, and V8 utes don't tip you off, the large bull statues around town let you know you're in the 'beef capital' of Australia. With over 2.5 million cattle within a 250km radius of Rockhampton, it's no surprise the smell of bulldust hangs thick in the air. This sprawling country town is the administrative and commercial centre of central Queensland, its wide streets and fine Victorian-era buildings reflecting the region's prosperous 19th-century heyday of gold and copper mining and the beef cattle industry.

Straddling the tropic of Capricorn, 'Rocky' marks the start of the tropics but lying 40km inland and lacking coastal sea breezes, summers here can be unbearably hot and humid. Rocky has a smattering of attractions but is best seen as the gateway to the coastal gems of Yeppoon and Great Keppel Island.

Orientation

Rockhampton is about 40km from the coast. Queensland's largest river, the Fitzroy, flows through the heart of the city, with the small commercial centre (the oldest part of Rocky) on the southern bank. The long Fitzroy Bridge connects the city centre with the newer northern suburbs. Coming in from the south, the Bruce Hwy skirts the centre and crosses the river via the Neville Hewitt Bridge.

EXPERIENCING THE GREAT BARRIER REEF

The Great Barrier Reef is one of Australia's World Heritage areas and one of the seven wonders of the natural world. Stretching 2000km from just south of the tropic of Capricorn (near Gladstone) to Torres Strait (just south of New Guinea), it is the most extensive reef system in the world.

The southern and fragmented end of the reef spreads itself as far as 300km from the mainland, but at the northern end the reef sits close to the coast in continuous stretches up to 80km wide. The lagoon between the outer reef and the mainland is dotted with smaller reefs, cays and islands. It's said you could dive here every day of your life and still not see the entire Great Barrier Reef. Consequently, selecting where to get wet can be quite bewildering. Some of the most popular ports providing good access to the reef are detailed here.

Agnes Water & Town of 1770

Tours (p380) take you to the beautiful reef lagoon at **Lady Musgrave Island**, for excellent snorkelling and diving.

Gladstone

Gladstone (p383) is the closest access point to the southern Reef islands and innumerable cays. Among these is **Lady Elliot Island** (p385).

Airlie Beach

The big attraction at Airlie Beach (p410) is spending two or more days aboard a boat and seeing some of the fringing coral reefs amid the **Whitsunday Islands**. There are, however, several fast catamarans that zoom out to pontoons moored on spectacular **Knuckle** and **Hardy Reefs**, which provide outstanding snorkelling and diving.

Townsville

Near Townsville (p424), **Kelso Reef** and the **Yongala shipwreck** are teeming with marine life. As well as overnight tours for divers, there are one- or two- day-trip options in glass-bottomed boats. The **Reef HQ Aquarium**, which is the Great Barrier Reef in a nutshell, is also here.

Mission Beach

Closer to the reef than any other gateway destination, Mission Beach (p440) is small and quiet and has a few boat and diving tours to the outer reef. Although the choice isn't big, neither are the crowds.

Cairns

The main launching pad for Great Barrier Reef tours: from Cairns (p450) you can do anything from relatively inexpensive day trips on huge, crowded boats to intimate five-day luxury charters. Some operators go as far north as **Lizard Island** for spectacular night diving and the famous Cod Hole.

Port Douglas

This swanky resort town (p463) is the gateway to the **Low Isles** and the **Agincourt Reef**, an outer ribbon reef with crystal-clear water and particularly stunning coral. Diving, snorkelling and cruising trips tend to be classier, pricier and less crowded than in Cairns.

Cooktown

The lure of Cooktown (p474) is its close proximity to **Lizard Island**. A handful of tour operators promise unrushed experiences, but operations pretty much shut down between November and May.

Information

Capricorn visitors centre (☎ 4927 2055; Gladstone Rd; ◷ 9am-5pm) Helpful centre on the highway beside the tropic of Capricorn marker, 3km south of the centre.

Cyber Oz Internet Café (☎ 4927 3633; 24 William St; ◷ 9am-5.30pm Mon-Thu, 9am-5pm Fri; per hr $5)
Post office (☎ 13 13 18; 150 East St; ◷ 9am-5pm Mon-Fri)

CAPRICORN COAST

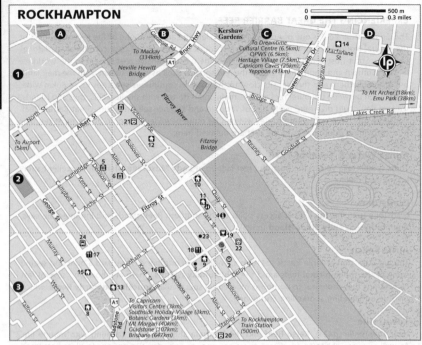

Sights & Activities

Rockhampton's **Botanic Gardens** (☎ 4922 1654; Spencer St; admission free; ☻ 6am-6pm) is a beautiful oasis with impressive banyan figs, tropical and subtropical rainforest, landscaped gardens and lily-covered lagoons just south of town. There's a formal Japanese garden, a café, and a small **zoo** (☻ 8am-5pm) with koalas, wombats, dingoes and a walk-through aviary.

In town, **Quay Street** has grand sandstone Victorian-era buildings dating back to the gold-rush days. You can pick up town walking maps from the visitors centres.

The excellent **Rockhampton City Art Gallery** (☎ 4927 7129; 62 Victoria Pde; admission free; ☻ 10am-4pm Tue-Fri, 11am-4pm Sat & Sun) boasts an impressive collection of Australian paintings, including works by Sir Russell Drysdale, Sir Sidney Nolan and Albert Namatjira. Contemporary indigenous artist Judy Watson also has a number of works on display. The permanent collection is supplemented by innovative temporary exhibitions, for which there are varying admission charges.

About 7km north of town, the **Dreamtime Cultural Centre** (☎ 4936 1655; www.dreamtimecentre .com.au; Bruce Hwy; adult/child $13.50/6.50; ☻ 10am-3.30pm Mon-Fri, tours 10.30am & 1pm) is an engaging exploration of regional indigenous heritage and includes an art gallery, a sporting hall of fame, interpretive walking trails and excellent 90-minute tours.

The **Archer Park Station & Steam Tram Museum** (☎ 4922 2774; Denison St; adult/child/family $6.60/4.50/15; ☻ 9am-4pm Sun-Fri) is housed in a former train station built in 1899. Through photographs and displays it tells the station's story, and that of the unique Purrey steam tram

Next door is the **Central Queensland Military & Artifacts Association Inc** (☎ 4921 0648; 40 Archer St; adult/concession $5/4; ☻ 9am-4pm), with dis-

INFORMATION		
Cyber Oz Internet Café.............1 C3	Coffee House.............................9 B3	Restaurant 98.......................(see 12)
Post Office...................................2 C3	Criterion Hotel.......................10 B2	Thai Tanee.................................18 B3
Rockhampton Library.................3 B3	Downtown Backpackers...........11 B2	
Rockhampton Visitors Centre......4 C2	Motel 98..................................12 B2	**DRINKING** 🍸
	Rockhampton	Ginger Mule..............................19 C3
SIGHTS & ACTIVITIES	Plaza Hotel..........................13 B3	
Archer Park Station & Steam Tram	Rockhampton YHA...................14 D1	**ENTERTAINMENT** 🎭
Museum.................................5 A2	Welcome Hotel Motel..............15 A3	Great Western Hotel.................20 C3
Central Queensland Military &		Pilbeam Theatre........................21 B1
Artifacts Association Inc..........6 B2	**EATING** 🍴	Stadium.....................................22 C3
Rockhampton City Art Gallery....7 B1	Bush Inn Bar	
	& Grill.................................(see 10)	**TRANSPORT**
SLEEPING 🛏	Coffee House..........................(see 9)	Kern Arcade.............................23 B3
Central Park Motel.....................8 A3	Gnomes...................................16 B3	Mobil Roadhouse.....................24 A3
	Pacino's...................................17 A3	Sunbus Terminus...................(see 23)

plays of Australian involvement in various military campaigns and wars. During WWII Rockhampton was home to 76,000 US servicemen and there's plenty of American memorabilia on display. Look out for some interesting 'trench art' pieces fashioned from discarded ammo casings, bullet shells and the like.

Rockhampton's **Heritage Village** (☎ 4936 1026; Bruce Hwy; adult/child/family $7.70/4.50/22.70; ⏰ 9am-4pm), 10km north of the city centre, is an interactive museum of replica historic buildings set in lovely landscaped gardens, and even has townspeople at work in period garb. There's also an visitors centre here.

Just north of the Fitzroy River, **Kershaw Gardens** (☎ 4936 8254; via Charles St; admission free; ⏰ 6am-6pm) is an excellent botanical park devoted to Australian native plants. Its attractions include artificial rapids, a rainforest area, a fragrant garden and heritage architecture.

As a backdrop to the city, **Mt Archer** rises 604m out of the landscape northeast of Rockhampton, offering stunning views of the city and hinterland from the summit, especially at night. It's an environmental park with walking trails weaving through eucalypts and rainforest.

Tours

Highly recommended is **Capricorn Dave's Beef n Reef Adventures** (☎ 1800 753 786, 0427-159 655; www .capricorndave.com.au; day trip $99). The whirlwind adventure tours around Rocky's hidden bush gems, swimming in billabongs, visiting an outback cattle station, and getting close to Australian wildlife. Lunch and transfers to and from your accommodation are included in the action-packed full-day tour. The random adventures continue on overnight trips with night-time wildlife spotting and cattle farm camping.

Sleeping

BUDGET

Downtown Backpackers (☎ 4922 1837; fax 4922 1050; Oxford Hotel, 91 East St; dm $20; 🖥) Located upstairs over a boisterous bar, Downtown Backpackers offers basic, budget accommodation right in the centre of town. YHA and VIP members receive discounts.

Southside Holiday Village (☎ 1800 075 911, 4927 3013; www.sshv.com.au; Lower Dawson Rd; unpowered/powered sites $20/26, cabins $45-85; 🏊) This is one of the city's best caravan parks. It has neat, self-contained cabins with elevated decking, large grassed camp sites, a courtesy coach and a good camp kitchen. It's about 3km south of the centre.

Rockhampton YHA (☎ 1800 617 194, 4927 5288; www .yha.com.au; 60 MacFarlane St; dm $22, d $50-59; 🔌 🖥 🏊) The Rocky YHA has a spacious lounge and dining area and a well-equipped kitchen. It has six- and nine- bed dorms as well as doubles and cabins with bathrooms and there's a large patch of lawn to toss a ball around. The hostel arranges tours, has courtesy pick-ups from the bus station, and is an agent for Premier and Greyhound buses.

Criterion Hotel (☎ 4922 1225; www.thecriterion .com.au; 150 Quay St; s/d $45/65, motel $108; 🔌) The Criterion is Rockhampton's grandest old pub with an elegant foyer and function room, a friendly bar and a great bistro (p390). Its top two storeys have dozens of period rooms, some of them beautifully restored, but although the rooms have showers the toilets are down the hall. The hotel also has a number of new 4.5-star motel rooms.

MIDRANGE & TOP END

Welcome Home Motel (☎ 4927 7800; 156 George St; s/d $78/85; 🔌) On a busy thoroughfare, this basic motel has large, quite comfortable rooms but has a curious lack of bench space or hand basins in the bathrooms.

Rockhampton Plaza Hotel (☎ 4927 5855; www
.rockhamptonplaza.com.au; 161-7 George St; d $105-115;
🅿 🖭 🖳 ; wi-fi) The Plaza has well-appointed,
pretty typical four-star hotel rooms that overlook a park. There's a bar and restaurant and
it's located a short stroll southwest of the centre and close to the train station.

Central Park Motel (☎ 4927 2333; CENPARK@bigpond
.com; 224 Murray St; s/d $106/121; 🅿 🖳) In a quiet
street opposite a park but close to the town
centre, this motel has large rooms and suites
catering for singles to families.

Coffee House (☎ 4927 5722; www.coffeehouse
.com.au; 51 William St; r from 155; 🅿 🖳) Generally
popular with the business traveller, the Coffee
House features beautifully appointed motel
rooms, self-contained apartments and spa
suites in central Rocky. There is a popular and
stylish café-restaurant-wine bar (see below)
on site.

Motel 98 (☎ 4927 5322; www.98.com.au; 98 Victoria
Pde; d $155; 🅿 🖭 🖳) The smart Motel 98 has
well-appointed, spacious rooms around a
pool. The restaurant (see right) has a terrace
overlooking the river, and a sound reputation
as one of the best restaurants in town.

Eating & Drinking

Thai Tanee (☎ 4922 1255; cnr William & Bolsover Sts; mains
$10-20; 🕒 dinner) This unpretentious restaurant
is recommended by the locals for consistently
good Thai food.

Bush Inn Bar & Grill (☎ 4922 1225; Criterion Hotel,
150 Quay St; dishes $10-20; 🕒 lunch & dinner) The Bush
Inn has a modern western theme with stone
floors, wooden booths and tables, and huge
steaks to match. It's a popular spot for a drink
and good pub grub.

Gnomes (☎ 4927 4713; 106 William St; mains $13-19;
🕒 lunch & dinner Tue-Sun) In this charming courtyard café, you'll find gluten-free and vegetarian dishes in a casual BYO setting.

Coffee House (☎ 4927 5722; 51 William St; mains
$20-30; 🕒 breakfast & lunch daily, dinner Mon-Sat) A
stylish though relaxed café-restaurant-wine
bar (with an extensive wine list – and big
Sunday brunches), this is also a popular spot
to indulge in local seafood and beef.

our pick Pacino's (☎ 4922 5833; cnr Fitzroy &
George Sts; mains $20-37; 🕒 dinner Tue-Sun) Oozing
Mediterranean warmth with its stone floors,
wooden tables and potted fig trees, this stylish
restaurant serves delicious Italian favourites
such as *osso bucco* and pasta cooked a dozen
different ways.

Restaurant 98 (☎ 4927 5322; www.98.com.au; 98
Victoria Pde; mains $22-37 🕒 lunch & dinner) One of
Rocky's finest, this licensed dining room features modern Australian versions of kangaroo,
steak, lamb and seafood. Sit inside or on the
terrace overlooking the Fitzroy River.

Ginger Mule (☎ 4927 7255; William St; 🕒 4pm-late
Wed-Sat) An urban-chic wine bar, this place
draws the Friday night crowd for a spot of
tapas and cocktails.

Entertainment

Great Western Hotel (☎ 4922 3888; 39 Stanley St)
Looking like a spaghetti western film set, this
grand old pub is home to Rocky's cowboys
and gals. Out back there's a rodeo arena where
every Friday night bucking bulls toss cowboys
in the air. Great entertainment!

Stadium (☎ 4927 9988; 234 Quay St; admission after
10pm $7; 🕒 late Fri & Sat) This is the place most
partygoers head after the pubs. It's a large,
flashy club with a sporty theme – you dance
on a mini basketball court.

Pilbeam Theatre (☎ 4927 4111; Victoria Pde)
This plush 967-seat theatre is located in the
Rockhampton Performing Arts Complex and
hosts a range of national and international
acts.

Getting There & Away
AIR
Jetstar, Qantas, Tiger Airways and Virgin Blue
connect Rockhampton with various cities. See
p379 for more details.

BUS
Greyhound Australia (☎ 13 20 30; www.greyhound.com
.au) has regular services from Rocky to Mackay
($60, four hours), Brisbane ($114, 11 hours)
and Cairns ($178, 18 hours). All services stop
at the **Mobil roadhouse** (91 George St). **Premier Motor
Service** (☎ 13 34 10; www.premierms.com.au) operates a Brisbane–Cairns service, stopping
at Rockhampton.

Young's Bus Service (☎ 4922 3813) to Yeppoon
($8.10, 45 minutes) includes a loop through
Rosslyn Bay and Emu Park. Buses departs
from the Kern Arcade in Bolsover St.

TRAIN
The **Queensland Rail** (☎ 1300 131 722, 4932 0453) *Tilt
Train* and *Sunlander* connect Rockhampton
with Brisbane (from $102) and Cairns ($167).
The journey takes seven to 11 hours, depend-
ing on which service you take. The *Spirit of*

CAPRICORN CAVES & BENT-WING BATS

In the Berserker Ranges, 24km north of Rockhampton near the Caves township, the amazing **Capricorn Caves** (☎ 4934 2883; www.capricorncaves.com.au; Caves Rd; adult/child $20/10; ☽ 9am-4pm) are not to be missed. These ancient caves honeycomb a limestone ridge and on a guided tour through the caverns and labyrinths you'll see cave coral, stalactites, dangling fig-tree roots, and little insectivorous bats. The highlight of the one-hour Cathedral tour is the beautiful natural rock cathedral where a haunting rendition of 'Amazing Grace' is played to demonstrate the cavern's incredible acoustics. Every December traditional Christmas carol sing-alongs are held in the cathedral. Also in December, around the summer solstice (1 December to 14 January), sunlight beams directly through a 14m vertical shaft into Belfry Cave creating an electrifying light show. If you stand directly below the beam, reflected sunlight colours the whole cavern with whatever colour you're wearing.

Daring spelunkers can book a two-hour adventure tour ($60) that takes you through tight spots with names such as 'Fat Man's Misery'. You must be at least 16 years old for this tour.

The Capricorn Caves complex has BBQ areas, a pool, kiosk, and **accommodation** (unpowered/powered sites $20/25, cabins from $90). Prices are for two people.

Nearby, **Mt Etna National Park** (☎ 4936 0511; adult/child $8/4; ☽ tours 5.30pm Mon, Wed, Fri & Sat Dec-Feb) is one of only five known maternity sites of the little bent-wing bat and accommodates 80% of the Australian population. There are no facilities and access is restricted. Rangers run night tours of the bat caves (bookings essential) from the Caves township.

---

the *Outback* also connects Rockhampton with Brisbane ($102, 10 hours), Emerald ($94, five hours), and Longreach ($111, 11 hours) twice weekly. The train station is 450m southwest of the city centre.

Getting Around

Rockhampton airport is 5km south of the centre. **Sunbus** (☎ 4936 2133) runs a reasonably comprehensive city bus network operating all day Monday to Friday and Saturday morning. All services terminate in Bolsover St, between William and Denham Sts. There's also a taxi service in town, **Rocky Cabs** (☎ 13 10 08).

YEPPOON

☎ 07 / pop 13,290

Pretty little Yeppoon is a small seaside town with a long beach, a calm ocean and an attractive hinterland of volcanic outcrops, pineapple patches and grazing lands. The handful of quiet streets, sleepy motels and beachside cafés attract Rockhamptonites beating the heat, and tourists heading for Great Keppel Island only 13km offshore.

Information

The extremely helpful **Capricorn Coast visitors centre** (☎ 1800 675 785, 4939 4888; www.capricorn coast.com.au; Scenic Hwy; ☽ 9am-5pm) is beside the Ross Creek roundabout at the entrance to the town.

Click On Central (☎ 4939 5300; cnr Mary & James Sts) has internet access for $5 per hour. The **Yeppoon library** (☎ 4939 3433; 78 John St) has free internet access.

Sights & Activities

Champions Brock Experience (☎ 1300 798 405; www .championsbrockexperience.com.au; 15 Jabiru Dr; adult/child $32/14; ☽ 10am-4pm Thu, Fri & Mon, 9.30am-5pm Sat & Sun) has the country's largest collection of racing legend Peter Brock's race and road cars. Entry is by guided tour only; tours commence on the hour and last 50 minutes.

Nearby, the **Horse & Carriage** (☎ 4939 5951; www.thehorseandcarriage.com; cnr Rockhampton Rd & Millroy Dr; adult/child $10/5; ☽ 10am-2pm Tue-Sun) has Queensland's largest collection of horse-drawn vehicles on display, as well as photographs and memorabilia of pioneering Australia.

Rosslyn Bay Marina, 7km south of Yeppoon, is the departure point for yacht charters, tours, and the ferry (see p394) to Great Keppel Island. **Funtastic Cruises** (☎ 0438-909 502; www .funtasticcruises.com; full-day cruise adult/child $90/75) operates full-day snorkelling trips to Middle Island on board its 17m catamaran, with a two-hour stopover on Great Keppel Island, morning and afternoon tea, and all snorkelling equipment. It can also organise camping drop offs to islands en route. **Sail Capricornia** (☎ 0402-102 373; www.keppelbaymarina.com.au) offers full-day snorkelling cruises on board a 12m yacht (adult/child $99/65 including lunch) as well as sunset and overnight cruises.

Golfers should check out Rydges Capricorn Resort (below).

Sleeping

Beachside Caravan Park (☎ 4939 3738; Farnborough Rd; unpowered/powered sites $18/21) This neat little camping park north of the town centre boasts an absolute beachfront location. It has good amenities and grassed sites with some shade but no cabins or on-site vans.

OURPICK Surfside Motel (☎ 4939 1272; surf sideptyltd@bigpond.com; 30 Anzac Pde; s/d $85/100; ✵ ☎) Across the road from the beach and close to town, this strip of lime green motel units epitomises Queensland summer holidays. The rooms have basic amenities but they're clean and cheerful. Great value.

Driftwood Motel & Holiday Units (☎ 4939 2446; www.driftwoodunits.com.au; 5-7 Todd Ave; s/d $95/150; ✵ ☎) Huge self-contained units at motel prices with absolute beach frontage make Driftwood a great bargain. There are good family units with separate bedrooms and there's a children's playground, but there's a four-night minimum stay in high season.

While Away B&B (☎ 4939 5719; www.whileaway bandb.com.au; 44 Todd Ave; s/d incl breakfast $100/120; ✵) With four good-sized rooms and an immaculately clean house with wheelchair access, this B&B is a perfect, quiet getaway – note that there are no facilities for kids. There are complimentary nibbles, tea, coffee, port and sherry as well as generous breakfasts.

Rosslyn Bay Inn (☎ 4933 6333; www.rosslynbayinn .com.au; Vin E Jones Dr; r from $115; ✵ ☎) At the marina. You'll find comfortable studio rooms and one- and two-bedroom units, as well as a bar and restaurant.

Beachfront 55 (☎ 4939 1403; www.beachfront55.com .au; 55 Todd Ave; units $129, villas from $285; ✵) The comfortable fully self-contained units have private BBQs and courtyards while the three-bedroom villa has a private pool, overlooks a garden and has ocean glimpses.

Rydges Capricorn Resort (☎ 1800 075 902, 4925 2525; www.capricornresort.com; Farnborough Rd; d $200-350; ✵ ☎) This large and lavish golf resort, about 8km north of Yeppoon, offers standard hotel rooms through to plush self-contained apartments. There's a huge pool, a gym and several bars and restaurants. The resort's two immaculate golf courses are open to the public at

$80 for 18 holes, which includes a motorised buggy. Club hire costs another $15.

Eating & Drinking

Shore Thing (☎ 4939 1993; 6 Normanby St; mains under $14; ☽ breakfast & lunch) At this breezy little café on the main street you can tuck into sandwiches, focaccias, wraps and big breakfasts.

Goosehorn (☎ 4939 5610; Normanby St; mains $10-28; ☽ 7am-late) A very metro-chic café-restaurant-wine bar with cool lighting, polished cement floors and a groovy atmosphere. You can nibble on tapas or nachos or something more substantial like pasta, steaks or Moreton Bay bugs. Also has an interesting cocktail list.

Keppel Bay Sailing Club (☎ 4939 9537; Anzac Pde; mains $10-34; ☽ lunch & dinner) Choose between the beachfront clubhouse and deck with good steaks and seafood or cross the road for a cheap buffet meal and the din of countless pokies at Spinnakers.

Thai Take-Away (☎ 4939 3920; 24 Anzac Pde; mains $12-20; ☽ dinner) A popular Thai BYO restaurant where you can sit outside on the sidewalk, catch a sea breeze, and satisfy those chilli and coconut cravings.

OURPICK Megalomania (☎ 4939 2333; Arthur St; mains $20-35; ☽ 11am-late) Another ultracool urban hang-out with a stone floor, slatted wooden blinds and an urban-islander vibe, this is a great place for a dinner or a drink. The menu changes weekly.

Michael's on Matthew Flinders (☎ 4930 2700; 105 Matthew Flinders Dr, Cooee Bay; mains $20-35; ☽ dinner Mon-Sun, breakfast Sat & Sun, lunch Fri-Sun) With a Mediterranean setting and breathtaking views of the bay, Michael's is the place for fine dining and intimate dinners.

Strand Hotel (☎ 4939 1301; 2 Normanby St; cnr Anzac Pde) The Strand has live music every weekend and is especially known for its Sunday afternoon Parilla, a South American themed BBQ with music to match.

Getting There & Away

Yeppoon is 43km northeast of Rockhampton. **Young's Bus Service** (☎ 4922 3813) runs frequent buses from Rockhampton ($8.10 one way) to Yeppoon and down to the Rosslyn Bay marina.

If you're heading for Great Keppel or the Reef, some ferry operators will transport you between your accommodation and Rosslyn Bay marina. If you're driving, there's a free day car park at the marina. For secure undercover parking, the **Great Keppel Island Security Car Park** (☎ 4933 6670; 422 Scenic Hwy; per day from $8), is on the Scenic Hwy south of Yeppoon, close to the turn-off to Rosslyn Bay marina.

AROUND YEPPOON
Emu Park
☎ 07 / pop 2970

The drive south from Yeppoon and Rosslyn Bay passes three fine headlands with good views – **Double Head**, **Bluff Point** and **Pinnacle Point**. After Pinnacle Point the road crosses **Causeway Lake**, a saltwater inlet where you can hire fishing boats, bait and tackle for a spot of estuary fishing. About 19km south of Yeppoon is Emu Park, a small seaside town with more good views and the **Singing Ship** memorial to Captain Cook – a curious monument of drilled tubes and pipes that emit mournful whistling and moaning sounds in the breeze.

Fifteen kilometres along the Emu Park–Rockhampton road, the **Koorana Crocodile Farm** (☎ 4934 4749; www.koorana.com.au; Coowonga Rd; adult/child $20/10; ⏰ 10am-3pm, tours 10.30am & 1pm) is a simple farm with lots of crocs destined to become fashion accessories or the odd restaurant meal.

If you plan on staying in this sleepy village, **Bell Park Caravan Park** (☎ 4939 6202; bellpark@primus.com.au; Pattinson St, Emu Park; unpowered/powered sites $18/22, cabins $84) has spacious sites, clean amenities and comfortable cabins a stone's throw from the beach.

Byfield
The hinterland north of Yeppoon is largely undeveloped state forest and national park bordering the large Shoalwater Bay Military Training Area (which is strictly off limits). The Byfield National Park and State Forest forms the **Byfield Coastal Area**, a wild and scenic region of rocky headlands, long sandy beaches, heath land, forest, mangrove-lined estuaries, rainforested creeks and granite mountains. There are five **camping grounds** (☎ 13 13 04; www.epa.gov.au; per person/family $4.50/18): Upper Stoney Creek, Red Rock, Waterpark Creek, Nine Mile Beach and Five Rocks. There's a self-registration stand at Red Rock but the other camp sites must be prebooked. Both Nine Mile Beach and Five Rocks are on the beach and you'll need a 4WD to access them. When conditions are right, there's decent surf at Nine Mile.

The tiny town of Byfield is a pleasant 40km drive north of Yeppoon and consists of a general store, a school and a cluster of houses.

Just south of Byfield, **Nob Creek Pottery** (☎ 4935 1161; 216 Arnolds Rd; admission free; ⏰ 9am-5pm) is an outstanding working pottery and gallery nestled in leafy rainforest where you can see the potters at work.

our pick **Waterpark Eco-Tours** (☎ 4935 1171; www.waterparkecotours.com; 201 Waterpark Creek Rd; 2-3hr tours $25; cabin $100; ⏰) Offers excellent river trips in a silent, electric-powered boat, and a horse-drawn carriage ride through a working tea-tree plantation. If you find it hard to leave the genuine hospitality on offer, there's a fully self-contained timber cabin on the 97-hectare farm where you can swing in a hammock, swim in the creek or just relax for a while.

Ferns Hideaway (☎ 4935 1235; www.fernshideaway.com.au; 67 Cahills Rd; unpowered sites $24, d $150; ⏰) , north of Byfield, is a secluded bush oasis in immaculate gardens that offers canoeing and nature walks. The timber homestead has a quality à la carte **restaurant** (mains $13-25; ⏰ lunch daily, dinner Sat, breakfast Sun), while nestled among the trees are cosy self-contained cabins with wood fires. Campers have hot showers included in the tariff.

The **Byfield General Store & Café** (☎ 4935 1190; 223 Byfield Rd; ⏰ 8am-6pm Wed-Mon, to 2pm Tue) has basic grocery supplies and a simple courtyard café serving pies, sandwiches and burgers. You can get fuel here and also some very good information about the national park.

GREAT KEPPEL ISLAND
Great Keppel Island has a stunning natural landscape of rocky headlands, forested hills, and a fringe of powdery white sand lapped by clear azure waters. Numerous 'castaway' beaches ring the 14-sq-km island while natural bushland covers 90% of the interior. A string of huts and accommodation options sit behind the trees lining the main beach but the developments are low-key and relatively unobtrusive. Only 13km offshore from Yeppoon, and with good snorkelling, swimming and bush walking, Great Keppel is an easily accessible and tranquil island retreat.

The sudden closure of Great Keppel Island Resort in February 2008 (at the time of research) has left tour operations and activities in a state of flux. Please check with the Capricorn Coast visitors centre (p391) on the current status.

Sights
Great Keppel's beaches are simply gorgeous. Take a short stroll from **Fisherman's Beach**, the

main beach, and you'll find your own deserted stretch of white sand. There is fairly good coral and excellent fish life, especially between Great Keppel and Humpy Island to the south. A 30-minute walk south around the headland brings you to **Monkey Beach**, where there's good snorkelling. A walking trail from the southern end of the airfield takes you to **Long Beach**, perhaps the best of the island's beaches.

There are several bushwalking tracks from Fisherman's Beach, the longest and perhaps most difficult leads to the 2.5m 'lighthouse' near **Bald Rock Point** on the far side of the island (three hours return).

You can see an **underwater observatory** off Middle Island, close to Great Keppel. A confiscated Taiwanese fishing junk was sunk next to the observatory to provide a haven for fish.

Activities
The **Watersports Hut** on the main beach hires out snorkelling equipment, kayaks and catamarans.

Keppel Reef Scuba Adventures (☎ 4939 5022; www .keppeldive.com; Putney Beach) offers introductory dives for $120, snorkelling trips (per person $38), and also hires out snorkelling gear (per day $15).

Tours
The ferry from Rosslyn Bay marina, **Freedom Fast Cats** (☎ 1800 336 244, 4933 6244; adult/child $63/42) operates a coral cruise to the best location of the day (depending on tides and weather), which includes viewing through a glass-bottomed boat and fish feeding. It also has full-day cruises (adult/child $130/85) including coral viewing, fish feeding, snorkelling, boom netting and a barbecue lunch.

Sleeping
Without Great Keppel Island Resort, accommodation options are severely limited. The resort is undergoing extensive renovations and refurbishments but will not re-open in the foreseeable future.

Holiday homes can be rented through the **Capricorn Coast visitors centre** (☎ 1800 675 785, 4939 4888; www.capricorncoast.com.au; Scenic Hwy, Yeppoon; ⏰ 9am-5pm) in Yeppoon. Six- and eight-bedroom homes can be rented in their entirety or the rooms can be rented as individual motel-style suites.

Great Keppel Island Backpackers & Holiday Village (☎ 4939 8655; www.gkiholidayvillage.com.au; dm $33, s/d tents $58/80, cabins with bathroom $130, 2-bedroom houses from $210) offers various types of good budget accommodation (including four-bed dorms and cabins that sleep three). It's a very friendly, relaxed place with shared bathroom facilities and a decent communal kitchen and BBQ area. Snorkelling gear is free and the village operates a water-taxi service for tours and island drop offs (from $20 per person) and motorised canoe trips around Middle Island ($35 per person).

Keppel Lodge (☎ 4939 4251; www.keppellodge .au; Fisherman's Beach; s/d $100/130, each additional person $50) is a pleasant open-plan house with four large bedrooms (with bathrooms) branching from a large communal lounge and kitchen. The house is available in its entirety – ideal for a group booking – or as individual motel-type suites.

our pick **Svendsen's Beach** (☎ 4938 3717; www .svendsensbeach.com; Svendsen's Beach; cabins per night $285, minimum 3 night stay) This secluded boutique cast-away retreat has two luxury tent-bungalows on separate elevated timber decks overlooking lovely Svendsen's Beach. The environmentally friendly operation has solar heating, wind generators, rainwater tanks and an ecofridge, and the communal beach-kitchen has a BBQ and stove-top. The artistic owner has fashioned decorative wooden sculptures and furnishings including a quaint candlelit bush-bucket shower. It's the perfect place for snorkelling, bushwalking and romantic getaways. Transfers from the ferry drop off on Fisherman's Beach are included in the tariff.

Eating
Self-caterers will need to bring all their supplies as there are no grocery stores, and only one restaurant, on the island.

Island Pizza (☎ 4939 4699; The Esplanade; dishes $6-30; ⏰ check blackboard for opening times) This friendly place prides itself on its gourmet pizzas with plenty of toppings. The pizzas are rather pricey but still tempting. Also available are hot dogs and pasta.

Getting There & Away
Freedom Fast Cats (☎ 1800 336 244, 4933 6244; www.keppel baymarina.com.au) departs the Keppel Bay marina in Rosslyn Bay (7km south of Yeppoon) at 9am Tuesday to Sunday, returning at 4pm. On Tuesday and Friday there's also a 10am ferry from the island, and a 3.30pm service from Rosslyn Bay to the island. The return

ISLAND CASTAWAY

'I love my castaway life.' Lyndie Malan sailed into Svendsen's Beach on Great Keppel Island 17 years ago and fell in love with the island…and a modern-day Robinson Crusoe, Carl Svendsen, who has lived his entire life on the island. This environmentally aware couple run a boutique ecotourist retreat at Svendsen's Beach (opposite) where guests can swim in secluded bays, snorkel the reefs or spend hours beachcombing for shells and driftwood.

'I love the bird life, the kookaburras and rainbow lorikeets, and the wonderful nocturnal birds like the curlews with their sad, plaintive cries. The walking tracks and fringing coral reefs give a 'desert island' feel to the place. We're a retreat not a resort, and we're trying really hard to cut our carbon footprint to almost nothing. But the thing I love the most is that turtles still lay their eggs on the island. Everything about turtles is kind of mysterious and magical, and if you're incredibly lucky you can encounter a girl laying her eggs on an evening walk.'

Lyndie's passion for her island life spills into her paintings and artistic driftwood pieces that decorate the retreat, and her passion for nature has inspired guided turtle tours, and books on local bushwalking and snorkelling hot spots for her guests.

A few days on Svendsen's Beach is a taste of modern-day castaway life, and like Lyndie you'll love the fact there are no neighbours and that you can sing as loud as you like.

fare is $41/22.50/107.50 per adult/child/family. If you have booked accommodation, check that someone will meet you on the beach to help with your luggage. Note that ferry departure times have been affected by the closure of Great Keppel Island Resort – ring to confirm times before planning your trip.

OTHER KEPPEL BAY ISLANDS

Great Keppel is the largest of 18 stunning continental islands dotted around Keppel Bay, all within 20km of the coast. Unlike coral cay islands, which are formed by the build-up of tiny fragments of coral, algae and other reef plants and animals, continental islands were originally rocky outcrops of the mainland ranges.

These beautiful islands feature clean, white beaches and impossibly clear water ranging from pale turquoise through to deep indigo blue. Several have fringing coral reefs excellent for snorkelling or diving. You can visit **Middle Island**, with its underwater observatory, or **Halfway** and **Humpy** Islands if you're staying on Great Keppel. Some of the islands are national parks where you can maroon yourself for a few days of self-sufficient camping.

To camp on a national park island, you need to take all your own supplies, including water. Camper numbers on each island are restricted. For information and permits call the **QPWS** (www.epa.gov.au) Rockhampton (☎ 4936 0511); Rosslyn Bay (☎ 4933 6608).

Whitsunday Coast

WHITSUNDAY COAST

Just the very word Whitsundays conjures images of everyone's idea of the perfect holiday. Go on, say it out loud. Don't be embarrassed. Whitsundays. Feels good doesn't it?

Now close your eyes and imagine yourself island hopping aboard a luxury yacht. Picture the dazzling white sand of Whitehaven Beach. Think about snorkelling amid pristine coral reefs among countless tropical fish. Feel the cool breeze dance over your skin as the sun warms you on a tropical island. Anticipate the throbbing nightlife and international cuisine at Airlie Beach.

The Whitsundays is not at all overhyped. If you can't enjoy yourself here, you don't have a pulse. And yet, the area is not all about the Whitsunday Islands themselves. What, there's more?

Mackay is a thriving regional city with a real heartbeat and plenty of soul; the Pioneer Valley and Eungella National Park offer cool respite, stunning scenery and cute platypuses; and Cape Hillsborough is rugged and largely untamed.

Tell someone you're heading to the Whitsunday Coast and prepare for a jealous response and cries of 'Can I come too?'. You've chosen wisely.

HIGHLIGHTS

- Being dazzled by the bright-white silicon sand at stunning **Whitehaven Beach** (p420)
- Gliding on top of the bright-blue ocean on a cruise to a secluded snorkelling spot on the **Great Barrier Reef** (p407)
- Waiting patiently for a glimpse of a shy platypus and walking in the misty rainforest at **Eungella National Park** (p404)
- Sharing the beach at dusk with the local kangaroos at ruggedly beautiful **Cape Hillsborough National Park** (p406)
- Hooking up with other travellers and planning a cruise trip over a beer at fun lovin' **Airlie Beach** (p410)

| TELEPHONE CODE: 07 | ■ www.queenslandholidays.com.au /whitsundays/index.cfm | ■ www.whitsunday.com |

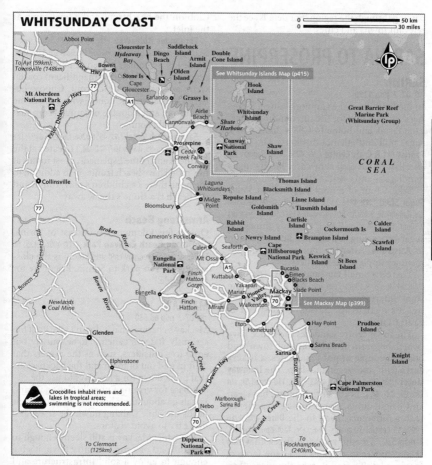

WHITSUNDAY COAST

(map)

See Whitsunday Islands Map (p415)

See Mackay Map (p399)

Crocodiles inhabit rivers and lakes in tropical areas; swimming is not recommended.

Getting There & Away

AIR

Mackay has a major domestic **airport** (www .mackayairport.com.au), and **Jetstar** (☎ 13 15 38; www .jetstar.com.au), **Qantas** (☎ 13 13 13; www.qantas.com .au) and **Virgin Blue** (☎ 13 67 89; www.virginblue.com .au) have regular flights to/from the major centres. **Tiger Airways** (☎ 03-9335 3033; www .tigerairways.com.au) flies to Mackay from Melbourne.

Jetstar and Qantas have frequent flights to Hamilton Island, from where there are boat/ air transfers to the other islands. All three fly into Proserpine (aka Whitsunday Coast) on the mainland; from there you can take a charter flight to the islands or a bus to Airlie Beach or nearby Shute Harbour.

BOAT

Airlie Beach and Shute Harbour are the launching pads for boat trips to the Whitsundays; see individual islands for details.

BUS

Greyhound (☎ 13 14 99; www.greyhound.com.au) and **Premier** (☎ 13 34 10; www.premierms.com.au) have coach services along the Bruce Hwy with stops at the major towns. They detour off the highway from Proserpine to Airlie Beach. For details see the relevant towns and cities.

TRAIN

Queensland Rail (www.traveltrain.com.au) has services between Brisbane and Townsville/Cairns passing through the region. For details see the relevant towns and cities.

SARINA TO PROSERPINE

SARINA

☎ 07 / pop 3290

In the foothills of the Connors Range, Sarina is a service centre for the surrounding sugarcane farms and home to CSR's Plane Creek sugar mill and ethanol distillery. The **Sarina Tourist Art & Craft Centre** (☎ 4956 2251; Railway Sq, Bruce Hwy; ❤ 9am-5pm) showcases locally made handicrafts and assists with information.

Take a tour of a minisugar mill at **Sarina Sugar Shed** (☎ 4943 2801; www.sarinasugarshed .au; Railway Sq; adult/child/concession $15/7.50/12; ❤ tours 9.30am, 10.30am, noon & 2pm), the only miniature sugar-processing mill and distillery of its kind in Australia. After the tour enjoy a complimentary tipple at the distillery.

There's a small **museum** (☎ 4943 1296; adult/child $4/3; ❤ 9.30am-2pm Tue, Wed & Fri) housing some interesting exhibits from times gone by. It's next to the Sarina Tourist Art & Craft Centre.

The town centre straddles the Bruce Hwy (which becomes Broad St through town) and boasts a couple of pubs and cafés, a bakery and a fruit-and-vegetable shop. The **Tramway Motel** (☎ 4956 2244; fax 4943 1262; 110 Broad St; s/d $80/95; 🅿 🖳), north of the centre, has clean and bright units. For a dining experience with a difference, head to the **Diner** (☎ 4956 1990; 11 Central St; mains $4-6; ❤ 4am-6pm Mon-Fri, 4-10am Sat), a rustic roadside shack that has served tucker to truckies and cane farmers for decades. To find it, take the turn-off to Clermont in the centre of town and look for the humble building on your left, just before the railway crossing.

AROUND SARINA

A short drive east from Sarina there are a number of low-key beachside settlements, where the clean, uncrowded beaches and mangrove-lined inlets provide excellent opportunities for relaxing, fishing, beachcombing and spotting wildlife such as nesting marine turtles.

Sarina Beach

On the shores of Sarina Inlet, this laid-back coastal village boasts a long beach, a general store/service station, a Surf Life Saving Club on the beachfront and a boat ramp at the inlet.

Fernandos Hideaway (☎ 4956 6299; www.sarina beachbb.com; 26 Captain Blackwood Dr; B&B s/d $100/125; 🅿 🖳) is a Spanish hacienda perched on a rugged headland offering magnificent coastal views and absolute beachfront. Choose between the panoramic double with a spa in the bathroom, and a double or family room that share a bathroom.

Sarina Beach Motel (☎ 4956 6266; fax 4956 6197; The Esplanade; s $75-95, d $80-107; 🅿 🖳) Located at the northern end of the Esplanade, most rooms at this motel have beach frontage. In addition to the pool, there's a children's playground and the beach is a stone's throw away.

Armstrong Beach

Only a few kilometres southeast of Sarina, **Armstrong Beach Caravan Park** (☎ 4956 2425; 66 Melba St; unpowered/powered sites $20/22) is the closest coastal van park to Sarina. Prices are for two people.

MACKAY

☎ 07 / pop 66,880

Mackay's charm is that it doesn't take itself too seriously. It doesn't attempt to be touristy, but embraces outsiders, such as the miners that drift in and out of town and the backpackers that bunk down for a few days to use the city as a base for visiting Eungella National Park. Locals go about their business, but hold their heads up while walking down the street and don't try to avoid visitors.

But while Mackay is still sleepy enough to play the part of a rural country town, it's big enough to enjoy a solid infrastructure and modern facilities. It's only a 1½-hour drive to the Whitsundays, a short flight to Brampton Island and a scenic drive among the sugarcane fields to Pioneer Valley and Eungella National Park. The new marina precinct is bustling with energy as people stroll the promenade in search of a seafood meal or a relaxing drink at an outdoor bar or café. It's up to you whether you like Mackay or not. The locals won't mind one way or another.

Orientation

Mackay's city centre is compact, with the main streets laid out in a grid south of the broad Pioneer River. Victoria, Wood and Sydney Sts are the places to go for restaurants, bars and pubs. The train station, airport, botanic

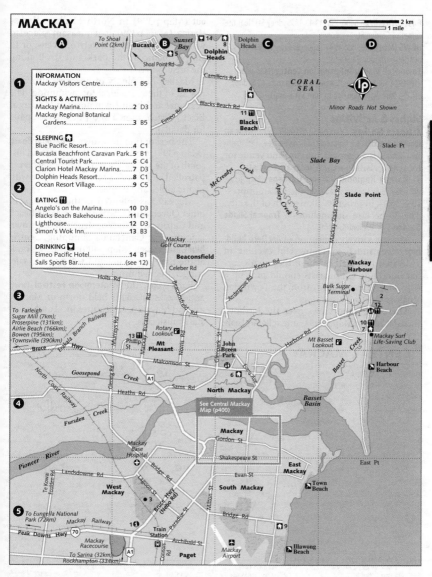

MACKAY

WHITSUNDAY COAST

gardens and visitors centre are about 3km south of the city centre.

Sydney St takes you across Forgan Bridge to North Mackay, the city's newer suburbs and the northern beaches. Mackay Harbour, 6km northeast of the centre, is dominated by a massive sugar terminal, while the adjacent marina has a select offering of waterfront restaurants.

Information

Mackay City Library (Map p400; ☎ 4957 1787; Gordon St; per 30min $2.50; ☼ 9am-5pm Mon, Wed & Fri, 10am-6pm Tue, 10am-8pm Thu, 9am-3pm Sat) Internet access.
Mackay visitors centre (Map p399; ☎ 4944 5888; www.mackayregion.com; 320 Nebo Rd; ☼ 8.30am-5pm Tue-Fri, 9am-5pm Mon, 9am-4pm Sat & Sun) About 3km south of the centre.

Post office (Map p400; ☎ 13 13 18; Sydney St) Near the corner of Gordon St.

QPWS (Map p400; ☎ 4944 7800; cnr River & Wood Sts; per person/family $4.50/18)

Town Hall Visitor Information Centre (Map p400; ☎ 4944 5888; townhall@mackayregion.com; 63 Sydney St; ⏰ 9am-5pm Mon-Fri, to 2pm Sat & Sun)

Sights & Activities

Artspace Mackay (Map p400; ☎ 4957 1722; www.art spacemackay.com.au; Gordon St; admission free; ⏰ 10am-5pm Tue-Sun) is a regional museum and venue for local and visiting exhibitions and artists.

Mackay Regional Botanic Gardens (Map p399; ☎ 4952 7300; Lagoon St; admission free) is an impressive 'work in progress' 3km south of the city. The 33-hectare site includes a **Tropical Shade Garden** (⏰ 8.45am-4.45pm).

Mackay's lovely collection of **Art Deco buildings** owes much to a powerful cyclone in 1918 that flattened many of the town's earlier buildings. Enthusiasts should pick up a copy of *Art Deco Mackay* from the Town Hall Visitors Centre.

There are good views over the harbour from **Mt Basset** (Map p399), and at **Rotary Lookout** (Map p399) in North Mackay. **Mackay Marina** (Map p399) is a pleasant place to wine and dine with a waterfront view, or to simply picnic in the park and stroll along the breakwater.

Mackay has plenty of beaches, although not all of them are ideal for swimming. The best ones are about 16km north of Mackay at Blacks Beach, Eimeo and Bucasia (see p403 for details).

The best option near town is **Harbour Beach** (Map p399), 6km north of the centre and just south of the Mackay Marina. The beach here is patrolled and there's a foreshore reserve with picnic tables and barbecues.

Mackay has followed in the footsteps of other Queensland towns, such as Airlie Beach and Cairns, with the construction of its own lagoon near Canelands Shopping Centre. **Bluewater Lagoon** (Map p400) was being built at the time of writing and will provide safe, stinger-free swimming.

Each year, the **Wintermoon Festival** (www .wintermoonfestival.com) is held north of Mackay around May/June. It features local and interstate musicians.

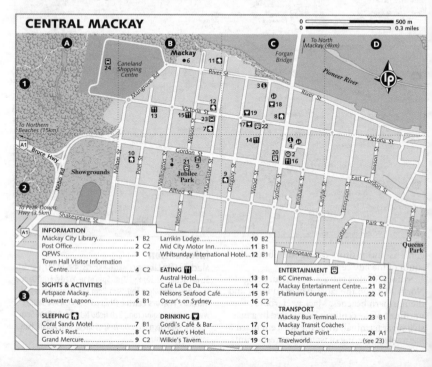

CENTRAL MACKAY

INFORMATION		
Mackay City Library	1	B2
Post Office	2	C2
QPWS	3	C1
Town Hall Visitor Information Centre	4	C2

SIGHTS & ACTIVITIES		
Artspace Mackay	5	B2
Bluewater Lagoon	6	B1

SLEEPING		
Coral Sands Motel	7	B1
Gecko's Rest	8	C1
Grand Mercure	9	C2

Larrikin Lodge	10	B2
Mid City Motor Inn	11	B1
Whitsunday International Hotel	12	B1

EATING		
Austral Hotel	13	B1
Café La De Da	14	C2
Nelsons Seafood Café	15	B1
Oscar's on Sydney	16	C2

DRINKING		
Gordi's Café & Bar	17	C1
McGuire's Hotel	18	C1
Wilkie's Tavern	19	C1

ENTERTAINMENT		
BC Cinemas	20	C2
Mackay Entertainment Centre	21	B2
Platinium Lounge	22	C1

TRANSPORT		
Mackay Bus Terminal	23	B1
Mackay Transit Coaches Departure Point	24	A1
Travelworld	(see 23)	

RUN FOR COVER

In February 2008 Mackay was hit by lashings of wind and rain that resulted in catastrophic floods. In three hours on 15 February, 625mm of rain was dumped on the city, causing chaos. Homes, schools and businesses were evacuated as the Pioneer River burst its banks and sent people scurrying for cover. Overwhelmed sewage stations overflowed into almost 200 homes. The city centre was the worst affected area. While most businesses were expected to recover, some listed in this section may still be feeling the effects of the damage by the time you read this.

Tours

Farleigh Sugar Mill (off Map p399; ☎ 4959 8360; adult/child/family $20/12/55; 2hr tours 1pm Mon-Fri Jun-Nov) In the cane-crushing season you can see how the sweet crystals are made. Learn all about the history, production and technology, but dress prepared for a working mill, which means long sleeves, long pants and enclosed shoes. The mill is 10km northwest of Mackay.

Jungle Johno Eco Tours (☎ 1800 611 953, 4951 3728; bookings@larrikinlodge.com.au; tours adult/child $75/40) The elusive platypus is the pot of gold at end of this rainbow. You'll be taken deep into the national park to spot these shy, amphibious creatures in their natural habitat. The seven-hour day trips, operating from Larrikin Lodge (right), include Finch Hatton Gorge and are a good way to see the best bits of Eungella and surrounds in one day. The popular tour includes pick-up, morning tea and lunch.

Mackay Water Taxi & Adventures (☎ 4942 7372, 0417-073 969; tjpic@mcs.net.au) Offers fishing charters (from $170 per person), day trips to Keswick and St Bee's Islands (from $140) and snorkelling and diving trips to the Great Barrier Reef and the Whitsunday and Cumberland Island groups. Trips leave from the marina.

Reeforest Adventure Tours (☎ 1800 500 353; www.reeforest.com) The day-long Platypus & Rainforest Eco safari (per person $105) explores Finch Hatton Gorge and visits the platypuses of Broken River. It includes lunch at a secluded bush retreat near the gorge and an interpretive walk. The tour also departs from Airlie Beach ($130).

Sleeping

BUDGET

There are plenty of motels strung along busy Nebo Rd, south of the centre. The budget options (around $50 for a double) post their prices out front and tend to suffer from road noise.

Central Tourist Park (Map p399; ☎ 4957 6141; Malcolm St, North Mackay; unpowered/powered sites $20/24, cabins $35-45, villas $55; 🔀 🖳) Rows of cabins (many with bathrooms) make this park, about 2km north of the centre, rather boring, but it's an inexpensive option relatively close to the city and accessible by buses 5 and 6. The villas, with bathroom, TV, fridge and air-con, are brilliant value, although this part of town is not anything to get as enthusiastic about.

Larrikin Lodge (Map p400; ☎ 1800 611 953, 4951 3728; www.larrikinlodge.com.au; 32 Peel St; dm $21, tw with/without air-con $50/48; 🔀 🖳 🖳) In a wonderfully quiet part of town, but close enough to all the action, this big old house oozes atmosphere. You'll feel like a guest here, not just another face passing through. The owners operate Jungle Johno Eco Tours (left) and will pick you up from the bus terminal if you ring ahead.

Gecko's Rest (Map p400; ☎ 4944 1230; www.geckosrest.com.au; 34 Sydney St; dm/s/d/f $22/35/50/80; 🔀 🖳) Bustling and busy, Gecko's almost bursts at the seams with adventurous travellers stopping over on their way up north or down the coast. The four-bed dorms all have a small fridge, the kitchen is clean and modern and there's a huge rooftop balcony area.

Whitsunday International Hotel (Map p400; ☎ 4957 2811; fax 4951 1785; 176 Victoria St; s/d $75/90; 🔀) The motel-style rooms here are decent enough, central and well priced although a tad on the small side. The bar downstairs facing Victoria St is probably not a place you'd want to linger for too long.

MIDRANGE

Ocean Resort Village (Map p399; ☎ 1800 075 144, 4951 3200; www.oceanresortvillage.com.au; 5 Bridge Rd, Illawong Beach; apt $85-95, 2-bedroom apt $130; 🔀 🖳) This is a good-value beachside resort comprising 34 self-contained apartments (studio, and one-and two-bedroom) set amid lush, tropical gardens in a cool, shady setting with two pools, barbecue areas and half-court tennis.

Coral Sands Motel (Map p400; ☎ 4951 1244; www.coralsandsmotel.com.au; 44 Macalister St; s/d $95/105; 🔀 🖳) One of the better midrange options in Mackay, the Coral Sands boasts ultrafriendly management and large rooms in a central location. The pool looks like it has seen better days, but with the river, shops, pubs and cafés so close to your doorstep, you won't care.

ourpick **Mid City Motor Inn** (Map p400; ☎ 4951 1666; stay@midcitymotel.com.au; 2 Macalister St; r $105-155; 🔀 🖳) Modern, comfortable and in a superb location beside the river promenade, the Mid City's name is slightly misleading although it can be forgiven as it's only a short stroll into the town centre.

TOP END

Grand Mercure (Map p400; ☎ 4969 1000; www .mackaygrandmercure.com.au; 9 Gregory St; r $170, ste $235; ✖ ▢ ▣ ; wi-fi) Mackay's long awaited addition to the top end of the scale in the city centre doesn't disappoint with its stylish décor and modern amenities. Lash out and try the spa suite ($280 to $350) with its huge plasma TV and balcony with panoramic vistas.

Clarion Hotel Mackay Marina (Map p399; ☎ 1800 386 386, 4955 9400; www.mackaymarinahotel.com; Mulherin Dr, Mackay Harbour; d $175-330; ✖ ▢ ▣ ; wi-fi) The Clarion is the darling of the rapidly developing marina precinct and it's not hard to see why. All rooms have spacious showers and balconies and all the mod-cons you'd expect of a hotel of international standing. Couples should try the Pamper Package ($395), which includes sparkling wine and chocolates, a 30-minute massage, hot breakfast and noon checkout in a spa suite.

Eating

RESTAURANTS

Angelo's on the Marina (Map p399; ☎ 4955 5600; Mulherin Dr, Mackay Marina; mains $16-30; ✖ 8am-late) A large, lively restaurant in a delightful marina setting, with an extensive range of pasta and a mouth-watering Mediterranean menu. It's fully licensed and there's a free courtesy bus for parties of six or more people, so join a group and enjoy.

Austral Hotel (Map p400; ☎ 4951 3288; 189 Victoria St; mains $17-23, steaks $21-39; ✖ lunch & dinner) You won't get a better cut of meat in Mackay than at the Austral. Huge plates of prime Aussie beef fill your plate in a genuine pub surrounding with cold draught beer to wash it down. Of course, there's the usual assortment of seafood and chicken dishes if cooked cow doesn't do it for you.

our pick Simon's Wok Inn (Map p399; ☎ 4942 0601; Phillips St, Mt Pleasant; mains $18-30; ✖ lunch & dinner) We'll let you in on a little secret that only locals know about. Let's just say, you'll be rewarded if you make the effort to get out here. The crispy skin coral trout is as close to perfection as you can get. Try the banquet (per person $35) and the genuinely good food just keeps coming until you've

had enough. It's located at Mt Pleasant Plaza shopping centre.

Lighthouse (Map p399; ☎ 4955 5022, takeaway 4955 5699; Mulherin Dr, Mackay Harbour; mains $22-29; ✖ 6am-late) A very popular seafood restaurant in a nautical setting that doubles as a takeaway next door. The generous plates of seafood in the main restaurant looked rather fetching when we were lining up for the cheaper takeaway option.

CAFÉS

Nelson's Seafood Café (Map p400; ☎ 4953 5453; cnr Victoria & Nelson Sts; mains $9-15; ✖ 10am-7.30pm Mon, Wed, Thu & Sun, to 8pm Fri & Sat) To call Nelson's a fish-and-chip shop would be a gross injustice. This is seafood with a twist. The crumbed scallops are as big as squash balls and the seafood fried rice and assorted salads are mouth-watering.

Oscar's on Sydney (Map p400; ☎ 4944 0173; cnr Sydney & Gordon Sts; mains $9-16; ✖ 7am-10pm Tue-Sat, to 9.30pm Sun & Mon) The delicious *poffertjes* (authentic Dutch pancakes with traditional toppings) are still going strong at this corner café, but don't be afraid to give the other dishes a go. The sweetcorn and capsicum frittata with smoked salmon and grilled asparagus ($14.50) may just hit the spot.

Café La De Da (Map p400; ☎ 4944 0203; 70 Wood St; meals $14-26; ✖ breakfast & lunch) Always busy, always good. True to its name, La De Da whiles away its time nonchalantly serving generous mains such as seafood, big steaks, curries, salads and the obligatory wraps and sandwiches.

Drinking

Sails Sports Bar (Map p399; ☎ 4955 5022; Mulherin Dr, Mackay Harbour) This outdoors bar with sports memorabilia on the walls can get rowdy at night, but most of the time it's mellow and a good place to knock back a beer or two.

Gordi's Café & Bar (Map p400; ☎ 4951 2611; 85 Victoria St) Order a $3 schooner and pull up a stool at this big open-air bar overlooking Victoria St's comings and goings.

McGuire's Hotel (Map p400; ☎ 4957 7464; 15 Wood St) Originally built in 1882, but demolished in 1938 and rebuilt, this big mustard-coloured building has good outdoor streetside seating.

Wilkie's Tavern (Map p400; ☎ 4957 2241; cnr Victoria & Gregory Sts) Usually has someone strumming a guitar on Thursday, Friday and Saturday nights.

Entertainment

Platinum Lounge (Map p400; ☎ 4944 1877; 83 Victoria St; ☺ 7pm-3am Wed-Sat, 5pm-2am Sun) On the 1st floor above the corner of Victoria and Wood Sts, the Platinum Lounge is a good place to unwind.

Cinema and theatre options:

BC Cinemas (Map p400; ☎ 4957 3515; 30 Gordon St; adult/child $14.50/10.50) This complex screens all the latest flicks.

Mackay Entertainment Centre (Map p400; ☎ 4957 2255; Gordon St; box office ☺ 9am-5pm Mon-Fri, 10am-1pm Sat) The city's main venue for live performances; phone the box office to find out what's on.

Getting There & Away

Located at the long-distance bus station, **Travelworld** (Map p400; ☎ 4944 2144; roseh@mkytworld .com.au; cnr Victoria & Macalister Sts; ☺ 7am-6pm Mon-Fri, to 4pm Sat) handles air, bus and train tickets and can help with transport connections.

AIR

The airport is about 3km south of the centre of Mackay.

Jetstar (☎ 13 15 38; www.jetstar.com.au) Flights to/from Brisbane and Sydney.

Qantas (☎ 13 13 13; www.qantas.com.au) Direct flights most days between Mackay and Brisbane.

Tiger Airways (☎ 03-9335 3033; www.tigerairways .com.au) Direct flights between Mackay and Melbourne.

Virgin Blue (☎ 13 67 89; www.virginblue.com.au) To/from Brisbane with flights connecting with services to several major centres.

BUS

Buses stop at Travelworld, where tickets can also be booked.

Greyhound (☎ 13 14 99; www.greyhound.com.au) Travels up and down the coast. Sample one-way adult fares and journey times are: Airlie Beach ($33, two hours), Townsville ($81, 6½ hours), Cairns ($139, 13 hours), Rockhampton ($60, 4½ hours), Hervey Bay ($128, 11 hours) and Brisbane ($164, 16 hours).

Premier (☎ 13 34 10; www.premierms.com.au) Cheaper but not as many services as Greyhound. Sample fares are: Airlie Beach ($21), Cairns ($103), Rockhampton ($37) and Brisbane ($120).

TRAIN

Queensland Rail (☎ 13 22 32, 1300 13 17 22; www .traveltrain.com.au) has several services stopping at Mackay on its way between Brisbane and Townsville/Cairns. The speedy *Tilt Train* departs at 7.25am on Monday, Wednesday and Friday, heading to Cairns ($162, 12 hours) via Townsville ($92, 5½ hours), and 8.25pm on Sunday, Wednesday and Friday heading to Brisbane ($222, 13 hours). Fares shown are adult business class.

The *Sunlander* departs at 2.10am heading to Cairns on Sunday and Tuesday and 5.35am on Thursday. Brisbane-bound, it departs Mackay at 11.10pm on Monday, Tuesday, Thursday and Saturday. There are several classes: sitting, economy berth, 1st-class berth and the luxurious Queenslander class. Adult fares between Mackay and Brisbane (17 hours) are $151/209/615 in sitting/economy berth/Queenslander.

Getting Around

Avis (☎ 4951 1266), **Budget** (☎ 4951 1400), **Europcar** (☎ 4952 6269; www.europcar.com.au) and **Hertz** (☎ 4951 3334) have counters at the airport. **Mackay Transit Coaches** (Map p400; ☎ 4957 3330) has several services around the city, and also connecting the city with the harbour and the northern beaches; pick up a timetable from one of the visitors centres. Routes begin from Canelands Shopping Centre and there are many signposted bus stops, but you can hail a bus anywhere along the route as long as there is room for it to pull over. There's a free service on Sunday, running to all the major tourist sights. Signal for the driver to pull over anywhere along the route on Gordon St and Nebo Rd. For a taxi, call **Mackay Taxis** (☎ 13 13 08). Count on about $15 for a taxi from either the train station or the airport to the city centre. **Con-X-ion** (☎ 1300 308718; www .con-x-ion.com) operates an airport service to your accommodation in Mackay for $10.

AROUND MACKAY
Mackay's Northern Beaches

The coastline north of Mackay is made up of a series of headlands and bays sheltering small residential communities with holiday accommodation.

At **Blacks Beach** the beach extends for 6km, so stretch those legs and claim a piece of Coral Sea coast for a day. If you are just passing through, you can grab a quick lunch or coffee at **Blacks Beach Bakehouse** (Map p399; ☎ 4969 5222; Shop 2, Blacks Beach Rd, Blacks Beach; meals $3-10; ☺ breakfast & lunch) and tuck into one of the huge rolls or hearty pies and then round it all off with slice of cake. For accommodation try **Blue Pacific Resort** (Map p399; ☎ 1800 808 386, 4954 9090; www

.bluepacificresort.com.au; 26 Bourke St, Blacks Beach; studios $145-170, 1-/2-bedroom units $165/185; ⊠ ⊠), which has self-catering facilities in all rooms.

At the north end of Blacks Beach is **Dolphin Heads**, where you can stay at the four-star **Dolphin Heads Resort** (Map p399; ☎ 1800 075 088, 4954 9666; www .dolphinheadsresort.com.au; Beach Rd, Dolphin Heads; d $150-170; ⊠ ⊠). The 80 comfortable motel-style units overlook an attractive (but rocky) bay.

North of Dolphin Heads is **Eimeo**, where the **Eimeo Pacific Hotel** (Map p399; ☎ 4954 6105; Mango Ave, Eimeo) crowns a headland commanding magnificent Coral Sea views. It's a great place for a beer.

Bucasia is across Sunset Bay from Eimeo and Dolphin Heads, but you have to head all the way back to the main road to get up there. **Bucasia Beachfront Caravan Resort** (Map p399; ☎ 4954 6375; www.bucasiabeach.com.au; 2 The Esplanade; caravan sites $29-33, cabins without bathroom $65, with bathroom $80-90; ⊠) has en-suite cabins right on the beach.

Pioneer Valley

Travelling west, Mackay's urban sprawl gives way to the lush greenness of the beautiful Pioneer Valley. The unmistakable smell of sugar cane wafts through your nostrils and loaded cane trains busily work their way along the roadside. The first sugar cane was planted here in 1867, and today almost the entire valley floor is planted with the stuff. The route to Eungella National Park (right), the Mackay–Eungella Rd, branches off the Peak Downs Hwy about 10km west of Mackay and follows the river through vast fields of cane to link up with the occasional small town or steam-belching sugar mill.

About 27km west of Mirani is the turnoff for Finch Hatton Gorge, part of Eungella National Park, and 1.5km past the turn-off is the pretty township of **Finch Hatton**. The historic **train station** (☒ 10am-3pm) doesn't see trains anymore but it has an interesting display on local history, and has internet access ($2 per half-hour). The friendly **Criterion Hotel** (☎ 4958 3252; 9 Eungella Rd; s/d $35/45; mains $7-18) has been refurbished and has spotless rooms and hearty, inexpensive counter meals. You'll be on the receiving end of some good, old country hospitality here.

From Finch Hatton, it's another 18km to Eungella, a quaint mountain village overlooking the valley. The last section of this road climbs suddenly and steeply, with several incredibly sharp corners – towing a large caravan up here is not recommended.

Eungella

Pretty little Eungella (*young*-gluh, meaning 'land of clouds') sits perched on the edge of the Pioneer Valley. There's a **General Store** (☎ 4958 4520) with snacks, groceries and fuel, and a couple of accommodation and eating options.

Eungella Holiday Park (☎ 4958 4590; unpowered/powered sites $20/22, cabins $85-120) is a small, friendly park located just north of the township, right on the edge of the escarpment. Prices are for two people. The owner is happy to shuttle guests to bushwalks in the national park and there's a kiosk with groceries, snacks and an ATM.

In its heyday, the rambling, old **Eungella Chalet** (☎ 4958 4509; fax 4958 4503; s without bathroom $38, d with/without bathroom $72/50, 1-/2-bedroom cabins $88/109; ⊠) would have been quite a sight and it still packs a punch today. The chalet is perched on the edge of a mountain and the views on a clear day, we're told, are amazing (it was drizzling and the clouds had hijacked the views when we visited). Upstairs rooms are clean and simple: the TVs look like they're on their last legs and the quaint heaters in the rooms are a reminder that it can get cold at night up here.

It's worth stopping in for lunch at the charming **Hideaway Café** (☎ 4958 4533; Broken River Rd; light meals $4-10; ☒ 9am-4pm). Sit on the picturesque little balcony and enjoy a decent home-cooked dish like Weiner schnitzel and potato salad or lentil vegetable casserole with 'lavish' bread. It's small, uncomplicated, unfussed and wholesome.

EUNGELLA NATIONAL PARK

Stunning Eungella National Park is 84km west of Mackay, and covers nearly 500 sq km of the Clarke Range, climbing to 1280m at Mt Dalrymple. The mountainous park is largely inaccessible, except for the walking tracks around Broken River and Finch Hatton Gorge. The large tracts of tropical and subtropical vegetation have been isolated from other rainforest areas for thousands of years and now boast several unique species.

Most days of the year you can be pretty sure of seeing a platypus or two in the Broken River. The best times to see them are the hours immediately after dawn and before dark; you must remain patiently silent and still. Platypus activity is at its peak from May to August, when the females are fattening themselves up in preparation for gestating their young. Other river life you're sure to see are the large northern snapping turtles and, flitting above the feeding platypuses, brilliant azure kingfishers.

Getting There & Away

There are no buses to Eungella or Finch Hatton, but Reeforest Adventure Tours and Jungle Johno Tours both run day trips from Mackay and will drop off and pick up those who want to linger (see p401).

Broken River

There's a **QPWS information office** (☎ 4958 4552; ☼ 8am-4pm), picnic area and **kiosk** (☼ 10am-5pm) near the bridge over the Broken River, 5km south of Eungella. A **platypus-viewing platform** has been built near the bridge, and bird life is prolific. There are some excellent walking trails between the Broken River picnic ground and Eungella; maps are available from the information office, which is (unfortunately) rarely staffed.

Fern Flat Camping Ground (☎ 4958 4552; fax 4958 4501; per person/family $4.50/18) was undergoing refurbishment at the time of writing and vehicle access was prohibited. Check with the QPWS before deciding to drive here. It's a lovely place to camp, though, with the shady sites adjacent to the river where the platypuses play. The camping ground is about 500m past the information centre and kiosk.

If you forgot the tent, **Broken River Mountain Retreat** (☎ 4958 4528; www.brokenrivermr.com.au; d $105-160; ☒ ☒) is a very comfortable alternative. Accommodation comprises cedar cabins ranging from small motel-style units to a large self-contained lodge sleeping up to six. There's a large guests' lounge with an open fire and the friendly **Platypus Lodge Restaurant & Bar** (mains $18.50-28.50) with a good selection of steak, seafood and chicken dishes, and a moderately priced wine list. The meals are seriously good. Bring an appetite.

Finch Hatton Gorge

About 27km west of Mirani, just before the town of Finch Hatton, is the turn-off to Finch Hatton Gorge. The last 2km of the 10km drive from the main road are on unsealed roads with several creek crossings that can become impassable after heavy rain. A 1.6km walking trail leads from the picnic area to **Araluen Falls**, with its tumbling waterfalls and swimming

holes, and a further 1km hike takes you to the **Wheel of Fire Falls**, another cascade with a deep swimming hole.

A fun and informative way to explore the rainforest here is to glide through the canopy on a cable with **Forest Flying** (☎ 4958 3359; www .forestflying.com; rides $45).

The following places are signposted on the road to the gorge.

The comfortable self-contained cabins at **Finch Hatton Gorge Cabins** (☎ 4958 3281; www.finch hattongorgecabins.com.au; d $95, extra person $20; ☒) sleep up to five, which is perfect if you're travelling with young kids or with a group. There's a wonderful view of the forest from all the cabins, and linen is provided. Although there are no longer any dorm or camping options, WWOOFers get three meals a day and accommodation in exchange for four hours work on the property or the nearby farm.

The friendly **Gorge Kiosk** (☎ 4958 3321) serves excellent ice creams (delicious mango plus other flavours), pies and lemonade – all home-made. Picnic and barbecue packs are available to take up the road to the national-park picnic ground.

CUMBERLAND ISLANDS
Brampton Island

Brampton Island proudly announces that there are no day-trippers to interrupt the peace and solitude. It's a classy resort that's popular with couples, honeymooners and those wanting a relaxed island experience. It's definitely not a party island, and kids (especially those under 12) are not catered for.

Brampton Island Resort (☎ 1300 134 044, 4951 4499; www.brampton-island.com; s $275-620, d $300-650; ☒ ☒ ☒) has four grades of room depending on the view and facilities and, naturally, the rates increase the closer you get to the ocean. The premium ocean-views are stunning, but even the standard rooms are classy. The Bluewater Restaurant serves a buffet breakfast and lunch and a scrumptious à la carte dinner as well as beach barbecues. Prices are often much cheaper if you book a five-night package or wait for stand-by rates.

Island transfers by either helicopter or launch from Mackay are organised through the resort when booking accommodation.

Other Cumberland Islands

If you have your own boat, or can afford to charter a boat or seaplane, most other islands in the Cumberland Group and the Sir James Smith Group to the north are also beautiful national parks.

Camp-site availability, bookings and permits for **Carlisle**, **Scawfell** and **Goldsmith Islands** and others can be made online at www.epa .qld.gov.au or at the Mackay **QPWS** (☎ 4944 7800; cnr River & Wood Sts; per person/family $4.50/18).

Carlisle Island can be reached from Brampton Island via the sand spit at low tide or by chartering a boat at Brampton resort. Scawfel and Goldsmith Islands are reached by charter boat, which can be organised through the **Mackay visitors centre** (☎ 4952 2677; www.mackay region.com; 320 Nebo Rd).

CAPE HILLSBOROUGH NATIONAL PARK

Despite being so easy to get to, this small coastal park feels like it's at the end of the earth. Ruggedly beautiful, it takes in the rocky, 300m-high Cape Hillsborough, and Andrews Point and Wedge Island, which are joined by a causeway at low tide. The park, 58km north of Mackay, features rough cliffs, a broad beach, rocky headlands, sand dunes, mangroves, hoop pines and rainforest. Kangaroos, wallabies, sugar gliders and turtles are common in the park; the roos are likely to be seen on the beach in the evening and early morning. There are also the remains of Aboriginal middens and stone fish-traps, which can be accessed by good walking tracks. On the approach to the foreshore area there's also an interesting boardwalk leading out through a tidal mangrove forest.

Smalleys Beach Campground (sites per person/ family $4.50/18) is a small, pretty, grassed camping ground hugging the foreshore and jumping with kangaroos. Self-register/pay at the camping ground.

Cape Hillsborough Nature Resort (☎ 4959 0152; www .capehillsboroughresort.com.au; MS 895 Mackay; unpowered/ powered sites $20/25, d $60-115; 🖳 🖳) is so low-key, you may find yourself checking your pulse. There's a huge array of cabin and motel accommodation, but the beach huts ($95) right on the foreshore steal the show in a rustic, run-down kind of way. Wallabies and lizards roam around the resort enjoying the cool sea breezes.

WHITSUNDAYS AREA

Everyone dreams of a holiday in the Whitsundays. But where to go? There are 74 islands that make up this stunning archipelago and choosing where to spend your time can be confusing. The truth is, no matter where you decide to go, it'll be worth it.

There is an island for every budget and whim from the basic accommodation at Hook Island to the exclusive luxury at Hayman Island. Families will love Lindeman Island while busy, bustling Hamilton Island caters to all. Daydream Island is small but fun, while South Molle and Long Islands will satisfy energetic types.

The islands, which are really the tips of mountain tops jutting out from the Coral Sea, are the perfect places to relax and unwind or be energetic, depending on your mood of the day. With several island resorts, from backpackers to five star, and Airlie Beach from which to base yourself, the turquoise waters, palm-fringed beaches and coral gardens beckon from your doorstep. It really is a magical part of the world.

Orientation & Information

Airlie Beach is the mainland centre for the Whitsundays, with a bewildering array of accommodation options, travel agents and tour operators. Shute Harbour, about 10km east of Airlie, is the port for most day-trip cruises and island ferries, while most of the yachts and some cruise companies berth at Abel Point Marina about 1.5km west of Airlie Beach.

The Whitsunday district office of the **QPWS** (☎ 4946 7022; fax 4946 7023; cnr Shute Harbour & Mandalay Rds; ◷ 9am-5pm Mon-Fri) is 3km past Airlie Beach on the road to Shute Harbour. This office deals with camping permits for the islands, and its staff are very helpful and a good source of information on a wide range of topics. This should be your first place to visit if you are interested in exploring the islands independently.

The official **Tourism Whitsundays Information Centre** (☎ 4945 3711, 1800 801 252; www.whitsunday tourism.com) is on the Bruce Hwy at the southern entry to Proserpine.

MAPS & BOOKS

100 Magic Miles of the Great Barrier Reef – The Whitsunday Islands by David Colfelt is sometimes referred to as the bible to the Whitsundays. It contains an exhaustive collection of charts with descriptions of all boat anchorages around the islands as well as articles on the islands and resorts, and features on diving, sailing, fishing, camping and natural history.

Two of the best maps to this region are the Travelog *Great Barrier Reef* map, which has a *Whitsunday Passage* map on the reverse side, and Sunmap's *Australia's Whitsundays*.

Activities

SAILING

The Whitsundays are a paradise of protected waters and numerous safe and picturesque anchorages. Here you can learn to sail, join an overnight tour on a racing maxi or a graceful tall ship, or charter a yacht and skipper it yourself. Read the boxed text (p408) before checking out what the following companies have on offer.

There are a number of bareboat charter companies around Airlie Beach, including the following:

Charter Yachts Australia (☎ 1800 639 520; www.cya .com.au; Abel Point Marina)

Cumberland Charter Yachts (☎ 1800 075 101; www .ccy.com.au; Abel Point Marina)

Queensland Yacht Charters (☎ 1800 075 013; www .yachtcharters.com.au; Abel Point Marina)

Sunsail (☎ 1800 803 988; www.sunsail.com.au; Hamilton Island Marina)

Whitsunday Escape (☎ 1800 075 145, 4946 5222; www.whitsundayescape.com; Abel Point Marina)

Whitsunday Rent A Yacht (☎ 1800 075 111; www .rentayacht.com.au; Trinity Jetty, Shute Harbour)

The following are some of the numerous sailing tours that have been recommended by readers:

Oz Adventure Sailing (☎ 1800 359 554; www.ozsail ing.com.au; Shute Harbour Rd, Airlie Beach) This company has a range of vessels including three tall ships, four racers and four sail-and-dive boats. There's also a sailing school if you catch the bug. Three-day, two-night packages start from $460 per person.

Maxi Action Ragamuffin (☎ 1800 454 777; www .maxiaction.com) *Ragamuffin* was a line honours winner in the famous Sydney to Hobart yacht race in 1979. Nowadays, she leads a more sedate existence and does two day trips: on Monday, Wednesday, Friday and Saturday she visits Hayman Island's Blue Pearl Bay for snorkelling; on Thursday and Sunday she heads for a Whitehaven Beach picnic cruise. Cruises depart Shute Harbour at 8.45am and return about 4.15pm (adult/child/concession/family $135/50/125/300).

Maxi Apollo (☎ 1800 635 334; Abel Point Marina) Another Sydney to Hobart winner, the *Apollo* does a three-day, two-night cruise to Whitehaven Beach and Blue Pearl Bay departing at 9.30am on Monday and Friday, returning at 4pm on Wednesday and Sunday for $460 per person.

Southern Cross Sailing Adventures (☎ 1800 675 790; www.soxsail.com.au; 4 The Esplanade, Airlie Beach) Southern Cross runs adventure sailing cruises on racing yachts such as *Siska* and *Southern Cross*, as well as more sedate cruises aboard the magnificent tall ship *Solway Lass*. You can also combine the racing yacht and tall ship experience. Three-day, two-night packages start from $429 per person.

The Whitsundays is also one of the best and most popular places to learn how to sail. Should this be your calling, the following are a selection of Airlie Beach sailing schools, each with several courses:

Whitsunday Marine Academy (☎ 4948 2350; www .whitsundaysailtraining.com; 277 Shute Harbour Rd) Run by Oz Adventure Sailing.

Whitsunday Sailing Club (☎ 4946 6138; Airlie Point)

DIVING

The ultimate diving experience to be had here is on the actual Great Barrier Reef, at places such as Black, Knuckle and Elizabeth Reefs. Dive boats should leave in the evening so that you wake up at your dive site. The following dive companies offer a good range of diving trips for certified divers, which combine the reef with the islands. These companies also offer dive courses; open-water courses with several ocean dives start at around $500.

Dive Time (☎ 4948 1211; www.divetime.com.au; Abel Point Marina)

Reef Dive & Sail (☎ 1800 075 120, 4946 6508; www .reefdive.com.au; 16 Commerce Close, Cannonvale)

Tropical Diving (☎ 1800 776 150, 4948 1029; www .tropicaldiving.com.au)

Apart from these companies, most of the island resorts also have their own dive schools and free snorkelling gear.

KAYAKING

Paddling serenely in search of an island with dolphins and turtles as company is one of the best ways to experience the Whitsundays. **Salty Dog Sea Kayaking** (☎ 4946 1388; www.saltydog .com.au) offers guided tours and kayak rental. Half-/full-day tours from Shute Harbour cost $70/125. There are also overnight trips ($365) and a brilliant six-day expedition ($1500) covering about 15km to 20km per day that's suitable for beginners. Kayak rental for a single kayak costs $50/60 for a half-/one day and $80/90 for a double.

Tours

It can be confusing figuring out the best and most convenient way to see the islands. There

SAILING THE WHITSUNDAYS

Bareboat Charters

These have become enormously popular in the Whitsundays. 'Bareboat' doesn't refer to what you wear on board; it simply means you rent the boat without skipper, crew or provisions. While you don't require formal qualifications to hire a yacht, you will need to prove to the company that at least one person in your group is fully competent in operating the vessel. On the first day you should receive around four hours of briefing and familiarisation with the yacht, during which time your own abilities will be assessed. If necessary you may be required to pay for additional tutoring for around $200 per day, or it may be necessary for you to hire a skipper for an hourly rate. If you lack experience, it's a good idea to hire an experienced skipper at least for the first day.

The operators usually require a booking deposit of $500 to $750 and a security bond of between $1000 and $2000 (depending on the kind of boat), payable on arrival and refunded after the boat is returned undamaged. Bedding is usually supplied and provisions can also be provided if you wish. Most companies have a minimum hire period of five days.

There's a wide range of yachts and cruisers available. You'll pay $500 to $800 a day in the high season (September, October, December and January) for a yacht that will comfortably sleep four to six passengers. It's worth asking if the company you choose belongs to the Whitsunday Bareboat Operators Association, a self-regulatory body that guarantees certain standards. Also check that the latest edition of David Colfelt's *100 Magic Miles* is stowed on board, and pick up a copy of the *Public Moorings and Anchoring* leaflet from QPWS.

Sailing Tours

These tours, which supply professional crew and catering, are all the rage in Airlie Beach. It can be hard work sorting through the glossy brochures, the stand-by rates and the word of mouth. Price can be a very good indication; we get stacks of letters complaining about the cheaper companies, everything from lengthy delays, boats breaking down, unsanitary conditions, even serious safety concerns. Look out for the tick of approval from the WCBIA (Whitsunday Charter Boat Industry Association) on the brochure. The usual package is three days and two nights, but longer cruises are possible, as are day tours, sailing courses and even ocean racing.

Crewing

A third option is to crew a private vessel by responding to 'Crew Wanted' notices pasted up in backpackers or at the marina and yacht club. Just like hitching a ride in a car, the experience could be life affirming or life threatening. Think about yourself stuck with someone you don't know on 10m of boat, several kilometres from shore, before you actually find yourself there. Be sure to let others know where you are going, with whom and when you expect to return.

---

are so many operators, but it needn't be too difficult. Not everyone has the time or the money to sail and therefore must rely on the faster catamarans to whisk them to several different islands on a day trip. If snorkelling or laying on the beach or exploring the rainforests of a few of the Whitsunday Islands appeals, then it's just a matter of hunting down the tour that will suit you.

Most day trips include activities such as snorkelling or boom netting, with scuba diving as an optional extra. Children generally pay half fare. Following are some (by no means all) of the day trips on offer and

bookings can be made at any of the tour agents in Airlie Beach:

Big Fury (☎ 4948 2201; Abel Point Marina; adult/child/family $110/55/310) Small operator with a maximum of 35 passengers that speeds out to Whitehaven Beach on an open-air sports boat followed by lunch and then snorkelling at a secluded reef nearby.

Cruise Whitsundays (☎ 4946 4662; www.cruise whitsundays.com; Shingley Dr, Abel Point Marina) This is one of the Whitsundays' largest operators. Cruise Whitsundays operates a huge wave-piercing catamaran that speeds out to a pontoon moored at Knuckle Reef Lagoon on the Great Barrier Reef for spectacular snorkelling opportunities.

Fantasea (☎ 4946 5111; www.fantasea.com.au; 11 Shute Harbour Rd, Jubilee Pocket) The largest tour operator in Airlie Beach, and the operator of the island ferries, offers a number of options. A high-speed catamaran cruises to its Reefworld pontoon on the Great Barrier Reef, where you can snorkel, take a trip in a semisubmersible and check out the underwater viewing chamber (adult/child/family $197/92/476). An overnight 'Reefsleep' costs from $400. There are several options for spending a day at one of the island resorts utilising Fantasea, as well as a Three Island Discovery Cruise that visits Long, Daydream and Hamilton (adult/child/family $80/44/227).

Mantaray Charters (☎ 1800 816 365; www.manta raycharters.com; adult/child/family $130/65/350) This tour allows you to spend the most time on Whitehaven Beach (about three hours), followed by a visit to Mantaray Bay; includes snorkelling and lunch.

Voyager 3 Island Cruise (☎ 4946 5255; adult/child $130/65) A good-value day cruise that includes snorkelling at Hook Island, beachcombing and swimming at Whitehaven Beach, and checking out Daydream Island.

Most of the cruise operators that operate from Shute Harbour do coach pick-ups from Airlie Beach and Cannonvale. You can take a public bus to Shute Harbour.

Sleeping
RESORTS
The rates quoted in this section are the standard rates, but hardly anyone pays these. Most travel agents can put together a range of discounted package deals that combine air fares, transfers, accommodation and meals.

CAMPING
QPWS (www.epa.qld.gov.au) manages national-park camping grounds on several islands for both independent campers as well as groups on commercial trips. Camping permits are available over the internet and from the Whitsunday QPWS office and cost $4.50 per person ($18 per family) per night. If you book online don't forget to pick up your permit/tag from the office.

There's a national parks leaflet, *Island Camping in the Whitsundays*, which describes the various sites, and provides detailed information on what to take and do. You must be self-sufficient, and are advised to take 5L of water per person per day, plus three days' extra supply in case you get stuck. You should also have a fuel stove; wood fires are banned on all islands.

Get to your island by Blue Ferry or a day-cruise boat; the booking agencies in Airlie

Beach will be able to assist. Or use an island-camping specialist such as **Island Camping Connections** (☎ 4948 2201), which leaves from Shute Harbour and can drop you at North or South Molle, Planton or Denman Islands ($40 return); Whitsunday Island or Henning Island ($99); Whitehaven Beach ($120); and Hook Island ($150). **Camping Whitsunday Islands** (☎ 4946 9330) has similar prices, and both operations can help with provisions and snorkelling gear.

Getting There & Around
AIR
The two main airports for the Whitsundays are at Hamilton Island (see p419) and Proserpine (see below). The Whitsunday airport, near Airlie Beach, has regular flights from the mainland to the islands by light plane, seaplane and helicopter; see p414 for details. Lindeman Island also has its own airstrip.

BOAT
Fantasea (☎ 4946 5111; www.fantasea.com.au; 11 Shute Harbour Rd, Jubilee Pocket) provides ferry transfers to the islands from Shute Harbour; see the individual islands for transfer details.

BUS
Greyhound (☎ 13 14 99; www.greyhound.com.au) and **Premier** (☎ 13 34 10; www.premierms.com.au) buses detour off the Bruce Hwy to Airlie Beach. **Whitsunday Transit** (☎ 4946 1800) connects Proserpine, Cannonvale, Abel Point, Airlie Beach and Shute Harbour.

PROSERPINE
☎ 07 / pop 3250
Proserpine airport decided on changing its name to Whitsunday Coast, no doubt in an effort to spruce up its image, but there's still no reason to linger in this industrial sugar-mill town, which is the turn-off point for Airlie Beach and the Whitsundays.. A quick stop just south of town at the helpful **Whitsunday Information Centre** (☎ 1800 801 252; www.whitsunday tourism.com.au; Bruce Hwy; ◷ 10am-6pm), the main source of information about the Whitsundays and surrounding region, is all you'll need.

Proserpine Airport is 14km south of town and is serviced from Brisbane as well as some other capitals by **Jetstar** (☎ 13 15 38; www.jetstar .com.au), **Qantas** (☎ 13 13 13; www.qantas.com.au) and **Virgin Blue** (☎ 13 67 89; www.virginblue.com.au).

In addition to meeting all planes and trains, **Whitsunday Transit** (☎ 4946 1800) has six scheduled bus services running daily from Proserpine to Airlie Beach. One way/return from the airport costs $15/28, and from the train station it's $8.20/15.20.

AIRLIE BEACH
☎ 07 / pop 6770

For such a small town, Airlie Beach positively hums with energy. You'll notice it as soon as you step onto the streets. Barely an Australian accent in earshot, Airlie bristles with holiday-makers from all corners of the globe. Can't blame them really.

Airlie itself is the base from which to explore the Whitsunday Islands. The cruise boats leave in the morning, letting the town finally catch up on some sleep. During this time, people meander the streets to shop, eat, sip coffee, make cruise bookings or laze about at the lagoon and it's then that the town manages to drift between lazy and energetic depending on her mood at the time.

Airlie Beach then awakens from her slumber when the day-trippers start to filter off the boats around late afternoon. It's closing in on party time now. Young travellers discuss the afternoon's snorkelling trip over a jug of beer and make plans to hook up with people they've met on the boat that day. Older travellers start preparing for a slap-up meal at a swish restaurant over a chilled bottle of wine. Families are getting the kids ready for a walk along the lagoon with the obligatory ice cream in hand. Couples of all ages stroll along Shute Harbour Rd holding hands, undecided on fish and chips, or steak and seafood.

By nightfall, people are roaming the streets in search of food, drink and each other. It's now time to do some serious partying. Never mind about the next boat trip tomorrow and the subsequent hangover. Live for the moment.

Orientation

Nearly everything lies along Shute Harbour Rd. Shute Harbour, where the island ferries depart from, is about 12km east, and Abel Point Marina, home to many of the cruising yachts, is about 1.5km west.

Information

The main drag is stacked with privately run tour agencies, all able to answer queries on island transport, and book tours and accommodation. Check out their notice boards for stand-by rates on sailing tours and resort accommodation. Internet access is widely available; many of the hostels have terminals and there are several dedicated internet cafés.

Airlie Beach Newsagency (☎ 4946 6410; 354 Shute Harbour Rd) Stocks interstate and overseas newspapers.
Airlie Beach visitors centre (☎ 4946 6665; 277 Shute Harbour Rd)
Destination Whitsundays (☎ 4946 7172; 297 Shute Harbour Rd) Tourist information.
Internet Centre (346 Shute Harbour Rd; per hr $4) The cheapest we found.
Post office (☎ 13 13 18; 372 Shute Harbour Rd; ⌚ 9am-5pm Mon-Fri, to 12.30pm Sat)
Where? What? How? Whitsundays (☎ 4946 5255; 283 Shute Harbour Rd) Tourist information.

Activities

For details on sailing, diving and kayaking around the islands, see p407.

SWIMMING & WATER SPORTS

The gorgeous lagoon on Airlie's foreshore provides year-round safe swimming and is an attractive, popular public space for those wanting to work on their tan. The beaches at Airlie Beach and Cannonvale are OK for swimming, but the presence of marine stingers means swimming in the sea isn't advisable between October and May. There are (seasonal) operators in front of the Airlie Beach Hotel that hire out jet skis, catamarans, windsurfers and paddle skis.

BUSHWALKS

The Conway Range behind Airlie Beach is part national park (see p415) and part state forest, and provides for some great walking in coastal rainforest. Try the 2.4km climb up Mt Rooper for great views, or the short Coral Beach Track at Shute Harbour, or the three-day Whitsunday Great Walk. For advice and track notes on these and other walks visit the QPWS.

SKYDIVING

Try tandem skydiving with **Tandem Skydive Airlie Beach** (☎ 4946 9115; from $249).

Tours
ISLAND CRUISES

A huge range of boats offer trips out to the Whitsundays and the Great Barrier Reef from

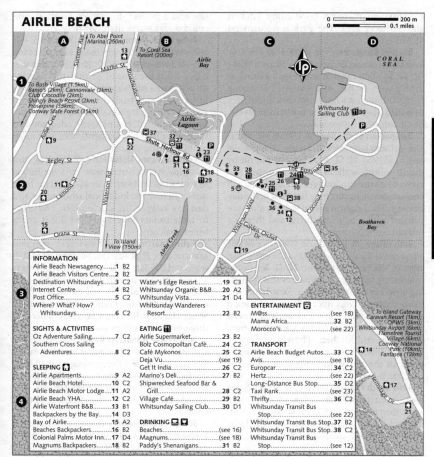

AIRLIE BEACH

the Abel Point Marina and Shute Harbour. See p407 for details of sailing tours and p407 for details of tour boats.

RAINFOREST/NATIONAL PARK TOURS
Fawlty's 4WD Tropical Tours (☎ 4946 6665) departs at 10.30am daily, and returns at 4pm. This tour is a great way to see the beautiful Cedar Creek Falls (when they're running that is) and some rainforest close up. Lunch and pick-ups are included in the price (adult/child $55/40).

Sleeping
BUDGET
Airlie Beach is a backpacker haven, but with so many hostels, standards vary. We heard of several reports of bedbugs being a problem here. Don't be afraid to speak up if you're not happy.

Magnums Backpackers (☎ 1800 624 634, 4946 6266; www.magnums.com.au; 366 Shute Harbour Rd; camp sites/ van sites $18/20, dm/d $17/52; ☒ ☐) All backpackers end up at Magnums one way or another. This huge, sprawling conglomerate is party central in more ways than one. Once you get past the hectically busy reception, you'll find simple beds set away from the main road. The outdoor bar area with its wooden tables and live music is incredibly popular.

Flametree Tourist Village (☎ 4946 9388; www.flame treevillage.com.au; Shute Harbour Rd; unpowered/powered sites $23/29, cabins from $85; ☒ ☒) Although not as glitzy as the other big parks, the spacious sites are scattered through lovely, bird-filled gardens and there's a good camp kitchen and barbecue area. The park is 6.5km west of Airlie.

Beaches Backpackers (☎ 1800 636 630; 4946 6244; www.beaches.com.au; 356 Shute Harbour Rd; dm/d $25/80; ✕ ☐ ☎) You must at least enjoy a drink at the big open-air bar, even if you're not staying here. Although it's busy, Beaches doesn't try to outdo Magnums in the boisterous stakes, but it comes close anyway.

Backpackers by the Bay (☎ 1800 646 994, ☎ /fax 4946 7267; www.backpackersbythebay.com; 12 Hermitage Dr; dm/d & tw $26/62; ✕ ☐ ☎) Don't be put off by the 10-minute walk to the town centre. The views from the sun lounges out the front will encourage you to stay here for most of the day anyway. The bright walls on the corridors are painted with a nautical theme and there's a relaxed barbecue area.

Bush Village (☎ 1800 8098 256, 4946 6177; www.bushvillage.com.au; 2 St Martins Rd; dm $27, d & tw with/without bathroom $108/78, all incl breakfast; ✕ ☐ ☎) Some interesting history accompanies this sprawling low-key hostel about 1.5km from the town centre. It was once a farm and then a brothel. Nowadays, it's a clean, safe haven with large four-bed dorms with their own bathroom and kitchen. There's a courtesy bus into town. Women travellers not interested in the party, pick-up scene will appreciate it here.

Airlie Beach YHA (☎ 1800 247 251, 4946 6312; airliebeach@yhaqld.org; 394 Shute Harbour Rd; dm $27.50, d with/without bathroom $77/71; ✕ ☐ ☎) Central, but just far enough removed from the hubbub, this good, clean hostel is small and reasonably quiet.

Island Gateway Caravan Resort (☎ 4946 6228; www.islandgateway.com.au; Shute Harbour Rd, Jubilee Pocket; unpowered/powered sites $30/37, cabins $78-100, chalets $135-145, villas $175; ✕ ☎) This is a big park about 1.5km east of Airlie Beach, making it the closest camping ground to the town centre. The sites are shady and the facilities are excellent and include a camp kitchen, a shop, half-court tennis and minigolf.

MIDRANGE

Airlie Beach Hotel (☎ 1800 466 233, 4964 1999; www.airliebeachhotel.com.au; cnr The Esplanade & Coconut Grove; s $119-249, d $129-249; ✕ ☎) Newly renovated with three-star motel units and four-star apartments, the ABH is now a slick, contemporary addition to the Airlie Beach accommodation scene. With three restaurants on

site and a perfect downtown location, you could do far worse than stay here.

Airlie Beach Motor Lodge (☎ 1800 810 925, 4946 6418; www.airliebeachmotorlodge.com.au; 6 Lamond St; d from $120-140, 2-bedroom apt $140-160; ✕ ☎) Undergoing a face-lift at the time of writing, this neat little place, tucked away in a residential area, is just a short walk from the Shute Harbour Rd action and the lagoon. The standard motel rooms are small, but perfectly adequate and the two-bedroom apartments offer a bit more room to swing your cat.

Colonial Palms Motor Inn (☎ 4946 7166; www.colonialpalms.bestwestern.com.au; cnr Shute Harbour Rd & Hermitage Dr; d from $120; ✕ ☎) The little ones will love the kids' pool while mum and dad laze away in the sun lounges. The comfortable rooms have cool tiled floors and a breezy balcony.

Airlie Apartments (☎ 4946 6222; www.airlieapartments.com; 22-24 Airlie Cres; 1-bedroom apt $120, 2-bedroom apt $125-160; ✕ ☎) Airlie Apartments is a good-value option that's ideal for families. The apartments are fully self-contained, there are views over Abel Point and the action on Shute Harbour Rd is not far away. There's a three-night minimum stay.

Whitsunday Wanderers Resort (☎ 1800 075 069, 4946 6446; www.whitsundaywanderers.com; Shute Harbour Rd; r $122-170; ✕ ☎) Resembling a small residential village, Wanderers has decent rooms with tiled floors among shaded gardens. The Melanesian rooms are the cheapest, but are good value.

Shingley Beach Resort (☎ 4948 8300; www.shingleybeachresort.com; 1 Shingley Dr; apt $140-240; ✕ ☎) These midrange, self-contained holiday apartments are close to Abel Point Marina and feature good views. There's four different room configurations, a bar and restaurant and two saltwater pools.

Whitsunday Organic B&B (☎ 4946 7151; www.whitsundaybb.com.au; 8 Lamond St; s/d $145/240) It's great to see that the new owners plan to keep this ecofriendly B&B just the way it was. Rooms are comfortable, but it's the organic garden walk and the orgasmic three-course organic breakfasts that everyone comes here for (nonguests $22.50). Lavender oil and fresh herbs surround the place to keep insects at bay and there's a 500L rainwater tank with fresh filtered water on offer as well as organic tea and coffee available all day. There are no TVs, ensuring your stay is all about peace and quiet.

TOP END

Most of the resorts here have package deals and stand-by rates that are much cheaper than their regular rates.

Whitsunday Vista (☎ 4948 4000; www.wentworth resorts.com.au; cnr Shute Harbour Rd & Hermitage Dr; apt $170-185; 🖭 🖳) The apartments vary here from very good to OK. Room 16S has a glass-enclosed spa bath overlooking the new marina precinct. There's an impressive Thai restaurant on the premises.

Water's Edge Resort (☎ 4948 2655; fax 4948 2755; www.watersedgewhitsundays.com.au; 4 Golden Orchid Dr; 1-bedroom apt $200-240, 2-bedroom apt $270-325; 🖭 🖳) The reception area immediately tells you that you're on holiday. Its open-air plan and gently revolving ceiling fans stir the languid, tropical heat. In the rooms, soft colours, cane headboards and shutters sealing off the bedroom from the living space immediately put your mind at ease.

Airlie Waterfront B&B (☎ 4946 7631; www.airlie waterfrontbnb.com.au; cnr Broadwater Av & Mazlin St; d $230-299; 🖭) Absolutely gorgeous views and immaculately presented from top to toe, this sumptuously furnished B&B oozes class and is a leisurely five-minute walk into town along the boardwalk. Some rooms have a spa and if you tire of the ocean views (how could you?) there are enough TVs, DVD and CD players to distract your attention.

Coral Sea Resort (☎ 1800 075 061, 4946 6458; www.coralsearesort.com; 25 Ocean View Ave; d $220-370, 1-bedroom apt $330, 2-bedroom apt $345-375; 🖭 🖳 ; wi-fi) At the end of a low headland overlooking the water just of the town centre, Coral Sea Resort has one of the best positions around. There's a huge range of well-appointed rooms that are motel style and self-contained, many with stunning views.

Eating

RESTAURANTS

Shute Harbour Rd abounds with restaurants; though also consider some of the resorts if you are after a quiet restaurant with a view.

Bolz Cosmopolitan Café (☎ 4946 7755; 7 Beach Plaza, The Esplanade; mains $12.50-26; 🕑 breakfast, lunch & dinner) You and everyone else will have the same idea at breakfast time on Sunday. It seems half the population of Airlie Beach pulls up a seat here. That doesn't mean lunch should be ignored either. Bolz has the usual array of dishes, but it's the gourmet pizzas that keep punters coming back.

Whitsunday Sailing Club (☎ 4946 7894; Airlie Point; mains $14-32; 🕑 lunch & dinner) The sailing-club terrace is a great place for a meal and a drink. Choose from the usual steak and schnitzel culprits off the inexpensive bistro blackboard. It's also a good place for a quiet drink.

Banjo's (☎ 4946 7220; cnr Shute Harbour Rd & Island Dr, Cannonvale; mains $16-30; 🕑 lunch & dinner) Order a drink from the bar and pull up a seat outside at this relaxed bar and grill that's popular with locals and tourists. The fare is stock-standard chicken, steak and seafood, but there's plenty to choose from. The public bus stops close to the front door at the Whitsunday Shopping Centre in Cannonvale.

Deja Vu (☎ 4948 4309; www.dejavurestaurant.com.au; Golden Orchid Dr; lunch mains $15-21, dinner mains $27-32; 🕑 lunch Tue-Sun, dinner Tue-Sat; 🖭) In a new location, Deja Vu is still one of Airlie's favourites. Try the crispy skin snapper, goat curry, or the tiger prawns and Moreton Bay bug *agnolotti*, but it's the famous long Sunday lunch (eight courses per person $35.50) that's the star of the show.

Shipwrecked Seafood Bar & Grill (☎ 4946 6713; www.shipwreckedbarandgrill.com.au; cnr Shute Harbour Rd & The Esplanade; lunch mains $18.50-25, dinner mains $30-44; 🕑 lunch & dinner; 🖭) One of the places to head if you want to go all-out for a special meal. Have a steak, chicken or duck if you absolutely must, but it would be a shame to miss out on the delectable fresh seafood, such as coral trout, swordfish, barramundi and salmon. Choose one of the 34 wines and settle back for a feast.

CAFÉS & QUICK EATS

If you're looking for a quick coffee, breakfast or light lunch, Airlie has plenty of places to go.

Marino's Deli (☎ 4946 4207; Shop 3b, 269 Shute Harbour Rd; dishes $6-15; 🕑 11am-8pm Mon-Fri, 10am-8pm Sat) Takeaway pasta, soup and gourmet rolls with delicious fillings dominate the menu at this unpretentious little deli-café. You can also get antipasto platters.

ourpick Café Mykonos (☎ 4946 5888; Shop 9, Shute Harbour Rd; mains $8-10; 🕑 11am-9pm) We stopped by for a quick lunch on the go and ended up coming back no less than three times (no, not on the same day!). Kebabs, *yiros* and other Greek faves are made right in front of you in minutes. Try going just once.

WHITSUNDAY COAST

Village Café (☎ 4964 1121; 351 Shute Harbour Rd; mains $10-16; 🕑 8am-5.30pm) Always busy with hungover backpackers, the breakfasts at this casual café are just the tonic to get the day started, even though it might be nearing lunchtime. If you've already done the brekky thing, the huge slabs of lasagne will do the trick for lunch.

Get it India (☎ 4948 1879; Shop 9, Beach Plaza, The Esplanade; mains $16-18; 🕑 11.30am-late) Quick, un-complicated and good. By all means eat at one of the plastic tables outside this small takeaway Indian café, but the best idea is to grab a feed early, take it back to your room and dig in after you've hit the bars and pubs.

SELF-CATERING
If you're preparing your own food, there's the small **Airlie Supermarket** (277 Shute Harbour Rd) in the centre of town and a larger one in Cannonvale, about 2km west of town.

Drinking
Airlie Beach is a hard drinking place, but it's also fun lovin'. People are here for a good time, not to cause trouble.

Paddy's Shenanigans (☎ 4946 5055; 352 Shute Harbour Rd; 🕑 5pm-3am) Paddy's has live music late at night, but before then it's a mellow place for a pint and a yarn.

The bars at **Magnums** (☎ 4946 6266; 366 Shute Harbour Rd) and **Beaches** (☎ 4946 6244; 356 Shute Harbour Rd), the two big backpackers, are always crowded, and everyone starts their night at one, or both, of them.

Entertainment
M@ss (☎ 4946 6266; 366 Shute Harbour Rd; 🕑 10pm-5am) The Gothic-inspired nightclub at Magnums plays crowd favourites and hosts foam parties.

Mama Africa (☎ 4948 0438; 263 Shute Harbour Rd; 🕑 10pm-5am) Huge dance floor and cool dance favourites keep this place rockin' all night.

Morocco's (☎ 4946 6446; Shute Harbour Rd; 🕑 10pm-late) Next door to, and affiliated with, Koala Beach Resort. There's rowdy dancing on a raised platform and theme nights.

Getting There & Away
AIR
The closest major airports are Proserpine and Hamilton Island.

Whitsunday airport (☎ 4946 9933), a small airfield 6km east of Airlie Beach, is midway between Airlie Beach and Shute Harbour. Half a dozen different operators are based here, and you can take a helicopter, light plane or seaplane out to the islands or the reef. **Air Whitsunday Seaplanes** (☎ 4946 9111; www.airwhitsunday.com.au) flies to Hayman and South Molle. **Helireef** (☎ 4946 9102) and Air Whitsunday Seaplanes offer joy flights over the Reef.

BOAT
Fantasea (☎ 4946 5111; www.fantasea.com.au; 11 Shute Harbour Rd, Jubilee Pocket) provides ferry transfers to/from the islands; see Getting There & Away under the individual islands for details.

BUS
Greyhound (☎ 13 20 30; www.greyhound.com.au) and **Premier Motor Service** (☎ 13 34 10; www.premierms.com.au) buses make a detour off the Bruce Hwy to Airlie Beach. There are buses between Airlie Beach and all the major centres along the coast, including Brisbane ($187, 19 hours), Mackay ($33, 2¼ hours), Townsville ($58, 4½ hours) and Cairns ($116, 11 hours).

Long-distance buses stop on The Esplanade, between the sailing club and the Airlie Beach Hotel. Any of the booking agencies along Shute Harbour Rd can make reservations and sell bus tickets.

Whitsunday Transit (☎ 4946 1800) connects Proserpine (Proserpine Airport), Cannonvale, Abel Point, Airlie Beach and Shute Harbour. Buses operate from 6am to 10.30pm.

Getting Around
Airlie Beach is small enough for you to cover it by foot, and most cruise boats have courtesy buses that will pick you up from wherever you're staying and take you to either Shute Harbour or Abel Point Marina. To book a taxi, call **Whitsunday Taxis** (☎ 13 10 08); there's a taxi rank on Shute Harbour Rd, opposite Magnums.

There are several car-rental agencies in town:

Airlie Beach Budget Autos (☎ 4948 0300; www.airliebudgetautos.com; 285 Shute Harbour Rd) In the courtyard of Whitehaven Holiday Units.

Avis (☎ 4946 6318; 366 Shute Harbour Rd)

Europcar (☎ 54946 4133; 398 Shute Harbour Rd)

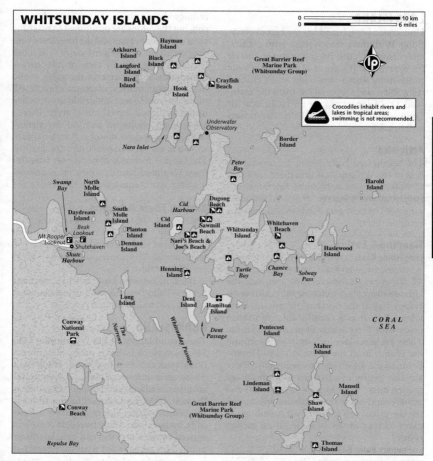

WHITSUNDAY ISLANDS

Crocodiles inhabit rivers and lakes in tropical areas; swimming is not recommended.

Hertz (☎ 4946 4687; Whitsunday Wanderers Resort)
Thrifty (☎ 4946 4300; 87 Shute Harbour Rd)

CONWAY NATIONAL PARK

The mountains of this national park and the Whitsunday Islands are part of the same coastal mountain range. The lower valleys of the region were flooded by rising sea levels following the last ice age, leaving only the highest peaks as islands, now cut off from the mainland.

The road from Airlie Beach to Shute Harbour passes through the northern section of the park. Several **walking trails** start from near the picnic and day-use area. About 1km past the day-use area, there's a 2.4km walk up to the **Mt Rooper lookout**, which provides

good views of the Whitsunday Passage and islands. Further along the main road, towards Coral Point (before Shute Harbour), there's a 1km track leading down to **Coral Beach** and **The Beak lookout**. This track was created with the assistance of the Giru Dala, the traditional custodians of the Whitsunday area; a brochure available at the start of the trail explains how the local Aborigines use plants growing in the area.

To reach the beautiful **Cedar Creek Falls**, turn off the Proserpine to Airlie Beach road on to Conway Rd, 8km north of Proserpine. It's then about 15km to the falls; the roads are well signposted. This is a popular picnic and swimming spot – when there's enough water, that is!

LONG ISLAND

Underrated Long Island has the best of everything. With three resorts, each with a different personality, this rugged island is suitable for everybody. It's about 11km long but not much more than 1.5km wide, and a channel only 500m wide separates it from the mainland. Day-trippers can use the facilities at the Long Island and Peppers Palm Bay resorts (see below).

Activities

The beaches on Long Island are among the best in the Whitsundays and there are 13km of walking tracks with some fine lookouts. **Long Island Dive & Snorkel** (☎ 0417 161 998) has a range of courses, gear for hire and trips for certified divers.

Sleeping & Eating

Long Island Resort (☎ 1800 075 125, 4946 9400; www .oceanhotels.com.au/longisland; d incl all meals $260-380; 🖭 🖳) A resort for everyone and, yep, the kids are more than welcome here. Sitting on Happy Bay at the north of the island, Long Island Resort is a comfortable, midrange place with three levels of accommodation. There are some fabulous short walks around the island, from the 600m stroll to Humpy Point, to the 4.4km walk to Sandy Bay. There are also plenty of activities to keep all age groups busy. The lodge units are small and austere, and bathroom facilities are shared; for the price, you're better off spending the extra to stay in the beachfront or garden rooms.

Peppers Palm Bay (☎ 1800 095 025, 4946 9233; www.peppers.com.au/palmbay; d $460-1200; 🖭 🖳) No phones, no TVs, no kids: Peppers guarantees relaxation and isolation. This intimate boutique resort houses a maximum of 42 guests in stylish comfort. The cabins, complete with swinging double hammock, sit around the pretty, sandy sweep of Palm Bay. The Platinum Suite has a wraparound deck and all the modern comforts you'd expect from such a hefty price tag. At the heart of the resort is a pool and a large, comfortable building that serves as the main dining area, bar and lounge.

South Long Island Nature Lodge (☎ 3839 7799; www.southlongisland.com; 5-night packages per person $2950) This secluded lodge on Paradise Bay consists of spacious, waterfront cabins made of Australian hardwood with high cathedral ceilings; there's no phone, no TV and no aircon, but the cabins are positioned to make the most of the sea breezes and the huge front window opens for magnificent views. The lodge is staffed by a friendly crew of just three – informality is the name of the game – and the maximum number of guests is just 12. All meals, beer, wine and soft drinks are included in the tariff and served buffet style. There's a five-night minimum stay, no day visitors or children, and no motorised water sports, so you're guaranteed peace and tranquillity. The tariff is inclusive of helicopter transfers from Hamilton Island, sailing tours and use of water-sports equipment.

Getting There & Around

Fantasea (☎ 4946 5111; www.fantasea.com.au) connects Long Island Resort to Shute Harbour by frequent daily services. The direct trip takes about 15 minutes, and costs $27/18 per adult/child.

It's 2km between Long Island Resort and Peppers Palm Bay and you can walk between them in about 25 minutes.

HOOK ISLAND

The second largest of the Whitsundays, the 53-sq-km Hook Island is predominantly national park and rises to 450m at Hook Peak. There are a number of good beaches dotted around the island, and Hook boasts some of the best diving and snorkelling locations in the Whitsundays. The resort itself is a no-frills, budget place. Many travellers come here enticed by the low prices and have left disappointed because it's not what they expected. If you want five-star luxury, don't come to Hook Island…try Hayman instead!

There are some wonderful camping opportunities in basic national-park **camping grounds** (per person/family $4.50/18) at Maureen Cove, Steen's Beach, Bloodhorn Beach, Curlew Beach and Crayfish Beach.

While it's basic, **Hook Island Wilderness Resort** (☎ 4946 9380; www.hookislandresort.com; camp sites $45, d with/without bathroom $120/150; 🖭 🖳) is also the cheapest resort in the Whitsundays, and its other advantage is that there's great snorkelling just offshore. The simple, adjoining units each sleep up to six or eight people; the bathrooms are *tiny*. Tea and coffee facilities are supplied in each room, and there's a camp kitchen strictly for the use of campers only, plus a couple of barbecues. There are no dorm facilities anymore, but there's around 60 camp sites with a superb beachfront location.

Transfers to the resort are arranged when you book your accommodation. Return transfers are by regular tour boat. The **Voyager** (☎ 4946 5255) does a daily three-island cruise (Hook Island, Whitehaven Beach and Daydream; see p409) as well as return transfers to Hook (adult/child $50/20). Transfers to other islands can be arranged. **Island Camping Connections** (☎ 4946 5255) or **Camping Whitsunday Islands** (☎ 4946 9330) can organise drop offs to the camping grounds for around $150.

SOUTH MOLLE ISLAND

South Molle Island offers an impressive array of short or long walks through gorgeous rainforest, making it an ideal destination for those wanting to put their legs to good use. The resort, which is decidedly nonglitzy, also has a nine-hole golf course, a gym, and tennis and squash courts. There is also a wide range of water-sports gear available for day-trippers to hire (nonmotorised water-sports equipment is free for resort guests). Of course, if relaxation is more your style, South Molle doesn't disappoint, with some superb beaches and a huge pool surrounded by inviting sun lounges.

Largest of the Molle group of islands at 4 sq km, South Molle is virtually joined to Mid Molle and North Molle Islands. Apart from the resort area and golf course at Bauer Bay in the north, the island is all national park. The island is crisscrossed by 15km of walking tracks, and has some superb lookout points. The highest point is Mt Jeffreys (198m), but the climb up Spion Kop is also worthwhile.

There are national park **camping grounds** (per person/family $4.50/18) located at Sandy Bay in the south and at Paddle Bay near the resort.

Full-board tariffs at **South Molle Island Resort** (☎ 1800 075 080, 4946 9433; www.southmolleisland.com.au; d $240-360, full board $360-440; ✺ ✉) include three buffet meals a day, and all tariffs include use of the golf course, tennis courts, nonmotorised water-sports equipment and nightly entertainment. The resort is far from luxurious and the rooms are pretty much your basic motel style, but they're clean, comfortable and functional.

Breakfast and lunch buffets are served in the main **Island Restaurant** (mains $20-30). The Discovery Bar is open until late and there's a small **café** (meals $5-20) that serves simple fare.

Backpackers can also get the Molle experience by cruising on the *Pride of Airlie*, which stops at South Molle for two nights on its three-day trip (adult $329). The journey also includes Whitehaven Beach. Guests stay in upmarket dorm rooms about 500m from the main resort and have exclusive access to their own bar. Book through **Koala Adventures** (☎ 1800 466 444; www.koalaadventures.com) in Airlie Beach.

Cruise Whitsundays (☎ 4946 4662; www.cruisewhitsundays.com) has connections to South Molle from Abel Point Marina (adult/child $26/17).

DAYDREAM ISLAND

Gorgeous little Daydream Island doesn't let her petite frame get her pushed to the back of the queue. At just more than 1km long and 200m wide, she is on the small side, but don't be fooled by her name. Daydream doesn't sit at the back of the class and stare out the window all day.

A steep and rocky path, taking about 20 minutes to walk, links the southern and northern ends of the island. There's another short walk to the tiny but lovely Sunlovers Beach, and a concreted path leads around the eastern side of the island. And once you've done these walks, you've just about covered Daydream Island from head to foot.

Surrounded by beautifully landscaped tropical gardens, and with a stingray-, shark- and fish-filled lagoon running through it, the large (296 rooms) **Daydream Island Resort & Spa** (☎ 1800 075 040, 4948 8488; www.daydreamisland.com; 3-night packages $990-1260; ✺ ✉) has tennis courts, a gym, catamarans, windsurfers and three swimming pools, all of which are included in the tariff. There are five grades of accommodation and most package deals include a buffet breakfast. There's a club with constant activities to keep children occupied, and they will love the fish-feeding sessions at the small coral reef pool near the main atrium. This is a large resort on a small island, so it's not the place to head if you're seeking isolation.

Breakfast is served buffet style at the Waterfalls Restaurant, which stays open all day, serving snacks, lunch and dinner. The **Boathouse bakery** (light meals $3-10) provides coffee, sandwiches and other lunchtime snacks. The casual **Fishbowl Tavern** (mains $19-31; ☽ Mon, Wed & Fri) offers the usual pizza, steak, risotto and salad. More formal is **Mermaids** (mains $24-35), which is on the beachfront.

Fantasea (☎ 4946 5111; www.fantasea.com.au; 11 Shute Harbour Rd, Jubilee Pocket) connects Daydream Island to Shute Harbour by frequent daily services (one way adult/child $27/18). Fantasea also does a three-island day-trip package (adult/child/family $80/44/227), which also visits Long and Hamilton Islands.

HAMILTON ISLAND
☎ 07 / pop 1840

Hamilton Island can come as quite a shock for the first-time visitor. Swarms of people and heavy development make Hamilton seem like a busy town rather than a resort island. Although this is not everyone's idea of a perfect getaway, it's hard not to be impressed by the sheer range of accommodation options, restaurants, bars and activities. The great thing about Hamilton is there's something for everyone here.

The sheer size of this resort means there are plenty of entertainment possibilities, which makes Hamilton an interesting day trip from Shute Harbour as you can use some of the resort facilities. The resort has tennis courts, squash courts, a gym, a golf driving range and a minigolf course. From **Catseye Beach**, in front of the resort, you can hire windsurfers, catamarans, jet skis and other equipment, and go parasailing or water-skiing.

A few dive shops by the harbour organise dives and certificate courses; you can take a variety of cruises to other islands and the outer reef. Half-day fishing trips cost around $125 per person, with fishing gear supplied.

There are a few **walking trails** on the island, the best being from behind the Reef View Hotel up to Passage Peak (230m) on the north-eastern corner of the island. Hamilton also has daycare and a Clownfish Club for kids.

Sleeping

Hamilton Island Resort (☎ 137 333, 4946 9999; www .hamiltonisland.com.au; ✕ 🖳 🐾) has options ranging from hotel rooms to self-contained apartments to penthouses. Rates listed are for one night although almost everyone stays for at least three nights, when the cheaper package deals come into effect. All bookings need to be made through the central reservations number.

Palm Terraces (d $290) These rooms are in low-rise complexes with big balconies overlooking the garden.

Palm Bungalows (d $315) These attractive individual units behind the resort complex are closely packed but buffered by lush gardens. Each has a double and single bed, and a small patio.

Self-Catering Accommodation (d $317-1245) Several types of fully self-contained units, from standard to luxury. There's a four-night minimum stay.

Reef View Hotel (d from $350-410) The large 20-storey, four-star hotel has 386 spacious rooms, mostly balconied; some have Coral Sea views, others garden views.

Whitsunday Holiday Apartments (d $350-430) These serviced one- to four-bedroom apartments are on the resort side of the island.

Beach Club (d $595) Flanking the main resort complex with its reception area, restaurants, bars, shops and pools, these 55 five-star rooms all enjoy absolute beachfront positions.

Eating & Drinking
RESORTSIDE

The following restaurants are found within the resort.

Toucan Tango Café & Bar (☎ 4946 8562; mains $15-29; ⊙ breakfast, lunch & dinner) Enjoy a casual poolside breakfast or a lazy lunch at this cool café overlooking Catseye Beach. Go for dinner, or just settle in for a drink and nibble from the snack menu while listening to live jazz.

Beach House (☎ 4946 8580; mains $39-49; ⊙ lunch & dinner) Modern Australian cuisine forms the basis of the menu at the Beach House, which enjoys absolute beachfront location. It's Hamilton's signature restaurant. Dishes include tuna, eye fillet and spatchcock.

HARBOURSIDE

These restaurants, all along the waterfront in what is known as Marina Village (or simply Harbourside), are independently run. There's also a supermarket-general store for those in apartments preparing their own meals.

Marina Deli (☎ 4946 8224; meals $5.50-12; ⊙ 7am-4pm) Simple, filling fare from croissants and muffins for breakfast to gourmet sandwiches, wraps and salads for lunch.

Marina Tavern (☎ 4946 8839; mains $14-20; ⊙ lunch & dinner) Formerly the yacht club, this busy seaside pub affords wonderful views of the marina. It's a great place for a decent pub feed or a drink. The T-bone steak ($28.50) will satisfy those with a hunger while the lasagne, chips and salad ($19.50) will do the trick for anyone else. There's also a snack menu ($6 to $9) if you just feel like grazing over a cold drink.

Manta Ray Café (☎ 4946 8213; mains $17-26; ⊙ breakfast, lunch & dinner) The food is popular here because it's simple and very tasty. The wood-fired gourmet pizzas are a favourite al-

WHITSUNDAY COAST

though the salt-and-pepper squid and Spanish paella provide worthy competition.

Mariners Seafood Restaurant (☎ 4946 8628; mains $26-38; ☺ dinner Mon, Tue & Thu-Sat) In a big, enclosed veranda overlooking the harbour, Mariners is both licensed and BYO. While the emphasis is on seafood, grills are also available; it's a stylish restaurant with a menu to match.

There's also a bakery, ice-cream shop and a supermarket/general store for those preparing their own meals.

Entertainment

The bars in the resort and Harbourside offer nightly entertainment. Toucan Tango (opposite) has live entertainment most nights, or you can head to Harbourside's **Boheme's NightClub** (☺ 9pm-late).

Getting There & Away
AIR

Hamilton Island airport is the main arrival centre for the Whitsundays. **Jetstar** (☎ 13 15 38; www.jetstar.com.au) has flights to/from Brisbane, Sydney, Melbourne and Adelaide. **Virgin Blue** (☎ 13 67 89; www.virginblue.com.au) has flights to/from Brisbane. **Island Air Taxis** (☎ 4946 9933) connect Hamilton with Airlie Beach.

BOAT

Fantasea (☎ 4946 5111; www.fantasea.com.au) connects Hamilton Island marina (adult/child $40/22) and airport ($50/28) to Shute Harbour by frequent daily services. Cruise Whitsundays connects Hamilton Island airport and Abel Point Marina in Airlie Beach (adult/child $49/27). Hamilton can be visited as part of a three-island day-trip package (adult/child/family $80/44/227) with Fantasea.

Getting Around

There's a free shuttle bus service operating around the island from 7am to 11pm.

Everyone hires a golf buggy (per one/two/three hours $45/55/60, all day $70) to whiz around the island. They are available from the office near reception or from the Charter Base near the ferry terminal.

HAYMAN ISLAND

The most northern of the Whitsunday group, Hayman is just 4 sq km in area and rises to 250m above sea level. It has forested hills, valleys and beaches but let's face it, it's the solitude and sheer luxury that you're here for.

It's no wonder that the private **Hayman Great Barrier Reef** (☎ 1800 075 175, 4940 1234; www.hayman .com.au; r $580-3900; ✖ ▣ ▣) is one of the world's best hotels. If you want exclusive five-star comfort then Hayman is for you.

An avenue of stately 9m-high date palms leads to the main entrance, and with its 212 rooms, seven restaurants, four bars, a hectare of swimming pools, landscaped gardens and grounds, an impressive collection of antiques and arts, and exclusive boutiques, Hayman is certainly impressive. If money is no object, the 11 lagoonside penthouses offer a resort-style relaxed ambience, but with all the luxurious trimmings of an international standard hotel, not to mention a glorious balcony furnished with an outdoor teakwood setting. Even the standard rooms in the pool wing are swish.

Guests flying to Hamilton Island are met by Hayman staff and escorted to one of the resort's fleet of luxury cruisers (one way adult/child $205/102.50) for a pampered transfer to the resort. **Air Whitsunday Seaplanes** (☎ 4946 9111) provides a seaplane charter service from Hamilton Island (per plane $725).

Flying is the only way to do day trips to Hayman. Check out **Air Whitsunday Seaplanes** (☎ 4946 9111; adult/child $195/175).

LINDEMAN ISLAND

Sitting snugly at the southern end of the Whitsundays, pretty little Lindeman Island is far enough away from the hubbub of Hamilton Island and Airlie Beach to be 'remote', but compensates with an energy all its own. Club Med took over the resort in 1992 and while it's a little dated in appearance, a vibrant, youthful atmosphere seems to radiate from everywhere you go. The 8-sq-km island is mostly national park and while the resort will appeal to travellers of all ages, those who don't have, or don't want to share the island with, lots of kids should look elsewhere.

Club Med (☎ 1800 258 2633, 4946 9333; www.clubmed .com; 3-night full-board packages per 2 people $1788; ✖ ▣) is all hustle and bustle and it's no secret that this resort will appeal to energetic types. However, it's not too difficult to slow the pace down if that's what you prefer. The GOs (that's what the staff call themselves – you're a GM) ensure there are plenty of activities to keep you entertained and the famous kids' club may well ensure you don't see the little ones all day (good news for most parents!). The accommodation serves a purpose, but don't expect luxury. Unless you want to hoof it up a mountain of steps, splash out a bit and ask for a resortside room.

All meals and drinks are included in the tariff. The Main Restaurant serves buffet-style breakfasts, lunches and dinners. The food is plentiful and varied.

Every night there's a live show in the main theatre performed by the young and energetic GOs. It's great fun, but put it into perspective. These are not highly paid actors and dancers. They're just young people making a couple of bucks while travelling and it's all very amateur in a fun kind of way. It's corny as hell, but that only adds to the appeal. There's usually a live band from 6.30pm and the 'disco' gets going from 10.30pm.

Club Med has its own launch that connects with flights from Hamilton Island and is included in your package.

WHITSUNDAY ISLAND

The largest of the Whitsunday group, this island covers 109 sq km and rises to 438m at Whitsunday Peak. There's no resort, but it has some fine bushwalking, and the 6km-long **Whitehaven Beach** on the southeastern coast is the longest and best beach in the group (some say in the country), with good snorkelling off its southern end. Many of the day-trip boats visit Whitehaven. The pure-white silicon sand can be dazzling on a sunny day, so make sure you wear your sunglasses!

There are national-park camping grounds at Dugong, Sawmill, Nari's and Joe's Beaches in the west; at Turtle Bay and Chance Bay in the south; at the southern end of Whitehaven Beach; and Peter Bay in the north.

OTHER WHITSUNDAY ISLANDS

The northern islands of the Whitsundays group are undeveloped and seldom visited by cruise boats or water taxis. Several of these – Gloucester, Saddleback, Olden and Armit Islands – have national-park camping grounds. The **QPWS office** (☎ 4946 7022; www.epa .qld.gov.au), 3km south of Airlie Beach, can issue camping permits and advise you on which islands to visit and how to get there.

North Queensland Coast

You've spent the morning hiking in a nearby rainforest. After a hearty brunch and a delicious coffee, you decide to work on your tan at a gorgeous stretch of palm-shaded beach. By midafternoon you're ready to browse the shops or take in a museum or cultural performance. As the sun decides to set, you enjoy a cold beer beside the pool and then wander the streets in search of a seafood meal over a bottle of wine. Grilled barramundi or Spanish mackerel? Or maybe fresh mud crab would go better with that sav blanc? After dinner, it's time to hit the pubs and meet up with friends.

This could be a typical day off for any north Queensland local. You may as well jump in and join them.

Of course, there's ample opportunity to play tourist as well. Buzz around Magnetic Island on a moped, search for an elusive cassowary at Mission Beach, speed around the waters of Dunk Island on a jet ski or hike the gruelling Thorsborne Trail on gorgeous Hinchinbrook Island.

NORTH QUEENSLAND COAST

HIGHLIGHTS

- Joining the full-moon party or lazing about in one of the pretty little villages on **Magnetic Island** (p430)
- Cheering on the Cowboys or partying in down-to-earth **Townsville** (p424)
- Spotting a cassowary in the rainforest behind **Mission Beach** (p440)
- Searching for a secluded beach all to yourself on **Dunk Island** (p443)
- Walking the **Thorsborne Trail** (p438) on stunning Hinchinbrook Island

- TELEPHONE CODE: 07
- www.townsvilleholidays.info
- www.tq.com.au/destinations/

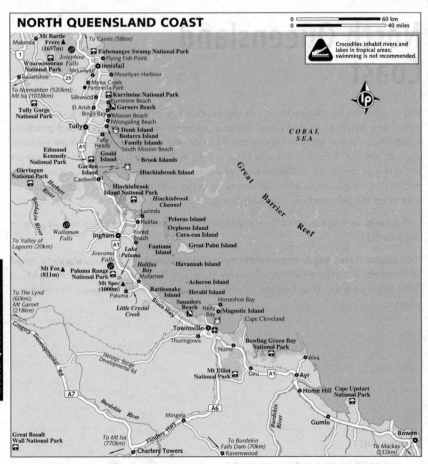

NORTH QUEENSLAND COAST

Dangers & Annoyances

Swimming in coastal waters is inadvisable from October to April due to the possible presence of marine stingers; see the boxed text, p381.

Saltwater crocodiles inhabit the mangroves, estuaries and open water in parts of north Queensland. Warning signs are posted around waterways where crocs may be present.

BOWEN TO TOWNSVILLE

BOWEN

☎ 07 / pop 7880

Bowen's 15 minutes of fame came in May 2007 when the cast and crew of Baz Luhrmann's epic movie *Australia* set-up shop here. Filming began in May/June 2007 (see boxed text, opposite), and the cast and crew were impressed with Bowen's low-key, unhurried atmosphere. You'll notice the sign 'Bowenwood' up on a hill as you approach town – quaint, in a cheesy sort of way. Although the town itself holds little of interest for travellers (except those here for fruit-picking work between April and November), there are some stunning beaches and bays northeast of the town centre.

Information

Tourism Bowen (☎ 4786 4222; www.tourismbowen .com.au; Bruce Hwy; ⏲ 8.30am-5pm) The usual trove of information, plus maps depicting the streets in which the movie *Australia* was filmed.

THERESE SAAD

Therese Saad was an extra on Baz Luhrmann's epic film *Australia*. The movie was filmed mostly in Bowen, between May and June 2007. The town was used in the film as a stand-in for Darwin in the 1930s. Starring Nicole Kidman, Hugh Jackman, Jack Thompson, Bryan Brown, David Gulpilil, Ben Mendelsohn and David Wenham, the cast reads like a who's-who of Australian cinema and TV.

Who did you play in the film? I played the part of an uptown girl…a high-society lady if you like. It was an amazing, once-in-a-lifetime experience.

What were the cast and crew like? Did they keep to themselves a lot? No, not at all – they were just normal Aussie people. Not one of them had a star's ego. They were lovely, all of them, and they loved Bowen. They were left to themselves, and weren't mobbed in the slightest. You could walk into the local supermarket and bump into Hugh or Nicole; they weren't precious at all.

Is Hugh Jackman as charming and good-looking in real life as he appears on screen? Yes, yes, yes! Hugh joined the local gym and a lot of the young girls in town decided it was time they joined as well!

What did the production do for the town? We called it 'Bazmania.' We couldn't believe what it did for the town: on every level it was beneficial, and it's something we'll cash-in on for years to come. Around 25,000 people visited Bowen in the six- to eight-week period when the cast and crew were here.

A lot of locals were used as extras in the film. What a great experience! It was funny because the film is set in the 1930s, and people were a lot smaller back then. They had to cast for short people! The production atmosphere started to rub off on the locals: people were looking after themselves; they dressed properly; they started treating each other a lot better. Young people's mannerisms, especially, started to change – it was an education for them.

Why do you think the cast and crew enjoyed filming in Bowen? It's a community with a lot of soul. It's a very stable place – definitely the best-kept secret of the Whitsundays!

As related to author Justin Flynn.

Sleeping & Eating

Bowen Backpackers (☎ 4786 3433; fax 4786 1073; cnr Herbet & Dalrymple Sts; dm with fan/air-con $25/26.50, d with air-con $53; 🐾) Has beds in four- and eight-bed dorms, with cheaper weekly rates available. The hostel can help find fruit-picking work in season.

Rose Bay Resort (☎ 4786 9000; www.rosebayresort .com.au; 2 Pandanus St, Rose Bay; r $130-230; 🐾 💻 🌐) You'll be happy here whether you choose the spacious studio units or the plush suites. Rooms are clean, stylish and modern, and with your own private beach there may be no need to leave the resort.

Horseshoe Bay Café (☎ 4786 2565; Horseshoe Bay; mains $14-25; 🕑 breakfast, lunch & dinner) If you walk away hungry from this busy, foreshore eatery, then it's your own fault. The huge all-day breakfasts are popular and the simple, yet substantial, lunches include big burgers and hearty pizzas. The extensive menu also includes mango chicken burgers, garlic prawns and a range of vegetarian meals.

360 on the Hill (☎ 4786 6360; Flagstaff Hill; mains $13-30; 🕑 breakfast, lunch & dinner) Browse through the small interpretive centre then take a seat outside at this brilliant café-restaurant, perched proudly on top of Flagstaff Hill. Amazing views accompany the excellent seafood mains, including the wildly popular coconut king prawns.

Getting There & Away

The long-distance bus stop is outside **Bowen Travel** (☎ 4786 2835; 40 Williams St), between Herbert and Gregory Sts. **Greyhound** (☎ 13 14 99; www.greyhound.com.au) and **Premier** (☎ 13 34 10; www.premierms.com.au) have a number of daily bus services along the coast stopping at destinations including Airlie Beach ($24, two hours) and Townsville ($40, four hours).

Queensland Rail (☎ 1300 131 722; www.traveltrain .com.au) operates the *Sunlander,* which runs four times a week between Brisbane and Cairns. It stops at Bootooloo Siding, 3km south of the centre.

AYR

☎ 07 / pop 8500

Ayr is on the delta of one of the biggest rivers in Queensland, the Burdekin, and is the major commercial centre for the rich farmlands of the Burdekin Valley. The local towns and territory are devoted to the production and harvesting of sugarcane, melons and mangos.

The **Burdekin visitors centre** (☎ 4783 5988; www
.burdekintourism.com.au; Plantation Park, Bruce Hwy; 9am-4pm) is on the southern side of town.

The **Billabong Sanctuary** (☎ 4778 8344; www
.billabongsanctuary.com.au; Bruce Hwy; adult/child/family $27/16/84; 8am-5pm), 17km south of Townsville, should not be underestimated. This 10-hectare wildlife park is definitely worth visiting. It's all about close-up and personal encounters with Australian wildlife, with shows and talks every 15 minutes or so. There's a café and a swimming pool, too.

TOWNSVILLE

☎ 07 / pop 143,330

Townsville might just be Australia's most underrated city. Don't believe us? Consider this: abundant sunshine, world-class diving, a lively restaurant and bar scene, two major sporting teams, a huge aquarium, excellent museums and a waterfront esplanade to rival that of any coastal paradise. That's a pretty impressive list for a capital city, let alone a regional hub.

With a large university and a strong military presence, Townsville knows how to let its hair down. Bars line bustling Flinders St, enticing thirsty locals and travellers with cheap drinks and nightly entertainment. The spruced-up Strand, Townsville's wonderful waterfront promenade, offers safe, year-round swimming and an excellent (free!) water park – the kids won't want to leave! The city is also home to the North Queensland Cowboys, the adored rugby league team, which dominates nearly every conversation on the streets.

ORIENTATION

Townville and its sister-city Thuringowa (a large suburb 15km southwest of central Townsville) are often referred to as the 'Twin Cities.' Dairy Farmers Stadium is in Thuringowa.

The arrival and departure point for long-distance buses is the Townsville Transit Centre on the corner of Palmer and Plume Sts – just south of Ross Creek. This is not to be confused with the Transit Mall on Stokes St (between Sturt St and Flinders St Mall), which is the departure point for local buses and taxis.

INFORMATION

Flinders Mall visitors centre (☎ 4721 3660; www
.townsvilleonline.com.au; Flinders St Mall, btwn Stokes & Denham Sts; 9am-5pm Mon-Fri, to 12.30pm Sat & Sun) Two desks: one provides general information, the other specialises in diving and reef tours (www.divecruise travel.com).

Internet Den (☎ 4721 4500; 265 Flinders St Mall; per hr $5; 9am-9pm Mon-Fri, 10am-8pm Sat & Sun) Friendly management and lots of computers.

Jim's Book Exchange (☎ 4771 6020; Shaw's Arcade) Wide range of secondhand books; off Flinders St Mall.

Mary Who? Bookshop (☎ 4771 3824; 414 Flinders St) Small but bountiful range of books and music.

Post office (☎ 13 13 18; www.australiapost.com.au; Post Office Plaza, Sturt St) Has a poste-restante window.

Townsville City Library (☎ 4727 9666; 272-278 Flinders St Mall; 9.30am-5pm Mon-Fri, 9am-noon Sat & Sun) Free Internet access, but you'll need to book hours in advance.

Townsville Enterprises visitors centre (☎ 4726 2700; www.townsvilleonline.com.au; 6 The Strand; 9am-5pm Mon-Fri) HQ for the booth in Flinders St Mall.

SIGHTS

It's no surprise that Townsville bills itself as an outdoors city. Undercover seating at Dairy Farmers Stadium was considered unnecessary because of the minimal rainfall during the rugby league season. The city boasts an average of 320 days of sunshine per year.

The Strand

Townsville's vibrant waterfront promenade, the Strand, flaunts a number of parks, pools, cafés and playgrounds. It's a busy place at any time of day or night. Walkers and joggers take to the paths from first light; beachgoers take over by midmorning; evening strollers are at it by late afternoon. The long stretch of beach is patrolled and protected by two stinger-proof enclosures in the danger months (November to May).

At the northeast tip is the **rock pool** (admission free; 24hr), an enormous artificial swimming pool surrounded by lawns and sandy beaches. A huge filtration system keeps it clean and stinger-free.

Kids will revel in the brilliant little **water park** (admission free; 10am-8pm Dec-Mar, to 6pm Sep-Nov, Apr & May, to 5pm Jun-Aug). Water is pumped through all sorts of tubes, culminating in a big bucket that fills up with water then dumps its load onto the squealing little ones below.

CENTRAL TOWNSVILLE

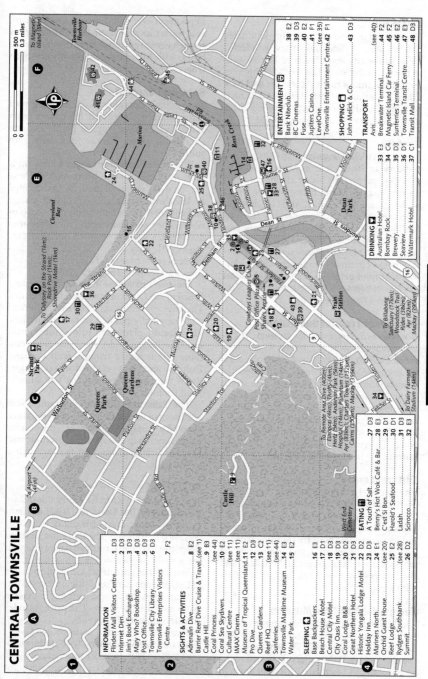

NORTH QUEENSLAND COAST

INFORMATION
Flinders Mall Visitors Centre.......1 D3
Internet Den.................................2 D3
Jim's Book Exchange......................3 D3
Mary Who? Bookshop......................4 D3
Post Office....................................5 D3
Townsville City Library...................6 D3
Townsville Enterprises Visitors
  Centre......................................7 F2

SIGHTS & ACTIVITIES
Adrenalin Dive..............................8 E2
Barrier Reef Dive Cruise & Travel..(see 1)
Castle Hill...................................9 B3
Coral Princess...........................(see 44)
Coral Sea Skydivers....................10 E2
Cultural Centre.........................(see 11)
IMAX Cinema............................(see 11)
Museum of Tropical Queensland..11 E2
Pro Dive...................................12 D3
Queens Gardens........................13 C2
Reef HQ.................................(see 11)
Sunferries..............................(see 44)
Townsville Maritime Museum......14 E3
Water Park...............................15 E2

SLEEPING
Base Backpackers.......................16 E3
Beach House Motel......................17 D1
Central City Motel.......................18 D3
City Oasis Inn.............................19 D3
Coral Lodge B&B........................20 D3
Great Northern Hotel....................21 D3
Historic Yongala Lodge Motel.......22 D2
Holiday Inn................................23 D3
Mariners North...........................24 E1
Orchid Guest House..................(see 20)
Reef Lodge................................25 E2
Rydges Southbank...................(see 28)
Summit.....................................26 D2

EATING
A Touch of Salt...........................27 D3
Benny's Hot Wok Café & Bar........28 E3
C'est Si Bon...............................29 D1
Harold's Seafood.........................30 D1
Ladah.......................................31 D3
Scirocco....................................32 E3

DRINKING
Australian Hotel..........................33 E3
Bombay Rock.............................34 C4
Brewery...................................35 D3
Seaview...................................36 D1
Watermark Hotel.........................37 C1

ENTERTAINMENT
Bank Niteclub.............................38 E2
BC Cinemas...............................39 D3
Fuse..40 E2
Jupiters Casino...........................41 F1
LevelOne................................(see 35)
Townsville Entertainment Centre..42 F1

SHOPPING
John Melick & Co........................43 D3

TRANSPORT
Avis.......................................(see 40)
Breakwater Terminal....................44 F2
Magnetic Island Car Ferry............45 F2
Sunferries Terminal......................46 E2
Townsville Transit Centre..............47 E3
Transit Mall................................48 D3

To Magnetic Island (8km)

Townsville Harbour

500 m
0.3 miles

To Odyssey on the Strand (1km);
Rock Pool (1km);
Shoredive Motel (1km)

To Airport (4km)

To Remote Area Dive (400m);
Ebropol (4km); Thrifty (4km);
Hertz (5km); Anderson Park (5km);
Hospital (14km); Palmetum (14km);
Ayr (83km); Charters Towers (132km);
Cairns (350km); Mackay (395km)

To Billabong
Sanctuary (17km);
Woodstock Trail
Rides (38km);
Ayr (82km);
Mackay (395km)

To Dairy Farmers
Stadium (14km)

West End
Cemetery

Castle
Hill

Queens
Park

Queens
Gardens

Strand
Park

Cleveland
Bay

Marina

Dean
Park

Cowboys Leagues Club

Post Office Plaza
Shaw's Arcade

Train
Station

Castle Hill

The big, red mound of Castle Hill dominates Townsville's skyline and offers wonderful views of the city and Cleveland Bay. A walk to the top of the 300m hill should be high on your list of things to do. Access the **goat track** (2km, 30 minutes) from Hillside Cres; or if walking sounds too energetic, you can drive up via Gregory St then Castle Hill Rd.

Reef HQ

This well-stocked **aquarium** (☎ 4750 0800; www .reefhq.com.au; Flinders St E; adult/child $21.50/10.50; 9.30am-5pm) proudly boasts a living coral reef on dry land. It's worth taking one (or a few) of the guided tours, which focus on different aspects of the reef and the aquarium. The fish-feeding display will excite younger guests, particularly seeing the sea snakes and the rather shy eels (impeccable table manners those guys!).

You can continue to experience life underwater without getting wet at the **IMAX cinema** (☎ 4721 1481; Flinders St E; adult/child/concession $13/8; 10.30am-4.30pm) next door.

Museum of Tropical Queensland

Not your ordinary, everyday **museum** (☎ 4726 0606; www.mtq.qld.gov.au; 70-102 Flinders St E; adult/child/ student $9/5/6.50; 9.30am-5pm), this place attempts to reconstruct scenes by using detailed models with interactive displays. The wreck of the *Pandora* is showcased at the museum, including some fascinating artefacts from the ship. Other galleries include the kid-friendly MindZone science centre, and displays on North Queensland's history from the dinosaurs to the rainforest and the reef.

Cultural Centre

The interactive Aboriginal dance and interpretive **centre** (☎ 4772 7679; www.cctownsville.com.au; 2/68 Flinders St E; adult/child $16.50/9; 9.30am-4.30pm) hosts a loud, entertaining session in which indigenous people perform traditional dance and music. There are some impressive art works and artefacts housed in the gallery, and the interpretive centre can be seen up close with a guided tour.

Townsville Maritime Museum

The highlight of a visit to this **museum** (☎ 4721 5251; www.townsvillemaritimemuseum.org.au; 42-68 Palmer St; adult/child/concession $6/3/5; 10am-4pm Mon-Fri, noon-4pm Sat & Sun) is the gallery dedicated to the wreck of the *SS Yongala*, which went down in a cyclone in 1911 with 125 passengers aboard, and wasn't located until 1958. Still, there's enough here to entertain more than just naval buffs, with historical exhibits on northern Queensland's maritime heritage.

Botanical Gardens

Townsville's Botanical Gardens are spread across three locations: each has its own character, but all have tropical plants and are abundantly green. They're open daily from sunrise to sunset, with free admission.

The **Queens Gardens** (cnr Gregory & Paxton Sts) is 1km northwest of the town centre. These are the town's original gardens, first planted in 1870 with trial plants (including mango and coffee) to potentially boost the local economy. They were thoroughly redesigned after 100,000 US soldiers squatted on them during WWII. They're now formal, ornamental gardens at the base of Castle Hill, with a children's playground and herb garden.

Anderson Park (Gulliver St, Mundingburra), established in 1932, is 6km southwest of the centre. The large gardens cover a 20-hectare site and were originally planted in taxonomic lots. They feature plants and palms from northern Queensland and Cape York Peninsula, lotus ponds and a tropical-fruit orchard. Don't be tempted to eat the fruits of the garden – no matter how enticing that Miracle Fruit sounds.

The **Palmetum** (University Rd), about 15km southwest of the centre, is a 17-hectare garden devoted to just one plant family – the humble palm. More than 300 species are represented here, including around 60 that are native to Australia.

ACTIVITIES

Well worth doing is a trail ride or cattle muster with **Woodstock Trail Rides** (☎ 4778 8888; www.wood stocktrailrides.com.au; Rowes Rd, Woodstock; half-/full-day rides $80/150; Apr-Nov). The trail rides take you deep into the huge farmstead where you stop for a barbecue lunch along Ross Creek. All riding abilities are catered for. Cattle musters ($150) include herding cattle on horseback, a camp-oven lunch, and learning to crack a whip and shear a sheep. The price includes transfers from/to Townsville.

Hurl yourself from a perfectly good aeroplane with **Coral Sea Skydivers** (☎ 4772 4889; www.coral seaskydivers.com.au; 181 Flinders St E; tandem jumps $315-415). Tandem jumps require no prior experience, just a lot of guts (but not too much: there's a weight limit of 95kg). The price gets more expensive the higher the plane takes you up.

Dive Courses

Two operators based in Townsville offer PADI-certified courses, where you'll learn to dive with two-days' training in the pool, plus three days and three nights living aboard the boat. Dive sites include a number of reefs, as well as the SS *Yongala* wreck and Wheeler Reef. In addition to the operator costs you'll need to obtain a dive medical and provide passport photos. Operators include the following:

Adrenalin Dive (☎ 4724 0600; www.adrenalindive .com.au; 9 Wickham St)

Pro Dive (☎ 4721 1760; www.prodive.com.au; 252 Walker St)

Great Barrier Reef

The booking agent **Barrier Reef Dive Cruise & Travel** (☎ 4772 5800; www.divecruisetravel.com) is part of the Flinders Mall visitors centre (p424), and has a comprehensive list of operators and offers. Most trips travel to the Great Barrier Reef as well as the famous SS *Yongala*.

The following operators run trips to the Reef; trips include lunch and snorkelling. If you want to just snorkel, take a day-trip that just goes to the Reef (the SS *Yongala* is for diving only). Multiday live-aboards are the best option for divers, with some operators offering advanced courses.

Adrenalin Dive (☎ 4724 0600; www.adrenalindive .com.au; 121 Flinders St E) *SS Yongala* day-trips including two dives (from $185). Also offers advanced diving certification courses and a snorkelling trip to Wheeler Reef ($155).

Coral Princess (☎ 4721 1673; www.coralprincess .com.au; Breakwater Terminal; ☽ 12.30pm Tue) Offers a four-day, three-night cruise between Townsville and Cairns, via Hinchinbrook and Dunk Islands (per person from $1500), departing from Breakwater Terminal.

Remote Area Dive (☎ 4721 4424; www.remotearea dive.com; 25 Ingham Rd) Diving ($195) and snorkelling ($150) trips to Orpheus and Pelorus Islands.

Sunferries (☎ 1800 447 333; www.sunferries.com.au; Breakwater Terminal) Day-trips to the Reef (adult/child $145/90) and certified dives ($70).

SLEEPING
Budget

Reef Lodge (☎ 4721 1112; www.reeflodge.com.au; 4 Wickham St; dm $21-23, tw & d with/without TV $57/54, motel r $72; ✖ ▣) The punters seem happy here and

are content to bask in Reef Lodge's unhurried and cruisy atmosphere. There's a sizeable kitchen, and people enjoy sitting in the courtyard area and meeting other travellers. The motel-style units are superb value, and there's a female-only dorm available.

Base Backpackers (☎ 1800 628 836, 4721 2322; www .basebackpackers.com; Townsville Transit Centre, 21 Plume St; dm/d $21/60; ✖ ▣) Base has fairly basic rooms and facilities, but includes the all-important one – the in-house bar. After sipping on a bright, alcoholic fizzy-drink, you could get lost in the maze of corridors here. Base is above the Townsville Transit Centre, close to both bus and ferry terminals.

our pick Orchid Guest House (☎ 4771 6683; 34 Hale St; dm $25, s with/without bathroom $60/45, d with bathroom $80; ✖) A guest house in every sense of the word. Fran will welcome you with free pick-up from anywhere in the city. The dorms are a surprise – hardly your everyday dorm rooms – with TV, fridge and air-con. The doubles are even better value. There's free laundry. Peace, quiet and value for money are guaranteed here.

Great Northern Hotel (☎ 4771 6191; fax 4771 6190; 496 Flinders St; s/d $50/65; ✖) A Townsville institution, this old pub has loads of character. The guest rooms upstairs are nothing special, but are clean and functional and all have access to the gorgeous old veranda overlooking Flinders St. If you're after something a bit different to backpackers hostels, this is a real, down-to-earth Aussie pub.

Coral Lodge B&B (☎ 1800 614 613, 4771 5512; www .corallodge.com.au; 32 Hale St; downstairs s/d $65/75, upstairs s/d $80/95; ✖) The upstairs self-contained units are as homy as you can get, while the downstairs guest rooms share male and female bathrooms. If staying in a safe, friendly, old-fashioned Aussie home appeals, then you've hit the spot.

Midrange

Shoredrive Motel (☎ 4771 6851; fax 4772 6311; 117 The Strand; s/d $85/95; ✖ ▣) The rooms here are functional and a little threadbare, but the location, right on the Strand's doorstep, is brilliant. The rooms are large and everything works fine, although the place lacks a bit of character.

Central City Motel (☎ 4724 0233; www.central citymotel.com; 164 Stanley St; s/d $95/105; ✖) The name doesn't tell fibs: it's the most central of Townsville's motels. While the rooms won't win any awards, they're functional and perfectly acceptable (if you're the type who reckons motel rooms are for sleeping only).

Beach House Motel (☎ 4721 1333; www.beachhouse motel.com.au; 66 The Strand; r $107-120; 🆒 🅿) A good option for those who just want a comfortable, decent and clean room without all the trimmings. Rooms are equipped with all the modern conveniences, such as a bar fridge, phone and TV, and the pool out the front is in an unusual location, allowing you to gawk at passers-by.

Historic Yongala Lodge Motel (☎ 4772 4633; www .historicyongala.com.au; 11 Fryer St; motel r $100-110, units from $115; 🆒 🅿) Comfortable as you can get and in a quiet, residential location (just a short stroll to the Strand and city), the Yongala has eight motel rooms and 10 self-contained, one- and two-bedroom apartments. The heritage restaurant is open daily for dinner.

Summit (☎ 4721 2122; www.summitmotel.com.au; 6-8 Victoria St; r $110-120; 🆒 🅿) There's not a lot of difference between the standard and executive rooms here, so save yourself $10 and go for the cheaper version. The rooms are standard, motel-style affairs, but are clean and comfortable.

Holiday Inn (☎ 4772 2477; www.townsville.holiday-inn .com; 334 Flinders St Mall; r $116-128; 🆒 🅿) The 'sugar shaker' is a prominent fixture of Townsville's skyline – a 20-storey circular building in the city's mall, housing 199 rooms. Guests have free use of a gym, located a short stroll away. There's a cool rooftop pool and the hotel is in a terrific part of town, smack-bang in the middle.

Rydges Southbank (☎ 4726 5265; www.rydges.com /townsville; 17-29 Palmer St; r from $135; 🆒 💻 🅿) The handsome rooms at this hotel cater mostly to business travellers, with practical, unfussy interiors; there are also separate meeting rooms available. Those on holiday will also appreciate the hotel's facilities, and whatever your reason for visiting, you'll love the opulent executive rooms with lounge areas and ocean views.

Top End
City Oasis Inn (☎ 1800 809 515, 4771 6048; www.cityoasis .com.au; 143 Wills St; r $170-200; 🆒 🅿 ; wi-fi) There are so many sparkling, white surfaces here that you'll have to allow time for your eyes to adjust upon entering. The fabulous loft apartments here have an upstairs bedroom separate from the downstairs kitchen, or opt for even more space between you and the kids in a two-bedroom apartment.

Mariners North (☎ 4722 0777; www.marinersnorth .com.au; 7 Mariners Dr; apt from $195; 🆒 🅿) Very nice, thank you very much. These large, self-contained apartments have brilliant balconies overlooking Cleveland Bay and big, clean bathrooms. The living areas are generously sized, and there's a big saltwater pool to frolic in.

EATING
Townsville is a superb place if you like your food. Seafood rules, but all palates will be satisfied.

Restaurants
Benny's Hot Wok Café & Bar (☎ 4724 3243; 17-21 Palmer St; mains $15-20; 🕑 lunch Thu, Fri & Sun, dinner daily) A little bit of everything Asian awaits at Benny's, which has fabulous outdoor seating and a good wine list. Whether your tastebuds fancy a quick trip to Japan, Thailand or China, Benny's will take you there for a fraction of the cost of an airline ticket.

Scirocco (☎ 4724 4508; 61 Palmer St; mains $16-30; 🕑 lunch Tue-Fri, dinner Tue-Sat) Mediterranean dining with a Greek twist greets you as you peruse the menu at Scirocco. Elegant and refined, the Greek-style lamb rack won't disappoint (that's if you can pass on the mud-crab lasagne).

our pick **A Touch of Salt** (☎ 4724 4441; cnr Stokes & Ogden St; mains $23-34; 🕑 lunch Fri, dinner Tue-Sat) A classy, family-run, riverside establishment serving delectable seafood accompanied by an extensive wine list and genuinely good service. If the price of evening waterside dining puts you off, try the Friday lunch (mains $15 to $17). A nice meal of Moreton Bay bugs for two and a bottle of wine shouldn't set you back much more than $60.

Cafés & Quick Eats
Harold's Seafood (☎ 4724 1322; cnr The Strand & Gregory St; meals $4-10; 🕑 lunch & dinner) More than your average fish-and-chip joint, Harold's also serves 'bug burgers' (of the Moreton Bay variety). Order at the counter, then pull up a seat outside and watch the goings-on along the Strand across the road.

Ladah (☎ 4724 0402; cnr Sturt & Stanley Sts; meals $10-16; 🕑 breakfast & lunch) The meals at this licensed café are sublime, and the energy radiating from the busy kitchen gives you every confidence in the food. Try the French toast with bacon and maple syrup for breakfast, or the smoked-cod and potato pie for lunch.

C'est Si Bon (☎ 4772 5828; 48 Gregory St; meals $11-23; 🕑 breakfast & lunch) Snappy, attentive serv-

RIDE 'EM COWBOY

You won't leave Townsville without hearing about Jonathon Thurston or Matt Bowen, the adored stars of the **North Queensland Cowboys** (☎ 4773 0700; www.cowboys.com.au) National Rugby League team. While the club represents the whole of North Queensland, its home is **Dairy Farmers Stadium** on Townsville's outskirts. The stadium was originally a harness-racing track, but was converted into a rugby league venue for the Cowboys' inaugural season in 1995. The stadium is a bit antiquated, but holds 26,500 people and the atmosphere is brilliant, especially if you score tickets to a game against hated rivals the Brisbane Broncos. It's worth seeing a game if you're here during the season, which runs from March to September. If you find yourself in a conversation with a local, you'll earn serious brownie points if you ask if JT is finally over his injury worries.

Courtesy buses to Dairy Farmers Stadium leave from the Cowboys Leagues Club on Flinders Mall and various other points throughout town. See the website for details.

Townsville's other major sporting team, the **Townsville Crocodiles** (☎ 4778 4222; www.crocodiles.com.au), competes in the National Basketball League and plays home games at Townsville Entertainment Centre.

ice greets you at this buzzing, licensed café-restaurant. It's a big, kitchen-like place where the friendly, energetic staff ensure that you'll enjoy the fresh produce on the Middle-Eastern influenced menu. For a light meal, you can't go past the roast butternut-pumpkin salad, while the authentic Israeli couscous will satisfy the fussiest of eaters.

Odyssey on the Strand (☎ 4724 1400; 120 The Strand; meals $12-30; ☯ breakfast & lunch daily, dinner Thu-Sat) The generously sized meals here have a Greek bias, but there's enough variety to keep everyone happy. Breakfasts are large enough to ward off the hunger pains until well after lunchtime. There's a good kids' menu and reasonable wine list. Our recommendation? The salt-and-pepper calamari and a glass of Marlborough sav blanc.

DRINKING

It must be the sunny climate, because Townsville sure loves a sip. There are bars spread out along Flinders St (where most of the action is), although Palmer St and the Strand also offer a few low-key spots.

Brewery (☎ 4724 2999; 252 Flinders St E; ☯ 10am-late) Drifting effortlessly between stylish and unpretentious, the Brewery is in the old post-office building and offers a little bit of everything, from casual dining, to outdoors drinking, a sports bar and nightclub. Try one of the award-winning, house-brewed beers: the Ned's Red Ale is delicious, but we were disappointed with the Belgian blonde.

Australian Hotel (☎ 4772 6999; 11 Palmer St; ☯ 11am-2am) A welcome addition to Townsville's rejuvenated and revamped Palmer St, the Australian boasts a stylish front bar with a good range of draught beers, while the big beer garden out the back is the place to knock back a few on a Sunday afternoon.

Watermark Hotel (☎ 4724 4281; 72-74 The Strand; ☯ noon-midnight) *The* place to be seen in Townsville (if it's good enough for Missy Higgins and silverchair, then it's good enough for the rest of us). Some serious Sunday sessions take place in the tavern bar, while there's also a more-upmarket bar and an excellent restaurant.

Seaview (☎ 4771 5005; cnr The Strand & Gregory Sts; ☯ 11am-midnight) Renowned for its Sunday sessions in the huge concrete beer 'garden', the Seaview serves ice-cold schooners and has live music and entertainment.

ENTERTAINMENT
Cinemas & Casinos

BC Cinemas (☎ 4771 4101; cnr Sturt & Blackwood Sts) If you fancy a flick, this place screens mainstream films.

Jupiters Casino (☎ 4722 2333; www.jupiterstownsville.com.au; Sir Leslie Thiess Dr) For a flutter head to this casino, flashing for your attention with its neon faux-fireworks.

Nightclubs

Bank Niteclub (☎ 4771 6148; 169 Flinders St E; admission $5; ☯ closed Mon) House and dance beats; slinky surrounds.

Bombay Rock (☎ 4724 2800; www.bombayrock.com.au; 719 Flinders St W; admission $6 after 10pm; ☯ 8pm-late Fri & Sat, 3pm-late Sun) Multilevel place with regular gigs and four bars.

Fuse (☎ 4771 3428; 87 Flinders St E; ☯ Fri & Sat) Get your fill of Guinness at Molly Malone's pub then slip around the back to this late-night club. Cover charge varies.

NORTH QUEENSLAND COAST

LevelOne (☎ 4724 2999; 252 Flinders St E; 🕑 Fri & Sat) Resident DJ spins dance and progressive house, as well as beats and breaks. Cover charge varies.

SHOPPING

Cotters Market (☎ 4727 9678; Flinders St Mall; 🕑 8.30am-1pm Sun) Cotters has about 200 craft and food stalls, as well as live entertainment. It's wheelchair-accessible.

John Melick & Co (☎ 4771 2292; 481 Flinders St) The place to go for a good range of camping and bushwalking gear, Driz-a-Bone oilskins, Akubra hats, boots and workwear.

Strand Night Market (☎ 4727 9678; The Strand; 🕑 5-9.30pm 1st Fri of month) Browse the stalls around the Strand Night Market for all sorts of curios, crafts and knick-knacks.

GETTING THERE & AWAY
Air

Virgin Blue (☎ 13 67 89; www.virginblue.com.au), **Qantas** (☎ 13 13 13; www.qantas.com.au) and **Jetstar** (☎ 13 15 38; www.jetstar.com) fly from Townsville to Brisbane, Sydney and Melbourne, with connections to other major cities.

Bus

The long-distance bus station is the **Townsville Transit Centre** (☎ 4721 3082; cnr Palmer & Plume Sts). You'll find agents for the major companies here, including:

Transit Centre Backpackers (☎ 4721 2322) Booking agents for Premier Motor Service.

Greyhound Australia (☎ 13 20 30, 4772 5100; www .greyhound.com.au) Services at least daily to Brisbane ($216, 23 hours), Rockhampton ($120, 12 hours), Airlie Beach ($58, 4½ hours), Mission Beach ($52, 3¾ hours) and Cairns ($67, six hours).

Car

The larger car-rental agencies are all represented in Townsville:

Avis (☎ 1300 137 498, 4721 2688; www.avis.com.au; 81 Flinders St) Also has an airport counter.

Europcar (☎ 1300 131 390, 4762 7050; www.delta europcar.com.au; 305 Ingham Rd, Garbutt) Also has an airport counter and rents 4WDs.

Hertz (☎ 13 30 30, 4775 5950; www.hertz.com; Stinson Ave, Garbutt)

Thrifty (☎ 4725 4600; www.thrifty.com.au; 289 Ingham Rd, Garbutt)

Train

The train station is about 1km south of the centre.

The Brisbane-to-Cairns **Sunlander** (☎ 1800 872 467; www.railaustralia.com.au) travels through Townsville three times a week en route to Brisbane (economy seat/sleeper $180/238, 1st-class sleeper $368, 24 hours), Proserpine (economy seat $28, four hours), Rockhampton (economy seat $61, 11 hours) and Cairns (economy seat $32, 7½ hours). Prices quoted here are for one-way adult fares. The more luxurious Queenslander class, which includes a sleeper and meals, is available on two services per week.

The **Inlander** (☎ 1800 872 467; www.railaustralia.com .au) heads from Townsville to Mt Isa (economy seat/sleeper $121/180, 1st-class sleeper $280, 21 hours, Thursday and Sunday) via Charters Towers (economy seat $26, three hours).

GETTING AROUND
To/From the Airport

Townsville Airport (☎ 4727 3211; www.townsvilleairport .com.au; cnr Halifax St & Stinson Ave, Garbutt) is 5km northwest of the city centre at Garbutt. A taxi to the centre costs about $15. The **Airport Shuttle** (☎ 4775 5544; one way/return $8/14) services all arrivals and departures, and will drop-off/pick-up anywhere within the central business district.

Bus

Sunbus (☎ 4725 8482; www.sunbus.com.au) runs local bus services around Townsville. Route maps and timetables are available from the Flinders Mall visitors centre (p424).

Taxi

Taxis congregate outside the Transit Mall near the corner of Sturt and Stokes Sts, or call **Townsville Taxis** (☎ 13 10 08, 4778 9555).

MAGNETIC ISLAND
☎ 07 / pop 2110

Magnetic Island's most attractive feature is that it doesn't pretend to be all glitz-and-glamour to draw you in. No spruced-up resorts here people, although five-star luxury is available if that's what you want.

'Maggie' is a 'real' island. People live and work here, and some even make the daily commute to Townsville. It's completely unpretentious, but staggeringly gorgeous at the same time (if Magnetic Island was a Hollywood film star, it'd probably be someone like Cate Blanchett…).

Captain Cook named Magnetic Island in 1770, when his ship's compass went peculiar as he sailed by. Nowadays, the ferries make

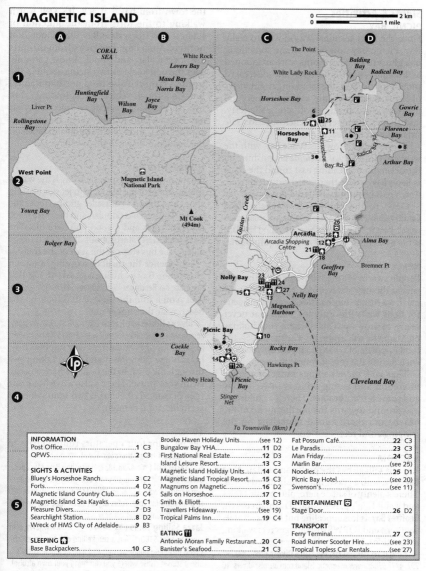

MAGNETIC ISLAND

a beeline to this spectacular holiday haven. Captain Cook missed out big-time!

Orientation & Information

The island is roughly triangular in shape. A sealed road follows the east coast for 10km from Picnic Bay, on the island's southern point, to Horseshoe Bay in the north. A local bus plies the route regularly. All ferries dock at Nelly Bay.

Post office (☎ 4778 5118; www.australiapost.com.au; Sooning St, Nelly Bay; ⏲ 9am-5pm Mon-Fri, to 11am Sat) With an ATM.

Queensland Parks & Wildlife Service (QPWS; ☎ 4778 5378; www.epa.qld.gov.au; Hurst St, Picnic Bay; ⏲ 7.30am-4pm)

Sights & Activities

PICNIC BAY

Since the ferry terminal was moved to Nelly Bay, Picnic Bay now has become something of a ghost town. Shopfronts were abandoned as businesses suffered from the decreased tourist traffic. Still, the twinkling night views of Townsville from the esplanade here are magical. It's a lovely stroll along the jetty, and there's a stinger-free enclosure for safe **swimming** on the beach.

To the west of town is **Cockle Bay**, with the wreck of HMS *City of Adelaide* languishing on the ocean floor. Heading east round the coast is **Rocky Bay**, where there's a short, steep walk down to a beautiful, sheltered beach.

Open to the public, the **Magnetic Island Country Club** (☎ 4778 5188; www.users.bigpond.net.au /migolf; Hurst St, Picnic Bay; 9/18 holes $15/20; ☼ from 8am) rents golf clubs, buggies and all equipment.

NELLY BAY

People swarm off the ferry and onto the marina at the newly developed Nelly Bay terminal. It's a rush to buy bus tickets, and the queue for taxis waits forlornly for a cab that never seems to show up. This is where your holiday on Magnetic will begin. It's a hectic place – the total opposite of what you'll probably experience during the rest of your stay here.

That said, there's a huge range of accommodation and eating options in Nelly Bay and some terrific **beaches**. There's a children's playground towards the northern end of the beach, and there's good **snorkelling** on the fringing coral reef.

ARCADIA

Arcadia village has the pretty and sedate **Alma Bay** cove, with a grassy hill and sheltered beach. There's plenty of shade here, plus picnic tables and a children's playground. The main beach, **Geoffrey Bay**, is less appealing but has a reef at its southern end (QPWS discourages reef walking at low tide). It's a very low-key place.

Learn to dive with **Pleasure Divers** (☎ 1800 797 797, 4778 5788; www.magnetic-island.com.au/plsr-divers; 10 Marine Pde; 3-/4-day PADI open-water courses from $299/799), which also offers advanced courses and dive trips to the *SS Yongala*.

RADICAL BAY & THE FORTS

Townsville was a supply base for the Pacific during WWII, and the **forts** on Magnetic Island were strategically designed to protect the town from naval attack. It's well worth walking to the forts from the junction of Radical and Horseshoe Bay Rds, about 2km north of Alma Bay. The views from the forts are spectacular, and you'll almost certainly spot the odd koala or two lazing about in the treetops. You can also head north to Radical Bay via a rough vehicle track, leading off of which are walking tracks to secluded **Arthur Bay** and **Florence Bay** (both or which are great for snorkelling), and the old **searchlight station** on the headland between the two bays.

HORSESHOE BAY

On the north coast, Horseshoe Bay is the watersports capital of the island, with jet skis blasting about and the odd parasailer gliding above the ocean. The beach is popular, and there are some excellent cafés and a good pub here too. The forts walk (left) starts about 2km north of the village; the bus stops at the start of the trail.

Experience the thrill of scooting about on Horseshoe Bay by hiring a **jet ski** (☎ 4758 1100; Horseshoe Bay Beach; per 15/30/60mins $45/80/150; ☼ Fri-Wed). You'll find the makeshift 'office' on the beach near the stinger net.

Bluey's Horseshoe Ranch (☎ 4778 5109; www.blueys horseranch.com; 38 Gifford St; rides per person $90) has been around for ages and offers very popular two-hour horse rides (9am and 3pm) taking you through the bush to the beach, where you can swim your horse. There's also a 3½-hour ride (per person $120, 9am) if two hours doesn't seem like long enough.

Tours

See p427 for tour operators running trips to the outer Great Barrier Reef.

Barnacle Bill (☎ 4758 1837; Horseshoe Bay; tours per person $85) Bill uses his 30 years of experience to ensure you'll end up with a healthy catch at the completion of his two-hour fishing tour. Tours depart Horseshoe Bay on Bill's 7m sport-fishing vessel; all gear is provided.

Jazza Sailing Tours (☎ 0404 875 530; www.jazza.com .au; day-trips $100) Offers a snorkelling day-trip on a 42ft yacht, including boom-netting and a pizza lunch. There's also a sunset cruise where you can bring your own alcohol.

Magnetic Island Sea Kayaks (☎ 4778 5424; www .seakayak.com.au; 93 Horseshoe Bay Rd, Horseshoe Bay; tours from $69) Has four-hour tours departing Horseshoe Bay, paddling to Balding Bay and back; includes breakfast and reef tax. Another option is to rent your own kayak (per day $55).

Reef EcoTours (☎ 0419-712 579; www.reefecotours .com; adult/child $70/60) A one-hour guided snorkelling tour, suitable for families.

Tropicana Tours (☎ 4758 1800; www.tropicanatours
.com.au; full-day tours adult/child $198/99) If you're
time-poor, this full-day tour with well-informed guides
takes in the island's best spots in a stretch 4WD. Enjoy
close encounters with wildlife, lunch at a local café and a
sunset cocktail (all included in the price). Shorter tours are
available if a full day sounds like too much effort.

Sleeping

Every budget is catered for on the island. It's especially popular with families and couples, but
seniors and backpackers are also catered for.

First National Real Estate (☎ 4778 5077; 21 Marine
Pde, Arcadia) and **Smith & Elliott** (☎ 4778 5570; 4/5
Bright Ave, Arcadia) can help with holiday rentals.

BUDGET
Picnic Bay

Travellers Hideaway (☎ 1800 000 290, 4778 5314;
www.travellersbackpackers.com; 32 Picnic St; dm $22, d $55;
🐾 🖥 🏊) If full-moon parties don't rock
your boat and peace and quiet is more your
go, then this basic backpackers moves to a
very slow beat. Dorms hold a maximum of
four, and while the whole place gives off a
rustic, bare-bones feel, the pool area is better
than average.

Nelly Bay

Base Backpackers (☎ 1800 242 273, 4778 5777; www
.stayatbase.com; 1 Nelly Bay Rd; unpowered sites $12-20, dm
$26-28, d with/without bathroom $110/95; 🖥 🏊) You
can feel the energy pumping through this huge
backpackers resort the moment you enter the
big, open-air foyer. It's a young, happening
place with a massive deck overlooking the
ocean. Base is famous for its wild full-moon
parties and great-value package deals.

Arcadia

Arcadia Resort (☎ 1800 663 666, 4778 5177; info@arkier
.com.au; 7 Marine Pde; dm $18-22, d & tw $65; 🐾 🖥 🏊)
A little worn around the edges, Arcadia
Resort no doubt tries its best to trade off
the success of its namesake at Airlie Beach.
All dorms have their own bathroom – make
sure you ask for one with an ocean view.
The doubles are great value and have a small
fridge and TV.

Horseshoe Bay

our pick **Bungalow Bay YHA** (☎ 1800 285 577, 4778
5577; www.bungalowbay.com.au; 40 Horseshoe Bay Rd; unpowered sites $12.50, dm $27, d $64; 🐾 🖥 🏊) It's al-
most worth coming to the island to stay at this
magical, award-winning resort-style hostel
and nature wonderland. Set among spacious
grounds backing onto national park, A-frame
bungalows house dorm rooms and simple
doubles. Take a guided nature-walk and hold
a koala at the mini wildlife sanctuary. There
are also two doubles with private bathrooms
($80; minimum two-night stay).

MIDRANGE & TOP END
Picnic Bay

Tropical Palms Inn (☎ 4778 5076; www.tropicalpalmsinn
.com.au; 34 Picnic St; s/d $95/105; 🐾 🏊) Self-con-
tained motel units are the go here, with a terrific little swimming pool right outside your
front door. The rooms are bright and comfortable and you can hire a 4WD from reception
($75 to $85 per day).

Magnetic Island Holiday Units (☎ 4778 5246;
www.magnetic-island.com.au/mi-units.htm; 16 Yule St;
1-/2-bedroom units $170/220; 🐾 🏊) These self-
contained units are in a secluded part of
the island, set amid leafy gardens and nicely
manicured lawns.

Nelly Bay

Magnetic Island Tropical Resort (☎ 1800 069 122,
4778 5955; www.magnetictropicalresort.com; 56 Yates St; d
$110; 🐾 🏊) A-frame cabins with bathrooms,
fridge and TV encircle large, bird-filled gardens here. This secluded resort often plays
host to wedding parties (if this is the first
place you visit, don't think taffeta and tuxes
are Magnetic Island's dress code).

Island Leisure Resort (☎ 4778 5000; www.island
leisure.com.au; 4 Kelly St; d $155, extra person $10; 🐾 🏊)
A block back from the bay, and with palm
trees sprouting up all over the place, Island
Leisure Resort is well situated. The self-contained rooms are spacious, and the pool is
large enough for a swim team to train in.

Arcadia

Brooke Haven Holiday Units (☎ 4778 5262; www
.brookehavenholidayunits.com; 5 Horden Ave; r $130; 🐾 🏊)
Set among tropical gardens, these units
sleep up to six people and are unbelievable
value. The only catch is they're not right on
the beach, but it's only a five-minute stroll
to find some sand, and at these prices, who
really cares?

Horseshoe Bay

Sails on Horseshoe (☎ 4778 5117; www.sailsonhorseshoe
.com.au; 13-15 Pacific Dr; 1-bedroom apt $225, 2-bedroom apt

$285-300; 🔀 🔊 ; wi-fi) Indulge in these beautiful self-contained apartments only metres from the beach. The rooms are spacious and have that lived-in, tropical feel. The undercover pool and barbecue area at the back is great for families. Try and snag one of the two-bedroom units at the front, with their own balconies overlooking the beach.

Eating
PICNIC BAY
Picnic Bay Hotel (☎ 4778 5166; Picnic Bay Mall; mains $14-26; 🕑 lunch & dinner) Settle in for an evening feed and a cold drink with Townsville's city lights sparkling just across the bay. It's a big, friendly pub where locals take great delight in sinking a few pots and enjoying a punt on the horses.

Antonio Moran Family Restaurant (☎ 4778 5018; 10 The Esplanade; mains $15-23; 🕑 breakfast, lunch & dinner) There's a little bit of everything at this sprawling cornerside eatery. Seafood is the norm (try the garlic mornay bugs), but huge serves of pasta and good pizzas and steaks are also on the menu. The coffee here is excellent, making breakfast an appealing option.

NELLY BAY
Fat Possum Café (☎ 4778 5409; 55 Sooning St; dishes $4-10; 🕑 breakfast & lunch) Names are not always accurate. Although the Fat Possum *is* a café, it serves its food with a twist, far from standard burger and chips staples. Try the grilled fish on a bed of salad, or the vegetarian and gluten-free options and you'll know what we mean.

Man Friday (☎ 4778 5658; 37 Warboy St; mains $14-35; 🕑 dinner Wed-Mon) Man Friday is the genuine article. Content locals and happy tourists leave here filled with delicious Mexican food, while the international menu is also deservedly popular. Bring your own wine and go for the Thai green curry.

Le Paradis (☎ 4778 5044; 8/98-100 Sooning St; mains $22-36; 🕑 lunch Sat & Sun, dinner daily) Mediterranean-inspired dishes dominate the extensive menu at this polished restaurant. Take a seat at the smart outside area on the corner of the street, settle in with a glass of wine and order the set lunch menu ($25).

ARCADIA
Banister's Seafood (☎ 4778 5700; 22 McCabe Cres; mains $10-30; 🕑 lunch & dinner) You can do the whole sit-down thing at this BYO joint, or grab some takeaways ($5 to $10) and scurry off to a

nearby beach. Whichever option you choose, the seafood here is fresh and hearty.

HORSESHOE BAY
Marlin Bar (☎ 4758 1588; 3 Pacific Dr; mains $10-24; 🕑 lunch & dinner) You can't leave Magnetic without at least enjoying a cold drink by the window of this busy, seaside pub and watching the sun sets across the bay. The meals are on the large side and (surprise!) revolve around seafood. The scallops with salad and the grilled mackerel are both brilliant value.

Noodies (☎ 4778 5786; 2/6 Pacific Dr; mains $14-25; 🕑 breakfast Sat & Sun, lunch & dinner Fri-Wed) While others have come and gone, Noodies has stood the test of time and has emerged in remarkably good shape. Mexican food dominates the menu, but you're welcome to enjoy a drink or maybe a breakfast burrito on weekends. Take home a souvenir Noodies beer to remember your meal.

our pick Swenson's (☎ 44778 5577; 40 Horseshoe Bay Rd; mains $16-30; 🕑 lunch & dinner) The restaurant at Bungalow Bay YHA hostel is renowned among Maggie's permanent residents, and travellers cotton-on pretty quickly that this is one of the best places to eat on the island. Pizzas and stir-fries are popular, but the curries are also worth coming for. We recommend the yellowfish curry with steaming jasmine rice, or there's a good selection of veg dishes to choose from.

Entertainment
Stage Door (☎ 4778 5448; www.stagedoortheatre .com.au; 5 Hayles Ave, Arcadia; dinner & show $60; 🕑 Fri & Sat) Comedy and cabaret while enjoying a sumptuous three-course dinner anyone? This theatre restaurant is popular, made so by its wonderful performing duo – Bernadette and Phill – who sing, dance and impersonate their way through a busy, entertaining show.

Getting There & Away
Sunferries (☎ 4771 3855; www.sunferries.com.au; return adult/child $27/13.50) operates a frequent passenger ferry between Townsville and Magnetic Island, which takes about 20 minutes each way. Ferries depart from the Breakwater terminal and pull-in at Nelly Bay on the island. Parking is available at the terminal.

Fantasea (☎ 4772 5422; www.magneticislandferry .com.au; Ross St, South Townsville; return car & 3 people $149, passenger only adult/child $23/14) operates a car ferry crossing to Magnetic Island eight times daily (seven on weekends) from the south side of Ross Creek.

Getting Around

BICYCLE

Magnetic Island is ideal for cycling, although some of the hills can be hard work. Most places to stay rent-out bikes for around $15 a day; some even offer them free to guests.

BUS

The **Magnetic Island Bus Service** (☎ 4778 5130; fares $3) ploughs between Picnic Bay and Horseshoe Bay at least 18 times a day, meeting all ferries and stopping at all major accommodation places. To book a wheelchair-accessible bus, call during office hours (8am to 4.30pm Monday to Friday, 8am to noon weekends).

MOKE & SCOOTER

Expect to pay around $50 per day (plus extras such as petrol and a per-kilometre fee) for a Moke. You'll need to be over 21 and carrying a current international (or Australian) driver's license. A credit-card deposit is required. Scooter hire starts at around $30 per day.

Road Runner Scooter Hire (☎ 4778 5222; 3/64 Kelly St, Nelly Bay) Also rents trailbikes.

Sails on Horseshoe (p433) Hires scooters.

Tropical Topless Car Rentals (☎ 4758 1111; Nelly Bay)

TOWNSVILLE TO MISSION BEACH

PALUMA RANGE NATIONAL PARK

Part of the **Wet Tropics World Heritage Area**, Paluma National Park and its teeny village provide a secluded respite from the drone of the Bruce Hwy.

Mt Spec Section

It's not uncommon for the lofty rainforest in this section of the park to be shrouded in mist or capped by cloud. Straddling the summit and escarpment of the Paluma Range, the Mt Spec Section stands over the Big Crystal Creek flood plain below.

There are two roads into this section of the park, both leading off a bypassed section of the Bruce Hwy: either 60km north of Townsville or 40km south of Ingham.

Take the northern access route to **Big Crystal Creek**. Goannas scamper away from your approaching footsteps as you walk the few hundred metres from the picnic area to the popular **Paradise Waterhole**. The self-registration **QPWS camping ground** (☎ 13 13 04; www.epa.qld.gov.au; per person/family $4.50/18) here is equipped with toilets, gas barbecues and drinking water. Access to Big Crystal Creek is via a 4km road, 2km north of Mt Spec Rd.

The southern access route, Mt Spec Rd, was built during the 1930s Depression. It's a dramatic, narrow road (with lose-your-lunch twists), weaving its way up the mountains to the village of **Paluma**. After 7km you come to **Little Crystal Creek**, where a pretty stone bridge (built in 1932) arches across the creek. This is a great swimming spot, with waterfalls and a couple of deep rock pools, and there's a small picnic area opposite the car park. From here it's another (steep) 11km up to Paluma.

PALUMA

Chimneys billow smoke in winter at the cosy little mountain-top village of Paluma – it can get chilly here in July and August. The town was founded in 1875 when tin was discovered in the area.

A number of walks lead through the surrounding rainforest. If not cushioned in cloud, **McClelland's Lookout**, 100m before Paluma village, provides humbling views. From the car park here a trail leads to **Witts Lookouts** (1.5km, 45 minutes return) and the steep **Cloudy Creek Falls** (3.5km, two hours return). Otherwise take the **H Track** (1.3km, 45 minutes) circuit walk, which leads from the rear of Lennox Cres along a former logging road.

Paluma Rainforest Inn (☎ 4770 8688; www .rainforestinnpaluma.com; 1 Mt Spec Rd; r $125-145; ❒) boasts large, stylish rooms with comfy beds. There are disabled-access facilities here, and an excellent bar-restaurant (mains $11 to $28, open for breakfast, lunch and dinner daily). The gardens contain more than 50 rhododendrons, which bloom throughout the year.

Approximately 11km beyond Paluma is **Lake Paluma**, a drinking-water storage dam with a dedicated foreshore area for swimming and picnicking. You can camp here with permission from **NQ Water** (☎ 4770 8526; www.nqwater .com.au) or stay in out-of-the-way log cabins at **Hidden Valley Cabins** (☎ 4770 8088; www.hiddenvalley cabins.com.au; backpacker s/d $30/40, s/d $55/75), which also has motel-style backpacker rooms and a licensed restaurant.

Jourama Falls Section

Jourama Falls and a series of cascades and rapids tumble along Waterview Creek, enclosed by palms and umbrella trees. It's a small but well-developed area, with a few lookouts, picnic areas and a **QPWS camping ground** (☎ 13 13 04; www.epa.qld.gov.au; per person/family $4.50/18) with drinking water, toilets and showers.

INGHAM

☎ 07 / pop 4610

Kick up your heels and get ready to party-on in wild Ingham! Well…no, not quite. Nowhere near it in fact. Sorry. Ingham is sleepy at the best of times, but positively comatose on weekends. Don't expect much to be going on from about 2pm on Saturday until Monday morning.

Ingham finds it difficult to awake from its seemingly perpetual slumber, but it's a nice enough town. It services the surrounding sugar-cane district where cane farms were established in the 1880s. There's a large population of Italian immigrants here, and for three days each May the **Australian-Italian Festival** (www.acecomp.com.au/Italian) gets the pasta flying with cooking displays, street markets, children's rides, fireworks and a troubadour competition.

Information

QPWS (☎ 4776 1700; www.epa.qld.gov.au; 49 Cassady St; ☼ 9am-5pm Mon-Fri) Handle permits for camping in the area.

Tyto Wetlands visitors centre (☎ 4776 5211; www .hinchinbrooknq.com.au; Bruce Hwy; ☼ 8.45am-5pm Mon-Fri, 9am-2pm Sat & Sun)

Sights

The Ingham **cemetery**, about 3km out of town via Forrest Beach Rd, is unique for its sprawl of ornate Italianate mausoleums, adorned with flamboyant statuary and tiles and shuttered with Venetian blinds.

The **Tyto Wetlands Nature Walk** starts close to the town centre and encompasses 90 hectares of carefully preserved natural environment. Spot a grass owl if you can!

Under an hour's drive west from Ingham (about 50km) are the dazzling heights of **Wallaman Falls** – the longest single-drop waterfall in Australia. The falls plunge around 300m off Seaview Range in the **Girringun National Park**, and have much more oomph in the wet season, after rains.

Further in to Girringun National Park is the dormant volcanic peak of **Mt Fox**, with its well-formed crater. A short scramble will allow you to peer over the edge; the 160m-long path is neither marked nor maintained, and so is reserved only for fit and experienced walkers (allow an hour).

Sleeping & Eating

Lees Hotel (☎ 4776 1577; info@leeshotel.com.au; 58 Lannercost St; s/d $55/65; ☒) Don't be put off by the dingy corridors. The rooms here, while not flash, are perfectly acceptable. The moulded

---

PUB WITHOUT BEER

Probably Ingham's best-known local is Dan Sheahan (1882–1977): a cane cutter, horseman and poet. Dan's poems carried on the Australian literary tradition, started by Banjo Paterson and Henry Lawson, of investigating Australian bush identity through verse. Sheahan's focus, though, was on examining the Australian identity during WWII. The **Ingham Library** (☎ 4776 4683; 25 Lannercost St; ☼ 9.30am-5pm Mon, 8.30am-5pm Tue-Fri, 9am-noon Sat) stocks a few titles of his collected works.

Though Sheahan enjoyed mild success from his poetry, one of his poems was to become wildly popular as a song. Sheahan penned *Pub Without Beer* (over a glass of wine) at Ingham's Day Dawn Hotel, after arriving to find that US troops had just been there and drained it dry of beer. The weekly *North Queensland Register* published the poem in 1944, but the Day Dawn was demolished in 1960. Lees Hotel (above) now stands in its place.

It wasn't until 1956 that Gordon Parsons used Sheahan's poem as inspiration to compose the song *Pub With No Beer* (over a whisky) at a pub in Taylors Arms, New South Wales (p251). The song was then immortalised by the late Australian country-music icon Slim Dusty, who went on to record *Duncan* ('I love to have a beer with…') in 1980, and whose album *Beer Drinking Songs* (1986) went gold within three weeks of its release.

All this goes a fair way towards proving that the humble beer is an integral part of the Australian identity.

horseman on the roof and talking dog out the front make it hard to miss Lees. On the same site as the Day Dawn Hotel, of *Pub Without Beer* fame (see boxed text, opposite), this is a good-old Aussie pub. Lees does decent counter meals in the bar and excellent sit-down meals in the bistro out the back.

Herbert Valley Motel (☎ 4776 1777; fax 4776 3646; 37 Townsville Rd; r $68-90; ✷ ✸) Undergoing a much-needed facelift at the time of research, this motel has functional rooms, but lousy air-con (made to work very hard in the heat of the day, but not too bad at night). Still, the beds are comfortable and management is friendly.

Elda's (☎ 4776 2039; 78 Lannercost St; sandwiches $4-5; ✻ breakfast & lunch Mon-Sat) Don't miss the chance to sample the delectable sandwiches at this mysterious deli-cum-fruit-shop. Walk past the imported Italian dry goods and fresh fruit and veg to the deli section, where your take away sandwich will be lovingly prepared.

Ingham Chinese Restaurant (☎ 4776 3522; 60 Lannercost St; meals $10-16; ✻ lunch & dinner) Definitely the place to go if you eat to live, rather than live to eat. This restaurant with an unremarkable name serves unremarkable (but OK) food, including a $10 lunch smorgasbord (Monday to Friday).

Getting There & Away

Greyhound Australia (☎ 13 14 99; www.greyhound.com .au) buses run between Townsville and Ingham ($34, 1½ hours), stopping in the centre of town on Townsville Rd, close to the corner of Lannercost St.

Ingham is on the **Queensland Rail** (☎ 1300 131 722; www.traveltrain.com.au) Brisbane-to-Cairns line. Trains run to/from Townsville (economy seat $29, 1¾ hours).

LUCINDA
☎ 07 / pop 450

Pretty little Lucinda draws in camera-wielding tourists eager to grab a snap of the 6km-long jetty. It's the world's longest bulk sugar-loading jetty, allowing enormous carrier ships to dock. It's certainly an impressive sight. With Hinchinbrook Island seemingly within touching distance, Lucinda boasts excellent fishing and a quiet, relaxed mood that only a small seaside village can produce.

Hinchinbrook Wilderness Safaris (☎ 4777 8307; www.hinchinbrookwildernesssafaris.com.au; 4 Waring St) runs four-hour tours down the Deluge Inlet (per person $60) and 2½-hour tours along the channel (per person $30). Transfers to/from Hinchinbrook are available (one way/return from $46/57).

Wanderer's Holiday Village (☎ 4777 8213; www .wanderers-lucinda.com.au; Bruce Pde; unpowered/powered sites $22/26, cabins $80-95; ✷ ✸) is a sprawling, well-equipped camping ground with a children's play area. It's a relaxed place (as is Lucinda).

Even if you're not staying at the **Lucinda Point Hotel-Motel** (☎ 4777 8103; cmusso@bigpond.com .au; cnr Halifax & Dungeness Rds; r with/without bathroom $95/60; ✷ ✸), it's worth being here for the Sunday afternoon (adult/child $14.50/5.50) or Saturday night (adult $23.50) barbecue smorgasbord. You get to use the pool, and the shaded beer garden is a perfect place to while away your time with a drink in hand. The motel rooms are comfortable and clean.

ORPHEUS ISLAND

Secluded Orpheus Island lies about 25km off the coast of Ingham. It's mostly national park, protecting macaranga trees (with huge, heart-shaped leaves), and eucalypts standing on a foundation of volcanic rocks. However it's the magnificent fringing reef that is the main attraction here.

Established in the 1940s, the luxurious **Orpheus Island Resort** (☎ 1800 077 167, 4777 7377; www.orpheus.com.au; d $1450-1700; ✷ ✸) trades on its isolation from the outside world: no interlopers, no phones, no TVs. Everything is included in the price: meals, snacks, snorkelling and tennis. The resort also runs diving trips and courses for guests. Children under 15 years of age aren't welcome.

There's **bush camping** at Yank's Jetty, South Beach and Pioneer Bay. There are toilets at Yanks Jetty and Pioneer Bay, and picnic tables at all sites, but you'll need to bring your own drinking water and a fuel stove. Permits can be obtained from **QPWS** (☎ 13 13 04; www.epa.qld .gov.au; per person/family $4.50/18).

The resort has a seaplane that handles transfers from Townsville ($450 return, 30 minutes) and Cairns ($780, one hour) to Orpheus.

CARDWELL
☎ 07 / pop 1250

Cardwell seems to suffer from an identity crisis: it can't quite work out whether it wants to be a bustling seaside resort town, or an idling, unhurried village. The truth lies somewhere in between, and to be honest, it's probably better-off this way – enjoying the best of both worlds.

The area offers superb **fishing** and the **beaches** are clean. It's also the stopping-off point for magnificent Hinchinbrook Island (right), and the new marina precinct has evolved from an unfinished conglomerate into a thriving, picturesque minivillage.

The **Cardwell Forest Drive** starts from the centre of town. It's a scenic, 26km round-trip, with excellent lookouts, walking tracks and picnic areas signposted along the way. There are super swimming opportunities at Attie and Dead Horse Creek, as well as Spa Pool.

Information

QPWS Reef & Rainforest Centre (☎ 4066 8601; www.epa.qld.gov.au; Main Jetty; ◯ 8am-4.30pm) Has an interactive rainforest display and information about Hinchinbrook Island and the nearby state and national parks.

Sleeping & Eating

Kookaburra Holiday Park (☎ 4066 8648; www.kookaburra holidaypark.com.au; 175 Bruce Hwy; unpowered/powered sites $22/26, dm/s/d $20/40/45, cabins without bathroom $60, units $105; ◯ ◯) More like a sprawling village than a caravan park, the Kookaburra's 1.2 hectares are green and tree-lined, and there's backpackers accommodation in a large Queenslander house out the back. You can borrow fishing rods, prawn nets and crab pots and attempt to catch dinner.

Mudbrick Manor (☎ 4066 2299; www.mudbrickmanor .com.au; Lot 13 Stony Creek Rd; d $120; ◯ ◯) This hand-built, mud-brick home is outstanding. You'll spend lazy days on the veranda overlooking the sprawling courtyard, soaking up the casual country finesse. The huge indoor lounge area has activities aplenty, or you can occupy yourself poking around the decorative interiors. Breakfast is included, but ask about the three-course dinners; they may entice you to stay another night.

Port Hinchinbrook Resort Hotel (☎ 4066 2000; www.porthinchinbrook.com.au; Bruce Hwy; d from $195; ◯ ◯ ; wi-fi) Located at the marina, the cabins here are more like luxury, open-plan villas. The front doors slide wide open to catch the cool breezes sliding off the marina waterfront, and there's a warm, earthy tone to the walls.

Annie's Kitchen (☎ 4066 8818; 107 Victoria St; mains $9-17; ◯ breakfast, lunch & dinner) Aside from the usual culprits like burgers and sandwiches, there are some wonderful main meal choices at this ultra-busy café-diner. Homemade rissoles, roast meats, mixed grills and big seafood plates all feature on the slightly-different-to-the-norm menu.

Muddy's (☎ 4066 8133; 221 Victoria St; mains $23-35; ◯ lunch & dinner Tue-Sun) For a slap-up meal, head to Muddy's for some of the best seafood in the north. It's not cheap, but at least you get what you pay for. Muddy's, not surprisingly, specialises in mud crab and has a pleasant decking area out the front.

Getting There & Away

Greyhound Australia (☎ 13 20 30; www.greyhound.com .au) buses stop at Cardwell en route to/from Townsville ($40, 2¼ hours) and Cairns ($38, 3¼ hours).

Cardwell is also on the Brisbane-to-Cairns train line; contact **Queensland Rail** (☎ 1300 131 722; www.traveltrain.com.au) for details.

HINCHINBROOK ISLAND

Hinchinbrook Island lives up to the hype. Australia's largest island national park, Hinchinbrook is somewhat of a holy grail for walkers. Indeed, hope that you're one of the fortunate 40 who are allowed to traverse the Thorsborne Trail at any one time. If not, there's a range of other ways to explore this stunning and unspoilt wilderness. Hinchinbrook's granite mountains rise dramatically from the sea. All 399 sq km of the island is national park, and rugged **Mt Bowen** (1121m) is its highest peak.

Walking opportunities here are excellent; however, some trails may close between November and March. The highlight is the **Thorsborne Trail**, a 32km coastal track from Ramsay Bay to Zoe Bay (with its beautiful waterfall) and on to George Point at the southern tip. It's recommended that you spend three nights to complete the trail. Return walks of individual sections are also possible. You'll need to wear a layer of insect repellent, protect your food from ravenous rats, draw water from creeks as you go and be alert to the possibility of crocs being present. The trail is ungraded and at times rough, including challenging creek crossings. You should carry a map, drinking water, fuel stove and trowel.

Bookings for the Thorsborne Trail need to be made in advance: for a place during the dry season, **QPWS** (☎ 13 13 04; www.epa.qld.gov.au; per person/family $4.50/18) recommends booking a year ahead (six months ahead for other dates). In

Cardwell the QPWS Reef & Rainforest Centre (opposite) stocks the imperative *Thorsborne Trail* brochure and screens the 15-minute *Without a Trace* video, which walkers are required to view.

Apart from the Thorsborne Trail, camping and short walks are available at **Macushla** (5km to 8km, 1½ to two hours), and the **Haven Circuit** (1km, 15 minutes).

Hinchinbrook Island Ferries (below) runs day tours (per person $85) to Hinchinbrook Island, departing from Cardwell's Hinchinbrook Marina. The tour includes exploration of mangroves, visiting the long stretch of beach at Ramsay Bay and the option of walking through the rainforest at Macushla.

Sleeping

QPWS camping grounds (☎ 13 13 40; www.epa.qld .gov.au; per person $4.50) There are six QPWS camping grounds along the Thorsborne Trail, plus the one at Macushla Bay and another at the Haven in the north.

Hinchinbrook Island Wilderness Lodge & Resort (☎ 4066 8270; www.hinchinbrookresort.com.au; Orchid Beach; beach cabins $275, tree houses $445; 🏊) Built into the steep hillside behind Orchid Beach in the island's north, these elevated tree houses feature floor-to-ceiling windows, a balcony, kitchenette and bathroom. Guests are free to use the resort's canoes, surf-skis and snorkelling gear, or just laze in the hammocks strung along the beach. All meals are available from the licensed restaurant and are not included in the accommodation rates (although full-board packages are available).

Getting There & Away

Hinchinbrook Island Ferries (☎ 4066 85 85; www .hinchinbrookferries.com.au) operates daily services (return $125, 50 minutes each way) between Cardwell's Port Hinchinbrook Marina and dock at the Hinchinbrook Resort. If you're walking the Thorsborne Trail, a one-way transfer costs $80. Walkers usually pick up the **Hinchinbrook Wilderness Safaris** (☎ 4777 8307; www .hinchinbrookwildernesssafaris.com.au; one way/return $46/57) service at the southern end of the trail.

GOOLD & GARDEN ISLANDS

These uninhabited islands provide the perfect setting for you to play castaway. Both are national parks and off the everyday tourist radar, so you could find you have the islands to yourself.

Goold Island, just 17km northeast of Cardwell, supports open forest, mangroves and sandy beaches on both its western and southern sides. There's a **QPWS camping ground** (☎ 13 13 04; www.epa.qld.gov.au; per person/family $4.50/18) on the island's west, with toilets, picnic tables and a gas barbecue. Bring drinking water.

Just south of Goold Island is tiny **Garden Island**, with a recreation reserve controlled by the local council. Permits to camp are required and available from the **Cardwell Newsagency** (☎ 4066 8622; 83 Victoria St; per person $3.85). The island has a good sandy beach but no fresh water; kids under six aren't permitted.

Hinchinbrook Island Ferries (☎ 4066 8270; www .hinchinbrookferries.com.au; return transfers $90) can ferry campers to/from Cardwell on request.

TULLY

☎ 07 / op 2460

Tully is proud of its reputation as the wettest place in Australia. Rather than cover it all up and deny it, the big 7.9m gumboot at the entrance to town announces to all that Tully received 7.9m of rain in 1950! Nothing like getting things out in the open straight away.

Tully is a sugar town with a big mill chimney. The surrounding banana plantations provide seasonal employment, attracting droves of young backpackers on working holidays. But really, it's the rapids that people are here for. The nearby Tully River provides thrilling **white-water rafting** year-round, thanks to the daily floodgate release by the local hydro-electricity company. Rafting trips are timed to coincide with the release of the floodgates.

Information

Tully visitors centre (☎ 4068 2288; Bruce Hwy; ⏱ 8.30am-4.45pm Mon-Fri, 9.30am-2.30pm Sat & Sun) On the highway just south of the Tully turn-off.

Sights & Activities

Book at the visitors centre for **Tully Sugar Mill Tours** (adult/child $12/8; ⏱ 10am, 11am & 1.30pm Mon-Fri & 11am Sat & Sun Jun-Nov). During the crushing season (June to November) the mill operates 24/7 and processes around two million tonnes of cane. The mill generates its own power by burning fibre residue. The 1½-hour tours must be booked at least 30 minutes before departure (as minimum numbers are required); wear closed-toe shoes and a shirt with sleeves.

There are good walking opportunities in the **Tully Gorge National Park**, located 40km from Tully along Cardstone Rd. There are picnic facilities here, as well as river access for swimming at **Tully Gorge** (though you may be converged upon by pumped-up, paddle-wheeling kayakers, and the gentle burble of the Tully River can turn suddenly into a rapid when the hydro-electricity company opens its floodgates).

There's excellent swimming at the unfortunately named **Alligator's Nest**, 7km north of town via Murray St. The visitors centre can provide leaflets detailing walks to the top of **Mt Tyson** (640m).

White-water rafting day-trips cost about $180 per person and include a barbecue lunch and transfers from Mission Beach, Cairns or Port Douglas. Operators include the following:

Raging Thunder Adventures (☎ 4030 7990; www .ragingthunder.com.au/rafting.asp)

R'n'R White Water Rafting (☎ 4051 7777; www .raft.com.au)

Sleeping & Eating

Banana Barracks (☎ 4068 0455; www.banana barracks.com; 50 Butler St; dm with/without bathroom $26/24, bungalows $60; 🖳) Often full of fruit-picking backpackers, this busy hostel has a fantastic public bar that serves icy-cold schooners of draught beer.

Tully Motel (☎ 4068 2233; tullymotel@bigpond.com; Bruce Hwy; r $75-87; 🖳) The superior rooms are worth the extra $12 at this good-value motel on the main highway.

Kanga Jacks (☎ 4068 2118; 51 Bryant St; meals $6-15; 🍽 breakfast & lunch Mon-Sat) One for early birds (it opens at 5am), Kanga Jacks serves hearty meals (lasagne, pork chops, steak, fish) with a crispy salad and hot chips. Look for the big red roller door at the entrance.

Getting There & Away

Greyhound Australia (☎ 13 14 99; www.greyhound.com .au) has services from Tully to Townsville ($46, 3¼ hours) and Cairns ($33, 2½ hours). Tully is also on the Brisbane-Cairns train line; contact **Queensland Rail** (☎ 1300 131 722; www.traveltrain .com.au) for details.

MISSION BEACH
☎ 07 / pop 2600

Mission Beach and its sister villages Wonpgaling Beach, Bingil Bay and South Mission Beach are like a big, happy family: four siblings who are similar in character and style, but live separate lives without being jealous of each other in the slightest. Each has a distinct vibe, but you can tell they're from the same pod.

Where rainforest meets the sea, Mission Beach has superb walking tracks and around 40 resident cassowaries that roam the rainforest on the town's back doorstep. The **beaches** here are world-class, there's a busy café and eating scene, and while it's primarily a tourist hub, the town effortlessly manages to stay low-key. Dunk Island (p443) is a mere 20-minute ferry ride away.

Information

Mission Beach has comprehensive services: internet access is available at a number of places on the main strip, ATMs are located in the newsagent and supermarket, and the post office is in the main group of shops.

Community for Cassowary & Coastal Conservation (C4; ☎ 4068 7197; www.cassowaryconservation.asn.au)

Intermission @ the Beach (☎ 4068 7117; David St) Internet access per 20 minutes/hour $2/5.

Mission Beach visitors centre (☎ 4068 7099; www .missionbeachtourism.com; Porters Promenade; 🕙 10am-4pm Mon-Sat, to 2pm Sun) Has a wall of pamphlets (in a number of languages).

Wet Tropics Environment Centre (☎ 4068 7179; www.wettropics.gov.au) In the visitors centre. Rainforest and cassowary conservation displays are curated by volunteers from the Community for Cassowary & Coastal Conservation. Proceeds from purchases go towards buying cassowary habitat, which is being depleted by development and threatens the survival of the species.

Sights & Activities

Dunk Island (p443) is a popular day-trip from Mission Beach. The **Great Barrier Reef** is just an hour away, and **rainforest walks** are extra exciting if you come across a cassowary!

DIVING & SNORKELLING

All boats depart from busy little Clump Point Jetty.

Day cruises to the outer reef with **Quick Cat** (☎ 4068 7289; www.quickcatscuba.com) include a 45-minute stop at Dunk Island, snorkelling, lunch and a glass-bottom boat jaunt ($140). Add $80 for an introductory dive; $55 for a certified dive. A return ferry to Dunk Island is also available ($40).

Calypso Dive & Snorkel (☎ 4068 8432; www .calypsodive.com; 20 Wongaling Beach Rd, Wongaling Beach)

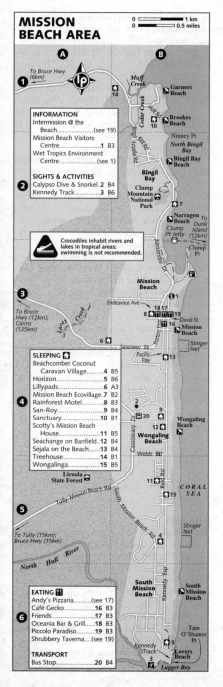

MISSION BEACH AREA

0 — 1 km
0 — 0.5 miles

To Bruce Hwy (6km)

Muff Creek

Cedar Creek

Garners Beach

Brookes Beach

Ninney Pt

North Bingil Bay

Bingil Bay Beach

Bingil Bay

Clump Mountain National Park

Narragon Beach
To Dunk Island (12km)
Clump Pt Jetty

Clump Pt

INFORMATION
Intermission @ the
 Beach......................(see 19)
Mission Beach Visitors
 Centre..........................1 B3
Wet Tropics Environment
 Centre...................(see 1)

SIGHTS & ACTIVITIES
Calypso Dive & Snorkel.2 B4
Kennedy Track.............3 B6

Crocodiles inhabit rivers and lakes in tropical areas; swimming is not recommended.

Mission Beach

Endeavour Ave

To Bruce Hwy (12km); Cairns (135km)

Lacey Creek

David St
Mission Beach

Stinger Net

Seaview St

Pacific Pde

SLEEPING
Beachcomber Coconut
 Caravan Village..........4 B5
Horizon.........................5 B6
Lillypads.......................6 A3
Mission Beach Ecovillage.7 B2
Rainforest Motel............8 B3
San-Roy........................9 B4
Sanctuary....................10 B1
Scotty's Mission Beach
 House........................11 B5
Seachange on Banfield..12 B4
Sejala on the Beach.....13 B4
Treehouse....................14 B1
Wongalinga..................15 B5

Wongaling Beach

Webb Rd

Licuala State Forest

Tully-Mission Beach Rd

South Mission Beach Rd

Cassowary Dr

Reid Rd

CORAL SEA

Stinger Net

To Tully (15km);
Bruce Hwy (15km)

North Hull River

EATING
Andy's Pizzaria.........(see 17)
Café Gecko...................16 B3
Friends.........................17 B3
Oceania Bar & Grill......18 B3
Piccolo Paradiso...........19 B3
Shrubbery Taverna....(see 19)

TRANSPORT
Bus Stop......................20 B4

South Mission Beach

South Mission Beach

Tam O'Shanter Pt

Kennedy Track

Lovers Beach

Lugger Bay

dives the *Lady Bowen* wreck with packages from $250. Introductory dives are from $65. Alternatively, there are trips out to the reef (per person $120) and jet-ski tours of Dunk Island ($195).

WALKING

Walkers should pick up the *Walking Guide* (40c) from the visitors centre, detailing the many trails in the area. Among them is the superb coastal **Kennedy Track** (7km, three hours return), which leads past secluded Lovers Beach and the Lugger Bay lookout. The inland walks through state park pass through tropical rainforest, where you're most likely to see a cassowary. **Licuala State Forest** has a number of rainforest walks, including a **children's walk** (10 minutes) marked with cassowary footprints, and the **Lacey Creek Track** (1.2km, 45 minutes) with interpretive signage and a cassowary display.

OTHER ACTIVITIES

Paddle over to Dunk Island for the day with **Coral Sea Kayaking** (☎ 4068 9154; www.coralseakayaking.com; half-/full-day tours $70/120) or juts bob around the coastline for half a day. Trips depart South Mission Beach.

Fancy a skydive? **Jump the Beach** (☎ 4031 1822; www.jumpthebeach.com; 9000/11,000/14,000ft tandem dives $210/244/295) uses the sand of Mission Beach to cushion your landing. There's a 100kg weight limit.

See opposite for details of white-water rafting trips on the Tully River, departing Mission Beach.

Tours

Informative wildlife-spotting tours along the Hull River (around four hours, including a light meal) are run by the following operators:
Hinchinbrook Explorer (☎ 4088 6154; www .hexplorer.com.au; adult/child $50/25)
River Rat Eco Cruises (☎ 4068 8018; www.riverrat cruises.com; adult/child $50/25)

Sleeping

BUDGET

Treehouse (☎ 4068 7137; www.yha.com.au; Frizelle Rd, Bingil Bay; unpowered sites $12, dm/d $23/55; 🏊) You'll be impressed by the big, poled-framed timber building here that merges effortlessly with the surrounding rainforest. The generous balcony space is dotted with heavy, wooden tables strewn with board games, international newspapers and books. Relaxed travellers

NORTH QUEENSLAND COAST

veg-out on sun lounges or hammocks under the shaded veranda.

Scotty's Mission Beach House (☎ 1800 665 567, 4068 8676; www.scottysbeachhouse.com.au; 167 Reid Rd, Wongaling Beach; 4-/6-/12-bed dm $21/23/26, d & tw with/without bathroom $59/49; ⚙ 🖳) Scotty's is perpetually abuzz with like-minded travellers catching some rays beside the well-grassed pool area, or eagerly tapping away at keyboards in the internet room. The dorms are clean and comfortable. The four-bed dorms have a bathroom, and the 12-bed ones are partitioned so they don't feel claustrophobic. All beds have new mattresses, making Scotty's a great place to stay.

ourpick Sanctuary (☎ 1800 777 012, 4088 6064; www .sanctuaryatmission.com; 72 Holt Rd, Bingil Bay; dm $33, huts s/d $61/65, cabins s/d $131/150; 🖳) Wow! If you want to sleep with nature on a platform within a real rainforest, surrounded only by flyscreen, then the huts here will fulfil your wish. If you prefer comfort, the cabins are exquisite, and even the shower cubicles provide floor-to-ceiling rainforest views. About 95% of the land here is set aside for conservation (the other 5% being the actual complex). Take one of the excellent yoga classes (one/five/10 classes $12/50/95), wander around the rainforest on the interpretive walk, or take refuge in the superb pool area. Sanctuary has its own sewage system, uses only rainwater throughout, flushes grey water down the toilet, uses biodegradable detergents and has no air-con (trust us, you won't need it – the breezes here are sublime).

Beachcomber Coconut Caravan Village (☎ 1800 008 129, 4068 8129; www.beachcombercoconut.com; Kennedy Esp, South Mission Beach; unpowered/powered sites $34/38, cabins with/without bathroom from $95/70, villas $160-170; ⚙ 🖳) Book early if you want to stay at this fabulous holiday park during school holidays. The Beachcomber has well-grassed camp sites and wonderful beachfront cabins overlooking Dunk Island. It's an excellent option for families, with a big swimming pool and a well-equipped playground.

MIDRANGE
Rainforest Motel (☎ 4068 7556; www.missionbeachrain forestmotel.com; 9 Endeavour Ave, Mission Beach; s/d $85/99; ⚙ 🖳) If only all motels could be like this! Each tidy, separate unit is surrounded by gorgeous faux-rainforest, and there's a path leading from the car park to the main street, 150m away.

San-Roy (☎ 4088 6699; 79 Banfield Pde, Wongaling Beach; unit $90; ⚙) It's not flash, but it's perfectly acceptable for a small family on a budget holiday. This cosy unit has a double bed in one bedroom, and three singles in the other.

Seachange on Banfield (☎ 4088 6699; 43 Banfield Pde, Wongaling Beach; house $130-150; ⚙) This cute, two-bedroom 1970s holiday house sports a big backyard and a sunroom overlooking the beach and Dunk Island. There's a big bench in the kitchen on which to prepare your own meals, with bar stools for those who want to prop themselves up and offer advice. It's a real home-away-from-home.

Mission Beach Ecovillage (☎ 4068 7534; www.eco village.com.au; Clump Point Rd, Mission Beach; d $178-190; ⚙ 🖳) With its own banana trees scattered around wonderful tropical gardens (including some spectacular cycads), the self-contained bungalows here are huge. The more-expensive rooms have a spa, and the brilliant free-form pool is perfect for all ages.

Sejala on the Beach (☎ 4088 6699; www.mission beachholidays.com.au/sejala; 26 Pacific Pde, Mission Beach; d $240; ⚙ 🖳) Your first tentative steps down into the cocoon-like bathrooms here will reveal shutter doors that you can open to shower with nature. These huts have loads of character, each with a kitchenette and a private barbecue on the front deck.

Lillypads (☎ 4088 6133; www.lillypads.com.au; 1375 Cassowary Dr, Mission Beach; house $300-350; ⚙ 🖳) You soon realise what the owners had in mind when they named this place – there's a beautiful lillypad pond out the front near the pool area. These two self-contained houses are the epitome of luxury, with a huge spa deck, polished floorboards throughout, plasma TV and open shower in the bathroom. There's a small rainforest 'body temple' a short walk away – relax in a hammock surrounded by mosquito netting and listen to the bubbling stream nearby.

TOP END
Wongalinga (☎ 4068 8221; www.wongalinga.com.au; 64 Reid Rd, Wongaling Beach; 1-/2-/3-bedroom apt $230/270/300; ⚙ 🖳) The three-bedroom apartments are so massive, you may need to take a whistle in case you get lost. The apartments have excellent air-con, but try opening up the shutters and letting the cool breezes waft through before you press any buttons.

Horizon (☎ 4068 8154; www.thehorizon.com.au; 1 Explorer Dr, South Mission Beach; std r $240, ste $285-460; ⚙ 🖳) The new owners (from Byron Bay) decided to revamp this secluded piece of paradise, and the results are impressive. The whole vibe is very contemporary, without compromising the natural beauty of the surroundings. Dunk Island looks like it's within touching distance of the huge, decked pool area.

Eating

Whether it's a quick bite on a romantic, candlelit dinner, Mission Beach exists for you, the traveller. There's pretty much nothing you can't have here! There are supermarkets for self-caterers at Mission Beach and Wongaling Beach.

Café Gecko (☎ 4068 7390; cnr Porters Promenade & Campbell Sts, Mission Beach; light meals $5-12; ☽ breakfast & lunch) The pies here are absolutely awesome – real chunks of steak and nothing artificial. The sandwiches are made fresh right in front of you at the hole-in-the-wall where you place your order. The bacon, eggs, tomato, toast and coffee breakfast goes down a treat after an early-morning swim.

Andy's Pizzaria (☎ 4088 6866; 2/45 Porter Promenade, Mission Beach; pizzas $7-15; ☽ dinner) Hole-in-the-wall pizza joint that's as simple as it is good. It's great for a quick meal, but accepts cash only.

Piccolo Paradiso (☎ 4068 7008; David St, Mission Beach; pizza from $12, pasta mains $12-17; ☽ lunch & dinner) There's a nice little bar area here – imbibe a beer while waiting for your pizza to cook. If you choose to eat-in, you'll do so in casual, relaxed surroundings.

Shrubbery Taverna (☎ 4068 7803; David St, Mission Beach; mains $18-30; ☽ lunch Fri-Sun, dinner Wed-Sun, bar open from 4.30pm Wed-Sun) Even if you're not interested in eating at this superb tavern, it's a great place to catch some live music on Sunday nights. Pull up a seat outside, order a drink and some Spanish mackerel and listen to the melody.

ourpick Oceania Bar & Grill (☎ 4088 6222; 52 Porter Promenade, Mission Beach; mains $21-34; ☽ lunch & dinner Sat-Mon, dinner Thu & Fri) Grab a draught beer or have a browse through the lengthy wine list before choosing your meal, which will inevitably consist of steak or seafood. The chilled seafood plate goes well with a sav blanc, or maybe the T-bone with a Stella or Barossa shiraz may be more to your liking.

Friends (☎ 4068 7107; Porter Promenade, Mission Beach; mains $26-33; ☽ dinner Tue-Sun) OK, so the menu may be limited, but with seafood-oriented starters and sumptuous dishes such

as pork-belly and duck, we think you'll like Friends. The atmosphere is elegant, but you won't need to wear your best frock or suit to dinner. Vegetarians may struggle here, although the seaweed option had good reviews from at least one traveller we met.

Getting There & Away

Greyhound Australia (☎ 13 20 30; www.greyhound.com.au) and **Premier** (☎ 13 34 10; www.premierms.com.au) buses stop in Wongaling Beach, and travel to/from Cairns ($31, two hours) and Townsville ($52, 3¾ hours).

The **Trans North** (☎ 4068 7400; www.transnorth bus.com; tickets from $3; ☽ Mon-Sat) local bus runs almost every hour between Bingil Bay and South Mission Beach; the visitors centre has timetables.

DUNK ISLAND

The water surrounding Dunk Island seems too blue to be true. It's the first thing you'll notice as you step off the ferry and onto the long jetty. As you make your way to terra firma and peer over the edge of the old wooden structure, myriad fish swarm below, taking it upon themselves to be the island's unofficial welcoming party. Whether you're a resort guest or a day-tripper, Dunk has heaps to offer.

Dunk's abundant species of birds (more than 100), butterflies, coral gardens and marine life were the inspiration for the transcendentalist EJ Banfield, who wrote four novels while living on the island between 1897 and 1923. Of them, *The Confessions of a Beachcomber* is probably the best known. **Banfield's grave** is a short walk from the jetty towards Muggy Muggy.

You can almost circumnavigate the island using the park's well-marked **walking trails** (9km, three hours). Otherwise, a walk to the top of **Mt Kootaloo** (271m, 5.6km, 1½ hours return) allows you to look back to the mainland and see Hinchinbrook Channel fanning out before you. There's good **snorkelling** over bommies at Muggy Muggy and great **swimming** at Coconut Beach.

Otherwise, day-trippers can utilise a limited number of the resort's facilities by purchasing a Resort Experience Pass (adult/child $40/20) available from the Watersports Centre just south of the jetty. This entitles you to lunch at one of the resort's cafés and an hour's use of a paddle ski.

NORTH QUEENSLAND COAST

Sleeping & Eating

Dunk Island Resort (☎ 1800 737 678, 4068 8199; www.dunk-island.com; s $311-551, d $366-628; ✖ 🖳) Rates vary depending on the standard of your room, and here's a tip: the standard beachfront rooms are just as nice as the more expensive beachfront suites. Stroll out your sliding door to the beautiful blue water only steps away. While-away your day in a sun lounge, then pack up and head to the bar and pool at dusk. There's a year-round kids' club (open 9am to noon and 5pm to 9pm; per child per session $30) for those aged between three and 12.

QPWS camping ground (☎ 4068 8199; www.epa.qld.gov.au; per person/family $4.50/18) QPWS has nine sites on a gravel patch just back from the jetty; there are toilets and showers.

Jetty Café (Dunk Island Jetty, meals $14-23) Daytrippers can buy decent meals like barramundi spring rolls, chicken burgers and steak sandwiches from this café on the end of the jetty.

Getting There & Away

Hinterland Air Transfer (☎ 1300 134 044, 8296 8010) runs return flights to/from Cairns (per adult/child from $198/100, 45 minutes, three daily).

Mission Beach Dunk Island Connections (☎ 4059 2709; www.missionbeachdunkconnections.com.au) runs combination bus-and-boat transfers between

Dunk and Cairns (return per adult/child $128/80, 2½ hours).

Dunk Island Express Water Taxi (☎ 4068 8310; Banfield Pde, Wongaling Beach; return adult/child $35/17.50) and **Dunk Island Ferry & Cruises** (☎ 4068 7211; www.dunkferry.com.au; Clump Point Jetty, Mission Beach; return adult/child $48/24) make the short trip from Mission Beach to Dunk Island.

BEDARRA ISLAND

Exclusive Bedarra Island is the sort of place you go whenever a 'who cares, it's only money' attitude grabs you. Yes, it's expensive, but they don't cut any corners here. It's worth it.

The 16 beachfront villas at **Bedarra Island Resort** (☎ 4068 8233; www.bedarraisland.com; 2-night packages $2792-5732, d $3300-6240; ✖ 🖳 🖳 ; wi-fi) are the very essence of luxury and seclusion. Indeed, the resort boasts that there are often more beaches here than guests! Each stunning, split-level villa overlooks Wedgerock Bay, has its own private plunge-pool and outdoor area with a day bed (to which a bucket of ice and plate of canapés are delivered daily). There's a bar open 24/7, and all meals are included. This is not a family resort – kids under 12 are not catered for. Access is via Dunk Island; contact Dunk Island Resort (p443) for details.

Far North Queensland Coast

Whether this is the beginning or the end of your East Coast journey, welcome to paradise. Basking in a tropical climate that draws travellers ever northwards in the winter months, Far North Queensland is bursting with natural highs. An extraordinary combination of reefs, rivers and rainforests make this one of Australia's most biologically diverse regions, all wrapped up in a neatly accessible corner of Queensland. Rainforest spills out onto stretches of pristine beach, mangroves crowd riverbanks, and coral gardens bloom out on the reefs. And although popular with travellers, this stretch of coast is nowhere near as crowded as places further down the coast, so you can always find a slice of solitude.

From Innisfail in the south to the frontier northern outpost of Cooktown, Far North Queensland has something for everyone. Cairns is the booming tourist hub, where an armada of boats waits to take you out diving and snorkelling on the reef. Port Douglas is the glitzy holiday playground, where you can swim all day and dine in style at night. But the adventure begins as you head further north through the sublime coastal rainforest of the Daintree National Park to the stunning beaches and alternative lifestyle around Cape Tribulation. Then embark on a 4WD adventure along the Bloomfield Track to Cooktown, where Captain Cook first set foot on Australia's shores.

The area's human landscape is equally diverse: Aboriginal communities, farmers and conservationists all live here, contributing boundless character and depth to this spectacular region.

FAR NORTH QUEENSLAND COAST

HIGHLIGHTS

- Snorkelling or diving on the stunning Great Barrier Reef from **Port Douglas** (p465), **Cairns** (p454) or, best of all, **Lizard Island** (p477)

- Taking the Skyrail up to **Kuranda** (p462), and visiting gallery at Djurri Dadagal Art Enterprises

- Taking an Aboriginal guided walk, then swimming in the clear water amid the ancient boulders of **Mossman Gorge** (p468)

- Scanning the riverbanks for saltwater crocs on cruises on the **Daintree River** (p469) or **Cooper Creek** (p470)

- Kayaking along the shoreline in search of turtles off **Myall Beach** (p472) at Cape Tribulation

- Tackling the 4WD **Bloomfield Track** (p473) from Cape Trib to Cooktown and stopping for a well-earned beer at the **Lion's Den Hotel** (p474)

- Join the locals fishing from the wharf at laid-back **Cooktown** (p474)

- Dining in style at one of the exquisite eateries at **Port Douglas** (p467)

- ★ Lizard Island
- ★ Cooktown
- ★ Lion's Den Hotel
- Bloomfield Track ★
- ★ Cape Tribulation
- Daintree River ★
- Mossman Gorge ★ ★ Port Douglas
- Great Barrier Reef
- Kuranda ★
- Cairns ★

■ TELEPHONE CODE: 07　　■ www.dctta.asn.au　　■ www.tropicalaustralia.com.au

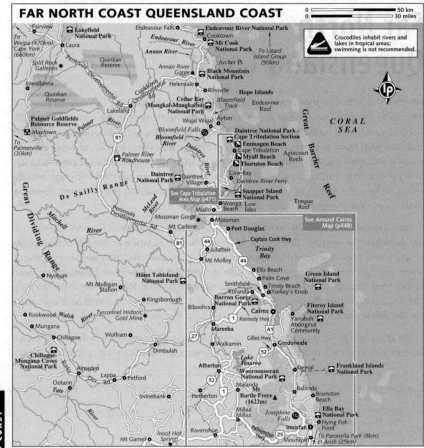

FAR NORTH COAST QUEENSLAND COAST

Crocodiles inhabit rivers and lakes in tropical areas; swimming is not recommended.

FAR NORTH QUEENSLAND COAST

MISSION BEACH TO CAIRNS

From Mission Beach the Bruce Hwy stays 20km or so inland of the coast, leading through a corridor of national parks, with burbling swimming holes and tranquil walking trails.

MISSION BEACH TO INNISFAIL

Back on the Bruce Hwy and about 5km north of the tiny township of El Arish, the Old Bruce Hwy (Japoonvale Rd) turns west and is a scenic detour on the route north. It runs along banana and sugar-cane plantations, with cane trains intermittently cutting across the road during harvest (June to December). Among this agricultural activity are the eccentric ruins of **Paronella Park** (☎ 4065 3225; www.paronellapark.com.au; Japoonvale Rd; adult/child $30/15; ◷ 9am-9.30pm), just south of Mena Creek. The rambling mossy Spanish castle, Lovers Tunnel and stunning gardens are testament to the owners' quest to bring a whimsical entertainment centre to the area's hard-working folk. Admission includes a range of cultural tours or you can wander the walking trails through stunning gardens past a waterfall and a swimming hole.

INNISFAIL

☎ 07 / pop 8262

Innisfail may come as a surprise to those who expect another ho-hum agricultural town. Innisfail buzzes, especially on Saturday mornings when outlying locals come to town to browse, shop, drink and eat. It has a real community feel and some gorgeous Art Deco architecture. Innisfail's cosmopolitan past credits Chinese settlers with establishing the area's banana plantations, and Italian immigrants arrived in the early 20th century to work the cane fields (during the 1930s there was even a local branch of the Mafia, called the Black Hand).

The **visitors centre** (☎ 4061 7422; Bruce Hwy; ⊙ 9am-5pm Mon-Fri, 10am-3pm Sat & Sun), about 3km south of town, has a town-walk brochure.

The **Local History Museum** (☎ 4061 2731; 11 Edith St; admission $3; ⊙ 10am-noon & 1-3pm Mon-Fri) displays various items evidencing Innisfail's history, while the puffs of incense from the **Lit Zing Khuong** (Temple of the Universal God; Owen St; admission by donation) are a gentle reminder of the area's Chinese heritage.

About 20km north of Innisfail on the Bruce Hwy is the turn-off to the bird-rich wetlands of **Eubenangee Swamp National Park**. During the Wet the water level of the Russell River rises such that it causes the Alice River to flow backwards, which floods the swamp.

Sleeping & Eating

The town's hostels cater to the banana pickers who work the surrounding plantations.

Innisfail Budget Backpackers (☎ 4061 7833; 125 Edith St; dm $25; ⌘ ⌨ ⌧) A rabbit-warren kind of place with a free bus to the beach on Sundays.

Barrier Reef Motel (☎ 4061 4988; www.barrierreefmotel.com.au; Bruce Hwy; s/d $90/100; ⌘ ⌧) The pick of Innisfail's motels, this comfortable place has 41 rooms (two of them self-catering) and a decent bar/restaurant.

Oliveri's Continental Deli (☎ 4061 3354; 41 Edith St; sandwiches $6; ⊙ 8.30am-5.30pm Mon-Fri, 8.30am-1pm Sat) Step back in time at this (almost) mini-museum. Apart from healthy lunch choices and delicious coffee, this authentic Italian delicatessen has 60 varieties of European cheese, hams, salamis and row upon row of smallgoods, and jarred goodies like antipasto, olives.

Roscoe's (☎ 4061 6888; 3b Ernest St; mains $22-30; ⊙ lunch & dinner) Roscoe's is a popular local haunt, serving pizza and pasta and has a buffet lunch ($16) daily.

Getting There & Around

Bus services operate at least daily with **Premier** (☎ 13 34 10; www.premierms.com.au) and **Greyhound**

Australia (☎ 13 14 99; www.greyhound.com.au) from Innisfail to Townsville ($58, 4½ hours) and Cairns ($27, 1½ hours), departing from the bus stop opposite King George Sq on Edith St.

Innisfail is on the Cairns–Townsville train line; contact **Queensland Rail** (☎ 1300 131 722; www.traveltrain.com.au; ⊙ 6am-9pm) for more information.

WOOROONOORAN NATIONAL PARK: JOSEPHINE FALLS SECTION

Fed by rain that collects around Queensland's highest mountain, Mt Bartle Frere (1622m), the **Josephine Falls** are a series of stepped clear-water pools fringed by giant tree roots. The turn-off is about 20km north of Innisfail and the falls are 8km inland from the highway. It's on the eastern fringe of Wooroonooran National Park, an enormous reserve of tropical rainforest. The lower swimming hole is a great place for a dip, but be careful after rain as flash flooding can occur. About 1km past the falls turn-off the road ends at **Golden Hole**, a lovely swimming hole with a picnic area and toilets.

Josephine Falls also marks the start of the demanding **Mt Bartle Frere Summit Track**, a two-day return trip for fit, experienced and well-equipped walkers only. The trail rises 1500m in 7.5km; cloud can close in suddenly and you're almost certain to experience rain. The track also branches to **Broken Nose** (962m; 10km return). Get advice on conditions and a copy of the *Mt Bartle Frere Trail Guide* from **QPWS** (☎ 13 13 04; www.epa.qld.gov.au) before you head off. You'll also need a camping permit ($4.50 per person), and you can self-register at the start of the walk.

BABINDA
☎ 07 / pop 1170

In the rush north to Cairns, few people stop at little ol' Babinda, but it's worth detouring past the veranda-fronted buildings and old timber pubs on the main street and into the rainforest to the mystical Babinda Boulders.

The **Babinda visitors centre** (☎ 4067 1008; cnr Munro St & Bruce Hwy; ⊙ 9am-4pm) has plenty of information on the area, including walking trails.

If you're in town on the weekend, try to catch a film at the timeless **Munro Theatre** (☎ 4067 1032; Munro St; ⊙ 7.30pm Fri, Sat & Sun), which dates back to the 1950s. Recline in a hessian-slung seat and enjoy the acoustics of its canvas-covered ceiling.

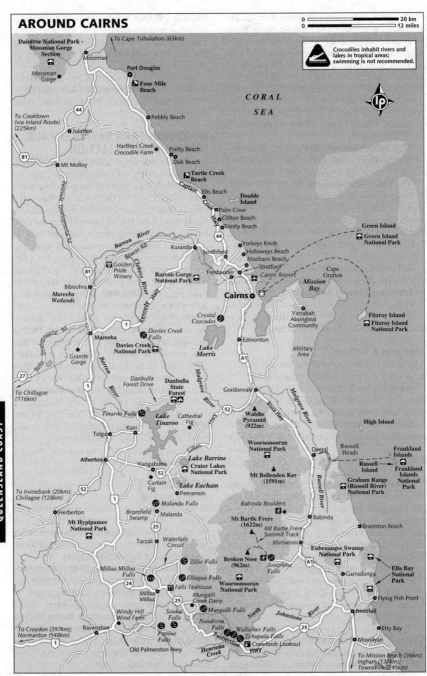

AROUND CAIRNS

0 — 20 km
0 — 12 miles

Crocodiles inhabit rivers and lakes in tropical areas; swimming is not recommended.

Daintree National Park - Mossman Gorge Section

To Cape Tribulation (63km)

Mossman

Mossman Gorge

Port Douglas

Four Mile Beach

CORAL SEA

Pebbly Beach

To Cooktown (via Inland Route) (225km)

Julatten

Hartleys Creek Crocodile Farm

Pretty Beach

Oak Beach

Mt Molloy

Turtle Creek Beach

Ellis Beach

Double Island

Palm Cove

Clifton Beach

Trinity Beach

Kuranda

Smithfield

Yorkeys Knob

Holloways Beach

Machans Beach

Stratford

Green Island

Green Island National Park

Barron River

Biboohra

Golden Pride Winery

Freshwater

Cairns Airport

Cape Grafton

Barron Gorge National Park

Mareeba Wetlands

Cairns

Mission Bay

Yarrabah Aboriginal Community

Fitzroy Island

Fitzroy Island National Park

Crystal Cascades

Mareeba

Davies Creek Falls

Davies Creek National Park

Lake Morris

Edmonton

Military Area

Granite Gorge

To Chillagoe (116km)

Danbulla Forest Drive

Danbulla State Forest

Gordonvale

High Island

Tinaroo Falls

Lake Tinaroo

Cathedral Fig

Walshs Pyramid (922m)

Russell Heads

Frankland Islands

Tolga

Kairi

Wooroonooran National Park

Deeral

Russell Island

Frankland Islands National Park

Atherton

Yungaburra

Lake Barrine

Crater Lakes National Park

Lake Eacham

Mt Bellenden Ker (1591m)

Graham Range (Russell River) National Park

To Irvinebank (20km); Chillagoe (128km)

Curtain Fig

Babinda Boulders

Peeramon

Herberton

Malanda Falls

Mt Bartle Frere (1622m)

Bramston Beach

Mt Hypipamee National Park

Bromfield Swamp

Malanda

Mt Bartle Frere Summit Track

Tarzali

Waterfalls Circuit

Mirriwinni

Eubenangee Swamp National Park

Ella Bay National Park

Zillie Falls

Broken Nose (962m)

Josephine Falls

Garradunga

Millaa Millaa Falls

Ellinjaa Falls

Falls Teahouse

Wooroonooran National Park

Flying Fish Point

Millaa Millaa

Mungalli Creek Dairy

Windy Hill Wind Farm

Soulta Falls

Mungalli Falls

North Johnstone River

Innisfail

To Croydon (397km); Normanton (548km)

Ravenshoe

Nandroya Falls

Papina Falls

Wallicher Falls

Tchupala Falls

Etty Bay

Old Palmerston Hwy

Henrietta Creek

Crawfords Lookout

Moutiyan

To Mission Beach (36km); Ingham (137km); Townsville (245km)

You can design and create your own didj-eridu at the excellent, family-run **Aboriginality** (☎ 4067 1660; 225 Howard Kennedy Hwy; $165). Start with an authentic, ready-to-use plain didj, come up with a design (you can paint or burn it) and finish with some expert playing lessons before taking it home. The day includes lunch and a trip to the Boulders with Dreamtime stories thrown in. Look for the sign just off the highway.

About 7km west of Babinda, in the Wooroonooran National Park, the **Babinda Boulders** are a stretch of massive granite boulders that have been sculpted by the fast-running creek. At the lower end is a grassy picnic area with a gentle clear-water swimming hole, while walking trails lead upstream to **Devil's Pool Lookout** (470m) and the **Boulders Gorge Lookout** (600m). Swimming is prohibited in the dangerous, fast-flowing upper reaches. If you cross the suspension bridge there's an 850m loop through a pretty section of rainforest.

There's a picnic area at the car park, and just before this is the **Boulders Camping Ground** (free, maximum two nights) with toilets and cold showers.

INNISFAIL TO GORDONVALE VIA THE ATHERTON TABLELAND

The detour west from Innisfail on the Palmerston Hwy is an excellent drive that takes you into the southern reaches of the Atherton Tableland via Wooroonooran National Park. The tableland is the fertile food bowl of the Cairns region, a lush pastoral place elevated from the coast, where lakes and waterfalls are set in pockets of rainforest and punctuated with patchwork fields and quaint villages. Here, altitude does its best to defeat humidity, and the abundant rainfall and rich volcanic soil combine to make this one of the greenest places in Queensland. There are some amazing B&Bs and ecoretreats out here, and a day or two spent detouring away from the coast is well worth the effort.

Wooroonooran National Park: Palmerston Section

Home to some of the oldest continually surviving rainforest in Australia, Wooroonooran's fertile soil and superwet climate (3500mm rainfall annually) make it one of the richest biological regions in the country.

Just inside the park boundary is **Crawfords Lookout**, with fine views of the coast; a 5km (2½-hour) walking track links it with the twin cascades of **Tchupala Falls**. The highlight of the area is a 7.5km loop walk (three to four hours) through superb high-canopied rainforest to the spectacular **Nandroya Falls**, which crash into a beautiful, deep swimming hole.

Millaa Millaa
☎ 07 / pop 289

Tiny Millaa Millaa is the gateway to the tableland from the south. Surrounded by rolling farmland dotted with black-and-white Friesian cows, this is also the centre of a thriving local dairy industry.

At **Mungalli Creek Dairy** (☎ 4097 2232; 254 Brooks Rd; ☽ 10am-4pm), about 6km southeast of the village, you can sample boutique biodynamic dairy products, including yogurt, cheese and sinfully rich cheesecake.

The **waterfalls circuit**, about 3km before Millaa Millaa, is a 16km loop that takes in three picturesque falls – 12m-high Millaa Millaa Falls are the best for swimming, with a large fenced swimming hole and a grassy picnic area.

Overlooking the rolling tableland where the Millaa Millaa Falls turn-off meets the highway, historic **Falls Teahouse** (☎ 4097 2237; www.fallsteahouse .com.au; Palmerston Hwy; s/d $65/110, meals $7-16; ☽ 10am-5pm) is a treat – the country-style kitchen serves Devonshire teas, salads, sandwiches made from home-baked bread, and pasta and barramundi dishes. The three guest rooms are individually furnished with period fixtures and fittings.

Tarzali Lakes Fishing Park (☎ 4097 713; www.tarzali lakes.com; adult/child fishing from $20/10; ☽ 10am-6pm, closed Wed), about halfway between Malanda and Millaa Millaa, is an aquaculture farm with several artificial lakes well stocked with jade perch and barramundi, so you're sure to catch something. There's plenty of bird-life here and the **platypus-spotting tours** (adult/child $10/5) have a 'no see, no fee' guarantee.

Malanda
☎ 07 / pop 1009

Milk runs through the proverbial veins of Malanda – ever since 500 bedraggled cattle made the arduous overland journey from New South Wales (taking 16 months) in 1908. There's still a working dairy here and a dairy research centre.

The **Malanda Falls visitors centre** (☎ 4096 6957; Atherton Rd; ☽ 9.30am-4.30pm) has thoughtful displays on the area's human and geological history, including its volcanic origins and the logging and dairy industry. Guided **rainforest**

WORTH A TRIP: YUNGABURRA

From Lake Eacham it's only 3km west to the chocolate-box quaintness of National Trust–registered village Yungaburra. Stroll along the creek in search of a platypus or simply wander around the heritage buildings. There's a fine old pub and some of the best boutique accommodation and restaurants on the tableland. Yungaburra is locally famous for its markets, held on the fourth Saturday of every month, when the village goes mad. Call in to the **visitors centre** (☎ 4095 2416; www.yungaburra.com; Cedar St; ✹ 10am-6pm) for details.

---

walks ($10; ✹ by appointment) led by members of the indigenous Ngadjonji community can be organised here. Next door are the **Malanda Falls**. They don't 'fall' so spectacularly, but the resulting pool, surrounded by lawns and forest, is a popular swimming spot.

CRATER LAKES NATIONAL PARK

Part of the Wet Tropics World Heritage Area, the two mirrorlike crater lakes of Lake Eacham and Lake Barrine are pleasant, forested areas.

The crystal-clear waters of **Lake Eacham** are great for swimming and spotting turtles. The 3km lake-circuit track is an easy walk and takes less than an hour. Stop in at the **Rainforest Display Centre** (McLeish Rd; ✹ 9am-1pm Mon, Wed, Fri) at the ranger station for information on the area, the history of the timber industry and the rebuilding of the rainforest.

Just off the Gillies Hwy, **Lake Barrine** is cloaked in thick old-growth rainforest; a 5km walking track around the lake takes about 1½ hours. The **Lake Barrine Rainforest Cruise & Tea House** (☎ 4095 3847; www.lakebarrine.com.au; Gillies Hwy; mains $6-14; ✹ breakfast & lunch) dominates the lakefront; book the 40-minute **lake cruise** (adult/child $13/6.50; ✹ 10.15am, 11.30am, 1.30pm, 2.30pm & 3.30pm) here. A short stroll from the tea house are two enormous, neck-tilting, 1000-year-old **kauri pines**.

From here it's a winding 35km drive down to Gordonvale where you can rejoin the Bruce Hwy to Cairns.

GORDONVALE & YARRABAH
☎ 07 / pop 5670

The drive back to the coast winds through striking ranges before popping out at **Gordonvale**, a rustic, old-fashioned town with a disproportionate number of timber pubs set around a central park, and with the obligatory sugar mill. It's all backed by the looming presence of Walsh's Pyramid. Gordonvale has the dubious honour of being the first place where cane toads were released in 1935.

Between Gordonvale and Edmonton is a turn-off to the Yarrabah Aboriginal Community, a scenic 37km drive through cane fields and hills. The **Yarrabah Menmuny Museum** (☎ 4056 9154; www.indiginet.com.au/yarrabah/museum.htm; Back Beach Rd; adult/child $6/4; ✹ 8am-4pm Mon-Fri) recounts Yarrabah's history and has a collection of Aboriginal artefacts and cultural exhibits. The museum also has spear-throwing demonstrations and a guided **boardwalk tour** (adult/child incl museum entry $14/10).

CAIRNS

☎ 07 / pop 98,981

Cairns is booming. As Queensland's most popular diving destination, a flotilla of cruise boats, catamarans and yachts heads out to the Great Barrier Reef from the marina each day. The compact centre is a miniurban jungle of tour shops, booking agents, car hire, internet cafés, restaurants and hostels, all aimed at wooing the stream of bewildered visitors.

This is unashamedly a tourist town, but it has an infectious holiday vibe and a tropical aura, it has come a long way from struggling cane town to international resort city. The mudflats and mangroves along the Esplanade foreshore have been replaced with a multimillion dollar development of parks and the dazzling saltwater lagoon. Old salts claim Cairns has lost some of its character and sold its soul, but it ticks to the tune of tourism. There's no limit to the activities you can organise here – apart from diving and snorkelling you can go bungee jumping, white-water rafting, ballooning or biking – and tours operate from Cairns to Cooktown, Cape Tribulation and Cape York.

Cairns thrives on its reputation as a party town, too. For many backpackers this is the end of the line on the east coast jaunt from Sydney. They like to hit the town hard and there are bars and nightclubs that seem to exist solely for their pleasure.

ORIENTATION

Cairns has a small centre running from the Esplanade on the waterfront back to Sheridan St, and bordered by Wharf and

Aplin Sts. Although it's referred to as the business district, it's really more boardshorts than briefcases.

Reef Fleet Terminal is the main point of departure for trips to the Reef and the transit centre for long-distance buses. The train station is behind Cairns Central Shopping Centre on McLeod St. The airport is about 7km north of the city centre.

Maps

For an impressive range of quality regional maps, topographic maps and nautical charts, head to **Absells Chart & Map Centre** (☎ 4041 2699; Main Street Arcade, 85 Lake St).

INFORMATION
Bookshops

Bookshelf (☎ 4051 8569; www.thebookshelfcairns.com .au; 95 Grafton St) Lots of secondhand books – proceeds go to a women's centre.

Exchange Bookshop (☎ 4051 1443; www.exchange bookshop.com; 78 Grafton St) New and secondhand books to buy and swap.

Emergency

Ambulance, Fire & Police (☎ 000; ⊗ 24hr)
Cairns Police Station (☎ 4030 7000)

Internet Access

Most tour booking agencies and many accommodation places have internet access; dedicated internet cafés are clustered along Abbott St, between Shields and Aplin Sts. They have fast connections, cheap international phone calls and CD burning, and charge between $2 and $5 per hour. Most of the public wi-fi hotspots in Cairns require payment: an exception is the McDonald's restaurant on the corner of Shields and the Esplanade.

Call Station (☎ 4052 1572; 123 Abbott St; ⊗ 8.30am-11.30pm; wi-fi)
Global Gossip (☎ 4031 6411; www.globalgossip.com; 125 Abbott St; ⊗ 9am-11.30pm; wi-fi)

Medical Services

Cairns Base Hospital (☎ 4050 6333; The Esplanade) Has a 24-hour emergency service.

Cairns City 24 Hour Medical Centre (☎ 4044 0444; cnr Florence & Grafton Sts) General practice and diving examinations.

Cairns Travel Clinic (☎ 4041 1699; 15 Lake St; ⊗ Mon-Fri 8.30am-5.30pm, 9am-noon Sat) Vaccinations, medical kits and advice.

Money

All major banks have branches with ATMs throughout central Cairns. Most banks exchange foreign currency; private currency exchange bureaux line the Esplanade and are open longer hours.

American Express (☎ 1300 139 060; 63 Lake St) In Westpac Bank.
Thomas Cook (☎ 4051 6255; 50 Lake St)

Post

Main post office (☎ 13 13 18; www.auspost.com; 13 Grafton St) Handles poste restante. There are branches in Orchid Plaza and in Cairns Central Shopping Centre.

Tourist Information

The glut of tourist information available in Cairns can either inspire you to do something wild, or baffle you with its sheer volume. Dozens of tour-booking agents operating in Cairns call themselves 'information centres' and fraudulently brandish the blue-and-white 'i' symbol; most places to stay also have tour-booking desks. The government-run **Gateway Discovery Centre** (☎ 4051 3588; www.tropicalaustralia .com.au; 51 The Esplanade; ⊗ 8.30am-6.30pm) offers impartial advice, books tours and houses an interpretive centre. It distributes the *Welcome to Cairns* directory with a map centrefold.

Other useful contacts:

Queensland Parks & Wildlife Service (QPWS; ☎ 4046 6602; www.epa.qld.gov.au; 5B Sheridan St) Information on national parks and state forests, walking trails and camping permits.

Royal Automobile Club of Queensland (RACQ; ☎ 4033 6433; www.racq.com.au; 537 Mulgrave Rd, Earlville) Maps and information on road conditions up to Cape York.

Wilderness Society (☎ 4051 6666; www.wilderness .org.au; 125 Abbott St) Advocacy organisation with information on local environmental issues; volunteers welcome.

SIGHTS

Hundreds of people flock around the shallow but dazzling 4800-sq-metre saltwater swimming **lagoon** (free; ⊗ 6am-10pm), and take up patches of grass right along the city's reclaimed foreshore. The lagoon is patrolled by lifeguards and illuminated at night. Strolling northwest from the lagoon, the 3km boardwalk **promenade** is popular with walkers, joggers and picnickers.

The **Cairns Regional Gallery** (☎ 4031 6865; www .cairnsregionalgallery.com.au; cnr Abbott & Shields Sts; adult/ child under 16 $5/free; ⊗ 10am-5pm Mon-Sat, 1-5pm Sun)

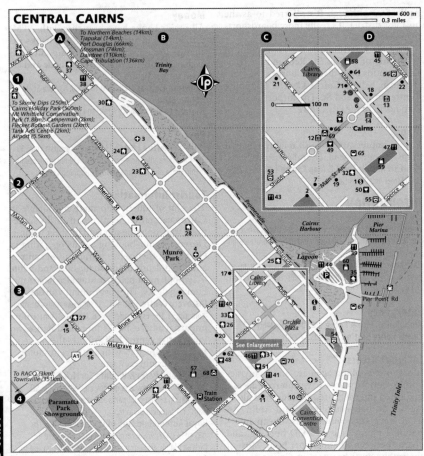

CENTRAL CAIRNS

has exhibitions reflecting the consciousness of the tropical north region, with an emphasis on local and indigenous works.

For contemporary works, visit the superb **Centre of Contemporary Arts** (☎ 4050 9401; www .coca.org.au; 96 Abbott St; ☉ 10am-5pm Tue-Sat), which houses the KickArts (www.kickarts.org.au) galleries of visual art, as well as the Jute theatre company and the End Credits Film Club.

Cairns Museum (☎ 4051 5582; www.cairnsmuseum .org.au; cnr Lake & Shields Sts; adult/child $5/2; ☉ 10am-4pm Mon-Sat) has displays on topics that have influenced Far North Queensland, including Aboriginal artefacts, construction of the Cairns–Kuranda railway and the contents of a now-demolished Chinese temple. There's an excellent bookshop and a café at street level.

It's worth a trip to the **Flecker Botanic Gardens** (☎ 4044 3398; www.cairns.qld.gov.au; Collins Ave, Edge Hill; ☉ 7.30am-5.30pm Mon-Fri, 8.30am-5.30pm Sat & Sun), 4km northwest of the centre. Wander around these lush tropical gardens, then cross the road to the **Rainforest Boardwalk** leading past Saltwater Creek to the twin **Centenary Lakes**, which showcase Far North Queensland's saltwater and freshwater ecosystems. Next door to the gardens is the stylish community **Tanks Arts Centre** (☎ 4032 2349; www.tanksartscentre.com; 46 Collins Ave, Edge Hill; ☉ gallery 10am-4pm Mon-Fri), where giant cylindrical WWII naval supply tanks have been transformed into exhibition and performance spaces.

Near the gardens is the entrance to the **Mt Whitfield Conservation Park**, the last remnant of

Cairns rainforest, with two more demanding walks: the Red Arrow Trail (one hour) and the Blue Arrow Trail (3½ hours), which climbs steeply and opens up to views over the city and coast.

Before heading out to the Reef, join one of the evening lectures at **Reef Teach** (☎ 4031 7794; www.reefteach.com.au; Main Street Arcade, 85 Lake St; adult/child $13/7; ☟ 10am-9pm Mon-Sat, lecture 6.30-8.30pm Mon-Sat), where marine experts explain how to identify specific types of coral and fish, and how to treat the Reef with respect.

Cairns' indigenous-owned cultural extravaganza **Tjapukai** (☎ 4042 9900; www.tjapukai.com.au; Kamerunga Rd, Smithfield; adult/child $31/15.50, incl transfers from Cairns & Northern Beaches $50/25; ☟ 9am-5pm) presents a variety of inspirational and educational performances combining interesting aspects of Aboriginal culture with show biz. It includes the Creation Theatre (which tells the story of creation using giant holograms and actors), the Dance Theatre and a gallery, as well as boomerang- and spear-throwing demonstrations set around an Aboriginal camp. You can also learn to paint a boomerang or take a canoe ride on the lake. **Tjapukai By Night** (adult/child $87/43.50, incl transfers $104/52; ☟ 7.30pm) is a dinner-and-show deal with a fireside corroboree. The park is just off the Captain Cook Hwy near the Skyrail terminal, about 15km north of the centre.

ACTIVITIES
Diving

Cairns is the scuba-diving capital of the Great Barrier Reef and a popular place to attain PADI open-water certification. There's a plethora of courses on offer, from budget four-day courses that combine pool training and reef dives (from $370) to five-day courses ($580 to $700) with two days' pool theory and three days aboard a boat. These live-aboard courses are generally more rewarding as you'll dive less-frequented parts of the Reef. The following outfits also offer live-aboard trips for certified divers lasting from one to three days:
Cairns Dive Centre (☎ 1800 642 591; 4051 0294; www.cairnsdive.com.au; 121 Abbott St)

Deep Sea Divers Den (☎ 1800 612223, 4046 7333; www.diversden.com.au; 319 Draper St)
Down Under Dive (☎ 1800 079 099, 4052 8300; www.downunderdive.com.au; 287 Draper St)
Pro Dive (☎ 1800 353 213; 4031 5255; www.prodive cairns.com; cnr Abbot & Shields Sts)
Tusa Dive (☎ 4031 1248; www.tusadive.com; cnr Shields St & The Esplanade)

If you really want to explore the Reef and visit the best sites, extended live-aboard trips are the way to go. These typically range from three to seven days and head to the outer reefs (including the renowned Cod Hole and Lizard Island). Recommended operators:

Explorer Ventures (☎ 4031 5566; www.explorer ventures.com) The *Nimrod Explorer* has four- to eight-day live-aboard trips diving the Ribbon Reef and the Cod Hole.
Mike Ball Dive Expeditions (☎ 4053 0500; www .mikeball.com; 143 Lake St) Three-day live-aboard expeditions (from $1385) head to the Cod Hole; four- and seven-day options also available.
Taka Dive (☎ 4051 8722; www.takadive.com.au; 131 Lake St; 4-/5-day tours from $1100/1300) Dives the Cod Hole and the Coral Sea. Also does speciality courses such as underwater photography.

White-Water Rafting

There's excellent white-water rafting down the Tully, Russell and Barron Rivers. The Tully River is probably the best of them; a day trip costs around $155. However, it's 140km from Cairns, so if you're heading to Mission Beach do the tour from there.

Major rafting companies in Cairns:

Foaming Fury (☎ 1800 801 540, 4031 3460; www .foamingfury.com.au) Full-day trips on the Russell; half-day on the Barron.
Raging Thunder (☎ 4030 7990; www.ragingthunder .com.au; Reef Fleet Terminal) Full-day Tully and half-day Barron trips.

Other Activities

AJ Hackett Bungee & Minjin (☎ 4057 7188; www .ajhackett.com; bungee jumps $99, minjin swing per person $45, bungee & minjin swing combo $140; ⏰ 10am-5pm) Bungee from the purpose-built tower or swing from the trees on the minjin (a harness swing).
Cable Ski (☎ 4038 1304; www.cableskicairns.com .au; Captain Cook Hwy, Smithfield; 1hr adult/child $34/29, day $59/68) Learn to water-ski, wakeboard or kneeboard without the boat at this water-sports park near the Skyrail (p463).
Hot Air Cairns (☎ 4039 9900; www.hotair.com.au; 30-/60min flights $180/280).

Skydive Cairns (☎ 1800 444 568, 4031 5466; www.skydivecairns.com.au; 59 Sheridan St; tandem jumps from 9000ft $210).

TOURS

There's a bewildering variety of tours on offer from Cairns, but the market's so tight that they're generally good value and have seasoned and entertaining guides.

Great Barrier Reef

Most of the operators working on the Reef include transport, lunch and snorkelling gear in their tour prices. When choosing a tour, consider the vessel (catamaran or sailing ship), its capacity (ranging from six to 300 people), what extras are offered and the destination. Generally, the outer reefs are more pristine; the inner reef areas can be patchy – showing signs of damage from humans, coral bleaching and crown-of-thorns starfish. Of course, operators who are only licensed to visit the inner reef have cheaper tours; in most cases you pay for what you get. The dive course operators also have day and live-aboard trips.

The majority of cruise boats depart from the Pier Marina and Reef Fleet Terminal at about 8am, returning around 6pm.

Great Adventures (☎ 1800 079 080, 4044 9944; www .greatadventures.com.au; adult/child from $174/87).
Passions of Paradise (☎ 1800 111 346, 4041 1600; www.passions.com.au; adult/child $119/70) Sexy sailing catamaran takes you to Michaelmas Cay and Paradise Reef.
Sunlover (☎ 1800 810 512, 4050 1333; www.sunlover .com.au; adult/child $175/90) Sunlover's fast catamaran takes day cruises to a pontoon on the outer Moore Reef.

Atherton Tableland

Most visitors take a trip on the Kuranda Scenic Railway and Skyrail, but there is a range of speciality tours to the highlands above Cairns.

Bandicoot Bicycle Tours (☎ 4055 0155; full-day tours $99; ⏰ Mon-Fri) Mountain bike tours of the Atherton Tableland.
Food Trail Tours (☎ 4032 0322; www.foodtrailtours .com.au; adult/child from $139/65; ⏰ 8am-5pm) Munch your way around the Highlands and the Mareeba area visiting farms producing macadamias, tropical-fruit wine, ice cream and coffee.
On the Wallaby (☎ 4050 0650; www.onthewallaby .com; day/overnight tours $95/165) Excellent activity-based tours around the Yungaburra area including cycling, hiking and canoeing.

Uncle Brian's Tours (☎ 4050 0615; www.unclebrian .com.au; tours $109; ⊗ 7.45am-8.30pm Mon-Wed, Fri & Sat) Popular small-group tours covering forests, waterfalls and lakes.

Cape Tribulation & the Daintree

After the Great Barrier Reef, Cape Trib is the next most popular day trip – usually taking in a cruise on the Daintree River.

Adventure Tours (☎ 1300 654 604; www.adventure tours.com.au; day tours $115; ⊗ 7.30am-5pm) Budget-oriented small-group tours include lunch, Mossman Gorge and a cruise on the Daintree River.

Billy Tea Bush Safaris (☎ 4032 0077; www.billytea .com.au; day trips adult/child $147/97; ⊗ 7.am-6.30pm) Ecotours that go beyond Cape Trib along the 4WD Bloom-field Track to Emmagen Creek.

Cape Trib Connections (☎ 4041 7447; www.capetrib connections.com; day trips $119; ⊗ 7.30am-6.30pm) Mossman Gorge, Cape Tribulation Beach and Port Douglas.

Cooktown & Cape York

Several companies run trips up to Cooktown, usually travelling up via Cape Tribulation and returning via the inland route.

Adventure North Australia (☎ 4053 7001; www .adventurenorthaustralia; day tour adult/child $199/159) Day trips with 4WD to Cooktown via coastal route, return-ing via inland route. Also two- and three-day tours, and fly-drive tours.

Wilderness Challenge (☎ 4055 4488; www.wilder ness-challenge.com.au; 3-day tours from $845; ⊗ Mon & Fri May-Nov) This 4WD tour goes to Cooktown via Cape Tribulation and the Bloomfield Track, returning via Cape York rock-art sites.

SLEEPING

Cairns has an excellent range of accom-modation in all budgets. Prices peak from 1 June to 31 October; prices quoted here are high-season rates. Even during this time, you may find reduced walk-in or stand-by rates for midrange and top-end places that otherwise advertise higher 'corporate rates'.

If you're planning on sticking around for a while to work or study (a minimum of four weeks), **Cairns Sharehouse** (☎ 4041 1875; www.cairns -sharehouse.com; cnr Draper & Minnie Sts; s/d from $100/200 per week) has a range of budget share accom-modation around the city.

Budget

There are literally dozens of backpacker hos-tels in Cairns, from intimate house-sized places to hangar-sized resorts.

Cairns Holiday Park (☎ 1800 259 977; 4051 1467; www .cairnscamping.com.au; 12-30 Little St; unpowered/powered sites $26/32; cabin $59; ⊠ ◻ ⊠ ; wi-fi) Closest park to the city centre with good facilities including backpacker cabins and free wi-fi internet.

Bellview (☎ 4031 4377; www.bellview.com.au; 85-87 The Esplanade; dm/s/d $22/35/54, motel units $55-75; ⊠ ⊠) Smack in the middle of the Esplanade, the family-run Bellview is a long-standing place that's part hostel, part budget guest-house – perfect if you're not into the rowdy backpacker scene.

our pick **Northern Greenhouse** (☎ 1800 000 541, 4047 7200; www.friendlygroup.com.au; 117 Grafton St; dm/tw/ apt $25/95/120; ⊠ ◻ ⊠) It fits into the budget category with dorm accommodation and a laid-back vibe, but this place is a cut above the backpackers. Neat studio-style apartments with kitchens and balconies are a great deal. The central deck, pool and games room is a good place to meet people.

Bohemia Central (☎ 1800 558 589, 4052 1818; 100 Sheridan St; www.bohemiacentral.com.au; dm $23-25, s/d $49/69; ⊠ ◻ ⊠) One of the newest of the cen-tral backpackers in a renovated two-storey timber building, Bohemia has spotless rooms, friendly staff and a cool pool and bar area at the back.

Gilligans (☎ 4041 6566; www.gilligansbackpackers.com .au; 57-89 Grafton St; dm $22-28, r $110-180) This enor-mous, upmarket backpackers deserves a men-tion for its size and ritzy facilities, but (apart from the dorms) it's pricey and also loud when the nightclub below is pumping. All rooms have en suite, and most have balconies.

Behind the train station, on and around Bunda St, is a group of colourful low-key backpacker hostels, with a laid-back, almost hippy vibe – great for travellers wanting to hang out but avoid the party scene. They all have similar facilities and prices.

Travellers Oasis (☎ 4052 1377; www.travoasis.com .au; 8 Scott St; dm/s/d $24/40/55; ⊠ ◻ ⊠) Boutique backpackers with a maximum of 50 guests. It has all the usual facilities (kitchen and laundry) painted primary cartoon colours.

Midrange

our pick **Floriana** (☎ 4051 7886; www.florianaguesthouse .com; 183 The Esplanade; d $75-110; ⊠ ⊠) Not inter-ested in hostels or flashy self-contained apart-ments? Floriana is a charismatic, family-run guesthouse oozing old-fashioned charm, with polished boards and original Art Deco fittings. The swirling staircase leads to individually decorated rooms, some with bay windows or balconies and all with en suites.

Fig Tree Lodge (☎ 4041 0000; www.figtreelodge.com.au; 253 Sheridan St; r $85-135, apt $125-155; ✖ 🖳 🛋) This resort-style accommodation is one of the better midrange places around. Rooms have a beachy blue-and-white theme, and self-contained apartments have full kitchens. There's nightly entertainment in the Irish-themed restaurant and bar.

Balinese (☎ 1800 023 331, 4051 9922; www.balinese.com.au; 215 Lake St; r $100; ✖ 🖳 🛋) Authentic wood furnishings and ceramic pieces bring a touch of Bali to Cairns at this neat, low-rise complex.

Reef Palms (☎ 1800 815 421, 4051 2599; www.reefpalms.com.au; 41-7 Digger St; apt $105-145; ✖ 🛋) The crisp white interiors of Reef Palms' apartments will have you wearing your sunglasses inside. All rooms in this traditional Queenslander-style place have kitchen facilities. Good for couples and families.

Cascade Gardens (☎ 1800 503 877, 4047 6300; www.cascadegardens.com.au; 175 Lake St; apt $135-185; ✖ 🛋) Cascade aims for the tropical Asian ambience with cane furniture and a palm-filled garden. It's a standard but well-equipped resort with spacious studios and self-contained apartments.

Bay Village (☎ 4051 4622; www.bayvillage.com.au; cnr Lake & Gatton Sts; r $145-165; ✖ 🖳 🛋) This sprawling resort has smart units encircling a central pool. It's popular with package tours but no worse for that. The pricier rooms are self-contained, with kitchens and lounges; the Bay Leaf Restaurant here serves well-regarded Balinese cuisine.

Inn Cairns (☎ 4041 2350; www.inncairns.com.au; 71 Lake St; apt $189; ✖ 🖳 🛋) Behind the unassuming facade, this is truly inner-city apartment living. Take the lift up to the 1st-floor pool or to the rooftop garden for a sundowner. The elegant self-contained apartments feature modern furnishings and fittings, and the staff are helpful.

Skinny Dips (☎ 1800 621 824, 4051 4644; www.skinnydips.com.au; 18 James St; s/d $135/170; ✖ 🖳 🛋) This intimate gay resort and spa is mostly for male guests – the central pool area is clothing-optional and you can meet around the bar or in the stylish restaurant, or in the 'chillout centre' (gym and sauna).

Top End

Waterfront Terraces (☎ 4031 8333; www.cairnsluxury.com; 233 The Esplanade; 1-/2-bedroom apt $195/269; ✖ 🛋) Right on the Esplanade, this low-rise

group of luxury apartments is set in neat and trim tropical grounds. Handsomely furnished one or two bedroom apartments have separate tiled lounges and kitchen areas and all the trimmings.

Shangri-la (☎ 4031 1411; www.shangri-la.com; Pier Point Rd; r from $270; ✖ 🖳 🛋 ; wi-fi) Towering over the marina, Shangri-la is Cairns' top hotel, an elegant five-star that ticks all the boxes for location, views, facilities (a gym, a pool bar and broadband internet) and service. The Horizon Club rooms are top notch.

EATING

Cairns has come a long way on the culinary front in recent years, and its status as an international city is reflected in its multicultural restaurants. Along with the usual seafood and steak, you'll find plenty of Asian restaurants, and cuisines from Indian to Italian. The latest development is the Pier waterfront. where half a dozen restaurants share a boardwalk overlooking the marina – just wander along and take your pick of French, Italian, seafood and Mod Oz.

If you want something cheap and quick, the **Night Markets** (btwn The Esplanade & Abbott St) has a busy Asian-style food court.

Restaurants

Rattle & Hum (☎ 4031 3011; 65-67 The Esplanade; mains $13-23; ⏰ 10am-midnight) From its prime people-watching position on the Esplanade you can watch the wood-fired pizzas being prepared or slip into the rustic 'outback saloon'–style restaurant with timber beams and low-slung lighting. Good, honest food and a laid-back atmosphere.

Pier Bar & Grill (☎ 4031 4677; www.pierbar.com.au; Pier Point Rd; mains $13-32; ⏰ lunch & dinner) For informal waterfront dining, the Pier is hard to beat. With a big deck overlooking the water and foreshore lagoon, it serves up exotic wood-fired pizzas, noodles, pasta and thick steaks, and is one of the most popular spots in town for a late-afternoon drink.

Green Ant Cantina (☎ 4041 5061; 183 Bunda St; mains $15-29; ⏰ dinner) This funky little slice of Mexico is tucked away behind the railway station but well worth seeking out for *quesadillas*, fajitas and 'mumbo gumbo'. Great cocktail list, cool tunes (live bands on Saturday) and cheap backpacker meals on Monday.

our pick **Donnini's Ciao Italia** (☎ 4051 1133; Marina Boardwalk; mains $18-35; ⏰ lunch & dinner) Locals rate

Donnini's as the best Italian in town and with its corner boardwalk location it's hard not to be lured in by the Mediterranean aromas. All delivered with swift service, classic pasta dishes include spaghetti marinara and prawn linguini, but many rate the traditional thin-crust pizzas.

M Yogo (☎ 4051 0522; www.matureyogo.com; Marina Boardwalk; mains $19-42; ☽ lunch & dinner) French-inspired cuisine from an award-winning Japanese chef makes M Yogo one of the most interesting dining experiences on the Pier boardwalk. Innovative seafood dishes with rich sauces, sassy young waiters and a breezy location.

Charlie's (☎ 4051 5011; 223-227 The Esplanade; buffet $28.50; ☽ 6-8.30pm) It's not the fanciest place in town but Charlie's, at the Acacia Court Hotel, is legendary for its nightly all-you-can-eat seafood buffet. Fill your plate (over and over) with prawns, oysters, clams or hot food and eat it out on the terrace by the pool.

Ochre Restaurant (☎ 4051 0100; www.redochregrill .com.au; 43 Shields St; mains $29-34; ☽ lunch Mon-Fri, dinner nightly) Serving modern Australian cuisine at its best, the Ochre's inventive menu utilises native Australian ingredients, artfully prepared to pioneer its own culinary genre. There are the animals (croc, roo and emu), but Aussie flora also appears on the menu. Try the tasting plates or platters, and finish with the wattleseed pavlova with plum sorbet and macadamia biscotti.

Cafés & Quick Eats

Gaura Nitai's (☎ 4031 2255; 55 Spence St; mains $5.50-10.90; ☽ 11.30am-2pm Mon-Fri, 6-8pm Tue-Sat) Hare Krishna restaurant serving simple but tasty and cheap vegetarian fare such as dhal and rice, soups and koftas. Very Zen.

Fusion Organics (☎ 4051 1388; cnr Grafton & Aplin Sts; dishes $5-15; ☽ Mon-Fri 7am-5pm, 7am-2pm Sat) From the wicker chairs in the breezy corner courtyard to the buckwheat waffles and the 'detox' juices, Fusion is inspiring to the core. As you settle in for brekky the choice is between sublime Genovese coffee and a host of pick-me-up juices. The quiches, frittata, corn fritters and filled breads are all organic, allergy-free and delicious.

Perrotta's at the Gallery (☎ 4031 5899; 38 Abbott St; mains $15-25; ☽ breakfast, lunch & dinner) With its fabulous covered deck and wrought-iron furniture, Perrotta's beckons you off the street for a breakfast of eggs, French toast with vanilla-roasted pear and superb coffee, but many return for lunch or dinner, when an inventive Mediterranean menu takes over.

Pubs

Serving a hungry but thrifty backpacker market, some of Cairns' pubs dish up amazingly cheap meals, and they're not half bad. For some you need a meal token available at hostels, or just ask about the special. Some of the best are the $5 evening meals at PJ O'Brien's, and the $10 meal-and-drink deals at the Woolshed and Shennanigans. See Drinking, below.

Self-Catering

There's a large **Woolworths** (btwn Lake & Abbott Sts; ☽ 8am-9pm Mon-Fri, 8am-5.30pm Sat, 9am-6pm Sun) supermarket in town stocking everything you can think of, and you'll find two supermarkets in **Cairns Central Shopping Centre** (McLeod St).

Cairns' main food market is **Rusty's Markets** (Grafton St, btwn Shields & Spence Sts; ☽ 5am-6pm Fri, 6am-3pm Sat, 6am-2pm Sun); in among the souvenirs, jewellery, crafts and clothing you'll find seafood, fresh fruit and veg, herbs and honey, as well as juice bars and food stalls.

DRINKING

Cairns is undoubtedly the party capital of the north coast and the number of places to go out for a drink is intoxicating. The most popular inner-city bars and clubs are geared towards the lucrative backpacker market – and they party hard! Most places are multipurpose, offering food, alcohol and some form of entertainment, and you can always find a beer garden or terrace to enjoy balmy evenings.

Pier Bar & Grill (☎ 4031 4677; www.pierbar.com.au, Pier Point Rd; ☽ 11.30am-midnight) The Pier is a local institution for its waterfront location; Sunday session is a must.

Grand Hotel (☎ 4051 1007; 33 McLeod St; ☽ 11am-1am) This laid-back local pub is worth a visit just so that you can rest your beer on the bar – an 11m-long carved crocodile!

Shenannigans (☎ 4051 2490; 48 Spence St) The huge beer garden with barrels for tables, big screens and a music stage is the stand-out at this marginally Irish-themed pub. Variety of entertainment from trivia nights and karaoke to live bands.

PJ O'Briens (☎ 4031 5333; cnr Lake & Shields St) It has sticky carpets and the smell of stale Guinness, but Irish-themed PJ's packs 'em in with party nights, pole dancing and dirt-cheap meals.

Woolshed Chargrill & Saloon (☎ 4031 6304; 24 Shields St; meals $12-16) Another backpacker favourite, a young crowd of travellers and attentive diving instructors get hammered and dance on the tables.

our pick **Sapphire Tapas Bar & Lounge** (☎ 4052 1494; 39 Lake St; tapas $9-16) Walk through the unassuming street entrance to the cathedral-like back room with funky artworks adorning the walls and couches in the corners. Sapphire is Cairns' most sophisticated lounge-bar – part restaurant, part dance club, with DJs on weekends. Great vibe and gay-friendly.

ENTERTAINMENT

12 Bar Blue (☎ 4041 7388; www.12barblue.com; 62 Shields St; ☽ 5pm-midnight Tue-Sun) The best place in Cairns for loungy live music, this intimate bar grooves to the beat of jazz, blues and swing.

Jute Theatre (☎ 4031 9555; www.jute.com.au; Centre of Contemporary Arts, 96 Abbott St; tickets from $15) Staging a variety of contemporary Australian works and indie plays, check out what's on at the Jute's sexy venue in the Centre of Contemporary Arts.

Reef Casino (☎ 4030 8888; www.reefcasino.com.au; 35-41 Wharf St; ☽ 10am-3am Sun-Thu, 10am-5am Fri & Sat) Gamble on table games such as blackjack, roulette and baccarat, or feed your coins into one of the 500 bling-bling poker machines. Also five restaurants, a lounge bar and a nightclub at the Velvet Rope.

Nightclubs

Nightclubs come and go in Cairns; ask locally about what's hot and not. Most places close at 3am or 5am, but it pays to get in by 1am. Cover charges usually apply.

Soho (☎ 4051 2666; cnr The Esplanade & Shields St; ☽ Wed-Sun) This Cairns institution – it's been going longer than most – features resident and touring DJs playing house, techno and hip-hop.

Rhino Bar (☎ 4031 2530; cnr Spence & Lake Sts; ☽ from 8pm) A young, high-energy crowd downs cocktails and shots, and spills out onto the enormous 1st-floor balcony overlooking Lake St. Can get messy.

Gilligan's (☎ 4041 6566; 57-89 Grafton St) You're guaranteed a crowd here, with 400-odd backpackers staying in this resort complex, but it's also popular with locals. The huge beer barn downstairs has live bands, and upstairs is Pure, with DJs spinning house tunes.

SHOPPING

Cairns offers the gamut of shopping opportunities, from exclusive boutiques such as Louis Vuitton to garishly kitsch souvenir barns, and everything in between. You'll have no trouble finding a box of macadamia nuts, some emu or crocodile jerky and tropical-fish fridge magnets.

Head to the **Night Markets** (cnr The Esplanade & Abbott St; ☽ 4.30pm-midnight) and **Mud Markets** (Pier Marketplace; ☽ Sat morning) if your supply of 'Cairns Australia' T-shirts is running low, or you need your name on a grain of rice.

Cairns has two multilevel shopping centres where you can peruse a big range of shops in a climate-controlled bubble: **Cairns Central Shopping Centre** (www.cairnscentral.com.au; McLeod St; ☽ 9am-5.30pm Mon-Wed & Fri & Sat, 9am-9pm Thu, 10am-4.30pm Sun) and **Pier Marketplace** (Pier Point Rd), which was developed as a waterfront shopping mall but at the time of writing many of the shops were vacant.

GETTING THERE & AWAY
Air

Departures for international cities leave frequently from **Cairns airport** (code CNS; ☎ 4052 9703; www.cairnsport.com.au/airport), with **Qantas** (www.qantas.com.au) heading to Tokyo and Singapore; **Jetstar** (www.jetstar.com.au) to Nagoya and Osaka; **Cathay Pacific** (www.cathaypacific.com) flying to Hong Kong; and **Air New Zealand** (www.airnewzealand.com) heading to Auckland three times a week.

Jetstar (☎ 13 15 38; www.jetstar.com.au); **Qantas** (☎ 13 13 13, 4050 4054; www.qantas.com.au; cnr Lake & Shield Sts) and **Virgin Blue** (☎ 13 67 89; www.virginblue.com.au) all fly the main domestic routes including Brisbane (two hours), Sydney (four hours), Melbourne (five hours), Adelaide (four hours) and Darwin (two hours). Perth and Hobart usually require a change in Sydney.

Skytrans (☎ 1800 818 405, 4046 2462; www.skytrans.com.au) services Cape York with regular flights to Cooktown, Coen and Lockhart River, as well as to Karumba in the Gulf and south to Townsville.

Bus

Cairns is the hub for Far North Queensland buses. **Greyhound Australia** (☎ 1300 473 946; www.greyhound.com.au; Reef Fleet Terminal) has four daily services down the coast to Brisbane ($255, 29 hours), via Townsville ($67, six hours), Airlie Beach ($116, 11 hours) and Rockhampton ($178, 18 hours). Departures are from outside

Reef Fleet Terminal at the southern end of the Esplanade.

Premier (☎ 13 34 10; www.premierms.com.au) also runs one daily service to Brisbane ($193, 29 hours) via Innisfail ($16, 1½ hours), Mission Beach ($16, two hours), Tully ($23, 2½ hours), Cardwell ($27, three hours), Townsville ($50, 5½ hours) and Airlie Beach ($84, 10 hours). Premier picks up from Stop D on the Lake St Transit Mall.

Sun Palm (☎ 4087 2900; www.sunpalmtransport .com) runs two morning services from Cairns to Cape Tribulation ($65, three hours) via Port Douglas ($30, 1½ hours) and Mossman ($40, 1¾ hours), with additional services direct to Port Douglas.

Country Road Coachlines (☎ 4045 2794; www.country roadcoachlines.com.au) runs a bus service between Cairns and Cooktown on the coastal route via Port Douglas and Cape Tribulation three times a week ($72) leaving Cairns Monday, Wednesday and Friday and returning from Cooktown Tuesday, Thursday and Saturday – depending on the condition of the Bloomfield Track. Another service takes the inland route via Mareeba on Monday, Wednesday and Friday ($72, same day return).

John's Kuranda Bus (☎ 0418-772 953) runs a service between Cairns and Kuranda ($3) at least twice a day and up to seven times between Wednesday to Friday. Buses depart from Cairns' Lake St Transit Centre. **Whitecar Coaches** (☎ 4091 1855) has regular bus services connecting Cairns with the tableland, departing from 46 Spence St and running to Kuranda ($4, 30 mins), Mareeba ($16.80, one hour), Atherton ($22, 1¾ hours), Herberton ($26, two hours) and Ravenshoe ($28.50, 2½ hours).

Car & Motorcycle

Hiring a car or a motorcycle is a good way to travel from Cairns to Far North Queensland. If you want to travel to Cooktown via the unsealed Bloomfield Track, hire a 4WD. Loads of hole-in-the-wall car rental companies can be found on Lake St and Abbott St.

Camperman (☎ 1800 216 223; www.camperman australia.com.au; 440 Sheridan St) Good-value campervans from $75 a day

Choppers Motorcycle Tours & Hire (☎ 0408-066 024; www.choppersmotocycles.com.au; 150 Sheridan St) Hire a Harley for $250 a day, or smaller bikes from $95 a day. Also offers motorcycle tours, from one hour to a full-day ride to Cape Trib.

Europcar (☎ 1300 13 13 90, 4051 4600; www.europcar .com.au; 135 Abbott St) With an airport desk.

Wicked Campers (☎ 1800 24 68 69; www.wicked campers.com.au; Abbott St) Colourful campers aimed at backpackers.

Train

The *Sunlander* departs Cairns on Tuesday, Thursday and Saturday for Brisbane (economy seat/sleeper $207/265, 31½ hours). It also operates the Scenic Railway to Kuranda. The train station is on the southwest side of the Cairns Central shopping centre. Contact **Queensland Rail** (☎ 1800 872 467; www.traveltrain.com.au).

GETTING AROUND
To/From the Airport

The airport is about 7km from central Cairns. **Australia Coach** (☎ 4040 1000; adult/child $10/5) meets all incoming flights and runs a shuttle bus to the CBD. A taxi will cost around $18.

Bicycle

You can hire bikes from the following:
Bike Man (☎ 4041 5566; www.bikeman.com.au; 99 Sheridan St; per day/week $15/50) Hire, sales and repairs.
Cairns Bicycle Hire (☎ 4031 3444; www.cairnsbicycle hire.com.au; 47 Shields St; per day/week $12/40, scooters per day from $35) Groovy bikes and scooters.

Bus

Sunbus (☎ 4057 7411; www.sunbus.com.au) runs regular services in and around Cairns from the Lake St Transit Centre, where schedules for most routes are posted.

Taxi

Black & White Taxis (☎ 131008) has ranks on the corner of Lake and Shields Sts, and on McLeod St in front of Cairns Central Shopping Centre.

ISLANDS OFF CAIRNS

Only a short skim across the water from Cairns, Green Island and Fitzroy Islands make for great day trips; spend the afternoon snorkelling in crystal waters, walking in patches of rainforest or just lazing on the beach. The picturesque Frankland Islands Group is another popular cruise – you can camp here (and on Fitzroy) and really leave the day-trippers behind.

Green Island

With a glamorous resort and stunning beaches, Green Island's long, doglegged jetty heaves under the weight of boatloads of day-trippers heading for its stunning beaches and offshore snorkelling opportunities. The island and its surrounding waters are protected by their national- and marine-park status. As well as taking gentle walks through the leafy interior, you can walk around the island in around \30 minutes.

The luxurious **Green Island Resort** (☎ 1800 673 366, 4031 3300; www.greenislandresort.com.au; ste $495-595; ✖ ✚) has stylish split-level suites, each with its own private balcony. Despite the exclusive feel it's partially open to day-trippers, so even if you're not staying you can enjoy the restaurants and water-sports facilities.

Great Adventures (☎ 1800 079 080, 4044 9944; www.greatadventures.com.au) has a fast catamaran (adult/child $67/33.50), departing Cairns' Reef Fleet Terminal at 8.30am, 10.30am and 1pm and returning at noon, 2.30pm and 4.30pm. Snorkelling gear and use of the resort's swimming pool are included.

Big Cat (☎ 4051 0444; www.bigcat-cruises.com.au; tours from $66/37) also runs half- and full-day tours departing Cairns' Reef Fleet Terminal at 9am and 1pm.

Fitzroy Island

A steep mountaintop peeping from the sea, Fitzroy Island has coral-strewn beaches, woodlands and walking tracks, camping and a flash refurbished resort.

Fitzroy Island is also known as Gabarra to the indigenous Gungandji people, who have hunted and fished from the island for centuries. Captain Cook named the island Fitzroy after the prime minister of the day when the *Endeavour* left for its Pacific journey. Today the island is national park, with the resort occupying a small portion. The most popular snorkelling spot is around the rocks at **Nudey Beach** (1.2km from the resort).

You can pitch a tent at the **Fitzroy Island Camping Ground** (☎ 4044 3044; camp sites $26), run by Cairns Regional Council. Bookings must be made in advance (10 sites available).

The Fitzroy Island Resort has been transformed into **Hunt Resort** (☎ 4051 9588; www.huntgroup.com.au; ✖ ✚), which was still under construction at the time of writing.

Raging Thunder (☎ 4030 7900; www.ragingthunder.com.au; adult/child $42/21) runs island transfers from Reef Fleet Terminal twice a day, leaving Cairns at 8.30am and 10.30am and returning at 3pm and 5pm.

Frankland Islands

If the idea of hanging out on one of five uninhabited coral-fringed islands with excellent snorkelling and stunning white sandy beaches perks your interest – and if not, why not? – cruise out to the Frankland Group National Park. These continental islands consist of High Island to the north and four smaller islands to the south: Normanby, Mabel, Round and Russell.

Campers can be dropped at High or Russell Islands, though numbers are limited on Russell and camping is only permitted on weekdays outside peak season. Permits must be obtained in advance from the Cairns **QPWS** (☎ 4046 6602; www.epa.qld.gov.au; 5B Sheridan St) or you can book online for High Island. You must be fully self-sufficient as there is no water on the islands.

Frankland Islands Cruise & Dive (☎ 4031 6300; www.franklandislands.com.au; adult/child $109/59) runs excellent day cruises, which include a cruise down the Mulgrave River, snorkelling and lunch.

CAIRNS' NORTHERN BEACHES

Cairns may not have its own beach, but you don't have to go far to find a patch of sand beneath the palms. A string of residential communities clings to the 26km stretch of coast north of Cairns, each separated by the twists and turns of the coastline, and reached by signposted turn-offs from the Captain Cook Hwy. There's a distinctive beach-holiday repose and each has its own feel: Yorkey's is popular with families and sailors, while Palm Cove is the upmarket honeymoon haven. There's not much opportunity for camping along the northern beaches these days – only Palm Cove and Ellis Beach have camping grounds.

Holloways Beach

The Coral Sea meets a rough ribbon of sand at low-key Holloways Beach. It's a mostly residential area, with beachside homes making way for a few tourist developments and the odd B&B.

The slick two-bedroom apartments at **Cairns Beach Resort** (☎ 1800 150 208, 4037 0400; www.cairnsbeachresort.com.au; 129 Oleander St; apt $125-145; ✖ ✚) are pure beachfront.

Coolum's on the Beach (☎ 4055 9200; cnr Hibiscus & Oleandar Sts; mains $22-32; ☽ breakfast Sat & Sun, lunch Fri-Sun, dinner daily) is renowned for its Sunday afternoon jazz sessions, and the beachfront location and Mod Oz menu make Coolum's the hottest spot in Holloway, especially on weekends.

Yorkeys Knob

In many ways the most appealing of the northern beaches, Yorkeys is a sprawling, low-key settlement on a white-sand beach. Nestled within the crescent-shaped Half Moon Bay is the marina, cradling 200 bobbing boats. The 'knob' is the rocky headland that cradles the bay to the north, allowing the wind to whip the water south. This wind is fuel for the many kite-surfers and windsurfers; Kite Rite (☎ 4055 7918; www.kiterite.com.au; 471 Varley St; per hr $79) is a professional outfit offering instruction, including gear hire, and a two-day certificate course ($499).

A couple of blocks back from the beach and sidled up against a little patch of rainforest, Villa Marine (☎ 4055 7158; www.villamarine .com.au; 8 Rutherford St; studio $79, units $119-149) is the best-value spot in Yorkeys.

York Beachfront Apartments (☎ 4055 8733; www .yorkapartments.com.au; 61-63 Sims Esplanade; apt $149-169; 🞑 🞑) is a stylish midsized complex offering apartments with fully equipped kitchens and laundries, and separate en suite bedrooms.

Yorkeys Knob Boating Club (☎ 4055 7711; 25 Buckley St; mains $12-25; 🕒 lunch & dinner daily, breakfast Sun) enjoys sea views overlooking the Half Moon Bay Marina and whips up grills, pastas and burgers. It's good for a drink on the deck and the bar is open late on Friday and Saturday nights.

Trinity Beach

Trinity Beach is a long stretch of sheltered white sand. High-rise hotel developments detract from the castaway ambience, but holidaymakers love it – turning their backs to the buildings and focusing on what is one of Cairns' prettiest beaches.

Castaways (☎ 4057 6699; www.castawaystrinitybeach .com.au; cnr Trinity Beach Rd & Moore St; apt $130; 🞑 🞑) has fully self-contained apartments close to the beach. Three pools, spas, tropical gardens and good stand-by rates.

L'unico Trattoria (☎ 4057 8855; 75 Vasey Esplanade; mains $18-28; 🕒 breakfast, lunch & dinner) is a stylish Italian restaurant basking in a stellar corner beachfront location.

Clifton Beach

Local and leisurely, Clifton Beach has a good balance of residential and resort accommodation and services. You can walk north along the beach about 2km to Palm Cove from here.

Clifton Palms (☎ 4055 3839; www.cliftonpalms .com.au; 35-41 Upolu Esplanade; cabins/units from $70/110, 2-bedroom apt $145; 🞑 🞑) has freestanding single-storey apartments backed by a curtain of green hills. There's a huge range of accommodation options to suit any budget or family group, and stand-by and low-season rates are jaw-droppingly good.

Palm Cove

The Saint Tropez of the northern beaches, Palm Cove is more intimate than Port Douglas and more ritzy than its southern neighbours. The holiday crowd promenades along Williams Esplanade, while the ribbon of white-sand beach lures sun lovers out of their luxury resorts. Of course, it's not all honeymooners and starlets: Palm Cove is for anyone willing to laze about on a decent beach, dine in top-notch restaurants and do some serious people-watching. There's even a camping ground for budget travellers.

Palm Cove Watersports (☎ 0402 861 011; www.palm covewatersports.com) has 1½-hour early morning sea-kayaking trips ($42) and half-day paddles to Double Island (adult/child $60/70).

Just out of Palm Cove on the highway, Cairns Tropical Zoo (☎ 4055 3669; www.cairnstropicalzoo.com .au; Captain Cook Hwy; adult/child $29/14.50; 🕒 8.30am-5pm) is an up-close wildlife experience with crocodiles and snakes, koala photo sessions and kangaroo feeding.

SLEEPING & EATING

Most accommodation and eating are found along Williams Esplanade, so wander along and see where the crowds are congregating.

Palm Cove Camping Ground (☎ 4055 3824; 149 Williams Esplanade; unpowered/powered sites $15.50/21) This council-run beachfront camping ground is ensconced among palms at the north end of the Esplanade near the jetty – no cabins but the only way to do Palm Cove on the cheap.

Palm Cove Accommodation (☎ 4055 3797; 19 Veivers Rd; d $75; 🞑) The only other truly budget option in Palm Cove, this small place opposite the tavern has just a few neat, self-contained rooms and a small garden.

Melaleuca Resort (☎ 1800 629 698, 4055 3222; www .melaleucaresort.com.au; 85-93 Williams Esplanade; apt $185-208; 🞑 🞑) Named after the melaleuca trees that line Palm Cove's esplanade, this charming boutique resort has 24 self-contained apartments, all with kitchens, balconies and laundry facilities.

Peppers Beach Club & Spa (☎ 4059 9200; www.pep pers.com.au; 123 Williams Esplanade; r from $322; ❄ ⓡ) Step through the opulent lobby at Peppers and into a wonderworld of swimming pools (there's a sand-edged lagoon pool and a leafy rainforest pool), tennis courts and all the spa treatments. Even the standard rooms have private balcony spas and the penthouse suites (from $550) have their own rooftop pool.

Apres Beach Bar & Grill (☎ 4059 2000; 119 Williams Esplanade; dishes $20-40; ⌚ 6.30am-11pm) Halfway along the Esplanade, Apres is the most happening place in Palm Cove, with regular live music and crowds spilling out to the open deck area. The menu runs the gamut of steaks, seafood, Asian and pasta – but it's all pretty pricey given the venue. The zany interior features old motorcycles, racing cars and a biplane hanging from the ceiling!

our pick **Nu Nu** (☎ 4059 1880; www.nunu.com.au; 123 Williams Esplanade; lunch $18-28, dinner $36-39; ⌚ breakfast, lunch & dinner) With one of the most innovative menus on the coast, retro Nu Nu specialises in 'wild foods' like beet-poached Angus tenderloin or roast chicken with leatherwood-honey grilled figs. Just about everything is intriguing so ask about the tasting menu.

Ellis Beach

Ellis Beach is the last of the northern beaches and the closest to the highway, which runs right past it. The long sheltered bay is a stunner and the view is spectacular as you drive in from the south. This is where the coastal road to Port Douglas really gets interesting.

Ellis Beach Oceanfront Bungalows (☎ 1800 637 036, 4055 3538; www.ellisbeachbungalows.com; Captain Cook Hwy; unpowered sites $26, powered sites $30-36, cabins $80, bungalows $145-180) is a lovely beachfront park with camping and cabins enjoying wide-screen |ocean TV.

One of the best opportunities in the north to see monster saltwater crocs, **Hartley's Crocodile Adventures** (☎ 4055 3576; www.crocodileadventures.com; adult/child $29/14.50; ⌚ 8.30am-5pm) is primarily a crocodile farm based around a large lagoon, but there's plenty of other wildlife here including native birds, koalas and snakes.

CAIRNS TO COOKTOWN

There are two routes to Cooktown from the south and most travellers with a 4WD do a loop, going up one way and back the other.

The most interesting route north is to Cape Tribulation along the Captain Cook Hwy, then continuing up the 4WD Bloomfield Track (known as the 'coast road') to Cooktown. This trip runs through the rainforest of Daintree National Park and past sublime beaches – don't miss it. To reach Cooktown by 2WD, turn inland off the Captain Cook Hwy to Kuranda and take the Kennedy Hwy to the sealed Peninsula and Cooktown Developmental Rds (known as the 'inland route'), which pass through the relatively arid southern reaches of Cape York Peninsula.

Prepare your camera for the coastal road between Palm Cove and Port Douglas, where the highway spectacularly hugs the coastline like a mini-far-north version of Victoria's Great Ocean Road.

KURANDA
☎ 07 / pop 1610

Reached by a winding 30km road, a scenic railway or Australia's longest gondola cableway from Cairns, Kuranda is easily the most popular day-tripping destination on the tableland. By day, this tiny village is crawling with tourists poking through the ever-expanding markets and lining up for various purpose-built nature attractions. Stay overnight to see it transform into the mellow village that made it so popular in the first place. While the markets and marketing can seem a bit tacky, this is a truly beautiful area with refreshing rainforest walks and an alternative feel.

The **Kuranda visitors centre** (☎ 4093 9311; www .kuranda.org; ⌚ 10am-4pm) is centrally located in Centenary Park.

Sights & Activities

The original **Kuranda Markets** (☎ 4093 7261; Therwine St; ⌚ 9am-3pm) started in 1978 and became famous for imaginative local art and craft products. It's still the place to see artists such as glassblowers at work, pick up hemp products and sample local produce such as honey and fruit wines. Across the road, the **Heritage Markets** (☎ 4093 8060; www.kurandamarkets .com.au; Rob Veivers Dr; ⌚ 9am-3pm) are made up of souvenirs and crafts such as ceramics, emu oil, jewellery, clothing, food, and figurines made from pistachio nuts.

Djurri Dadagal Art Enterprises (☎ 0428-645 945; Coondoo St; ⌚ 9.30am-3.30pm) is an excellent indigenous art cooperative where the paintings, artefacts, screen prints and textiles are produced on site by local artists. You can see artists at work most days.

The Kuranda region has half a dozen nature and wildlife parks showing off bats, birds, butterflies, koalas, snakes and spiders that are certain to keep kids amused, but it's just as much fun (and free) to wander off into the surrounding rainforest. There are a number of easy **walking trails** in and around the village. Across the train line by the station a path leads down to the Barron River. Follow the path downstream to the railway bridge (1km, 20 minutes). This bridge marks the start of the Jungle Walk section (800m, 15 minutes), which is a paved track that runs between Barron Gorge Rd meeting the Jumrum Creek Walk (800m, 15 minutes), which starts/ finishes on Coondoo St and links to a 2km walk to **Barron Falls**.

Sleeping

Kuranda Rainforest Park (☎ 4093 7316; www .kurandarainforestpark.com.au; Kuranda Heights Rd; unpowered/powered sites $22/26, s/d $25/45, units $85-100; 🖭 🖳 🗐) This excellent park lives up to its name with grassy camping sites enveloped in rainforest. The park is a 10-minute walk from town via a forest trail.

Kuranda Backpackers Hostel (☎ 4093 7355; www .kurandabackpackershostel.com; cnr Arara & Barang Sts; dm/ s/d $19/46/49; 🖳) This rambling, semi-fallingapart, double-storey home is surrounded by a large garden. It has an old and slightly bleak feel with creaky floorboards and steel-frame bunks but there are spacious common areas.

ourpick **Kuranda Resort & Spa** (☎ 4093 7556; www .kurandaresortandspa.com; 3 Green Hills Rd; dm $40, d $129-169; 🖭 🖳 🖳) You'll feel as though you've stepped inside a magazine spread when you enter the exotic, stylish apartments on offer here. From Asian-inspired two-storey loft villas to spacious self-contained apartments, the accommodation is top notch, and the ecofriendly resort has a spectacular pool, a tennis court, an in-house theatre, a gym and a superb restaurant. The day spa has the full range of pampering therapies.

Eating

There are dozens of busy cafés along Coondoo and Therwine Sts, and also tucked away in the markets.

Nevermind Cafe (☎ 4093 8448; Shop 1, 24 Coondoo St; meals $5-12; 🕑 breakfast & lunch) Epitomising that slightly hippy vibe that still exists up here,

Nevermind has organic smoothies, herbal teas, toasted sandwiches and great coffee.

Banjo's Bar & Grill (☎ 4093 9399; 17 Therwine St; mains $10-22; 🕑 breakfast & lunch daily, dinner Thu-Sat; 🖳) Kuranda's liveliest restaurant serves up organic mango crepes for brekky, gourmet burgers, focaccias and pizzas with occasional live music.

Getting There & Away

It's about the journey as much as the destination with Kuranda. The Skyrail and Scenic Railway between Kuranda and Cairns are themselves big attractions and most people go up one way and down the other. If that's not for you, it's only a 20-minute drive or a cheap bus ride up from Cairns.

Kuranda Scenic Railway (☎ 4036 9333; www.kuranda scenicrailway.com.au; Cairns train station, Bunda St; adult/ concession/child one way $39/31/19.50, return $56/50/27) winds 34km from Cairns to Kuranda through picturesque mountains and no less than 15 tunnels. The line took five years to build, and was opened in 1891. The trip takes 1¾ hours and trains depart Cairns at 8.30am and 9.30am daily, returning from pretty Kuranda station (known for its floral displays) at 2pm and 3.30pm.

Skyrail Rainforest Cableway (☎ 4038 1555; www .skyrail.com.au; adult/child one way $39/19.50, return $56/28; 🕑 8.15am-5.15pm) is one of the world's longest gondola cableways at 7.5km. From Smithfield, a northern suburb of Cairns, it includes two stops with boardwalks and interpretive panels. Transfers to/from the terminal and combination (Scenic Railway and Skyrail) deals are available.

John's Kuranda Bus (☎ 0418-772 953) runs a service to Kuranda ($3) from Lake St Transit Centre. **Whitecar Coaches** (☎ 4091 1855) has five departures ($5) from 46 Spence St, Cairns.

PORT DOUGLAS

☎ 07 / pop 948

Port Douglas is the flashy playground of Far North Queensland. Like a spoilt child it thumbs its nose at Cairns by being more sophisticated, more intimate and, perhaps most of all, by having a beautiful white-sand beach.

There's no question this is a manicured, purpose-built holiday town so there's a happy, relaxed vibe and clearly plenty of money floating around. While those swish seafood restaurants, boutique clothing stores and four-star apartments soften the edges of the far-north

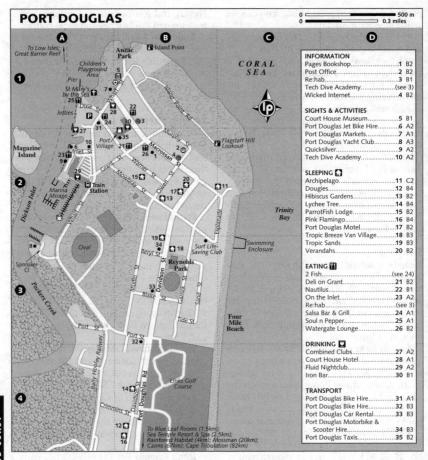

PORT DOUGLAS

0 — 500 m
0 — 0.3 miles

CORAL SEA

Trinity Bay

Four Mile Beach

To Blue Leaf Rooms (1.5km);
Sea Temple Resort & Spa (2.5km);
Rainforest Habitat (4km); Mossman (20km);
Cairns (67km); Cape Tribulation (82km)

frontier image, Port Douglas retains an endearing character with all the comforts of a big city condensed into a surprisingly small town. The town centre is built on a spit of land jutting out into the Coral Sea with Dickson Inlet and the gleaming marina on the west side and Four Mile Beach on the east. The Great Barrier Reef is less than an hour away and getting there is as easy as choosing which boat to hop on.

Information

There's no 'official' (ie noncommercial) tourist information centre in Port Douglas. There are lots of signs alerting you to tourist information, but they're all basically booking agencies.

All the major banks have branches with ATMs along Macrossan St. The main post office is on Owen St.

Pages Bookshop (☎ 4099 5094; Shop 3, 35 Macrossan St; ⊗ 9am-6pm) Stocks a range of fiction and nonfiction titles.

Re:hab (☎ 4099 4677; www.rehabportdouglas.com.au; 3/18 Macrossan St; per hr $4; wi-fi) Chic internet café.

Wicked Internet (☎ 4099 6900; 48 Macrossan St; per hr $5) Internet café and ice-cream parlour.

Sights

Most people put in a few hours or days strolling or sunning on delightful **Four Mile Beach**, a broad band of squeaky white-sand beach backed by palms that reaches as far as your squinting eyes can see. For a fine view over the beach and bay, follow Wharf St and the steep Island Point Rd to **Flagstaff Hill Lookout**.

The **Court House Museum** (☎ 4098 5395; 18 Wharf St; admission $2; ⏲ 10am-1pm Tue, Thu, Sat & Sun) near Anzac Park dates back to 1879 and has an interesting display on the town's early history, including the 1887 trial of Ellen Thomson, the only woman legally hanged in Queensland.

The **Port Douglas Markets** (Anzac Park, bottom of Macrossan St; ⏲ 8.30am-1.30pm Sun) make for a leisurely Sunday morning browse along the grassy foreshore of Anzac Park.

There's no shortage of wildlife tourist parks in north Queensland, but **Rainforest Habitat** (☎ 4099 3235; www.rainforesthabitat.com.au; Port Douglas Rd; adult/child/family $29/14.50/72.50; ⏲ 8am-5pm) is up there with the best. The sanctuary endeavours to keep and showcase native animals in enclosures that closely mimic their natural environment – wetlands, grasslands and rainforest – but also allow you to get up close and personal. As well as koalas, kangaroos, crocs and tree kangaroos, Rainforest Habitat is home to parrots, wading birds, kookaburras, flying foxes and the prehistoric-looking cassowary. Take your time as the ticket is valid for three days. Come early for **Breakfast with the Birds** (adult/child incl admission $39/19.50; ⏲ 8-10.30am) or **Lunch with the Lorikeets** ($39/19.50; ⏲ noon-2pm).

Activities

The **Port Douglas Yacht Club** (☎ 4099 4386; www .portdouglasyachtclub.com.au; Spinnaker Close) offers free sailing with club members every Wednesday from 4pm – you might have to do some sweet-talking if places are limited, but it's a great way to get out on the water and meet some locals.

Port Douglas Jet Bike Hire (☎ 4099 3175; www .reefsprinter.com.au; per 30min/hr $85/140), at the Wharf St jetty, rents jet bikes.

Sea Temple Golf Club (☎ 4087 2222; www.seatemple golfclub.com.au; Old Port Rd; 18 holes $115; ⏲ 6.30am-4pm), at Sea Temple Resort & Spa, south of town, is a championship links course rated in the top 50 in Australia.

Port Douglas doesn't have the range of dive companies that Cairns has, but a few operators offer PADI open-water courses and advanced dive certificates. **Tech Dive Academy** (☎ 4099 6880; www.tech-dive-academy.com; 3/46 Wharf St; 4-day open-water courses from $750) has high-quality personalised instruction with limited numbers per class (one to three). **Quicksilver Dive School** (☎ 4055 3255; www.silverseries.com.au/diveschool.htm;

Marina Mirage; 4-day open water courses $595) is based at the Novotel in Palm Cove where the first two days are held; transfers from Port Douglas included. It also runs cruises and sailing trips (see below).

Tours

Port Douglas is a hub for tours, either out to the Reef or north to the rugged rainforests of Daintree and Cape Tribulation.

GREAT BARRIER REEF

Port Douglas is closer to the outer reef than Cairns is, and the unrelenting surge of visitors has had a similar impact on its condition here. Access to the majority of sites that operators visit is around an hour from Port Douglas. Day tours usually make two to three stops on the outer and ribbon reefs, including St Crispins, Agincourt, Chinaman and Tongue Reefs. Several operators visit the Low Isles: an idyllic little island with a lighthouse and fringing coral just 15km offshore.

Aristocat (☎ 4099 4727; www.aristocat.com.au; adult/child $159/115) Fast cat to three snorkelling sites. Maximum 45 passengers.

Haba (☎ 4098 5000; www.habadive.com.au; Marina Mirage; adult/child $155/95) Long-standing local dive company; visits two sites.

Poseidon (☎ 4099 4772; www.poseidon-cruises.com .au; adult/child $165/125) Luxury catamaran with trips to Agincourt reefs.

Quicksilver (☎ 4087 2100; www.quicksilver-cruises .com) Major operator with fast cruises to Agincourt Reef aboard *Wavepiercer* (adult/child $186/93) and family-oriented sailing trips to the Low Isles on the *Wavedancer* (adult/child from $122/61). It also operates a dive school (left).

LOW ISLES

Ragamuffin III (☎ 0415-874 202; snorkelling trip $135) This well-known exracing yacht does day trips to the Low Isles.

Shaolin (☎ 4099 4772; www.shaolinportdouglas.com; adult/child $150/90) A refitted Chinese junk, the *Shaolin* has snorkelling cruises to the Low Isles.

OTHER TOURS

There are numerous operators offering day trips to Cape Tribulation, some via Mossman Gorge.

Fine Feather Tours (☎ 4094 1199; www.finefeather tours.com.au; half-/full-day tours $165/225) Serious ornithologists and amateur twitchers alike will love these bird-watching tours led by an expert guide.

Lady Douglas (☎ 4099 1603; 1½hr cruises adult/child $25/12; lunch cruise $45) A paddlewheeler that runs afternoon and sunset croc-spotting cruises down the Dixon Inlet.

Reef and Rainforest Connections (☎ 4099 5333; www.reefandrainforest.com.au) A big range of day-long ecotours that combine a number of attractions. There's a Cape Trib and Bloomfield Falls 4WD safari (adult/child $159/124), a trip to Kuranda including the Skyrail and the Scenic Railway (adult/child $125/63) and various wildlife tours to the region's parks and sanctuaries.

Skysafari (☎ 4099 3666; www.skysafari.com.au) Scenic helicopter flights from 10 minutes over Port Douglas ($95 per person) to an hour taking in the reef and rainforest ($429). You can also arrange drop-offs to remote waterfalls or islands, which can work out cheaper as a day trip (less flying time).

Sleeping

Befitting a holiday town, Port Douglas is swimming in accommodation, most of it in self-contained apartments or upmarket resorts. There are a few good budget options, but nothing like the scale of that in Cairns, and price brackets here generally move up a notch. Discounts are often available online or as stand-by rates, and prices can drop significantly during the low season.

BUDGET

Tropic Breeze Van Village (☎ /fax 4099 5299; 24 Davidson St; unpowered/powered sites $26/28, cabins $75; 🖭) The closest van park to Port central, with a path straight through to the beach, Tropic Breeze is a little cramped but has grassy sites and basic cabins (no en suite).

ourpick ParrotFish Lodge (☎ 1800 995011, 4099 5011; www.parrotfishlodge.com; 37-39 Warner St; dm $25-33, d $85-95; 🗱 🖳 🖭) Mural-sized contemporary art covers the walls in this cheery, central backpackers. The décor is extreme beach, with bright-yellow walls and iridescent-blue swirling floors. The restaurant and bar is a great meeting place.

Dougies (☎ 1800 996 200, 4099 6200; www.dougies .com.au; 111 Davidson St; tent sites per person $13; dm $26, d & tw $75; 🗱 🖳 🖭) Set in spacious grounds south of the centre, Dougies is a backpacker resort where it's easy to hang about the grounds in a hammock by day and move to the bar at night.

Port Douglas Motel (☎ 4099 5248; www.portdouglas motel.com; 9 Davidson St; d $95-110; 🗱 🖭) For value and location this little motel is hard to beat and is often full. Rooms are bright and well furnished (no views); some are self-contained with basic kitchen facilities.

MIDRANGE

Blue Leaf Rooms (☎ 4099 5414; www.blueleafrooms.com .au; 316 Port Douglas Rd; d $99-109; 🗱 🖳 🖭) These excellent-value rooms are independently owned but part of the Mantra Treetops Resort – you get to use the resort facilities without paying the full whack. It's about 4km south of town and a short walk to Four Mile Beach.

Archipelago (☎ 4099 5387; www.archipelago.com .au; 72 Macrossan St; d $113-190; 🗱 🖳 🖭) Close to the beach and the town centre, the 12 self-contained rooms spread over three levels – the upper rooms have 'filtered' views to the beach. Rooms are neat and functional, with a balcony and cane furniture.

Pink Flamingo (☎ 4099 6622; www.pinkflamingo.com .au; 115 Davidson St; r $125-185; 🗱 🖳 🖭) The pink-flamingo statue at the entrance to your room holds your 'Do Not Disturb' sign at this gay-friendly resort. The bright primary-coloured interiors are a bit arresting, but the giant beds, oversized spas and heated garden pool are pure relaxation. The resort has a gym and outdoor movie nights.

Lychee Tree (☎ 4099 5811; www.lychee-tree.com.au; 95 Davidson St; apt $135-160; 🗱 🖭) Families will fit right in at these single-storey self-contained apartments (one or two bedrooms). They're simply decorated and well equipped with kitchens, washing machines and dryers, and balconies overlooking tropical gardens.

ourpick Hibiscus Gardens (☎ 1800 995 995, 4099 5315; www.hibiscusportdouglas.com.au; 22 Owen Sts; r $165; 🗱 🖳 🖭) Balinese influences of teak furnishing and fixtures, bi-fold doors and plantation shutters – as well as the occasional Buddha – give this stylish resort an exotic ambience. The in-house day spa specialises in indigenous healing techniques and products.

Tropic Sands (☎ 4099 4533; www.tropicsands.com .au; 21 Davidson St; apt $175; 🗱 🖳 🖭) The handsome open-plan rooms here are in a beautiful, white, colonial-style building. From your private balcony you can catch a whiff of the sea or whatever's cooking in your fully equipped kitchen.

TOP END

Verandahs (☎ 4099 6650; www.verandahsportdouglas .com.au; 7 Davidson St; r from $245; 🗱 🖭) These stylish two-bedroom, two-bathroom apartments are serviced daily and come with stainless-steel kitchens, polished floorboards and modern furnishings. The namesake verandas have barbecues and are great for entertaining.

Sea Temple Resort & Spa (☎ 1800 833 762, 4084 3500; www.mirvachotels.com.au; Mitre St; r $310-608; 🐾 🖳 🐕) Port Douglas' most luxurious five-star is set in lush tropical gardens near the southern end of Four Mile Beach and is part of a superb 18-hole golf course. Take a studio with a spa, a two-bedroom apartment or the opulent 'swim out' penthouse with direct access to the enormous lagoon pool. The day spa has a full range of treatments, including hot stones.

Eating

For a town of its size, Port Douglas has some of the best dining north of Noosa. Chairs and tables spill out of cafés along Macrossan St, candlelit gardens make for romantic evening dinners and fresh seafood highlights many a menu.

RESTAURANTS

our pick On the Inlet (☎ 4099 5255; www.portdouglas seafood.com; 3 Inlet St; mains $18-37; 🕑 lunch & dinner) With a sublime location on Dickson Inlet, tables here are spread along a sprawling deck, where you can wave to the passing boats and gather around to await the 5.30pm arrival of near-resident George the grouper, who comes to feed most days (take up the early-dinner deal of a bucket of prawns and a drink for $19). The menu is big on seafood and you can select live crayfish and mud crabs from a large tank. Great service, cool atmosphere.

2 Fish (☎ 4099 6350; www.2fishrestaurant.com.au; 7/20 Wharf St; mains $22.50-40; 🕑 lunch & dinner) Seafood dominates many a menu in Port Douglas, but 2 Fish takes it to new levels. More than 15 types of fish, from coral trout to red emperor and wild barramundi, can be prepared in a variety of innovative ways, or you could try a dish of bay bugs, king prawns and yabbies.

Salsa Bar & Grill (☎ 4099 4922; www.salsaportdouglas .com.au; 26 Wharf St; mains $26-34; 🕑 lunch & dinner) Set in a white Queenslander across from Dickson Inlet, Salsa Bar & Grill is a local favourite, offering an imaginative range of Mediterranean-inspired dishes and a casual vibe. Try the jambalaya, a Cajun concoction of rice with prawns, yabby, crocodile and smoked chicken. Leave room for the soft cheeses that are produced on site.

Watergate Lounge (☎ 4099 6665; www.watergate lounge.com.au; 31 Macrossan St; mains $28-36; 🕑 lunch & dinner) Flashy and fashionable, Watergate is a '70s retro bar-restaurant with squishy white leather couches in the bar opening out to a flame-lit alfresco garden. Worth dropping in for a drink and a plate of tapas in the bar, but the restaurant menu is also enticing.

Nautilus (☎ 4099 5330; www.nautilus-restaurant.com .au; 17 Murphy St; mains $32-49; 🕑 dinner) Nautilus has been a dining institution in Port Douglas for more than 50 years. Its tables are in two lush outdoor settings amid tall palms, and stiffly dressed in white linen. Seafood is a speciality, such as mud crab with kaffir lime and lemongrass laksa.

CAFÉS & QUICK EATS

Re:hab (☎ 4099 4677; 3/18 Macrossan St; 🕑 8am-10pm) You can smell the fresh-roasted coffee aromas from the street, though most people inside have their noses buried in a computer.

Deli On Grant (☎ 4099 5852; 11 Grant St; meals $8-12; 🕑 7.30am-5pm) A range of boutique produce and home-cooked meals to take away are on offer here. With three hours' notice the Deli will put together sensational ready-to-go picnic hampers (plates, cutlery and all).

Soul n Pepper (☎ 4099 4499; 2 Dixie St; mains $16-28; 🕑 breakfast, lunch & dinner) Right opposite the pier; there's a soulfulness in the sea breeze at this laid-back outdoor café. It's especially popular for breakfast and lunch.

Drinking & Entertainment

Drinking and eating go hand in hand in Port Douglas and the local pubs are as much casual restaurants as they are watering holes.

Iron Bar (☎ 4099 4776; 5 Macrossan St; mains $18-30; 🕑 lunch & dinner) A bit of whacky outback shearing-shed décor never goes astray in Queensland. It's well done – all rustic iron and aging timber. After polishing off your T-bone or Don Bradman eye fillet (the steaks are named after famous Aussies), head upstairs for a flutter on the cane-toad races ($5).

Court House Hotel (☎ 4099 5181; cnr Macrossan & Wharf Sts; mains $15-25; 🕑 lunch & dinner) Commanding a prime corner location, the Court is a bubbling local with cover bands providing entertainment on weekends.

Combined Clubs (☎ 4099 5553; Ashford Ave; 🕑 10am-10pm) It looks a bit like a tin shed from the outside, but locals love this relaxed club for cheap drinks and a sundowner on the waterfront deck. Also serves up good-value bistro meals for lunch and dinner.

Fluid Nightclub (☎ 4099 5200; Shop 54, Marina Mirage; ☾ 10pm-5am) Fluid is the heart of Port's late, late-night scene. The party usually starts at casual Henry's Bar or the lounge bar Mez, then moves upstairs to the dance floor at Fluid. Tuesday night is backpacker night, and there are occasional touring bands and DJs.

Getting There & Away

Sun Palm (☎ 4087 2900; www.sunpalmtransport.com) has frequent daily services between Port Douglas and Cairns ($30, 1½ hours) via the northern beaches and the airport, and up the coast to Mossman ($10, 20 minutes), Mossman Gorge ($15, 30 minutes), Daintree ($25, one hour) and Cape Tribulation ($35, three hours).

Airport Connections (☎ 4099 5950; www.tnq shuttle.com; one way $30; ☾ 3.30am-4.30pm) runs an hourly shuttle-bus service between Port Douglas and Cairns airport, continuing on to Cairns CBD.

Country Road Coachlines (☎ 4045 2794; www.country roadcoachlines.com.au) has a bus service from Port Douglas to Cooktown on the coastal route via Cape Tribulation three times a week ($72).

Getting Around

BICYCLE

Port Douglas Bike Hire (www.portdouglasbikehire; per day/week $19/89; ☾ 9am-5pm) corner Wharf & Warner Sts (☎ 4099 5799); corner Davidson & Port Sts (☎ 4099 4303) has two locations in town; free delivery for multiday hire.

BUS

Sun Palm (☎ 4087 2900; www.sunpalmtransport.com; ☾ 7am-midnight) runs in a continuous loop every half-hour from the Rainforest Habitat (near the Captain Cook Hwy turn-off) to the Marina Mirage, stopping regularly. Flag the driver down at the marked bus stops. Also runs twice-daily service between Port Douglas and Mossman.

CAR & MOTORCYCLE

Port Douglas has plenty of small local car-hire companies, most lined up on Warner St. One-way rental to Cairns or the airport is no problem. If you're planning to continue north up the Bloomfield Track to Cooktown, Port Douglas is the last place you can hire a 4WD vehicle for the job. With less cutthroat competition, vehicle hire is pricier here than in Cairns. Expect to pay $60 a day for a small car and $130 a day for a 4WD, plus insurance.

Port Douglas Car Rental (☎ 4099 4988; www .portdouglascarrental.com.au; 81 Davidson St)
Port Douglas Motorbike & Scooter Hire (☎ 4099 4000; www.plazaportdouglas.com.au; 37 Davidson St) Based at Plaza Port Douglas, it rents out scooters from $75 a day and motorbikes from $155 a day.

Taxi

Port Douglas Taxis (☎ 131 008) offers 24-hour service and has a rank on Warner St.

MOSSMAN

☎ 07 / pop 1740

After the holiday hype of Port Douglas, Mossman – only 20km north – brings you back to earth. It's a pleasant, unpretentious cane town with a working sugar mill and cane trains to prove it. Mossman should be an obligatory stop to visit Mossman Gorge, and it's also a good place to fill up the tank and stock up on supplies if you're heading north. **Mossman Sugar Mill Tours** (☎ 4030 4190; www.mos sag.com.au; Mill St; adult/child $20/15; ☾ 11am & 1.30pm Mon-Fri Jun-Oct) will show you how all that giant tropical grass gets turned into sugar.

Mossman Gorge

Inspiring Mossman Gorge, 5km west of town, is in the southeast corner of Daintree National Park and forms part of the traditional lands of the Kuku Yalanji indigenous people. Walking tracks loop from the car park along the boulder-strewn Mossman river to a swimming hole where you can take a dip with the slow-moving jungle perch (identified by two black spots on their tails) – take care here, particularly after downpours, as the currents can be swift. There's a picnic area here but no camping.

Mossman Gorge Gateway (☎ 4098 2595; www.yal anji.com.au; ☾ 8.30am-5pm Mon-Sat) is a cultural and visitors centre, 1km before the gorge car park, run by the Kuku Yalanji community. To truly appreciate the cultural significance of Mossman Gorge, join the excellent 1½-hour guided walks run by **Kuku-Yalanji Dreamtime Walks** (adult/child $27.50/15; ☾ 9am, 11am, 1pm & 3pm Mon-Sat). Indigenous guides lead you through the rainforest point ing out and explaining the significance of rock-art sites, plants and natural features.

DAINTREE VILLAGE

☎ 07 / pop 80

After passing the relaxed beach communities of Newell and Wonga Beach, the road swings towards the Daintree River crossing and the

DAINTREE NATIONAL PARK: THEN & NOW

The greater Daintree rainforest, now protected as part of Daintree National Park, has a controversial history. In 1983 the Bloomfield Track was bulldozed through sensitive lowland rainforest from Cape Tribulation to the Bloomfield River, attracting international attention to the fight to save the lowland rainforests. The conservationists lost that battle, but the publicity generated by the blockade indirectly led to the federal government's moves in 1987 to nominate Queensland's wet tropical rainforests for World Heritage listing.

One of the key outcomes was a total ban on commercial logging in the area, but World Heritage listing doesn't affect land-ownership rights or control. In 1994, the Daintree Rescue Program, a state and federal government buy-back scheme, attempted to consolidate and increase public land ownership in the area, lowering the threat of land clearing and associated species extinction. They spent $23 million repurchasing large properties, adding them to the Daintree National Park and installing visitor interpretation facilities such as Marrdja and Dubuji boardwalks. Sealing the road to Cape Tribulation (eventually completed in 2002) opened the area to rapid settlement, activating attempts to buy back freehold blocks to reduce settlement pressures.

Coupled with stringent development controls, it looks as though the adage of *Paradise Lost* is being reversed by local and state efforts, and the Daintree just could be *Paradise Regained*. Check out www.austrop.org.au, which welcomes volunteers to assist at the Cape Tribulation Tropical Research Station (Bat House; p472).

What can I do?

When visiting this impossibly beautiful part of the world, *leave only footsteps behind*. That's as easy as taking your rubbish with you, sticking to the designated trails and driving slowly to avoid hitting wildlife. Consider the following:

- Does the tour I'm going on have ecocertification (www.ecotourism.org.au)?
- Are tour participants encouraged to take their rubbish with them when visiting World Heritage sites?
- Are there any volunteer opportunities for me to assist with cleaning up beaches or wildlife monitoring etc?
- Is my accommodation choice encouraging guests to recycle rubbish and reduce water consumption?

route to Cape Trib, but it's worth taking the left-hand (straight ahead) detour to the tiny settlement of Daintree for a croc-spotting tour on the broad Daintree River. Neither Daintree Village nor the surrounding countryside is part of the Wet Tropics World Heritage Area – it's mostly cleared farmland – but there are still pockets of untouched rainforest.

Tours

It's all about cruising on the Daintree River here. Sightings of resident saltwater crocodiles are frequent but not guaranteed. Tours can be booked at the two agencies in the village.

Chris Dahlberg's Daintree River Tours (☎ 4098 7997; www.daintreerivertours.com.au; Daintree Village; adult/child $35/55; ☎ 6.30am Feb-Oct, 6am Nov-Jan) Two-hour tours specialising in bird-watching.

Crocodile Express (☎ 4098 6120; www.daintree connection.com.au; Daintree Village; 1hr cruise adult/child $22/11) Eight departures from Daintree Village and 12 from the Daintree ferry crossing. Also a lunch cruise (adult/child $69/34).

Daintree River Experience (☎ 4098 7480; www .daintreecruises.com.au; 2hr cruise adult/child $50/36; ☺ 6am & 4pm) Serene two-hour sunrise and sunset cruises specialising in bird-watching.

Electric Boat Cruises (☎ 1800 686 103; www.electric boatcruises.com; 1hr cruise adult/child $20/10; ☺ 7 daily Mar-Jan) Also offers a 1½-hour tour at 8am including muffins and coffee (adult/child $35/17).

Sleeping & Eating

Daintree boasts some superb B&Bs and boutique accommodation in the village and the surrounding forest and farmland.

Red Mill House (☎ 4098 6233; www.redmillhouse .au; 11 Stewart St; s/d $140/180; ❄ 🖵 ❀) Birdwatchers will love the Red Mill. The owners of this lovely old cedar home are enthusiastic birders and the large veranda overlooking the rainforest garden is a great place to enjoy breakfast and observe the resident wildlife.

River Home Cottages (☎ 4098 6225; www.riverhome cottages.com.au; Upper Daintree Rd; d $140; ⌨) Drive 5km down an unsealed road to reach these secluded self-contained cottages. The owners can show you to a secluded waterfall and swimming hole at the back of the property, or just relax in the spa fitted in each cabin.

Daintree Eco Lodge & Spa (☎ 1800 808 010, 4098 6100; www.daintree-ecolodge.com.au; 20 Daintree Rd; s/d from $510/550; ⌨ 🖳 🖳) The 15 boutique villas (10 with private spas) prop on stilts in the rainforest canopy a few kilometres south of Daintree Village. It's a luxurious retreat and the spa here uses its own range of organic products and methods borrowed from the indigenous community. The superb Julaymba Restaurant specialises in dishes of barramundi and steak prepared using local produce, incorporating indigenous berries, nuts, leaves and flowers. Try the Flaming Green Ant cocktail – made with crushed green ants!

Papaya (☎ 4098 6173; 3-5 Stewart St; mains $7-25; ⌨ lunch & dinner Wed-Sun) The tempting 'Taste of the Daintree' platter with treats such as crocodile wontons and sugar-cane prawns is a signature dish at this snappy little bar and bistro in the village.

DAINTREE RIVER TO CAPE TRIBULATION

Crossing the Daintree River by the cable ferry gives the feeling that you're about to enter a frontier wilderness. From here the road narrows and winds north for 35km, hugging the coast for most of the way to Cape Tribulation. Along the way are smatterings of tiny hamlets, isolated beaches and attractions that make getting to Cape Trib half the fun.

The indigenous Kuku Yalanji people called the area Kulki; the name Cape Tribulation was given by Captain Cook after his ship ran aground on an outlying reef.

Part of the Wet Tropics World Heritage Area, this extraordinarily beautiful stretch is one of the few places in the world where the tropical rainforest meets the sea. In recognition of this unique environment, much of the area is protected as the Daintree National Park, which was declared in 1981.

Cow Bay and Cape Tribulation are loosely termed 'villages', but the length of Cape Tribulation Rd is peppered with secluded

places to stay and eat. There's no mains power north of the Daintree River – electricity is supplied by generators or, increasingly, solar power. The only fuel between the Daintree River and Cape Trib is at **Rainforest Village** (☎ 4098 9015; ⌨ 7am-7pm).

The lovable **Daintree River ferry** (car/motorcycle/bicycle & pedestrian one way $10/4/1; ⌨ 6am-midnight), a cable ferry, carries you and your vehicle across the river every 15 minutes or so.

Sights & Activities

About 3km beyond the Daintree River crossing, a 5km unsealed road leads to Cape Kimberley Beach, a quiet beach with **Snapper Island** just off shore. The island is national park, with a fringing reef. Access is by private boat; Crocodylus Village takes a sea-kayaking tour there.

On the steep, winding road between Cape Kimberly and Cow Bay is the **Walu Wugirriga (Alexandra Range) lookout**, with an information board and superb views over the Range and the Daintree River inlet.

The **Daintree Discovery Centre** (☎ 4098 9171; www .daintree-rec.com.au; Tulip Oak Rd; adult/child/family $25/10/58 valid for seven days; ⌨ 8.30am-5pm) is an award-winning rainforest interpretive centre. Its aerial walkway takes you high into the forest canopy via a 23m tower. You can spend about an hour meandering along the boardwalks and looking out for wildlife, but if you hire an audio guide ($5), expect to spend at least a couple of hours. The audio guide also offers an excellent Aboriginal tour, interpreting the rainforest from an indigenous viewpoint.

Just past the centre, **Jindalba Boardwalk** is a 700m circuit walk that snakes through the rainforest.

The tiny village of **Cow Bay** clings to the main road, but turn east down a sealed 5km road to the lovely secluded beach.

Book ahead for a place on one of the **Cooper Creek Wilderness** (☎ 4098 9126; www.ccwild.com; Cape Tribulation Rd; guided walks $40) walks, which take you through Daintree rainforest and include a dip in Cooper Creek. Night walks (departing at 8pm) focus on spotting nocturnal wildlife.

Cape Tribulation Wilderness Cruises (☎ 4033 2052; www.capetribcruises.com; Cape Tribulation Rd; adult/child $25/17.50) has one-hour mangrove cruises down Cooper Creek in search of crocs.

Marrdja Botanical Walk is a beautiful 540m (30-minute) interpretive boardwalk that follows the creek through a section of rainforest packed with fan palms and past mangroves to a look-

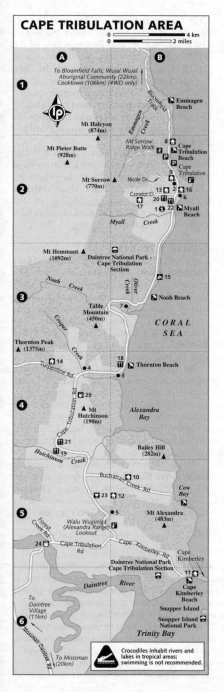

CAPE TRIBULATION AREA

out over Noah Creek. Wear insect repellent to beat the mildly annoying midges.

Sleeping & Eating

There's basic camping at Snapper Island and Noah Beach – book online through **QPWS** (www.epa.qld.gov.au).

   Daintree Koala Beach Resort (☎ 4090 7500; www.koalaadventures.com; Cape Kimberley; unpowered/powered sites per person $10/13, dm $25, d $50-120; ✕ ⓢ) At Cape Kimberley Beach, this is a spacious camping ground with secluded sites among the trees, small 'jungle huts' with bunk beds, air-con cabins, and a bar and restaurant.

   Crocodylus Village (☎ 4098 9166; www.crocodyluscapetrib.com; Buchanan Creek Rd; dm/d $20/75; ⓛ ⓢ) Associated with the YHA, it has cramped safari-style tents at Cow Bay and runs adventurous two-day sea-kayaking tours to Snapper Island ($199).

   Epiphyte B&B (☎ 4098 9039; www.rainforestbb.com; 22 Silkwood Rd; s/d/tr/cabin $70/95/120/140) Set on a lush 3.5-hectare property, spectacularly laid-back Epiphyte has individually styled rooms

Crocodiles inhabit rivers and lakes in tropical areas; swimming is not recommended.

of varying sizes. From the front deck of the house you can kick back with views of imposing Thornton's Peak.

Heritage Lodge & Spa (☎ 4098 9138; www.heritage lodge.net.au; Turpentine Rd; r from $215; 🗶 🖭) In a secluded rainforest location, the Heritage Lodge overlooks a beautiful stretch of Cooper Creek – the swimming holes in the 'back yard' are sensational. As well as comfortable individual cabins, spa treatments (www.daintreespa.com) are on offer.

Fan Palm Boardwalk Cafe (☎ 4098 9119; Cape Tribulation Rd, Cow Bay; mains $5-18; ☼ breakfast, lunch & dinner) Alfresco dining on the edge of the rainforest with perky wraps, sandwiches, burgers and breakfast fare.

Daintree Ice Cream Company (☎ 4098 9114; Cape Tribulation Rd; ice cream $5; ☼ 11am-5pm) Exotic tropical flavours like wattleseed, black sapote, macadamia, mango, coconut or jackfruit are on offer here.

Cafe on Sea (☎ 4098 9718; mains $10-15; ☼ breakfast & lunch) Fronting Thornton Beach, this licensed place is a soothing spot for a light lunch or a drink.

Cow Bay Hotel (☎ 4098 9011; Bailey Creek Rd; mains $10-30; ☼ dinner) If you have a hankering for a basic pub counter meal and a pot of beer, this is the only real pub in the whole Daintree region; takeaway alcohol is available.

CAPE TRIBULATION

Walking along beautiful Cape Tribulation Beach in the gathering sunset, it's hard not to wonder what Captain Cook was thinking when he gave this little piece of paradise such a depressing name. Of course, he was too busy weaving his way through (and eventually running aground on) the reef to be awed by this dramatic coastline.

Here the rainforest tumbles right down to two magnificent beaches – Myall and Cape

Trib – separated by a knobby cape. The village of Cape Tribulation marks the end of the road, literally, and the beginning of the 4WD-only coastal route along the Bloomfield Track. Discovered by hippies in the '70s, backpackers in the '80s and everyone else in the '90s, Cape Trib retains a frontier quality, with low-key development, road signs alerting drivers to cassowary crossings, and crocodile warnings that make beach strolls that little bit less relaxing.

Stop in at **Mason's Store** (☎ 4098 0070; Cape Tribulation Rd; ☼ 8am-6pm), about 1.5km south of the cape, for information on the region including the Bloomfield Track. There's internet access here and at PK's Jungle Village and the Dragonfly Cafe. There's an ATM in the IGA supermarket next to PK's Jungle Village.

Sights & Activities

Long walks on the stunning swathes of **Cape Tribulation Beach** or **Myall Beach** are a favourite pastime and you can swim safely in the shallows of the Coral Sea outside stinger season, though you should heed any warning signs and local advice about croc sightings. Just south of PK's Jungle Village is the **Dubuji Boardwalk**, an easy 1.8km wheelchair-accessible loop through mangroves and rainforest.

Bat House (☎ 4098 0063; Cape Tribulation Rd; www .austrop.org.au; admission $2; ☼ 10.30am-3.30pm Tue-Sun) is an information and education centre run by volunteers from Austrop, a local conservation organisation. As the name suggests, it's also a nursery for injured or orphaned fruit bats (flying foxes), and there's always one hanging around (sorry) for you to meet.

Serious, fit walkers should lace-up early for the **Mt Sorrow Ridge Walk** (7km, five to six hours return); it's strenuous but worth it. The start of the marked trail is about 150m north of the Kulki picnic area car park, on your left.

THE CASSOWARY'S PRECIOUS POO

Looking like something out of *Jurassic Park*, a flightless bird struts through the rainforest. It's as tall as a grown man, has three razor-sharp clawed toes, a blue-and-purple head, red wattles (the fleshy lobes hanging from its neck), a helmet-like horn and unusual black feathers that look more like ratty hair, much like an emu. Meet the cassowary, the shy native of these northern forests.

The endangered cassowary is considered an important link in the rainforest ecosystem. It is the only animal capable of dispersing the seeds of more than 70 species of trees whose fruit is too large for other rainforest animals to digest and pass. Cassowaries swallow fruit whole and excrete the fruit's seed intact in large piles of dung, which acts as fertiliser encouraging growth of the seed. Without them, the rainforest as we know it would look very different.

Other activities in Cape Trib include horse-riding, sea kayaking, yoga and 'jungle surfing' on a flying fox, all of which can be booked through your accommodation.

Tours

The Great Barrier Reef is just 45 minutes to an hour off shore, but at the time of writing only one outfit was running trips to the reef. The sailing catamaran **Rum Runner** (☎ 1300 556 332, 4098 0016; www.rumrunner.com.au; adult/child $120/90; ☼ Apr-Feb) takes a maximum of 40 passengers for snorkelling and diving.

Mason's Tours (☎ 4098 0070; www.masonstours.com.au, Cape Tribulation Rd) offers interpretive walks lasting two hours (adult/child $38/29) or a half-day ($45/35), and a croc-spotting night walk ($38). They also run 4WD tours up the Bloomfield Track (from $106/66).

Sleeping & Eating

PK's Jungle Village (☎ 4098 0040; www.pksjunglevillage.com; unpowered sites per person $10, dm $22-25, budget s/d $44/66, d $88-110; ❄ 🖳 🞸) A short boardwalk back from Myall Beach, PK's is a long-time budget favourite, staffed by overworked backpackers. There's a whole range of accommodation, and its boozy bar and restaurant is the entertainment hub of Cape Trib.

Cape Trib Beach House (☎ 4098 0030; www.capetribbeach.com.au; dm $25, d $79-189; ❄ 🖳 🞸) A low-key backpackers' alternative to PK's party house, neat rainforest huts range from air-con dorms to overpriced private timber cabins. Access the beach down some stairs leading from the restaurant.

Ferntree Rainforest Resort (☎ 4098 0033; www.ferntreerainforestlodge.com.au; Camelot Close, Cape Tribulation; dm $30, d $138-174; ❄ 🞸) This resort combines slick budget dorms (air-con and en suite) with upmarket rooms and timber lodges, the best of which are poolside.

our pick **Rainforest Hideaway** (☎ 4098 0108; www.rainforesthideaway.com; 19 Camelot Close; d $95-135) This colourful, rambling B&B was single-handedly built by the owner – even the furniture and the beds are handmade. Best is the self-contained rustic cabin with an outdoor shower open to the rainforest.

Cape Trib Farmstay (☎ 4098 0042; www.capetribfarmstay.com; Cape Tribulation Rd; d $110; ❄) These neat, private timber cottages are set in a lovely 30-hectare fruit orchard yielding mangosteen, rambutan, breadfruit and bananas – which you might find on your breakfast plate. The cute stilted cabins (one with wheelchair access) have joyous views of Mt Sorrow from their verandas.

Dragonfly Gallery Cafe (☎ 4098 0121; Lot 9, Camelot Close; mains $13-28; ☼ lunch & dinner; 🖳) The timber pole-house, lush garden, and turtle-filled lily pond are serene surrounds for afternoon coffee and cakes or an evening meal of jungle lamb curry or barramundi in coconut.

our pick **Whet Restaurant** (☎ 4098 0007; 1 Cape Tribulation; tapas $7, mains $27-32; ☼ 10am-11pm) Whether you're munching on a plate of tapas with a tropical-fruit cocktail or dining by candlelight on tiger-prawn linguini, loungy Whet is Cape Trib's coolest address. Sink into the black leather couches for a late night – this is the only place you can get a meal much after 8pm.

Getting There & Around

See p458 for details of buses between Cape Tribulation, Cairns and Cooktown.

The **Cape Trib Shuttle Bus** (☎ 4098 0121; one way $5; ☼ 10am, 11am, noon & 1pm) runs between Coconut Beach Resort and Cape Trib Beach four times a day.

CAPE TRIBULATION TO COOKTOWN: THE COAST ROAD

The Bloomfield Track from Cape Tribulation to Cooktown is the great adventure drive of the far north coast. It's a 4WD-only route that traverses creek crossings, diabolically steep climbs and patchy surfaces. It can be impassable for many weeks on end during the Wet, and even in the Dry you should ask about road conditions locally at Mason's Store (opposite). The Track runs for about 80km before linking up with the sealed Cooktown Developmental Rd 30km south of Cooktown. Although this is a remote region, there are a few accommodation places and attractions along the way – you don't need to do the trip in a single day.

It's 5km from Cape Trib to Emmagen Creek, which is the official start of the Bloomfield Track. Just before you reach Emmagen Creek, you'll see a huge strangler fig. From beside the tree, a walking path leads down to the pretty crescent-shaped **Emmagen Beach**.

A little way beyond the Emmagen Creek crossing, the road climbs and dips steeply and turns sharp corners over fine, slippery bulldust. This is the most challenging section of the drive, especially after rain. The road then follows the broad tidal Bloomfield River before crossing it 30km north of Cape Trib.

Turn left immediately after the bridge to see the **Bloomfield Falls**. The falls are for looking only: crocs inhabit the river and the site is significant to the indigenous Wujal Wujal community located just north of the river. Residents of Wujal Wujal, the **Walker Family** (☎ 4060 8069; walkerfamilytours@bigpond.com; adult/child $15/7.50) run recommended half-hour walking tours of the falls and surrounding forest departing daily from the car park, as well as half-day safaris ($106/66). Bookings are essential.

North of Bloomfield, the road conditions steadily improve and you pass through the tiny hamlets of Ayton, Rossville and finally Helenvale. Nearly everyone stops in at the **Lion's Den Hotel** (☎ 4060 3911; www.lionsdenhotel.com .au; Helensvale; unpowered/powered sites $16/22, s/d $40/50, d safari tents $66; 🐾). This well-known watering hole dates back to 1875 and always attracts a steady stream of travellers and local characters. There's fuel, ice-cold beer and a restaurant, as well as camping and safari-style cabins on stilts.

About 4km north, the Bloomfield Track meets the sealed Cooktown Developmental Rd and from there it's a dust-free 28km to Cooktown.

CAIRNS TO COOKTOWN: THE INLAND ROUTE

The main route between Cairns and Cooktown is sealed all the way, but remains stoically arid whatever the season. It's 332km long (4½ to five hours' drive), winding over a small range before flattening out and passing through half-forgotten mining towns.

After heading north out of Cairns, take the turn-off to Kuranda and climb over the Atherton Tableland. At Mareeba you meet the Peninsula Developmental Rd, which takes you north through the small township of **Mt Molloy** and the former wolfram (tungsten) mining town of **Mt Carbine** before the road climbs through the De Sailly Range, where there are surprising panoramic views over the savannah. Stop in for a beer at the **Mt Carbine Hotel** to see the world's longest playable didjeridu.

It's another 115km (passing the Palmer River Roadhouse) to **Lakeland**, a hamlet that produces sugar, grain, coffee and bananas, and sits at the junction of the Peninsula Developmental Rd and the Cooktown Developmental Rd. Turning left takes you

on the road to Cape York, and straight ahead is 80km to Cooktown. Not far past the Bloomfield Track turn-off you pass the jumble of basalt boulders that form the **Black Mountain National Park**. Home to unique species of frogs, skinks and geckoes, it was formed 260 million years ago by a magma intrusion below the surface, which then solidified and was gradually exposed by erosion.

COOKTOWN
☎ 07 / pop 1336

A far-north frontier town with a breezy coastal outlook, Cooktown is a small place with a big history. It was here that Captain Cook first set foot on the Australian continent. Technically on Cape York Peninsula and the biggest town on the Cape, Cooktown has a laid-back, tropical nature where happiness is a fishing rod and an esky full of beer.

The inland route was finally sealed all the way in 2005, and tourism is a growing industry, but the town remains unadorned and unfussed by the attention, and years of isolation and hard living have imbued the locals with a matter-of-fact, laconic character and a great sense of humour. As well as historical sites relating to early European contact, there's increasing recognition for the area's indigenous community and unspoilt natural environment of wetlands, mangroves, rainforest and long, lonely beaches. From here you can take off by 4WD through Lakefield National Park (p478), or take a trip out to spectacular Lizard Island (p477).

History
On 17 June 1770 Cooktown became the site of Australia's first nonindigenous settlement, however transient, when Captain James Cook beached his barque, the *Endeavour*, on the banks of its estuary. The *Endeavour* had earlier struck a reef off shore from Cape Tribulation, and Cook and his crew spent 48 days here while they repaired the damage.

In 1874 Cooktown became a large and unruly port town at the centre of the Palmer River gold rush. At its peak there were no fewer than 94 pubs and the population was more than 30,000. A large percentage of this population was Chinese, and their industrious presence led to some wild race-related riots. And here, as elsewhere in the country, the indigenous population was overrun and outcast, with much bloodshed.

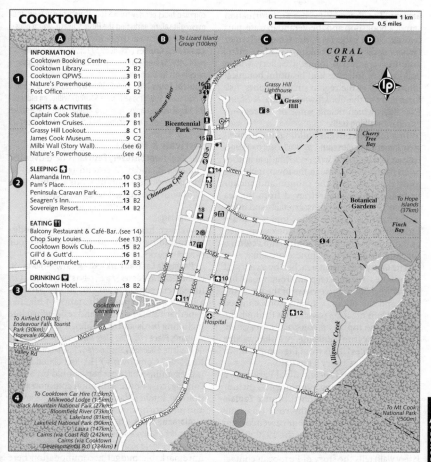

COOKTOWN

INFORMATION	
Cooktown Booking Centre	**1** C2
Cooktown Library	**2** B2
Cooktown QPWS	**3** B1
Nature's Powerhouse	**4** D3
Post Office	**5** B2

SIGHTS & ACTIVITIES	
Captain Cook Statue	**6** B1
Cooktown Cruises	**7** B1
Grassy Hill Lookout	**8** C1
James Cook Museum	**9** C2
Milbi Wall (Story Wall)	(see 6)
Nature's Powerhouse	(see 4)

SLEEPING	
Alamanda Inn	**10** C3
Pam's Place	**11** B3
Peninsula Caravan Park	**12** C3
Seagren's Inn	**13** B2
Sovereign Resort	**14** B2

EATING	
Balcony Restaurant & Café-Bar	(see 14)
Chop Suey Louies	(see 13)
Cooktown Bowls Club	**15** B2
Gill'd & Gutt'd	**16** B1
IGA Supermarket	**17** B3

DRINKING	
Cooktown Hotel	**18** B2

Orientation & Information

Cooktown is on the inland side of a headland sheltering the mouth of the Endeavour River. The main street is Charlotte St, which runs south from the wharf. Overlooking the town from the northern end of the headland is Grassy Hill, and east of the town centre are Cherry Tree Bay and Finch Bay, the Botanic Gardens and Mt Cook National Park.

Cooktown has a post office, an ATM and internet access. Information services include:

Cooktown Booking Centre (☎ 4069 5381; www .cooktownbookings.com.au; 132 Charlotte St) Information and bookings for tours, transport and accommodation.

Cooktown Library (☎ 4069 5009; Helen St) Internet access per hour $4.

Cooktown QPWS (☎ 4069 5777; Webber Esplanade; ☻ 8am-3pm Mon-Fri) Information and camping permits for national parks, including Lizard Island.

Nature's Powerhouse (☎ 4069 6004; www.natures powerhouse.info; Walker St; ☻ 9am-5pm) Information centre.

Sights & Activities

For a northern outpost Cooktown has its share of sights, including historical attractions in town, gardens, beaches, waterfalls and natural settings that are worth the legwork or 4WD trip involved to reach them.

Nature's Powerhouse (☎ 4069 6004; www.naturespower house.info; Walker St; galleries adult/child $3/free; ☻ 9am-5pm) is an environment interpretive and information centre at the entry to Cooktown's public **Botanic**

Gardens. The Powerhouse has an information stand, a bookshop and the Verandah Cafe, plus two excellent galleries – the Charlie Tanner Gallery dedicated to Cooktown's 'snake man', and the Vera Scarth-Johnson Gallery, with a collection of intricate and beautiful botanical illustrations of the region's native plants. Ask for a copy of the *Cooktown Heritage & Scenic Rim* flyer, which details some of the region's excellent **walking trails**.

In a former convent building, the impressive **James Cook Museum** (☎ 4069 5386; cnr Helen & Furneaux Sts; adult/child $7.50/3; ☷ 9.30am-4pm) houses relics from Cook's time in the town, including journal entries, and the cannon and anchor from the *Endeavour*, retrieved from the sea floor in 1971. Photographs, artefacts and interpretive panels explain other topics that are influential to the shaping of Cooktown, such as indigenous Guugu Yimithirr Bama culture, the gold rush and the Chinese presence.

The **Grassy Hill Lookout**, reached by a very stiff 15-minute walk or a steep and rough road, has sensational 360-degree views of the town, the river and the ocean. Captain Cook climbed this hill looking for a passage out through the reefs. At the top sits a compact, corrugated, 19th-century iron **lighthouse**. A 1½km **walking trail** (45 minutes) leads from the summit down to the beach at Cherry Tree Bay.

Charlotte St and Bicentennial Park have a number of interesting monuments, including the much-photographed bronze **Captain Cook statue**. There's also the rock (marking the spot where the *Endeavour* careened) and the Queen's Steps, built for the 1970 visit of Queen Elizabeth II. Nearby, the **Milbi Wall (Story Wall)** tells the story of European contact from the local Gungarde (Guugu Yimithirr) indigenous community's perspective.

Tours

Some interesting tours operate out of Cooktown daily from May to October, with scaled-back versions in the low season from November to at least April. But this is not Cairns or Port Douglas, and although the reef is not far away, there are no regularly scheduled dive or snorkelling trips.

Ahoy Plane-Sailing (☎ 4069 5232; www.ahoyplane -sailingseaplanes.com.au) Scenic reef flights (from $140) and an extraordinary Lizard Island tour ($330), which lands in Watson's Bay by seaplane.

Barts Bush Adventures (☎ 4069 6229; www.barts bushadventures.com.au; days tours adult/child $165/85, camping tours per day from $300) Variety of day tours and overnight safaris, including the Bush & Beach, which goes to Coloured Sands and Elim Beach.

Cooktown Cruises (☎ 4069 5712; 2hr cruises adult/ child $40/25) Scenic cruises up the Endeavour River; also hires boats by the hour.

Guurrbi Tours (☎ 4069 6259; www.guurrbitours.com; 2-/4hr tours $90/115, self-drive $60/80) Willie, an elder of the Nugal-warra family, runs two unique tours that use the physical landscape to describe the emotional landscape.

Festivals & Events

The **Cooktown Discovery Festival** is held over the Queen's Birthday Weekend (early June) to commemorate Captain Cook's landing in 1770 with a costumed re-enactment.

Sleeping

Cooktown has accommodation in all budgets, including two standard motels and four caravan parks.

Peninsula Caravan Park (☎ 4069 5107; 64 Howard St; unpowered/powered sites $24/27, cabin s $80; ☷ ☷) On the eastern edge of town, this simple park has a lovely bush setting with stands of big, old paperbark and gum trees, and resident wildlife including birds and wallabies.

Pam's Place (☎ 4069 5166; www.cooktownhostel.com; cnr Charlotte & Boundary Sts; dm/s/d $25/55/60, motel d $90- 100 ☷ ☷) Cooktown's YHA-associated hostel is everything a backpackers should be: a welcoming, cosy house with good common areas (lounge, kitchen, laundry etc), a leafy garden and an assortment of neurotic parrots.

Alamanda Inn (☎ 4069 5203; phscott@tpg.com .au; cnr Hope & Howard Sts; guesthouse s/d $40/50, motel s/d $50/60, unit s/d $65/75; ☷ ☷) The friendly but unremarkable budget accommodation here ranges from rooms in the guesthouse (share a bathroom and kitchen) to basic motel rooms and units with kitchenettes.

Seagren's Inn (☎ 4069 5357; seagrens-inn@bigpond .com; Charlotte St; d $95-140; ☷ ☷) Upstairs in a century-old heritage building, Seagren's is all about old-style atmosphere. The small front rooms open onto the second-level veranda but the pick is room 9, a huge three-room apartment at the rear with private balcony.

ourpick **Milkwood Lodge** (☎ 4069 5007; www .milkwoodlodge.com; Annan Rd; s/d $110/130; ☷ ☷) In a patch of rainforest 2.5km south of town, these six breezy, self-contained, timber-pole cabins are beautifully designed with bushland views opening out from each private balcony. The spacious spilt-level apartments have king beds and kitchenette, but are not suitable for kids.

Sovereign Resort (☎ 4043 0500; www.sovereignresort.com.au; cnr Charlotte & Green Sts; d $165-200; ☒ 🖳 ☒) Cooktown's top resort hotel is right on the main street and is a warren of comfortable tropical-style rooms with wooden-slat blinds and tile floors. Kick back in the fine garden pool area or the Balcony Restaurant & Bar (mains $30 to $34; open for breakfast, lunch and dinner).

Eating & Drinking

It might not be *haute cuisine*, but eating out in Cooktown these days is more than just a counter meal in the local pub (there's also the bowls club, of course!). Drinking is a favourite pastime here too, and the local pubs and clubs are a good place to mix it with the locals. There's an IGA supermarket on Hogg St.

Gill'd & Gutt'd (☎ 4069 5863; Fisherman's Wharf, Webber Esplanade; meals $4-10; ☼ lunch & dinner) Fish and chips the way it should be – fresh and right on the waterside wharf.

Cooktown Bowls Club (☎ 4069 5819; Charlotte St; mains $10-22; ☼ lunch & dinner Mon-Sat) Sign in at the door, and join the club for the night. As well as big servings of bistro meals such as fish or steak, you can revisit the salad bar at will. You can join in social bowls on Wednesday and Saturday afternoon and barefoot bowls on Wednesday evening.

Chop Suey Louies (☎ 4069 5357; Seagren's Inn, Charlotte St; mains $17-27; ☼ lunch & dinner from 5pm Wed-Mon Apr-Sep) With Cooktown's Chinese heritage it's only right that you should be able to get a decent chicken chow mein or beef in blackbean sauce. This stylish licensed restaurant with low-cut cream furniture is downstairs from the Seagren's Inn.

Cooktown Hotel (☎ 4069 5308; 96 Charlotte St; mains $12.50-22; ☎ lunch & dinner) The double-storey timber 'Top Pub' is hard to miss at the top end of Charlotte St. Plenty of character, plenty of locals and a nice side beer garden to sit in with a beer or counter meal.

Getting There & Around

Cooktown's airfield is 10km west of town along McIvor Rd. **Skytrans** (☎ 1800 818 405; www.skytrans.com.au) flies twice a day between Cooktown and Cairns (from $95, 45 minutes).

Country Road Coachlines (☎ 4045 2794; www.countryroadcoachlines.com.au) runs a bus service between Cairns and Cooktown on the coastal route via Port Douglas and Cape Tribulation three times a week ($72) leaving Cairns Monday, Wednesday and Friday and returning from Cooktown Tuesday, Thursday and Saturday. Another service takes the inland route via Mareeba on Monday, Wednesday and Friday ($72, same day return).

To get to sights outside town, **Cooktown Car Hire** (☎ 4069 5007; www.cooktown-car-hire.com) at Milkwood Rainforest Lodge rents 4WDs.

LIZARD ISLAND GROUP

Famed for their marine life and bird-watching, the spectacular islands of the Lizard Island Group are clustered just 27km off the coast about 100km from Cooktown. Besides Lizard Island there are four smaller islands in the Lizard group: **Osprey Island**, with its nesting birds, **Palfrey Island**, with an automatic lighthouse, **South Island** and **Seabird Islet**, home to a tern colony. The island group is renowned for its diving, in particular the famous Cod Hole and Pixie Bommie sites.

Lizard Island

Lizard Island's **beaches** are nothing short of sensational, and range from long stretches of white sand to idyllic little rocky bays. The water is crystal clear and magnificent coral surrounds the island – snorkelling here is superb. The island is a national park with good bushwalking – the climb to the top of **Cook's Look** is a great walk (three hours return) with amazing views. Near the top there are traces of stones marking an Aboriginal ceremonial area.

Sleeping

Accommodation is only available on Lizard Island, and the choice is either bush camping or supreme five-star luxury!

The **QPWS camping ground** (☎ 13 13 04; www.epa.qld.gov.au; per person/family $4.50/18) on Watson's Bay has toilets, gas barbecues and untreated water. Book in advance and bring all supplies as there are no shops on the island.

You really don't need us to tell you whether **Lizard Island Resort** (☎ 1300 134 044; www.lizardisland.com.au; Anchor Bay; 2 nights s/d from $2792/3300; ☒ ☒) is any good or not. You'll be one of a maximum of 80 guests in 40 villas on one of the most exclusive and luxurious resorts in Far North Queensland – expect to see someone rich and famous sharing the

---

DETOUR: LAKEFIELD NATIONAL PARK

With a 4WD and a sense of adventure, the route from Cooktown through Lakefield National Park to Laura (or further north to Musgrave) will give you a taste of remote Cape York Peninsula. It's an isolated route without any facilities or fuel stops along the way; plan ahead and carry enough supplies and water to get you through. This detour skirts the southern end of the park, emerging at Laura on the Peninsula Developmental Rd then heading back south.

Leaving Cooktown on the McIvor Rd, **Endeavour Falls** is 33km down a mostly sealed road. Stop in at the tourist park where there's a grocery store, fuel and a good year-round swimming hole. Further north is the **Hopevale Aboriginal Community**, established as a Lutheran Mission in 1949. The community has an arts centre and a couple of shops. Back on the Cooktown road, turn northwest to continue to **Battle Camp** and **Lakefield National Park**. The 542,000-hectare park encompasses a wide variety of country around the flood plains of the Normanby, Kennedy, Bizant, Morehead and Hann Rivers, and is generally only accessible between June and November. Self-registration bush camp sites are scattered throughout the park but only Kalpowar Crossing and Hann Crossing sites have facilities.

The Laura River is crossed 25km from the park boundary (112km from Cooktown). The abandoned **Old Laura Homestead** is on the far bank. Take the left at the T-junction and it's 28km to Laura on the Peninsula Developmental Rd. From here it's 36km southwest to **Jowalbinna Rock Art Safari Camp** (☎ 4035 4488; www.jowalbinna.com.au; camping $9, cabins with meals from $125) with secluded camping and accommodation and guided walks of ancient Quinkan rock-art sites. From Laura it's 60km south to Lakeland and the road back to Cairns.

Osprey Restaurant or indulging in spa treatments. Rates include all meals and a range of activities.

Getting There & Away

Unless you have your own boat or can con someone in Cooktown into an expensive charter, flying is the easiest way to Lizard Island.

Hinterland Aviation has two scheduled flights a day from Cairns to Lizard Island (one way/return $225/450) that must be booked through **Voyages** (☎ 1300 134 044; www.lizardisland.com.au).

From Cooktown **Ahoy Plane-Sailing** (☎ 4069 5232; www.ahoyplane-sailingseaplanes.com.au) has an exciting day tour ($330), which lands in Watson's Bay by seaplane; camping drop-off can also be arranged.

Directory

CONTENTS

PRACTICALITIES

- Plugs have angled pins; voltage is 220V to 240V, 50Hz.

- Broadsheet dailies include the *Sydney Morning Herald,* Melbourne's *Age* and the national *Australian*.

- The metric system is used for weights and measures.

- Free-to-air TV is provided by the government-sponsored Australian Broadcasting Corporation (ABC) and multicultural SBS, and three commercial stations, namely Seven, Nine and Ten.

- Video players use the PAL system.

- Most interior spaces in the ACT, NSW, Queensland and Victoria are nonsmoking.

ACCOMMODATION

The East Coast is a well-trodden route with plenty of accommodation options to suit all budgets. Endowed with Australia's largest cities and most famous holiday resorts, the coast boasts abundant motels, guesthouses, B&Bs, hostels, pubs and caravan parks with camp sites. There are also lots of less conventional possibilities such as farm-stays, houseboats and yachts.

The listings in this guidebook are ordered from budget to midrange to top end, with the cheapest options within each category listed first. Any place that charges up to $100 per room has been categorised as budget accommodation. Midrange prices are from $100 to $160 per room, while the top-end tag is applied to places charging more than $160 per room. As Sydney is a more expensive destination, our price ranges for it differ slightly, with budget stretching to $120 a double and midrange places going up to $180 a room.

In many regions prices don't vary dramatically from season to season, and we have simply listed the prices that are charged for the majority of the year. In other areas there are dramatic seasonal price variations; in these cases we have listed high-season prices but not the short peak season around Christmas, when many coastal resorts have a short-lived price spike in the middle of the high season. Along the southeastern coast, the summer months (December to February) are high season, particularly the school holidays that begin just before Christmas. The southern winter coincides with the mild northern dry season, and the northern migration (particularly during school holidays) keeps prices high in the north.

B&Bs

In country areas, guesthouses and B&Bs are the fastest-growing segment of the accommodation market. New places are opening all the time, and the options include everything from a room in a restored Victorian-era mansion or a rambling Queenslander to a contemporary purpose-built cottage.

FAVOURITE CAMP SITES

Here's some favourite camp sites of this book's authors:

- Cape Conran Coastal Park, Gippsland, Victoria (p135)

- Murramarang National Park, South Coast NSW (p163)

- Myall Lakes National Park, Central Coast NSW (p238)

- Bundjalung National Park, North Coast NSW (p267)

- Fraser Island Beach, Fraser Coast, Queensland (p377)

- Dunk Island, North Queensland (p444)

- Frankland and Fitzroy Islands, Far North Queensland (p460 and p460)

Tariffs cover a wide price range. They're typically in the $80 to $150 (per double) bracket, but can be much higher in areas that attract weekend getaways and romantic escapes from the cities.

Local tourist offices usually have a list of places.

Online resources:

Australian B&B (www.australianbandb.com.au)

Bed & Breakfast (www.babs.com.au)

OZ Bed and Breakfast (www.ozbedandbreakfast.com)

Camping

If you want to explore the East Coast on a shoestring, camping is the way to go. Camping in national parks can cost from nothing to $14 per person – nights spent around a campfire under the stars are unforgettable. Tent sites at private camping and caravan parks cost around $12 to $30 per couple per night, and a few dollars more with electricity.

National parks and their camping areas are administered by each state. Contact details include:

New South Wales www.nationalparks.nsw.gov.au

Queensland www.epa.qld.gov.au/parks_and_forests

Victoria www.parkweb.vic.gov.au

When it comes to urban camping, remember that most city caravan parks are a long way from the centre of town. Most caravan parks are good value, with almost all of them equipped with hot showers, toilets and laundry

facilities, and usually a pool. Many have on-site cabins. The size of these cabins and the facilities offered vary but expect to pay $50 to $90 for two people in a cabin with a kitchenette – about the same as a cheap motel. If you intend to do a lot of caravanning or camping, it's not a bad idea to join one of the major chains such as **Big 4 Holiday Parks** (☎ 03-9421 0100, 1800 632 444; www.big4.com.au). It gives you discounts on accommodation at member parks as well as various other tourist discounts.

Note that all camping and cabin rates quoted throughout this guide are for two people.

Farm-stays

Many coastal and hinterland farms offer a bed for the night and the chance to see rural Australia at work. At some you sit back and watch other people raise a sweat, while others like to get you involved in day-to-day activities. Check out the options on the website for **Australian Farmhost Holidays** (www.australiafarmhost .com). For travellers who don't mind getting their hands dirty, there's **Willing Workers on Organic Farms** (WWOOF; ☎ 03-5155 0218; www .wwoof.com.au). Regional and town tourist offices should also be able to tell you what's available in their area.

Hostels

Hostels or 'backpackers' are a highly social, low-cost fixture of the East Coast accommodation scene. There is a staggering number, ranging from family-run places in converted houses to huge, custom-built resorts replete with bars, nightclubs and a party attitude. Standards range from outstanding to awful, and management from friendly to scary.

Dorm beds typically cost $20 to $30, with single rooms hovering around $50 and doubles costing $60 to $90.

Useful organisations:

Nomads Backpackers (☎ 02-9299 7710; www.no madsworld.com) Membership ($39 for 12 months) entitles you to numerous discounts.

VIP Backpacker Resorts (☎ 07-3395 6052; www .vipbackpackers.com) Membership ($43 for 12 months) entitles you to various discounts.

YHA (☎ 02-9261 1111; www.yha.com.au) Membership (from $32 for 12 months) entitles you to discounts at YHA and many independent hostels.

A warning for Australian and Kiwi travellers: some hostels will only admit overseas backpackers, mainly because they've had problems with locals sleeping over and bothering the backpackers. Fortunately it's only a rowdy minority that makes trouble, and often hostels will only ask for identification in order to deter potential troublemakers.

Hotels & Motels

Hotels in cities or places visited by lots of tourists are generally of the business or luxury variety where you get a comfortable, anonymous and mod-con-filled room. These places tend to have a pool, a restaurant or café, room service and other facilities. We quote 'rack rates' (official advertised rates) throughout this book, but often hotels will offer regular discounts and special deals.

For comfortable midrange accommodation, motels (or motor inns) are a reliable option. Almost every country town has at least one, and the larger towns have many. Prices vary, and there's rarely a cheaper rate for singles, so they tend to be better for couples. Most motels have similar features (tea- and coffee-making facilities, fridges, TVs, air-con, bathrooms) but the price will indicate the standard. You'll mostly pay between $50 and $120 for a room.

The travel booking websites useful for finding airfares (p495) are usually also good for rooms. The following are room-specific and often have excellent deals:

Lastminute.com (www.lastminute.com.au)
Quickbeds.com (www.quickbeds.com.au)
Wotif.com (www.wotif.com.au)

Pubs

For the budget traveller, rooms in pubs (more formally known as public houses) aka hotels, aka 'the local', can be a good option. In the cities they are less attractive, and the rooms are either noisy or run down or both. In the country, however, pubs usually make for a convenient and often interesting choice. In tourist areas some of these pubs have been restored as they are often in outstanding heritage buildings, but generally the rooms remain small and old-fashioned, with a long amble down the hall to the bathroom. Never book a room above the bar if you're a light sleeper.

Pubs usually have single/double/twin rooms with shared facilities from around $35/60/60, obviously more if you want a private bathroom. The website www.pubstay.com.au lists an array of the better places.

Rental Accommodation

Rental accommodation is found in the form of holiday flats (in tourist areas) and serviced apartments (in cities). A holiday flat is much like a motel unit but has a serviceable kitchen. Holiday flats are often rented on a weekly basis; expect to pay anywhere from $80 to $140 per night for a one-bedroom flat. Ask a local real-estate agent about holiday rentals.

If you want to stay for a longer period, the first place to look for a shared flat or a room in the cities is the classified-advertisements sections of daily newspapers. Wednesday and Saturday are the best days for these ads. Notice boards at universities, hostels and cafés are also good places to look for flats and houses to share or rooms to rent.

Useful websites:

Couch Surfing (www.couchsurfing.com) Hooks you up with spare couches and new friends around the world.
Domain.com.au (www.domain.com.au) Lists holiday and long-term rentals.

Flatmate Finders (www.flatmatefinders.com.au) Good site for long-term share accommodation in Sydney and Melbourne.

Sleeping with the Enemy (www.sleepingwiththe enemy.com) Another good site for long-term accommodation in Sydney and Cairns.

Keep in mind that some long-term lodgings require deposits (or bonds) and don't come furnished.

ACTIVITIES

See the East Coast Australia Outdoors chapter, p63.

BUSINESS HOURS

Most shops and businesses open at 9am and close at 5pm or 5.30pm weekdays, and at either noon or 5pm on Saturday. Sunday trading is becoming increasingly common, but it's mostly limited to the larger cities or main tourist towns. In most towns there are usually one or two late shopping nights each week, when the doors stay open until 9pm or 9.30pm. Usually it's Thursday and/or Friday night. Supermarkets are generally open till 8pm and sometimes for 24 hours in cities. You may also find milk bars (general stores) and convenience stores that open late. In tourist resort areas (eg Cairns and the Gold Coast) shops may stay open later and all day on Saturday. Conversely, many small towns – even those that subsist on tourists – may be locked up so tight by 10pm that you can't even buy a chocolate bar.

Banks are generally open from 9.30am to 4pm Monday to Thursday, and until 5pm on Friday. Post offices open from 9am to 5pm Monday to Friday.

Restaurants typically open at noon for lunch and 6pm for dinner. Restaurants stay open until at least 9pm, but tend to serve food much later on Friday and Saturday nights. Cafés tend to be all-day affairs, opening at 7am and closing around 5pm, unless they simply continue their business into the night. Pubs usually serve food from noon to 2pm and from 6pm to 8pm. Pubs and bars often open at lunchtime and continue well into the evening, particularly from Thursday to Saturday.

CHILDREN

Practicalities

All cities and most major towns have centrally located public rooms where parents can go to nurse their baby or change its nappy (dia-

per); check with the local tourist office or city council for details. While many Australians have a relaxed attitude about breast-feeding or nappy changing in public, others frown upon it.

In Victoria it is illegal for anyone to discriminate against someone breast-feeding in public.

Most motels and better-equipped caravan parks supply cots and baby's baths; many also have playgrounds, swimming pools and in-house videos for children, as well as child-minding services. Many B&Bs, on the other hand, market themselves as sanctuaries from all things child-related.

If you want to leave Junior behind for a few hours, licensed childcare agencies have places set aside for casual care, or many of the larger hotels have contacts. Licensed centres are subject to government regulation and usually have a high standard; visitors centres can also often help you find childcare.

Child concessions (and family rates) often apply for such things as accommodation, tours, admission fees, and air, bus and train transport, with some discounts as high as 50% of the adult rate. However, the definition of 'child' can vary from under 12 to under 18 years.

Medical services and facilities in Australia are of a high standard, and items such as baby food, formula and disposable nappies are widely available in urban centres. Major car-hire companies will supply and fit booster seats for you.

Sights & Activities

There's plenty to keep kids occupied along the East Coast. Theme parks such as Sea World and Movie World on the Gold Coast are popular, but there are many cheaper and free options as well. Websites www.sydneyschild .com.au and www.melbourneschild.com.au have useful information.

CLIMATE

Australia's size means there's a lot of climatic variation along the entire East Coast, but without severe extremes. From Melbourne to Sydney the coast has cold (though generally not freezing), wet winters (June to August). Summers (December to February) are pleasant and warm, sometimes quite hot and usually dry. Violent electrical storms and sudden downpours are likely culminations

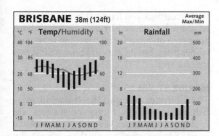

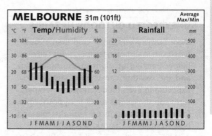

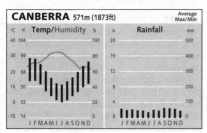

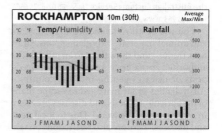

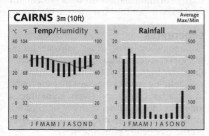

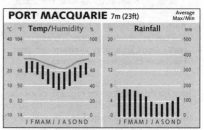

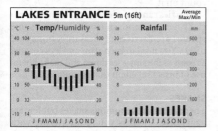

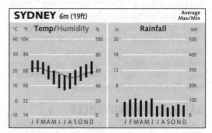

to a period of hot summer weather along the coast. Spring (September to November) and autumn (March to May) are transition months, much the same as in Europe and North America.

As you head north of Sydney and into the subtropics, seasonal variation becomes less dramatic. In Far North Queensland, however, you enter the monsoon belt of the tropics where there are two seasons: hot and very wet (ie the wet season), and hot and dry (the dry season).

See p23 for more information on Australia's East Coast seasons.

CUSTOMS

When entering Australia you can bring most articles in free of duty provided that customs is satisfied they are for personal use and you'll be taking them with you when you leave.

DIRECTORY

UNEXPECTED OUTDOOR HAZARDS

More bushwalkers die of cold than in bush-fires. Even in summer, temperatures can drop below freezing at night in the mountains and the weather can change very quickly. Exposure in even moderately cool temperatures can sometimes result in **hypothermia**; for more information on hypothermia and how to minimise its risk, see p509.

And although you will hear this often, it bears regular repeating: use plenty of sunscreen and wear a hat. The Australian sun can be very strong, especially as you go north. Don't let a nasty **sunburn** ruin your holiday or cause long-term damage.

There's a duty-free quota of 2.25L of alcohol, 250 cigarettes and dutiable goods up to the value of $900 per person. For comprehensive information on customs regulations, contact the **Australian Customs Service** (ACS; ☎ 02-6275 6666, 1300 363 263; www.customs.gov.au).

You will be asked to declare all food, plant and animal material – wooden spoons, straw hats, the lot – and show them to an official. The authorities are naturally keen to prevent weeds, pests or diseases getting into the country – Australia has so far managed to escape many of the agricultural pests and diseases prevalent in other parts of the world. Due to local pests and diseases, there are also restrictions on taking fruit and vegetables between states (see the boxed text, p499). If you have any doubts about what you can bring into Australia, ring the closest Australian embassy or check the government's customs information under the ACS website. For further information on quarantine regulations contact the **Australian Quarantine & Inspection Service** (AQIS; www.aqis.gov.au).

DANGERS & ANNOYANCES

Generally Australia is a safe place to travel. W.ith simple precautions, you should have no worries.

Animal Hazards

Australia is often marvelled at for its profusion of dangerous creatures. Nothing strikes fear into the hearts of visiting campers and hikers more than stories of spiders in sleeping bags and snakes on walking trails. Australia has also had its share of shark and crocodile attacks. Of course, unless you go looking for

these creatures, you'll probably never see one, let alone be attacked by one. Hospitals have antivenin on hand for all common snake and spider bites, but it helps to know what it was that bit you.

MARINE STINGERS

The Chironex box and the Irukandji jellyfish, also known as sea wasps or 'stingers', are found north of Agnes Water on Queensland's coast. For information on these potentially fatal hazards see the boxed text, p381.

CROCODILES

Commonly known as 'salties', saltwater (or estuarine) crocodiles are a real danger up north – they have been known to sample humans. As well as living around the coast they are found in estuaries, creeks and rivers, sometimes a long way inland. Observe safety signs or ask locals whether an inviting waterhole or river is croc-free before plunging in.

INSECTS

For four to six months of the year you'll have to cope with those two banes of the Australian outdoors – the fly and the mozzie (mosquito).

In the cities the flies aren't too bad; it's in the bush they start getting out of hand. The humble fly net, which fits on a hat, is very effective even if it looks ridiculous. Repellents may help to deter the little bastards but don't count on it.

Mozzies can be a problem in summer, especially near wetlands in tropical areas – some species are carriers of viral infections (see p509). You need to keep arms and legs covered as soon as the sun goes down and make liberal use of insect repellent that contains DEET.

SNAKES

There are many venomous snakes but few are aggressive – unless you're interfering with one, or have the misfortune to stand on one, it's unlikely that you'll be bitten. The most common venomous snakes in Australia are the brown and tiger snakes. The golden rule is 'if you see a snake leave it alone'. Don't try to catch or kill it. See p508 for information on treating snake bites.

SPIDERS

Nasty spiders include the funnel-web, the redback and the white-tailed spider. The deadly funnel-web spider is found in NSW (including Sydney) and its bite is treated in the same way as snake bite. The redback spider is black with a distinctive red stripe on its body; for bites, apply ice and seek medical attention. The white-tailed is a long, thin black spider with, you guessed it, a white tail, and has a nasty bite that can lead to local inflammation and ulceration. The large and frightening huntsman spider, which often enters homes, is harmless.

Bushfires

Bushfires happen every year along the East Coast, especially as some areas suffer ongoing drought. In hot, dry and windy weather, be extremely careful with any flame – cigarette butts thrown out of the windows of cars have started many a fire. On a total fire ban day it is forbidden even to use a camping stove. The locals won't be amused if they catch you; they'll happily dob you in, and the penalties are severe.

Take local advice before setting out on a bushwalk. On a day of total fire ban, don't go; delay your trip until the weather has changed. If you're out in the bush and you see smoke, even a long way away, take it seriously. Go to the nearest open space, downhill if possible. A forested ridge is the most dangerous place to be. Bushfires move very quickly and change direction with the wind.

Crime

Don't leave hotel rooms or cars unlocked, and don't leave your valuables unattended or visible through a car window. Sydney, the Gold Coast, Cairns and Byron Bay all get a dishonourable mention when it comes to theft, so keep a careful eye on your belongings in these areas. Make use of lockers or hotel safes.

Some pubs in Sydney and other cities popular with travellers carry posted warnings about drugged drinks, after several reported cases in the past few years of women accepting a drink from a stranger only to later fall unconscious and be sexually assaulted. Women are advised to refuse drinks offered by strangers in bars and to drink bottled alcohol rather than from a glass.

Driving

Australian drivers are generally fairly courteous, but there are some particular dangers on the open road in rural areas. See p501 for more information.

Swimming

Be aware that many surf beaches can be dangerous places to swim if you are not used to the conditions. Rips (undertows) are the main problem, and a number of people are paralysed each year by diving into waves in shallow water and hitting a sand bar – check first.

Many beaches are patrolled by surf lifesavers, and patrolled areas are marked off by flags. If you swim between the flags, help should arrive quickly if you get into trouble; raise your arm (and yell) if you need help. Outside the flags and on unpatrolled beaches you are more or less on your own.

If you find yourself being carried out by a rip, the important thing to do is just keep afloat; don't panic or try to swim against the rip. In most cases the current stops within a couple of hundred metres of the shore; swim parallel to the shore for a short way to get out of the rip and then make your way to shore.

Getting Around

The international wheelchair symbol (blue on a white background) for parking in allocated bays is recognised. Maps of central business districts showing accessible routes, toilets etc are available from major city councils, some regional councils and at information centres.

Most of the taxi companies in major cities and towns have modified vehicles to accommodate wheelchairs. Avis and Hertz offer hire cars with hand controls at no extra charge for pick up at capital cities and the major airports, but advance notice is required.

DISCOUNT CARDS
Senior Cards

Australian senior travellers with some form of identification are often eligible for concession prices. Overseas pensioners are entitled to discounts of at least 10% on most express bus fares and bus passes with Greyhound. Travellers over 60 years of age (both Australian residents and visitors) will simply need to present current age-proving identification to be eligible for discounts off regular air fares.

Student & Youth Cards

Carrying a student card entitles you to a wide variety of discounts throughout Australia. The most common card is the International Student Identity Card (ISIC), which is issued to full-time students aged 12 years and over, and gives the bearer discounts on accommodation, transport and admission to some attractions. It's available from student unions, hostelling organisations and some travel agencies; for more information, see the website of the **International Student Travel Confederation** (ISTC; www.istc.org).

The ISTC is also the body behind the International Youth Travel Card (IYTC or Go25), which is issued to people between 12 and 26 years of age who are not full-time students, and gives equivalent benefits to the ISIC. A similar ISTC brainchild is the International Teacher Identity Card (ITIC), available to teaching professionals.

EMBASSIES & CONSULATES

The website of the **Department of Foreign Affairs & Trade** (www.dfat.gov.au) provides a full listing of all Australian diplomatic missions overseas.

Embassies & Consulates in Australia

The principal diplomatic representations to Australia are in Canberra. There are also representatives of some countries in Brisbane, Melbourne and Sydney; look in the *Yellow Pages* directory for a complete listing.

Canada Canberra (Map p158; ☎ 02-6270 4000; http://geo.international.gc.ca/asia/australia/; Commonwealth Ave, Canberra, ACT 2600); Sydney (Map pp186-7; ☎ 02-9364 3000; Level 5, 111 Harrington St, Sydney, NSW 2000)

France Canberra (Map p158; ☎ 02-6216 0100; www.ambafrance-au.org; 6 Perth Ave, Yarralumla, ACT 2600); Sydney (Map pp186-7; ☎ 02-9261 5779; www.consulfrance-sydney.org; Level 26, St Martins Tower, 31 Market St, Sydney, NSW 2000)

Germany Canberra (Map p158; ☎ 02-6270 1911; www.germanembassy.org.au; 119 Empire Circuit, Yarralumla, ACT 2600); Sydney (Map pp182-3; ☎ 02-9328 7733; 13 Trelawney St, Woollahra, NSW 2025); Melbourne (Map pp76-7; ☎ 03-9864 6888; 480 Punt Rd, South Yarra, Vic 3141)

Ireland Canberra (Map p158; ☎ 02-6273 3022; irish emb@cyberone.com.au; 20 Arkana St, Yarralumla, ACT 2600); Sydney (Map pp186-7; ☎ 02-9231 6999; Level 30, 400 George St, Sydney, NSW 2000)

Japan Canberra (Map p158; ☎ 02-6273 3244; www.japan.org.au; 112 Empire Circuit, Yarralumla, ACT 2600); Sydney (Map pp186-7; ☎ 02-9231 3455; Level 34, Colonial Centre, 52 Martin Pl, Sydney, NSW 2000)

Netherlands Canberra (Map p158; ☎ 02-6220 9400; www.netherlands.org.au; 120 Empire Circuit, Yarralumla, ACT 2600); Sydney (Map pp182-3; ☎ 02-9387 6644; Level 23, Tower 2, 101 Grafton St, Bondi Junction, NSW 2022)

New Zealand (www.nzembassy.com/australia) Canberra (Map p158; ☎ 02-6270 4211; Commonwealth Ave, Canberra, ACT 2600); Sydney (Map pp186-7; ☎ 02-8256 2000; Level 10, 55 Hunter St, Sydney, NSW 2001)

Singapore (Map p158; ☎ 02-6271 2000; www.mfa.gov.sg/canberra; 17 Forster Cres, Yarralumla, ACT 2600)

South Africa (Map p158; ☎ 02-6272 7300; www.sahc.org.au; cnr Rhodes Pl & State Circle, Yarralumla, Canberra, ACT 2600)

UK Canberra (Map p158; ☎ 02-6270 6666; www.britaus.net; Commonwealth Ave, Yarralumla, ACT 2600); Sydney (Map pp186-7; ☎ 02-9247 7521; 16th fl, 1 Macquarie Pl, Sydney, NSW 2000); Melbourne (Map pp78-9; ☎ 03-9652 1600; 11th fl, 90 Collins St, Melbourne, Vic 3000)

USA Canberra (Map p158; ☎ 02-6214 5600; http://usembassy-australia.state.gov; 21 Moonah Pl, Yarralumla, ACT 2600); Sydney (Map pp186-7; ☎ 02-9373 9200; Level 59, 19-29 Martin Pl, Sydney, NSW 2000); Melbourne (Map p92; ☎ 03-9526 5900; Level 6, 553 St Kilda Rd, Melbourne, Vic 3004)

FESTIVALS & EVENTS

Some of the most enjoyable festivals are also the most typically Australian, such as surf lifesaving competitions on beaches during summer. There are also some big city-based street festivals, sporting events, and arts festivals that showcase comedy, music and dance.

The following is a snapshot of some of the many festivals and special events held along the East Coast during the year. Tourist offices should be able to give precise dates of these and other events.

January

Midsumma (www.midsumma.org.au) Melbourne's gay, lesbian and transgender festival runs through January and February, starts with a street party, includes the famous Red Raw dance party and ends with the Midsumma Carnival in early February.

Big Day Out (www.bigdayout.com) This huge open-air music concert tours Sydney, Melbourne and the Gold Coast (as well as Adelaide and Perth), stopping over for one day in each city. It attracts big-name international acts and dozens of local bands.

Australian Open Tennis Championships (www.australianopen.com) Melbourne, late January (see p90).

February

Sydney Gay & Lesbian Mardi Gras (www.mardigras.org.au) One of Australia's biggest and wildest festivals, the month-long Mardi Gras has an amazing street parade down Oxford St and a riotous Mardi Gras party.

March/April

Australia Formula One Grand Prix (www.grandprix.com.au) Melbourne reels in early March to the roar of engines and the smell of exhaust.

East Coast Blues and Roots Festival (www.bluesfest
.com.au) There's an explosion of music over the Easter long
weekend when artists from all over the world set up camp
in lovely Byron Bay.
Melbourne International Comedy Festival (www
.comedyfestival.com.au) Just over three weeks of laughs can
be had at one of the largest comedy festivals in the world.

May
Nimbin Mardi Grass The alternative community of
Nimbin swells for this mother-of-all-hippy-festivals – pitch
a tent and chill out, man.
Wintermoon Festival (www.wintermoonfestival.com)
Held 70km north of Mackay each year around May/June,
this festival is a great opportunity to hear local and
interstate musicians strut their stuff.
Sorry Day (www.journeyofhealing.com) On 26 May each
year, the anniversary of the tabling in 1997 of the *Bringing
Them Home* report, Australians acknowledge the continuing
pain and suffering of indigenous Australians affected by
Australia's one-time child-removal practices and policies.

June
Cooktown Discovery Festival Commemorating Captain
Cook's landing in 1770, this knees-up is held over the
Queen's Birthday weekend.

July
Queensland Music Festival (www.queenslandmusic
festival.com.au) Originally known as the Brisbane Festival
of Music. Held biennially (odd-numbered years), this
festival features Australian and international musicians and
styles: jazz, rock, indigenous, classical and world music.

August
Hervey Bay Whale Festival (www.herveybaywhale
festival.com.au) Held over a fortnight, this festival celebrates the return of these magnificent creatures.

September
AFL Grand Final (www.afl.com.au) The football season
culminates with one of Australia's biggest sporting events:
the AFL Grand Final at the MCG in Melbourne on the last
Saturday in September.

October
IndyCar (www.indy.com.au) Rev your engine for the
IndyCar race and the parties that follow in its tailwind.
Surfers Paradise is manic at the best of times but during this
three-day celebration it really goes off. See p298 for more.
Melbourne International Arts Festival (www.mel
bournefestival.com.au) This annual festival offers some of
the best of opera, theatre, dance and the visual arts from
around Australia and the world. It starts in early October
and runs to early November.

November
Melbourne Cup (www.melbournecup.com.au) Australia's premier horse race is in Melbourne, but the whole
country shuts down while the race is run. Many country
towns schedule race meetings to coincide with it; people
take the afternoon off work and wear posh hats at the pub.

December
Sydney to Hobart Yacht Race (rolexsydneyhobart.com)
Sydney Harbour is a sight to behold on Boxing Day (26 December), when boats of all shapes and sizes crowd its waters
to farewell the yachts competing in this gruelling race.
Woodford Folk Festival (www.woodfordfolkfestival
.com) Held between Christmas and New Year, this five-day
festival in Queensland's Glass House Mountains is Australia's largest folk festival (see the boxed text, p338).

FOOD
There's an impressive range and quality of
food in the major cities of the East Coast,
largely thanks to the immigrants who flooded
into Australia in the late 20th century, bringing their cuisines with them. The eating
recommendations provided in this book are
grouped into restaurants, cafés, quick eats,
and self-catering.

Quality restaurants charge from $15 to
$40 or more for a main course. The best
value can be found in ethnic restaurants and
modern cafés, where a good meal in casual
surroundings can cost less than $20 and a
cooked breakfast will set you back about $10.
A number of inner-city pubs offer upmarket
restaurant-style fare, but most serve standard
(often large-portion) bistro meals, usually in
the $10 to $20 range. Bar (or counter) meals,
which are eaten in the public bar, usually cost
between $6 and $10. Generally, opening hours
for breakfast are between 6am and 11am,
lunch is served from around noon to 3pm
and dinner usually starts after 6pm.

See p51 for more on what makes the East
Coast such a dining delight.

GAY & LESBIAN TRAVELLERS
The East Coast of Australia – Sydney especially –
is a popular destination for gay and lesbian
travellers. Certain areas are the focus of the gay
and lesbian communities: Cairns and Noosa
in Queensland; Sydney's Oxford St and Kings
Cross; the Blue Mountains, Hunter Valley and
the NSW north-coast hinterland; and the
Melbourne suburbs of Prahran, St Kilda and
Collingwood are all popular areas. As well as
Sydney's Mardi Gras (opposite) in February to

early March, there's Melbourne's Midsumma Festival (p486) in January and February.

In general Australians are open-minded about homosexuality, but the further out of the big towns and cities you get, the more likely you are to run into homophobia. Homosexual acts are legal in all states but the age of consent between males varies. In the Australian Capital Territory, Victoria and NSW it is 16 years, and in Queensland it is 18.

Australia's gay community produces a wide range of publications including *DNA, Lesbians on the Loose* and the art magazine *Blue*.

Useful websites:

Gay & Lesbian Tourism Australia (Galta; www.galta .com.au) General info.

Pink Board (www.pinkboard.com.au) Sydney-based, with useful forums.

Queer Australia (www.queeraustralia.com) More general info.

HOLIDAYS
Public Holidays

Public holidays vary quite a bit from state to state. The following is a list of the main national and state public holidays; for precise dates (which may vary from year to year), check locally (* indicates holidays are only observed locally).

NATIONAL
New Year's Day 1 January
Australia Day 26 January
Easter (Good Friday to Easter Monday) March/April
Anzac Day 25 April
Queen's Birthday Second Monday in June
Christmas Day 25 December
Boxing Day 26 December

NEW SOUTH WALES
Bank Holiday First Monday in August
Labour Day First Monday in October

QUEENSLAND
Labour Day First Monday in May
RNA Show Day (Brisbane) August*

VICTORIA
Labour Day Second Monday in March
Melbourne Cup Day First Tuesday in November*

School Holidays

The Christmas holiday season, from mid-December to late January, is part of the summer school vacation; it's the time you are most likely to find East Coast accommodation booked out and long queues at tourist attractions. There are three shorter school-holiday periods during the year, but they vary by a week or two from state to state. They fall from early to mid-April, late June to mid-July, and late September to early October.

INSURANCE

Don't underestimate the importance of a good travel-insurance policy that covers theft, loss and medical problems. Most policies offer lower and higher medical-expense options; the higher ones are chiefly for countries that have extremely high medical costs, such as the USA. There is a wide variety of policies available, so compare the small print.

Some policies specifically exclude designated 'dangerous activities' such as scuba diving, parasailing, bungee jumping, motorcycling, skiing and even bushwalking. If you plan on doing any of these things, make sure the policy you choose fully covers you for your activity of choice.

See p505 for information on health insurance and p500 for information on insurance related to car travel and rental.

INTERNET ACCESS

Most East Coast towns have places where you can access the internet, usually for about $6 to $8 an hour. In really popular places, you'll find access in convenience stores, travel agencies, visitors centres and more. Hostels almost always have internet access.

Wi-fi is finally becoming more widespread in Australia. Popular tourist towns often have cafés with wireless access – often for free (with purchase). Ask at visitors centres. Hotels are catching up with other parts of the world as well and you can usually find a place that will let you get online with your laptop or other device in most towns. Beware, however, many chain hotels and more expensive places charge outrageous prices for wi-fi access, often as much as $20 an hour. In this book, we've noted places that let you surf with wi-fi in the listings.

Also see Internet Resources, p26.

LEGAL MATTERS

Most travellers will have no contact with the Australian police or any other part of the legal system. Those that do are likely to experience it while driving. The country's roads have a significant police presence, with the power

---

TAX REFUNDS

If you purchase new or secondhand goods with a total minimum value of $300 from any one supplier no more than 30 days before you leave Australia, you are entitled under the Tourist Refund Scheme (TRS) to a refund of any GST paid (usually 10%). The scheme only applies to goods you take with you as hand luggage or wear onto the plane or ship. Also note that the refund is valid for goods bought from more than one supplier, but only if at least $300 has been spent at each. For more information, contact the **Australian Customs Service** (☎ 1300 363 263; www.customs.gov.au).

---

to stop your car and ask to see your licence (you're required to carry it), check your vehicle for roadworthiness, and also to insist that you take a breath test to check your blood-alcohol level – needless to say, drink-driving offences are taken very seriously here.

First offenders who are caught with small amounts of illegal drugs are likely to get a fine rather than go to jail, but nonetheless the recording of a conviction against you may affect your visa status.

If you are arrested, it's your right to phone a friend, a relative or a lawyer before any formal questioning begins. Legal Aid is available only in serious cases and only to the truly needy (for links to Legal Aid offices see www.nla.aust.net.au). However, many solicitors do not charge for an initial consultation.

MAPS

You'll find plenty of maps available when you arrive in Australia. Visitors centres usually have free maps of the region and towns, although quality varies. Automobile associations (p499) are a good source of reliable road maps.

City street directories such as those produced by Ausway and UBD are very useful but they're expensive, bulky and usually only worth getting if you intend to do a lot of driving in one city.

For bushwalking and other outdoor activities for which large-scale maps are essential, browse the topographic sheets put out by **Geoscience Australia** (☎ 02-6249 9111, 1800 800 173; www.ga.gov.au). Many of the more popular sheets are usually available over the counter at outdoor-equipment shops.

MONEY

In this book, unless otherwise stated, all prices given in dollars refer to Australian dollars. Exchange rates are listed inside the front cover. For an idea of the costs of travel in East Coast Australia, see p23. Many purchases have a 10% goods and services tax (GST) included in the price.

ATMs & Eftpos

ANZ, Commonwealth, National and Westpac bank branches are found nationwide and most have 24-hour ATMs. Of course, you won't find ATMs everywhere – not off the beaten track or in very small towns – so make sure you've got cash if you're heading well away from population centres. Most ATMs now accept cards from other banks and are linked to international networks.

Eftpos (Electronic Funds Transfer at Point of Sale) is a very convenient service that many Australian businesses have embraced. It means you can use your bank card to pay for services or purchases direct, and often withdraw cash as well. Eftpos is available practically everywhere these days, but many places demand a minimum purchase of about $10.

Credit Cards

Visa and MasterCard credit cards are accepted widely along the East Coast. Charge cards such as Diners Club and American Express are not as widely accepted. Credit cards can also be used to get cash advances over the counter at banks and from many ATMs, depending on the card. Fees for using your credit card at a foreign bank or ATM can be high; ask before you leave.

The most flexible option is to carry both a credit and a debit card; some banking institutions link the two to one card.

Currency

Australia's currency is the Australian dollar, made up of 100 cents. There are 5¢, 10¢, 20¢, 50¢, $1 and $2 coins, and $5, $10, $20, $50 and $100 notes. Although the smallest coin in circulation is 5¢, prices are often still marked in single cents, and then rounded to the nearest 5¢ when you come to pay.

Exchanging Money

Changing travellers cheques or foreign currency usually isn't a problem at banks in the region. Licensed moneychangers such as

American Express will only be found in major cities; most large hotels will change currency or travellers cheques for guests, but the rates are generally poor.

Tipping

In Australia, tipping is not mandatory as it is in the USA. As in the UK and most of continental Europe, it's customary to tip in restaurants and also in upmarket cafés. This applies more in the cities, particularly Melbourne and Sydney. Out in the sticks, a tip might be received with a level of surprise. Tip if you think the service warrants it; 5% to 10% of the bill is usually enough. Taxi drivers don't expect tips as such but many of them do expect you to round up to the nearest dollar and may fuss over the handing out of change if you don't offer.

Travellers Cheques

Amex, Thomas Cook and other well-known international brands of travellers cheques are easily exchanged. You need to present your passport for identification when cashing them.

Increasingly, international travellers simply withdraw cash from ATMs, enjoying the convenience and the usually decent exchange rates.

POST

Australia's postal services are efficient and reasonably cheap. **Australia Post** (www.auspost.com .au) has offices in almost every town although some are part of larger commercial establishments and it may seem easier to buy a card than actually mail it.

All post offices will hold mail for visitors, and some city GPOs (main or general post offices) have very busy poste restante sections. You need to provide some form of identification (such as a passport) to collect mail. Post office opening hours are generally 9am to 5pm Monday to Friday.

SOLO TRAVELLERS

People travelling alone along the East Coast face the unpredictability that is an inherent part of making contact with entire communities of strangers: sometimes you'll be completely ignored, and other times you'll be greeted with such enthusiasm it's as if you've been spontaneously adopted. Suffice to say that the latter moments will likely become highlights of your trip.

Solo travellers are a common sight in Australia and there is certainly no stigma attached to lone visitors. In some places you may find there's an expectation that solo visitors should engage in some way with the locals, particularly in rural pubs where keeping to yourself can prove harder than it sounds. Women travelling on their own should exercise caution when in less-populated areas.

TELEPHONE

The two main telecommunication companies are **Telstra** (www.telstra.com.au) and **Optus** (www.optus .com.au). Both are also major players in the mobile (cell) market, along with **Vodafone** (www .vodafone.com.au), **Virgin** (www.virginmobile.com.au) and **3** (www.three.com.au).

Domestic & International Calls
INFORMATION & TOLL-FREE CALLS

Numbers starting with ☎ 190 are usually recorded-information services, charged at anything from 35¢ to $5 or more per minute (more if dialled from mobiles and payphones). To make a reverse-charge (collect) call from any public or private phone, just dial ☎ 1800-REVERSE (738 3773) or ☎ 12 550.

Toll-free numbers (prefix ☎ 1800) can be called free of charge from anywhere in Australia, though they may not be accessible from interstate or from mobile phones. Calls to numbers beginning with ☎ 13 or ☎ 1300 are charged at the rate of a local call. Telephone numbers beginning with ☎ 1800, ☎ 13 or ☎ 1300 cannot be dialled from outside Australia.

INTERNATIONAL CALLS

If dialling from overseas, the country code is ☎ 61 and you need to drop the 0 (zero) in the area codes.

Most payphones allow ISD (International Subscriber Dialling) calls; the cost and international dialling code will vary depending on which provider you're using. International calls from Australia are very cheap and subject to specials that reduce the rates even more, so it's worth shopping around.

The **Country Direct service** (☎ 1800 801 800) connects callers in Australia with operators in nearly 60 countries to make reverse-charge or credit-card calls.

When calling overseas you need to dial the international access code from Australia (☎ 0011 or ☎ 0018).

INTERNET CALLS

Many internet places let you make cheap international calls; sometimes for as little 1¢ per minute. It's also common at the more savvy places for the computers to be equipped so you can use Skype (www.skype.com) and other voice-over-internet (VoIP) services.

LOCAL CALLS

Local calls from private phones cost 15¢ to 30¢ while local calls from public phones cost 50¢; both involve unlimited talk time. Calls to mobile phones attract higher rates and are timed.

LONG DISTANCE CALLS & AREA CODES

For long-distance calls, East Coast Australia uses four Subscriber Trunk Dialling (STD) area codes. STD calls can be made from virtually any public phone and are cheaper during off-peak hours, generally between 7pm and 7am. Long-distance calls (ie to more than about 50km away) within these areas are charged at long-distance rates, even though they have the same area code. The following are the area codes in East Coast Australia:

State/Territory	Area code
Australian Capital Territory	☎ 02
New South Wales	☎ 02
Queensland	☎ 07
Victoria	☎ 03

Mobile Phones

Local numbers with the prefixes ☎ 04xx or ☎ 04xxx belong to mobile phones. Australia's mobile networks service more than 90% of the population, but vast tracts of Australia's interior are not covered. The East Coast gets good reception, but away from the major towns it can be haphazard or nonexistent.

Australia's digital network is compatible with GSM 900 and 1800 (used in Europe), but generally not with some CDMA systems used in the USA or Japan. It's easy and cheap enough to get connected short-term, though, as the main service providers all have prepaid mobile schemes. If you have an unlocked GSM phone, you can get a local SIM card and phone number for under $30 (with a basic phone $60); try any of the carriers listed above.

Phonecards

A wide range of phonecards is available; these can be bought at newsagents and post offices for a fixed dollar value (usually $10, $20,

$30 etc) and can be used with any public or private phone by dialling a toll-free access number and then the PIN number on the card. Once again, it's well worth shopping around. Some public phones also accept credit cards, although this can be a ripoff.

TIME

Victoria, NSW and Queensland keep Eastern Standard Time, which is 10 hours ahead of Greenwich Mean Time (UTC). When it's noon in Sydney, the time in London is 3am (April to October) or 1am (November to March); 5pm/7pm the previous day in Los Angeles, 8pm/10pm the previous day in New York and 2pm in Auckland.

Daylight savings – for which clocks are put forward an hour – operates in Victoria and NSW from the last Sunday in October to the first Sunday in April. Queensland doesn't have daylight-savings time.

TRAVELLERS WITH DISABILITIES

Disability awareness in Australia is reasonably high. Legislation requires that new accommodation must meet accessibility standards and tourist operators must not discriminate.

Reliable information is the key ingredient for travellers with disabilities, and the best place to start is the **National Information Communication & Awareness Network** (Nican; ☎ /TTY 02-6241 1220, TTY 1800 806 769; www.nican.com.au). It's an Australia-wide directory providing information on access, accommodation, sporting and recreational activities, transport and specialist tour operators.

The website of the **Australian Tourist Commission** (ATC; www.australia.com) publishes detailed, downloadable information for people with disabilities, including travel and transport tips and contact addresses of organisations in each state.

TOURIST INFORMATION

Tourist information is provided in Australia by various regional and local offices, details of which are given in the relevant city and town sections throughout this book. Each state has a government-run tourist organisation ready to inundate you with information. Check out the following:

Tourism New South Wales (www.visitnsw.com)
Tourism Queensland (☎ 13 88 33; www.queensland holidays.com.au)
Tourism Victoria (☎ 13 28 42; www.visitvictoria.com)

DIRECTORY

The **Australian Tourism Commission** (www.aus tralia.com) is the government body charged with luring foreign visitors; the website has information in eight languages. For ATC branches in other countries visit www.tourism .australia.com.

VISAS

All visitors to Australia need a visa. Only New Zealand nationals are exempt, and even they receive a 'special category' visa on arrival.

Visa application forms are available from Australian diplomatic missions overseas, travel agents and the website of the **Department of Immigration & Citizenship** (☎ 13 18 81; www .immi.gov.au). There are several types of visa, as explained following.

Electronic Travel Authority

Many visitors can get an Electronic Travel Authority (ETA) through travel agents registered with the International Air Transport Association (IATA) or through an overseas airline. They make the application direct when you buy a ticket and issue the ETA, which replaces the usual visa stamped in your passport; it's common practice for travel agents to charge a fee for issuing an ETA (usually US$25). This system is available to passport holders of some 32 countries, including the UK, the USA and Canada, most European and Scandinavian countries, Malaysia, Singapore, Japan and Korea. You can also make an online ETA application at www.eta.immi.gov.au, which costs $20.

Tourist Visas

Short-term tourist visas have largely been replaced by the ETA. However, if you are from a country not covered by the ETA, or you want to stay longer than three months, you'll need to apply for a visa. Standard Tourist Visas (which cost $70) allow one entry (in some cases multiple entries), for a stay of up to 12 months, and are valid for use within 12 months of issue.

Visa Extensions

A Further Stay visa can be applied for within Australia through the Department of Immigration and Citizenship. It's best to apply at least two or three weeks before your visa expires. The application fee is $205 and is nonrefundable, even if your application is rejected.

Working Holiday Makers Visas

Young (aged 18 to 30) visitors from Belgium, Canada, China, Cyprus, Denmark, Estonia, Finland, France, Germany, Hong Kong, Ireland, Italy, Japan, Korea, Malta, the Netherlands, Norway, Sweden, Taiwan and the UK are eligible for a WHM visa, which allows you to visit for up to one year and gain casual employment.

The emphasis of this visa is on casual and not full-time employment, so you're only supposed to work for any one employer for a maximum of six months. This visa can only be applied for at Australian diplomatic missions abroad and you can't change from a tourist visa to a WHM visa once you're in Australia. You can also apply for this visa online at www.immi.gov.au/visitors/working-holiday.

You can apply for this visa up to a year in advance, which is worthwhile as there's a limit on the number issued each year. Conditions include having a return air ticket or sufficient funds for a return or onward fare, and an application fee of $185 is charged. For details of what sort of employment is available and where, see p493.

VOLUNTEERING

There are a lot of opportunities to volunteer your time and expertise in Australia. Resources include:

Conservation Volunteers Australia (CVA; ☎ 1800 032 501, 03-5330 2600; www.conservationvolunteers.com.au) Organises practical conservation projects such as tree planting, walking-track construction and flora and fauna surveys.

Go Volunteer (www.govolunteer.com.au) National website listing volunteer opportunities.

i-to-i (www.i-to-i.com) Conservation-based volunteer holidays in Australia.

Volunteering Australia (www.volunteeringaustralia .org) Support, advice and volunteer training.

Willing Workers on Organic Farms (WWOOF; ☎ 03-5155 0218; www.wwoof.com.au) Work on a farm in return for bed and board.

You will also find local opportunities listed in chapters throughout this book. For a list of opportunities in Brisbane and Queensland, see p318.

WOMEN TRAVELLERS

Australia is generally a safe place for women travellers, although the usual sensible precautions apply. It's best to avoid walking alone late at night in any of the major cities and towns. And if you're out on the town, always keep enough money aside for a taxi back to your accommodation. Lone women should be wary of staying in basic pub accommodation unless it looks safe and well managed.

WORK

New Zealanders can work in Australia without having to apply for a special visa or permit, but other short-term visitors can only work in Australia if they have a Working Holiday Makers (WHM) visa (see opposite). Major tourist centres such as the resort towns along the Queensland coast and the ski fields of Victoria and NSW are all good prospects for casual work during peak seasons.

Seasonal fruit-picking (harvesting) relies on casual labour, and there is something to be picked, pruned or farmed somewhere in Australia all year round. It's hard work that involves early-morning starts, and you're usually paid by how much you pick (per bin/bucket); expect to earn A$50 to A$60 a day to start with, more when you get quicker at it.

Other options for casual employment include factory work, labouring, bar work and waiting on tables. People with computer, secretarial, nursing and teaching skills can find work temping in the major cities by registering with a relevant agency. See the websites below for contact details of some agencies.

Information

Backpacker accommodation, magazines and newspapers are good resources for local work opportunities.

Useful websites:

Career One (www.careerone.com.au) General employment site, good for metropolitan areas.

Face2Face Fundraising (www.face2facefundraising.com.au) Fundraising jobs for charities and not-for-profits.

Good Cause (www.goodcause.com.au) Fundraising jobs for charities and not-for-profits.

Harvest Trail (www.jobsearch.gov.au/harvesttrail) Harvest jobs around Australia.

Seek (www.seek.com) General employment site, good for metropolitan areas.

Workabout Australia (www.workaboutaustralia.com.au) By Barry Brebner; it gives a state-by-state breakdown of seasonal work opportunities.

Work Oz (www.workoz.com) Visa, travel, bank account and other practical information regarding working in Australia.

Taxes

If you have a WHM visa, you should apply for a tax file number (TFN). Without it, tax will be deducted from any wages you receive at the maximum rate (around 47%). Apply for a TFN online via the **ATO** (www.ato.gov.au); it takes about four weeks to be issued. The office can provide additional info about paying taxes and refunds.

Transport

CONTENTS

GETTING THERE & AWAY

This section covers how to get to and from major cities along the East Coast for visitors to Australia. For information about travelling along the East Coast see p497.

ENTERING THE COUNTRY

Disembarkation in Australia is generally a straightforward affair, with only the usual customs declarations (p483) and the race to the luggage carousel to endure. However, global instability in the last few years has resulted in conspicuously increased security in Australian airports, and you may find that customs procedures are now more time-consuming. Morning immigration lines at Sydney Airport's international terminal can seem endless.

THINGS CHANGE...

The information in this chapter is particularly vulnerable to change. Check directly with the airline or a travel agent to make sure you understand how a fare (and ticket you may buy) works and be aware of the security requirements for international travel. Shop carefully. The details given in this chapter should be regarded as pointers and are not a substitute for your own careful, up-to-date research.

Passport

There are no restrictions when it comes to foreign citizens entering Australia. If you have a visa (p492) you should be fine.

AIR

Domestic

The domestic airline industry has undergone some major upheavals in recent years, with intense competition among airlines. Few people pay full fare as the airlines continue to offer a wide range of discounts. These come and go and there are regular special fares, so keep your eyes open.

See p497 for a list of carriers flying within Australia.

International

There are lots of competing airlines and a wide variety of air fares to choose from if you're flying in from Asia, Europe or North America, but you'll still pay a lot for a flight. If you plan to fly at a particularly popular time of year (Christmas is notoriously difficult for Sydney and Melbourne) or on a particularly popular route (such as Hong Kong, Bangkok or Singapore to Sydney or Melbourne), make your arrangements well in advance of your trip.

The high season for flights into Australia is roughly over the country's summer (December to February), with slightly less of a premium on fares over the shoulder months (October/November and March/April). The low season generally tallies with the winter months (June to August).

Airlines

The East Coast's Sydney and Melbourne airports (Australia's busiest international gateways), as well as those in Brisbane and Cairns have international service.

Air Canada (☎ 1300 655 767; www.aircanada.ca) Flies to Sydney.

Air New Zealand (☎ 13 24 76; www.airnz.com.au) Flies to Brisbane, Cairns, Melbourne and Sydney.

British Airways (☎ 1300 767 177; www.britishairways.com.au) Flies to Sydney.

Cathay Pacific (☎ 13 17 47; www.cathaypacific.com) Flies to Brisbane, Cairns, Melbourne and Sydney.

CLIMATE CHANGE & TRAVEL

Climate change is a serious threat to the ecosystems that humans rely upon, and air travel is the fastest-growing contributor to the problem. Lonely Planet regards travel, overall, as a global benefit, but believes we all have a responsibility to limit our personal impact on global warming.

Flying & Climate Change

Pretty much every form of motor travel generates CO_2 (the main cause of human-induced climate change) but planes are far and away the worst offenders, not just because of the sheer distances they allow us to travel, but because they release greenhouse gases high into the atmosphere. The statistics are frightening: two people taking a return flight between Europe and the US will contribute as much to climate change as an average household's gas and electricity consumption over a whole year.

Carbon Offset Schemes

Climatecare.org and other websites use 'carbon calculators' that allow jetsetters to offset the greenhouse gases they are responsible for with contributions to energy-saving projects and other climate-friendly initiatives in the developing world – including projects in India, Honduras, Kazakhstan and Uganda.

Lonely Planet, together with Rough Guides and other concerned partners in the travel industry, supports the carbon offset scheme run by climatecare.org. Lonely Planet offsets all of its staff and author travel.

For more information check out our website: lonelyplanet.com.

Emirates (☎ 1300 303 777; www.emirates.com) Flies to Brisbane, Melbourne and Sydney.

Garuda Indonesia (☎ 1300 365 330; www.garuda -indonesia.com) Flies to Brisbane, Melbourne and Sydney.

Japan Airlines (☎ 02-9272 1111; www.au.jal.com) Flies to Brisbane, Cairns, Melbourne and Sydney.

Malaysian Airlines (☎ 13 26 27; www.malaysiaair lines.com.au) Flies to Brisbane, Melbourne and Sydney.

Qantas (☎ 13 13 13; www.qantas.com.au) Flies to all major Australian cities.

Singapore Airlines (☎ 13 10 11; www.singaporeair .com.au) Flies to Brisbane, Melbourne and Sydney.

Thai Airways International (☎ 1300 651 960; www .thaiairways.com.au) Flies to Brisbane, Melbourne and Sydney.

Tiger Airways (www.tigerairways.com; 03-9335 3033) Flies to Melbourne via Darwin and Perth and then on to numerous East Coast destinations.

United Airlines (☎ 13 17 77; www.unitedairlines.com .au) Flies to Melbourne and Sydney.

Virgin Atlantic (☎ 1300 727 340; www.virgin-atlantic .com) Flies to Sydney.

Tickets

Travel agents may offer good fares to Australia but with airline commissions down, you may have to pay a service fee to buy a ticket.

Plenty of websites exist to find the best airfares to Australia. It's usually a good idea to compare the results (both fares and routings) from several sites. In addition airline websites often have web-only fares unavailable elsewhere.

Cheap Flights (www.cheapflights.com) Compares the fares found on several sites.

Cheapest Flights (www.cheapestflights.co.uk) Cheap worldwide flights from the UK.

Expedia (www.expedia.com) Large mainstream site; has international variations for several countries.

Flight Centre International (www.flightcentre.com) Respected operator handling direct flights, with sites for Australia, Canada, New Zealand, the UK and the USA.

Kayak (www.kayak.com) Good site; compares results from airline and booking sites.

Opodo (www.opodo.com) Has localised French, German and UK sites.

Orbitz (www.orbitz.com) Large mainstream site serving travellers from the US.

STA (www.statravel.com) Prominent in international student travel, but you don't have to be a student; site linked to worldwide STA sites.

Travel.com.au (www.travel.com.au) Good Australian site; look up fares and flights into and out of the country.

Travelocity (www.travelocity.com) Large mainstream site; has international variations for several countries.

Roundtheworld.com (www.roundtheworldflights.com) Allows you to build your own multiflight trip from the UK.

Zuji (www.zuji.com.au) Good Asia Pacific–based site.

ROUND-THE-WORLD TICKETS

If you are flying to Australia from the other side of the world, round-the-world (RTW) tickets can be real bargains. They're generally put together by the three biggest airline alliances – **Star Alliance** (www.staralliance.com), **Oneworld** (www.oneworldalliance.com) and **Skyteam** (www.skyteam.com) – and give you a limited period (usually a year) in which to circumnavigate the globe. You can go anywhere the participating airlines go, as long as you stay within the prescribed kilometre extents or number of stops and don't backtrack when flying between continents. See the relevant websites for details.

An alternative type of RTW ticket is one put together by a travel agent. These are usually more expensive than airline RTW fares but allow you to devise your own itinerary.

Asia

Most Asian countries offer competitive airfare deals, but Bangkok, Singapore and Hong Kong are the best places to shop around for discount tickets.

Flights between Hong Kong and Australia are notoriously heavily booked. Flights to and from Bangkok and Singapore are often part of the longer Europe-to-Australia route so they are also in demand. Plan your preferred itinerary well in advance.

Tiger Airways, a Singapore-based budget carrier, has services from Asia via Singapore to Darwin and Perth and then on to Melbourne, where it has a burgeoning network of domestic flights.

Canada

The air routes from Canada are similar to those from mainland USA, with most passengers stopping in a US gateway such as Los Angeles or San Francisco, although Air Canada now has nonstop Vancouver–Sydney service.

Continental Europe

From major European destinations, most flights travel to Australia via one of the Asian capitals. Some flights are also routed through London before arriving in Australia via Singapore, Bangkok, Hong Kong or Kuala Lumpur.

New Zealand

Air New Zealand and Qantas operate a network of flights linking key New Zealand cities with most major Australian gateway cities, while a few other international airlines include New Zealand and Australia on their Asia–Pacific routes.

Pacific Blue, a subsidiary of budget airline Virgin Blue, flies between both Christchurch and Wellington and several Australian cities, including Perth, Hobart and Adelaide.

There's usually not a significant difference in price between seasons, as this is a popular route year-round, although prices can increase over the Christmas period.

UK & Ireland

There are two routes from the UK: the western route via the USA and the Pacific; and the eastern route via the Middle East and Asia. Flights are usually cheaper and more frequent on the latter. Some of the best deals around are with Emirates, Gulf Air, Malaysia Airlines, Japan Airlines and Thai Airways International. British Airways, Singapore Airlines and Qantas generally have higher fares but may offer a more direct route.

USA

Most of the flights between the North American mainland and Australia travel to and from the USA's west coast, with Los Angeles and San Francisco the gateways.

Partial deregulation of the Australian and US air market in 2008 will allow some new carriers on these routes that will hopefully bring lower fares to what have been overpriced routes (Qantas and United have enjoyed a duopoly). The first airline to announce service is **V Australia** (www.vaustralia.com.au), an offshoot of Virgin Blue.

Numerous airlines offer flights via Asia or various Pacific islands.

SEA

It's possible (though by no means easy or safe) to make your way between Australia and countries such as Papua New Guinea and Indonesia, and between New Zealand and Australia and some smaller Pacific islands, by hitching rides or crewing on yachts – usually you have to at least contribute towards food. Try asking around at harbours, marinas and sailing clubs.

Good places on the Australian East Coast include Coffs Harbour, Great Keppel Island, Airlie Beach and the Whitsundays, and Cairns – basically anywhere boats call.

GETTING AROUND

AIR

East Coast Australia is well serviced by airlines. The following have service throughout the region and across Australia.

Jetstar (☎ 13 15 38; www.jetstar.com.au) Budget offshoot of Qantas has extensive service.

Qantas/QantasLink (☎ 13 13 13; www.qantas.com .au) Service across Australia.

Tiger Airways (www.tigerairways.com) Budget airline with Melbourne as a hub. Serves a swath of East Coast destinations from Mackay to Canberra.

Virgin Blue (☎ 13 67 89; www.virginblue.com.au) Has service throughout Australia.

The following small airlines offer limited regional service within East Coast Australia.

Macair (☎ 13 13 13; www.macair.com.au) Flies to small Queensland towns from Cairns, Townsville and Brisbane.

Regional Express (Rex; ☎ 13 17 13; www.regional express.com.au) Serves primarily small towns from Melbourne and Sydney.

Skytrans (☎ 1800 818 405, 07-4046 2462; www .skytrans.com.au) Flies between Cairns, Cooktown, Brisbane and Palm Island.

BICYCLE

Whether you're hiring a bike to ride around a city or wearing out your chain wheels on a long-distance haul, the East Coast is a great place for cycling. There are bike paths in most major cities, and in the country you'll find thousands of kilometres of good roads. In many areas along the coast the countryside is flat or composed of gently rolling hills.

Much of eastern Australia was settled on the principle of not having more than a day's horse ride between pubs, so it's possible to plan even ultralong routes and still get a shower at the end of each day. Most cyclists carry camping equipment but it's feasible to travel from town to town staying in hostels, hotels or caravan parks.

No matter how fit you are, water is vital. Dehydration is no joke and heatstroke can be life threatening (see p508). It can get very hot in summer, and you should take things easy, wear a helmet with a peak (or a cap under your helmet) and plenty of sunscreen, avoid cycling in the middle of the day and drink lots of water. Remember that it can get very cold in the mountains, so pack appropriately. In the south, be aware of the blistering hot 'northerlies' that can make a northbound cyclist's life hell in summer.

Bicycle helmets are compulsory, as are white front lights and red rear lights for riding at night. Most good-sized towns will have a shop stocking at least basic bike parts.

INFORMATION

The national cycling body is the **Bicycle Federation of Australia** (☎ 02-6249 6761; www.bfa .asn.au). Each state and territory has a touring organisation that can also help with cycling information and put you in touch with touring clubs.

Bicycle New South Wales (☎ 02-9218 5400; www .bicyclensw.org.au)

Bicycle Queensland (☎ 07-3844 1144; www.bq.org.au)

Bicycle Victoria (☎ 03-8636 8888; www.bv.com.au)

Pedal Power ACT (☎ 02-6248 7995; www.pedalpower .org.au)

For more information see p67, and Lonely Planet's *Cycling Australia* (new edition due September 2009).

PURCHASE & HIRE

It can be surprisingly difficult to find places that hire out bikes for longer than a day or two, so if you're coming specifically to tour, it makes sense to bring your own; check with your airline for costs and the degree of dismantling and packing required.

If you arrive in the country without a set of wheels and want to buy a reliable new road cycle or mountain bike, your absolute bottom-level starting point is $400 to $550. To set yourself up with a new bike, plus all the requisite on-the-road equipment such as panniers, helmet etc, your starting point becomes $1500 to $2000. Second-hand bikes are worth checking out in the cities, as are the post-Christmas sales and midyear stocktakes/clearances, when newish cycles can be heavily discounted.

Your best bet for reselling your bike is via the **Trading Post** (www.tradingpost.com.au), which is distributed in newspaper form in many urban centres and also has a busy online trading site.

The rates charged by most outfits for renting road or mountain bikes (not including the discounted fees offered by budget accommodation places to their guests) are anywhere from $10 to $15 per hour and $15 to $40 per day. Security deposits can range from $50 to $200, depending on the rental period.

BUS

Other than hitching, bus travel is generally the cheapest way to get around and it gives you the greatest coverage. But it can be a tedious form of transport and requires a bit of planning if you intend to do more than straightforward city-to-city trips. Travelling by bus also means you can miss out on seeing off-the-beaten-track highlights away from the main coastal highways. Local services can be very hit or miss. See individual city listings in this book to see what bus options exist.

There's only one national bus network, **Greyhound Australia** (☎ 13 14 99; www.greyhound .com.au). The next biggest player on the East Coast is **Premier Motor Service** (☎ 13 34 10; www .premierms.com.au). Premier is the main competitor to Greyhound on the East Coast route and is the only major carrier that still makes the Princes Hwy (Hwy 1) run south of Sydney. It has fewer services per day but usually costs a few dollars less on most routes and goes the distance from Melbourne to Cairns.

There are also many smaller bus companies either operating locally or specialising in one or two main intercity routes. These often offer the best deals – **Firefly Express** (☎ 1800 631 164; www.fireflyexpress.com.au) charges $65 for a Sydney-to-Melbourne express (via the Hume Hwy) for example. In Victoria, **V/Line** (☎ 13 61 96; www.vlinepassenger.com.au) operates bus services to places trains no longer go, and in NSW **Countrylink** (☎ 13 22 32; www.countrylink.nsw.gov.au) does the same.

In most towns up the East Coast there is just one bus terminal, and in very small towns there might not even be a terminal – just a drop-off/pick-up point.

Backpacker Buses

While the companies offering transport options for budget travellers in East Coast Australia are pretty much organised-tour operators, they do also get you from A to B (sometimes with hop-on, hop-off services) and so can be a cost-effective alternative to the big bus companies. The buses are usually smaller, you'll meet lots of other travellers, and the drivers sometimes double as tour guides; conversely, some travellers find the tour-group mentality and inherent limitations don't suit them.

Discounts for card-carrying students and members of hostel organisations are usually available.

Autopia Tours (☎ 1800 000 507; www.autopiatours .com.au) The 3-day Melbourne–Sydney tour goes via Wilsons Prom, the Snowy Mountains and Canberra ($400).

Oz Experience (☎ 1300 300 028; www.ozexperience .com) A hop-on, hop-off service you will either love or hate. Travellers have complained about seat availability and a boozy culture, while others love the social experience. The network covers central, northern and eastern Australia. Travel is one-directional and passes are valid for up to six months with unlimited stops. A Melbourne–Cairns pass is $770.

Bus Passes

Bus passes are a good option if you plan plenty of stopovers. You should book or phone at least a day ahead to reserve a seat if you're using any of the following passes.

Greyhound (☎ 13 14 99; www.greyhound.com.au) offers many passes and it's worth checking its website or brochures, available at travel agents and Greyhound offices, for full details. There's a 10% discount for members of YHA, VIP, Nomads and other approved organisations, as well as card-carrying students.

The Aussie Kilometre Pass is the simplest and gives you a specified amount of travel, starting at 500km ($99) and going up in increments to 20,000km ($2209). The pass is valid for 12 months; you can travel where and in what direction you like, and stop as many times as you like. A 2000km pass ($360) will get you from Brisbane to Cairns, or 4000km ($657) will get you from Melbourne to Cairns.

Greyhound also has several Aussie Explorer Passes, with several covering much of the East Coast. With these passes you don't get the go-anywhere flexibility of the Aussie Kilometre Pass (you can't backtrack), but if you can find a route that suits you it generally works out cheaper.

Premier (☎ 13 34 10; www.premierms.com.au) offers several passes for travel along the East Coast. One good for six months of travel between Melbourne and Cairns costs $320. There are 10% discounts for members of YHA, VIP, Nomads and other approved organisations, as well as card-carrying students.

Classes

There are no separate classes on buses, and the vehicles of the different companies all look pretty similar and are equipped with air-con, toilets and videos. Smoking isn't permitted on Australian buses.

Costs

Following are average, nondiscounted, one-way bus fares on some well-travelled Australian routes. Look for web specials.

Melbourne to Canberra (adult/child/concession $75/65/70)

Melbourne to Sydney (adult/child/concession $80/60/70)

Sydney to Byron Bay (adult/child/concession $90/80/85)

Sydney to Brisbane (adult/child/concession $90/80/85)

Brisbane to Airlie Beach (adult/child/concession $150/130/140)

Brisbane to Cairns (adult/child/concession $200/170/180)

Reservations

During summer, school holidays and public holidays, you should book well ahead, especially on the intercity services. At other times you should have few problems getting onto your preferred service. But if your long-term travel plans rely on catching a particular bus, book at least a day or two ahead.

You should make a reservation at least a day in advance if you're using a travel pass.

CAR & MOTORCYCLE

The best way to see the East Coast is by car – it's certainly the only way to get to those interesting out-of-the-way places without taking a tour.

Diesel and unleaded fuel is available from service stations. LPG (gas) is also available in the populated areas but not always at more remote service stations – if you're on gas it's safer to have dual fuel capacity. Prices vary according to place and time. On main East Coast highways there's usually a small town or a petrol station roughly every 50km or so.

Motorcycles are very popular, as the climate is just about ideal for bikes for much of the year. Bringing your own motorcycle into Australia will entail an expensive shipping exercise, valid registration in the country of origin and a *Carnet De Passages en Douanes*. This is an internationally recognised customs document that allows you to import your vehicle without paying customs duty or taxes. To get one, apply to a motoring organisation/association in your home country. You'll also need a rider's licence and a helmet. A fuel range of 350km will easily cover fuel stops up the East Coast and, for that matter, around the continent. The long, open roads are really made for large-capacity machines above 750cc.

Automobile Associations

The national **Australian Automobile Association** (www.aaa.asn.au) is an umbrella organisation for the various state associations and maintains links with similar bodies throughout the world. Day-to-day operations are handled by the state organisations, which provide emergency breakdown services, literature, excellent touring maps and detailed guides to accommodation and camp sites.

The state organisations have reciprocal arrangements with other states and with similar organisations overseas. So, if you're a member of the National Roads and Motorists Association (NRMA) in NSW, you can use the facilities of the Royal Automobile Club of Victoria (RACV). Similarly, if you're a member of the AAA in the USA, or the RAC or AA in the UK, you can use any of the Australian state organisations' facilities (the maps are worth it alone). Bring proof of membership with you.

The main state association contact details:

NSW & ACT NRMA (☎ 13 21 32; www.nrma.com.au)
Queensland RACQ (☎ 13 19 05; www.racq.com.au)
Victoria RACV (☎ 13 19 55; www.racv.com.au)

INTERSTATE QUARANTINE

When travelling in Australia, whether by land or air, you'll come across signs (mainly in airports, in interstate train stations and at state borders) warning of the possible dangers of carrying fruit, vegetables and plants (which may be infected with a disease or pest) from one area to another. Certain pests and diseases – such as fruit fly, curcubit thrips, grape phylloxera and potato cyst nematodes, to name a few – are prevalent in some areas but not in others, and so for obvious reasons authorities would like to limit them spreading.

There are quarantine inspection posts on some state borders and occasionally elsewhere. While quarantine control often relies on honesty, many posts are staffed and officers are entitled to search your car for undeclared items. Generally they will confiscate all fresh fruit and vegetables, so it's best to leave shopping for these items until the first town past the inspection point.

Driving Licence

You can use your home country's driving licence in Victoria, NSW and QLD, as long as it is written in English (if it's in another language, a certified translation must be carried) and carries your photograph for identification.

Hire

There are plenty of car-rental companies ready and willing to put you behind the wheel. Between a group, car hire can be reasonably economical. The main thing to remember is distance – if you want to travel far, you need unlimited kilometres.

Major companies:

Avis (☎ 13 63 33; www.avis.com.au)
Budget (☎ 1300 362 8484; www.budget.com.au)
Hertz (☎ 13 30 39; www.hertz.com.au)
Thrifty (☎ 13 61 39; www.thrifty.com.au)

These companies have offices or agents in most major towns. There is a vast number of local firms which are sometimes cheaper than the big operators, but cheap car hire often comes with serious restrictions.

The big firms sometimes offer one-way rentals; pick up a car in Melbourne and leave it in Sydney, for example. There are, however, a variety of restrictions on this and sometimes there's a substantial drop-off fee.

The major companies offer a choice of deals, either unlimited kilometres or 100km or so a day free plus so many cents per kilometre over this. Daily rates are typically from $50 a day for a small car, from $75 to $80 a day for a medium car, or $85 to $100 a day for a big car, not including insurance. Note that booking your car through one of the large travel websites (or directly with the majors) can often save you quite a bit of money rather than waiting to do so in Australia. From the US, for instance, rates under US$40 per day with unlimited kilometres are common.

You must be at least 21 years old to hire from most firms; if you're under 25 you may only be able to hire a small car or have to pay a surcharge. It gets cheaper if you rent for a week or more and there are often low-season and weekend discounts. Credit cards are the usual payment method.

4WD & CAMPERVAN

Having a 4WD enables you to get right off the beaten track and out to some of the natural wonders that most travellers miss. Check the insurance conditions carefully, especially the excess, as they can be onerous. Even for a 4WD, the insurance offered by most companies does not cover damage caused when travelling 'off-road', which basically means anything that is not a maintained bitumen or dirt road. Off-peak, you can find campervan deals starting at $40 per day.

Hertz, Budget and Avis have 4WD rentals. Specialist rental firms include:

Backpacker Campervans (☎ 1800 670 232; www .backpackercampervans.com.au) Rents campervans.
Britz Rentals (☎ 1800 331 454; www.britz.com) Hires fully equipped 4WDs fitted out as campervans.
Wicked Campers (☎ 07-3634 9000, 1800 246 869; www.wickedcampers.com.au) Has vehicles emblazoned with profane commentary such as 'Lawyers come from anal intercourse'. Your tastes may vary.

Insurance

In Australia, third-party personal injury insurance is included in the vehicle-registration cost, ensuring that every registered vehicle carries at least minimum insurance. We recommend extending that minimum to at least third-party property insurance – minor collisions can be amazingly expensive.

When it comes to hire cars, understand your liability in the event of an accident. Rather than risk paying out thousands of dollars, you can take out your own comprehensive car insurance or pay an additional daily amount (often ridiculously high) to the rental company for an 'insurance excess reduction' policy. This reduces the excess you must pay in the event of an accident from between $2000 and $5000 to a few hundred dollars. Check with your credit-card company as many provide this coverage for free with use of your card.

Be aware that if travelling on dirt roads you will not be covered by insurance unless you have a 4WD. Also, most companies' insurance won't cover the cost of damage to glass (including the windscreen) or tyres. Although, again, your credit-card company may cover this. Check.

Purchase

If you're planning a stay of several months with plenty of driving, buying is much cheaper than renting. But remember that reliability is all-important. You'll probably get any car cheaper by buying privately through newspaper classifieds rather than through a car dealer. Buying through a dealer does have the advantage of some sort of guarantee, but this might not be much use if you plan to take the car to another state.

There's plenty of debate among travellers about where the best place is to buy and sell used cars. Sydney is a particularly good place to buy cars from backpackers who have finished their trips. These vehicles will have done plenty of kilometres but they often come complete with camping gear, Eskies (large insulated containers for food or drink), water containers, tools and road maps. The best place to look is on hostel noticeboards or at car markets. Sydney is also well set up for travellers to sell vehicles; see p215 for more information. Twenty-year-old Toyotas will go for about $2000.

When you come to buy or sell a car, every state has its own regulations, particularly with rego (registration). In Vic, for example, a car has to have a compulsory safety check (Road Worthy Certificate; RWC) before it can be registered in the new owner's name. In NSW safety checks are compulsory every year when you come to renew the registration.

Note that it's much easier to sell a car in the same state that it's registered in, otherwise you (or the buyer) must re-register it in the new state, and that's a hassle.

Before you buy any vehicle, regardless of who the seller is, we strongly recommend that you have it thoroughly checked by a competent mechanic. The state automobile associations have lists of reputable mechanics.

The **Register of Encumbered Vehicles** (REVS; ☎ 13 32 20; www.revs.nsw.gov.au) is a NSW government organisation that can check to ensure the car you're buying is fully paid-up and owned by the seller.

BUY-BACK DEALS

One way of getting around the hassles of buying and selling a vehicle privately is to enter into a buy-back arrangement with a car or motorcycle dealer; make sure you read the small print and don't accept any verbal guarantees – get it in writing. However, some dealers may find ways of knocking down the price when you return the vehicle, even if it was agreed to in writing – sometimes by pointing out expensive repairs that allegedly will be required to gain the dreaded RWC needed to transfer the registration.

A company that specialises in buy-back on cars and campervans is **Travellers Autobarn**

(☎ 02-9360 1500, 1800 674 374; www.travellers-autobarn .com.au). It has offices in Brisbane, Cairns, Melbourne and Sydney, and offers a range of vehicles.

Road Conditions & Hazards

Australia has few multilane highways, although there are stretches of divided road (four or six lanes) in some particularly busy areas such as the tollroads of Sydney, Melbourne and Brisbane.

However, if you think this is the case from Sydney to Brisbane, you are mistaken. Much of the Pacific Hwy (Hwy 1) in NSW is a clogged, trucky mess. Going south from Sydney, the Hume Hwy in NSW and Victoria is modern but misses the coast. The Princes Hwy (Hwy 1), which runs on the coast from Sydney to Melbourne, is mostly two lanes, but traffic is normally not a problem.

You don't have to get far off the beaten track to find yourself on dirt roads. In fact, anybody who sets out to see the countryside in reasonable detail should expect some dirt-road travelling. The problem here is that if you have a hire car, the company's insurance won't cover you unless you've hired an expensive 4WD.

ANIMAL HAZARDS

Kangaroos are common hazards on country roads. If you're travelling at any sort of speed, hitting one can make a real mess of your car, not to mention the kangaroo. They are most active at dawn and dusk, and often travel in groups. Many Australians avoid travelling altogether after dark in country areas because of the hazards posed by animals.

If you are travelling at night and a large animal appears in front of you, hit the brakes (if there isn't a car right behind you), dip your lights (so you don't continue to dazzle and confuse it) and only swerve if it's safe to do so. Numerous travellers have been killed in accidents caused by swerving to miss animals. It's better to damage your car and perhaps kill the animal than cause the death of yourself and your passengers and other motorists on the road.

Road Rules

Driving in Australia holds few surprises, other than the odd animal caught in your headlights. Australians drive on the left-hand side of the road and all cars are right-hand drive. An important road rule is 'give way to the

TRANSPORT

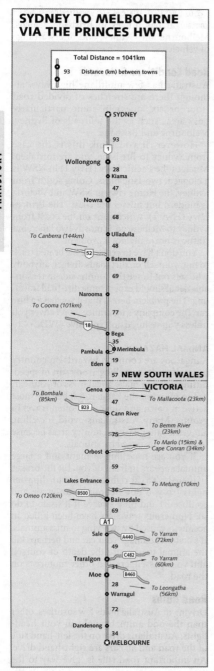

SYDNEY TO MELBOURNE VIA THE PRINCES HWY

Total Distance = 1041km

93   Distance (km) between towns

- SYDNEY
- 93
- Wollongong
- 28
- Kiama
- 47
- Nowra
- 68
- Ulladulla
- 48   To Canberra (144km)
- Batemans Bay
- 69
- Narooma
- 77   To Cooma (101km)
- Bega
- 35
- Pambula / Merimbula
- 19
- Eden
- 57   **NEW SOUTH WALES / VICTORIA**
- Genoa   To Bombala (85km)
- 47   To Mallacoota (23km)
- Cann River
- 75   To Bemm River (23km)
- To Marlo (15km) & Cape Conran (34km)
- Orbost
- 59
- Lakes Entrance   To Metung (10km)
- 36
- Bairnsdale   To Omeo (120km)
- 69
- Sale   To Yarram (72km)
- 49
- Traralgon   To Yarram (60km)
- 31
- Moe
- 28
- Warragul   To Leongatha (56km)
- 72
- Dandenong
- 34
- MELBOURNE

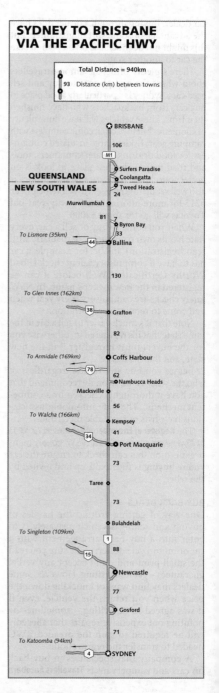

SYDNEY TO BRISBANE VIA THE PACIFIC HWY

Total Distance = 940km

93   Distance (km) between towns

- BRISBANE
- 106
- **QUEENSLAND / NEW SOUTH WALES**
- Surfers Paradise
- Coolangatta
- Tweed Heads
- 24
- Murwillumbah
- 81
- Byron Bay
- 7
- 33
- Ballina   To Lismore (35km)
- 130
- Grafton   To Glen Innes (162km)
- 82
- Coffs Harbour   To Armidale (169km)
- 62
- Nambucca Heads
- Macksville
- 56
- Kempsey   To Walcha (166km)
- 41
- Port Macquarie
- 73
- Taree
- 73
- Bulahdelah
- 88   To Singleton (109km)
- Newcastle
- 77
- Gosford
- 71
- SYDNEY   To Katoomba (94km)

BRISBANE TO CAIRNS VIA THE BRUCE HWY

Total Distance = 1705km

93 Distance (km) between towns

To Mossman (75km)

44 ✪ **CAIRNS**
88
To Ravenshoe (94km)
25 **Innisfail**
52
Tully
96
Ingham
A1 110
Townsville
A6 87
To Charters
Towers (135km)
Ayr
115
Bowen To Airlie Beach (36km)
66
Proserpine
123
Mackay
70
To Clermont (274km)
332
To Emerald (270km) To Yeppoon (40km)
A1
A4 **Rockhampton**
171
33
Gladstone
Calliope 19
To Bundaberg (53km)
155
3
Childers
33
57 **Hervey Bay**
Maryborough 34
89
Gympie
60 To Noosa (21km)
6
Nambour
To Kingaroy (164km)
17
104
✪ **BRISBANE**
To Toowoomba (128km)

right' – if an intersection is unmarked (unusual), you must give way to vehicles entering the intersection from your right.

The general speed limit in built-up areas is 60km/h, although this has been reduced to 50km/h on many residential streets. Near schools, the limit is 40km/h in the morning and afternoon. On the open highway it's usually 100km/h or 110km/h. Keep an eye out for signs. The police have radar and cameras, and are very fond of using them in strategically concealed locations.

Seatbelt usage is compulsory. Small children must be belted into an approved safety seat.

DRINK-DRIVING

Along the East Coast, drink-driving is a real problem, especially in country areas. Serious attempts are being made to reduce the road toll, and random breath tests are not uncommon in built-up areas. If you're caught with a blood-alcohol level of more than 0.05% be prepared for a hefty fine and the loss of your licence. In Vic you must be *under* 0.05%.

PARKING

One of the big problems with driving around big cities like Sydney and Melbourne (or popular tourist towns like Byron Bay) is finding somewhere to park. Even if you do find a spot there's likely to be a time restriction, a meter (or ticket machine) or both. Parking officers in Australia are like parking officers the world over – they'd put a ticket on a fire hydrant if it had wheels. Parking fines range from about $50 to $120 and if you park in a clearway your car will be towed away or clamped – look for signs. If your rental car draws the ticket, the fine will be charged to your credit card, sometimes months later.

In the cities there are large multistorey car parks where you can park all day for $15 to $30.

HITCHING

Hitching is never entirely safe in any country in the world, and we don't recommend it. Travellers who decide to hitch should understand that they are taking a small but potentially serious risk. People who do choose to hitch will be safer if they travel in pairs and let someone know where they are planning to go.

In Australia, the hitching signal can be a thumbs up, but a downward-pointed finger is more widely understood.

LOCAL TRANSPORT

Brisbane, Melbourne and Sydney have public-transport systems utilising buses, trains, ferries and/or trams. Larger regional towns and cities along the East Coast have their own local bus systems. These usually operate from the main train station, or, where there isn't one, from the main long-distance coach terminal. If the town is large enough to warrant having a taxi fleet, taxis are found here as well. Local buses often are timed for school runs, making weekend travel tough. There's almost no service north of Cairns.

TRAIN

Train travel is a comfortable option for short-haul sectors along the East Coast – but it's also a few dollars more than travelling by bus and it may take a few hours longer. XPT stands for Express Passenger Train. These NSW trains link Sydney with Melbourne, Brisbane, Dubbo, Grafton and Casino.

Rail services within each state are run by that state's rail body, either government or private.

CityRail (☎ 13 15 00; www.cityrail.nsw.gov.au) Covers the NSW coast around Sydney and as far north as Newcastle; also to the Blue Mountains.

CountryLink (☎ 13 22 32; www.countrylink.info) In NSW, operates from Sydney south to Canberra and Melbourne and along the coast north to Brisbane (but *not* Byron Bay).

Queensland Rail (☎ 1300 131 722; www.qr.com.au) Operates various train services from Brisbane to Cairns.

V/Line (☎ 13 61 96; www.vline.com.au) Has train services in Victoria, including between Melbourne and Bairnsdale.

Costs

Children can travel for reduced fares; purchasing fares in advance saves you 30% to 50%. First class costs about 40% more than economy. Discounted tickets usually require advance purchase. Australian and foreign students (with an ISIC) get a 50% discount on economy fares. Some standard one-way train fares:

Melbourne to Sydney (adult economy $130)
Canberra to Sydney (adult economy $60)
Sydney to Brisbane (adult economy $130)
Brisbane to Cairns (adult economy $220)

Reservations & Classes

During national holidays, school holidays and weekends it can be a good idea to book a seat. You can do this at railways stations or through the railway companies. Many discount fares require you to reserve well in advance.

Extra-cost sleeper service is available between Melbourne, Sydney, Brisbane and Cairns. Some trains also carry 1st-class seats.

Train Passes

Coverage of the East Coast by rail isn't bad. Several useful passes are sold. **Rail Australia** (www.railaustralia.com.au) provides information on train passes available from the various rail companies.

Austrail Flexipass Allows travel across Australia for a set number of economy-class travelling days within a six-month period: $950 for 15 days, $1330 for 22 days and $1570 for 29 days.

Backtracker Gives unlimited travel on Countrylink trains linking Sydney with Canberra, Melbourne and Brisbane. It costs $220 for 14 days, $255 for one month and $275 for three months (your best value). It is only sold to non-Australians.

East Coast Discovery Pass Allows travel with unlimited stops over a designated route in one direction during a six-month period. The entire Melbourne to Cairns route costs $500. You can buy shorter segments, such as Sydney to Brisbane ($130).

Health Dr David Millar

CONTENTS

East Coast Australia is a remarkably healthy region in which to travel, considering that such a large portion of it lies in the tropics. Tropical diseases such as malaria are extremely rare, while others such as yellow fever are unknown; diseases of poor sanitation such as cholera and typhoid are unheard of. Thanks to Australia's isolation and quarantine standards, even some animal diseases such as rabies and foot-and-mouth disease have yet to be recorded.

Few travellers to this area will experience anything worse than an upset stomach or a bad hangover, and if you do fall ill the standard of hospitals and health care is high.

BEFORE YOU GO

Since most vaccines don't produce immunity until at least two weeks after they're given, visit a physician four to eight weeks before departure. Ask your doctor for an International Certificate of Vaccination (otherwise known as 'the yellow booklet'), which will list all the vaccinations you've received. This is mandatory for countries that require proof of yellow fever vaccination upon entry (sometimes required in Australia, see right), but it's a good idea to carry a record of all your vaccinations wherever you travel.

Bring medications in their original, clearly labelled containers. A signed and dated letter from your physician describing your medical conditions and medications, including generic names, is also a good idea. If carrying syringes

---

REQUIRED & RECOMMENDED VACCINATIONS

Proof of yellow-fever vaccination is required only from travellers entering Australia within six days of having stayed overnight or longer in a yellow-fever-infected country. For a full list of these countries visit the websites of the **World Health Organization** (WHO; www.who.int) or the **Centers for Disease Control and Prevention** (CDC; www.cdc.gov).

If you're really worried about health when travelling, there are a few vaccinations you could consider. The World Health Organization recommends that all travellers should be covered for diphtheria, tetanus, measles, mumps, rubella, chickenpox and polio, as well as hepatitis B, regardless of their destination. When you're planning to travel it's a great time to ensure that all routine vaccination cover is complete. The consequences of these diseases can be severe and while Australia has high levels of childhood-vaccination coverage, outbreaks of these diseases do occur.

---

or needles, be sure to have a physician's letter documenting their medical necessity.

If your health insurance doesn't cover you for medical expenses abroad, consider extra insurance; check www.lonelyplanet.com for more information. Find out in advance if your insurance will make payments directly to providers or reimburse you later for overseas health expenditures. In Australia, as in many countries, doctors expect payment at the time of consultation. Make sure you get a receipt detailing the service and keep the contact details of the health provider. See p506 for details of health care in Australia.

INSURANCE

Health insurance is essential for all travellers. While health care in Australia is of a high standard and is not overly expensive by international standards, considerable costs can build up and repatriation is extremely expensive. Make sure your existing health insurance will cover you; if not, organise extra insurance.

HEALTH

MEDICAL CHECKLIST

- antibiotics
- antidiarrhoeal drugs (eg loperamide)
- acetaminophen/paracetamol or aspirin
- anti-inflammatory drugs (eg ibuprofen)
- antihistamines (for hay fever and allergic reactions)
- antibacterial ointment in case of cuts
- steroid cream or cortisone (for poison ivy and other allergic rashes)
- bandages, gauze, gauze rolls
- adhesive or paper tape
- scissors, safety pins, tweezers
- thermometer
- pocketknife
- DEET-containing insect repellent
- permethrin-containing insect spray for clothing, tents and bed nets
- sunblock
- oral rehydration salts
- iodine tablets or water filter (for water purification)

INTERNET RESOURCES

There is a wealth of travel health advice to be found on the internet. For further information, the Lonely Planet website (www.lonelyplanet.com) is a good place to start. The **World Health Organization** (www.who.int/ith) publishes a superb book called *International Travel and Health*, which is revised annually and is available online at no cost. Another website of general interest is **MD Travel Health** (www.mdtravelhealth.com), which provides complete travel-health recommendations for every country and is updated daily.

FURTHER READING

Lonely Planet's *Healthy Travel Australia, New Zealand & The Pacific* is a handy, pocket-sized guide packed with useful information including pretrip planning, emergency first aid, immunisation and disease information and what to do if you get sick on the road. Other recommended references include *Traveller's Health*

by Dr Richard Dawood (Oxford University Press) and *International Travel Health Guide* by Stuart R Rose, MD (Travel Medicine Inc).

IN TRANSIT

DEEP VEIN THROMBOSIS

Blood clots may form in the legs (deep vein thrombosis) during plane flights, chiefly because of prolonged immobility. The longer the flight, the greater the risk. Though most blood clots are reabsorbed uneventfully, some may break off and travel through the blood vessels to the lungs, where they could cause life-threatening complications.

The chief symptom of deep vein thrombosis is swelling or pain of the foot, ankle or calf, usually – but not always – on just one side. When a blood clot travels to the lungs, it may cause chest pain and breathing difficulties. Travellers with any of these symptoms should immediately seek medical attention.

To prevent the development of deep vein thrombosis on long flights, you should walk about the cabin, perform isometric contractions of the leg muscles (ie flex the leg muscles while sitting), drink plenty of fluids and avoid alcohol and tobacco.

JET LAG & MOTION SICKNESS

Jet lag is common when crossing more than five time zones, resulting in fatigue, malaise, insomnia or nausea. To avoid jet lag drink plenty of (nonalcoholic) fluids and eat light meals. Upon arrival, expose yourself to sunlight and readjust your schedule (for meals, sleep etc) as soon as possible.

Antihistamines such as dimenhydrinate and meclizine are usually the first choice for treating motion sickness. Their main side effect is drowsiness. A herbal alternative is ginger, which works like a charm for some people.

ON THE EAST COAST OF AUSTRALIA

AVAILABILITY & COST OF HEALTH CARE

Australia has an excellent health-care system. It's a mixture of privately run medical clinics and hospitals alongside a system of public hospitals funded by the government. The Medicare system covers Australian residents for some health-care costs. Visitors

---

TRAVEL HEALTH WEBSITES

It's usually a good idea to consult your government's travel-health website before departure, if one is available.

Australia (www.smartraveller.gov.au)
Canada (www.hc-sc.gc.ca/english)
UK (www.doh.gov.uk)
USA (www.cdc.gov)

from countries with which Australia has a reciprocal health-care agreement are eligible for benefits specified under the Medicare programme. Agreements are currently in place with New Zealand, the UK, Ireland, the Netherlands, Sweden, Finland, Italy and Malta; check the details before departing these countries. In general, agreements provide for any ill-health that requires prompt medical attention. For further details visit www.health.gov.au/pubs /mbs/mbs3/medicare.htm.

There are excellent, specialised public-health facilities for women and children in Australia's major centres.

Self-care

In Australia's remote locations it is possible there'll be a significant delay in emergency services reaching you in the event of serious accident or illness. Don't underestimate the distance between towns; an increased level of self-reliance and preparation is essential.

Consider taking a wilderness first-aid course, such as those offered at the **Wilderness Medicine Institute** (www.wmi.net.au); take a comprehensive first-aid kit that is appropriate for the activities planned; and ensure that you have adequate means of communication. Australia has extensive mobile-phone coverage but additional radio communication is important for remote areas. The **Royal Flying Doctor Service** (www.rfds.org.au) provides an important backup for remote communities.

Pharmaceutical Supplies

Over-the-counter medications are widely available at chemists (pharmacies) throughout Australia. These include painkillers, antihistamines for allergies and skin-care products.

You may find that medications readily available over the counter in some countries are only available in Australia by prescription. These include the oral contraceptive pill, most medications for asthma and all antibiotics. If you take medication on a regular basis, bring an adequate supply and ensure you have details of the generic name as brand names may differ between countries.

INFECTIOUS DISEASES

Bat lyssavirus Related to rabies; some deaths have occurred after bites. The risk is greatest for animal handlers and vets. Rabies vaccine is effective, but the risk to travellers is low.

Dengue fever Occurs in northern Queensland, particularly during the wet season (November to April). Also known as

'breakbone fever', because of the severe muscular pains that accompany it, this viral disease is spread by a species of mosquito that feeds primarily during the day. Most people recover in a few days but more severe forms of the disease can occur, particularly in residents who are exposed to another strain of the virus (there are four types) in a subsequent season.

Giardiasis Widespread in the waterways around Australia. As such, drinking untreated water from streams and lakes is not recommended. Water filters and boiling or treating water with iodine are effective in preventing the disease. Symptoms consist of bad-smelling diarrhoea, abdominal bloating and wind. Treatment is available (tinidazole or metronidazole).

Hepatitis C A growing problem among intravenous drug users. Blood transfusion services screen all blood before use.

HIV Rates in Australia have stabilised and levels are similar to other Western countries. Clean needles and syringes are widely available through all chemists.

Malaria Not an ongoing problem in the region although isolated cases have occurred in northern Queensland. The risk to travellers is low.

Meningococcal disease Occurs worldwide and is a risk with prolonged dorm-style accommodation. A vaccine exists for some types (meningococcal A, C, Y and W). No vaccine is presently available for the viral type of meningitis.

Ross River fever Widespread throughout Australia. The virus is spread by mosquitoes living in marshy areas. In addition to fever it causes headache, joint and muscular pains and a rash, and resolves after five to seven days.

Sexually transmitted diseases Occur at rates similar to most other Western countries. The most common symptoms are pain while passing urine and a discharge. Infection can also be present without symptoms. Throughout the country, you'll find sexual health clinics in all of the major hospitals. Always use a condom with any new sexual partner. Condoms are readily available in chemists and through vending machines in many public places including toilets.

Tick typhus Cases have been reported throughout Australia, but predominantly in Queensland and New South Wales. A week or so after being bitten, a dark area forms around the bite, followed by a rash and possible fever, headache and inflamed lymph nodes. The disease is treatable with antibiotics (doxycycline). See a doctor if you suspect you have been bitten.

Viral encephalitis (Murray Valley encephalitis virus) Spread by mosquitoes and is most common in northern Australia, especially during the wet season (October to March). This potentially serious disease is normally accompanied by headache, muscle pains and light sensitivity. Residual neurological damage can occur and no specific treatment is available. However, the risk to most travellers is low.

TRAVELLER'S DIARRHOEA

Tap water is universally safe in Australia. All water other than tap or bottled water should be boiled, filtered or chemically disinfected (with iodine tablets) to prevent traveller's diarrhoea and giardia.

If you develop diarrhoea, drink plenty of fluids, preferably an oral rehydration solution containing lots of salt and sugar. A few loose stools don't require treatment but if you have more than four or five stools a day, you should take an antibiotic (usually a quinolone drug) and an antidiarrhoeal agent (such as loperamide). If diarrhoea is bloody, persists for more than 72 hours or is accompanied by fever, shaking chills or severe abdominal pain you should seek medical attention.

ENVIRONMENTAL HAZARDS
Animal Bites & Stings
MARINE ANIMALS

Marine spikes, such as those found on sea urchins, stonefish, scorpion fish, catfish and stingrays, can cause severe local pain. If this occurs, immediately immerse the affected area in hot water (as high a temperature as can be tolerated). Keep topping up with hot water until the pain subsides and medical care can be reached. The stonefish is found only in tropical Australia, including northern Queensland. Antivenin is available.

Marine stings from jellyfish such as Chironex box and Irukandji also occur in Australia's tropical waters, particularly during the wet season (November to April). The box jelly has an incredibly potent sting and has been known to cause fatalities. Warning signs exist at affected beaches and stinger nets are in place at the more popular beaches. Never dive into water unless you have checked it's safe with local beach lifesavers. 'Stinger suits' (full-body Lycra swimsuits) prevent stinging, as do wetsuits. If you are stung, first aid consists of washing the skin with vinegar to prevent further discharge of remaining stinging cells, followed by rapid transfer to a hospital; antivenin is widely available.

SHARKS & CROCODILES

The risk of shark attack in Australian waters is no greater than in other countries with extensive coastlines. There's also low risk of an attack by tropical sharks on scuba divers in northern Australian waters. Great White Sharks are now few in number in the temperate southern waters. Check with surf-lifesaving groups about local risks.

The risk of crocodile attack in tropical northern Australia is real but predictable and largely preventable. Discuss the local risk with police or tourist agencies before swimming in rivers, water holes and in the sea.

SNAKES

Australian snakes have a fearful reputation that is justified in terms of the potency of their venom, but unjustified in terms of the actual risk to travellers and locals. Snakes are usually quite timid and in most instances will move away if disturbed. They have small fangs, making it easy to prevent bites to the lower limbs (where 80% of bites occur) by wearing protective clothing (such as gaiters) when bushwalking. The bite marks are very small and may even go unnoticed.

For all confirmed or suspected bites, prevent the spread of venom by applying pressure to the wound and immobilising the area with a splint or sling before seeking medical attention. Firmly wrap an elastic bandage (you can improvise with a T-shirt) around the entire limb, but not so tight as to cut off the circulation. Along with immobilisation, this is a life-saving first-aid measure.

SPIDERS

Australia has a number of poisonous spiders. The Sydney funnel-web spider causes severe local pain, as well as generalised symptoms (vomiting, abdominal pain and sweating). Antivenin exists, so apply pressure to the wound and immobilise the area before transferring to a hospital.

Redback spiders are found throughout the country. Bites cause pain at the site followed by profuse sweating and generalised symptoms (including muscular weakness, sweating at the site of the bite and nausea). First aid includes application of ice or cold packs to the bite, then transfer to hospital.

White-tailed spider bites may cause an ulcer that is difficult to heal. Clean the wound thoroughly and seek medical assistance.

Heatstroke

There's very hot weather year-round in northern Queensland and during the summer months for most of the country. When arriving from a temperate or cold climate, it takes about two weeks for acclimatisation to occur. Before the body is acclimatised an excessive amount of salt is lost in perspiration, so increasing the salt in your diet is essential.

Heat exhaustion occurs when fluid intake does not keep up with fluid loss. Symptoms include dizziness, fainting, fatigue, nausea or vomiting. On observation, the skin is usually pale, cool and clammy. Treatment consists of rest in a cool, shady place and fluid replacement with water or diluted sports drinks.

Heatstroke is a severe form of heat illness that occurs after fluid depletion or extreme heat challenge from heavy exercise. This is a medical emergency, with heating of the brain leading to disorientation, hallucinations and seizures. Heatstroke is prevented by maintaining an adequate fluid intake to ensure the continued passage of clear and copious urine, especially during physical exertion.

A number of unprepared travellers die from dehydration each year in outback Australia. This can be prevented by following these simple rules:

- Carry sufficient water for any trip including extra in case of breakdown.
- Always let someone, such as the local police, know where you are going and when you expect to arrive.
- Carry communications equipment of some form.
- Stay with the vehicle rather than walking for help.

Hypothermia

Hypothermia is a significant risk, especially during the winter months in southern parts of Australia. Despite the absence of high mountain ranges, strong winds produce a high chill factor that can result in hypothermia even in moderately cool temperatures. Early signs include the inability to perform fine movements (such as doing up buttons), shivering and a bad case of the 'umbles' (fumbles, mumbles, grumbles, stumbles). The key elements of treatment include moving out of the cold, changing out of wet clothing into dry clothes with wind- and waterproof layers, adding insulation and providing fuel (water and carbohydrate) to allow shivering, which builds the internal temperature. With severe hypothermia, shivering actually stops; this is a medical emergency requiring rapid evacuation in addition to the above measures.

Insect-Borne Illness

Various insects can be a source of irritation and, in Australia, may be the source of specific diseases (dengue fever, Ross River fever).

Protection from mosquitoes, sandflies, ticks and leeches can be achieved by a combination of the following strategies:

- wear loose-fitting long-sleeved clothing
- apply 30% DEET on all exposed skin and repeat every three to four hours
- impregnate clothing with permethrin (an insecticide that kills insects but is completely safe to humans).

Surf Beaches & Drowning

The East Coast has exceptional surf, but beaches vary in their conditions: the slope off-shore can result in changeable and often powerful surf. The ground underwater may also hide depressions and sand bars. Check with local surf-lifesaving organisations and be aware of your expertise and limitations before entering the water.

Ultraviolet-Light Exposure

Australia has one of the highest rates of skin cancer in the world. Monitor your exposure to sunlight closely. UV is strongest between 10am and 4pm so avoid skin exposure during these times year-round north of Coffs Harbour; spring to autumn between Coffs Harbour and Sydney; and from mid-spring to mid-autumn south of Sydney. Always use 30+ sunscreen, applied 30 minutes before going into the sun and repeated regularly, to minimise damage. Wear good sunglasses that filter out UV radiation.

Water-Borne Illness

Tap water is universally safe in the region. Increasing numbers of lakes, streams and rivers, however, are contaminated by bugs that cause diarrhoea, making water purification essential. The simplest way for you to purify water is to boil it thoroughly.

Consider purchasing a water filter. It's very important to read the specifications, so that you know exactly what it removes from the water and what it doesn't. Filtering will not remove all dangerous organisms, so if you can't boil water it should be treated chemically. Chlorine tablets will kill many pathogens, but not some parasites such as giardia and amoebic cysts. Iodine is more effective in purifying water and is available in tablet form. Follow the directions carefully and remember that too much iodine can be harmful.

Glossary

4WD – four-wheel-drive vehicle

ACT – Australian Capital Territory
ALP – Australian Labor Party
Anzac – Australian and New Zealand Army Corps
award wage – minimum pay rate

banana bender – resident of Queensland
bastard – form of address that can mean many things, from high praise or respect ('He's the bravest bastard I know') to dire insult ('You rotten bastard!'); avoid using if unsure!
BBQ – barbecue
bêche-de-mer – sea cucumber
bevan – mildly abusive Queensland term for an unsophisticated youth (elsewhere known as a *bogan*)
billabong – ox-bow bend in a river cut off by a changed watercourse; a water hole
billy – tin container used to boil tea in the *bush*
bitumen – road with this surface
bogan – mildly abusive term for an unsophisticated youth
bombora – isolate patch of offshore reef ('bommie')
boogie board – half-sized surfboard
boom netting – riding through the surf on nets in the front or rear of a travelling boat
boomerang – curved, flat, wooden implement traditionally used by Aboriginal people for hunting
booner – mildly abusive *ACT* term for an unsophisticated youth
bora ring – circular area ringed with banked earth used for Aboriginal ceremonial purposes, created mainly in *NSW* and southeastern Queensland
bottle shop – liquor store, off-licence
box jellyfish – species of deadly jellyfish; also known as sea wasp, box jelly, sea jelly, stinger
brekkie – breakfast
budgie smuggler – small, tight men's bathing suit
bug – Moreton Bay/Balmain bug, a small edible crustacean
bunyip – mythical *bush* animal or spirit
bush, the – countryside, usually covered with trees or shrubs; anywhere away from the city
bush tucker – native foods, usually in the *outback*
bushranger – Australia's equivalent to the outlaws of the Wild West (some goodies, some baddies)
BYO – bring your own; a restaurant licence that permits customers to drink alcohol they have purchased elsewhere

camp-o-tel – semipermanent tent with beds and lights
chook – chicken
counter meal – pub meal, usually eaten at the bar
cuppa – 'cup of' tea, coffee etc

dag – dirty lump of wool at the back end of a sheep; affectionate or mildly abusive term for an unfashionable or socially inept person
damper – bush loaf made from flour and water and cooked in a fire or camp oven
DEET – N, N diethyl-*m*-toluamide (a broad-spectrum insect repellent)
didjeridu, didj – cylindrical wooden musical instrument traditionally played by Aboriginal men. Sometimes spelt didgeridoo.
donga – sugar-cane cutter's cabin (archaic); prefabricated transportable cabin
Dreamtime, the – concept that forms the basis of Aboriginal spirituality, incorporating the creation of the world and spiritual energies around us
Dry, the – dry season in northern Australia
dunny – outdoor lavatory

Eftpos – electronic funds transfer at point of sale (method of paying for goods or services and withdrawing cash)
EPA – Environmental Protection Agency (in Queensland this government department runs the *QPWS*)
Esky – large insulated container for food or drink

flake – shark meat, often served in fish-and-chip shops
freshie – freshwater crocodile; see also *saltie*

galah – noisy cockatoo; noisy idiot
grog – general term for alcoholic drinks
gum tree – eucalyptus tree

jackeroo – young male trainee on a *station*
jillaroo – young female trainee on a *station*
jumper – sweater; pullover

Koorie – collective term used to identify Aboriginal people from southeastern Australia; in NSW spelt Koori; see also *Murri*

lamington – square of sponge cake covered in chocolate icing and coconut
larrikin – someone who is playfully mischievous
lay-by – a deposit on an article so the shop will hold it for you
live-aboard – cruise or dive boat offering accommodation
long black – double shot of espresso poured over hot water

mal – Malibu surfboard
mangrove – coastal tree that grows in salt water
middy – small (285ml) glass of beer, *NSW*; see also *pot*

milk bar – general store
Mod Oz – modern Australian cuisine, influenced by a wide range of foreign cuisines, but with a definite local flavour
mozzies – mosquitoes
Murri – collective term used to identify Aboriginal people from northeastern Australia; see also *Koorie*

NRMA – National Roads and Motorists Association (*NSW* automobile club)
NSW – New South Wales

outback – remote part of the *bush*

paddock – fenced area of land, usually intended for livestock
PADI – Professional Association of Diving Instructors (an international diving organisation that provides scuba training)
pokies – poker machines
pot – small (285ml) glass of beer, Victoria and Queensland; see also *middy*

QPWS – Queensland Parks & Wildlife Service (parks division of the *EPA* in Queensland)
Queenslander – traditional raised timber dwelling; resident of Queensland

RACQ – Royal Automobile Club of Queensland
RACV – Royal Automobile Club of Victoria
rashie – 'rash-vest' (UV-resistant skin-tight surfing top)
road train – a truck pulling a number of linked trailers (semitrailer-trailer-trailer)
RSL – Returned Servicemen's League; community venue operated by same

saltie – saltwater or estuarine crocodile; see also *freshie*
scar tree – a tree from which bark has been removed and treated to make canoes, dishes, shields or other items

schoolies – the weeks in late November or December when freshly graduated Australian teens head to the beach and drink themselves stupid
schooner – large glass of beer, NSW
scrub – *bush*; trees, shrubs and other plants growing in an arid area
sea wasp – deadly *box jellyfish*
sealed road – hard-surfaced or *bitumen*-covered road
shout – buy a round of drinks (as in 'It's your shout')
SLSC – Surf Life Saving Club, a branch of the *Surf Life Saving Association*; community venue operated by same
station – large farm
stinger – deadly *box jellyfish*
Stolen Generations – generations of indigenous children forcibly removed from their parents
stubby – 375ml bottle of beer
Surf Life Saving Association – a water-safety and rescue authority primarily staffed by volunteers
swag – canvas-covered bed-roll used in the *outback*; a large quantity
swagman – vagabond (archaic); itinerant labourer

terra nullius – legal concept that Australia was uninhabited at the time of British colonisation
thongs – flip-flops (footwear)
tinny – 375ml can of beer; small aluminium fishing dinghy
tucker – food

veggie – vegetable; vegetarian

walkabout – lengthy walk away from it all
wattle – Australian acacia species with furry yellow flowers
Wet, the – wet season in northern Australia

yabbie – freshwater crayfish
yum cha – classic southern Chinese dumpling feast

GLOSSARY

The Authors

RYAN VER BERKMOES
Coordinating Author, Sydney, North Coast New South wales

Whether it is the sand of the shore or a twig in the forest, Ryan Ver Berkmoes is always happy to have a bit of East Coast Australia caught in his shorts. A native of California, Ryan has covered a fair bit of the world during his long writing career. Since his first blissful introduction to Byron, he's had a special fondness for New South Wales (especially Sydney!). In fact two of the best things about doing this book are losing oneself on an endless beach and losing oneself in a Woolara pub with pals.

PETER DRAGICEVICH
South Coast New South Wales, Central Coast New South wales

The New South Wales coast often beckoned during the years Peter spent chasing deadlines on the various publications he managed in Sydney. He has fond memories of sanity-preserving breaks spent drinking wine and playing cards with mates in various spectacular locales. This is the eighth book he's coauthored for Lonely Planet, and as one of his most recent was the *Sydney City Guide*, he's currently plotting ways to explore the entire coast one book at a time.

JUSTIN FLYNN
Whitsunday Coast, North Coast Queensland

Justin's first venture to the Sunshine State was as a seven-year-old when the family packed up and headed for the Gold Coast to escape the dreary Victorian winter. Like most southerners, he has been lured back several times and can never resist the prospect of feasting on fresh Queensland seafood with a cold XXXX in hand under a tropical sun. There aren't many parts of coastal Queensland that Justin hasn't been to now, but a tour of the Bundaberg Rum factory remains at large...for now.

LONELY PLANET AUTHORS

Why is our travel information the best in the world? It's simple: our authors are passionate, dedicated travellers. They don't take freebies in exchange for positive coverage so you can be sure the advice you're given is impartial. They travel widely to all the popular spots, and off the beaten track. They don't research using just the internet or phone. They discover new places not included in any other guidebook. They personally visit thousands of hotels, restaurants, palaces, trails, galleries, temples and more. They speak with dozens of locals every day to make sure you get the kind of insider knowledge only a local could tell you. They take pride in getting all the details right, and in telling it how it is. Think you can do it? Find out how at **lonelyplanet.com**.

THE AUTHORS

PAUL HARDING — Far North Coast Queensland

Over the past two decades Melbourne-born Paul has travelled to almost every corner of the Australian continent, but has a particular love for the most remote places. For this edition he travelled to the beautiful corner of Far North Queensland (as far north as the tip of Australia on Cape York), diving on the reef, marvelling at the rainforest, dutifully investigating Cairns' nightlife, and meeting plenty of characters. A freelance writer, editor and occasional photographer, Paul has also contributed to Lonely Planet's *Australia*, *Northern Territory* and *New South Wales* guides.

CATH LANIGAN — Southeast Coast Victoria

Cath has lived in East Gippsland for the past eight years, where she is deeply immersed in the local community and infatuated with the Southeast Coast region. She explores Gippsland's national parks, beaches and coastal towns regularly with her partner and two children, preferably camping along the way. Cath lived in South Gippsland for three years where she worked as a journalist on the *South Gippsland Sentinel Times* newspaper and enjoyed calling Inverloch home. When she's not doing the occasional authoring job, Cath works from home recruiting Lonely Planet's new authors.

ROWAN MCKINNON — Melbourne

Rowan grew up in Frankston in the 1970s, on the big-city fringe at the end of the train line. It was a time of sharpies and surfies, souped-up panel vans with shagpile and mirrored interiors, Thin Lizzy and Led Zeppelin, when Bon Scott headed AC/DC at the dance in the Frankston High School hall. Rowan surfed all over the Mornington Peninsula as a teenager and young adult before a love of music and the lure of the big city drew him into the punk/new wave music scene of inner Melbourne. Rowan's authored many Lonely Planet guidebooks, specialising in the island states of the South Pacific.

ALAN MURPHY — Brisbane

Alan loves exploring a new part of the Sunshine state every time he makes a foray north. On this occasion he got to immerse himself in the urban jungle of Brisbane and was delighted to discover a cosmopolitan city basking in a tropical climate and packed with cultural offerings, world-class cuisine and... koalas. When tired of discovering wonderful institutions like the Breakfast Creek Hotel, he packed up his bags and headed to the island bliss of Moreton Bay. He was very happy to be given the opportunity of contributing to the *East Coast Australia* guide, and always finds writing about his home country a unique challenge.

THE AUTHORS

OLIVIA POZZAN
Gold Coast, Sunshine Coast,
Fraser Coast, Capricorn Coast

Raised on the Fraser Coast in the Sunshine State, Olivia's sun-soaked beach-side upbringing shaped a life-long addiction to balmy days and gorgeous beaches. Before her veterinary career led her around the Outback and eventually to the deserts of the Middle East, her bikini collection graced every sandy shore from the rainforest-fringed northern Reef to the glitzy Gold Coast. After years of travelling the globe, a craving for sand between her toes finally drew her back to Queensland, where she lives on the glorious Sunshine Coast. Sporting a new bikini collection, Olivia revisited her favourite coastal hotspots while researching her chapters.

CONTRIBUTING AUTHORS

Michael Cathcart wrote the History chapter. Michael presents history programs on ABC TV and teaches history at the Australian Centre, University of Melbourne. He is also noted as the man who abridged *A History of Australia* by Australia's best-known historian, Manning Clark, turning the six-volume classic into one handy book.

Matthew Evans cowrote the Food & Drink chapter. Matthew was originally a chef before crossing to the dark side as food writer and restaurant critic. After five years as chief reviewer for *The Sydney Morning Herald,* he has opted out, growing chooks and making Berkshire pork sausages in foodies' paradise, Tasmania

Tim Flannery wrote the Environment chapter. Tim is a naturalist, explorer, writer and climate-change activist. He was named Australian of the Year in 2007, and is currently an adjunct professor at Macquarie University in NSW. He is the author of a number of award-winning books, including *The Future Eaters* and *Throwim Way Leg* (an account of his adventures as a biologist working in New Guinea) and the landmark ecological history of North America, *The Eternal Frontier*. His most recent book is *Chasing Kangaroos* (2007).

Donna Wheeler helped research the Melbourne chapter. Donna has commissioned food guides and online features for Lonely Planet and has worked as a digital producer, content strategist and art director. She has studied visual arts, English literature and is a graduate of RMIT's Professsional Writing and Editing programme. She now devotes her time to freelance writing and editing.

Behind the Scenes

THIS BOOK

This is the 3rd edition of East Coast Australia. The 1st edition was published in 2002, the result of work by authors Verity Campbell, Pete Cruttenden, Kate Daly and Chris Rowthorn. The 2nd edition was coordinated by Linsday Brown, and his coauthors were Simone Egger, Sandra Bao, Ryan Ver Berkmoes, Simon Sellars, Cath Lanigan, Michael Cathcart, Tim Flannery and Matthew Evans, with research assistance from Justine Vaisutis, Paul Smitz, Sally O'Brien and Nina Rousseau.

For this 3rd edition, Ryan Ver Berkmoes took over the coordinating role, also writing the Destination, Itineraries, Culture, East Coast Australia Outdoors, Sydney and North Coast New South Wales chapters. He was joined by coauthors Rowan McKinnon, Cath Lanigan, Peter Dragicevich, Olivia Pozzan, Alan Murphy, Justin Flynn and Paul Harding. Donna Wheeler helped research the Melbourne chapter. Michael Cathcart wrote the History chapter, Matthew Evans wrote the Food & Drink chapter, and Tim Flannery wrote the Environment chapter. Dr David Millar contributed the Health chapter. See The Authors on p512 for further details on who wrote which chapters.

This guidebook was commissioned in Lonely Planet's Melbourne office, and produced by the following:

Commissioning Editors Kerryn Burgess, Emma Gilmour
Coordinating Editors Sasha Baskett, Averil Robertson, Gina Tsarouhas
Coordinating Cartographers Hunor Csutoros, Anthony Phelan
Coordinating Layout Designer Jacqui Saunders
Managing Editors Bruce Evans, Geoff Howard
Managing Cartographer David Connolly
Managing Layout Designer Celia Wood
Assisting Editors David Andrew, Gennifer Ciavarra, Daniel Corbett, Peter Cruttenden, Evan Jones, Anne Mulvaney, Rosie Nicholson, Charlotte Orr, Charles Rawlings-Way
Assisting Cartographers Barbara Benson, Joshua Geoghegan, Corey Hutchison, Tadhgh Knaggs, Erin McManus, Mandy Sierp
Assisting Layout Designers Paul Iacono, Jim Hsu
Cover Designer Vicki Beale
Cover Artwork Pablo Gastar
Colour Designer Indra Kilfoyle
Project Manager Sarah Sloane

Thanks to Trent Paton, Lisa Knights, Katie Lynch, Adam McCrow, Helen Christinis, Jennifer Garrett, Darren O'Connell, Eoin Dunlevy

---

THE LONELY PLANET STORY

Fresh from an epic journey across Europe, Asia and Australia in 1972, Tony and Maureen Wheeler sat at their kitchen table stapling together notes. The first Lonely Planet guidebook, *Across Asia on the Cheap*, was born.

Travellers snapped up the guides. Inspired by their success, the Wheelers began publishing books to Southeast Asia, India and beyond. Demand was prodigious, and the Wheelers expanded the business rapidly to keep up. Over the years, Lonely Planet extended its coverage to every country and into the virtual world via lonelyplanet.com and the Thorn Tree message board.

As Lonely Planet became a globally loved brand, Tony and Maureen received several offers for the company. But it wasn't until 2007 that they found a partner whom they trusted to remain true to the company's principles of travelling widely, treading lightly and giving sustainably. In October of that year, BBC Worldwide acquired a 75% share in the company, pledging to uphold Lonely Planet's commitment to independent travel, trustworthy advice and editorial independence.

Today, Lonely Planet has offices in Melbourne, London and Oakland, with over 500 staff members and 300 authors. Tony and Maureen are still actively involved with Lonely Planet. They're travelling more often than ever, and they're devoting their spare time to charitable projects. And the company is still driven by the philosophy of *Across Asia on the Cheap*: 'All you've got to do is decide to go and the hardest part is over. So go!'

THANKS
RYAN VER BERKMOES
Emma Gilmour in Lonely Planet's Melbourne office is a dream commissioning editor *and* her tongue knows its way around a good Al Swearingen quote. Among the many, many people who deserve thanks for this fab road trip, Jo Stiebel, helped me keep my lefts right and rights, well, correct. Best of all, she didn't dick around in Coffs Harbour. In Sydney, Jane Mathews was simply a dream. Everything good about that chapter is thanks to her passion for the city. (And thank you Jane for telling me back in 1990 that I should work for Lonely Planet.) Thanks to Erin Corrigan who helped me love more than just Byron Bay back in our days of innocence.

Finally, I dedicate this book to my father, Peter Ver Berkmoes. In 1942, as a young lad from Indiana, he was sent to fly in Australia-based bombers when WWII still hung in the balance. His sacrifice got him a drawer full of medals he has never liked to talk about, but he does like to talk about Australia. Although he hasn't been back since 1944, mention Oz to him and he says: 'Great people. Every time I'd take a sip of beer, they'd buy me another one.'

PETER DRAGICEVICH
Working on this book was a great opportunity to catch up with dear friends, while blatantly taking advantage of their local knowledge and comfortable spare rooms. On that front I owe a huge debt of gratitude to David Mills, Barry Sawtell, Jo Brook, Michael Woodhouse, Marcus O'Donnell, Ben Preston and Linda Dragicevich.

JUSTIN FLYNN
Thanks to the ever-helpful tourist office staff who answered my never-ending and annoying questions. Thanks to all the travellers for their helpful suggestions on how to improve this book. Big thanks to my Essex mate Louise – a reluctant snorkelling buddy but enthusiastic drinking companion in Airlie Beach. Thanks to Jess for helping me research Townsville's pubs. Cheers to Ryan for cobbling this thing together. Massive thanks to Emma at LP for trusting me with this gig and for remaining patient. Huge thanks to Wendy, Brit Brit and Liv Liv for being yourselves.

PAUL HARDING
Thanks go to the many people who helped out with company, advice and information while I was in Queensland. In Cairns, thanks to Karen Doane at Tourism Tropical North Queensland; to Bram Collins at Undara; Chrystal Mantyka at Reef Teach; and Willie Gordon in Cooktown for cultural insights. Big thanks to Hannah for company and good times from Cairns to Cape Trib. At Lonely Planet, thanks to Emma Gilmour and Ryan Ver Berkmoes.

CATH LANIGAN
A big thanks to Gippsland friends who shared their local knowledge: Amanda Hack, Andrew Sharpe, Daya Jepsen, Fiona Maud, Gavin van Eede, Joel Orenstein, Kate McAnergney, Kathryn Goller, Kerri-anne Crane, Kylie Greenaway, Liz Cook, Noel Maud, Phil Sewell, Shannyn van der Nol and Uli Hasel. Much appreciation goes to Parks Victoria staff Andrew Schulze, Carla and Josh Puglisi, Daryl Burns, Drue Shultz, Graeme Baxter and Wing Hagger; and to LP commissioning editor Emma Gilmour and coauthor Rowan McKinnon. Special thanks to my family: John for all the driving and Zoe and Jarno for extensive playground and kids' meals research.

ROWAN MCKINNON
Thanks to Donna Wheeler for great work on Melbourne Encounter. Thanks to my commissioning editor Emma Gilmour and to cartographic guru David Connelly. To my partner Jane, thanks for reading my roughs and bringing me tea and toast. And to my kids Lewis, Eadie, Lauren and the Wesonator – big love!

ALAN MURPHY
A very big thanks to my friend Tundra Gorza, who was a fountain of information on all things Brisbane, my tour guide, and detective on follow-up research. Kudos to Pete for popping up to Brizzie for a day's cricket at the GABBA and fine German beers afterwards. Thank you to all the travellers and members of the tourism industry in and around Brisbane that were kind enough to spend time imparting their local knowledge to me. And lastly, my appreciation to Meg and Emma at LP for giving me the opportunity of working on this guide.

OLIVIA POZZAN
The generosity and friendly smiles I encountered on my road trips through Queensland, even after the devastating floods of an unusually wet summer, reflect the warm-heartedness of Queenslanders in general. It was a pleasure to meet so many diverse and interesting characters and to immerse myself in the beautiful Queensland landscape (so lush and green after the rains). A

huge thanks to everyone I met, especially the helpful staff at the visitor information centres. And a special thanks to Emma, Ryan, and my coauthors.

OUR READERS
Many thanks to the travellers who used the last edition and wrote to us with helpful hints, useful advice and interesting anecdotes:

Ray Abbott, Robyn Abbott, Kevin Barker, Shane Bibby, Douglas Boulton, Claire Brandon, Eileen Cancella, Adrian Cole, Ruari Cormack, Helen Crump, Jacky Dale, Margaret Dickson, Theresa Engberg, Willy A Flegel, Ron Forster, Peter Hattinger, David Hawkins, Richard Hemming, Shawn Hiatt, Susan Holgate, Angela Luckett, Hannah Mcquilkan, Stammbach Melanie, Niall O'Callaghan, Clare O'Donoghue, Pauli Ojea, Sarah Porritt, Elizabeth Pratt, Nancy Shneiderman, Ken Simpson, Katja Tessmann, Vivek Thoppay, Dan Walsh, Chelsea Webber, Maggie Weiley, Anne Westad, Emma Wilson, Geoff Wilson, Louise Wolff, Luka Zupan.

ACKNOWLEDGMENTS
Many thanks to the following for the use of their content:

Globe on title page ©Mountain High Maps 1993 Digital Wisdom, Inc.

SEND US YOUR FEEDBACK
We love to hear from travellers – your comments keep us on our toes and help make our books better. Our well-travelled team reads every word on what you loved or loathed about this book. Although we cannot reply individually to postal submissions, we always guarantee that your feedback goes straight to the appropriate authors, in time for the next edition. Each person who sends us information is thanked in the next edition – and the most useful submissions are rewarded with a free book.

To send us your updates – and find out about Lonely Planet events, newsletters and travel news – visit our award-winning website: **www.lonelyplanet.com/contact**.

Note: we may edit, reproduce and incorporate your comments in Lonely Planet products such as guidebooks, websites and digital products, so let us know if you don't want your comments reproduced or your name acknowledged. For a copy of our privacy policy visit www.lonelyplanet.com/privacy.

Index

000 Map pages
000 Photograph pages

INDEX

INDEX

GreenDex

The following attractions, accommodation, cafés, pubs and restaurants have been selected by Lonely Planet authors because they demonstrate a commitment to sustainability. We've selected cafés, pubs and restaurants for their support of local producers or their devotion to the 'slow food' cause, meaning they serve mainly seasonal, locally sourced produce on their menus. We've also highlighted farmers markets and the local producers themselves. In addition, we've covered accommodation that we deem to be environmentally friendly for its commitment to energy conservation, recycling or some other element of sustainability. Attractions are listed because they're involved in conservation or environmental education. Some are indigenously owned or operated, thereby maintaining and preserving local identity and culture. For more tips about travelling sustainably in East Coast Australia, see p24. We're continuously developing our sustainable-travel content. If you think we've omitted someone who should be listed here, or if you disagree with our choices, email us at talk2us@lonelyplanet .com.au and set us straight for next time. For more information about sustainable tourism and Lonely Planet, see www.lonelyplanet.com/responsibletravel.

GREENDEX